Dictionary of Literary Biography

1. *The American Renaissance in New England*, edited by Joel Myerson (1978)
2. *American Novelists Since World War II*, edited by Jeffrey Helterman and Richard Layman (1978)
3. *Antebellum Writers in New York and the South*, edited by Joel Myerson (1979)
4. *American Writers in Paris, 1920–1939*, edited by Karen Lane Rood (1980)
5. *American Poets Since World War II*, 2 parts, edited by Donald J. Greiner (1980)
6. *American Novelists Since World War II, Second Series*, edited by James E. Kibler Jr. (1980)
7. *Twentieth-Century American Dramatists*, 2 parts, edited by John MacNicholas (1981)
8. *Twentieth-Century American Science-Fiction Writers*, 2 parts, edited by David Cowart and Thomas L. Wymer (1981)
9. *American Novelists, 1910–1945*, 3 parts, edited by James J. Martine (1981)
10. *Modern British Dramatists, 1900–1945*, 2 parts, edited by Stanley Weintraub (1982)
11. *American Humorists, 1800–1950*, 2 parts, edited by Stanley Trachtenberg (1982)
12. *American Realists and Naturalists*, edited by Donald Pizer and Earl N. Harbert (1982)
13. *British Dramatists Since World War II*, 2 parts, edited by Stanley Weintraub (1982)
14. *British Novelists Since 1960*, 2 parts, edited by Jay L. Halio (1983)
15. *British Novelists, 1930–1959*, 2 parts, edited by Bernard Oldsey (1983)
16. *The Beats: Literary Bohemians in Postwar America*, 2 parts, edited by Ann Charters (1983)
17. *Twentieth-Century American Historians*, edited by Clyde N. Wilson (1983)
18. *Victorian Novelists After 1885*, edited by Ira B. Nadel and William E. Fredeman (1983)
19. *British Poets, 1880–1914*, edited by Donald E. Stanford (1983)
20. *British Poets, 1914–1945*, edited by Donald E. Stanford (1983)
21. *Victorian Novelists Before 1885*, edited by Ira B. Nadel and William E. Fredeman (1983)
22. *American Writers for Children, 1900–1960*, edited by John Cech (1983)
23. *American Newspaper Journalists, 1873–1900*, edited by Perry J. Ashley (1983)
24. *American Colonial Writers, 1606–1734*, edited by Emory Elliott (1984)
25. *American Newspaper Journalists, 1901–1925*, edited by Perry J. Ashley (1984)
26. *American Screenwriters*, edited by Robert E. Morsberger, Stephen O. Lesser, and Randall Clark (1984)
27. *Poets of Great Britain and Ireland, 1945–1960*, edited by Vincent B. Sherry Jr. (1984)
28. *Twentieth-Century American-Jewish Fiction Writers*, edited by Daniel Walden (1984)
29. *American Newspaper Journalists, 1926–1950*, edited by Perry J. Ashley (1984)
30. *American Historians, 1607–1865*, edited by Clyde N. Wilson (1984)
31. *American Colonial Writers, 1735–1781*, edited by Emory Elliott (1984)
32. *Victorian Poets Before 1850*, edited by William E. Fredeman and Ira B. Nadel (1984)
33. *Afro-American Fiction Writers After 1955*, edited by Thadious M. Davis and Trudier Harris (1984)
34. *British Novelists, 1890–1929: Traditionalists*, edited by Thomas F. Staley (1985)
35. *Victorian Poets After 1850*, edited by William E. Fredeman and Ira B. Nadel (1985)
36. *British Novelists, 1890–1929: Modernists*, edited by Thomas F. Staley (1985)
37. *American Writers of the Early Republic*, edited by Emory Elliott (1985)
38. *Afro-American Writers After 1955: Dramatists and Prose Writers*, edited by Thadious M. Davis and Trudier Harris (1985)
39. *British Novelists, 1660–1800*, 2 parts, edited by Martin C. Battestin (1985)
40. *Poets of Great Britain and Ireland Since 1960*, 2 parts, edited by Vincent B. Sherry Jr. (1985)
41. *Afro-American Poets Since 1955*, edited by Trudier Harris and Thadious M. Davis (1985)
42. *American Writers for Children Before 1900*, edited by Glenn E. Estes (1985)
43. *American Newspaper Journalists, 1690–1872*, edited by Perry J. Ashley (1986)
44. *American Screenwriters, Second Series*, edited by Randall Clark, Robert E. Morsberger, and Stephen O. Lesser (1986)
45. *American Poets, 1880–1945, First Series*, edited by Peter Quartermain (1986)
46. *American Literary Publishing Houses, 1900–1980: Trade and Paperback*, edited by Peter Dzwonkoski (1986)
47. *American Historians, 1866–1912*, edited by Clyde N. Wilson (1986)
48. *American Poets, 1880–1945, Second Series*, edited by Peter Quartermain (1986)
49. *American Literary Publishing Houses, 1638–1899*, 2 parts, edited by Peter Dzwonkoski (1986)
50. *Afro-American Writers Before the Harlem Renaissance*, edited by Trudier Harris (1986)
51. *Afro-American Writers from the Harlem Renaissance to 1940*, edited by Trudier Harris (1987)
52. *American Writers for Children Since 1960: Fiction*, edited by Glenn E. Estes (1986)
53. *Canadian Writers Since 1960, First Series*, edited by W. H. New (1986)
54. *American Poets, 1880–1945, Third Series*, 2 parts, edited by Peter Quartermain (1987)
55. *Victorian Prose Writers Before 1867*, edited by William B. Thesing (1987)
56. *German Fiction Writers, 1914–1945*, edited by James Hardin (1987)
57. *Victorian Prose Writers After 1867*, edited by William B. Thesing (1987)
58. *Jacobean and Caroline Dramatists*, edited by Fredson Bowers (1987)
59. *American Literary Critics and Scholars, 1800–1850*, edited by John W. Rathbun and Monica M. Grecu (1987)
60. *Canadian Writers Since 1960, Second Series*, edited by W. H. New (1987)
61. *American Writers for Children Since 1960: Poets, Illustrators, and Nonfiction Authors*, edited by Glenn E. Estes (1987)
62. *Elizabethan Dramatists*, edited by Fredson Bowers (1987)
63. *Modern American Critics, 1920–1955*, edited by Gregory S. Jay (1988)
64. *American Literary Critics and Scholars, 1850–1880*, edited by John W. Rathbun and Monica M. Grecu (1988)
65. *French Novelists, 1900–1930*, edited by Catharine Savage Brosman (1988)
66. *German Fiction Writers, 1885–1913*, 2 parts, edited by James Hardin (1988)
67. *Modern American Critics Since 1955*, edited by Gregory S. Jay (1988)
68. *Canadian Writers, 1920–1959, First Series*, edited by W. H. New (1988)
69. *Contemporary German Fiction Writers, First Series*, edited by Wolfgang D. Elfe and James Hardin (1988)
70. *British Mystery Writers, 1860–1919*, edited by Bernard Benstock and Thomas F. Staley (1988)

71 *American Literary Critics and Scholars, 1880–1900,* edited by John W. Rathbun and Monica M. Grecu (1988)

72 *French Novelists, 1930–1960,* edited by Catharine Savage Brosman (1988)

73 *American Magazine Journalists, 1741–1850,* edited by Sam G. Riley (1988)

74 *American Short-Story Writers Before 1880,* edited by Bobby Ellen Kimbel, with the assistance of William E. Grant (1988)

75 *Contemporary German Fiction Writers, Second Series,* edited by Wolfgang D. Elfe and James Hardin (1988)

76 *Afro-American Writers, 1940–1955,* edited by Trudier Harris (1988)

77 *British Mystery Writers, 1920–1939,* edited by Bernard Benstock and Thomas F. Staley (1988)

78 *American Short-Story Writers, 1880–1910,* edited by Bobby Ellen Kimbel, with the assistance of William E. Grant (1988)

79 *American Magazine Journalists, 1850–1900,* edited by Sam G. Riley (1988)

80 *Restoration and Eighteenth-Century Dramatists, First Series,* edited by Paula R. Backscheider (1989)

81 *Austrian Fiction Writers, 1875–1913,* edited by James Hardin and Donald G. Daviau (1989)

82 *Chicano Writers, First Series,* edited by Francisco A. Lomelí and Carl R. Shirley (1989)

83 *French Novelists Since 1960,* edited by Catharine Savage Brosman (1989)

84 *Restoration and Eighteenth-Century Dramatists, Second Series,* edited by Paula R. Backscheider (1989)

85 *Austrian Fiction Writers After 1914,* edited by James Hardin and Donald G. Daviau (1989)

86 *American Short-Story Writers, 1910–1945, First Series,* edited by Bobby Ellen Kimbel (1989)

87 *British Mystery and Thriller Writers Since 1940, First Series,* edited by Bernard Benstock and Thomas F. Staley (1989)

88 *Canadian Writers, 1920–1959, Second Series,* edited by W. H. New (1989)

89 *Restoration and Eighteenth-Century Dramatists, Third Series,* edited by Paula R. Backscheider (1989)

90 *German Writers in the Age of Goethe, 1789–1832,* edited by James Hardin and Christoph E. Schweitzer (1989)

91 *American Magazine Journalists, 1900–1960, First Series,* edited by Sam G. Riley (1990)

92 *Canadian Writers, 1890–1920,* edited by W. H. New (1990)

93 *British Romantic Poets, 1789–1832, First Series,* edited by John R. Greenfield (1990)

94 *German Writers in the Age of Goethe: Sturm und Drang to Classicism,* edited by James Hardin and Christoph E. Schweitzer (1990)

95 *Eighteenth-Century British Poets, First Series,* edited by John Sitter (1990)

96 *British Romantic Poets, 1789–1832, Second Series,* edited by John R. Greenfield (1990)

97 *German Writers from the Enlightenment to Sturm und Drang, 1720–1764,* edited by James Hardin and Christoph E. Schweitzer (1990)

98 *Modern British Essayists, First Series,* edited by Robert Beum (1990)

99 *Canadian Writers Before 1890,* edited by W. H. New (1990)

100 *Modern British Essayists, Second Series,* edited by Robert Beum (1990)

101 *British Prose Writers, 1660–1800, First Series,* edited by Donald T. Siebert (1991)

102 *American Short-Story Writers, 1910–1945, Second Series,* edited by Bobby Ellen Kimbel (1991)

103 *American Literary Biographers, First Series,* edited by Steven Serafin (1991)

104 *British Prose Writers, 1660–1800, Second Series,* edited by Donald T. Siebert (1991)

105 *American Poets Since World War II, Second Series,* edited by R. S. Gwynn (1991)

106 *British Literary Publishing Houses, 1820–1880,* edited by Patricia J. Anderson and Jonathan Rose (1991)

107 *British Romantic Prose Writers, 1789–1832, First Series,* edited by John R. Greenfield (1991)

108 *Twentieth-Century Spanish Poets, First Series,* edited by Michael L. Perna (1991)

109 *Eighteenth-Century British Poets, Second Series,* edited by John Sitter (1991)

110 *British Romantic Prose Writers, 1789–1832, Second Series,* edited by John R. Greenfield (1991)

111 *American Literary Biographers, Second Series,* edited by Steven Serafin (1991)

112 *British Literary Publishing Houses, 1881–1965,* edited by Jonathan Rose and Patricia J. Anderson (1991)

113 *Modern Latin-American Fiction Writers, First Series,* edited by William Luis (1992)

114 *Twentieth-Century Italian Poets, First Series,* edited by Giovanna Wedel De Stasio, Glauco Cambon, and Antonio Illiano (1992)

115 *Medieval Philosophers,* edited by Jeremiah Hackett (1992)

116 *British Romantic Novelists, 1789–1832,* edited by Bradford K. Mudge (1992)

117 *Twentieth-Century Caribbean and Black African Writers, First Series,* edited by Bernth Lindfors and Reinhard Sander (1992)

118 *Twentieth-Century German Dramatists, 1889–1918,* edited by Wolfgang D. Elfe and James Hardin (1992)

119 *Nineteenth-Century French Fiction Writers: Romanticism and Realism, 1800–1860,* edited by Catharine Savage Brosman (1992)

120 *American Poets Since World War II, Third Series,* edited by R. S. Gwynn (1992)

121 *Seventeenth-Century British Nondramatic Poets, First Series,* edited by M. Thomas Hester (1992)

122 *Chicano Writers, Second Series,* edited by Francisco A. Lomelí and Carl R. Shirley (1992)

123 *Nineteenth-Century French Fiction Writers: Naturalism and Beyond, 1860–1900,* edited by Catharine Savage Brosman (1992)

124 *Twentieth-Century German Dramatists, 1919–1992,* edited by Wolfgang D. Elfe and James Hardin (1992)

125 *Twentieth-Century Caribbean and Black African Writers, Second Series,* edited by Bernth Lindfors and Reinhard Sander (1993)

126 *Seventeenth-Century British Nondramatic Poets, Second Series,* edited by M. Thomas Hester (1993)

127 *American Newspaper Publishers, 1950–1990,* edited by Perry J. Ashley (1993)

128 *Twentieth-Century Italian Poets, Second Series,* edited by Giovanna Wedel De Stasio, Glauco Cambon, and Antonio Illiano (1993)

129 *Nineteenth-Century German Writers, 1841–1900,* edited by James Hardin and Siegfried Mews (1993)

130 *American Short-Story Writers Since World War II,* edited by Patrick Meanor (1993)

131 *Seventeenth-Century British Nondramatic Poets, Third Series,* edited by M. Thomas Hester (1993)

132 *Sixteenth-Century British Nondramatic Writers, First Series,* edited by David A. Richardson (1993)

133 *Nineteenth-Century German Writers to 1840,* edited by James Hardin and Siegfried Mews (1993)

134 *Twentieth-Century Spanish Poets, Second Series,* edited by Jerry Phillips Winfield (1994)

135 *British Short-Fiction Writers, 1880–1914: The Realist Tradition,* edited by William B. Thesing (1994)

136 *Sixteenth-Century British Nondramatic Writers, Second Series,* edited by David A. Richardson (1994)

137 *American Magazine Journalists, 1900–1960, Second Series,* edited by Sam G. Riley (1994)

138 *German Writers and Works of the High Middle Ages: 1170–1280,* edited by James Hardin and Will Hasty (1994)

139 *British Short-Fiction Writers, 1945–1980,* edited by Dean Baldwin (1994)

140 *American Book-Collectors and Bibliographers, First Series,* edited by Joseph Rosenblum (1994)

141 *British Children's Writers, 1880–1914,* edited by Laura M. Zaidman (1994)

142 *Eighteenth-Century British Literary Biographers,* edited by Steven Serafin (1994)

143 *American Novelists Since World War II, Third Series,* edited by James R. Giles and Wanda H. Giles (1994)

144 *Nineteenth-Century British Literary Biographers,* edited by Steven Serafin (1994)

145 *Modern Latin-American Fiction Writers, Second Series,* edited by William Luis and Ann González (1994)

146 *Old and Middle English Literature,* edited by Jeffrey Helterman and Jerome Mitchell (1994)

147 *South Slavic Writers Before World War II,* edited by Vasa D. Mihailovich (1994)

148 *German Writers and Works of the Early Middle Ages: 800–1170,* edited by Will Hasty and James Hardin (1994)

149 *Late Nineteenth- and Early Twentieth-Century British Literary Biographers,* edited by Steven Serafin (1995)

150 *Early Modern Russian Writers, Late Seventeenth and Eighteenth Centuries,* edited by Marcus C. Levitt (1995)

151 *British Prose Writers of the Early Seventeenth Century,* edited by Clayton D. Lein (1995)

152 *American Novelists Since World War II, Fourth Series,* edited by James R. Giles and Wanda H. Giles (1995)

153 *Late-Victorian and Edwardian British Novelists, First Series,* edited by George M. Johnson (1995)

154 *The British Literary Book Trade, 1700–1820,* edited by James K. Bracken and Joel Silver (1995)

155 *Twentieth-Century British Literary Biographers,* edited by Steven Serafin (1995)

156 *British Short-Fiction Writers, 1880–1914: The Romantic Tradition,* edited by William F. Naufftus (1995)

157 *Twentieth-Century Caribbean and Black African Writers, Third Series,* edited by Bernth Lindfors and Reinhard Sander (1995)

158 *British Reform Writers, 1789–1832,* edited by Gary Kelly and Edd Applegate (1995)

159 *British Short-Fiction Writers, 1800–1880,* edited by John R. Greenfield (1996)

160 *British Children's Writers, 1914–1960,* edited by Donald R. Hettinga and Gary D. Schmidt (1996)

161 *British Children's Writers Since 1960, First Series,* edited by Caroline Hunt (1996)

162 *British Short-Fiction Writers, 1915–1945,* edited by John H. Rogers (1996)

163 *British Children's Writers, 1800–1880,* edited by Meena Khorana (1996)

164 *German Baroque Writers, 1580–1660,* edited by James Hardin (1996)

165 *American Poets Since World War II, Fourth Series,* edited by Joseph Conte (1996)

166 *British Travel Writers, 1837–1875,* edited by Barbara Brothers and Julia Gergits (1996)

167 *Sixteenth-Century British Nondramatic Writers, Third Series,* edited by David A. Richardson (1996)

168 *German Baroque Writers, 1661–1730,* edited by James Hardin (1996)

169 *American Poets Since World War II, Fifth Series,* edited by Joseph Conte (1996)

170 *The British Literary Book Trade, 1475–1700,* edited by James K. Bracken and Joel Silver (1996)

171 *Twentieth-Century American Sportswriters,* edited by Richard Orodenker (1996)

172 *Sixteenth-Century British Nondramatic Writers, Fourth Series,* edited by David A. Richardson (1996)

173 *American Novelists Since World War II, Fifth Series,* edited by James R. Giles and Wanda H. Giles (1996)

174 *British Travel Writers, 1876–1909,* edited by Barbara Brothers and Julia Gergits (1997)

175 *Native American Writers of the United States,* edited by Kenneth M. Roemer (1997)

176 *Ancient Greek Authors,* edited by Ward W. Briggs (1997)

177 *Italian Novelists Since World War II, 1945–1965,* edited by Augustus Pallotta (1997)

178 *British Fantasy and Science-Fiction Writers Before World War I,* edited by Darren Harris-Fain (1997)

179 *German Writers of the Renaissance and Reformation, 1280–1580,* edited by James Hardin and Max Reinhart (1997)

180 *Japanese Fiction Writers, 1868–1945,* edited by Van C. Gessel (1997)

181 *South Slavic Writers Since World War II,* edited by Vasa D. Mihailovich (1997)

182 *Japanese Fiction Writers Since World War II,* edited by Van C. Gessel (1997)

183 *American Travel Writers, 1776–1864,* edited by James J. Schramer and Donald Ross (1997)

184 *Nineteenth-Century British Book-Collectors and Bibliographers,* edited by William Baker and Kenneth Womack (1997)

185 *American Literary Journalists, 1945–1995, First Series,* edited by Arthur J. Kaul (1998)

186 *Nineteenth-Century American Western Writers,* edited by Robert L. Gale (1998)

187 *American Book Collectors and Bibliographers, Second Series,* edited by Joseph Rosenblum (1998)

188 *American Book and Magazine Illustrators to 1920,* edited by Steven E. Smith, Catherine A. Hastedt, and Donald H. Dyal (1998)

189 *American Travel Writers, 1850–1915,* edited by Donald Ross and James J. Schramer (1998)

190 *British Reform Writers, 1832–1914,* edited by Gary Kelly and Edd Applegate (1998)

191 *British Novelists Between the Wars,* edited by George M. Johnson (1998)

192 *French Dramatists, 1789–1914,* edited by Barbara T. Cooper (1998)

193 *American Poets Since World War II, Sixth Series,* edited by Joseph Conte (1998)

194 *British Novelists Since 1960, Second Series,* edited by Merritt Moseley (1998)

195 *British Travel Writers, 1910–1939,* edited by Barbara Brothers and Julia Gergits (1998)

196 *Italian Novelists Since World War II, 1965–1995,* edited by Augustus Pallotta (1999)

197 *Late-Victorian and Edwardian British Novelists, Second Series,* edited by George M. Johnson (1999)

198 *Russian Literature in the Age of Pushkin and Gogol: Prose,* edited by Christine A. Rydel (1999)

199 *Victorian Women Poets,* edited by William B. Thesing (1999)

200 *American Women Prose Writers to 1820,* edited by Carla J. Mulford, with Angela Vietto and Amy E. Winans (1999)

201 *Twentieth-Century British Book Collectors and Bibliographers,* edited by William Baker and Kenneth Womack (1999)

202 *Nineteenth-Century American Fiction Writers,* edited by Kent P. Ljungquist (1999)

203 *Medieval Japanese Writers,* edited by Steven D. Carter (1999)

204 *British Travel Writers, 1940–1997,* edited by Barbara Brothers and Julia M. Gergits (1999)

205 *Russian Literature in the Age of Pushkin and Gogol: Poetry and Drama,* edited by Christine A. Rydel (1999)

206 *Twentieth-Century American Western Writers, First Series,* edited by Richard H. Cracroft (1999)

207 *British Novelists Since 1960, Third Series,* edited by Merritt Moseley (1999)

208 *Literature of the French and Occitan Middle Ages: Eleventh to Fifteenth Centuries,* edited by Deborah Sinnreich-Levi and Ian S. Laurie (1999)

209 *Chicano Writers, Third Series,* edited by Francisco A. Lomelí and Carl R. Shirley (1999)

210 *Ernest Hemingway: A Documentary Volume,* edited by Robert W. Trogdon (1999)

211 *Ancient Roman Writers,* edited by Ward W. Briggs (1999)

212 *Twentieth-Century American Western Writers, Second Series*, edited by Richard H. Cracroft (1999)

213 *Pre-Nineteenth-Century British Book Collectors and Bibliographers*, edited by William Baker and Kenneth Womack (1999)

214 *Twentieth-Century Danish Writers*, edited by Marianne Stecher-Hansen (1999)

215 *Twentieth-Century Eastern European Writers, First Series*, edited by Steven Serafin (1999)

216 *British Poets of the Great War: Brooke, Rosenberg, Thomas. A Documentary Volume*, edited by Patrick Quinn (2000)

217 *Nineteenth-Century French Poets*, edited by Robert Beum (2000)

218 *American Short-Story Writers Since World War II, Second Series*, edited by Patrick Meanor and Gwen Crane (2000)

219 *F. Scott Fitzgerald's The Great Gatsby: A Documentary Volume*, edited by Matthew J. Bruccoli (2000)

220 *Twentieth-Century Eastern European Writers, Second Series*, edited by Steven Serafin (2000)

221 *American Women Prose Writers, 1870–1920*, edited by Sharon M. Harris, with the assistance of Heidi L. M. Jacobs and Jennifer Putzi (2000)

222 *H. L. Mencken: A Documentary Volume*, edited by Richard J. Schrader (2000)

223 *The American Renaissance in New England, Second Series*, edited by Wesley T. Mott (2000)

224 *Walt Whitman: A Documentary Volume*, edited by Joel Myerson (2000)

225 *South African Writers*, edited by Paul A. Scanlon (2000)

226 *American Hard-Boiled Crime Writers*, edited by George Parker Anderson and Julie B. Anderson (2000)

227 *American Novelists Since World War II, Sixth Series*, edited by James R. Giles and Wanda H. Giles (2000)

228 *Twentieth-Century American Dramatists, Second Series*, edited by Christopher J. Wheatley (2000)

229 *Thomas Wolfe: A Documentary Volume*, edited by Ted Mitchell (2001)

230 *Australian Literature, 1788–1914*, edited by Selina Samuels (2001)

231 *British Novelists Since 1960, Fourth Series*, edited by Merritt Moseley (2001)

232 *Twentieth-Century Eastern European Writers, Third Series*, edited by Steven Serafin (2001)

233 *British and Irish Dramatists Since World War II, Second Series*, edited by John Bull (2001)

234 *American Short-Story Writers Since World War II, Third Series*, edited by Patrick Meanor and Richard E. Lee (2001)

235 *The American Renaissance in New England, Third Series*, edited by Wesley T. Mott (2001)

236 *British Rhetoricians and Logicians, 1500–1660*, edited by Edward A. Malone (2001)

237 *The Beats: A Documentary Volume*, edited by Matt Theado (2001)

238 *Russian Novelists in the Age of Tolstoy and Dostoevsky*, edited by J. Alexander Ogden and Judith E. Kalb (2001)

239 *American Women Prose Writers: 1820–1870*, edited by Amy E. Hudock and Katharine Rodier (2001)

240 *Late Nineteenth- and Early Twentieth-Century British Women Poets*, edited by William B. Thesing (2001)

241 *American Sportswriters and Writers on Sport*, edited by Richard Orodenker (2001)

242 *Twentieth-Century European Cultural Theorists, First Series*, edited by Paul Hansom (2001)

243 *The American Renaissance in New England, Fourth Series*, edited by Wesley T. Mott (2001)

244 *American Short-Story Writers Since World War II, Fourth Series*, edited by Patrick Meanor and Joseph McNicholas (2001)

245 *British and Irish Dramatists Since World War II, Third Series*, edited by John Bull (2001)

246 *Twentieth-Century American Cultural Theorists*, edited by Paul Hansom (2001)

247 *James Joyce: A Documentary Volume*, edited by A. Nicholas Fargnoli (2001)

248 *Antebellum Writers in the South, Second Series*, edited by Kent Ljungquist (2001)

249 *Twentieth-Century American Dramatists, Third Series*, edited by Christopher Wheatley (2002)

250 *Antebellum Writers in New York, Second Series*, edited by Kent Ljungquist (2002)

251 *Canadian Fantasy and Science-Fiction Writers*, edited by Douglas Ivison (2002)

252 *British Philosophers, 1500–1799*, edited by Philip B. Dematteis and Peter S. Fosl (2002)

253 *Raymond Chandler: A Documentary Volume*, edited by Robert Moss (2002)

254 *The House of Putnam, 1837–1872: A Documentary Volume*, edited by Ezra Greenspan (2002)

255 *British Fantasy and Science-Fiction Writers, 1918–1960*, edited by Darren Harris-Fain (2002)

256 *Twentieth-Century American Western Writers, Third Series*, edited by Richard H. Cracroft (2002)

257 *Twentieth-Century Swedish Writers After World War II*, edited by Ann-Charlotte Gavel Adams (2002)

258 *Modern French Poets*, edited by Jean-François Leroux (2002)

259 *Twentieth-Century Swedish Writers Before World War II*, edited by Ann-Charlotte Gavel Adams (2002)

260 *Australian Writers, 1915–1950*, edited by Selina Samuels (2002)

261 *British Fantasy and Science-Fiction Writers Since 1960*, edited by Darren Harris-Fain (2002)

262 *British Philosophers, 1800–2000*, edited by Peter S. Fosl and Leemon B. McHenry (2002)

263 *William Shakespeare: A Documentary Volume*, edited by Catherine Loomis (2002)

264 *Italian Prose Writers, 1900–1945*, edited by Luca Somigli and Rocco Capozzi (2002)

265 *American Song Lyricists, 1920–1960*, edited by Philip Furia (2002)

266 *Twentieth-Century American Dramatists, Fourth Series*, edited by Christopher J. Wheatley (2002)

267 *Twenty-First-Century British and Irish Novelists*, edited by Michael R. Molino (2002)

268 *Seventeenth-Century French Writers*, edited by Françoise Jaouën (2002)

269 *Nathaniel Hawthorne: A Documentary Volume*, edited by Benjamin Franklin V (2002)

270 *American Philosophers Before 1950*, edited by Philip B. Dematteis and Leemon B. McHenry (2002)

271 *British and Irish Novelists Since 1960*, edited by Merritt Moseley (2002)

272 *Russian Prose Writers Between the World Wars*, edited by Christine Rydel (2003)

273 *F. Scott Fitzgerald's Tender Is the Night: A Documentary Volume*, edited by Matthew J. Bruccoli and George Parker Anderson (2003)

274 *John Dos Passos's U.S.A.: A Documentary Volume*, edited by Donald Pizer (2003)

275 *Twentieth-Century American Nature Writers: Prose*, edited by Roger Thompson and J. Scott Bryson (2003)

276 *British Mystery and Thriller Writers Since 1960*, edited by Gina Macdonald (2003)

277 *Russian Literature in the Age of Realism*, edited by Alyssa Dinega Gillespie (2003)

278 *American Novelists Since World War II, Seventh Series*, edited by James R. Giles and Wanda H. Giles (2003)

279 *American Philosophers, 1950–2000*, edited by Philip B. Dematteis and Leemon B. McHenry (2003)

280 *Dashiell Hammett's The Maltese Falcon: A Documentary Volume*, edited by Richard Layman (2003)

281 *British Rhetoricians and Logicians, 1500–1660, Second Series*, edited by Edward A. Malone (2003)

282 *New Formalist Poets*, edited by Jonathan N. Barron and Bruce Meyer (2003)

283 *Modern Spanish American Poets, First Series*, edited by María A. Salgado (2003)

284 *The House of Holt, 1866–1946: A Documentary Volume*, edited by Ellen D. Gilbert (2003)

285 *Russian Writers Since 1980,* edited by Marina Balina and Mark Lipoyvetsky (2004)

286 *Castilian Writers, 1400–1500,* edited by Frank A. Domínguez and George D. Greenia (2004)

287 *Portuguese Writers,* edited by Monica Rector and Fred M. Clark (2004)

288 *The House of Boni & Liveright, 1917–1933: A Documentary Volume,* edited by Charles Egleston (2004)

289 *Australian Writers, 1950–1975,* edited by Selina Samuels (2004)

290 *Modern Spanish American Poets, Second Series,* edited by María A. Salgado (2004)

291 *The Hoosier House: Bobbs-Merrill and Its Predecessors, 1850–1985: A Documentary Volume,* edited by Richard J. Schrader (2004)

292 *Twenty-First-Century American Novelists,* edited by Lisa Abney and Suzanne Disheroon-Green (2004)

293 *Icelandic Writers,* edited by Patrick J. Stevens (2004)

294 *James Gould Cozzens: A Documentary Volume,* edited by Matthew J. Bruccoli (2004)

295 *Russian Writers of the Silver Age, 1890–1925,* edited by Judith E. Kalb and J. Alexander Ogden with the collaboration of I. G. Vishnevetsky (2004)

296 *Twentieth-Century European Cultural Theorists, Second Series,* edited by Paul Hansom (2004)

297 *Twentieth-Century Norwegian Writers,* edited by Tanya Thresher (2004)

298 *Henry David Thoreau: A Documentary Volume,* edited by Richard J. Schneider (2004)

299 *Holocaust Novelists,* edited by Efraim Sicher (2004)

300 *Danish Writers from the Reformation to Decadence, 1550–1900,* edited by Marianne Stecher-Hansen (2004)

301 *Gustave Flaubert: A Documentary Volume,* edited by Éric Le Calvez (2004)

302 *Russian Prose Writers After World War II,* edited by Christine Rydel (2004)

303 *American Radical and Reform Writers, First Series,* edited by Steven Rosendale (2005)

304 *Bram Stoker's* Dracula: *A Documentary Volume,* edited by Elizabeth Miller (2005)

305 *Latin American Dramatists, First Series,* edited by Adam Versényi (2005)

306 *American Mystery and Detective Writers,* edited by George Parker Anderson (2005)

307 *Brazilian Writers,* edited by Monica Rector and Fred M. Clark (2005)

308 *Ernest Hemingway's* A Farewell to Arms: *A Documentary Volume,* edited by Charles Oliver (2005)

309 *John Steinbeck: A Documentary Volume,* edited by Luchen Li (2005)

310 *British and Irish Dramatists Since World War II, Fourth Series,* edited by John Bull (2005)

311 *Arabic Literary Culture, 500–925,* edited by Michael Cooperson and Shawkat M. Toorawa (2005)

312 *Asian American Writers,* edited by Deborah L. Madsen (2005)

313 *Writers of the French Enlightenment, I,* edited by Samia I. Spencer (2005)

314 *Writers of the French Enlightenment, II,* edited by Samia I. Spencer (2005)

315 *Langston Hughes: A Documentary Volume,* edited by Christopher C. De Santis (2005)

316 *American Prose Writers of World War I: A Documentary Volume,* edited by Steven Trout (2005)

317 *Twentieth-Century Russian Émigré Writers,* edited by Maria Rubins (2005)

318 *Sixteenth-Century Spanish Writers,* edited by Gregory B. Kaplan (2006)

319 *British and Irish Short-Fiction Writers 1945–2000,* edited by Cheryl Alexander Malcolm and David Malcolm (2006)

320 *Robert Penn Warren: A Documentary Volume,* edited by James A. Grimshaw Jr. (2006)

321 *Twentieth-Century French Dramatists,* edited by Mary Anne O'Neil (2006)

Dictionary of Literary Biography Documentary Series

1 *Sherwood Anderson, Willa Cather, John Dos Passos, Theodore Dreiser, F. Scott Fitzgerald, Ernest Hemingway, Sinclair Lewis,* edited by Margaret A. Van Antwerp (1982)

2 *James Gould Cozzens, James T. Farrell, William Faulkner, John O'Hara, John Steinbeck, Thomas Wolfe, Richard Wright,* edited by Margaret A. Van Antwerp (1982)

3 *Saul Bellow, Jack Kerouac, Norman Mailer, Vladimir Nabokov, John Updike, Kurt Vonnegut,* edited by Mary Bruccoli (1983)

4 *Tennessee Williams,* edited by Margaret A. Van Antwerp and Sally Johns (1984)

5 *American Transcendentalists,* edited by Joel Myerson (1988)

6 *Hardboiled Mystery Writers: Raymond Chandler, Dashiell Hammett, Ross Macdonald,* edited by Matthew J. Bruccoli and Richard Layman (1989)

7 *Modern American Poets: James Dickey, Robert Frost, Marianne Moore,* edited by Karen L. Rood (1989)

8 *The Black Aesthetic Movement,* edited by Jeffrey Louis Decker (1991)

9 *American Writers of the Vietnam War: W. D. Ehrhart, Larry Heinemann, Tim O'Brien, Walter McDonald, John M. Del Vecchio,* edited by Ronald Baughman (1991)

10 *The Bloomsbury Group,* edited by Edward L. Bishop (1992)

11 *American Proletarian Culture: The Twenties and The Thirties,* edited by Jon Christian Suggs (1993)

12 *Southern Women Writers: Flannery O'Connor, Katherine Anne Porter, Eudora Welty,* edited by Mary Ann Wimsatt and Karen L. Rood (1994)

13 *The House of Scribner, 1846–1904,* edited by John Delaney (1996)

14 *Four Women Writers for Children, 1868–1918,* edited by Caroline C. Hunt (1996)

15 *American Expatriate Writers: Paris in the Twenties,* edited by Matthew J. Bruccoli and Robert W. Trogdon (1997)

16 *The House of Scribner, 1905–1930,* edited by John Delaney (1997)

17 *The House of Scribner, 1931–1984,* edited by John Delaney (1998)

18 *British Poets of The Great War: Sassoon, Graves, Owen,* edited by Patrick Quinn (1999)

19 *James Dickey,* edited by Judith S. Baughman (1999)

See also DLB 210, 216, 219, 222, 224, 229, 237, 247, 253, 254, 263, 269, 273, 274, 280, 284, 288, 291, 294, 298, 301, 304, 308, 309, 315, 316, 320

Dictionary of Literary Biography Yearbooks

1980 edited by Karen L. Rood, Jean W. Ross, and Richard Ziegfeld (1981)

1981 edited by Karen L. Rood, Jean W. Ross, and Richard Ziegfeld (1982)

1982 edited by Richard Ziegfeld; associate editors: Jean W. Ross and Lynne C. Zeigler (1983)

1983 edited by Mary Bruccoli and Jean W. Ross; associate editor Richard Ziegfeld (1984)

1984 edited by Jean W. Ross (1985)

1985 edited by Jean W. Ross (1986)

1986 edited by J. M. Brook (1987)

1987 edited by J. M. Brook (1988)

1988 edited by J. M. Brook (1989)

1989 edited by J. M. Brook (1990)

1990 edited by James W. Hipp (1991)

1991 edited by James W. Hipp (1992)

1992 edited by James W. Hipp (1993)

1993 edited by James W. Hipp, contributing editor George Garrett (1994)

1994 edited by James W. Hipp, contributing editor George Garrett (1995)

1995 edited by James W. Hipp, contributing editor George Garrett (1996)

1996 edited by Samuel W. Bruce and L. Kay Webster, contributing editor George Garrett (1997)

1997 edited by Matthew J. Bruccoli and George Garrett, with the assistance of L. Kay Webster (1998)

1998 edited by Matthew J. Bruccoli, contributing editor George Garrett, with the assistance of D. W. Thomas (1999)

1999 edited by Matthew J. Bruccoli, contributing editor George Garrett, with the assistance of D. W. Thomas (2000)

2000 edited by Matthew J. Bruccoli, contributing editor George Garrett, with the assistance of George Parker Anderson (2001)

2001 edited by Matthew J. Bruccoli, contributing editor George Garrett, with the assistance of George Parker Anderson (2002)

2002 edited by Matthew J. Bruccoli and George Garrett; George Parker Anderson, Assistant Editor (2003)

Concise Series

Concise Dictionary of American Literary Biography, 7 volumes (1988–1999): *The New Consciousness, 1941–1968; Colonization to the American Renaissance, 1640–1865; Realism, Naturalism, and Local Color, 1865–1917; The Twenties, 1917–1929; The Age of Maturity, 1929–1941; Broadening Views, 1968–1988; Supplement: Modern Writers, 1900–1998.*

Concise Dictionary of British Literary Biography, 8 volumes (1991–1992): *Writers of the Middle Ages and Renaissance Before 1660; Writers of the Restoration and Eighteenth Century, 1660–1789; Writers of the Romantic Period, 1789–1832; Victorian Writers, 1832–1890; Late-Victorian and Edwardian Writers, 1890–1914; Modern Writers, 1914–1945; Writers After World War II, 1945–1960; Contemporary Writers, 1960 to Present.*

Concise Dictionary of World Literary Biography, 4 volumes (1999–2000): *Ancient Greek and Roman Writers; German Writers; African, Caribbean, and Latin American Writers; South Slavic and Eastern European Writers.*

Dictionary of Literary Biography® • Volume Three Hundred Twenty-One

Twentieth-Century French Dramatists

Dictionary of Literary Biography® • Volume Three Hundred Twenty-One

Twentieth-Century French Dramatists

Edited by
Mary Anne O'Neil
Whitman College

A Bruccoli Clark Layman Book

THOMSON
GALE

ST. PHILIP'S COLLEGE LIBRARY

Detroit • New York • San Francisco • San Diego • New Haven, Conn. • Waterville, Maine • London • Munich

THOMSON

GALE

Dictionary of Literary Biography
Volume 321: Twentieth-Century French Dramatists
Mary Anne O'Neil

Editorial Directors
Matthew J. Bruccoli and Richard Layman

© 2006 Thomson Gale, a part of The Thomson Corporation.

Thomson and Star Logo are trademarks and Gale is a registered trademark used herein under license.

For more information, contact
Thomson Gale
27500 Drake Rd.
Farmington Hills, MI 48331-3535
Or you can visit our Internet site at
http://www.gale.com

ALL RIGHTS RESERVED
No part of this work covered by the copyright hereon may be reproduced or used in any form or by any means—graphic, electronic, or mechanical, including photocopying, recording, taping, Web distribution, or information storage retrieval systems—without the written permission of the publisher.

For permission to use material from this product, submit your request via Web at http://www.gale-edit.com/permissions, or you may download our Permissions Request form and submit your request by fax or mail to:

Permissions Department
Thomson Gale
27500 Drake Rd.
Farmington Hills, MI 48331-3535
Permissions Hotline:
248-699-8006 or 800-877-4253, ext. 8006
Fax: 248-699-8074 or 800-762-4058

While every effort has been made to ensure the reliability of the information presented in this publication, Thomson Gale does not guarantee the accuracy of the data contained herein. Thomson Gale accepts no payment for listing; and inclusion in the publication of any organization, agency, institution, publication, service, or individual does not imply endorsement of the editors or publisher. Errors brought to the attention of the publisher and verified to the satisfaction of the publisher will be corrected in future editions.

LIBRARY OF CONGRESS CATALOGING-IN-PUBLICATION DATA

O'Neil, Mary Anne, 1945–
   Twentieth-century French dramatists / Mary Anne O'Neil.
      p. cm. — (Dictionary of literary biography ; v. 321)
   "A Bruccoli Clark Layman book."
   Includes bibliographical references and index.
   ISBN 0-7876-8139-3 (hardcover : alk. paper)
   1. French drama—20th century—Bio-bibliography—Dictionaries. 2. Dramatists, French—20th century—Biography—Dictionaries. I. Title. II. Series.
   PQ556064 2005
   842'.9109'03—dc22
                                                           2005023691

Printed in the United States of America
10 9 8 7 6 5 4 3 2 1

*To the contributors, many of whom are colleagues and former students,
with thanks for their help in creating this volume*

Contents

Plan of the Series xv
Introduction xvii

Arthur Surenovitch Adamov (1908–1970) 3
Klaus Engelhardt

Jean Anouilh (1910–1987) .18
Michel Rocchi

Guillaume Apollinaire (1880–1918) 31
Mary Anne O'Neil

Fernando Arrabal (1932–) 42
Klaus Engelhardt

Antonin Artaud (1896–1948) 54
Martine Antle

Jacques Audiberti (1899–1965) 63
Christophe Lagier

Samuel Beckett (1906–1989) 71
Culley Jane Carson

Albert Camus (1913–1960) 85
Dale Cosper

Aimé Césaire (1913–) 94
Meredith Goldsmith

Paul Claudel (1868–1955) 103
Madhuri Mukherjee

Jean Cocteau (1889–1963) 120
Drew Jones

Lucette Desvignes (1926–) 138
Jerry L. Curtis

Marguerite Duras (Marguerite Donnadieu)
(1914–1996) 145
Elizabeth M. Anthony

Jean Genet (1910–1986) 161
Kristy Clark Koth

Michel de Ghelderode
(Adolphe-Adhémar Martens)
(1898–1962) 175
Susan McCready

André Gide (1869–1951) 186
Catharine Savage Brosman

Jean Giono (1895–1970) 203
Guy F. Imhoff

Jean Giraudoux (1882–1944) 214
Catharine Savage Brosman

Eugène Ionesco (1909–1994) 234
Jeanine Teodorescu-Regier

Bernard-Marie Koltès (1948–1989) 251
Martine Antle

Philippe Minyana (1946–) 257
Nicole Simek

Henry de Montherlant (1896–1972) 265
Henriette Javorek

Marcel Pagnol (1895–1974) 276
Brett Bowles

Henri Pichette (1924–2000) 287
Jason Owens

Roger Planchon (1931–) 292
Francine Heather Conley

Yasmina Reza (1959–) 304
Inas Messiha

Jules Romains (Louis Farigoule)
(1885–1972) 309
Susan McCready

Armand Salacrou (1899–1989) 317
Rosemary Plater-Zyberk Clark

Nathalie Sarraute (1900–1999) 325
Sarah Hurlburt

Jean-Paul Sartre (1905–1980) 334
   John Ireland

Georges Schéhadé (1905–1989) 353
   Kristin M. Vining-Stauffer

Jean Tardieu (1903–1995) .360
   Patricia Lancaster

Boris Vian (1920–1959) 372
   Alexander Hertich

Michel Vinaver (Michel Grinberg) (1927–) 381
   Kevin Elstob

Roger Vitrac (1899–1952) 392
   Alexander Hertich

Jean-Paul Wenzel (1947–) 402
   Christine E. B. Moritz

Checklist of Further Readings 411
Contributors 413
Cumulative Index 417

Plan of the Series

...Almost the most prodigious asset of a country, and perhaps its most precious possession, is its native literary product—when that product is fine and noble and enduring.

Mark Twain*

The advisory board, the editors, and the publisher of the *Dictionary of Literary Biography* are joined in endorsing Mark Twain's declaration. The literature of a nation provides an inexhaustible resource of permanent worth. Our purpose is to make literature and its creators better understood and more accessible to students and the reading public, while satisfying the needs of teachers and researchers.

To meet these requirements, *literary biography* has been construed in terms of the author's achievement. The most important thing about a writer is his writing. Accordingly, the entries in *DLB* are career biographies, tracing the development of the author's canon and the evolution of his reputation.

The purpose of *DLB* is not only to provide reliable information in a usable format but also to place the figures in the larger perspective of literary history and to offer appraisals of their accomplishments by qualified scholars.

The publication plan for *DLB* resulted from two years of preparation. The project was proposed to Bruccoli Clark by Frederick G. Ruffner, president of the Gale Research Company, in November 1975. After specimen entries were prepared and typeset, an advisory board was formed to refine the entry format and develop the series rationale. In meetings held during 1976, the publisher, series editors, and advisory board approved the scheme for a comprehensive biographical dictionary of persons who contributed to literature. Editorial work on the first volume began in January 1977, and it was published in 1978. In order to make *DLB* more than a dictionary and to compile volumes that individually have claim to status as literary history, it was decided to organize volumes by topic, period, or genre. Each of these freestanding volumes provides a biographical-bibliographical guide and overview for a particular area of literature. We are convinced that this organization—as opposed to a single alphabet method—constitutes a valuable innovation in the presentation of reference material. The volume plan necessarily requires many decisions for the placement and treatment of authors. Certain figures will be included in separate volumes, but with different entries emphasizing the aspect of his career appropriate to each volume. Ernest Hemingway, for example, is represented in *American Writers in Paris, 1920–1939* by an entry focusing on his expatriate apprenticeship; he is also in *American Novelists, 1910–1945* with an entry surveying his entire career, as well as in *American Short-Story Writers, 1910–1945, Second Series* with an entry concentrating on his short fiction. Each volume includes a cumulative index of the subject authors and articles.

Between 1981 and 2002 the series was augmented and updated by the *DLB Yearbooks*. There have also been nineteen *DLB Documentary Series* volumes, which provide illustrations, facsimiles, and biographical and critical source materials for figures, works, or groups judged to have particular interest for students. In 1999 the *Documentary Series* was incorporated into the *DLB* volume numbering system beginning with *DLB 210: Ernest Hemingway*.

We define literature as the *intellectual commerce of a nation:* not merely as belles lettres but as that ample and complex process by which ideas are generated, shaped, and transmitted. *DLB* entries are not limited to "creative writers" but extend to other figures who in their time and in their way influenced the mind of a people. Thus the series encompasses historians, journalists, publishers, book collectors, and screenwriters. By this means readers of *DLB* may be aided to perceive literature not as cult scripture in the keeping of intellectual high priests but firmly positioned at the center of a nation's life.

DLB includes the major writers appropriate to each volume and those standing in the ranks behind them. Scholarly and critical counsel has been sought in deciding which minor figures to include and how full their entries should be. Wherever possible, useful refer-

---

*From an unpublished section of Mark Twain's autobiography, copyright by the Mark Twain Company

ences are made to figures who do not warrant separate entries.

Each *DLB* volume has an expert volume editor responsible for planning the volume, selecting the figures for inclusion, and assigning the entries. Volume editors are also responsible for preparing, where appropriate, appendices surveying the major periodicals and literary and intellectual movements for their volumes, as well as lists of further readings. Work on the series as a whole is coordinated at the Bruccoli Clark Layman editorial center in Columbia, South Carolina, where the editorial staff is responsible for accuracy and utility of the published volumes.

One feature that distinguishes *DLB* is the illustration policy—its concern with the iconography of literature. Just as an author is influenced by his surroundings, so is the reader's understanding of the author enhanced by a knowledge of his environment. Therefore *DLB* volumes include not only drawings, paintings, and photographs of authors, often depicting them at various stages in their careers, but also illustrations of their families and places where they lived. Title pages are regularly reproduced in facsimile along with dust jackets for modern authors. The dust jackets are a special feature of *DLB* because they often document better than anything else the way in which an author's work was perceived in its own time. Specimens of the writers' manuscripts and letters are included when feasible.

Samuel Johnson rightly decreed that "The chief glory of every people arises from its authors." The purpose of the *Dictionary of Literary Biography* is to compile literary history in the surest way available to us—by accurate and comprehensive treatment of the lives and work of those who contributed to it.

The *DLB* Advisory Board

Introduction

The twentieth century was the greatest age of French theater since the neoclassical period of the mid 1700s, with every decade producing noteworthy playwrights. In fact, the enthusiasm for dramatic literature that energized the French stage in the early 1900s has continued unabated into the twenty-first century. Twentieth-century French drama was cosmopolitan, experimental, and eclectic, and it attempted to appeal to a much wider audience than past theater. Dramatists came not only from Paris—the center of French culture—but also from the provinces and the French states of the Caribbean, as well as from Francophone countries such as Belgium. Still others were foreigners who had immigrated to France for political or cultural reasons and who chose either to write in French instead of their mother tongue or to have their works translated and staged in France rather than in their native lands. The most important French play of the century, *En attendant Godot* (published 1952, produced 1953; translated as *Waiting for Godot*, 1954), is by the Irishman Samuel Beckett. French dramatists of this era often came from the working class, but they generally developed their skills in educated or artistic milieus.

Twentieth-century French playwrights were largely influenced by non-French traditions, especially classical Greek theater and the Balinese theater, as well as by major dramatists such as William Shakespeare, Luigi Pirandello, and Bertolt Brecht. Most writers felt the need to innovate: they experimented, often audaciously, with themes, characterization, and language. Even those playwrights of the 1930s, 1940s, and 1950s who revived Greek myths transformed their classical subject matter into contemporary political allegories. Throughout the century, playwrights incorporated the visual arts, dance, music, and technology into their works, so that plays were no longer speeches declaimed by actors to a distant audience but highly sensual, multimedia spectacles, the goals of which were not simply to entertain but also to involve the spectator.

Theater directors played an unusually active role in the development of twentieth-century French theater. As David Bradby's *Modern French Drama, 1940–1980* (1984) and Dorothy Knowles's *French Drama of the Inter-war Years, 1918–1939* (1967) explain, directors often collaborated closely with a single playwright, rewrote or adapted existing dramatic texts, and even composed their own works. With financial support from the French government, directors opened theaters in the provinces, produced contemporary plays, and subsidized first-time playwrights in an effort to remake theater into a popular art form, as it had been in the England of Shakespeare.

The roots of twentieth-century French drama lie in the Romantic theater. In the 1820s and 1830s, a generation of young, independent-minded theorists and playwrights, with Victor Hugo in the forefront, successfully broke with the neoclassical conventions that had dominated French dramatic literature for almost two hundred years. In his 1827 *Préface de Cromwell* (Preface to Cromwell), Hugo argued for a *mélange des genres* (blend of genres) instead of the strict division between comedy and tragedy. He also rejected the classical unities of time, place, and action, as well as the notion of *bienséance* (decorum), which set strict limits on the type of actions that could take place onstage. His verse plays, with their sets, costumes, and characters drawn from history rather than Greek mythology, did much to create a popular audience for theater in France.

Later, in the 1840s, at the decline of the Romantic movement, the *pièces bien faites* (well-made plays) of Eugène Scribe and Victorien Sardou shifted the focus of drama from character development to plot construction, while in the 1880s André Antoine's Théâtre Libre (Free Theater) introduced radically realistic topics, decors, and acting techniques. Maurice Maeterlinck's symbolist plays, such as his well-known *Pelléas et Mélisande* (1892; translated 1894), integrated scenery, music, dance, and dialogue. According to Knowles, beginning in the 1890s, Paul Fort's Théâtre d'Art (Theater of Art) countered realistic drama with a theater of aesthetics and ideas. Throughout the nineteenth century, innovations in written plays and in methods of play production freed French theater from the strictures of neoclassicism and prepared readers and audiences for a truly revolutionary theatrical experience. Finally, as if to signal that the new century would feature even more audacious approaches to theater, in 1896 Alfred Jarry offered his *Ubu Roi* (1896, Ubu the King; translated, 1951) to the Parisian public. This farce filled with vulgar language and nonsensical events was consciously designed to shock and anger its audience, and it paved the way for the absurdist theater of the 1950s.

In the early years of the twentieth century, Paris was the center of French intellectual life, including drama. According to Knowles, two distinct categories of theater dominated the capital: the state-subsidized Comédie-Française and the commercial *théâtres du boulevard* (boulevard theaters). More than an outlet for creative works, the Comédie-Française was an educational institution concerned with preserving France's cultural patrimony. As such, it specialized in staging European masterpieces of the past performed by classically trained actors. It neither sought out nor welcomed young French playwrights. Meanwhile, serious modern plays could not find a market in boulevard theaters, which offered light entertainment to middle-class audiences more interested in attractive sets and clever acting than in intellectual stimulation.

This situation changed after 1910, however, with the advent of a new theatrical avant-garde composed of aspiring directors, most of whom had been actors. Jacques Copeau founded the first of the studio theaters, the Théâtre du Vieux Colombier, in Paris's Latin Quarter in 1913, with the intention of countering both the profit-seeking boulevard theaters and the state theater. According to Bradby and Knowles, Copeau hired actors with no background in the classical traditions, trained them for versatility in the interpretation of texts, created simple sets with symbolic decors, and staged plays that made the audience think. His repertory included classical Greek and Elizabethan drama as well as the works of modern foreign playwrights and contemporary French authors. The *Cartel des quatre* (Cartel of Four) of Charles Dullin, Louis Jouvet, Georges Pitoëff, and Gaston Baty followed his example in the 1920s. In their small, independent theaters, they experimented not only with new texts and acting techniques but also with the shape of the stage, lighting, and the integration of music, dance, and sculpture into their productions. At this time theaters became known for their directors. The director became the interpreter of texts, a creative artist equal to the playwright. These directors and their independent theaters produced some permanent changes in the French theatrical world by forming an audience eager for intellectually challenging plays and by creating a need for original works that encouraged young writers. Hence, in this case innovative writers followed the lead of innovative directors.

The period between World War I and World War II also featured the influence of foreign theatrical traditions and playwrights on French theater. Dissatisfied with the restrictions on audience involvement produced by the proscenium stage–the traditional stage area located between the curtain and the orchestra–directors tried open stages in the manner of Elizabethan England. The Balinese theater, a total theatrical experience that brought music, dance, and gesture into play, greatly influenced Antonin Artaud, the most important French theoretician of drama of the early twentieth century. Similarly, Paul Claudel was greatly affected by Asian theater. Additionally, influential works by the contemporary Italian playwright Pirandello appeared on the French stage as early as the 1920s. Pirandello's uses of the contrast between appearance and reality and the play within the play provided fresh approaches for the French theater, as did the German Brecht's notion of a theater of alienation in the 1950s. Foreign models suggested new possibilities and stimulated a willingness to experiment among French dramatists.

Many playwrights of the interwar years found their subjects in contemporary intellectual movements. A spirit of revolt against bourgeois values and rationality characterized the Dadaism and Surrealism that inspired Guillaume Apollinaire, Roger Vitrac, Artaud, and the early theater of Jean Cocteau. Jules Romains translated his Unanimist philosophy into plays about the formation of group identities, while François Mauriac's theater takes up Sigmund Freud's theories of the subconscious. Claudel's Christian dramas belong to the *renouveau catholique* (Catholic revival) that began in the 1870s and continued until World War II. Claudel's works also demonstrate the persistence of symbolist thought, as does the *théâtre de l'inexprimé* (theater of the unspoken), a drama of suggestion and emotion that elicited considerable interest in the 1920s. Other dramatists foreshadow existentialist thought of the 1940s. Armand Salacrou and Jean Anouilh, for example, both wrote about the human condition as well as the conflict between the individual and society.

Among the other important trends of this period is what Knowles calls the literary or "well-written" play. Jean Giraudoux, perhaps the most noteworthy French playwright of the 1930s, composed works whose principal value lay in their poetic language and the verve of the dialogue. Claudel offers another instance of such a playwright. His verse allegories were too lengthy to be produced in their original versions and were first read and admired for their poetry. Yet, other playwrights of this kind, such as Cocteau, clearly wrote with performance in mind. Cocteau incorporated sets by Pablo Picasso and music by Erik-Alfred-Leslie Satie and Igor Fyodorovich Stravinsky to create a complete artistic spectacle. A final theatrical genre of this period worth noting is the revival of the *comédie de moeurs* (comedy of manners), which explores social relations. The Provençal writer Marcel Paul Pagnol is a master of this form, especially in his plays about life in Marseille that were later adapted for the cinema.

One of the most revolutionary figures of the interwar years was Artaud, an actor, director, playwright, and theoretician. Heir to the ambitions of the nineteenth-century poet Jean-Nicolas-Arthur Rimbaud, Artaud rejected the entire Western tradition of drama, which he considered corrupted by bourgeois morality and rationality, in favor of a total theater of sound, gesture, and visual shock. His concept of a *théâtre de la cruauté* (theater of cruelty) envisioned the theatrical performance as a powerful ritual, in the manner of a magic spell or primitive religious ceremony, capable of transforming the audience spiritually. Although Artaud's ideas influenced Parisian director Jean-Louis Barrault in the 1940s, according to Bradby, his radical theories were not really understood or accepted in France until the 1950s.

The defeat of France at the beginning of World War II and the ensuing Nazi Occupation of the country had consequences for the French theater, as well as for every other aspect of French life. Except for the beginning of the Occupation, theaters remained open, and they continued to attract audiences from every class of French society as people sought both relief from the horrors of war and a communal experience in a time of isolation. Many important dramatists of the 1920s and 1930s, such as Anouilh, Cocteau, Claudel, and Giraudoux, continued to write for the stage. They were joined by the novelists Henry de Montherlant, Jean-Paul Sartre, and Albert Camus, who now tried their hands at playwriting. During this period there was a predilection for subjects drawn from Greek literature that is partially explained by German censorship. However, plays featuring characters and situations from classical mythology often included barely veiled references to World War II or Nazi tyranny. In fact, French drama from 1940 to 1945, like the clandestinely published poetry of the same period, offers many examples of politically committed literature.

Another important phenomenon of the war years was the emergence of plays that concentrated on metaphysics rather than psychology. Both Sartre and Camus wrote works that staged their philosophies, with characters and situations embodying existentialist and absurdist concepts. Surprisingly, many of these plays revived the unities of time, place, and action from the tradition of neoclassical tragedy, but they also borrowed techniques of the nineteenth-century melodrama, such as exaggerated characters and surprise events. Sartre's plays, especially, were successful in interesting the Parisian public in the importance of responsibility, choice, revolt, and action in the search for an authentic life.

The modern French plays that have attracted the most attention appeared in the 1950s. The works of this period have been called variously "avant-garde theater," "the theater of the absurd," "the new French theater," "experimental theater," and even "antitheater." All of these terms are valid. These plays were avant-garde because they provided future playwrights with models of a theater that depended much less on dialogue and story line than had classical or realist theater. They were absurd in the sense that their predominant theme is the struggle to give meaning to human existence in an irrational world. They are antitheater since they forgo the staples of all traditional theater—character development, conflict, plot, suspense, revelation. Often nothing happens over the course of these plays, or actions repeat themselves. Characters have no individual personality, or they disintegrate physically or emotionally, or they metamorphose into someone else. Rebelling against Molière's dictum that the first rule of all theater is to please, these writers often angered audiences with the illogical nature of their plays. Additionally, they sometimes berated the audience, and even attacked the spectators, either with loud noises and unpleasant scenes or by actually venturing into their midst. Since few of these playwrights were trained in the theater, they relied on new and unusual models of performance, including the circus, mime, vaudeville, cinema, religious rituals, and even language textbooks. The results were a transformation of French theater and, eventually, of theater throughout the Western world.

The four most important French dramatists of this avant-garde are Beckett, Eugène Ionesco, Arthur Adamov, and Jean Genet. Among these playwrights, only Genet is a native Frenchman. Beckett was born in Ireland and had published poetry and novels in English before deciding to write his first and most significant play, *En attendant Godot*, in French. Ionesco, a Romanian reared and educated in France, abandoned a university career for playwriting after being inspired, he claimed, by an English conversation manual. Adamov left his birthplace in Russia to immigrate to Paris as a teenager. A friend and student of Artaud, Adamov first wrote plays that plunge the reader into nightmare worlds. Meanwhile, Frenchman Genet was an orphan and criminal who also wrote fiction before attempting theatrical works. His prototype was the Catholic Mass, and he insisted upon ritual and alienation. All four dramatists are different, yet they share common characteristics, especially a preoccupation with language, a critique of rational thinking, and reflections on what constitutes drama. Many lesser playwrights of the 1950s and 1960s, including Fernando Arrabal, Jacques Audiberti, Marguerite Duras, Michel de Ghelderode, Henri Pichette, Georges Elias Schéhadé, Jean Tardieu, and Boris Vian, demonstrate affinities in theme or technique with these four great innovators of French drama, and they also deserve recognition as noteworthy contributors to the midcentury avant-garde.

A combination of circumstances explains why Paris became the mecca for new theater in the 1950s. After the liberation of France at the end of World War II, writers fleeing from politically repressive states, such as fascist Spain and communist Eastern Europe, flocked to Paris. The experience of life under a totalitarian regime had brought home the value of intellectual freedom and stimulated the impulse for revolutionary changes. Consequently, a desire to experiment was in the air. Although the avant-garde dramatists worked independently rather than as a school of artists, they shared this general outlook and attitude. Existentialism, with its emphasis on action and choice, certainly contributed to the willingness of these playwrights to take risks. As in the interwar period, Parisian theatrical directors played a key role in the popularization of new drama without regard for financial success or concern about unfavorable reviews. Their unflagging support of nontraditional authors succeeded in arousing interest in difficult and odd dramatic texts. The fame of these texts soon spread to England and America. Hence, the collaboration between playwrights and directors again forged artistic triumphs that could not have been realized by the playwrights alone.

Around the time that avant-garde theater became recognized in Paris, other movements began to encourage theatrical life in the provinces. According to Bradby, beginning in 1947, the French cultural ministry revived a plan conceived before World War II for decentralizing artistic life through the creation of *centres dramatiques nationaux* (national dramatic centers). In this plan, an economic collaboration between the ministry in Paris and the mayoralties of large provincial cities encouraged experienced theatrical directors to establish theaters and permanent acting troupes in areas formerly served only by traveling companies. By 1952 five such centers had been set up in Alsace, Saint-Etienne, Rennes, Toulouse, and Aix-en-Provence. Other centers emerged during the later 1950s. Notably, Lyon, the metropolis of southeastern France, became a hub of theatrical activity. In the 1960s the novelist André Malraux, cultural minister under President Charles de Gaulle, expanded this program through his *maisons de la culture* (community arts centers), which promoted music and the visual arts as well as theater. Regional centers did much to break the stronghold of Paris on French cultural life. An added benefit of decentralization was that provincial theaters offered the possibility for local playwrights, whose works could not find producers in Paris, to begin their careers.

Festivals further encouraged decentralization. As Bradby explains, in 1947 the Parisian director Jean Vilar inaugurated an outdoor festival in Avignon, a medieval city of lower Provence that had housed the Roman Catholic popes of the fourteenth century. Still immensely popular in the new millennium, this oldest and most prestigious of French summer festivals attracts both the local population and an international audience during the vacation period when Parisian theaters close. Acting troupes from throughout France perform contemporary works, at least a few by new playwrights, as well as European and American classics. Here theater also has proved to be a rallying point for all the creative arts, as drama and workshops on acting and literature are accompanied by music, dance, and street painters.

The popular-theater movement arose during roughly the same years as decentralization. According to Knowles, the idea of popular theater began, like decentralization, in the waning years of the Third Republic in the late 1930s, when both the central government and individual playwrights envisioned a type of drama with great popular appeal that would create a sense of community, especially among the urban masses. In 1920 the French government subsidized the establishment of the Théâtre National Populaire (National Popular Theater), or TNP, with the intention of providing low-cost performances by established theatrical troupes to the Parisian working classes. According to Knowles, the first director of TNP, Firmin Gémier, conceived of theater as a spectacle and incorporated athletic displays or circus acts into his productions. In the 1950s Vilar, the creator of the Avignon festival, took over the directorship of the TNP. Vilar brought plays into working-class Parisian districts in what Bradby has called "TNP weekends" that, along with the performance of plays, included inexpensive meals, lectures on dramatic literature, and music. Later, Vilar provided transportation to bring working-class audiences to his theater situated across from the Eiffel Tower. As Bradby explains, by the late 1960s there were two branches of the TNP, one in Paris and another at Villeurbanne, a suburb of Lyon, under the directorship of Roger Planchon, a disciple of Brecht and firm believer in decentralized theater. Alongside these national theaters, smaller theaters cropped up throughout the 1960s in the suburbs of Paris, where much of the working-class population of France lived.

One of the truly fascinating aspects of the popular-theater movement was its concentration on methods of performance rather than on the creation of new texts specifically written for a popular audience. For Gémier, as both Knowles and Bradby have pointed out, a theater for the masses meant a theater of massive means, full of entertainment and excitement. He felt that contemporary texts, such as avant-garde works, were not appropriate for such theater. Yet, Vilar and Planchon, on the contrary, often staged difficult French and foreign plays, contemporary as well as classical. They conceived of their goal as educational, and they attempted to render intellectually challenging plays comprehensible to a general audience of workers, the middle class, and students. Inevitably, however, the project of popular theater led to the composition of new plays that reflected contemporary interests and subjects.

Given the French experience of World War II and the leftist leanings of so many French intellectuals of the postwar years, it was inevitable that some dramatists turned to politics. The plays Sartre, Camus, and Anouilh had written during the Occupation already had political overtones. Sartre's works of the 1950s and 1960s, especially *Les Séquestrés d'Altona* (produced 1959, published 1960; translated as *Loser Wins,* 1960, and as *The Condemned of Altona,* 1961), discussed Marxism openly but always in a philosophical context. In the 1950s Brecht was highly regarded in France as a political playwright, and, according to Bradby, his theater was immensely popular in the provinces as well as in Paris. Yet, French dramatists were slow to write Brechtian political plays at this time, probably because the avant-garde, or absurdist, theater of this period was the dominant theatrical movement that overshadowed all other experiments. As Martin Esslin explains in *Theatre of the Absurd* (1969), this situation began to change after 1955, when Adamov altered the direction of his theater to reflect historical and political concerns, using the stage to condemn capitalism. Beginning in the late 1950s, other authors—including Michel Vinaver and the director-turned-playwright Planchon—also turned their attention to politics in plays on the history of colonialism and its effects on society. Their theater, grounded in real historical events with an emphasis on their social consequences, was far removed from the metaphysical concerns in the avant-garde works of a Beckett or Ionesco. Political theater continued to be developed through the 1960s and 1970s in the racially conscious plays of the Martinican Aimé Césaire. Such politically committed literature, often inspired by Marxism, deserves more attention from an international audience than it has received thus far. Perhaps because these plays focus mainly on French history and French social problems, they have seemed less worthy of attention outside of France. However, this drama may represent the only successful attempts anywhere in the Western world at a theater of socialist realism, the type of literature envisioned by the founders of the Soviet Union to spread the values of communism but that, ironically, took root in democratic France rather than in totalitarian Russia.

In May 1968 a general strike paralyzed France and provoked a great deal of reflection on the appropriate role of the artist in society. The theater was especially affected by *les événements de mai* (the events of May). According to Bradby, directors of popular theaters in Paris became conscious of the ethical dilemma posed by accepting money from the state to stage left-leaning political plays. Moreover, most French theaters operated in a way that was no model of equality. The director had become all-powerful. He chose texts, adapting them as he wished, controlled the actors' interpretations, designed sets, and managed finances. The crisis initiated by the general strike quickly gave rise to a new idea of theater, one that would be a group effort and truly democratic.

More than the work of any individual playwright, the *créations collectives* (collective creations) of the Théâtre du Soleil (Theater of the Sun) stand out as the most important innovation of the 1970s. Founded by Ariane Mnouchkine and university students from Paris, the Théâtre du Soleil was conceived as a radical experiment in theater. There were no stars; instead, all of the actors took turns playing important and minor roles. All members of the troupe received the same salary and were required to participate in menial tasks, such as housecleaning. Mnouchkine herself rejected the role of imperious director to become more of a coordinator of the troupe's efforts. The troupe members considered themselves artistic revolutionaries and composed their own, original scenarios on the French Revolution in an effort to bring actors and spectators together in an understanding of the historical roots of contemporary society. The performance of such plays was designed to be a transformative experience for the troupe and audience alike and one that might incite political action. According to Bradby, in an effort to demystify the theater and to wipe out the barrier between artist and spectator, actors dressed, applied makeup, and rehearsed in front of the audience, and they led spectators to their seats and engaged them in conversation during the play.

Hence, the Théâtre du Soleil's most important works, *1789* (1970) and *1793* (1973), were dramatic experiences rather than simple productions of plays. The *texts programmes* (text-programs) of *1789* and *1793* were the results of months of documentation and group work. Troupe members were required to read deeply in French history and attend historical lectures. Teams of actors then improvised scenes that concentrated on the people's experience of the Revolution and the Reign of Terror as well as on the rise of capitalism. The final text is a compilation of the successful improvisations that became the plays' scripts. As Bradby explains, large sections of the scripts actually transcribe the words of revolutionary figures drawn from historical documents of the period. These plays are truly collective works, not only composed by a community of actors but also bringing together voices from the past and present and inviting an active audience reaction. Quite unlike the sometimes incomprehensible, often alienating French avant-garde theater of the 1950s and 1960s, the Théâtre du Soleil offers an uplifting, communal experience, one that draws heavily from the popular traditions of farce and the circus.

The success of the Théâtre du Soleil did not, however, signal the demise of the individual author. To the contrary, the last three decades of the twentieth century in France featured the emergence of dozens of new playwrights in Paris and in the provinces. The openness and the push for innovation that have characterized French theater from the early 1900s are, in part, responsible for continuing to attract writers to the stage. Additionally, the French cultural ministries, especially those of the Fifth Republic, deserve a considerable share of the credit. Their program of decentralization, including their funding of regional and suburban theaters, directors, and acting troupes, and especially the subsidies they have awarded to first-time authors, have encouraged young artists to turn their talents to drama. French playwrights of the last third of the century often write novels and poetry as well as plays, and more and more commonly, they are moviemakers. Many women playwrights have emerged, including the novelists Duras and Natalie Sarraute.

While it is difficult to generalize about the varied playwrights who emerged at the end of the century, some of whom are in mid career at the beginning of the twenty-first century, it can be said that most are socially conscious. For their subject matter, many turn to contemporary history, including problems they trace to male domination, racism, anti-Semitism, colonialism, and capitalism. The *théâtre du quotidien* (theater of the everyday) of Jean-Paul Wenzel portrays the experience of ordinary life for working-class people who must struggle, often unconsciously, with the aftermath of wars, the breakdown of the family, and economic constraints. These plays differ from the political plays of Camus and Sartre in that they have no metaphysical bias and do not celebrate the individual will. Their appeal lies in their attempt to present ordinary people caught up in forces far beyond their control that have fashioned their personalities and their worlds. Such works demonstrate an abiding interest among French writers in drama that appeals to the general populace rather than an intellectual or artistic elite, and they suggest that the democratization of dramatic subjects will continue into the twenty-first century.

–*Mary Anne O'Neil*

Acknowledgments

This book was produced by Bruccoli Clark Layman, Inc. C. Bryan Love was the in-house editor. He was assisted by Penelope M. Hope and R. Bland Lawson.

Production manager is Philip B. Dematteis.

Administrative support was provided by Carol A. Cheschi.

Accountant is Ann-Marie Holland.

Copyediting supervisor is Sally R. Evans. The copyediting staff includes Phyllis A. Avant, Caryl Brown, Melissa D. Hinton, Philip I. Jones, Rebecca Mayo, and Nancy E. Smith.

Pipeline manager is James F. Tidd Jr.

Editorial associates are Elizabeth Leverton, Dickson Monk, and Timothy C. Simmons.

In-house vetter is Catherine M. Polit.

Permissions editor is Amber L. Coker. Permissions assistant is Crystal A. Gleim.

Layout and graphics supervisor is Janet E. Hill. The graphics staff includes Zoe R. Cook and Sydney E. Hammock.

Office manager is Kathy Lawler Merlette.

Photography editor is Mark J. McEwan.

Digital photographic copy work was performed by Joseph M. Bruccoli.

Systems manager is Donald Kevin Starling.

Typesetting supervisor is Kathleen M. Flanagan. The typesetting staff includes Patricia Marie Flanagan and Pamela D. Norton.

Library research was facilitated by the following librarians at the Thomas Cooper Library of the University of South Carolina: Elizabeth Suddeth and the rare-book department; Jo Cottingham, interlibrary loan department; circulation department head Tucker Taylor; reference department head Virginia W. Weathers; reference department staff Laurel Baker, Marilee Birchfield, Kate Boyd, Paul Cammarata, Joshua Garris, Gary Geer, Tom Marcil, Rose Marshall, and Sharon Verba; interlibrary loan department head Marna Hostetler; and interlibrary loan staff Bill Fetty and Nelson Rivera.

I wish to thank Catharine Brosman, who interested me initially in this project and guided me in its realization from start to finish. My daughter Anne O'Neil-Henry performed the Web and library searches that located many of the contributors. Student assistant Meredith Hyslop worked on the editing and formatting of the entries.

I would also like to thank the Camargo Foundation in Cassis, France, where I had the privilege of living as a fellow in 1995. The cultural opportunities offered by the foundation revived my fascination with modern French theater that had lapsed since my undergraduate days.

Dictionary of Literary Biography® • Volume Three Hundred Twenty-One

Twentieth-Century French Dramatists

Dictionary of Literary Biography

Arthur Surenovitch Adamov

(23 August 1908 – 15 March 1970)

Klaus Engelhardt
Lewis and Clark College

PLAY PRODUCTIONS: *La Grand et la petite manœuvre,* Paris, Théâtre des Noctambules, 11 November 1950;

L'Invasion, Paris, Studio des Champs-Elysées, 14 November 1950;

La Parodie, Paris, Théâtre Lancry, 5 June 1952;

Le Professeur Taranne, Lyons, Théâtre de la Comédie, 18 March 1953;

Le Sens de la marche, Lyons, Théâtre de la Comédie, 18 March 1953;

Tous contre tous, Paris, Théâtre de l'Œuvre, 1953;

Comme nous avons été, Paris, Théâtre de l'Œuvre, May 1954;

Le Ping-Pong, Paris, Théâtre des Noctambules, 3 March 1955;

Paolo Paoli, Lyons, Théâtre de la Comédie, 17 May 1957;

Les Ames mortes, adapted from Nikolai Vasil'evich Gogol's *Pokhozhdeniia Chichikova, ili Mertyve dushi,* Villeurbanne, Théâtre de la Cité, 22 January 1960;

Le Printemps 71, translated as *Spring '71,* London, Unity Theatre, June 1962; Saint-Denis, Théâtre Gérard Philipe, 26 April 1963;

La Politique des restes, London, Unity Theater, 1967; Saint-Denis, Théâtre Gérard Philipe, 1967;

M. le Modéré, Paris, Théâtre des Mathurins, September 1968;

Off Limits, Aubervilliers, Théâtre de la Commune, 18 January 1969;

Si l'été revenait, Vincennes, La Cartoucherie, 17 May 1972.

BOOKS: *L'Aveu* (Paris: Sagittaire, 1946); excerpt translated by Richard Howard as *The Endless Humilia-*

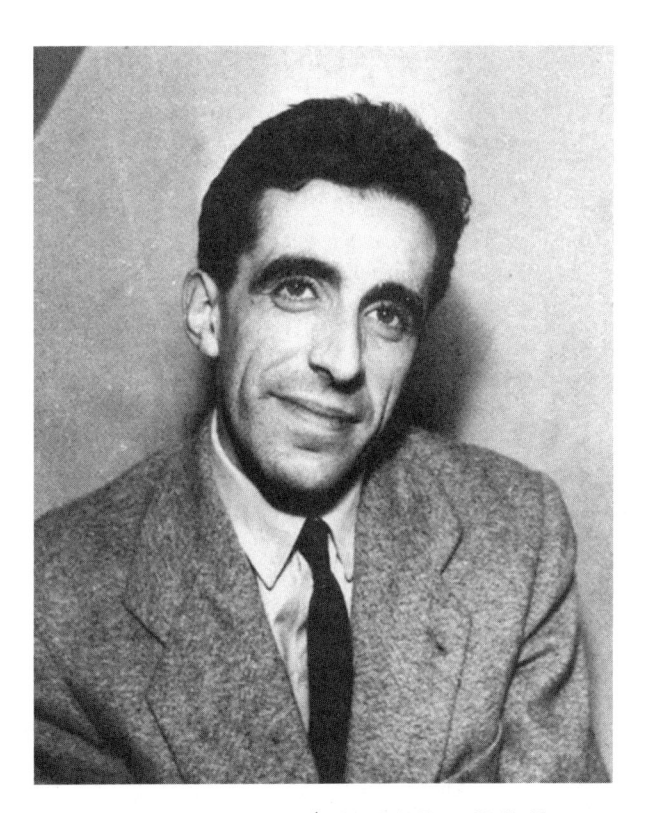

Arthur Surenovitch Adamov (© Lipnitzki/Roger-Viollet/Getty Images; from the frontispiece for John H. Reilly, Arthur Adamov, *1974; Thomas Cooper Library, University of South Carolina)*

tion, Evergreen Review, 2, no. 8 (Spring 1959): 64–95;

La Grande et la petite manœuvre (Paris: Cahiers de la Pléiade, 1950);

La Parodie; L'Invasion (Paris: Charlot, 1950); *L'Invasion* translated by Robert Doan as *The Invasion* (University Park: University of Pennsylvania Press, 1968);

Théâtre I (Paris: Gallimard, 1953)–comprises *La Parodie, L'Invasion, La Grande et la petite manœuvre, Le Professeur Taranne,* and *Tous contre tous; Le Professeur Taranne* translated by A. Bermel as *Professor Taranne,* in *Four Modern French Comedies,* introduction by Wallace Fowlie (New York: Putnam, 1960), pp. 127-149;

Théâtre II (Paris: Gallimard, 1955)–comprises *Le Sens de la marche, Les Retrouvailles,* and *Le Ping-Pong; Le Ping-Pong* translated by Richard Howard as *Ping Pong* (New York: Grove, 1959);

August Strindberg, dramaturge, by Adamov and Maurice Gravier (Paris: L'Arche, 1955);

Paolo Paoli (Paris: Gallimard, 1957); translated by Geoffrey Brereton as *Paolo Paoli: The Years of the Butterfly* (London: Calder, 1959);

Théâtre de Société (scènes d'actualité), by Adamov, Guy Demoy, and Maurice Regnaut (Paris: Editeurs français réunis, 1958)–comprises *Intimité, Je ne suis pas français,* and *La Complainte du ridicule;*

Les Ames mortes, adapted from Nikolai Vasil'evich Gogol's *Pokhozhdeniia Chichikova, ili Mertyve dushi* (Paris: Guilliarme, 1960); translated by Peter Mayer as *Dead Souls* (New York: Studio Duplicating Service, 1961);

Le Printemps 71 (Paris: Gallimard, 1961);

Ici et maintenant (Paris: Gallimard, 1964);

Théâtre III (Paris: Gallimard, 1966)–comprises *Paolo Paoli, La Politique des restes,* and *Sainte Europe;*

L'Homme et l'enfant (Paris: Gallimard, 1968); translated by Jo Levy as *Man and Child* (London & New York: Calder, 1991);

Théâtre IV (Paris: Gallimard, 1968)–comprises *M. le Modéré* and *Le Printemps 71;*

Antonin Artaud et le théâtre de notre temps (Paris: Gallimard, 1969);

Off Limits (Paris: Gallimard, 1969);

Je, ils (Paris: Gallimard, 1969);

Si l'été revenait (Paris: Gallimard, 1970).

PRODUCED SCRIPTS: *La Logeuse,* adapted from Fyodor Dostoevsky's *Khoziaika,* radio, Organisation de Radio Télévision Française 3, 9 December 1950;

Polly, adapted from John Gay's *Beggar's Opera,* radio, Organisation de Radio Télévision Française 3, 3 March 1951;

L'Eternel mari, adapted from Fyodor Dostoevsky's *Vechnyi muzh,* radio, Organisation de Radio Télévision Française 3, 19 January 1952;

Le Potier politicien, adapted from Ludvig Holberg's *Den politiske Kandstøber,* radio, Organisation de Radio Télévision Française 3, 5 July 1952;

La Parole est au poète, radio, by Adamov and Bernard Brecht, Organisation de Radio Télévision Française 3, 1952;

L'Agence universelle, radio, Organisation de Radio Télévision Française 3, 15 March 1953;

Lady Macbeth au village, adapted from Nikolai Leskov's *Ledi Makbet mtsenkogo uezda,* radio, Organisation de Radio Télévision Française 3, 30 April 1953;

Parallèlement, adapted from Georg Kaiser's *Nebeneinander,* radio, Organisation de Radio Télévision Française 3, 16 June 1954;

Les Trois Sœurs, adapted from Chekhov's *Tri sestry,* television, 1958;

L'Autre Rive, adapted from Ivan Goncharov's *Obryv,* radio, Organisation de Radio Télévision Française 3, 5 December 1959;

En fiacre, translated by Humphrey Hare, radio, BBC 3, 10 December 1959; original French version, radio, Organisation de Radio Télévision Française 3, 9 February 1963;

Pierre et Jean, adapted from Guy de Maupassant's *Pierre et Jean,* radio, Organisation de Radio Télévison Française 3, 13 February 1960;

Le Temps vivant, radio, Organisation de Radio Télévision Française 3, 12 January 1963;

Finita la commedia, radio, Organisation de Radio Télévision Française 3, 1 March 1964;

Du matin à minuit, adapted from Georg Kaiser's *Van morgens bis mitternachts,* television, Télévision Française 3, 17 October 1966;

La Mort d'Ivan Ilitch, adapted from Leo Tolstoy's *Smert' Ivana Il'icha,* German television, 1967;

La Cigale, adapted from Chekhov's *Kuznechitsa,* television, 1970;

Entretiens et théatre radiophonique, 5 CDs and 2 books, Marseille, Dimanche, 1997.

OTHER: Claudine Chonez, *Il est tempts,* edited by Adamov (Rodez: Les Feuillets de l'Ilot, 1941);

August Strindberg, *Inferno,* preface by Adamov (Paris: Griffon, 1947);

Roger Gilbert-Lecomte, *Testament: poèmes et textes en prose,* introduction by Adamov (Paris: Gallimard, 1955);

La Commune de Paris, 18 mars–28 mai 1871: anthologie, edited by Adamov (Paris: Editions sociales, 1959);

"Une Pièce progressiste quand même," in *Connaissance de Don Ramón María del Valle-Inclan* (Paris: Julliard, 1963), pp. 56-58.

TRANSLATIONS: Carl Jung, *Le Moi et l'inconscient* (Paris: Gallimard, 1938);

Rainer Maria Rilke, *Le Livre de la pauvreté et de la mort* (Alger: Charlot, 1941);

Georg Büchner, *La Mort de Danton* (Paris: Le Monde illustré, 1948);

Büchner, *Theatre Complet*, translated by Adamov and Marthe Robert (Paris: L'Arche, 1953);

Heinrich von Kleist, *La Cruche cassée, Théâtre populaire*, 6 (March–April 1954): 49–92;

August Strindberg, *Le Pélican*, translated by Adamov and C. G. Bjurström, *Théâtre populaire*, 17 (1 March 1956): 37–62;

Nikolai Vasil'evich Gogol, *Les Ames mortes: ou les aventures de Tchitchikov* (Lausanne: La Guilde du livre, 1956);

Maksim Gor'ky, *Les Ennemis, Théâtre populaire*, 27 (November 1957): 33–58; 28 (January 1958): 27–75;

Anton Pavlovich Chekhov, *L'Esprit des bois* (Paris: Gallimard, 1958);

Gogol, *Le Revizor*, in *Répertoire pour un théâtre populaire*, volume 14 (Paris: Arche, 1958);

Strindberg, *Le Père*, in *Répertoire pour un théâtre populaire*, volume 17 (Paris: L'Arche, 1958);

Gor'ky, *La Mère* (Paris: Club Français du livre, 1958);

Gor'ky, *Vazna Geleznova (seconde version)* (Paris: L'Arche, 1958);

Chekhov, *Théâtre* (Paris: Club Français du livre, 1958);

Gor'ky, *Les Petits bourgeois, L'Avant-Scène*, 206 (15 October 1959);

Ivan Aleksandrovich Goncharov, *Oblomov* (Paris: Club Français du livre, 1959);

Gogol, *Cinq Récits* (Paris: Club des libraires de France, 1961);

Erwin Piscator, *Le Theatre politique*, translated by Adamov and Claude Sebisch (Paris: L'Arche, 1962);

Strindberg, *La Sonate des spectres* (Paris: L'Arche, 1962);

Gor'ky, *Theatre complet*, 4 volumes, translated by Adamov and others (Paris: L'Arche, 1963–1964);

Fyodor Dostoevsky, *Crime et Châtiment* (Paris: Club Français du livre, 1964);

Max Frisch, *La Grande Muraille*, translated by Adamov and Jacqueline Autrusseau (Paris: Gallimard, 1969);

Chekhov, *Ivanov: (Suivi de) La mouette,* revised, with an introduction, by Michel Cadot (Paris: Flammarion, 1996).

SELECTED PERIODICAL PUBLICATIONS–UNCOLLECTED: *Le Désordre, Eléments*, 1 (1 January 1951): 25–37;

Comme nous avons été, La Nouvelle Revue Francaise, 1, no. 3 (1 March 1953): 431–445; translated by Richard Howard as *As We Were, Evergreen Review*, 1, no. 4 (1957): 113–126;

Les Apolitiques, La Nouvelle Critique, 101 (December 1958): 124–131;

"De quelques faits," *Théâtre populaire*, 46 (1962): 46–60;

En fiacre, L'Avant-Scène, 294 (1 September 1963): 39–46.

Although he has been eclipsed in reputation by Eugène Ionesco and Samuel Beckett, Arthur Surenovitch Adamov was among the first to embrace the theater of the absurd that emerged in Parisian theater repertories in the early 1950s. Adamov's early plays implement Antonin Artaud's advice of doing away with the traditional "psychological" theater and facile entertainment offered to the educated, theatergoing bourgeoisie. Barely situated in time and space, Adamov's plays are meant to articulate, in a way that might be described as autotherapeutic, Adamov's own neuroses and nightmarish obsessions, some of which he confessed in his autobiographical work *L'Aveu* (1946, The Confession): "Je veux en ces pages, faire à la fois le proces et l'apologie de la névrose . . . Apologie de la névrose qui donne à sa victime une lucidité suraiguë–inaccessible à l'homme dit normal" (I would like, in these pages . . . to justify the neurosis that . . . grants the victim a peracute lucidity, inaccessible to the so-called normal) (translation by Martin Esslin).

In 1955, however, Adamov began criticizing and rejecting some of his early plays. He took a new direction, addressing social and political issues in a way that placed him, both in ideology and dramatic technique, within the realm of Bertolt Brecht's left-leaning epic theater. This period of Adamov's career includes plays ranging from the dream-based *Le Professeur Taranne* (produced and published in 1953; translated as *Professor Taranne*, 1960), a forerunner of *littérature engagée* (committed literature), and *Le Printemps 71* (Spring '71; published 1961, produced 1963), an historical tableau of the Paris Commune of 1871. In his later plays, up to and including *Sainte Europe* (1966, Holy Europe), Adamov combines the psychological elements of his earlier plays with historical and social themes, but he also makes increasing use of satire and parody, placing himself at an ironic distance from his characters.

Besides his production as a playwright, Adamov published a series of translations ranging from Carl Jung's *Le Moi et l'inconscient* (1938, The Id and the Unconscious) to the complete dramatic works of August Strindberg, Maksim Gor'ky, and Anton Chekhov. Additionally, Adamov is credited with approximately twenty radio plays, most adaptations of works by writers such as Chekhov, Fyodor Dostoevsky, Nikolai Leskov, Georg Kaiser, Ivan Goncharov, Guy de Maupassant, Leo Tolstoy, John Gay, Ludwig Hol-

Scene from a 1955 performance of Adamov's Le Ping-Pong *at Théâtre des Noctambules (photo by Bernard; from* Ici et maintenant, *1964; Thomas Cooper Library, University of South Carolina)*

berg, and Jules Vallès. Adamov's choice of writers for his translations and adaptations reveals some of his literary interests. Other keys to understanding Adamov's dramatic oeuvre lie in his autobiographical works, including *L'Aveu, L'Homme et l'enfant* (1968; translated as *Man and Child,* 1991), and *Je, ils* (1969, I, They); in his critical essays collected in *Ici et maintenant* (1964, Here and Now); and in the various prefaces and *notes preliminaries* (preliminary notes) to the four-volume Gallimard edition of his plays. These works provide windows into the mind of a complicated and innovative artist.

Arthur Surenovitch Adamov was born on 23 August 1908 at Kislovodsk, in the Caucasus region. His father, Sourene Adamov, was a wealthy Armenian businessman, owner of several oil wells on the shores of the Caspian Sea near Baku; his mother was Helene Bagaturov Adamov. Adamov was cared for by a French governess and from childhood spoke both Russian and French. The first book he read was Honoré de Balzac's *Eugénie Grandet* (1833; translated as *Eugenia Grandet,* 1843), initiating him to a literature he would come to know intimately and consider his own.

At the outbreak of World War I, the Adamov family traveled in the Black Forest region in southwestern Germany. Although they were citizens of Russia, an enemy state, and therefore faced the threat of immediate internment, they were able to use their political connections to escape to Geneva. Since the Russian Revolution, Geneva had become the refuge of many Russian emigrant families, but Adamov never warmed to the milieu. In 1918 the Soviet Union "socialized"–or confiscated–the entire estate of Adamov's family. Their only source of income was the gradual sale of their portable possessions, such as jewelry. Impoverished, the family decided to move to Wiesbaden, Germany, in 1922, and Adamov was enrolled in the International French Lycée at Mainz.

In 1924 the Adamov family relocated to Paris. During the 1920s and 1930s the French capital teemed with literary and artistic talent and activity. Many young writers and artists were interacting in literary circles, many of them committed to Surrealist experiments and other innovative techniques and styles. Still in high school, Adamov mingled with this milieu, frequenting, among other places, the Dôme (Dome), a café-restaurant, where he was able to associate with many young artists and intellectuals, including Paul Eluard, André Breton, Roger Blin, and Alberto Giacometti.

Perhaps the most influential among the artists that Adamov encountered was Artaud. Inspired by the performance of a Balinese theater group that visited Paris in 1931, Artaud dismissed Western "literary" theater. He sought to establish drama as an autonomous medium of artistic expression and metaphysical significance, emphasizing dialogue as only one component among many, including costumes, acting, lighting, colors, sounds, dance, pantomime, and stage props. In his seminal work *Le Théâtre et son double* (1938; translated as *The Theater and Its Double,* 1958), Artaud tried to restore to the theater its metaphysical meaning by invoking its origins in religion and magic: "lier le théâtre aux possibilities de l'expression par les formes, et par tout ce qui est gestes, bruits, couleurs, plastiques, etc., c'est le rendre à sa destination primitive, c'est le replacere dans son aspect religieux et métaphysique, c'est le réconcilier avec l'univers" (to tie the theater to the possibilities of expressing itself through forms and through all that is gestures, noises, colors, plastic forms, etc., is to return it to its primary destination, to place it back into its religious and metaphysical dimension, to reconcile it with the universe). Adamov's relationship with Artaud was such that when Artaud was confined to a mental hospital in Rodez for four years, Adamov raised funds among his fellow artists and friends in order to have Artaud released in 1943.

After several false starts, including dabbling in Surrealist poetry and editing the short-lived avant-garde review *Discontinuité* (Discontinuity), the only issue of which appeared in June 1928, Adamov did not publish for several years. Meanwhile, the notoriously truant high-school student grew into a problem-ridden, neurotic young adult. Unable to establish physical relationships with women, he acted out his sexual obsessions and his fetishism in brothels and in the back alleys of Paris. According to *L'Homme et l'enfant,* at the age of twenty he attempted suicide for the first time: "je joue au suicide, me jette sous un taxi, me relève à temps" (I pretend to commit suicide, throw myself under a cab, get up in time). In 1933 Adamov's father committed suicide while Adamov was asleep in the adjacent room. Twenty-five years later, in *L'Homme et l'enfant,* Adamov noted: "Je détestais mon père, c'est donc moi qui l'ai tué. Pendant au moins une année, j'en étais sûr. Je ne suis pas jusqu'à présent sûr du contraire" (I detested my father; hence it is I who killed him. For at least one year I was certain of it. Until this day I am not certain of the contrary).

Although Adamov was not an active member of the French Resistance during World War II, he was briefly interned by the Nazis at Argelès on two separate occasions. After the war and before Adamov made his mark as a playwright, he published an astonishingly clear-sighted, analytical confession of his years of anguish: *L'Aveu.* This "avowal" renders more than a frank account of his unsavory personal lifestyle—written in clear, rational language, it constitutes an attempt to deal with the psychological problems that haunted him, and it provides indispensable clues for the understanding of his life and early work. The titles of the four chapters of *L'Aveu* convey a general idea of its gist and tenor: "Ce qu'il y a" (What Is), "L'Humiliation sans fin" (The Endless Humiliation), "Le Temps de l'ignominie" (The Time of Ignominy), "Journal terrible" (Terrible Journal). Esslin says of *L'Aveu* that this "small book . . . must be among the most terrifying and ruthless documents of self-revelation in the whole of world literature," but "in this document of ruthless self-revelation, Adamov outlined a whole philosophy of the theater of the absurd, long before he started to write his first play." Inside the dust jacket of *Je, ils,* Adamov calls *L'Aveu* the secret place of his work, a little bit like its water closet.

Adamov was also influenced by the works of Strindberg. He explains Strindberg's importance in the essay "August Strindberg, dramaturge" (1955) and in the preliminary note to *Théâtre II* (1955, Theater II): "Il y a dix ans que j'ai commencé à écrire pour le théâtre. Les véritables raisons de mon choix, je les connais mal. . . . Tout ce que je veux dire, c'est qu'à cette époque je lisais beaucoup Strindberg—notamment *Le Songe,* dont la grande ambition m'avait aussitôt séduit" (I began writing for the theater ten years ago. I don't know the real reasons for this choice. . . . All I can say is that, at that time, I was reading a lot of Strindberg—especially *The Dream,* whose great ambition seduced me). The influence of Strindberg, especially his *Ett droemspel* (1901; translated as *A Dream Play,* 1912–1916), accounts for the dreamlike atmosphere that is the hallmark of all of Adamov's absurdist plays. Additionally, Adamov owed a great deal to Russian writers such as Chekhov, Nikolai Vasil'evich Gogol, and Gor'ky. With Chekhov he shares the frequent use of indirect dialogue. His link to Gor'ky is their communist-inspired ideology. Finally, Gogol's strategic distribution of characters and his technique of matching character flaws with various trades and occupations is mirrored in Adamov's *Paolo Paoli* (produced and published 1957; translated as *Paolo Paoli: The Years of the Butterfly,* 1959).

Adamov emerged on the dramatic scene in 1950. That year two plays by Adamov, *La Parodie* (The Parody, produced 1952) and *L'Invasion* (translated as *The Invasion,* 1968), were published with endorsements by such illustrious personalities as André Gide, Jacques Lemarchand, Jean Vilar, René Char, Roger Blin, Henri Thomas, and Jacques Prévert. These endorsements were meant to augment the chances of the plays' being picked up by a Parisian theater director. The first of Adamov's plays to be performed on stage, however, was *La Grande et la petite manœuvre* (1950, The Big and the Little Maneuver). Adamov's emergence at this time indicates that he belongs to the very first generation to create absurdist theater in France. Ionesco's groundbreaking *La Cantatrice chauve* (translated as *The Bald Soprano* and *The Bald Prima Donna,* 1958) premiered in May 1950, preceding *La Grande et la petite manœuvre* by only six months. Ionesco's *La Leçon* (translated as *The Lesson,* 1958) was staged in February 1951, and Beckett's classic *En attendant Godot* (translated as *Waiting for Godot,* 1954) followed in January 1953.

All of Adamov's absurdist plays—*La Parodie, L'Invasion, La Grande et la petite manœuvre, Tous contre tous* (1953, All against All), and *Le Sens de la marche* (1953, The Direction of the March)—are set in the context of an oppressive police state, but Adamov carefully avoids any direct allusion to the Nazi-friendly Vichy Regime or the German occupation of northern France. He does, however, acknowledge that social unrest is afoot, caused by the presence of too many refugees streaming into the country. The closest Adamov comes to a political statement is in *Tous contre tous,* where the alien refugees can be recognized by an external sign, namely the fact that they all limp. In keeping with Artaud's theories, the refugees' "otherness" is not based on their mental structures or on their language, but on *physical* characteristics, a theatrical device that every spectator can see and understand. In the preliminary note of *Théâtre II,* Adamov freely acknowledges that "les réfugiés, en fin de compte, sont tout de même les Juifs" (the refugees, in the final analysis, are, of course, the Jews) who fled to France from the Holocaust in large numbers. Adamov's emphasis on the physical differences, as well as the revolutionary agitation of *Tous contre tous*, constitutes what Esslin identifies as "la petite manoeuvre," the external part of the self that can be "cured" by social action. However, Adamov's main focus, especially in his earlier plays, is the "grande manoeuvre," the private psychic dilemmas and obsessions of his characters and the inevitability of death–the aspect of the human condition that remains essentially "incurable."

In *La Parodie*, a wall-mounted clock without hands, ever increasing in size, suspends time, much like Ionesco's unpredictable clock in *La Cantatrice chauve*. In contrast, the space in which the action takes place grows smaller as the play progresses, creating a sense of imprisonment or claustrophobia. Over the course of the play the spectator is confronted with a group of individuals who have little in common and essentially fail to communicate with each other. Two contrasting protagonists, N. and the Employee, pursue the same woman, named Lili, who remains indifferent to both of them. The Employee is constantly trying–and failing–to set up dates with her, whereas N. awaits her passively, lying indolently in the street. In the end he is run over by a car, and his body is disposed of by garbage collectors. Ultimately, while both the activist and his indolent counterpart seek the same goal, neither is rewarded with success, establishing a pattern of failure found in many of Adamov's subsequent plays.

Not only is the plot of *La Parodie* unconventional, but N. and the Employee, conceived as archetypal abstractions, do not invite the spectator to identify with them. Nevertheless, in *La Parodie*, as in later plays, Adamov identified with the inactive role that often leads to physical destruction. As he explains in *Théâtre II*: "Ceci dit, *La Parodie* n'a pas été seulement pour moi une tentative de justification (j'ai beau être comme N., je ne serai plus puni que l'Employé), mas aussi un acte de rébellion" (For me, *La Parodie* was not only a tentative act of self-justification [I may well be like N., I will not be punished any more than the Employee], it was also an act of rebellion).

The dialogue of *La Parodie*, which features everyday language, is dispassionate and consists of short, flat, and often incomplete sentences. As Adamov explains in *Théâtre II*:

> je découvrais, dans les scènes les plus quotidiennes, en particulier celles de la rue, des scènes de théâtre. Ce qui me frappait alors surtout, c'était le défilé des passants, la solitude dans le cotoîement, l'effrayante diversité des propos, dont je me plaisais à n'entendre que des bribes,
> celles-ci me semblant constituer, liées à d'autres bribes, un ensemble dont le caractère fragmentaire garantissait la vérité symbolique.

> (I discovered in the most common, everyday scenes, especially those occurring in the streets, scenes of the theater. What struck me above all was pedestrians passing each other, the solitude in their encounters, the frightening diversity of their speech of which I heard only fragments. These fragments, tied together with others, seemed to constitute new groupings whose fragmentary character guaranteed their symbolic truth.)

A similar approach to language is found in portions of Ionesco's drama.

Published with *La Parodie*, *L'Invasion* shares many features with its companion piece. The plot centers on the members of one family. One of the characters, Pierre, is trying to sort the unpublished manuscripts of his deceased brother-in-law, Jean. Pierre has to contend with ownership claims by Jean's family. In the meantime, Pierre's wife Agnes leaves him temporarily for a virtual stranger, identified only as le Premier-venu (the first comer). This new relationship fails, however, and she returns to her husband in order to "borrow a typewriter." The subtext is that she would like to return to him, but she never actually conveys this critical message. Adamov explains in *Théâtre II* that he initially took pride in having "invented" Pierre's wife's mode of indirect communication: "A fin de réussir la gageure, je cherchai désespérément des phrases-clefs qui, apparemment, se rapporteraient à la vie quotidienne, mais, au fond, signifieraient 'tout autre chose'" (In order to succeed in this wager, I looked with desperation for key-phrases that, apparently, would have to do with everyday language, but, in fact, would mean "something quite different"). Later, however, he admits having discovered "Que l'œuvre de Tchékhov . . . abonde en dialogues de ce genre, et que ces dialogues constituent même, pour une grande part, son originalité" (that Chekhov's work . . . abounds with dialogues of this kind, and that the latter constitute, in fact, a large part of [Chekhov's] originality). In the end Pierre fails to complete his project, tears up the manuscript pages that have "invaded" and disrupted his life, and commits suicide. While *L'Invasion* is a little more structured than *La Parodie*, both plays end in failure, leaving the audience without the satisfaction of a familiar, neatly resolved plot.

Adamov's first play to be seen on stage, *La Grande et la petite manœuvre*, is placed in a broader social context. As in both *La Parodie* and *L'Invasion*, the protagonists are two contrasting characters: le Militant (the Militant), who has overthrown a dictatorial regime only to assume dictatorial powers for himself, and le Mutilé

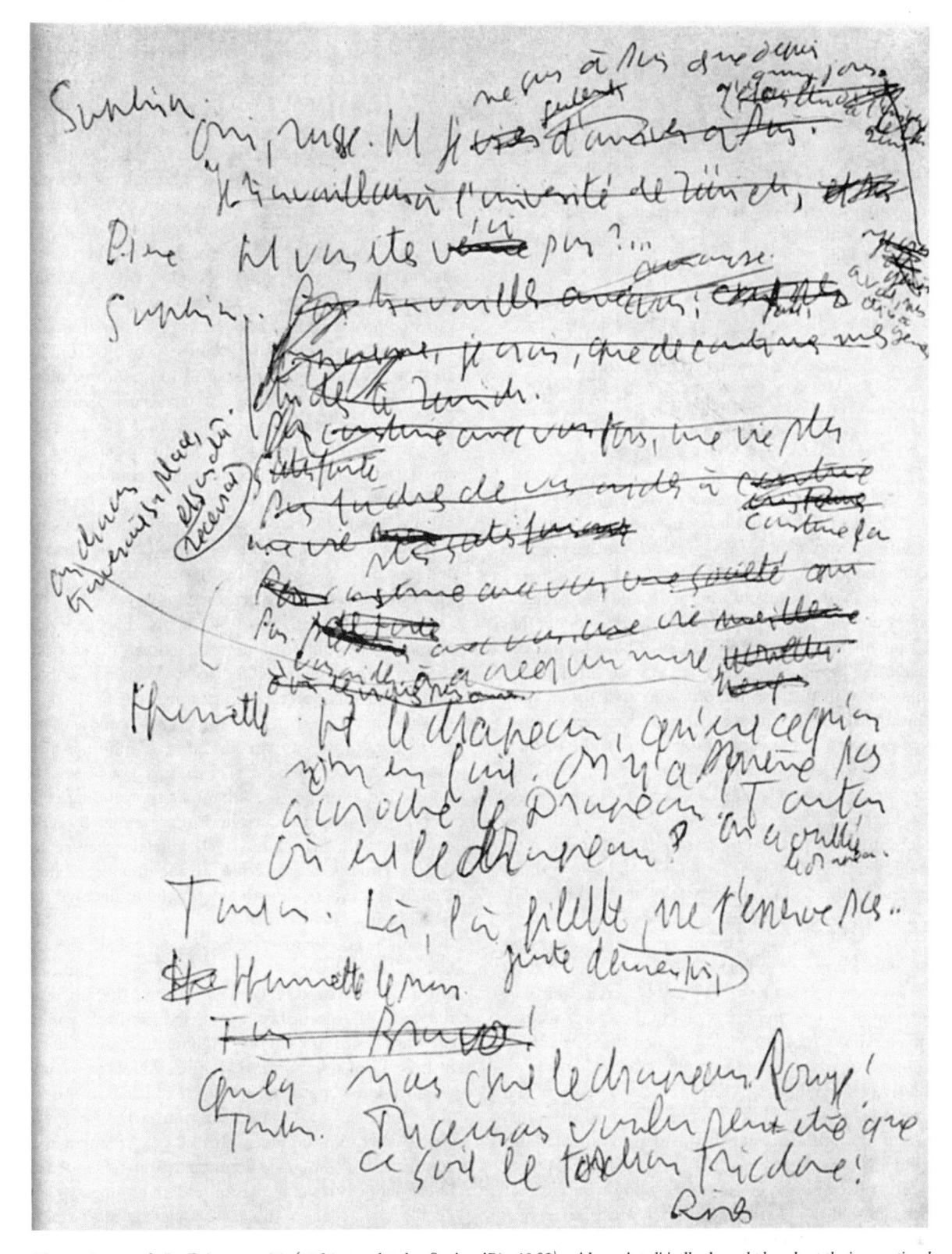

Manuscript page for Le Printemps 71 *(1961; translated as* Spring '71, *1962), Adamov's politically charged play about the insurrectional Paris government at the close of the Franco-Prussian War of 1870–1871 (from* Ici et maintenant, *1964; Thomas Cooper Library, University of South Carolina)*

(the Mutilated One). According to the author commentary in *Théâtre II,* le Mutilé reflects a frightening dream experienced by Adamov himself:

> j'étais assis sur un parapet devant la mer, en compagnie de ma soeur, ou plutôt d'une soeur; je savais que, d'un instant à l'autre, j'allais devoir la quitter pour obéir à un appel; quelque part, des Moniteurs m'attendaient pour m'imposer de terribles séances tenant à la fois de l'entraînement militaire et de la gymnastique, séances au terme desquelles je serai motile, puis détruit, je le savais
>
> (I was seated at a railing by the sea, accompanied by my sister. I knew that, from one moment to the next, I would have to leave in order to follow a call. Somewhere, "les Moniteurs" were expecting me, in order to subject me to some terrible training sessions, part military, part gymnastic. I knew that at the end of these sessions, I would be mutilated, then destroyed.)

Le Mutilé, who embodies Adamov's confessed indolence, is placed in this predicament: he follows a series of self-destructive commands given to him by mysterious supernatural authorities identified as les Moniteurs. They cause him to lose both his arms in a work-related accident and later push him into two car accidents that cost him his legs. Erna, the woman whose love could silence these pernicious voices and save le Mutilé from his masochist instincts, is the one who ends up pushing his mutilated body into the street and to his demise. Brecht and Strindberg used mutilation in some of their plays, but for Adamov mutilation becomes, among other things, a metaphor for his sexual impotence. As he explains in *L'Aveu:* "Tout ce que je sais de moi, c'est que je souffre. Et si je souffre c'est qu'à l'origine de moi-même il y a mutilation, séparation" (All I know about me is that I suffer. And if I suffer, it is because at the origin of myself lies mutilation, separation). As in his earlier plays, both protagonists of *La Grande et la petite manœuvre* are doomed to fail.

Adamov's next absurdist play, *Le Sens de la marche,* is very similar to its predecessors and therefore, according to Adamov, does not really broaden the scope of his work. For this reason, he severely criticizes the play. Similarly, although *Les Retrouvailles* (1955, The Reunion) extends Adamov's series of absurdist works, it too left the author dissatisfied. Adamov even admitted having consciously invented the dream that purportedly caused him to create the play. He observes that the images and the characters in *Les Retrouvailles* have a predetermined meaning and are therefore deprived of their effectiveness. On the other hand, writing *Les Retrouvailles* made him understand that it was time to move on: "je crois avoir, grâce aux *Retrouvailles,* liquidé tout ce qui, aprés m'avoir permis d'écrire, finissait par m'en empêcher" (Thanks to *Les Retrouvailles,* I believe to have liquidated everything that, having permitted me to write, ended up preventing me from doing so).

While he was engaged in writing *Le Sens de la marche,* Adamov interrupted his work in order to record one of his nightmares in the form of a play, *Le Professeur Taranne.* Adamov claims to have completed this play in two days and two nights. In the plot Professor Taranne is being accused of having undressed in front of children at a public beach. Interrogated by the police, he denies the charge, insisting that he is not only a respected member of the community but also a distinguished professor and researcher of "international" reputation. None of these claims can be confirmed. Instead, Taranne's contact and supposed host at a Belgian university sends him a letter accusing him of plagiarism. Additionally, a notebook that Taranne claims as his own contains mostly blank pages, and he is unable to decipher the entries it does contain. A further claim that Taranne is booked on an overseas cruise cannot be substantiated, either. Before the final curtain, Taranne is seen beginning to take off his clothes, which suggests that the original accusation may be accurate without, however, proving it irrefutably.

In *Théâtre II,* Adamov claims that *Le Professeur Taranne* sent him in a new direction. Transcribing a dream without altering the least detail did not allow him to introduce archetypal characters who share in his private obsessions or to use the play to demonstrate any particulars of the human condition. Taranne is a three-dimensional person who may or may not be an exhibitionist and an impostor. Adamov's typical dual complementary protagonists are here represented by a single character with a complex psychological structure. In the dream Taranne is identical with the dreamer. The only change Adamov claims to have made to his own dream is replacing the original sentence he uttered in the dream: "Je suis l'auteur de *La Parodie!*" (I am the author of *La Parodie!*) with "Je suis le Professeur Taranne!" (I am Professor Taranne!). Beyond that, the language of the play is ostensibly a transcription of what the dreamer heard himself say, untainted by any didactic or technical consideration. Taranne, therefore, is not an allegory but a character with a life of his own. Additionally, because of Adamov's approach, *Le Professeur Taranne* became the first of his plays to name a specific country. In *Théâtre II,* Adamov explains: "Transcrivant fidèlement un rêve, je fus forcé de n'en négliger aucun detail; ayant, par exemple, reçu dans le rêve une lettre qui venait de Belgique et qui portrait sur son timbre le 'lion royal', je nommai dans la pièce la Belgique et son lion" (Transcribing a dream truthfully, I was forced not to neglect a single detail. Having, for instance, in the dream, received a letter from Belgium with a stamp

Poster advertising Adamov's play at the Unity Theatre in London in 1962 (from Ici et maintenant, *1964; Thomas Cooper Library, University of South Carolina)*

showing the "Royal Lion," I named Belgium and her lion in the play).

Adamov was satisfied with *Le Professeur Taranne*. Critics have called it a turning point in his evolution from an absurdist playwright to the author of such critical social analyses as *Le Ping-Pong* (produced and published 1955; translated as *Ping Pong*, 1959), *Paolo Paoli*, and *Le Printemps 71*. In his monograph on Adamov, John H. Reilly places *Le Professeur Taranne* on the same level as *L'Aveu*: "it is an honest and relatively direct expression of a tortured soul. *Professeur Taranne* is a powerful play and is the one work written by Adamov which communicates the sense of inner sadness as effectively as *The Confession*."

Le Ping-Pong owes its name to the final scene, the first part of the play Adamov wrote, in which two quarreling old men named Arthur and Victor are shown arguing and playing a game of table tennis. The majority of the play, however, is set at a much earlier time. The play's centerpiece is an electric pinball machine located in Madame Duranty's café. Arthur, an art student, and Victor, a future physician, are drawn to the newly installed pinball machine that soon becomes the center of their lives—as well as the lives of Sutter, an agent of the pinball consortium, of Arthur's girlfriend Annette, of Madame Duranty, and of two other representatives of the consortium, the employee Roger and the director, Mr. Constantine. Rather than becoming addicted players of the pinball machine, Arthur and Victor approach Mr. Constantine with a proposal for improving it. They are unsuccessful but leave the meeting with the hope that future ideas of enhancing the machine may meet with a better reception. Meanwhile, the state moves to take over the pinball machine business, which spells the decline of the consortium. Annette dies in an automobile accident, and Sutter ends up a beggar. The director, after trying to save the consortium, dies as well. Arthur takes over the consortium, and Victor finishes his medical studies and becomes a physician. Years later the two friends meet in the ping-pong match that concludes the play. Gradually, Arthur and Victor change the rules of the game, doing away with the net and then the rackets. After an extreme physical effort, Victor succumbs to a heart attack.

According to Esslin, *Le Ping-Pong* is "one of the masterpieces of the Theatre of the Absurd." Most notably, the central role of an object (what Geneviève Serreau describes as a "personnage-objet") dedicated to a futile form of entertainment underscores the "absurd" nature of *Le Ping-Pong*. In keeping with many of his earlier plays, Adamov creates two complementary protagonists, one bearing his own first name, and the other bearing the name of a close friend from his early school days. But some of the features of *Le Ping-Pong* point toward a new phase in Adamov's development as a writer. The two friends actually take the decision to dedicate their lives to the pinball machine, whereas many of his earlier protagonists find themselves in situations with which they have to cope, situations that ultimately destroy them. Additionally, the capitalist motive of material gain (money, power, influence over women) is portrayed in a critical light throughout the play, as is the all-encompassing fascination with material objects, as represented by the pinball machine. Such themes are important to Adamov's later drama.

Throughout his career Adamov avoided the carefully structured five-act model of the classical French theater. Most of his plays are of dual structure, with two parts subdivided into five or six tableaux of unequal length. His plotlines are relatively weak; the various tableaux seem rather like successive snapshots of the underlying, implied action. In a sense, then, Adamov's theater was never far from Brecht's epic theater. Although Brecht had already been introduced in France with plays such as *Die Ausnahme und die Regel* (1937; translated as *The Exception and the Rule*, 1961) and *Mutter Courage und Ihre Kinder* (1949; translated as *Mother Courage and Her Children*, 1949), in 1954 Brecht's own Berliner Ensemble (Berlin Ensemble) presented *Mutter Courage und Ihre Kinder* in Paris. At this time the French public took note of the German playwright, both his innovative theatrical technique and his communist political stance. The Brecht debate that was kindled in France coincided with a new impulse, furthered by Jean Vilar, director of the Théâtre National Populaire (National Popular Theater) since 1951, to attract a new nontraditional, non-Parisian public to the theater.

While the explicit political theater of Jean-Paul Sartre, Albert Camus, and others flourished in the late 1940s, the absurdist aesthetics that informed Adamov's early plays precluded him from introducing social and political issues in any way other than through heavily veiled allusions to the presence of oppressive government forces, the refugee problems caused by the Holocaust, and similar events. However, in the mid 1950s, as he reached a point in his life where the dominance of his personal neuroses subsided somewhat, Adamov embraced the new possibilities of a politically engaged theater situated in a defined historical and social context. Hence, Adamov became part of a new trend, as there was an increase in political drama generally in this period. An important contributing factor was the French intelligentsia's increasing concern with France's ill-fated attempt to maintain its presence as a colonial power in Algeria by military means.

Paolo Paoli is Adamov's first bold step in political drama. The play is set in pre–World War I Europe, beginning in 1900 and leading up to the event that triggered World War I, the murder of Archduke Franz Ferdinand, heir to the Austro-Hungarian throne, at Sarajevo in the summer of 1914. Paoli's father, born a Corsican, works in the administration of the French prison at Devil's Island off the shore of French Guiana. Paoli, an entomologist, has the prisoners catch exotic butterflies for him for a token compensation, and he sells them profitably in Europe to manufacturers who use their wings in the production of fashion accessories and other luxury trinkets. One of his best customers, Florent Hulot-Vasseur, a collector of rare butterflies himself, deals in ostrich feathers, a precious commodity for the hat industry. Hulot-Vasseur courts Stella, Paoli's German-born wife, who buys ostrich feathers from him for her hat boutique. One of Paoli's suppliers is the falsely incarcerated and later escaped prisoner Marpeaux, whose wife, Rose, becomes, for a time, Paoli's mistress. In order to have Marpeaux's status as escaped prisoner revoked, Paoli and Hulot-Vasseur call on the well-connected Catholic clergyman Saulnier, who not only is benefiting from the butterfly trade but also becomes an active player by providing contacts to his brother, a missionary in China, in order to keep the supply of rare butterflies flowing. Entirely at Saulnier's mercy, Marpeaux is placed in Hulot-Vasseur's factory, where he is expected to militate for the Catholic "yellow" trade unions against their Communist counterparts. In the end, however, Marpeaux sides with the Communist trade unions, and Paoli decides—against his own and Hulot-Vasseur's commercial interests—to opt out of the capitalist game and to dedicate himself to the betterment of the working class's social condition.

Each of the play's twelve episodes is preceded by the projection of historical and political information, accompanied by the sound of contemporary popular songs. This device, inspired by Erwin Piscator, a German theater director (and Brecht associate), allowed Adamov to demonstrate the impact of international politics on society without having to burden the dialogue of the characters with political discourse. The commerce of frivolous commodities such as butterflies and ostrich feathers at first may seem as absurd and trivial

Scene from a performance of Le Printemps 71 *at Théâtre national de Bratislava in November 1962 (from* Ici et maintenant, *1964; Thomas Cooper Library, University of South Carolina)*

as the central role of a pinball machine in *Le Ping-Pong*. A closer analysis reveals, however, that by shrewdly choosing his topic and by judiciously selecting the main characters, Adamov is able to relate a commentary on contemporary French society through many of the international issues and social developments that led to World War I. Reference is made to the Dreyfus affair that ended in 1906; the Morocco crises of 1906 and 1911, which pitted the German Empire against the colonial powers England and France; French colonialism; the corrupt French penal system; the Boer Wars in South Africa from 1899 to 1902; the questionable political role of the Church, which was separated from the state in 1906; the competition between Germany and France in prewar international trade; the rise of nationalism in Germany and France; and the struggle between capitalist interests on the one hand and the Catholic and Communist forces within organized labor on the other. Through these allusions Adamov creates politically engaged theater. Human exploitation in the name of capitalism is critically highlighted in the fate of Marpeaux and his wife, the play's only two positive characters, both members of the working class. Additionally, as Sartre did two years later in *Les Séquestrés d'Altona* (1959, The Condemned of Altona; translated as *Loser Wins*, 1960), Adamov essentially equates the attitude of the French government toward the Algerian conflict with an unreformed Nazi dynasty in postwar Germany.

In 1958 Adamov published *Théâtre de Société*. In the three short plays published in the volume—*Intimité* (Intimacy), *Je ne suis pas français* (I Am Not French), and *La Complainte du ridicule* (The Complaint of Ridicule)— Adamov advanced his politically engaged drama a step further than before, taking aim directly at French president Charles de Gaulle's constitutional reform (the creation of the Fifth Republic in 1958) and the French army's controversial opposition to the liberation of Algeria. Even here, however, Adamov elevates at least the first and the last of these three satires above the level of direct political discourse by creating allegorical playlets.

Adamov occasionally returned to the sequestered, mad world of his absurdist plays, as he did with his radio play *En fiacre* (1959, In the Cab), a dialogue among three crazed sisters during a cab ride, at the end of which one of them is murdered. Nevertheless, after *Le Ping-Pong,* and especially after *Paolo Paoli,* Adamov was perceived as a committed political playwright, aligned yet never fully identified with the ideology and goals of the French Communist Party.

In 1961 Adamov married his long-time friend and collaborator Jacqueline Autrusseau Adamian ("le Bison"), who preserved his legacy until her own death in January 2004. The perception of Adamov as a political playwright was enhanced by the 1961 publication of his historical docudrama titled *Le Printemps 71* and its performance at the Théâtre Gérard Philipe in Saint-Denis in 1963. In this play Adamov presents his vision of the short-lived insurrectional Paris government at the close of the Franco-Prussian War of 1870–1871. Brecht had written a play on the same topic, *Tage der Kommune* (1957; translated as *The Days of the Commune,* 1971). Although Adamov acknowledged Brecht's influence on his drama in interviews (reprinted in *Ici et maintenant*), Brecht's play focuses mostly on the leaders of the Commune and their innovative legislative work, while Adamov's main interest is in the common people and their reaction to the political upheaval and their eventual military defeat.

Rather than being represented by two characters as in *Paolo Paoli,* the common people in *Le Printemps 71* are represented by the vast majority of the forty-person cast of characters. Their plight is reinforced by the presence of two women who are young sympathizers from Poland and Russia. Although Adamov refrains from idealizing his characters, their engaging, often spirited demeanor leaves no doubt about their creator's sympathies.

In order to convey the wider-ranging political scenario of *Le Printemps 71,* Adamov resorts to a two-tier structure. Twenty-six street-level tableaux are interspersed with nine *guignols* (puppet plays) in which Bismarck, the victor of the war, and Adolphe Thiers, who will defeat the insurrection, interact with allegorical representations—inspired by Honoré Daumier's political caricatures—of the Bank of France, the National Assembly, and the Commune. Additionally, the decrees and ordinances of the insurrectional government are broadcast anonymously, during the so-called transitions of the play, through a loudspeaker. In the last phase of the seventy-three-day existence of the Commune, the notorious Bloody Week, most of the insurgents die on the barricades. Adamov makes clear his hopes for a world-wide Communist revolution: in the short epilogue, the map of Paris that is presented at the beginning and throughout the play is replaced by a world map on which Communist countries are marked in red. Then, *Le Printemps 71* closes with an intonation of the Communist Internationale Anthem.

In order to write *Le Printemps 71,* Adamov conducted extensive research on the Paris Commune. As a by-product of this effort, he published a separate work titled *La Commune de Paris, 18 mars–28 mai 1871: anthologie* (1959, The Paris Commune, 18 March–28 May 1871: Anthology). This book opens with a selection of pertinent posters and public proclamations. Then Adamov proceeds to reproduce samples of texts by the leading insurgents as well as their opponents at Versailles. Short works by Gustave Flaubert, Emile Zola, and Victor Hugo, followed by works by Karl Liebknecht, Karl Marx, Friedrich Engels, and Vladimir Lenin conclude the volume. Prefatory and contextual remarks leave no doubt about Adamov's pro-communist political stance.

While some of Adamov's critics, such as Julius Wilhelm, see *Le Professeur Taranne, Le Ping-Pong, Paolo Paoli,* and *Le Printemps 71* as the most accomplished examples of his work, others give him credit for evolving his art beyond these plays, for having searched beyond the posture of a militant writer of anticapitalist, anti-authoritarian, antiracist inspiration. They argue that Adamov successfully incorporated social and historical themes into his expanded repertory, but his profound, firsthand experience with human neuroses always informed his theater as well. It is in this synthesis, according to many critics, that Adamov found his very own, unmistakable voice.

For example, in *La Politique des restes* (The Politics of Leftovers; published 1966, produced 1967), the curable sociopolitical aspect of human nature and its incurable spiritual dimension are intricately intertwined. The white South African Johnnie Brown is the victim of a psychosis, the frightening proliferation of material objects, that also plays a key role in several of Ionesco's plays, including *Les Chaises* (1952; translated as *The Chairs,* 1958) and *Tueur sans gages* (1958; translated as *The Killer,* 1960). In Johnnie Brown's clinically documented case the psychosis involves all sorts of objects, including an excess of theater tickets, ticket booths, and kitchen garbage. No longer satisfied with describing this psychosis in the abstract, as he might have done in the early 1950s, Adamov situates his subject in a country where the proliferation of blacks represents an explosive social problem. As he explains in "De quelques faits" (1962): "I have chosen . . . South Africa, the country of apartheid, where the Whites tremble before the ceaselessly growing excess of the black population . . . and I imagined the transformation of a personal neurosis into a collective one." Driven by his own idée fixe and the influence of apartheidist propaganda, Brown has killed the black citizen Tom Guinness and is being tried in court. Flashbacks showing the murder and the circumstances leading up to it are enacted simultaneously on a different part of the stage. The lawyer for the accused, the state attorney, and the presiding judge try to exculpate the defendant, until he, in an uncontrolled outburst, accuses everybody around him of wishing him ill and threatens them with murder as well. Now considered a public menace, Brown is condemned to confinement at a psychiatric clinic.

After publishing another autobiographical work, *Ici et maintenant,* in 1964, Adamov published a new play, *Sainte Europe,* in which contemporary European politics are represented as anything but saintly. This work furnishes the most striking example of his synthetic approach to drama. During a state visit at the old Carolingian imperial residence of Aachen, Agha of Irania, the perpetually inebriated Muslim ruler of the East, meets with Charlemagne, Emperor of "le Pays Franc" (the Frankish country), Alemania, and Castilia. The purpose of the meeting is the negotiation of a major grant to be extended by the empire to Irania in order to reform and develop the country. However, bad news about an earthquake in Irania and labor unrest in the West complicate the transaction. The funds for the grant have to be raised with the help of the banker Honoré de Rubens and the rich province of Brabant, represented by its king, Crépin the Short, whose wife, Teresa, is one of Honoré de Rubens's daughters. Other characters include Pope Innocent XXV; Mr. Henderson, Ambassador of Nord-Centre-Amérique (North-Center-America); and Mœller van der See, Duke of Cobourg, Magdebourg, and Brandebourg, who at one moment sports an armband featuring a swastika. Adamov's frequent use of anachronisms, of medieval-sounding, bombastic titles and ceremonial language, and his deliberate distortion of historical and geographical names lift the play out of any specific historic context. For example, "Brabant" is the name of the wealthy Benelux countries; Charlemagne is Charles de Gaulle, but he also shares some features with Emperor Charles V; Teresa identifies herself with St. Theresa of Avila; and Pope Innocent XXV is invented. In terms of the plot of the play, the concept of granting development funds to a Third World nation in exchange for political loyalty in the battle against *bolchévisme* (Bolshevism) is reminiscent of postcolonial practices during the Cold War—especially once it becomes clear that the necessary resources, as well as a botched military intervention, originate in Nord-Centre-Amérique. None of the relationships between the play world and the real world are made explicit, however, and the "reality" of the plot is

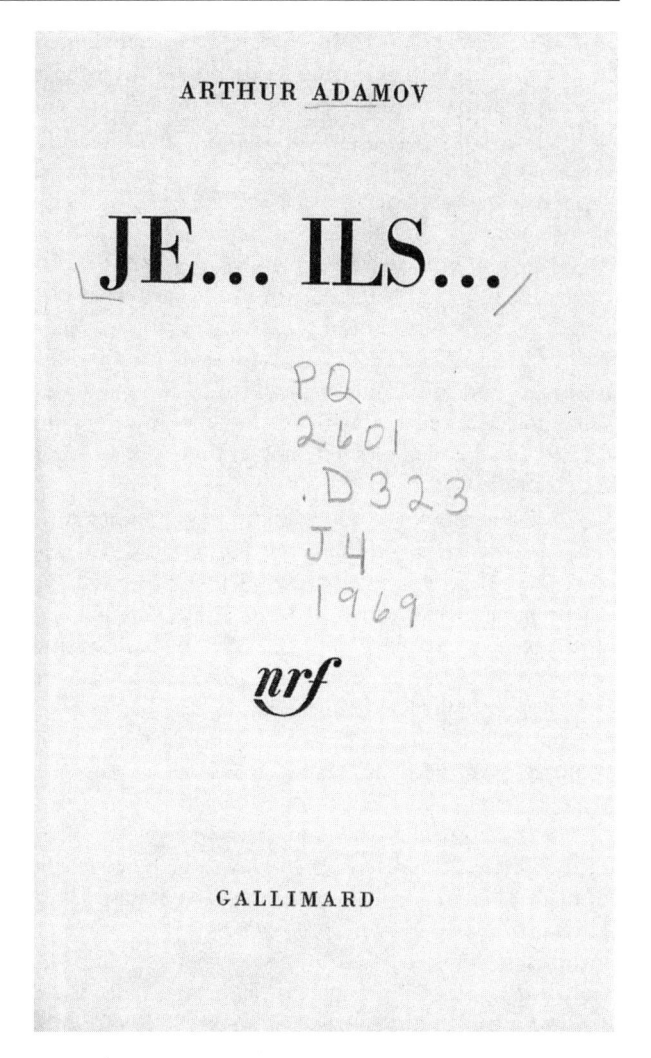

Title page for the last of Adamov's autobiographical works (Thomas Cooper Library, University of South Carolina)

further diluted by dream sequences attributed to Charlemagne and Teresa.

The common people with which Adamov explictly sympathizes in earlier plays do not appear in the palaces of Aachen and Istanbul. Their political unrest is, however, present throughout the political intrigue, expressed repeatedly in shouts for freedom from offstage. Furthermore, in the epilogue, the last two characters on stage, Francesca and Mœller van der See, are wounded by stray bullets as a full-scale revolution has broken out in the street. In an unexpected twist, Adamov associates their deaths with those of the medieval-romance characters Tristan and Yseult: "Car ils ont bu leur destruction et leur mort" (Because they drank their destruction and their death). Hence, Adamov couples the militant, crusading aspects of Charlemagne's medieval empire with the introspective, self-destructive quality of courtly love that has informed Western European literature since the twelfth century. Meanwhile, outside of the palace the people shout: "Liberté! Liberté!" (Liberty! Liberty!).

Adamov admitted that he worked for three years on *Sainte Europe* and that he was particularly fond of it. Nevertheless, some critics, such as Konrad Schoell, have called the play difficult, while others, such as Wilhelm, have expressed doubts about its artistic quality. Nevertheless, this vitriolic satire focusing on the Fifth Republic and de Gaulle's leadership, the emerging Common Market, the Vatican, and the power of the United States constitutes yet another dimension of Adamov's dramatic art.

Adamov oversaw the publication of another autobiographical writing, *L'Homme et l'enfant,* in 1968. His next play, *M. le Modéré* (Mister Moderate; produced and published in 1968), further demonstrates his political bent. *M. le modéré* maintains the radical social criticism and comical tenor introduced in *Sainte Europe,* although it is less complex and wide-ranging. In this *clownerie* (Adamov's own designation for acting like a clown), Maurice Dupré, a hotel manager in Paris, is obsessed with the notion of moderation, which leads him to a pathological inability to make decisions on his own. Pushed by an American named Havas, he becomes the head of a fantasy Switzerland called the State of Jura. He is unable to put down an insurrection, however, and as a result, he is deposed by his own police chief and exiled in London. Through his daughter Mado, a victim of his incestuous sexual overtures, he becomes the father-in-law of the Prince of Wales, but he simultaneously gives himself over to drinking and ends up half paralyzed and confined to a wheelchair. Here and elsewhere, Adamov draws on images and objects that he used during his absurdist phase. Thus, the baby carriage/hospital gurney used in *M. le modéré* as a sign of Dupré's decline is reminiscent of a similar vehicle with similar significance in *La Grande et la petite manœuvre*. At the same time, the play is situated in modern European politics. Adamov includes references to Dean Rusk, foreign secretary under John F. Kennedy, and American president Lyndon B. Johnson.

Adamov was most successful in blending the individual and the social givens of human existence in *Off Limits* (performed and published in 1969), a play set in New York. Adamov had visited New York twice, and he included a disclaimer in the preface to the book: "je n'ai pas voulu découvrir ici l'Amérique entière, mais un certain milieu social hétéroclite, qui s'étend à New York, entre Washington Square, la General Motors et la villa de Katherine Hepburn" (here I did not intend to discover America as a whole, but only a certain heterogeneous milieu that extends, in New York, between Washington Square, General Motors and Katherine Hepburn's villa). Each of the five tableaux of the play reflects a party filled with social games (semispontaneous "happenings" in the tradition of New York's The Living Theater) and casual conversations, based, according to the author, on scenes and events he actually witnessed. Sex, drugs, and alcohol are all pervasive in his portrait of a decaying society. Adamov portrays the catalyst for social decline as America's military involvement in the Vietnam conflict. The broader social flaws to which Adamov alludes include racial discrimination, capitalist exploitation, colonialism, and the commercialism of the media. On one level the characters castigate these abuses, but on another they contribute to them through their actions. Two young, relatively innocent characters, seventeen-year-old Jim and sixteen-year-old Sally, get shot during an attempt to escape to Mexico, and the epilogue ends with the announcement that ten students at Yale have torn up their draft notices. The closing projected image is of multiple Statues of Liberty breaking up into pieces.

In 1970 Adamov returned one last time to Strindberg's *Ett droemspel* in order to write *Si l'été revenait* (If Summer Returned; published 1970, produced 1972). Set in Stockholm, the play consists of four dreams by four related characters. Lars and Brit are married, but Lars and his sister Thea have been in an incestuous relationship. The fourth character is the hermaphrodite Alma, who introduced Lars to Brit. These characters' dreams reflect a complicated web of relationships, each from the dreamer's perspective. Links to the external world—student unrest at the university, the missionary work with the miners of Kiruna performed by Lars' and Thea's mother, Alma's social work in the Third World—are secondary.

In his preliminary notes to *Si l'été revenait,* Adamov describes the essentially circular trajectory of his career as an artist:

Qu'est-ce qui ressort de tout cela? En tout cas que j'étais bien léger à l'époque où je voulais 'bannir' la psychologie du théâtre. Mais tout ou Presque tout est psychologie, le corps lui-même est un objet quasiment psychique, alors? Alors, je confondais le formalisme psychologique idiot, boulevardier, et la psychologie profonde. Quiconque sait l'influence que Strindberg a exercée jadis sur moi, verra que cette influence, il l'a aujourd'hui, bien que d'une toute autre manière, reconquise.

(The upshot of all this? Certainly the fact that I was rather careless when I wished to "ban" psychology from the theater. Everything, or almost everything is psychology. Even the body is practically a psychic entity. So? So I confused the formalistic, idiotic boulevard psychology with profound psychology. Whoever knows the influence Strindberg once had on me will see that this influence, although in a different manner, has regained its strength.)

Adamov did not witness the premiere of his last play. The drug and alcohol abuse and disease he portrayed in *Off Limits* were integral to his last years, and on 15 March 1970 he ended his life by ingesting an overdose of barbiturates. *Si l'été revenait* was produced posthumously at the Cartoucherie in Vincennes, on the outskirts of Paris, on 17 May 1972.

Arthur Surenovitch Adamov was among the most innovative playwrights of his time. Although he was a pioneer of the theater of the absurd in the 1950s, he was also among the first to call the dramatic trend into question by rejecting some of his own absurdist plays and critiquing those by his fellow playwrights. Early in his career, Adamov took to writing as a way of spiritual survival, of exorcizing his own nightmares. For a time Adamov seemed to have some success in healing his own neuroses, and he turned his analytical skills to the social and political issues that beleaguered the early years of de Gaulle's presidency, including the constitution of the Fifth Republic, the liberation of Algeria, and the Cold War. In his politically engaged drama he employed formal elements of Brecht's epic theater and the analytical tools provided by Marxist social theory. At the end of his career, Adamov was able to weave his early interest in human psychology and his later interest in politics into an unusual kind of political satire. Many critics consider this innovation to be his greatest contribution to French drama.

References:

Antonin Artaud, *Le Théâtre et son double* (Paris: Gallimard, 1938);

David Bradby, *Adamov* (London: Grant & Cutler, 1975);

Martin Esslin, *The Theatre of the Absurd* (Garden City, N.Y.: Doubleday, 1961);

Leonard Cabell Pronko, *Avant-Garde: The Experimental Theater in France* (Berkeley: University of California Press, 1962);

John H. Reilly, *Arthur Adamov* (New York: Twayne, 1974);

Konrad Schoell, *Das französische Drama seit dem zweiten Weltkrieg*, volume 2: *Das neue Theater von Ionesco bis Gatti* (Göttingen: Vandenhoeck & Ruprecht, 1970);

Geneviève Serreau, *Histoire du "nouveau théâtre"* (Paris: Gallimard, 1966);

Julius Wilhelm, *Nouveau Roman und Anti-Théâtre* (Stuttgart: Kohlhammer, 1972).

Jean Anouilh
(23 June 1910 – 3 October 1987)

Michel Rocchi
University of Puget Sound

PLAY PRODUCTIONS: *L'Hermine,* Paris, Théâtre de l'Œuvre, 26 April 1932;

Y'avait un prisonnier, Paris, Théâtre des Ambassadeurs, 21 March 1935;

Le Voyageur sans bagage, Paris, Théâtre des Mathurins, 16 February 1937;

La Sauvage, Paris, Théâtre des Mathurins, 10 January 1938;

Le Bal de voleurs, Paris, Théâtre des Arts, 17 September 1938;

Léocadia, Paris, Théâtre de la Michodière, 28 November 1940;

Le Rendez-vous de Senlis, Paris, Théâtre de l'Atelier, 30 January 1941;

Eurydice, Paris, Théâtre de l'Atelier, 18 December 1941;

Antigone, Paris, Théâtre de l'Atelier, 4 February 1944;

L'Invitation au château, Paris, Théâtre de l'Atelier, 4 November 1947;

Ardèle, Paris, Comédie des Champs-Elysées, 3 November 1948;

La Répétition, Paris, Théâtre Marigny, 25 October 1950;

Colombe, Paris, Théâtre de l'Atelier, 11 February 1951;

La Valse des toréadors, Paris, Comédie des Champs-Elysées, 9 January 1952;

L'Alouette, Paris, Théâtre Montparnasse-Gaston Baty, 14 October 1952;

Médée, Paris, Théâtre de l'Atelier, 26 March 1953;

Cécile, ou L'école des pères, Paris, Comédie des Champs-Elysées, 29 October 1954;

Pauvre Bitos, ou Le dîner de têtes, Paris, Théâtre Montparnasse-Gaston Baty, 12 October 1956;

L'Hurluburlu, Paris, Comédie des Champs-Elysées, 5 February 1959;

Becket, ou L'Honneur de Dieu, Paris, Théâtre Montparnasse-Gaston Baty, 1 October 1959;

Le Songe du critique, Paris, Comédie des Champs-Elysées, 5 November 1960;

La Grotte, Paris, Théâtre Montparnasse-Gaston Baty, 6 October 1961;

L'Orchestre, Paris, Comédie des Champs-Elysées, 10 February 1962;

Jean Anouilh (courtesy of Agence Enguerand-Bernard; from Leonard Cabell Pronko, The World of Jean Anouilh, *1961; Thomas Cooper Library, University of South Carolina)*

Le Boulanger, la boulangère, et le petit mitron, Paris, Comédie des Champs-Elysées, 14 November 1968;

Cher Antoine, ou L'amour raté, Paris, Comédie des Champs-Elysées, 1 October 1969;

Les Poissons rouges, ou Mon père, ce héros, Paris, Théâtre de l'Œuvre, 21 January 1970;

Ne Réveillez pas Madame, Paris, Comédie des Champs-Elysées, 21 October 1970;

Tu étais si gentil quand tu étais petit, Paris, Théâtre Antoine, 17 January 1972;

Le Directeur de l'Opéra, Paris, Comédie des Champs-Elysées, 27 October 1972;

Monsieur Barnett, Paris, Café-Théâtre des Halles, 29 October 1974;

Le Scénario, Paris, Théâtre de l'Œuvre, 1 October 1975;

Chers zoiseaux, Paris, Comédie des Champs-Elysées, 3 December 1976.

BOOKS: *Y'avait un prisonnier* (Paris: L'Illustration, 1935);

Le Voyageur sans bagage (Paris: L'Illustration, 1937); translated by John Whiting as *Traveler without Luggage* (London: Methuen, 1959);

Les Bal des voleurs (Paris: Fayard, 1938);

Antigone (Paris: Didier, 1942); translated by Lewis Galantière as *Antigone* (New York: Random House, 1946);

Pièces roses (Paris: Calmann-Lévy, 1942)—comprises *Le Bal des voleurs, Le Rendez-vous de Senlis,* and *Léocadia; Le Bal des voleurs* translated by Lucienne Hill as *Thieves' Carnival* (London: Methuen, 1952); *Le Rendez-vous de Senlis* translated by Edwin O. Marsh as *Dinner with the Family* (London: Methuen, 1958); *Léocadia* translated by Patricia Moyes as *Time Remembered* (London: S. French, 1954);

Pièces noires (Paris: Calmann-Lévy, 1942)—comprises *L'Hermine, La Sauvage, Le Voyageur sans bagage,* and *Eurydice; L'Hermine* translated by Miriam John as *The Ermine,* in *Jean Anouilh . . . Plays,* volume 1 (New York: Hill & Wang, 1958); *La Sauvage* translated by Hill as *Restless Heart* (London: Methuen, 1957); *Eurydice* translated by Kitty Black as *Point of Departure* (London: S. French, 1951); republished as *Legend of Lovers* (New York: Coward-McCann, 1952);

Nouvelles pièces noires (Paris: La Table Ronde, 1946)—comprises *Jézabel, Antigone, Roméo et Jeannette,* and *Médée; Roméo et Jeannette* translated by John as *Romeo and Jeannette,* in *Jean Anouilh . . . Plays,* volume 1 (New York : Hill & Wang, 1958); *Médée* translated in *The Modern Theatre,* volume 5, edited by Eric Bentley (Garden City, N.Y.: Doubleday, 1957);

Pièces brillantes (Paris: La Table Ronde, 1951)—comprises *L'Invitation au château, Colombe, La Répétition, ou L'Amour puni,* and *Cécile, ou L'Ecole des pères; L'Invitation au château* translated by Christopher Fry as *Ring round the Moon* (London: Methuen, 1950); *Colombe* translated by Louis Kronenberger as *Mademoiselle Colombe* (New York: Coward-McCann, 1954);

L'Alouette (Paris: La Table Ronde, 1953); translated by Fry as *The Lark* (London: Methuen, 1955);

Pièces grinçantes (Paris: La Table ronde, 1956)—comprises *Ardèle, ou La Marguerite, La Valse des Toréadors, Ornifle, ou Le Courant d'air,* and *Pauvre Bitos, ou Le Dîner de têtes; Ardèle, ou La Marguerite* translated by Hill as *Ardèle* (London: Methuen, 1951); *La Valse des Toréadors* translated by Hill as *Waltz of the Toreadors* (London: Elek, 1953; New York: Coward-McCann, 1953); *Ornifle, ou Le Courant d'air* translated by Hill as *It's Later Than You Think* (Chicago: Dramatic, 1970); *Pauvre Bitos, ou Le dîner de têtes* translated by Hill as *Poor Bitos* (London: Methuen, 1956);

Humulus le muet, by Anouilh and Jean Aurenche (Grenoble: Françaises Nouvelles, 1958);

Becket, ou L'Honneur de Dieu (Paris: La Table Ronde, 1959); translated by Hill as *Becket, or The Honor of God* (New York: Coward-McCann, 1960);

La Petite Molière (Paris: L'Avant-Scène, 1959);

L'Hurluberlu, ou Le Réactionnaire amoureux (Paris: La Table Ronde, 1959); translated by Hill as *The Fighting Cock* (London: Methuen, 1967);

Madame de . . . , translated by Whiting (London: S. French, 1959);

Le Songe du critique, edited by Richard Fenzl (Dortmund: Lensing, 1960);

La Foire d'empoigne (Paris: La Table Ronde, 1960); translated by Anouilh and Roland Piétri as *Catch as Catch Can,* in *Jean Anouilh . . . Plays,* volume 3 (New York: Hill & Wang, 1967);

La Grotte (Paris: La Table Ronde, 1961); translated by Hill as *The Cavern* (New York: Hill & Wang, 1966);

Fables (Paris: La Table Ronde, 1962);

Le Boulanger, la boulangère, et le petit mitron (Paris: La Table Ronde, 1969);

Cher Antoine, ou L'Amour rate (Paris: La Table Ronde, 1969); translated by Hill as *Dear Antoine, or The Love That Failed* (New York: Hill & Wang, 1971; London: Eyre Methuen, 1971);

Les Poissons rouges, ou Mon Père, ce héros (Paris: La Table Ronde, 1970);

Ne Réveillez pas Madame (Paris: La Table Ronde, 1970);

Nouvelles Pièces grinçantes (Paris: La Table Ronde, 1970)—includes *L'Hurluberlu, ou Le Réactionnaire amoureux, La Grotte, L'Orchestre, Le Boulanger, la boulangère, et le petit mitron,* and *Les Poissons rouges, ou Mon Père, ce héros; L'Orchestre* translated by John as *The Orchestra,* in *Jean Anouilh . . . Plays,* volume 3 (New York: Hill & Wang, 1967);

Tu étais si gentil quand tu étais petit (Paris: La Table Ronde, 1972);

Le Directeur de l'opéra (Paris: La Table Ronde, 1972); translated by Hill as *The Director of the Opera* (London: Eyre Methuen, 1973);

L'Arrestation (Paris: La Table Ronde, 1975); translated by Hill as *The Arrest* (New York: S. French, 1978);

Le Scénario (Paris: La Table Ronde, 1976);

Chers Zoiseaux (Paris: La Table Ronde, 1977);

La Culotte (Paris: La Table Ronde, 1978);

La Belle vie suivi de Episode de la vie d'un auteur (Paris: La Table Ronde, 1980);

Le Nombril (Paris: La Table Ronde, 1981); translated by Michael Frayn as *Number One* (London & New York: S. French, 1985);

Oedipe, ou Le Roi boiteux: d'après Sophocle (Paris: La Table Ronde, 1986);

La Vicomtesse d'Eristal n'a pas reçu son balai mécanique: Souvenirs d'un jeune homme (Paris: La Table Ronde, 1987);

En marge du théâtre, edited by Efrin Knight (Paris: La Table Ronde, 2000).

Editions in English: *Jean Anouilh . . . Plays*, translated by Lewis Galantière and others, 3 volumes (New York: Hill & Wang, 1958–1967)–volume 1: *Five Plays* (1958) comprises *Antigone, Eurydice, The Ermine, The Rehearsal,* and *Romeo and Jeannette;* volume 2: *Five Plays* (1959) comprises *Restless Heart, Time Remembered, Ardele, Mademoiselle Colombe,* and *The Lark;* and volume 3: *Seven Plays* (1967) comprises *Thieves' Carnival, Medea, Cecile, or The School for Fathers, Traveler without Luggage, The Orchestra, Episode in the Life of an Author,* and *Catch as Catch Can;*

Collected Plays, 2 volumes (London: Methuen, 1966, 1967)–volume 1 comprises *The Ermine*, translated by Miriam John; *Thieves' Carnival*, translated by Lucienne Hill; *Traveller without Luggage*, translated by Hill; and *Dinner with the Family*, translated by Edwin O. Marsh; volume 2 comprises *Time Remembered*, translated by Patricia Moyes; *Point of Departure*, translated by Kitty Black; *Antigone*, translated by Galantière; *Romeo and Jeannette*, translated by John; and *Medea*, translated by Luce Klein and Arthur Klein;

Five Plays, introduction by Ned Chaillet (London: Methuen, 1987)–comprises *Léocadia*, translated by Timberlake Wertenbaker; *Antigone*, translated by Barbara Bray; *The Waltz of the Toreadors*, translated by Hill; *The Lark*, translated by Christopher Fry; and *Poor Bitor*, translated by Hill.

PRODUCED SCRIPTS: *Les Dégourdis de la onzième*, by Anouilh and others, motion picture, 1936;

Vous n'avez rien à déclarer? by Anouilh and others, motion picture, 1937;

La Citadelle du silence, by Anouilh and others, motion picture, Impérial Film, 1937;

Les Otages, by Anouilh and others, motion picture, Nero-Film AG, 1938;

Calvacade d'amour, by Anouilh and Jean Aurenche, motion picture, Pressburger Films, 1940;

Marie-Martine, by Anouilh (uncredited) and Jacques Viot, motion picture, Eclair-Journal, 1943;

Le Voyageur sans bagages, by Anouilh and Aurenche, motion picture, Eclair-Journal, 1944;

Monsieur Vincent, by Anouilh, Jean Bernard-Luc, and Maurice Cloche, motion picture, EDIC/Union Générale Cinématographique, 1947;

Anna Karenina, by Anouilh, Guy Morgan, and Julien Duvivier, motion picture, London Film Productions, 1948;

Pattes blanches, by Anouilh and Bernard-Luc, motion picture, Majestic Films, 1949;

Caroline chérie, by Anouilh and Michel Audiard (uncredited), motion picture, Cinéphonic/Gaumont, 1950;

Deux sous de violettes, by Anouilh (uncredited) and Monelle Valentin (uncredited), motion picture, Gaumont, 1951;

Le Rideau rouge, by Anouilh and André Barsacq, motion picture, Gaumont, 1952;

Monsoon, by Anouilh and others, motion picture, CFG Productions/Film Group Judd, 1952;

Un caprice de Caroline chérie, by Anouilh and Cécil Saint-Laurent, motion picture, Cinéphonic, 1953;

Le Chevalier de la nuit, motion picture, Telenet Film, 1954;

La Mort de Belle, motion picture, Cinéphonic/Odeon, 1961;

La Ronde, motion picture, Interopa Film/Paris Film Productions/Société Nouvelle Pathé Cinéma, 1964;

Piége pour Cendrillon, by Anouilh and others, television, Gaumont International/Jolly Film, 1965;

A Time for Loving, motion picture, London Screenplays, 1971;

Le Jeune Homme et le lion, television, 1976;

Histoire du chevalier des Grieux et de Manon Lescaut, television miniseries, Hungarian TV/TF1/Télécip, 1978;

La Belle vie, television, 1979;

Le Diable amoureux, by Anouilh and others, television, Bayerischer Rundfunk/France2/La Sept-Arte/Radiotelevisão Portuguesa/Telmondis/Westdeutscher Rundfunk, 1991.

OTHER: *Michel-Marie Poulain,* by Anouilh, Pierre Imbourg, and André Warnod, preface by Michel Mourre (Paris: Braun, 1953);

Le Loup, ballet scenario by Anouilh and Georges Neveux, music by Henri Dutilleux (Paris: Ricordi, 1953);

Le Dossier Molière, by Léon Thoorens, Anouilh, and others (Verviers: Gerard, 1964).

TRANSLATIONS: William Shakespeare, *Trois comédies: Comme il vous plaira, La Nuit des rois, Le Conte d'hiver,* translated by Anouilh and Claude Vincent (Paris: La Table Ronde, 1952);

Graham Greene, *L'Amant complaisant,* translated by Anouilh and Nicole Anouilh (Paris: Laffont, 1962);

Oscar Wilde, *Il est important d'être aimé,* translated by Anouilh and Nicole Anouilh (Paris: Papiers, 1985).

Considered among the most important and influential twentieth-century French dramatists, Jean Anouilh had a life and approach to literature that were far from ordinary. His exclusive concentration on theater was particularly unusual: most French dramatists of the 1930s and 1940s, including Anouilh's most significant contemporary influence, Jean Giraudoux, not only wrote for the stage but also composed poetry, novels, or essays. Among Anouilh's other distinguishing features are his claims that he was apolitical and the fact that he rarely commented formally on his work. Dedicated neither to philosophical elaborations nor to theorization about drama, he instead labored over the exact wording, gestures, and situations of his characters.

Anouilh always guarded his privacy and rarely granted interviews. In a letter addressed to the Belgian critic Hubert Gignoux in 1946 (and reprinted by Paul Ginestier), Anouilh wrote, " Je n'ai pas de biographie et j'en suis très content . . . Le reste de ma vie, et tant que le Ciel voudra que ce soit encore mon affaire personnelle, j'en réserve les détails." (I do not have a biography and I am very happy about it. The rest of my life, as long as God wills it, will remain my personal business, and I will withhold the details of it). Yet, Anouilh's plays provide important clues about his life, and after his death important biographical information came to light, especially through Caroline Anouilh's biography of her father, *Drôle de Père* (1990, Odd Father).

Jean Anouilh was born in Bordeaux on 23 June 1910. He had Franco-Basque origins. His father, François Anouilh, was a tailor, and his mother, Marie-Magdeleine, was a pianist. They exposed Anouilh to the world of entertainment at an early age. In Arcachon, near Bordeaux, Marie-Magdeleine Anouilh's night shifts in music-hall orchestras and accompanying stage presentations imbued her son with the love of theater. Anouilh often heard dramatic performances from backstage, attended rehearsals, and read scripts until bedtime.

Caroline Anouilh claims that in his preteen years Anouilh discovered a dark family secret: his mother had a lover who was actually his biological father. This secret weighed heavily on him for the rest of his life. Anouilh started to write plays by the age of twelve, but his earliest efforts have not survived. When his family moved to Paris in 1918, Anouilh became the classmate of Jean-Louis Barrault, who eventually became one of France's most renowned actor-producers. In 1927 Anouilh entered law school, but he soon dropped out and pursued employment in advertising.

By age eighteen, Anouilh was the enthusiastic acolyte of Louis Jouvet, director of the privately owned Comédie des Champs-Elysées in Paris. Anouilh had an epiphany when he attended a performance of Giraudoux's *Siegfried* (1928): he realized that theater would be his vocation. In 1929 Anouilh was called to military service, but after returning to civilian life in 1931 he began working as Jouvet's secretary at the Comédie des Champs-Elysées.

Around this time Anouilh married an actress fifteen years his elder, Monelle Valentin, who starred as female lead in most of his early plays. In 1934 they had a daughter, named Catherine, who followed the family career in theater. Monelle, however, had several adulterous affairs, which caused Anouilh much pain and suffering.

In her biography of her father, Caroline Anouilh (a daughter from a second, later marriage) provides a sympathetic image of the reclusive writer. She portrays Anouilh as a color-blind, myopic man who never thought himself handsome, and describes him as a doting father and husband who was overly protective of his family. Caroline Anouilh re-creates episodes of her family life in vivid details. Some passages of her biography, written in the form of a discourse with her deceased father, provide comic scenes that humanize Anouilh. She evokes the man who fully trusted children's instincts and was more at ease in their world than with adults. Anouilh's prankster side emerges in the biography as well. He enjoyed practical jokes and child's play, deriving pleasure from the laughter of the family that he wanted always at his side.

Anouilh was also full of contradictions, particularly when it came to finances. He was capable, for example, of purchasing lavish dwellings in France and Switzerland for his family, only to balk at the end-of-month bills. He could swing from extreme generosity to embarrassing avarice, and throughout his life he disliked the financially comfortable class, even as he joined it.

Title page for the first in a series of Anouilh's thematically organized play collections. This one, published in 1942, features his "rosy" plays (Thomas Cooper Library, University of South Carolina).

A diligent worker, Anouilh labored daily at his craft on a rigid schedule. He was reluctant to travel far from home and asked his family to make needed trips on his behalf. From his childhood days, Anouilh struggled through indecision and a fear of risk that he only overcame in his work, where he did not shy away from innovation. Yet, he took criticism of his work personally and with difficulty.

Caroline Anouilh claims that beyond his family life and work regimen her father was a solitary man comfortable with only a few close friends. He was afflicted by a morbid shyness, particularly with strangers, that brought him to the point of panic. Even Anouilh's closest friends, such as the writer Marcel Aymé, knew little of his personal life. According to Pol Vandromme, Aymé once hesitatingly answered persistent requests for biographical anecdotes on Anouilh by explaining:

> Il est des gens qui ont tout livré d'eux-mêmes au bout d'un quart d'heure de conversation sans qu'ils soient pour autant des imbéciles, d'autres qu'on pratique depuis des années et dont on ne sait rien que d'extérieur. Pour moi Jean Anouilh est de ceux-ci. A l'abord, il a une trompeuse apparence qui, on s'en aperçoit vite, ne laisse deviner que l'existence d'un mystère.
>
> (There are those who would reveal all about themselves after a fifteen-minute conversation, others that we know for years but only superficially. For me Jean Anouilh is among the latter. At first he has a tricky appearance that we soon realize reveals nothing but a mystery.)

Although he was an extremely private person, Anouilh's beliefs were reflected in his plays. Recurring themes in his scripts, such as the corrupting power of money, the incongruities of society, sympathy for the working class, the lauding of youthful idealism, and the intricacies of family ties, reveal much about the playwright. Anouilh's characters seem to engage in the polemics he wanted to launch against his critics.

By the 1920s, the ideal in playwriting was *la pièce bien faite* (the well-made play), which was rooted in nineteenth-century realist theater. Such plays featured carefully arranged scenes with an orderly exposition and climax. Alhough Anouilh favored the well-made play, he gave primacy to theme and characters, subordinating plot. Molière was the playwright Anouilh admired most, especially, according to Philip Thody, his use of "dramatic action to depict character and evoke laughter." Anouilh also admired the early-twentieth-century Italian playwright Luigi Pirandello. According to Alba Marie della Fazia, several of Anouilh's plays employ Pirandello's trademark use of the play within a play and the confusion of reality and illusion. The works of fellow French playwright Giraudoux are also echoed in Anouilh's plays, particularly in the characters. According to della Fazia, "Giraudoux's young heroines, pure, virtuous, innocent, radiant, and intransigent, who spin magic webs around themselves in order to shut out the prosaism of routine existence, find sister souls in Anouilh's lonely heroines."

Humulus le muet (Humulus the Mute), Anouilh's first play, written in 1929 with his friend Jean Aurenche, remained unpublished until 1958 and was not staged. In it, Humulus, a young mute, is helped by a British doctor to be able to utter a daily word. By abstaining from speaking one day, he can say two words the next. When Humulus falls in love with Hélène, he practices his word economy, remaining silent for a month. On the day he intends to reveal his love, he offers an elaborate declaration only to have Hélène respond by reaching into her bag, pulling out a cone, holding the cone up to her ear, and urging Humulus to speak louder so she can hear. Of this play, Caroline Anouilh says, "Si papa n'était pas le roi des parleurs, il savait aussi que les paroles ne suffisent pas toujours à provoquer la communication" (If my father was not the king of talkers, he did know that words are not enough to enable communication). *Mandarine,* also written in 1929, was staged only briefly in 1933. Anouilh was dissatisfied with its artistic direction and never published it, and the manuscript has been lost.

In the period between World War I and World War II and in the postwar period, playwriting in France was closely identified with play producing. Managers and producers working at independent art theaters in Paris, such as Marigny, Athénée, Atelier, Oeuvre, and Vieux Colombier, assumed the role of partners with playwrights in the creation of plays. Hence, Anouilh collaborated throughout his career, first with the director-designer André Barsacq, and later with artistic director Roland Piétri, who took over Jouvet's theater, the Athénée, in the early 1930s. Anouilh was also faithful to a group of actors and set and costume designers, including actors Michel Bouquet and Marcel Perès and costume designer Jean-Denis Malclès. These people constituted Anouilh's virtual troupe.

Written and staged successfully at the Théâtre de l'Œuvre in Paris in 1932, *L'Hermine* (published 1942; translated as *The Ermine,* 1958) marks Anouilh's first stage production. Pierre Fresnay, who remained one of Anouilh's favorite actors, played Frantz, a man obsessed with his financial misery and in love with a woman named Monime. The play treats one of Anouilh's perennial themes: the corrupting influence of money. Frantz equates freedom and happiness only with financial security. He decides to kill Monime's surrogate mother, who is rich and opposes their marriage, thereby eliminating two obstacles to his happiness. However, the murder inevitably provokes not only criminal consequences but also psychological realizations. Although Monime still loves Frantz, she cannot deal with the atrocity of the crime.

In 1932, a year after writing the gloomy *L'Hermine,* Anouilh wrote *Le Bal des voleurs* (produced and published 1938; translated as *Thieves' Carnival,* 1952), in which he mixes marionettes, musical interludes, and scene changes. Almost twenty years later in an interview with *Arts* (16 November 1951), Anouilh attributed the origin of his dramaturgy to this play: "You know, it seems to me that everything is in *Le Bal des voleurs*. My characters, my themes." In the play three thieves disguise themselves as nobles in order to gain access to the world of Lord Edgar and Lady Hurf, who are vacationing in Vichy with their two nieces, Eva and Juliette. Not duped by their stratagem, Lady Hurf invites them to a masked ball during which her house is actually robbed. Two bankers disguised as robbers are arrested and taken for the real robbers. When Juliette falls in love with Gustave, one of the three thieves, Lord Edgar claims to have found in him his long-lost son, and the play ends happily. The play is a rare work in that it lacks Anouilh's characteristic pessimism. It was successful in Paris and in 1954–1955 when it played in New York at the Cherry Lane Theater.

In 1932 Anouilh also wrote *Jézabel*. The title character is named after the slayer of prophets and wife of Ahab, King of Israel. The play portrays parents exploiting their children, the alcoholic and crude mother poisoning the father, economic inequality, and a son conflicted over his love for his mother despite her crime and many lovers. Motivated by his shame of his own financial status, Marc, the young protagonist, shuns Jacqueline, the girl he loves, because she is too perfect. Anouilh establishes a dichotomy between the two female characters: Jacqueline, who is pure, sincere, and unselfish, and the unfaithful Jézabel, who, in her desperation to find love, pursues men. The father becomes apathetic to his wife when he discovers her adultery. At the end of the play, Marc villifies himself to destroy any possibility of marriage with Jacqueline, but after some hesitation he also leaves his mother. Anouilh never staged this somber commentary on family life, particularly motherhood, and it was not published until 1946.

Written in 1934, *La Sauvage* (The Savage; produced 1938, published 1942; translated as *Restless Heart,* 1957) shows Anouilh's continued refinement of his recurring character: the young woman who defies bourgeois values and whose purity is at stake. *La Sauvage* indicates the way that nature's primitive purity has been soiled by mankind. The action, punctuated by the passage of time from night to daytime, tells of Thérèse's quest for a happiness beyond her grasp. The play begins during the midnight hour as Thérèse celebrates her twentieth birthday, and it concludes a week later when she breaks up with her lover, Florent, and leaves her family to affirm her independence. In act 3, Thérèse tells Florent: "Tu es un riche: un vainqueur qui n'a pas combattu" (You are rich: a winner who has not fought). She gives up both her father's lower-class lifestyle and the comfortable, bourgeois milieu of her lover, recognizing that she cannot escape the one nor belong to the other. She departs, closing the door on her past. The

Scene from a 1947 production of L'Invitation au château *(translated as* Ring round the Moon, *1950) at the Théâtre de l'Atelier (© Lipnitzki/Roger-Viollet/Getty Images)*

conclusion of the play is presented as a positive one because Thérèse gains self-knowledge through detachment from material objects and family ties. Her silence at the end of the play reveals her newfound serenity. She compares herself to a snake that has lost its venom ("Je suis comme un petit serpent qui a perdu ses dents venimeuses" [I am like a small snake who lost its venomous teeth]), and to a wild horse that will not be missed ("Il ne faut pas le regretter, c'était sûrement une mauvaise bête" [No use regretting it, it was surely a bad animal]). *La Sauvage* premiered in Paris at the Théâtre des Mathurins on 10 January 1938.

Anouilh's next play, *Y'avait un prisonnier* (There Was a Prisoner; performed and published 1935), was rarely performed, and it was eventually eclipsed by the better-constructed *Le Voyageur sans bagage* (performed and published 1937; translated as *Traveler without Luggage,* 1959). These two plays share the theme of an adult refusing to accept his past and rejecting his family. In *Y'avait un prisonnier,* Ludovic, out of prison after a fifteen-year sentence for failed financial dealings, discovers his family members have become pretentious bourgeois. Disillusioned, he opts for an escape with his mute prison mate, La Brebis. His friend's muteness and name (which means "The Sheep") contrast with the elegant yacht anchored in Cannes where his family is waiting to receive him. Ludovic and La Brebis jump overboard in an attempt to begin a new life in a less tainted location. By his escape, Ludovic avoids being placed in an asylum by his ashamed family. Ludovic is one of Anouilh's many protagonists who refuses compromises, preferring his own version of freedom despite the consequences.

Ahouilh's first major stage success was *Le Voyageur sans bagage,* a story of lost identity. After an eighteen-year sojourn in an asylum, Gaston, a wounded soldier with amnesia, returns to confront several families that claim him as their own. Having been content without any memories—or "luggage"—to encumber him, he is suddenly thrown into turmoil by society and repulsed by the atrocities ascribed to him. He is told he was a drunkard who slept with his brother's wife, raped the underage maid, despised and abused his mother, conspired to murder his best friend (whom he has paralyzed for life), and sadistically tortured and killed animals. Gaston must especially reckon with two sets of people: those who embrace the past and those who seek monetary gain. A philanthropic duchess upholds the value of the past, saying, "Et notre passé, c'est le meilleur de nous-même!" (And our past, it's the best part of us!). Meanwhile, a greedy lawyer envisions the financial advantages for the family that can claim a wounded veteran. Gaston must either accept his past and assume his identity and his place in his family or return to the asylum.

Throughout *Le Voyageur sans bagage*, Anouilh highlights the difficulty of distinguishing reality from fiction. Gaston evaluates the cruelty of the first eighteen years of his life against the kind and serene adult he has become. Once he recognizes who he was, he rejects his former self, a man who was unloved and without friends. He also rejects the family that never understood him. By rejecting his past, Gaston assumes his freedom in an illusion of his own making. He confides to an English boy an identifying scar that allows the boy to claim Gaston as his kin. Gaston then begins a new life with a new family, a fresh start. David I. Grossvogel, in his analysis of Anouilh's characters, describes this type of situation as the restoration of a childhood paradise lost.

Successfully staged in 1941, *Le Rendez-vous de Senlis* (The Rendezvous of Senlis; published 1942; translated as *Dinner with the Family*, 1958) is another play about escape from the past. Georges, who has compromised himself by marrying for convenience, is ashamed of his parents' avarice and hypocrisy, his wife's adultery and hysterical fits of jealousy, and his own psychological degeneration. He seeks love with the pure, naive Isabelle, for whom he constructs an elaborate illusion. He arranges for Isabelle to meet "his family" at Senlis. Hired actors play the attentive and loving father and mother Georges wishes he had. Although Isabelle discovers the lie, she chooses to indulge the illusion. During the rendezvous, each character struggles to play his or her role to the end, and the illusion becomes reality.

Léocadia (produced 1939, published 1942; translated as *Time Remembered*, 1954) is pure fantasy in the lineage of *Le Bal des voleurs* or *Le Rendez-vous de Senlis*. Although it is less famous than its predecessors and rarely staged, *Léocadia* was one of the more successful theatrical achievements of Anouilh during the prewar period. Heartbroken at the sudden suicide of his beloved Léocadia, Prince Albert is comforted by the Duchess, his aunt. The Duchess meticulously re-creates the idyllic setting where Albert and Léocadia lived their brief interlude, reproducing the architectural details and decor and enlisting the service staff to pretend that Léocadia is still alive. She replaces Léocadia with Amanda, a look-alike from peasant stock. Anouilh employs some of his favorite devices and themes in this play: role-playing, the distance between social classes, the unmasking of the stratagem, the power of love to conquer appearances, and the inability to communicate. Here, as in several other plays, dance and music (particularly by French composers such as Darius Milhaud and Francis Poulenc) are intrinsic elements of the action. In fact, Anouilh prepared choreography and musical accompaniments for other plays as well, including *Le Bal des voleurs* and *L'Invitation au Château* (Invitation to the House; produced 1947, published 1951; translated as *Ring round the Moon*, 1950). A graceful dancer, Anouilh carefully conceived the steps and movements of his characters so that he could call these plays "ballet." Originally performed briefly in 1939 at the Atelier, *Léocadia* was revived by André Barsacq, who staged it in Paris on 28 November 1940 at the Théâtre de la Michodière, beginning a run of 150 performances. For the American debut, the play was given the Proustian title *Time Remembered*. It was produced in New York City at the Morosco Theater in 1957 with Helen Hayes in the role of the Duchess, Richard Burton as Prince Albert, and Susan Strasberg as Amanda. Both the Parisian revival and the New York staging were highly successful.

During World War II and the German occupation, Anouilh continued writing. He declared, as della Fazia explains, "that he cared nothing about politics." Like two other contemporary playwrights, Jean Cocteau and Jean-Paul Sartre, his plays of the war years begin to reinterpret historical and mythological characters. In *Eurydice* (produced 1941, published 1942; translated as *Point of Departure*, 1951), Anouilh's first experimental play to make use of mythological figures, Eurydice and Orpheus anachronistically inhabit the modern world. The second-class musicians meet in a train-station cafeteria and fall in love at first sight. Yet, their love is hindered by Eurydice's promiscuous past and Orpheus's jealousy. Unable to overcome her past, Eurydice commits suicide in an attempt to redeem herself. The legendary aspects of the myth are reworked to allow Orpheus one more chance at being reunited with his lover on the condition he not look into her eyes until the following morning, but Orpheus disobeys because he senses that their earthly love is impossible. The religious themes of sin, confession, redemption, and afterlife dominate the play. Orpheus cannot forgive Eurydice's sins in this world but joins her in an eternal life unfettered by the judgment of mortals. While poetry is not generally considered to be Anouilh's strength, in this play he produced some unexpectedly powerful poetic scenes exalting everyday life and evoking the simplicity of love. Although the earthly love of Orpheus and Eurydice is condemned by the past to perish, Anouilh relays the power of the love that will be reborn in a blissful afterlife.

Scene from Anouilh's La Valse des toréadors *(translated as* Waltz of the Torreadors, *1953), at the Comédie de Champs-Elysées in Paris, January 1952 (© Lipnitzki/Roger-Viollet/Getty Images)*

By the 1940s Anouilh began to group and publish his plays in thematic classifications that he felt represented the phases of his evolution and loosely resembled the distinction between comedy and tragedy. The titles are *Pièces roses* (1942, Rosy Plays), *Pièces noires* (1942, Dark Plays), *Nouvelles Pièces noires* (1946, New Dark Plays), *Pièces brillantes* (1951, Bright Plays), *Pièces grinçantes* (1956, Gritty Plays), *Nouvelles Pièces grinçantes* (1970, New Gritty Plays), and *Pièces baroques* (1976, Baroque Plays). The starkest contrast in groupings occurs between *Pièces roses,* which includes three early plays, *Le Bal des voleurs, Le Rendez-vous de Senlis,* and *Léocadia,* and *Pièces noires,* which includes *L'Hermine, La Sauvage, Le Voyageur sans baggage,* and *Eurydice.* Except for the relatively "rosy" endings of the *Pièces roses,* Anouilh's plays have lighthearted beginnings and then gradually darken and end gloomily. Many plays evoke the theme of death. Very few of his characters derive pleasure in any daily activities, whether it be their work, their families, their food, or their leisure. Their milieu is intolerant, arbitrary, and often cruel. The characters' struggles usually involve financial or social obstacles. Many of them are young idealists burdened by lost innocence and hardened by their situations. Yet, for all the grimness that characterizes their condition, Anouilh's characters never truly despair. They attenuate the dimness of their fate with flickering moments of genuine love, unwavering honesty, and deep trust in humanity.

Although Anouilh established himself on the theatrical scene during the 1930s, it was mainly during World War II and the German occupation that he achieved fame. Premiering at the end of the occupation, *Antigone* (published 1942, performed 1944; translated, 1946) was a great success because the audiences identified with Antigone's resistance to her uncle Creon, the ruler of Thebes. Anouilh's reinterpretation of Aeschylus's and Sophocles' *Antigone* intertwines calls for personal freedom in the context of the family with a political revolt against authority. Antigone is the first of Anouilh's protagonists who are intransigently ruthless in their defiance and rejection of mediocrity, abhorring compromise and assuming the full burden of their acts. In the prologue, Anouilh speaks of the tragedy of characters about to replay their Sartrean hell by repeating their acts in endless absurdity. Hence, in a review for *Horizon* (November 1960), Germaine Brée insightfully asserts that the essence of Anouilh's characters is a "fidelity to the role one is designated to play, the acceptance of oneself in a given part whatever its essential absurdity."

Similar to Gaston of *Le Voyageur sans bagage,* Antigone seeks the simple happiness of her youth when confronted by the imposition of political order. Antigone knows from the start that she will die for her attempt to bury her brother, but she takes full responsibility for her act and accepts the consequences of her choice. When Creon asks her for whom she defiantly disobeys him by burying her brother's body, she answers, "Pour personne. Pour moi" (For no one. For myself). Creon is both family and politician, determined to maintain the family's peace and the state's law. Antigone is equally unbending in her insistence upon preserving the purity of an uncompromised choice. She tells Creon, "Nous sommes de ceux qui posent les questions jusqu'au bout" (We are of those who ask questions up to the very end). Convinced of his power to save Antiogone, Creon tries to reason with her and tells her that he was once a similar idealist before becoming the responsible king he is now. Critic John Edmond Harvey lucidly captures the core of the conflict:

> heroine and spectator alike uncover the true meaning of her role. Her destiny is not, as everyone has believed all along, to subordinate civil obligations to those of family and religion. Creon lets slip a few words in praise of everyday happiness and all is over: Antigone pounces on these words, and in a flurry of rhetoric she suddenly understands that her role is to reject compromise, to spurn all life which is less than perfection.

After this epiphany, there is no retreat for Antigone. For a French public a few months away from liberation, the sobriety of Barsacq's original staging in Paris on 4 February 1944 heightened the tragedy of Antigone's negation. Antigone represents the strife of the human condition and the desire to be true to oneself. She is one of Anouilh's best-known characters.

In 1945 Anouilh wrote *Roméo et Jeannette* (translated as *Romeo and Jeannette*, 1958), his reinterpretation of William Shakespeare's *Romeo and Juliet*, set in postwar France and published in *Nouvelles pièces noires*. Death looms heavily in this play, in which Anouilh returns to the motifs of the dishonesty of the family and people's fears of their past. The following year Anouilh reworked the character of Medea in *Médée* (published 1946, performed 1953; translated, 1957), also published in *Nouvelles pièces noires*. In this play Jason confronts Medea, the woman who, in a jealous and vengeful rage, has just killed the two children she bore him. Anouilh's Jason strikes the pose of the hero who can be reconciled to the real world despite such atrocities. While Medea holds to her ideals, Jason comes to terms with life's imperfections. Although a literary success, the play failed when it was produced in 1953.

Written a year or two after the liberation of Paris, Anouilh's next play, *L'Invitation au château,* involves a reworking of many of his previous characters and motifs. It is a pastiche of *Le Bal des voleurs,* featuring the use of masks, ballet, mistaken identities, caricatures, and the Pygmalion story. The English translation of the play by Christopher Fry, *Ring round the Moon,* received international acclaim.

During this period Anouilh presented a pair of vaudeville farces centered on the misfortunes of the General Saint-Pé, who cares for his bedridden wife. In *Ardèle* (produced 1948; published 1956; translated, 1951), the General finds disconcerting the passion of his hunchbacked sister, Ardèle, for a hunchbacked tutor. Consequently, he locks his sister in her room, where she remains for the entire play. In *La Valse des toréadors* (produced 1952; translated as *Waltz of the Toreadors,* 1953), the General reminisces about his first love, the beautiful Mademoiselle Sainte-Euverte, for whom he fell seventeen years ago when he danced a waltz with her at a military ball. Both *Ardèle* and *La Valse des toréadors* share depictions of lovers who, despite the exaggerated situations, suffer genuine emotions. Ardèle dies in her room after a hunger strike, and the General is forced by his ailing wife to dance with her as she trips the waltz of his lost love.

In 1950 Anouilh presented *La Répétition* (translated as *The Rehearsal,* 1961), a Pirandellian play within a play in which Anouilh's characters rehearse Pierre Carlet de Chamblain de Marivaux's eighteenth-century drama *La Double Inconstance* (1723, Double Infidelity). In this rehearsal, Anouilh transforms his actors into Marivaux's characters so effortlessly that they become indistinguishable. The following year, Anouilh returned to the mix of farce and horror of the General Saint-Pé plays with *Colombe* (1951; translated as *Mademoiselle Colombe,* 1954), in which the flashback technique is used. Julien, a soldier, loves his wife despite the distance between them. Upon his return, when he discovers his wife's adultery with his own brother, he refuses to relinquish the romantic image he has of her. He even insists on kissing his brother on the mouth to attempt to comprehend his wife's pleasure. Failing to understand, he nevertheless clings to the Colombe he loved.

Anouilh's version of the Joan of Arc story, *L'Alouette* (produced 1952, published 1953; translated as *The Lark,* 1955), is indicative of a trend away from comedy toward more serious drama. The choice of an historical episode involving issues of Christianity and national identity appealed to French theater audiences of the time. Like Antigone, Jeanne is defiant as she faces death alone, but whereas Antigone rebels against Creon's secular order, Jeanne's rebellion is against her family and religious order. Jeanne rejects any compromise to preserve peace and harmony. She owes allegiance to her individual values instead of blind obedience to the church. During her trial for heresy, no amount of reasoning makes her recant her act.

After divorcing Monelle, on 30 July 1953 Anouilh married Nicole Lançon, also known as Char-

Scene from a 1953 performance of L'Alouette *(translated as* The Lock, *1955) at Théâtre Montparnasse-Gaston Baty (© Lipnitzki/Roger-Viollet/Getty Images)*

lotte Chardon. The press did not discover Anouilh's discreet second marriage until three years later. According to Caroline Anouilh's biography, Anouilh was excessively jealous with his second wife and his daughters, who were all faithful and unflinching in their love and devotion.

Anouilh followed *L'Alouette* with three plays that were tributes to Molière. Anouilh's *Ornifle* (translated as *It's Later Than You Think,* 1970), published 1956, pays homage to Molière's *Dom Juan* (1665). Although Anouilh's Ornifle dresses like Molière's character, he is much less successful than Dom Juan. He juggles his amorous adventures with his quest for the ideal, which he persists in pursuing in spite of his failures. In *Pauvre Bitos* (produced and published 1956; translated as *Poor Bitos,* 1956) Anouilh re-creates Molière's *Tartuffe* (1664). This play takes on the subject of assassination by reviving the revolutionary figure of Maximilien Robespierre. It denounces hatred and, more particularly, those who become embittered by their own hateful ideologies. Anouilh then wrote another political play, *L'Hurluburlu* (The Misanthrope; produced and published 1959; translated as *The Fighting Cock,* 1967), a version of Molière's *La Misanthrope* (1666). In this play the selfish protagonist is a General who, having lost touch with reality, clings to an exaggerated sense of honor for his country.

Anouilh returned to the flashback technique in 1959 with one of his best-known plays, *Becket, ou L'Honneur de Dieu* (translated as *Becket, or The Honor of God,* 1960), the story of conflict between church and state and between two friends who become foes. The play is based on the history of Thomas à Becket, the newly ordained archbishop of Canterbury, who declares his allegiance to the church, and thus goes against his friend, the English king Henry Plantagenet. Becket takes on the role of upholding God's honor, while Henry pleads with his friend to abandon these convictions. Although Becket does not harbor a deep faith in God, he defends the honor he has chosen to champion.

After *Becket,* Anouilh produced a series of less successful plays. *La Petite Molière* (1959), which starred his daughter Catherine, features autobiographical elements. *La Foire d'empoigne* (1960, Game of Grab; translated as *Catch as Catch Can,* 1967) caused a rift between Anouilh and Charles de Gaulle. Anouilh's play por-

Scene from a production of Anouilh's Pauvre Bitos, ou Le Diner de têtes *(translated as* Poor Bitos, *1956) at the Théâtre Montparnasse-Gaston-Baty in 1956 (courtesy of Agence Enguerand-Bernard; from Leonard Cabell Pronko,* The World of Jean Anouilh, *1961; Thomas Cooper Library, University of South Carolina)*

trays de Gaulle as a despot who exploits historical events to govern the victimized French. Following his feud with de Gaulle, Anouilh is reported to have become much less interested in playwriting. In 1961 Anouilh returned to Pirandellian themes with *La Grotte* (translated as *The Cavern,* 1966), in which a fictional playwright's efforts to complete his drama are suspended as a detective solves a murder committed on the stage.

Although Anouilh began to concentrate on directing after 1963, he still wrote many plays. He had another success in 1968 with *Le Boulanger, la boulangère, et le petit mitron* (The Baker, His Wife, and His Little Apprentice; published 1969), a play in which the characters' dreams are actualized on stage. In *Cher Antoine* (performed and published in 1969; translated as *Dear Antoine, or The Love That Failed,* 1971), characters act out directions that the deceased Antoine left for them. A play on the same theme, *Les Poissons rouges, ou Mon père, ce héros* (Gold Fish, or My Father, The Hero; performed and published 1970), initially got a lukewarm reception but fared better when it was revived in 1994. Meanwhile, *Ne Réveillez pas Madame* (Don't Wake Me Madame; performed and published 1970) stages Anouilh's reminiscences about the theater, and *Le Directeur de l'Opéra* (performed and published 1972; translated as *The Director of the Opera,* 1973) consists of sketches on the theme of the decaying family.

In 1971 Anouilh produced a play titled *L'Arrestation* (published 1975; translated as *The Arrest,* 1978), a satire of the bourgeois family featuring adulterous and manipulative mothers, a hardened scoundrel, and the scoundrel's newly discovered bastard child. *L'Arrestation* was Anouilh's last successful effort on stage. Later, in *Tu étais si gentil quand tu étais petit* (You Were So Nice When You Were Little; produced and published 1972), Anouilh returned to Greek mythology, specifically the Orestes myth.

Anouilh spent time in his elegant apartments in Paris or in Pully, near Lausanne, until his death on 3 October 1987. Over his long career Anouilh's love of the stage was unwavering, and this love extended to second-rate musicians and struggling actors, people who had his sympathy and were often portrayed in his plays. Anouilh associated such people with the plight of the masses from the Depression era to postwar poverty. They served as a reminder of the childhood poverty he experienced and never forgot. Anouilh was appalled by modern society's excesses, and he was given to pessimism about the future.

Anouilh insisted, however, on a private life where he could live according to his personal code of moral values, and he avoided direct involvement in the political controversies of his day. He was inclined to let his art convey his ideas and content to cede his voice to actors while maintaining his privacy. For scholars, then, the plays are a vital reflection of the man who composed them. They portray heroism under difficult circumstances, insist upon the values of solidarity and courage but, most of all, emphasize individual freedom, even against impossible odds.

In terms of literary style, Jean Anouilh is difficult to categorize. He was not an absurdist, an existentialist, a Surrealist, or an avant-gardist; yet, crosscurrents of all the major twentieth-century French artistic trends may be seen in his work. Since he collaborated with France's greatest directors, actors, and designers, the complexity of his work is unsurprising. Anouilh wrote more than fifty plays in fifty years, and the most significant of them have been performed on international stages and made into movies. With such a large sphere of influence, Anouilh's place in the history of French theater is undeniably secure.

Bibliography:

Kathleen White Kelly, *Jean Anouilh: An Annotated Bibliography* (Metuchen, N.J.: Scarecrow Press, 1973).

References:

Caroline Anouilh, *Drôle de père* (Paris: Lafon, 1990);

Francesca Balladon, "Exercice d'application d'un modèle d'organisation éducative. L'OBE et l'*Antigone* d'Anouilh," *French Studies in Southern Africa*, 30 (2001): 13–22;

Harold Clurman, *The Naked Image: Observations on the Modern Theatre* (New York: Macmillan, 1966);

Robert de Luppé, *Jean Anouilh* (Paris: Editions universitaires, 1959);

Alba Marie della Fazia, *Jean Anouilh* (Boston: Twayne, 1969);

Wallace Fowlie, *Dionysus in Paris: A Guide to Contemporary French Theater* (New York: Meridian, 1960);

Hubert Gignoux, *Jean Anouilh* (Paris: Temps Présent, 1946);

Paul Ginestier, *Jean Anouilh: Textes de Anouilh, points de vue critique témoignages, chronologie* (Paris: Seghers, 1969);

David I. Grossvogel, *The Self-Conscious Stage in Modern French Drama* (New York: Columbia University Press, 1958);

John Edmond Harvey, *Anouilh: A Study in Theatrics* (New Haven: Yale University Press, 1964);

Christophe Mercier, *Pour saluer Jean Anouilh* (Etrépilly: Bartillat, 1995);

Val Morgan, "Translation and Performance: Anouilh's Becket," *New Comparison*, 29 (Spring 2000): 66–80;

Leonard Cabell Pronko, *The World of Jean Anouilh* (Berkeley: University of California Press, 1961);

Philip Thody, *Anouilh* (Edinburgh & London: Oliver & Boyd, 1968);

Pol Vandromme, *Un auteur et ses personages: Essai suivi d'un recueil de textes critiques de Jean Anouilh* (Paris: La Table Ronde, 1965);

Mary Ann Frese Witt, *The Search for Modern Tragedy: Aesthetic Fascism in Italy and France* (Ithaca, N.Y.: Cornell University Press, 2001).

Guillaume Apollinaire

(26 August 1880 – 9 November 1918)

Mary Anne O'Neil
Whitman College

See also the Apollinaire entry in *DLB 258: Modern French Poets.*

PLAY PRODUCTIONS: *Les Mammelles de Tirésias,* Paris, Conservatoire Renée Maubel, 21 June 1917;

Couleur du temps, Paris, Conservatoire Renée Maubel, 24 November 1918;

La Température, Stavelot, Belgium, Théâtre de l'Escalier, 2 September 1975;

A la cloche de bois, Stavelot, Belgium, Théâtre Universitaire de Liège, 30 August 1990.

BOOKS: *Mirely, ou Le Petit Trou pas cher* (N.p., 1900);

Les Exploits d'un jeune Don Juan, as G.A. (Paris, 1907; Philadelphia, 1944; London, 1949); translated as *Amorous Exploits of a Young Rakehell* (Paris: Olympia, 1953);

Les Onze mille verges, as G. . . . A. . . . (Paris, 1907); republished as *Les Onze mille verges, ou Les Amours d'un hospodar* (Paris, 1911); translated by Alexander Trocchi (as Oscar Mole) as *The Debauched Hospodar* (Paris: Olympia, 1953);

L'Enchanteur pourrissant (Paris: Kahnweiler, 1909);

L'Hérésiarque et cie (Paris: Stock, 1910); translated by Rémy Inglis Hall as *The Heresiarch and Co.* (Garden City, N.Y.: Doubleday, 1965); translation republished as *The Wandering Jew, and Other Stories* (London: Hart-Davis, 1967);

Le Bestiaire, ou Cortège d'Orphée (Paris: Deplanche, 1911; republished, with translations by Lauren Shakely, New York: Metropolitan Museum of Art, 1977);

Pages d'histoire–Chroniques des grands siècles de la France (Vincennes: Les Arts graphiques, 1912);

Les Peintres cubistes: Méditations aesthétiques (Paris: Figuière, 1913); translated by Lionel Abel as *The Cubist Painters: Aesthetic Meditations, 1913* (New York: Wittenborn, 1944; revised edition, New York: Wittenborn, Schultz, 1949);

Alcools, poèmes 1898–1913 (Paris: Mercure de France, 1913); translated by William Meredith as *Alcools:*

Guillaume Apollinaire (from Pierre-Marcel Adéma, Guillaume Apollinaire, le mal-aimé, *1952; Collection of E. M. Poullain; Thomas Cooper Library, University of South Carolina)*

Poems, 1898–1913, introduction and notes by Francis Steegmuller (Garden City, N.Y.: Doubleday, 1964);

L'Antitradition futuriste: Manifeste-synthèse (Milan: Direction du Mouvement futuriste, 1913);

L'Enfer de la Bibliothèque nationale; icono-bio-bibliographie descriptive, critique, complète à ce jour, de tous les ouvrages, composant cette célèbre collection, avec un index alphabétique des titres et noms d'auteurs, by Apollinaire, Fernand Fleuret, and Louis Perceau (Paris: Mercure de France, 1913);

Les Trois Don Juan, L'Histoire romanesque (Paris: Bibliothèque des Curieux, 1914); translated by Harold Winner as *Three Don Juans* (Calcutta: Susil Gupta, 1944);

Le Poète assassiné (Paris: Bibliothèque des Curieux, 1916); translated and edited, with a biographical notice, by Matthew Josephson as *The Poet Assassinated* (New York: Broom, 1923);

Vitam impendere amori: Poèmes et dessins (Paris: Mercure de France, 1917);

Les Mamelles de Tirésias: Drame surréaliste en deux actes et un prologue (Paris: Sic, 1918); translated by Maya Slater as *The Mammaries of Tiresius,* in *Three Pre-Surrealist Plays,* edited, with an introduction, by Slater (Oxford & New York: Oxford University Press, 1997);

Calligrammes, poèmes de la paix et de la guerre, 1913–1916 (Paris: Mercure de France, 1918); translated by Anne Hyde Greet as *Calligrammes, Poems of Peace and War (1913–1916),* introduction by S. I. Lockerbie and commentary by Greet and Lockerbie (Berkeley & London: University of California Press, 1980);

Le Flâneur des deux rives, Collection des tracts, no. 2 (Paris: La Sirène, 1918);

La Femme assise (Paris: Nouvelle Revue Française, 1920);

Le Verger des amours (Monaco, 1924);

Cortège priapique (Havana [i.e., Paris]: Au Cabinet des Muses [i.e., Bonnel & Picart], 1925);

Il y a, preface by Ramón Gomez de la Serna (Paris: Messein, 1925);

Anécdotiques (Paris: Stock, 1926);

Julie, ou La Rose (Hamburg, 1927); translated by Chris Tysh and George Tysh as *Julie or the Rose* (Deal, U.K.: Transgravity Press, 1978);

Ombre de mon amour, introduction by Pierre Cailler (Vésenaz, Switzerland: Cailler, 1947);

Couleur du temps, drame en trois actes et en vers, preface by Edouard Autant-Lara and Louise Autant-Lara (Paris: Editions du Bélier, 1949);

Que faire? Roman, edited by Noëmi Onimus-Blumenkranz, preface by Jean Marcenac (Paris: La Nouvelle Edition, 1950);

Casanova, comédie parodique, preface by Robert Mallet (Paris: Gallimard, 1952);

Le Guetteur mélancolique: Poèmes inédits, preface by André Salmon (Paris: Gallimard, 1952);

Textes inédits: Guillaume Apollinaire, introduction by Jeanine Moulin, Textes littéraires français, no. 50 (Geneva: Droz / Lille: Giard, 1952);

Chroniques d'art, 1902–1918, edited, with a preface, by LeRoy C. Breunig (Paris: Gallimard, 1960); translated and enlarged by Susan Suleiman as *Apollinaire on Art: Essays and Reviews, 1902–1918* (London: Thames & Hudson, 1972; New York: Viking, 1972);

Les diables amoureux, edited by Michel Décaudin (Paris: Gallimard, 1964);

Œuvres complètes, 4 volumes, edited by Décaudin (Paris: Balland & Lecat, 1965–1966);

Apollinaire et la Démocratie sociale, edited by Pierre Caizergues, Archives des Lettres modernes, no. 101 / Archives Guillaume Apollinaire, no. 1 (Paris: Minard, 1969);

La Bréhatine, Cinéma-drame, by Apollinaire and André Billy, edited, with an introduction, by Claude Tournadre, with a critical essay by Alain Virmaux, Archives des letters Modernes, no. 126 / Archives Guillaume Apollinaire, no. 5 (Paris: Lettres Modernes, 1971);

Œuvres en prose complètes, 3 volumes, edited by Décaudin and Caizergues, Bibliothèque de la Pléiade, nos. 267, 382, and 399 (Paris: Gallimard, 1977–1993);

Petites merveilles du quotidian, edited, with an introduction, by Caizergues (Montpellier: Fata Morgana, 1979)—comprises writings published from 1909 to 1912 in *L'Intransigeant* and *Paris-Journal;*

A Quelle heure un train partira-t-il pour Paris?: Pantomime, by Apollinaire, Francis Picabia, Marius de Zayas, and Alberto Savinio, edited, with an afterword, by Willard Bohn (Montpellier: Fata Morgana, 1982);

Soldes, poèmes inédits de Guillaume Apollinaire, edited by Gilbert Boudar, Caizergues, and Décaudin (Saint-Clément-la-Liviere: Fata Morgana, 1985);

Journal intime 1898–1918, edited by Décaudin (Paris: Limon, 1991);

L'Arbre à soie et autres échos du "Mercure de France," edited by Caizergues and Décaudin, Collection L'Imaginaire, no. 347 (Paris: Gallimard, 1996).

Editions and Collections: *Les Œuvres érotiques complètes de Guillaume Apollinaire,* 3 volumes (Paris: Barcelonnette, 1934)—comprises volume 1, *Poésies: Cortège priapique, Julie, ou La Rose,* and *Le Verger des amours;* volume 2, *Les Exploits d'un jeune Don Juan;* and volume 3, *Les Onze mille verges, ou Les Amours d'un hospodar;*

Choix de poésies: Guillaume Apollinaire, edited, with an introduction in English, by C. M. Bowra (London: Horizon, 1945)—comprises selections from *Calligrammes* and *Alcools;*

Il y a, preface by Paul Léautaud (Paris: Editions Grégoire, 1947);

Alcools, edited by Tristan Tzara (Paris: Le Club du Meilleur Livre, 1955);

Calligrammes: Poèmes de la paix et de la guerre (1913–1916), edited by Michel Décaudin (Paris: Le Club du Meilleur Livre, 1955);

Œuvres poétiques, edited by Marcel Adéma and Décaudin, preface by André Billy, Bibliothèque de la Pléiade, no. 121 (Paris: Gallimard, 1956);

Le Poète assassiné, edited and annotated by Décaudin (Paris: Le Club du Meilleur Livre, 1959);

Le Dossier d'alcools, edited, with introduction and notes, by Décaudin (Geneva: Droz / Paris: Minard, 1960);

L'Hérésiarque et cie (Paris: Le Livre Club du Libraire, 1963);

Les Onze Mille Verges, afterword by Toussaint Médecin-Molinier (Paris: Cercle du Livre Précieux, 1963);

Alcools, edited, with an introduction and notes in English, by A. E. Pilkington (Oxford: Blackwell, 1970);

L'Enchanteur pourrissant, edited, with an introduction, by Jean Burgos, Paralogue, no. 5 (Paris: Lettres Modernes, 1972);

L'Enchanteur pourrissant, svivi de Les Mamelles de Tirésias et du Couleur du Temps, edited, with a preface, by Décaudin (Paris: Gallimard, 1972);

Alcools; et, Calligrammes, edited by Claude Debon (Paris: Imprimerie Nationale, 1991);

Tendre comme le souvenir, preface by Madeleine Pagès (Paris: Gallimard, 1997).

Editions in English: *Selected Writings of Guillaume Apollinaire,* translated, with an introduction, by Roger Shattuck (New York: James Laughlin, 1948; London: Harvill, 1950);

Alcools, translated by Anne Hyde Greet, with a foreword by Warren Ramsey and commentary by Greet (Berkeley & Los Angeles: University of California Press, 1965);

Selected Poems: Apollinaire, translated, with an introduction, by Oliver Bernard (Harmondsworth, U.K.: Penguin, 1965); enlarged bilingual edition published as *Apollinaire: Selected Poems* (London: Anvil Press, 1986);

The Debauched Hospodar and Memoirs of a Young Rakehell, introduction by David B. Lewis (Los Angeles: Holloway House, 1967);

The Poet Assassinated, translated by Ron Padgett, illustrated by Jim Dine (New York: Holt, Rinehart & Winston, 1968; London: Hart-Davis, 1968); republished as *The Poet Assassinated and Other Stories* (San Francisco: North Point Press, 1984; Manchester, U.K.: Carcanet, 1985);

Apollinaire: Calligrams, translated by Greet, Unicorn French Series, volume 10 (Santa Barbara, Cal.: Unicorn Press, 1970)—comprises selections from *Calligrammes* in French and English;

Hunting Horns: Poems of Apollinaire, translated by Barry Morse (South Hinksey, U.K.: Carcanet, 1970)—comprises translations of poems from *Alcools* and *Calligrammes;*

Zone, translated by Samuel Beckett (Dublin: Dolmen Press / London: Calder & Boyars, 1972);

Les Onze mille verges, or The Amorous Adventures of Prince Mony Vibescu, translated by Nina Rootes, introduction by Richard N. Coe (London: Owen, 1976; New York: Taplinger, 1979);

Bestiary, or, The Parade of Orpheus, translated by Pépé Karmel (Boston: Godine, 1980);

Century of Clouds: Selected Poems from the French of Guillaume Apollinaire, translated by Geoff Page and Wendy Coutts (Canberra: Leros, 1985);

The Amorous Exploits of a Young Rakehell, translated by Reaves Tessor (New York: Blue Moon, 1994; Ware, U.K.: Wordsworth Classics, 1995);

Alcools: Poems, translated by Donald Revell (Hanover, N.H.: University Press of New England for Wesleyan University Press, 1995);

Apollinaire, edited by Robert Chandler, translated by Chandler and others, Everyman's Poetry, no. 75 (London: Everyman, 2000).

OTHER: Marquis de Sade, *L'Œuvre du Marquis de Sade: Zoloe; Justine; La Philosophie dans le boudoir; Les crimes de l'amour; Aline et Valcour. Pages choisies, comprenant des morceaux inédits et des lettres publiées pour la première fois, tirées des archives de la Comédie-Française,* edited, with an introduction and bibliographical essay, by Apollinaire, Les Maîtres de l'amour, first series (Paris: Bibliothèque des Curieux, 1909);

Pietro Aretino, *L'Œuvre du divin Arétin,* 2 volumes, translated and edited, with an introduction, by Apollinaire, Les Maîtres de l'amour, first series (Paris: Bibliothèque des Curieux, 1909, 1910);

Andréa de Nerciat, *Julie philosophe, ou Le Bon patriote: Histoire à peu près veritable d'une citoyenne active, qui a été tour à tour agent et victime dans les dernières revolutions de la Hollande, du Brabant et de la France,* 2 volumes, edited, with an introduction and bibliographical essay, by Apollinaire, Le Coffret du bibliophile: Les Romans libertins, first series, no. 4 (Paris: Bibliothèque des Curieux, 1910);

Giorgio Baffo, *L'Œuvre du Patricien de Venise, Giorgio Baffo: Sonnets, madrigaux, canzoni, capitoli. Traduction nouvelle,* translated and edited, with an introduction and bibliographical essay, by Apollinaire, Les

Maîtres de l'amour, first series (Paris: Bibliothèque des Curieux, 1910);

L'Œuvre libertine des conteurs italiens, 2 volumes, translated and edited, with an introduction and bibliographical essay, by Apollinaire, Les Maîtres de l'amour, first series (Paris: Bibliothèque des Curieux, 1910, 1911);

John Cleland, *Mémoires de Fanny Hill, femme de plaisir; avec des documents sur la vie à Londres au XVIIIe siècle, et notamment la vie galante d'après les Sérails de Londres,* translated and edited, with an introduction and bibliographical essay, by Apollinaire, Les Maîtres de l'amour, first series (Paris: Bibliothèque des Curieux, 1910);

Ernest Feydeau, *Souvenirs d'une cocodette, écrits par elle-même,* edited, with an introduction and bibliographical essay, by Apollinaire, Le Coffret du bibliophile, second series, no. 3 (Paris: Bibliothèque des Curieux, 1910);

Abbot Jouffreau de Lazeraie, *Le Joujou des demoiselles: Le calembourg en action,* edited, with an introduction and bibliographical essay, by Apollinaire, Le Coffret du bibliophile (Paris: Bibliothèque des Curieux, 1910);

Honoré-Gabriel de Riquetti, comte de Mirabeau, *L'Œuvre du comte de Mirabeau,* 2 volumes, edited, with an introduction and bibliographical essay, by Apollinaire, Les Maîtres de l'amour (Paris: Bibliothèque des Curieux, 1911, 1913);

Claude-Prosper Jolyot de Crébillon, *L'Œuvre de Crébillon le fils,* 2 volumes, edited, with an introduction and bibliographical essay, by Apollinaire, Les Maîtres de l'amour (Paris: Bibliothèque des Curieux, 1911, 1913);

Pierre Corneille Blessebois, *L'Œuvre de Pierre-Corneille Blessebois: Le Rut, ou La Pudeur éteinte; Histoire amoureuse de ce temps; Le Zombi du Grand-Pérou,* edited, with an introduction and bibliographical essay, by Apollinaire, Les Maîtres de l'amour (Paris: Bibliothèque des Curieux, 1912);

Louis Charles Fougeret de Monbron, *Le Canapé couleur de feu: Histoire galante par Fougeret de Montbron, suivie de La Belle sans chemise, ou Eve ressuscitée,* introduction by Apollinaire, Le Coffret du bibliophile (Paris: Bibliothèque des Curieux, 1912);

Etienne de Jouy, *La Galerie des femmes: Collection incomplete de huit tableaux recueillis par un amateur,* edited, with an introduction and bibliographical essay, by Apollinaire, Le Coffret du bibliophile, third series, no. 6 (Paris: Bibliothèque des Curieux, 1912);

Parnasse satyrique du XVIIIe siècle, introduction by Apollinaire (Paris: Bibliothèque des Curieux, 1912);

La Philosophie des courtisanes: Ouvrage imité de l'italien, edited, with an introduction and bibliographical essay, by Apollinaire, Le Coffret du bibliophile (Paris: Bibliothèque des Curieux, 1913);

Pierre Albert-Birot, *Trente et un poèmes de poche,* preface by Apollinaire (Paris: Sic, 1917);

Charles Baudelaire, *Les Fleurs du mal: Texte définitif avec les variants de la première édition (1857), les pièces ajoutées dans les Editions de 1861, 1866, 1868, suivies des poèmes publiés du vivant et après la mort de l'auteur,* edited, with an introduction, by Apollinaire, Les Maîtres de l'amour (Paris: Bibliothèque des Curieux, 1917);

Très plaisante et récréative hystoire du très preulx et vaillant chevalier Perceval le Galloys, jadis chevalier de la Table Ronde, lequel acheva les aventures de Sainct Graal, au temps du noble Roy Arthurs, edited by Apollinaire, Nouvelle Bibliothèque beleue (Paris: Payot, 1918);

Le Festin d'ésope: Revue des belles lettres, edited by Apollinaire and others (Geneva: Slatkine, 1971).

One of the most important French literary figures of the early twentieth century, Guillaume Apollinaire is best known for his poetry and art criticism. During his short but prolific career, however, he also worked as a journalist specializing in cultural and artistic commentary, and he wrote a novel, short stories, pornographic works, translations, and several plays. In his literary works Apollinaire harks back to Romanticism with many of his recurrent themes, including love, nostalgia for childhood, and solitude. His techniques, however, are very different from those of his Romantic predecessors. Living in an age that fostered inventions such as the airplane and cinema, Apollinaire was fascinated by technology and its potential for changing culture. He was also greatly influenced by innovations in contemporary art and music. He enjoyed the irreverent attitudes of Dadaism, the use of fragmentation and multiple perspectives in Cubist painting, and the flexible structures of jazz.

Apollinaire's fame as a playwright rests upon a single play, *Les Mamelles de Tirésias* (produced 1917, published 1918; translated as *The Mammaries of Tiresias,* 1997), often considered the original avant-garde play of the new century, a work in which the word "surréaliste" (Surrealist) appears for the first time. Yet, Apollinaire's interest in the theater was abiding. He wrote plays from his late adolescence until just before his death, and, had he lived longer, he may have established a greater reputation as a dramatist. Apollinaire's most noteworthy characteristic as a playwright is his ability to incorporate the discoveries of contemporary intellectual movements, especially Futurism, Dadaism, and Cubism, into traditional comic genres, such as the farce, the sex comedy, and the comedy of manners.

Guillaume Apollinaire was born Wilhelm Apollinaris de Kostrowitzky in Rome on 26 August 1880, the illegitimate child of an impoverished Polish demimondaine, Angeliska (or Angelika) Alexandrina Kostrowitzky, and an Italian army officer, Francesco-Constantino-Camillo Flugi d'Aspermont. After Flugi d'Aspermont abandoned Kostrowitzky in 1882, Apollinaire spent his youth with his mother and younger brother, Albert, moving around the French Riviera, where he attended schools in Monaco, Cannes, and Nice. Interested in literature but not in studying, Apollinaire never passed the *baccalauréat,* the national examination permitting entrance to a university at the end of secondary education. In 1899 the family moved to Paris, where Apollinaire tried his hand at journalism and parody but also at the more serious literary endeavors of poetry and the short story. He left Paris for two years, 1901–1902, to work in the Rhineland as a private tutor for an aristocratic family. During this sojourn in Germany, he read widely in Romantic literature and developed his literary sensibilities, and he had the first of many unrequited love experiences, an infatuation with the English governess and Sunday-school teacher Annie Playden.

Apollinaire's first complete play, probably written between 1899 and 1902, is the one-act comedy *A la cloche de bois* (On the Sly), which was never published and was performed for the first time in 1990 at the University of Liège in Belgium. This youthful work is in the tradition of the Spanish *sainete,* a short, comic play with very few characters that satirizes social types and customs. In *A la cloche de bois,* two young Parisian demimondaines have gambled away the money needed to pay their hotel bills at a fashionable European spa. They decide to leave the resort town *à la cloche de bois:* they will sneak away as silently as the sound coming "from a wooden bell." Their flight is interrupted, however, by two local policemen who hope to advance their careers by stopping a crime. Predictably, the young ladies' physical charms change the arrest into a rescue. All ends happily as the policemen and the women embrace before the women board the last train for Paris. Beyond the comic turns of the plot, Apollinaire also offers some lighthearted political criticism. The owner of the hotel from which the women escape is dubbed a follower of "internationalism." Far from a communist, however, this proprietor is a consummate capitalist, swindling without prejudice people of every nationality. The ballad appearing in the third and final scenes is filled with puns on the title, evoking both bells, from those used to cover cheese plates to death knells, and wood, including *la gueule de bois,* a wooden mouth,

Cover for a later edition of Apollinaire's collection of short stories (translated as The Heresiarch and Co., *1965). First published in 1910, the book was nominated for the prestigious Goncourt Prize (Thomas Cooper Library, University of South Carolina).*

or hangover. The outrageous humor of *A la cloche de bois* suggests the direction Apollinaire took in subsequent dramatic works. Additionally, as in his later plays, Apollinaire mixes verse and prose.

Upon his return to Paris, Apollinaire earned his living as a bank clerk. At the same time, he became actively involved in the intellectual world of the French capital. He became acquainted with well-established Symbolist poets and playwrights, including Alfred Jarry, the author of *Ubu roi* (1896, King Turd; translated, 1951), as well as younger, unknown writers who were seeking to make their mark in the new century, including his close friend André Salmon. Additionally, in 1904 Apollinaire struck up a friendship with Pablo Picasso, who had moved to Paris soon after Apollinaire's return from Germany. This relationship marked a turning point in Apollinaire's career. He became a defender of experimenta-

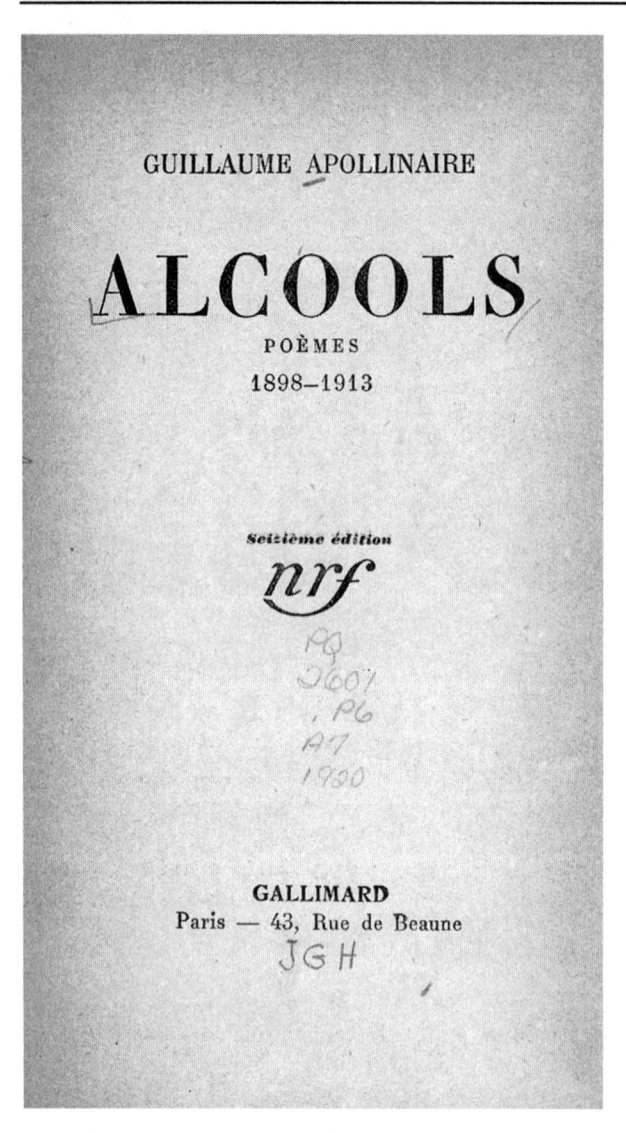

Title page for a later edition of Apollinaire's first significant poetry collection, originally published in 1913 (Thomas Cooper Library, University of South Carolina)

tion and innovation in the arts, a celebrator of technology and the future. His essays on Cubism, composed for the most part between 1904 and the beginning of World War I, remain pertinent for art critics.

From the early days of his career, the outgoing and affectionate Apollinaire frequently collaborated with other artists. Between 1903 and 1905 he participated in the founding of a series of literary magazines intended to showcase his writings and those of his friends. During the next decade Apollinaire worked not only with journalists and creative writers but also with visual artists, musicians, and even choreographers in the composition and production of a ballet, an unproduced (and perhaps unfinished) movie script, and dramatic works.

Between 1906 and 1912 Apollinaire collaborated with his friend Salmon on three short dramatic works in the hopes that they would bring the struggling writers some income. However, none of the plays were published or performed successfully during Apollinaire's lifetime. *La Température* (produced 1975, The Fever) is little more than a one-act spoof, in which a male patient wins the affections of his lascivious nurse and a large sum of money from a rakish friend. The second of these plays, *Jean-Jacques,* is a series of fourteen tableaux evoking real and imagined historical events. It was written for the bicentenary of Jean-Jacques Rousseau's birth. The last of these works, *Le Marchand d'anchois* (The Anchovy Merchant), was principally composed by Apollinaire. It is more of an operetta than a play: dialogue conveys a vague plot that is constantly interrupted by satirical or risqué poems set to the tunes of popular songs. Jonas, a Norwegian anchovy merchant, decides to sell his wares to Parisian ladies as well as to menageries of the French capital for feeding their polar animals. Meanwhile, his Norwegian workers, equally desirous to leave Scandinavia for Paris, disguise themselves as exotic animals and sail in hot-air balloons to France. In Paris, Jonas meets and successfully woos the female animal trainer Layouchka, and the animals reveal their true human identities after fleecing a naive public of its money. *Le Marchand d'anchois* is remarkable for its surprising characters: anchovies leap out of their barrels to sing; the midnight sun and the aurora borealis speak encouragingly to the voyagers; even nature, in the guise of a strongman, puts on a weight-lifting demonstration. The dialogue and songs are filled with puns and conscious slips of the tongue but also comment on current politics and technological innovations. The result is a combination of the ridiculous and the serious that is very much in line with the notion of the modern temperament Apollinaire later outlined in "L'Esprit moderne et les poètes" (1917, The New Spirit and Poets).

In 1910 Apollinaire published a collection of short stories, *L'Hérésiarque et cie* (translated as *The Heresiarch and Co.,* 1965), that was nominated for the prestigious Goncourt Prize, and in 1913 he published his first important collection of poetry, *Alcools* (translated, 1964). Another project from this period, *A Quelle heure un train partira-t-il pour Paris?* (At What Time Will a Train Leave for Paris?), is a pantomime created in 1914 by Apollinaire, painters Francis Picabia and Marius de Zayas, and the musician Alberto Savinio. It was intended as a touring piece for performance in America, a plan that was scrapped at the onset of World War I. Apollinaire tried to revive the work as a ballet in 1917, but neither the pantomime nor the ballet reached the stage, and the manuscript was not published until 1982. The six short scenes of *A Quelle heure un train partira-t-il pour Paris?* are based on a poem by Apollinaire, "Le Musicien de Saint-Merry" (The Musician of Saint-Merry), from his 1918 book *Calligrammes, poèmes de la paix et de la guerre, 1913–1916* (translated as *Calligrammes, Poems of Peace and War [1913–1916]*, 1980). During the play, verses from the poem are shouted through a megaphone or spoken by characters in two scenes. In both poem and play, a man without eyes, nose, or ears enchants the women of Paris with his flute, in the manner of Orpheus or the Pied Piper of Hamlin, and leads them into an abandoned house, where the musician and the women disappear. In the final scene, Napoleon III, who has made a brief appearance in scene 4, shoots himself to death. Willard Bohn has suggested that this play is the first theatrical example of Dadaism, a movement officially launched two years later in 1916. Like all Dadaist works, *A Quelle heure un train partira-t-il pour Paris?* is intended to shock and express the artist's revolt against corrupt social institutions, such as monarchy and war. In another sense, the play seems typical of the experimentation Apollinaire engaged in after 1910, especially with regard to using other arts to perform the function of words. Lines of the poem appear on colored posters; monuments of modern Paris and landscapes from throughout the world are projected on screens; and women of all sizes, shapes, and colors crowd the stage. Words are reduced to their sound and cadence, and the human voice becomes another urban noise, like the automobile horn. Despite the suicide at the conclusion, this play conveys the excitement of life in Paris.

At the onset of World War I, Apollinaire joined the French infantry and served on the front lines until he suffered a head wound during combat in March 1916. He then returned to Paris and continued to pursue a career in literature. At the Théâtre du Vieux Colombier in Paris on 26 November 1917, Apollinaire gave a lecture titled "L'Espirt nouveau et les poètes" that was published in the literary review *Le Mercure de France* (1 December 1918). In this lecture Apollinaire offers the best explanation of what avant-garde artists—whose unofficial leader he became by the advent of World War I—might accomplish in the new century. Far from a rebel bent on destroying European literary traditions, Apollinaire felt obliged to maintain order at a time when popular art was moving in new directions with the development of photography, cinema, and the phonograph. If writers enjoyed a greater liberty than in any other age, they also bore the responsibility of creating a literature that conveyed the spirit of this new age. Apollinaire calls on artists to draw subjects from all areas of human experience, especially daily life. Literature should be as experimental as science and take risks. It should also be synthetic, incorporating the elements and techniques of the other fine arts, such as sound, image, and color. Finally, Apollinaire asserts his right to incorporate ridiculous and unexpected situations into literature. He posits that laughter and surprises furnish the best translations of the modern artist's enthusiasm for life and distinguish twentieth-century art from earlier artistic and literary movements.

In their notes to "L'Esprit nouveau et les poètes," in *Œuvres en prose complètes* (1977–1993, Complete Works in Prose), Pierre Caizergues and Michel Décaudin point out that Apollinaire's conception of realistic art, as well as his adventurous spirit, date from his earliest writings: "Sa conception de la poésie comme une création de l'imagination toujours en prise avec le réel est . . . sa constante référence" (His conception of poetry as a creation of the imagination that always has its finger on the pulse of reality is . . . his constant reference). Following his own advice, Apollinaire engaged in daring experimentation in his poetry: "Zone" (1912) imitates jazz improvisation, while the posthumous collection *Calligrammes* features early examples of visual poetry in which the words form designs, and collage poems reminiscent of Cubist creations. Similarly, Apollinaire's dramatic works, from the one-act plays composed during his adolescence to the longer works finished shortly before his death, combine the ridiculous with the serious in an effort to portray the complicated and often contradictory realities of the twentieth century.

The final two years of Apollinaire's life included the production of his play *Les Mamelles de Tirésias*. In his preface to the 1918 edition of *Les Mamelles de Tirésias*, Apollinaire claimed that he wrote the play in 1903, fourteen years before its first performance. However, the theme of the play, the need to repopulate France, suggests that the actual date of composition is much closer to the war years. The subtitle of the play is *Drame surréaliste en deux actes et un prologue* (Surrealist Drama in Two Acts and a Prologue). By "Surrealist," Apollinaire meant a representation of reality that surpassed the traditional facile use of realistic detail or overly sentimental topics to imitate life for the stage. He felt that the theater should suggest the infinite possibilities of the modern world, where science made miracles possible. He proposed a mixture of good sense, fantasy, and laughter, much like that outlined in "L'Esprit nouveau et les poètes," that might shock or outrage traditional theatergoers but would appeal to the modern mind that understands life as an inextricable blend of tragedy, comedy, and surprises.

The prologue to *Les Mamelles de Tirésias* is a lengthy poem in free verse. The Troupe's Manager both criticizes nineteenth-century French drama, in which playwrights presented "a slice of life" to the audience,

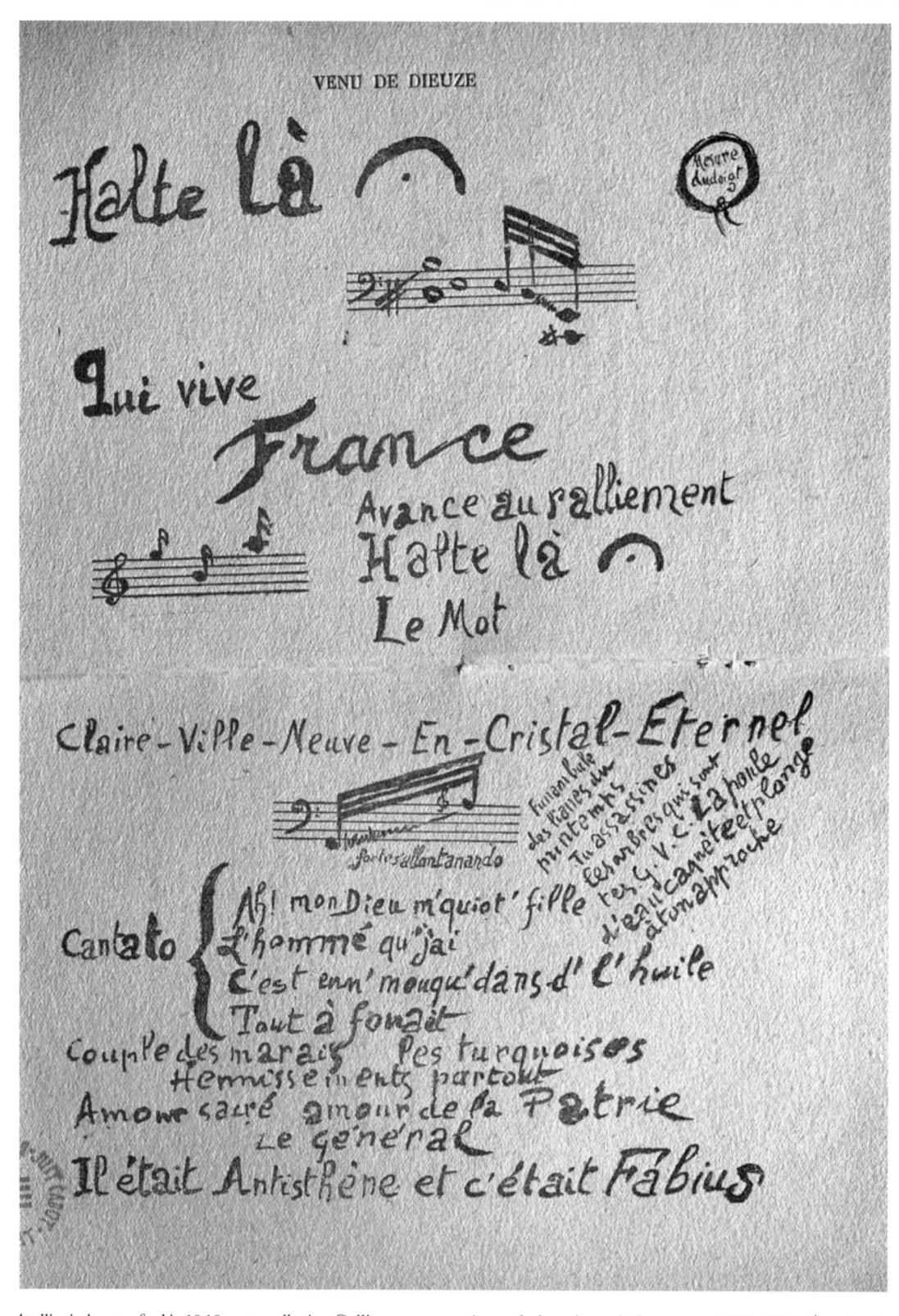

Apollinaire's notes for his 1918 poetry collection, Calligrammes, poèmes de la paix et de la guerre, 1913–1916 *(translated as* Calligrammes, Poems of Peace and War, *1980; © Archivo Iconografico, S.A./CORBIS)*

and promises a totally modern theatrical experience filled with action, music, art, and acrobatics. On the island of Zanzibar, Thérèse, a new feminist, refuses to bear children. Her breasts, colored balloons, liberate themselves and facial hair magically appears. Thérèse becomes Tiresias, the sexually unstable sage of antiquity, and leaves her home. Meanwhile, a character named "Le Mari" (The Husband) decides to assume his patriotic duty to repopulate society assisted only by an incubator. In the second act, he produces 40,049 children in a single day. Although still in the cradle, each extraordinarily precocious infant contributes to Le Mari's wealth and the general economy, principally through literary and journalistic activity. Ultimately, Thérèse/Tiresias returns to seek the loving embrace of her mate, who rescues her airborne breasts. The play ends with Thérèse, once again a woman, relaunching her breasts and exhorting them to feed the new generation of children produced by her husband. Music, juggling, and slapstick comedy, performed by gamblers, a policeman, a journalist, and a single character called "Le Peuple de Zanzibar" (The People of Zanzibar), fill the middle scenes of the play. Each act concludes with song and dance by a chorus of all characters.

The vast majority of the dialogue of *Les Mamelles de Tirésias* is written in various verse forms, ranging from rhyming alexandrine couplets to free verse. Carefully lettered placards repeating lines of poetry appear frequently, as if to echo the dialogue. Stage directions require characters to shout their lines through a megaphone. All manner of sounds, from the strains of popular instruments to breaking dishes and noisemaking by the actors, punctuate the dialogue. Costumes include painted faces and electric lighting, and the sexual transformations of Thérèse take place quickly and onstage. Stage directions call for the actors to move about constantly, not only dancing and performing acrobatics but also doing magic tricks, cutting hair, and throwing objects at the audience. Yet, Apollinaire does not create a nonsense play; rather, in a radical break with nineteenth-century theater, he creates a highly experimental work that juxtaposes music, painting, literature, and everyday objects, turning the performance into a rich, multidimensional spectacle that involves the spectator.

Also among Apollinaire's late flurry of dramatic writings is *Casanova* (published 1952), which was written between 1917 and 1918. According to the editor of the play, Roger Mallet, Apollinaire was inspired by the Russian ballet to write a musical. This three-act verse play resembles the Italian opera buffa in its use of stock characters, disguises, carnival setting, and comic reversals.

Apollinaire's last play, *Couleur du temps* (Color of the Times), was performed after his death in Paris in 1918. This play approaches the author's earlier themes but is more skillfully composed. The three acts are written in a variety of verse forms. As in his earlier dramatic works, Apollinaire draws from a variety of myths, including those of Faust, Sleeping Beauty, and Pygmalion, to explore the contemporary topics of war and aviation. This play also has an international setting, moving from the unnamed capital of a country at peace but threatened by war to an equatorial desert island to the South Pole. The main characters are symbolic. A rich man who has organized an escape by airplane represents the past; an engineer convinced of the supremacy of science represents the present; while an

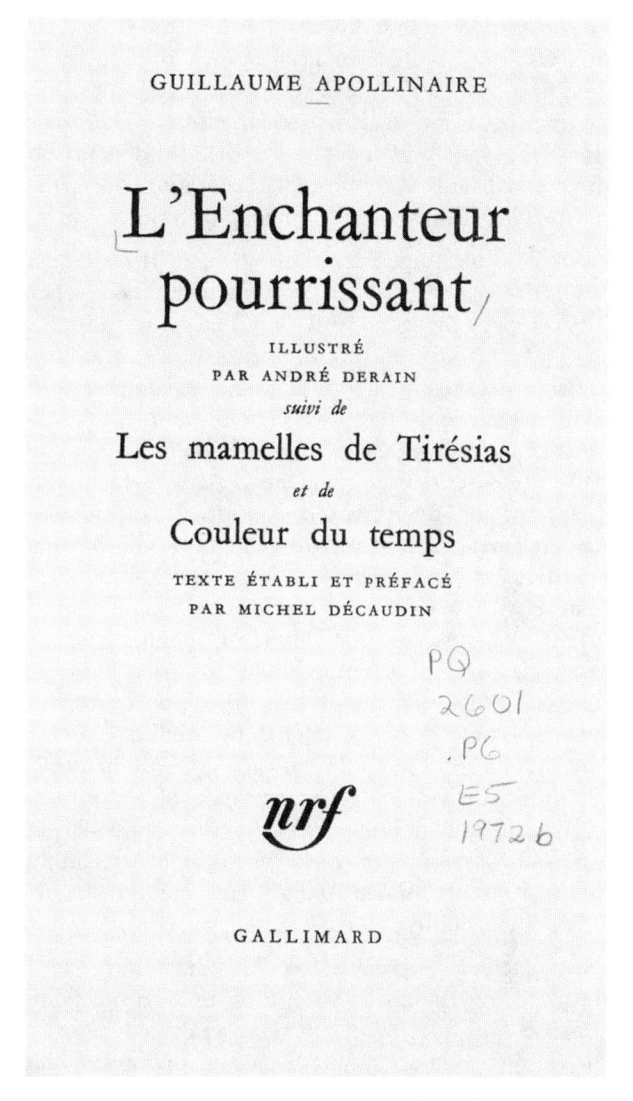

Title page for a 1972 edition of several of Apollinaire's plays, including Les Mamelles de Tirésias *(1917; translated as* The Mammaries of Tiresias*), his surrealistic play about a woman's transformation into a man and then back into a woman, generally considered to be the first avant-garde play of the twentieth century (Thomas Cooper Library, University of South Carolina)*

idealistic poet stands for the future. *Couleur du temps* reveals both Apollinaire's fascination with modern life and his nostalgia for the past, but the play is markedly more pessimistic than his earlier efforts. There is a sense that humanity is set on a course for destruction: love and beauty are outmoded aspirations incapable of resisting the onslaught of money or technology.

The play opens as the rich man, the scientist, and the poet prepare to fly from civilization. Their first stop is the graveyard of a battlefield, where a mother and fiancée mourn the death of a soldier. Their voices are joined by a chorus of the dead proclaiming the end of all love. The three men take the women away from the graveyard in their plane on the false pretense of protecting them. Act 2, which takes place on the desert island and involves emotional entanglements among the women and two of the men, questions the possibility of peace and happiness in nature. A new character, "Le Solitaire" (The Solitary Man), demonstrates that solitude is as unsatisfactory as civilization and sets off with the group. Act 3 begins in midair but soon descends to frozen polar reaches, where all four men lay claim to a beautiful woman frozen in a block of ice and fight each other to the death. Stranded, the women decry their inevitable demise as well as the folly of humans who pursue impossible ideals. They are joined by a chorus of the living and the dead in saying, "Adieu Adieu il faut que tout meure" (Goodbye goodbye all must die).

Such a pessimistic ending may have been inspired by Apollinaire's sense of his own mortality. Indeed, his battle injuries had so weakened him that he would soon become another victim of the war. The poet who had mockingly dubbed himself *le mal aimé* (the poorly loved one) married Jacqueline Kolb, a woman to whom he had written during the war, in May 1918. However, the marriage was short; Apollinaire died of Spanish influenza on 9 November of the same year.

Guillaume Apollinaire is a transitional figure in the history of twentieth-century French theater. He was well educated in European drama of the past, such as the Italian commedia dell'arte, medieval farce, and classical Greek and French tragedy. He preferred writing in verse, but his plays are not simply exercises in declamation. Apollinaire was committed to the notion of the stage as a common ground for all artistic forms, not only literature but also music, painting, and dance. He was the first twentieth-century artist to incorporate everyday objects, posters, technology, and the noises of common life into his plots and scenery. His main themes are romantic love and childhood, as well as the strange attractions of the city, war, and technology. At almost a century's distance, Apollinaire's theater appears every bit as innovative and seminal as his often-celebrated poetry.

Letters:

Lettres à sa marraine, 1915–1918, edited, with an introduction, by Pierre-Marcel Adéma (Paris: Pour les Fils du Roi, 1948);

Lettres de Guillaume Apollinaire envoyées à Jane Mortier (Liège, Belgium: Dynamo, 1950);

Lettres à Lou, edited by Michel Décaudin (Paris: Gallimard, 1969);

Guillaume Apollinaire, André Level: Lettres, edited, with an introduction, by Brigitte Level (Paris: Lettres Modernes, 1976);

Six lettres d'Apollinaire: Avec des réponses de Saint-Georges de Bouhélier, Raymond de La Tailhède et André Fontainas, afterword by Décaudin (Muizon: A l'Ecart, 1982);

Correspondance avec son frère et sa mère: Guillaume Apollinaire, edited by Gilbert Boudar and Décaudin (Paris: José Corti, 1987);

Correspondance Guillaume Apollinaire, Jean Cocteau, edited by Pierre Caizergues, Décaudin, and Boudar (Paris: Jean-Michel Place, 1991);

Picasso/Apollinaire: Correspondance, edited by Caizergues and Hélène Seckel (Paris: Gallimard, 1992);

Guillaume Apollinaire. Corrispondenza I, edited by Lucia Bonato (Rome: Bulzone, 1992);

Correspondance Jules Romains/Guillaume Apollinaire, edited by Claude Martin (Paris: Jean-Michel Place, 1994);

Correspondance 1913–1917: Guillaume Apollinaire, Mireille Havet, edited by Dominique Tiry (Montpellier: Centre d'Etude du XXe Siècle, Université Paul-Valéry, 2000).

Bibliographies:

La Revue des Lettres Modernes, special Apollinaire issues, 1–14 (1962–1978);

Scott Bates, "Guillaume Apollinare," in *A Critical Bibliography of French Literature,* volume 6: *The Twentieth Century,* part 2: *Principally Poetry, Theater, and Criticism before 1940, and Essay,* edited by Douglas W. Alden and Richard A. Brooks (Syracuse, N.Y.: Syracuse University Press, 1980), pp. 882–907;

Carnets bibliographiques de La Revue des Lettres Modernes—Guillaume Apollinaire, edited by Peter C. Hoy (Paris: Minard, 1983).

Biographies:

André Billy, *Apollinaire vivant* (Paris: La Sirène, 1923);

Philippe Soupault, *Guillaume Apollinaire, ou Reflets de l'incendie* (Marseille: Cahiers du Sud, 1927);

Christian Fettweis, *Apollinaire en Ardenne* (Brussels: Henriquez, 1934);

Ernst Wolf, *Guillaume Apollinaire und das Rheinland* (Dortmund: Husen, 1937);

Louise Faure-Favier, *Souvenirs sur Guillaume Apollinaire* (Paris: Grasset, 1945);

Pierre-Marcel Adéma, *Guillaume Apollinaire, le mal-aimé* (Paris: Plon, 1952);

Cecily Mackworth, *Guillaume Apollinaire and the Cubist Life* (London: Murray, 1961; New York: Horizon, 1963);

Francis Steegmuller, *Apollinaire: Poet among the Painters* (New York: Farrar, Straus, 1963; London: Hart-Davis, 1964);

Margaret Davies, *Apollinaire* (Edinburgh & London: Oliver & Boyd, 1964; New York: St. Martin's Press, 1965);

Pierre-Marcel Adéma, *Guillaume Apollinaire* (Paris: La Table Ronde, 1968);

Pierre Caizergues, *Apollinaire journaliste: Les Débuts et la formation du journaliste, 1900–1909* (Paris: Minard, 1981);

André Parinaud, *Apollinaire 1880–1918: Biographie et Relecture* (Paris: Editions Jean-Claude Lattès, 1994).

References:

Scott Bates, *Guillaume Apollinaire* (New York: Twayne, 1967; revised edition, Boston: Twayne, 1989);

Claude M. Bégué and Pierre Latigue, "*Alcools*," in *Apollinaire: Analyse critique*, Profil d'une œuvre, no. 25 (Paris: Hatier, 1972);

David Berry, *The Creative Vision of Guillaume Apollinaire: A Study of Imagination* (Saratoga, Cal.: Anma Libri, 1982);

Willard Bohn, *Modern Visual Poetry* (Newark: University of Delaware Press, 2001);

Madeleine Boisson, *Apollinaire et les Mythologies antiques* (Fasano, Italy: Schena / Paris: Nizet, 1989);

Claude Bonnefoy, *Apollinaire*, Classiques du XXe siècle, no. 100 (Paris: Editions Universitaires, 1969);

Laurence Campa, *L'Esthétique d'Apollinaire* (Paris: Société d'Edition d'Enseignement Supérieur, 1996);

Blaise Cendrars, *Jéroboam et La Sirène*, preface by Hughes Richard (Dole: Canevas, 1992);

Claude Debon, ed., *Les Critiques de notre temps et Apollinaire* (Paris: Garnier Frères, 1971);

Martin Esslin, *The Theatre of the Absurd* (Garden City, N.Y.: Doubleday/Anchor, 1961);

Antoine Fongaro, *Apollinaire poète: Exégèses et discussions, 1957–1987* (Toulouse: Presses Universitaires du Mirail-Toulouse, 1988);

Alfred Jarry, *Tout Ubu* (Paris: Livre de Poche, 1962);

Raymond Jean, "L'Erotique de Guillaume Apollinaire," *Cahiers du Sud*, 386 (1966): 13–21;

James Lawler, "Music and Poetry in Apollinaire," *French Studies*, 10 (1956): 339–346;

Marie-Louise Lentengre, *Apollinaire: Le nouveau lyrisme*, revised edition (Paris: Jean-Michel Place, 1996);

Roger Little, *Guillaume Apollinaire* (London: Athlone, 1976);

Timothy Mathews, *Reading Apollinaire: Theories of Poetic Language* (Manchester: Manchester University Press, 1987);

Henri Meschonnic, "Apollinaire illuminé au milieu des ombres," *Europe*, 451–452 (1966): 141–169;

Catherine Moore, *Apollinaire en 1918: La poétique de l'enchantement* (Paris: Minard, 1995);

Leonard Pronko, *Avant-Garde: The Experimental Theatre in France* (Berkeley: University of California Press, 1964);

Peter Read, *Apollinaire et "Les Mammelles de Tirésias": La Revanche d'Eros* (Rennes: Presses Universitaires de Rennes, 2000);

Read, *Picasso et Apollinaire: Les Métamorphoses de la mémoire, 1905–1973* (Paris: Jean-Michel Place, 1995);

André Rouveyre, *Amour et poésie d'Apollinaire* (Paris: Seuil, 1955);

Pénélope Sacks-Galey, *Calligramme, ou Ecriture figurée: Apollinaire inventeur de formes* (Paris: Minard, 1988);

Pierre Souyris, "Les Deux Versions du *Pont Mirabeau*," *Le Flâneur des deux rives*, 7–8 (1955): 19–26;

Jean Starobinski, *L'Œil vivant: Essai* (Paris: Gallimard, 1961);

Stefan Themerson, *Apollinaire's Lyrical Ideograms* (London: Gaberbocchus, 1968);

Margareth Wijk, *Guillaume Apollinaire et l'esprit nouveau*, Etudes romanes de Lund, no. 36 (Lund, Sweden: C. W. K. Gleerup, 1982);

Sergio Zoppi, *Apollinaire teorico* (Naples: Edizioni Scientifiche Italiane, 1970).

Papers:

Manuscripts of Guillaume Apollinaire's works are held in the Fonds Jacques Doucet, Bibliothèque Ste-Geneviève, Paris.

Fernando Arrabal
(11 August 1932 –)

Klaus Engelhardt
Lewis and Clark College

PLAY PRODUCTIONS: *Le Tricycle,* Madrid, Teatro de Bellas Artes, February 1958;

Pique-nique en campagne, Paris, Théâtre de la Lutèce, 25 April 1959;

Fando et Lis, Liège, Théâtre expérimental de la Cambre, 21 September 1959;

Guernica, Celle, Germany, Schloßtheater Celle, May 1960;

Les Deux Bourreaux, New York, Première Jazz Gallery, 15 May 1960;

Le Cimetière des voitures, New York, 41st Street Theatre, 13 November 1961;

Strip-tease de la jalousie, Paris, Centre américain, 1964;

Le Couronnement, Paris, Théâtre Mouffetard, 10 January 1965;

Les Amours impossibles, Paris, Centre américain, 25 May 1965;

Oraison, Berlin, Galerie Diogenes, July 1965;

Le Grand Cérémonial, Paris, Théâtre des Mathurins, March 1966;

Cérémonie pour un noir assassiné, Nancy, France, Nancy Festival, May 1966;

La Jeunesse illustrée, Paris, Théâtre du Bilboquet, 19 June 1966;

La Communion solennelle, Paris, Théâtre de Poche Montparnasse, 8 July 1966;

La Bicyclette du condamné, Paris, Festival de l'Union Nationale des étudiants de France, September 1966;

Concert dans un œuf, Bordeaux, France, Théâtre-Français, 19 November 1966;

Le Labyrinthe, Vincennes, Théâtre Daniel Sorano, January 1967;

L'Architecte et l'empereur d'Assyrie, Paris, Théâtre Montparnasse-Gaston-Baty, 15 March 1967;

Bestialité érotique, Paris, Théâtre Alpha, March 1968;

Une Tortue nommée Dostoïevski, Paris, Théâtre Alpha, March 1968;

L'Aurore rouge et noire, Brussels, Théâtre de poche, 26 December 1968;

Le Jardin des délices, Amsterdam, De Bakke Grand Theater, 5 March 1969;

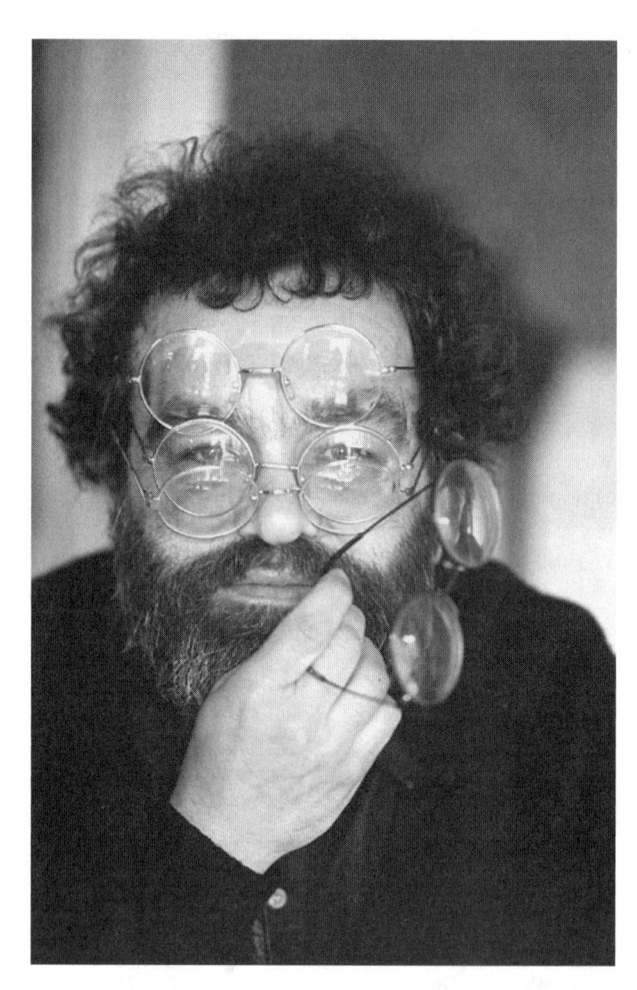

Fernando Arrabal (© Sophie Bassouls/CORBIS SYGMA)

. . . Et ils passèrent des menottes aux fleurs, Paris, Théâtre de l'Epée-de-Bois, 26 September 1969;

La Ballade du train phantôme, Paris, Théâtre de l'Atelier, 1975;

Le Ciel et la merde II, Paris, Théâtre de Plaisance, 5 June 1976;

Vole-moi un petit milliard, Paris, 30 January 1977;

Le Ciel et la merde, Paris, Théâtre de Plaisance, 1978;

Le Roi de Sodome, Paris, Théâtre d'Edgar, 25 January 1979;

Apokalyptica, Graz, Schauspielhaus, 10 October 1979;

Carta de amor (Como un suplicio chino), Madrid, Centro de Arte Reina Sofia, January 2002;

Lettre d'amour: Comme un supplice chinois, Paris, Théâtre du Rond-Point, 22 January 2004.

BOOKS: *Théâtre,* volume 1 (Paris: Julliard, 1958)–comprises *Oraison; Les Deux Bourreaux; Fando et Lis;* and *Le Cimetière des voitures; Oraison* translated by Barbara Wright, in *Plays,* volume 1 (London: Calder & Boyars, 1962), pp. 9–21; *Les Deux Bourreaux* translated by Wright and Richard Howard as *The Two Executioners,* in *The Automobile Graveyard, a Play in Two Acts, and The Two Executioners, a Melodrama in One Act* (New York: Grove, 1960), pp. 9–71; *Fando et Lis* translated by Wright, in *Plays,* volume 1 (London: Calder & Boyars, 1962), pp. 43–90; *Le Cimetière des voitures* translated by Howard as *The Automobile Graveyard,* in *The Automobile Graveyard, a Play in Two Acts, and The Two Executioners, a Melodrama in One Act* (New York: Grove, 1960), pp. 73–94;

Baal Babylone (Paris: Julliard, 1959); translated by Howard as *Baal Babylon* (New York: Grove, 1961);

Théâtre, volume 2 (Paris: Julliard, 1961)–comprises *Guernica; Le Labyrinthe; Le Tricycle; Pique-nique en campagne;* and *La Bicyclette du condamné; Guernica* translated by Wright, in *Plays,* volume 2 (London: Calder & Boyars, 1967), pp. 7–27; *Le Labyrinthe* translated by Wright as *The Labyrinth,* in *Plays,* volume 2 (London: Calder & Boyars, 1967), pp. 29–66; *Le Tricycle* translated by Wright as *The Tricycle,* in *Plays,* volume 2 (London: Calder & Boyars, 1967), pp. 67–108; *Pique-nique en campagne* translated by James Hewitt as *Picnic on the Battlefield, Evergreen Review,* 4, no. 15 (1960): 76–90; *La Bicyclette du condamné* translated by Wright as *The Condemned Man's Bicycle,* in *Plays,* volume 2 (London: Calder & Boyars, 1967), pp. 127–149;

L'Enterrement de la sardine: Livre du nain Hieronymus (Paris: Julliard, 1961); translated by Patrick Bowles as *The Burial of the Sardine* (London: Calder & Boyars, 1966);

La Pierre de la folie (Paris: Julliard, 1963);

Théâtre, volume 3 (Paris: Julliard, 1965)–comprises *Le Grand Cérémonial* and *Cérémonie pour un noir assassiné; Le Grand Cérémonial* translated by Jean Benedetti as *The Grand Ceremonial,* in *Plays,* volume 3 (London: Calder & Boyars, 1970), pp. 97–215;

Cérémonie pour une chèvre et un nuage (La Louvière, Belgium: Daily Bul, 1965);

Théâtre, volume 4 (Paris: Bourgois, 1966)–comprises *Le Couronnement* and *Concert dans un œuf; Le Couronnement* reprinted as *Le Lai de Barrabas* (Paris: Bourgois, 1969);

Arrabal celebrando la ceremonia de la confusion (Madrid: Alfaguara, 1966);

Théâtre, volume 5: *Théâtre panique* (Paris: Bourgois, 1967)–comprises *La Communion solennelle; Les Amours impossibles; Une Chevre sur un nuage; La Jeunesse ilustrée; Dieu est-il devenu fou?; Strip-tease de la jalousie; Les Quatre Cubes;* and *L'Architecte et l'empereur d'Assyrie; La Communion solennelle* translated by Bettina Knapp as *Solemn Communion, Drama Review,* 13 (1968); *Les Amours impossibles* translated by Knapp as *Impossible Lovers, Drama Review,* 13 (1968); *Strip-tease de la jalousie* translated by Knapp as *Striptease of Jealousy,* in *Drama Review,* 13 (1968); *L'Architecte et l'empereur d'Assyrie* translated by Everard d'Harnoncourt and Adele Shank as *The Architect and the Emperor of Assyria* (New York: Grove, 1969);

Fêtes et rites de la confusion (Paris: Le Terrain vague, 1967);

Théâtre, volume 6 (Paris: Bourgois, 1969)–comprises *Le Jardin des délices; Bestialité érotique;* and *Une Tortue nommée Dostoïevski; Le Jardin des délices* translated by Helen Gary Bishop and Tom Bishop as *The Garden of Delights* (New York: Grove, 1974);

Théâtre, volume 7 (Paris: Bourgois, 1969)–comprises ... *Et ils passèrent des menottes aux fleurs* and *L'Aurore rouge et noire; ... Et ils passèrent des menottes aux fleurs* translated by Charles Marowitz as *And They Put Handcuffs on the Flowers* (New York: Grove, 1973);

Théâtre, volume 8 (Paris: Bourgois, 1970)–comprises *Ars amandi: Opéra comique* and *Dieu tenté par les mathématiques: Orchesration théâtrale;*

Théâtre, volume 9 (Paris: Bourgois, 1970)–comprises *Le Ciel et la merde* and *La Grande Revue du XXème siècle;*

Lettre au General Franco: Texte intégral de la lettre envoyée par Arrabal à Franco le 18 mars 1971, includes translation from Spanish into French by Dominique Sevrain (Paris: Union générale d'éditions, 1972);

Le New York d'Arrabal, poems and photographs by Arrabal (Paris: Balland, 1973);

Sur Fischer: Intitiation aux échecs (Monte Carlo: Rocher, 1974);

Fêtes et rites de la confusion (Paris: Union générale d'éditions, 1974);

Jeunes Barbares d'aujourd'hui (Paris: Bourgois, 1975);

Théâtre, volume 10 (Paris: Bourgois, 1976)–comprises *Bella ciao, ou La Guerre de mille ans* and *Sur le fil, ou La Ballade du train fantôme; Sur le fil, ou La Ballade du train fantôme* translated by Andrew Steven Gordon, dissertation, Columbia University, 1981;

Théâtre, volume 11 (Paris: Bourgois, 1978)–comprises *La Tour de Babel; La Marche royale; Une Orange sur le mont de Vénus;* and *La Gloire en images;*

Lettre aux militants communistes espagnols: Songe et mensonge de l'eurocommunisme = Carta a los militantes comunistas españoles: Sueño y mentira del eurocomunismo, translated from Spanish into French by Sevrain (Paris: Bourgois, 1978);

Théâtre, volume 12: *Théâtre bouffe* (Paris: Bourgois, 1979)–comprises *Vole-moi un petit milliard; Le Pastaga des loufs, ou Ouverture orang-outan;* and *Punk et punk et colégram;*

Théâtre, volume 13 (Paris: Bourgois, 1980)–comprises *Mon Doux Royaume saccagé; Le Roi de Sodome;* and *Le Ciel et la merde II;*

Les échecs féeriques et libertiares: Chroniques de "L'Express" (Monaco: Rocher, 1980);

Inquisición (Granada: Don Quijote, 1982);

Théâtre, volume 14 (Paris: Bourgois, 1982)–comprises *L'Extravagante Réussite de Jésus-Crist, Karl Marx et William Shakespeare* and *Lève-toi et rêve;*

1984, carta a Fidel Castro (Madrid: Playor, 1983); translated into French as *Lettre à Fidel Castro: an 1984* (Paris: Bourgois, 1983);

El Rey de Sodoma (Madrid: MK, 1983);

Le Cheval-jument ou hommage à John Kennedy T. (Paris: Bourgois, 1983);

La Torre herida por el rayo (Barcelona: Destino, 1983); translated into French as *La Tour prends garde* (Paris: Grasset, 1983); translated into English by Anthony Kerrigan as *The Tower Struck by Lightning* (New York: Viking, 1988);

Théâtre, volume 15 (Paris: Bourgois, 1984)–comprises *Les Délices de la chair* and *La Ville dont le prince était une princesse;*

Echecs et mythe (Paris: Payot, 1984);

Humbles Paradis: Première anthologie poétique (Paris: Bourgois, 1985);

La piedra iluminada (Barcelona: Destino, 1985); translated by Andrew Hurley as *The Compass Stone* (New York: Grove, 1987);

Théâtre, volume 16 (Paris: Bourgois, 1985)–comprises *Bréviaire d'amour d'un haltérophile; Apokalyptica;* and *La Charge des centaures; Bréviaire d'amour d'un haltérophile* translated by Lorenzo Mans as *The Body-Builder's Book of Love* (New Brunswick, N.J.: Estreno Plays, 1999);

La Reverdie (Paris: Acropole, 1985);

La Vierge rouge (Paris: Acropole, 1986); translated by Hurley as *The Red Virgin* (New York: Penguin, 1993);

La Fille de King Kong (Paris: Acropole, 1988);

Théâtre, volume 17 (Paris: Actes Sud, 1988)–comprises *Les "Cucarachas" de Yale; Une Pucelle pour un gorille; La Madonne rouge;* and *La Traversée de l'empire;*

L'Extravagante Croisade d'un révolutionnaire obèse (Luxembourg: Phi, 1989);

L'Extravagante Croisade d'un castrat amoureux, ou Comme un lys entre les épines (Paris: Actes Sud, 1989);

Théâtre, volume 18 (Paris: Actes Sud, 1990)–comprises *La nuit est aussi un soleil* and *Roues d'infortune;*

El Greco, translated from Spanish by Hurley, Secret Museums, no. 3 (Paris: Flohic, 1991); reprinted as *Le Frénétique du spasme: El Greco* (Charenton: Flohic, 1997);

El sueño de los insectos, by Arrabal and Jorge Camacho (Huelva: Disputación Provincial de Huelva, 1992);

Carta a José Maria Aznar: Con copia a Filipe González (Madrid: Espasa Calpe, 1993);

Genios y Figueras: —mis idolatrados genios, prologue by Angel Berenguer (Madrid: Espasa Calpe, 1993);

Lettres à Julius Baltazar, preface by Michel Déon, afterword by Milan Kundera (Mortemart: Rougerie, 1993);

Liberté couleur de femme, ou Adieu Babylone: Poeme cinematographique (Mortemart: Rougerie, 1993);

La dudosa luz del día (Madrid: Espasa Calpe, 1994);

El mono, o Enganchado al caballo, Colección Autores españoles e hispanoamericanos (Barcelona: Planeta, 1994);

La Tueuse du jardin d'hiver, introduction by Kundera, translated from Spanish into French by Luce Moreau-Arrabal (Paris: Ecriture, 1994);

Carta al rey de España (Madrid: Espasa Calpe, 1995);

Têtes de mort dans l'armoire = Cabezas de muerto en el armario (Paris: Jannink, 1995);

Théâtre, volume 19 (Paris: Actes Sud, 1996)–comprises *Le Fou Rire des Lilliputiens* and *Comme un lis entre les épines;*

Un esclavo llamado Cervantes (Madrid: Espasa, 1996); translated into French by Arrabal and Moreau-Arrabal as *Un Esclave nommé Cervantès* (Paris: Plon, 1996);

Ceremonia por un teniente abandonado (Madrid: Espasa, 1998);

Diccionario pánico: jaculatorias y arrabalescos (España: Excritos, 1998);

Le funambule de Dieu (Paris: Ecriture, 1998);

Le Peintre et l'Aborigène; suivi de Arènes gelées de Olivier O. Olivier (Creil: Dumerchez, 1998);

Porté disparu (Paris: Plon, 2000);

Carta de amor (Como un suplicio chino), introduction by Berenguer (Alcalá de Henares, Madrid: Universidad de Alcalá, Servicio de Publicaciones, 2002); translated into French in *Lettre d'amour: Comme un supplice chinois; suivi de Claudel et Kafka* (Arles: Actes Sud, 2004), pp. 1–36;

Claudel y Kafka (Saragossa, Spain: Libros del Innombrable, 2002); translated into French in *Lettre d'amour: Comme un supplice chinois; suivi de Claudel et Kafka* (Arles: Actes Sud, 2004), pp. 37–83;

Champagne pour tous! (Paris: Stock, 2002);

Carta a Stalin (Madrid: Esfera de los Libros, 2003); translated into French as *Lettre à Staline* (Paris: Flammarion, 2004).

Editions and Collections: *Arrabal,* edited by Jacques Roman (Yverdon: Kesselring, 1977);

L'Architecte et l'empereur d'Assyrie (Paris: Union generale d'éditions, 1986);

Le Grande Cérémonial (Paris: Union generale d'éditions, 1986);

Arrabal Espace, edited by Ante Glibota (N.p.: Studio di Val Cervo / P.A.C., 1993);

Teatro completo, 2 volumes, edited, with an introduction, by Francisco Torres Monreal (Madrid: Espasa Calpe / Melilla: Consejería de Cultura de le Ciudad Autónoma de Melilla, 1997).

Edition in English: *Guernica and Other Plays,* translated by Barbara Wright (New York: Grove, 1969).

PRODUCED SCRIPTS: *Viva la muerte,* motion picture, adapted by Arrabal from his novel *Baal Babylone,* motion picture, Isabelle Films/S.A.T.P.E.C., 1970; subtitled English version, Max L. Raab Productions, 1971;

J'irai comme un cheval fou, motion picture, Babylone Films, 1973;

L'Arbre de Guernica, motion picture, Babylone Films/Ci-Le Films/Les Productions Jacques Roitfeld/Luso Films, 1975;

La Traversée de la Pacific, by Arrabal and Roger Lemelin, motion picture, Babylone Films/Ciné Pacific/Films A2, 1980; released in English as *The Emperor of Peru,* 1982;

Le Cimetière des voitures, adapted by Arrabal from his play, motion picture, Babylone Films/Antenne 2, 1981;

Adieu Babylone! Liberté coleur de femme, motion picture, France 2/Cinécim, 1993.

OTHER: "Biografia de Andre Breton, poeta," in *La revolution surrealista a traves de Andre Breton* (Caracas: Monte Avila, 1970), pp. 11–12;

"Avant-propos," "L'Homme panique," "Le Théâtre comique cérémonie," "Olivier Oliveir," and "Topor peintre," in *Le "Panique,"* edited by Arrabal (Paris: Union générale d'éditions, 1973), pp. 7, 37–55, 97–100, 124–126, 141–142;

"La Mémoire et le temps et ses accouchements prodigieux," in *La sexualité. D'ou vient l'Orient? Ou va l'Occident?: Documents du Congres de Tokyo "La Deuxième Renaissance" (avril 1984),* edited by Armando Verdiglione (Paris: Belfond, 1984), pp. 27–31;

Devoirs devacances été 85, by Jean Miotte and Arrabal (Paris: Galilee, 1986);

Miotte, by Arrabal and others (Paris: La Différence, 1987);

Metamorfosi del nihilisme, by Arrabal and others (Barcelona: Fundació Caixa de Pensions, 1989);

Opera écrit pour le bicentenaire de la Révolution Française (Paris: L'Opéra de la Bastille, 1990);

Lucien Clergue, *Passion passions,* preface by Arrabal (Arles: Actes Sud, 1997);

Le roman, pour quoi faire? by Arrabal and others (Paris: Flammarion, 2004), pp. 7–17.

Fernando Arrabal is generally associated with the Theater of the Absurd that developed in the early 1950s, but his overall body of work defies this categorization. In 1962 Arrabal, working with like-minded writers and artists, founded the short-lived but influential "Panic" movement that provides the best parameters for understanding his complex theater: a mixture of different types and styles of drama and themes that ultimately serves as a celebration of the theater. Beyond his career as a playwright, Arrabal has published volumes of poetry and novels, and he has been involved in the production of several movies, especially adaptations of his own works. His nonfiction includes open letters to political leaders and critical works on El Greco and Miguel de Cervantes. A passionate chess player, Arrabal has published material on the art of playing chess, the chess novel *La Torre herida por el rayo* (1983; translated into French as *La Tour prends garde,* 1983; translated into English as *The Tower Struck by Lightning,* 1988); and an introduction to the game analyzing Bobby Fischer's technique.

Until the end of Francisco Franco's dictatorship over Spain in 1975, Arrabal's works could not be published in his native Spain. Instead, he lived in exile in France, writing in Spanish while his wife, French native Luce Moreau-Arrabal, translated his works into French. With the 1986 novel *La Vierge rouge* (translated as *The Red Virgin,* 1993), however, Arrabal began composing works in French. Because of these circumstances, specialists in both French and Spanish literature have claimed Arrabal as belonging to their respective national literatures. His writings have been translated into many languages, and he has become a leading–if controversial–figure within French and international literature and politics.

Fernando Arrabal Terán was born on 11 August 1932 in Melilla, Spanish Morocco, where his father, Fernando Arrabal Ruiz, an officer in the Spanish army,

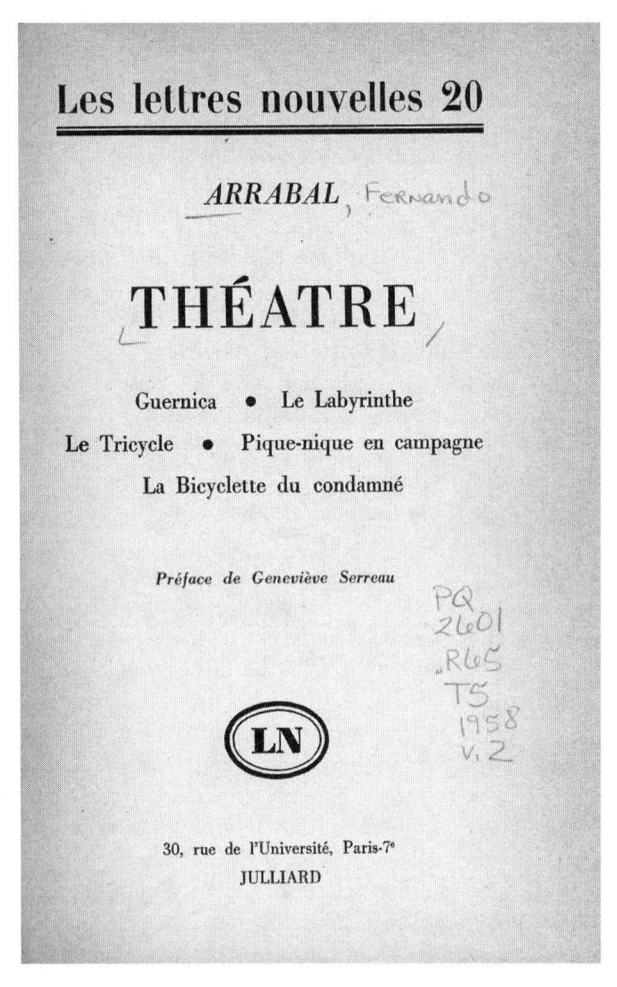

Title page for the 1961 second volume of Arrabal's theater collection, which includes the antiwar Pique-nique en campagne *(1959; translated as* Picnic on the Battlefield, *1960), his most frequently performed play (Thomas Cooper Library, University of South Carolina)*

was temporarily stationed. In July 1936, at the beginning of the civil war, his father was denounced to the Spanish police for his political opposition to Franco's military coup. Initially condemned to death, he was transferred to several prisons and finally sent to a psychiatric prison at Burgos in Spain. Arrabal's mother, Carmen Terán, disagreed with her husband's political stance. In fact, she may have been responsible for informing against her husband. At Arrabal's home, Arrabal's father was presumed dead, and his name was no longer pronounced. Much later, in 1961, Arrabal investigated his father's disappearance and discovered that he had probably escaped from prison in the winter of 1941, never to be heard from again.

In 1940 Arrabal's family settled in Madrid. Arrabal was sent to the boarding school of the Escolapios Fathers at Getafe, not far from Madrid. This institution was known for the quality of its literary instruction. Two years later, Arrabal's talent earned him the Premio de Superdotato Courtes (Courtes Prize for the Exceptionally Gifted). Arrabal's first efforts in drama and poetry date from as far back as 1945. After earning his baccalaureate in 1951, Arrabal lived in Madrid, dedicating his free time to reading and writing. He established a circle of likeminded friends, where he began to recite his early works, some of which are still unpublished.

In 1952 Arrabal wrote *Pique-nique en campagne* (produced 1959, published 1961; translated as *Picnic on the Battlefield,* 1960), which became his most frequently performed play. Written during the Korean War, the play is one of Arrabal's most categorical condemnations of warfare. The two soldier-protagonists, Zapo and Zépo, fighting on opposite sides, stumble upon each other between the front lines. Before long they discover that each is subject to nationalistic propaganda in his respective army. As the play progresses, they become increasingly similar. Meanwhile, Zapo's parents show up in the midst of the battlefield in order to hold a picnic with their son. Their conversation consists exclusively of the commonplaces and platitudes that characterize their petty bourgeois milieu. Zapo's parents are in denial about the seriousness and significance of the war. As they are all dancing the fandango, they are mowed down by a machine-gun salvo. The banality of their deaths reinforces Arrabal's antiwar stance.

As the recipient of a three-month scholarship awarded by the French government for the study of French theater, Arrabal traveled to Paris in 1955, the year in which he wrote *Fando et Lis* (published 1958, produced 1959, translated 1962). The setting is similar to that of Samuel Beckett's *En attendant Godot* (published 1952, produced 1953; translated as *Waiting for Godot,* 1954). Two adolescent lovers, Fando and Lis, the latter partially paralyzed and confined to an old-fashioned baby carriage, take a futile journey to the mythical city of Tar. Although the influence of *En attendant Godot* is evident throughout the play, unlike Beckett's protagonists Vladimir and Estragon, Fando and Lis are lovers. Their love anticipates the sadomasochism that characterizes many couples in Arrabal's theater. The play ends with the murder of Lis by Fando.

Shortly after arriving in France, Arrabal was diagnosed with tuberculosis and sent to the Sanatorium Bouffémont, near Paris, where between 1955 and 1957 he wrote such works as *Le Labyrinthe* (published 1961, produced 1967; translated as *The Labyrinth,* 1967), *Cérémonie pour un noir assassiné* (published 1965, produced 1966), and *Oraison* (published 1958, translated 1962, produced 1965). Arrabal welcomed his confinement because it afforded him the chance to stay in France indefinitely.

The scenario of *Le Labyrinthe,* a mock trial situated in a court filled with a maze of clotheslines draped with blankets, places Arrabal in the tradition of Franz Kafka's surrealistic novels. Accusations are proffered and reversed, and characters contradict themselves. The plot is overshadowed by the sinister power and inscrutable paternal "wisdom" of Justin, the originator of the labyrinth. Micaëla, Justin's daughter, both guides and confuses him through an array of promises, accusations, and countercharges.

The Kafkaesque themes of betrayal, prison, torture, and death also prevail in *Les Deux Bourreaux* (published 1958, produced 1960; translated as *The Two Executioners,* 1960). In this play Arrabal deals explicitly with his father's arrest by Franco's political police and subsequent disappearance in the Spanish prison system, and with his ambivalent feelings for his mother. Meanwhile, *Le Cimetière des voitures* (published 1958; translated as *The Automobile Graveyard,* 1960; produced 1961) presents the nightmarish vision of a community of marginal characters living in an assemblage of wrecked cars. The community is led by a couple, Milos and his wife, Dila. Dila is available to their guests for sexual favors. This static environment is interrupted by the periodic appearance of the coach-and-athlete couple Lasca and Tiossido, and it is jeopardized by three jazz musicians, Emanou (Jesus), Topé (Judas), and Fodère (Peter), who defy an ordinance against playing music in public venues. Later, Lasca and Tiossido appear in police uniforms and try to help enforce the ordinance. The three musicians act out a caricature of Christ's Passion: Emanou's Christ-like behavior and teachings are misunderstood, Topé betrays him and joins the hunt by the police, and Fodère renounces him. Emanou is eventually dragged across the stage, his dying body tied to a bicycle in the form of a cross. Unlike in the Gospels, there is no hint of a resurrection, and life in the car cemetery returns to its normal, subhuman state. *Le Cimetière des voitures* ultimately presents a horrifying metaphor of urban decay. Signs of humanity and hope emerge when a newborn child is welcomed into the community, only to be dashed as the child is stabbed to death before the final curtain. During the production of *Le Cimetière des voitures* in New York in April 1966, the producer J. H. Dunn placed the spectators in the same space as the actors who not only performed the play inches away from the audience but also interacted with individual spectators, creating an atmosphere of total theater. Three years later, Arrabal used a similar technique when he directed his own play . . . *Et ils passèrent des menottes aux fleurs* (produced 1969, published 1969; translated as *And They Put Handcuffs on the Flowers,* 1973).

In the summer of 1957 Arrabal, in collaboration with the composer J. Yves Brossard, created *Orchestration théâtrale* (Theatrical Orchestration), which was later published as "Panic Opera" under the title *Dieu tenté par les mathématiques* (1970, God Tempted by Mathematics). It features no human actors and no dialogue. Instead, Arrabal provides detailed instructions, complete with diagrams, explaining that human emotions, such as surprise or confusion, occur also between certain objects (colored spheres and other geometric objects) and can be expressed by moving and configuring these objects on stage in specific ways. After witnessing a production of this experiment, however, Arrabal expressed dissatisfaction. *Les Quatre Cubes* (1967, The Four Cubes), which features two mute actors ("A" and "B"), represents another (although less complex) attempt to have the spectator focus on the successive movements of inanimate objects on stage.

Arrabal's political convictions have been more consistent than his approach to stagecraft. From his early experiences, Arrabal developed a steadfast opposition to all forms of oppression. This position is laid out in a series of open letters addressed to powerful public figures: the Spanish dictator Franco (*Lettre au General Franco,* 1972); Cuba's dictator Fidel Castro (*1984, carta a Fidel Castro,* 1983); the Spanish prime minister José María Aznar with a copy to the Portuguese leader Felipe González (*Carta a José Maria Aznar,* 1993); and Juan Carlos I, king of Spain (*Carta al rey de Espana,* 1995).

Arrabal's literary works also have conveyed his political convictions. Following a path set out by *Pique-nique en campagne, Guernica* (produced 1960, published 1961, translated 1967) is an uncompromising antiwar statement, featuring a clear reference to the widely known antiwar mural Pablo Picasso painted in 1937 for the Spanish Pavilion of the World Fair at Paris. Both the painting and the play are political statements expressing outrage over the atrocities perpetrated during the Spanish Civil War (1936–1939). *Guernica* is set during the historic bombardment of the Basque town of Guernica by German warplanes. The survival of the elderly protagonists, Fanchou and Lira, is jeopardized by falling debris. Their dialogue suggests that they are caught in the chaos of modern warfare without even beginning to comprehend the significance of this historic cataclysm. As the play progresses, however, the parallel between the couple in *Guernica* and Mr. and Mrs. Tépan in *Pique-nique en campagne* ends: whereas the Tépans are simply killed by gunfire, in *Guernica* the oak tree that symbolizes the liberty of the Basque nation miraculously survives the fiery, unprovoked attack. After Fanchou and Lira are completely buried under debris and presumably dead, two colored balloons rise triumphantly above the smoking ruins of the town, announcing, in Arrabal's own words, the advent of *les lendemains qui chantent* (singing tomorrows). At the close

Covers for later editions of Arrabal's 1966 and 1967 plays (translated as The Grand Ceremonial *and* The Architect and the Emperor of Assyria*), one exploring the dysfunctional relationship between a hunchback named Cavanosa and his mother, and the other depicting the chaotic relationship between "L'Empereur," the lone survivor of a plane crash on an isolated island, and "L'Architecte," the island's lone inhabitant (Thomas Cooper Library, University of South Carolina)*

of the play, the noise of gunfire and bombing runs is drowned out by the unofficial Basque national anthem "Gernikako arbola" (The Basque tree).

Franco's dictatorial regime and his oppression of civic and intellectual liberties influenced Arrabal's writings throughout his literary career. Works such as *Les Deux Bourreaux,* the novel *Baal Babylone* (1959; translated as *Baal Babylon,* 1961) and the movie adaptation of it, *Viva la muerte* (1970, Long Live Death), deal directly with the political situation in Spain, including Arrabal's childhood trauma. Furthermore, the conditions in Spanish prisons and the Spanish justice system are denounced in . . . *Et ils passèrent des menottes aux fleurs,* which is a loosely connected series of gruesome episodes of prison life. The last part of the play presents the desperate attempts of a woman to save the life of her condemned husband. She appeals in vain to the president's confessor, to a banker, and to a general, representing the Church, big business, and the military, the three social forces with which Franco colluded and from which he derived his dictatorial power. As late as in 2000, sixty-four years after his father's arrest, Arrabal dedicated an autobiographical essay, *Porté disparu* (Reported Missing), to this event from his troubled childhood.

Meanwhile, Arrabal's representations of women's relationships with their male partners and sexuality in general often have been considered offensive and scandalous and have given rise to violent reactions against his plays. Sadomasochistic and incestuous forms of love as well as amorous frustration prevail in the two-act play *Le Grand Cérémonial* (published 1965, produced 1966; translated as *The Grand Ceremonial,* 1970). The crippled hunchback and social reject Cavanosa daily sits on a park bench and strives to attract women. Sil, his latest victim, falls under his spell. She forsakes her "normal" lover and consents to Cavanosa's sadistic forms of love. She also agrees to help Cavanosa with his matricidal plans, promising to remove the corpse of his mother from his apartment after the deed is done. Cavanosa's room is filled with life-size female dolls, provided by his mother in an effort to shield her adolescent son from contact with the opposite sex. He uses them for mock wedding ceremonies and sadoerotic games. Expecting eventually to be murdered by her son, Cavanosa's mother acts out her incestuous passion for her son. At the end of the first act, he ceremoniously undresses one of the dolls and lies down with her, while Sil is heard groaning, offstage, under the torturous acts of the mother. Cavanosa's infantile exclamation "Maman, maman!" (Mama, Mama!) at the end of each scene underscores his sexual atrophy. The last part of the play mirrors the themes of the beginning: Cavanosa finds another woman, Lys, who has experienced an upbringing similar to his own. With her he finally succeeds in escaping from the horrors of his earlier existence, leaving behind his distressed mother.

Sexual oppression in women's education is the subject of *Le Jardin des délices* (published and produced 1969; translated as *The Garden of Delights,* 1974), a complex play constructed on two time levels, the life of a famous actress, Laïs, alternated with oneiric flashbacks to her formative years in a religious boarding school. As Laïs and her best friend, Miharca, discover their sexuality, they manage to escape from the convent, but Miharca comes back to haunt Laïs's adult life. The ritual murder of Miharca concludes the play and frees Laïs from her past. Sexual initiation, violence, and death are linked, culminating in the consenting woman's death.

Confused memories, flashbacks, rites of passage, initiation rituals, and complementary female characters are at the center of *Le Couronnement* (produced 1965, published 1966), later reprinted as *Le Lai de Barrabas* (1969, The Poem of Barrabas). Giafar finds Lys's dead body in a puddle of blood in her bed. With a kiss he is able to bring her back to life. Thanks to a magical flashback, Giafar witnesses Lys's birth and the carefully orchestrated coming-of-age ceremony she experienced. The objective of the esoteric, and often obscene, initiation ritual is for Lys, seated on a portable throne and wearing an iron crown, to become acquainted with the content of a parchment titled "Supreme Violence." In a parallel version of this ritual, depicted later in the play, she submits willingly to be disemboweled by Kardo, one of two Grand Guignolesque characters, reminiscent of K.'s assistants Arthur and Jeremiah in Kafka's *Das Schloss* (1926; translated as *The Castle,* 1930). Kardo kills her with a large knife shaped like a phallus. "Supreme Violence," whose contents are never revealed, is later presented to Giafar, whose education through love is the ultimate goal of the play.

An emphasis on aesthetic over moral values is often apparent in Arrabal's body of work. Not only did Arrabal publish biographical material on painters (such as *El Greco,* 1991), but he also had contemporary artists do paintings of him that he suggested by providing his own sketches. He then incorporated these paintings into his autobiographical writings. In his play *Concert dans un œuf* (Concert in an Egg; produced 1966, published 1966), Arrabal demonstrates the link between theater and the visual arts by having projected at the end of each tableau images such as the triptych *The Garden of Earthly Delights* by Hieronymus Bosch, various images by Pieter Brueghel, as well as photographs of modern skyscrapers and leading public figures.

Arrabal readily acknowledges that both Dadaism and Surrealism have had a profound influence upon his work, but he resists being classified—as Martin Esslin does in *The Theater of the Absurd* (1961)—as an "Absurdist" writer. According to Bernard Gille's 1970 study, Arrabal has explained that his plays "viennent d'horizons plus sauvages et moins spéculatifs" (come from more savage horizons). Hence, Arrabal has offered other labels for his plays, including "théâtre de cérémonie" (Theater of Ceremony) and "théâtre panique" (Panic theater). Of these, the latter is perhaps the best way to classify his works.

Panic theater was part of an orchestrated artistic agenda. At a meeting in the Paris Café de la Paix in February 1962, Arrabal, the Chilean writer and moviemaker Alexandre Jodorowsky, and the French writer and painter Roland Topor discovered a close affinity and decided to create the Panic movement (after rejecting the designation "burlesque"). In the years immediately following, these men published several works featuring the designation "panique": Arrabal's *Cinq récits paniques* (Five Panic Narratives), published in the first issue of Breton's Surrealist review *La Brèche* (1962); Arrabal's lecture at the University of Sydney, titled *L'Homme panique* (August 1963, Panic Man); Jodorowsky's *Les Nouvelles paniques* (1963, Panic News); and Topor's *Panic* (1965).

It is difficult, however, to provide a concise definition of Panic theater. The highly individualistic creators of the Panic movement have written about aspects of it, but some of their statements are contradictory or vague. Gille suggests that "*L'Homme panique* est une théorie de la connaissance issue d'une réflexion sur la création artistique et ses hasards, ce qui lui ôte tout caractère rationnel et logique" (*Panic Man* is a theory of

Raymond Gérôme in Arrabal's L'Architecte et l'empereur d'Assyrie, *at the Théâtre Montparnasse in Paris, March 1967 (© Lipnitzki/Roger-Viollet/Getty Images)*

knowledge generated from a reflection on artistic creation and its hazards, which rules out any rational and logical characteristics). While the Panic movement's founders openly acknowledged their debts to Dadaism and Surrealism, they intended their style to be more comprehensive, if less defined. In the fourth volume of the Bourgois edition of *Théâtre* (1967), Arrabal offers the following description of the movement: "Malgré d'enormes différences entre nos tentatives, nous faisons du théâtre une fête, une cérémonie d'une ordonnance rigoreuse. La tragédie et le guignol, la poésie et la vulgarité, la comédie et le mélodrame, l'amour et l'érotisme, le happening et la théorie des ensembles, le mauvais goût et le raffinement esthétique, le sacrilège et le sacré, la mise à mort et l'exaltation de la vie, le sordide et le sublime s'insèrent tout naturellement dans cette fête, cette cérémonie 'panique'" (Despite enormous differences between our efforts, we transform theater into a celebration, a ceremony of rigorous order. Tragedy and clownery, poetry and vulgarity, comedy and melodrama, love and eroticism, happenings and set theory, bad taste and aesthetic refinement, sacrilege and the sacred, putting to death and the exaltation of life, the sordid and the sublime, all get infused quite naturally into this feast, this "panic" ceremony).

In July 1967 Arrabal was jailed in Madrid for three weeks because of a provocative dedication he had written into one of his books during a book promotion: "Me cago en Dios, en la Patra (misspelled for Patria) y en todo lo demás" (Damn God, the fatherland and everything else). An array of internationally known writers, including Beckett, Eugène Ionesco, François Mauriac, and Henry Miller, came to his defense. Beckett addressed the Spanish court in these terms: The court "va juger un écrivain espagnol qui, dans le bref espace de dix ans, s'est hissé jusqu' au premier rang des dramaturges d'aujourd'hui, et cela par la force d'un talent profondément espagnol" (will judge a Spanish writer who, in the short period of ten years, has elevated himself to the first rank of today's playwrights, and this he owes to a talent which is essentially Spanish). Arrabal was acquitted in September of the same year.

One of Arrabal's most successful plays, *L'Architecte et l'empereur d'Assyrie* (translated as *The Architect and the Emperor of Assyria*, 1969), was produced and published in 1967. In the first act, the "Emperor," the only survivor of a plane wreck, meets the "Architect," the lone inhabitant of an unknown island. The Emperor is in reality a nameless office worker who has killed his mother, while the Architect has yet to learn the use of human language but possesses magic powers over animals and natural phenomena. After two years of isolated cohabitation, reminiscent of that portrayed in Daniel Defoe's *The Life and Strange Surprizing Adventures of Robinson Crusoe* (1719), they are able to communicate. In a dizzying sequence of role-playing episodes, the Emperor begins to act out his megalomaniacal, erotic, and perverse dreams of ruling, unopposed, over a powerful empire; in short, he pretends to bring the blessings of civilization to the primitive island. At first, the Architect plays along with this game, but soon the Architect leaves the island on a makeshift canoe. The Emperor is left to interact with an effigy that he has erected of himself, during which he reflects on his existence prior to the plane wreck. Facing a tribunal of his own conscience, he can no longer maintain the lies and exaggerations he used while entertaining the Architect. In the second act, the Architect returns, and what begins as just another episode of role-playing becomes an actual trial for matricide. The Architect-Judge-Executioner interrogates and condemns the Emperor to die. In the next-to-last scene, after the Emperor's execution, the Architect fulfills the last wish of the condemned and eats his body. Through this cannibalistic act, both characters are fused into one: gradually the Architect metamorphoses into the Emperor. The last scene mirrors the beginning of the play, only this time it is the Architect who emerges from the plane crash. The unpredictable oneiric sequences of *L'Architecte et l'empereur d'Assyrie,* although carefully constructed and orchestrated, reflect a chaotic universe. Both the Emperor and the Architect assume, in turn, multiple roles (the accused, various witnesses, animal characters, and so on), but the role-play can be broken up at any time, deliberately leaving the spectator in a state of confusion. Gille calls *L'Architecte et l'empereur d'Assyrie* "la demonstration la plus libre du théâtre Panique" (the freest

Cover for a 1969 collection of Arrabal's plays translated into English. The title play, 1960, expresses Arrabal's outrage at atrocities committed during the Spanish Civil War (Thomas Cooper Library, University of South Carolina).

demonstration of Panic theater), and the Architect "le plus convaincant de tous les personnages Paniques" (the most convincing of all Panic people). The English version of the play was staged in New York at La Mama Theater in May 1976 to enthusiastic reviews and in Barcelona in April of the following year. It remains one of Arrabal's most popular plays.

The late 1960s and the 1970s were years of travel and intense political and literary activity for Arrabal. In 1968 he participated in the Paris student uprising that led to a general strike throughout France. The following year Arrabal traveled to New York, where he wrote . . . *Et ils passèrent les menottes aux fleurs*. In 1970 he went to Tunisia to film *Viva la muerte*. That year his daughter Lelia was born, and a son, Samuel, was born in 1972. Arrabal returned to the United States in 1974 to visit Madrid, New Mexico, where he found inspiration for

Spanish painter Crespo's montage of the play L'extravagante reussite de Jésus-Christ, Karl Marx et William Shakespeare *(The Crazy Success of Jesus Christ, Karl Marx, and William Shakespeare), featuring Arrabal on the right (from Albert Chesneu and Angel Berenguer,* Plaidoyer pour une différence: Entretiens recueillis à Coucerault, *1978; Thomas Cooper Library, University of South Carolina)*

En la cuerda floja (On the Tightrope; published as *Sur le fil, ou La Ballade du train fantôme* [On the Tightrope, or The Ballad of the Phantom Train], 1976). He followed this experience with a journey to Tokyo in 1975.

... Et ils passèrent les menottes aux fleurs is representative of Arrabal's works of the 1970s, which were, according to Peter L. Podol, "indirectly inspired by Arrabal's incarceration in Spain and his contact with the May revolution in Paris." Arrabal followed the shocking torture and suffering in *... Et ils passèrent les menottes aux fleurs* with the brutality of *Le Ciel et la merde* (Heaven and Shit; published 1970, produced 1978). Based on the Manson murders of 1969, this play explores the close ties between religious ritual and all forms of sexual expression, including sadism.

Arrabal's next work, *La Grande Revue du XXème siècle* (1970, The Great Revue of the Twentieth Century), critiques modern technology in six separate sketches on subjects including the atom bomb, flying saucers, and the *Titanic,* and figures ranging from the Virgin of Fatima to Sigmund Freud. Podol suggests the play is "perhaps Arrabal's wittiest drama" because it succeeds in combining humor and politics. Other examples of Arrabal's politically-driven drama are *Bella ciao, ou La Guerre de mille ans* (published 1976, Bella Ciao, or The Thousand-Year War), a condemnation of capitalism and militarism; *La Marche royale* (published 1978, The Royal March), a satire of Franco; *Sur le fil, ou La Ballade du train fantôme,* a play that explores the theme of exile; and *Les Jeunes barbares d'aujourd'hui* (1975, Today's Young Barbarians), which provides a Marxist perspective on bicycle racing. *La Tour de Babel* (published 1978, The Tower of Babel) brings together the author's obsession with his native land and his Leftist convictions in a series of tableaus interpreting Spanish history as a fall into decadence after the civil war of the 1930s.

After the fall of Franco's regime in 1975, Arrabal's plays began to be staged more frequently in Spain. He began to publish original works in Spanish while his wife continued producing French translations. Many of Arrabal's plays of the 1980s and 1990s, such as *Mon Doux Royaume saccagé* (published 1980, My Sweet Kingdom Sacked) and *Bréviaire d'amour d'un haltèrophile* (published 1985; translated as *The Body Builder's Book of Love*, 1999), treat subjects similar to those of his earlier plays. *Carta de amor (Como un suplicio chino)* (2002, Love Letter [Like Chinese Torture]), which premiered in Madrid in January 2002, returns to the theme of the mother-son relationship explored in Arrabal's earlier plays. However, in this monologue spoken by "la madre" (the mother), it is not the actual mother but rather "la madrasta historia" (the wicked stepmother of history) that has destroyed the family and the son's connection to the father. The play suggests that Arrabal's mother was as much a victim of Franco as his father, and that Arrabal has reconciled himself to both his mother and Spain.

Because Fernando Arrabal's works were neither published nor performed in Spain during the Franco years, many literary historians classify Arrabal as a French playwright, often neglecting his narrative and lyrical works, as well as his political writings. Other scholars see him as one of the most significant contemporary Spanish writers, claiming that many essentially Spanish themes prevail in his oeuvre—especially his works portraying the Spanish Civil War and Spanish prisons (the latter reflecting not only his father's plight but also his own experience). Regardless, Arrabal consistently has broken taboos and caused his audiences to rethink many comforting moral and aesthetic commonplaces, and his profound impact on both the French and the Spanish literary scenes might be said to call into question the need for a conventional national category for his work.

Interviews:

Alain Schifres, *Entretiens avec Arrabal* (Paris: Belfond, 1969);

Albert Chesneu and Angel Berenguer, *Plaidoyer pour une différence: Entretiens recueillis à Coucerault* (Grenoble: Presses universitaires de Grenoble, 1978);

Karl Kohut, *Escribir en París: Entrevistas con Fernando Arrabal, Adelaïde Blasquez, José Corrales Egea, Julio Cortázar, Agustín Gómez Arcos, Juan Goytisolo, Augusto Roa Bastos, Severo Sarduy, Jorge Semprúm* (Frankfurt: Vervuert / Barcelona: Hogar del Libro, 1983).

References:

Jean-Jacques Daetwyler, *Arrabal* (Lausanne: Editions L'Age d'homme, 1975);

Thomas John Donahue, *The Theater of Fernando Arrabal: A Garden of Earthly Delights* (New York: New York University Press, 1980);

Martin Esslin, *The Theatre of the Absurd* (Garden City, N.Y.: Doubleday, 1961);

Deborah B. Gaensbauer, *The French Theatre of the Absurd* (Boston: Twayne, 1991);

Bernard Gille, *Fernando Arrabal,* Théâtre de tous les temps, no. 12 (Paris: Seghers, 1970);

Peter L. Podol, *Fernando Arrabal* (Boston: Twayne, 1978);

Harald Wentzlaff-Eggebert, "Fernando Arrabal's *Baal Babilonia.* Das Enfant terrible des französischen Nachkriegstheaters als meisterhafter spanischer Erzähler," *Romanistische Zeitschrift für Literaturgeschichte,* 21 (1997): 147–177.

Antonin Artaud

(4 September 1896 – 4 March 1948)

Martine Antle
University of North Carolina at Chapel Hill

See also the Artaud entry in *DLB 258: Modern French Poets.*

PLAY PRODUCTIONS: *Ventre Brûlé, ou La Mère folle,* Paris, Théâtre Alfred Jarry, 1 June 1927;
Les Cenci, adaptation of Percy Bysshe Shelley's *The Cenci,* Paris, Théâtre des Folies-Wagram, 7 May 1935.

BOOKS: *Tric Trac du Ciel* (Paris: Galerie Simon, 1923);
L'Ombilic des Limbes (Paris: La Nouvelle Revue Française, 1925); translated by Victor Corti as "Umbilical Limbo," in *Collected Works,* volume 1 (London: Calder & Boyars, 1968), pp. 49–65;
Le Pèse-Nerfs (Paris, 1925); enlarged as *Le Pèse-Nerfs, suivi des Fragments d'un Journal d'Enfer,* Collection Critique, no. 5 (Marseille: Les Cahiers du Sud, 1927); *Le Pèse-Nerfs* translated by Corti as "Nerve Scales," in *Collected Works,* volume 1 (London: Calder & Boyars, 1968), pp. 69–86; selections from the enlarged edition translated by Helen Weaver as "From *The Nerve Meter*" and *Fragments of a Diary in Hell,* in *Antonin Artaud: Selected Writings,* edited, with an introduction, by Susan Sontag (New York: Farrar, Straus & Giroux, 1976), pp. 77–96;
A la grande nuit, ou Le Bluff surréaliste (Paris: Antonin Artaud, 1927);
L'Art et la Mort (Paris: A l'Enseigne des Trois Magots/ Denoël, 1929); translated by Corti as "Art and Death," in *Collected Works,* volume 1 (London: Calder & Boyars, 1968), pp. 89–116;
Le Théâtre Alfred Jarry et l'Hostilité Publique, by Artaud and Roger Vitrac (Paris, 1930);
Le Moine de M. G. Lewis, raconté par Antonin Artaud (Paris: Denoël, 1931);
Héliogabale ou l'Anarchiste couronné (Paris: Denoël & Stelle, 1934); translated as *Heliogabalus: The Crowned Anarchist* (New York & London: Creation, 2003);
Les Nouvelles Révélations de L'Etre, as Le Révélé (Paris: Denoël, 1937); excerpt translated by Weaver as "From *The New Revelations of Being,*" in *Antonin*

Antonin Artaud (© Martinie/Roger-Viollet/Getty Images)

Artaud: Selected Writings, edited, with an introduction, by Sontag (New York: Farrar, Straus & Giroux, 1976), pp. 411–414;
Le Théâtre et son double (Paris: Gallimard, 1938); translated by Mary Caroline Richards as *The Theater and Its Double* (New York: Grove, 1958);
D'un Voyage au pays des Tarahumaras, Collection L'Age d'Or, no. 9 (Paris: Fontaine, 1945); translated by David Rattray as "Concerning a Journey to the Land of the Tarahumaras," *City Lights Journal,* no. 2 (1964): 69–84; *D'un Voyage au pays des Tarahumaras*

enlarged as *Les Tarahumaras* (Décines, Isère: L'Arbalète, 1955; revised edition, Paris: Gallimard, 1974); translated by Weaver as *The Peyote Dance* (New York: Farrar, Straus & Giroux, 1976);

Lettres de Rodez (Paris: Guy Lévis Mano, 1946); translated by Weaver as "Letters from 1943–45 (Rodez)," in *Antonin Artaud: Selected Writings*, edited, with an introduction, by Sontag (New York: Farrar, Straus & Giroux, 1976), pp. 443–465;

Xylophone contre la grande presse et son petit public, by Artaud and Henri Pichette (Paris: Imprimerie Davy, 1946);

Artaud le Mômo (Paris: Bordas, 1947); translated by Clayton Eshleman and Norman Gless as *Artaud The Momo* (Santa Barbara, Cal.: Black Sparrow, 1976);

Van Gogh, le suicidé de la société (Paris: K Editeur, 1947); translated as "Van Gogh: The Man Suicided by Society," in *The Tiger's Eye: On Arts and Letters* (1949);

Ci-gît, précédé de La Culture Indienne (Paris: K Editeur, 1947); translated by Weaver as "Indian Culture and Here Lies," in *Antonin Artaud: Selected Writings*, edited, with an introduction, by Sontag (New York: Farrar, Straus & Giroux, 1976), pp. 535–551;

Pour en finir avec le jugement de Dieu, émission radiophonique enregistrée le 28 novembre 1947 (Paris: K Editeur, 1948); translated by Guy Wernham as *To Have Done with the Judgment of God: Words for Radio Dated Nov. 28, 1947* (San Francisco: Bern Porter, 1956);

Lettre contre la Cabbale: Adressé à Jacques Prevel (Paris: Haumont, 1949);

Supplément aux Lettres de Rodez, suivi de Coleridge le traître (Paris: Guy Lévis Mano, 1949);

Vie et mort de Satan le feu, suivi de Textes Mexicains pour un Nouveau Mythe, preface by Serge Berna (Paris: Arcanes, 1953); translated by Alastair Hamilton and Corti as *The Death of Satan and Other Mystical Writings* (London: Calder & Boyars, 1974);

Galapagos: Les Iles du bout du monde (Paris: Broder, 1955);

Œuvres Complètes, edited by Paule Thévenin, 26 volumes (Paris: Gallimard, 1956–1994)—comprises volume 1, *Préambule; Correspondance avec Jacques Rivière; L'Ombilic des limbes; Le Pèse-nerfs; L'Art et la mort; Textes et poèmes inédits* (1956); revised and enlarged in 2 parts: part 1, *Préambule; Adresse au pape; Adresse au Dalaï-Lama; Correspondance avec Jacques Rivière; L'Ombilic des limbes; Le Pèse-nerfs, suivi des Fragments d'un journal d'enfer; L'Art et la mort; Premiers poèmes, 1913–1923; Premières proses; Tric trac du ciel; Bilboquet; Poèmes, 1924–1935;* and part 2, *Textes surréalistes; Lettres* (1970; revised and enlarged, 1976; revised and enlarged, 1984); volume 2, *L'Evolution du décor; Théâtre Alfred Jarry; Trois œuvres pour la scène; Deux projets de mise en scène; Notes sur les tricheurs de Steve Passeur; Comptes rendus, Apropos d'une pièce perdue, A propos de la littérature et des arts plastiques* (1961; revised and enlarged, 1980); volume 3, *Scenari; A propos du cinéma; Lettres; Interviews* (1961; revised and enlarged, 1978); volume 4, *Le Théâtre et son double; Le Théâtre de Séraphin; Les Cenci* (1964; revised and enlarged, 1978); *Les Cenci* translated by Simon Watson Taylor as *The Cenci* (London: Calder & Boyars, 1969; New York: Grove, 1970); *Le Théâtre de Séraphin* translated by Weaver as "The Theater of the Seraphim," in *Antonin Artaud: Selected Writings*, edited, with an introduction, by Sontag (New York: Farrar, Straus & Giroux, 1976), pp. 271–276; volume 5, *Autour du "Théâtre et son double" et des "Cenci"* (1964; revised and enlarged, 1979); volume 6, *Le Moine de Lewis raconté par Antonin Artaud* (1966; revised and enlarged, 1982); volume 7, *Héliogabale ou l'Anarchiste couronné; Les Nouvelles révélations de l'être* (1967; revised and enlarged, 1982); volume 8, *De "Quelques problèmes d'actualité" aux "Messages révolutionnaires"; Lettres du Mexique* (1971; revised and enlarged, 1980); volume 9, *Les Tarahumaras; Lettres de Rodez* (1971; revised and enlarged, 1979); volume 10, *Lettres écrites de Rodez: 1943–1944* (1974); volume 11, *Lettres écrites de Rodez: 1945–1946* (1974); volume 12, *Artaud le Mômo; Ci-gît, précédé de La Culture indienne* (1974); volume 13, *Van Gogh, le suicidé de la société; Pour en finir avec le jugement de dieu; Le Théâtre de la cruauté; Lettres à propos de "Pour en finir avec le jugement de dieu"* (1974); volume 14, *Suppôts et suppliciations,* 2 parts (1978); volume 15, *Cahiers de Rodez: Février–avril 1945* (1981); volume 16, *Cahiers de Rodez: Mai–juin 1945* (1981); volume 17, *Cahiers de Rodez: Juillet–août 1945* (1982); volume 18, *Cahiers de Rodez: Septembre–novembre 1945* (1983); volume 19, *Cahiers de Rodez: Décembre 1945–janvier 1946* (1984); volume 20, *Cahiers de Rodez: Février–mars 1946* (1984); volume 21, *Cahiers de Rodez: Avril–25 mai 1946* (1985); volume 22, *Cahiers du retour à Paris: 26 mai–juillet 1946* (1986); volume 23, *Cahiers du retour à Paris: Août–septembre 1946* (1987); volume 24, *Cahiers du retour à Paris: Octobre–novembre 1946* (1988); volume 25, *Cahiers du retour à Paris: Décembre 1946–janvier 1947* (1990); and volume 26, *Histoire vécue d'Artaud-Mômo: Tête-à-tête* (1994);

Autre chose que l'enfant beau (Paris: Broder, 1957);

Voici un endroit (Alès: P.A.B., 1958);

México, Spanish version, edited, with an introduction, by Luis Cardoza y Aragón (Mexico City: Universidad Nacional Autónoma de México, 1962); enlarged French version published as *Messages Révolutionnaires* (Paris: Gallimard, 1979; republished, 1998);

Collected Works, 4 volumes, translated by Victor Corti (London: Calder & Boyars, 1968–1974)–volume 1 (1968) includes "Cup and Ball" and "Unpublished Prose and Poetry";

Antonin Artaud: 1896–1948, dessins, Cahiers de l'Abbaye Sainte-Croix, no. 37 (Sables d'Olonne, France: Musée de l'Abbaye Sainte-Croix, 1980);

Antonin Artaud: Dessins (Paris: Editions du Centre Georges-Pompidou, 1987);

L'Arve et l'aume, suivi de 24 lettres à Marc Barbezat (Décines, Isère: L'Arbalète, 1989);

Antonin Artaud: Œuvres sur papier (Marseille: Musées de Marseille / Paris: Réunion des Musées Nationaux, 1995); translated by Margit Rowell as *Works on Paper* (New York: Museum of Modern Art/Harry N. Abrams, 1996).

Edition: *Van Gogh, le suicidé de la société,* "deluxe edition" (Paris: Gallimard, 1990).

Editions in English: *Antonin Artaud Anthology,* translated by Bernard Brechtman and others, edited by Jack Hirschman (San Francisco: City Lights Books, 1965);

To Have Done with the Judgment of God, translated by Clayton Eshleman and Norman Gless (Los Angeles: Black Sparrow, 1975);

Antonin Artaud: Selected Writings, translated by Helen Weaver, edited, with an introduction, by Susan Sontag (New York: Farrar, Straus & Giroux, 1976);

Antonin Artaud: Four Texts, translated by Eshleman and Glass (Los Angeles: Panjandrum Books, 1982)–comprises "To Georges Le Breton (Draft of a Letter)," "Artaud the Mômo," "To Have Done with the Judgment of God," and "The Theater of Cruelty and an Open Letter to the Reverend Father Laval";

Artaud on Theatre, edited and translated by Claude Schumacher (London: Methuen, 1989); revised and enlarged, edited and translated by Schumacher and Brian Singleton, 2001);

Watchfiends and Rack Screams: Works from the Final Period by Antonin Artaud, edited and translated by Eshleman and Bernard Bador (Boston: Exact Change, 1995).

PRODUCED SCRIPT: *La Coquille et le clergyman,* motion picture, 1927.

RECORDING: *Pour en finir avec le jugement de Dieu,* read by Maria Casarès, Roger Blin, Paule Thévenin, and Artaud, 2 CDs, P. Doan and M. Chalosse, 2001.

TRANSLATIONS: Matthew Gregory Lewis, *Le Moine* (Paris: Denoël & Stelle, 1931);

Ludwig Lewisohn, *Crime passionel,* translated by Artaud and Bernard Steele (Paris: Denoël, 1932).

SELECTED PERIODICAL PUBLICATIONS–UNCOLLECTED: "Le Visage humain," *Mercure de France,* no. 1017 (May 1948): 98–102;

"Aliéner l'acteur" and "Le Théâtre et la science," *L'Arbalète,* no. 13 (Summer 1948): 7–14;

"Notes pour une 'Lettre aux Balinais,'" *Tel Quel,* no. 46 (Summer 1971): 10–34;

"La Force du Mexique," *Nouvelle Revue Française,* no. 345 (August 1982): 3–7.

Antonin Artaud is the most original and controversial dramatist of the twentieth century. His posthumously published *Œuvres Complètes* (1956–1994, Complete Works), edited by Paule Thévenin, features works that are complex, difficult, at times obscure, and often beyond categorization. Artaud challenges Western thought and Western modes of representation through a questioning of the origins of language and the roles of art and metaphysics in contemporary societies. His exploration of oriental theater and mysticism and the changes he brought to the French stage place him as a leader among theorists and stage directors in modern French theater.

Antonin Marie Joseph Artaud was born in Marseille, France, on 4 September 1896, the son of Antoine-Roi Artaud, an import-export merchant, and Euphrasie Nalpas, a woman of Greek origin his father met through business connections. Artaud received a French Catholic education. At the age of five he survived acute meningitis, which caused permanent nerve damage. For the rest of his life he suffered intense cerebral pain, depression, and drug addiction, and he spent portions of his childhood and adult life in rest homes and mental-health wards in Rouen, Paris, and Rodez.

In 1920 Artaud's parents sent him to Paris, where he could be under the care of Doctor Toulouse, a psychotherapist who specialized in alternative therapies. Artaud moved in with the Toulouse family, who readily accepted him, although he eventually adopted an itinerant lifestyle. At this time he began correspondence with Jacques Rivière, the editor of *La Nouvelle Revue Française* (The New French Review). These letters, later published as *Correspondance avec Jacques Rivière* (1927), are the best surviving

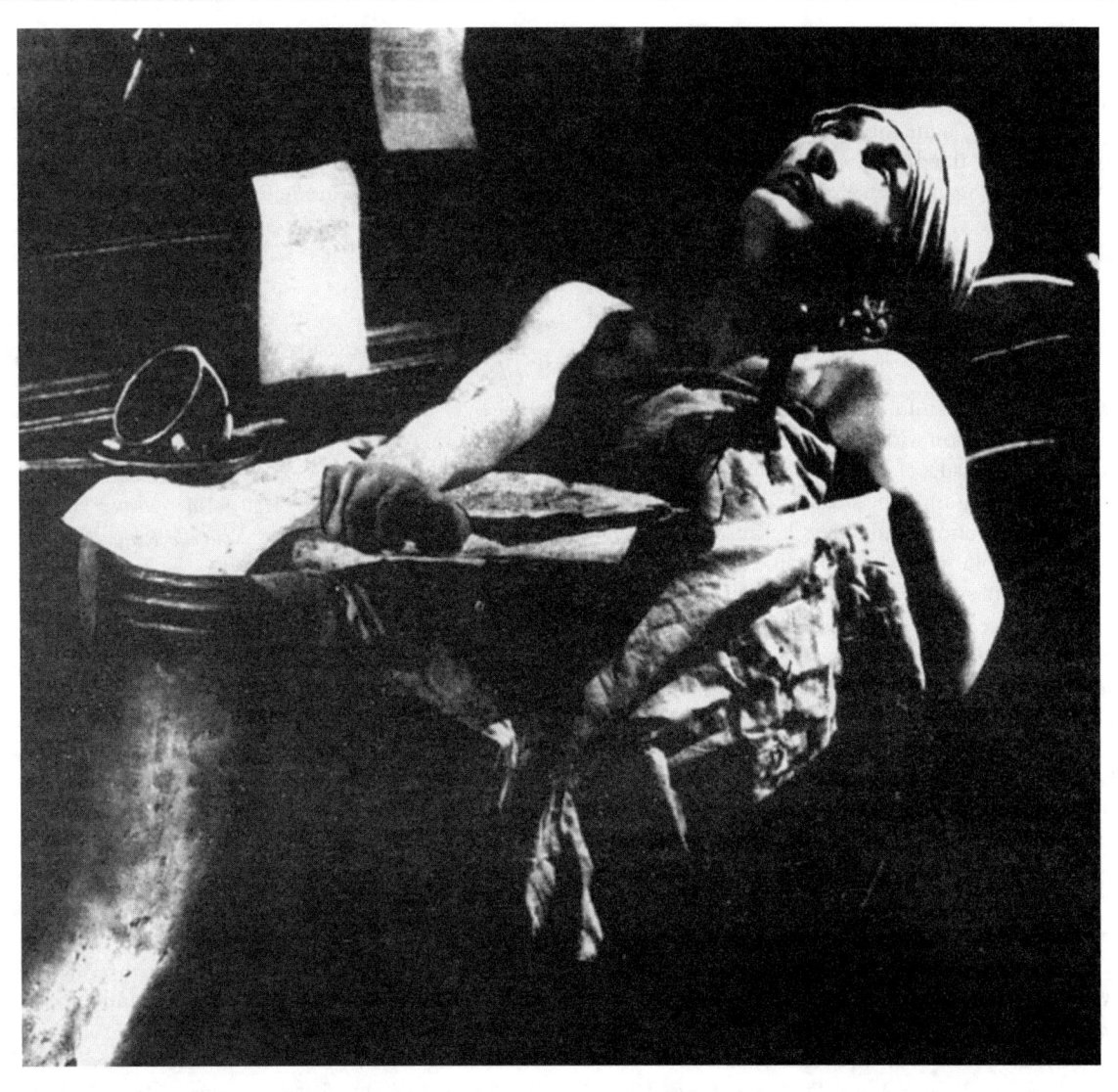

Artaud in the role of Jean-Paul Marat in Abel Gance's movie Napoléon *(1927) (photograph © Snark International; from Mark. V. Rose,* The Actor and His Double, *1986; Thomas Cooper Library, University of South Carolina)*

testimony of Artaud's genius as a writer, his acute sensitivity to the process of writing, and the pain he suffered during his youth. On several occasions in his correspondence he refers to the "maladie d'l'esprit" (sickness of the mind). A letter to Rivière dated 25 May 1924 furnishes a vivid example of Artaud's self-consciousness about his troubled mind and his urgent need to communicate. Artaud describes the suffering of living, which he calls a veritable "poison de l'être . . . Une maladie qui vois enlève la parole, le souvenir, qui vous déracine la pensée" (poison of being . . . a sickness that affects the soul in its deepest reality and that infects its manifestation . . . A veritable *paralysis*. A sickness that deprives you of speech, of memory, that uproots your thinking [translation by Bernard Frechtman]).

Artaud's move to Paris in 1920 marked the beginning of a rich, active, and productive artistic life. He lived among the leading Parisian intellectual and artistic circles of his time, developed skills as a writer, poet, artist, dramaturge, actor, and stage director, and began collaborating with many poets, artists, playwrights, and members of the Surrealist movement such as Max Jacob, Michel Leiris, André Masson, and Jean Dubuffet. In 1920 he began publishing poems and poetic prose pieces in reviews. Over the next several years came a flurry of book publications: *Tric Trac du Ciel* (1923, Backgammon of Heaven); *L'Ombilic des Limbes* (1925; translated as "Umbilicus Limbo," 1968); *Le Pèse-Nerfs* (1925; translated as "Nerve Scales," 1968); and *A la grande nuit, ou Le Bluff surréaliste* (1927, In the Great Darkness, or The Surrealist Bluff).

Soon after his move to Paris in 1920, Artaud was introduced to Aurélien Lugné-Poë, the director of the Théâtre de l'Œuvre, and in 1921 he took on his first work as an actor, a minor role in a play written by Henri de Régnier titled *Les Scrupules de Sganarelle* (1908, The Scruples of Sganarelle). From then on he collaborated on and acted in many plays. He also composed sketches of costumes for Francisco de Castro's *L'Hôtellerie* (1897, The Inn) and Jacinto Grau's *Le Comte Alarcos* (1917, Count Alarcos). In October 1924 Artaud joined a group of Surrealist artists, with whom he shared common views about the need to revolutionize literature and the need to search for a new poetic language. During his short affiliation with the Surrealist movement, he edited the third issue of *La Révolution Surréaliste* (The Surrealist Revolution), which featured scathing attacks on Western institutions and letters lauding Eastern culture. Artaud broke with the Surrealist group in 1925, when the Surrealists joined the Communist Party.

During his years in Surrealist circles in Paris in the 1920s, Artaud wrote a scenario for the first Surrealist movie script, *La Coquille et le clergyman* (The Shell and the Clergyman), which was produced in 1927 by the experimental moviemaker Germaine Dulac. Artaud worked as an actor and collaborated with the major producers and actors of his time, including Lugné-Poë, Charles Dullin, and Georges Pitoëff. He also took roles in experimental movies by Abel Gance, G. W. Pabst, Carl Theodor Dreyer, and Fritz Lang. Artaud's performance in the role of Marat in Gance's movie *Napoléon* (1927) brought him recognition onscreen. Another success was his performance as Brother Krassien in *La Passion de Jeanne d'Arc* (The Passion of Joan of Arc), directed by Dreyer in 1927 and released in 1928.

In June 1927 Artaud and Dadaists Roger Vitrac and Robert Aron cofounded the Théâtre Alfred Jarry (Alfred Jarry Theater), named after the late-nineteenth-century author of *Ubu Roi* (1896; translated, 1951). The main objective of this collaboration was a search for a new theatrical aesthetic. Artaud believed that the new aesthetic should be based on the notion of *spectacle intégral* (total theater), a new form of performance in which communication with the audience is based on visual signs (including gestures and props), noises, and other nonverbal means. In this new theatrical experience, the mise-en-scène becomes an essential part of theater. Hence, Artaud broke with the tradition of mimetic drama, favoring a minimalist stage in which objects, accessories, and props convey meaning to the audience. He relied on the use of large mannequins, taller than the human body, to create the *langage de la cruauté* (language of cruelty) he advocated, a cruelty he identified as the conflict, and even violence, that theater must portray in order to awaken the irrational, dark side of human nature. He also aspired to eliminate the four-walled performance space and place the spectator in the center of the action. Throughout his writings on theater, Artaud envisioned and advocated a *langage théâtral pur* (pure theatrical language) that was free of verbal discourse. This new aesthetic would alter the influence of the playwright, who would take a secondary role in the representation of his plays. Ultimately, the mission of Théâtre Alfred Jarry was *réveiller et secouer* (to wake up and shake up) the spectator and make him an active participant as prescribed in the preface of Alfred Jarry's *Ubu Roi*. Artaud sought to produce a cathartic experience, a trance; the experience was to act as a revelation, uncovering the mysteries of the psyche.

On 1 and 2 June 1927 the Théâtre Alfred Jarry produced Vitrac's *Les Mystères de l'amour* (1924; translated as *The Mysteries of Love,* 1964), Max Robur's [Aron's] *Gigogne*, and Artaud's *Ventre Brûlé, ou La Mère folle* (Burned Belly, or the Crazy Mother), the text of which has been lost. These performances were well received by the public and the Parisian intellectual elite. However, because of an approximately 8,000-franc deficit and other financial constraints, the Théâtre Alfred Jarry's repertoire was reduced to a dozen performances. On 14 January 1928 the theater featured a performance of *La Mère* (The Mother), an adaptation of the Maksim Gor'ky novel; Paul Claudel's *Partage de Midi* (1906; translated as *Break of Noon,* 1960); and Vitrac's *Victor ou les enfants au pouvoir* (1929, Victor, or The Children Are in Power), an important example of Surrealist drama. In his work for the theater, Artaud was often criticized for his choice of plays because, despite his advocacy of theater in which the text takes a secondary role in the performance, all the plays he selected relied heavily on dialogue. In spite of its short career, the Théâtre Alfred Jarry was the most important experimental theatrical enterprise of the interwar period, and it played a crucial role in the development of theater in France and elsewhere from the 1950s onward. Artaud's theatrical philosophy had an especially profound impact on theories of performance. Play directors such as Jean-Louis Barrault, Roger Blin, Peter Brook, John Cage, and Ariane Mnouchkine have been influenced by him.

In August 1931 Artaud visited the "Exposition Coloniale" (Colonial Exhibition) in Paris, and his experiences there marked a turning point in his ideas about a new theater. Balinese theater, which relies on dance, song, facial expressions, pantomime, and a complex, rigorous, coded gestural language, fascinated Artaud. He felt that it represented the possibility to renew contact with the origins of theater, *un théâtre pur* (a pure theater), and had the potential to renew theatrical conventions in the West. Working from his experience with Balinese ritual theater and dance, Artaud began to theorize about the functions of the human body and the ways in which theater could transform the body and allow it to transcend its ordinary form. Artaud believed that the multiple facets of the body and its masks could take on many meanings and represent the "doubles" of theater. The body remained a constant preoccupation during Artaud's life, a recurring theme in his writings on theater and poetry, in his correspondence, and in his drawings.

Artaud continued to contest the supremacy of the text onstage. In 1935 he created and directed a full-length play inspired by Percy Bysshe Shelley's tragedy *Les Cenci* (The Cenci). It opened on 7 May 1935 at the Théâtre des Folies-Wagram (The Folies-Wagram Theater) in Paris and was performed seventeen times. In this production Artaud put into practice his philosophy of theater and especially his idea of a theater of cruelty based on nonverbal communication; he experimented with gigantic mannequins, a wheel, shadows, loud discordant sounds, and visual effects in order to dramatize the scenes of Beatrice's torture.

Artaud's essays on theater, including articles and lectures, were published throughout the 1930s in *La Nouvelle Revue Française* and were reprinted in 1938 in a single volume titled *Le Théâtre et son double* (translated as *The Theatre and Its Double*, 1958). This book features many of Artaud's arguments for the fundamental renewal of the form and content of theater. In 1931 Artaud presented a reading of *Le Théâtre et son double* at the Sorbonne in Paris, at which the writer Anaïs Nin was present. In her journal Nin recalled the agonizing tone of his voice and the theatricality of his reading. Considered by some a visionary and poetic work, this collection of essays went largely unnoticed for several decades until the emergence of the Beat movement in the United States in the 1960s; it has since brought Artaud recognition throughout the world.

Artaud's early collaboration with the Théâtre Alfred Jarry and the stage innovations it introduced were crucial to the establishment of the Nouveau Théâtre (New Theater) of postwar France. Artaud's stage innovations introduced the idea that a live theatrical performance should create a religious and therapeutic experience. The performance should transform the spectator and direct him away from the rationalistic aims of traditional Western theater, which relied too heavily on the written word. In *Le Théâtre et son double*, Artaud compared theater to the plague. He believed that theater, like the plague, should upset the usual order of life and provide an experience powerful enough to dissolve the social order: "Une vraie pièce de théâtre bouscule le repos des sens, libère l'inconscient comprimé, pousse à une sorte de révolte virtuelle et qui d'ailleurs ne peut avoir tout son prix que si elle

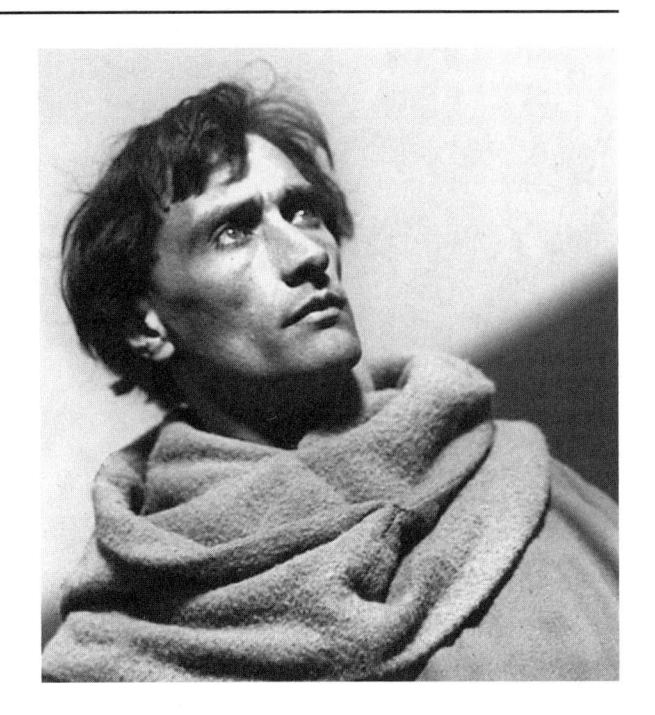

Photograph of Artaud playing Brother Krassien in the movie La Passion de Jeanne d'Arc *(1928) (photograph by Henry Guttmann; © Getty Images)*

demeure virtuelle, impose aux collectivités rassemblées une attitude héroïque et difficile" (A true play shakes up the repose of the senses, liberates the constricted unconscious, pushes to a type of virtual revolt and which, besides, can only have its full value if it remains virtual, imposes on assembled collectivities an heroic and difficult attitude).

Researching the cabala, Artaud developed a new philosophy of acting, including a method of breathing for actors, since Artaud firmly believed that each movement or gesture was directly connected to breath. In Artaud's new vision of theatrical performance, the actor took part in a complex network of visual and auditory sign systems in which his or her body language resembled that of an "hiéroglype animé" (animated hieroglyph). In a chapter of *Le Théâtre et son double* titled "Un Athlétisme affectif" (An Emotional Athletics), Artaud rewrote the teachings of the cabala for the theater: henceforth, voice and music took on an incantatory rhythm in order to reveal "la vérité intérieure" (the inner truth), and theater became a radical social force with the potential for bringing change. The most important mission of theatricality for Artaud was to purge Western civilization of its evils and ailments. Artaud was thus among the first artists and intellectuals to oppose Western thought.

In his search for a new language that would best convey the mythic, spiritual, and ritualistic essence of

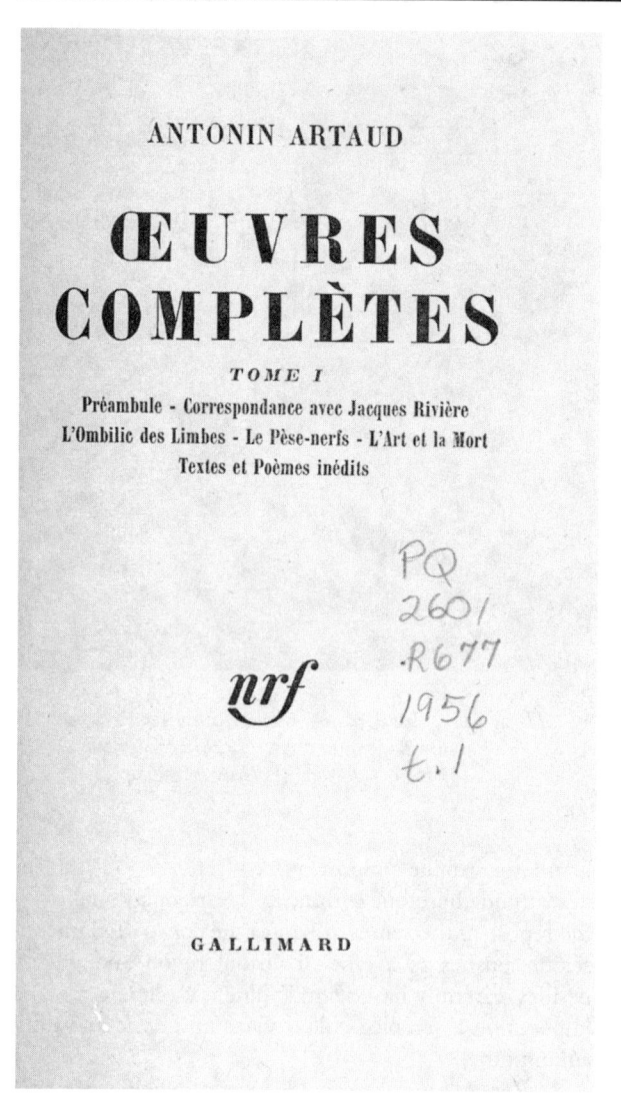

Title page for the first volume of Artaud's complete works, published in twenty-six volumes between 1956 and 1994 (Thomas Cooper Library, University of South Carolina)

theater, Artaud studied Tibetan philosophy extensively and traveled to Mexico in 1936 to experience the effects of peyote and explore the ritual theater of the Tarahumaras Indians. In his writings on the Tarahumaras, *D'un Voyage au pays des Tarahumaras* (1945), Artaud revealed his idealized vision of Mexico and his perception of nature. To him, the mountains of the Tarahumaras appeared as rich signs and "éffigies naturelles" (natural effigies) that provoked sensorial and quasi-religious experiences. Just like in theater, he claimed, "all true effigies have a double, a shadowed self," and the Sierra opened up to a deep, mysterious symbolism: "De la montagne ou de moi-même, je ne peux dire ce qui était hanté, mais un miracle optique analogue, je l'ai vu, dans ce périple à travers la montagne, se présenter au moins une fois par journée" (Whether it was the mountain or myself which was haunted, I cannot say, but I saw similar optical miracles during this journey across the mountain, and they confronted me at least once a day [translation by David Rattray]). Yet, despite his genuine interest in the indigenous culture of the Tarahumaras Indians and his fascination with the *Ciguri* (peyote dance), Artaud did not engage in dialogue with the indigenous populations. Cross-cultural exchanges with the Tarahumaras remained limited, and even though Artaud participated in the rituals, he remained an outsider.

Another artistic experience played a fundamental role in the shaping of Artaud's philosophy on theater and its "doubles." Artaud became captivated by the multiple visual and auditory signs evoked by Lucas van Leyden's painting *Lot and His Daughters* (circa 1520), on display at the Louvre Museum in Paris. Artaud drew parallels between Balinese dance, the theatricality of the canvas, and the new type of theatrical language he was still trying to articulate. He often referred to Leyden's painting and its unusual pictorial architecture in order to redefine the notion of "cruelty" in his theater. This painting, according to Artaud's reading in *Le Théâtre et son double,* communicated "rigeur cosmîque et nécessité implacable (cosmic rigor and implacable decision). For "cruelty" in this painting, just like in theater, was not exclusively dependent on the main theme (incest in this case), but rather on the apocalyptic portrayal (or "staging") of nature and the visual and aural signs animating the pictorial landscape. Ultimately, Artaud's concept of "cruelty" and his theatrical reading of *Lot and His Daughters* resonated in art criticism and critical theory. Because of Artaud, theatricality was no longer solely an issue in theater but could also be applied to other forms of artistic expression such as painting, drawing, and writing.

Artaud developed his theories through works such as *Héliogabale ou L'Anarchiste couronné* (1934; translated as *Heliogabalus: The Crowned Anarchist,* 2003). In this play Artaud uses the figure of the Roman emperor Heliogabalus, renowned for his sexual deviance and immense brutality, to explore the *langage de la cruauté* (language of cruelty) and the mysteries of astrology and numerical symbolism.

In 1937 a delusional Artaud, who believed he would play a significant role in the Apocalypse, set off on a mission to Ireland. Soon he was expelled from the country, and on the return trip he had to be restrained. Back in France, Artaud was moved through a series of asylums before being placed in the asylum in the city of Rodez from 1943 until 1946. His mental health deteriorated rapidly beginning in 1944, when Dr. Gaston Ferdière attempted to cure him with a series of electroshocks.

After Artaud was released from the asylum in Rodez in 1946, he returned to Paris, where he started to gain notoriety. The publisher Gallimard began considering the publication of his complete works. A Vincent van Gogh exhibit in Paris in 1947 had a deep impact on Artaud, who wrote an essay on Van Gogh titled *Van Gogh, le suicidé de la société* (1947; translated as "Van Gogh: The Man Suicided by Society," 1949). In this essay Artaud speaks highly of Van Gogh's artistic vision and talent and defends him from a French psychiatrist's charge of degeneracy: "En face de la lucidité de Van Gogh qui travaille, la psychiatrie n'est plus qu'un réduit de gorilles eux-mêmes obsédés et persécutés et qui n'ont, pour pallier les plus épouvantables états de l'angoisse et de la suffocation humaines, qu'une ridicule terminologie" (Faced with Van Gogh's lucidity, always active, psychiatry becomes nothing less but a den of gorillas, so obsessed and persecuted that it can only use a ridiculous terminology to palliate the most frightful anxiety and human suffocation [translated by Mary Beach and Lawrence Ferlinghetti]). Artaud received the 1947 Sainte-Beuve literary prize for his essay.

Labeled at once as a genius, a madman, and a *poète maudit* (a cursed poet), Artaud continued to be a marginalized figure until the last years of his life. In 1948 he produced three short radio programs adapted from one of his prose texts titled *Pour en finir avec le jugement de Dieu* (recorded in 1947 for a 2 February 1948 airing that was canceled; published in 1948; translated as *To Have Done with the Judgment of God*, 1956; mass-market edition of recording produced in 2001). In this work, Artaud embodies the alienation of the individual in society and expresses his urge to seek an elementary form of consciousness.

Artaud died of cancer on 4 March 1948 at the Ivry Hospice in Paris. At the time of his death he was largely ignored by critics, who rarely moved beyond considering whether or not he was mad. When Artaud's works started to gain recognition in the 1960s, however, he quickly became a cult figure, a legend in the world of theater and art.

Artaud produced relatively few plays and was mostly a visionary theorist. His *Le Théâtre et son double* was the first major theoretical text on theater. However, his writings and work in theater proved controversial. His detractors took him to task for producing few plays, for being too abstract, and for dreaming of an impossible theater. His followers, meanwhile, praised him for his visionary theories that played a major role in the development of theater in France and around the world. His artistic manifestos attracted the attention of philosophers, poststructuralists, and critics. His drawings, sketches, and self-portraits continue to be exhibited in special collections and museums worldwide.

Antonin Artaud remains an important point of reference in the world of twentieth-century theater. During the 1990s new studies investigating his works and legacy materialized in France and on the international scene. For example, in 1993 a movie titled *La véritable histoire d'Artaud le Momô* (The True Story of Artaud-Momô) challenged the conven-

Cover for the first American edition of Artaud's 1938 collection of essays on theater (Thomas Cooper Library, University of South Carolina)

tional understanding of Artaud. Produced by Gérard Mordillat and Jérôme Prieur, this documentary follows Artaud's trajectory from 26 May 1946 to 4 March 1948. It offers a fresh look at Artaud through biographical data, interviews, recordings of Artaud's voice, photographs, and Artaud's drawings. The juxtaposition of biographical elements, unpublished photographs taken by Georges Pastier, and the reading of Artaud's texts by friends who accompanied him during the last years of his life reveal the humanity and dignity of Artaud. Additionally, a Fonds de Recherche (Research Center) focusing on Artaud was established at the University Paris III in 1997, led by Olivier Penot-Lacassagne and a new generation of young researchers. The mission of this research center is to develop a comprehensive archival database dedicated to Artaud studies. The center started a new journal in 2000 titled *Bulletin Antonin Artaud*. Such efforts will further illuminate Arlaud's role in theatre and influence future generations of scholars and writers.

Letters:

Correspondance avec Jacques Rivière (Paris: La Nouvelle Revue Française, 1927);

"Lettres (à Maurice Bataille d'octobre 1947)," *France-Asie,* no. 30 (September 1948): 1049–1058;

Lettres d'Antonin Artaud à Jean-Louis Barrault, edited, with a preface, by Paul Arnold, notes by André Frank (Paris: Bordas, 1952);

"Lettre (à Pierre Loeb du 23 avril 1947)," *Les Lettres nouvelles,* no. 6 (April 1958): 481–486;

"Lettre (à Albert Camus)," *Nouvelle Revue Française,* no. 89 (May 1960): 1012–1020;

"Lettre (à Roger Karl du 1er mars 1939)," *Lettre ouverte,* no. 2 (March 1961): 59–60;

"Onze lettres à Anaïs Nin," *Tel Quel,* no. 20 (Winter 1964): 3–11;

"Lettres inédites (de 1930 à 1933)," *Opus International,* no. 3 (1967): 62–69;

Lettres à Génica Athanasiou: Précédées de deux poèmes à elle dédiés (Paris: Gallimard, 1969);

"La dernière lettre de Rodez," *Magazine littéraire,* no. 95 (December 1974): 51;

Lettres à Annie Besnard, edited by Françoise Buisson (Paris: Le Nouveau Commerce, 1977);

Nouveaux écrits de Rodez: Lettres au docteur Ferdière, 1943–1946, et autres textes inédits, suivis de six lettres à Marie Dubuc, 1935–1937, edited by Pierre Chaleix, preface by Gaston Ferdière (Paris: Gallimard, 1977);

"Lettres à Janine," *Nouvelle Revue Française,* nos. 316–317 (May–June 1979): 177–191, 167–179;

"Lettres (à Pierre Bordas)," *Nouvelle Revue Française,* no. 364 (May 1983): 170–188;

"Lettres (à A. Adamov et J. Lemarchand)," *Nouvelle Revue Française,* no. 413 (June 1987): 112–119.

Bibliography:

Claude-Jean Rameil, "Bibliographie," *Obliques,* nos. 10–11 (1976): 257–283.

Biographies:

Otto Hahn, *Portrait d'Antonin Artaud* (Paris: Le Soleil Noir, 1968);

Jacques Prevel, *En compagnie d'Antonin Artaud,* edited by Bernard Noël (Paris: Flammarion, 1974);

Thomas Maeder, *Antonin Artaud* (Paris: Plon, 1978);

Stephen Barber, *Antonin Artaud: Blows and Bombs* (London: Faber & Faber, 1993);

André Roumieux, *Artaud et l'asile,* 2 volumes (Paris: Séguier, 1996);

Barber, *Blows and Bombs: Antonin Artaud, the Biography* (London: Creation, 2002).

References:

Stephen Barber, *Artaud, The Screaming Body* (London: Creation, 1999);

Jacques Derrida, *Artaud le Moma* (Paris: Galilée, 2002);

Derrida and Paule Thévenin, *The Secret Art of Antonin Artaud* (Cambridge, Mass.: MIT Press, 1998);

Camille Dumoulie, *Les Théâtres de la cruauté: Hommage à Antonin Artaud* (Paris: Desjonquières, 2000);

Thierry Galibert, *Antonin Artaud, écrivain du Sud* (Aix-en-Provence: Edisud, 2002);

Armand Laroche, *Antonin Artaud et son double* (Périgueux: Fanlac, 1964);

Olivier Penot-Lacassagne, *Antonin Artaud en revues* (Paris: Sheer, 2004);

Penot-Lacassagne, *Antonin Artaud 1: Modernités d'Antonin Artaud* (Paris: Minard, 2000);

Penot-Lacassagne, *Antonin Artaud 2: Artaud et les avant-gardes théâtrales* (Paris: Minard, 2004);

Gene A. Plunka, ed., *Antonin Artaud and the Modern Theater* (Rutherford, N.J.: Fairleigh Dickinson University Press, 1994);

Jonathan Pollock, *Le Rire du Mômo: Antonin Artaud et le littérature anglo-américaine* (Paris: Kimé, 2002);

Edward Scheer, ed., *Antonin Artaud: A Critical Reader* (New York & London: Routledge, 2003);

Manohar Sethi, *The Theatre of Cruelty* (New Delhi: Commonwealth, 1993);

La véritable histoire d'Artaud le Momô, motion picture, Laura Productions/La Sept Arte/Les Films d'Ici/Arcanal/Centre Georges Pompidou, 1993;

Alain Virmaux, *Antonin Artaud et le théâtre* (Paris: Seghers, 1970).

Papers:

A collection of Antonin Artaud's papers is held at the Bibliotéque Nationale in Paris.

Jacques Audiberti
(25 March 1899 – 10 July 1965)

Christophe Lagier
California State University, Los Angeles

PLAY PRODUCTIONS: *Quoat-Quoat,* Paris, Théâtre de la Gaité-Montparnasse, 28 January 1946;
Le Mal court, Paris, Théâtre de Poche, 17 June 1947;
Les Femmes du bœuf, Paris, Comédie-Française, 23 November 1948;
La Fête noire, Paris, Théâtre de la Huchette, 3 December 1948;
L'Ampélour, Paris, Théâtre des Noctambules, 17 February 1950;
Sa Peau, Paris, Théâtre des Noctambules, 11 April 1950;
Pucelle, Paris, Théâtre de la Huchette, 1 June 1950;
Les Naturels du Bordelais, Paris, Théâtre La Bruyère, 30 September 1953;
La Mégère appcivoisée, adapted from William Shakespeare's *The Taming of the Shrew,* Paris, Théâtre de l'Athénée, 1957;
La Hobereaute, IVème Festival des Nuits de Bourgogne, 28 June 1957; Paris, Théâtre du Vieux-Colombier, 25 September 1958;
Le Ouallou, Paris, Théâtre La Bruyère, 26 April 1958;
L'Effet Glapion, Paris, Théâtre La Bruyère, 9 September 1959;
La Logeuse, Paris, Théâtre de l'Oeuvre, 3 October 1960;
La Fourmi dans le corps, Paris, Comédie-Française, 27 March 1962;
Pomme, pomme, pomme, Paris, Théâtre La Bruyère, 7 September 1962;
La Brigitta, Paris, Théâtre de l'Athénée, 23 September 1962;
Le Cavalier seul, Lyon, Théâtre du Cothurne, 5 December 1963;
L'Opéra du monde, Lyon, Théâtre du Cothurne, 11 June 1964.

BOOKS: *L'Empire et la trappe* (Paris: Librairie du Carrefour, 1930);
Elisabeth-Cécile-Amélie (Paris: Guy Lévis-Mano, 1936);
Race des hommes (Paris: Gallimard, 1937);
Abraxas (Paris: Gallimard, 1938);
Septième (Paris: Gallimard, 1939);

Jacques Audiberti (© Lipnitzky/Roger-Viollet/Getty Images)

Paroles d'éclaircissement (Aurillac: La Pomme de Sapin, 1940);
Des Tonnes de semence (Paris: Gallimard, 1941);
Urujac (Paris: Gallimard, 1941);
Carnage (Paris: Gallimard, 1942);
La Nouvelle Origine (Paris: Gallimard, 1942);
Le Retour du divin (Paris: Gallimard, 1943);
Toujours (Paris: Gallimard, 1943);
La Fin du monde (Paris: Société parisienne de librairie et d'éditions, 1944);
La Nâ (Paris: Gallimard, 1944);
La Bête noire (Paris: Les Quatre Vents, 1945);
Vive Guitare (Paris: Robert Laffont, 1946);
Monorail (Fribourg & Paris: Egloff, 1947);

Talent (Fribourg & Paris: Egloff, 1947);
L'Opéra du monde (Paris: Fasquelle, 1947);
Le Victorieux (Paris: Gallimard, 1947);
Théâtre, 5 volumes (Paris: Gallimard, 1948–1962)—comprises volume 1 (1948), *Quoat-Quoat; L'Ampélour; Les Femmes du bœuf; Le Mal court;* volume 2 (1952), *La Fête noire; Pucelle; Les Naturels du Bordelais;* volume 3 (1956), *La Logeuse; L'Opéra parlé; Le Ouallou; Altanima;* volume 4 (1961), *Coeur à cuire; Le Soldat Dioclès; La Fourmi dans le corps; Les Patients; L'Armoire classique; Un Bel Enfant;* and volume 5 (1962), *Pomme, pomme, pomme; Bâton et ruban; Boutique fermée; La Brigitta;*
Les médecins ne sont pas des plombiers (Paris: Gallimard, 1948);
Cent jours (Paris: Gallimard, 1950);
Le Maître de Milan (Paris: Gallimard, 1950);
La Pluie sur les boulevards (Angers: Au Masque d'or, 1950);
Le Globe dans la main I: L'amour (Paris: Foret, 1950);
Le Globe dans la main II: La médecine (Paris: Foret, 1951);
L'Ouvre-boîte: Colloque abhumaniste, by Audiberti and Camille Bryen (Paris: Gallimard, 1952);
Marie Dubois (Paris: Gallimard, 1952);
Rempart, un poème (Paris: Gallimard, 1953);
Molière (Paris: L'Arche, 1954);
Les Jardins et les fleuves (Paris: Gallimard, 1954);
L'Abhumanisme (Paris: Gallimard, 1955);
Le Cavalier seul (Paris: Gallimard, 1955);
La Beauté de l'amour (Paris: Gallimard, 1955);
La Poupée: Roman (Paris: Gallimard, 1956);
Les Enfants naturels (Paris: Fasquelle, 1956);
Le Sabbat ressucité, by Audiberti and Leonor Fini (Paris: Société des amis des livres, 1957);
Infanticide préconisé (Paris: Gallimard, 1958);
Lagune hérissée (Paris: Société des Cent-Une, 1958);
L'Effet Glapion: Parapsychocomédie (Paris: Gallimard, 1959);
Scénario et dialogues de La Poupée (Paris: Gallimard, 1962);
Les Tombeaux ferment mal (Paris: Gallimard, 1963);
Ange aux entrailles (Paris: Gallimard, 1964);
Dimanche m'attend (Paris: Gallimard, 1965);
La Poupée: Comédie en 6 tableaux (Paris: Gallimard, 1969);
La Forteresse et la marmaille: 1938–1964, afterword by Josiane Fournier, L'Ecole des Lettres (Paris: Le Seuil, 1996);
Le Mur du fond: Ecrits sur le cinéma (Paris: Cahiers du cinéma, 1996);
Paris fut: Ecrits sur Paris 1937–1953, edited by Fournier (Paris: Editions Claire Paulhan, 1999);
Chiens écrasés (Saint-Clément: Fata Morgana, 2000);
Le Poète (Saint-Clément: Fata Morgana, 2001).

PRODUCED SCRIPT: *La Poupée,* motion picture, Ajace Produzioni Cinematografiche/Films Franco-Africains/Procinex, 1962.

OTHER: Jacques Bourgeat, *Au petit trot de Pégase,* preface by Audiberti (Paris: Union des Bibliophiles de France/Vox, 1945);
Marcel Franck, *Notre-Dame de la C.G.T.,* preface by Audiberti (Paris: Chaillot, 1947);
Suzanne de Verneilh, *Deux pilotes,* preface by Audiberti (Paris: Foret, 1950);
Géa Augsbourg, *Mes Amériques: 78 dessins accompagnés de notes de voyage,* preface by Audiberti (Bâle: Vineta, 1951);
Geneviève Laporte, *Les Cavaliers d'ombre 7,* preface by Audiberti (Paris: Foret, 1954);
Pierre de Ronsard, *Pierre de Ronsard et ses musiciens, sélection des meilleurs poèmes de Ronsard, textes musicaux de l'époque,* edited by France Igly, preface by Henri Busser, introduction by Audiberti (Paris: Debresse, 1955);
Les Jardins de Priape: Poésies erotiques du seizième siècle, edited by Robert Arnaut, introduction by Audiberti (Paris: Cercle du livre prècieux, 1960);
Igly, *Troubadours et trouvères,* prefaces by Audiberti and William Rime (Paris: Seghers, 1960);
Pierre Osenate, *Passage des vivants: poèmes,* preface by Audiberti (Paris: Source, 1962).

TRANSLATIONS: Gabriela Mistral, *Désolation: Poèmes,* translated by Audiberti and others (Paris: Nagel, 1946);
Le Tasse, *Les Flèches d'Armide* (Paris: Le Seuil, 1946);
Benjamin Joppolo, *Les Chevaux de bois* (Paris: Chêne, 1947);
Valentino Bompiani, *Albertina* (Paris: Théâtre de la Huchette, 1948);
Eduardo de Filippo, *Madame Filoumé* (Paris: Théâtre de la Renaissance, 1952);
Joppolo, *Le Chien, le photographe et le tram* (Paris: Corréa, 1953);
William Shakespeare, *La Mégère apprivoisée* (Paris: Gallimard, 1957).

Jacques Audiberti had already proved himself as a novelist, poet, and essayist when after World War II he began concentrating on plays. By the time of his death in 1965, he was widely known as an innovative dramatist whose work was almost impossible to classify: his theater, like his writing in other genres, fell in line with neither traditional models nor the avant-garde trends of his day. Hence, many labels crafted by contemporary critics, including "theater of the absurd," "new theater," and "poetic theater," are not quite appropriate for Audiberti's extraordinarily rich and complex plays. The adjective most frequently applied to his plays is "baroque," but even that description is problematic. Audiberti's theater is original, poetic, and sometimes humorous; it questions the origin of evil and social power structures as reflected in language. It is a philosophical enterprise and a reflection on theater itself inspired by Friedrich Nietzsche and Antonin Artaud.

Jacques Séraphin-Marie Audiberti was born on 25 March 1899, in the home of his paternal grandparents in the Vauban district of Antibes, a fortified town between Cannes and Nice on the French Riviera. Until the age of six Audiberti lived in this house on rue du Saint-Esprit with his parents, Louis Audiberti, a master mason, and his wife, Victorine. He spent the remainder of his childhood in a home his father built in another district of town, the anse Saint Roch. Audiberti was always attached to his city of birth and the two houses in which he grew up: Antibes's beautiful, rugged coastline and the dwellings of his youth are often depicted in his novels. The historical significance of the town, where a memorable battle marked Napoleon's return to France from Elba in 1815 and the beginnings of his last-ditch effort to recover his empire, fostered an appreciation of the weight and violence of history, themes that recur in Audiberti's literary work. Throughout his life, Audiberti frequently returned to stroll the famous ramparts of Antibes.

Audiberti's father was alternately stern and whimsical, and he often intimidated his son. His mother, meanwhile, was overly protective of her only child. As a teenager at Collège d'Antibes, the local junior high school that now bears his name, Audiberti had difficulty adjusting to the scholarly environment and developed a particular aversion to mathematics. He abandoned his studies in 1914 for health reasons, and although he resumed them in 1916, he never took the *baccalauréat,* the diploma that marks the end of high school in France. From an early age Audiberti was shy toward women, and his literary work became a means for expressing his bourgeoning adolescent desires. The power of sexuality became a recurring theme in his drama.

As a youth, Audiberti became fascinated by the new medium of cinema. He was also an avid reader of "classical" contemporary authors, including Anatole France and Victor Hugo, who had a significant and consistent influence on his writings. He also read Guillaume Apollinaire, but evidently found little of interest in the work of the radical poet. As a teenager, Audiberti submitted his first collection of poetry to the playwright Edmond Rostand, creator of *Cyrano de Bergerac* (performed 1897, published 1898, translated 1898). Rostand encouraged the budding author with a supportive letter and an autographed picture, and from 1914 on, Audiberti contributed short articles and poetry to a local daily paper, the *Réveil d'Antibes* (Antibe's Awakening).

In 1918 poor health exempted Audiberti from compulsory yearlong military service, and he took a job as a clerk at the Antibes courthouse. Then, after a short stint living in or near Marseille, Audiberti left for Paris in 1924 to join a school acquaintance, Emile Condroyer, who was making a name for himself as a reporter of picturesque and adventurous stories. At the time, writings like Condroyer's were fashionable in journalism, and he became the first recipient of the prestigious Albert Londres Award in 1933. A friend of Audiberti's father helped place Audiberti in a junior position at the daily *Journal,* but in the fall of 1924 he transferred to the *Petit Parisien* (Little Parisian), where for the next five years he served as an anonymous "tourneur": a scavenger of items for the "news in brief" section of the paper. Audiberti haunted police stations of the capital and suburbs to get the latest on fires, suicides, muggings, and other crimes. He later referred humorously to this period of his life in terms of "the school of the poetry of the suburbs," where he developed an appreciation for the grotesque and trivial aspects of life that manifested itself in his drama.

During this time Audiberti met Benjamin Péret, a friend and proponent of André Breton, the young leader of the Surrealist movement. Péret introduced Audiberti to the ambiguities of Pablo Picasso's art and to the potential benefits of the Surrealist revolution. Although Audiberti met Breton and probably read some of his books, he never subscribed to his ideology and resented the authoritarian ways of the Surrealist leader. Some years later he told Paul Guth in *Quarante contre un* (1947, Forty against One): "Je ne suis pas entré dans le groupe. Ce n'était pas mon chemin. Je n'avais rien à leur apporter" (I did not enter the group. It was not my path. I had nothing to give them). Audiberti was suspicious of artistic movements and political causes throughout his life and never affiliated himself with them; nevertheless, his contact with the Surrealists did influence his work.

Around this time Audiberti met Elisabeth, a young primary-school mistress from the Caribbean Islands. They married in 1926 and had two daughters, Jacqueline (born in 1926) and Marie-Louise (born in 1928). After 1937, however, Audiberti chose to live alone, not settling in any one place, but moving constantly from one hotel to another, or from one friend's apartment to another.

In 1930 Audiberti, with the help of money borrowed from his father, self-published his first book of poetry, *L'Empire et la trappe* (The Empire and the Trap).

Cover for the first volume in Audiberti's five-volume play collection, published between 1948 and 1962 (Thomas Cooper Library, University of South Carolina)

The book was favorably reviewed by Jean Cassou in *Les Nouvelles Littéraires* (Literary News) and by Maurice Fombeure in *La Nouvelle Revue Française* (The New French Review), commonly called *NRF*, two well-known literary journals of the time. These reviews caught the attention of Valéry Larbaud, who introduced the poet to the major writers of Paris, including Leon-Paul Fargue, Drieu la Rochelle, and, later, Jean Cocteau, Louis Aragon, André Malraux, and Jean Paulhan, an *NRF* figure with whom Audiberti established a correspondence that lasted more than thirty years. In 1933 one of Audiberti's poems was published in *NRF*, the most sought-after public validation in French literature, and Audiberti decided to associate himself with the group of literary intellectuals involved with the magazine. In 1935 he was promoted to senior reporter at the *Petit Parisien,* where he now got a byline.

In 1937 two major events occurred in Audiberti's literary career. First, he was awarded a prize for "best one-act play" for *L'Ampélour* (published in 1948). Despite the honor, the play was not produced until 1950, when André Reybaz staged it at the small avant-garde Théâtre des Noctambules. *L'Ampélour* revolves around a group of early-nineteenth-century commoners who are gathered at a local inn. Strange characters gradually appear, including a Napoleon look-alike. The second important event of 1937 was Gallimard's publication of Audiberti's second book of poetry, *Race des hommes* (Race of Men), accomplished with the help of Paulhan. In 1938 Audiberti became the first recipient of the Mallarmé Award for poetry, and Gallimard published his ambitious first novel, *Abraxas*. After receiving positive reviews by Marcel Arland in *NRF* and by Henri Callet in *Europe,* Audiberti's career flourished, and he regularly published poetry, novels, and essays and continued to contribute to dailies (such as *Aujourd'hui* [Today]), literary magazines, and cinema magazines, including *Comoedia* (Comedy) and *Les Cahiers du Cinéma* (Cinema Notebooks). Through his work with *Les Cahiers du Cinéma* in the 1950s, Audiberti befriended movie director Jacques Baratier, with whom he collaborated later on a screenplay, and François Truffaut, who became one of the leaders of the French movie *Nouvelle-Vague* (New Wave).

Audiberti's most prolific period was from 1939 to 1947, when he produced nine novels, including *Carnage* (1942) and *La Nâ* (1944), and two essays, including *La Nouvelle Origine* (1942, The New Origin), a sort of poetry manifesto in which he explored a new philosophical theory he called "l'abhumanisme" (abhumanism). This theory was influenced by Nietzschean concepts: language creates a screen between a person and the horrors and weight of history that can only be penetrated by abhumanist language. This language can break through the shield of illusion and bring one closer to an ahistorical reality where the true self resides. During this period Audiberti also published three collections of poetry and two translations from Italian, including a work by Sicilian author Benjamin Joppolo. In 1942 L'Académie Française (The French Academy) awarded Audiberti the Jean Reynaud Prize, which honors creative and inventive literary works.

Although Audiberti continued to publish novels, essays, poetry, and translations until his death, theater became a major part of his literary production beginning in 1945. At the time he lived at the Hôtel Taranne in Saint Germain-des-Prés and established a friendship with absurdist playwright Arthur Adamov, who also lived there. Audiberti began writing plays or stories that were dramatized, including *Quoat-Quoat* (performed 1946, published 1948). The production of *Quoat-Quoat* at the Théâtre de la Gaité-Montparnasse, a former music hall, was a risky venture for Reybaz, who is named as the director on the playbill. The production was a collaborative effort between Audiberti and Reybaz, who, along with his fiancée, actress Catherine Toth, acted in the play. It was produced on a low budget, especially since the nation had been devastated by World War II. In a 1964 radio interview with Georges Charbonnier, later published in *Entretiens avec Georges Charbonnier* (1965, Interviews with George Charbonnier), Audiberti explained that the actors painted the sets themselves and resolved technical problems as best as they could. He recalled, for example, that one character's beard was connected to his cap, which prohibited him from taking it off, creating some unexpected gags.

The premiere of *Quoat-Quoat* took place on 28 January 1946, and the performance received reviews ranging from encouraging to negative. Reviewing the piece for the conservative daily *Le Figaro* (2 February 1946), André Warnod wrote: "C'est une pièce pour théâtre d'essai, de laboratoire. On sent que son auteur est un poète, qu'il a une personalité. Il parle une langue riche en images colorées et hardies, mais son dialogue fait songer parfois à une épaisse forêt vierge" (It is a play designed for avant-garde, laboratory-like theater. One can feel that its author is a poet, that he has personality. He speaks a language rich in bold and colored images, but his dialogue sometimes reminds one of a dense virgin forest). Overall, Warnod was troubled by the exuberance and vividness of Audiberti's style.

Quoat-Quoat established the major recurring themes of Audiberti's theater: the ways that history and Catholicism imprison one's mind and create a division between the outer and the inner self; the manner in which one's reintegration with nature through sexuality brings one closer to the primordial source that is deeply connected to evil and suffering; and how the freer use of language has the potential to bridge the gap between one's lost true self and one's present uncomfortable state of being. These themes echo precepts expressed in Artaud's *Le Théâtre et son double* (1938; translated as *The Theater and its Double,* 1958), which Audiberti read and appreciated. Audiberti even attended Artaud's famous last conference at the Théâtre du Vieux-Colombier in 1947.

Quoat-Quoat is set on a steamer, *Le Mirmidon,* at sea between France and Mexico during the French Second Empire. The young protagonist, Amédée, poses as an archaeologist specializing in the prehistoric culture of the Aztecs, but he is actually a spy secretly trying to recover the treasure of Emperor Maximilian. The captain of the ship, aware of Amédée's true identity, informs the young man of a strange maritime rule: if a spy starts flirting with a woman onboard, he must suffer by having his nails pulled, then be shot and dumped into the sea. Despite this warning and the panic that follows it, Amédée cannot resist telling Clarisse, the captain's daughter, that he has loved her since childhood. He is arrested but escapes with the help of a revolutionary Mexican woman and her magic stone, which is imbued with the power of the Aztec god Quoat-Quoat. The real French government spy, a female disguised as a ragged stowaway, suddenly appears to bail him out by revealing her true identity and explaining that Amédée had been a decoy. The captain declares Amédée "free," but Amédée, taking his destiny into his own hands, goes up to the deck, where the firing squad, unaware of the captain's change of heart, shoots him. Dismayed, the captain uses the magic Aztec stone to destroy the vessel.

A common scholarly interpretation of *Quoat-Quoat* describes the ship as a microcosm of the world, a metaphysical and real prison from which death is the only escape: the absurd regulations established by tradition—and interpreted and implemented by the paternal, yet authoritative, captain—must be questioned and dismissed by any human being who strives for freedom. But resisting unfair traditional rules or morals and trying to liberate oneself comes at a high cost, and sometimes the cost is life itself. Hence, Amédée is the only character who truly escapes, and he does so by choosing death. Such resistance to established norms is an important feature of many of Audiberti's later plays.

In 1946 Audiberti met Georges Vitaly, a budding young director interested in promoting and producing avant-garde plays, especially those he liked to call "théâtre de choc" (shock theater). In 1947 Vitaly directed Audiberti's most famous play, *Le Mal court* (The Evil Runs; published 1948), at the Théâtre de Poche, a tiny Left Bank venue. Suzanne Flon, a then-unknown young actress, played the lead role and soon became a close friend of the author. Though the audience was small and the play did not initially attract much attention, it won the Prix des Jeunes Comapagnies (Young Companies Prize), an award aimed at encouraging theater companies that had just started and were between amateur and professional status. The 1955 revival of *Le Mal court* at the Théâtre La Bruyère, with Vitaly again directing and Flon in the lead role, was a triumph, and Audiberti broke out of his small literary circle into the mainstream.

Set in eighteenth-century Europe, *Le Mal court* mixes fictional characters and thinly disguised historical figures in a plot that is complicated, involving real and fake spies and dual identities. It is a distorted fairy tale in which Princess Alarica, a beautiful, naive virgin from the poor little Kingdom of Courtland, is traveling with

Title page for Audiberti's play (1959, The Glapion Effect) that portrays a woman's flashback during a dinner party (Thomas Cooper Library, University of South Carolina)

her small entourage to marry a rich young king from a powerful land. She is trapped in a sexually compromising situation by a wicked cardinal from the prince's land who wants to prevent the marriage for political reasons. She learns that not only has she been used as a decoy, so that the king can attract a more appropriate bride, but also that she has been deceived by her trusted old spinster nanny. Awakened to such malice, Alarica abandons her naive illusions about the decency and reliability of people and realizes the true nature of the world. To survive as a governing power she has no choice but to use evil to fight evil, and therefore let "evil run": she deposes her genteel but weak father and sets to rule with no mercy, using a newfound socially inferior lover as an acolyte.

Audiberti scholars generally agree that Alarica's quest for purity is prohibited by the politics of the real world. She is awakened to that hard fact through eroticism, as if sexuality brought her closer to the source of evil—not a biblical evil, but a pagan notion of separation from nature that can only be perceived when acting freely on one's sexual desires.

Reviews of *Le Mal court* ranged from negative to unqualified praise. Francis Ambrière, writing for *Opéra* (25 June 1947), claimed: "Si vous goûtez la poésie dans sa liberté, allez au Théâtre de Poche. On vous y offre l'occasion d'une délectation vive et claire" (If you like poetry in its freedom, go to Théâtre de Poche. You will be privy to a clear and vivacious delectation). Conversely, André Ransan, in *Ce Matin* (21 June 1947, This Morning), wrote: "Il est regrettable à mon avis que l'ouvrage soit aussi cérébral. Derrière chaque réplique, on devine l'intellectuel et le penseur" (It is regrettable in my opinion that the work is too cerebral. Behind each line, one can feel the intellectual and the thinker).

In 1950 Reybaz directed Audiberti's *Sa Peau* (Her Skin) at the tiny Théâtre des Noctambules. *Sa Peau* is a one-act sketch that depicts a disenchanted forty-something actress, Frimoussa, who mentors a younger actress named Gabrielle. Frimoussa soon seems to be living vicariously through her protégée. In 1950 Audiberti collaborated for the last time with Reybaz in the staging of *L'Ampélour*. Meanwhile, Audiberti continued to work with Vitaly until 1962. *La Fête noire* (The Black Feast), a dramatic version of *La Bête noire* (1945, The Black Beast), was produced in 1948 and *Pucelle* (Maiden) in 1950, both at the small Théâtre de la Huchette in the Latin Quarter. *La Fête noire* is a play set in the seventeenth century in a mountainous desert countryside occupied by a terrible beast who is killing local virgin girls. Doctor Felicien, a frustrated Don Juan type, is called upon to try to solve the problem. *Pucelle* is a farcical version of the Joan of Arc story. In 1957 Vitaly mounted *La Mégère apprivoisée*, Audiberti's adaptation of William Shakespeare's *The Taming of the Shrew* (circa 1595), at the Théâtre de l'Athénée. The cast featured Pierre Brasseur. In 1958 Le Théâtre du Vieux-Colombier revived *La Hobereaute* (The Falcon Squiress), originally played at the Festival des Nuits de Bourgogne in 1957 and adapted from an Audiberi text originally published in 1956 as *L'Opéra parlé* (Spoken Opera). The title character is a mysterious ninth-century girl possessing the ancient magical powers of druids and confronted by a new Christian way of life.

In the 1950s and early 1960s Audiberti expanded his presence on the theatrical scene through his friendship with Ludmila Vlasto, director of the newly reinstituted Théâtre La Bruyère. Vlasto booked five productions of Audiberti's plays: *Les Naturels du Bordelais* (The Bordeaux Naturals; published 1952, performed 1953), a fiasco that provoked a short-lived quarrel between Audiberti and Vitaly; Vitaly's 1955 revival of *Le Mal court; Le Ouallou* (The Nadalotta; published 1956, performed 1958); *L'Effet Glapion* (The Glapion Effect; published and performed in 1959), which nearly matched the success of the revival of *Le Mal court;* and *Pomme, pomme, pomme* (Apple, Apple, Apple; published and performed in 1962), also directed by Vitaly. *Les Naturels du Bordelais* is the story of Guy-Loup, a libertine who is accused of murder. *Le Ouallou* tells the story of Glinglin-les-Dormantes, a feared criminal who reigns over the underworld of a police station basement. *Pomme, pomme, pomme* is a parody of the Adam and Eve myth set in twentieth-century Paris.

L'Effet Glapion, which was subtitled "parapsycho-comedy," combined elements of vaudeville and Surrealism and provided a bridge between the "anti-theater" of the period and more traditionally commercial theatre. With this production, Audiberti publicly distanced himself from the avant-garde of the 1950s, leaving room for a more indefinite theatrical genre like that René de Obaldia endorsed with his *Genousie* (1960; translated as *Jenousia,* 1966). The plot of *L'Effet Glapion* mixes realism and fantasy, science fiction and a distorted sense of history. Physician Blaise Agrichant and his wife, Monique, are entertaining a captain of the constabulary at their Sunday meal. Everything seems normal at first, but soon through Monique's (apparent) reminiscence, the scene shifts to the same room exactly a year earlier. A rapid succession of convoluted events, including multiple transformations of characters, creates havoc, and the play ends almost where it began, with the three original characters finishing their Sunday repast. The reviews of *L'Effet Glapion* were almost unanimously positive. Even in the conservative Catholic *La Croix* (19 September 1959, The Cross), Henri Rabine wrote: "Maître incontesté du 'mot' Audiberti possède le pouvoir démiurgique de le multiplier à la mesure d'une fantaisie dont la caractéristique est justement d'être démesurée" (Undisputed master of the "word," Audiberti possesses the half-god power to multiply it and to moderate it in a fantasy that is paradoxically immoderate).

Other directors rarely matched Vitaly's success in producing Audiberti's plays. Neither Jean Le Poulain's staging of *La Hobereaute* at the fourth Festival des Nuits de Bourgogne (Festival of Nights of Bourgogne) in 1957 nor a production directed by Michel de Ré at the Théâtre du Vieux-Colombier in 1958 received much positive attention. Pierre Valde's production of Audiberti's *La Logeuse* (The Lodgeress; published in 1956) at the Théâtre de l'Oeuvre in 1960 did not fare any better.

Title page for Audiberti's final play (1969, The Doll), an adaptation of his 1956 novel, written for director Marcel Maréchal (Thomas Cooper Library, University of South Carolina)

This play depicts the troublesome ways of Madame Cirqué, who rents the many rooms of her apartment to males in order to satisfy her voracious sexual appetite. Next, André Barsaq's controversial direction of Audiberti's *La Fourmi dans le corps* (The Embodied Ant; published in 1961) at the conservative Comédie-Française in 1962 was hissed and booed during its premiere. Set in the seventeenth century, the plot revolves around the character of Barthélémy de Pic-Saint-Pop, a virgin noblewoman, who has decided to preserve herself from evil by becoming the head of the Royaumont Abbey. But the war rages, and she has to engage her forces in the battle. Also unsuccessful was François Maistre's 1962 effort to direct Audiberti's *La Brigitta* (published in 1962) at the Théâtre de l'Athénée. In *La Brigitta* two maniacs exploit the weaknesses of a girl who wants to become a movie star. Audiberti's plays were finally given a second life through Marcel Maréchal's production of Audiberti's *Le Cavalier seul* (The Lone Knight) at Théâtre du Cothurne in Lyon in 1963. This success was facilitated by the director's love for the author's work and his involvement in and connections with prestigious summer theater festivals such as that at Avignon. *Le Cavalier seul* depicts the adventures of Mirtus, a courageous and intelligent medieval colossus who engages in the Crusades.

In 1964 Audiberti's health worsened significantly. He busied himself finishing novels, poetry books, essays, and a movie scenario, and he wrote only one more play before his death from cancer on 10 July 1965: an adaptation of his 1956 novel *La Poupée* (The Doll; published in 1969) that he wrote for Maréchal.

Critics have often noted the rich expression of Audiberti's plays, but they often qualify them as poetic and linguistic games. Audiberti's wordplay was excluded from the critical discussions about the functions of communication that were generated by absurdist theater in the 1950s, making theater of the absurd appear even more innovative than it was. Whereas in the absurdist plays of *le nouveau théâtre* (The New Theater) the crisis of communication frequently seemed to be the result of an atrophy of discourse, there is an inverted will in Audiberti's work to explore the limits of the creative potential of language, a phenomenon that translates into logorrhea.

Since his death, Jacques Audiberti's theater regularly has been produced in France, partly through the efforts and recognition of Maréchal. His plays have been performed in many countries, including Germany, Holland, Belgium, and the United States. Testifying to Audiberti's profound impact on drama, the conservative *Le Quotidien de Paris* (The Paris Daily) devoted an article to a successful staging of *Le Mal court* at the Théâtre de l'Atelier in 1993, declaring that in an "intelligent series devoted to 'Classic playwrights of the 20th Century,' Audiberti had naturally to be included next to [Luigi] Pirandello, [Harold] Pinter, [Henri de] Montherlant."

Letters:

Lettres à Jean Paulhan, 1933–1965 (Paris: Gallimard, 1993).

Interview:

Entretiens avec Georges Charbonnier (Paris: Gallimard, 1965).

Biography:

André Deslandes, *Audiberti* (Paris: Gallimard, 1964).

References:

Gérard-Denis Farcy, *Les Théâtres d'Audiberti* (Paris: Presses Universitaires de France, 1988);

Jeanyves Guérin, *Le Théâtre d'Audiberti et le baroque* (Paris: Klincksieck, 1976);

Paul Guth, *Quarante contre un* (Paris: Corrêa, 1947);

Christophe Lagier, *Le Théâtre de la Parole-spectacle: Jacques Audiberti, René de Obaldia et Jean Tardieu* (Birmingham, Ala.: Summa, 2000);

Constantin Toloudis, *Jacques Audiberti* (Boston: Twayne, 1980).

Papers:

Manuscripts and unpublished materials by Jacques Audiberti are archived at L'Institut Mémoires de l'Edition (Institute of Contemporary Publishing Archives) in Paris.

Samuel Beckett

(13 April 1906 – 22 December 1989)

Culley Jane Carson
Austin Peay State University

See also the Beckett entries in *DLB 13: British Dramatists Since World War II; DLB 15: British Novelists, 1930–1959; DLB 233: British and Irish Dramatists Since World War II, Second Series; DLB 319: British and Irish Short Fiction Writers, 1945–2000;* and *DLB Yearbook: 1990.*

PLAY PRODUCTIONS: *Le Kid,* by Beckett and Georges Pelorson, Dublin, Peacock Theatre, February 1931;

En attendant Godot, Paris, Théâtre de Babylone, 5 January 1953; produced in English as *Waiting for Godot,* London, Arts Theatre Club, 3 August 1955; Miami, Coconut Grove Playhouse, 3 January 1956; New York, John Golden Theatre, 19 April 1956;

Fin de partie and *Acte sans paroles I,* London, Royal Court Theatre, 3 April 1957; Paris, Studio des Champs Elysées, 26 April 1957; *Fin de partie* produced in English as *Endgame,* New York, Cherry Lane Theatre, 28 January 1958;

Krapp's Last Tape (produced with *Endgame*), London, Royal Court Theatre, 28 October 1958; New York, Provincetown Playhouse, 14 January 1960; translated into French by Beckett and Pierre Leyris as *La Dernière Bande,* Paris, Théâtre Recamier, 22 March 1960;

Act Without Words II, London, Institute of Contemporary Arts, 25 January 1960;

Happy Days, New York, Cherry Lane Theatre, 17 September 1961; London, Royal Court Theatre, 1 November 1962; produced in French as *Oh les beaux jours,* Paris, Odéon-Théâtre de France, 29 October 1963;

Spiel, translated into German by Elmar Tophoven, Ulm-Donau, Germany, Ulmer Theater, 14 June 1963; original English version produced as *Play,* New York, Cherry Lane Theatre, 4 January 1964; London, Old Vic Theatre, 7 April 1964; produced in French as *Comédie,* Paris, Pavillion de Marsan, 14 June 1964;

Samuel Beckett (photograph by Beppe Arvidsson; © AFP/ Getty Images)

Kommen und Gehen, translated into German by Tophoven, Berlin, Schiller Theater, 14 January 1966; produced in French as *Va et vient,* Paris, Odéon-Théâtre de France, 28 February 1966; original English version produced as *Come and Go,* Dublin, Peacock Theatre, 28 February 1968;

Breath, New York, Eden Theater, 16 June 1969; Oxford, Oxford Playhouse, 8 March 1970;

Not I, New York, Lincoln Center, 7 December 1972; London, Royal Court Theatre, 16 January 1973; produced in French as *Pas moi,* Paris, D'Orsay Petite Salle, 3 April 1975;

The Lost Ones, New York, Theatre for the New City, 7 April 1975;

That Time, London, Royal Court Theatre, 20 May 1976;

Footfalls, London, Royal Court Theatre, 20 May 1976;

A Piece of Monologue, New York, La MaMa Experimental Theatre Club, 14 December 1979;

Texts for Nothing, New York, Public Theatre, 24 February 1981;

Rockaby, Buffalo, State University of New York at Buffalo, 8 April 1981; produced in French as *Berceuse,* Paris, Centre Georges Pompidou, 14 October 1981;

Ohio Impromptu, Columbus, Ohio State University, 7 May 1981;

Catastrophe, Avignon, Avignon Festival, 21 July 1982;

What Where, New York, Harold Clurman Theatre, 15 June 1983.

BOOKS: *Whoroscope* (Paris: Hours, 1930);

Proust (London: Chatto & Windus, 1931; New York: Grove, 1957);

More Pricks Than Kicks (London: Chatto & Windus, 1934; New York: Grove, 1970);

Echo's Bones and Other Precipitates (Paris: Europa, 1935);

Murphy (London: Routledge, 1938; New York: Grove, 1957); translated into French by Beckett (Paris: Bordas, 1947);

Molloy (Paris: Minuit, 1951); translated by Beckett and Patrick Bowles (Paris: Olympia, 1955; New York: Grove, 1955);

Malone meurt (Paris: Minuit, 1951); translated by Beckett as *Malone Dies* (New York: Grove, 1956; London: Calder, 1958);

En attendant Godot (Paris: Minuit, 1952); translated by Beckett as *Waiting for Godot* (New York: Grove, 1954; London: Faber & Faber, 1956); revised edition, edited by Douglas McMillan and James Knowlson (London: Faber & Faber, 1993);

L'Innommable (Paris: Minuit, 1953); translated by Beckett as *The Unnamable* (New York: Grove, 1958; London: Calder & Boyars, 1975);

Watt (Paris: Olympia, 1953; New York: Grove, 1959; London: Calder, 1963); translated into French by Beckett, Ludovic Janvier, and Agnès Janvier (Paris: Minuit, 1968);

Nouvelles et Textes pour rien (Paris: Minuit, 1955); translated by Beckett as *Stories and Texts for Nothing* (New York: Grove, 1967);

Fin de partie, suivi de Acte sans paroles (Paris: Minuit, 1957); translated by Beckett as *Endgame, Followed by Act Without Words* (New York: Grove, 1958; London: Faber & Faber, 1958);

All That Fall (New York: Grove, 1957; London: Faber & Faber, 1957); translated into French by Beckett and Robert Pinget as *Tous ceux qui tombent* (Paris: Minuit, 1957);

From an Abandoned Work (London: Faber & Faber, 1958); translated into French by Beckett, Ludovic Janvier, and Agnès Janvier as *D'un ouvrage abandonné,* in *Têtes-Mortes* (Paris: Minuit, 1967), pp. 9–30;

Krapp's Last Tape and Other Dramatic Pieces (New York: Grove, 1960)–comprises *Krapp's Last Tape, All That Fall, Embers, Act Without Words I,* and *Act Without Words II; Krapp's Last Tape* and *Embers* translated into French by Beckett and Pierre Leiris as *La Dernière Bande, suivi de Cendres* (Paris: Minuit, 1960); original French version of *Act Without Words II* published as *Acte sans paroles II,* in *Dramatische Dichtungen,* volume 1 (Frankfurt am Main: Suhrkamp, 1963), pp. 332–337;

Comment c'est (Paris: Minuit, 1961); translated by Beckett as *How It Is* (New York: Grove, 1964; London: Calder, 1964);

Happy Days (New York: Grove, 1961; London: Faber & Faber, 1962); translated into French by Beckett as *Oh les beaux jours* (Paris: Minuit, 1963);

Poems in English (London: Calder, 1961; New York: Grove, 1963);

Play and Two Short Pieces for Radio (London: Faber & Faber, 1964)–comprises *Play, Words and Music,* and *Cascando; Play* and *Words and Music* translated into French by Beckett as *Comédie* and *Parole et Musique,* in *Comédie et actes divers* (Paris: Minuit, 1966), pp. 9–35, 63–78;

Imagination morte imaginez (Paris: Minuit, 1965); translated by Beckett as *Imagination Dead Imagine* (London: Calder & Boyars, 1965);

Assez (Paris: Minuit, 1966); translated by Beckett as *Enough,* in *No's Knife: Collected Shorter Prose, 1945-1966* (London: Calder & Boyars, 1967);

Bing (Paris: Minuit, 1966); translated by Beckett as *Ping,* in *No's Knife: Collected Shorter Prose, 1945-1966* (London: Calder & Boyars, 1967);

Comédie et actes divers (Paris: Minuit, 1966)–comprises *Comédie, Va et vient, Parole et Musique, Dis Joe,* and *Acte sans paroles II; Dis Joe* translated by Beckett as *Eh Joe,* in *Eh Joe and Other Writings* (London: Faber & Faber, 1967); original English version of *Va et vient* published as *Come and Go* (London: Calder & Boyars, 1967), pp. 15–21;

Eh Joe and Other Writings (London: Faber & Faber, 1967)–comprises *Eh Joe, Act Without Words II,* and

Film; Film translated into French by Beckett (Frankfurt am Main: Suhrkamp, 1968);

No's Knife: Collected Shorter Prose, 1945–1966 (London: Calder & Boyars, 1967);

Poèmes (Paris: Minuit, 1968);

Sans (Paris: Minuit, 1969); translated by Beckett as *Lessness* (London: Calder & Boyars, 1970);

Le Dépeupleur (Paris: Minuit, 1970); translated by Beckett as *The Lost Ones* (London: Calder & Boyars, 1972; New York: Grove, 1972);

Mercier et Camier (Paris: Minuit, 1970); translated by Beckett as *Mercier and Camier* (London: Calder & Boyars, 1974; New York: Grove, 1975);

Premier amour (Paris: Minuit, 1970); translated by Beckett as *First Love* (London: Calder & Boyars, 1973);

Breath and Other Shorts (London: Faber & Faber, 1972)—comprises *Breath, Come and Go, Act Without Words I, Act Without Words II,* and *From an Abandoned Work; Breath* translated into French by Beckett as *Souffle,* in *Film, suivi de Souffle* (Paris: Minuit, 1972);

Not I (London: Faber & Faber, 1973); translated into French by Beckett as *Pas moi,* in *Oh les beaux jours, suivi de Pas moi* (Paris: Minuit, 1975);

That Time (London: Faber & Faber, 1976); translated into French by Beckett as *Cette fois* (Paris: Minuit, 1978);

Fizzles (New York: Grove, 1976); translated into French by Beckett in *Foirade: Fizzles* [bilingual edition] (London & New York: Petersburg / Paris: Fequet & Baudier, 1976);

All Strange Away (New York: Gotham Book Mart, 1976; London: Calder, 1979);

Pour finir encore et autres foirades (Paris: Minuit, 1976); translated by Beckett as *For to End Yet Again and Other Fizzles* (London: Calder, 1976);

Footfalls (London: Faber & Faber, 1976); translated into French by Beckett as *Pas* (Paris: Minuit, 1977);

Ends and Odds: Eight New Dramatic Pieces (New York: Grove, 1976)—comprises *Not I, That Time, Footfalls, Ghost Trio, Theatre I, Theatre II, Radio I,* and *Radio II;* enlarged as *Ends and Odds: Plays and Sketches* (London: Faber & Faber, 1977)—includes *. . . but the clouds . . . ;*

Four Novellas (London: Calder, 1977)—comprises *First Love, The Expelled, The Calmative,* and *The End;* republished as *The Expelled, and Other Novellas* (Harmondsworth, U.K. & New York: Penguin, 1980);

Poèmes suivi de Mirlitonnades (Paris: Minuit, 1978);

Compagnie, translated into French by Beckett (Paris: Minuit, 1979); original English version published as *Company* (New York: Grove, 1980);

Nohow On: Three Novels (New York: Grove, 1980)—comprises *Company; Ill Seen, Ill Said;* and *Worstward Ho; Ill Seen, Ill Said* translated into French by Beckett as *Mal vu mal dit* (Paris: Minuit, 1981);

Rockaby and Other Short Pieces (New York: Grove, 1981)—comprises *Rockaby, Ohio Impromptu, All Strange Away,* and *A Piece of Monologue; Rockaby* and *Ohio Impromptu* translated into French by Beckett as *Berceuse, suivi de Impromptu d'Ohio* (Paris: Minuit, 1982); *A Piece of Monologue* translated by Beckett as *Solo,* in *Solo, suivi de Catastrophe* (Paris: Minuit, 1982);

Catastrophe et autres dramaticules (Paris: Minuit, 1982); *Catastrophe* translated by Beckett, in *Three Plays* (New York: Grove, 1984);

Three Plays (New York: Grove, 1984)—comprises *Ohio Impromptu, Catastrophe,* and *What Where;*

As the Story Was Told (Cambridge: Rampant Lions, 1987);

Stirrings Still (New York: Blue Moon, 1988; London: Calder, 1988);

Dream of Fair to Middling Women, edited by Eoin O'Brien and Edith Fournier (Dublin: Black Cat Press, 1992);

Eleuthéria (Paris: Minuit, 1995); translated by Michael Brodsky as *Eleutheria: A Play in Three Acts* (New York: Foxrock, 1995).

Editions and Collections: *The Collected Works of Samuel Beckett,* 16 volumes (New York: Grove, 1970);

I Can't Go On, I'll Go On: A Selection from Samuel Beckett's Work, edited, with an introduction, by Richard W. Seaver (London: Faber & Faber, 1976; New York: Grove, 1976);

Collected Poems in English and French (New York: Grove, 1977; London: Calder, 1977);

Disjecta: Miscellaneous Writings and a Dramatic Fragment, edited by Ruby Cohn (London: Calder, 1983; New York: Grove, 1983);

Collected Shorter Plays (New York: Grove, 1984; London: Faber & Faber, 1984);

Collected Poems 1930–1978 (London: Calder, 1984);

Collected Shorter Prose, 1945–1980 (London: Calder, 1984);

The Complete Dramatic Works (London: Faber & Faber, 1986);

Samuel Beckett's Company/Compagnie and A Piece of Monologue/Solo, edited by Charles Krance (London & New York: Garland, 1993);

Samuel Beckett: The Complete Short Prose, 1929–1989, edited, with an introduction, by S. E. Gontarski (New York: Grove, 1995);

Poems 1930–1989 (London: Calder, 2002).

Edition in English: *Eleuthéria,* translated by Barbara Wright (London: Faber & Faber, 1996).

PRODUCED SCRIPTS: *All That Fall,* radio, BBC Third Programme, 13 January 1957;

Embers, radio, BBC Third Programme, 24 June 1959;

Words and Music, radio, BBC Third Programme, 13 November 1962;

Cascando (in French), radio, Office de la radio et de la télévision française, 13 October 1963; English version, BBC Third Programme, 6 October 1964;

Film, motion picture, Evergreen Theatre, Inc., 1965;

Eh Joe (in German), television, Süddeutscher Rundfunk, 1966; original English version, BBC2, 4 July 1966;

Rough for Radio II (originally written in French in the early 1960s), radio, BBC 3, 13 April 1976;

Ghost Trio, television, BBC2, 17 April 1977;

. . . but the clouds . . . , television, BBC2, 17 April 1977;

Quadrat 1+2, television, Süddeutscher Rundfunk, 1982; English version as *Quad,* BBC2, 16 December 1982;

Nacht und Träume, television, Süddeutscher Rundfunk, 19 May 1983;

Was Wo, television, Süddeutscher Rundfunk, 13 April 1986.

Although he began as a poet and reached his fullest expression as a novelist, Samuel Beckett is nevertheless best remembered as a dramatist with internationally acclaimed dramatic works that changed twentieth-century theater. His prose was intensely poetic, increasingly terse, and acutely attentive to the sound and patterns of verbal composition. He was obsessed by structure, and all his works are clearly organized by the use of repetition: words and phrases are repeated to create an echo effect, certain passages are repeated to punctuate and partition the work, and in one of his plays the entire work is repeated from beginning to end.

The impact of *En attendant Godot* (published 1952; produced 1953; translated as *Waiting for Godot,* 1954) on twentieth-century theater cannot be exaggerated. The metaphor of life as waiting for something to happen appealed to a vast audience, and it was performed in theaters before the intellectual class and in prisons for socially rejected inmates. *En attendant Godot* features grim humor and equivocal language that have allowed it to retain its popularity through decades of revivals and reinterpretations. After this success, Beckett continued to write and direct plays intended to appeal to the intellect through the senses, with music and lighting effects displacing characterization and plot.

Beckett wrote in both French and English, and he translated most of his works into the other language himself. As he gained more experience in the theater, he collaborated more and more closely with the directors of his plays. Over the course of his career Beckett's works tended to become shorter, as if he had taken to heart the conclusion of his novel *L'Innommable* (1953; translated as *The Unnamable,* 1958) and resolved that since words were ineffectual, the fewer the better. He took his inspiration from works of art, biblical and classical literature, popular music-hall performances, his acquaintance with the common folk and the downtrodden of Ireland and France, and most of all from memories and personal experience.

Samuel Barclay Beckett was born on 13 April 1906, in Foxrock, a suburb of Dublin, Ireland. He was the second son of May and William Frank Beckett. His father, a quantity surveyor, was descended from French Huguenots; his mother was, until marriage, a nurse and an interpreter for the Irish Red Cross. Like his older brother, Frank, Beckett attended local schools until the age of fourteen, when he left for the boarding school of Portora Royal. Beckett excelled at sports and was popular, although not outgoing. At seventeen he entered Trinity College, where he became interested in modern languages and achieved fluency in French, Italian, and German. After graduating first in his class, he won a fellowship as an exchange lecturer in Paris, where he was introduced to James Joyce, who became his mentor. Because of Beckett's close relationship with Joyce, critics have often classified his early works as derivative. Meanwhile, Beckett developed a rather tangled relationship with Joyce's daughter, Lucia. She apparently pursued the young writer, causing many misunderstandings until Beckett finally told her that he did not love her. In 1932 Lucia was placed in an asylum for the mentally disturbed.

In 1929 Beckett published a critical article and a short story in the periodical *transition.* Around this time he also wrote *Whoroscope,* a prize-winning poem published in 1930, and *Proust,* a work of criticism published in 1931. When he returned to Ireland from Paris, he took a promising teaching position at Trinity College, but he disliked it so intensely that he did not finish the second year, sending his letter of resignation from Germany, where he was visiting relatives.

During the following decade Beckett spent most of his time in Paris and began to establish himself as a novelist. Drawing from the first novel he wrote, *Dream of Fair to Middling Women,* which was rejected and published only posthumously in 1992, he published the collection of short stories *More Pricks Than Kicks* (1934). He also produced a collection of poems, *Echo's Bones and Other Precipitates* (1935), and the novel *Murphy* (1938).

Beckett was close to his family, although his relationship with his mother was tempestuous. In

Scene from the 1953 world premiere of En attendant Godot *(performed as* Waiting for Godot, *1955), featuring Jean Martin as Lucky and Roger Blin as Pozzo (© Collection Roger-Viollet/Getty Images)*

1933 he was devastated by two deaths in the family: his cousin Peggy, one of his first loves, died of tuberculosis, and his father died of a heart attack. During the following months Beckett experienced serious health problems that appeared to be stress related, and he eventually moved to London, where he underwent two years of psychotherapy.

In 1937 Beckett permanently settled in Paris. While walking home with friends on 7 January 1938 Beckett was stabbed by a pimp. A passerby solicited by his friends for help, a piano student named Suzanne Deschevaux-Dumesnil, not only came to Beckett's aid but remained involved with him. Suzanne was six years older than Beckett. They began living together in 1939 and eventually married.

During World War II, Beckett was active in the French Resistance both in Paris and later in Roussillon, where he retreated with Suzanne. He continued writing prose fiction in English until 1946, when, in the middle of writing a story in English, he changed the language of composition to French. This change was momentous, and it introduced a period of intense productivity.

Early in 1947 Beckett wrote his first complete play, *Eleuthéria* (1995; translated as *Eleutheria,* 1995). It is a relatively conventional three-act play about a man named Victor Krapp who seeks to escape the bourgeois life his family expects of him. There was some interest in producing the play in the early 1950s, but nothing came of it, and Beckett never published it during his lifetime. That year Beckett also began writing the trilogy *Molloy* (1951; translated, 1955), *Malone meurt* (1951; translated as *Malone Dies,* 1956), and *L'Innommable,* his major works of fiction.

In 1949 Beckett completed *En attendant Godot*. It was only with great difficulty, and chiefly because of Suzanne's persistence in acting as his agent, that Beckett found both a director and a theater in which to present the play. Roger Blin agreed to take on the work in 1950, and Beckett and Blin developed a working relationship. After a difficult search for a venue and actors, the play was finally performed at the Théâtre de Babylone, a converted shop with 230 folding seats. At first the play was poorly received, but it generated controversy and eventually began playing to full houses.

En attendant Godot consists of two acts summed up by Vivian Mercier's famous phrase, "nothing happens, twice." Two tramps, Vladimir (Didi) and Estragon (Gogo), are waiting in a barren countryside for someone named Godot, with whom they have an appointment, but who never appears, merely sending a message boy to defer the appointment to the next day. They pass the time telling jokes, contemplating suicide, and talking to another unlikely pair, Pozzo and Lucky, who are traveling through. The clothing, gestures, and broad humor are aspects of the play that Beckett borrowed from the music hall, circus, and silent movies. His characters are obsessed by the physical and psychological impossibility of living ("going on"); yet, they are incapable of doing anything else. They are tormented by both the brevity of existence and the intolerable, interminable waiting game of life. Although Beckett's vocabulary is direct, the language is at times lofty and poetic. Most of the dialogue is made up of short sentences in which the characters complete each other's thoughts or that take up and repeat key elements in a style that is almost musical. (In fact, Beckett's lifelong love of music informed much of his writing for theater and movies.) Allusions stemming from the author's classical and Christian education and his fascination with philosophy abound.

Beckett masterfully stages the interaction of the characters in *En attendant Godot*. The master-slave relationship of Pozzo and Lucky provides a contrast to the egalitarian friendship of Vladimir and Estragon, who quarrel and tease each other like an old married couple. Vladimir and Estragon discuss hanging themselves on the bare tree onstage, but they are unable to make up their minds for fear that if the first succeeds while the second, slightly heavier one causes the branch to break, the second will be left utterly alone. Bored as they are, they enjoy the diversion of Pozzo's visit, although they are outraged at his treatment of Lucky. For their entertainment, Pozzo offers to have Lucky dance, sing, or think. His dance is a charade interpretation of human life in which he acts out the illusion of being caught in a net. When ordered to think, he pronounces in a monotone voice a parody of a scientific treatise sprinkled with nonsense syllables and linguistic jokes, such as fictitious researchers named Fartov and Belcher or Testu and Conard. One of the humorous devices of the play is the juxtaposition of clichés and popular expressions in unusual and often socially inappropriate combinations, creating startling, absurd, and comical images.

In the second act, the only change in the set is that the tree is covered with leaves. Although the stage directions indicate that it is the following day, there is a feeling that much time has passed. One of the strengths of the play is an atmosphere of timelessness, an insistence that the passage of time is both unbearably slow and infinite. When Pozzo and Lucky arrive in this scene, the question of time comes up again: Pozzo is now blind and completely dependent on Lucky, who is mute. The changes in these characters are too dramatic to have occurred overnight, and Vladimir is curious about the chronology of events. Pozzo derides him for his need to think in terms of time, reminding him that life is a single brief day between two dark nights. After they depart, Estragon falls asleep, and Vladimir offers a soliloquy summing up the action of the play, predicting that the next day will be the same as today, speculating on the nature of truth and dreams, and enlarging his view to reveal an awareness of an audience watching him watch his friend. The last words of the play, in which Vladimir and Estragon agree to leave yet remain in place, are identical to the closing words of the first act, although the characters have traded lines. Their immobility as the curtain falls physically expresses the "I can't go on; I must go on" that we encounter throughout Beckett's work.

Within the year, *En attendant Godot* premiered in Berlin, and Beckett's translation into English was presented in London in 1955 and in the United States in 1956. In later years, Beckett frequently directed the play himself. He consistently refused to discuss the meaning of the play or the motivation of the characters, preferring to shape a precise presentation that he found visually, aurally, and intellectually satisfying.

Beckett visited his mother every year, and he was with her in Dublin when she died on 25 August 1950. Her death was emotionally traumatic for him, and scenes from the event were introduced into his later writings. In 1954 Beckett learned that his brother, Frank, was dying of lung cancer, and he returned to Ireland to help care for him until his death on 13 September.

Beckett's next play, *Fin de partie* (published 1957; translated as *Endgame*, 1958), was completed in 1956 and produced in 1957. The title refers to the final moves of a chess game, and the main character, Hamm, talks about his existence as if he were playing a game. Like *En attendant Godot,* the play features a dreary setting and

Donald Davis as Krapp in a 1960 production of Krapp's Last Tape *(first produced in 1958) in Provincetown, Massachusetts. In the play Krapp listens to messages he recorded when he was younger, especially those regarding the death of his mother and an experience with a lover, and comments on them (photograph by Avery Willard; New York Public Library).*

two pairs of linked characters. Hamm, blind and in a wheelchair, bullies Clov, his servant. Hamm's legless parents, Nagg and Nell, live in garbage cans and pop out to speak from time to time. The bleak setting is established by Clov, who looks out the window and describes the surrounding area as devoid of life. Clov constantly threatens to leave and in fact appears with his suitcase in hand at the end, but he never actually departs. Hence, the end of the play recalls the final words of *En attendant Godot,* where Vladimir suggests they leave, and Estragon agrees, yet they do not move.

Hamm's day is divided into ritual actions. He has a time to take his tranquilizer and a time to tell his tale, for which he adopts a narrator's tone of voice, changing back to his usual tone in order to comment on his own narration. His father, Nagg, also tells a story in which he not only employs Hamm's method of using storyteller and commentary tones but also adopts the voices of two characters. Nagg's story explicitly equates the creation of a pair of pants with the creation of the world, which is in a sorry state. The storytelling functions as the creation of an alternate (though joyless) reality in response to the misery of existence. The themes of *Fin de partie,* including waiting, filling time, and the need to tell stories, recur in Beckett's plays.

In 1956 Beckett also wrote two short dramatic pieces, *Acte sans paroles I* (published and produced 1957; translated as *Act Without Words,* 1958) and *Acte sans paroles II* (produced 1960; translated as *Act Without Words II,* 1960; original French version published 1963), and a radio play in English, *All That Fall* (published and produced 1957). As their titles indicate, the theater pieces are without dialogue, and each conveys a powerful vision of despair. In the first part of *Acte sans paroles* the audience sees a man in a situation resembling that of a laboratory animal. Trapped on the stage that he is unable to leave, he visibly contemplates suicide, but he is not able to carry out his plans because the objects he needs (branch, rope, scissors) are mysteriously withdrawn. Part 2 features two characters, A and B, with completely different personalities, one brisk and businesslike, the other slow and brooding. Each is awakened separately by a goad, performs a daily routine in solitude, then retires to a sack until the goad reappears. These people are subject to forces beyond their comprehension, but the "greater power" is by no means benign.

Much of Beckett's writing tends toward the conclusion that words are meaningless and futile (as in *L'Innommable*). The *Acte sans paroles* plays are an early expression of the uselessness of the word. Significantly, Beckett's later works for television also have no dialogue, and in some of the speeches in his plays the words are intentionally difficult to discern. Lucky's long speech in *En attendant Godot* is an early example.

All That Fall, written for the BBC, was broadcast on 13 January 1957. Beckett was intrigued by the dramatic possibilities of sound effects and voice, and this radio play has more characterization and plot than any of his works for the theater. Mr. and Mrs. Rooney are an infirm elderly Irish couple. Mrs. Rooney goes to surprise her husband at the train station, but Mr. Rooney's train has arrived late because a child fell (or was pushed by Mr. Rooney) under the wheels. For Mr. and Mrs. Rooney, the fear of falling is a daily concern. They laugh with scorn at the announced text for the next day's sermon, "The Lord upholdeth all that fall and raiseth up all those that he bowed down." The grim view of life that the play symbolizes, merely the painful time preceding the inevitable fall, is characteristic of Beckett's work, where physical incapacity and degeneration of the body are frequent themes.

Krapp's Last Tape (produced 1958, published 1960) was written in English and translated into French as *La Dernière Bande* (1960). In this play the title character listens to and comments on the messages he recorded in previous years, particularly descriptions of his mother's death and a scene where he makes love to a woman in a rowboat. Now that he is old and decrepit, chronically constipated, and turning to prostitutes, Krapp criticizes his younger self and his fascination with women and love. He asserts that he would not want to return to that earlier time, although he seems to have little in the present to live for. He listens again—for the third time—to the lovemaking scene in the boat, which stands out in his memory as the happiest moment in his life. Humor is generated through clownish byplay (Krapp literally slips on a banana peel) and by Krapp's references to his bowels and openly vulgar gestures (he repeatedly caresses a banana and holds the tip of it in his mouth). Krapp's quasi dialogue with his younger self by means of the tape recorder is generally considered a theatrical tour de force.

During the late 1950s Beckett wrote another radio play in English titled *Embers* (produced 1959, published 1960; translated into French as *Cendres,* 1960). The main character, Henry, is obsessed with the sound of the sea, which he hears even when he is far from it; he talks constantly to himself to drown out the sound. Henry talks at length to his dead father, who does not answer, and to his presumably dead wife, who does. He orders sound effects, such as the sound of horses' hooves, to accompany his own voice. He seems to be orchestrating the sounds of his life to fill an otherwise empty existence. Like Hamm, he believes that storytelling is an important way to spend time, and certain elements of his story are repeated—the dying fire, the white snow-filled world—to create a visually striking scene.

Beckett owed much of his success to Suzanne's persistent calls on publishers and theater directors. In order to ensure that she would inherit the rights to his work, they married secretly in England in 1961. Although Beckett had many close women friends over the years, he and Suzanne continued to live together and to take long vacations together until shortly before they died. They built a house in Ussy-sur-Marne, a village about sixty kilometers from Paris, where Beckett withdrew, usually alone, to write.

Beckett's next play was *Happy Days* (produced and published 1961; translated into French as *Oh les beaux jours,* 1963). It features a middle-aged woman named Winnie who is buried up to her waist in a mound of scorched grass. She spends her day sorting through the contents of her handbag and talking to her husband, Willie, who rarely answers and is often not even visible to the audience. Despite the constraints of her situation, she is optimistic and repeatedly announces that this is another happy day. Although Winnie is buried up to her neck in act 2, she remains animated and grateful for small blessings, such as the fact that the voices in her head cease from time to time. She is one of the most striking examples in Beckett's theater of futility, portraying an existence in which talking merely makes the time pass. Awakened each morning by an alarm that also sounds if she closes her eyes during the day, Winnie spends the day in useless chatter, reassuring her husband that she could not survive if he were to leave her. In her handbag she has a revolver, but neither she nor Willie uses it. Winnie, like the man in *Acte sans paroles I,* appears to be the victim of some sort of cruel joke, subjected to a pointless experiment, like an insect whose legs have been ripped off.

Beckett's next two radio plays, *Words and Music* (produced 1962; published 1964; translated into French as *Parole et Musique,* 1966) and *Cascando* (produced in French in 1963; published in English in 1964), are distinctive in that music becomes a voice, making it a

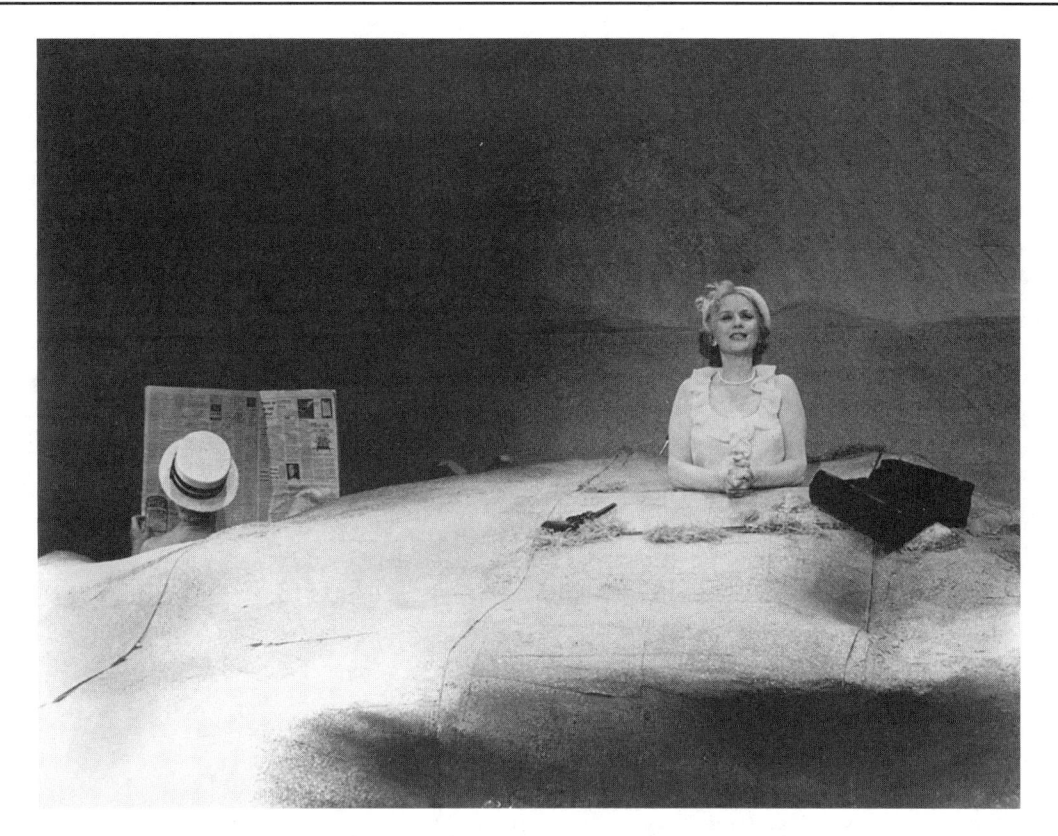

Hume Cronyn and Jessica Tandy in Beckett's Happy Days *at the Lincoln Center, New York, 1972 (photograph by Martha Swope; New York Public Library)*

radio-play character. The theme of *Cascando* is a desire to find the right story, the one that will end the necessity for telling stories, a theme that will reappear in *Not I* (produced 1972; published 1973; translated into French as *Pas moi,* 1975). As early as in *En attendant Godot,* Beckett's dramatic personae were preoccupied with storytelling, but in *Cascando* readers and spectators are introduced to the idea that there exists a particular story–a story to end all stories–that in the telling will satisfy the need to tell stories and end the obsession. *Cascando* was the last published dramatic work Beckett composed in French for almost twenty years, and the next-to-last overall.

Beckett was often asked to direct or assist with the production of his plays, and by the end of his career he had taken charge of many performances in France, Germany, and England. As he became more experienced, he experimented more and more with light, sound, and unusual sets. *Play* (published 1964; translated into French as *Comédie,* 1966) was written in English but premiered in German translation as *Spiel* at the Ulmer Theater in Germany in 1963. The heads of two women and a man appear from three urns; each speaks only when the spotlight illuminates his or her head. Hence, the light itself is almost a fourth character, commanding the others to speak or be silent. Each voice, unaware of the others, recounts essentially the same story of a love triangle. Beckett makes use of multiple musical techniques, with phrases taken up, repeated, and answered by other voices, until the entire work is repeated from the beginning. The da capo effect helps to unite the three monologues and allows the viewer to reexperience the movement of the play with the same appreciation as the concertgoer savoring a favorite sonata.

In 1963, during his only visit to the United States, Beckett participated in the filming of his scenario, *Film* (1965), in New York, with Buster Keaton playing the principal role, a character who does not speak. Beckett's theater pieces written after this period are generally very short, and the speaking–when there is any speaking at all–is mostly monologue. The three women in *Come and Go* (first published in French translation as *Va et vient,* 1966; first produced in German translation as *Kommen und Gehen,* 1966; original version published 1967) are so similar they appear to be three versions of the same woman, and their dialogue consists of variations on a theme. Their clothing is similar; all three names are flower related; and their concerns and movements are almost identical. The device of

Scene from Beckett's Play *performed at the Cherry Lane Theatre, New York, 1964 (photograph by Alix Jeffry; New York Public Library)*

replaying the same brief scene three times with interchangeable actors is used again and more fully played out in his last play, *What Where* (performed 1983, published 1984).

Beckett's shortest work is the famous *Breath* (performed 1969; published 1972; translated into French as *Souffle,* 1972), his forty-second contribution to the revue *Oh! Calcutta!* The brevity of life is evoked in an inhalation and increase of light, followed by an exhalation and decrease of light, with a brief cry at either end. The stage is littered with unidentifiable rubbish. Beckett was angry when his script was tampered with so that the stage directions included naked people among the clutter, and he was eventually able to stop productions that did not follow his script.

By the late 1960s, Beckett's eyesight was rapidly deteriorating, eventually requiring surgery in 1970–1971. While vacationing in Tunisia in 1969, he learned that he had been awarded the Nobel Prize in literature. He did not seek such honors, and he was concerned that the devastating news meant that his need for privacy would be disrupted. He asked his friend Jerome Lindon to travel to Norway to accept the prize in his place.

The following year Beckett wrote *Not I,* which features a woman's lighted mouth delivering a long monologue in which the speaker repeatedly denies that she is talking about herself. Also present onstage is a dimly seen auditor who gestures rarely. Mouth experiences an imperative that she is unable to define. She believes she has something to tell, or something to think, or something to be forgiven. The story she tells is that of a speechless woman; she seems to be addressing an unheard interlocutor, and the curtain falls while she is still speaking. Like all of Beckett's later plays, this one is technically difficult to produce and requires unusual talents of his actors. While the actress of *Happy Days* can only express herself with her face, the range of expression is further reduced in *Not I,* where only her mouth is visible.

The actor in *That Time* (published and produced 1976; translated into French as *Cette fois,* 1978), which was written in 1974–1975, appears as a disembodied head listening to his own voice in three versions (labeled A, B, and C by the author). Unlike in *Krapp's Last Tape,* where there is interaction between the stage character and his recorded voice, the movement of the old man in *That Time* is limited to opening and closing his eyes and smiling. The voices deliver intertwined monologues focusing on memories from three different periods. The emphasis is on aging and loneliness; in the final image all turns to dust, and the final words "come and gone in no time gone in no time" summarize the life cycle concisely and draw out the *vita brevis* theme of the title, a favorite with Beckett since the time of his celebrated "they give birth astride of a grave" in *En attendant Godot.* Beckett returns to this theme again in *Footfalls* (1976), in which the protagonist, May, paces continually and speaks, first to her mother, and then to herself. She invents a story about a girl named Amy (an anagram of her own name) who vanishes from the story ("I was not there") just as May vanishes from the stage at the end. By juxtaposing the end of the tale with the fading away of May, Beckett has extended his expression of the brevity and uselessness of life to include the ephemeral nature of art itself.

Beginning in the late 1960s, Beckett wrote a series of scripts for television: *Eh Joe* (1966), *Ghost Trio* (1977), . . . *but the clouds* . . . (1977), *Quad* (1982), and *Nacht und Träume* (1983). None of these scripts have any dialogue. One hears either a single voice that is clearly not that of the character in view or no words at all. *Ghost Trio* and . . . *but the clouds* . . . include voice-overs, while in *Quad* four different types of percussion accompany the four actors as they pace out a pattern with an audible shuffling of feet. Meanwhile, *Nacht und Träume* uses a twice-hummed and twice-sung portion of Franz Peter Schubert's lied of the same name; there is no other sound.

Beckett's final works for the theater are for the most part concerned with aging and death. *A Piece of Monologue* (performed 1979, published 1981; translated into French as *Solo,* 1982) brings to the stage an old man whose speech is reminiscent of the woman's in *Not I.* The monologue is actually a dramatic reading of a prose passage with minimal set and lighting requirements. The opening words, "Birth was the death of him," are yet another expression of the brevity of life. The speaker has destroyed the photographs on his wall one by one as death has taken the people they depict. The old man's solitude is extreme, and, as he puts it, he is facing a blank wall, "Dying on."

Rockaby (performed and published 1981; translated into French as *Berceuse,* 1982) features another dying figure, this time a woman who bears a resemblance to May in *Footfalls.* In this play the rocking of the chair is coordinated with the recorded voice of the woman offering short, repetitive phrases that form a long poem. This poem describes a life of seeking a kindred soul to replace the mother, and the final acceptance that she is, as she says, "her own other" as she rocks herself toward her own death. The *rockaby* of the title links the rocking of the baby with the slow winding down of the old woman, and the chair represents, even in the stage directions, the embrace of the mother.

Beckett was asked to write a play for an international symposium that was to take place in May 1981 at Ohio State University. Although he did not generally accommodate requests or write for specific occasions, he tried to please his friends. *Ohio Impromptu* (published 1981; translated into French as *Impromptu d'Ohio,* 1982) seems to show the last moments of an old man. In this case the man is sitting at a table with his double, who is reading aloud from a book what is clearly the story of the end of the old man's life. He finishes the story, closes the book, and the two stare at each other until the lights fade out. The last spoken words are, "Nothing is left to tell." The link between the end of the story and the end of life emphasizes the fact that the old man is an artistic creation and that the life of the play is over when the lights go out.

In 1982 Beckett wrote his last play in French, *Catastrophe* (published and produced 1982; translated, 1984). In this play Beckett returns to the theme of *Acte sans paroles I* and *II,* that of a malevolent force that manipulates the individual. In this case the malevolent force is a play director dressed as a party boss who works with an intermediary, an assistant; these characters control the protagonist. Beckett dedicated *Catastrophe* to Czech writer Václav Havel. The parallels between the play and the treatment of Havel, who became a political prisoner in Czechoslovakia after being charged with subverting the Communist republic, are explicit. Beckett had been especially horrified to learn that the imprisoned Havel was deprived of writing materials. At the conclusion of *Catastrophe,* the protagonist lifts his head and looks at the audience in a silent but powerful act of defiance. Conversely, the writing that takes place onstage is in the form of production notes, the assistant's notes about whitening the protagonist's skin and seeing that his hands are not clenched. Words become the weapon of the tyrant, while the protest is wordless. Apart from being an overt political statement, the play is a straightforward expression of Beckett's own feelings as a director. He always sought to mold the actor's performance to his own exacting standard; any independent move could be a catastrophe.

Scene from a 1996 New York production of Beckett's 1966 play Come and Go, *which features three virtually identical women whose roles are interchangeable (© Getty Images)*

Beckett's last play, *What Where,* was first performed in New York in 1983. It was also translated as *Was Wo* and cut for a television performance in Germany in 1985 that was broadcast the following year. *What Where* takes up many of the same themes as Beckett's other plays. It features a spare, repetitive monologue by the voice of the main character, Bam, as he and the three other characters (Bom, Bem, and Bim) reenact, over and over, a short scene referring to torture and a refusal to reveal information. The entire story is acted out "first without words" and then "with words." The dictatorial voice of Bam describes the passing of the seasons and halts the action when he is not satisfied, even replaying the last few words with a slight change that he finds more satisfactory. The characters are all very similar in appearance, and it is likely that they are meant to represent aspects of a single individual. The play implies that the tortured individual did not reveal the information ("what" and "where") because he did not know it. It is tempting to see *What Where* as referring to Beckett as an author, since he consistently refused to "reveal" the meaning of his works. The final lines of the play, "That is all. Make sense who may. I switch off," are remarkably appropriate as an end to Beckett's career as a dramatist.

In the late 1980s, after a lifetime of smoking, Beckett developed emphysema and needed to use oxygen. His wife, Suzanne, was also in poor health, and she died in July 1989. Beckett spent the last months of his life in a nursing home and died on 22 December 1989. He was buried with his wife in the Cimetière du Montparnasse in Paris.

Samuel Beckett's artistry is widely admired, and his landmark plays transformed the theater not only in France but across the world. Drawing on a vast background in philosophy, languages, and the visual arts, Beckett created dialogue with a realistic feel that is nevertheless highly poetic. His humor, imagery, and grim message that the business of life is "dying on" continue to resonate with audiences.

Interview:

Mel Gussow, *Conversations with and about Beckett* (London: Hern, 1996).

Bibliographies:

Raymond Federman and John Fletcher, *Samuel Beckett: His Work and His Critics* (Berkeley: University of California Press, 1970);

Robin J. Davis, *Samuel Beckett: Checklist and Index of His Published Works* (Stirling, Scotland: The Compiler, 1979).

Biographies:

Deirdre Bair, *Samuel Beckett: A Biography* (New York: Harcourt Brace Jovanovich, 1978; London: Cape, 1978);

James Knowlson, *Damned to Fame: The Life of Samuel Beckett* (New York: Simon & Schuster, 1996).

References:

James Acheson, *Samuel Beckett's Artistic Theory and Practice: Criticism, Drama, and Early Fiction* (Basingstoke, U.K.: Macmillan, 1997; New York: St. Martin's Press, 1997);

Acheson and Kateryna Arthur, eds., *Beckett's Later Fiction and Drama: Texts for Company* (New York: St. Martin's Press, 1987);

Richard Admussen, *The Samuel Beckett Manuscripts: A Study* (Boston: G. K. Hall, 1979);

A. Alvarez, *Samuel Beckett* (New York: Viking, 1973);

Cathleen Culotta Andonian, *Samuel Beckett: A Reference Guide* (Boston: G. K. Hall, 1989);

Arthur N. Athanason, *Endgame: The Ashbin Play* (New York: Twayne, 1993);

Morris Beja, S. E. Gontarski, and Pierra Astier, eds., *Samuel Beckett: Humanistic Perspectives* (Columbus: Ohio State University Press, 1982);

Linda Ben-Zvi, *Samuel Beckett* (Boston: Twayne, 1986);

Leo Bersani, *Arts of Impoverishment: Beckett, Rothko, Resnais* (Cambridge, Mass.: Harvard University Press, 1993);

Harold Bloom, ed., *Samuel Beckett: Modern Critical Views* (New York: Chelsea, 1985);

Enoch Brater, *Beyond Minimalism: Beckett's Late Style in the Theater* (New York: Oxford University Press, 1987);

Brater, *The Drama in the Text: Beckett's Late Fiction* (New York: Oxford University Press, 1994);

Brater, ed., *Beckett at 80 / Beckett in Context* (New York: Oxford University Press, 1986);

Susan D. Brienza, *Samuel Beckett's New Worlds: Styles of Metafiction* (Norman: University of Oklahoma Press, 1987);

Mary Bryden, *Women in Samuel Beckett's Prose and Drama: Her Own Other* (Lanham, Md.: Barnes & Noble, 1993);

Lance St. John Butler and Robin J. Davis, eds., *Rethinking Beckett: A Collection of Critical Essays* (New York: St. Martin's Press, 1990);

John Calder, ed., *As No Other Dare Fail: For Samuel Beckett on His 80th Birthday by His Friends and Admirers* (London: Calder, 1986);

Calder, ed., *Beckett at Sixty: A Festschrift* (London: Calder & Boyars, 1967);

Bell Gale Chevigny, ed., *Twentieth Century Interpretations of Endgame* (Englewood Cliffs, N.J.: Prentice-Hall, 1969);

Richard N. Coe, *Samuel Beckett* (New York: Grove, 1964; revised, 1970);

Ruby Cohn, *Back to Beckett* (Princeton: Princeton University Press, 1973);

Cohn, *A Beckett Canon* (Ann Arbor: University of Michigan Press, 2001);

Cohn, "A Checklist of Beckett Criticism," *Perspective*, 11 (Autumn 1959): 193–196;

Cohn, *Samuel Beckett: The Comic Gamut* (New Brunswick, N.J.: Rutgers University Press, 1962);

Cohn, ed., *Casebook on Waiting for Godot* (New York: Grove, 1967);

Cohn, ed., *Samuel Beckett: A Collection of Critical Essays* (New York: McGraw-Hill, 1975);

Steven Connor, *Samuel Beckett: Repetition, Theory and Text* (Oxford: Blackwell, 1988);

Thomas J. Cousineau, *Waiting for Godot: Form in Movement* (Boston: Twayne, 1990);

Anthony Cronin, *Samuel Beckett: The Last Modernist* (London: HarperCollins, 1996);

Paul Davies, *The Ideal Real: Beckett's Fiction and Imagination* (Rutherford, N.J.: Fairleigh Dickinson University Press / London: Associated University Presses, 1994);

Colin Duckworth, *Angels of Darkness: Dramatic Effect in Samuel Beckett with Special Reference to Eugène Ionesco* (London: Allen & Unwin, 1972; New York: Barnes & Noble, 1972);

Gerry Dukes, *Samuel Beckett* (New York: Overlook, 2001);

Martin Esslin, *The Theater of the Absurd* (Harmondsworth, U.K.: Penguin, 1968);

Esslin, ed., *Samuel Beckett: A Collection of Critical Essays* (Englewood Cliffs, N.J.: Prentice-Hall, 1969);

Anthony Farrow, *Early Beckett: Art and Allusion in More Pricks than Kicks and Murphy* (Troy, N.Y.: Whitston, 1991);

Raymond Federman and John Fletcher, *Samuel Beckett: His Works and His Critics* (Berkeley: University of California Press, 1970);

Beryl Fletcher and others, *A Student's Guide to the Plays of Samuel Beckett* (London: Faber & Faber, 1978);

John Fletcher, *Samuel Beckett's Art* (London: Chatto & Windus, 1967);

Fletcher and John Spurling, *Beckett: A Study of His Plays* (New York: Hill & Wang, 1972);

Alan Warren Friedman, Charles Rossman, and Dina Sherzer, eds., *Beckett Translating/Translating Beckett* (University Park: Pennsylvania State University Press, 1987);

S. E. Gontarski, *The Intent of Undoing in Samuel Beckett's Dramatic Texts* (Bloomington: Indiana University Press, 1985);

Gontarski, ed., *The Beckett Studies Reader (1976–1991)* (Gainesville: University Press of Florida, 1993);

Gontarski, ed., *On Beckett: Essays and Criticism* (New York: Grove, 1986);

Lois G. Gordon, *The World of Samuel Beckett, 1906–1946* (New Haven: Yale University Press, 1996);

Lawrence Graver and Raymond Federman, eds., *Samuel Beckett: The Critical Heritage* (London & Boston: Routledge, 1979);

Ihab Hassan, *The Literature of Silence: Henry Miller and Samuel Beckett* (New York: Knopf, 1967);

Gerhard Hauck, *Reductionism in Drama and the Theatre: The Case of Samuel Beckett* (Potomac, Md.: Scripta Humanistica, 1992);

David Hesla, *The Shape of Chaos: An Interpretation of the Art of Samuel Beckett* (Minneapolis: University of Minnesota Press, 1971);

Frederick J. Hoffman, *Samuel Beckett: The Language of Self* (Carbondale: University of Southern Illinois Press, 1962);

Jonathan Kalb, *Beckett in Performance* (Cambridge: Cambridge University Press, 1989);

Hugh Kenner, *A Reader's Guide to Samuel Beckett* (New York: Farrar, Straus & Giroux, 1973);

Kenner, *Samuel Beckett: A Critical Study* (Berkeley: University of California Press, 1968);

Hwa Soon Kim, *The Counterpoint of Hope, Obsession, and Desire for Death in Five Plays by Samuel Beckett* (New York: Peter Lang, 1996);

James Knowlson and John Pilling, *Frescoes of the Skull: The Later Prose and Drama of Samuel Beckett* (New York: Grove, 1979);

Charles R. Lyons, *Samuel Beckett* (New York: Grove, 1984);

Anna McMullan, *Theatre on Trial: Samuel Beckett's Later Drama* (New York: Routledge, 1993);

Pierre Mélèse, *Beckett* (Paris: Seghers, 1966);

Vivian Mercier, *Beckett/Beckett: The Truth of Contradiction* (New York: Oxford University Press, 1977);

Lawrence Miller, *Samuel Beckett: The Expressive Dilemma* (New York: St. Martin's Press, 1992);

Edouard Morot-Sir, Howard Harper, and Dougald McMilan III, eds., *Samuel Beckett: The Art of Rhetoric,* North Carolina Studies in the Romance Languages and Literatures, no. 5 (Chapel Hill: University of North Carolina Press, 1976);

Kristen Morrison, *Canters and Chronicles: The Use of Narrative in the Plays of Samuel Beckett and Harold Pinter* (Chicago: University of Chicago Press, 1983);

Lois Oppenheim and Marius Buning, eds., *Beckett On and On* (Madison, N.J.: Fairleigh Dickinson University Press, 1996);

John Pilling, *Samuel Beckett* (London: Routledge, 1976);

Pilling, ed., *Cambridge Companion to Beckett* (Cambridge & New York: Cambridge University Press, 1993);

Pilling and Mary Bryden, eds., *Ideal Core of the Onion: Reading Beckett Archives* (London: Beckett International Foundation, 1992);

Rosemary Pountney, *Theatre of Shadows: Samuel Beckett's Drama 1956–76* (Gerrards Cross, U.K.: Smythe, 1998);

Christopher B. Ricks, *Beckett's Dying Words: The Clarendon Lectures, 1990* (Oxford: Clarendon Press, 1993; New York: Oxford University Press, 1993);

Jeremy Robinson, *Samuel Beckett Goes into the Silence* (Kidderminster, U.K.: Crescent Moon, 1992);

Alan Schneider, *Entrance: An American Director's Journey* (New York: Viking, 1986);

Nathan A. Scott Jr., *Samuel Beckett* (Hewlett, N.Y.: Hillary House, 1965);

Bennett Simon, *Tragic Drama and the Family: Psychoanalytic Studies from Aeschylus to Beckett* (New Haven: Yale University Press, 1968);

Joseph H. Smith, ed., *The World of Samuel Beckett* (Baltimore: Johns Hopkins University Press, 1991);

Bert O. States, *The Shape of Paradox: An Essay on Waiting for Godot* (Berkeley: University of California Press, 1978);

James T. F. Tanner and J. Don Vann, *Samuel Beckett: A Checklist of Criticism* (Kent, Ohio: Kent State University Press, 1969);

Eugene Webb, *The Plays of Samuel Beckett* (Seattle: University of Washington Press, 1974);

S. E. Wilmer, ed., *Beckett in Dublin* (Dublin, Ireland: Lilliput, 1992);

Katherine Worth, *Revolutions in Modern English Drama* (London: Bell, 1972);

Worth, ed., *Beckett the Shape Changer: A Symposium* (London: Routledge, 1975);

Catharina Wulf, ed., *Ge Eye = L'oeil Fauve: New Essays on Samuel Beckett's Television Plays* (Amsterdam & Atlanta: Rodopi, 1995).

Albert Camus
(7 November 1913 – 4 January 1960)

Dale Cosper
Whitman College

See also the Camus entry in *DLB 72: French Novelists, 1930-1960*.

PLAY PRODUCTIONS: *Le Malentendu,* Paris, Théâtre des Mathurins, 24 August 1944;

Caligula, Paris, Théâtre Hébertot, 26 September 1945;

L'Etat de siège, Paris, Théâtre de Marigny, 27 October 1948;

Les Justes, Paris, Théâtre Hébertot, 15 December 1949;

Les Esprits, adapted from Pierre de Larivey's play, Angers, Festival d'Art Dramatique, 16 June 1953;

Réquiem pour une nonne, adapted from William Faulkner's novel, Paris, Théâtre des Mathurins, 22 September 1956;

Les Possédés, adapted from Fyodor Dostoevsky's novel, Paris, Théâtre Antoine, 30 January 1959.

BOOKS: *Révolte dans les Asturies,* by Camus and others (Algiers: Charlot, 1936);

L'Envers et l'endroit (Algiers: Charlot, 1937); translated by Philip Thody as "Betwixt and Between," in *Lyrical and Critical* (London: Hamilton, 1967); translated by Ellen Conroy Kennedy as "The Wrong Side and the Right Side," in *Lyrical and Critical Essays* (New York: Knopf, 1968), pp. 5-61;

Noces (Algiers: Charlot, 1939); translated by Kennedy as "Nuptials," in *Lyrical and Critical Essays* (New York: Knopf, 1968), pp. 63-92;

L'Etranger (Paris: Gallimard, 1942); translated by Stuart Gilbert as *The Outsider* (London: Hamilton, 1946); republished as *The Stranger* (New York: Knopf, 1946); translated by Matthew Ward as *The Stranger* (New York: Knopf, 1988);

Le Mythe de Sisyphe (Paris: Gallimard, 1942); translated by Justin O'Brien as "The Myth of Sisyphus," in *The Myth of Sisyphus and Other Essays* (London: Hamilton, 1955), pp. 3-91;

Le Malentendu suivi de Caligula (Paris: Gallimard, 1944); translated by Gilbert as *Caligula and Cross Purpose* (New York: New Directions, 1947);

Albert Camus (photograph by Central Press; © Getty Images)

Lettres à un ami allemand (Paris: Gallimard, 1945); translated by O'Brien as "Letters to a German Friend," in *Resistance, Rebellion and Death* (New York: Knopf, 1961; London: Hamilton, 1961), pp. 1-32;

La Peste (Paris: Gallimard, 1947); translated by Gilbert as *The Plague* (New York: Knopf, 1948);

L'Etat de siège (Paris: Gallimard, 1948); translated by Gilbert as *State of Siege,* in *Caligula and Three Other*

Plays (New York: Random House, 1958), pp. 135–232;

Actuelles: Chroniques 1944–1948 (Paris: Gallimard, 1950); partially translated by O'Brien as "The Liberation of Paris," "The Flesh," and "Pessimism and Tyranny," in *Resistance, Rebellion and Death* (New York: Knopf, 1961; London: Hamilton, 1961), pp. 33–65;

Les Justes (Paris: Gallimard, 1950); translated by Gilbert as *The Just Assassins*, in *Caligula and Three Other Plays* (New York: Random House, 1958), pp. 233–302;

L'Homme révolté (Paris: Gallimard, 1951); translated by Anthony Bower as *The Rebel* (London: Hamilton, 1953; New York: Knopf, 1954);

Actuelles II: Chroniques 1948–1953 (Paris: Gallimard, 1953); partially translated by O'Brien as "The Unbeliever and Christians," "Why Spain," and "Defense of Freedom," in *Resistance, Rebellion and Death* (New York: Knopf, 1961; London: Hamilton, 1961), pp. 67–107;

Les Esprits, adapted from Pierre de Larivey's play (Paris: Gallimard, 1953);

L'Eté (Paris: Gallimard, 1954); translated by Kennedy as *Summer*, in *Lyrical and Critical Essays* (New York: Knopf, 1968), pp. 107–186;

Réquiem pour une nonne, adapted from William Faulkner's novel (Paris: Gallimard, 1956);

La Chute (Paris: Gallimard, 1956); translated by O'Brien as *The Fall* (New York: Knopf, 1957);

L'Exil et le royaume (Paris: Gallimard, 1957); translated by O'Brien as *Exile and the Kingdom* (London: Hamilton, 1958; New York: Knopf, 1958);

Actuelles III: Chronique algérienne 1939–1958 (Paris: Gallimard, 1958); partially translated by O'Brien as "Algeria," in *Resistance, Rebellion and Death* (New York: Knopf, 1961; London: Hamilton, 1961), pp. 109–171;

Discours de Suède (Paris: Gallimard, 1958); translated by O'Brien as *Speech of Acceptance upon the Award of the Nobel Prize for Literature, Delivered in Stockholm on the Tenth of December, Nineteen Hundred and Fifty-seven* (New York: Knopf, 1958);

Les Possédés, adapted from Fyodor Dostoevsky's novel (Paris: Gallimard, 1959); translated by O'Brien as *The Possessed* (New York: Knopf, 1960);

Carnets, mai 1935–février 1942 (Paris: Gallimard, 1962); translated by Thody as *Notebooks*, volume 1: *1935–1942* (New York: Knopf, 1963);

Carnets, janvier 1942–mars 1951 (Paris: Gallimard, 1964); translated by O'Brien as *Notebooks*, volume 2: *1942–1951* (New York: Knopf, 1965);

Essais (Paris: Gallimard, 1965);

La Mort heureuse, Cahiers Albert Camus, no. 1 (Paris: Gallimard, 1971); translated by Howard as *A Happy Death,* edited, with an afterword, by Jean Sarocchi (London: Hamilton, 1972; New York: Knopf, 1972);

Le Premier Camus, suivi de Ecrits de jeunesse d'Albert Camus, by Camus and Paul Viallaneix, Cahiers Albert Camus, no. 2 (Paris: Gallimard, 1973); translated by Kennedy as *Youthful Writings* (New York: Knopf, 1976; London: Hamilton, 1977);

Fragments d'un combat: 1938–1940, Alger Républicain, Le Soir Républicain, 2 volumes, edited by Jacqueline Lévi Valensi and André Abou (Paris: Gallimard, 1978);

Journaux de voyage (Paris: Gallimard, 1978); translated by Hugh Levick as *American Journals* (New York: Paragon, 1987; London: Hamilton, 1988);

Caligula, version de 1941, suivi de La Poétique du premier Caligula, edited by A. James Arnold (Paris: Gallimard, 1984);

Le Premier homme, edited by Catherine Camus (Paris: Gallimard, 1994); translated by David Hapgood as *The First Man* (London: Hamilton, 1995; New York: Knopf, 1995).

Collections: *Théâtre, récits, nouvelles* (Paris: Gallimard, 1962);

Oeuvres complètes d'Albert Camus, 5 volumes (Paris: Club de L'Honnête Homme, 1983).

Editions in English: *Caligula: A Drama in Two Acts,* translated by Justin O'Brien (New York & London: S. French, 1961);

Summer, translated by Philip Thody, Penguin 60s (London: Penguin, 1995);

The Outsider, translated by Joseph Laredo, introduction by Peter Dunwoodie, Everyman's Library, no. 139 (London: Campbell, 1998);

The Fall, translated by O'Brien, introduction by Oliver Todd (London: Penguin, 2000);

The Myth of Sisyphus, translated by O'Brien, introduction by James Wood (London: Penguin, 2000);

The Plague, translated by Robin Buss (New York: Knopf, 2001);

Summer in Algiers, Pocket Penguin, no. 4 (London: Penguin, 2005).

OTHER: Sébastien-Roch Nicolas de Chamfort, *Maximes et anecdotes,* preface by Camus, biography by Pierre-Louis Ginguené (Monaco: DAC, 1944);

André Salvet, *Le Combat silencieux,* preface by Camus (Paris: Sceaux, 1945);

Jean Camp and others, *L'Espagne libre,* preface by Camus (Paris: Calmann-Lévy, 1946);

Pierre-Eugène Clairin, *Dix Estampes originales,* introduction by Camus (Paris: Rombaldi, 1946);

Jacques Méry, *Laissez passer mon peuple,* preface by Camus (Paris: Seuil, 1947);

Jeanne Héon-Canone, *Devant la mort,* preface by Camus (Angers: Siraudeau, 1951);

"Herman Melville," in *Les Ecrivains célèbres,* volume 3 (Paris: Mazenod, 1952);

Daniel Mauroc, *Contre-Amour,* preface by Camus (Paris: Minuit, 1952);

Oscar Wilde, *Ballade de la geôle de Reading,* preface by Camus (Paris: Falaize, 1952);

Alfred Rosmer, *Moscou sous Lénine: Les Origines du communisme,* preface by Camus (Paris: Horay, 1953);

Désert vivant: Images et couleurs de Walt Disney, texts by Camus, Marcel Aymé, Louis Bromfield, Julian Huxley, François Mauriac, André Maurois, and Henry de Montherlant (Paris: Société Française du Livre, 1954);

Konrad Ferdinand Bieber, *L'Allemagne vue par les écrivains de la Résistance française,* preface by Camus (Geneva: Droz / Lille: Giard, 1954);

"L'Enchantement de Cordes," in Claire Targuebayre, *Cordes-en-Albigeois* (Toulouse: Privat, 1954);

Roger Martin du Gard, *Oeuvres complètes,* 2 volumes, preface by Camus (Paris: Gallimard, 1955);

"Réflexions sur la guillotine," in *Réflexions sur la peine capitale,* by Camus and Arthur Koestler (Paris: Calmann-Levy, 1957), pp. 123–180; Camus's contribution translated by Richard Howard as *Reflections on the Guillotine: An Essay on Capital Punishment* (Michigan City, Ind.: Fridtjof-Karla, 1960 [i.e., 1959]);

La Vérité sur l'affaire Nagy, preface by Camus, afterword by François Fejtö (Paris: Plon, 1958);

La Postérité du soleil, text by Camus, photographs by Henriette Grindat (Geneva: Engelberts, 1965).

TRANSLATIONS: James Thurber, *La Dernière Fleur* (Paris: Gallimard, 1952);

Pedro Calderón de la Barca, *La Dévotion à la croix* (Paris: Gallimard, 1953);

Dino Buzzati, *Un Cas intéressant, Avant-Scène,* no. 105 (1955): 1–25;

Félix Lope de Vega Carpio, *Le Chevalier d'Olmedo* (Paris: Gallimard, 1957).

Albert Camus was a French-Algerian novelist, essayist, dramatist, and journalist whose concepts of absurdity and revolution made his writings among the most famous in postwar literature. A Nobel laureate, Camus analyzed and offered solutions to the apparent meaninglessness of modern life. His four original plays, written between 1944 and 1949, move away from social realism and psychology to stage a philosophy of freedom, rebellion, and action against a background of history and politics.

In the autobiographical *Le Premier homme* (1994; translated as *The First Man,* 1995), Camus describes his birth on 7 November 1913 in Mondovi, Algeria, to Lucien Auguste Camus and his wife, Catherine Sintès. Camus's father descended from Bordeaux stock on the paternal side and from the Ardèche region of south-central France on the maternal side. Camus's mother was a descendant of Spanish emigrants from Majorca. Although no one in the family spoke Spanish, Camus was always proud of his *espagnolisme* (Spanish roots), and he learned the language on his own.

Lucien Auguste Camus grew up fatherless and was placed in a Protestant orphanage at a young age. Called to serve in the army in 1914, he was gravely injured at the battle of the Marne. He died of his wounds on 11 October of that year, and he was buried at Saint-Brieuc in Brittany. Hence, like their father, Camus and his older brother, Lucien Jean Etienne, grew up fatherless. The boys lived with their mother, grandmother, and maternal uncle, Etienne Sintès, in a three-room apartment in Belcourt, a working-class Algerian neighborhood not far from the sea. Camus's mother worked as a cleaning lady, and the household survived on her meager earnings and those of her brother. Camus's entire life and work was marked by the influence of his mother, who was illiterate, hearing impaired, and largely silent. By all accounts she was unable to show or express affection. For the young Camus, she epitomized a silent and indifferent universe.

In his youth Camus developed a deep love of nature, especially of the Mediterranean Sea and its coasts. This landscape is the subject of his early lyrical essay *Noces* (1939; translated as "Nuptials," 1968). Camus was also athletic, and he thrived on physical activities. He was an avid and excellent soccer goalie, but he eventually had to curtail his athletic activities when he was diagnosed with tuberculosis at age seventeen.

As a *pupille de la nation* (a war orphan), Camus qualified for money from the French government to help with his education. At the *école communale* (public elementary school) he attracted the attention of a teacher, Louis Germain, who convinced Camus's controlling grandmother to allow him to pursue his studies at the lycée (senior high school) level. Camus later dedicated his Nobel Prize acceptance speech to Germain. At the lycée another teacher, Jean Grenier, recognized Camus's considerable literary and philosophical gifts. Already a published author himself, Grenier influenced Camus's ideas, especially his notion of the absurd. Camus dedicated his first philosophical essay, *Le Mythe de Sisyphe* (1942; translated as "The Myth of Sisyphus,"

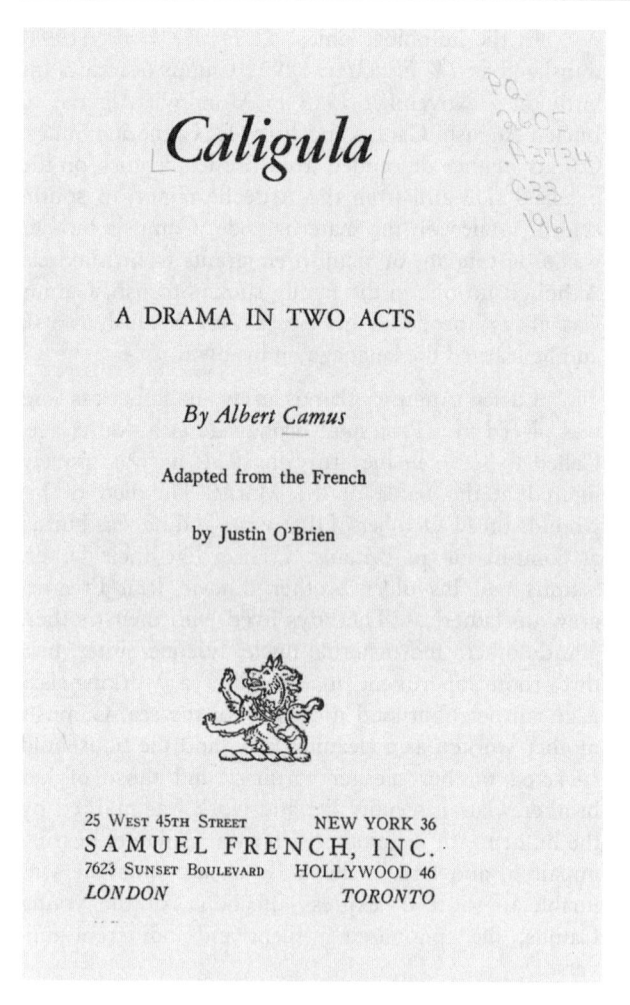

Title page for a 1961 English translation of Camus's 1945 play that explores the concept of absurd art in an absurd universe (Thomas Cooper Library, University of South Carolina)

1955), to Grenier and then immortalized him with the character Victor Mallan in *Le Premier homme*.

Just as Germain encouraged Camus to go to the lycée, Grenier convinced him to pursue university studies. In 1933 Camus enrolled at the University of Algiers. The following year, Camus joined the local Communist Party. In Algiers, Camus met his first wife, Simone Hié, whom he wed on 16 June 1934; however, Simone's morphine addiction and infidelities caused the marriage to break up in less than two years. In 1936 Camus completed a *diplôme d'études supérieures* (Diploma of Higher Education) with a thesis on Augustine and Plotinus, but his health prevented him from taking the *agrégation*, the competitive examination that would have qualified him for teaching.

While studying at the University of Algiers and participating in Communist Party politics, Camus organized the theatrical group Le Théâtre du Travail (The Workers' Theater), which in its inaugural program on 25 January 1936 presented, with the consent of the author, a dramatization of André Malraux's *Le Temps du mépris* (1936, The Time of Scorn; translated as *Days of Wrath* and also as *Days of Contempt*, 1936). A second play, *Révolte dans les Asturies* (1936, Revolt in Asturia), was purportedly written collaboratively by the troupe, but it is primarily the work of Camus, who was the director, chief actor, and stage manager. The play was inspired by the suppression of an uprising of miners in Spain in September 1934. *Révolte dans les Asturies* was banned, but a copy survives thanks to the publisher, Edmond Charlot of Algiers.

Camus left the Communist Party after becoming disenchanted with its role in the Spanish Civil War and its policy regarding the indigenous population of Algeria. In 1937 he founded a new theatrical group, Le Théâtre de l'Equipe (The Team Theater). This organization disavowed any political affiliation or agenda and, inspired by the work of Jacques Copeau at his Nouveau Colombier theater in Paris and Julien Duvivier's movie *La Belle Equipe* (1936, The Beautiful Team), they offered in 1937–1938 the medieval Spanish play *La Celestina*, André Gide's *Retour de l'enfant prodigue* (1907; translated as *The Return of the Prodigal*, 1953), Charles Vildrac's *Le Paquebot Tenacity* (1920, The Ocean-liner Tenacity, translated as *S.S. Tenacity*, 1929), and an adaptation of Fyodor Dostoevsky's *Brat'ia Karamazovy* (1881; translated as *The Brothers Karamazov*, 1912). John Millington Synge's *Playboy of the Western World* (1907), translated as *Baladin du monde occidental*, was added to the repertoire for the 1938–1939 season.

Along with his theatrical activity, Camus began to work as a journalist in 1937 at the *Alger Républicain (Republican Algiers)*, covering subjects as varied as politics and literature. That year Camus also published his first collection of short stories, the autobiographical *L'Envers et l'endroit* (The Wrong Side and the Right Side; translated as "Betwixt and Between," 1967). In 1939 Camus published *Noces*. Both of these works were published by Charlot in Algiers.

The outbreak of World War II in 1939 had major political consequences for the French colony of Algeria. *Alger Républicain* changed hands to become *Soir Républicain* (The Republican Evening News), and it was now subject to censorship. Rather than submit to such control, Camus left Algeria–leaving behind his second wife, Francine Faure, whom he wed in 1940–to write for the newspaper *Paris-Soir* (The Paris Evening News). When Paris fell to the Germans in June 1940, Camus returned to Algeria, to the city of Oran, his wife's birthplace, where he taught in a private school. In 1942, after discovering that his tuberculosis had spread to both lungs, he again returned to France, this time to the southeastern Cévennes region for treatment and rest. Francine joined him there in the summer of 1942, but she returned to her teaching duties in Oran in the fall. By November 1942, all of France was occupied by the Germans, and North Africa had fallen to the Allies; hence, Camus was unable to rejoin his wife in Algeria, and they remained separated until the end of the war. In 1943 Camus moved to Paris, where he worked as a reader for the Gallimard publishing house. His most important activity of the final years of the war was his collaboration with his friend Pascal Pia on the clandestine newspaper *Combat* (1943–1947). Unable to enlist in the army because of his poor health, Camus found in *Combat* a means of political engagement and resistance.

The publication of Camus's novel *L'Etranger* (1942, The Stranger; translated as *The Outsider*, 1946) and his philosophical essay *Le Mythe de Sisyphe* during the war established him as one of the most important contemporary French writers. When it was discovered after the liberation of France that the editor of *Combat* and the author of *L'Etranger* and *Le Mythe de Sisyphe* were the same person, Camus quickly gained the esteem and affection of his countrymen and worldwide fame.

In *Le Mythe de Sisyphe,* Camus articulates his philosophy of the absurd. It is at once a feeling and a concept resulting from the encounter between human demands for rationality, clarity, order, and immortality, and a universe offering indifference, obscurity, chaos, and death. The Greek mythological figure Sisyphus, who was condemned to roll a rock repeatedly up a mountain, is for Camus the absurd hero incarnate. Meanwhile, *L'Etranger* illustrates this absurd human condition. The hero of the novel, Meursault, condemned to death for an accidental murder, rejects the false consolations of religion and affirms the joys of earthly life.

Camus's first play produced in Paris was *Le Malentendu* (The Misunderstanding, published 1944; translated as *Cross Purpose*, 1947). It premiered at the Théâtre des Mathurins on 24 August 1944 under the direction of Marcel Herrand. The role of Martha was played by Maria Casarès, the daughter of the former Spanish minister of war. From their first encounter, Maria became the great love of Camus's life. The play, however, was not a success. Although the critics praised Casarès, they found the play cold and plodding, and complained that the ending was implied from the beginning.

The basic plot of *Le Malentendu* is given in *L'Etranger,* specifically, in the newspaper article that the fictional hero Meursault finds under his mattress in his jail cell. It is an absurdist version of the story of the prodigal son. Jan is returning to his home in Czechoslovakia, having left his mother and sister there years before to seek his fortune in the outside world. He wants to arrive unannounced, without identifying himself or being recognized by his family, in order to create within himself a sense of belonging to the place and to the people. He leaves his wife, Maria, in the village and goes to the inn his family keeps. He does not know that his mother and his sister Martha are in the habit of killing and robbing their guests to finance their projected move to a southern clime where they can live happily in the sun. The women do not recognize Jan and serve him poisoned tea. When Maria comes in search of her husband, Martha learns of the true identity of the murdered guest and goes off to drown herself. The "misunderstanding" is twofold: the women do not recognize their guest, and Jan does not understand that human

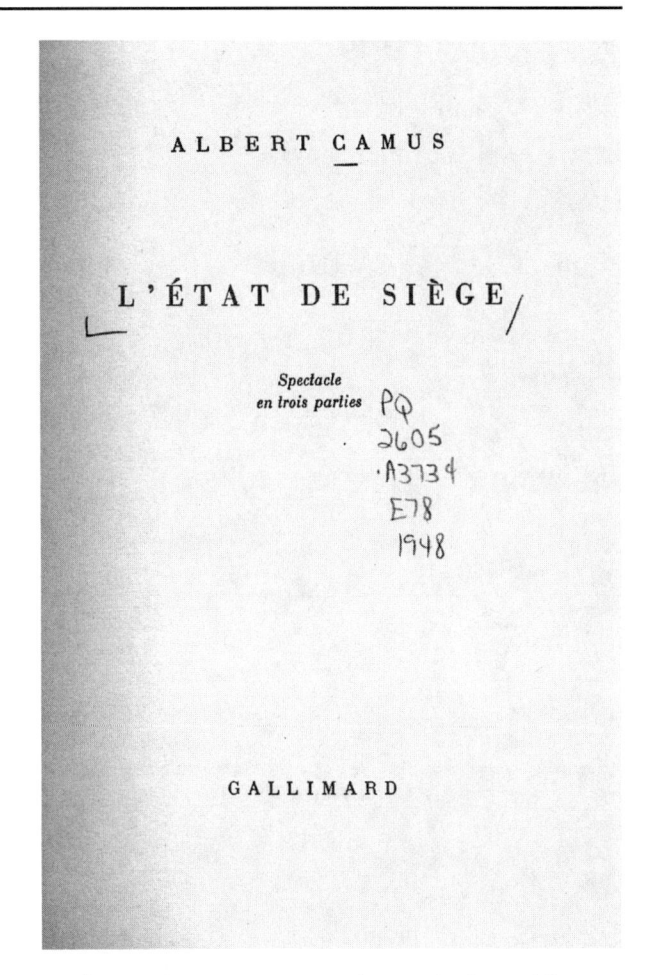

Title page for Camus's 1948 play (translated as State of Siege, *1958), an allegory set in early modern Spain that was roundly rejected by audiences and critics (Thomas Cooper Library, University of South Carolina)*

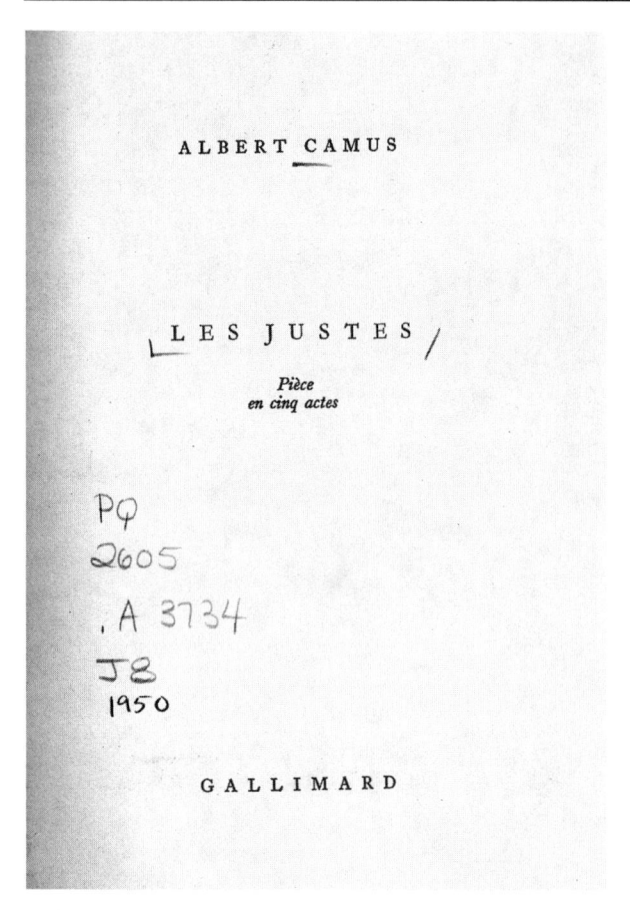

Title page for Camus's 1950 play (translated as The Just Assassins, *1958) that explores the relationship between means and ends in revolutionary activity (Thomas Cooper Library, University of South Carolina)*

beings are constantly at risk and should never take chances. Jan's desire to be recognized and to feel at home blinds him to the role chance plays in human affairs.

The existentialist philosopher Jean-Paul Sartre and Camus became friends during the Nazi occupation of France and remained so for nearly a decade. Sartre originally asked Camus to play the male lead in *Huis clos* (1945, No Exit; translated as *In Camera*, 1946), but this project did not come to fruition. Through Sartre, Camus became acquainted with the prominent Parisian directors Herrand, Jean-Louis Barrault, and Jean Vilar.

Paul Oettly produced Camus's next play, *Caligula* (published 1944; translated, 1947), at the Théâtre Hébertot in Paris on 26 September 1945. Camus began working on *Caligula* in 1939. The original three-act version was part of what Camus had planned as his "cycle of the absurd," a philosophical essay, a novel, and a play: *Le Mythe de Sisyphe, L'Etranger,* and *Caligula*. The final, four-act version starred the popular actor Gérard Philippe in the title role. In the play, the young Roman emperor Caligula has encountered the absurdity of human existence at least in part because of the death of his sister and lover Drusilla. He becomes aware that human desires for meaning, clarity, and immortality are absurd in a world where human life is apparently meaningless, indifferent, incoherent, and doomed to death and oblivion. Caligula has decided to teach what he has learned to his subjects through drama, violence, and arbitrary murder. In league against him is a man of real merit, Cherea, a young admirer, Scipio, and an increasing band of notables who realize that they will all perish if they do not revolt. With Caligula are his aging mistress, Caesonia, and the cynic Helicon. Finally, Caligula's terror provokes the rebels to slay him. Based primarily on Camus's concept of the absurd, including plays within the play that raise the issues of the role of art in an absurd universe and what might constitute "absurd art," *Caligula* also explores the theme of revolt. Audiences appreciated the caustic wit and brilliant production, and *Caligula* was an immediate success.

At the end of the war Francine Camus rejoined her husband in Paris, but Camus remained involved with Maria Casarès. On 5 September 1945 the twins Jean and Catherine were born to Francine. Now a recognized member of the Parisian intelligensia, Camus continued his work at *Combat*. He also wrote a series of letters published as *Lettres à un ami allemand* in 1945 (translated as "Letters to a German Friend," 1961) and traveled to New York in 1946. Camus's most important work of the postwar years was the novel *La Peste* (1947; translated as *The Plague*, 1948), a thinly veiled allegory of the German occupation. The fictional plague of Oran in Algeria reminded his French readers of the Nazi occupation, recalling occupied Paris in particular. The novel was a huge success on both sides of the Atlantic.

La Peste was followed by two plays, *L'Etat de siège* (published 1948; translated as *State of Siege*, 1958) and *Les Justes* (published 1950; translated as *The Just Assassins*, 1958). *L'Etat de siege* is an allegorical play featuring characters called Plague and Death set in early modern Spain. David Bradby describes the play as "an attempt to create a modern myth . . . It traces the establishing of a dictatorship by Plague followed by its overthrow, which only becomes possible when enough citizens are prepared to band together." Imagined by Camus as "total theater" with sets and costumes by Balthus and music by Arthur Honneger, it consists of lyrical monologue, dialogues between humans and abstractions, choral recitation, and elements of farce. Presented for

The wreck of the car in which Camus was killed at Villeblevin, France, in 1960 (© Getty Images)

the first time at the Théâtre de Marigny on 27 October 1948, *L'Etat de siège* was a stunning failure.

Les Justes was produced on 15 December 1949 at the Théâtre Hébertot under the direction of Oettly and starring Casarès in the role of Dora. Inspired by the history of Russian terrorists in 1905, the play dramatizes the question of means and ends in revolutionary activity. Reminiscent of the political realism of Sartre's *Les Mains sales* (1948; translated as *Dirty Hands*, 1949), the action of the play turns on the question of whether the terrorists should bomb the Duke Serge's carriage despite the presence of his children. The main characters Kaliayev and Stepan hold different views on the matter. While Stepan regards the children's deaths as acceptable because the terrorist act will eliminate political oppression, Kaliayev cannot condone the deaths of the innocent. Kaliayev ultimately throws the bomb that kills the duke, but only when the duke is alone. Kaliayev pays for this assassination with his own life, a punishment he accepts because he considers his act necessary but unjustifiable. The play has little action and consists largely of the disputes among the characters. *Les Justes* enjoyed a successful run of a year.

The last decade of Camus's life featured both turmoil and success. His critique of Stalinism and communism in general turned the Parisian political Left against him. Sartre's protégé Francis Jeanson wrote a negative review of Camus's *L'Homme révolté* (1951; translated as *The Rebel*, 1953) for *Le Temps modernes* (Modern Times), touching off a heated public exchange between Camus and Sartre, who was the editor of the journal. This episode involved the first in a series of attacks that made Camus miserable.

L'Homme révolté is Camus's most ambitious philosophical essay. A meditation on the history of rebellion, revolt, and revolution in Western history, it addresses the theme of murder in a manner reminiscent of the way in which *Le Mythe de Sisyphe* considers the problem of suicide. Camus strongly felt that the most pressing issue of modern times was totalitarianism and terrorism.

Camus's novel *La Chute* (1956; translated as *The Fall,* 1957) and his collection of stories *L'Exil et le royaume* (1957; translated as *Exile and the Kingdom,* 1958) were well received throughout the world. In 1957 Camus also published "Réflections sur la peine capitale" (translated as *Reflections on the Guillotine,* 1960). Although he received the Nobel Prize in literature in 1957, the award was tarnished by the suggestion in the Parisian left-wing press that it crowned a career that was already finished.

Hounded by his enemies among the Parisian intelligentsia for his critique of communism and his refusal to take a new stand on the Algerian War, Camus found refuge and consolation in the theater. While he composed no more original plays, he adapted several works for the stage, including the Renaissance playwright Pierre de Larivey's *Les Esprits* (1579, The Spirits). In the foreword he wrote for his adaptation of Larivey's comedy (1953), Camus claims it was the model for Molière's *L'Avare* (1668, The Miser). Two more adaptations, *Réquiem pour une nonne,* an adaptation of William Faulkner's *Requiem for a Nun* (1951), and *Les Possédés,* an adaptation of Dostoevsky's *Besy* (1873, The Devils; translated as *The Possessed,* 1913), followed in 1956 and 1959. Camus's other translations and adaptations of plays date from the 1950s, including works by Pedro Calderón de la Barca, Dino Buzzati, and Lope de Vega.

During the last years of his life Camus began work on what he intended to be the saga of Algeria, *Le Premier homme.* The unfinished manuscript was found in his briefcase on the highway after the automobile accident that ended his life on 4 January 1960. Camus was on his way to Paris to meet with the minister of cultural affairs, Malraux, who wanted to entrust the Algerian author with the direction of a national theater.

Although the theater was Albert Camus's passion, literary critics have been nearly unanimous in their negative assessment of his talent in this genre. During Camus's lifetime critics often found his plays "defective." For example, Henry Popkin concludes, "except in *Caligula,* we miss the theater's equivalents for the sophisticated method of his fiction." Camus's biographer Olivier Todd essentially agrees with Popkin, writing, "Camus se voulait dramaturge. A mon sens, *Caligula* tient toujours la scène avec force, les autres pièces moins" (Camus thought of himself as a playwright. In my opinion *Caligula* is still a powerful play, the other plays less so). In this vein, Anthony Rizzuto reluctantly concludes that "the root problem in Camus's love scenes in general and dialogue in particular is that he had little or no talent for dramatic art."

Nevertheless, Camus's dramatic renderings of absurdity and revolution through characters that embody philosophical concepts appealed to French audiences of the postwar period and influenced other writers. Bradby sums up the importance of Camus's theater when he judges that it corresponds to Sartre's definition of a "theater of situations," claiming that Camus's drama "portrays" the contemporary realities of suffering and death" with characters that are less interesting for their psychological motivations than for the choices they make.

Letters:

Camus and Jean Grenier, *Correspondance, 1932–1960,* edited by Marguerite Dobrenn (Paris: Gallimard, 1981);

Camus and Pascal Pia, *Correspondance, 1939–1947,* edited by Yves Marc Ajchenbaum (Paris: Fayard, 2000).

Interview:

Robert Donald Spector, "A Final Interview," *Venture,* 3-4 (20 December 1959).

Bibliographies:

Maurice Beebe, "Criticism of Albert Camus: A Selected Checklist of Studies in English," *Modern Fiction Studies,* 10 (Autumn 1964): 303–314;

Peter C. Hoy, *Camus in English* (Wymondham, U.K.: Brewhouse Press, 1968);

Robert F. Roeming, *Camus: A Bibliography* (Madison: University of Wisconsin Press, 1968);

Brian T. Fitch and Hoy, *Essai de bibliographie des études en langue française consacrées à Albert Camus (1937–1971)* (Leece, Italy: Milella, 1973);

Raymond Gay-Crosier, *Camus* (Darmstadt, Germany: Wissenschaftliche Buchgesellschaft, 1976).

Biographies:

Philip Thody, *Albert Camus: A Study of His Work* (New York: Grove, 1959);

Herbert R. Lottman, *Albert Camus: A Biography* (Garden City, N.Y.: Doubleday, 1979);

Patrick McCarthy, *Camus* (New York: Random House, 1982);

Olivier Todd, *Camus: Une vie* (Paris: Gallimard, 1996); translated by Benjamin Irvy as *Albert Camus: A Life* (London: Chatto & Windus, 1997).

References:

Alex Argyros, *Crimes of Narration: Camus' "La Chute"* (Toronto: Paratexte, 1985);

David Bradby, *Modern French Drama 1940–1990* (Cambridge: Cambridge University Press, 1991);

Germaine Brée, *Camus* (New Brunswick: Rutgers University Press, 1959);

Brée, *Camus and Sartre: Crisis and Commitment* (New York: Delta, 1972);

Brée, ed., *Camus: A Collection of Critical Essays* (Englewood Cliffs, N.J.: Prentice-Hall, 1962);

Robert Champigny, *A Pagan Hero: An Interpretation of Mersault in Camus' The Stranger* (Philadelphia: University of Pennsylvania Press, 1959);

Ilona Coombs, *Camus, homme de théâtre* (Paris: Nizet, 1968);

John Cruickshank, *Albert Camus and the Literature of Revolt* (London: Oxford University Press, 1959);

Peter Cryle, *The Thematics of Commitment: The Tower and the Plain* (Princeton: Princeton University Press, 1985);

Brian T. Fitch, *The Narcissistic Text: A Reading of Camus' Fiction* (Toronto: University of Toronto Press, 1982);

Edward Freeman, *The Theater of Albert Camus: A Critical Study* (London: Methuen, 1971);

Raymond Gay-Crosier, *Albert Camus 1980* (Gainesville: University Presses of Florida, 1980);

Gay-Crosier, *L'Envers d'un échec: Etude sur le théâtre d'Albert Camus* (Paris: Lettres Modernes, 1967);

Jacques Guicharnaud, *Modern French Theater from Giraudoux to Genet* (New Haven: Yale University Press, 1967);

Thomas Hanna, *The Thought and Art of Albert Camus* (Chicago: Regnery, 1958);

Rosemarie Jones, *Camus' "L'Etranger" and "La Chute"* (London: Grant & Cutler, 1980);

Adele King, *Albert Camus* (New York: Grove, 1964);

Donald Lazere, *The Unique Creation of Albert Camus* (New Haven: Yale University Press, 1973);

Connor Cruise O'Brien, *Albert Camus of Europe and Africa* (New York: Viking, 1970);

Jean Onimus, *Albert Camus and Christianity,* translated by Emmett Parker (University: University of Alabama Press, 1970);

Emmett Parker, *Albert Camus, the Artist in the Arena* (Madison: University of Wisconsin Press, 1965);

Henry Popkin, "Camus as Dramatist," *Partisan Review* (Summer 1959): 499–503;

Phillip H. Rhein, *Albert Camus* (New York: Twayne, 1969);

Anthony Rizzuto, *Camus: Love and Sexuality* (Gainesville: University Presses of Florida, 1998);

David Sprintzen, *Camus: A Critical Examination* (Philadelphia: Temple University Press, 1988);

B. F. Stoltzfus, "Caligula's Mirrors: Camus' Reflexive Dramatization of Play," *French Forum,* 8 (January 1983): 75–86.

Aimé Césaire
(26 June 1913 -)

Meredith Goldsmith
Whitman College

PLAY PRODUCTIONS: *La Tragedie du roi Christophe,* Salzburg, Austria, Salzburg Festival, 4 August 1964;

Une Tempête, Hammamet, Festival d'Hammamet, Summer 1969;

Une Saison au Congo, Paris, Theater de l'Est, 4 October 1976.

BOOKS: *Cahier d'un retour au pays natal,* translated into Spanish by Lydia Cabrera as *Retorno al país natal,* preface by Benjamin Peret, illustrated by Wilfredo Lam (Havana: Molina y Cía, 1942); original French version (Paris: Brodas, 1947); *Cahier d'un retour au pays natal: Memorandum on My Martinique,* French and English edition, English translation by Lionel Abel and Ivan Goll, preface by André Breton (New York: Brentano's, 1947); definitive edition, preface by Petar Guberina (Paris: Présence Africaine, 1956);

Les Armes miraculeuses (Paris: Gallimard, 1946);

Soleil cou-coupé (Paris: Editions K, 1948);

Corps perdu, with illustrations by Pablo Picasso (Paris: Fragrance, 1950); translated by Clayton Eschleman and Annette Smith as *Lost Body* (New York: Braziller, 1986);

Discours sur le colonialisme (Paris: Réclame, 1950); translated by Joan Pinkham as *Discourse on Colonialism* (New York: Monthly Review, 1972);

Et les chiens se taisaient (Paris: Présence Africaine, 1956); translated by Eshleman and Smith as *And the Dogs Were Silent,* in *Aimé Césaire: Lyric and Dramatic Poetry, 1946–1982* (Charlottesville: University of Virginia Press, 1990), pp. 1–74;

Lettre à Maurice Thorez, foreword by Alioune Diop (Paris: Présence Africaine, 1956);

Ferrements (Paris: Seuil, 1960);

Toussaint Louverture: La Révolution française et le problème colonial (Paris: Le Club français du livre, 1960); revised and enlarged edition, preface by Charles André Julien (Paris: Présence Africaine, 1962);

Aimé Césaire (from the frontispiece for Aimé Césaire: The Collected Poetry, *1983; Thomas Cooper Library, University of South Carolina)*

Cadastre (Paris: Seuil, 1961); translated by Emile Snyder and Sanford Upson, introduction by Snyder (New York: Third World Press, 1973);

La Tragédie du roi Christophe (Paris: Présence Africaine, 1963); translated by Ralph Manheim as *The Tragedy of King Christophe* (New York: Grove, 1970);

Une Saison au Congo (Paris: Seuil, 1965); translated by Manheim as *A Season in the Congo* (New York: Grove, 1968; revised edition, Paris: Seuil, 1973);

Une Tempête, d'après "La tempête" de Shakespeare–Adaptation pour un théâtre nègre (Paris: Seuil, 1969); translated by Richard Miller as *A Tempest, Based on Shakespeare's The Tempest–Adaptation for a Black Theatre* (New York: Borchardt, 1985);

Moi, laminaire (Paris: Seuil, 1982).

Editions and Collections: *Aimé Césaire, écrivain martiniquais*, edited by Monique and Simon Battestini (Paris: Nathan, 1967);

La Tragédie du roi Christophe (Paris: Présence Africaine, 1970);

Œuvres complètes, 3 volumes (Fort-de-France, Martinique: Editions Désormeaux, 1976)—comprises volume 1, *Poésie;* volume 2, *Théâtre;* and volume 3, *Œuvre historique et politique;*

Tropiques, by Césaire, René Ménil, and others, 2 volumes, edited by Césaire (Paris: Jean-Michel Place, 1978);

Et les chiens se taisaient (Paris: Présence Africaine, 1989);

La Poésie, edited by Daniel Maximin and Gilles Carpentier (Paris: Seuil, 1994).

Editions in English: *State of the Union: Poems*, translated by Clayton Eshleman and Denis Kelly, Caterpillar, no. 1 (Bloomington, Ind. & Cleveland, Ohio: Asphodel Book Shop, 1966);

Aimé Césaire: The Collected Poetry, edited and translated by Eshleman and Annette Smith (Berkeley: University of California Press, 1983);

Non-Vicious Circle: Twenty Poems of Aimé Césaire, translated and edited, with an introduction, by Gregson Davis (Stanford, Cal.: Stanford University Press, 1984);

Aimé Césaire: Lyric and Dramatic Poetry: 1946–82, translated by Eshleman and Smith (Charlottesville: University Press of Virginia, 1990);

A Tempest, Based on Shakespeare's The Tempest–Adaptation for a Black Theatre, translated by Philip Crispin (London: Oberon, 2000).

PRODUCED SCRIPT: *Et les chiens se taisaient*, radio, Radio France, 1956.

OTHER: "Poésie et connaissance," *Tropiques*, 12 (1945): 157–170;

Victor Schoelcher, *Esclavage et colonisation*, edited by Emile Tersen, introduction by Césaire (Paris: Presses universitaires de France, 1948);

Commémoration du centenaire de l'abolition de l'esclavage: Discours prononcés à la Sorbonne, le 27 avril 1948, by Césaire and others, introduction by Edouard Depreux (Paris: Presses universitaires de France, 1948);

René Depestre, *Végétations de clarté*, preface by Césaire (Paris: Seghers, 1951);

"Décolonisation pour les Antilles," *Présence africaine* (April–May 1956): 7–12;

"Culture et colonisation," *Présence africaine* (September 1956): 190–205;

Daniel Guérin, *Antilles décolonisées*, preface by Césaire (Paris: Présence Africaine, 1956);

Sékou Touré, *Expérience Guinéenne et unité africaine*, preface by Césaire (Paris: Présence Africaine, 1959);

"L'Homme de culture et ses responsabilités," *Présence africaine* (March–April 1959): 116–122;

"Deuil aux Antilles," *Présence africaine* (Third Trimester 1962): 221–222;

"Société et littérature dans les Antilles," "Discours sur l'art africain," and "Esthéthique césairienne," *Etudes littèraires*, 6, no. 1 (1973): 9–20, 99–109, 111–112.

Martinican author Aimé Césaire is not only responsible for *Cahier d'un retour au pays natal* (first published in Spanish 1942; original French version 1947; translated as *Memorandum on My Martinique*, 1947), a widely acknowledged masterpiece documenting the twentieth-century colonial condition, but he is also an accomplished playwright. Like his poetry and polemical essays, Césaire's plays explore the paradox of black identity under French colonial rule. Césaire's shift to drama in the late 1950s and 1960s allowed him to integrate the modernist and Surrealist techniques of his poetry and the polemics of his prose. In what Césaire describes as his "triptych" of plays, *La Tragédie du roi Christophe* (published 1963, produced 1964; translated as *The Tragedy of King Christophe*, 1970), *Une Saison au Congo* (published 1965; translated as *A Season in the Congo*, 1968; produced 1976), and *Une Tempête* (published and produced 1969; translated as *A Tempest*, 1985), he explores a series of related themes, especially the efforts of blacks—whether in Africa, the United States, or the Caribbean—to resist the powers of colonial domination.

The life of Aimé Césaire spans the twentieth century and its anticolonial movements. He was born in Basse-Pointe, in the north of the island of Martinique, the second of the six children of Fernand Césaire, a minor government official, and his wife, Eléonore, a seamstress. Although the family was poor, Césaire received a good education and early showed his aptitude for studies. He first attended the Lycée Schoelcher in Fort-de-France, the capital of Martinique, and then he received a scholarship to attend the prestigious Lycée Louis le Grand in Paris.

There he met a Senegalese student, the future poet and African politician Léopold Senghor. In 1934 Césaire, with Senghor and Guyanan poet Léon Damas, founded the student journal *Etudiant Noir* (Black Student). This group of black Francophone intellectuals developed the concept of "Negritude," the embrace of blackness and Africanness as a counter to a legacy of colonial self-hatred.

In 1935 Césaire entered the Ecole Normale Supérieure in Paris, where he studied American black writers, especially the poets of the Harlem Renaissance. During this time he traveled to Dalmatia and began work on his *Cahier d'un retour au pays natal*. With Senghor, Césaire read and discussed the ethnologist Leo Frobenius's *Kulturgeschichte Afrikas* (1933, History of African Culture; translated into French as *Histoire de la civilization africaine,* 1936). Césaire eventually passed the *agrégation des lettres,* the national competitive examination that leads to a career in teaching. In 1937 he married fellow Martinican student Suzanne Rossi. Their son, Jacques, the first of Césaire's four sons and two daughters, was born in 1938. In 1939 Césaire and Suzanne returned to Martinique to take up teaching positions at Lycée Schoelcher. Among Césaire's students were the writer Edouard Glissant and the critic of colonialism Frantz Fanon.

In 1939 Césaire published his first version of *Cahier d'un retour au pays natal* in the journal *Volontés* (Intentions). In this long autobiographical poem, Césaire rejected European culture, accepting his African and Caribbean roots. Juxtaposing historical data, descriptions of nature, and dream imagery, he praises the contributions of the black race to world civilization. The poem was first published as a book in Spanish in 1942, then in French in 1947. Césaire revised the poem considerably before finally publishing the definitive version in 1956. *Cahier d'un retour au pays natal* has become one of the best-known French poems of the twentieth century.

Césaire and his wife returned to the Caribbean as World War II began. Although Martinique was far removed from Europe, as a French territory it suffered economically from a German blockade, then later from censorship imposed by a representative of the Vichy government. During the war Césaire became increasingly critical of the Vichy government and established himself as a political voice in Martinique. In 1941 he and Suzanne founded the anticolonialist journal *Tropiques* (Tropics) to promote Martinican culture; he was able to publish the journal in spite of the censor. That year Césaire received a visit from André Breton, the founder of Surrealism, who had read Césaire's poetry and crossed the Atlantic to try to convince him to join his movement.

Under the influence of Surrealism, Césaire wrote his second collection of poetry, *Les Armes miraculeuses* (1946, Miraculous Arms), and later *Soleil cou-coupé* (1948, Sun Cut Throat), a title taken from Guillaume Apollinaire's poem "Zone" (1912). Césaire's essay "Poésie et connaissance" (Poetry and Knowledge), published in *Tropiques* in 1945, espouses the Surrealist principle of poetry as a means of liberating subconscious truth.

Césaire became active in regional politics and was elected mayor of Fort-de-France and deputy to the Constituent National Assembly on the French Communist Party ticket in 1945. He then successfully fought to have Martinique and Guadeloupe recognized as overseas departments of France, which, as scholar Janis Pallister explains, the Communists believed would give the islands greater power within the political system. Henceforth, Césaire divided his time between Paris and Martinique. In 1947 he became cofounder of another journal, *Présence africaine* (African Presence), which published the works of black Francophone writers, notably those of Césaire's Martinican compatriot Joseph Sobel. In the 1960s the journal evolved into a publishing house of the same name.

Césaire turned his attention to the African diaspora in his poetry collection *Corps perdu* (1950; translated as *Lost Body,* 1986). During the 1950s and 1960s, Césaire remained active in both politics and literature. In the 1950s he wrote several important political essays, including *Discours sur le colonialisme* (1950; translated as *Discourse on Colonialism,* 1972) and *Lettre à Maurice Thorez* (1956, Letter to Maurice Thorez), the latter of which explains his break with the Communist Party after the Soviet invasion of Hungary. In 1957 Césaire founded the Parti Progressiste Martiniquais (Martinique Progressive Party), and in 1959 he participated in the Second Congress of Negro Writers and Artists in Rome. While maintaining his duties as the elected deputy from Martinique to the French National Assembly in Paris, he wrote two collections of poetry on Africa and the slave experience, *Ferrements* (1960, Iron Chains) and *Cadastre* (1961; translated, 1973).

The year that Césaire left the Communist Party coincides with his earliest experiment in drama, *Et les chiens se taisaient* (published and broadcast 1956; translated as *And the Dogs Were Silent,* 1990). Césaire turned to theater in an effort to make his literary themes more accessible. His plays oscillate between lyricism, realism, and allegory, manipulating the conventions of the theater to provide a commentary on the politics of racism, colonialism, and decolonization.

Et les chiens se taisaient is adapted from a long poem of the same title that appeared at the end of *Les armes miraculeuses;* hence, the play clearly marks Césaire's transition from poetry to theater. According to Davis, Césaire described this work as a "lyric oratorio." The play features the Surrealism of his poetry and is difficult to stage. *Et les chiens se taisaient* was aired as a radio drama in France, but unlike later plays, it has not enjoyed revivals. Nevertheless, it was an important precursor to Césaire's later theatrical works, featuring many recurring themes: anger against colonial power; the painful memories of slavery and the middle passage; placing the West Indies within a global pan-African context; and the impossible situation of black political leadership in the age of decolonization.

Et les chiens se taisaient features two highly distinct styles of speech. The dense, lyrical monologues of Césaire's postcolonial hero, the Rebel, and the other Caribbean characters contrast with the rhetorically calculating style of the white colonial executives. The play also demonstrates Césaire's mastery of ancient mythology and classical dramatic traditions, drawing consciously on the myth of Osiris and Aeschylean tragedy. Additionally, as throughout Césaire's writing, dogs have a complex symbolic function. Barking dogs evoke slave masters, who used dogs against rebellious slaves; however, the image of the dog is also linked with the Egyptian god Anubis, described by Gregson Davis as "a dog-headed deity who presided over cemeteries." Césaire employs both aspects of canine imagery in this play, which centers on the death of the Rebel, Césaire's first dramatic model for the postcolonial revolutionary leader.

The beginning of the play kills much of the suspense, as the Echo (which, like the Chorus, supplies commentary on the play's events) informs the audience that "Bien sûr qu'il va mourir le Rebelle" (the Rebel will surely die). Moving the scene to a colonial prison, Césaire re-creates the appropriation of the island by the French, the horrors of the slave trade, and the arrival of white colonial bureaucrats, all through the exchange of voices among two narrators (one male and one female), madwomen, bishops, and a colonial administrator. Then the chorus reenacts a scene of black revolution, marked by "chants monotones et sauvages, piétinements confus" (wild and monotonous chants, confused stamping of feet), and rowdies crying for death to the whites. It is in this chaotic atmosphere that the Rebel emerges, depicted through the imagery of Osiris, with a dog's head and sandals resembling pale suns on his feet. As Davis explains, writers of the Negritude movement appropriated "Egyptian culture as 'black,'" and thus Césaire foregrounds the Osiris and Anubis myths rather than the Christian myths many critics have located in the play.

The second act of *Et les chiens se taisaient* focuses on the isolation of the Rebel, who explains that his participation in the slave revolt was motivated by his desire for equality. He imagines the world as a forest, with trees of different woods growing together in harmony. However, his refusal to be a slave was realized through violent means, and he accepts responsibility for joining—despite his denial of racial hatred—the cry of "Mort aux Blancs" (death to the whites). His mother and lover urge him to reject death, which would necessitate a tacit acceptance of colonial authority. The Rebel rejects the urging of both women, who, like other black women in Césaire's plays, represent compromise in the name of survival. Act 3 returns to the prison, where the Rebel is increasingly weakened as he is beaten by the jailer and his wife, who mock the juxtaposition of black skin and red blood. The tone of the play—and of the Rebel's monologues in particular—becomes increasingly apocalyptic and hallucinatory. Tom-toms beat as the play moves backward into an African cultural past. As the two narrators indicate, the Rebel dies in the middle of growing, fecund plants and flowers. With the death of the Rebel, the Echo's assertion at the beginning of the play is realized, but there are hints of a possible rebirth.

Although *Et les chiens se taisaient* is a political play, its critiques remain largely on the level of allegory and are deliberately obscure. In contrast, Césaire's next dramatic efforts, the plays of his explicitly "political triptych," comment more directly on specific historical situations of the 1950s and 1960s, especially in the context of postcolonial nationhood, leadership, and identity. The first of these plays, *La Tragédie du roi Christophe,* is also the first of Césaire's plays to be written expressly for the theater. It was directed by the avant-gardist Jean-Marrie Serreau, who, as Davis reports, "master-minded the première production at the Salzburg festival" in 1964 "and subsequently took it to the Théâtre de l'Odéon in Paris." Césaire's relationships with French left-wing intellectuals and artists Michel Leiris and Pablo Picasso helped the play circumvent bureaucratic obstacles, and it was a huge success. It was performed in North America, Europe, and Africa, and it was restaged at the Comédie-Française in 1991 under the government of French president François Mitterrand.

In *La Tragédie du roi Christophe,* Césaire provides an ironic commentary on postcolonial leadership, beginning a critique that he develops further in *Une Saison au Congo.* Throughout the drama he explores

Cover for a 1989 edition of Césaire's first experiment in drama (And the Dogs Were Silent), produced for Radio France in 1956 (Thomas Cooper Library, University of South Carolina)

the fallacy of colonial imitation of the *métropole* (that is, France) as the protagonist, Christophe, moves from an emulation of French royalty to an embrace of his African roots that occurs only as he nears death.

The play opens with a cockfight whose participants are Christophe and Pétion, named after the rulers of divided Haiti in the early nineteenth century. A commentator describes the Haitian Revolution, in which Christophe served as a general under Toussaint L'Ouverture. Christophe is appointed the president of the republic, but he abandons the city of Port-au-Prince to Pétion and the mulatto class, establishing himself as a king in the northern region of Haiti. Césaire thus begins to demonstrate how swiftly the ideals of the revolution can be betrayed. From the beginning of the play Christophe's character vacillates between his commitment to black freedom and his embrace of the legacy of black slavery and exploitation in Haiti. Christophe attests to his countrymen that "de noms de gloire je veux couvrir vos noms d'esclaves" (with names of glory I will cover your slave names), vowing to reclaim a black identity erased by slavery. Meanwhile, he wants to build a citadel as a symbol of freed Haiti but, ironically, can only do so by putting demands on his workers reminiscent of slavery. Césaire makes it clear that Christophe's drives, imitative of white oppression, are part of his undoing.

In Acts 2 and 3, the optimism at first associated with Christophe's leadership rapidly dissipates. One of the ladies of the court realizes that Christophe's path to liberty closely resembles the path to slavery, "Si bien que celle de la liberté et celle de l'esclavage se confondraient" (So well that those of liberty and slavery could be mistaken for each other). It soon emerges that Christophe, despite his desire for black freedom, is deeply invested in the logic and rhetoric of slavery. As he forcibly marries a group of men and women, his language begins to resemble that of a slave master as he praises the bodies of the women and their potential for work. Obsessed by fears of betrayal, Christophe orders the death of Archbishop Brelle, who threatens to expose the growing corruption in Haiti. Then, as labor continues on the citadel—work the stage directions compare with the building of the pyramids—a storm strikes Christophe's garrison and treasury; here, as in *Une Tempête,* a storm symbolizes an impending social and political crisis. This crisis comes to a head in the progressively surreal third act. At a lavish state event, Christophe brings in five African men dressed in their native country's robes. He claims to have bought them from a slave ship and purchased their freedom. However, as Christophe parades the Africans through the court, it becomes clear that he has only perpetuated their enslavement. During the Feast of the Assumption, which celebrates the ascension of the Virgin Mary into heaven, the ghost of Brelle appears in the church and curses Christophe, who collapses, paralyzed. As the play draws to a close, Christophe appears as a mad, old, feeble king, betrayed by his own soldiers, and with his people in revolt. Invoking Africa and speaking in Creole, Christophe commits suicide.

Christophe's political agent, Hugonin, appears alone on stage after Christophe's death. In evening clothes, Hugonin apologizes for his lateness and drunkenness. He then reveals himself to be Baron Samedi, the voodoo god associated with death and funerals. Here Césaire suggests that under the veneer of Frenchness and officiality associated with Hugonin there lies an authentic vestige of Haitian culture. Both Hugonin and Christophe have repressed their African and Caribbean heritages beneath a veneer of Frenchness with similarly tragic results. For Césaire, the task of the postcolonial writer is to synthesize these heritages.

The second play of Césaire's political triptych is *Une Saison au Congo,* which recounts the rise, fall, and assassination of Congolese political leader Patrice Lumumba. Published in 1965, the play recounts the Congo's declaration of independence from Belgian colonial rule, its rise to independence as Zaire under the leadership of Lumumba, and its neocolonial subjection under the ambitious but corrupt Mokutu, a thinly veiled portrayal of Mobutu Sésé Seko, the former president of Zaire. The play's topical nature affected its production history: as Davis reports, the Belgian authorities tried to suppress the production of the play, which was first staged in Brussels. Césaire's supporters among the intellectuals of Paris intervened and, according to Davis, "succeeded in circumventing these obstacles." When the play was staged in Paris under the direction of avant-garde director Serreau, Davis claims that it "provoked unease" among the "educated Zairean population."

The title of the play carries a double purpose: it makes clear that the true subject matter of the play is not simply that of the tragic hero Lumumba but the tragedy of the Congo and all of its people. Additionally, the title associates the Congo with hell through its allusion to Arthur Rimbaud's prose poem *Une Saison en enfer* (1873; translated as "A Season in Hell," 1931). Césaire introduces his audience to the Congo/hell through Lumumba, who begins the play as a *bonimenteur* (beer seller). By beginning with the image of Lumumba selling beer, Césaire exploits the irony of politics as salesmanship. As he tells the audience that "le bock de bière est désormais le symbole de notre droit congolais et de nos libertés congolaises" (in the Congo a mug of beer is the symbol of all our rights and liberties), Lumumba emphasizes the artificial nature of rights under colonialism. Here, as in *Une Tempête,* Césaire emphasizes how colonizers bring the pleasures of alcohol, which is a means for keeping a subject population in its place. The introductory scene also foregrounds the gender politics of the play when a heckler cries that Polar Beer, the brand of beer Lumumba is selling, threatens to make men impotent. Lumumba's appeal to the women in the audience to disprove that claim underscores his masculine authority. The scene also introduces a *sanza* (mbira) player, who like a wandering Greek chorus figure, comments on events. For example, as the Belgian police watch Lumumba with concern, the *sanza* player, whom they dismiss as a "nuisance," sings "*Ata-ndele*" (Sooner or Later).

As the play depicts Lumumba's rise to power, it reveals the colonial and neocolonial forces working to undercut the Congo's bid for independence. Césaire uses poetic form to underscore the control colonial forces exercise over the fate of the newly independent state. In caricatures of a series of bankers, the dialogue moves into sustained rhymed couplets; in their speeches, the bankers make it clear that avarice and economic corruption will cause the downfall of the free Congo's leaders. In contrast, Lumumba's long monologue evoking the Congo as both mother and child, perhaps the most beautiful of the play, is written in lyrical free verse.

Césaire next exposes the false rhetoric of the "civilizing mission" the Belgian colonizers used to justify their appropriation of the Congo: the departing president reminds the crowd that King Leopold came to the Congo in the name of civilization rather than diamonds or gold mines. Then Césaire expands his critique of the colonizers to include both the ostensibly neutral forces of the United Nations, embodied in the character of Dag Hammarskjöld, and those of the "Ambassadeur Grand Occidental," a figure for American political power. The Ambassador justifies his country's authority through the belief that it is the watchdog of the world and has a particular mandate to guard against Communism. Underscoring the American role in the tragedy of the Congo, Césaire radicalizes the argument of the play, moving past the conflict between colonizer and colonized to mete out global culpability.

The last two acts of *Une Saison au Congo* chart the political fall of Lumumba and, ultimately, his murder. Act 2 demonstrates how rapidly Lumumba's authority is threatened by outside forces as well as by competition within the newly independent Congo. Lumumba is betrayed by those he trusts the most, especially his soldier and supporter Mokutu. He is also denied use of the radio to communicate with his people, which Césaire, like fellow Martinican intellectual and contributor to *Présence africaine* Fanon, identifies as central to the effectiveness of resistance movements. Having distributed the responsibility for Lumumba's downfall onto the range of forces established in act 1, in the third act Césaire has an unnamed white mercenary serve as Lumumba's murderer. At this juncture the play goes from being realistic to increasingly impressionistic. Hammarskjöld, Mokutu, and Lumumba's other enemies step onstage to admit their complicity in Lumumba's death.

The original edition of the play ends on a slightly optimistic note: the final moments take place at the Independence Day celebrations in Kinshasa. Although Mokutu, lacking Lumumba's natural eloquence, harangues the audience, it is the *sanza* player who has the last word, exhorting the newly independent nation, and its leaders, to "grow straight" and "to keep it clean." However, Césaire added a scene for the 1973 edition of the play in which Mokutu admits his betrayal of Lumumba and openly acknowledges his manipulation of the people of the newly independent Congo. This ending is much darker than the original. After Mokutu exhorts the crowd, he bids his soldiers to fire into the throng, killing the *sanza* player and others. As the smoke dissipates, Mokutu leaves the stage. With the new ending Césaire offers an increasingly skeptical perspective on neocolonial power: with the rise of the dictator, a new reign of terror has begun. Hence, Césaire's use of the indefinite article in the play's title, which corresponds to the indefinite article in the last play of Césaire's triptych, *Une Tempête:* Lumumba's rise and fall is just one season of many in the Congo's struggle for freedom, just as the "tempest" of the third play's title is only one storm of many in the history of colonial confrontation.

The title page of *Une Tempête* announces its revisionary relationship with Shakespeare's play *The Tempest* and its overturning of what Pallister calls the "master-slave dynamic" of that play: "d'après 'la Tempête' de Shakespeare–Adaptation pour un théâtre nègre" (according to *The Tempest* of Shakespeare–An Adaptation for Black Theater). Césaire's use of the phrase "black theater" is significant in its claim for a black transnational identity. The play makes reference to the postcolonial relations of the French Caribbean and the *métropole;* the postcolonial struggles of Africa; and the struggles of the Black Power and Civil Rights movements in the United States. With this play Césaire argues for a diasporic black identity that works to reverse the stifling binary of colonizer and colonized.

In contrast to *Une Saison au Congo,* which is largely realist in style, *Une Tempête* establishes itself as self-consciously theatrical from the beginning. Le Meneur du jeu (the Master of Ceremonies) enters the stage, inviting each actor to take up his own character and mask. Nature is identified as a vital character in the play, and the storm and the wind are invited to take up their own parts. By beginning the play in this manner, Césaire inverts the culture/nature dyad endemic to colonialism: not only are humans unable to control nature, but they are equal to nature as performers in the drama. Significantly, when Prospero enters the stage, he reminds Miranda that the shipwreck they are witnessing is only a play.

Césaire revises, racializes, and politicizes the relationships Shakespeare creates among Prospero, Ariel, and Caliban. Ariel is characterized as a mulatto slave, while Caliban is a black slave. By figuring Ariel as a mulatto, Césaire presents him as an ambivalent intermediary between white and black and colonizer and colonized, representing the position of the mulatto class in the Martinique of Césaire's upbringing. Caliban, on the other hand, is presented as a black nationalist: he enters the stage crying "Uhuru," the Swahili word for "freedom." Césaire depicts the relationship between Prospero and Caliban as analogous to that between the colonizer and colonized as portrayed in *Une saison au Congo:* Prospero congratulates himself for having given Caliban language, yet characterizes him as an ape. Caliban, however, understands the gift of language in an explicitly anticolonial and ironic manner: "Tu ne m'as rien appris du tout. Sauf, bien sûr, à baragouiner ton langage pour comprende tes ordres" (You didn't teach me a thing. Except to jabber in your own language so that I could understand your orders).

Césaire introduces an element of environmental anticolonialism as well: Caliban says to Prospero, "tu crois que la terre est chose Mort . . . C'est tellement commode! Morte, alors on la piétine, on la souille, on la foule d'un pied vanqueur" (you think the earth is dead . . . it's so much simpler that way! Dead, you can walk on it, pollute it, you can tread upon it with the steps of a conqueror). As in *Une Saison au Congo,* in which Lumumba characterizes the Congo as both mother and child, here the land is both feminized and personified, and to respect the land implies a rejection of the patriarchal and hierarchical objectives of colonial power.

Where Shakespeare's play makes Prospero the sorcerer, in Césaire's play Caliban also has the powers of sorcery. Césaire presents Caliban as agent in the relationship rather than simply a slave: Prospero has given Caliban language, and Caliban teaches Prospero about the natural world of the island. Caliban is also linked with the destructive forces of nature, invoking the thunder god Shango to increase his power. The initial conflict between the two characters staged in act 1 concludes with Caliban's renunciation of his colonial identity and claiming the radical identity of black nationalism: "Appelle-moi X . . . l'homme dont on a *volé* le nom" (Call me X . . . a man whose history has been *stolen*). All of Caliban's dialogue with Prospero make use of *tu,* the familiar second-person pronoun, which means that Caliban addresses his ostensible master as an equal. Ariel, however, uses the *vous* form, underscoring his inability to reject his master and his liminal position between colonizer and colonized.

As the play progresses, Césaire further alters Shakespeare's original by demystifying the love relationship between Fernando and Miranda; Fernando cheats Miranda at cards, claiming that his deceptions will provide her a good introduction to the less innocent world she will encounter upon leaving the island. However, Fernando and Miranda disappear from the plot shortly before the play's conclusion.

Césaire continues emphasizing the play's racial politics with the Shakespearean fools Stephano and Trinculo, who both wish to turn Caliban into a museum piece and exhibit him in Europe. Such abuses not only happened during Shakespeare's lifetime, but throughout the nineteenth and early twentieth centuries many colonial subjects had been turned into museum exhibits and freak shows. Finally, the play moves toward a reversal of the colonial binary. Prospero's staging of a performance of the Roman gods—ostensibly to instruct his daughter and future son-in-law in beauty and harmony—is disrupted by the entrance of the African god Eshu, the priapic trickster god who signifies reversal in ancient African cultures. Ultimately, Caliban and Prospero stay together on the island, but not until Caliban makes an impassioned speech for his freedom. As the play nears its close, Caliban and Prospero seem locked in unresolvable conflict, as Caliban damns the colonial enterprise, and Prospero vows to fight back. In the brief final speech, which occurs after the curtain is half-raised to indicate the passage of time, Prospero appears physically aged and weary. Despite his efforts to defend civilization on the island, it appears that nature is winning; the island is overrun with animals, and even the climate has changed. Just as Césaire begins the play by making storm and wind active characters in the drama, he ends the play by suggesting that nature has overwhelmed even the force of colonial power.

After 1970 Césaire published another volume of poetry, *Moi, laminaire* (1982, I, Laminary) and several more political and historical essays. In 1982 Mitterrand appointed him president of the regional council for the French *départements d'outremer* (Overseas Departments), a position that allowed him to encourage the economic and cultural development of his native Martinique. In 1993 he retired from national political life in Paris to Fort-de-France, Martinique, which acknowledged the island's debt to a great champion of its liberation and culture with a municipal celebration of his ninetieth birthday in 2003.

Cover for a 1970 edition of Césaire's 1963 play (translated as The Tragedy of King Cristophe, *1970), the first in his political "triptych" dealing with colonialism and its effects on both the colonizers and their subjects (Thomas Cooper Library, University of South Carolina)*

Pallister has stated that Aimé Césaire's writing "expresses the need for revolution, for change in a flawed and prejudiced world." All of his plays, especially the triptych, draw on history, African myth, and European literature to create a portrait of the Caribbean that both avows the damage done by capitalism and colonialism and underlines the difficulty of achieving liberation from this legacy. The latter problem is indicated in the fact that neither Césaire nor his characters choose to speak Creole in a sustained way. Additionally, each play offers a version of the postcolonial black male intellectual coming of age and taking responsibility for his people but hesitating to cut ties with France. Césaire's move from poet to dramatist at the time when he broke his ties with the Communist Party in the 1950s was motivated, in Davis's words, "by a sincere desire on his part to narrow the gap in communication between avant-garde writer and provincial audience," to reach the Martinican people with his vision of Caribbean civilization through a literary form more accessible than his poetry. Thus, Césaire's plays continue to be performed and studied as both political activism and popular theater.

References:

Lillian Pestre de Almaida, "Le Bestiaire symbolique dans *Une Saison au Congo:* Analyse stylistique des images zoomorphes dans la piece de Cesaire," *Présence francophone,* 13 (Fall 1976): 93–105;

Almaida, "Les Deux textes de *Et les chiens se taisaient,*" *Œuvres et critiques,* 4 (Fall 1979): 203–211;

Albert James Arnold, *Modernism and Negritude: The Poetry and Poetics of Aimé Césaire* (Cambridge, Mass.: Harvard University Press, 1981);

Charlotte Brow, "The Meaning of Caliban in Black Literature Today," *Comparative Literature Studies,* 13 (September 1976): 240–253;

Frederick Ivor Case, "Aimé Césaire et l'Occident chrétien," *Esprit créateur,* 10 (Fall 1970): 242–256;

Marc-A. Christophe, "Totalitarianism and Authoritarianism in Aimé Césaire's *La Tragédie du roi Christophe,*" *CLA Journal,* 22 (1978): 31–45;

Guy Daninos, "*Une Tempête* de Césaire ou le prélude d'une nouvelle renaissance," *Licorne,* 9 (1985): 153–160;

Gregson Davis, *Aimé Césaire* (New York: Cambridge University Press, 1997);

Hervé Fuyet and others, "Décolonisation et classes sociales dans *La Tragédie du roi Christophe,*" *French Review,* 46 (May 1973): 1101–1106;

Clément Mbom, *Le Théâtre d'Aimé Césaire, ou La primauté de l'universalité* (Paris: Nathan, 1979);

Ernest Moutoussamy, *Aimé Césaire: député à l'Assemblé nationale, 1945–1993* (Paris: L'Harmattan, 1993);

Georges Ngal, *Aimé Césaire, un homme à la recherche d'une patrie* (Dakar: Nouvelles éditions africaines, [1975]; republished, Paris: Présence Africaine, 1994);

Albert Owusu-Sarpong, *Le Temps historique dans l'œuvre théâtrale d'Aimé Césaire* (Sherbrooke, Quebec: Naaman, 1986; Paris: L'Harmattan, 2002);

Janis L. Pallister, *Aimé Césaire* (New York: Twayne, 1991);

Ernstpeter Ruhe, *Aimé Césaire et Janheinz Jahn, les débuts du théâtre césairien: La nouvelle version de "Et les chiens se taisaient"* (Würzburg, Germany: Königshausen & Neumann, 1990).

Paul Claudel

(6 August 1868 – 23 February 1955)

Madhuri Mukherjee
William Paterson University

PLAY PRODUCTIONS: *L'Annonce faite à Marie,* Paris, Théâtre de l'Oeuvre, 23 December 1912;

L'Otage, London, Scala Theatre, 1913; Paris, Théâtre de l'Oeuvre, 5 June 1914;

L'Echange, Paris, Théâtre du Vieux-Colombier, 15 January 1914;

Protée, music by Darius Milhaud, Salzburg, 1914;

La Nuit de Noël 1914, read by Eve Francis, Paris, Université des Annales, March 1915;

Tête d'or, Paris, Théâtre du Gymnase, 30 May 1919; revised, Paris, Laboratoire de Théâtre, 25 April 1924;

Le Pain dur, act 2, scene 2, read by Francis and Jean Hervé, Paris, Théâtre du Gymnase, 30 May 1919; full version, Canada, 1943; Paris, Théâtre de l'Atelier, 12 March 1949;

L'Homme et son désir, music by Milhaud, Paris, Théâtre des Champs-Elysées, 6 June 1921;

Partage de midi, Paris, Groupe Art et Action, 12 November 1921; revised, Paris, Théâtre Marigny, 17 December 1948;

La Femme et son ombre, Tokyo, Imperial Theater of Tokyo, 16 March 1923;

La Ville, reading at the "Palais de Bois," 1926; translated into Dutch by Urbain Van de Voorde, Brussels, Salle Patria, 25 February 1931; French original, Paris, Théâtre National Populaire, 1955;

Sous le rempart d'Athènes, music by Germaine Tailleferre, Paris, Opéra, 26 October 1927;

Le Père humilié, Dresden, Schauspielhaus, 26 November 1928; Paris, Théâtre de l'oeuvre, 1941;

Christophe Colomb, as opera, music by Milhaud, Berlin, Staatsopera Unter den Linden, 30 June 1930; Paris, Salle Gustave Doré, 1937; as *Le Livre de Christophe Colomb,* without music, Paris, Théâtre du Vieux-Colombier, 1947;

L'Agamemnon d'Eschyle, Les Choéphores d'Eschyle, Les Euménides d'Eschyle, adapted from Aeschylus's *Agamemnon, Choephoroi, Eumenides,* Brussels, Théâtre de la Monnaie, 27–28 March 1935;

Paul Claudel (Hulton Archive / © Getty Images)

Jeanne d'Arc au bûcher, translated into German, Basel, 12 May 1938; French original, music by Arthur Honegger, Orléans, Théâtre Municipal d'Orléans, 6 May 1939;

La Danse des morts, music by Honegger, Paris, Claudel's residence, 2 February 1939;

Le Soulier de satin, Paris, Comédie-Française, 23 November 1943;

La Jeune Fille Violaine, Paris, Salle d'Iéna, 14 March 1944;

L'Histoire de Tobie et de Sara: Moralité en trois actes, Roubaix, Central Théâtre, 28 February 1947;

L'Ours et la lune, Algiers, 2 May 1948;

Le Festin de la sagesse, music by Milhaud, Rome, 15 February 1950;

La Cantate à trois voix, Marseille, Groupe Théâtral Universitaire d'Aix-Marseille, 27 May 1955.

BOOKS: *Tête d'or,* anonymous (Paris: Librairie de l'Art Indépendant, 1890); revised edition, as Claudel, in *L'Arbre* (Paris: Mercure de France, 1901); revised edition translated by John Strong Newberry as *Tête d'or: A Play in Three Acts* (New Haven: Yale University Press / London: Milford, 1919);

La Ville, anonymous (Paris: Librairie de l'Art Indépendant, 1893); revised edition, as Claudel, in *L'Arbre* (Paris: Mercure de France, 1901); translated, based on both editions, by Newberry as *The City: A Play* (New Haven: Yale University Press, 1920);

Connaissance de l'Est (Paris: Mercure de France, 1900; expanded, 1907); expanded edition translated by Teresa Frances and William Rose Benét as *The East I Know* (New Haven: Yale University Press, 1914);

L'Arbre (Paris: Mercure de France, 1901)–comprises *Tête d'or* (revised version), *La Ville* (revised version), *L'Echange, Le Repos du septième jour,* and *La Jeune Fille Violaine* (revised version); original version of *La Jeune Fille Violaine,* preface by Jean Royère (Paris: Excelsior, 1926); revised edition of *L'Echange* (Paris: Mercure de France, 1954); original edition of *L'Echange* translated by Donald L. Holley and Jean-Pierre Krémer as *The Trade/L'Echange* (Woodbridge, Ont.: Editions Albion Press, 1995);

Connaissance du temps (Fou-Tchou, China: Rozario, 1904);

Ode: Les Muses (Paris: Bibliothèque de l'Occident, 1905); translated by Edward Lucie-Smith as *The Muses* (London: Turret, 1967);

Partage de midi (Paris: Bibliothèque de l'Occident, 1906; republished, with a new preface, Paris: Mercure de France, 1948; revised edition, Paris: Gallimard, 1949); translated by Wallace Fowlie as *Break of Noon,* in *Two Dramas: Break of Noon, The Tidings Brought to Mary* (Chicago: Regnery, 1960);

Art Poétique (Paris: Mercure de France, 1907); translated by Renée Spodheim as *Poetic Art* (New York: Philosophical Library, 1948);

Cinq Grandes Odes, suivies d'un processional pour saluer le siècle nouveau (Paris: Bibliothèque de l'Occident, 1910); translated by Lucie-Smith as *Five Great Odes* (London: Rapp & Carroll, 1967; Chester Springs, Pa.: Dufour, 1970);

Théâtre, first series, 4 volumes (Paris: Mercure de France, 1910–1912)–volume 4 (1912) comprises *Le Repos du septième jour, l'Agamemnon d'Eschyle,* and *Vers d'exil;*

L'Otage: Drame en trois actes (Paris: Nouvelle Revue Française, 1911); translated by Pierre Chavannes as *The Hostage: A Drama* (New Haven: Yale University Press / London: Oxford University Press, 1917);

Le Chemin de la Croix (Brussels: Durendal, 1911; Paris: Librairie de l'Art Catholique, 1914); translated by John J. Burke as *Stations of the Cross* (New York: Paulist Press, 1937);

L'Annonce faite à Marie: Mystère en quatre actes et un prologue (Paris: Nouvelle Revue Française, 1912); translated by Louise Morgan Sill as *The Tidings Brought to Mary: A Mystery* (New Haven: Yale University Press, 1916; London: Chatto & Windus, 1916);

Cette Heure qui est entre le printemps et l'été: Cantate à trois voix (Paris: Nouvelle Revue Française, 1913);

Deux poèmes d'été: La Cantate à trois voix; Protée: Drame satirique (Paris: Nouvelle Revue Française, 1914);

Corona benignitatis anni Dei (Paris: Nouvelle Revue Française, 1915); translated by Sister Mary David as *Coronal* (New York: Pantheon, 1943);

La Nuit de Noël 1914 (Paris: Librairie de l'Art Catholique, 1915);

Trois Poèmes de guerre (Paris: Nouvelle Revue Française, 1915); translated by Edward J. O'Brien as *Three Poems of the War,* introduction by Chavannes (New Haven: Yale University Press / London: Oxford University Press, 1919);

Autres Poèmes durant la guerre (Paris: Nouvelle Revue Française, 1916);

Sainte Thérèse (Paris: Bertrand, 1916);

L'Homme et son désir (Paris: Nouvelle Revue Française, 1918);

Le Pain dur: Drame en trois actes (Paris: Nouvelle Revue Française, 1918); translated by John Heard as *Crusts,* in *Three Plays: The Hostage, Crusts, The Humiliation of the Father* (Boston: Luce, 1945);

Sainte Cécile: Poème (Paris: Librairie de l'Art Catholique, 1918);

La Messe là-bas (Paris: Nouvelle Revue Française, 1919);

Protée: Drame satyrique en deux actes (Paris: Nouvelle Revue Française, 1919); revised, in *Deux farces lyriques* (Paris: Gallimard, 1927);

L'Ours et la lune: Farce pour un théâtre de marionnettes (Paris: Nouvelle Revue Française, 1919);

Introduction à quelques oeuvres: Conférence faite le 30 mai 1919 au Théâtre du Gymnase pour la maison des amis des livres (Paris: Monnier, 1920);

Le Père humilié: Drame en quatre actes (Paris: Nouvelle Revue Française, 1920; revised edition, Paris: Gallimard, 1945); original edition translated by Heard as *The Humiliation of the Father,* in *Three Plays: The Hostage, Crusts, The Humiliation of the Father* (Boston: Luce, 1945);

Ode jubilaire: Pour le six-centième anniversaire de la mort de Dante (Paris: Nouvelle Revue Française, 1921);

Verlaine (Paris: Nouvelle Revue Française, 1922);

Un Coup d'oeil sur l'âme japonaise: Discours aux étudiants de Nikko (Paris: Nouvelle Revue Française, 1923);

Sainte Geneviève (Tokyo: Chinchiocha, 1923);

A travers les villes en flammes: Note d'un témoin (Paris: Champion, 1924);

Morceaux choisis, avec un portrait et un autographe de l'auteur (Paris: Gallimard/Nouvelle Revue Française, 1925);

Feuilles de saints (Paris: Nouvelle Revue Française, 1925);

L'Endormie (Paris: Champion, 1925);

Le Soulier de satin, première journée (Paris: Plon, 1925); revised and expanded as *Le Soulier de satin, ou Le pire n'est pas toujours sûr: Action espagnole en quatre journées,* 4 volumes (Paris: Gallimard, 1928–1929); translated by John O'Connor and Claudel as *The Satin Slipper; or, The Worst Is Not the Surest: Spanish Action in Four Days* (New York & London: Sheed & Ward, 1931);

La Parabole du festin, as Delachapelle (Paris: Davis, 1926); republished as *La Sagesse, ou La Parabole du festin* (Paris: Gallimard, 1939);

La Philosophie du livre (Maastricht, The Netherlands: Stols, 1926; Paris: Aveline, 1926);

Cent phrases pour éventails (Tokyo: Koshiba, 1927; Paris: Gallimard, 1942);

L'Oiseau noir dans le soleil levant (Paris: Excelsior, 1927; enlarged edition, Paris: Gallimard/Nouvelle Revue Française, 1929);

Le Viellard sur le mont Omi (Paris: Le Livre, 1927);

Sous le rempart d'Athènes (Paris: Gallimard/Nouvelle Revue Française, 1928);

Positions et propositions: Art et littérature, 2 volumes (Paris: Gallimard, 1928, 1934); volume 1 translated by O'Connor and Claudel as *Ways and Crossways* (New York & London: Sheed & Ward, 1933);

Le Livre de Christophe Colomb (Vienna: Universelle, 1929; enlarged edition, Paris: Gallimard, 1935); original edition translated by Claudel, Agnes Meyer, and Darius Milhaud as *The Book of Christopher Columbus: A Lyrical Drama in Two Parts* (New Haven: Yale University Press / London: Oxford University Press, 1930);

Le Voleur volé, suivi du Bon Samaritain (Paris: Emile-Paul Frères, 1930);

Cantate à trois voix; suivie de Sous le rempart d'Athènes, et de traductions diverses (Paris: Gallimard, 1931);

Sur la présence de Dieu (Vienna & Ligugé: Aubin, 1932);

Jean Charlot (Paris: Gallimard, 1933);

Note sur l'art chrétien (Paris: Desclée de Brouwer, 1933);

Le Jardin aride: Parabole (Paris: Nouvelle Revue Française, 1934);

La Légende de Prâkriti (Paris: Gallimard, 1934);

Ecoute, ma fille (Paris: Gallimard, 1934);

Conversations dans le Loir-et-Cher (Paris: Gallimard, 1935);

Introduction à la peinture hollandaise (Paris: Gallimard, 1935);

Figures et paraboles (Paris: Gallimard, 1936);

Les Aventures de Sophie (Paris: Gallimard, 1937);

Introduction au Livre de Ruth (Paris: Desclée de Brouwer, 1938);

Un Poète regarde la Croix (Paris: Gallimard, 1938); translated by Fowlie as *A Poet Before the Cross* (Chicago: Regnery, 1958);

La Mystique des pierres précieuses (Paris: Cartier, 1938);

Jeanne d'Arc au bûcher (Paris: Gallimard, 1939);

L'Epée et le miroir (Paris: Gallimard, 1939);

Contacts et circonstances (Paris: Gallimard, 1940);

Ainsi donc une fois (Paris: Gallimard, 1940);

L'histoire de Tobie et de Sara: Moralité en trois actes (Paris: Gallimard, 1942);

Présence et prophétie (Fribourg, Switzerland: Editions de la Librairie de l'Université, 1942; Paris: Egloff, 1947);

Seigneur, apprenez-nous à prier (Paris: Gallimard, 1942); translated by Ruth Bethell as *Lord, Teach Us How to Pray* (London: Dobson, 1947; New York: Longmans, Green, 1948);

Prière pour les paralysés, suivie des Quinze Psaumes graduels CXIX à CXXIII (Paris: Horizons de France, 1944);

Poèmes et paroles durant la guerre de trente ans (Paris: Gallimard, 1945);

Visages radieux (Paris: Egloff, 1945; revised, 1947);

Dodoitzu: Poèmes de Paul Claudel (Paris: Gallimard, 1945);

Le Livre de Job (Paris: Plon, 1946);

Les Révélations de la Salette (Paris: Table Ronde, 1946);

Un Hommage à la poésie (Nantes: Fleuve, 1946);

L'Œil écoute (Paris: Gallimard, 1946); translated by Elsie Pell as *The Eye Listens* (New York: Philosophical Library, 1950);

Introduction à l'Apocalypse (Paris: Egloff, 1946);

La Rose et le rosaire (Paris: Egloff, 1946);

Chine (Geneva: Skira, 1946);

Saint François (Paris: Gallimard, 1946);

Discours et remerciements (Paris: Gallimard, 1947);

Du côté de chez Ramuz (Neuchâtel, Switzerland: Ides et Calendes, 1947);

Laudes (Brussels: Girouette, 1947);

Vézelay (Paris: Challamel, 1948);

Paul Claudel interroge le Cantique des cantiques (Paris: Egloff, 1948);

Sous le signe du dragon (Paris: Table Ronde, 1948);

Paul Claudel répond les psaumes (Neuchâtel, Switzerland: Ides et Calendes, 1948);

Accompagnements (Paris: Gallimard, 1949);

Emmaüs (Paris: Gallimard, 1949);

Une Voix sur Israël (Paris: Gallimard, 1950);

Saint Thérèse de Lisieux vous parle, edited by the Benedictines of l'Abbaye Notre-Dame-du-Pré (Lisieux: L'Abbaye Notre-Dame-du-Pré, 1950);

Œuvres complètes, 29 volumes, edited by Robert Mallet (Paris: Gallimard, 1950–1986);

L'Evangile d'Isaïe (Paris: Gallimard, 1951);

Paul Claudel interroge l'Apocalypse (Paris: Gallimard, 1952);

Le Symbolisme de la Salette (Paris: Gallimard, 1952);

Trois Figures saintes pour le temps actuel: Le Frère Charles, Sainte Thérèse de Lisieux, Eve Lavallière (Paris: Amyot-Dumont, 1953);

Mémoires improvisés, edited by Jean Amrouche (Paris: Gallimard, 1954);

J'aime la Bible (Paris: Arthème Fayard, 1955); translated by Wade Baskin as *The Essence of the Bible* (New York: Philosophical Library, 1957);

Conversation sur Jean Racine (Paris: Gallimard, 1956);

Qui ne souffre pas . . . réflexions sur le problème social (Paris: Gallimard, 1958);

Cahiers Paul Claudel, 15 volumes (Paris: Gallimard, 1959–)—comprises volume 1: *"Tête d'or" et les débuts littéraires* (1959); volume 2: *Le Rire de Paul Claudel* (1960); volume 3: *Correspondance Paul Claudel–Darius Milhaud (1912–1953),* preface by Henri Hoppenot, introduction by Jacques Petit (1961); volume 4: *Paul Claudel diplomate* (1962); volume 5: Claudel and Aurélian François Lugné-Poe, *Claudel homme de théâtre: Correspondance avec Lugné-Poe, 1910–1928,* edited by René Farabet, foreword by Jacques Robichez, introduction by Pierre Moreau (1964); volume 6: Claudel, Jacques Copeau, Charles Dullin, and Louis Jouvet, *Claudel homme de théâtre: Correspondances avec Copeau, Dullin, Jouvet,* edited by Henri Micciollo and Petit (1966); volume 7: *La figure d'Israël,* introduction by Jacques Madaule (1968); volume 8: Gilbert Gadoffre, *Claudel et l'univers chinois* (1968); volume 9: *Prague* (1971); volume 10: Paul Claudel and Jean-Louis Barrault, *Correspondance,* edited, with an introduction, by Michel Lioure, preface by Jean-Louis Barrault (1974); volume 11: *Claudel aux Etats-Unis (1927–1933),* edited by Lucile Garbagnati, foreword by Petit (1982); volume 12: Claudel and Jacques Rivière, *Correspondance (1907–1924),* edited by Auguste Anglès and Pierre de Gaulmyn (1984); volume 13: *Lettres de Paul Claudel à Elisabeth Sainte-Marie Perrin et à Audrey Parr,* edited by Michel Malicet and Lioure, introduction by Marlène Sainte-Marie Perrin (1990); volume 14: *Correspondance diplomatique (Tokyo, 1921–1927),* edited by Garbagnati, preface by Malicet (1995); and volume 15: *Une visite à Brangues: Conversation entre Paul Claudel, Jacques Madaule, et Pierre Schaeffer en février 1944,* includes 2 CDs (2005);

Je crois en Dieu, edited by Agnès du Sarment (Paris: Gallimard, 1961); translated by Helen Weaver as *I Believe in God: A Meditation on the Apostles' Creed,* edited by du Sarment (New York: Holt, Rinehart & Winston, 1963; London: Harvill, 1965);

Bréviare poétique (Paris: Gallimard, 1962);

Sainte Agnès, et poèmes inédits (Paris: Wesmael-Charlier, 1963);

Mes idées sur le théâtre, edited by Petit and Jean-Pierre Kempf (Paris: Gallimard, 1966); translated by Christine Trollope as *Claudel on the Theatre* (Coral Gables, Fla.: University of Miami Press, 1972);

Journal, 2 volumes, edited by François Varillon and Petit (Paris: Gallimard, 1968, 1969);

Magnificat, bilingual edition, Spanish translation by Alfonso Rubic (Monterey, Mexico: Sierra Madre, 1969);

Poésies (Paris: Gallimard, 1970);

Supplément aux Œuvres complètes, 4 volumes, edited by Malicet, Jacques Houriez, and others (Lausanne, Switzerland & Paris: L'Age d'Homme / Besançon: Centre Jacques Petit de l'Université de Besançon, 1990–1997);

Les Agendas de Chine, edited by Houriez (Lausanne, Switzerland & Paris: L'Age d'Homme, 1991);

L'Arsenal de Fou-Tchéou: Œuvres consulaires, Chine 1895–1905, edited by Houriez (Lausanne, Switzerland & Paris: L'Age d'Homme, 1995);

Le poëte et la Bible, 2 volumes, edited by Malicet, Dominique Millet, and Xavier Tilliette (Paris: Gallimard, 1998, 2004)—comprises volume 1: *1910–1946;* and volume 2: *1945–1955;*

Conversations écologiques, edited by Jean Bastaire (Cognac: Le Temps Qu'Il Fait, 2000);

Bible de Paul Claudel, 2 volumes, edited by Maryze Bazaud, introduction by Houriez (Besançon: Presses universitaires franc-comtoises / Paris: Les Belles Lettres, 2000).

Editions and Collections: *Poèmes de guerre 1914–1916* (Paris: Nouvelle Revue Française, 1922)–

includes *Trois poèmes de guerre, Autres poèmes durant la guerre,* and *La Nuit de Noël, 1914;*

Paul Claudel dans ses plus beaux textes (Montreal: Varin, 1940);

Pages de prose, selected and edited by André Blanchet (Paris: Gallimard, 1944);

La Perle noire, edited by Blanchet (Paris: Gallimard, 1947);

Théâtre, second series, 2 volumes, edited by Jacques Madaule (Paris: Gallimard, 1947, 1948);

Le Bestiare spirituel (Lausanne, Switzerland: Mermod, 1949);

Réflexions sur la poésie, Collection Idées, no. 29 (Paris: Gallimard, 1963);

Œuvres en prose, edited by Petit and Charles Galpérine (Paris: Gallimard, 1965);

Au milieu des vitraux de l'Apocalypse, edited by Pierre Claudel and Petit (Paris: Gallimard, 1966);

Œuvre poétique, edited by Jacques Petit (Paris: Gallimard, 1967);

Poèmes de Paul Claudel: Le Monde de Vézélay (Saint-Léger-Vauban: Zodiaque, 1967);

Le Poète et le Shamisen; Le Poète et le vase d'encens; Jules, ou, l'Homme-aux-deux-cravates, edited by Michel Malicet (Paris: Les Belles Lettres, 1970);

Richard Wagner: Rêverie d'un poète français, edited by Malicet (Paris: Les Belles Lettres, 1970);

Paul Claudel en verse, compiled and edited by Hubert Juin (Paris: Horay, 1971);

Partage de midi: Un Drame revisité, 1948–1949, edited by Gérald Antoine (Paris: L'Age d'Homme, 1997);

Paul Claudel en verse, edited by Juin (Paris: Horay, 2005).

Edition in English: *Knowing the East,* translated by James Lawler (Princeton & Oxford: Princeton University Press, 2004).

PRODUCED SCRIPTS: *Les Eumenides d'Eschyle,* radio, Radio Belge, 18 November 1929;

Le Repos du septième jour, radio, music by Darius Milhaud, Radio Marseille, 2 November 1942;

Le Soulier de satin, radio, Radiodiffusion Française, 1942;

L'Otage, radio, Radiodiffusion Française, April 1947;

Les Choéphores d'Eschyle, radio, music by Milhaud, Radiodiffusion Française, 29 March 1949;

Tête d'or, radio, music by Arthur Honegger, Radiodiffusion Française, 24 January 1950;

L'Echange, radio, Radiodiffusion Française, 14 February 1950;

Protée, radio, music by Milhaud, Radiodiffusion Française, 16 May 1950;

Le Livre de Christophe Colomb, radio, music by Milhaud, Radiodiffusion Française, 10 October 1950;

L'Histoire de Tobie et de Sara, radio, music by Gaston Litaize, Radiodiffusion Française, 13 December 1951;

Jeanne d'Arc au bûcher, radio, Radiodiffusion Française, 26 September 1952;

L'Agamemnon d'Eschyle, radio, music by Jean Wiener, Radiodiffusion Française, 13 December 1952.

OTHER: Aeschylus, *L'Agamemnon d'Eschyle,* translated by Claudel (Fou-Tchou, China: Rozario, 1896);

Aeschylus, *Les Choéphores d'Eschyle,* translated by Claudel (Paris: Nouvelle Revue Française, 1920);

Aeschylus, *Les Euménides d'Eschyle,* translated by Claudel (Paris: Nouvelle Revue Française, 1920);

Vitraux des cathédrales de France, XIIe et XIIIe siècles, edited by H. M. Zbinden, preface by Claudel (Paris: Plon, 1937);

Paul Claudel traduit librement Les sept psaumes de la pénitence, avec un Examen de conscience (Paris: Seuil, 1945);

Le Mal est parmi nous, by Claudel and others (Paris: Plon, 1948);

Eve Francis, *Temps héroïques: Théâtre, cinéma,* preface by Claudel (Paris: Denoël, 1949);

Jacques Madaule, *Le Drame de Paul Claudel,* preface by Claudel (Paris: Desclée de Brouwer, 1964);

Psaumes: Traductions 1918–1959, translated by Claudel, edited by Renée Nantet and Jacques Petit (Paris: Desclée de Brouwer, 1966).

The dramatic works of Paul Claudel have an unusual place in modern French literature and theater. Aesthetically, Claudel's plays are generally associated with symbolist drama, but most of his works were written in the twentieth century, years after symbolism had waned as a movement, and years after most symbolist writers (such as Villiers de l'Isle-Adam and Maurice Maeterlinck) had written their most important plays. While Claudel's plays are steeped in symbol and metaphor, they also feature elements that may be described as burlesque, pastoral, psychological, naturalist, theological, historical, spiritual, religious, and melodramatic.

In terms of poetic form, Claudel employs the *verset*, a verse form inaugurated by Claudel and subsequently adopted by poets such as Charles Péguy, Victor Ségalen, and Saint-John Perse. The *verset* is neither verse nor prose: it is a free-flowing, lyrical phrase well suited for expressing spiritual, religious, and cosmic yearnings. As developed by Claudel, the *verset* is based on the rhythm of human respiration *(le souffle)*. It also reflects poetic inspiration, with the varying lengths of the *verset* translating the poet's spontaneous grasp of ideas.

Thematically, Claudel's work is heavily informed by his religious beliefs. Born and raised in a family that

PAUL CLAUDEL

L'OTAGE

DRAME

nrf

ÉDITION DE LA
NOUVELLE REVUE FRANÇAISE
MARCEL RIVIÈRE & C_{IE}
31, RUE JACOB, PARIS

Title page for Claudel's 1911 play (The Hostage) about the efforts of Sygne de Coûfontaine to hide the freed Pope Pius XII, who had been imprisoned by Napoleon (Thomas Cooper Library, University of South Carolina)

was not particularly religious, Claudel became staunchly and fervently Catholic following an experience he had in the Cathedral of Notre-Dame-de-Paris when he was eighteen years old. So complete was his conversion, and so unshakeable his faith thereafter, that Claudel saw Catholicism as the only valid religion possible. His faith made him intolerant of other creeds, especially Eastern religions such as Buddhism and Hinduism. In *L'Asie et le démon* (1986, Asia and the Devil), published in *Œuvres complètes*, Claudel wrote of the more than two decades he spent in diplomatic service in the Orient: "J'ai habité longtemps l'Asie, mais je n'avais pas la vocation de l'Asie. Elle représentait simplement pour moi cet 'ailleurs' à quoi mon métier de consul et de diplomate me donnait droit. Je n'avais pas de lumière à en attendre et de questions à lui poser. J'étais chrétien et j'en savais plus qu'elle" (I've lived in Asia for a long time, but I did not have a vocation for Asia. Asia simply represented, for me, an "elsewhere" to which my career as a consul and a diplomat entitled me. I did not expect any revelations from her, nor did I have questions to ask of her. I was Christian, and I knew more than she did). While Claudel was receptive to some oriental influences and forms, his intransigence in matters of religion prevented him from fully embracing anything non-Catholic.

Claudel's literary work–including his theater–reflects his yearning to evangelize the world and to supplant the geographical Orient with a biblical East. His evangelical impulse is evident in both his first full-length play, *Tête d'or* (Head of Gold, published 1890, revised 1901, original version performed 1919, revised version performed 1924; translated, 1919), written in 1889, and his last great dramatic work, *Le Livre de Christophe Colomb* (published 1929; translated as *The Book of Christopher Columbus*, 1930), written in 1927 and first performed as an opera in Berlin in 1930. In *Tête d'or*, a Western army led by the title character is pitted against the peoples of the East, whereas *Christophe Colomb* is a saga glorifying the explorer who seeks to conquer the New World. Claudel's entire dramatic cycle is framed by these two figures–one fictional, one historical–representing invasion, conquest, appropriation, and evangelization, the dominant themes of his theater. Meanwhile, personal struggles are depicted through other characters of Claudel's drama, including Pierre de Craon and Violaine from *L'Annonce faite à Marie* (performed and published 1912; translated as *The Tidings Brought to Mary*, 1916) and Prouhèze from *Le Soulier de satin* (published 1925, revised and expanded as *Le Soulier de satin, ou Le pire n'est pas toujours sûr: Action espagnole en quatre journées*, 1928–1929, performed 1943; translated as *The Satin Slipper; or, The Worst Is Not the Surest: Spanish Action in Four Days*, 1931). These characters attempt to elevate the divine within them to triumph over the yearnings of the flesh and the attractions of the material world.

Paul-Louis-Charles-Marie Claudel was born on 6 August 1868 in the village of Villeneuve-sur-Fère-en-Tardenois. He was the third child of Louis-Prosper Claudel, an employee in the government fiscal services, and Louise-Athenais Cerveaux. The couple's first son, Henri, born in 1863, did not survive. A daughter, the sculptor Camille, was born in 1864, and a second daughter, Louise, was born in 1870. In July 1870 the family moved to Bar-le-Duc, where they remained for six years. In October 1875 Claudel enrolled as a day student in the school run by the Sisters of Doctrine Chrétienne, where he was an excellent pupil, winning all the prizes at the annual award ceremony. In August

1876 Claudel's father was transferred to Nogent-sur-Seine, where the family lived until September 1879, when they moved to Wassy-sur-Blaise (Claudel always spelled it as "Vassy"). By this time, Claudel's sister Camille had already begun to model clay and exhibit signs of her talent as a sculptor. Consequently, Claudel's mother moved to Paris with the children—while his father remained in the provinces—so that Camille could enroll in the Colarossi studio. The family first lived at 111 rue Notre-Dame-des-Champs, then in 1886 moved to the Boulevard de Port-Royal.

Claudel had some difficulty adjusting to life in the capital. In October 1882 he began to study rhetoric at the Lycée Louis-le-Grand, where he remained for "trois années affreuses; je répète, affreuses" (three frightful years; I repeat, frightful), as he confided to Henri Guillemin in 1942. Accustomed to small provincial schools with small class sizes, and used to being scholastically more advanced than his peers, Claudel was unprepared for the competition required in a class of forty to fifty students. Nevertheless, in 1883 he won the first prize for French discourse, a prize he received from the hands of influential historian and critic Ernest Renan. Claudel made friends with classmates Marcel Schwob and Léon Daudet, and he was greatly influenced by his philosophy teacher, the Kantian scholar Auguste Burdeau.

Claudel's first literary effort was composed in 1884 and discovered years later in one of his notebooks. It is a poem titled "Août" (August) that consists of twelve alexandrines, the traditional twelve-syllable meter of French verse. The poem evokes landscapes and nature. In 1885 Claudel observed the national funeral held for Victor Hugo, a writer he did not particularly admire because he considered him more a professional man of letters than an inspired writer. The following year Claudel read seer-poet Jean-Nicolas-Arthur Rimbaud's collection of prose poems, *Les Illuminations* (1886; translated as "Illuminations," 1953), which had been published in Félix Fénélon's journal *La Vogue* (The Vogue). Rimbaud exercised a major influence on Claudel, who found in the iconoclastic nineteenth-century poet, as Harold Waters explains, "a suffering individual deeply touched with divine grace." In the summer of 1886 Claudel took a trip to the Isle of Wight with his sister Camille. An essay based on this journey appeared in the 1 August 1889 issue of *Revue Illustrée* (Illustrated Review)—Claudel's first published text.

While attending mass at the Cathedral of Notre-Dame-de-Paris on Christmas Day 1886 Claudel experienced a conversion that altered the course of his life. In an essay titled "Ma Conversion" (My Conversion), which first appeared in the 13 October 1913 issue of *La Revue de la jeunesse* (The Youth Review), Claudel explains: "En un instant mon coeur fut touché et *je crus*. Je crus d'une telle force d'adhésion, d'un tel soulèvement de tout mon être, d'une conviction si puissante, d'une telle certitude ne laissant place à aucune espèce de doute que, depuis, tous les livres, tous les raisonnements, tous les hasards d'une vie agitée, n'ont pas pu ébranler ma foi, ni à vrai dire la toucher" (In an instant my heart was touched, and *I believed*. I believed with such a force of adhesion, with such an upheaval of my entire being, with so powerful a conviction, with such certainty leaving no room for any kind of doubt that, from then on, no book, no reasoning, none of the whims of a busy life have been able to shake my faith, nor even, truth be told, touch it). Despite his claims for the immediacy of his conversion, four more years passed before Claudel officially entered the Church and received its sacraments.

From 1886 to 1890 Claudel studied at the Faculté de Droit (Law School). He graduated in 1890 and enrolled in the Ecole des Sciences Politiques. Claudel met Stéphane Mallarmé and became a regular participant in the Tuesday meetings at Mallarmé's home. Mallarmé, the head of the symbolist movement, taught Claudel to reject traditional verse forms, and he also taught him the importance of the senses in the creation of poetry that is suggestive rather than rhetorical.

In 1887 Claudel wrote his first complete dramatic work, the poetic burlesque *L'Endormie* (1925, The Sleeper). It is a short, lyrical one-act play in which Volpilla, a young female faun, incites the Poet to conquer the most beautiful of nymphs, Galaxaure. After a frantic and breathless chase, the Poet discovers that the "nymph" he has awakened is actually the old, ugly, and drunken monster Strombo. *L'Endormie* was followed by Claudel's second dramatic work, a play titled *Une Mort prematurée* (A Premature Death). Claudel subsequently destroyed the text of this play; all that has survived is the fourth act, published as "Fragment d'un drame" in *Bibliographie des oeuvres de Paul Claudel . . . Précédée de "Fragment d'un drame," 1891* (1931, Bibliography of the works of Paul Claudel . . . Preceded by "Fragment of a Play," 1891).

Claudel's first major play, *Tête d'or,* written in 1889, is a lengthy, three-act play with action spread over several locations and an indeterminate period of time. In the first act, Simon Agnel returns to his homeland to bury his wife. While digging her grave, he meets his alter ego, Cébès, a pale and weak adolescent. The two men swear an oath of fidelity. The second act is set in the emperor's palace. Barbarian hordes are threatening the kingdom, and the people are resigned to defeat. Agnel arrives, his golden locks blazing, and he is dubbed "Tête d'or." Tête d'or shakes the populace out of its stupor and leads the people to victory. He then

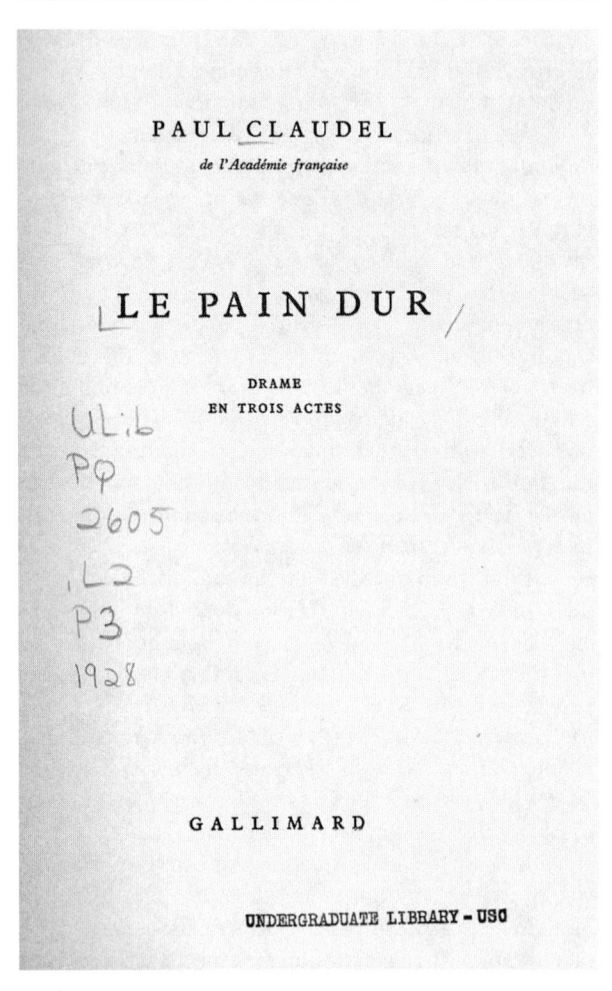

Title page for a later edition of Claudel's 1918 play (translated as Crusts, *1945), which begins thirty years after the story of* L'Otage *(The Hostage) and portrays the struggles of Sygne's son, Louis (Thomas Cooper Library, University of South Carolina)*

murders the old emperor, usurps the throne, proclaims himself king of men, and sends the emperor's beautiful daughter into exile. In the third act, consumed by an insatiable desire for power, Tête d'or sets out to conquer the earth. With all of Europe subjugated, Tête d'or turns toward Asia, facing the Asiatic hordes in the mountains of the Caucasus. He eventually declares victory but is fatally wounded. Left alone to die, he hears a whimper: it is the daughter of the former emperor, who has been crucified on a tree by a deserter. Summoning his ebbing strength, Tête d'or manages to pull out the nails with his teeth. Before dying, he appoints her his successor, but she dies shortly after he does.

In this complex work, two themes dominate: the psychological and spiritual evolution of Tête d'or and the clash between East and West, culminating in the battle between Tête d'or's army and the Asian troops.

Although Tête d'or dies, victory is declared. Yet, the play ends on an ambiguous note, for the victors do not continue their march to claim the land or the altars of the vanquished enemy they have sent fleeing. On the contrary, *Tête d'or* ends with a retreat, although the about-face of Tête d'or's army is represented as a forward march: "En avant! chez nous! vers l'Ouest!" (Forward march! Back to our homes! Westward bound!). Tête d'or has failed to conquer Asia, and the lesson of this failure is culled by Cassius: "Car voici que l'homme a terminé sa suprême entreprise, tout est fini / Et il ne prévaudra point / Contre la Puissance qui maintient les choses en place" (For look, man has finished his supreme undertaking, everything is over / And he will not prevail / Against the Power that keeps things in place). The end of the play underscores the importance of preserving the status quo, of maintaining the equilibrium between Europe and "sa soeur antique" (her antique sister), Asia.

Claudel's next play was *La Ville* (1893, revised 1901; translated as *The City,* 1920), written in 1890. It features two brothers, Isidore and Lambert de Besme, who govern a strange and frightening city. In the first version of the play, the city in question is Paris, while in the second it is called Besme. In the second version, which has many fewer characters than the first, Isidore is a thinker and an engineer, while Lambert is a politician. Although Isidore is in charge of running the machinery that makes the city function, he is profoundly unhappy; his science has revealed to him the emptiness and vanity of life. His refrain is "Rien n'est" (There is nothing). Lambert, too, is searching for meaning, which he believes he would find if only the young Lâla would reciprocate his love. However, Lâla is in love with Coeuvre, the poet. She marries him, and they have a son, Yvors. But Lâla leaves Coeuvre, taking their son with her, and joins Avare, the leader of a revolution, while Coeuvre disappears underground. Rejected by Lâla, Lambert collapses. Meanwhile, Isidore is killed by rebels. Avare appoints Yvors the new leader of the city, but Yvors is not sure what to do with the power invested in him. Coeuvre then emerges from his underground retreat dressed in bishop's garb and accompanied by many clergy. He has converted to Christianity, and he brings the answer that his son is seeking: men will no longer reign—the city shall henceforth be governed by God.

Deciding on a career in the diplomatic corps, Claudel prepared for and passed the foreign-service examination and was appointed attaché, a post he held at the Quai d'Orsay from 1890 to 1892. During this time, he wrote *La Jeune Fille Violaine* (original version 1926, revised version 1901, The Young Girl Violaine), a play he later turned into *L'Annonce faite à Marie*. This first version of *La Jeune Fille Violaine* was not published until much later because Claudel put it aside to write a second version in 1898. *La Jeune Fille Violaine* is in the style of a medieval morality play, a Christian drama enacting the confrontation between two figures, the sisters Violaine and Bibiane (Claudel rechristened the latter as Mara for the second version and *L'Annonce faite à Marie*). The four-part play opens in a medieval farm, Combernon, where two sisters, Violaine and Bibiane, are both in love with the same man, Jacquin Uri. Bibiane misleads Jacquin into believing that Violaine is in love with Eloi Baube (Pierre de Craon in the second version), who is betrothed to Lidine. Violaine elects not to deny Bibiane's claim and leaves Combernon. As she departs, Bibiane throws cinders into Violaine's eyes, blinding her. Bibiane and Jacquin then marry and have a son, Aubin, who is born blind. Understanding that her child's blindness is a divine punishment, Bibiane goes into the forest to seek the help of a blind healer, whom she discovers to be none other than Violaine. Bibiane asks Violaine to cure Aubin's blindness. Aubin receives the gift of sight, certainly through Violaine's saintly intercession, but more on account of Bibiane's adamant faith. Bibiane then returns to Jacquin with their son. However, Jacquin is still in love with Violaine, and the jealous Bibiane goes back and fatally wounds her sister, leaving her to die. The play is a meditation on the themes of faith and pardon. In the end, Bibiane confesses her actions to both her husband and her father and obtains their pardon.

In February 1892 Claudel was named vice-consul to France's consulate in New York. Over the next four decades Claudel pursued his diplomatic career across four continents—Europe, Asia, and North and South America—while continuing his prodigious literary output.

Claudel's next play, *L'Echange* (published 1901, performed 1914, revised 1954; translated as *The Exchange*, 1995), is set in America, with the action taking place somewhere on the east coast. It is a psychological drama involving four characters who find themselves in a house by the sea and who "exchange" places and partners. Thomas Pollock Nageoire is a businessman and the rich proprietor of the house. Lechy Elbernon is an actress and Nageoire's mistress. Marthe is a young Frenchwoman newly married to Louis Laine, a half Indian employed as Nageoire's groundskeeper. Louis finds marriage confining, and Marthe is unhappy in the foreign land to which her husband has brought her. Meanwhile, Nageoire is attracted to Marthe and offers to buy her. Marthe is shocked by the idea, but money has already changed hands. Meanwhile, Louis is seduced by Lechy and becomes her lover. When Louis decides to leave with the money Nageoire has given him, Lechy hires someone to kill him. She then sets fire to the bungalow where Nageoire's fortune is hidden. Nageoire makes no attempt to save his fortune—he seems to have found some sort of peace in Martha's company. The plot of *L'Echange* is simple, and the play is classical in structure, respecting *les bienséances*, the conventions of classical theater. Nevertheless, Claudel orchestrates many ideas and symbols in the play, and his four characters are partly autobiographical, revealing different facets of their creator's personality.

In October 1894 Claudel left New York for Boston. The following year he was appointed to a post in China, to which he traveled after a brief vacation in Paris. The crossing to China by sea took more than a month, with the ship stopping at several ports of call, including Aden and Colombo. Claudel used this time to write some of the works that would later be published under the title *Connaissance de l'Est* (1900, expanded 1907; translated as *The East I Know*, 1914). During his sojourn in China, Claudel continued to add texts to this work and began a second version of *La Jeune Fille Violaine*. He also wrote the play *Le Repos du septième jour* (1901, The Seventh Day's Rest), the story of a mythical Christian emperor who descends into the underworld to save his people from being invaded by the dead. The play ponders metaphysical and religious questions involving being, nothingness, and death.

The central action of *Le Repos du septième jour*, that of the Emperor's descent into hell, parallels the legend of Maudgalyayana, a disciple of the Buddha who descends into hell in order to rescue his mother, who has been relegated there to expiate the sin of eating meat, a sin she committed unknowingly. The legend of Maudgalyayana has been adopted by theaters of all Buddhist countries, especially Japan and China, where it is usually performed as an opera. There are many parallels between the plot of Claudel's play and the oriental legend. In both a sin is committed in ignorance and a living person agrees to descend into hell in order to rescue and deliver the tormented soul or souls. In the legend Maudgalyayana offers to take his mother's place in hell, while in Claudel's play the Emperor sacrifices himself in order to save his people. And although Maudgalyayana undertakes his journey out of filial devotion while Claudel's Emperor seeks to save all of his subjects from being haunted and harassed by the dead, when the Emperor enters hell he first encounters his mother.

The theological issue in both the legend and the play is the question of redemption. In the Indian legend, the Buddha appears before Maudgalyayana and reveals how his mother may be delivered: by the performance of a ritual ceremony for the dead, to be accomplished in the seventh month, a month when the earth enters its period of rest. Similarly, in *Le Repos du*

Claudel on the cover of the American newsmagazine the year he was named ambassador to the United States, a post he held from 1928 to 1933 (© Time & Life Pictures; Getty Images)

septième jour, the people are reminded, after a week of hard work, to put aside their wealth and material possessions, to rest from their labors, and to devote themselves to praising God. Despite this parallel, *Le Repos du septième jour* expresses one of Claudel's criticisms of Buddhism. The anti-Buddhist lesson is recited at length to the Emperor by the Demon, who seems to be Lucifer. It is ironic that Claudel uses the fallen angel to explain Christian theology. In long verses of biblically inspired poetry, the Demon discourses upon the mysteries of hell—death, suffering, punishment—and impresses upon the Emperor that Buddhism is "la Connaissance invertie, la Fin retournée sur la cause" (Knowledge inverted, the End turned round on the cause).

After serving in China for four years, Claudel returned to France on home leave and contemplated retiring from the world and entering a religious order. Ultimately deciding against monastic life, Claudel settled on returning to China in 1900. During this crossing he became involved with Rosalia (Rose) Vetch, a married woman of Polish and Scottish origin, whose husband conducted business in the Far East. For four years Rose lived in Claudel's home with her children, and when she left in August 1904, she was pregnant with Claudel's daughter, Louise.

Partage de Midi (published 1906, performed 1921, revised version performed 1948, revised version published 1949; translated as *Break of Noon,* 1960) has been seen as the dramatic transposition of Claudel and Rose's liaison and subsequent separation. It is one of Claudel's most celebrated plays and perhaps the most autobiographical, and he returned to it several times, writing different versions. The principal characters in the first version, Ysé and Mesa, meet on a boat bound for the Orient. Mesa is a customs official who has just been denied what he had hoped would be his vocation, the priesthood, and Ysé is the wife of an engineer, De Ciz, who expects to make his fortune in the Orient. De Ciz and Ysé's children are with them. Also on board is Amalric, a friend of Mesa. Ysé and Mesa discover their love for each other, and the exchanges between them are among the most beautiful passages in all of Claudel's writings. Their love, however, is perceived as sinful and wrong. Worsening matters, Ysé becomes pregnant with Mesa's child. Ysé leaves Mesa to live with Amalric in the south of China, where she gives birth to Mesa's child. When Mesa arrives at their house to rescue Ysé from falling into the hands of Chinese revolutionaries, Amalric attacks him and leaves him to die. Amalric plans to board a ship with Ysé, hoping it will be their ticket to freedom. Before departing, Ysé kills her child in an attempt to sever ties with the past. However, she changes her mind and abandons Amalric, returning to Mesa as he revives. Mesa and Ysé make peace with each other and prepare to die.

Claudel wrote no plays between 1900 and 1904, but he did work on and publish other important works, namely, *Connaissance du temps* (1904, Knowledge of the Times), written between 1902 and 1903, and *De la connaissance du monde et de soi-même* (1904), first published in his *Art poétique.* Additionally, between 1900 and 1908 Claudel wrote his most powerful poetic works, the *Cinq Grandes Odes* (1910; translated as *Five Great Odes,* 1967).

Two years after Rose's departure, Claudel was still suffering from the end of his liaison with her, so he took the advice of his confessor and decided to marry and raise a Catholic family. On 15 March 1906 he married Reine Sainte-Marie-Perron, the daughter of the architect of Notre-Dame-de-Fourvières Cathedral in Lyons. He then returned to China with his wife, and they formed a conservative household and raised five children together.

Claudel left China for Paris in 1909, where he learned that his sister Camille suffered from madness. His *Journal* (1968, 1969) captures the anguish that Camille's insanity caused him. In the years immediately preceding World War I, Claudel was in Germany, first in Frankfurt, then in Hamburg, after which he was posted to Rome as the *attaché commercial* (commercial attaché). This move was followed by a posting in Rio de Janeiro, Brazil. He went on this assignment without his family, but he was accompanied by his secretary, the composer Darius Milhaud, who collaborated with Claudel on several projects. A brief posting in Denmark was followed by Claudel's appointment as ambassador to Japan.

In 1909–1910 Claudel worked on his most famous play, *L'Annonce faite à Marie,* and he wrote *L'Otage* (published 1911; performed 1913; translated as *The Hostage,* 1917), the first of a trilogy generally known as the Coûfontaine cycle. *L'Otage* is an historical drama set in 1812. The action takes place in the old monastery of Coûfontaine, recently purchased by one of the central characters, Sygne de Coûfontaine. Sygne's cousin, Georges Coûfontaine, has freed Pope Pius VII, who had been imprisoned by Napoleon, and hidden him on Sygne's estate. To prevent the Pope's hiding place from being exposed, Sygne is forced to marry Toussaint Turelure, a baron who had pillaged the estate during the French Revolution. *L'Otage* continues Claudel's exploration of the theme of sacrifice, probing the contradictory duties (fraternal loyalty, loyalty to her husband, loyalty to the Church, and loyalty to the state) that Sygne must resolve. Her very name, Sygne (sign) is symbolic: on her deathbed, she refuses to forgive Turelure, even after bearing his son, and her refusal is con-

Title page for the 1929 revised and expanded version of Claudel's play (The Satin Slipper) set in Spain and Morocco in the late sixteenth century. The plot features a tragic love story amid the Spanish conflict with the Moors (Thomas Cooper Library, University of South Carolina).

veyed not through words but through a gesture, a slow, sweeping, emphatic sign of negation.

The second play of the trilogy, *Le Pain dur* (published 1918, performed 1919; translated as *Crusts*, 1945), is set thirty years later and revolves around Sygne's son, Louis. Having lost all the fortune he had invested in a plantation in Africa, Louis is bankrupt, and he holds his father responsible for his losses. Hailed by the African politician and poet Léopold Senghor, this play is an expression of Claudel's anticolonial stance. At the same time the play examines the effects of the industrial revolution, the vices of greed and avarice, and the exploitation of human beings by other human beings.

The third and final play of the Coûfontaine trilogy is *Le Père humilié* (published 1920, produced 1928, revised version published 1945; original version translated as *The Humiliation of the Father*, 1945). Louis Turelure is now an old man, serving as France's ambassador in Rome, where he lives with his wife, Sichel (formerly his father's mistress), and their daughter, Pensée. Brothers Orian and Orso, nephews of Pope Pius, are both in love with Pensée. She loves Orian and conceives his child, but when Orian dies on the battlefield, she agrees to marry Orso in order to give her child a father and a family name.

Claudel's most famous play, and possibly his greatest, *L'Annonce faite à Marie*, was first published in book form in 1912. Essentially a new version of *La Jeune Fille Violaine*, the play consists of a prologue and four acts and evokes the themes of faith and sacrifice. In the prologue, Violaine and Pierre de Craon, a mason and builder of churches, talk about an encounter they had a year earlier, when Pierre had attempted to possess Violaine physically but had only succeeded in cutting her arm with a blunt knife. Now Pierre is afflicted with leprosy, and he seeks Violaine's forgiveness for his actions of a year ago. Violaine pardons him, giving him a solemn kiss that is observed by her sister Mara, who is in love with Violaine's fiancé Jacques Hury. Mara conspires against Violaine and succeeds in arousing Jacques's suspicions about Violaine's chastity. When Violaine reveals that she, in turn, has contracted leprosy, Jacques turns away from her and marries Mara. Violaine retires into the forest of Le Géyn, a leper colony, and devotes her life to God. Mara and Jacques have a child, who dies. Mara carries the corpse to her sister, hoping that Violaine can revive the child. Violaine performs the miracle: the child comes back to life, with eyes the same blue as Violaine's, although they were originally as dark as Mara's. As she is dying, Violaine is carried back to Combernon, where Jacques understands his mistake. Violaine, however, insists that he accept Mara's love and persuades Jacques to forgive her.

L'Annonce faite à Marie has become one of the most frequently performed plays in the world. The force and intensity of this play derive from the absolute faith Mara has in her sister's saintliness. Holding the corpse of her child in her arms, Mara demands that the child be brought back to life. The miracle of the child's resurrection can only be effected through Violaine's spiritual powers. Violaine is thus the instrument of the miracle, but Mara's unshakeable faith provides the driving force and participates equally in it.

While *L'Annonce faite à Marie* is Claudel's most popular play, *Le Soulier de satin* is the most complex. Claudel began writing this play in 1919 and completed it in 1924 while serving as French ambassador to Japan. The action begins in Spain at the end of the sixteenth century, against the background of the Renaissance and Spain's exploration of Africa. It is the story of Doña love with Don Rodrigue. Don Pélage sends Prouhèze to Morocco as his emissary to take command of the fortress of Mogador, constantly besieged by the Moors. However, this mission is only a pretext: he really wants to test her virtue. Prouhèze is accompanied by a lieutenant, Don Camille, who is also in love with her. Rodrigue follows Prouhèze to Mogador and pleads with her to leave Morocco with him. Prouhèze resists the temptation, armed with the resolve instilled in her by the Virgin Mary, to whom she has devoted herself, offering one of her satin slippers as a symbol of this consecration. When her husband, Pélage, dies, however, Prouhèze writes to Rodrigue and summons him to Mogador. However, the letter strangely takes ten years to reach Rodrigue. Meanwhile, not having heard from Rodrigue, Prouhèze marries Don Camille, and they have a daughter whom they name Sept-Epées (Seven Swords). When Rodrigue finally arrives in Morocco, Mogador is under attack by the Moors. Prouhèze refuses to be rescued from the danger, entrusts her daughter to Rodrigue's care (Sept-Epées looks like Rodrigue, a detail that underlines the spiritual bond between them), and dies.

Claudel left Japan in 1927 and was named ambassador to the United States, a post he held from 1928 to 1933. During this time he wrote *Le Livre de Christophe Colomb,* which dramatizes Christopher Columbus's vision for the world and the trials and tribulations he had to undergo in order to attempt its realization. In Claudel's play, Columbus is more a missionary than an explorer, sailor, or merchant, burning with a desire to unite all the peoples of the earth under the banner of Catholicism. He finds an ardent champion in "Her Most Catholic Majesty," Queen Isabelle. The play opens with a solemn processional in which the book recounting the life and voyages of Columbus is installed on the stage. This first brief scene sets the tone for the rest of the play:

> L'EXPLICATEUR. – Le Livre de la Vie et des voyages de Christophe Colomb qui a découvert l'Amérique!
>
> Au Nom du Père et du Fils et du Saint-Esprit.
>
> LE CHOEUR, *d'une voix tonnante.* – Ainsi soit-il!
>
> (THE EXPLICATOR. – The Book of the Life and voyages of Christopher Columbus who discovered America!
>
> In the name of the Father, the Son, and the Holy Ghost.
>
> THE CHOIR, *in a thunderous voice.* – Amen!)

L'Explicateur is the narrator who recounts what transpires between scenes. Both part of and external to the action of the play, he sometimes describes decor and provides stage directions. He also directs Le Choeur and, jointly with them, represents the voice of posterity and its judgment of Columbus. Throughout the play much is made of the fact that the explorer has such a seemingly preordained name, being "the Dove that bears Christ" to the New World. Doves appear in several scenes of the play; in a scene titled "Irruption des Colombes" (Irruption of Doves) the playwright calls for a whole host of white doves to engulf the stage.

Claudel's last diplomatic posting was in Brussels, after which he retired to a château he had purchased in Brangues. Dividing his time between Brangues and Paris, he concentrated on biblical commentary. He was elected to the Académie française (French Academy) in 1947. Claudel died at Brangues on 23 February 1955 after suffering a heart attack. A funeral service was held at Notre-Dame Cathedral in Paris.

Claudel left much of himself in his dramatic oeuvre, projecting aspects of himself or his biography into each play through one or more characters. Claudel the consul for France embarking for the Orient is Tête d'or, the Jeune Consul; Claudel the poet is Coeuvre, the poet of *La Ville;* the Claudel who ploughed the Indian Ocean and indulged in illicit love is Mesa of *Partage de Midi.* Claudel the Catholic is Pierre de Craon in *L'Annonce faite à Marie;* Claudel is also Rodrigue of *Le Soulier de satin,* whose peregrinations across the globe recall Claudel's own. In *Mémoires improvisés* (1954, Improvised Memoirs), Claudel emphasizes how much of his own persona is invested in each of his characters, citing *L'Otage* as his first example:

> Mes états d'esprit successifs ont été plutôt toujours exprimés par un ensemble de personnages différents. C'est ainsi que . . . je me reconnais aussi bien dans, disons, dans Sygne, que je me reconnais dans Toussaint Turelure, ou dans Georges: tous ces trois, je reconnais des traits particuliers de mon caractère. Et de même dans *Violaine,* évidemment, le personnage de Pierre de Craon et le personnage d'Anne Vercors.
>
> (My successive states of mind have almost always been expressed by a cast of different characters. Thus . . . I recognize myself as much in, let's say, Sygne as I do in Toussaint Turelure, or in Georges: in all three I recognize specific traits of my character. And similarly, in *Violaine,* obviously, the character of Pierre de Craon, and the character of Anne Vercors).

Claudel's theater is structured around what may be described as a profound desire for the unity of the universe. In *Mémoires improvisés,* Claudel describes Christopher Columbus in the context of his fascination for

Title page for the English translation of Claudel's 1929 play that depicts Christopher Columbus as a Catholic missionary, with the author's inscription (Rare Books Collection, Thomas Cooper Library, University of South Carolina)

the explorer: "Ce personnage . . . me hantait depuis assez longtemps. C'était le héros d'une idée que j'aie toujours eue, cette idée du rassemblement de la terre, de la réunion des différentes parties de l'humanité, et Christophe Colomb me semblait, à ce sujet, un véritable champion et, on peut dire, un saint" (This character . . . has haunted me for a long time. He was the hero of an idea I've always had, the idea of bringing together the Earth, of uniting humanity's different parts, and Christopher Columbus seemed to me, on this subject, a true champion, one might say a saint). Hence, Western conquerors, explorers, and missionaries recur in Claudel's writings: beyond Christopher Columbus, there are figures such as Alexander the Great, Saint Francis Xavier, and Napoleon, who dreamed of conquests in the Orient. In *Mémoires improvisés*, Claudel describes Napoleon as "un romantique échevelé, un homme pourvu par une idée presque mystique qui ne lui laisse pas de repos" (a frenzied romantic, a man imbued with an almost mystical idea that leaves him no rest).

Ultimately, Claudel believed that his dream of universal unity had to be achieved by "the conquest of souls," by the invasion and evangelization of the Other (the East) by the Self (the West). The only universality he could admit is Catholicism. This position generally has been seen by critics as a fatal flaw. For example, Jean Biès comments on Claudel's apparent arrogance in *Littérature française et pensée hindoue* (1974, French Literature and Hindu Thought): "A voir tant de mépris (de l'Autre) et une telle sûreté de soi, l'on se pose la question: l'un de nos plus grands poètes chrétiens, et peut-être le plus grand, était-il vraiment chrétien?" (In the face of so much scorn [for the Other] and such sureness of oneself, one has to ask the question: one of our greatest Christian poets, and perhaps the greatest, was he really Christian?).

Although he has many critics, Paul Claudel remains the most important French Catholic playwright of the twentieth century. He was the playwright who best brought to the modern stage the symbolist aesthetic of musicality, suggestion, and nuance. Claudel was fortunate in his collaboration with director Jean-Louis Barrault, who was willing to take risks with lengthy and complicated plays that demanded much of the actor and of the audience. Barrault deserves much of the credit for popularizing Claudel in Paris in the 1950s.

Letters:

Paul Claudel et Jacques Rivière, Correspondance, 1907–1914 (Paris: Plon, 1926); translated by Henry Longan Stuart as *Letters to a Doubter* (New York: Boni, 1927; London: Burns, Oates & Washbourne, 1927);

Dust jacket for the 1960 English translations of two of Claudel's most popular plays (Richland County Public Library)

Correspondance avec Jacques Rivière, 2 volumes, edited by Henri Alain Fournier (Paris: Gallimard, 1948);

Correspondance, 1899–1926: Paul Claudel et André Gide (Paris: Gallimard, 1949); translated by John Russell as *The Correspondence, 1899–1926, between Paul Claudel and André Gide*, edited by Robert Mallet (London: Secker & Warburg / Boston: Beacon, 1952);

Paul Claudel, Francis Jammes, Gabriel Frizeau, Correspondance 1897–1938; Avec les lettres de Jacques Rivière, edited, with a preface, by André Blanchet (Paris: Gallimard, 1952);

Lettres de P. Claudel sur la Bible, au R. P. R. Paroissin (17 août 1949–11 octobre 1954) (Paris: Nouvelles Editions Debresse, 1955);

Lettres inédites de mon parrain Paul Claudel, edited by Agnès du Sarment (Paris: Gabalda, 1959); translated by William Howard as *Letters from My Godfather, Paul Claudel* (Dublin: Clonmore & Reynolds, 1964);

Correspondance Paul Claudel–Darius Milhaud (1912–1953), preface by Henri Hoppenot, introduction by Jacques Petit, Cahiers Paul Claudel, no. 3 (Paris: Gallimard, 1961);

Claudel and Aurélian François Lugné-Poe, *Claudel homme de théâtre: Correspondance avec Lugné-Poe, 1910–1928,* edited by René Farabet, foreword by Jacques Robichez, introduction by Pierre Moreau, Cahiers Paul Claudel, no. 5 (Paris: Gallimard, 1964);

Claudel, Jacques Copeau, Charles Dullin, and Louis Jouvet, *Claudel homme de théâtre: Correspondances avec Copeau, Dullin, Jouvet,* edited by Henri Micciollo and Petit, Cahiers Paul Claudel, no. 6 (Paris: Gallimard, 1966);

Claudel et l'Amérique II: Lettres de Paul Claudel à Agnès Meyer, 1928–1929: Note-book d'Agnès Meyer, 1929, edited, with an introduction and notes, by Eugène Roberto (Ottawa: Editions de l'Université d'Ottawa, 1969);

La porte ouverte: lettres inédites de Paul Claudel, edited by Maurice Zundel and Jacques Madaule (La Pierre-qui-Vire: Presses Monastiques, 1970);

Martha Bibesco, *Echanges avec Paul Claudel: Nos lettres inédites* (Paris: Mercure de France, 1972);

Paul Claudel, Louis Massignon (1908–1914): Correspondance, edited by Michel Malicet (Paris: Desclée de Brouwer, 1973);

Claudel and Jean-Louis Barrault, *Correspondance,* edited, with an introduction, by Michel Lioure, preface by Jean-Louis Barrault, Cahiers Paul Claudel, no. 10 (Paris: Gallimard, 1974);

La Tristesse d'un automne sans été: Correspondance de Gabrielle Vulliez avec André Gide et Paul Claudel (1923–1931), edited by Wanda Laparra Vulliez (Lyon: Centre d'Etudes Gidiennes, Université Lyon II, 1981);

Claudel and Jacques Rivière, *Correspondance (1907–1924),* edited by Auguste Anglès and Pierre de Gaulmyn, Cahiers Paul Claudel, no. 12 (Paris: Gallimard, 1984);

Lettres de Paul Claudel à Elisabeth Sainte-Marie Perrin et à Audrey Parr, edited by Malicet and Lioure, introduction by Marlène Sainte-Marie Perrin, Cahiers Paul Claudel, no. 13 (Paris: Gallimard, 1990);

Lettres à sa fille Reine, edited by Malicet (Lausanne, Switzerland: L'Age d'Homme, 1991);

Correspondance, 1911–1954: Paul Claudel, Gaston Gallimard, edited by Bernard Delvaille (Paris: Gallimard, 1995);

Correspondance diplomatique (Tokyo, 1921–1927), edited by Lucile Garbagnati, preface by Malicet, Cahiers Paul Claudel, no. 14 (Paris: Gallimard, 1995);

Claudel and Jacques Madaule, *Connaissance et reconnaissance: Correspondance 1924–1954,* edited by Andrée Hirschi and Pierre Madaule (Paris: Desclée de Brouwer, 1996);

Paul Claudel, Stanislas Fumet, Correspondance 1920–1954: Histoire d'une amitié, edited by Marianne Malicet (Lausanne, Switzerland: L'Age d'Homme, 1997);

Lettres à une amie: Correspondance avec Francoise de Mercilly, 1935–1954, edited by Xavier Tilliette (Paris: Bayard, 2002);

Lettres de Paul Claudel à Jean Paulhan (1925–1954) (Bern, Berlin & Brussels: Lang, 2004).

Interview:

Mémoires improvisés: Quarante et un entretiens avec Jean Amrouche, edited by Louis Fournier (Paris: Gallimard, 1969).

Bibliographies:

Bibliographie de la littérature française, volume 3 (Paris: Chronique des Lettres françaises, 1931), pp. 146–160;

Jacques Benoist-Méchin and Georges Blaizot, *Bibliographie des oeuvres de Paul Claudel . . . Précédée de "Fragment d'un drame," 1891* (Paris: Blaizot, 1931);

S. Dreher and M. Rolli, *Bibliographie de la littérature française de 1930 à 1938* (Geneva: Droz, 1948), pp. 95–96;

Marguerite L. Drevret, *Bibliographie de la littéraire française de 1940 à 1949* (Geneva: Droz, 1954), pp. 145–150;

Jacques Petit and Andrée Hirschi, eds., *Bibliographie des œuvres de Paul Claudel* (Paris: Les Belles Lettres, 1973);

Jacqueline de Labroille, *Claudel and the English Speaking World* (London: Grant & Cutler, 1973).

Biographies:

Daniel Rops, *Claudel tel que je l'ai connu* (Strasbourg: Le Roux, 1957);

Henri Mondor, *Claudel plus intime* (Paris: Gallimard, 1960);

Louis Chaigne, *Vie de Paul Claudel par lui-même* (Paris: Seuil, 1961);

Paul-André Lesort, *Paul Claudel par lui-même* (Paris: Seuil, 1963).

References:

Pascale Alexandre-Bergues, *L'Echange de Paul Claudel* (Besançon, France: Presses Universitaires Franc-Comtoises, 2002);

André Alter, *Textes de Claudel: Points de vue critiques, témoignages, bibliographie* (Paris: Seghers, 1968);

François Angelier, *Paul Claudel: Un mystique à l'état civil* (Paris: Pygmalion, 2000);

Gérald Antoine, *Paul Claudel, ou L'Enfer du génie* (Paris: Robert Laffont, 1988);

Louis Barjon, *Paul Claudel* (Paris: Editions universitaires, 1953);

Jean-Louis Barrault, *Nouvelles réflexions sur le théâtre* (Paris: Flammarion, 1959);

Ernest Beaumont, *The Theme of Beatrice in the Plays of Paul Claudel* (London: Rockliff, 1954);

Jean-Claude Berton, *Shakespeare et Claudel: Le Temps et l'espace au théâtre* (Geneva: La Palatine, 1958);

Jean Biès, *Littérature française et pensée hindoue, des origines* (Paris: Librairie C. Klincksieck, 1974), pp. 166–169;

André Blanc, ed., *Les critiques de notre temps et Claudel* (Paris: Garnier Frères, 1970);

Pierre Brunel, ed., *Paul Claudel* (Paris: L'Herne, 1997);

Georges Cattaui, *Claudel: Le cycle des Coûfontaine et le mystère d'Israel* (Paris: Desclée de Brouwer, 1968);

Cattaui and Jacques Madaule, eds., *Entretiens sur Paul Claudel* (Paris: Mouton, 1968);

René Farabet, *Le Jeu de l'acteur dans le théâtre de Claudel* (Paris: Lettres modernes, 1960);

Wallace Fowlie, *Paul Claudel*, Studies in Modern European Literature and Thought (London: Bowes & Bowes, 1957);

Stanislas Fumet, *Claudel* (Paris: Gallimard, 1958; second edition, 1968);

Gilbert Gadoffre, *Claudel et l'univers chinois,* Cahiers Paul Claudel, no. 8 (Paris: Gallimard, 1968);

Henri Gouhier, "La trilogie," in *Paul Claudel, IV, l'Histoire,* edited by Jacques Petit (Paris: Minard, 1967), pp. 31–42;

Richard Griffiths, ed., *Claudel: A Reappraisal* (London: Rapp & Whiting, 1968);

Henri Guillemin, *Claudel et son art d'écrire* (Paris: Gallimard, 1955);

Bernard Hue, *Littérature et arts de l'orient dans l'oeuvre de Paul Claudel* (Paris: Librairie C. Klincksieck, 1978);

Bettina Liebowitz Knapp, *Paul Claudel* (New York: Ungar, 1982);

Jacqueline de Labriolle, *Les "Christophe Colomb" de Paul Claudel* (Paris: Librairie C. Klincksieck, 1972);

James R. Lawler, "Claudel's art of provocation," *Essays in French Literature,* 1 (November 1964): 30–55;

Paul-André Lesort, *Paul Claudel par lui-même* (Paris: Seuil, 1963);

Michel Lioure, *L'esthétique de Paul Claudel* (Paris: Armand Colin, 1971);

Aurélien Lugné-Poë, *Dernière pirouette* (Paris: Sagittaire, 1946);

Jacques Madaule, *Claudel et le langage* (Paris: Desclée de Brouwer, 1968);

Michel Malicet, *Lecture psychanalytique de l'oeuvre de Claudel,* 3 volumes, Annales littéraires de l'Université de Besançon, nos. 221, 226, and 227 (Paris: Belles Lettres, 1978–1979);

Gabriel Marcel, *Regards sur le théâtre de Paul Claudel* (Paris: Beauchesne, 1964);

Marianne Mercier-Campiche, *Le Théâtre de Claudel: ou la Puissance du grief et de la passion* (Paris: Pauvert, 1968);

Jacques Petit, *Le Premier Drame de Claudel: Une Mort prematurée* (Paris: Belles Lettres, 1970);

Petit and Jean-Pierre Kemp, *Claudel on the Theatre* (Coral Gables, Fla.: University of Miami Press, 1972);

Henri Peyre, "Le Classicisme de Paul Claudel," *Nouvelle Revue française* (1 September 1932): 432–441;

Georges Poulet, "Oeuf, semence, bouche ouverte, zéro," *Nouvelle Revue Française,* special Claudel issue: *Hommage à Paul Claudel* (1 September 1955): 445–466;

Jean Rousset, "La Structure du drame claudélien: l'écran et le face à face," in *Forme et signification* (Paris: Corti, 1964), pp. 171–189;

Joseph Samson, *Paul Claudel poète-musicien* (Geneva & Paris: Milieu du Monde, 1947);

Marie-Louise Tricaud, *Le Baroque dans le théâtre de Paul Claudel,* Histoire des idées et critique littéraire (Geneva: Droz, 1967);

André Vachon, *Le Temps et l'espace dans l'oeuvre de Paul Claudel: Expérience chrétienne et imagination poétique* (Paris: Seuil, 1965);

François Varillon, *Claudel,* Les Ecrivains devant Dieu, no. 14 (Paris: Desclée de Brouwer, 1967);

Harold A. Waters, *Paul Claudel,* Twayne's World Authors Series, no. 92 (New York: Twayne, 1970);

Harold Watson, *Claudel's Immortal Heroes: A Choice of Deaths* (New Brunswick, N.J.: Rutgers University Press, 1971).

Papers:

Some of Paul Claudel's letters and manuscripts, including the manuscript for *L'Annonce faite à Marie,* are held by the Bibliothèque nationale, Paris; Claudel's letters and postcards to Audrey Parr are on deposit as Add. MS 9591, Cambridge University Library.

Jean Cocteau

(5 July 1889 – 11 October 1963)

Drew Jones
Queens College, The City University of New York

See also the Cocteau entries in *DLB 65: French Novelists, 1900–1930* and *DLB 258: Modern French Poets.*

PLAY PRODUCTIONS: *Le Dieu bleu,* ballet, scenario by Cocteau and Frédéric de Madrazo, music by Reynaldo Hahn, Paris, Théâtre du Châtelet, June 1912;

Parade, ballet, scenario by Cocteau, music by Erik Satie, Paris, Théâtre du Châtelet, 18 May 1917;

Le Boeuf sur le toit, ou The Nothing Doing Bar, farce, scenario by Cocteau, music by Darius Milhaud, Paris, Théâtre des Champs-Elysées, 21 February 1920;

Les Mariés de la Tour Eiffel, music by Germaine Tailleferre, Georges Auric, Arthur Honegger, Milhaud, and Francis Poulenc, Paris, Théâtre des Champs-Elysées, 18 June 1921;

Antigone, adapted from Sophocles' play, music by Honegger, Paris, Théâtre de l'Atelier, 20 December 1922;

Roméo et Juliette, adapted from William Shakespeare's *Romeo and Juliet,* Paris, Théâtre de la Cigale, 2 June 1924;

Le Train bleu, ballet, scenario by Cocteau, music by Milhaud, Paris, Théâtre des Champs-Elysées, 20 June 1924;

Orphée, Paris, Théâtre des Arts, 17 June 1926;

Œdipus Rex, opera-oratorio, libretto adapted by Cocteau from Sophocles' play, music by Igor Stravinsky, Paris, Théâtre Sarah-Bernhardt, 30 May 1927;

La Voix humaine, Paris, Comédie-Française, 17 February 1930;

La Machine infernale, Paris, Comédie des Champs-Elysées, 10 April 1934;

Œdipe-roi, adapted by Cocteau from Sophocles' play, Paris, Nouveau Théâtre Antoine, June 1937;

Les Chevaliers de la Table Ronde, Paris, Théâtre de l'Oeuvre, 14 October 1937;

Les Parents terribles, Paris, Théâtre des Ambassadeurs, 14 November 1938;

Jean Cocteau (photograph by Arnold Newman/© Getty Images)

Les Monstres sacrés, Paris, Théâtre Michel, 17 February 1940;

Le Bel indifférent, Paris, Théâtre des Bouffes-Parisiens, 1940;

La Machine à écrire, Paris, Théâtre Hébertot, 29 April 1941;

Rénaud et Armide, Paris, Comédie-Française, 13 April 1943;

Le Jeune homme et la mort, ballet, scenario by Cocteau, music by J. S. Bach, Paris, Théâtre des Champs-Elysées, 25 June 1946;

L'Aigle à deux têtes, Paris, Théâtre Hébertot, November 1946;

Un Tramway nommé Désir, adapted from Tennessee Williams's *A Streetcar Named Desire,* Paris, Théâtre Edouard VII, 17 October 1949;

Bacchus, Paris, Théâtre Marigny, Paris, 20 December 1951;

La Dame à la Licorne, ballet, libretto by Cocteau, music by Jacques Chailley, Munich, Theaters am Gartnerplatz, 9 May 1953;

L'Impromptu du Palais-Royal, Tokyo, 1 May 1962.

BOOKS: *La Lampe d'Aladin: Poèmes* (Paris: Société des Editions, 1909);

Le Prince frivole (Paris: Mercure de France, 1910);

La Danse de Sophocle: Poèmes (Paris: Mercure de France, 1912);

Dans le ciel de la patrie (Paris: Société Spad, 1918);

Le Coq et L'arlequin: Notes autour de la musique, Collection des tractes, no. 1 (Paris: La Sirène, 1918); translated by Rollo H. Myers as *Cock and Harlequin: Notes Concerning Music* (London: Egoist Press, 1921);

Le Cap de Bonne-Espérance: Poème (Paris: La Sirène, 1919);

L'Ode à Picasso: Poème 1917 (Paris: A La Belle Edition, 1919);

Le Potomak, 1913-1914: Précédé d'un Prospectus, 1916, et suivi des Eugènes de la guerre, 1915 (Paris: Société Littéraire de France, 1919; revised edition, Paris: Stock, 1924);

Carte Blanche: Articles parus dans "Paris-Midi" du 31 mars au 11 août 1919 (Paris: La Sirène, 1920); expanded as *Carte Blanche: Orné de dessins, aquarelles, photographies* (Lausanne, Switzerland: Mermod, 1953);

Escales, by Cocteau and André Lhote (Paris: La Sirène, 1920);

Poésies, 1917-1920 (Paris: La Sirène, 1920);

La Noce massacrée (Souvenirs): 1. Visites à Maurice Barrès (Paris: La Sirène, 1921);

Le Secret professionnel (Paris: Stock, 1922); enlarged as *Le Secret professionnel, suivi des Monologues de l'Oiseleur* (Paris: Au Sans Pareil, 1925); translated by Margaret Crosland as "Professional secrets," in her *Cocteau's World: An Anthology of Writings by Jean Cocteau* (London: Owen, 1972; New York: Dodd, Mead, 1973), pp. 341-382;

Vocabulaire: Poèmes (Paris: La Sirène, 1922);

Dessins (Paris: Stock, 1923);

Le Grand Ecart (Paris: Stock, 1923); translated by Lewis Galantière as *The Grand Ecart* (New York & London: Putnam, 1925);

Les Mariés de la Tour Eiffel (Paris: Nouvelle Revue Française, 1923); translated by Dudley Fitts as *The Eiffel Tower Wedding Party,* in *The Infernal Machine and Other Plays* (Norfolk, Conn.: New Directions, 1963), pp. 151-178;

Picasso (Paris: Stock, 1923);

Plein-chant: Poème (Paris: Stock, 1923);

La Rose de François: Poème inédit, Collection Alter Ego, no. 5 (Paris: A la Belle Edition, 1923);

Thomas l'Imposteur (Paris: Nouvelle Revue Française, 1923); translated by Galantière as *Thomas the Imposter* (New York & London: Appleton, 1925);

Férat (Paris: Crès, 1924);

Poésie 1916-1923 (Paris: Nouvelle Revue Française, 1924);

Cri écrit (Montpellier: Montane, 1925);

Le Mystère de Jean l'Oiseleur: Monologues, 1924 (Paris: Champion, 1925);

Prière mutilée, Collection de l'horloge: Une heure, un poète, no. 1 (Paris: Cahiers Libres, 1925);

L'Ange Heurtebise: Poème (Paris: Stock, 1926);

Lettre à Jacques Maritain (Paris: Stock, 1926);

Maison de Santé (Paris: Briant-Robert, 1926);

Le Rappel a l'ordre: Le Coq et l'Arlequin; Carte Blanche; Visites à Maurice Barrès; Le Secret professionnel; D'un ordre considéré comme une anarchie; Autour de l'imposteur; Picasso (Paris: Stock, 1926); translated by Myers as *A Call to Order: Written Between the Years 1918 and 1926 and Including "Cock and Harlequin," "Professional Secrets," and Other Critical Essays* (London: Faber & Gwyer, 1926; New York: Holt, 1926);

Roméo et Juliette: Prétexte à mise en scène par Jean Cocteau d'après le drame de William Shakespeare (Paris: Au Sans Pareil, 1926);

Opéra, oeuvres poétiques 1925-1927 (Paris: Stock, 1927);

Orphée: Tragédie en un acte et un intervalle (Paris: Stock, 1927); translated by Carl Wildman as *Orphée: A Tragedy in One Act and an Interval* (London: Oxford University Press, 1933);

Le Pauvre Matelot: Complainte en trois actes, with music by Darius Milhaud (Paris: Heugel, 1927);

Le Livre blanc, anonymous (Paris: Sachs & Bonjean, 1928); enlarged edition, with a preface and illustrations by Cocteau (Paris: Signe, 1930); enlarged again as *Le Livre blanc, suivi de quatorze textes érotiques inédits* (Paris: Persona, 1981); first enlarged edition translated as *The White Paper* (Paris: Olympia, 1957; New York: Macaulay, 1958);

Le Mystère laïc–Giorgio de Chirico: Essai d'étude indirecte (Paris: Quatre Chemins, 1928); enlarged as *Essai de critique indirecte: Le Mystère laïc–Des Beaux-arts considérés comme un assassinat,* introduction by Bernard Grasset (Paris: Grasset, 1932);

Œdipe-roi; Roméo et Juliette (Paris: Plon, 1928);

25 Dessins d'un dormeur (Lausanne, Switzerland & Geneva: Mermod, 1928);

Antigone; Les Mariés de la Tour Eiffel (Paris: Gallimard, 1928); *Antigone* translated by Carl Wildman, in

Four Plays (London: MacGibbon & Kee, 1962), pp. 9–30;

Les Enfants terribles (Paris: Grasset, 1929); translated by Samuel Putnam as *Enfants Terribles* (New York: Brewer & Warren, 1930);

Carnet de l'amiral (Paris: Grasset, 1930);

Opium: Journal d'une désintoxication (Paris: Stock, 1930); translated by Ernest Boyd as *Opium: The Diary of an Addict* (London & New York: Longmans, 1932);

La Voix humaine: Pièce en un acte (Paris: Stock, 1930); translated by Wildman as *The Human Voice* (London: Vision, 1951);

La Machine infernale: Pièce en 4 actes (Paris: Grasset, 1934); translated by Wildman as *The Infernal Machine: A Play in Four Acts* (London: Oxford University Press, 1936);

Mythologie (Paris: Quatre Chemins, 1934);

Soixante dessins pour "Les Enfants Terribles" (Paris: Grasset, 1934 [i.e., 1935]);

Portraits-Souvenir, 1900–1914 (Paris: Grasset, 1935); translated by Crosland as *Paris Album, 1900–1914* (London: W. H. Allen, 1956);

Le Fantôme de Marseille (Paris: Gallimard, 1936);

Les Chevaliers de la Table Ronde: Pièce en trois actes (Paris: Gallimard, 1937); translated by W. H. Auden as *The Knights of the Round Table*, in *The Infernal Machine and Other Plays* (New York: New Directions, 1963), pp. 179–292;

Mon Premier Voyage (Tour du monde en 80 jours) (Paris: Gallimard, 1937); translated by Stuart Gilbert as *Round the World Again in Eighty Days* (London: Routledge, 1937);

Les Parents terribles: Pièce en trois actes (Paris: Gallimard, 1938); translated by Charles Frank as *Intimate Relations*, in *Four Plays* (London: MacGibbon & Kee, 1962), pp. 31–120;

Enigme: Poème (Paris: Réverbères, 1939);

La Fin du Potomak (Paris: Gallimard, 1940);

Les Monstres sacrés: Portrait d'une pièce en trois actes (Paris: Gallimard, 1940); translated by Edward O. Marsh as *The Holy Terrors*, in *Four Plays* (London: MacGibbon & Kee, 1962), pp. 121–196;

Allégories (Paris: Gallimard, 1941);

Desseins en marge des Chevaliers de la Table Ronde (Paris: Gallimard, 1941);

La Machine à écrire: Pièce en trois actes (Paris: Gallimard, 1941); translated by Ronald Duncan as *The Typewriter: A Play in Three Acts* (London: Dobson, 1947);

Le Gréco (Paris: Au Divan, 1943);

Rénaud et Armide: Tragédie (Paris: Gallimard, 1943);

Serge Lifar à l'Opéra, by Cocteau and Paul Valéry (Paris: Champrosay, 1944);

Poèmes écrits en allemand (The Hague: H. van Krimpen, 1944);

Léone (Paris: Gallimard, 1945); translated by Alan Neame as "Leoun," *Agenda,* 2, nos. 1–2 (1961);

Portrait de Mounet-Sully: Prose inédite, illustrated by Cocteau (Paris: Bernouard, 1945);

L'Aigle à deux têtes: Trois actes (Paris: Gallimard, 1946); translated by Duncan as *The Eagle Has Two Heads* (London: Vision, 1948; New York: Funk & Wagnalls, 1948);

La Belle et la Bête, Journal d'un film (Paris: Janin, 1946); translated by Duncan as *Diary of a Film (La Belle et la Bête)* (London: Dobson, 1950; New York: Roy, 1950);

La Crucifixion: Poème (Paris: Morihien, 1947); translated by Jack Hirschman as *The Crucifixion* (Bethlehem, Pa.: Quarter, 1976);

Deux Travestis, illustrated by Cocteau (Paris: Fournier, 1947)–comprises *Le Fantôme de Marseille* and *Le Numéro Barbette;*

La Difficulté d'être (Paris: Morihien, 1947); translated by Elizabeth Sprigge as *The Difficulty of Being* (London: Owen, 1966; New York: Coward-McCann, 1967);

L'Eternel retour (Paris: Nouvelles Editions Française, 1947);

Le Foyer des artistes (Paris: Plon, 1947);

Ruy Blas: Adapté pour l'écran par Jean Cocteau (Paris: Morihien, 1947);

Drôle de menage: Textes et dessins (Paris: Morihien, 1948);

Poèmes: Jean Cocteau (Paris: Gallimard, 1948)–comprises *Léone, Allégories, La Crucifixion,* "Neiges," and "Un ami dort";

Le Sang d'un poète, film (Paris: Marin, 1948); translated by Lily Pons as *The Blood of a Poet: A Film* (New York: Bodley, 1949);

Reines de la France (Paris: Darantière, 1949);

Dufy (Paris: Flammarion, 1949);

Lettre aux Américains (Paris: Grasset, 1949);

Maalesh: Journal d'une tournée de théâtre (Paris: Gallimard, 1949); translated by Mary C. Hoeck as *Maalesh: A Theatrical Tour in the Middle-East* (London: Owen, 1956; Westport, Conn.: Greenwood Press, 1978);

Théâtre de Poche (Paris: Morihien, 1949); enlarged as *Nouveau Theatre de Poche* (Monaco: Rocher, 1960);

Modigliani (Paris: Hazan, 1950);

Orson Welles, by Cocteau and André Bazin (Paris: Chavane, 1950);

Orphée: Film (Paris: La Parade, 1950);

Jean Marais (Paris: Calmann-Lévy, 1951);

Bacchus: Pièce en trois actes (Paris: Gallimard, 1952); translated by Hoeck, in *The Infernal Machine and Other*

Plays (New York: New Directions, 1963), pp. 293–404;

Le Chiffre sept (Paris: Seghers, 1952);

Gide vivant: Paroles de Jean Cocteau, edited by Jean-Claude Colin-Simard (Paris: Amiot-Dumont, 1952);

Journal d'un inconnu (Paris: Grasset, 1952); translated by Alec Brown as *The Hand of a Stranger* (London: Elek, 1956; New York: Horizon, 1959);

La Nappe du Catalan: Soixante-quatre poèmes et seize lithographies en couleurs, by Cocteau and Georges Hugnet (Paris: Fequet & Baudier, 1952);

Appogiatures (Monaco: Rocher, 1953);

Démarche d'un poète / Der Lebensweg eines Dichters, bilingual edition, translated into German by Friedhelm Kemp (Munich: Bruckmann, 1953);

Dentelle d'éternité (Paris: Seghers, 1953);

Clair-Obscur: Poèmes (Monaco: Rocher, 1954);

Colette: Discours de réception à L'Académie Royale de langue et de littérature française (Paris: Grasset, 1955);

Discours de réception à L'Académie Française et Réponse d'André Maurois (Paris: Gallimard, 1955);

Le Dragon des mers (Paris: Guillot, 1955);

Adieu à Mistinguett (Liège, Belgium: Dynamo, 1956);

Le Discours de Strasbourg (Metz: SMEI, 1956);

Le Discours d'Oxford, edited by Jean Seznec (Paris: Gallimard, 1956); translated by Jean Stewart as "Poetry and Invisibility," *London Magazine* (January 1957);

Témoignage (Fleurs-de-l'Orne, France: Bertrand, 1956);

La Chapelle Saint-Pierre, Villefranche-sur-Mer (Monaco: Rocher, 1957);

La Corrida du Premier Mai (Paris: Grasset, 1957);

Erik Satie (Liège, Belgium: Dynamo, 1957);

Paraprosodies, précédées de 7 dialogues (Monaco: Rocher, 1958);

La Salle des mariages, Hôtel de Ville de Menton (Monaco: Rocher, 1958);

La Canne blanche (Paris: Estienne, 1959);

Gondole des morts (Milan: Pesce d'oro, 1959);

Guide à l'usage des visiteurs de la chapelle Saint Blaise-des-Simples (Monaco: Rocher, 1960);

Le Testament d'Orphée, Brimborions, no. 71 (Liège, Belgium: Dynamo, 1960);

Notes sur "Le Testament d'Orphée" (Liège, Belgium: Dynamo, 1960);

Cérémonial espagnol du Phénix, suivi de La Partie d'échecs (Paris: Gallimard, 1961); translated by Margaret Crosland as *The Palais Royal Impromtu,* in *Cocteau's World: An Anthology of Writing by Jean Cocteau* (London: Owen, 1972; New York: Dodd, Mead, 1973), pp. 180–204;

Le Cordon ombilical: Souvenirs (Paris: Plon, 1962);

Discours à l'Académie royale de langue et de littérature françaises, Brimborions, no. 99 (Liège, Belgium: Dynamo, 1962);

L'Impromptu du Palais-Royal: Divertissement (Paris: Gallimard, 1962);

Picasso de 1916 à 1961 (Monaco: Rocher, 1962);

Le Requiem (Paris: Gallimard, 1962);

La Comtesse de Noailles: Oui et non (Paris: Perrin, 1963);

Entre Picasso et Radiguet, edited by André Fermigier (Paris: Hermann, 1967);

Faire-Part, edited by Pierre Chanel, preface by Claude Michel Cluny (Paris: Chambelland, 1968);

La Belle et la Bête / Beauty and the Beast, bilingual edition of the script, edited by Robert M. Hammond (New York: New York University Press, 1970);

Du Cinématographe, edited by André Bernard and Claude Gauteur (Paris: Belfond, 1973); translated by Robin Buss as *The Art of Cinema,* introduction by Buss (London: Boyars, 1992);

Paul et Virginie, by Cocteau and Raymond Radiguet (Paris: Edition Spéciale, 1973);

Le Portrait surnaturel de Dorien Gray: pièce fantastique en quatre actes et 5 tableaux, adapted from Oscar Wilde's *The Picture of Dorian Gray* (Paris: Orban, 1978);

Mes monstres sacrés: Jean Cocteau, edited by Edouard Dermithe and Bertrand Meyer, introduction by Milorad (Paris: Encre, 1979);

Tapisseries d'Aubusson (Aubusson: Société d'édition pour la Tapisserie d'Aubusson, 1983);

Le Mystère de Jean l'Oiseleur, edited by Milorad (Paris: Persona, 1983);

Le Passé défini: Journal, 3 volumes, edited by Pierre Chanel (Paris: Gallimard, 1983–1989); volumes 1 and 2 translated by Richard Howard as *Past Tense: Diaries,* introduction by Ned Rorem (San Diego & New York: Harcourt Brace Jovanovich, 1987; volume 1, London: Hamilton, 1987; volume 2, London: Methuen, 1990);

Jean Marais: Textes inédits de Jean Cocteau (Paris: SPAG, 1984);

Embarcadères: Poèmes inedits, edited by Pierre Caizergues (Fontfroide: Fata Morgana, 1986);

Journal: 1942–1945, edited by Jean Touzot (Paris: Gallimard, 1989);

Une Encre de lumière: Textes retrouvés et textes inédits, edited by François-Amy de la Bretèque and Caizergues (Montpellier: Centre d'études littéraires du XXe, 1989).

Editions and Collections: *Morceaux choisis: Poèmes* (Paris: Gallimard, 1932);

Poésie critique, edited by Henri Parisot (Paris: Quatre Vents, 1945 [i.e., 1946]); republished, 2 volumes (Paris: Gallimard, 1959, 1960)–comprises volume 1, *Poésie critique* (1959); and volume 2, *Monologues* (1960);

Oeuvres complètes de Jean Cocteau, 11 volumes (Lausanne, Switzerland: Marguerat, 1947–1951);

Théâtre, 2 volumes (Paris: Gallimard, 1948);

Poèmes, 1916–1955 (Paris: Gallimard, 1956);

Théâtre (Paris: Grasset, 1957);

Poésie de journalisme, 1935–1938, edited by Pierre Chanel (Paris: Belfond, 1973);

Orphée: The Play and the Film, edited, with an introduction and notes in English, by Edward Freeman (Oxford: Blackwell, 1976);

Le Mystère de Jean l'Oiseleur, edited by Milorad (Paris: Persona, 1983);

La Machine infernale: Pièce en 4 actes, edited, with an introduction, by Gérard Lieber (Paris: Librairie Générale Française, 1992);

Carnet de l'amiral X, edited, with an introduction, by Pierre Caizergues (Saint-Clément-de-Rivière: Fata Morgana, 1997);

La Machine infernale, edited by Thanh-Vân Ton-That (Paris: Larousse-Bordas, 1998);

Le Livre blanc et autres textes, edited, with an introduction, by Bernard Benech, preface by Dominique Fernandez (Paris: Librairie Générale Française, 1999);

Oeuvres poétiques complètes, edited by Michel Décaudin and others (Paris: Gallimard, 1999);

Le Potomak: 1913–1914; précédé d'un Prospectus 1916, preface by Serge Linares (Paris: Passage du Marais, 2000);

28 autoportraits: écrits et dessinés, textes et entretiens (1928–1963), edited by Caizergues (Paris: Ecriture, 2003)–includes *Cocteau par Cocteau: Entretiens avec Pierre Brive, juillet-août 1962*, supplementary CD, L'Archipel, 2003;

Théâtre complet, edited by Décaudin and others (Paris: Gallimard, 2003).

Editions in English: *Children of the Game*, translated by Rosamund Lehmann (London: Harvill, 1955); republished as *Les Enfants Terribles* (London: Harvill, 1955); republished again as *The Holy Terrors* (New York: New Directions, 1957);

The Journals of Jean Cocteau, edited and translated by Wallace Fowlie (New York: Criterion, 1956);

The Imposter, translated by Dorothy Williams (London: Owen, 1957; New York: Citadel, 1960);

Opium: The Diary of a Cure, translated by Margaret Crosland and Sinclair Road (London: Owen, 1957; New York: Grove, 1958); republished, with a new introduction by Crosland, as *Opium: The Illustrated Diary of His Cure* (London: Owen / Chester Springs, Pa.: Dufour, 1990);

The Miscreant, translated by Williams (London: Owen, 1958); republished, with an introduction by Serena Thirkell (London: Brilliance Books, 1986);

My Journey Round the World, translated by W. J. Strachan (London: Owen, 1958);

Five Plays: Jean Cocteau (New York: Hill & Wang, 1961)–comprises *Orphée*, translated by Carl Wildman; *Antigone*, translated by Wildman; *Intimate Relations (Les Parents terribles)*, translated by Charles Frank; *The Holy Terrors (Les Monstres sacrés)*, translated by Edward O. Marsh; and *The Eagle with Two Heads (L'Aigle à deux têtes)*, translated by Wildman; abridged as *Four Plays: Jean Cocteau* (London: MacGibbon & Kee, 1962)–comprises *Antigone; Intimate Relations; The Holy Terrors;* and *The Eagle with Two Heads;*

Orpheus; Oedipus Rex; The Infernal Machine: Jean Cocteau, translated by Wildman (London & New York: Oxford University Press, 1962);

The Infernal Machine and Other Plays (New York: New Directions, 1963)–comprises *The Infernal Machine*, translated by Albert Bermel; *Orpheus*, translated by John Savacool; *The Eiffel Tower Wedding Party*, translated by Dudley Fitts; *The Knights of the Round Table*, translated by W. H. Auden; and *Bacchus*, translated by Mary C. Hoeck;

The Wedding on the Eiffel Tower, translated by Michael Benedikt, in *Modern French Plays*, edited by Benedikt and George Wellwarth (London: Faber & Faber, 1965);

My Contemporaries, edited and translated, with an introduction, by Crosland (London: Owen, 1967; Philadelphia: Chilton, 1968);

Two Screenplays: The Blood of a Poet; The Testament of Orpheus, translated by Carol Martin-Sperry (New York: Orion, 1968; London: Calder & Boyars, 1970);

Le Livre blanc, translated, with an introduction, by Crosland (London: Owen, 1969);

Professional Secrets: An Autobiography of Jean Cocteau Drawn from His Lifetime Writings, edited by Roger Phelps, translated by Richard Howard (New York: Farrar, Straus & Giroux, 1970; London: Vision, 1972);

Beauty and the Beast: Diary of a Film, translated by Ronald Duncan, introduction by George Amberg (New York: Dover, 1972);

Three Screenplays: L'Eternel Retour, Orphée, La Belle et la Bête, translated by Martin-Sperry (New York: Grossman, 1972);

Cocteau's World: An Anthology of Writings by Jean Cocteau, edited and translated by Crosland (London: Owen, 1972; New York: Dodd, Mead, 1973);

Souvenir Portraits: Paris in the Belle Epoque, translated by Jesse Browner (New York: Paragon House, 1990; London: Robson, 1991);

Tempest of Stars: Selected Poems, bilingual edition, translated by Jeremy Reed (London: Enitharmon, 1992);

Les Parents Terribles, translated by Jeremy Sams, introduction by Simon Callow (London: Hern, 1994);

Thirteen Monologues, by Cocteau and Georges Feydeau, translated by Peter Meyer (London: Oberon, 1996);

Round the World Again in 80 Days, translated by Stuart Gilbert, introduction by Callow (London: Tauris Parke, 2000).

PRODUCED SCRIPTS: *Le Sang d'un poète,* motion picture, Vicomte de Noailles, 1932; released with English subtitles as *The Blood of a Poet,* Edward T. Ricci, 1933;

Ecco la felicità, motion picture, adapted from Nicolas Evreinoff by Cocteau, Andre Cerf, and Marcel L'Herbier, Scalera Film S.P.A./DisCina, 1940; released in France as *La Comédie du bonheur,* 1942;

L'Eternel Retour, motion picture, Films André Paulvé, 1943; subtitled version released in the United States as *The Eternal Return,* DisCina, 1948; subtitled version released in the United Kingdom as *Love Eternal,* n.d.;

Le Baron fantôme, motion picture, by Louis Chavance and Serge de Poligny, with additional dialogue by Cocteau, Consortium de Productions de Films, 1943; released with English subtitles as *The Phantom Baron,* n.d.;

Les Dames du Bois de Boulogne, motion picture, adapted by Robert Bresson from Denis Diderot's novel *Jacques le Fataliste et son maître,* with additional dialogue by Cocteau, Les Films Raoul Ploquin, 1945; subtitled version released in the United States as *The Ladies of the Bois de Boulogne,* Brandon Films, 1964; subtitled version released elsewhere as *The Ladies of the Park,* n.d.;

La Belle et la Bête, motion picture, Films André Paulvé, 1946; released with English subtitles as *Beauty and the Beast,* Lopert, 1948;

L'Aigle à deux têtes, motion picture, Les Films Vog, 1947; released with English subtitles as *The Eagle Has Two Heads,* 1948;

Ruy Blas, motion picture, adapted by Cocteau from Victor Hugo, Pierre Billon, 1947; released with English subtitles as *Ruy Blas,* DisCina, 1948;

Les Parents terribles, motion picture, Films Ariane, 1948; released with English subtitles as *The Storm Within,* DisCina, 1950;

Ce siècle a cinquante ans, motion picture, by Cocteau, Marcel Achard, Françoise Giroud, and Andre Roussin, SEPIC/UGC Images, 1949; dubbed in English and released in the United States as *Days of Our Years,* Souvaine Selective Pictures, 1951;

Orphée, motion picture, Films André Paulvé/Films du Palais Royal, 1950; released with English subtitles as *Orpheus,* DisCina, 1950;

Les Enfants terribles, motion picture, adapted from the Cocteau novel by Cocteau and Jean-Pierre Melville, Melville Productions, 1950; released with English subtitles as *The Strange Ones,* Arthur Mayer-Edward Kingsley, 1952;

La Corona negra, motion picture, adapted from a Cocteau story by Cocteau, Luis Saslavsky, and Charles de Peyret-Chappuis, Spanish dialogue by Miguel Mihura, Suevia Films S.A., 1951; French version released as *La Couronne noire,* n.d.; English version released as *Black Crown,* n.d.;

Le Bel indifférent, short motion picture, 1957;

Le Testament d'Orphée, motion picture, Editions Cinégraphiques, 1960; released with English subtitles as *The Testament of Orpheus,* Films Around the World, 1962;

Princesse de Clèves, motion picture, adapted from Marie-Madeleine de La Fayette's novel by Cocteau and Jean Delannoy, Enalpa Film/Produzioni Cinematografiche Mediterranee/Silver Films, 1960; in English as *Princess of Cleves,* n.d.;

Thomas l'imposteur, motion picture, adapted from Cocteau's novel by Cocteau, Georges Franju, and Michel Worms, Filmel, 1964.

OTHER: Jean Desbordes, *J'adore,* preface by Cocteau (Paris: Grasset, 1928);

Tennessee Williams, *Un Tramway nommé Désir,* translated by Paule de Beaument, adapted by Cocteau (Paris: Bordas, 1949).

Novels, poetry, lyrics, painting, movies, plays, and acting were all among Jean Cocteau's artistic pursuits. Cocteau was also a conversationalist, dandy, and outspoken public personality, and he considered these elements of his life to be artistic expressions as well. Consequently, while his critics claimed his art suffered from inordinate attention to his public persona, Cocteau believed his art and his life were inextricably bound. Like Oscar Wilde, Cocteau championed style in matters of great importance, and this emphasis affected many writers who developed their voices in his wake.

Cocteau's attention to style served him well in all areas of artistic production, but most notably in the theater. In a career as a dramatist that spanned forty years, Cocteau wrote plays set in such disparate locales as

Two scenes from the 1921 Paris production of Les Mariés de la Tour Eiffel *(Wedding on the Eiffel Tower) (courtesy of Cocteau; from Dominique Païni, François Nemer, and Valérie Loth, eds.,* Jean Cocteau, sur le fil du siècle, *2004; Richland County Public Library)*

ancient Greece, King Arthur's court, and contemporary Paris. Throughout his drama there is an emphasis on the status of the play as an event rather than as a text. Cocteau was a contemporary of Antonin Artaud, who played the role of Tirésias in the first production of Cocteau's *Antigone* (performed 1922, published 1928, translated 1961). In the 1920s and 1930s Cocteau was experimenting in the ways that Artaud later proposed in his essay *Le Théâtre et son double* (1938; translated as *the Theater and Its Double,* 1958). In the theater, as in most of his artistic endeavors, Cocteau was part of the avant-garde, producing works that were fresh and contemporary. Yet, after an initial period of dramatic rule breaking that is important to theater history, Cocteau began writing plays that conformed more closely to the standards established by traditional French dramaturgy. This change of approach may have made his later plays more palatable to the audiences of his day, but they were not truly innovative, and most are no longer performed.

Jean Cocteau was born at Maisons-Lafitte, outside Paris, on 5 July 1889, to Georges and Eugénie Cocteau. Cocteau was born into the easy existence of the bourgeois capitalists of the early Third Republic: he was supported by family wealth through his youth and into his early forties. The Cocteaus' country house was in Maisons-Laffite; they also maintained a Parisian apartment in the rue La Bruyère.

Although his family was financially comfortable, Cocteau's youth was not trouble free: when he was only ten years old, his father took his own life. Little is known about this event, and Cocteau did not speak much of his youth, or his family, including his mother, his sister Marthe, and his brother Paul. Biographers have speculated that the more macabre elements of Cocteau's work are related to the trauma of his father's suicide.

Beyond this event, Cocteau's youth was largely unexceptional. He attended the Lycée Condorcet in Paris, where he developed erotic fantasies about his friends. Cocteau recounts the eroticism that the lycée held for him in a memoir titled *Le Livre blanc* (1928; translated as *The White Paper,* 1957). Though the book was unsigned, the text was accompanied by fluid line drawings that were unmistakably Cocteau's. In this book he describes the character of Dargelos for the first time. This type of character later resurfaced in what is widely regarded as Cocteau's supreme achievement in the novel genre, *Les Enfants terribles* (1929; translated as *Enfants Terribles,* 1930), as well as in the movie *Le Sang d'un poète* (1932; script published 1948; script translated as *Blood of a Poet,* 1949). The Dargelos type has become a stock character in gay male literature: the rough-and-tumble classmate or peer whose virility attracts a narrator character. *Les Enfants terribles* gained Cocteau renown for capturing the zeitgeist of a generation of disaffected youth. He later adapted this novel for a movie production in 1950.

Cocteau was attracted to the theater at a young age. He remembered the spectacle of his mother dressing for the theater and later returning to recount to him the adventures of the evening. He read the programs that she brought home, and played with toy theaters, creating scenery and imagining the action on stage. He also staged productions with his siblings in the garden at Maisons-Lafitte. During high school, Cocteau devoted more energy to attending theater matinees than to his studies. He failed the baccalaureate examination three times before abandoning his studies.

Cocteau's *entrée en scène* (entrance on the scene) in Paris literary society occurred at the age of nineteen at the Théâtre Fémina on the Champs Elysées. The occasion was not a play, but an afternoon poetry recital arranged by the actor Edouard de Max. De Max was one of the most famous actors of his time, belonging to the permanent troupe of the Comédie-Française. Like many of Cocteau's other acquaintances (among whom were Marcel Proust, André Gide, Sergey Diaghilev, Gertrude Stein, and Reynaldo Hahn), de Max belonged to the demimonde of gays and lesbians that flourished in the shadows of Parisian society during the early decades of the twentieth century. Although the recital of April 1908 was successful and drew attention to Cocteau, he later referred to his early poetry as unworthy of being revisited. Cocteau refused later in life to see the verses he wrote for his first three volumes reproduced in his complete works, preferring to begin with *Le Potomak* (1919, The Potomac; revised 1924), an unusual hybrid work written in 1914 but not published until after World War I.

The most important result of Cocteau's poetry debut was that it added to his growing circle of connections. His acquaintance with Gide earned him an early, although unfavorable, review in the *Nouvelle Revue Française,* the most important literary magazine of the day. Such articles kept Cocteau's name circulating: a model for celebrity in the twentieth century, he is a member of the group of artists who grew to increasing fame in part because of negative publicity. Though Cocteau was hurt by criticism, which often came from those he considered friends, he was a master at manipulating his public reputation and ensuring that even negative criticism contributed to his fame.

As he began to establish himself on the literary scene, Cocteau became friends with the poet Anna de Noailles and collaborated with Maurice Rostand, son of

Cover for the video of Cocteau's 1946 movie La Belle et la Bête, *a commercial and critical success (© Lopert Films, Inc.; Richland County Public Library)*

Edmond, on a literary review titled *Shéhérazade*. This review was published out of Cocteau's *garçonnière* (bachelor flat) in the Hôtel Brion, an artists' compound whose famous residents included Rainer Maria Rilke and Auguste Rodin. Eventually, this building was occupied solely by the sculptor and has become the permanent home of the Musée Rodin (Rodin Museum).

Perhaps the most valuable connection that Cocteau established during this time was with the Ballets Russes. He ingratiated himself into the troupe and obtained a *carte de circulation* (circulation card), which allowed him to witness the creation of their spectacles from backstage. The Ballets Russes was a creation of Diaghilev and performed a "season" each year in Paris beginning in 1909. The troupe helped resuscitate ballet in France, which had been stagnant for several decades. A favorite composer for the troupe was Igor Stravinsky. The most revolutionary ballet performed in France at that time was the *Rite of Spring,* a collaboration between Stravinsky and Diaghilev; on its premiere in 1913 the audience rioted, objecting to the unusual choreography and music.

Cocteau owed much to the Ballets Russes in his formation as an artist. It was with them that he began his life in the plastic arts by painting, creating sets, and designing publicity posters for the company. In 1912 he created his first ballet scenario for the company, *Le Dieu Bleu.* It was not a great success, but it helped prepare Cocteau for his breakthrough theater work, *Parade,* five years later. During his association with the Ballet Russes, Cocteau had his first artistic epiphany when Diaghilev commanded him, "Etonne-moi" (Surprise me). Cocteau said repeatedly during his life that it was from this moment on that he began to think seriously about his art, about what it could do, and about the effects that he could have in shaping perceptions of art, rather than simply following fashion.

World War I left a deep impression on Cocteau. Although he had been exempted from obligatory military service because of family connections, Cocteau volunteered to participate in a Red Cross ambulance corps at the front. A friend had commandeered delivery vans from Parisian fashion houses to serve as ambulances for the wounded, and couturier Paul Poiret designed a special outfit for Cocteau to wear. Later, at elegant Parisian luncheons, Cocteau enjoyed recounting his adventures at the front lines. Although this treatment of the war as spectacle offended Gide, who described Cocteau's behavior in his journal, Cocteau later reflected on the atrocities of the war in his novel *Thomas l'Imposteur* (1923; translated as *Thomas the Imposter,* 1925).

During this time Cocteau befriended famed aviator Roland Garros and accompanied him on several test flights. Garros flew many successful missions before being shot down and killed by the German army late in the war. This friendship inspired Cocteau's first widely acclaimed book of poems, *Le Cap de Bonne-Espérance* (1919, Cape of Good Hope), which appeared, like *Le Potomak,* just after the war.

Although the dissemination of many of Cocteau's artistic productions during this period were delayed until after the war, his first important artistic statement came during the conflict. In 1917 the controversial ballet *Parade* appeared on stage in Paris. Cocteau's role in this production has been the subject of debate. For example, according to Francis Steegmuller, Gide said of Cocteau's participation, "He is perfectly aware that the sets and costumes are by [Pablo] Picasso, and that the music is by Satie, but he wonders whether Picasso and Satie aren't by him." The principal role played by Cocteau, however, was as the director of a group of artists that included choreographer Léonide Massine in addition to Picasso and Satie. Cocteau was responsible for the original concept of the ballet and the scenario, and he contributed ideas to each of the three other principals. According to Steegmuller, French-Russian dancer and choreographer Serge Lifar emphasized the importance of Cocteau's ideas to ballet: "Everything that is now current in ballet . . . was invented by Cocteau for *Parade.*"

Parade debuted at the Théâtre du Châtelet on 18 May 1917. The backdrop curtain, painted by Picasso, represented Parisian houses. A fair is under way in the street. A group of dancers represent "the parade." The word "parade" is used in the sense of a promotional spectacle designed to entice clients into the main show, and the dancers responsible for the enticement include a Chinese magician, a young American girl, and acrobats. Three managers responsible for selling tickets comment on how the crowd has taken the publicity act for the real show, and they try to communicate to the audience that the real show lies within. But no one enters. Exhausted, the managers collapse on the stage, and the magician, girl, and acrobats attempt to lure the audience inside, but to no avail.

One of the key elements of the scenario is described by a term used on the theater program in 1917: *ballet réaliste* (Realistic Ballet). This term emphasizes the originality of the ballet in presenting life-like rather than stylized or idealized characters. In the last line of the scenario, which appears in *Théâtre de Poche* (1949, Pocket Theater) Cocteau says that "the gestures of life were, for the first time, amplified and magnified into dance." Elements of the music hall were brought onto the formal ballet stage for the first time; when combined with Picasso's daring cubist costumes and sets and Satie's music, they created a provocative spectacle. Opening night ended in chaos: Cocteau claimed to have been threatened by a theatergoer who tried to stab him with a hat pin. Guillaume Apollinaire stepped in and calmed the woman. Apollinaire's short introduction to the ballet, included in the 1917 program, furnished the first use of the term *surréaliste* (Surrealist) to describe an artwork.

The extent of the scandal created by this production is hard to judge. Cocteau believed that the public reacted immediately to the genius in the work, and remembered an artistic scandal that engrossed the Parisian theater industry. Others have claimed that the public was unimpressed and indifferent. Whatever the cause may have been, the production clearly proved unpopular, shutting down a week after opening.

Although Diaghilev and others recognized *Parade* as original and exciting, it was not until the first revival in 1920 that it gained a wide appreciation. It was performed many times in the 1920s by the Ballets Russes in Paris, London, and across Europe.

The years following the war were some of the most productive of Cocteau's life. In addition to theater work and poetry, Cocteau wrote his first novels, *Thomas L'Imposteur* and *Le Grand Ecart* (1923; translated as *The Grand Ecart*, 1925). He wrote these works in tandem with Raymond Radiguet's *Le Diable au corps* (1923; translated as *The Devil in the Flesh*, 1932) and *Le Bal du Comte d'Orgel* (1924, Count d'Orgel's Ball; translated as *The Count's Ball*, 1929). During this period Cocteau and Radiguet lived and worked together in a productive personal and professional relationship. During a vacation to Toulon, however, Radiguet ate some bad oysters, contracted typhoid, and died shortly thereafter in Paris in 1923. Cocteau was so grief stricken that he was unable to attend the funeral.

During his affair with Radiguet, Cocteau produced two spectacles for the Paris stage. The first was *Le Boeuf sur le toit, ou The Nothing Doing Bar* (1920), which Cocteau conceived from a musical sketch provided by Darius Milhaud. Milhaud, who had just returned from Brazil, had composed pieces based on traditional Brazilian songs. He wanted to present them in their original context, but Cocteau convinced Milhaud to let him write a farce to accompany the music. Cocteau's connections again proved useful when Raoul Dufy, the Fauvist painter, agreed to produce the scenery. In the production Cocteau again borrows from the music-hall stage. The action takes place in a bar, the "Nothing Doing Bar" of the subtitle, and the time setting is Prohibition-era America. The characters wear cardboard heads three times normal size that serve, as Cocteau underscores in the scenario, as "moving scenery." The characters move in slow motion and "against the music." As they go about their business, there is a police raid. The bottles of booze are hidden, and milk is produced. A policeman begins to dance, and the barman flips a switch, lowering the ceiling fan and decapitating the policeman. The policeman falls dead, but the party continues as if nothing happened. The policeman's head is presented to a ballerina who dances while smoking, drinking, and shaking the head "like a cocktail." She then leaves, walking off stage on her hands, and the rest of the patrons follow. Finally, the barman resuscitates the "dead" policeman with gin and presents him with the three-meter-long bill for the evening's festivities. To the chagrin of Milhaud, who felt Cocteau's light and humorous text diminished his music, *Le Boeuf sur le toit* was a success; the production ran for one hundred performances, a significant number for a ballet. More

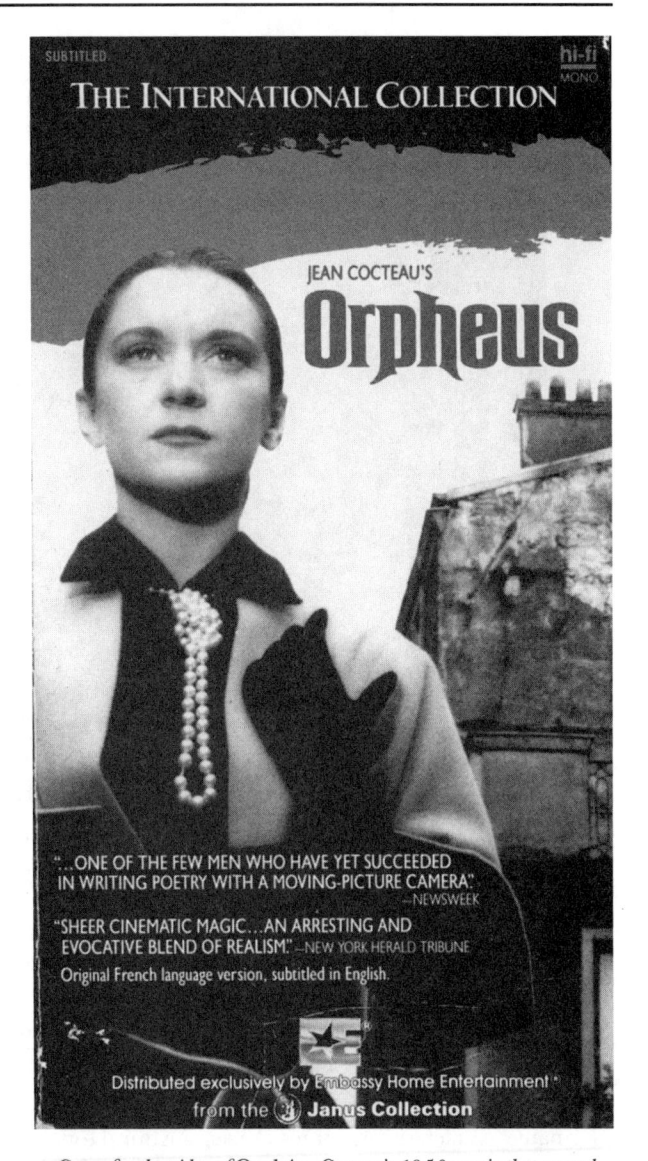

Cover for the video of Orphée, *Cocteau's 1950 movie that earned awards at the 1950 Venice Film Festival and the 1951 Cannes Film Festival (© Embassy Home Entertainment; Richland County Public Library)*

important for Cocteau's career, the spectacle established him as a serious collaborator for contemporary composers.

Cocteau's early hybrid spectacles feature important innovations. Cocteau wanted to introduce spoken words into *Parade,* but this idea was rejected because many people in the dance world saw it as incongruous to the ballet. That this position is no longer held in modern ballet owes a great deal to Cocteau's next work, *Les Mariés de la Tour Eiffel* (performed 1921, published 1923; translated as *The Eiffel Tower Wedding Party*, 1963).

For this production Cocteau collaborated with five of the most dynamic young French composers:

Poster advertising Cocteau's 1950 movie, which he adapted from his 1929 novel that resonated with a generation of disaffected youth (© Bettmann/CORBIS)

Germaine Tailleferre, Georges Auric, Arthur Honegger, Milhaud, and Francis Poulenc. Along with Louis Durey, this group would become internationally known as "Les six" (The Six). Although they did not form a cohesive musical movement because their composition styles did not adhere to any central principle, they presumably recognized the publicity value of this grouping. Cocteau was a lifelong supporter of these composers, and their careers are strongly associated with his.

The innovative musical numbers of *Les Mariés de la Tour Eiffel* are interspersed with Cocteau's text. The spectacle offers a farcical take on the bourgeois tradition of getting married on the main platform of the Eiffel Tower. Narrators are hidden in two massive phonographs on either side of the stage. (Cocteau sat in one of these contraptions during the first production.) These narrators describe a scene that would otherwise be somewhat incomprehensible to the audience. First, an ostrich runs across the set, chased by a hunter. Then, a dancing telegraph arrives and is killed by the hunter. The audience learns that the ostrich has jumped out of a camera as a photographer was getting ready to take a picture. A cyclist appears, having lost his way, and is guided in the right direction. The wedding party poses for a picture, and as the photo is being taken, a person in a bathing suit pops out of the camera, and performs a dance. The dancer then returns to the camera, and the wedding party poses again, but this time a baby emerges from the camera. Photographic puns abound: for example, the baby is the very "picture" of his father. There are more dancing telegraphs, another picture, and then a lion jumps out of the camera and general chaos ensues. The ostrich eventually returns to the camera, and the photo is taken, freezing the wedding party in a timeless "tableau," which is offered for sale for "1,000,000,000,000" of an undefined currency. A final photo is taken, and this time a dove emerges from the camera, indicating that there is peace at last. Finally, the manager arrives, announcing the closure of the Eiffel Tower.

Although Cocteau refused to classify himself as belonging to any literary movement, his early career was greatly influenced by Surrealism and Dadaism. *Les Mariés de la Tour Eiffel* features many Surrealist elements. However, Surrealists such as André Breton disdained Cocteau's dandyism and refused to take him seriously. In fact, Breton became one of Cocteau's harshest critics throughout the 1920s. Cocteau's constant need to justify himself to his critics caused him to make many pronouncements on his art, and his most famous writing on theater appeared as the preface to *Les Mariés de la Tour Eiffel*. Here, Cocteau describes his goals for the theater. He writes: "J'essaie donc de substituer une 'poésie de théâtre' à la 'poésie au théâtre'" (I am attempting to substitute a "poetry of the theater" for "poetry in the theater"). Cocteau wants to bring out elements of theater other than language—motion, music, sets, costumes—to create a more visceral experience for the audience. Cocteau emphasizes that one must take full advantage of modern innovations and listen to all of the voices in the theater. He takes one of the photographer's lines as the organizing principle for his play: "Puisque ces mystères me dépassent, feignons d'en etre l'organisateur" (Because these mysteries surpass me, let's pretend to be their organizer). Cocteau also emphasized the importance of collaboration in the theater. He explains that while it might seem ideal for one person to take charge of all aspects of a theatrical representation, this method is actually impossible: a group effort is required. He goes on to indicate the emergence of a new genre, suitable neither for opera houses nor the popular theaters. All sorts of new combinations of dance, acrobatics, pantomime, drama, satire, orchestral music, and the spoken word are possible. Such drama will emerge, Cocteau argues, as the "l'expression plastique de la poésie" (plastic expression of poetry).

Cocteau insisted that he be called "poet" above all. In fact, he called his dramaturgy "poésie de théâtre" (Theater Poetry) and his novels "poésie de roman" (Novel Poetry). Cocteau was wary of labels that would limit his capacity as an artist. This concern is one of the reasons he never allied himself with any of the major artistic movements of his day. Cocteau believed that poets existed in a realm removed from politics, a theory that was beneficial to his art but led to criticism for some of his actions during World War II.

After his early dance collaborations, nothing Cocteau did in the theater was revolutionary. He continued to incorporate music into his dramatic works, but they became more text based. Cocteau turned first to ancient Greece for inspiration, producing a one-act version of *Antigone* with incidental music by Honegger, sets by Picasso, and costumes by Gabrielle "Coco" Chanel. This play had a run of one hundred performances beginning in December 1922.

Cocteau remained despondent over Radiguet's death. In January 1924 he left Paris for Monte Carlo, where he met the musicologist Louis Laloy. This meeting marks a turning point in Cocteau's life: Laloy suggested that opium might ease Cocteau's depression, and, while there is evidence that Cocteau had tried opium before, during this period it became an addiction. The rest of his life was punctuated by "cures" and returns to this habit. While some artists have lauded the inspiration provided them by drug-induced states, the effect of opium on Cocteau was not always beneficial to his artistic production. In fact, Cocteau was often at his most productive during sanatorium visits when he was trying to overcome his habit. For example, he wrote the novel *Les Enfants terribles* in two weeks during a cure paid for by his friend Chanel (as was customary).

After *Antigone*, Cocteau turned to William Shakespeare for inspiration. In June 1924 *Roméo and Juliette* (published 1926) debuted. Cocteau played the role of Mercutio in this production. Cocteau's last ballet collaboration with Diaghilev, *Le Train bleu* (1924, The Blue Train), debuted at the same time as *Roméo et Juliette*. Cocteau wrote the libretto and designed the sets, and the music was by Milhaud. The ballet was named after the famed express train that took tourists to the newly popular French Riviera. The action was a beach scene, with bathers dancing in costumes by Chanel. It was not a great success, and by the time of its debut Cocteau was involved in further projects set in ancient Greece: a libretto for Fyodorovich Stravinsky's one-act opera, *Oedipus Rex* (1927, King Oedipus), and his first version of the Orpheus myth, *Orphée* (Orpheus; produced 1926, published 1927, translated 1933).

During the time he was preparing *Orphée*, Cocteau experienced his first withdrawal from opium, an event that coincided with his return to Catholicism. Although Cocteau had been baptized in the Catholic Church, he had not been a practicing Catholic. Whether religion was responsible for his giving up opium, Cocteau did for a time attempt to live an austere life. During this time he composed a letter to the friend responsible for leading him back to the church. This work, *Lettre à Jacques Maritain* (1926), celebrates sobriety and the church. However, by the time Cocteau was editing it for publication he had already returned to opium and was distancing himself from the church.

Orphée takes place in a contemporary setting, and the characters are modernized. The traditional myth tells of Orpheus's descending into Hades to retrieve his

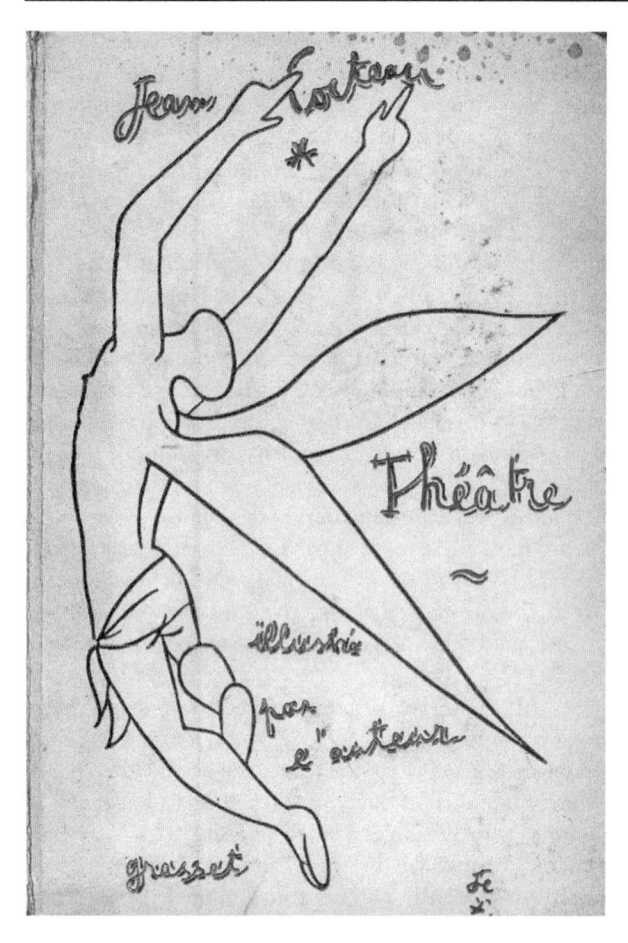

Cover for a 1957 collection of Cocteau's plays (Thomas Cooper Library, University of South Carolina)

dead wife, Eurydice, whom he is allowed to bring back to Earth on the condition that he not look at her until they have arrived. Orpheus does look, however, and Eurydice is lost to him forever. This story is one of the most popular Greek myths, and it has been revisited many times in the theater and opera.

Cocteau's *Orphée* is remarkable for its stagecraft. Heurtebise floats onstage, and characters descend into the underworld by passing through mirrors. The latter effect was to become a trademark of Cocteau, who used it again in the movie version of *Orphée* (1950) and in the movie *La Belle et la Bête* (1946, Beauty and the Beast). For Cocteau, the act of looking at oneself in the mirror was akin to seeing the progression of death, and thus mirrors represent the gateway to what lies beyond. By passing through mirrors, mortals may go over to the other side, and Death, personified by a beautiful young woman, is allowed to come and circulate among the living. There are magic rubber gloves that permit one to cross from one realm to another, prefiguring the role of magic gloves in the movies *Orphée* and *La Belle et la Bête*. Orpheus takes up Eurydice, begins to bring her back, looks at her, and then Eurydice is dead again. The Bacchantes come to kill Orpheus, and he is decapitated. Breaking the boundary between stage and life, the decapitated head of Orpheus reveals itself to be that of Jean Cocteau, and he gives his address. Finally, Orpheus and Eurydice are born again into a new existence. Cocteau departs from the tragedy of the Greek myth and mixes in comic elements, including a horse that communicates near-obscene messages by tapping his foot in code.

Orphée did not have a long run, but it was successful in bringing Cocteau more serious consideration from the Parisian literary and theatrical communities. Shortly after its debut Cocteau was invited to write a work for the Comédie-Française. His submission, a one-act monologue titled *La Voix humaine* (published 1930; translated as *The Human Voice*, 1951), was accepted and staged in 1930. The play features a jilted woman's phone conversation with the lover who is leaving her. The audience sees only the woman's side of the conversation; she is alone on stage with a telephone receiver in hand. The play takes advantage of the multiple interruptions because of the use of a party line and the unreliable service of the phone company to sustain the drama, and Cocteau's words convey the tragic and harrowing condition of this woman. Of all Cocteau's plays, *La Voix humaine* has had the greatest sustained success. It has been filmed in several countries and languages, and in the late 1950s it was adapted by Poulenc as a one-act opera, a version that continues to be produced frequently.

Around the time Cocteau composed *La Voix humaine*, he again fell in love with a young writer, Jean Desbordes. As with Radiguet, Cocteau was an active admirer and promoter of Desbordes's work, although the critical consensus is that Desbordes's work did not approach the quality of Radiguet's. The late 1920s were productive for Cocteau—not only did he write the scenario for Stravinsky's *Oedipus Rex* but also a play based on the same story, *Œdipe-roi*, that was produced for the first time in 1937. He next published *Le Livre blanc* and, during one of his many cures, *Les Enfants terribles*. Cocteau also began plans for his first movie, *Le Sang d'un poète*, which is now recognized as a classic of the cinema.

In 1934 Cocteau wrote his last major play based on Greek mythology. *La Machine infernale* (produced and published 1934; translated as *The Infernal Machine*, 1936) is an adaptation of the Oedipus myth, and it is generally considered to be one of Cocteau's finest dramas. It was directed by Louis Jouvet, the famous French director who also produced major plays by Jean Giraudoux and Jean Genet. The sets by Christian Bérard were widely praised by critics. Cocteau delivered the narration for the debut production.

La Machine infernale is a tragedy into which Cocteau mixes elements of comedy. Jocasta is a libertine, flirting with her guards, who have purported to see the ghost of her dead husband, Laius. Laius has returned to warn Jocasta of her destiny, but he is not able to appear before her directly. In a departure from the Sophoclean drama, the Sphinx is given a prominent role, and she is shown to be complicit in her own fall, providing Oedipus with the answer to the famous riddle. She takes this action because she has fallen in love with Oedipus and will not see him killed. Rather than feeling gratitude to and love for the Sphinx, however, Oedipus rushes off to Thebes to meet his fate. Jocasta and Oedipus marry, and the clues to Oedipus's true identity proliferate until it is no longer undeniable. Jocasta hangs herself, and Oedipus tears out his eyes.

The period between the composition of *La Machine infernale* and the end of World War II is generally considered to be a low point in Cocteau's career as an artist. During this time his opium addiction grew more severe, and he began to have financial trouble. These events coincided with a move toward plays with greater commercial appeal. While critics found Cocteau's plays less original and appealing, his fame continued to grow, especially thanks to *Les Chevaliers de la Table Ronde* (performed and published 1937; translated as *The Knights of the Round Table*, 1963) and *Les Parents terribles* (produced and published 1938; translated as *Intimate Relations*, 1961). A major factor in both these productions was the participation of Jean Marais, who became Cocteau's lover and one of the biggest stage and screen stars of the next twenty years. Marais was first brought to Cocteau's attention during auditions for *Œdipe-roi* in 1937. Cocteau was attracted to Marais and wanted to cast him as Oedipus. The producers, however, objected to an unknown in the lead, and Marais was cast in the smaller role of the Chorus, which Cocteau had reduced to one individual.

Marais's Parisian debut in a leading role came when he appeared as Galahad in *Les Chevaliers de la Table Ronde*. His acting talent was still undeveloped at this point, but he proved a handsome and popular matinee star. In *Les Chevaliers de la Table Ronde,* Cocteau revisits the great Anglo-Norman tradition of the Arthurian legend. Most of Cocteau's characters, such as Guinevere, Merlin, Arthur, Lancelot, and Galahad, are directly taken from the myth. Cocteau's innovation is the introduction of a character named Ginifer who collaborates with Merlin and whose primary characteristic is an ability to take on the appearance of the other characters in the play. No actor plays Ginifer; instead, from time to time the actor playing a given character shifts into a different demeanor and speaks with a peasant accent to show that the character is actually Ginifer in disguise. Gawain, Guinevere, and Galahad are alternately inhabited by this mischievous spirit.

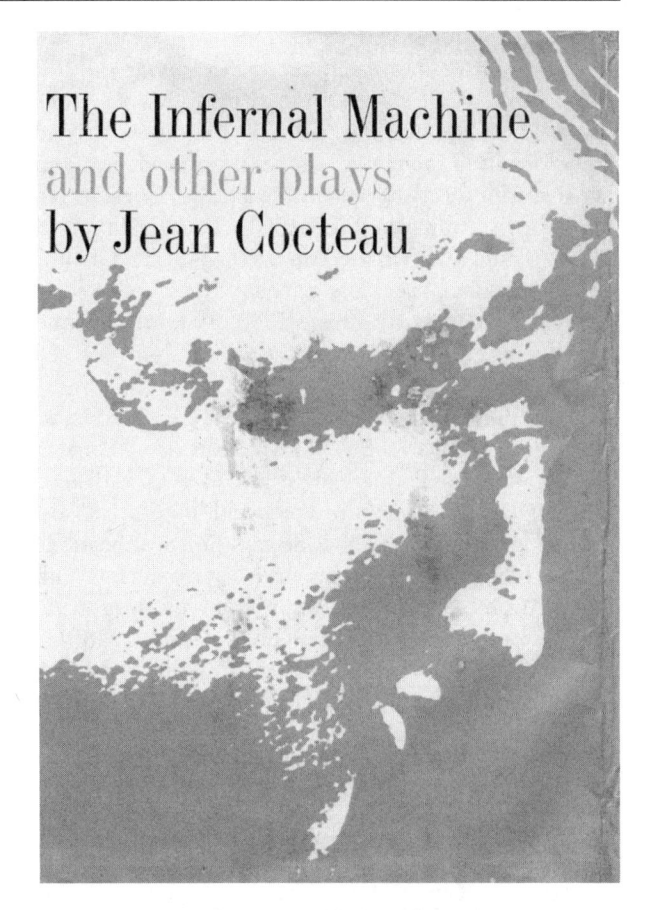

Dust jacket for a 1963 collection of Cocteau's plays in English translation, featuring his last major play based on Greek mythology, an adaptation of the Oedipus myth (Richland County Public Library)

In Cocteau's plot, Arthur's castle is bewitched, a result of the absence of the Holy Grail. Merlin is happy about the disequilibrium; consequently, he is troubled by the arrival of Galahad, who promises to put everything right in Arthur's kingdom. With the help of Ginifer, Merlin tries to maintain the disorder that gives him an advantage, but he is ultimately unable to do so. Arthur eventually discovers the secret of Guinevere and Lancelot's love and kills Lancelot. Guinevere cannot allow Lancelot to go to his death alone and joins him, saying to Arthur that her death is a necessary condition of the Grail's return. With her death, the Grail is revealed, and Merlin is banished. Peace and prosperity return to the kingdom, but at great personal cost to Arthur.

This play was originally written in 1934, and it took Cocteau three years to get the play produced. In the intervening period, he earned money through journalism, and one of his projects was a journalistic re-creation of Jules Verne's *Le Tour du monde en quatre-vingts jours* (1872; translated as *The Tour of the World in Eighty Days,* 1873). Cocteau and a friend, Marcel Khill, managed to retrace the path of Phileas Fogg and Passepartout in the requisite time. By coincidence, during this trip, on a steamer in the Pacific, Cocteau ran into British actor and director Charlie Chaplin. Cocteau's writings about the trip were published in the newspaper *Paris Soir* (Paris Evening), then collected in the volume *Mon Premier Voyage* (1937, My Journey round the World; translated as *Round the World Again in Eighty Days,* 1937).

At this time Cocteau also discovered *poésie de la boxe* (Boxing Poetry). In 1937 Cocteau met "Panama Al" Brown at a Parisian nightclub. Brown had been bantamweight champion of the world, but he had lost his title in Valencia in 1934. Seeing theatrical possibilities in boxing, Cocteau became his manager. With money from Chanel and a program of drug withdrawal, Brown won back his title in March 1938. He then retired from the ring to perform shadowboxing dance acts in Parisian nightclubs. He and Cocteau grew apart, and Brown again became a drug addict, eventually dying on the streets of Harlem in 1951.

Despite repeated "cures," Cocteau's own opium addiction was at its worst during the 1930s. Marais, who became Cocteau's life partner, rescued him from his deepest addiction. Marais abhorred opium and pressured Cocteau to give it up, athough Cocteau never did so entirely.

During their time together Marais inspired Cocteau to create plays and movies for him to star in. The third Cocteau play to feature Marais was the playwright's greatest popular success: *Les Parents terribles,* the story of a mother's jealousy at seeing her son fall in love with a young woman. Yvonne wants to forbid her son Michel from seeing the girl in order to keep him for herself. She is aided in this task by her husband, Georges, who, unbeknownst to the family, has had an affair with the very same girl.

Les Parents terribles had been considered unproducible by Jouvet, who turned it down. Cocteau obtained funding from Roger Capgras, and the play debuted in the fall of 1938 to instant success. The intrigue and plot twists matched the conventions of the *théâtre de boulevard* (Boulevard Theater) and pleased a wide audience familiar with such drama. Beyond its conventional construction, the success of the play largely stemmed from its contemporary setting, its Oedipal undercurrent, and the memorable performances of Marais. However, the play was shut down after one hundred performances by the Conseil Municipal de Paris (Municipal Council of Paris) on the grounds that the subject matter was immoral. Production was then moved to another theater, the Bouffes Parisiennes, where the play continued its run. Only when Marais fell ill and had to withdraw did the play close. It was revived in 1941, and although Marais did not participate, the role of the mother was played by Yvonne de Bray, for whom it initially had been written (de Bray had been replaced in the first run because of illness). Although this production was quickly shut down by the occupation government, de Bray, along with Marais, performed in the movie version in 1948.

De Bray was a muse for Cocteau, who wrote his next play, *Les Monstres sacrés* (produced and published 1940; translated as *The Holy Terrors,* 1961), for her. De Bray played the role of Esther, an actress and leader of a theater company. Esther's husband, Florent, is with the Comédie-Française. Florent's leading lady in the current production of *Britannicus* is a young ingénue named Liane. Liane appears in Esther's dressing room one evening to confess an affair with Florent, a confession that she immediately retracts, claiming that she made it up to get attention. Esther then takes pity on Liane and invites her to share the family home. The three live together for about five months, during which time Florent and Liane inevitably have an affair. At the end of the play, however, Florent and Esther reunite, and Liane goes off to Hollywood.

Cocteau's next plays followed a path away from classical sources toward contemporary issues. In 1941 Cocteau wrote *La Machine à écrire* (produced and published 1941; translated as *The Typewriter,* 1947), which was yet another vehicle for Marais. In this production Marais got to display his developing talent by playing a dual role, that of the twins Pascal and Maxime. The plot is a particularly complicated provincial murder mystery. People in a small town are sent threatening letters by an anonymous person signing himself as "la machine à écrire." The story centers around a family: Didier, the father; Pascal and Maxim, his sons; and Margot, his adopted daughter. Fred, a friend of the family, works for the police and investigates the crime. First, Margot confesses to the crime, then Maxime, and then a young employee of the post office. In a final coup de théâtre, Solange, a friend of the family, reveals her guilt. As Neal Oxenhandler explains, Cocteau tries to use the detective plot to examine family relationships, but he does not pay sufficient attention to the plot demands of the genre. One expects the revelation of a convincing motive at the end of a detective story, but Cocteau fails to provide one.

Rehearsals for the first run of *La Machine à écrire* were closed down by the occupation government. Cocteau's reputation as a homosexual and a drug addict was not seen favorably by the Vichy censors, who closed the play largely because he was the author. Furthermore, Cocteau was singled out for having written articles early in the war against the racism of the Nazi regime. He had

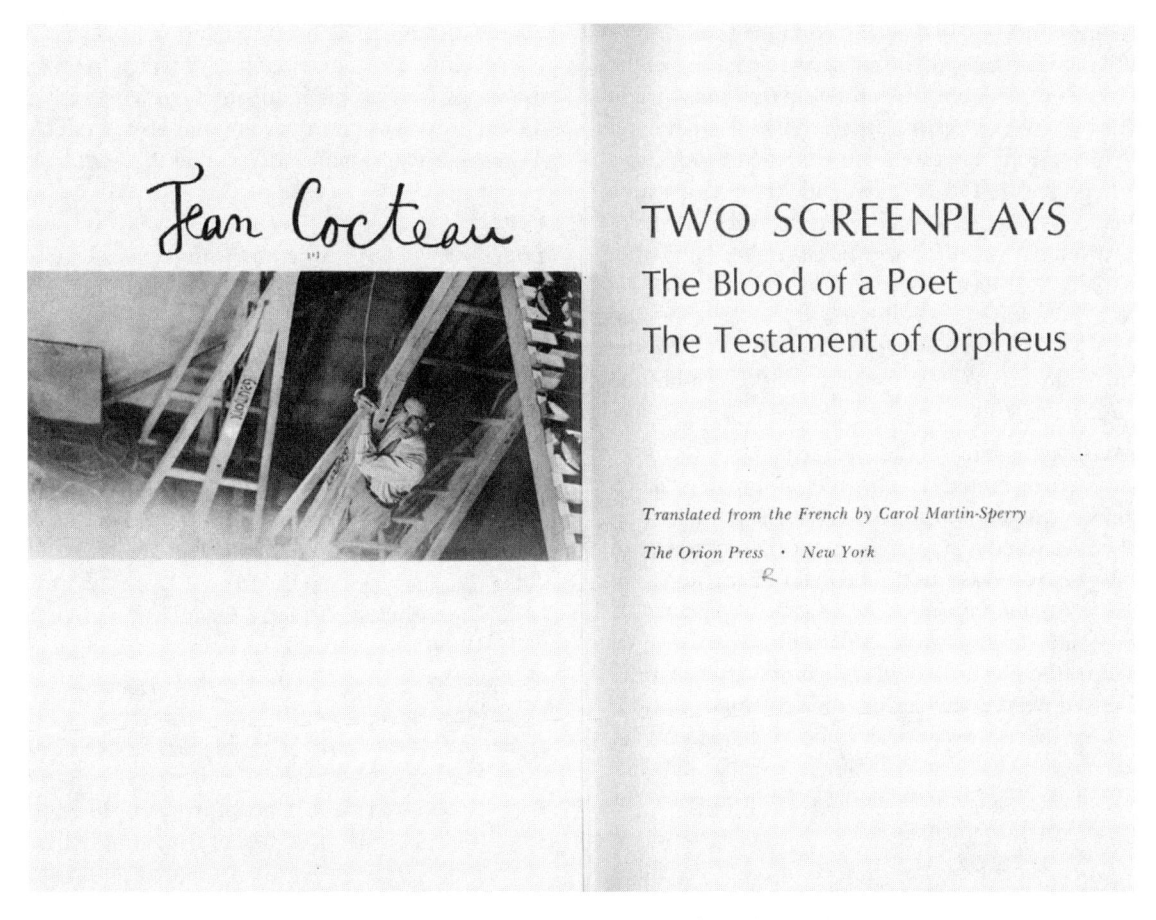

Frontispiece and title page for a 1968 English edition of two of Cocteau's screenplays (Richland County Public Library)

also published an article praising Gide and defending the "decadent" writings of the interwar years, the very writings used by Nazi sympathizers as examples of France's moral laxity. Hence, Cocteau felt increasingly endangered, and he began to cultivate some connections within the Vichy government as a means of self-preservation. Cocteau was a longtime Germanophile and spoke German fluently. He genuinely admired the German sculptor Arno Breker and wrote a salute to him in 1943. Because Breker was a favorite of Adolf Hitler, Cocteau was criticized by many of his fellow writers for this work; to them, praising Breker was the equivalent of embracing National Socialism.

Cocteau's wartime reputation is a complicated matter. All artists required government approval for licenses to produce work during the occupation. Rather than stop working, Cocteau agreed to work under these conditions. He held the position that the poet was above politics, a position that Jean-Paul Sartre's writing in particular showed to be untenable. Cocteau viewed his refusal to participate in political questions as similar to his refusal to belong to Surrealism or any other organized body of thought.

In 1942 a copy of Genet's novel *Notre-Dame-des-fleurs* (1943; translated as *Our Lady of the Flowers*, 1949) came into Cocteau's possession, and he immediately recognized its beauty, writing about it in his journal. It is largely because of Cocteau's promotion that Genet began to find an audience. *Notre-Dame-des-fleurs* is openly homoerotic and was published covertly; possession of the novel at the time probably would have been justification for arrest for immorality. Yet, Cocteau felt his duty was to art, and he defended Genet. After the war Cocteau signed, with Sartre, a petition to have Genet excused from what would have been a life prison sentence as a repeat offender.

Despite his declining professional reputation and questionable wartime politics, Cocteau emerged after the war as one of France's most admired moviemakers. He returned to screenwriting during the war with *La Comédie du bonheur* (The Comedy of Happiness; first released as *Ecco la felicità*, 1940; released in French, 1942) and then the popular *L'Eternel retour* (1943, The Eternal Return). In 1946 he wrote and directed *La Belle et la Bête*, which managed the rare combination of commercial and critical success.

During this period Cocteau continued to produce plays. Perhaps because of the conservative nature of the occupation government, he produced his most traditional play in 1943, *Rénaud et Armide* (1943, Rénaud and Armide), a tragedy in verse for the Comédie-Française. Marie Bell appeared as Armide, and Maurice Escande as Rénaud. After the war Cocteau returned to melodrama, producing *L'Aigle à deux têtes* (produced and published 1946; translated as *The Eagle Has Two Heads*, 1948), a convoluted story about a queen who falls in love with her would-be assassin. His final work for the Parisian stage was *Bacchus* (produced 1951, published 1952, translated 1963).

Although some of the characters of Cocteau's later works reveal interesting aspects of human psychology, they generally inhabited untidy plots that prevented critical success. One reason for the sloppiness of Cocteau's drama was that he had shifted his attention to cinema. After *La Belle et la Bête*, Cocteau produced a movie version of *Les Parents terribles* in 1948. He then returned to the Orpheus myth one more time: in 1950 he produced what many consider his cinematic masterpiece, *Orphée*, which won prizes at the 1950 Venice Film Festival and the 1951 Cannes Film Festival. Thus, Cocteau added universally acclaimed motion pictures to his list of artistic achievements.

Cocteau spent the last thirteen years of his life in semiretirement on the French Riviera. He had charmed a wealthy patroness, Francine Weissweiller, and she invited Cocteau and his last companion, Edouard Dermithe, to live with her at her villa in Saint Jean Cap Ferrat. Cocteau decorated the house with his murals and engaged in several municipal projects. He wrote less, and he produced only one more movie, *Le Testament d'Orphée* (1960; released with English subtitles as *The Testament of Orpheus*, 1962), which was partially financed by François Truffaut. It received mostly negative reviews.

During his last years, Cocteau saw his career celebrated. He was honored as one of France's great living literary figures, was elected to the Académie française (The French Academy), and received an honorary doctorate at Oxford. He was knighted, becoming a Chevalier de la Légion d'honneur (Knight of the Legion of Honor) in 1949, and he was made a member of the Belgian Académie Royale de Langue et de Littérature françaises (Belgian Royal Academy of French Literature and Language). He died on 11 October 1963, and his passing was widely mourned.

Jean Cocteau was a true visionary, producing acclaimed works in more genres than any other single artist of the twentieth century, but his career as a dramatist was uneven. While his later theatrical pieces are widely dismissed, he left an enduring legacy built upon his revolutionary contributions to ballet, spectacle, and drama as well as his innovative work in cinema, and these efforts had an important and lasting effect on the dramatic arts in France and around the world.

Letters:

Lettres à André Gide, edited by Jean-Jacques Kihm (Paris: La Table Ronde, 1970);

Lettres à Milorad 1955–1963, edited by Milorad (Paris: Saint-Germain-des-Prés, 1975);

Correspondance avec Jean-Marie Magnan (Paris: Belfond, 1981);

Lettres à Jacques Maritain (Paris: Stock, 1984);

Lettres à Jean Marais (Paris: Albin Michel, 1987);

Correspondance: Jean Cocteau, Anna de Noailles, edited by Claude Mignot-Ogliastri (Paris: Gallimard, 1989);

Lettres à sa mère, volume 1: *1989–1918*, edited by Pierre Caizergues and Pierre Chanel (Paris: Gallimard, 1989);

Correspondance Jean Cocteau–Lucien Clergue (Arles: Actes Sud, 1989);

Lettres de l'Oiseleur, edited by Manuel Burrus (Monaco: Rocher, 1989);

Correspondance Guillaume Apollinaire–Jean Cocteau, edited by Caizergues and Michel Décaudin (Paris: Place, 1991);

Cocteau and Jean Hugo, *Correspondance*, edited by Brigitte Borsaro and Caizergues (Montpellier: Centre d'études du XXe siècle, Université Paul Valéry, 1995);

Lettres à Jean-Jacques Kihm, edited by Françoise Bibolet and Chanel (Mortemart: Rougerie, 1996);

Correspondance Georges Auric–Jean Cocteau, edited by Caizergues (Montpellier: Centre d'études du XXe siècle, Université Paul Valéry, 1999);

Correspondance Jean Cocteau–Darius Milhaud, edited by Caizergues and Josiane Mas (Paris: Massalia, 1999);

Cocteau and Louise de Vilmorin, *Correspondance croisée*, edited by Olivier Muth (Paris: Gallimard, 2003).

Interviews:

Maurice Rouzaud, *Une Entrevue sur la critique avec Maurice Rouzaud*, Les Amis d'Edouard, no. 145 (Paris: Champion, 1929);

André Fraigneau, *Entretiens autour du cinématographe* (Paris: A. Bonne, 1951); translated by Vera Traill as *Cocteau on the Film: An Interview Recorded by André Fraigneau* (New York: Roy, 1954);

William Fifield, "Jean Cocteau: An Interview," *Paris Review*, 32 (Summer–Fall 1964): 13–37;

Fraigneau, *Entretiens avec André Fraigneau* (Paris: Union Générale, 1965);

Fraigneau, interview with Cocteau, in *Entretiens sur le cinématographe,* edited by André Bernard and Claude Gauteur (Paris: Belfond, 1973).

Biographies:

Margaret Crosland, *Jean Cocteau: A Biography* (London: Nevill, 1955; New York, Knopf, 1956);

André Fraigneau, *Cocteau par lui-même* (Paris: Seuil, 1957); translated by Donald Lehmkuhl as *Cocteau,* Evergreen Profile Book, no. 24 (New York: Grove / London: Evergreen, 1961);

Frederick Brown, *An Impersonation of Angels: A Biography of Jean Cocteau* (New York: Viking, 1968; Harlow: Longman, 1969);

Elizabeth Sprigge and Jean-Jacques Kihm, *Jean Cocteau: The Man and the Mirror* (New York: Coward-McCann, 1968; London: Gollancz, 1968);

Francis Steegmuller, *Cocteau: A Biography* (Boston: Little, Brown, 1970);

Julie Saul, ed., *Jean Cocteau–The Mirror and the Mask: A Photo-Biography,* with an essay by Steegmuller (Boston: Godine, 1992);

Henry Gidel, *Jean Cocteau* (Paris: Flammarion, 1997).

References:

Clément Borgal, *Cocteau, Dieu, la mort, la poésie* (Paris: Centurion, 1968);

Borgal, *Cocteau: Poète de l'au delà* (Paris: Tequi, 1977);

Brigitte Borsaro, *Cocteau, le cirque et le music-hall,* Cahiers Jean Cocteau, Nouvelle série, no. 2 (Paris: Passage du Marais, 2003);

Monique Bourdin, ed., *Poésie critique et critique de la poésie, Revue de lettres modernes,* special Cocteau issue, 4 (2003);

Jacques Brosse, *Cocteau* (Paris: Gallimard, 1970);

Oliver Cariguel, "Jean-Pierre Millecam: Jean Cocteau n'a écrit qu'un poéme, celui de sa vie," *Magazine Littéraire,* 423 (September 2003): 37–38;

Danielle Chaperon, *Jean Cocteau: La Chute des angles* (Lille: Press Universitaires de Lille, 1990);

Henry Cohen, "Cocteau's *Les parents terribles* as an Ironic Remaniement of Racine's Phèdre," *Dalhousie French Studies,* 59 (2002): 56–66;

Georgiana M. M. Colvile, "*Parade* and Its Double(s)," *PTL: A Journal for Descriptive Poetics and Theory,* 2 (1977): 221–226;

Lydia Crowson, *The Esthetic of Jean Cocteau* (Hanover, N.H.: University Press of New England, 1978);

Carol A. Cujec, "Modernizing Antiquity: Jean Cocteau's Early Greek Adaptations," *Classical and Modern Literature,* 17, no. 1 (1996): 45–56;

Pierre Dubourg, *La Dramaturgie de Jean Cocteau* (Paris: Grasset, 1954);

Arthur B. Evans, *Jean Cocteau and His Films of Orphic Identity* (Philadelphia: Art Alliance Press, 1975);

William Fifield, *Jean Cocteau* (New York: Columbia University Press, 1974);

Daniel Fischlin, "Queer Margins: Cocteau, *La Belle et la Bête,* and the Jewish Differend," *Textual Practice,* 12, no. 1 (1989): 69–88;

Wallace Fowlie, *Jean Cocteau: The History of a Poet's Age* (Bloomington: Indiana University Press, 1966);

Laura Doyle Gates, "Jean Cocteau and 'la poésie du théâtre,'" *Romance Quarterly,* 35 (November 1988): 435–441;

Catherine M. Jones, "S/X: Fictions of Embodiment in Cocteau's *Les Chevaliers de la Table Ronde,*" *French Review,* 72 (March 1999): 687–695;

Bettina Liebowitz Knapp, *Jean Cocteau* (Boston: Twayne, 1989);

Annette Shandler Levitt, "Jean Cocteau's Theatre: Idea and Enactment," *Theatre Journal,* 45 (October 1993): 363–372;

Jean-Marie Magnan, *Cocteau* (Paris: Desclée de Brouwer, 1968);

James P. McNab, "Mythical Space in *Les Enfants terribles,*" *French Review,* 47 (Spring 1974): 162–170;

Judith G. Miller, "Jean Cocteau and Hélène Cixous: Oedipus," in *Drama, Sex and Politics,* edited by James Redmond (Cambridge: Cambridge University Press, 1985), pp. 203–211;

Gérard Mourgue, *Jean Cocteau* (Paris: Editions Universitaires, 1965);

Neal Oxenhandler, *Scandal and Parade: The Theater of Jean Cocteau* (New Brunswick, N.J.: Rutgers University Press, 1957);

H. Dwight Page, "The Resurrection of the Sophoclean Phoenix: Jean Cocteau's *La Machine Infernale,*" *Classical and Modern Literature,* 18 (Summer 1998): 329–343;

Dominique Païni, François Nemer, and Valérie Loth, eds., *Jean Cocteau, sur le fil du siècle* (London: Holberton, 2004);

Frank W. D. Ries, *The Dance Theatre of Jean Cocteau* (Ann Arbor: University of Michigan Research Press, 1986);

Cornelia Tsakiridou, ed., *Bucknell Review,* special Cocteau issue: *Reviewing Orpheus: Essays on the Cinema and Art of Jean Cocteau,* 41, no. 1 (1997).

Papers:

Jean Cocteau's papers are held at Archives Jean Cocteau, Milly-la-Forêt (Essonne), France.

Lucette Desvignes
(1 May 1926 -   )

Jerry L. Curtis
Ohio State University—Newark

PLAY PRODUCTIONS: *La Grange aux rencontres,* Lyon, Théâtre de la Baleine, 13 April 1964; performed as *Strange Encounters,* Columbus, Ohio, Riffe Center, 28 September 1996;

L'Editeur et la dame, Beaune, Fête du Livre de Beaune, 18 October 1988;

Le Cri du ventre, Lyons-Feyzin, Mairie, 12 October 1989;

Eurydice, Eurydice, translated into English, Newark, Ohio, Black Box Theater of the Ohio State University, Newark, 25 September 1998.

BOOKS: *Marivaux et l'Angleterre: Essai sur une création dramatique originale* (Paris: Klincksieck, 1970);

Les Nœuds d'argile, Collection dirigée par Sophie Leroy (Dijon: Civry, 1982); revised edition, introduction by Jacques Lacarrière, Les Mains nues, no. 1 (Paris: Mazarine, 1985);

Clair de nuit: Roman (Paris: Fayard, 1984);

Le Grain du chanvre ou l'Histoire de Jeanne, introduction by Lacarriére, Les Mains nues, no. 2 (Paris: Mazarine, 1985);

Le Livre de Juste, Les Mains nues, no. 3 (Paris: Mazarine-Fayard, 1986);

Canicule: Nouvelle (Dijon: Aléï, 1987);

Famille, familles: nouvelles (Dijon: Aléï, 1988);

Vent debout: Roman, Les Mains libres, no. 1 (Paris: Bourin, 1991);

La Maison sans volets: Roman (Paris: Bourin, 1992);

Le Marché aux Bœufs de St-Christophe-en-Brionnais, photographs by Jean-Marc Biry (Strasbourg: Chambre à Part, 1992);

La Brise en poupe: Roman, Les Mains libres, no. 2 (Paris: Bourin, 1993);

Contes du vignoble (Dijon: Bourgogne-Rhône-Loire, 1993);

Le Miel de l'aube: Une enfance en Bourgogne sous l'Occupation (Précy-sous-Thil: Armançon, 1999);

Le Père Noël est un chien: Contes de Noël, preface by Jacqueline Sessa (Précy-sous-Thil: Armançon, 2000);

La Nuit de la chouette, Petit nuit (Auxerre: NYKTA, 2001);

Affaires de familles: nouvelles, preface by Sessa (Précy-sous-Thil: Armançon, 2001);

Lucette Desvignes (photograph by Evelyne Proriol; from Le Miel de L'aube, *1999; Skillman Library, Lafayette College)*

A Translation of Three Plays by Lucette Desvignes: Eurydice, Eurydice; Strange Encounters; and Marsyas, or the Rebellious Flautist, edited and translated by Jerry L. Curtis, preface by Brian E. Rainey, Studies in French Literature, no. 57 (Lewiston, N.Y.: Edwin Mellen Press, 2002);

La Seconde visite (Précy-sous-Thil: Armançon, 2003);

Le Journal indien, illustrations by Michel Dufour (Précy-sous-Thil: Armançon, 2003);

La Poésie de Lucette Desvignes / The Poetry of Lucette Desvignes: A Bilinqual Edition, edited and translated by Curtis (Potomac, Md.: Scripta Humanistica, 2005).

Edition in English: *Telling It Like It Was: Seven Short Stories and a Modern Tale*, edited by Jerry L. Curtis, translated by Brian E. Rainey and others (Columbus: Center for Studies on Lucette Desvignes, The Ohio State University Printing Facility, 2002).

PRODUCED SCRIPT: *Eurydice, Eurydice*, radio, *France Culture*, Radio France 1, 6 June 1986.

OTHER: *Travaux comparatistes*, edited, with a preface, by Desvignes (Saint-Etienne: Centre d'études comparatistes et de recherche sur l'expression dramatique, Université de Saint-Etienne, 1978);

André Mareschal, *La Cour Bergère, ou L'Arcadie de Messire Phillippes Sidney: Tragi-Comédie*, 2 volumes, edited by Desvignes (Saint-Etienne: Editions de l'Université de Saint-Etienne, 1981);

"Conversation entre chien et loup," *Droits de l'Homme, Paroles de Poètes* (Dijon: Aléï, Le Dé bleu, 1989), pp. 61–64;

Dessins, Maquettes, Sculptures, Cocqueberg, Sculpteur, preface by Desvignes (Dijon : ICO, 1996);

"Destined to be Ohioans," *Out Behind the Barn*, edited by Jerry L. Curtis and Shirley Curtis (Columbus, Ohio: AARP Ohio Impact Alliance, 2003);

Marianne Benkö: Red and Blue Fires, with an introduction and commentary by Desvignes (The Hague: Terra Promessa Art Gallery, 2004);

Jean-Yves Debreuille, *Salvator Gurrieri: Hommage*, preface by Desvignes (Lyon: Bachès, 2005).

SELECTED PERIODICAL PUBLICATIONS–
UNCOLLECTED:
FICTION
"Le Défilé," *Travaux du Centre d'études comparatistes et de recherche sur l'expression dramatique*, 14 (1976): 159–166; reprinted, *Contre-Ciel*, 7 (November 1984): 51–55; reprinted again, in *Coïncidences* (Montreal: Aléï, 1990), pp. 17–27;

"Le Chat blanc," *Nouvelles Nouvelles*, 2 (1986): 30–35;

"Le Noël de Grosminet Mouton," *Le Bien Public* and *Le Courrier de Saône-et-Loire* (Christmas 1986): 24, 36; reprinted, *La Protection des Animaux (Revue trimestrielle de la Confédération des SPA de France)*, 120, no. 4 (Christmas 1988): 22–23;

"La Lampe," *NYX*, 9, no. 1 (1989): 29–31;

"Diptyque," *Greffes* (1990): 73–108;

"Lui," *Studies on Lucette Desvignes and the Twentieth Century*, 2 (1992): 175–178;

"La Chienne de Pompéi," *Studies on Lucette Desvignes and the Twentieth Century*, 2 (1992): 179–187;

"La Lucarne," *Studies on Lucette Desvignes and the Twentieth Century*, 3 (1993): 179–188;

"Matinée au Jardin," *Studies on Lucette Desvignes and the Twentieth Century*, 4 (1994): 143–156;

"Kermesse," *Studies on Lucette Desvignes and the Twentieth Century*, 5 (1995): 151–166;

"La Chatte anonyme," *Studies on Lucette Desvignes and the Twentieth Century*, 6 (1996): 145–154;

"La Passion n'a pas d'âge," *Studies on Lucette Desvignes and the Twentieth Century*, 7 (1997): 117–132;

"Chère Maman," *Studies on Lucette Desvignes and the Twentieth Century*, 8 (1998): 137–160;

"Les Faraglioni à la portée de tous," *Studies on Lucette Desvignes and the Twentieth Century*, 9 (1999): 133–162;

"Après la noce," *Studies on Lucette Desvignes and the Twentieth Century*, 10 (2000): 117–134;

"Rue du Lycée," *Studies on Lucette Desvignes and the Twentieth Century*, 11 (2001): 147–158;

"Promenade sur l'eau," *Studies on Lucette Desvignes and the Twentieth Century*, 12 (2002): 127–133;

"Le Chat triste," *Studies on Lucette Desvignes and Contemporary French Literature*, 13 (2003): 127–150;

"Prima Lezione: Al Ristorante," *Studies on Lucette Desvignes and Contemporary French Literature*, 14 (2004): 121–128;

"Le Gouteur de Livarots," *Studies on Lucette Desvignes and Contemporary French Literature*, 14 (2004): 137–149;

"Le Troisième Age," *Studies on Lucette Desvignes and Contemporary French Literature*, 15 (2005): 109–115.

POETRY
"Cœur, mon cœur," published as "Ecrit I," *Travaux du Centre d'études comparatistes et de recherche sur l'expression dramatique*, 7 (1974): 37;

"Hymne I," published as "Ecrit II," *Travaux du Centre d'études comparatistes et de recherche sur l'expression dramatique*, 7 (1974): 69–70;

"Un Printemps de plus," published as "Ecrit III," *Travaux du Centre d'études comparatistes et de recherche sur l'expression dramatique*, 7 (1974): 193–195;

"Naufrage," published as "Ecrit XXIII," *Travaux du Centre d'études comparatistes et de recherche sur l'expression dramatique*, 14 (1976): 9–10;

"Cœur, mon cœur," "Lettre morte," "Le Cri," "Advienne, advienne," "Zodiaque," and "Faits-divers," *Studies on Lucette Desvignes and the Twentieth Century*, 2 (1992): 167–173;

"Mycène," *Studies on Lucette Desvignes and the Twentieth Century*, 5 (1995): 195–198;

"La passante" and "Image," *Studies on Lucette Desvignes and the Twentieth Century*, 6 (1996): 203–207;

"Ananké" and "Tyrinthe," *Studies on Lucette Desvignes and the Twentieth Century*, 7 (1997): 145–152;

"Peinture" and "La Ballade des petits nuages," *Studies on Lucette Desvignes and the Twentieth Century*, 8 (1998): 187–190;

"L'Idylle," "Les Couleurs de la lune," and "Dialogue avec Pan," *Studies on Lucette Desvignes and the Twentieth Century*, 9 (1999): 171–186;

"La Ballade des petits chats," *Studies on Lucette Desvignes and the Twentieth Century*, 10 (2000): 167–170;

"Méditation," *Studies on Lucette Desvignes and the Twentieth Century*, 11 (2001): 171–172;

"Epidaure," *Studies on Lucette Desvignes and the Twentieth Century*, 12 (2002): 179–180.

NONFICTION

"A Few Words about *Strange Encounters*," *Studies on Lucette Desvignes and the Twentieth Century*, 7 (1997): 83–94.

Celebrated French author Lucette Desvignes has incorporated her vast knowledge of European dramatic literature into successful original works for the theater. She has been inspired above all by ancient Greek tragedy and its obsessions with pride, rebellion, fate, and choice. Her use of classical theater as a model places her in the tradition of some of the most influential French playwrights of World War II, such as Jean Anouilh, Jean-Paul Sartre, and Albert Camus. These writers usually re-created the mythology and situations of Greek literature in order to allegorize the political crises of the Nazi occupation or dramatize philosophical concepts. Desvignes's drama, however, is not so much political or philosophical as psychologically and aesthetically inspired. The rigor of her plots trains the focus of the reader or playgoer on her contemporary portrayals of aspects of the human condition. In Desvignes's dramatic universe, twentieth-century people suffer the same ills, the same passions, and the same conflicts as their Greek predecessors. These parallels are especially obvious in *Marsyas, ou le rebelle à la flûte* (translated as *Marsyas, or the Rebellious Flautist*, 2002) and *Eurydice, Eurydice* (produced for radio, 1986; translated, 2002), but even *La Grange aux rencontres* (performed 1964; translated as *Strange Encounters*, 2002) plays out the ancient search for self-knowledge—embodied in the Socratic dictum "know thyself"—in the guise of a detective story. Themes of Orphean descent and confrontation between the human and the divine appear in all of Desvignes's plays, including *L'Editeur et la dame* (performed 1988; The Editor and the Lady), where the battle between mortals and gods is transposed into the comic mode as an aspiring author overcomes an unapproachable, imperious editor. Throughout her dramatic oeuvre Desvignes moves beyond the regional characters and history that characterize much of her prose fiction, portraying topics of universal appeal and relevance.

Lucette Desvignes was born Lucienne Jeanne Parent on 1 May 1926 in Mercurey, a small village in Saône-et-Loire. Her parents, Jean Parent and Marie-Germaine Barraud, were both schoolteachers. In September 1929 the family moved to Chalon when her father was named headmaster of the Ecole de Garçons du Centre (City Center Elementary School for Boys). Here Parent grew up with her brother Bobby and half sister Simone in the highly charged intellectual atmosphere created by her parents, who were known throughout the area as progressive teachers. She attended the Collège de Jeunes Filles (High School for Young Girls).

During the Nazi occupation of France, the school where Parent lived was regularly requisitioned by the military to house French soldiers going to the front, then Nazi troops occupying Chalon, then French prisoners of war, then soldiers of the Liberation Army. Hence, it became a locus of war, a place where, as Desvignes explains in her autobiography *Le Miel de l'aube* (1999, The Honey of Dawn), "L'histoire non seulement nous atteignait depuis l'extérieur, mais bien s'installait dans nos murs" (History not only reached us from the outside, but also made itself at home within our walls).

Eighteen-year-old Parent earned her *baccalauréat* in Langues et Philosophie (Languages and Philosophy) the year World War II ended. She then pursued graduate studies at the University of Dijon and earned master's degrees in classical English in 1946 and law in 1947. On 1 September 1948, just after beginning a teaching career that lasted for thirty-seven years, she married André Desvignes at the City Hall of Chalon.

Lucette Desvignes's first assignment as an English teacher was at the Lycée Paul Bert in Auxerre, Yonne, in 1947–1948. She then transferred to the Collège Classique de Jeunes Filles (Classical High School for Young Girls) in Louhans, Saône-et-Loire, for 1948–1949. Desvignes was next appointed to her former *collège* in Chalon, which had become a coeducational institution renamed the Lycée Pontus de Thyars, after a famous local bishop and friend of Pierre de Ronsard who was a member of the Pléiade circle of poets during the French Renaissance. She remained there from 1949 until 1959. During this time her two children, Yves-Antoine and Jean, were born, and in 1956 she passed her *agrégation*, a competitive national exam allowing her to teach at state secondary schools.

In October 1959 Desvignes was appointed assistant in comparative literature at the Faculté des Lettres (Faculty of Letters) of the University of Lyon (currently Lyon-2, Université Lumière). After eight years in Lyon as a senior assistant, she was appointed lecturer at the University Literary Center of the University of Saint-Etienne. Desvignes completed two dissertations, the first a critical edition of Pierre Carlet de Chamblain de Marivaux's *Les Sincères* (1739, The Sincere Ones) and the second a monumental comparative study of English influences on French theater titled *Marivaux et l'Angleterre* (Marivaux and England), published in 1970. That year she received her doctorate at the University of Paris (Paris-IV Sorbonne) and taught comparative literature and history of theater at the University of Saint-Etienne. She eventually rose to the position of full professor, in the process creating the Centre d'études comparatistes et de recherche sur l'expression dramatique (Center for Comparative Studies and Research on Dramatic Expression).

André Desvignes, meanwhile, worked from 1950 to 1968 for the Société Gros et Compagnie, first in Chalon, then in Lyon, before being named director of Valor, the Dijon branch in the business of selling steel from the province of Lorraine. In 1976 the Desvignes' twenty-five-year-old son, pianist and composer Yves-Antoine Desvignes, drowned in the canal at Plombières-les-Dijon. André Desvignes nearly died of a heart attack from the shock and, as a result, took early retirement in 1981. Lucette was obliged to commute from her family home in Dijon to teach at the University of Saint-Etienne from 1969 until she took early retirement in 1983 to devote herself exclusively to writing.

Desvignes's writing ability stems from a combination of her creative intuition and her academic training. She developed a passion for literature within the pedagogical atmosphere created by her parents. Desvignes was also influenced by the painful experiences of the war years when her father's school was taken over by the Nazis. This period of her childhood both imbued her with a decidedly humanistic perspective and caused her to become a "militant pacifist." Following the liberation, she determined to dedicate herself to the life of the mind. Then, as she readily admits, her teaching career provided a rigorous apprenticeship for the writing career she has chosen.

During Desvignes's academic career there were some manifestations of her literary talents, including the composition of two of her plays: *Marsyas, ou le rebelle à la flûte* in 1957 and *La Grange aux rencontres* in 1964. She also wrote a short story, "Le Défilé" (The Lineup), published in three different reviews in 1976, 1987, and 1991. Throughout her teaching career she wrote essays, short stories, poems, and plays without intending to publish them. In fact, her first three plays, all of which were written during her academic career, have only been published in English translations in 2002, and only *La Grange aux rencontres* and *Eurydice, Eurydice* have been performed in France.

Desvignes's drama transcends any of the classifications or definitions proposed by traditional schools of literary thought. Her plays often voice contemporary concerns within the framework of tragic circumstances derived from classical myths and legends. These works are essentially theatrical metaphors of universal dilem-

Cover for Desvignes's monumental 1970 study of English influences on French drama (Marivaux and England; Thomas Cooper Library, University of South Carolina)

mas. For instance, there is the clash of human aspirations with the whimsical edicts of fate in *Marsyas, ou le rebelle à la flûte,* the impact of the past on the present in *La Grange aux rencontres,* and the wrenching loss of a loved one in *Eurydice, Eurydice.*

In *Marsyas, ou le rebelle à la flûte,* Desvignes is more concerned with compelling dialogue than with action. The onstage exchanges pit the poetic and musical talents of a proud but gifted satyr, Marsyas, against the divine but dubious wisdom of Apollo. This encounter symbolizes a clash of cosmic proportions between humanity and fate. The play is enhanced by background music by French impressionists Claude Debussy, Maurice Ravel, and Albert Roussel. This music is used to celebrate the forces of nature. The play begins with Marsyas surrounded by a quartet of dancing nymphs (Irene, Charis, Thymia, and Carteria), and the scene quickly achieves a high level of eroticism and sensuality. As the nymphs thread together disjointed exclamations, the script attains a fluidity that resembles the musical background and becomes a choral statement designed to echo the sentiments of the spectators.

The idyllic setting created by the playing of Marsyas's flute and the dancing of the nymphs is disrupted when an august quartet enters the scene: Pan (the musical mentor of Marsyas), Bacchus (the great lover of wine), Sylenus (a wood spirit in human form), and Midas (the king of Phrygia). Marsyas plays his flute, paying homage to Pan and his guests, until a disguised Apollo arrives and tells him he plays "like a god." When Marsyas fails to be astonished with such a comparison, he offends Apollo, who challenges Marsyas to a musical duel based on the notion that infinite beauty—that of the gods—is far superior to the beauty produced on divine instruments in the hands of mortals. In opposing Apollo, Marayas transforms his passions into beauty—beauty he believes equal to that of the gods.

The two begin to play, and the tribunal judging them listens, then votes, fearing divine retribution, for Apollo. Impenitent, Marsyas rebels against their judgment and, as he does so, evolves from an animal into the spokesperson for humanity: he refuses the edict that humans are but servants of the gods. Although he knows he will be subdued and punished by the gods, he believes his music will live on: his rebellious art will be seen as a sacred venture, a challenge to divine authority, and a religion for modern times. *Marsyas* has never been performed.

La Grange aux rencontres was a veritable tour de force when it was written in 1948 and later staged by Lyon's Théâtre de la Baleine in 1964. In this play Desvignes uses flashback techniques that permit her to illuminate past and present scenarios simultaneously on two different stages. The effect she achieves would have been impossible to stage using more traditional techniques, such as verbal allusions to the past, *apartés* (asides), actions supposedly taking place in the wings, and entr'actes to permit costume changes and alternating scenes. For Desvignes, these techniques were theatrical tricks, all lacking in verisimilitude and hence diminishing the audience's ability to participate in the willing suspension of disbelief.

La Grange aux rencontres is a psychodrama featuring two ragged beggars, Gus and Hanna, coming to terms with their criminal past and their lifelong flight from it. Gus and Hanna's unexpected reckoning occurs when they spend the night in a shed used for storage in a small village. On the primary stage they are welcomed by the condescending secretary of the mayor, and then they are guided through their consciences by a mysterious character named The Vagabond. The two main characters simultaneously appear on two separate stages, one representing their present, the other their past. By means of spotlight and blackout, the audience is able to witness the reenactment of four murders that occurred fifteen years earlier and piece together the fragmented lives of the two protagonists. On the illuminated stage representing their past, "Young Gus" stabs Niels, and "Young Hanna" poisons Martha, thus murdering their respective rivals; their retarded daughter Simplice poisons the coffee of Maria, the fiancée of their son George, who then strangles Simplice, stuffs her body down a well, and flees through a swamp to escape punishment. Hence, on the second stage the spectators and the protagonists witness a cinematographic replay of the repressed memories of Gus and Hanna—a "camera-eye" technique found in all of Desvignes's writings.

Desvignes's use of the "camera-eye" technique demonstrates that she was keenly aware of a synergy among art forms during the 1950s. Moviemakers were seeking to legitimize cinema by imitating the *littérarité* ("literarity") of written forms. While some novelists began to doubt the continued relevance of fiction and turned to journalism, others turned to the "silver screen" or to television to dramatize their narratives. Meanwhile, some dramatists became cinematographers, and some cinematographers set out to be the sole authors of their movies. The cross-fertilization that occurred in this time of uncertainty and change in the literary world proved fruitful. Additionally, Desvignes engaged contemporary dramatic theory: during this era theoreticians of modern theater attempted to justify the onstage creation of an archetypical collective unconscious where memory could be invoked as a premonition of the present. When she wrote *La Grange aux rencontres,* Desvignes became one of the first French playwrights to anticipate and apply these techniques, trends, and theories.

Eurydice, Eurydice is a one-act play that offers further insight into Desvignes's dramatic skills. While the stage setting is that of "an old-fashioned provincial park overlooking the fracas of the city," the play derives its title and theme from the Orphic myth, recast in modern times (the 1920s) in order to dramatize the cosmic workings behind our self-inflicted losses and the fateful results of our failure to communicate with those we love. The cast includes The Lady, The Man, The Man's Wife, a woman in search of cats, Henrietta's mother, a child in search of a kite, and two paramedics. Each character represents a quest for something or someone.

Desvignes portrays the fortuitous encounter between a distinguished blind man about fifty-five years of age and a woman he once loved and lost. When The Man's Wife goes off on a walk to escape her husband's acerbic remarks, The Man has the fateful meeting and conversation with his lost love, The Lady. They meet in the same public park where years ago they fell in love. The Lady has returned after years of absence, and their meeting enables both to "see" the day of their separation and to reconstruct, through animated dialogue that revives the past, the misunderstanding that led to the dissolution of their relationship, her departure, and the different paths they took as a result of their failure to pronounce the words that might have altered their destinies. The dialogue between them constitutes an Orphic descent into memory, an encounter with the failure that changed their lives—a cathartic illumination that allows each of them to accept the bitter truths that neither had been able fully to comprehend. A love story of mythical proportions, the play represents the frailty of the human spirit and the power of words to reward or to thwart efforts to achieve individual happiness. Radio France 1 first aired a performance of the play on 6 June 1986. *Eurydice, Eurydice* was first performed in English translation at Ohio State University at Newark on 25 September 1998.

L'Editeur et la dame was read publicly at the Fête du Livre de Beaune (Book Festival of Beaune) on 18 October 1988. Based on an unpublished short story by Desvignes, this play is set in the head office of a Parisian publishing firm. An eccentric gate-crasher manages to reach the Executive's desk. She sits on the desk and imperiously gives the Executive a summary of the manuscript she has brought and demands that he accept it. During the exchange she explains how she progressively turned into a cannibal. The fight between a publisher weakened by digestive problems and a harpy who has carefully planned that she will have the upper hand is obviously unequal. In the end, the apostle of cannibalism succeeds in extorting a profitable contract from the publishing firm. The publisher accepts the manuscript about cannibalism on the premise that such a scandalous story can ensure the book's success.

Desvignes's play *Le Cri du ventre* (The Cry of the Stomach) closely resembles some of her major prose works in her use of an historical subject. It was commissioned for the bicentennial of the French Revolution in conjunction with an exhibit on the history of bread in France. *Le Cri du ventre* was performed from 12 to 22 October 1989 at Lyons-Feyzin as one of three forty-five-minute plays produced in a triptych, the others featuring a supper among the nobility and a bourgeois dinner among a charity parish board. Desvignes's theme was hunger among the people during the French Revolution. In her play the people of the provinces of France echo the sentiments and pleas of the famished Parisians who marched on the Court at Versailles in October 1789 and brought back to Paris "the Baker, the Baker's Wife and the Baker's Assistant" (meaning the royal family, who was supposed to put an end to the shortage of bread by their mere presence in the capital). The historical facts are presented to hungry villagers through a glove-puppet show by an itinerant peddler, an event that spreads the idea of revolution as necessary to fight the abject misery of the people. Once again, clever dramatic effects are produced by Desvignes: this time her

Cover for the 2002 translations of three of Desvignes's plays, all of which rework ancient Greek myths. These works have not been published in French (Howard-Tilton Memorial Library, Tulane University).

use of "a play within a play" through the onstage performance of the puppet show.

Desvignes was promoted to the rare distinction of Commandeur dans l'Ordre des Palmes académiques (Commander in the Order of Academic Palms) in 1978. That year her career as a writer of fiction began when she purchased a Rhodia No. 16 writing pad and proceeded to compose at one sitting the opening thirty pages of her first novel, *Les Nœuds d'argile* (Bonds of Clay). The manuscript eventually filled several writing pads, and the typescript was published in 1982 by Alain Schrotter in Dijon under the Editions de Civry imprint. The novel received the 1982 Prix Roland Dorgelès (Roland Dorgelès Prize). *Les Nœuds d'argile* became the first part of *Les Mains nues* (Naked Hands), a three-volume, two-thousand-page saga that traces the history of Desvignes's Burgundian ancestors. The other two novels in the series are *Le Grain du chanvre, ou L'Histoire de Jeanne* (1985, The Texture of Linen, or The Story of Jeanne) and *Le Livre de Juste* (1986, The Book of Juste). *Le Grain du Chanvre, ou l'Histoire de Jeanne* and the

1985 republication of *Les Nœuds d'argile* feature laudatory prefaces by Jacques Lacarrière. In 1986 the three volumes of Desvignes's family saga were collected as *Les Mains nues*, and that year they received the Prix Bourgogne (Burgandy Award).

In a subsequent two-volume saga, *Les Mains libres* (Free Hands), Desvignes romanticizes the history of her husband's ancestors who migrated from Luxembourg to "The Americas." The abject poverty of Luxembourg and the devastating effect poverty had on André Desvignes's ancestors is recounted in *Vent debout* (1991, Head Winds). Their migration across the Atlantic to Pennsylvania is then depicted in *La Brise en poupe* (1993, Tail Winds).

Desvignes also has authored more difficult-to-classify novels. In 1984 the Parisian publishing house Fayard published *Clair de nuit* (Night Glow), which is at once a murder mystery, an interior monologue, a love story, and the anatomy of a dying man. It was awarded presentation on the literary television show by Bernard Pivot called *Apostrophes,* a French cultural event and institution for nearly twenty years. Desvignes's 1992 novel *La Maison sans volets* (The House without Shutters) combines a murder mystery, a psychological novel, and a political statement on urban renewal. *La Nuit de la chouette* (2001, The Night of the Owl) is a detective story, and *La Seconde visite* (2003, The Second Visit) tells a tale of vengeance in a southern Burgundian village and the failure of the locals to participate wholeheartedly in a reconciliation with a German tour operator, a former Nazi occupier.

In 1984 Desvignes received the Prix de l'Humour Alexis Piron (Alexis Piron Humor Award) for "Une Consultation" (A Consultation), a short story that was published later in her 1988 short-story collection *Famille, familles* (Family, Families). In 1991 a literary prize for the short story, the Prix Lucette Desvignes de la Nouvelle (Lucette Desvignes Prize for the Short Story), was created in her honor in Chalon-sur-Saône. In 2001 Desvignes published a second short-story collection, *Affaires de familles* (Family Matters). Many of these works had been published in *Studies on Lucette Desvignes* between 1992 and 2000. Desvignes's storytelling abilities are also on display in *Contes du vignoble* (1993, Tales of the Vine) and *Le Père Noël est un chien: Contes de Noël* (2000, Santa Claus is a Dog: Christmas Tales). *Contes du vignoble* is dedicated to the villages and villagers of Saône-et-Loire and the Côte d'Or. In the book Desvignes describes villagers she and her husband knew, capturing the character of her native Burgundy. In *Le Père Noël est un chien*, Desvignes creates a collection of animal characters that think and talk and behave like humans.

Desvignes has also written the first volume of an autobiography, *Le Miel de l'aube*. In it she recounts her youth and adolescence in Burgundy during the German occupation of France. Her desire to portray life in the provinces accurately, on display both in the autobiography and in *Les Mains nues*, explains the title Patrick Brady has given to his critical study of Desvignes's oeuvre: *Daughter of Burgundy: Lucette Desvignes and the French Tradition* (1995).

After Desvignes and her husband retired in 1984, they traveled often, mainly to Italy and the United States, where they visited more than forty-five states including Hawaii. Desvignes currently resides in Dijon, where she still actively pursues her literary career. She has completed a five-act play titled *Encore toi, Electre!* (You Again, Electra!) and the first two volumes of her diary, covering 1992–1993 and 1994–1995, named *A Caustic View of Things in This World*. These works are in the hands of the publisher, together with two novels, *Voyage en Botulie* (A Journey to Botuly) and *Ravello, ou Le 13éme Jour* (Ravello, or The 13th Day).

Lucette Desvignes's work has been included in the curricula of several foreign universities, including schools in Athens, Bucharest, and Mainz. In North America, her work has been part of the curricula at Rice University, Ohio State University, and the University of Tennessee, as well as Regina University in Saskatchewan, Canada. Desvignes has been honored at two international conferences, and since 1991 a scholarly journal, *Studies on Lucette Desvignes and the Twentieth Century,* has focused on her work. Additionally, a Center for Studies on Lucette Desvignes was established on the Newark Campus of Ohio State University in September 1997.

References:

Patrick Brady, *Daughter of Burgundy: Lucette Desvignes and the French Tradition* (Knoxville, Tenn.: New Paradigm, 1995);

Jerry L. Curtis, *The Imprisoned Hero in Camus, Beckett, and Desvignes* (Knoxville, Tenn.: New Paradigm, 1995);

Curtis, *Lucette Desvignes sur le chemin de la vendage* (Précy-sous-Thil: Armançon, 2004);

Curtis, ed., *Essays on the Work of French Author Lucette Desvignes* (New York: Edwin Mellen Press, 2000);

Sharon Diane Nell, Bernadette C. Lintz, George Poe, and Brady, eds., *The French Novel: from Lafayette to Desvignes: Collected Essays to Mark the 60th Birthday of Patrick Brady* (Knoxville, Tenn.: New Paradigm, 1995);

Jacqueline Sessa, "Passion et Catharsis dans le Théâtre de Lucette Desvignes," *Studies on Lucette Desvignes and the Twentieth Century,* 7 (1997): 103–116;

Sessa, "Temps et Espace dans le Théâtre de Lucette Desvignes," *Studies on Lucette Desvignes and the Twentieth Century,* 12 (2002): 23–45;

Sessa, "L'Arbre, l'insecte . . . et l'Homme dans l'œuvre de Lucette Desvignes," *Studies on Lucette Desvignes and the Twentieth Century,* 13 (2003): 31–46.

Marguerite Duras
(Marguerite Donnadieu)
(4 April 1914 – 3 March 1996)

Elizabeth M. Anthony
Wake Forest University

See also the Duras entry in *DLB 83: French Novelists Since 1960.*

PLAY PRODUCTIONS: *Le Square,* Paris, Studio des Champs-Elysées, 17 September 1956; revised version, Paris, Théâtre Daniel-Sorano, 15 January 1965;

Les Viaducs de la Seine-et-Oise, Paris, Théâtre de Poche, 1960;

Les Papiers d'Aspern, adapted by Duras and Robert Antelme from Michael Redgrave's stage adaptation of Henry James's "The Aspern Papers," Paris, Théâtre des Mathurins, 1961;

La Bête dans la jungle, Paris, Théâtre de l'Athénée, September 1962;

Les Eaux et forêts, Paris, Théâtre Mouffetard, 14 May 1965;

La Musica, Paris, Studio des Champs-Elysées, 8 October 1965;

Des Journées entières dans les arbres, Paris, Odéon-Théâtre de France, 1 December 1965; revised version, Paris, Théâtre d'Orsay, 15 October 1975;

"Yes," peut-être and *Le Shaga,* Paris, Théâtre Gramont, 5 January 1968;

L'Amante anglaise, Paris, Théâtre National Populaire, Salle Gémier, 16 December 1968;

Suzanna Andler, Paris, Théâtre des Mathurins, December 1969;

La Danse de mort, adapted from August Strindberg's play, Paris, Théâtre du Palais de Chaillot, 21 February 1970;

L'Eden cinéma, Paris, Théâtre d'Orsay, 25 October 1977;

Le Navire Nuit, Paris, Théâtre Edouard VII, 1978;

Savannah Bay, revised version, Paris, Théâtre du Rond-Point, 1983; original version, Paris, Théâtre du Palais de Chaillot, January 1995;

Véra Baxter, Paris, Théâtre de Poche Montparnasse, 1983;

Marguerite Duras (from the cover for L'Amante anglaise, *translated by Barbara Bray, 1968; Richland County Public Library)*

La Musica deuxième, Paris, Théâtre du Rond-Point, Salle Renaud-Barrault, 20 March 1985.

BOOKS: *Les Impudents* (Paris: Plon, 1943);

La Vie tranquille (Paris: Gallimard, 1944);

Un Barrage contre le Pacifique (Paris: Gallimard, 1950); translated by Herma Briffault as *The Sea Wall* (New York: Pellegrini & Cudahy, 1953); translated by Antonia White as *A Sea of Troubles* (London: Methuen, 1953);

Le Marin de Gibraltar (Paris: Gallimard, 1952); translated by Barbara Bray as *The Sailor from Gibraltar* (London: Calder & Boyars, 1966; New York: Grove, 1967);

Les Petits Chevaux de Tarquinia (Paris: Gallimard, 1953); translated by Peter Duberg as *The Little Horses of Tarquinia* (London: Calder, 1960; London: Calder / New York: Riverrun, 1985);

Des Journées entières dans les arbres, suivi de Le Boa, Madame Dodin, Les Chantiers (Paris: Gallimard, 1954); translated by Anita Barrows as *Whole Days in the Trees and Other Stories* (London: Calder / New York: Riverrun, 1984);

Le Square (Paris: Gallimard, 1955); translated by Sonia Pitt-Rivers and Irina Morduch as *The Square* (London: Calder, 1959; New York: Grove, 1959);

Moderato Cantabile (Paris: Minuit, 1958); translated by Richard Seaver (New York: Grove, 1960; London: Calder & Boyars, 1966);

Les Viaducs de le Seine-et-Oise (Paris: Gallimard, 1960); translated by Bray and Sonia Orwell as *The Viaducts of Seine and Oise*, in *Three Plays* (London: Calder & Boyars, 1967), pp. 117–159;

Dix Heures et demie du soir en été (Paris: Gallimard, 1960); translated by Anne Borchardt as *Ten-Thirty on a Summer Night* (London: Calder, 1962; New York: Grove, 1963);

Hiroshima mon amour (Paris: Gallimard, 1960); translated by Seaver (New York: Grove Weidenfeld, 1961; republished, 1966);

Une Aussi Longue Absence, by Duras and Gérard Jarlot (Paris: Gallimard, 1961); translated by Barbara Wright, in *Hiroshima mon amour; Une Aussi Longue Absence* (London: Calder & Boyars, 1966);

L'Après-midi de Monsieur Andesmas (Paris: Gallimard, 1962); translated by Borchardt as *The Afternoon of Monsieur Andesmas*, in *The Afternoon of Monsieur Andesmas; The Rivers and Forests* (London: Calder, 1964);

Miracle en Alabama, adapted by Duras and Jarlot from William Gibson's *The Miracle Worker,* published with *L'Homme qui se taisait* by Pierre Gaillot (Paris: Avant-Scène, 1962);

Le Ravissement de Lol V. Stein (Paris: Gallimard, 1964); translated by Seaver as *The Ravishing of Lol V. Stein* (New York: Grove, 1967); translated by Eileen Ellenbogen as *The Rapture of Lol V. Stein* (London: Hamilton, 1967);

Théâtre I: Les Eaux et forêts, Le Square, La Musica (Paris: Gallimard, 1965); *Les Eaux et forêts* translated as *The Rivers and Forests*, in *The Afternoon of Monsieur Andesmas; The Rivers and Forests* (London: Calder, 1964); *Le Square* translated by Bray and Orwell as *The Square*, in *Three Plays* (London: Calder & Boyars, 1967), pp. 7–64; *La Musica* translated by Bray, in *Suzanna Andler; La Musica; & L'Amante anglaise* (London: Calder, 1975);

Des Journées entières dans les arbres (Paris: Avant-Scène, 1966); translated by Bray and Orwell as *Days in the Trees,* in *Three Plays* (London: Calder & Boyars, 1967), pp. 65–116;

Le Vice-Consul (Paris: Gallimard, 1966); translated by Ellenbogen as *The Vice-Consul* (London: Hamilton, 1968; New York: Pantheon, 1987);

L'Amante anglaise (novel) (Paris: Gallimard, 1967); translated by Bray (London: Hamilton, 1968; New York: Grove, 1968);

L'Amante anglaise (play) (Paris: Cahiers du Théâtre National Populaire, 1968); revised as *Le Théâtre de l'amante anglaise* (Paris: Gallimard, 1991); original version translated by Bray, in *Suzanna Andler; La Musica; & L'Amante anglaise* (London: Calder, 1975);

Théâtre II: Suzanna Andler; Des Journées entières dans les arbres; Yes, peut-être; Le Shaga; Un Homme est venu me voir (Paris: Gallimard, 1968); *Suzanna Andler* translated by Bray, in *Suzanna Andler; La Musica; & L'Amante anglaise* (London: Calder, 1975), pp. 1–66;

Détruire, dit-elle (Paris: Minuit, 1969); translated by Bray as *Destroy, She Said* (London: Hamilton, 1970; New York: Grove, 1970);

Abahn, Sabana, David (Paris: Gallimard, 1970);

Les Papiers d'Aspern, adapted by Duras and Robert Antelme from Michael Redgrave's stage adaptation of Henry James's "The Aspern Papers" (Paris: Paris-Théâtre, 1970);

L'Amour (Paris: Gallimard, 1971);

Ah Ernesto (Paris: François Ruy-Vidal, 1971);

India Song: Texte-théâtre-film (Paris: Gallimard, 1973); translated by Bray (New York: Grove, 1976; London: Oberon, 1992);

Nathalie Granger, suivi de La Femme du Gange (Paris: Gallimard, 1973);

Home, adapted from the play by David Storey (Paris: Gallimard, 1973);

Le Camion, suivi de Entretien avec Michelle Porte (Paris: Minuit, 1977);

L'Eden cinéma (Paris: Mercure de France, 1977); translated by Bray as *Eden Cinema*, in *Four Plays* (London: Oberon, 1992), pp. 48–95;

Le Navire Night; Césarée; Les Mains négatives; Aurélia Steiner, Aurélia Steiner, Aurélia Steiner (Paris: Mercure de France, 1979);

Véra Baxter, ou Les Plages de l'Atlantique (Paris: Albatros, 1980);

L'Homme assis dans le couloir (Paris: Minuit, 1980); translated by Mary Lydon as *The Seated Man in the Passage, Contemporary Literature,* 24 (Summer 1973): 259–275;

L'Eté 80 (Paris: Minuit, 1980);

Les Yeux verts (Paris: Cahiers du cinéma, 1980); translated by Carol Barks as *Green Eyes* (New York: Columbia University Press, 1990);

Agatha (Paris: Minuit, 1981); translated by Howard Limoli, in *Agatha; Savannah Bay: Two Plays* (Sausalito: Post-Apollo, 1992);

Outside: Papiers d'un jour (Paris: Michel, 1981); translated by Arthur Goldhammer as *Outside: Selected Writings* (Boston: Beacon, 1986);

L'Homme atlantique (Paris: Minuit, 1982); translated by Alberto Manguel as *The Atlantic Man*, in *Two by Duras* (Toronto: Coach House Press, 1993), pp. 31-58;

Savannah Bay (Paris: Minuit, 1982; revised, 1983); translated by Bray, in *Four Plays* (London: Oberon, 1992); translated by Limoli in *Agatha; Savannah Bay: Two Plays* (Sausalito: Post-Apollo, 1992);

La Maladie de la mort (Paris: Minuit, 1982); translated by Bray as *The Malady of Death* (New York: Grove, 1986);

Théâtre III: "La Bête dans le jungle," d'après Henry James, adaptation de James Lord et Marguerite Duras; "Les Papiers d'Aspern," d'après Henry James, adaptation de Marguerite Duras et Robert Antelme; "La Danse de mort," d'après August Strindberg, adaptation de Marguerite Duras (Paris: Gallimard, 1984);

L'Amant (Paris: Minuit, 1984); translated by Bray as *The Lover* (New York: Pantheon, 1985; London: Flamingo, 1986);

La Douleur (Paris: POL, 1985); translated by Bray as *The War: A Memoir* (New York: Pantheon, 1986; London: Collins, 1986);

La Musica deuxième (Paris: Gallimard, 1985); translated by Bray, in *Four Plays* (London: Oberon, 1992), pp. 9-46;

La Mouette de Tchekov (Paris: Gallimard, 1985);

Les Yeux bleus, cheveux noirs (Paris: Minuit, 1986); translated by Bray as *Blue Eyes, Black Hair* (New York: Pantheon, 1987; London: Collins, 1987);

La Pute de la côte normande (Paris: Minuit, 1986); translated by Manguel as *The Slut of the Normandy Coast*, in *Two by Duras* (Toronto: Coach House Press, 1993), pp. 9-27;

Emily L. (Paris: Minuit, 1987); translated by Bray (New York: Pantheon, 1989; London: Collins, 1989);

La Vie matérielle: Marguerite Duras parle a Jérôme Beaujour (Paris: POL, 1987); translated by Bray as *Practicalities: Marguerite Duras Speaks to Jérôme Beaujour* (New York: Grove Weidenfeld, 1990; London: Collins, 1990);

La Pluie d'été (Paris: POL, 1990); translated by Bray as *Summer Rain* (New York: Scribners, 1992);

L'Amant de la Chine du nord (Paris: Gallimard, 1991); translated by Leigh Hafrey as *The North China Lover* (New York: New York Press, 1992; London: Flamingo, 1992);

Yann Andréa Steiner (Paris: POL, 1992); translated by Bray as *Yann Andrea Steiner* (New York: Scribners, 1993);

Ecrire (Paris: Gallimard, 1993);

Le Monde extérieur (Paris: POL, 1993);

C'est tout (Paris: POL, 1995);

Théâtre IV: Véra Baxter; L'Eden cinéma; Le théâtre de l'amante anglaise; adaptations de "Home" par David Storey et "La Mouette" par Anton Tchékov (Paris: Gallimard, 1999).

Collection: *Romans, Cinéma, Théâtre, Un parcours 1943-1993* (Paris: Gallimard, 1997).

Edition in English: *The Man Sitting in the Corridor*, translated by Barbara Bray (New York: Blue Moon Books, 1991).

PRODUCED SCRIPTS: *Hiroshima mon amour*, motion picture, Argos, 1959;

Une Aussi Longue Absence, motion picture, by Duras and Gérard Jarlot, Galatea, 1961;

La Musica, motion picture, Raoul Plaquin Films, 1966;

Détruire, dit-elle, motion picture, Ancinex & Madeleine Films, 1969;

Jaune le soleil, motion picture, Albina, 1971;

Nathalie Granger, motion picture, Mouflet, 1972;

La Femme du Gange, motion picture, Albina, 1973;

India Song, motion picture, Armorial & Sunchild, 1975;

Baxter, Vera Baxter, motion picture, Institut National de l'Audiovisuel, 1976;

Son Nom de Venise dans Calcutta desert, motion picture, 1976;

Des Journées entières dans les arbres, motion picture, Antenne 2/Duras Films/Théâtre d'Orsay, 1976;

Le Camion, motion picture, Auditel/Cinéma 9, 1977;

Le Navire Night, motion picture, Losange, 1978;

Césarée, motion picture, 1979;

Les Mains négatives, motion picture, 1979;

Aurélia Steiner, dite Aurélia Melbourne, motion picture, 1979;

Aurélia Steiner, dite Aurélia Vancouver, motion picture, 1979;

Agatha ou les lectures illimitées, motion picture, Institut National de l'Audiovisuel/Berthemont, 1981;

L'Homme atlantique, motion picture, Des Femmes Filment/Institut National de l'Audiovisuel/Berthemont, 1981;

Dialogue de Rome, motion picture, Rai Cinecitta, 1982;

Les Enfants, motion picture, 1985.

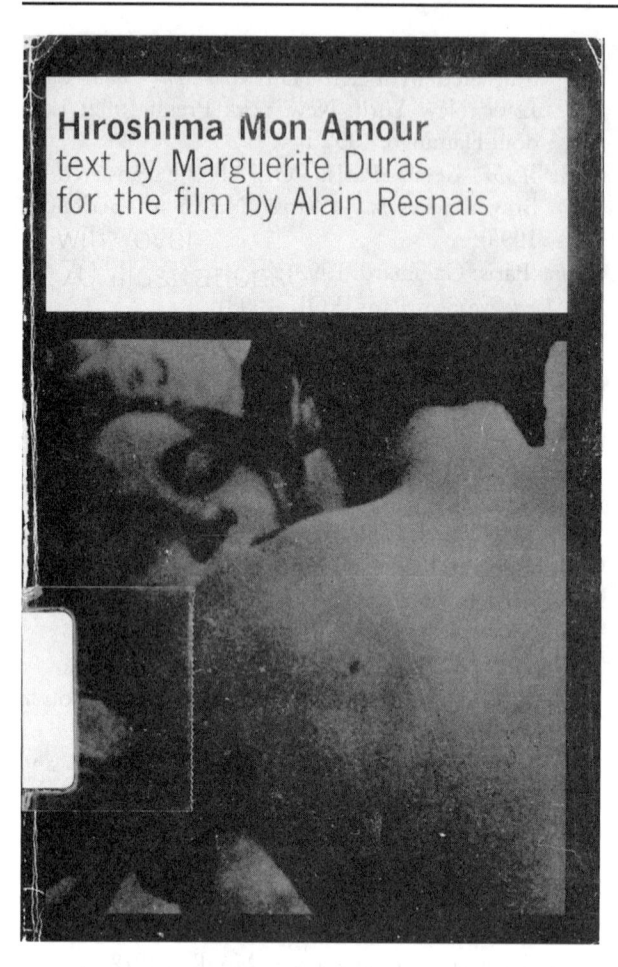

Cover for the English translation (1961) of Duras's script for the 1959 movie about a French actress who tells a Japanese architect about her affair with a German soldier during World War II (Richland County Public Library)

OTHER: "Notes on *India Song,*" in *Marguerite Duras,* by Duras, François Barat, and Joël Farges (Paris: Albatros, 1975).

Marguerite Duras published more than seventy works during her lifetime, making her one of the most prolific French writers of the twentieth century. She began her literary career as a novelist and eventually turned to theater and movies, but whether she was working as a novelist, journalist, playwright, stage director, or moviemaker, she always considered herself a writer. Duras's novels, short stories, plays, scenarios, and motion pictures are all marked by her distinctive voice. Her poetic and enigmatic style of writing often mixes literary genres. In fact, much of the innovation in her work stems from the way in which she borrows properties from one genre to expand the boundaries of another. Additionally, Duras frequently reworked and rewrote material. She transformed several of her works from the page to the stage to the screen, and she challenged the very notion of autobiography by writing multiple versions of the story of her childhood in her novels. Duras's fictional works feature recurring characters, settings, and motifs. The themes she frequently explores include memory and forgetting, love and desire, poverty, injustice, insanity, silence, and death.

Duras's plays underscore the power of narrative in the theater. They often unfold in the aftermath of an event. There are rarely more than two or three characters on Duras's stage, and minimal settings and subtle movements emphasize the importance of the characters' words. The gaps and omissions in Duras's scripts require the reader or spectator to play an active role in the construction of her narratives, and her plays frequently end on a note of uncertainty. Her characters include storytellers who relate past events; investigators who try to understand a criminal psyche; and individuals once intimately involved who come together to discuss a shared past. In other works, friends or strangers simply join one another in conversation. These characters' discussions rarely shed light on their relationships, but they do raise questions about relationships in general. Duras often weaves complex ideas into daily conversation, shedding light on painful aspects of human existence.

Duras was born Marguerite Donnadieu on 4 April 1914 in Gia-Dinh, north of Saigon. Her father, Henri Donnadieu, was a professor of mathematics from Lot-et-Garonne who left France in 1905 to teach in French Colonial Indochina (Vietnam). Her mother, Marie Legrand, the daughter of poor farmers in northern France, was a schoolteacher who had been appointed to teach in Indochina. The couple married in 1909. In 1918 they moved to Phnom Penh, Cambodia, with their three children, Pierre (born in 1910), Paul (born in 1911), and Marguerite. Marguerite was only four years old when her father became ill and returned to France. By the time he died in 1921, Marie Donnadieu had already assumed the financial responsibility of raising her three children. She taught in a native school in Phnom Penh for two years before moving to Sadec, then Vinh Long, a town on the Mekong.

In order to support her family, Marie Donnadieu continued teaching and began to play piano in a silent-movie house. Looking for a way to enhance her income, she purchased some property at Prey Nop in Cambodia in 1928, only to discover that the land could not be cultivated. Each year her crops were washed away by the Pacific Ocean. With the help of local peasants she attempted to construct a seawall, but it crumbled, unable to withstand the force of the waters in the floodplain.

Distraught by her financial ruin, Marie Donnadieu began to focus on her daughter's education. Unlike her brothers, Marguerite had done well in school, showing a great deal of potential. At fifteen years old Marguerite left her home to attend the Lycée Chasseloup-Laubat in Saigon. There Marguerite met a wealthy Chinese man who became her lover. This relationship figured in Duras's most celebrated novel, *L'Amant* (1984; translated as *The Lover*, 1985), and also in *L'Amant de la Chine du nord* (1991; translated as *The North China Lover*, 1992).

The places and people of Duras's childhood and adolesence figure predominantly in all of her works. Throughout her "Indochinese Cycle," which includes *Un Barrage contre le Pacifique* (1950; translated as *The Sea Wall*, 1953), *L'Eden cinéma* (1977; translated as *Eden Cinema*, 1992), *L'Amant*, and *L'Amant de la Chine du nord*. Duras portrays aspects of her family life. She writes of a mother who loves her eldest son more than her other children. She portrays a thieving, violent older brother. She describes the younger of her two brothers as someone she loves deeply. Additionally, *Un Barrage contre le Pacifique* and *L'Eden cinéma* describe her mother's determination and her struggle to provide for her children.

Duras also relies on her memories of life in French Colonial Indochina in her "India Cycle," which comprises *Le Ravissement de Lol V. Stein* (1964; translated as *The Ravishing of Lol V. Stein*, 1967), *Le Vice-Consul* (1966; translated as *The Vice-Consul*, 1968), *L'Amour* (1971, Love), *La Femme du Gange* (published and produced as movie 1973, The Woman of the Ganges), *India Song* (published 1973; produced as movie 1975; translated, 1976), and the movie *Son Nom de Vénise dans Calcutta desert* (1976, Her Venetian Name in Deserted Calcutta). In 1926 Duras's mother took in a beggar who was trying to sell her baby, and the image of the poverty-stricken woman and the sounds of her pain mark the India Cycle. Later, while traveling to school in Saigon, Duras took note of the new general administrator's wife, Elisabeth Striedter. Elegant and elusive, Striedter became Anne-Marie Stretter of *India Song* and a recurring figure in Duras's oeuvre. The brief description of Duras that appeared in several of her published novels and plays underscores the importance of the setting of her youth: "Marguerite Duras est née en Indochine où son père était professeur de mathématiques et sa mère institutrice. A part un bref séjour en France pendant son enfance, elle ne quitta Saigon qu'à l'âge de dix-huit ans" (Marguerite Duras was born in Indochina where her father was professor of mathematics and her mother, a teacher. Aside from a short stay in France during her childhood, she lived in Saigon until the age of eighteen).

In 1932 Duras traveled to Paris, France, where she passed the *baccalauréat* in philosophy with Vietnamese as a foreign language and studied mathematics, law, and political science. During this time she became an avid theatergoer, and she was particularly enamored with Georges Pitoëff's productions at the Théâtre des Mathurins. At the Faculté de droit (law school) she met Robert Antelme, a member of the French Communist Party. They married in 1939 and moved into an apartment on the Left Bank. Their address, 5 rue Saint-Benoît, became well known among Parisian intellectuals. The couple hosted gatherings attended by writers, philosophers, and politicians for many years. Duras, who had worked for the Ministry of Colonies since 1937, left her job in 1940 and began to write.

Her first novel, *Les Impudents* (The Shameless), was published by Plon in 1943 under the nom de plume Duras, taken from the name of a small town in Lot-et-Garonne where she had vacationed as a child. That same year, Duras, Antelme, and their close friend Dionys Mascolo entered the French Resistance. Antelme and Duras's apartment became a meeting place for members of the Resistance, including the young François Mitterand. Following the publication of Duras's second novel, *La Vie tranquille* (1944, The Tranquil Life), her husband was arrested by the Gestapo and sent to a concentration camp. In the fall of 1944 Duras joined the French Communist Party. She was an active member for six years, hosting many meetings at her home. With the help of Mitterand, Duras eventually located her husband at Dachau. He was sent home in 1945, but he was barely alive. Duras nursed him back to health before they divorced the following year. Despite the end of their marriage, the couple maintained a friendly relationship and kept their apartment together for many years. In 1947 Duras had a son, Jean, with Mascolo, with whom she had fallen in love. Between 1950 and 1955 she published four novels and a collection of short stories before turning her attention to the theater.

Duras's first play, *Le Square* (expanded version published 1965; translated as *The Square*, 1967), premiered in Paris in 1956. According to Gilles Costaz, Duras had not considered writing for the theater until director Claude Martin asked her to collaborate with him on a theatrical adaptation of her recent novel, *Le Square* (1955; translated as *The Square*, 1959). She then reworked the narrative with such ease that she claimed she had originally written a play without knowing it. Duras attended rehearsals and was so pleased with the performances of Ketty Albertini and R.-J. Chauffard that she interfered little in the staging of the play. The play received little attention from critics, although one admirer, Samuel Beckett, attended four performances. In 1965 Duras lengthened the play for director Alain Astruc; she published this version of *Le Square* that year in *Théâtre I*.

As the title suggests, the play is set in a quiet square, with the action occurring between 4:30 in the afternoon and nightfall. The nameless characters, a

Dust jacket for the 1968 English translation of Duras's 1967 novel, in which the parts of a dismembered body are found on trains in various parts of France. Duras rewrote the narrative as a play in 1968 (Richland County Public Library).

twenty-year-old young woman and a forty-year-old man, sit inconspicuously on a bench in the square. The man is a traveling salesman and the woman is a maid looking after her employer's young child. The child's request for a snack prompts the man to speak, and he begins to do so freely. The young woman asks many questions, and he answers her in a polite and cautious manner. He describes his life as a traveling salesman. Although he is sometimes lonely and afraid, he accepts his lifestyle and is resistant to change. His job, like any other, requires perseverance, patience, and endurance. He is able to eat regular meals, and he enjoys the small pleasures in life–reading the newspaper, conversing in cafés, and seeing beautiful landscapes. The young woman listens and tries to imagine a lifestyle so unlike her own. Unlike the salesman, she views her job as a temporary situation; she dreams of the day she will tell her employer she is leaving. She does not wish to travel. She longs to marry and have a home of her own. In fact, the hope that someone will ask for her hand in marriage keeps her going. Meanwhile, she works dutifully and does all that is asked of her. She feels that if she were to refuse to perform a task, it would be as if she viewed her situation as something permanent.

Throughout the play the child plays independently. He interrupts the dialogue on two occasions, once announcing that he is thirsty and once announcing that he is tired, and his voice actually divides the play into three parts. At first, the man and the young woman have different points of view and their situations seem to be incompatible. As their conversation develops in the second part of the play, the audience learns they have much in common. They speak of love, death, loneliness, hope, and incidents from the past that continue to haunt them. They develop an understanding of one another, and they share many opinions. Both agree that conversation is an essential part of life: as the young woman claims, "Oui, je sais, il semble alors qu'on pourrait se passer de tout, de manger, de dormir, plutôt que de bavarder" (Yes, I know, it seems as if it would be easier to give up eating and sleeping, than talking). As night falls the audience is prompted to wonder if the man and the young woman will meet again, but at the close of the play it remains uncertain whether he will join her on Saturday night at a local dance and whether he will be the one to take her hand in marriage. While a happy ending is possible, the sadness of the characters suggests that their conversation in the square will be their last.

After her first foray into theater, Duras became a journalist for *France-Observateur* (France Observer). She continued to pursue her literary interests, however, and in 1958 she published one of her most successful novels, a crime story titled *Moderato Cantabile* (translated, 1960). The following year her script *Hiroshima Mon Amour* (Hiroshima My Love, published 1960; translated, 1961) was produced as a movie.

Duras chose a crime story for her next play, *Les Viaducs de la Seine-et-Oise* (published and produced 1960; translated as *The Viaducs of Seine and Oise*, 1967). The plot was based on the account of a crime Duras had followed in *France-Observateur,* a story that was also covered by *Le Monde* (The World) in January 1950. Local authorities had pieced together a mutilated body in the town of Savigny-sur-Orge. The victim was a retired employee of the National Railway Company (La Société Nationale des Chemins de Fer [SNCF]) whose wife murdered him at home while he was reading the newspaper. She dismembered his body and disposed of his remains by dropping them onto trains as they passed under a bridge in Savigny-sur-Orge. She then reported the disappearance of her husband, but after being questioned by the authorities, she confessed to the crime.

Duras was fascinated by this story and returned to it on four different occasions. Her first version of it, *Les Viaducs de la Seine-et-Oise,* premiered in Paris in 1960 and was awarded the Prix de la Jeune Critique (The Young Critics' Prize). In this play Duras altered the facts of the crime: both the husband and wife commit murder, and their victim is the wife's cousin, Marie-Thérèse, who had lived with them for twenty-seven years. Before the curtain rises, a voice describes the evidence that led the investigators to the couple. The authorities were able to identify both the victim and the location of the crime by putting together the pieces of the body and locating a viaduct under which all the trains in the region travel. The voice identifies the criminals as retired SNCF employees in their sixties. Their motive is never determined, yet they are both found guilty. The man is condemned to death, and the woman is sentenced to life in prison.

In act 1, the couple, Claire and Marcel, are biding their time at home. They have been following the investigation of their crime in the newspaper—mirroring the public's fascination with crime stories that disrupt the social order—and they expect to be interrogated. Meanwhile, they discuss the murder and how they disposed of the body. Although they try to understand what led them to commit such an unspeakable act, they cannot explain their actions. They do not know why they killed the deaf and mute Marie-Thérèse, who had prepared their meals and had never given them reason to complain. Marcel hopes that if the jury understands that they cannot explain their actions, the judgment will be more lenient. He searches for a way to avoid the death penalty. Claire, on the other hand, retreats into the past. She recalls the joy of hearing Giuseppe Verdi's *La Traviata* (1853, The Wayward Woman) in concert. The overture of *La Traviata* subsequently plays on a radio in the distance. The melodious sound of the music is juxtaposed with the sound of passing trains, which haunts the characters and interrupts the dialogue nine times in act 1.

Act 2 takes place in a local bar. Claire and Marcel are having an after-dinner drink. Bill, the owner of the bar, and Alphonso, a local farmer, discuss the crime that is in all the newspapers. They remark that the head is still missing and that without this crucial piece of evidence, it will be difficult to identify the victim. A young couple dances in the background, evoking notions of love and youth for the elderly couple. Claire and Marcel watch the couple dance as Bill watches Claire and Marcel. This spectatorship or voyeurism is typical of Duras's work and becomes more pronounced in her later plays. It often suggests a displaced or mediated desire. The young lover soon steps away from his companion and joins the conversation about the crime. The night wears on and the sound of passing trains serves as a constant reminder of the murder.

Through their conversation with the others Claire and Marcel admit their guilt. Claire argues that even murder may seem like a natural act when one is committing it. The young lover, an undercover detective, is the first to understand their confession. He waits until the final moments of the play to handcuff Claire and Marcel. The opening movement of *La Traviata* sounds in the theater as the curtain falls. Duras invites her audience to ponder the couple's motives—perhaps boredom or fear of aging and death led them to kill Marie-Thérèse, or perhaps her presence was somehow unbearable for them—but she confirms nothing. In later versions of the story Duras altered the story line and the sequence of events. Ultimately preferring her novel and play titled *L'Amante anglaise* (novel published 1967; play published and produced 1968; novel translated, 1968; play translated, 1975), she later withdrew publication and production rights of *Les Viaducs de la Seine-et-Oise.*

Following *Les Viaducs de la Seine-et-Oise,* Duras adapted two stories by Henry James for the theater. Written in collaboration with Antelme, *Les Papiers d'Aspern,* an adaptation of "The Aspern Papers" (1888), was performed for a sellout crowd at the Théâtre des Mathurins in Paris in 1961. In 1962 James Lord staged *La Bête dans la jungle,* Duras's successful adaptation of Henry James's "The Beast in the Jungle" (1903). This play was revived in 1981, and both adaptations of James's works were published by Gallimard in Duras's *Théâtre III* (1984). Duras and her friend Gérard Jarlot adapted William Gibson's *The Miracle Worker* (published and produced for television, 1957, produced as play 1959) as *Miracle en Alabama* (published 1962, Miracle in Alabama) in 1963.

After the premiere of her third adaptation in three years, Duras embarked on an original project. *Les Eaux et forêts* (published 1965; translated as *The Rivers and Forests,* 1964), Duras's first comic play, premiered in 1965 during her most prolific period as a playwright. It had a moderately successful run, but there has been little interest in the play since. Like *Le Square,* the play is set in a public space where the characters meet. The nature of their relationship is unclear: perhaps they are meeting for the first time, perhaps they have met before, or perhaps they know each other well. Nothing is certain because the man and the two women who convene on a sidewalk engage in nonsensical dialogue replete with wordplay and inanities, punctuated by the sound of a barking dog.

In the opening moments of the one-act play, the man cries out, for he has just been bitten by a dog. Two women come to his aid. The owner of the dog shows great concern. She later reveals that her dog has developed a habit of biting passersby. She tries to escort the man to the Pasteur Institute, where she is secretly compensated for her referrals. The man refuses treatment, however, claiming that his wound is minor. During their conversation the characters construct truths that they unravel in the end. Their names are as uncertain as their words and biographies. Zigou the dog answers to Toto and Mirza. The other characters address the dog's owner as Mrs. Thompson, Mrs. Johnson, Mrs. Simpson, and Marguerite-Victoire Sénéchal. The second woman recalls the story of Marguerite-Victoire Sénéchal's husband, who fell into a canal and died. She then speaks of her own husband, Duvivier, from whom she has kept a secret. The man, whose name may be Mr. Thompson, seems to know what the first woman did in 1932 on the shores of the Lac des Settons. He may be the man with whom she once danced the tango. The man claims that he is now wealthy, has many children, and works at the Mazarine Library.

The characters fabricate these claims as much for themselves as for their listeners. In the end, the first woman reveals, "c'est moi qui l'ai foutu dans le canal de la Marne au Rhin, mon mari" (I am the one who pushed my husband into the Marne au Rhin canal). The second woman announces, "Moi, c'est pire. J'ai pas de secret ni dedans, ni dehors, zéro. J'ai seulement Duvivier" (My case is worse. I don't have any kind of secret at all, nothing. I only have Duvivier). The man ultimately declares, "Moi, je ne suis de rien à la Mazarine, j'ai jamais été le moindre rouage dans la marche quelconque du moindre établissement public" (As for me, I am nothing to the Mazarine, I have never been the least little cog in the functioning of even the tiniest public establishment). As the play draws to a close, the man sings a tune and the women tap their feet in unison as if they are ready to invent new biographies and continue their conversation. In Duras's absurdist play, language and wordplay serve as an escape from a dreary existence.

Les Eaux et forêts marked the beginning of Duras's affiliation with actors Claire Deluca and René Erouk. They appeared in three other plays by Duras during the 1960s: *Yes, peut-être* (Yes, Maybe, 1968), *Le Shaga* (The Shaga, produced and published 1968), and *La Musica* (published and produced 1965; translated 1975). In *La Musica,* Deluca and Erouk play a couple who meet to finalize their divorce. Originally written for a British television station, *La Musica* premiered in Paris in 1965 at the Studio des Champs-Elysées.

La Musica takes place in a hotel lobby. Anne-Marie Roche and Michel Nollet, a couple in their mid thirties, have come to the town of Evreux to sign their divorce papers. Hence, the play opens at the end of their relationship. They did not need to come to Evreux to settle their affairs, however, and it soon becomes clear that they wanted to see one another again. They remain in the hotel lobby well into the night discussing their lives, including their past and the future. The quiet town in which they once lived has changed. There are even plans to build an airport. Anne-Marie and Michel then begin to share their lives with other people. The audience hears the voice of Michel's companion on the telephone as she awaits his return. Anne-Marie receives a telegram from her fiancé. She then tells Michel of her and her fiancé's plans to move to America after the wedding. He cannot bear the possibility of not running into her by chance, yet he could never leave France because of his work. Consequently, Anne-Marie comes to understand that he is still as preoccupied with his career as he was when they were married. The past seeps through their conversation in fragments. They recall their happiest moments together when they were living in the hotel. Once they moved into the house and tried to do as others do, they grew apart. She would go driving, go to bars, and go to movies in the afternoons. He had many affairs. She too had an affair. He recalls waiting for her return in a fit of jealousy: "Sur le quai de la gare j'ai voulu vous tuer. J'avais acheté une arme, j'attendais que vous descendiez du train pour vous tuer" (I wanted to kill you on the platform at the station. I had bought a gun, I was waiting for you to get off the train so I could kill you). Now they wonder what led them to commit adultery. Their painful love story is not over: they will always be in love. *La Musica,* like so many of Duras's plays, ends on a note of uncertainty. Michel remarks that the beginning and ending of their relationship seem somehow indistinguishable: "Maintenant. Le commencement ou la fin?" (Now. The beginning or the end?). The play was well received by the public and helped establish Duras's reputation as a playwright. In 1966 Duras wrote and co-directed a cinematic version, also titled *La Musica*. Then in 1985, twenty years after the premiere of the play, she added a second act and titled the new version *La Musica deuxième* (La Musica II, produced and published 1985; translated, 1992).

Beginning with *La Musica,* Duras's plays feature many stage directions. She pays great attention to detail, describing scenery and lighting as well as the actors' movements, facial expressions, emotions, gestures, and intonation. In fact, the plays published in *Théâtre II* (1968) reveal that Duras is a playwright concerned not just with dialogue but with the way it is spoken and with the silences and pauses that fall between the words. These works require a careful reading, for much of the narrative takes place in the characters' tone of voice, in their silences, and in their movements.

Duras's *Des Journées entières dans les arbres* (produced 1965, published 1966; translated as *Days in the Trees,* 1967), adapted from her 1954 short story of the same title (translated as "Whole Days in the Trees," 1984), illustrates her attention to detail. Through dialogue and explicit stage directions, Duras reveals the inner struggles of each of the three characters. She intermittently notes how and why the three main characters enter and exit the stage. At times a character's movement enables him or her to overhear conversations, and at other times it allows a character to speak freely in the absence of others. Throughout the text Duras describes how the characters react to one another and the emotions that accompany their words.

Des Journées entières dans les arbres tells the story of an aged mother who has returned to France to visit her grown son. It is a semi-autobiographical sketch in which Duras explores the relationship between her older brother and her mother. In the three-act play the preferred son, Jacques, is one of six children. He lives in a sparsely furnished apartment with a young woman named Marcelle. The play is a character study of the mother, her son, and Marcelle, and it is entirely set in the son's apartment and in the bar where he and Marcelle work. The characters eat, drink, play cards, and converse as they reveal their inner struggles. In the opening scene the mother tells Marcelle that she has traveled from her home in a former French colony. She adds, "Il me fallait revoir mon fils avant de mourir" (I had to see my son again before I die). The mother is dressed in black, and gold bracelets adorn her arms. She explains that she became wealthy late in life, and the irony is that she does not have time to spend her money. She is the owner of a factory, and her house is so large she simply wanders from room to room. Meanwhile, her son, now in his forties, has never really grown up. As a child Jacques spent his days climbing trees instead of attending school. While he thought that his truancy was a secret, his mother reveals that she always knew. Jacques has not changed his wild ways: he sleeps all day and spends his nights working in a club, gambling and womanizing. His thin frame and haggard eyes confirm his lifestyle. The mother is secretly pleased to find that Jacques is as dependant on her as ever. Marcelle is also weak and dependant. She speaks of her unfortunate childhood, and she does not expect Jacques to love her—she simply does not want to be abandoned. Duras establishes an important metaphor when all of the characters claim that they are hungry. The *choucroute* (sauerkraut) served at midday only seems to satisfy part of their hunger, and they all clearly crave something more from life. When *Des Journées entières dans les arbres* premiered at the Odéon-Théâtre in December 1965, critics applauded Duras's writing,

Title page for Duras's 1971 novel (Love), part of her "India Cycle" that included several scripts produced as movies in the mid 1970s (Thomas Cooper Library, University of South Carolina)

Jean-Louis Barrault's direction, and Madeline Renaud's memorable performance as the mother. In fact, the play is one of Duras's most critically acclaimed, largely because of Renaud's stunning performance.

Duras assumed the role of stage director for her next two plays, *Le Shaga* and *Yes, peut-être*. These dark comedies premiered in a double billing in January 1968, each with the same cast: Marie-Ange Dutheil, Deluca, and Erouk. Neither play was well received, however, and Duras abandoned this style of theater.

Yes, peut-être is an antiwar play. According to Duras's directions, the stage is uniformly beige, and the characters reside in the aftermath of a nuclear catastrophe. Two women, A and B, carry Geiger counters to detect radioactivity. Duras notes, "On entendra ou non battre ces compteurs" (These counters may or may not be heard). One of the women discovers a semiconscious man whose tattered clothing bears the emblems of the American flag, the Legion of Honor, and the *coq gaulois* (the French rooster), a national symbol. The words "l'honneur" (honor), "la patrie" (fatherland), and "God" adorn his clothing as well. He is the object of much of the women's conversation, although, as the last surviving soldier, he is a symbol of a shameful past to which they can only refer in a vague manner. Duras employs many adjectives to describe the women, including "innocents, insolents, tendres et gaies" (innocent, insolent, tender, and gay). They are also "sans malice, sans intelligence, sans mémoire" (without malice, without intelligence, without memory). The dialogue is as alienating as the setting, for it is as if the women must reinvent language. The masculine form of the pronoun "eux" (they) no longer exists; the word "guerre" (war) is difficult to pronounce; and "héros" (hero) is pronounced as "Eros." On one hand, the play appears to be about the impossibility of representing war. On the other, the intermittent use of English words and syntax, a reference to "Asios," and current events at the time of the inception of the play suggest that Duras may be deriding American involvement in Vietnam.

More language play occurs in *Le Shaga*. In fact, "Shaga" is a language of its own. In this play two women and a man are gathered in a courtyard. Duras notes, "Il est vraisemblable que se sont des fous dans une cour d'asile" (It is likely they are patients in the courtyard of an insane asylum). One of the women, B, speaks only Shaga. Her words must be translated by the other woman, A, so that the man, H, can follow their conversation. The audience soon learns that B has only been speaking Shaga since early that morning, but the only French word she recalls is "terminé" (finished). In general, the man is not satisfied with A's translations. They often consist of sentences such as, "Elle ne sait pas pourquoi elle rit" (She does not know why she is laughing) and "Elle ne sait pas si elle veut qu'on l'aide à trouver ce qu'elle veut" (She does not know if she wants us to help her figure out what she wants). At times, H can figure out what B is saying on his own since her language begins to follow a recognizable pattern. Regardless, H's words are no more lucid than those of the women. The man claims that he ran out of gas down the road two years ago. He is still carrying an oil can with holes. They all try to imagine how he could possibly fill the can. The man speaks of traveling to places such as Monte Carlo and Liverpool. He is particularly preoccupied with the story of a bird that he never quite manages to tell. At one point in the middle of the play, all three characters begin scratching themselves in a farcical manner. The play ends with all three characters laughing and uttering a greeting in Shaga that sounds much like the French phrase, "Ça va?" (How are you?). While patients in a mental institution might have the freedom to speak of serious matters, the characters in *Le Shaga* never do. They are too busy applauding one another's gags and reinventing language.

Duras's next play, *Suzanna Andler* (translated, 1975), was published in 1968 but not staged until 1969. It is a painful love story reminiscent of *La Musica*. Suzanna and Jean Andler are still married, yet they have been estranged for an indefinite period of time. Jean is a wealthy entrepreneur who has had a series of affairs over the years. Suzanna, now in her forties, claims that she bears the burden of being one of the most betrayed women in Saint-Tropez. For the first time in her life she has a lover, an associate of Jean's, who has accompanied her on her quest to rent a villa in Saint-Tropez for the summer. Her husband, she learns, is out of town with another woman while a governess looks after their young daughter in Paris. The plot unfolds at a villa by the sea. It is winter, and the gusty winds blow across the terrace and the deserted beach. Through a succession of conversations between Suzanna and the other characters, Duras begins to paint a portrait of a wistful woman. Whether she is speaking to the realtor Rivière, her friend Monique, or her lover Michel, Suzanna has difficulty telling the truth. Lying seems to come second nature to her as she tries to hide her unhappiness and suicidal thoughts from everyone except her husband. During a phone conversation with her husband, Suzanna appears to be truthful. Despite their painful history, she and Jean still respect one another. There is still intimacy and tenderness between them that she does not share with the other characters in the play. Their relationship is perhaps the most puzzling aspect of *Suzanna Andler:* there is no indication that Suzanna and Jean will ever stop having affairs, and it seems unlikely that they will divorce in the near future. Suzanna's final words addressed to Michel, "Peut-être que je t'aime" (Maybe I love you), have little impact.

Suzanna Andler also touches on the topic of alcohol. Earlier in the play Suzanna confesses to her husband that her lover encourages her to drink each night, and it often scares her. The presence and power of alcohol in the play reflects the playwright's life. Duras's ongoing preoccupation with alcohol began to seep into her plays and greatly affected the latter part of her career.

Suzanna Andler was not well received by the critics and was soon repudiated by Duras as well. Never able to abandon a text, however, Duras later returned to the story of Suzanna Andler, changing a few details and renaming her heroine Véra Baxter. Her motion picture, *Baxter, Véra Baxter,* starring Delphine Seyrig and Gérard Depardieu, premiered in 1976. Duras subsequently published a work titled *Véra Baxter, ou Les Plages de l'Atlantique* (Véra Baxter, or the Beaches of the Atlantic,

1980). A play version of *Véra Baxter* premiered in Paris in 1983, the text of which was published in *Théâtre IV* (1999).

The last play published in *Théâtre II* was never staged. *Un homme est venu me voir* (A Man Came to See Me) is the tale of an encounter between two men who have not seen each other in eighteen years. Steiner, a man in his fifties, receives a knock at the door. The visitor reluctantly enters, and he and Steiner begin to discuss their mutual past. They were once members of a Communist Party: for ten years they were like brothers devoted to the same cause. Then, the party split and they joined opposing sides. The visitor indicates that he remained with the faction in power while Steiner was tried and condemned to prison. Steiner later escaped by paying off a prison guard, and he eventually married and had children. His comfortable home and the distant voice of his wife confirm that he has chosen a bourgeois lifestyle. He reveals that he has severed his political ties and is now content to follow political currents passively. Meanwhile, the visitor never left the party, but new leaders have long since taken over, and he is now in a subservient position. As the conversation continues, the audience realizes that the play is about the importance of remembering a painful moment in history. In response to the visitor's question, "La mémoire, c'est vous?" (You are memory?), Steiner replies, "Je crois, oui" (I believe so, yes). The visitor subsequently describes himself as a black mark on a white page. In fact, his name is Marker and he was apparently a monster in his youth.

All but two of the historical references in the play are vague. Marker speaks of being a witness at the 1933 Moscow trials, a reference to the repressive purge of the Communist Party. He also describes Steiner as a refugee from a Nazi concentration camp. This critical reference to Steiner's past, along with the ethnicity of his name, evokes the horrors of the Holocaust. In fact, for Duras, the name Steiner is distinctly Jewish. It recurs in several of her texts and movies and embodies notions of individual and collective suffering, otherness, marginality, and oppression. Hence, through key historical references *Un homme est venu me voir* underscores both the failures of communism and the atrocities of World War II. However, unlike most of Duras's characters who delve into a painful past, Steiner and Marker remain stoic and detached. Their intermittent angry outbursts are followed by an impassiveness that has developed over time.

In December 1968, Duras's theatrical adaptation of her novel *L'Amante anglaise* premiered in Paris to rave reviews. Director Claude Régy and actors Renaud, Claude Dauphin, and Michael Lonsdale all contributed to the success of the performance. In 1970 Duras

Title page for the script for Duras's unproduced-play-turned-movie (1973), about a lavish but troubled party at the French Embassy in India, set against the backdrop of beggars and lepers who line the banks of the Ganges (Thomas Cooper Library, University of South Carolina)

received the Prix Ibsen (Ibsen Prize) for the play, and critically acclaimed revivals in 1976, 1977, and 1989–1990 confirm its place as one of Duras's most notable contributions to French theater. In 1991 Duras decided to make the text of her play more widely available. She added a new preface and published *Le Théâtre de l'amante anglaise* (The Play of the English Lover). This version also appears in *Théâtre IV*.

L'Amante anglaise differs from the earlier play upon which it is based, *Les Viaducs de la Seine-et-Oise*, both structurally and thematically. The main characters are now called Claire and Pierre Lannes. Before the play begins, a recorded voice describes what is known of the crime. Parts of a human body were found on several trains in various regions of France. One part of the body is, however, missing: the head. The voice adds that this piece of the puzzle will never be found. Detectives discover that all of the trains on which they found pieces of the victim's body passed beneath a bridge in the town of Viorne. As the authorities descend on the small town, one woman, Claire Lannes, confesses to murdering and dismembering her deaf and mute cousin, Marie-Thérèse Bousquet.

The play is structured as an interrogation. The interrogator, however, is never identified. He is neither a police officer nor a detective. He is simply someone who, like the spectator, is trying to understand Claire Lannes, her state of mind, and the nature of her crime. Like the interrogator, the spectator must piece together the incongruous fragments of the story. In act 1, the interrogator questions Pierre Lannes about his wife. They speak of Claire's relationship with Marie-Thérèse, her past, and her daily routine. Pierre claims that Claire would spend hours just sitting and staring in the garden, and he says that Claire and Marie-Thérèse seemed to get along well. He admits that he did not find the disappearance of Marie-Thérèse particularly odd—he assumed that she had had enough of Claire's unconventional ways. Pierre also speaks of Claire's past, of her relationship with a man from Cahors, and of her attempted suicide following the end of their affair. Pierre admits, as if for the first time, that he once loved Claire deeply, but he is now relieved to be rid of her. During act 2, Claire Lannes takes center stage. Claire is willing to speak, but her words never unveil her motive. Many of her statements about her habits, her feelings, and her past contradict those of Pierre, and it becomes clear that Pierre never really knew his wife. Claire's sanity comes into question on several occasions, but her madness is neither confirmed nor explained. The interrogator searches for the right question to ask about the crime, but he ultimately realizes that there is no right question. Claire's crime remains inexplicable, and the location of the head remains unknown. If she were to reveal its whereabouts, no one would continue to listen to her.

Although the stage remains bare throughout the play, the dialogue in *L'Amante anglaise* evokes several spaces, each associated with a character or a specific element of the story. For instance, the garden is Claire's haven. She sits for hours, even days, on a bench next to her favorite plant, *la menthe anglaise* (English mint). The name of the plant is a play on words: "l'amante en glaise" refers to a female lover in clay. Claire tells the interrogator that she chewed the mint leaves to remove the taste of the heavy sauces used in Marie-Thérèse's cooking. "Cahors" is at once the town of Claire's youth and the lover she never forgot. Meanwhile, the orderly house is linked to Marie-Thérèse before her death; the cave is the location of the crime, the dark space where Claire dismembers her cousin's body; and the forest is linked to Alphonso, a local lumberjack in whom Claire often confides. Additionally, the Balto is the local bar where the news of the crime circulates among the citizens of Viorne, and it is also the site of Claire's confession. Hence, despite the bare stage, the characters' words evoke a series of settings.

Over the next decade, Duras devoted most of her time to the cinema, releasing fifteen motion pictures between 1971 and 1981. Nevertheless, she continued her work in the theater, adapting August Strindberg's *La Danse de mort* (1970, The Dance of Death) and David Storey's *Home* (1973). In 1973 she published *India Song* with the designation *Texte-théâtre-film* (Text-Play-Movie). Originally commissioned as a stage play by Peter Hall, the director of the National Theater in London, *India Song* was never staged. Duras began working on the movie version almost immediately, and when it was released in 1975 she declared it to be the definitive performance of the text. In her preface to *India Song*, Duras notes, "Les personages évoqués dans cette histoire ont été délogés du livre intitulé *Le Vice-Consul* et projetés dans de nouvelles régions narratives" (The characters evoked in this story have been dislodged from the book titled *Le Vice-Consul* and projected into new narrative regions). She adds that the structure of *India Song* owes much to the narration of *La Femme du Gange*: "En réalité, *India Song* est consecutive de *La Femme du Gange*. Si *La Femme du Gange* n'avait pas été écrit, *India Song* ne l'aurait pas été" (In truth, *India Song* follows *La Femme du Gange*. If *La Femme du Gange* had not been written, *India Song* would not exist).

In *India Song* four disembodied voices recall the story of the French ambassador's wife, Anne-Marie Stretter. They relate the tale of her infamous affair with Michael Richardson, the man who followed her to India after abandoning his fiancée, Lol V. Stein. They also relate a parallel story of a beggar woman who walked from Savannakhet, Laos, to Calcutta. Her native song now resounds along the banks of the Ganges.

A reception takes place at the French embassy, the home of Anne-Marie Stretter. One of the guests, the vice-consul, professes his love for her. In a manner that is familiar to readers of Duras, he claims he loves her despite her love for Michael Richardson. The other guests at the reception shun the vice-consul. They recall the scandalous incident when, in a moment of folly, he stood on his balcony and shot at the lepers along the river. In *India Song*, Duras evokes an India where loss, pain, and suffering typify the lives of both those at embassy balls and the population of beggars and lepers who line the banks of the delta. Memory is a constant motif. Not only do the narrative voices attempt to recall the stories of the now-dead characters, but they also continually invite Duras's audience to revisit other works from her corpus.

In her next play, Duras returned to the setting of her youth. *L'Eden cinéma,* adapted from her novel *Un Barrage contre le Pacifique,* tells the story of Duras's mother and her financial and emotional struggles as a widow raising her young children in French Colonial Indochina. When the play premiered in 1977, critics cited the memorable performances of Renaud and Bulle Ogier in the roles of mother and daughter. Additionally, the music of Carlos d'Alessio captured the nostalgic mood of the play. *L'Eden cinéma* is one of Duras's most innovative plays: using techniques borrowed from the cinema, she expands the boundaries of stage production.

As the play opens, the mother is already dead. Her children, Suzanne and Joseph, are storytellers who look to the audience and speak of their mother's trials and determination. At times the characters perform a type of pantomime, imitating images on a silent-movie screen. The disembodied "Voice of Suzanne" often complements the movements and gestures of the characters onstage. On occasion, the "Voice of Suzanne" appears to be that of an older Suzanne. Elsewhere "the Voice" seems to belong to the young girl onstage. There are also traditional scenes with dialogue in the play. Each style of narration is thematically linked to a specific part of the story.

In the opening sequence, the children tell their mother's story. They explain that after working as a pianist in a silent-movie house for ten years, she purchased a plot of land with her savings. Her plans to cultivate the land, however, were unsuccessful because the tides of the Pacific Ocean periodically washed away her crops. Even the seawall that she and the local peasants constructed crumbled under the force of the ocean. Ultimately, it was as if the mother had thrown ten years of savings into the ocean.

Following this initial narrative sequence, the mother joins the other characters and plays her role until the scene of her death. Early on, Suzanne meets a wealthy man, Mr. Jo. He offers her several gifts in exchange for the time she spends with him. One of the objects he gives her is a diamond ring. This object changes hands several times throughout the play, confirming that it does not represent a bond between Suzanne and Mr. Jo. Suzanne initially gives the ring to her mother, who tries to sell it in Saigon. Unfortunately, the ring has a flaw, and the mother refuses to sell it for a reduced price. Throughout the play, characters sell the ring for more or less than it is worth, and it becomes an object that links all of the characters, including Joseph and the wealthy woman with whom he has an affair.

Duras with Bruno Nuytten, to whom she dedicated L'Amour, *on the set of* India Song *(1973) at the Trianon Palace, Versailles (© Erica Lennard)*

Near the end of the play the mother stands up and reads a letter that she wrote to the cadastral officials before her death. She decries the corruption and injustice that reigns in the French colony. She accuses the officials of knowingly stealing her youth, her children's future, and the hope of the poverty-stricken peasants who live on the plain. The reading of the letter is one of the most powerful moments of the play as the mother convincingly conveys her anger and despair. The play concludes with a description of the mother's death. Joseph defines his mother's plight as he speaks to the peasants who have come to pay their respects: "Blanche, elle était blanche. Même si son espoir était le vôtre et si elle a pleuré les enfants de la plaine, elle est restée une étrangère à votre pays" (White, she was white. Even though she shared your hopes and cried for the loss of the children on the plain, she remained a foreigner in your country). Ironically, the mother will be buried in the colonial cemetery in Saigon.

Poster for the 1978 movie from Duras's script (The Ship Night), based on a story related to her by a man who was having an erotic telephone relationship with a woman who refused to meet him (from Christiane Blot-Labarrère, Marguerite Duras, *1992; Thomas Cooper Library, University of South Carolina)*

Duras came across the topic for her next play by chance: she received a story from a man who had been having an erotic telephone relationship with a woman who refused to meet him. In fact, when the man attempted to meet the woman, she claimed that she was ill. Duras quickly turned this tale into a script for *Le Navire Night* (1978, The Ship "Night"). The play premiered in 1978, coinciding with the release of her movie of the same title. Both the movie, which featured few images, and the poorly constructed play were panned by the critics. Duras was drinking heavily at this time, and her alcoholism affected her ability to work on her projects with others.

In 1981 Duras published *Agatha* (translated, 1992). Inspired by Robert Musil's *Der Mann ohne Eigenschaften* (1930–1943; translated as *The Man without Qualities*, 1995), *Agatha* describes an incestuous relationship between a brother and sister. The text, composed of dialogue and stage directions, resembles a play, but it has never been staged. The conversation between the brother and sister before they part is tender and erotic. They speak of an unfathomable love and a desire of mythic proportions. They recall moments of their youth spent by the sea. They speak of the force and constant presence of "la mer" (the sea), referring at once to the ocean and to "la mère" (the mother), who knew of their relationship. The recurring verbs "dire" (to speak) and "voir" (to see) underscore the power of words to evoke images in the text. Duras admits that she was drawn to this story since it was inspired in part by her intense love for the younger of her two brothers. Upon completion of her text, Duras began working on a cinematic version that premiered in 1981 as *Agatha ou les lectures illimitées* (Agatha or The Limitless Text).

Duras wrote her next play, *Savannah Bay* (translated, 1992), for Renaud in 1982. Duras staged the play with the help of her assistants, Yann Andrea and Roberto Plate, the following year. During the initial rehearsals, Duras began to rewrite her original script. In light of several conversations she had with Plate, she transformed the setting from a "realistic" decor to a "mythic space." She reorganized the narrative fragments that make up the story told and retold by the storyteller-characters, Madeleine and the Young Woman. Duras even altered verb tenses, shifting passages of her play from the past conditional to the present tense. Hence, when *Savannah Bay* premiered in Paris in 1983, it was no longer a performance of the text that had been published under the same name. Shortly after the play premiered, Duras transcribed her performance notes and published both versions of *Savannah Bay* in her newly expanded edition of 1983. Readers then had access to the revised version and the original version that had never been staged. In 1995, however, director Jean-Claude Amyl further complicated the history of *Savannah Bay* by staging the original version of Duras's play at the Théâtre du Palais de Chaillotin in Paris.

In both versions of *Savannah Bay,* Madeleine and the Young Woman express their love for one another as they piece together a tragic love story from the past. A recording of Edith Piaf's song *Les Mots d'amour* (The Words of Love) sounds in the theater in the opening moments of the play. When the recorded music fades, the Young Woman sings the song as Madeleine repeats the words *comme sous dictée* (as if dictated). Together the women sing and chant the lyrics about an immeasurable love that is at once their own and the one that may have brought them together. In the following "scene," Madeleine and the Young Woman begin their tale of love and loss. They speak of a young girl who may have been Madeleine's daughter and the Young Woman's mother. They describe how, after giving birth, she left her child behind and headed for the marshes. They then explain that although "He" was with "Her" when she swam out too far, he was unable to save her from being drawn into the sea. From time to time, Madeleine and the Young Woman assume the roles of the characters within their story. They speak for the young couple who meet in the warm waters of Savannah Bay. They also speak for a man from Madeleine's past whose story resembles their own. In other words, Madeleine and the Young Woman construct a series of "plays within the play." Other innovative features of *Savannah Bay* include Madeleine's antics. Madeleine frequently disrupts the narrative by claiming that she does not remember the events of the story. She also occasionally pauses to reflect upon her life in the theater, the costumes she has worn, and the roles that she has performed. The play also functions as a celebration of Duras's work. Madeleine and the Young Woman reveal that their story exists in many genres: as they speak of the book, the play, and the cinematic versions of their tale, they nod to Duras's works and to her penchant for rewriting her stories. Furthermore, like many of Duras's characters, Madeleine and the Young Woman are vessels of sadness, and their story is marked by the painful eroticism that had become familiar to Duras's audiences.

La Musica Deuxième premiered in Paris in 1985. In the postscript of this play Duras explains that she had been thinking of adding a second act to *La Musica* since the inception of the play in 1965. *La Musica Deuxième* continues where the first play ends. Anne-Marie Roche and Michel Nollet, the couple who have come together to sign their divorce papers, continue their conversation through the night until dawn. During the second act they delve further into their memories of the past, further exploring their pain. In the end, they affirm that while they may have other relationships, nothing will ever compare to the love they shared. Critics responded favorably to Duras's staging of the play, and some felt that it was one of her greatest contributions to the French stage. With *La Musica Deuxième,* Duras seems to have found the ideal situation and setting for two of her recurring motifs: pain and desire. The play balances silence and repetition and conveys feelings for which there are no words. It was her last major production.

Duras died on 3 March 1996 in her home in Paris on the Rue St. Benôit. During the latter part of her life, she suffered from health problems related to alcoholism and emphysema. Duras shared her final years with a young writer, Yann Andrea, whom she met in 1980. Andrea cared for Duras until her death. She is buried in the Montparnasse cemetary in Paris. Immediately following her death, the Parisian newspaper, *Le Monde,* devoted five pages to her life and works.

Over the course of her career Marguerite Duras continually posed the question, "What is theater?" Her plays feature traditional elements, but they also have many innovative aspects, many of them involving borrowings from other genres. Duras also privileges the voice in her theater. The musicality of the names of her characters and settings are as important as any other element in the dialogue. She even experiments with disembodied voices, a characteristic of many modern plays. Duras's theater bears the traces of oral and written narrative traditions. She blends languages and invents new forms of communication. It is a theater of verbal constructs where fragments of a story echo from the stage and the rest is left to the audience's imagination. Furthermore, rewriting was an integral part of her work. By periodically reworking her stories, she interrogated the links between writing and remembering, and memory and reception. Thematically, her stories are at once personal and universal. Her characters are generally marginal figures who suffer from madness, loneliness, boredom, or injustice, and they often relate dark and painful stories about love or loneliness or crime. Like other influential artists of her time, Duras stretched dramatic conventions and illuminated new ways to create rich and powerful drama exploring the human condition.

Interviews:

Xavière Gauthier, *Les Parleuses* (Paris: Editions de Minuit, 1974); translated by Katharine A. Jensen as *Woman to Woman* (Lincoln & London: University of Nebraska Press, 1987);

Susan Husserl-Kapit, "An Interview with Marguerite Duras," *Signs: Journal of Women and Culture in Society,* 1 (Winter 1975): 423–434;

Michelle Porte, *Les Lieux de Marguerite Duras* (Paris: Minuit, 1977).

Bibliographies:

Alain Vircondelet, *Marguerite Duras: Une Etude* (Paris: Seghers, 1972);

Robert Harvey and Hélène Volat, *Marguerite Duras: A Bio-Bibliography* (Westport, Conn.: Greenwood Press, 1997).

Biographies:

Alain Vircondelet, *Duras: Biographie* (Paris: Bourin, 1991); translated by Thomas Buckley as *Duras: A Biography* (Normal, Ill.: Dalkey Archive, 1994);

Laure Adler, *Marguerite Duras: Une Vie* (Paris: Gallimard, 1998); translated by Anne-Marie Glasheen as *Marguerite Duras: A Life* (Chicago: University of Chicago Press, 2000; London: Gollancz, 2000).

References:

Sanford S. Ames, ed., *Remains to Be Seen: Essays on Marguerite Duras* (New York: Peter Lang, 1988);

Yann Andréa, *M.D.* (Paris: Minuit, 1983);

Christiane Blot-Labarrère, *Marguerite Duras* (Paris: Seuil, 1992);

Cahiers de la Compagnie Madeleine Renaud-Jean-Louis Barrault, special Duras issues, no. 52 (December 1965); no. 89 (October 1979); no. 106 (September 1983);

Claire Cerasi, *Marguerite Duras de Lahore à Auschwitz* (Geneva: Slatkine, 1993);

Alfred Cismaru, *Marguerite Duras* (New York: Twayne, 1971);

Gabrielle Cody, *Impossible Performances: Duras as Dramatist* (New York: Peter Lang, 2000);

Susan D. Cohen, *Women and Discourse in the Fiction of Marguerite Duras: Love, Legends, Language* (Amherst: University of Massachusetts Press, 1993);

Laurie Corbin, *The Mother Mirror: Self-Representation and the Mother-Daughter Relation in Colette, Simone de Beauvoir, and Marguerite Duras* (New York: Peter Lang, 1996);

Gilles Costaz, "Théâtre: La Plainte-chant des amants," *L'Arc,* special Duras issue, 98 (1985): 58–67;

Mechthild Cranston, ed., *In Language and in Love, Marguerite Duras: The Unspeakable; Essays for Marguerite Duras* (Potomac, Md.: Scripta Humanistica, 1992);

Deborah N. Glassman, *Marguerite Duras: Fascinating Vision and Narrative Cure* (Rutherford, N.J.: Fairleigh Dickinson University Press / London & Cranbury, N.J.: Associated University Press, 1991);

Leslie Hill, *Marguerite Duras: Apocalyptic Desires* (London & New York: Routledge, 1993);

Carol Hofmann, *Forgetting and Marguerite Duras* (Niwot: University Press of Colorado, 1991);

Karen Kaivola, *All Contraries Confounded: The Lyrical Fiction of Virginia Woolf, Djuna Barnes, and Marguerite Duras* (Iowa City: University of Iowa Press, 1991);

Julia Kristeva, "The Pain of Sorrow in the Modern World: The Works of Marguerite Duras," *PMLA,* 102 (March 1987): 138–152;

Suzanne Lamy and André Roy, *Marguerite Duras à Montréal* (Montreal: Spirale, 1981);

Marcelle Marini, *Territoires du féminin avec Marguerite Duras* (Paris: Minuit, 1977);

Lucy Stone McNeece, *Art and Politics in Duras' "India Cycle"* (Gainesville: University Press of Florida, 1996);

Carol J. Murphy, *Alienation and Absence in the Novels of Marguerite Duras* (Lexington, Ky.: French Forum Monographs, 1982);

Liliane Papin, *L'autre scène: Le théâtre de Marguerite Duras* (Saratoga, Cal.: ANMA Libri, 1988);

Jean Pierrot, *Marguerite Duras* (Paris: Corti, 1986);

Raylene L. Ramsey, *The French New Autobiographies: Sarraute, Duras, and Robbe-Grillet* (Gainesville: University Press of Florida, 1996);

Rencontre des "Cahiers Renaud-Barrault" avec Marguerite Duras, Madeleine Renaud, Jean-Louis Barrault, Claude Régy, les spectateurs et les comédiens de la compagnie, Cahiers de la Compagnie Renaud-Barrault, no. 91 (September 1976);

Revue des Sciences Humaines, special Duras issue, 202 (April–June 1986);

Marilyn R. Schuster, *Marguerite Duras Revisited* (New York: Twayne, 1993);

Trista Selous, *The Other Woman: Feminism and Femininity in the Work of Marguerite Duras* (New Haven: Yale University Press, 1988);

Jean-Luc Seylaz, *Les Romans de Marguerite Duras* (Paris: Minard, 1963);

Eleanor Honig Skoller, *The In-Between of Writing: Experience and Experiment in Drabble, Duras, and Arendt* (Ann Arbor: University of Michigan Press, 1993);

Raynalle Udris, *Welcome Unreason: A Study of "Madness" in the Novels of Marguerite Duras* (Amsterdam & Atlanta: Rodopi, 1993);

David Walker, "Consuming Passions: Marguerite Duras," in his *Outrage and Insight: Modern French Writers and the "Fait Divers"* (Oxford: Berg, 1995), pp. 187–202;

Sharon Willis, *Marguerite Duras: Writing on the Body* (Urbana & Chicago: University of Illinois Press, 1987).

Jean Genet
(19 December 1910 – 15 April 1986)

Kristy Clark Koth

See also the Genet entry in *DLB 72: French Novelists, 1930–1960* and the Genet obituary in *DLB Yearbook: 1986*.

PLAY PRODUCTIONS: *Les Bonnes,* Paris, Théâtre de l'Athénée, 19 April 1947; translated as *The Maids,* New York City, Tempo Playhouse, 6 May 1955; London, New Lindsay Theatre Club, 5 June 1956;

'Adame Miroir, ballet, music by Darius Milhaud and choreography by Janine Charrat, Paris, Théâtre Marigny, 31 May 1948;

Haute Surveillance, Paris, Théâtre des Mathurins, 26 February 1949; translated as *Deathwatch,* New York, East Theater, 1958;

The Balcony, London, Arts Theatre, 22 April 1957; New York, Circle in the Square, 3 March 1960; produced in the original French as *Le Balcon,* Paris, Théâtre du Gymnase, 18 May 1960;

Les Nègres, clownerie, Paris, Théâtre de Lutèce, 28 October 1959; translated as *The Blacks: A Clown Show,* New York City, Saint Mark's Playhouse, 4 May 1961;

Les Paravents, translated into German as *Wände überall,* Berlin, Schlosspark Staatsteater, 19 May 1961; Paris, Théâtre de l'Odéon, 16 April 1966;

"Elle," Parma, Festival de Parme, 24 April 1990; Gennevilliers, Théâtre de Gennevilliers, 1990;

Splendid's, Nanterre, Théâtre Nanterre-Amandiers, 1995; translated, London, Lyric Hammersmith, 15 July 1995;

Le Bagne, Nice, Théâtre National de Nice, 23 May 2004.

BOOKS: *Le condamné à mort* (Fresnes, 1942); translated by Diane de Prima as *The Man Sentenced to Death* (N.p., 1950);

Notre-Dame-des-Fleurs, anonymous (Paris: Denoël & Morihien, 1943); as Genet (Monaco: Aux dépens d'un amateur, 1944); translated by Bernard Frechtman as *Our Lady of the Flowers* (Paris: Morihien, 1949; New York: Grove, 1963; London: Blond, 1964); definitive French version, in *Œuvres complètes,* volume 2 (Paris: Gallimard, 1951), pp. 7–207;

Chants secrets (Lyon: L'Arbalète, 1945);

Jean Genet (photograph by Rajak Ohanian; from Jeremy Reed, Jean Genet: Born to Lose, *2005; Thomas Cooper Library, University of South Carolina)*

Miracle de la rose (Lyon: L'Arbalète, 1946); definitive version, in *Œuvres complètes,* volume 2 (Paris: Gallimard, 1951), pp. 221–469; translated by Frechtman as *Miracle of the Rose* (London: Blond, 1965; New York: Grove, 1966);

La Galère (Paris: Loyau, 1947);

Pompes funèbres (Bikini: Aux dépens de quelques amateurs, 1947; revised edition, Paris: Gallimard, 1948); definitive version, in *Œuvres complètes,* volume 3 (Paris: Gallimard, 1953), pp. 7–162; translated by Frechtman as *Funeral Rites* (London: Blond, 1969; New York: Grove, 1969);

Querelle de Brest (Paris, 1947); definitive version, in *Œuvres complètes,* volume 3 (Paris: Gallimard, 1953), pp. 171–350; translated by Gregory Streatham as *Querelle of Brest* (London: Blond, 1966);

Poèmes (Lyon: L'Arbalète, 1948); translated by Steven Finch as *Treasures of the Night: Collected Poems* (San Francisco: Gay Sunshine Press, 1981);

Journal du voleur (Geneva, 1948); translated by Frechtman as *The Thief's Journal* (Paris: Olympia Press, 1954; New York: Grove, 1964; London: Blond, 1965);

Haute Surveillance (Paris: Gallimard, 1949); translated as *Deathwatch,* in *The Maids; Deathwatch: Two Plays* (New York: Grove, 1954), pp. 101–164; definitive French edition (Paris: Gallimard, 1965);

L'Enfant criminel et 'Adame Miroir (Paris: Morihien, 1949);

Lettre à Leonor Fini (Paris: Loyau, 1950); translated by Frechtman as "Mademoiselle," *Flair,* 1 (April 1950): 82–83, 114;

Œuvres complètes, 6 volumes (Paris: Gallimard, 1951–1991)–includes volume 6, *L'Ennemi déclaré,* edited by Albert Dichy (1991), translated by Jeff Fort as *The Declared Enemy* (Stanford: Stanford University Press, 2004);

Les Bonnes: Pièce en un acte. Les Deux versions précédées d'une lettre de l'auteur (Sceaux: Jean-Jacques Pauvert, 1954); translated as *The Maids,* in *The Maids; Deathwatch: Two Plays* (New York: Grove, 1954), pp. 33–100; definitive French version, in *Œuvres complètes,* volume 4 (Paris: Gallimard, 1968), pp. 137–176;

Le Balcon (Lyon: L'Arbalète, 1956); revised by Genet and translated by Frechtman as *The Balcony* (London: Faber & Faber, 1957; New York: Grove, 1958); revised French version (Lyon: L'Arbalète, 1960); definitive French version, preface by Genet (Lyon: L'Arbalète, 1962); translated by Frechtman (New York: Grove, 1960; London: Faber & Faber, 1966);

Les Nègres, clownerie (Lyon: L'Arbalète, 1958); translated by Frechtman as *The Blacks: A Clown Show* (London: Faber & Faber, 1960; New York: Grove, 1960);

L'Atelier d'Alberto Giacometti; Les Bonnes, suivi d'une letter; L'Enfant criminel; Le Funambule (Lyon: L'Arbalète, 1958);

Les Paravents, translated by Hans Georg Brenner as *Wände überall* (Hamburg: Merlin Verlag, 1960); first French edition (Lyon: L'Arbalète, 1961); translated by Frechtman as *The Screens* (New York: Grove, 1962; London: Faber & Faber, 1963); definitive French version, in *Œuvres complètes,* volume 5 (Paris: Gallimard, 1979), pp. 157–375;

Les Bonnes & "Comment jouer Les Bonnes" (Lyon: L'Arbalète, 1963);

Lettres à Roger Blin (Paris: Gallimard, 1966); translated by Richard Seaver as *Letters to Roger Blin: Reflections on the Theater* (New York: Grove, 1969);

Here and Now for Bobby Seale: Essays by Jean Genet (New York: Committee to Defend the Panthers / San Francisco: Black Panther Party Ministry of Information, 1970);

Un Captif amoureux (Paris: Gallimard, 1986); translated by Barbara Bray as *Prisoner of Love* (Hanover, N.H.: Wesleyan University Press, 1991);

"Elle" (Lyon: L'Arbalète, 1989);

Fragments . . . , et autres texts, preface by Edmund White (Paris: Gallimard, 1990); translated by Charlotte Mandell as *Fragments of the Artwork* (Stanford: Stanford University Press, 2003);

Splendid's: Pièce en 2 actes (Lyon: L'Arbalète, 1993); translated by Neil Bartlett as *Splendid's* (London: Faber & Faber, 1995);

Le Bagne (Décines: L'Arbalète, 1994).

Editions and Collections: *Journal du voleur; Querelle de Brest; Pompes funèbres* (Paris: Gallimard, 1993);

Rembrandt: Le secret de Rembrandt, suivi de Ce qui est resté d'un Rembrandt déchiré en petits carrés bien réguliers, et foutu aux chiottes (Paris: Gallimard, 1995);

Le Condamné à mort et autres poèmes: (suivi de) Le Funambule (Paris: Gallimard, 1999);

Théâtre complet (Paris: Gallimard, 2002).

Editions in English: *Reflections on the Theatre and Other Writings,* translated by Richard Seaver (London: Faber & Faber, 1972);

Querelle, translated by Anselm Hollo (New York: Grove, 1974);

The Man Sentenced to Death, translated by Steven Finch (San Francisco: Gay Sunshine Press, 1981);

The Complete Poems of Jean Genet, translated by David Fisher (San Francisco: ManRoot, 1981);

Treasures of the Night: The Collected Poems of Jean Genet, translated by Finch (San Francisco: Gay Sunshine Press, 1981);

The Selected Writings of Jean Genet, edited by Edmund White (Hopewell, N.J.: Ecco, 1993);

The Complete Poems, translated by Jeremy Reed and George Messo (Kent, U.K.: Intimacy, 2001).

PRODUCED SCRIPT: *Un Chant d'amour,* motion picture, 1950.

SELECTED PERIODICAL PUBLICATIONS–UNCOLLECTED: "Jean Cocteau," *Empreintes,* nos. 7–8 (May–July 1950): 23–25;

"'What I Like About the English Is That They Are Such Liars . . . ,'" *Sunday Times Colour Magazine,* 24 February 1963, p. 11;

"D'un bout à l'autre, une tornade," *Le Monde,* 19 April 1963, p. 15;

"To a Would-Be Producer . . . ," translated by Bernard Frechtman, *Tulane Drama Review,* 7 (Spring 1963): 80–81;

"Something Which Seemed to Resemble Decay . . . ," translated by Frechtman, *Art and Literature,* 1 (March 1964): 77–86;

"The Members of the Assembly," translated by Richard Seaver, *Esquire* (November 1968): 86–89;

"A Salute to 100,000 Stars," translated by Seaver, *Evergreen Review,* 12 (December 1968): 51–53, 87–88;

"Bobby Seale, the Black Panthers and U.S. White People," *Black Panther,* 4 (28 March 1970): 7;

"Une Lettre de Jean Genet," *Les Lettres Francaises* (29 March 1972): 14;

"Jean Genet et la condition des immigrés," *L'Humanité* (3 May 1974): 12;

"'Des espirits moins charitables que le mien pourraient croire déceler une assez piètre operation politique,'" *L'Humanité* (13 August 1975): 6.

Jean Genet was one of the most controversial French writers of the twentieth century, and his contributions to the French language are generally considered to be as important as those of Marcel Proust, Arthur Rimbaud, and Paul Verlaine. While representing relations of power and dominance in his highly polemical works, Genet speaks consistently from the margins. His theatrical themes include ritual, role-playing, and the opposition between appearance and reality. His blending of argot and proper French, his emphasis on how one says something over what one says, and his preference for the gesture over the act all combined to create a style unprecedented in French theater.

Genet's writing career can be divided into three periods. He began by writing novels, the first in December 1941 and the last in 1948. While Genet may have been working on play scripts as early as 1942, the genre did not receive his full attention until around 1946. The first productions of his plays took place in 1947 and 1949, followed by a five-year break, and then a renewed devotion to the theater that did not wane until the mid 1960s. By 1968 Genet had renounced all creative writing and focused his attention on political struggles, particularly those of the American Black Panthers and the Palestinians. Although he wrote two movie scripts during this period, he abandoned both projects before their completion. Genet finished only one more literary work, *Un Captif amoureux* (1986; translated as *Prisoner of Love,* 1991), featuring autobiographical memoirs and political reportage that he wrote over the last years of his life. This work was published posthumously.

Recording Genet's biographical information was once a difficult task. Many of his literary works are autobiographical but feature multiple intentional or unintentional inaccuracies. Additionally, Genet often gave false information in interviews and on legal documents. However, because of the extensive research of Edmund White for his 1993 biography of Genet, many errors have been found and corrected.

Jean Genet was born on 19 December 1910 at a birthing clinic in Paris. On his birth certificate, his mother, Camille Gabrielle Genet, claimed she was twenty-one years old, single, and a governess. His father was not named and remains unknown to this day. Camille Genet kept her son for seven months before abandoning him to the public welfare system on 28 July 1911. Genet never saw his mother again. She died eight years later, probably the victim of an epidemic of influenza in Paris.

As a baby Genet was placed with a foster family in the village of Alligny-en-Morvan. His foster parents, Eugénie and Charles Regnier, were modest but well-respected members of the community. The Morvan region was home to a great many foster children, most of whom were placed in farm families where they were expected to do manual labor from a young age, but Genet was placed in a family of artisans. Although they were in good company, the foster children were always seen as outsiders. They never were allowed to feel that they belonged. Genet seemed to exaggerate his difference by spurning Morvan patois despite having moved into the region before speaking his first word. His insistence on speaking proper French gave him an air of superiority that aggravated the other foster children.

Genet was a good student and a member of the church choir, but his career as a petty thief began in these years. According to Jean-Paul Sartre's study titled *Saint Genet, comédien et martyr* (1952; translated as *Saint Genet, Actor and Martyr,* 1963), Genet was accused of being a thief at the age of ten. To Genet, this appellation seemed unjust, and his defense was to take pride in this new identity. He was known to steal small coins, pencils, and other school supplies, which he usually shared with the other children. By the age of twelve this pastime seems to have dissipated, but he took up the habit again later as an adult, stealing mostly books, but also cloth, clothing, and money.

In 1923 Genet took the Certificat d'Etudes (Certificate of Studies) exam. He was one of only five children from the Alligny area who qualified to take the exams, and, of those five, he was the only child from the public welfare system. Genet passed the exam with honors, receiving the highest score in his region, which earned him a printing apprenticeship in the Paris area. The privilege was short-lived, however, since Genet ran away only two weeks after his arrival. He was eventually sent to work in the home of the blind composer

Title page for Genet's 1949 play (translated as Deathwatch, *1954), about jealousy and mutual fascination among three homosexual prison inmates (Thomas Cooper Library, University of South Carolina)*

René de Buxeuil. There he learned about rhythm, rhyme, and prosody and first showed an interest in writing. Seven months after arriving, however, Genet stole money from his employer. De Buxeuil turned Genet over to the authorities, throwing him into a long-term struggle with the French penal system.

For the next year and a half Genet moved from one psychiatric or disciplinary institution to another. In September 1926 he was brought to an agricultural penitentiary colony in Mettray, where he stayed until adulthood. Mettray made a lasting impression on Genet and became the setting of his second novel, *Miracle de la Rose* (1946, definitive version 1951; translated as *Miracle of the Rose,* 1965). In this harsh and hierarchical world Genet learned the joys of sexual relations with other boys. Although his later writing glorified his experiences at Mettray, the reality of life there was less than glorious. Genet escaped briefly in 1927, and in 1929 he signed up for the army in order to gain an early release from Mettray. He spent most of the next seven years in the military, the main exception being the second half of 1933, which he spent as a vagabond traveling through France and Spain. During his military service Genet encountered the Arab world, serving in Syria, Morocco, and Algeria. He remained attached to the Arab peoples for the rest of his life.

In mid 1936 Genet deserted the military and began a long journey through Europe. As he later reported in *Journal du voleur* (1948; translated as *The Thief's Journal,* 1954), he falsified the name on his passport and traveled through Italy, Albania, Yugoslavia, Austria, Czechoslovakia, Poland, Nazi Germany, and Belgium. Several times he was arrested for traveling without the proper documents or for vagabondage. Returning to France in 1937, Genet spent the next seven years in and out of prison, variously charged with theft, carrying an illegal weapon, desertion from the military, vagrancy, and traveling on a train without a valid ticket. His thefts most often involved books. When asked by a judge in 1943 if he knew the price of the edition of Verlaine's *Fêtes galantes* (1869, Gallant Festivals) that he had stolen, Genet replied that he did not know its price, but he knew its value.

Genet began to write in prison. In 1941 he started *Notre-Dame-des-Fleurs* (1943; translated as *Our Lady of the Flowers,* 1949; definitive French version 1951), and he finished it the following year. During this period he also wrote the poem *Le condamné à mort* (translated as *The Man Sentenced to Death,* 1950) and published it at his own expense in September 1942. Dedicated to Maurice Pilorge, a twenty-year-old murderer whose execution Genet had read about in a newspaper article, *Le condamné à mort* features themes that became the trademark of Genet's novels: homosexual desire among convicts, the confusion of genders, and the exaltation of the penis. His style combines romantic imagery with sexually explicit description, eloquent discourse with slang, and pious devotion with blasphemous symbolism.

In 1943 Genet met the poet, novelist, and moviemaker Jean Cocteau, who greatly admired *Le condamné à mort*. Cocteau became not only a good friend to Genet but also his promoter. It was through Cocteau that Genet's first novel was published. Cocteau twice rescued Genet from trouble. The first occasion was after Genet was arrested in May 1943 for stealing the expensive book of Verlaine's writings. Because of his repeated convictions, Genet was eligible for a life sentence, but Cocteau arranged for the famous lawyer Maurice Garçon to defend the young writer. In court Cocteau took the stand and declared that Genet was the greatest writer of the modern era. Cocteau's influence was effective, and Genet was given only a three-month sentence. Just one month after being released from prison, Genet was arrested for theft again and was sent back to prison. This last prison sentence was for four months, but before his term was up, Genet was transferred to the Tourelles prison, which was run by the militia and used as a relay center for the Nazi concentration camps. Under the Nazi Occupation a new law had been created that allowed the state to intern political prisoners and anyone without a profession, residence, or means of financial support, and Genet's financial situation was in question. Cocteau and the Swiss publisher Marc Barbezat contacted everyone they knew who might have some influence on Genet's case. Barbezat agreed to publish several works by Genet, thus ensuring his income, and Cocteau's friends spoke out in Genet's favor. In March 1944 Genet was released from prison for the last time. Five years later, through the support of Cocteau and Sartre, Genet was officially pardoned by President Vincent Auriol.

Genet's first four novels were all published clandestinely and in limited editions. These first editions were circulated within literary circles and never made their way beyond those elite groups until they were republished in the 1950s. Their effect, however, was to make Genet famous almost overnight. *Notre-Dame-des-Fleurs* was written mostly in prison in 1941 and 1942. On Cocteau's recommendation it was published clandestinely by Paul Morihien and Robert Denoël at the end of 1943. Only about 30 books were actually bound that year. The rest of the 350 copies, in which Monaco was falsely listed as the place of publication, were not bound or circulated until 1944. In this novel the narrator named Jean Genet, awaiting trial in prison, recounts the histories of characters whose lives intertwine. The style is similar to cinematic montage, in which scenic units are presented in disarray. The dominant themes in the novel are the conflation of sanctity and debauchery and the interdependence of normal society and marginalized figures. These themes recur throughout Genet's writings.

Genet's second novel, *Miracle de la rose*, was also written mostly in prison in 1943–1944 and was published in March 1946 by Barbezat in a run of 475 copies. It is also narrated by a character named Jean Genet, and it continues the themes of his first novel, this time in the context of his stays in Mettray and in prison. The hero, Harcamone, is a two-time murderer and the most respected member of the prison population. He does not regret his acts and bravely accepts his upcoming execution.

Genet wrote his third novel as a free man in 1945 and 1946. *Pompes funèbres* (1947, revised 1948, definitive version 1953; translated as *Funeral Rites*, 1969) is a tribute to and glorification of Genet's companion Jean Decarnin, a member of the French underground during the Occupation who was killed by militiamen during the liberation of Paris on 19 August 1944. Despite the dedication Genet wrote to this war hero, the book was a scandal that outraged most of its readers because it appeared to glorify the militiamen. Genet's fourth novel, *Querelle de Brest* (1947, definitive version 1953; translated as *Querelle of Brest,* 1966), written in 1946 and 1947, is the only one that is not autobiographical. *Querelle de Brest* presents a society without control where criminals go unpunished.

By the time Genet had finished *Querelle de Brest,* he had developed an interest in theater. He wrote *Haute Surveillance* (produced and published 1949; translated as *Deathwatch,* 1954; definitive French version 1965) and *Les Bonnes* (produced 1947, published 1954, definitive version 1968; translated as *The Maids,* 1954) simultaneously with *Querelle de Brest,* and he was preparing to have his plays staged as the novel was published. As he worked on the staging of *Les Bonnes,* Genet again turned his focus to his own life to write the last novel published during his lifetime, *Journal du voleur*. Most critics refer to this work as an autobiographical novel, acknowledging both the literary style and the distorted history it features. In the "journal" Genet chronicles his life from his birth to the mid 1940s. While the events recounted are for the most part true, Genet changed the chronology, romanticized events, people, and places, and introduced fantasies.

Unlike his novels, Genet's plays have no apparent connection to the events of his life. Although they are often categorized with the works of Eugène Ionesco and Samuel Beckett as Theater of the Absurd, Genet's plays are significantly different from other absurdist drama. Unlike Ionesco, Genet avoids satire: his plays are confrontational rather than humorous. And the richness of Genet's dialogue and decor is in stark contrast to Beckett's minimalism. Although Genet insisted that art could never create political change, his plays demand the political engagement of his audience.

Haute Surveillance was Genet's first attempt at theater, although it was not the first of his plays staged. He began writing it in 1943 and rewrote it four times before its publication in *La Nef* in March 1947, one month before the premiere of *Les Bonnes*. The setting is a prison cell, and the play presents the jealousy and fascination among three homosexual inmates. Yeux-Verts has been sentenced to death for the murder of a young girl. He is admired by the other inmates for his heinous crime and his cool demeanor as he awaits his execution. Lefranc, a petty thief, is ridiculed by another cell mate, Maurice, who finds him unworthy of respect. Lefranc responds to this harassment by strangling Maurice in an attempt to raise himself to the status of Yeux-Verts. Yet, Lefranc understands too late that he cannot will himself to Yeux-Verts's position. The dialogue of the play pro-

Cover for Genet's 1956 play (revised and translated as The Balcony, *1957), about a brothel in which people act out sexual fantasies of control (Thomas Cooper Library, University of South Carolina)*

vides a realistic depiction of life in prison, yet Genet implies in his notes that the actors should avoid a realistic representation. For example, he indicates that the actors should move in geometric patterns, use heavy or lightning-quick gestures, and appear to have aged thirty to forty years by halfway through the play.

Haute Surveillance was first performed on 26 February 1949 at the Théâtre des Mathurins in Paris, codirected by Genet and Jean Marchat. The reviews were mainly negative: Genet's attempt at antirealism had not been clear. One particularly disparaging review by Jean-Jacques Gautier for *Le Figaro Littéraire* (The Figaro Literary Magazine) led the novelist and respected journalist François Mauriac to respond in Genet's defense. Although Mauriac contrasted Genet's work with the geniuses of Proust, Rimbaud, and André Gide, he declared Genet a poet. Mauriac's defense gave Genet's work legitimacy. Translated as *Deathwatch,* the play was not performed in the United States until 1958, when it was directed by Leo Garen at the East Theater in New York. The American production met with generally positive reviews, but those closest to Genet (such as his agent and translator Bernard Frechtman) complained that the director had misunderstood Genet's work and turned it into a realistic psychological drama. Genet was ultimately displeased with *Haute Surveillance,* and in 1967 he asked that it never be staged again. True to his contradictory ways, however, he collaborated at the end of his life with the director Michel Dumoulin on a revised version of the play, which Dumoulin produced at New York University in May 1988, two years after Genet's death.

The publication of *Haute Surveillance* was followed closely by the premiere of *Les Bonnes,* considered Genet's most accomplished work. White writes that "*The Maids* represents a real departure in modern theatre: a new interest in ritual, exalted language, and the portrayal of psychological violence that may or may not stand for a veiled political struggle." Genet recognized the importance of this work to his literary career in 1946, as he was reworking the script in preparation for production. In his transition from novelist to playwright, Genet shifted his interest from homosexual passion and the cult of the criminal to power relations, racial divisions, and colonialism. Hence, *Haute Surveillance* was a dramatic piece with the thematic material of the novels while *Les Bonnes* began a new trend.

Les Bonnes presents the story of two sisters, Claire and Solange, who are employed as maids by a bourgeoise known only as Madame. They plot the murder of their mistress but end by completing this task in absentia, as Claire plays the role of Madame and drinks the poisoned tea. Genet might have been inspired to write this play by a news story from 1933 that was also the subject of a report by the well-known psychoanalyst Jacques Lacan. The story concerns two sisters, Christine and Léa Papin, domestic servants who were treated harshly by their bourgeois employers. Eventually the sisters, thrown into a rage by the latest reproach, killed their mistress and her daughter, tearing out their eyes in the process. They then mutilated the bodies further, washed themselves up, and went to bed together in their room. The uncontrolled violence shocked the country, but the sisters could not explain their act.

Les Bonnes is a one-act play set entirely in Madame's bedroom, and it occurs in real time, which has led critics to note the classical nature of the play. The long, elevated speeches, the unity of action, and the disciplined passions of the characters are further reminders of classical theater. The play opens with Claire and Solange playing a game of mimicry in which Solange takes the role of Claire and Claire becomes Madame. The scene climaxes as the aggression of the maid turns into a violent attack on Madame, which ends just short of strangulation as an alarm clock sounds, and the two characters end their ritual. Claire and Solange have been rehearsing the murder of their employer. A brief phone call heightens the urgency of the task, and Claire takes control, insisting that she will be able to kill Madame. Madame enters the bedroom, bemoaning her condition and noting how lucky the maids are to have such uncomplicated lives. Claire brings Madame her poisoned tea, but before she drinks it, Madame gets word that she is to meet her husband at the Bilboquet restaurant. She sends Solange out to flag down a cab, and Claire is left behind to watch as Madame uncovers clue after clue about her maids' inappropriate behavior while refusing to drink her tea. In the final scene Claire and Solange are left to resolve their situation. The maids take turns coercing each other back into their role-playing. Finally, Claire, in the role of Madame, drinks the tea given to her by Solange, in the role of Claire, who now becomes "La femme Lemercier. La Lemercier. La fameuse criminelle" (That Lemercier woman. The Lemercier. The infamous criminal). In his 1963 preface to the play, titled "Comment jouer *Les Bonnes*" (How to Perform *The Maids*), Genet wrote, "il ne s'agit pas d'un plaidoyer sur le sort des domestiques. Je suppose qu'il existe un syndicat des gens de maison—cela ne nous regarde pas" (this is not a discourse on the fate of domestic workers. I suppose there is a union for domestic help—that is not our concern). Genet never expected his theater to effect political change, but he nevertheless used his plays to comment on the relationship between the powerful and the dominated.

Les Bonnes premiered in Paris on 19 April 1947. Cocteau had contacted the famous actor and director Louis Jouvet in the summer of 1946 and asked him to look at Genet's work. Jouvet liked Genet's play but made him rewrite it several times, trimming the original four acts to one with a powerful final scene. The relationship between writer and director was turbulent: Genet resented Jouvet's emphasis on producing a play that would be a commercial success, while Jouvet was frustrated by the playwright's lack of commitment to the project. By the time the play opened Genet had ceased communicating with Jouvet. Reactions to the premiere were mixed. Whistles and boos were heard alongside the occasional cheer during most of the ninety-two performances. A few critics recognized the play's originality, but most of the reviews were negative. Sartre felt that Jouvet had misunderstood Genet's play and wrote an appendix to *Saint Genet* defending the work. Although it met with mixed reviews, the play helped to advance Genet's career. It was his first work to reach a wide public, and it brought him his first literary award, Le Prix de la Pléiade, which he officially won for both *Les Bonnes* and *Haute Surveillance*. Since its premiere *Les Bonnes* has been performed all over the world. In the 1954 publication of the play Genet included a letter to the editor, Jean-Jacques Pauvert, that discussed what he saw as the problems with the Jouvet production, and in the 1963 publication he added "Comment jouer *Les Bonnes*."

In May 1948 the ballet *'Adame Miroir* was presented by Les Ballets Roland Petit at the Théâtre Marigny in Paris. The music was composed by Darius Milhaud, the choreography was created by Janine Charrat, and the text and story line were written by Genet. This work was Genet's only excursion into ballet. *'Adame Miroir* presents the narcissistic relationship between a sailor and his reflection. A third dancer is covered in a veil and portrays death. Genet expands on the theme of the double, this time relating it to homoerotics. The title *'Adame* reflects both the male name "Adam" and the female title "Madame" (as pronounced in a working-class Parisian dialect). The ballet was a success, but Genet was disappointed in it. In 1950 he claimed to be abandoning the theater, ashamed of the vanity he felt in seeing his works performed onstage. He had been disgusted by the fashionable Parisian productions of *'Adame Miroir* and *Les Bonnes,* and he was increasingly uncomfortable with his fame. Genet took a long break from literary exploits.

The lone exception to Genet's break was his work in cinema. He was infatuated with movies, and in his novels he adopted the montage technique of cinema, a style in which scenes are presented in a scattered array of flashbacks, jump cuts, broken sequences, and repetitions. In 1950 Genet wrote and directed his only motion picture, *Un Chant d'amour*. The movie takes place in the criminal world and depicts violent homosexual passions. A prison guard notices a bouquet of flowers being swung from one barred window to the next, where a hand tries in vain to grasp it. On closer inspection, the guard finds all of the prisoners masturbating in their cells and witnesses the erotic exchanges of two prisoners separated by a cell wall. Overcome yet disgusted by his own homosexual desire, the guard thrashes one of the prisoners, triggering a fantasy sequence in which the beaten prisoner imagines a romantic interlude with his neighbor. The guard finally places his gun in the mouth of his victim. In the final scene, the guard leaves the prison. He again sees the swinging bouquet, but he turns away just before the struggling hand finally makes the catch.

Initially *Un Chant d'amour* could not be shown in public, for the material was considered pornographic. Several private copies were made that were quickly pirated. The first public showings were in 1964 in the United States, and they met consistently with (at times violent) police intervention. That year, the American Civil Liberties Union backed a lawsuit brought by Saul Landau, who wanted the courts to guarantee his right to show the movie under the First Amendment. The case was eventually reviewed by the United States Supreme Court, which upheld an earlier decision condemning the movie. It was first shown publicly in Paris and London in the early 1970s. *Un Chant d'amour* was one of the first cinematic depictions of homosexual eroticism, and it is now regarded as a minor masterpiece.

The artistic silence that followed this movie was broken in 1955 with an intense period of writing. Over the course of one year, Genet wrote *Le Balcon* (1956; revised and translated as *The Balcony,* 1957; produced in English 1957; produced in French 1960; definitive version 1962); *Les Nègres, clownerie* (published 1958, produced 1959, revised 1960; translated as *The Blacks: A Clown Show,* 1960), "Elle" ("She," published 1989, produced 1990), and the first drafts of *Les Paravents* (published in German as *Wände überall,* 1960; produced in Germany 1961; original version published 1961; translated as *The Screens,* 1962; original version produced 1966; definitive French version published 1979). He also worked on a movie script that he eventually abandoned.

Le Balcon is set in a brothel called Le Grand Balcon (The Grand Balcony), where people live out sexual fantasies of control. With the aid of a mysterious apparatus Madame Irma voyeuristically looks into the salons where these fantasies are enacted and reflected in all directions through multiple mirrors placed onstage. In the first four of the nine tableaux that make up *Le Balcon,* the audience witnesses the clients playing out sadomasochistic fantasies in the roles of bishop, general, judge, and beggar. The clients often interrupt the action to comment on the process of the performance, insisting that the roles be acted out properly and that a script outlining a ritual be followed. The scenes are further disrupted by a rebellion taking place outside the walls of the brothel. Clients stop their role-playing to ask about the state of the rebellion, and the gunfire in the background is a reminder of the reality beyond the stage.

In the fifth and longest tableau Irma explains the function of the bordello: visitors come to live out their erotic fantasies of power in a pure form. In the real world the position of the judge, bishop, or general becomes tainted by daily life, but in the house of illusions the representation remains static and true. The customers repeat the same ritual again and again to maintain its purity.

In the second half of the play the clients of the bordello use the revolution to usurp the power and positions of their fallen counterparts in the outside world. Irma will take on the role of the queen, and the Chief of Police will be the hero who has saved her. The Chief alone is displeased with his new role. In the final tableau Roger, a failed revolutionary, enters the brothel to play the Hero in a salon created by Irma for the glorification of the Chief of Police. It is a mausoleum. As the scene ends, the Hero castrates himself. He is dragged out of the mausoleum, and the Chief replaces him there, intending to stay forever. Gunfire is heard again, indicating that the rebellion has started anew. Madame Irma reassumes her initial identity and sends home the figures as if they were nothing more than clients, indicating to them, as is her habit, the safest way to exit the brothel. She then addresses the audience in precisely the same manner, making the spectators aware of their collusion in the struggle for power.

The audience's attention is continually drawn to the mechanisms of Genet's play, either in the salon scenes, which function as plays within the play, in the placement of mirrors that allow the audience to see things that would otherwise be hidden, or, as in Madame Irma's final comment, in moments of direct address that make the playgoers participants in the action. Genet avoids realism through such metatheatrical devices as well as stage directions that encourage exaggerated acting.

Le Balcon was first produced in English at a small London theater club in April 1957. It was directed by Peter Zadek, who previously had staged *Les Bonnes.* To appease the censors, Zadek cut several religious references and the castration scene. Genet came to London during rehearsals and was infuriated; he felt that Zadek had turned some of the tableaux into satires and cheapened others with superfluous additions. He asked that opening night be delayed and offered to stay and work until the play was properly performed. Rather than accept Genet's offer, Zadek asked him to leave and had him barred from the theater on opening night. Genet publicly denounced the production in a press conference in Paris and composed "Comment jouer *Le Balcon*" (How to Perform *The Balcony*) in response to Zadek's production. Genet was never satisfied with the play. From the completion of the first draft in 1955 until 1961, when his fifth version of the play was published, Genet continually rewrote *Le Balcon.* According to Barbezat, Genet weakened the play with his own obsessive revisions.

Le Balcon was produced in Paris only after great struggle. Both the theater and director were changed several times. A script of the play was handed to a high officer of the police who warned the director of the Théâtre Antoine, where the play was expected to run, not to stage the play. However, *Le Balcon* continued to intrigue the French public because of continuing debate about it within theatrical circles and reports of productions abroad. Finally, the appointment by Charles de Gaulle of André Malraux to arts minister paved the way for the play to be produced. Malraux gave permission to Peter Brook to stage *Le Balcon,* which he did in May 1960. Genet was again disappointed by the staging and performance of his play. Audiences were confused and often appalled, and they generally responded coolly. *Le Balcon* was most successful in New York at the Off-Broadway Circle in the Square, where an abridged version opened in March 1960 under the direction of José Quintero. The play generated controversy, and it was performed 672 times before closing in 1962–at that time it was the longest-running play in Off-Broadway history.

Genet's next play, *Les Nègres, clownerie,* developed out of three inspirations. The first inspiration was a documentary movie by Jean Rouch, *Les Maîtres-Fous* (1954, The Mad Masters), about an exoricism ritual performed by a group of men in Ghana. Genet saw this movie in 1955. The second was an eighteenth-century music box Genet had been given as a present. The figures on the music box were four blacks dressed in livery and bowing before a little white princess. It occurred to Genet that, although the music box was old, the image was still a standard in his day, and he thought about how the inverse image would be met with great surprise. The third inspiration was the request by the director Raymond Rouleau that Genet write a play for an all-black cast. Hence, Genet set aside *Le Balcon,* which he had been working on, and wrote the first draft of *Les Nègres, clownerie* almost overnight.

As the curtain is drawn, four black men and four black women in formal dress are dancing a minuet to Mozart around a catafalque in the center of the stage. A white court then enters the stage and takes its place on a raised tier from which it can observe the actions of the blacks. The white court comprises the Queen, her valet, a governor, a judge, and a missionary. These characters are played by black actors who are wearing white masks that do not completely cover their faces (making it obvious that black actors are playing the whites). Archibald, the director of the blacks' performance, addresses both the court and the audience to introduce the dancers, who, he says, are there for the entertainment of the whites. But he also makes it clear that it will all be very confusing and uncomfortable for the audience: "Mais . . . afin que vous soyez assurés qu'un tel drame ne risque pas de pénétrer dans vos vies précieuses, nous aurons encore la politesse, apprise parmi vous, de rendre la communication impossible" (But . . . in order that you can rest assured that there is no risk of such a drama penetrating into your precious lives, we will have

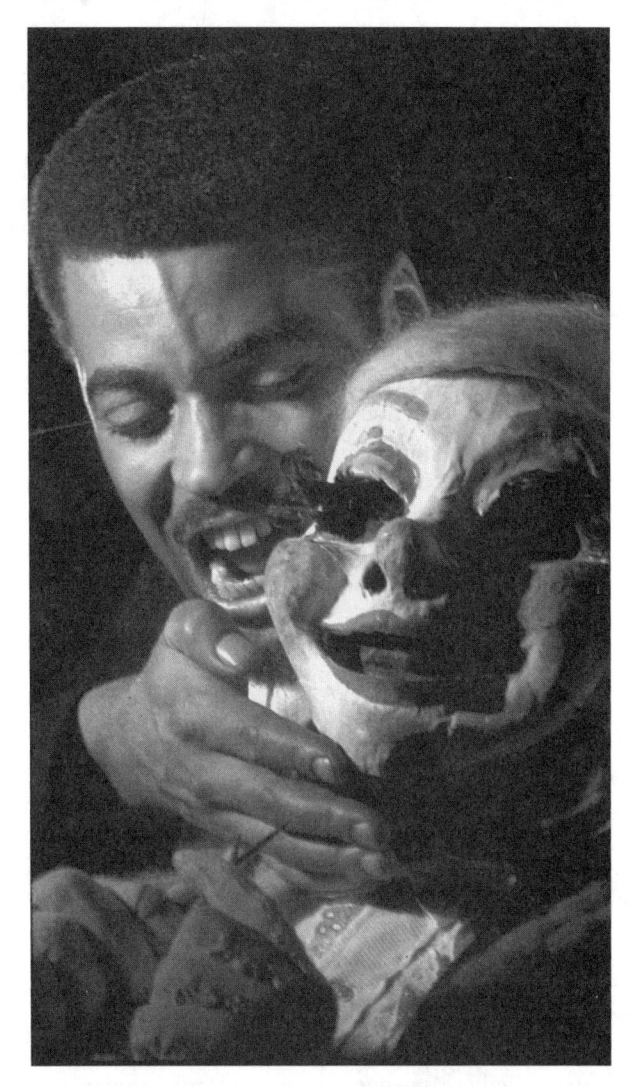

James Earl Jones in the first American production of Genet's Les Nègres, clownerie *(1958; translated as* The Blacks: A Clown Show, *1960) at Saint Mark's Playhouse, New York, 1 July 1961 (photograph by Gjon Milli; © Time Life Pictures/Getty Images)*

the courtesy, which we have learned from you, to render communication impossible).

The audience and the court learn that the catafalque contains the body of a white woman, killed by the blacks to entertain the whites. What follows is a ritual trial in which the blacks struggle to prove to the whites that they are as savage and criminal as the whites expect and want them to be. Parallel to this trial are repeated attempts by two of the black characters, Village and Virtue, to declare their love to each other. This love is rebuked by the other blacks, who insist that Village and Virtue play their roles properly, according to the script written by the whites, a script in which there is no space for the expression of black love. When the white court finally descends onto the stage to punish the blacks for their crime, the whites are massacred. But they are not truly white, so they are not truly massacred. It has all been a game. The whites raise their masks, exposing their blackness, and the catafalque is shown to be empty. This ritual trial has been nothing more than a diversionary tactic to distract the audience from a real trial occurring elsewhere. In the "real" world offstage, a black man is being tried and executed for having betrayed his own people. This real execution of a black traitor paves the way for a new form of expression that will allow Virtue and Village to express their love in terms that are free of white conventions.

Many of the themes in *Les Nègres, clownerie* are found in Genet's earlier plays: the interdependence of opposing forces, including master and servant, judge and criminal, white and black; the masquerade that throws into question any stable identity; and the sexual and emotional repression of marginalized people. However, the aggressiveness of *Les Nègres, clownerie* is new. Genet often mentioned that he was asked by blacks to write this play, but he also stressed that he did not write it for blacks but against whites. Continual references to the audience—through direct address, finger-pointing, and targeted lighting—make it impossible for the spectators to feel uninvolved. The audience is, as Archibald has promised, confused. The plot is difficult to follow since much has happened leading up to the opening scene, and the usual exposition of the backstory is nearly absent. Furthermore, the pieces of exposition that do appear are at times contradictory and are constantly interrupted or cut short by comments about how the play should unfold, questions about whether someone is playing his role properly, or by unrelated comments from the court. As Una Chaudhuri maintains in her 1986 work, *No Man's Stage: A Semiotic Study of Jean Genet's Major Plays*, the emphasis is moved by force away from the plot, focusing audience attention on the verbal attack.

The language of *Les Nègres, clownerie* ranges from obscene to eloquent. Genet taunts the audience at first with a discussion of the consecrated wafer of the Eucharist as being black, or gray, or black on one side and white on the other. As the play proceeds, the notion of things being turned around becomes real and threatening, for white depends on black:

> Félicité: Si vous êtes la lumière et que nous soyons l'ombre, tant qu'il y aura la nuit où vient sombrer le jour . . .
>
> La Reine: Je vais vous faire exterminer.
>
> Félicité, *ironique:* Sotte, que vous seriez plate, sans cette ombre qui vous donne tant de relief.

> (Felicity: If you are the light and we the shadow, as long as there is night into which the day darkens . . .
>
> The Queen: I'm going to have you exterminated.
>
> Felicity, *ironically:* Idiot! How flat you'd be without that shadow that gives you so much depth.)

The blacks—and the spectators—are able to imagine a world where black dominates white: "Ce qui est doux, bon, aimable et tender sera noir. Le lait sera noir, le sucre, le riz, le ciel, les colombes, l'espérance, seront noirs—l'opéra aussi, où nous irons, noires dans des Rolls noires, saluer des rois noirs, entendre une musique de cuivre sous les lustres de cristal noir" (Whatever is gentle, good, kind, and tender will be black. Milk will be black, sugar, rice, the sky, doves, hope will be black—the opera, too, where we will go, black in our black Rolls Royces, to salute black kings, to listen to brass bands under chandeliers of black crystal).

Despite having encouraged its creation, Rouleau did not direct the premiere of *Les Nègres, clownerie*. Rouleau and Genet had trouble finding enough French-speaking black actors to fill the roles. Instead, Roget Blin, who had directed Beckett's *En attendant Godot* (published 1952; translated as *Waiting for Godot*, 1954) to great acclaim in 1953, was searching for an appropriate play for a troupe of black actors called Les Griots when he heard about Genet's work. He and Genet spent one month tightening the plot. Genet's collaboration with a man of the theater improved *Les Nègres, clownerie*, and it is considered one of Genet's best works. Nevertheless, staging the play was not an easy task. The actors, some of whom were professional and some of whom were amateur, were at first shocked, even offended, by the aggressive tone and vulgar language of the play. Additionally, a few of the actors were African, two were Haitian, one came from Guyana, and the rest were Antillean, which meant that there were several different accents that needed to be standardized and minimized so that the actors could be easily understood. According to some critics, this task was not entirely accomplished. Despite their difficulties, the dedicated cast and crew worked without recompense for six months to produce a success.

Les Nègres, clownerie opened on 28 October 1959 at the Théâtre de Lutèce in Paris to stunned audiences: white spectators did not know if they should applaud the beauty of the play or defend themselves against its attack. Regardless, *Les Nègres, clownerie* drew a full house night after night. The production was, according to Genet, close to perfect. The play, which had a run of 169 performances, was eventually moved into the Théâtre de la Renaissance in order to accommodate larger audiences. It was awarded the Grand Prix de la Critique for the best play of 1959. In the United States the play was an even greater success. The first American production of *The Blacks* opened at St. Mark's Playhouse in New York City on 4 May 1961 under the direction of Gene Frankel. The cast included artists who eventually became well known: James Earl Jones, Cicely Tyson, Godfrey Cambridge, Louis Gossett, and Maya Angelou. *The Blacks: A Clown Show* ran for four years straight, setting a record for an Off-Broadway production.

While *Les Nègres, clownerie* was playing regularly to full houses in Paris, Genet was in Greece working on his final play, *Les Paravents*. Genet may have started forming the outline for this play as early as 1955, but he did not begin writing it until 1957. By mid 1958 the first version was completed, but like Genet's other plays it was rewritten many times over several years. In 1960 *Les Paravents* was published in German translation, and an expurgated version was staged for the first time that year in Berlin. The original version of the play was published in 1961, but it was not performed in France until 1966.

Critics agree that *Les Paravents* is an accomplished work, but its length and staging requirements make it a difficult choice for theater directors. It has, therefore, not been produced as often as Genet's other major plays. As published, the play takes approximately five hours to perform. There are almost one hundred roles to be distributed among approximately twenty actors. The stage must be large enough to accommodate multiple, large screens that can be moved freely on and off the stage as well as at least four different platform levels. A theater director who followed Genet's instructions precisely would only produce this play in an open-air theater built in the middle of a cemetery.

Les Paravents depicts the development of revolutionary events in a colonized country (a loosely disguised Algeria). The plot revolves around an Arab man, Saïd, who is an outcast and so poor that he cannot afford a beautiful bride. He must marry the ugliest woman in the community, Leila, who covers her face in shame with a hood. In the opening tableau, Saïd and his mother are making their way to the wedding, bringing a suitcase of presents. The mother dances proudly before her son in mismatched high-heeled shoes, then falls into hysterical laughter. The suitcase opens, revealing that it is empty. Laughter will be the mother's weapon against life's injustices: "Je suis le Rire . . . celui qui apparaît quand tout va mal" (I am Laughter . . . the kind that appears when everything goes wrong). Saïd's revolt is more personal. He accepts his wife's ugliness and asks her to display it proudly. He accepts his poverty and status as an outcast. He unwittingly inspires the revolutionary rebels, but when they want to turn him into a hero and the symbol of their struggle, he refuses to participate. By the end of the play, as they are trying Saïd for treason, the rebels have assumed the roles of their oppressors.

Cover for the video of the 1974 movie adaptation of Genet's 1947 play Les Bonnes, *about two servants who plot the death of their bourgeois employer (Thomas Cooper Library, University of South Carolina)*

According to their names and dress, the colonialists are alternately French, English, German, Italian, and Spanish. They are symbols rather than real people. Sir Harold, for example, is able to leave an oversized stuffed glove in his stead to remind the workers of his control over them. Meanwhile, the screens of the title not only serve as scenery but also represent the line between life and death. Over the course of the play characters die and pass through the screens to the upper tier of the stage. In this place beyond life they are united in rollicking laughter: the colonialists laugh with the Arab rebels, and Saïd's mother laughs with the soldier she accidentally strangled. All of the dead lose their political associations, and together they enjoy the spectacle of life that is continuing onstage.

The subject of *Les Paravents,* the revolt of a colonized Arab people, was unpopular in France following Algeria's fight for independence. The play opened in Paris at the government-supported Théâtre de l'Odéon on 16 April 1966 and created the greatest scandal in the history of French theater since the premiere of Victor Hugo's *Hernani, ou l'Honneur castillan* (published and produced, 1830; translated as *Hernani; or, The Honor of a Castilian*, 1830). Night after night, the play was attended by right-wing militants who stormed the stage or interrupted the play in protest. The strongest reactions came in response to a scene in which a fallen French lieutenant is honored by his men with a symphony of flatulence. Later in 1966 *Les Paravents* became a central issue in a budget debate in Parliament. Christian Bonnet, a conservative from Brittany, attacked the practice of subsidizing theaters that presented works such as Genet's and asked that the Théâtre de l'Odéon's funds be cut as punishment. The minister of culture, Malraux, fiercely defended the theater, reminding the members of Parliament that the geniuses of Charles Baudelaire and Rimbaud were also misunderstood during their lifetimes.

Les Paravents was the last literary work Genet published during his lifetime. In February 1964, after the publication of *Les Paravents* but before its debut in Paris, one of Genet's closest friends, a trapeze artist named Abdallah Bentaga, committed suicide. Although Genet and Bentaga were no longer lovers at the time of his death, Genet was devastated by the loss. The following month he told friends that he had torn up all of his remaining manuscripts and had given up writing. Three years later, still suffering over Bentaga's death and fearing old age, Genet wrote a new will and attempted to take his own life through an overdose of sleeping pills.

Over the next two decades Genet dedicated himself to politics, using his fame to draw the world's attention to the injustices practiced against minorities and the politically weak. But he did not attempt to rally people through art, which he maintained could not create political change, but through activism. He spoke out in support of the student protests in France in 1968; the antiwar demonstrations in Vietnam-era America; the anti-American leftist Zengakuren group in Japan; the Black Panthers movement in the United States; the terrorist organization Baader-Meinhoff in West Germany; and the Palestinian Liberation Organization in the Middle East. This last group retained Genet's undying support, although he admitted that he could only support the PLO as long as there was no Palestinian state. Consistent in his politics, Genet would have given up his support of the Palestinians had they gained independence, for they would then have become part of the power structure.

In 1983 Genet began writing his final literary work. He had been diagnosed with cancer four years earlier, and although he had responded well to chemotherapy he knew that his cancer was terminal. The previous year Genet had witnessed atrocities that had stunned him and compelled him to write. In September 1982 he had traveled to the Near East and was in Beirut when the city was invaded by the Israeli army. The Christian Lebanese militia massacred hundreds of those in the Palestinian refugee camps at Sabra and Shatila. Genet was one of the first Westerners to enter Shatila after the massacre, an experience that he documented in his article for the *Journal of Palestine Studies* (1 January 1983), titled "Quatre heures à Shatila," later republished in volume six of *Œuvres complètes* (1991).

Genet's last work, *Un Captif amoureux,* is a collection of memories and commentaries about his involvement with two homeless groups, the Black Panthers and the Palestinians. It is also a reflection on Genet's own life, a philosophical examination of his politics, a condemnation of the power of the media, and an acceptance of the inevitability of death. He completed *Un Captif amoureux* in late 1985 and was correcting the proofs in the days before his death on 15 April 1986. Gallimard published the book the next month.

Although he had been suffering from cancer for years, Genet died from a fall in the hotel room in Paris where he was staying. On the morning of 15 April, his friends found his body lying on the threshold to the bathroom. Genet's death came one day after the passing of Simone de Beauvoir, but unlike the massive funeral held for her in Paris, Genet's friends decided to bury him quietly. Following his expressed wish to be interred in Morocco, they laid him to rest just outside of the town of Larache, in an old Spanish cemetery.

Since Genet's death, two further plays and one screenplay have been published: *"Elle," Splendid's* (1993; translated, 1995), and *Le Bagne* (1994, The Penal Colony). *"Elle"* was first staged in Parma, Italy, at the Festival de Parme in April 1990. The first French production was staged that autumn at the Théâtre de Gennevilliers under the direction of Bruno Bayen and starring Maria Casarès, a veteran of Genet's plays. The English-language premiere (also as *"Elle"*) was staged in July 2002 at The Zipper, an Off-Broadway theater. *Splendid's* was first performed in 1995 at the Théâtre de Nanterre-Amendiers and that same year in English at the Lyric Hammersmith in London. *Le Bagne* has never been filmed, but it was performed onstage for the first time on 23 May 2004 at the Théâtre National de Nice.

Splendid's is a two-act play Genet began perhaps as early as 1942 and finished in 1948. He thought about staging the play in 1952 and again in 1956, but he ultimately refused to allow its production. After having rewritten the play several times, Genet finally decided he didn't like it and abandoned the project. However, not everyone shared his negative opinion of the play: Frechtman admired the piece and tried repeatedly to convince Genet to stage it, and Sartre found it superior to *Les Bonnes*. Despite Genet's attempts to destroy all copies of the manuscript, it survived. Barbezat had a copy and a contract to publish it, and his company, L'Arbalète, did so in 1993.

In the plot a gang of seven thugs called La Rafale kidnap a young American heiress and hold her captive on the seventh floor of the luxury hotel Splendid's. The gang is joined by a former police officer who has, for philosophical reasons, turned to a life of crime. When one of the thugs, overwhelmed by the seductive feminine presence, strangles the heiress, the gang realizes their fate has been sealed. Knowing that the police will not raid the building as long as they believe the heiress is still alive, the gang leader dons the clothes of the dead girl and convincingly poses as her on the balcony. Then the gang members dress in the clothes of the hotel guests to reenact an elegant party and their own trial. Treason moves the plot forward, as the former policeman shoots the gang leader, still dressed as a woman, in full view of the police, who then storm the building. In an attempt at self-preservation, the shooter reassumes his policeman's identity and arrests the gang members before the police enter. Although not as powerful as his full-length plays, *Splendid's* features the themes and stylistic properties characteristic of Genet's plays: the transformation of identity, impersonation, the interdependency of good and evil, treason, ritual, and slang mixed with poetry.

Little is known about the writing of *"Elle."* Genet mentioned the play in 1955, when he was working on *Le Balcon, Les Nègres, clownerie,* and *Les Paravents,* and, according to White, it was most likely completed that year. *"Elle"* is in reference to the Pope, who is referred to respectfully in French as Sainteté (Holiness), a word of feminine gender. It is a one-act play in which a photographer has been summoned to the Vatican to take a picture of the Pope that will be disseminated to the faithful. But as the Pope enters the scene, the play turns into a meditation on imagery and authenticity. Can an image represent the Pope? And if so, can any image represent the Pope? The meditation leads to the conclusion that the Pope is nothing more than a sanctified image and therefore the best thing to represent him is *nothing*.

Genet's last published work, *Le Bagne,* was originally written as a screenplay in 1952. Genet attempted to rewrite it in 1955 but eventually abandoned the work entirely and destroyed his revisions. The original movie script that Genet gave to Barbezat survived. The story takes place in a romanticized world of the French penal colonies (which were phased out beginning in 1938). Three convicts who are defined by courage and toughness are trapped in rivalry and jealousy. Santo Fortano is a new prisoner whose reputation has preceded him to the penal colony. He is well known for his heinous crimes, but in this prison from which no man returns, past crimes are meaningless. The criminals must commit new crimes in order to maintain their identities. A fellow prisoner, Rocky, uses a needle Fortano has passed to him to blind and kill a guard. The needle falls to the floor between the cell doors of Fortano and Rocky. Another prisoner, Roger, tells the warden the needle belonged to Fortano, who is then sent to the guillotine. In extensive notes Genet defines the smallest details of the set, costumes, and camera angles. The set is stark, and the prisoners are naked. The elimination of anything that could distract draws attention to the characters' gestures.

With nineteenth-century poets Verlaine and Baudelaire, Jean Genet is respected as a *poète maudit* (cursed poet). He is also considered, along with Proust and Louis-Ferdinand Céline, one of the most expressive French writers of the twentieth century. While Genet's novels earned him a place among France's greatest authors, his theater originally brought him to the attention of the general public. His plays continue to be performed and appreciated throughout the world. With the shift from novels to theater, Genet moved his audience from the world of criminals, outsiders, and homosexuals to the world of power relations. As Genet predicted, his theater was incapable of changing society, but it provided a vision of how power relations function. In the process Genet has shown his audiences that they are all playing roles in a great theater. As Madame Irma of *Le Balcon* says, "il faut rentrer chez vous, où tout, n'en doutez pas, sera encore plus faux qu'ici" (You must go home, where everything, without a doubt, will be more false than here).

Letters:

Lettres à Olga et Marc Barbezat (Lyon: L'Arbalète, 1988);

Lettres au Petit Franz (1943–1944) (Paris: Gallimard, 2000).

Interviews:

Robert Poulet, "Jean Genet: 'Fouillez l'ordure, vous trouverez mon secret,'" *Le Bulletin de Paris,* 145 (19 July 1956): 10–11;

"Interview with Jean Genet," *Playboy* (April 1964): 45–55;

Pierre Démeron, "Conversation with Jean Genet," *Oui,* 1 (November 1972): 62–64, 99–100, 102;

Hubert Fichte, "Jean Genet Talks to Hubert Fichte," translated by Patrick McCarthy, *New Review,* 4 (April 1977): 9–21.

Bibliography:

Richard C. Webb and Suzanne A. Webb, *Jean Genet and His Critics: An Annotated Bibliography* (Metuchen, N.J. & London: Scarecrow Press, 1982).

Biographies:

Harry E. Stewart and Rob Roy McGregor, *Jean Genet: A Biography of Deceit, 1910–1951* (New York: Peter Lang, 1989);

Edmund White, *Genet: A Biography* (New York: Vintage, 1993);

Jeremy Reed, *Jean Genet: Born to Lose* (London: Creation, 2005).

References:

Odette Aslan, *Jean Genet* (Paris: Seghers, 1973);

Georges Bataille, "Jean Genet," in his *La Littérature et le mal* (Paris: Gallimard, 1957), pp. 185–226; translated by Alastair Hamilton as *Literature and Evil* (London: Calder & Boyars, 1973);

Véronique Bergen, *Jean Genet, entre mythe et réalité* (Brussels: De Boeck University, 1993);

Gisèle Bickel, "Crime and Revolution in the Theater of Jean Genet," in *Myths and Realities of Contemporary French Theater*, edited by Patricia M. Hopkins and Wendell M. Aycock (Lubbock: Texas Tech University Press, 1985), pp. 169–180;

Bickel, *Jean Genet: Criminalité et transcendence*, Stanford French and Italian Studies, no. 55 (Saratoga, Cal.: Anma Libri, 1987);

Claude Bonnefoy, *Genet*, Classiques du XXe siècle, no. 76 (Paris: Editions Universitaires, 1965);

Roger Borderie and Henri Ronse, eds., *Obliques*, special Genet issue, no. 2 (1972);

Peter Brooks and Joseph Halpern, eds., *Genet, A Collection of Critical Essays* (Englewood Cliffs, N.J.: Prentice-Hall, 1979);

Lewis T. Cetta, *Profane Play, Ritual and Jean Genet: A Study of His Drama* (University: University of Alabama Press, 1974);

Una Chaudhuri, *No Man's Stage: A Semiotic Study of Jean Genet's Major Plays* (Ann Arbor: University of Michigan Research Press, 1986);

Richard N. Coe, *The Theatre of Jean Genet: A Casebook* (New York: Grove, 1970);

Coe, *The Vision of Jean Genet: A Study of his Poems, Plays and Novels* (New York: Grove, 1968);

Derek F. Connon, "Confused? You Will Be: Genet's *Les Nègres* and the Art of Upsetting the Audience," *French Studies: A Quarterly Review*, 50 (October 1996): 425–438;

Bernard Dort, *Théâtre reel* (Paris: Seuil, 1971);

Scott Durham, ed., *Genet: In the Language of the Enemy*, Yale French Studies, no. 91 (New Haven: Yale University Press, 1997);

Jane Giles, *The Cinema of Jean Genet: Un Chant d'Amour* (London: BFI Publishing, 1991);

David I. Grossvogel, "Jean Genet," in his *Four Playwrights and a Postscript* (Ithaca, N.Y.: Cornell University Press, 1962), pp. 133–174;

Jacques Guicharnaud, *Modern French Theatre: From Giraudoux to Genet*, revised edition (New Haven: Yale University Press, 1967);

Robert Hauptman, *The Pathological Vision. Jean Genet, Louis-Ferdinand Céline and Tennessee Williams* (New York: Peter Lang, 1983), pp. 1–50;

Josephine Jacobsen and William R. Mueller, *Ionesco and Genet: Playwrights of Silence* (New York: Hill & Wang, 1968);

Bettina Knapp, *Jean Genet* (New York: Twayne, 1968);

Magazine littéraire, special Genet issue, no. 313 (September 1993);

Joseph H. McMahon, *The Imagination of Jean Genet* (New Haven: Yale University Press, 1963);

Laura Oswald, *Jean Genet and the Semiotics of Performance* (Bloomington: Indiana University Press, 1989);

Gene A. Plunka, *The Rites of Passage of Jean Genet: The Art and Aesthetics of Risk Taking* (Rutherford, N.J.: Fairleigh Dickinson University Press / London: Associated University Presses, 1992);

Jean-Paul Sartre, *Saint Genet, comédien et martyr*, Œuvres complètes de Jean Genet, volume 1 (Paris: Gallimard, 1952); translated by Bernard Frechtman as *Saint Genet, Actor and Martyr* (New York: George Braziller, 1963);

Jeannette L. Savona, *Jean Genet* (New York: Grove, 1982);

Savona, "Théâtre et univers carcéral: Jean Genet et Michel Foucault," *French Forum*, 10 (May 1985): 201–213;

H. E. Stewart, "You Are What You Wear: Appearance and Being in Jean Genet's Works," *Francofonia: Studi e ricerche sulle letterature di lingua francese*, 10 (Spring 1986): 31–40;

Philip Thody, *Jean Genet: A Study of His Novels and Plays* (New York: Stein & Day, 1969);

Jean Verdeil, "Double et dédoublement dans le théâtre de Jean Genet," in *Doubles et dédoublements en literature*, edited by Gabriel A. Pérouse (Saint-Etienne: Publications de l'Université de Saint-Etienne, 1995), pp. 219–226.

Papers:

Some of Jean Genet's letters, film scripts, plays, poems, and other texts are held in the Genet Collection at the Institut Mémoires de l'Edition Contemporaine in Paris.

Michel de Ghelderode
(Adolphe-Adhémar Martens)
(3 April 1898 – 1 April 1962)

Susan McCready
University of South Alabama

PLAY PRODUCTIONS: *La Mort regarde à la fenêtre,* Brussels, Théâtre de la Bonbonnière, 29 April 1918;

Le Repas des fauves, Brussels, January 1919;

Oude Piet, Anvers, Les Œuvriers de la Renaissance d'Occident, 23 January 1925;

La Farce de la mort qui faillit trépasser, Brussels, Vlaamsche Volkstooneel, 19 November 1925;

Images de la vie de Saint François d'Assise, Brussels, Vlaamsche Volkstooneel, 2 February 1927;

La Mort du Docteur Faust, Paris, Art et Action, 27 January 1928;

Le Miracle dans le faubourg, Brusssels, Concours de littérature dramatique de la Province de Brabant, 16 December 1928;

Escurial, Brussels, Koninklijke Vlaamsche Schouwburg, 12 January 1929;

Barabbas, Ostende, Vlaamsche Volkstooneel, 4 March 1929;

Christophe Colomb, Paris, Art et Action, 25 October 1929;

Pantagleize, Saint-Trond, Vlaamsche Volkstooneel, 22 April 1930;

Atlantique, Brussels, Vlaamsche Volkstooneel, 29 November 1930;

Trois acteurs, un drame . . . , Brussels, Théâtre Royal du Parc, 2 April 1931;

Le Voleur d'étoiles, Vlaamsche Volkstooneel, 28 March 1932;

Le Mystère de la Passion de Notre-Seigneur Jésus-Christ, Brussels, Toone IV, 30 March 1934;

Magie rouge, Brussels, Le "Plateau 33," 30 April 1934;

Le Ménage de Caroline, Brussels, Universal Exposition, 26 October 1935;

Sire Halewyn, Brussels, Théâtre communal, 21 January 1938;

Adrian et Jusemina and *Arc-en-ciel,* Paris, Compagnie de la Rose, 27 May 1939;

Hop Signor!, Brussels, Théâtre Royal du Parc, 23 April 1942;

Michel de Ghelderode (from Jean Decock, Le Théâtre de Michel de Ghelderode, *1969; Thomas Cooper Library, University of South Carolina)*

Mademoiselle Jaïre, Paris, Compagnie Roger Iglésis, 4 July 1949;

Fastes d'enfer, Paris, Compagnie du Myrmidon, 11 July 1949;

Marie la misérable, Woluwe-Saint-Lambert, L'Eglise de Woluwe-Saint-Lambert en Brabant, 14 June 1952;

La Farce des ténébreux, Paris, Compagnie Georges Vitaly, 12 November 1952;

La Balade du Grand Macabre, Lyon, Théâtre de la Comédie, 18 February 1953;

Les Femmes au tombeau, Paris, Compagnie Théâtrale de la Cité, 7 May 1953;

L'Ecole des bouffons, Paris, Théâtre de l'Œuvre, 13 October 1953;

Le Cavalier bizarre, Paris, Compagnie Roger Jourdan, 10 November 1953;

Masques ostendais, Liège, L'Equipe des Rats Morts, Théâtre de l'Etuve, 5 April 1954;

Le Club des menteurs, Paris, Comédiens du cours Berthon, 16 November 1957;

La Transfiguration dans le cirque, Rotterdam, Rotterdams Toneel, 10 April 1959;

Sortie de l'acteur, Kraków, Teatr Studencki 38, 27 November 1960;

Don Juan ou les Amants chimériques, Brussels, Atelier du Théâtre National de Belgique, 22 October 1962;

D'un Diable qui prêcha merveilles, Brussels, Groupe Ratures, 2 November 1964;

Le Sommeil de la raison, Korbach, Germany, Le Mascaret, 24 May 1968;

La Pie sur le gibet, Brussels, Toone VII, 16 July 1969;

Vénus and *Un soir de pitié,* Brussels, Athalyc, 14 March 1970;

Le Siège d'Ostende, Montreal, Ecole nationale de Théâtre du Canada, 20 March 1984;

Tête de bois, Brussels, Compagnie Michel de Ghelderode, 19 December 1985;

La Couronne de fer-blanc, Kinshasa, Republic of Congo, Théâtre des Intrigants, 18 October 2001.

BOOKS: *La Halte catholique* (Brussels: L'Edition, 1922);

L'Histoire comique de Keizer Karel: Telle que la perpétuèrent jusqu'à nos jours les gens de Brabant et de Flandre, preface by Max Deauville (Brussels: La Renaissance d'Occident, 1923; definitive edition, Brussels: Carrefour, 1943);

L'Homme sous l'uniforme (Brussels: L'Edition, 1923);

Le Mystère de la Passion de Notre-Seigneur Jésus-Christ: Avec tous les personnages, pour les théâtres des marionnettes reconstitué d'après le spectacle (Brussels: La Renaissance d'Occident, 1925);

Oude Piet, Théâtre, no. 1 (Brussels: Editions de La Renaissance d'Occident, 1925);

Les Vieillards: Farce mystique en 1 acte (Brussels: La Vache Rose, 1925); translated by Samuel Draper as *The Old Men,* in *The Strange Rider and Seven Other Plays* (New York: American Friends of Ghelderode, 1964), pp. 93–107;

La Corne d'Abondance (Brussels: La Vache Rose, 1925);

Kwiebe-Kwiebus (Brussels: La Renaissance d'Occident, 1926); republished as *Voyage autour de ma Flandre* (Bruges: Stainforth, 1947);

La Mort du Docteur Faust, preface by Camille Poupeye (Ostende-Bruges: Editions de La Flandre littéraire, 1926); translated by George Hauger as *The Death of Doctor Faust,* in *Seven Plays,* volume 2 (New York: Hill & Wang, 1964), pp. 95–150;

Vénus, preface "de l'éditeur" by Ghelderode (Ostende-Bruges: Editions de La Flandre littéraire, 1927); translated by David Willinger, in *Theatrical Gestures from the Belgium Avant-Garde* (New York: New York Literary Forum, 1987), pp. 115–126;

La Transfiguration dans le cirque; Escurial, Théâtre, no. 2, preface by Maurice Gauchez (Brussels: La Renaissance d'Occident, 1928); *La Transfiguration dans la cirque* translated by Willinger as *Transfiguration in the Circus,* in *The Siege of Ostend, The Actor Makes His Exit, Transfiguration in the Circus* (Austin: Host, 1990), pp. 254–284; *Escurial* translated by Lionel Abel, in *The Modern Theatre,* volume 5, edited by Eric Bentley (Garden City, N.Y.: Doubleday, 1957), pp. 161–178;

Don Juan: Drama-Farce pour le music-hall; Christophe Colomb: Féerie dramatique, Théâtre, no. 3 (Brussels: La Renaissance d'Occident, 1928); *Christophe Colomb* translated by Hauger as *Christopher Columbus,* in *Seven Plays,* volume 2 (New York: Hill & Wang, 1964), pp. 151–175;

Ixelles, mes amours, as Philostène Constable (Ostend: Cahiers de la Flandre Littéraire, 1928);

Trois acteurs, un drame (Brussels: La Renaissance d'Occident, 1929); translated by Hauger as *Three Actors and Their Drama,* in *Seven Plays,* volume 1 (New York: Hill & Wang, 1960), pp. 125–141;

Barabbas: Tragédie en trois actes (Brussels: Labor, 1932); translated by Hauger, in *Seven Plays,* volume 1 (New York: Hill & Wang, 1960), pp. 45–123;

Arc-en-ciel: Féerie (Verviers: L'Avant-Poste, 1933);

Pantagleize: Un coeur innocent dans le monde (Brussels: Le Vrai, 1934); translated by Hauger, in *Seven Plays,* volume 1 (New York: Hill & Wang, 1960), pp. 143–222;

Les Femmes au tombeau (Brussels: Tréteaux, 1934); translated by Draper as *The Women at the Tomb,* in *The Strange Rider and Seven Other Plays* (New York: American Friends of Ghelderode, 1964), pp. 9–43;

Adrian et Jusemina (Brussels: Tréteaux, 1935);

La Balade du grand Macabre: Farce pour rhétoriciens (Brussels: Tréteaux, 1935);

Magie rouge: Farce en 3 actes (Brussels: Tréteaux, 1935); translated by Draper as *Red Magic*, in *The Strange Rider and Seven Other Plays* (New York: American Friends of Ghelderode, 1964), pp. 109–175;

Le Ménage de Caroline (Brussels: Tréteaux, 1935);

Masques Ostendais (Anvers: Ça ira, 1935);

Le Cavalier bizarre (Anvers: Ça ira, 1938); translated by Draper as *The Strange Rider*, in *The Strange Rider and Seven Other Plays* (New York: American Friends of Ghelderode, 1964), pp. 45–65;

Hop Signor!: Tragédie (Brussels: Cahiers du Journal des Poètes, 1938); translated by Hauger, in *Seven Plays*, volume 2 (New York: Hill and Wang, 1964), pp. 47–94;

Sortilèges (Paris: L'Essor, 1941; definitive edition, preface by Franz Hellens, Paris: Maréchal, 1947)—comprises *L'écrivain public*; *Le diable à Londres*; *Le jardin malade*; *L'amateur de reliques*; *Eliah le peintre*; *Rhotomago*; *Sortilèges*; *Voler la mort*; *Nuestra Senora de la Soledad*; *Brouillard*; *Un crépuscule*; and *Tu fus pendu!*;

Théâtre Complet, 3 volumes (Brussels: Houblon, 1942)—comprises volume 1, *La Farce des ténébreux*, *Hop Signor!*, *Don Juan, ou les Amants chimériques*, *Mademoiselle Jaïre*; *Mademoiselle Jaïre* translated by Hauger as *Mademoiselle Jairus*, in *Seven Plays*, volume 2 (New York: Hill & Wang, 1964), pp. 203–271; volume 2, *L'Ecole des bouffons*, *Magie rouge*, *Sortie de l'acteur*, *D'un Diable qui prêcha merveilles*, and *Le Soleil se couche*; *L'Ecole des bouffons* translated by Kenneth S. White as *School for Buffoons* (San Francisco: Chandler, 1968); and volume 3, *La Pie sur le gibet*, *La Balade du Grand macabre*, *Les Aveugles*, *Fastes d'enfer*, *Le Ménage de Caroline*, and *Pantagleize*; *Les Aveugles* translated by Hauger as *The Blind Men*, in *Seven Plays*, volume 1 (New York: Hill & Wang, 1960), pp. 223–233; *Fastes d'enfer* translated by Hauger as *Chronicles of Hell*, in *Seven Plays*, volume 1 (New York: Hill & Wang, 1960), pp. 235–273;

L'Hôtel de Ruescas: Nouvelle (Anvers: Le Papegay, 1943);

Choses et gens de chez nous (Brussels: Maréchal, 1943);

Mes statues (Liège: Carrefour, 1943);

Théâtre, 6 volumes (Paris: Gallimard, 1950–1982)—comprises volume 1 (1950), *Hop Signor!*, *Escurial*, *Sire Halewyn*, *Magie rouge*, *Mademoiselle Jaïre*, and *Fastes d'enfer*; *Sire Halewyn* translated by Gerard Hopkins as *Lord Halewyn*, in *Seven Plays*, volume 1 (New York: Hill & Wang, 1960), pp. 275–304; volume 2 (1952), *Le Cavalier bizarre*, *La Balade du grand macabre*, *Trois acteurs, un drame*, *Christophe Colomb*, *Les Femmes au tombeau*, and *La Farce des ténébreux*; volume 3 (1953), *La Pie sur le gibet*, *Pantagleize*, *D'un Diable qui prêcha merveilles*, *Sortie de l'acteur*, and *L'Ecole des bouffons*; *Sortie de l'acteur* translated by Willinger as *The Actor Makes His Exit*, in *The Siege of Ostend, The Actor Makes His Exit, Transfiguration in the Circus* (Austin: Host, 1990), pp. 172–253; volume 4 (1955), *Un soir de pitié*, *Don Juan, ou Les Amants chimériques*, *Le Club des menteurs*, *Les Vieillards*, *Marie la misérable*, and *Masques ostendais*; *Un soir de pitié* translated by Hauger as *A Night of Pity*, in *Seven Plays*, volume 2 (New York: Hill & Wang, 1964), pp. 177–191; volume 5 (1957), *Le Soleil se couche*, *Les Aveugles*, *Barabbas*, *Le Ménage de Caroline*, *La Mort du Docteur Faust*, *Adrian et Jusemina*, and *Piet Bouteille*; *Piet Bouteille* translated by Hauger, in *Seven Plays*, volume 2 (New York: Hill & Wang, 1964), pp. 193–201; and volume 6 (1982), *Le Sommeil de la raison*, *Le Perroquet de Charles-Quint*, *Le Singulier trépas de Messire Ulenspiegel*, *La Folie d'Hugo van der Goes*, *La Grande Tentation de Saint-Antoine*, and *Noyade des songes*; *Noyade des songes* translated by Willinger as *Dreams Drowning*, in *Theatrical Gestures from the Belgium Avant-Garde* (New York: New York Literary Forum, 1987), pp. 127–136;

La Farce de la mort qui faillit trépasser (Brussels: A l'Enseigne de la Sirène, 1952);

La Flandre est un songe (Brussels: Durendal, 1953);

A propos de Franz Hellens (Liège: Dynamo, 1964);

Ultimes boutades (Liège: Dynamo, 1965);

Le Siège d'Ostende (Brussels: Musin, 1980); translated by Willinger as *The Siege of Ostende*, in *The Siege of Ostend, The Actor Makes His Exit, Transfiguration in the Circus* (Austin: Host, 1990), pp. 42–171.

PRODUCED SCRIPTS: *Sire Halewyn*, radio, I.N.R., 29 October 1930;

Le Cavalier bizarre, radio, 1932;

Le Cœur Révélateur, radio, 1932;

Annibal, speaker futur, radio, 1933;

Bureau ouvert de neuf à midi, radio, 1933;

Plaisir d'amour, radio, 1933;

La ronde des prisonniers, radio, 1933;

Cinq mai 1835, radio, 1934;

Payül dans le beffroi, radio, 1934;

Payül champion, radio, 1934;

Payül lauréat, radio, 1934;

Payül au paradis, radio, 1934;

Payül reporter, radio, 1934;

L'Oiseau chocolat, radio, 1937;

Comment l'empereur Charles devint voleur des chiens, radio, 1939;

D'un fou qui se coryait empereur, radio, 1939;

Scènes de la vie d'un bohème: Franz Schubert, radio, 1941;

Il Fiammingo, radio, 1942.

OTHER: "Sous le lustre aux ciquante flames," in Jean Francis, *Michel de Ghelderode, dramaturge des pays de par deça* (N.p.: Labor, 1949);

Magdeleine E. Cluzel, *Glimpses of the Theatre and Drama*, introduction by Ghelderode, translated by Lily Hastings and Baird Hastings (New York: Kamin, 1953);

"Jozef Czapski mon frère humain," in *Galerie M. Bénézit . . . Czapski, peintures, du 24 février au 11 mars 1961* (Paris: Galerie M. Bénézit, 1961);

Franz Hellens, *Le Dernier jour du monde: Nouvelles fantastiques,* preface by Ghelderode (Paris: Belfond, 1967);

Le Sommeil de la raison, Marginales: Revue bimestrielle des idées et des lettres, 22, nos. 112–113 (May 1967): 118–144;

Daniel Van Damme, *Le Glouton des lettres,* preface by Ghelderode (Brussels: Musin, 1972);

"Rue de l'Arbre Bénit," in Francis, *La Chanson des rues d'Ixelles* (Brussels: Musin, 1975);

Death Looks in the Window (La Mort regarde à la fenêtre), translated by David Willinger, in *Theatrical Gestures from the Belgium Avant-Garde* (New York: Literary Forum, 1987), pp. 97–110.

SELECTED PERIODICAL PUBLICATIONS–
UNCOLLECTED: *Têtes de bois, La Flandre littéraire* (15 November 1924): 33–35; translated by David Willinger as *Blockheads,* in *Theatrical Gestures from the Belgium Avant-Garde* (New York: New York Literary Forum, 1987), pp. 111–114;

La Tentation de St-Antoine, La Renaissance d'Occident (June 1925): 814–819;

Le Massacre des Innocents, La Renaissance d'Occident (November 1926): 232–237;

Duvelor, ou La Farce du diable vieux, Le Rouge et le Noir (27 May 1931);

Le Chagrin d'Hamlet, Le Rouge et le Noir (22 March 1933);

Atlantique, Magie rouge (first trimester 1984): 13–23.

Michel de Ghelderode was among the most influential twentieth-century dramatists working in French, earning an international reputation as an avant-garde playwright. Although he lived his entire life in his native Belgium, Ghelderode achieved his critical and commercial success in postwar Paris. His plays are often set in surreal, dystopic fantasylands, and they are often peopled by grotesques, dwarves, and marionettes; nevertheless, they exhibit psychological realism. Sex, death, religion, and the theater itself were Ghelderode's most cherished themes, and he addressed them while testing the limits of social mores and contemporary dramaturgy. Although he sometimes achieved notoriety through scandal, Ghelderode felt he never received the recognition nor achieved the financial success he deserved. However, unbeknownst to Ghelderode, he was under consideration for the Nobel Prize in literature at the time of his death.

Ghelderode was born Adolphe-Adhémar Martens in Ixelles, Belgium, on 3 April 1898. He was the fourth child of a middle-class couple, Henri-Adolphe Martens, a clerk at the general archives at Brussels, and his wife, Jeanne-Marie. Although the family were Dutch speakers, the Martens chose to educate their children in French, the only official language of Belgium at the time. In fact, Ghelderode published all of his works in French, and he apparently never mastered written Dutch. Martens attended school at the Institut St-Louis in Belgium until 1914, when he was forced to leave after a bout with typhus. His adolescence was deeply affected by his illness and the death of his brother in World War I. Martens attempted suicide at least once and was never entirely stable. He became something of a hypochondriac, always suffering from one ailment or another. Some biographers believe Martens's symptoms may have been feigned, while more sympathetic biographers argue that his symptoms were real but perhaps psychosomatic.

After a brief period studying viola at the Conservatoire Royal de Bruxelles (Royal Conservatory of Music in Brussels), Martens turned his attention toward literature with his first play, *La Mort regarde à la fenêtre* (published in English translation 1987, *Death Looks in the Window*), which was performed only once in April 1918 at the Théâtre de la Bonbonnière. Inspired by the works of Edgar Allan Poe, this drama tells of a ghostly feast in eighteenth-century Rome. Martens's next performed play was the antiwar satire *Le Repas des fauves* (The Feast of the Wild Beasts). It was never published, and there is no manuscript record of it: all that is known is that it was performed briefly in 1919, and it was well received by the audience. Ghelderode later disparaged his early work as facile and flat, and, though his mature works are often satirical, they are never as directly polemical as *Le Repas des fauves* seems to have been.

Martens's budding theatrical career was briefly interrupted by his military service from 1919 to 1921. After returning to civilian life, he was hired by the city of Schaarbeek as a clerk, a job that allowed him to spend a large portion of his day writing. His first works during this period were fiction rather than plays. Although he was writing in French, Martens chose to publish all his prose works under the name Ghelderode, which he legally adopted in 1930 to show his deep connection to his Flemish roots. The name is from his father's maternal line, and it is also a place in Holland. Ghelderode published *La Halte catholique* (The

Catholic Retreat) in 1922 and *L'Homme sous l'uniforme* (The Man Beneath the Uniform) and *L'Histoire comique de Keizer Karel* (The Comic History of Keizer Karel) in 1923. These early works of fiction testify to Ghelderode's pessimism in the years immediately following his military service in World War I and demonstrate his nostalgia for medieval Flanders, themes that he often broached in his theatrical works.

In 1924 Ghelderode married Jeanne Gérard, whom he had met two years earlier while he was working as a salesman in a bookstore, and he began to publish more frequently. Two kinds of early works established him as a literary trickster of sorts: the poetry of Philostène Constable and a series of works published as restored medieval plays for marionettes. More than a mere pseudonym, the mortician-turned-poet Philostène Constable was an alter ego for Ghelderode, who insisted that Constable was a real person: on one occasion going so far as to hire an actor to play the poet in order to keep the hoax alive. Ghelderode began work in 1924 on the poetry collection *Ixelles, mes amours* (Ixelles, my loves) published under the name Philostène Constable in 1928. In 1925 Ghelderode published the medieval puppet play *Le Mystère de la Passion de Notre-Seigneur Jésus-Christ* (The Mystery of the Passion of Our Lord Jesus Christ), claiming it was reconstituted from puppet plays performed in certain working-class neighborhoods of Brussels. Over the next two years he published similar works in periodicals: *La Tentation de St-Antoine* (1925, The Temptation of Saint Anthony), *Le Massacre des Innocents* (1926, The Massacre of the Innocents), and *La Farce de la mort qui faillit trépasser* (The Farce of Death, Who Nearly Passed Away, performed 1925, published 1952). Only the last of these works was ever included in a collection of Ghelderode's theater. Nevertheless, these early puppet plays were important in the development of Ghelderode's aesthetic, which often drew from popular theatrical forms, including the mystery play, farce, music hall, and the circus, and which aimed to free the theater from the strictures of the psychological and naturalist conventions that dominated the stage in the late nineteenth and early twentieth centuries.

Ghelderode also published two theatrical works in 1925: *Oude Piet* (performed 1925, Bottle Foot; known also by its French title *Piet Bouteille*), for which he won the dramatic literature prize awarded by *La Renaissance d'Occident* (The Occidental Renaissance), and *Les Vieillards* (translated as *The Old Men*, 1964), which he described in the subtitle as a *farce mystique* (mystical farce). In both of these works Ghelderode explores old age, death, and the way religious authorities engender and profit from superstition, themes to which he returned frequently.

Scene from the initial 1929 run of Christophe Colomb, *in which Ghelderode depicts Christopher Columbus as a dreamer and fantasist rather than as an explorer (from Jean Decock,* Le Théâtre de Michel de Ghelderode, *1969; Thomas Cooper Library, University of South Carolina)*

Although he was not particularly religious, Ghelderode's work testifies to his lasting fascination with religion, particularly religion as practiced by the common Flemish folk, who often became characters in his plays. Several of Ghelderode's minor dramas from the 1920s and early 1930s demonstrate the intersection of his interests in religion and popular theater: *Duvelor, ou La Farce du diable vieux* (1931, Duvelor, or the Farce of the Aging Devil); *Le Siège d'Ostende* (published 1980, produced 1984; translated as *The Siege of Ostend*, 1990), which is described in the text as an "épopée militaire pour marionettes" (military epic for puppets); *Les Aveugles* (1942; translated as *The Blind Men*, 1960), a morality play "d'après Bruegel, dit l'ancien" (after Bruegel the Elder) written in 1933; *Les Femmes au tombeau* (published 1934, performed 1953; translated as *The Women at the Tomb*, 1964), a "tragédie pour marionettes" (tragedy for marionettes) recounting the days following the Crucifixion; and *D'un Diable qui prêcha merveilles* (Of a Devil Who Preached Wonders, published 1942, performed 1964), a "mystère pour marionettes" (mystery for marionettes) set in "Brugelmonde" and written in 1934.

Other early plays show Ghelderode's developing fascination with old age, death, and theater. For example, *Le Cavalier bizarre* (radio play 1932, produced 1953; translated as *The Strange Rider*, 1964) is a minor play

Poster for Ghelderode's 1930 play, among his last to be performed in collaboration with the Vlaamsche Volkstooneel (The Flemish Popular Theater) (from Jean Decock, Le Théâtre de Michel de Ghelderode, *1969; Thomas Cooper Library, University of South Carolina)*

written in 1920 but not published until 1938 that represents a retirement home as Death (the "strange rider" of the title) approaches. Another early play that deals with old age is *Don Juan* (published 1928, produced 1962). Additionally, two plays from 1927–1928 demonstrate Ghelderode's developing interest in theater as subject as well as genre: *Vénus* (1927; translated, 1987), the story of an actress who has her arms removed in order to resemble the Venus de Milo, and *La Transfiguration dans le cirque* (published 1928, produced 1959; translated as *Transfiguration in the Circus,* 1990), which stages a clown uprising. Although most of these minor works were not performed during Ghelderode's lifetime, they reveal the development of his theatrical aesthetic.

During this early period Ghelderode's collaboration with the Vlaamsche Volkstooneel (The Flemish Popular Theater), known as the VVT, further shaped his drama. The VVT was an avant-garde, Catholic theater troupe performing plays in Dutch throughout Belgium in the 1920s and early 1930s. They produced Ghelderode's *Farce de la mort qui faillit trépasser* to critical and popular acclaim in 1925. Through this production Ghelderode came to the attention of many more avant-garde playgoers, and his theatrical career arguably began in earnest at this point. In a speech delivered in 1956, Ghelderode referred to his association with the VVT as "la généreuse aventure" (the generous adventure). During his partnership with the VVT, which lasted into the early 1930s, he developed as a playwright, creating colorful plays full of movement and music. Still, Ghelderode was somewhat removed from the productions of his plays at the VVT because they were performed in Dutch and not French. This arrangement was necessary, however, because avant-garde theater in French had not gained a foothold in Belgium during the time Ghelderode began writing plays. Hence, the language Ghelderode's parents had chosen for his education became an obstacle rather than a vehicle for him, and the young author had to submit to seeing his plays performed in translations in which he had no hand.

In 1927 the VVT had a major success with Ghelderode's *Images de la vie de Saint François d'Assise* (Images from the Life of Saint Francis of Assisi), which stages the life of St. Francis and hints at the revolutionary possibilities of his mystically inspired doctrine of poverty. In 1929 the VVT produced *Barabbas* (published 1932; translated, 1960), which tells the story of the Passion from the point of view of the criminal released in Jesus' place by Pilate. *Pantagleize* (published 1934; translated 1960), produced in 1930, and *Le Voleur d'étoiles* (The Star Thief), a *comédie féerique* (a fairy comedy) from 1932, were the last of Ghelderode's plays produced by the VVT. Both of these works demonstrate the influence of German expressionism and Surrealism on Ghelderode, and both satirize contemporary politics and courts of law in the context of absurd situations in fantastical settings.

Ghelderode's relationship with the VVT was formative, but it was not exclusive. *Le Miracle dans le faubourg* (Miracle in the suburbs) was performed in 1928 as part of the Concours de littérature dramatique de la Province de Brabant (Dramatic Literature Competition for the Province of Brabant). Additionally, *Trois acteurs, un drame* (1929; translated as *Three Actors and Their Drama,* 1960) was staged at the Théâtre Royal du Parc in 1931. *Le Miracle dans le faubourg* is the story of a child's resurrection brought about by the intercession of a slow-witted but compassionate family friend. *Trois acteurs, un drame* is a Pirandellian fantasy about the relationship between an actor and his role. A playwright disparages three actors whose performances he finds inadequate; the resentful actors then plan to commit suicide on stage, and their staged deaths are followed by the suicide of the author.

Another play, *Sortie de l'acteur* (published 1953; produced 1960; translated as *The Actor Makes His Exit*, 1990), is very much the product of Ghelderode's experience with the VVT, although it was never performed by that troupe. The play was written between 1933 and 1935 as an homage to Ghelderode's recently deceased friend, actor Renaat Verheyen, who had played the lead role in the VVT productions of *Images de la vie de St-François d'Assise, Barabbas,* and *Pantagleize.* Similar to *Trois acteurs, un drame,* the play explores the actor's relationship to his role and to the playwright. Renatus, the lead actor in a play by Jean-Jacques, learns that his character is to die onstage and takes it as an omen of his own death. When Renatus really does fall ill, Jean-Jacques pays no attention to his friend but rather tries to seduce Renatus's lover. Renatus finally dies reciting lines from Jean-Jacques' plays, and the playwright is left to his remorse. In a final scene Jean-Jacques asks forgiveness of the actor's ghost. Of all of Ghelderode's plays, this one most supports an autobiographical reading, as material mined from the author's own relationship with his lead actor becomes the source for the complicated relationship between Jean-Jacques and Renatus.

Around the same time that Ghelderode was beginning to achieve fame in Belgium, the prominent Parisian theater critic Camille Poupeye presented Ghelderode to a French audience when he wrote the preface to *La Mort du Docteur Faust* (translated as *The Death of Doctor Faust,* 1964), which appeared in 1926. Two years later the play was produced at the small but influential Art et Action theater in Paris, marking Ghelderode's debut on the French stage. Set in both the sixteenth and twentieth centuries, Ghelderode's retelling of the Faust legend opposes the "real" Faust from the past with an actor playing the role of Faust in the present. Confronted by his double, the "real" Faust founders, and as he struggles to kill the actor playing him, he accidentally kills himself. Once again Ghelderode uses a theatrical setting both to experiment with theatrical form and to explore the psychological negotiation between real and make-believe that must take place in the minds of both actor and audience.

In 1929 Louise Lara, director of Art et Action, produced *Christophe Colomb* (published 1928; translated as *Christopher Columbus,* 1964). This play, in which the hero famously blows soap bubbles in the opening scene, is characterized in the subtitle as a *Féerie dramatique* (a dramatic fairy tale). A dreamer rather than an explorer, Columbus decides to embark on his voyage not out of ambition but because "Il faut partir car quel sort me réserve la société si je continue de faire des bulles, des bulles que je ne peux pas expliquer?" (I have to go, because what does society have in store for me if I continue to make bubbles, bubbles that I cannot explain?). His voyages consist of a series of fantastical anachronisms, and in the end he is frozen, a statue in a sideshow attraction, criticized for, among other things, not having been an American citizen.

The year that *Christophe Colomb* was produced in Paris, a Dutch version of *Escurial* (published 1928; translated, 1957) debuted in Brussels. This dark one-act play is often paired with *Christophe Colomb* in performance and in published collections. This combination has occurred because the two plays, perhaps the most performed and most frequently collected of Ghelderode's oeuvre, mark his transition from the hue and cry of his puppet-inspired plays to a more abstract, language-oriented dramaturgy. *Escurial* stages a struggle of wills between a king and his fool, Folial, a character that appears again in Ghelderode's *L'Ecole des bouffons* (published 1942, produced 1953; translated as *School for Buffoons,* 1968). As they watch over the dying queen, it becomes clear that the king has poisoned her because she has been unfaithful, and then it becomes clear that the queen has been unfaithful with Folial. Out of boredom the king suggests a carnival game, familiar in the theater, in which he and his fool trade places. When Folial refuses to relinquish his borrowed power as "king," the king has him killed. Here Ghelderode again explores the relationship between fantasy and reality and hints at what many critics later called the "dramaturgy of cruelty" apparent in his later plays.

Despite the appeal of some of Ghelderode's plays among the avant-garde in interwar Paris, he did not attain celebrity status in France until after World War II. Ghelderode scholar and bibliographer Roland Beyen summarizes the author's career in theatrical performance by dividing it into a Flemish period (1925–1932), a French period (1947–1953), and an international period (after 1951). However, most of Ghelderode's plays were written before the war, although many remained unproduced until later; furthermore, the majority of those plays that had been performed were staged only in Dutch translation.

Two more important plays of Ghelderode's transitional period debuted in Brussels in the mid 1930s, but this time they were performed in French: *Magie rouge* (published 1935; translated as *Red Magic,* 1964) at the experimental "Plateau 33" in 1934, and *Le Ménage de Caroline* (produced and published 1935, Caroline's Household) as part of the Universal Exposition in 1935. Written in 1931, *Magie rouge* is considered typical

Scene from a 2000 performance in Warsaw of Duvelor, ou La Farce du diable vieux *(Duvelor, or the Farce of the Aging Devil), one of Ghelderode's many puppet plays (photograph by Pawel Stankiewicz, Warsaw Theatre Academy; from <puppet.man.bialystok.pl>)*

of this period of Ghelderode's work. It combines the folkloric figures of the miser and the alchemist with a modern tale of greed, jealousy, and vengeance. Hyéronimus, the miser, hatches a plan to force Armador, the alchemist, to reveal his secrets. Little does Hyéronimus know that he is himself the object of a scheme, set up by his wife and Armador, who is her lover. Hyéronimus is robbed of his treasure, he loses his wife, and he is finally led to the scaffold for a crime committed by Armador. In this play Ghelderode enhances the verbal richness and sharpens the cruel wit of *Escurial* and *Christophe Colomb*.

Like many of Ghelderode's plays written in the 1920s and early 1930s, *Le Ménage de Caroline* draws on the popular theater for inspiration. This macabre tale of puppets that come to life represents both what made Ghelderode famous in Belgium–his rich and colorful tales inspired by Flemish popular tradition–and what kept him from being immediately accessible to audiences outside of Belgium, namely what David Parsell calls his "irreducible Flemishness."

Throughout the 1930s Ghelderode experimented in radio drama, with some success. His most important play for radio was *Sire Halewyn,* which debuted in 1930 and was later produced as a stage play in Brussels in 1938. Three of Ghelderode's other radio dramas are collected in the last volume of the *Théâtre* (1982): *Le Perroquet de Charles-Quint* (The Parakeet of Charles V), *Le Singulier trépas de Messire Ulenspiegel* (The Strange Death of Mister Ulenspiegel), and *La Folie d'Hugo van der Goes* (The Madness of Hugo van der Goes), all written in 1934 and 1935.

During World War II, Ghelderode continued to write, and although performances of his plays were less frequent, an important premiere took place in 1942 when *Hop Signor!* (published 1938; translated 1964) was staged by the Théâtre Royal du Parc in Brussels. Written in 1936, the play takes its odd title from a Belgian children's game, "Opisnoorke," in which children holding the four corners of a blanket toss a doll up into the air and catch it in an apparent re-creation of a medieval torture and execution technique. The play, which takes place "en Flandres d'antan" (in Flanders of yore) and tells the story of a disillusioned and impotent sculptor who is abused by his cruel, sexually unsatisfied wife, has often been read autobiographically. The usual

Ghelderodian cast of monks, dwarves, and grotesques inhabit the dark play. *Hop Signor!* marks Ghelderode's first serious foray into the theater of cruelty.

Around this time Ghelderode wrote what became his last great play, *L'Ecole des bouffons,* in which he directly articulates the aesthetic of cruelty. In this play, set in sixteenth-century Flanders, the king's fool Folial passes on the secrets of his art to a cohort of ungrateful student clowns: "Le secret de notre art, de l'art, du grand art, de tout art qui veut durer? (un silence, et à voix basse, mais distinctement) C'est la CRU-AU-TE!" (The secret of our art, of art, of great art, of all art which hopes to last? [a silence, and in a low voice but distinctly] It is CRU-EL-TY!). It is not clear to what extent Ghelderode had been influenced by Antonin Artaud's articles on the theater of cruelty that were collected in 1938 as *Le Théâtre et son double* (translated as *The Theater and Its Double,* 1958). It is known, however, that Ghelderode wished to downplay the connection, because he claimed to have written *L'Ecole des bouffons* in 1937 and not in 1942.

During the Occupation, Radio-Bruxelles broadcast a series of Ghelderode's chronicles of sixteenth-century Flanders called *Choses et gens de chez nous* (Things and Folks from Home). These works were collected in a volume in 1943. Although the broadcasts were generally apolitical, the fact that he contributed to Radio-Bruxelles during the Nazi occupation was enough to label Ghelderode a "collaborator" and to precipitate his dismissal from his civil service job without a pension. Despair followed, and over the next few years as he fought, with eventual success, to regain his reputation and pension, Ghelderode contemplated murder-suicide.

Although Ghelderode had for the most part ceased writing plays, in the late 1940s his career in theater found its second wind. In the summer of 1949 two plays by Ghelderode, *Fastes d'enfer* (published 1942, produced 1949; translated as *Chronicles of Hell,* 1960) and *Mademoiselle Jaïre* (published 1942, produced 1949; translated as *Mademoiselle Jairus,* 1964), won first and third prizes, respectively, in the Grand Prix des Jeunes Compagnies (Grand Prize for Young Companies), a theater competition for young troupes in Paris. *Mademoiselle Jaïre* was written in 1934. Set against the backdrop of a carnival, it is the story of a dying girl whose parents appeal to a witch called Antiqua Mankabena, and then to a magical preacher, to heal their daughter. The preacher succeeds in part, but the girl is not entirely alive. Instead, she remains suspended between life and death, unable to recognize anyone. She meets a young man who, like her, is neither fully alive nor dead, and they kiss, but in the noise and excitement of the carnival, the girl dies in the arms of the witch Antiqua.

The other play, *Fastes d'enfer,* was written during 1936 and 1937. It is also set in Flanders, and it too stages a resurrection of sorts: Jan Eremo, the bishop of Flanders, revives to accuse priests who have tried to poison him with a communion wafer. Vénéranda, the bishop's mother, discovers the poisoned wafer, which had been stuck in his throat, and then insists that her son absolve the plotting priests so that he can die in peace. After the bishop dies, Vénéranda is poisoned with the same communion wafer by the evil Simon Laquedeem, the bishop's assistant. The conclusion of the play is punctuated by scatological humor. Playwright Jean Genet, who later wrote some of the most scandalous works of postwar France, attended the premiere and exclaimed, "Il y a tout, là. Tout ce qu'on fera" (It is all there. Everything that we will do).

Following the Ghelderode sensation of the summer of 1949 and the publication of the first of the six-volume *Théâtre* by Gallimard in 1950, theater critic Guy Dornand announced that the Paris theater scene was suffering from "ghelderodite aiguë" (acute ghelderotitis.) Recovery was slow. Over the course of the 1950s many previously unperformed plays by Ghelderode found their way onto the stage in Paris.

In 1952 Jean-Louis Barrault, by this time a major figure in Paris, was set to produce *La Farce des ténébreux* (published 1942, The Farce of The Shadowy Ones) at the Théâtre Marigny. Sets were already built and posters already printed when Barrault abandoned the play, fearing the scandal it might cause. Georges Vitaly's company finally took the honor and notoriety of producing *La Farce des ténébreux* in late 1952, on the sets that Félix Labisse had designed for Barrault. The play, part of which is set in a brothel frequented by the bishop (among others), is deliberately shocking. Fernand d'Abcaude is suicidal after the death of his fiancée, Azurine. Well-meaning friends try to cure his depression by hiring the actress Emmanuèle to appear as Azurine's putrid cadaver. When this ploy fails to move Abcaude, they take him to a brothel belonging to the cult of the "Ténébreux" (The Shadowy Ones). There they witness a sacrilegious ceremony in honor of Putrégina, queen of prostitutes, after which Abcaude unveils the statue of Putrégina to reveal the figure of Azurine. Horrified, Abcaude couples with Emmanuèle in the play's final scene.

Other Paris premieres in 1953 included *Les Femmes au tombeau,* performed by the Compagnie Théâtrale de la Cité; *L'Ecole des bouffons,* performed at the Théâtre de l'Œuvre; and *Le Cavalier bizarre,* performed by the Compagnie Roger Jourdan. That year *La Balade du Grand Macabre* (published 1935, Death Takes a Stroll), written in 1934, premiered in Lyon at the Théâtre de la Comédie. It is another of Ghelderode's plays set in Breugelmonde. Labeled a *farce pour rhétoriciens* (farce for rhetoricians) by the author, the play stages the strange announcement of the end of time by Porprenaz and Nekrozotar and the madcap preparations for doomsday undertaken by the stuttering prince Goulave and his corrupt ministers.

Meanwhile, Ghelderode's plays continued to be performed in Belgium. His last play, *Marie la misérable* (published 1955, Mary the Poor), was commissioned to be performed at the church of Woluwe-Saint-Lambert in Brabant on the feast day of the local saint. Written and performed in 1952, the play is considered by most critics to be inferior to Ghelderode's earlier work.

At the time Ghelderode began to be internationally acclaimed, he had long completed the writings that earned him that recognition. Throughout the 1950s many of Ghelderode's previously performed plays, such as the popular *Escurial* and *Christophe Colomb*, were revived from Buenos Aires to Helsinki. Among the important premieres abroad during this period were *La Transfiguration dans le cirque* in Rotterdam in 1959 and *Sortie de l'acteur* in Kraków in 1960.

In 1951 Ghelderode gave a series of interviews to Roger Iglésis and Alain Trutat that were published under the title *Les Entretiens d'Ostende* (Interviews from Ostende) in 1956. These interviews, which were broadcast on Belgian and French radio in 1951 and 1952, feature important descriptions of Ghelderode's career and his writing process. Yet, they must not be taken at face value, as Beyen has demonstrated that—as with all of Ghelderode's accounts of his life and writing—the author erred, exaggerated, and even injected fabrications throughout the interviews. Most notably, Ghelderode's claims about when plays were written (preserved also in the otherwise definitive *Théâtre* published by Gallimard) have been shown to be highly inaccurate. Hence, the interviews reveal Ghelderode as a complicated figure. Just as in his plays he re-created a mythical past for his beloved Flanders, he sometimes tried to remake his own past as he wished it had been.

When Michel de Ghelderode died on 1 April 1962, he was probably the most influential playwright in French and among the most influential worldwide. Unlike many of his contemporaries in the theater, Ghelderode, who penned more than fifty plays, focused almost exclusively on writing drama: his oeuvre includes only a handful of published works that are not plays. In the *Entretiens d'Ostende,* Ghelderode said, "je suis allé vers le théâtre par nécessité . . . Cette forme je ne l'ai pas prise, elle m'a pris—voilà la vérité! On ne choisit pas. Ou si peu" (I went toward the theater by necessity . . . This genre that I didn't take, took me—there's the truth! We don't choose. Or so little). Compelled by this deep-seated sense of necessity,

Scene from a 1949 performance of Mademoiselle Jaïre, *the story of parents who turn to a witch and then a magical preacher in attempts to save their dying daughter (from Jean Decock,* Le Théâtre de Michel de Ghelderode, *1969; Thomas Cooper Library, University of South Carolina)*

Ghelderode wrote plays that shocked audiences, challenged convention, and employed popular theatrical traditions that had been neglected by artists of the elite. Ghelderode redefined the possibilities of the theater and prepared the way for postwar playwrights such as Genet and Samuel Beckett. Jean Cocteau, an author to whom Ghelderode is often compared, lavished praise upon his contemporary, saying, "Ghelderode, c'est le diamant qui ferme le collier de poètes que la Belgique porte au cou. Ce diamant noir jette des feux cruels et nobles. Ils ne blessent que les petites âmes. Ils éblouissent les autres" (Ghelderode is the diamond clasp of the necklace of poets that Belgium wears around her neck. This black diamond shines with cruel and noble flames. They wound only petty souls. They dazzle the others).

Letters:

Correspondance de Michel de Ghelderode, 5 volumes, edited by Roland Beyen (Brussels: Labor, 1991–1998).

Interview:

Roger Iglésis and Alain Trutat, *Les Entretiens d'Ostende* (Paris: L'Arche, 1956).

Bibliography:

Roland Beyen, *Bibliographie de Michel de Ghelderode* (Brussels: Académie Royale de Langue et de Littérature Française, 1987).

Biographies:

Roland Beyen, *Michel de Ghelderode, ou La Hantise du masque: Essai de biographie critique* (Brussels: Palais des Académies, 1971);

David B. Parsell, *Michel de Ghelderode* (New York: Twayne, 1993);

Michel de Ghelderode, "Le Diamant noir," Fondation internationale Michel de Ghelderode <www.ghelderode.be>.

References:

Roland Beyen, *Ghelderode: présentation, choix de textes, chronologie, bibliographie* (Paris: Seghers, 1974);

Beyen, Michel Otten, and others, *Michel de Ghelderode et le Théâtre contemporain, Actes du Congrès international de Gênes 22–25 novembre 1978* (Brussels: Société Internationale des études sur Michel de Ghelderode, 1980), pp. 11–22;

Beyen, ed., *Michel de Ghelderode, ou La Comédie des apparences* (Paris & Brussels: Laconti, 1980);

Jacqueline Blancart-Cassou, *Le Rire de Michel de Ghelderode* (Paris: Klincksieck, 1987);

Elisabeth Deberdt-Malaquais, *La Quête de l'identité dans le théâtre de Ghelderode* (Paris: Editions Universitaires, 1967);

Jean Decock, *Le Théâtre de Michel de Ghelderode: Une dramaturgie de l'anti-théâtre et de la cruauté* (Paris: Nizet, 1969);

David I. Grossvogel, *20th-Century French Drama* (New York: Columbia University Press, 1961);

Jacques Guicharnaud and June Guicharnaud, *Modern French Theater from Giraudoux to Genet* (New Haven: Yale University Press, 1967);

Leonard Cabell Pronko, *Avant-Garde: The Experimental Theater in France* (Berkeley: University of California Press, 1962);

Raymond Trousson, ed., *Michel de Ghelderode, dramaturge et conteur: Actes du Colloque de Bruxelles (22–23 octobre 1982)* (Brussels: Editions de l'Université de Bruxelles, 1983);

George E. Wellworth, *The Theater of Protest and Paradox: Developments in the Avant-Garde Drama* (New York: New York University Press, 1964).

Papers:

A collection of Ghelderode's papers is held at the Fondation internationale Michel de Ghelderode in Brussels.

André Gide

(22 November 1869 – 19 February 1951)

Catharine Savage Brosman
Tulane University

See also the Gide entry in *DLB 65: French Novelists, 1900–1930.*

PLAY PRODUCTIONS: *Le Roi Candaule,* Paris, Nouveau Théâtre, 9 May 1901;

Philoctète, Paris, private performance, 3 April 1919; reading, Paris, Comédie des Champs-Elysées, 16 October 1937;

Saül, Paris, Théâtre du Vieux-Colombier, 16 June 1922;

Le Retour de l'enfant prodigue, Monte Carlo, Théâtre de Monte-Carlo, 4 December 1928; Paris, Théâtre de l'Avenue, 23 February 1933;

Œdipe, Antwerp, Cercle Artistique, 10 December 1931; Paris, Théâtre de l'Avenue, 18 February 1932;

Les Caves du Vatican, adapted by Gide from his novel, Montreux, Société des Belles-Lettres, 9 December 1933; revised, Paris, Comédie-Française, 13 December 1950;

Perséphone, libretto by Gide, Paris, Opéra, 30 April 1934;

Le Treizième Arbre, Marseille, Rideau Gris, 8 May 1935; Paris, Théâtre Charles de Rochefort, 13 January 1939;

Robert ou L'Intérêt général, Tunis, Théâtre Municipal, 30 April 1946.

SELECTED BOOKS: *Les Cahiers d'André Walter,* anonymous (Paris: Didier-Perrin, 1891); translated by Wade Baskin as *The Notebooks of André Walter* (New York: Philosophical Library, 1968; London: Owen, 1968);

Le Traité du Narcisse (Paris: Librairie de l'Art Indépendant, 1891); translated by Dorothy Bussy as *Narcissus,* in *The Return of the Prodigal . . .* (London: Secker & Warburg, 1953);

Les Poésies d'André Walter, anonymous (Paris: Librairie de l'Art Indépendant, 1892);

La Tentative amoureuse (Paris: Librairie de l'Art Indépendant, 1893); translated by Bussy as *The Lovers'*

André Gide (© Hulton/Getty Images)

Attempt, in *The Return of the Prodigal . . .* (London: Secker & Warburg, 1953);

Le Voyage d'Urien (Paris: Librairie de l'Art Indépendant, 1893); translated by Baskin as *Urien's Voyage* (New York: Philosophical Library, 1964; London: Owen, 1964);

Paludes (Paris: Librairie de l'Art Indépendant, 1895); translated by George D. Painter as *Marshlands,* in *Marshlands and Prometheus Misbound: Two Satires* (New York: New Directions, 1953; London: Secker & Warburg, 1953);

Les Nourritures terrestres (Paris: Mercure de France, 1897); translated by Bussy as *The Fruits of the*

Earth, in *The Fruits of the Earth* (New York: Knopf, 1949; London: Secker & Warburg, 1949);

Le Prométhée mal enchaîné (Paris: Mercure de France, 1899); translated by Lilian Rothermere as *Prometheus Illbound* (London: Chatto & Windus, 1919);

Philoctète (Paris: Mercure de France, 1899)—comprises *Philoctète, Le Traité du Narcisse, La Tentative amoureuse,* and *El Hadj*; *Philoctète* translated by Jackson Mathews as *Philoctetes,* in *My Theater* (New York: Knopf, 1952); *El Hadj* translated by Bussy, in *The Return of the Prodigal . . .* (London: Secker & Warburg, 1953);

Feuilles de route, 1895–1896 (Brussels: Vandersypen, 1899);

Lettres à Angèle, 1898–1899 (Paris: Mercure de France, 1900);

Le Roi Candaule (Paris: Revue Blanche, 1901); translated by Mathews as *King Candaules,* in *My Theater* (New York: Knopf, 1952), pp. 161–235;

L'Immoraliste (Paris: Mercure de France, 1902); translated by Bussy as *The Immoralist* (New York: Knopf, 1930; London: Cassell, 1930);

Saül (Paris: Mercure de France, 1903; enlarged, adding a preface by the author and his "De l'évolution du théâtre," 1904); enlarged edition translated by Mathews as *Saul* and *The Evolution of the Theater,* in *My Theater* (New York: Knopf, 1952), pp. 1–107, 259–275;

Prétextes: Réflexions sur quelques points de littérature et de morale (Paris: Mercure de France, 1903; enlarged, 1913); translated by Angelo P. Bertocci and others as *Pretexts: Reflections on Literature and Morality,* edited by Justin O'Brien (London: Secker & Warburg, 1959; New York: Meridian, 1959);

Amyntas (Paris: Mercure de France, 1906); translated by Villiers David (London: Bodley Head, 1958);

Le Retour de l'enfant prodigue (Paris: Vers et Prose, 1907); translated by Bussy as *The Return of the Prodigal,* in *The Return of the Prodigal . . .* (London: Secker & Warburg, 1953);

La Porte étroite (Paris: Mercure de France, 1909); translated by Bussy as *Strait Is the Gate* (New York: Knopf, 1924; London: Jarrolds, 1924);

Oscar Wilde: In Memoriam (souvenirs); Le "De Profundis" (Paris: Mercure de France, 1910); translated by Bernard Frechtman as *Oscar Wilde: In Memoriam (Reminiscences); "De Profundis"* (New York: Philosophical Library, 1949);

Nouveaux Prétextes: Réflexions sur quelques points de Littérature et de Morale (Paris: Mercure de France, 1911);

C.R.D.N., anonymous (Bruges: Sainte-Catherine, 1911); enlarged as *Corydon* (1920); trade edition, as Gide (Paris: Gallimard, 1924; enlarged, 1929); translated (New York: Farrar, Straus, 1950; London: Secker & Warburg, 1952); republished (Paris: Gallimard, 1977);

Isabelle (Paris: Nouvelle Revue Française/Marcel Rivière, 1911); translated by Bussy, in *Two Symphonies* (New York: Knopf, 1931; London: Cassell, 1931), pp. 1–137;

Bethsabé (Paris: Bibliothèque de l'Occident, 1912); translated by Mathews as *Bathsheba,* in *My Theater* (New York: Knopf, 1952), pp. 109–127;

Souvenirs de la cour d'assises (Paris: Nouvelle Revue Française, 1914);

Les Caves du Vatican, 2 volumes (Paris: Nouvelle Revue Française, 1914); translated by Bussy as *The Vatican Swindle* (New York: Knopf, 1925); translation republished as *Lafcadio's Adventures* (New York: Knopf, 1927); republished again as *The Vatican Cellars* (London: Cassell, 1952);

La Symphonie pastorale (Paris: Gallimard, 1919); translated by Bussy as *The Pastoral Symphony,* in *Two Symphonies* (New York: Knopf, 1931; London: Cassell, 1931), pp. 139–233;

Si le grain ne meurt, 2 volumes (Bruges: Sainte-Catherine, 1920, 1921); translated by Bussy as *If It Die . . .* (New York: Random House, 1935; London: Secker & Warburg, 1950);

Morceaux choisis (Paris: Gallimard, 1921);

Pages choisise (Paris: Crès, 1921);

Numquid et tu . . . ? anonymous (Bruges: Sainte-Catherine, 1922); trade edition, as Gide (Paris: Pléiade/Schiffrin, 1926); translated by O'Brien as *Numquid et tu . . . ?* in *The Journals of André Gide,* volume 2: *1914–1927* (New York: Knopf, 1948; London: Secker & Warburg, 1948), pp. 169–190;

Dostoïevsky (Paris: Plon-Nourrit, 1923); translated by Arnold Bennett as *Dostoyevsky* (London & Toronto: Dent, 1925; New York: Knopf, 1926);

Incidences (Paris: Gallimard, 1924);

Caractères (Paris: A l'Enseigne de la Porte étroite, 1925);

Les Faux-Monnayeurs (Paris: Gallimard, 1925); translated by Bussy as *The Counterfeiters* (New York: Knopf, 1927; London & New York: Knopf, 1928); translation republished as *The Coiners* (London: Cassell, 1950);

Le Journal des Faux-Monnayeurs (Paris: Eos, 1926); translated by O'Brien as *Logbook of the Coiners* (London: Cassell, 1952);

Voyage au Congo (Paris: Gallimard, 1927); translated by Bussy as *Travels in the Congo,* in *Travels in the Congo* (New York: Knopf, 1929), pp. 1–199;

Le Retour du Tchad: Carnets de route (Paris: Gallimard, 1928); translated by Bussy as *Return from Lake Chad,* in *Travels in the Congo* (New York: Knopf, 1929), pp. 201–375;

L'Ecole des femmes (Paris: Gallimard, 1929); translated by Bussy as *The School for Wives* (New York: Knopf, 1929);

Essai sur Montaigne (Paris: Schiffrin/Pléiade, 1929); translated by Stephen H. Guest and Trevor E. Blewitt as *Montaigne: An Essay in Two Parts* (London: Blackamore / New York: Liveright, 1929);

Un Esprit non prévenu (Paris: Kra, 1929);

Robert (Paris: Gallimard, 1930); translated by Bussy, in *The School for Wives; Robert; Geneviève, or The Unfinished Confidence* (New York: Knopf, 1950; London: Cassell, 1953);

Œdipe (Paris: Gallimard, 1931); translated by Russell as *Oedipus*, in *Two Legends: Theseus and Oedipus* (New York: Knopf, 1950), pp. 1–43; translation republished as *Oedipus and Theseus* (London: Secker & Warburg, 1950);

Œuvres complètes d'André Gide, 15 volumes, edited by Louis Martin-Chauffier (Paris: Gallimard, 1932–1939);

Pages de journal (1929–1932) (Paris: Gallimard, 1934);

Les Nouvelles Nourritures (Paris: Gallimard, 1935); translated by Bussy as *Later Fruits of the Earth*, in *The Fruits of the Earth* (New York: Knopf, 1949; London: Secker & Warburg, 1949);

Nouvelles pages de journal (1932–1935) (Paris: Gallimard, 1935);

Geneviève (Paris: Gallimard, 1936); translated by Bussy as *Geneviève, or The Unfinished Confidence*, in *The School for Wives; Robert; Geneviève, or The Unfinished Confidence* (New York: Knopf, 1950; London: Cassell, 1953);

Retour de l'U.R.S.S. (Paris: Gallimard, 1936); translated by Bussy as *Return from the U.S.S.R.* (New York: Knopf, 1937; London: Secker & Warburg, 1937); translation republished as *Back from the U.S.S.R.* (London: Secker & Warburg, 1937);

Retouches à mon Retour de l'U.R.S.S. (Paris: Gallimard, 1937); translated by Bussy as *Afterthoughts: A Sequel to "Back from the U.S.S.R."* (London: Secker & Warburg, 1938); translation republished as *Afterthoughts on the U.S.S.R.* (New York: Dial, 1938);

Journal 1889–1939 (Paris: Gallimard, 1939); translated by O'Brien, in *The Journals of André Gide*, volume 1: *1889–1913*; volume 2: *1914–1927*; and volume 3: *1928–1939* (New York: Knopf, 1947–1949; London: Secker & Warburg, 1947–1949);

Découvrons Henri Michaux (Paris: Gallimard, 1941);

Théâtre (Paris: Gallimard, 1942)—comprises *Saül; Le Roi Candaule; Œdipe; Perséphone;* and *Le Treizième Arbre; Perséphone* translated by Mathews as *Persephone*, in *My Theater* (New York: Knopf, 1952);

Interviews imaginaires (Paris: Gallimard, 1942); enlarged as *Interviews imaginaires; La Délivrance de Tunis, pages de journal, mai 1943* (New York: Schiffrin, 1943); translated by Malcolm Cowley as *Imaginary Interviews* (New York: Knopf, 1944);

Pages de journal (1939–1942) (New York: Schiffrin, 1944; Algiers: Charlot, 1944; enlarged edition, Paris: Gallimard, 1946); translated by O'Brien, in *The Journals of André Gide,* volume 4: *1939–1949* (New York: Knopf, 1951; London: Secker & Warburg, 1951);

Poussin (Paris: Au Divan, 1945);

Thésée (New York: Schiffrin, 1946; Paris: Gallimard, 1946); translated by John Russell as *Theseus* (London: Horizon, 1948; New York: New Directions, 1949);

Le Retour (Neuchâtel & Paris: Ides et Calendes, 1946);

Et nunc manet in te (Neuchâtel: Richard Heyd, 1947); translated by Keene Wallis as *The Secret Drama of My Life* (Paris & New York: Boar's Head Books, 1951); original French enlarged as *Et Nunc manet in te, suivi de Journal intime* (Neuchâtel: Ides et Calendes, 1951); translated by O'Brien as *Madeleine* (New York: Knopf, 1952) and as *Et nunc Manet in te and Intimate Journal* (London: Secker & Warburg, 1952);

Paul Valéry (Paris: Domar, 1947);

Poétique (Neuchâtel & Paris: Ides et Calendes, 1947);

Le Procès; Pièce tirée du roman de Kafka, by Gide and Jean-Louis Barrault (Paris: Gallimard, 1947); translated by Jacqueline and Frank Sundstrom as *The Trial, from the Novel of Franz Kafka* (London: Secker & Warburg, 1950);

Préfaces (Neuchâtel & Paris: Ides et Calendes, 1948);

Rencontres (Neuchâtel & Paris: Ides et Calendes, 1948);

Les Caves du Vatican: Farce en trois actes (Neuchâtel & Paris: Ides et Calendes, 1948);

Eloges (Neuchâtel & Paris: Ides et Calendes, 1948);

Notes sur Chopin (Paris: L'Arche, 1948); translated by Frechtman as *Notes on Chopin* (New York: Philosophical Library, 1949);

Feuillets d'automne (Paris: Mercure de France, 1949); translated by Elsie Pell as *Autumn Leaves* (New York: Philosophical Library, 1950);

Littérature engagée, edited by Yvonne Davet (Paris: Gallimard, 1950);

Journal, 1942–1949 (Paris: Gallimard, 1950); translated by O'Brien, in *The Journals of André Gide*, volume 4: *1939–1949* (New York: Knopf, 1951; London: Secker & Warburg, 1951);

Ainsi soit-il ou les jeux sont faits (Paris: Gallimard, 1952); translated by O'Brien as *So Be It, or The Chips Are Down* (New York: Knopf, 1959; London: Chatto & Windus, 1960);

Ne jugez pas (Paris: Gallimard, 1969);

Le Récit de Michel, edited by Claude Martin (Neuchâtel: Ides et Calendes, 1972);

Les Cahiers et les Poésies d'André Walter, avec des fragments inédits du Journal, edited by Martin (Paris: Gallimard, 1986);

Fragment des Faux-Monnayeurs: Edition critique du manuscrit de Londres, edited by David Keypour (Sainte-Foy-lès-Lyon: Centre d'Etudes Gidiennes, 1990);

A Naples: Reconnaissance à l'Italie, edited, with an afterword, by Martin (Fontfroide: Fata Morgana, 1993);

Le Grincheux (Fontfroide: Fata Morgana, 1993);

L'Oroscope, ou Nul n'évite sa destinée: Scénario, fac-similé et transcription, edited by Daniel Durosay (Paris: Jean-Michel Place, 1995);

Le Scénario d'Isabelle, by Gide and Pierre Herbart, edited by Cameron D. E. Tolton (Paris: Lettres Modernes, 1996);

Journal, I: 1887–1925, edited by Eric Marty (Paris: Gallimard, 1996);

Journal, II: 1926–1950, edited by Martine Sagaert (Paris: Gallimard, 1997);

Essais critiques, edited by Pierre Masson (Paris: Gallimard, 1999);

Le Ramier, foreword by Catherine Gide, preface by Jean-Claude Perrier, afterword by David H. Walker (Paris: Gallimard, 2002).

Editions and Collections: *Le Théâtre complet d'André Gide,* 8 volumes, edited by Richard Heyd (Neuchâtel & Paris: Ides et Calendes, 1947–1949);

Romans, récits et soties, oeuvres lyriques, edited by Yvonne Davet and Jean-Jacques Thierry (Paris: Gallimard, 1958);

Le Roi Candaule, edited by Patrick Pollard (Bron: Centre d'Etudes Gidiennes, 2000);

Souvenirs et voyages, edited by Masson, Daniel Durosay, and Martine Sagaert (Paris: Gallimard, 2001).

Editions in English: *The Journals of André Gide,* 4 volumes, translated by Justin O'Brien (New York: Knopf, 1947–1951; London: Secker & Warburg, 1947–1955);

Two Legends: Theseus and Oedipus, translated by John Russell (New York: Knopf, 1950); republished as *Oedipus and Theseus* (London: Secker & Warburg, 1950);

The School for Wives; Robert; Geneviève, or The Unfinished Confidence, translated by Dorothy Bussy (New York: Knopf, 1950; London: Cassell, 1953);

Oscar Wilde (London: Kimber, 1951);

My Theater, translated by Jackson Mathews (New York: Knopf, 1952)—comprises *Saul; Bathsheba; Philoctetes; King Candaules; Persephone;* and *The Evolution of the Theater;*

Marshlands and Prometheus Misbound: Two Satires, translated by George D. Painter (New York: New Directions, 1953; London: Secker & Warburg, 1953);

The Return of the Prodigal, Preceded by Five Other Treatises, with Saul, A Drama in Five Acts, translated by Bussy (London: Secker & Warburg, 1953)—comprises *The Return of the Prodigal; Narcissus; The Lovers' Attempt; El Hadj; Philoctetes; Bathsheba;* and *Saul;*

The Immoralist, translated by Richard Howard (New York: Modern Library, 1983);

Amyntas, translated by Howard (New York: Ecco Press, 1988);

The Immoralist, translated by David Watson (New York: Penguin, 2001).

OTHER: Emmanuel Signoret, *Poésie complètes,* preface by Gide (Paris: Mercure de France, 1908);

Stendhal, *Armance,* preface by Gide (Paris: Champion, 1925);

Antoine de Saint-Exupéry, *Vol de nuit,* preface by Gide (Paris: Gallimard, 1931);

Henry Monnier, *Morceaux choisis,* preface by Gide (Paris: Gallimard, 1935);

Thomas Mann, *Avertissement à l'Europe,* preface by Gide (Paris: Gallimard, 1937);

Henry Fielding, *Tom Jones, histoire d'un enfant trouvé,* edited, with a preface, by Gide (Paris: Gallimard, 1938);

William Shakespeare, *Théâtre Complet,* 2 volumes, preface by Gide (Paris: Nouvelle Revue Française, 1938);

Johann Wolfgang von Goethe, *Théâtre,* introduction by Gide (Paris: Nouvelle Revue Française, 1942);

Jean Schlumberger, *Saint-Saturnin,* preface by Gide (Zurich: Oprecht, 1946);

Hermann Hesse, *Voyage en Orient,* preface by Gide (Paris: Calmann-Lévy, 1947);

Stendhal, *Lamiel,* preface by Gide (Paris: Livre Français, 1947);

Taha Hussein, *Le Livre des jours,* preface by Gide (Paris: Gallimard, 1947);

Anthologie de la poésie française, edited, with a preface, by Gide (Paris: Gallimard, 1949; New York: Pantheon, 1949);

Knut Hamsun, *La Faim,* preface by Gide (Paris: Chaix, 1950).

TRANSLATIONS: Rabindranath Tagore, *L'Offrande lyrique (Gitanjali)* (Paris: Nouvelle Revue Française, 1914);

Joseph Conrad, *Typhon* (Paris: Nouvelle Revue Française, 1918);

Photograph of Gide in his youth (© Albion-Guillot/Roger-Viollet/ Getty Images)

Walt Whitman, *Œuvres choisies,* translated by Gide and others (Paris: Nouvelle Revue Française, 1918);

William Shakespeare, *Antoine et Cléopâtre* (Paris: Vogel, 1921);

Tagore, *Amal et la lettre du roi* (Paris: Vogel, 1922);

William Blake, *Le Mariage du Ciel et de l'Enfer* (Paris: Claude Aveline, 1923);

Aleksandr Sergeevich Pushkin, *La Dame de pique,* translated by Gide, Jacques Schiffrin, and Boris de Scholezer (Paris: Pléiade, 1923);

Pushkin, *Nouvelles,* translated by Gide and Schiffrin (Paris: Pléiade/Schiffrin, 1928);

Shakespeare, *Hamlet, Acte premier* (Paris: La Tortue, 1930; Brussels: Décagone, 1944);

Johann Wolfgang von Goethe, "*Second Faust:* Fragment," *Nouvelle Revue Française,* 38 (March 1932);

Anonymous, *Arden de Feversham* (partial translation), *Cahiers du Sud* (June–July 1933);

Shakespeare, *Hamlet,* bilingual edition (New York: Schiffrin, 1944; Paris: Gallimard, 1946);

Goethe, *Prométhée* (Paris: Jonquière, 1951).

According to Maria van Rysselberghe, in 1921 André Gide said, "Au fond, le théâtre ne m'intéresse pas beaucoup; il me semble qu'il n'a de sens que dans un milieu aristocratique, comme ce fut le cas à la cour de Louis XIV, à Weimar; le théâtre anglais pourtant fait exception, qui s'adressait à tous" (Basically, the theater does not interest me much; it seems to me that it has meaning only in an aristocratic milieu, as in Louis XIV's court, at Weimar; English theater is an exception, however, being directed toward all). Despite this claim, Gide devoted considerable creative energy to composing plays and arranging them for production. He remains, however, less known for his theater than for his other literary endeavors, especially his fiction, *Journals* (Diaries), and autobiography. Even critics who generally express admiration for Gide's works have frequently dismissed his drama as untheatrical. In fact, until 1992 only two book-length studies of his drama had appeared in print. That year, Jean Claude published *André Gide et le théâtre* (André Gide and the Theater), his two-volume examination of the aesthetics, background, production, and reception of Gide's plays. Since that time, critical editions and related studies have shed further light on Gide's career in the theater.

Although few in number, Gide's plays include three that belong in any collection of major twentieth-century French drama: *Le Roi Candaule* (produced and published 1901; translated as *King Candaules,* 1952), *Saül* (published 1903, produced 1922; translated as *Saul,* 1952), and *Œdipe* (published and produced 1931; translated as *Oedipus,* 1950). Each of these plays was produced by an eminent director. Innovative and expressing deeply felt moral impulses, they reflect Gide's desire to create a modern drama beyond realism. René Lalou, a mid-century literary critic, recognized the contributions of these plays to dramatic renewal in France. Gide further enriched French drama with his translations, librettos, and adaptations, and he made important critical statements, including his lecture, "De l'évolution du théâtre" (translated as *The Evolution of the Theater,* 1952), delivered in Brussels in 1904 and published that year. Gide was also a supporter of the Théâtre du Vieux-Colombier, founded by his close friend Jacques Copeau in 1913. In fact, the year Gide claimed disinterest in the theater, he was anxious that Copeau's proposed staging of *Saül,* already postponed twice, might be canceled. He admitted wishing for popular success and took great interest in matters of production, deploring what he considered actors' misinterpretations and other blunders.

Gide's life was full of internal conflict. In the note he appended to the first part of his autobiography, *Si le grain ne meurt* (1920, 1921; translated as *If It Die . . . ,* 1935), he wrote: "Je suis un être de dialogue; tout en moi combat et se contredit" (I am a being of dialogue; everything in me fights and contradicts itself). One person who saw this existence in dramatic terms was the Catholic poet Paul Claudel, long one of Gide's correspondents despite their disagreements. Claudel wrote in a letter dated July 1926: "Vous êtes l'enjeu, l'acteur et le théâtre d'une grande lutte" (You are the stakes, actor, and theater of a great struggle). Drawing from these characterizations, critic Daniel Durosay, in his introduction to Gide's *L'Oroscope* (1995, The Mountain Watcher), suggests that Gide's existence was "fondée sur le mal-être et son dépassement" (founded on ill-being and its surpassing).

Born on 22 November 1869, Gide was the only child of Paul Gide, a Paris law professor from a southern family, and his wife Juliette (née Rondeaux), who came from Normandy and had considerable personal wealth. Both parents were from Calvinist families, although the Rondeaux family had been Catholic until the late eighteenth century, and one branch reverted to the Roman church. In *Si le grain ne meurt,* Gide stresses his dual and opposing heritages, northern and southern, Catholic and Protestant. In practice, however, a severe Protestant morality dominated his boyhood, and in some ways he never freed himself entirely from its legacy, which both enriched and burdened him. Gide's highly developed individualism derived in part from belonging to a tiny minority: the French population was approximately 2 percent Protestant around 1900.

From 1877 until late October 1880 Gide attended the Ecole Alsacienne, a private school. His studies were interrupted, however, by illness and a three-month suspension for unseemly conduct. Upon his father's death in late October 1880, Gide went with his mother to Normandy, then Montpellier. When they returned to Paris he reenrolled in the Ecole Alsacienne, but he was soon withdrawn because of nervous troubles. After studying with private tutors, he returned to school again and earned a baccalaureate in 1889. During this time Gide was surrounded by women–his mother, his aunt, his mother's former governess, and various Norman cousins. Among the latter was Madeleine Rondeaux, who later became his wife. Gide favored her for her reserve, tact, and intelligence. As a boy, he had glimpsed Madeleine's mother languidly stretched out on a sofa, taking smelling salts. At the time he did not understand the significance of this scene, that she was having an affair. When he found his cousin in tears immediately afterward, Gide learned that Madeleine was deeply wounded and that her hurt was connected to her mother's conduct. It was then that she became, as he wrote in *Si le grain ne meurt,* "un nouvel orient de ma vie" (a new orientation of my life), and he vowed to protect her.

Gide's literary talent was recognized by his contemporaries, among them Pierre Louÿs at the Ecole Alsacienne, and Paul Valéry, a lifelong friend he met in Montpellier in 1890. Gide began contributing to little magazines, and in 1891 he anonymously published his first work, *Les Cahiers d'André Walter* (translated as *The Notebooks of André Walter,* 1968), a highly romantic, overblown, but occasionally brilliant confessional work in diary form. Gide's motivation for this book was to induce Madeleine to marry him; instead, it apparently frightened her. During this period Gide continued publishing short works.

In 1893 Gide left for North Africa, accompanying a friend who had won a traveling fellowship. This journey, the first of many to Algeria and Tunisia, allowed Gide to discard the Calvinist sexual code with which he had been raised and acknowledge the homosexuality that he had already suggested in his writings, largely through negative references to female sexuality and homoerotic imagery in *Les Cahiers d'André Walter* and *Le Voyage d'Urien* (1893; translated as *Urien's Voyage,* 1964). As Gide explained in the second part of *Si le grain ne meurt,* during these travels he laid the foundation for a lifetime personal ethic, "un idéal d'équilibre, de plénitude et de santé" (an ideal of balance, fullness, and health). He left his Bible at home, although he later asked his mother to send it to him. For many years he oscillated between belief and nonbelief. He disliked all organized religion, but he remained devoted to his image of Christ as a vagabond, a freethinking rebel. As he explained in his journal in 1907, "Je ne suis qu'un petit garçon qui s'amuse, doublé d'un pasteur protestant qui le regarde" (I am just a little boy having fun, doubled by a Protestant pastor watching him).

Like his Protestantism, Gide's homosexuality set him apart from others. He insisted always that he was not a sodomist, but a pederast, drawn to young boys and adolescents. While he did not announce his sexual proclivity until the 1920s, it is expressed obliquely in several works, and the desire to "manifest" (tell the truth about) himself, sexually and otherwise, was a major motivation throughout his career. He assigned great importance, both personal and social, to his confessional autobiography and to a treatise on homosexuality published at first anonymously under the title *C.R.D.N.* (1911; translated, 1950) and then in 1920 under the full title, *Corydon.*

Gide rapidly embarked on two further trips to North Africa. Although Gide's family was ignorant about his exact conduct, they were uneasy about him. Shortly after his mother's death in 1895, Madeleine

Gide during his travels in Africa in the 1890s (© Martinie/Roger-Viollet/Getty Images)

agreed to marry him. Gide's uncle Charles Gide was among those who considered the marriage a precautionary move. It was, however, a failure: evidence suggests that Madeleine became aware of her husband's sexual proclivities early in the marriage, which remained unconsummated. Personal writings by Gide and the testimony of others indicate that it was an unhappy arrangement. Although Gide and Madeleine initially traveled together, they soon began living apart, he traveling or staying in Paris, she living at their estate in Cuverville, Normandy. Such a relationship was facilitated by the fact that they were both independently wealthy.

The long list of works Gide published over the course of his career demonstrates his creative vigor. He published fiction (short narratives and one long novel), essays in literary criticism, essays on social matters, and works that defied generic categorization. Perhaps his greatest literary achievement is his journal, kept from 1887 until the very end of his life. Over the years these writings have been published both in fragments and as books. Both personal diary and writer's notebook, these volumes feature incisive prose and keen insight. Additionally, Gide was influential as a critic, editor, and friend to other writers.

Gide's overriding literary concerns were chiefly aesthetic, not edifying or mimetic. As he explained in a letter to Jules Renard, published in *Nouveaux Prétextes* (1911, New Pretexts), "L'oeuvre d'art ne doit rien prouver; ne peut rien prouver sans tricherie" (A work of art must not prove anything; cannot prove anything without cheating). In his "Chroniques de l'Ermitage" (1905, Chronicles of The Hermitage), published in volume 4 of *Œuvres complètes* (1933, Complete Works), Gide asserts that morality is "une dépendance de l'esthétique" (dependent upon aesthetics). He prized style and argued for discipline, difficulty, and formalism in art. In "De l'evolution du théâtre," Gide states that "l'art naît de contrainte, vit de lutte, et meurt de liberté" (Art is born of constraint, lives on struggle, and dies from freedom). He was interested in the individual and particular circumstances, but many of his works are characterized by great stylization and generalization, or what in *Les Faux-Monnayers* (1925; translated as *The Counterfeiters*, 1927) he called an "érosion des contours" (erosion of contours) characteristic of classicism. He viewed the theater as "le lieu de caractères" (the place of characters) where individual truths are pretexts for generalization. In his view, Christianity discouraged characters—strong individual personalities—and no entirely Christian theater could exist.

Gide's drama is largely based on pagan Greek and biblical material, both treated freely. Critic Paul Surer, in his *Cinquante ans de théâtre* (1969, Fifty Years of Theater), asserts that Gide was "le premier à deviner le parti qu'un dramaturge pouvait tirer des légendes bibliques ou des fictions antiques pour exprimer son éthique personnelle ou des préoccupations toutes modernes" (the first to perceive the advantage that a playwright could draw from biblical legends or ancient tales to express his personal ethic or quite modern concerns). While Gide drew on mythology in his other writings, notably in his last narrative, *Thésée* (1946; translated as *Theseus*, 1948), his drama best illustrates its rich potential for modern applications.

Gide's plays share with his other works themes of happiness, freedom, individualism, destiny, self-discovery, desire, chastisement, and religion, as well as his characteristic moral rigor. A further feature of Gide's plays is self-projection. Major characters not only speak for the author but serve as varied selves, illustrating potentialities and contradictions, displaying his protean personality. His major works feature characters with traits that, when not counterbalanced or controlled, possess them and lead to extraordinary conduct. In a letter to Ary Scheffer, written soon after Scheffer had spoken in print of Gide's novel *L'Imora-*

liste (1902; translated as *The Imoralist*, 1930) and later published in *Œuvres complètes*, Gide explained his method:

> Que de bourgeons nous portons en nous, cher Scheffer, qui n'écloront jamais que dans nos livres! . . . Mais si, par volonté, on les supprime tous, *sauf un*, comme il croît aussitôt, comme il grandit! . . . Pour créer un héros ma recette est bien simple: Prendre un de ces bourgeons, le mettre en pot–tout seul–on arrive bientôt à un individu admirable.
>
> (How many buds we bear within ourselves, dear Scheffer, which will never blossom except in our books! . . . But if, by design, one suppresses them all, *except one*, how it grows at once, how it gets big! . . . To create a hero my recipe is very simple: Take one of these buds, put it in a pot–all alone–and soon one has a wondrous individual.)

Here Gide describes the artist as a kind of horticulturalist who removes most of the buds from a stalk so that those remaining can develop and blossom extraordinarily, but he is also interested in the passions that consume human beings: "Je n'aime pas les hommes; j'aime ce qui les dévore" (I do not love men; I love what devours them), says Prometheus in *Le Prométhée mal enchaîné* (1899; translated as *Prometheus Illbound*, 1919).

According to author and close friend Roger Martin du Gard, the first play Gide wrote, *Saül*, is one of his finest works. In a missive included in *Lettres* (1930, Letters), Gide explained that, like *L'Immoraliste*, it is a warning against the hedonism and self-indulgence expressed in *Les Nourritures terrestres* (1897; translated as *The Fruits of the Earth*, 1949). Such swings between renunciation and self-gratification are characteristic of Gide's oeuvre. Written in 1896, *Saül* was published in 1903 and produced in 1922 by Copeau (who played the title role) at the Vieux-Colombier. The premiere was, in Gide's own word, "un four" (a flop). Attendance was good throughout the run, but reviews were generally negative. The dramaturgy is neither classical nor that of nineteenth-century "well-made plays." Instead, it recalls Romantic practice, with multiple settings (palace, desert, grotto) and Shakespearean touches, including supernatural elements. Yet, Saül is not a Romantic hero, but a deranged personality struggling for self-knowledge and self-control, torn between strength and weakness. (Gide had encountered writings by Friedrich Nietzsche in the 1890s and was drawn to, or had developed independently, elements of their ethics.) As a psychological drama involving an individual struggle for identity and meaning, the play is modern, despite the biblical basis. Saül exclaims: "Je deviens très étonnant!–Ma valeur est dans ma complication" (I am becoming very astonishing!–My value lies in my complexity).

In *Saül*, Gide rearranges and develops material from 1 Samuel 17, 18, and 28 in a five-act drama depicting King Saül's personal and political undoing. As the Philistines besiege his kingdom, Saül, having exterminated the soothsayers, has attempted vainly to read the stars himself. Ignorance of destiny is paralleled with ignorance about himself. Saül is beset by demons–actual actors representing his temptations and weaknesses. The queen and others try to manipulate him by introducing as their spy the handsome shepherd David, who shortly kills Goliath. Then, when David befriends Jonathan, the king's weak son, the king feels jealousy. The love between the young men, which is biblically based, is never explicitly sexual, yet suggests homoerotic attraction, as does Saül's obvious fascination with David. The suggestion of homosexuality often has been noted. For example, according to Martin du Gard, his friend Pierre Margaritis wrote that, despite his admiration for the play, he was bothered by its "côté pédéraste" (pederastic side).

Concerned about the kingdom, which is once again besieged, Saül attempts unsuccessfully to teach Jonathan to reign. Unseen, he observes David with Jonathan, who fantasizes (as Saül does later) about becoming a goatherd with David and places the crown on David's head. Saül is both intrigued and disturbed by this scene and its implications. In a symbolic act, he has his beard shaved and goes to consult the lone remaining witch, the aged pythoness of Endor. She conjures up the shade of Samuel, who says it is not the Philistines who worry him but something else. Samuel predicts Saül's defeat by the Philistines, his death and Jonathan's, and David's assumption of the throne. Angered by the prediction, the king strikes the witch, but not before she warns him about desire: "Tout ce qui t'est charmant t'est hostile" (Everything that is charming to you is hostile to you). Saül's self-ignorance makes him vulnerable: "Ils veulent savoir mon secret et je ne le sais pas moi-même!" (They want to know my secret and I don't know it myself!). Like the character Michel in *L'Immoraliste*, Saül tries to cultivate his will; instead, it disintegrates. Demons, having assumed attractive forms, settle in his tent. He asks: "Avec quoi l'homme se consolera-t-il d'une déchéance? sinon avec ce qui l'a déchu" (With what will a man be consoled after a downfall? if not with what brought him down). The end of the personal crisis is Saül's death at the hands of a treacherous courtier; the solution to the political crisis finally comes when David replaces Saül as king.

Cover for Gide's 1901 play about a king who shares his wife's beauty with a poor fisherman by giving him a ring of invisibility and the dire consequences of their actions (Zimmerman Library, University of New Mexico)

Philoctète (published 1899, private performance 1919; translated as *Philoctetes*, 1952), a subject treated also by Sophocles, is, according to Gide's prefatory note, a moral treatise not intended for presentation. It has been staged both privately and publicly, however, first at the Comédie des Champs-Elysées on 16 October 1937, with the renowned actor Marcel Herrand in the cast. With its elevated tone, long speeches, simple plot involving a moral dilemma, and few characters, this short five-act work resembles certain French classical dramas inspired by Greek models, such as Jean Racine's *Andromaque* (1668; translated as *Andromache*, 1675) and *Mithridate* (1673; translated as *Mithridates*, 1926). The plot turns on the question of duty. Bitten by a serpent and suffering a stinking wound, Philoctète has been abandoned on a frozen, deserted island by his compatriots, his only weapons a bow and arrows, a legacy from Heracles. The gods have decreed that those arms alone can prevail against the Trojans, and the old warrior Ulysse and young Néoptolème, Achilles' son, have been sent to wrest them from Philoctète by ruse. The play includes themes typical of Gide's work: competing rights and duties and individual self-discipline and self-sacrifice. Néoptolème protests the use of treachery toward his father's friend, while Ulysse argues that reasons of state outweigh, and must prevail over, individual rights and ethics, following divine will. Finally, the characters cannot agree on the ideal for which one should fight and sacrifice. For Ulysse, it is the fatherland and its gods. But Philoctète observes: "Au-dessus des dieux . . . il y a quelque chose" (Above the gods . . . there is something else). The crux of the problem is identifying the higher good. In the end, trickery is not necessary, as Philoctète surrenders the bow and arrows willingly, not out of patriotism but devotion to something he cannot name–an internal rather than external imperative: "Ce que l'on entreprend au-dessus de ses forces . . . voilà ce qu'on appelle vertu" (What one undertakes beyond one's strength . . . that's what's called virtue). In a departure from the myth, Philoctète remains on the island. Flowers pierce the snow, and birds come down to nourish him.

Gide's next play, *Le Roi Candaule*, was first produced in 1901 at the Nouveau Théâtre by Aurélien Lugné-Poe, who resisted realism in favor of poetic drama. The play closed after its first performance; the few laudatory reviews were offset by many attacks. Greatly disappointed, Gide, in "De l'evolution du théâtre," indicted his contemporaries by observing that drama can flourish only in the absence of public hypocrisy.

The plot of *Le Roi Candaule* is derived from both fact and fable. Sources include Herodotus's *Clio* (late fifth century B.C.) and Plato's *Republic* (circa 380–360 B.C.). The historical character Gyges was king of Lydia in the seventh century B.C. According to Plato, Gyges, a humble shepherd in the royal service, discovered a ring with the power to make its wearer invisible. Armed with the ring, he slipped into the palace of King Candaules, seduced the queen, and murdered the king. Then Gyges acceded to the throne and married the queen. In contrast, Herodotus presents Gyges as a trusted member of the king's bodyguard. The king, having often praised his wife's beauty to Gyges, asks him to observe her in her bedchamber. For this betrayal, the queen compels Gyges to kill Candaules and take the throne. His assumption of power is then justified by the Delphic oracle. This story already had been treated in French by the poet Théophile Gautier (*Le Roi Candaule*, 1844), and among the stage presentations based on the legend was Henri Meilhac and Ludovic Halévy's *Le Roi Candaule* (produced and published 1873; translated as *The Realm of Joy*, 1969). Additionally, a version of the story by Friedrich Hebbel, *Gyges und sein Ring* (published 1856; translated as *Gyges and His Ring*, 1914), was staged in Berlin in 1856.

Gide's *Le Roi Candaule* is a three-act play written in occasionally rhymed free verse. Gide employs both Plato's and Herodotus's stories, but the emphasis is on character and motivation, not the marvelous. Like *Saül, Le Roi Candaule* illustrates self-destruction. Candaule's excessive and misplaced generosity actually amounts to manipulating and experimenting with others. The theme of voluntary divestiture, intended to create greater freedom and enjoyment, appears also in *Les Nourritures terrestres* and *L'Immoraliste,* and in his own life Gide displayed contradictory impulses toward acquisition and divestiture, thrift and expenditure. Candaule seeks to dazzle those around him, including Gygès, a poor fisherman, with his wealth and happiness. He imposes these things on others under the pretext that they are not complete unless shared. However, such imposition is a means of controlling others; the king's annoyance when his gifts are not thoroughly appreciated shows that his generosity is really directed toward himself.

Candaule's scheme to have Gygès observe Queen Nyssia's beauty by becoming invisible succeeds. Gygès observes her, unseen, and then he proceeds to share her bed without her discovering his identity. When Nyssia tells Candaule that it was their finest night of love, he is shaken: his gift has backfired on him. Gide is less interested, however, in Candaule's sexual discomfiture than in questions of power and conduct. Learning how her husband has betrayed her, Nyssia, as in the legend, compels Gygès's to kill him. Gygès then assumes the throne and obliges the queen, who has removed her veils since her modesty was mocked, to replace them. Power under Gygès's reign will be exercised directly, not through mediation. Contemporary and later readings of the play as a socialist manifesto conflict with Gide's aesthetics. In his preface to the play, published in volume 3 of *Œuvres complètes,* Gide noted that it might be interpreted simply as the defeat of an aristocracy dismantled by too-noble impulses.

Nearly thirty years passed before Gide wrote another major drama. During this period he undertook various dramatic projects, some of which were published, while others were dropped. In 1901 he wrote one act of a libretto titled *Le Retour* (1946, The Return) before abandoning it for a comic opera composed by Raymond Bonheur.

In 1907 Gide published the short work *Le Retour de l'enfant prodigue* (translated as *The Return of the Prodigal,* 1953), which consists almost entirely of dialogue. Although Gide called it a poem, it has been staged, and it is included in Gide's *Le Théâtre complet d'André Gide* (1947–1949, The Complete Theater of André Gide). Furthermore, both James C. McLaren and

ANDRÉ GIDE

THE RETURN OF THE PRODIGAL

Preceded by Five Other Treatises
with
SAUL
A Drama in Five Acts

Translated by
DOROTHY BUSSY

London
SECKER & WARBURG
1953

Title page for a collection of Gide's works in English, featuring his 1907 dramatic-poem version of the parable of the prodigal son (Howard-Tilton Memorial Library, Tulane University)

Claude included this work in their studies of Gide's drama. Following Gide's conviction that institutions have distorted Christ's message, the evangelical material upon which *Le Retour de l'enfant prodigue* is based is treated idiosyncratically: the parable becomes an indictment of the Roman Catholic Church, the "house" to which the prodigal son, weakened by hardship, returns. While his mother receives him with love and forgiveness and his father with understanding, the elder brother, with his pretension to exclusive truth, speaks harshly of his brother: his formula is "Hors la Maison, point de salut pour toi" (Outside the house, there is no salvation for you). Gide further develops the parable by adding a younger brother who idolizes the prodigal and will imitate him. While others denounce the ethic of freedom, discovery, self-development, and what Gide called "vagabondage," the boy's imminent departure signals their validity. As the boy leaves, the prodigal holds the lamp–his legacy of illumination.

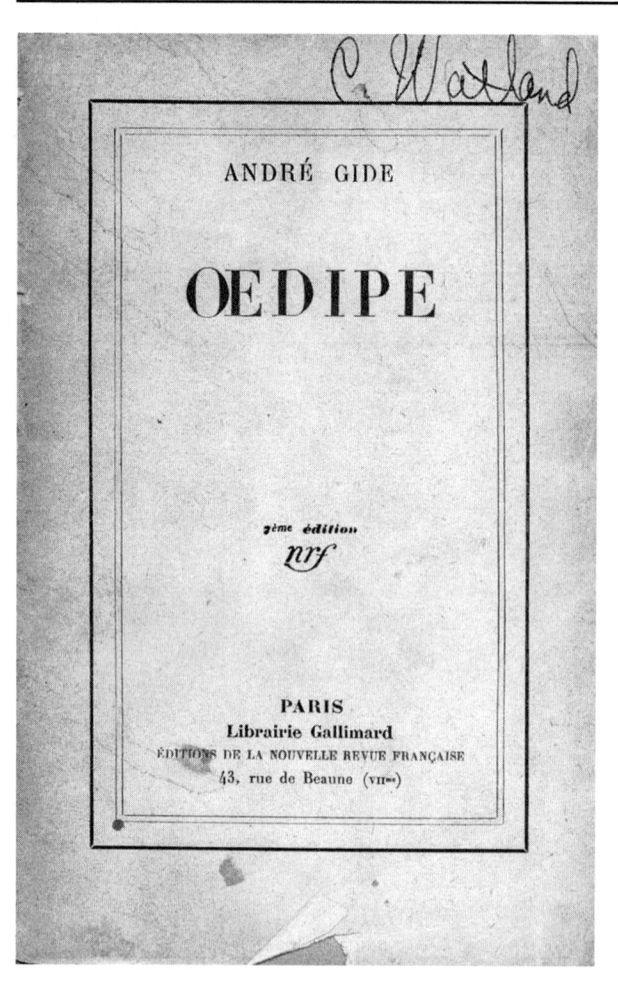

Cover for Gide's 1931 version of the Oedipus story, which met with mixed reviews when it premiered in Paris in 1932 (Thomas Cooper Library, University of South Carolina)

Another work from this period, *Bethsabé* (published 1912; translated as *Bathsheba*, 1952), is a short free-verse play that Gide called a dramatic poem. It initially appeared in magazines, with two scenes published in *L'Ermitage* (1903, The Hermitage) before the whole work was published in *Vers et prose* (1908–1909, Verse and Prose). *Bethsabé* has rarely been performed. Based on 2 Samuel 11, the dramatic poem tells the story of David's adultery with Bathsheba, the wife of his Hittite warrior Uriah. The majority of the work consists of David's monologues. While tasteful, they are poetically and thematically sensuous, recalling the passages from *Les Nourritures terrestres* involving desire and the ambivalence of desire when the object is threatened by fulfillment. The prophet Nathan, discovering David's adultery, reveals God's displeasure. David asks, "Que fera l'homme / Si derrière chacun de ses désirs se cache Dieu?" (What will man do / If behind each of his desires God hides?). He arranges for Uriah's death in battle but realizes (in a departure from the Bible) that it was less the woman he desired than the moment, the setting, the essence of Uriah's happiness. David dismisses Bathsheba roughly: he cannot achieve another's unique experience.

In 1909 Gide participated in the founding of the preeminent literary monthly in twentieth-century France, *La Nouvelle Revue Française* (The New French Review), where he was an important behind-the-scenes figure. He wrote little during World War I. For some months, he worked for a charitable organization, the Foyer Franco-Belge (The French-Belgian Hostel), which cared for refugees. In 1916 Gide experienced a religious and moral crisis, recorded in his journal. This crisis apparently was caused by profound discouragement about the war, his inability to control his sensual appetite, and perhaps also a lack of creative activity. Gide feared that he was possessed by the Devil. To combat his sense of possession by a skilled demonic dialectician able to enter his mind, he turned to the Gospels and attempted to recover a child-like belief in the presence of Christ and truth of his Word. His efforts were, however, always self-conscious; the interior voice of faith in him was always offset by doubt, and his desire to reform was always offset by the knowledge that he eventually would fall back into sensual gratification. This period was Gide's last period of profound religious feeling. Around this time he translated William Shakespeare's *Antony and Cleopatra* (circa 1606) as *Antoine et Cléopâtre* (performed with music 1920; published 1921). In 1918 Gide left for England with Marc Allégret, a young protégé and lover. In an act of revenge and finality, Madeleine burned Gide's lengthy correspondence with her.

With the disintegration of his relationship with Madeleine, Gide established a close relationship with Maria (Madame Théo) van Rysselberghe, an older friend of long standing. For nearly twenty-five years they resided in adjoining flats in Paris. From 1918 on, she kept a diary (published as *Les Cahiers de la Petite Dame* [The Notebooks of the Little Woman], 1973–1977) recording Gide's conversations and activities and assessing his figure. In 1923 van Rysselberghe's daughter, Elisabeth, gave birth to Gide's child, named Catherine. The child was chiefly a pedagogical and feminist experiment. Gide's penchant for contradiction, opposition, and self-dialogue continued to manifest itself in his divided private life: he was a married homosexual, "devoted" to Madeleine, but attracted to the freethinking van Rysselberghe circle, and thereby compelled to father a child with a woman not his wife. Similarly, in his fifties he began proclaiming his atheism while still honoring the figure of Christ. Attacked for his immorality, he nevertheless was widely admired; critic André Rouveyre called him "le contemporain capital" (the key contemporary).

Gide's continued interest in antiquity is illustrated by his "Considérations sur la mythologie grecque" (Considerations on Greek Mythology), published in *Morceaux choisis* (1921, Selected Passages), and an unfinished drama, *Ajax,* published in volume 4 of *Œuvres complètes*. Additional dramatic undertakings of the early interwar years include beginning a translation of Shakespeare's *Hamlet* (circa 1599) in 1922. That year Gide's translation of Rabindranath Tagore's *Dak-Ghar* (1912; translated as *The Post Office*, 1914), titled *Amal et la lettre du roi* (Amal and the Letter from the King), appeared.

In 1925, after finishing his long novel *Les Faux-Monnayeurs*, Gide was invited by the French government to inspect timber-growing concessions in French colonies, and he promptly left with Allégret for an eleven-month journey to Africa. Allégret filmed their travels. The human misery and injustices Gide observed led him to publish two documentary works and turn to communism. He was never a party member, however, and with scant interest in political theory, he claimed it was Christ, not Marx, that drew him to Soviet-style socialism. With fellow travelers such as André Malraux he participated in many left-wing activities during the 1930s.

Gide's major dramatic work from the interwar period, *Œdipe,* was composed in 1930. Here Gide again reworked a story from antiquity. Noteworthy French versions of the Oedipus tragedy, following those by Sophocles (*Oedipus Rex,* late fifth century B.C.) and Seneca (*Oedipus,* early first century A.D.), had been written by Pierre Corneille (*Œdipe,* published and produced 1659), Voltaire (*Œdipe,* produced 1718, published 1719), and Jean Cocteau (*Œdipe-Roi,* published 1928, performed 1937), who later took up the story again in *La Machine infernale* (published and produced 1934; translated as *The Infernal Machine,* 1936). Gide was particularly drawn to the Oedipus story because his notion of a pagan theater was fulfilled in the hero's individualism offset by fatality. His three-act prose drama was staged first in Antwerp in 1931, then in Paris in 1932 by Georges Pitoëff, who played the title role. The reception in Paris was mixed overall, but there were many unfavorable assessments. Nevertheless, Gide believed that later critics would recognize the excellence of the play.

In *Œdipe,* Gide expresses his social concerns of the 1930s and the humanism of his maturity, including his anticlericalism, his belief in progress, and his belief that God is a human concept: "Dieu, c'est tout simplement ce que tu mets au bout de cet élan de ta pensée" (God is simply what you place at the end of that thrust of your thought). Popular credulity and priestly manipulation are mocked repeatedly in the play, although priest and gods have the last word. Contemporary diction, anachronisms (such as references to Freudian repression), and wit give the play a modern flavor.

Gide's Œdipe is a hero flawed by hubris, pride in his accomplishments, happiness, and independent thinking. Knowing he was found in the wild, he supposes he is a bastard, introducing a theme, illegitimacy, that recurs in Gide's work. But rather than proclaim "Familles, je vous hais" (Families, I despise you), as Gide writes in *Les Nourritures terrestres,* or flee attachments, as does Bernard of *Les Faux-Monnayeurs* after discovering his illegitimacy, Œdipe is pleased to have no family precedents to follow. He has invented himself: "Qu'importe, dès lors, si je suis Grec or Lorrain?" (What does it matter, then, if I am Greek or from Lorraine?). (Gide's anachronistic allusion to Lorraine echoes his quarrel in the 1890s with Maurice Barrès, a writer born in Lorraine who emphasized provincial roots.) Œdipe's adversaries and critics are Créon, who argues on pragmatic grounds for a solid conservatism built on tradition; the priest Tirésias, who exercises power by inspiring fear and warns Œdipe repeatedly against arrogance; and Œdipe's daughter Antigone, who intends to take the veil, sacrificing herself to offset her father's impiety. Meanwhile, the Chorus, expressing Gide's social concerns, offers warnings, noting the king's indifference to his people's suffering.

Before discovering his secret, Œdipe proclaims his humanistic creed. Humanity's goal is ahead, and it is not the fulfillment of some preordained model but a process of self-discovery and improvement for the entire species. For Œdipe, there can be no divine answer and no universal model: "Je me sentais une réponse à je ne savais encore quelle question" (I felt I was an answer to a question yet unknown). Yet, he acknowledges a great difficulty in the process of self-discovery and improvement: things are not always what they seem. Œdipe's uneasiness multiplies as pieces of the puzzle accumulate. Upon learning that he has killed his father and married his mother–thereby fulfilling the oracle–he is appalled by his deeds while simultaneously recognizing that the disaster was predestined by fate. (The theme of destiny is echoed in Gide's posthumously published movie scenario, *L'Oroscope*.)

Œdipe does not, however, repent as Tirésias demands because he was not free to do anything other than what he did. After Jocasta is found hanged, Œdipe blinds himself. (Blindness is another important theme in Gide's work, seen especially in *La Symphonie*

Jeanne Moreau in the 1950 production of Gide's Les Caves du Vatican *(1933, The Vatican Cellars), adapted from his 1914 novel of the same title (© Lipnitzki/Roger-Viollet/Getty Images)*

pastorale [1919; translated as *The Pastoral Symphony*, 1931].) This deed does not indicate that he blames himself, but rather serves as an acknowledgment of his previous blindness and his desire to go beyond it: "C'est volontiers que je m'immole. J'étais parvenu à ce point que je ne pouvais plus dépasser qu'en prenant élan contre moi-même" (I immolate myself willingly. I had reached the point where I go farther only in taking impetus against myself). He desires, he says, only what is difficult. He will leave Thebes and thereby end the plague. Antigone, fulfilling her destiny of self-sacrifice, will accompany him. Learning that his bones will bring blessings to those in whose land he is buried, he says, "Quels qu'ils soient, ce sont des hommes. Au prix de ma souffrance, il m'est doux de leur apporter du bonheur" (Whoever they are, they are men. At the price of my suffering, it pleases me to bring happiness to them). Thus redeemed, he departs as a humanistic hero. The figure of Oedipus later reappears in Gide's *Thésée*.

Gide's translation of a portion of Johann Wolfgang von Goethe's *Faust II* (1832; translated, 1838) appeared in the *Nouvelle Revue Française* in 1932. The following year an unfinished drama by Gide, *Proserpine*, was published in volume 4 of *Œuvres complètes*. That year a stage adaptation of his farcical *Les Caves du Vatican* (novel published 1914; translated as *The Vatican Swindle*, 1925; drama published 1948) was first performed in Switzerland. In 1934 *Perséphone* (published 1942; translated as *Persephone*, 1952), a verse libretto related to *Proserpine*, was staged in Paris with Ida Rubinstein in the title role and music by Igor Stravinsky. The work testifies to Gide's social concerns at the time: Persephone returns to Hades to relieve the distress of the shades and bring respite to their sufferings. Another play, a farce titled *Le Treizième Arbre* (published 1942, The Thirteenth Tree), was staged in 1935. It attacked the influence of priests and mocked Freudian psychology through reductio ad absurdum.

In 1936 Gide visited the Soviet Union. This visit led to disappointment. The social and political realities were far from what he imagined. He was especially incensed by policies restricting sexual freedom. Two short works published after his return denounced Soviet errors, causing his estrangement from the left wing, and he gradually abandoned his socialist views.

Madeleine died in 1938, and Gide appears to have felt genuine grief and guilt. She had been his moral center. During World War II Gide resided in the south with friends, then in Tunis and Algiers, where he kept his diary, helped found a literary magazine, and pursued other projects. He was too controversial to be elected to the Académie française (French Academy), but in 1947 he received an honorary doctorate from Oxford University and the Nobel Prize in literature. His postwar dramatic activities include *Le Procès; Pièce tirée du roman de Kafka* (1947; translated as *The Trial, from the Novel of Franz Kafka*, 1950), based on Franz Kafka's *Der Prozeß* (1925; translated as *The Trial*, 1937) and written in collaboration with Jean-Louis Barrault. He also worked on various scenario projects. Gide's translation of *Hamlet*, published in 1944, was first performed in 1946. His play *Robert ou L'Intérêt général* (Robert: or, General Interest), a work he began in 1935, was also produced in 1946. The timely topics of this play—conflict between industrialists and workers, and a son's rebellion against his conservative father—place it in a category of works Gide and Sartre called *littérature engagée* (committed literature). In December 1950 an expanded stage version of *Les Caves du Vatican* was produced at the Comédie-Française in Paris. Gide attended rehearsals with great interest and attended the premiere, which was widely considered a triumph.

Gide died on 19 February 1951 and was buried at Cuverville. In 1952 his works were placed on the Roman Catholic Church's Index Librorum Prohibitorum (Index of Prohibited Books), defining them as a threat to faith and morals, yet also indicating their impact and influence. The inexpensive reprints, critical editions, and abundance of scholarship produced in subsequent years testify to the lasting importance of Gide's works.

André Gide earned a place of significance in twentieth-century French drama for renewing ancient plots; for offering psychological insight, moral complexity, and challenging positions; and for working in a searching style, by turns witty, elevated, and direct. In 1903 he stated, "L'artiste ne peut se passer d'un public; et quand le public est absent, que fait-il? Il l'invente et . . . attend du futur ce que lui dénie le présent" (The artist cannot do without a public; and when the public is absent, what does he do? He invents it and . . . awaits from the future what the present denies him). Gide barely had an audience for his theater until *Œdipe* was produced, but since that time his plays have been widely recognized for their poetry and poignancy.

Letters:

Lettres (Liège: A la Lampe d'Aladdin, 1930);

Correspondance Francis Jammes–André Gide, 1893–1938, edited by Robert Mallet (Paris: Gallimard, 1948);

Marcel Proust, *Lettres à André Gide* (Neuchâtel & Paris: Ides et Calendes, 1949);

Correspondance, 1899–1926, Paul Claudel–André Gide, edited by Mallet (Paris: Gallimard, 1949); translated by John Russell as *The Correspondence, 1899–1926, between Paul Claudel and André Gide* (New York: Pantheon, 1952);

Correspondance, 1909–1926, Rainer Maria Rilke–André Gide, edited by Renée Lang (Paris: Corrêa, 1952);

Correspondance Paul Valéry–André Gide, 1890–1942, edited by Mallet (Paris: Gallimard, 1955); abridged and translated by June Guicharnaud as *Self-Portraits: The Gide-Valéry Letters, 1890–1942* (Chicago: University of Chicago Press, 1966);

Rilke, Gide, et Verhaeren: correspondance inédite, edited by Carlo Bronne (Paris: Messein, 1955);

Correspondance André Gide–Charles Péguy 1905–1912, edited by Alfred Saffrey (Persan: Imprimerie de Persan-Beaumont, 1958);

The Correspondance of André Gide and Edmund Gosse, 1904–1928, edited by Linette F. Brugmans (New York: New York University Press, 1959; London: Owen, 1960);

Correspondance André Gide–Arnold Bennett, 1911–1931: Vingt ans d'amitié littéraire, edited by Brugmans (Geneva & Paris: Droz & Minard, 1964);

Correspondance André Gide–Roger Martin du Gard, 1913–1951, 2 volumes, edited by Jean Delay (Paris: Gallimard, 1968);

Jean Cocteau, *Lettres à André Gide,* edited by J. J. Kihm (Paris: La Table Ronde, 1970);

Correspondance André Gide–François Mauriac, 1912–1950, edited by Jacqueline Morton (Paris: Gallimard, 1971);

Correspondance d'André Gide et Georges Simenon, edited by Francis Lacassin and Gilbert Sigaux (Paris: Plon, 1973);

Charles Brunard, *Correspondance avec André Gide et souvenirs* (Paris: La Pensée Universelle, 1974);

Gide and Albert Mockel, *Correspondance (1891–1938),* edited by Gustave Vanwelkenhuyzen (Geneva: Droz, 1975);

Henri Ghéon and Gide, *Correspondance,* 2 volumes, edited by Jean Tipi and Anne-Marie Moulènes, (Paris: Gallimard, 1976);

Correspondance André Gide–Jules Romains, edited by Claude Martin (Paris: Flammarion, 1976);

Gide and Jacques-Emile Blanche, *Correspondance: 1892–1939,* edited by Georges-Paul Collet (Paris: Gallimard, 1979);

André Gide–Justin O'Brien, Correspondance 1937–1951, edited by Morton (Lyon: Centre d'Etudes Gidiennes, 1979);

Correspondance André Gide–Dorothy Bussy, 1918–1951, 3 volumes, edited by Jean Lambert, notes by Richard Tedeschi (Paris: Gallimard, 1979–1982); translated by Tedeschi as *Selected Letters of André Gide and Dorothy Bussy* (London: Oxford University Press, 1983);

Deutsch-französische Gesprache 1920–1950: La Correspondance de Ernst Robert Curtius avec André Gide, Charles Du Bos, et Valery Larbaud, edited by Herbert Dieckmann and Jane M. Dieckmann (Frankfurt: Klostermann, 1980);

Gabrielle Vulliez, *La Tristesse d'un automne sans été: Correspondance de Gabrielle Vulliez avec André Gide et Paul Claudel (1923–1931)* (Bron: Centre d'Etudes Gidiennes, Université Lyon II, 1981);

Gide and François-Paul Alibert, *Correspondance: 1907–1950,* edited by Martin (Lyon: Presses Universitaires de Lyon, 1982);

André Gide–Jean Giono, Correspondance 1929–1940, edited by Roland Bourneuf and Jacques Cotnam (Lyon: Centre d'Etudes Gidiennes, 1984);

D'un monde à l'autre. La Correspondance André Gide–Harry Kessler (1903–1933), edited by Claude Foucart (Lyon: Centre d'Etudes Gidiennes, Université Lyon II, 1985);

Gide, *Correspondance avec Jef Last (1934–1950),* edited by C. J. Greshoff (Lyon: Presses Universitaires de Lyon, 1985);

Gide and Anna de Noailles, *Correspondance (1902–1928),* edited by Claude Mignot-Ogliastri (Lyon: Centre d'Etudes Gidiennes, Université Lyon II, 1986);

Gide and Thea Sternheim, *Correspondance (1927–1950),* edited by Foucart (Lyon: Centre d'Etudes Gidiennes, Université Lyon II, 1986);

Gide, *Correspondance avec Francis Vielé-Griffin (1891–1931),* edited by Henry de Paysac (Lyon: Presses Universitaires de Lyon, 1986);

Gide and Jacques Copeau, *Correspondance,* 2 volumes, edited by Jean Claude (Paris: Gallimard, 1987);

Gide, *Correspondance avec André Ruyters (1895–1950),* edited by Martin and Victor Martin-Schmets (Lyon: Presses Universitaires de Lyon, 1987);

Gide, *Correspondance avec sa mère, 1880–1895,* edited by Martin (Paris: Gallimard, 1988);

Gide and Jean Schlumberger, *Correspondance 1901–1950,* edited by Pascal Mercier and Peter Fawcett (Paris: Gallimard, 1993);

Gide and Henri de Régnier, *Correspondance (1891–1911),* edited by David J. Niederauer and Heather Franklyn (Lyon: Presses Universitaires de Lyon, 1997);

Franz Blei and Gide, *Briefwechsel (1904–1933)* (Darmstadt: Wissenschaftliche Buchgesellschaft, 1997);

Gide and Jacques Rivière, *Correspondance 1909–1925: Lettres d'André Gide, Juliette Gide, Madeleine Rondeaux, et Elie Allégret,* edited by Pierre de Gaulmyn and Alain Rivière, with the collaboration of Kevin O'Neill and Stuart Barr (Paris: Gallimard, 1998);

L'Enfance de l'art: Correspondances avec Elie Allégret, 1886–1896, edited by Daniel Durosay (Paris: Gallimard, 1998);

Gide and Georges Simenon, *Sans trop de pudeur: Correspondance, 1938–1950; Suivie du Dossier G. S. d'André Gide,* edited by Benoît Denis, preface by Dominique Fernandez (Paris: Omnibus, 1999);

Gide and Jean Malaquais, *Correspondance 1935–1950, précédée de Historique de ma rencontre avec André Gide . . . ,* edited by Pierre Masson and Geneviève Millot-Nakach (Paris: Phébus, 2000);

Gide and Pierre de Massot, *Correspondance 1923–1950,* edited by Jacques Cotnam (Nantes: Centre d'Etudes Gidiennes, 2001);

Gide and Edouard Ducôté, *Correspondance 1895–1921,* edited by Pierre Lachasse (Nantes: Centre d'Etudes Gidiennes, 2002);

Gide, "Cher vieux: Lettres à Marcel Drouin (1895–1925)," *La Nouvelle Revue Française,* nos. 560, 561, 562 (January, April, June 2002): 1–29, 332–352, 338–360;

Gide and Aline Mayrisch, *Correspondance 1903–1946,* edited by Masson and Cornel Meder (Paris: Gallimard, 2003);

Gide, Valéry, and Pierre Louÿs, *Correspondances à trois voix, 1888–1920,* edited by Fawcett and Mercier (Paris: Gallimard, 2004).

Interviews:

Entretiens avec Jean Amrouche (Paris: Gallimard, 1949); as 2 CDs (Paris: INA/Radio France, 1996);

Eric Marty, *André Gide, qui êtes-vous? Avec les entretiens André Gide–Jean Amrouche* (Paris: La Manufacture, 1987).

Bibliographies:

Arnold Naville, *Bibliographie des écrits d'André Gide 1891–1952* (Paris: Guy le Prat, 1949);

Jacques Cotnam, *Bibliographie chronologique de l'oeuvre d'André Gide, 1889–1973* (Boston: G. K. Hall, 1974);

Cotnam, *Inventaire bibliographique et index analytique de la correspondance d'André Gide, publiée de 1897 à 1971* (Boston: G. K. Hall, 1975);

"Inventaire des traductions des oeuvres d'André Gide," *Bulletin des Amis d'André Gide,* nos. 28, 29, 30, 31, 35, 42, 46, 58 (1975–1983);

Claude Martin and others, *André Gide, correspondence générale (1879–1951): Répertoire, préface, chronologie, index et notices,* nos. 1–8 (Lyon: Centre d'Etudes Gidiennes, Université Lyon II, 1985);

Catharine Savage Brosman, *An Annotated Bibliography of Criticism on André Gide, 1973–1988* (New York & London: Garland, 1990).

Biographies:

Jean Schlumberger, *Madeleine et André Gide* (Paris: Gallimard, 1956); translated by Richard H. Akeroyd as *Madeleine and André Gide* (Tuscaloosa, Ala.: Portals Press, 1980);

Jean Delay, *La Jeunesse d'André Gide,* 2 volumes (Paris: Gallimard, 1956, 1957); abridged and translated by June Guicharnaud as *The Youth of André Gide* (Chicago: University of Chicago Press, 1963);

Claude Martin, *André Gide par lui-même* (Paris: Seuil, 1963);

George D. Painter, *André Gide, A Critical Biography* (New York: Atheneum, 1968);

Pierre de Boisdeffre, *Vie d'André Gide 1869–1951: Essai de biographie critique* (Paris: Hachette, 1970);

Maria van Rysselberghe, *Les Cahiers de la Petite Dame,* 4 volumes, Cahiers André Gide, nos. 4–7 (Paris: Gallimard, 1973–1977);

Martin, *La Maturité d'André Gide: De "Paludes" à "l'Immoraliste" 1895–1902* (Paris: Klincksieck, 1977);

Auguste Anglès, *André Gide et le premier groupe de "La Nouvelle Revue Française,"* 3 volumes (Paris: 1978–1986);

Pierre Lepape, *André Gide le messager: Biographie* (Paris: Seuil, 1997);

Martin, *Gide, ou, La vocation du bonheur* (Paris: Fayard, 1998);

Alan Sheridan, *André Gide: A Life in the Present* (Cambridge: Harvard University Press / Oxford: Oxford University Press, 1999);

Raphaël Dupouy, *André Gide, homme solaire* (Le Lavandou: Réseau Lalan, 2001);

Alain Goulet, *André Gide: Ecrire pour vivre* (Paris: Corti, 2002).

References:

André Gide, special issues of *Revue des Lettres Modernes,* nos. 1–11 (1970–   );

Emily Apter, *André Gide and the Codes of Homotextuality* (Saratoga, Cal.: Anma Libri, 1987);

Christopher D. Bettinson, *Gide: A Study* (Totowa, N.J.: Rowman & Littlefield, 1977);

Bettinson, *Gide–Les Caves du Vatican* (London: Arnold, 1972);

Germaine Brée, *André Gide, l'insaisissable Protée* (Paris: Les Belles Lettres, 1953); revised, enlarged, and translated as *André Gide* (New Brunswick: Rutgers University Press, 1963); French version of revised and enlarged edition (Paris: Les Belles Lettres, 1970);

Bulletin des Amis d'André Gide, 31 volumes (Lyon: Centre d'Etudes Gidiennes, Université de Lyon II, 1968–April 1985; Montpellier: Centre d'Etudes Littéraires du XXᵉ Siècle, Université de Montpellier III, July 1985–1988; Nanterre: Centre d'Etudes des Sciences de la Littérature, Université de Paris X, 1989–1990; Nanterre: Centre de Sémiotique/Recherches Interdisicplinaires sur les textes modernes, Université de Paris X, 1991; Lyon: Centre d'Etudes Gidiennes, 1992–April 1994; Nantes: Centre d'Etudes Gidiennes, July–October 1994–   );

Elaine D. Cancalon, *Techniques et personnages dans les récits d'André Gide,* Archives André Gide, no. 2 (Paris: Lettres Modernes, 1970);

Karin Nordenhaug Ciholas, *Gide's Art of the Fugue: A Thematic Study of "Les Faux-Monnayeurs"* (Chapel Hill: University of North Carolina Press, 1974);

Jean Claude, *André Gide et le théâtre,* 2 volumes, Cahiers André Gide, nos. 15–16 (Paris: Gallimard, 1992);

Thomas Cordle, *André Gide* (New York: Twayne, 1969);

Pamela Antonia Genova, *André Gide dans le labyrinthe de la mythotextualité* (West Lafayette, Ind.: Purdue University Press, 1995);

Alain Goulet, *"Les Caves du Vatican": Etude méthodologique* (Paris: Larousse, 1927);

Goulet, *Fiction et vie sociale dans l'œuvre d'André Gide,* 2 volumes (Paris: Minard, 1984, 1985);

W. Wolfgang Holdheim, *Theory and Practice of the Novel* (Geneva: Droz, 1968);

G. W. Ireland, *Gide: A Study of His Creative Writings* (London: Oxford University Press, 1970);

N. David Keypour, *Gide, écriture et réversibilité dans "Les Faux-Monnayeurs"* (Paris: Didier/Erudition / Montreal: Presses de l'Université de Montréal, 1980);

Philippe Lejeune, *Exercices d'ambiguïté: Lectures de "Si le grain ne meurt" d'André Gide* (Paris: Lettres Modernes, 1974);

David Littlejohn, ed., *Gide: A Collection of Critical Essays* (Englewood Cliffs, N.J.: Prentice-Hall, 1970);

Martine Maisani-Léonard, *Gide, ou l'ironie de l'écriture* (Montreal: Presses de l'Université de Montréal, 1976);

Roger Martin du Gard, *Notes sur André Gide, 1913–1951* (Paris: Gallimard, 1951); republished in Martin du Gard, *Œuvres complètes,* volume 2 (Paris: Gallimard, 1955); translated by John Russell as *Notes on André Gide* (London: Deutsch, 1953);

James C. McLaren, *The Theatre of André Gide: Evolution of a Moral Philosopher* (Baltimore: Johns Hopkins University Press, 1953);

Daniel Moutote, *Les Images végétales dans l'œuvre de Gide* (Paris: Presses Universitaires de France, 1970);

Moutote, *Index des idées, images et formules du "Journal" d'André Gide* (Lyon: Centre d'Etudes Gidiennes, 1985);

Moutote, *Le Journal d'André Gide et les problémes du moi 1889–1925* (Paris: Presses Universitaires de France, 1968);

Maurice Nadeau and Philippe Clerc, *Album Gide* (Paris: Gallimard, 1985);

H. J. Nersoyan, *André Gide. The Theism of an Atheist* (Syracuse, N.Y.: Syracuse University Press, 1969);

Justin O'Brien, *Index détaillé des quinze volumes de l'Edition Gallimard des "Œuvres complétes" d'André Gide* (Asnières-sur-Seine: Prétexte, 1954);

Kevin O'Neill, *André Gide and the "Roman d'aventure"* (Sydney: Sydney University Press, 1969);

Patrick Pollard, *André Gide, Homosexual Moralist* (New Haven: Yale University Press, 1991);

Vinio Rossi, *André Gide: The Evolution of an Aesthetic* (New Brunswick, N.J.: Rutgers University Press, 1967);

Catharine H. Savage [Brosman], *André Gide: L'évolution de sa pensée religieuse* (Paris: Nizet, 1962);

Ben Stoltzfus, *Gide's Eagles* (Carbondale & Edwardsville: Southern Illinois University Press / London & Amsterdam: Feffer & Simons, 1969);

Susan M. Stout, *Index de la Correspondance André Gide–Roger Martin du Gard* (Paris: Gallimard, 1971);

Paul Surer, *Cinquante ans de théâtre* (Paris: Société d'édition d'enseignement supérieur, 1969);

Wylie Sypher, "Gide's Cubist Novel," *Kenyon Review,* 11 (Spring 1949): 291–309;

Michael J. Tilby, *Gide, "Les Faux-Monnayeurs"* (London: Grant & Cutler, 1981);

C. D. E. Tolton, *Gide and the Art of Autobiography: A Study of "Si le grain ne meurt"* (Toronto: Maclean-Hunter Press, 1975);

David H. Walker, ed., *André Gide* (London & New York: Longman, 1996);

Helen Watson-Williams, *André Gide and the Greek Myth: A Critical Study* (Oxford: Clarendon Press, 1967).

Papers:

Fifty of André Gide's manuscripts and approximately twelve thousand letters are deposited at the Bibliotheque Littéraire Jacques Doucet, Paris. These manuscripts, including the manuscript for *Œdipe,* are listed in the *Catalogue de Fonds Spéciaux de Ia Bibliothèque Littéraire Jacques Doucet* (Boston: G. K. Hall, 1972). Additionally, Bibliothèque nationale de France purchased the manuscript of *Les Faux-Monnayeurs* from a private collection in 2001. Other manuscripts are located in the Harry Ransom Humanities Research Center, University of Texas at Austin, while still others remain in private hands.

Jean Giono
(30 March 1895 – 9 October 1970)

Guy F. Imhoff
Saint Bonaventure University

See also the Giono entry in *DLB 72: French Novelists, 1930–1960.*

PLAY PRODUCTIONS: *Lanceurs de graines,* Geneva, Compagnie des Quinze, 30 September 1932; Paris, Théâtre de l'Atelier, 10 November 1932; English translation by Joan Smith, London, June 1933;

Le Bout de la route, Paris, Théâtre des Noctambules, 30 May 1941;

La Femme du boulanger, Paris, Théâtre des Ambassadeurs, 11 May 1944;

Le Voyage en calèche, Paris, Théâtre du Vieux Colombier, 21 December 1947; revised as *La Calèche,* Paris, Théâtre Sarah Bernhardt, 15 December 1965;

Joseph à Dothan, by Joost Van den Vondel, adapted by Giono, Orange, Théâtre d'Orange, 29 July 1952;

J'ai connu Jean-Pierre Grenier, by Giono and others, Paris, Théâtre Marigny, 1959;

Domitien, Canseneuve, Vaucluse, August 1964.

BOOKS: *Accompagnés de la flûte* (Manosque: Les Cahiers de l'Artisan, 1924);

Colline, Collection Cahiers Verts (Paris: Grasset, 1929); translated by Jacques Le Clerq as *Hill of Destiny* (New York: Brentano's, 1929);

Un de Beaumugnes (Paris: Grasset, 1929); translated by Le Clerq as *Lovers Are Never Losers* (New York: Brentano's, 1931; London: Jarolds, 1932);

Manosque-des-Plateaux (Paris: Emile-Paul, 1930);

Naissance de l'Odyssée (Paris: Kra, 1930; Paris: Grasset, 1938);

Présentation de Pan, Collection Les Amis des Cahiers Verts (Paris: Grasset, 1930);

Regain (Paris: Grasset, 1930); translated by Henri Fluchère and Geoffrey Myers as *Harvest* (New York: Viking, 1939; London: Heinemann, 1940);

Solitude de la pitié (Paris: Cahiers Libres, 1930); translated as *The Solitude of Compassion,* afterword by Henry Miller (New York: Seven Stories, 2002);

Eglogues (Manche: Pou-qui-Grimpe Coutances, 1931);

Jean Giono (© AP Photo)

Le Grand Troupeau (Paris: Gallimard, 1931); translated by Norman Glass as *To the Slaughterhouse* (London: Owen, 1969);

Jean le Bleu (Paris: Grasset, 1932); translated by Katherine A. Clarke as *Blue Boy* (New York: Viking, 1946; London: Routledge, 1948);

Le Serpent d'étoiles (Paris: Grasset, 1933);

Le Chant du monde (Paris: Gallimard, 1934); translated by Fluchère and Myers as *The Song of the World* (New York: Viking, 1937; London & Toronto: Heinemann, 1938);

Que Ma joie demeure (Paris: Grasset, 1935); translated by Clarke as *Joy of Man's Desiring* (New York: Viking, 1940; London: Routledge & Kegan Paul, 1949);

Rondeur des jours (Alger: Les Vraies Richesses, 1936);

Les Vraies richesses (Paris: Grasset, 1936);

Batailles dans la montagne (Paris: Gallimard, 1937);

Le Bout de la route ([Alger]: La Société les Vraies Richesses, 1937);

Jean Giono et la Provence (Paris, 1937);

Jofroi de La Maussan (Paris: L'Ecole Municipale Estienne, 1937);

Refus d'Obéissance (Paris: Gallimard, 1937);

Entrée du Printemps (Paris: Gonin, 1938);

Lettres aux Paysans sur la pauvreté et la paix (Paris: Grasset, 1938);

Le Poids du ciel (Paris: Gallimard, 1938);

Premiers Poèmes-Eglogues, Premières Proses (Cannes: Cahiers du Contadour, 1938);

Précisions, Vivre libre, no. 2 (Paris: Grasset, 1939);

Provence (Paris: Plas, 1939; Vendée: La Source Perrier, 1939);

Pour saluer Melville (Paris: Gallimard, 1941);

Triomphe de la vie (Neuchâtel, Switzerland: Ides et Calendes, 1941; Paris: Grasset, 1942);

L'Eau vive (Paris: Gallimard, 1943);

Théâtre de Jean Giono (Paris: Gallimard, 1943)—comprises *Le Bout de la route; Lanceurs de graines; La Femme du boulanger;* and *Esquisse d'une mort d'Hélène;*

Du Côté de Baumugnes (Liège: Aelberts, 1945);

Le Voyage en calèche (Monaco: Rocher, 1946 [i.e., 1947]);

Noé (Paris: La Table Ronde, 1947);

Un Roi sans divertissement (Paris: La Table Ronde, 1947; Paris: Gallimard, 1947);

Fragments d'un déluge (Villeneuve-Saint-Georges: Fonteinas, 1948);

Fragments d'un paradis (Paris: G. Déchalotte, 1948);

Mort d'un personnage (Paris: Grasset, 1949);

Les Ames fortes (Paris: Gallimard, 1949);

Le Poids du ciel (Paris: Gallimard, 1949);

Village (Paris: Prochaska, 1950);

Les Grands chemins (Paris: Gallimard, 1951);

Le Hussard sur le toit (Paris: Gallimard, 1951); translated by Jonathan Griffin as *The Hussar on the Roof* (London: Museum Press, 1953); republished as *The Horseman on the Roof* (New York: Knopf, 1954);

Le Moulin de Pologne (Paris: Gallimard, 1952); translated by Peter de Mendelssohn as *The Malediction* (New York: Criterion, 1955; London: Museum Press, 1955);

Arcadie, Arcadie! (Manosque: Rico L'Artisan, 1953);

Recherche de la pureté, by Giono and Bernard Buffet, commentary by Pierre Bergé (Paris: Creuzevault, 1953);

Voyage en Italie (Paris: Gallimard, 1953); translated by John Cummings as *An Italian Journey* (Evanston, Ill.: Marlboro Press/Northwestern University Press, 1998);

Provence (Paris: Hachette, 1954; Paris: Klein, 1954);

L'Ecossais, ou La Fin des héros (Manosque: Aux Dépens du Rotary-Club de Manosque, 1955);

Notes sur l'affaire Dominici suivies de Essai sur le caractère des personnages (Paris: Gallimard, 1955); translated by Mendelssohn as *The Dominici Affair* (London: Museum Press, 1956);

La Pierre (La Chaux-de-Fonds, Switzerland: Méroz "pierres," Fabrique de pierres d'horlogerie, 1955);

Bernard Buffet (Paris: Hazen, 1956);

Giono par lui-même, edited by Claudine Chonez, Ecrivains de toujours, no. 32 (Paris: Seuil, 1956);

Lundi (Paris: Dutilleul, 1956);

Le Bonheur fou (Paris: Gallimard, 1957); translated by Phyllis Johnson as *The Straw Man* (New York: Knopf, 1959; London: Redman, 1961);

Provence (Manosque: Rico et Auphan, 1957);

Provence (Paris: Belle, 1957);

Angélo (Paris: Gallimard, 1958); translated by Alma E. Murch (London: Owen, 1960);

Hortense, ou L'Eau vive, by Giono and Alain Allioux (Paris: France-Empire, 1958);

Oppède le vieux (Manosque: Rico et Auphan, 1959);

Sur Des Oliviers morts (Périgueux: Fanlac, 1959);

Domitien, suivi de Joseph à Dothan (Paris: Gallimard, 1959);

Peintres de la réalité du XXe siècle (Paris: Hadès, 1960);

Camargue (Lausanne: Clairefontaine, 1960);

Images de Provence (Paris: Heures Claires, [1960s]);

Crésus: Livre de conduite du metteur en scène (Manosque: Rico et Auphan, 1961);

Ménagerie énigmatique (Paris: Aux dépens d'un Amateur, 1961);

Routes et Chemins avec Jean Giono et 56 peintres témoins de leur temps: Edition des peintres témoins de leurs temps à l'occasion de leur XIe exposition au Musée Galliera en 1962 (Paris: Les Presses artistiques, 1961);

Chroniques romanesques (Paris: Gallimard, 1962);

Le Désastre de Pavie, 24 février 1525, Collection Trente Journées qui ont fait la France (Paris: Gallimard, 1963); translated by Murch as *The Battle of Pavia, 24th February 1525* (London: Owen, 1965);

Manosque (Manosque: Rico, 1964);

Animalités (Paris: Klein, 1965);

Le Bal; L'Ecossais; Angélo; Le Hussard sur le toit (Paris: Gallimard, 1965);

Deux Cavaliers de l'orage (Paris: Gallimard, 1965); translated by Alan Brown as *Two Riders of the Storm* (London: Owen, 1967);

La Charge du roi (Paris: Maeght, 1965);

Le Haut pays (Paris: Editions d'Art les Heures claires, 1965);

Le Déserteur (Paudex, Switzerland & Lausanne, Switzerland: Fontainemore, 1966);

Le Génie du sud, edited by Claude-Annick Jacquet, Les Classiques de la civilisation française (Montreal, Paris & Brussels: Didier, 1967);

Préface à l'Iliade (Paris: Ecole Estienne, 1967);

Provence perdue (Manosque: Rotary-Club de Manosque, 1967);

Terre d'Or (Paris: Leiger, 1967);

Ennemonde et autres caractères (Paris: Gallimard, 1968); translated by David Le Vay as *Ennemonde* (London: Owen, 1970);

La Chute des anges; Un Délug; Le Cœur-cerf (Manosque: Rico, 1969);

Une Histoire d'amour (Manosque: Manosque, 1969);

L'Oiseau bagué: Contes (Paris: Le Livre de Poche, 1969);

L'Iris de Suse (Paris: Gallimard, 1970);

La Mission (Manosque: Manosque, 1971);

Les Récits de la demi-brigade (Paris: Gallimard, 1972);

Le Déserteur et autres récits (Paris: Gallimard, 1973);

Le Cheval fou: "Le Chant du monde," by Giono and Jean-Pierre Grenier, Collection Le manteau d'Arlequin (Paris: Gallimard, 1974);

Les Terrasses de l'Ile d'Elbe (Paris: Gallimard, 1976);

Faust au village (Paris: Gallimard, 1977);

Ecrits Pacifistes, Collection Idées, no. 387 (Paris: Gallimard, 1978);

Angélique (Paris: Gallimard, 1980);

Œuvres cinématographiques, edited by Jacques Mény (Paris: Gallimard, 1980);

Voilà le pays magique!: Textes choisis, preface by André Tillieu (Manosque: Mont-d'Or, 1980);

Cœurs, Passions, Caractères (Paris: Gallimard, 1982);

Dragoon, suivi de Olympe (Paris: Gallimard, 1982);

Les Trois arbres de Palzem (Paris: Gallimard, 1984);

De Homère à Machiavel, notes by Henri Godard, Cahiers Giono, no. 4 (Paris: Gallimard, 1986);

Manosque-des-Plateaux suivi de Poème de l'olive (Paris: Gallimard, 1986);

Les Images d'un jour de pluie, et autres récits de jeunesse (Paris: Auzou, 1987);

Nous avons tous fait des crèches, Collection Voilà le pays magique, no. 3 (Manosque: Mont-d'Or, 1987);

La Chasse au bonheur (Paris: Gallimard, 1988);

Il n'y avait plus qu'à marcher: Texte pour Jean Garcia (Cognac: Le Temps qu'il fait, 1989);

Le Bestiaire (Paris: Ramsay/De Cortanze, 1991);

Giono, l'humeur bell: Recueil d'articles, edited by Jacques Chabot (Aix-en-Provence: Université de Provence, 1992);

Le Noyau d'abricot (Paris: Jeanne, 1993);

Provence, edited by Godard (Paris: Gallimard, 1993);

Description de Marseille: Le 16 octobre 1939 (Entremont-le-Vieux: Quatuor, 1995);

Dans L'Odeur des collines, ou De l'Olympe à Manosque, Collection Grand pollen (Paris: Alternatives, 1998);

De Monluc à la "Série Noire," edited by Godard, Les Cahiers de la NRF, Cahiers Giono, no. 5 (Paris: Gallimard, 1998);

Virgile, ou Les palais de l'Atlantide, Eux & eux, no. 2 (Paris: Les Belles Lettres, 2001).

Collections: *Romans* (Paris: Gallimard, 1956);

Chroniques Romanesques (Paris: Gallimard, 1962);

Les Oeuvres de Jean Giono, 5 volumes, Collection Les Immortels Chefs-d'œuvres (Paris: Rombaldi, 1965–1967);

Œuvres romanesques complètes, 6 volumes, edited by Robert Ricatte, Bibliothèque de la Pléiade, nos. 230, 237, 256, 268, 285, and 312 (Paris: Gallimard, 1971–1983)–volume 5 (1980) includes *L'Homme qui plantait des arbres,* translated as *The Man Who Planted Trees,* afterword by Norma L. Goodrich (Chelsea, Vt.: Chelsea Green, 1985);

Les Oeuvres de Jean Giono, 10 volumes (Bièvres: Tartas, 1974–1977);

Récits et essais, edited by Pierre Citron and others, Bibliothèque de la Pléiade, no. 351 (Paris: Gallimard, 1988);

Romans et Essais 1928–1941, edited by Godard (Paris: Librairie générale française, 1992);

Journal–Poèmes–Essais, edited by Citron and others, Bibliothèque de la Pléiade, no. 415 (Paris: Gallimard, 1995).

Editions in English: *The Man Who Planted Trees,* translated by Barbara Bray, afterword by Aline Giono (London: Harvill, 1995);

Second Harvest, translated by Henri Fluchere and Geoffrey Myers (London: Harvill, 1999).

PRODUCED SCRIPTS: *L'Eau vive,* by Giono and Alain Allioux, motion picture, Caravelle, 1957; dubbed into English as *Girl and the River;*

La Duchesse, motion picture, 1959;

Le Foulard de Smyrne, motion picture, 1959;

Crésus, motion picture, Les Films Jean Giono, 1959;

Un Roi sans divertissement, motion picture, Les Films Jean Giono, 1963;

"Le Chevelure d'Atalante," television, *Provinces,* Office de Radiodiffusion Télévision Française, 1968.

OTHER: Maria Borrély, *Le Dernier feu,* preface by Giono (Paris: Gallimard, 1931);

Catalogue de l'Exposition du peintre M.-O. Coubine, preface by Giono (N.p., 1934);

Antoon Coolen, *Le Bon assassin,* preface by Giono (Paris: Grasset, 1936);

Marcel Pagnol, *Regain,* adapted from Giono's novel, preface by Giono (Paris & Marseille: Pagnol, 1937);

Jacques Lucien, Catalogue de l'exposition à Aix-en-Provence, preface by Giono (N.p., 1938);

Jacques Lucien, *Carnets de moleskine,* preface by Giono (Paris: Gallimard, 1939);

Léon Isnardy, *Géographie du départment des Basses-Alpes,* preface by Giono (Manosque: Mollet, 1939);

Herman Melville, *Moby Dick,* translated by Giono, Jean Smith, and Lucien (Paris: Gallimard, 1941);

J. Poucel, *A la découverte des orchidées de France,* preface by Giono (Paris: Stock, 1942);

Samivel, *L'Opéra de pics,* preface by Giono (Grenoble: Arthaud, 1944);

Anton Hansen Tammsaare, *La terre-du-voleur,* preface by Giono (Paris: Trémois, 1946);

L'exposition d'Edith Berger à la Galerie Pelletan-Helleu, preface by Giono (Paris, 1947);

Les Pages immortelles de Virgile (Paris: Corrêa, 1947; Paris: Buchet-Chastel, 1960);

Exposition du peintre Bourdil, preface by Giono (1948);

L'Iliade d'Homère, preface by Giono (Paris: Bordas, 1950);

Maurice Chauvet, *La Route du vin,* preface by Giono (Montpellier: Arceaux, 1950);

Charles Agniel, *Les Compagnons de la bonne auberge,* preface by Giono (Paris: Table Ronde, 1952);

Niccolò Machiavelli, *Œuvres complètes,* preface by Giono (Paris: Gallimard, 1952);

Albert Detaille, *La Provence merveilleuse,* preface by Giono (Marseille: Detaille, 1953);

Exposition de Geneviève Gallibert, preface by Giono (N.p.: Maison Française d'Oxford, 1954);

Ernest Borrély, *Basses-Alpes, Haute Provence, aspect géographique, historique, touristique, économique et administratif du département,* introduction by Giono (Paris: Alépée, 1955);

Félix Leclerc, *Moi, mes souliers,* preface by Giono (Paris: Amiot-Dumont, 1955);

Jacques Meuris, *Le Journal de Provence,* preface by Giono (Brussels & Paris: Dutilleul, 1955);

Exposition de Bernard Buffet, preface by Giono (Aix-en-Provence, 1955);

Maurice Pezet, *Les Alpilles au cœur de la Provence,* preface by Giono (Paris: Horizons de France, 1955);

Niccolò Machiavelli, *Toutes les lettres officielles et familières, celles de ses seigneurs, de ses amis et des siens,* edited by Edmond Barincou, preface by Giono (Paris: Gallimard, 1955);

Bernard Buffet, *Horreur de la guerre,* preface by Giono (Paris: Parenthèses, 1955);

Lucien Jacques, Catalogue de l'exposition à Marseille, preface by Giono (N.p., 1956);

Lucien Jacques aquarelles, preface by Jean Giono (Manosque: Editions de l'artisan, 1956);

Romée de Villeneuve, *Dix Ans d'erreurs,* preface by Giono (Avignon: Presses Universelles, 1956);

Lucien Jacques, Catalogue de l'exposition à la Galerie d'Orsay, preface by Giono (N.p., 1957);

Exposition de Bernard Buffet à la Galerie Charpentier, preface by Giono (Paris, 1958);

Maurice Chevaly, *Fleurs artificielles,* preface by Giono (Aix-en-Provence: Editions de la Pensée Universitaire, 1958);

Georges Pillement, *Rome que j'aime,* preface by Giono (Paris: Sun, 1958);

Régina Wallet, *Le Sang de la vigne,* preface by Giono (Paris: Scorpion, 1958);

René Héron de Villefosse, *L'Epopée bohémienne,* preface by Giono (Paris: Klein, 1959);

Charles Dickens, *De Grandes Espérances,* translated by Pierre Leyris, preface by Giono (Paris: Le Livre de Poche, 1959);

Maximilien Vox, *Conversations de Napoléon Bonaparte,* preface by Giono (Paris: Planète, 1959);

Georges Navel, *Chacun son royaume,* preface by Giono (Paris: Gallimard, 1960);

Fernand Dartigues, *En vers . . . mais contre tous!* preface by Giono (Cannes: Dartigues, 1961);

François Morénas and Claude Morénas, *Circuits de découverte des Monts de Vaucluse, Gordes et le Haut-Pays lavandier,* preface by Giono (Saignon: Auberge de Jeunesse, 1961; republished, 1970; republished, Le Coudrayacouard: Cheminements en Provence, 1997); preface reprinted in François Morénas, *L'Hôtel des renards* (Paris: Calmann-Lévy, 1980);

Tableau de la littérature française de Rutebeuf à Descartes, volume 1, preface by Giono (Paris: Gallimard, 1962);

Michel de Montaigne, *Journal de voyage en Italie par la Suisse et l'Allemagne en 1580 et 1581,* afterword by Giono (Paris: Mazenod, 1962);

Exposition de Willy Eisenschitz à la galerie Montmorency, preface by Giono (Paris, 1964);

Tristan: La Merveilleuse Histoire de Tristan et Yseut, preface by Giono (Paris: Grasset, 1964);

Blaise de Monluc, *Commentaires,* preface by Giono (Paris: Gallimard, 1964);

Juan Ramón Jiménez, *Platero et moi,* preface by Giono (Paris: Rombaldi, 1964);

Pierre Mélet, *Antonaves, mille ans d'histoire,* preface by Giono (Antonaves, Hautes-Alpes: Les Amis du Village, 1965);

Raymond Collier and others, *Monuments et art de Haute-Provence,* preface by Giono (Digne: Société scientifique et littéraire des Basses-Alpes, 1966);

Sëi Shonagon, *Les notes de chevet,* Connaissance de l'Orient, no. 22, preface by Giono (Paris: Gallimard, 1966);

Yves Brayer, preface by Giono (Paris: La Bibliothèque des Arts, 1967);

Marius Audier, *La Vie du cardiaque,* preface by Giono (Paris: Hachette, 1968);

Claude Frégnac, *Merveilles des palais italiens,* preface by Giono (Paris: Hachette, Collections "Réalités," 1968); translated by Frégnac as *Great Houses of Italy* (London: Weidenfeld & Nicolson, 1968);

Catalogue de l'Exposition de Renée Arbour à Manosque, preface by Giono (Manosque, 1969);

Pavillon de Vendôme: Paysages du Midi, de Cézanne à Derain, preface by Giono (Aix-en-Provence: Pavillon de Vendôme, 1969);

Catalogue des Expositions d'Anne-Marie Avon-Campana, preface by Giono (N.p., 1969; reprinted, 1985);

Antoon Coolen, *La Faute de Jeanne Le Coq,* preface by Giono (Paris: Autrement, 1995).

Jean Giono is best known as a novelist who rejected the modern, industrialized world and advocated a return to a simple existence in harmony with nature. His characters are often peasants who love the earth and artisans who find their satisfaction in work well done. His early novels teach the need for personal happiness, achievable only through separation from society and its evils, while his later works adopt a collective notion of happiness. Giono admitted that he found writing for the theater difficult. According to Maxwell A. Smith, Giono wrote his plays quickly for fear that they would become novels if he did not do so. Yet, he managed to introduce important characters and plots to the French stage, many of them related to the work he accomplished in his novels as he explored the types of people and situations faced by modern man.

Antoine Jean Giono was born on 30 March 1895, in Manosque, the largest city of La Haute Provence (Upper Provence), to Antoine Jean Giono, a shoemaker, and Pauline Pourcin, a laundress. His paternal grandfather, an Italian exile who loved to tell stories, was the inspiration for many of Giono's fictional characters. Giono never finished his formal education. In 1911, because his father contracted a lengthy illness, Giono took a job as an office boy at a bank to help support his parents. However, he educated himself in literature during lunch break by reading the Latin and Greek classics, as well as Dante, Miguel de Cervantes, and Johann Wolfgang van Goethe. He wrote and published poems in a local newspaper between 1913 and 1916. His experiences in the trenches of World War I at the battles of the Somme and the Kemmel made him a believer in pacifism, which became a major theme of his literary work.

Cover for a late American edition of Giono's 1932 novel, a narrative thread of which formed the basis for Marcel Pagnol's movie La Femme du boulanger (The Baker's Wife), *as well as for Giono's 1943 play of the same title (Bruccoli Clark Layman Archives)*

After his discharge from the army in 1920, Giono returned to Manosque and his work at the bank, where he eventually became undermanager. That year Giono's father died, and Giono married a local woman, Elise Maurin, a hairdresser's daughter. Giono continued publishing poems during the years 1921 to 1923, and in 1926 he made his first attempt at writing for the theater, *Esquisse d'une mort d'Hélène* (Sketch of Helen's Death). The work was never produced. According to Pierre Citron, it is not really a play but rather a dialogue. Francis Rouillet-Renouleau describes it as a suite of "lyrical modulations." The dialogue describes the death of Helen of Troy and the mourning of her nurse. Giono employs natural imagery in the scene: a peach flower slowly falls as two pigeons kiss and disappear in the shadow of a pillar.

Giono's daughter Aline was born on 25 October 1926. In 1929 Giono, after having met some of the leading French literary figures of the time, including André Gide and André Chamson, decided to earn his living as a writer. He resigned from the bank, where he had just been promoted to branch manager. Giono soon experienced success. In 1930 he won the American Brentano Prize for his novel *Colline* (1929; translated as *Hill of Destiny*, 1929) and the Northcliffe Prize for the novel *Regain* (1930; translated as *Harvest*, 1939), for which he also won the Prix Corrard (Corrard Prize) in 1931. Giono's pacifist ideals made him the leader of Le Contadour, a group of Provençal writers and others known for their promotion of peace and love of the earth, many of whom lived collectively on a plot of land at Contadour beginning in 1935. Giono and a friend, painter Lucien Jacques, founded *Cahiers du Cantadour* (Notebooks of the Cantadour), which lasted from 1936 to 1939, when the group was dissolved on the eve of war.

Giono's second dramatic effort, *Le Bout de la route* (published in 1931, produced in 1941, The End of the Road), is set on a small farm. It opens with a man named Jean arriving late at night after a long trip. He left his village because of the unfaithfulness of his wife, whom he still loves, and is traveling in search of a place where he can live in peace, alone with the memory of his spouse. Albert, a visiting shepherd, welcomes him to the farm. Rosine, a hard-working widow, owns the farm and lives there with both her mother and her daughter Mina, whom Albert loves.

The scenic directions for *Le Bout de la route* are a mixture of straightforward detail and poetry. At the beginning of act 1, Giono specifies the setting as a peasant home, and he describes the age, physical characteristics, and clothing of the characters. In act 1, scene 8, Giono explains that the audience should hear the grandfather clock "live," and in scene 9, he directs the grandmother to wear a dress embossed with flowers of gold and blue "like an old dream." Although the protagonist, Jean, is a peasant, he speaks more like a poet, using emotional, imagistic language to praise the natural world, the need for contact with the earth, and the value of love. He encourages Mina to enjoy life, listen to the waters sing, and hear the blood of her lover, Albert. Meanwhile, Jean is attached to his past, including his wife–both he and the grandmother exchange memories of their lost loved ones. For Citron, Jean resembles Giono himself, and W. D. Redfern similarly argues that Jean demonstrates a superior knowledge that makes him Giono's spokesman.

At the beginning of the play Rosine appears to champion work alone. However, as Jean settles on the farm and indicates that he wants nothing more than to work and live alone, she suggests that he find a wife in order to establish an equilibrium among the conflicting demands of work, love, and family. According to Rosine, this situation is Jean's only chance for happiness: "La terre sait ce qu'elle fait. Si tu es vivant, c'est que tu dois faire ton travail. C'est l'ordre. Et l'ordre, mon petit gars, quand on est bâti comme tu l'es, c'est la femme. C'est l'enfant. Les enfants. La vie!" (Earth knows what it does. If you are alive, that means that you must do your work. It is the order. And order, my friend, when one is built like you, is the wife. It is the child. Children! Life!) But after his wife's infidelity, Jean feels that love has abandoned him. When he understands that Mina has fallen in love with him, he decides to leave the farm because too many *les vivants* (living people) are around him. Jean hopes that the end of the road is a little bit further along. The play was first produced in May 1941 at the Théâtre des Noctambules in Paris and enjoyed great success during the German Occupation because, according to Rouillet-Renouleau, it generally evoked the values of work, family, and homeland supported by the Vichy government.

Lanceurs de graines (produced in 1932, published in 1943, Sowers of Seeds) is also set on a farm and takes as its subject the clash of the old and modern worlds. In the opening scene, Aubert has decided to leave the family farm because he cannot accept the fact that his widowed mother Delphine has married Maître Antoine, a man who wants to introduce more modern methods of agriculture that will harm nature. While the mother takes the side of the husband, Aubert and a young servant named Catherine become allies. After Aubert's departure, Antoine and his men undertake the destruction of an old oak tree and a small lake. Afterward, a storm approaches and the domesticated animals run away from the farm. Antoine gets lost in the woods, and Delphine, who goes after her husband during the storm, does not recognize the way back home. When Antoine finds his way back, he is feverish but remorseful for his attack on nature. He dies as Aubert returns to declare his love to Catherine and vows to take care of the farm in the old, traditional ways.

Lanceurs de graines contributed significantly to Giono's international reputation. The first production in Geneva, Switzerland, in September 1932 was followed by Parisian productions at the Théâtre de l'Atelier in November and the Théâtre Montmartre in December. It was later staged in London, Brussels, Oslo, Frankfurt, Prague, and Vienna. As in *Le Bout de*

Portrait of Giono painted by Serge Fiorio in 1933, around the time Giono became active among Le Contadour, a group of writers and intellectuals devoted to peace and love of the earth (© 2004 Artists Rights Society [ARS], New York/BONO, Oslo)

la route, the setting is realistic. The language is less poetic than in Giono's other plays and allows the reader to concentrate on the conflict between the two male characters at the center of the story. Aubert, like Jean of *Le Bout de la route,* is a solitary figure, but his separation from society stems from his love of nature, his dislike of capitalism, and his championship of the artisan, all of which make him unable to accept his new family situation and the destruction of the traditional farm. Antoine, on the contrary, is a capitalist who wants to make money out of nature. Aubert sees Antoine's emphasis on profit as selfish and improper: "Toi, tu veux raser tout ce qui existe et semer des graines pour ton plaisir . . . tout arracher ce qu'est la nature naturelle" (You want to destroy what is, and sow grain for your pleasure . . . against what is natural). Meanwhile, nature becomes an active character in the play. Because water screamed when they started their work, the workers admit that "C'est une maline. J'ai entendu là-bas dedans que ça ballotait sourdement" (It has intelligence. I heard it boil underground). Nature takes revenge against the workers in the form of the storm and the animals' flight. When Antoine returns home from the storm, he seeks a way to talk to the trees and apologize for his actions, but he knows it is too late to learn their language. He dies without reconciling himself to nature; yet, he has learned that humanity and nature must cooperate because nature is also capable of destruction.

Finally, the relationship between men and women emerges as an important secondary theme of *Lanceurs de graines.* The young servant Catherine asks Delphine if a woman's love has any importance to a man. Delphine does not answer the question, ministering instead to her dying husband's needs. Nevertheless, in the play's conclusion, Catherine indicates her willingness to cooperate with Aubert for the good of the farm by agreeing to marry him. This ending represents the hope for a young couple, symbolizing a future generation, to start anew and save the world

Title page for the first edition of Giono's only play (The Barouche Trip) that deals explicitly with war. Set in Italy during Napoleon's invasion, the background and action parallel the German occupation of France during World War II (Howard-Tilton Memorial Library, Tulane University).

from the destructive forces of capitalism and greed. This hope for another Eden is essential to Giono's work.

Like other French writers of the period, Giono was attracted to communism. In the early 1930s Giono wrote articles for *Vendredi* (Friday), a left-wing antifascist newspaper. On 11 August 1934 he and his wife had another daughter, Sylvie. Giono stopped writing for *Vendredi* around 1935, after the Communist Party advocated military intervention against Adolf Hitler, Benito Mussolini, and Francisco Franco. Because of his opposition to war and unwillingness to serve, Giono was arrested and held for two months in Marseille in 1939, enduring solitary confinement for twenty days. Upon his release, he received a certificate of demobilization that excused him from military service. After World War II, Giono was arrested in 1945 and imprisoned for six months in Fort St. Vincent in the Alps, this time by Communists who accused him of Nazi sympathies because he continued to publish during the war. Giono was put on *La liste noire du Comité national des écrivains* (The Black List of the National Committee of Writers), which prevented him from publishing anything for two years.

During the war Giono composed *La Femme du boulanger* (published 1943, The Baker's Wife), which premiered in Paris at the Théâtre des Ambassadeurs on 11 May 1944. The play evokes a popular Gionian subject, the artisan and his important role in the life of a village. A baker named Honoré and his wife, Aurélie, live a simple life in a small town. Honoré works hard to provide bread for the community and, through these efforts, a comfortable life for his wife. Aurélie, however, longs for something more. Honoré tries to understand her melancholia, but his simplicity cannot penetrate his spouse's sadness. Aurélie soon decides to run away with a shepherd, and the baker stops baking bread because he has no more reason to live. The whole village starts to suffer, and soon everyone tries to find the baker's wife so he will start baking bread again.

The story of the baker's wife originated in Giono's novel *Jean le Bleu* (1932; translated as *Blue Boy*, 1946), but it was made famous by Marcel Pagnol in his movie *The Baker's Wife* (1938). Giono staged his play after a disagreement with Pagnol concerning the rights to movie scripts that Pagnol had written based on Giono's books. They argued about their level of participation in the writing of these scripts, and Giono sued Pagnol, but lost. Critics agree that the play was not a success. Citron considers the dialogue obscure, while Rouillet-Renouleau states that Giono could not forget the movie while writing the play. The language is uncharacteristic of Giono, especially the sexual allusions at the opening of the play. There are few stage directions beyond the description of Madame Perotte, the Baron's stewardess, in act 2.

Jean le Bleu features a series of long dialogues. In act 1, Honoré and his wife have a lengthy conversation in which the husband tries to understand what is bothering his wife. When she disappears from the bakery, several characters come onstage to speak with Honoré: three women dressed in black, three men who talk about the charms of the baker's wife, and a young woman willing to give herself to the baker to help him forget his sorrow. The first act ends with these characters trying to convince the baker to bake bread, but he will not change his mind until his wife is found.

The second act takes place at a castle, where Giono re-creates the social structure of a typical French village of his time, with a baron, his stewardess, his three nieces, a priest, and a teacher. The play takes an unexpected turn as Honoré arrives drunk and explains why he believes he and all those around him have died. Although more comical than the protagonists of *Le Bout de la route* and *Lanceurs de graines*, Honoré resembles them in his role as an artisan: he exercises power in the village, and, without his bread, the village cannot survive. His idealistic view of love—he simply wants his wife back, in spite of her infidelity—sets him apart from the other villagers. His cleverness gives him superiority over nobility, church, and social institutions, since all acquiesce to his will. At the end of the play Aurélie comes back to her husband as he waits for her in the marshes. He has brought something warm for her to wear while they return home to begin life anew.

Le Voyage en calèche (published and performed, 1947, The Barouche Trip) is the only play in which Giono deals with the subject of war. The action takes place in Italy in 1797, during the invasion of the Napoleonic armies. Consalvo, a young Italian outlaw, takes the name Julio and pretends to be a servant in the castle of an opera singer named Fulvia. In the search for Consalvo, Colonel Vincent and his troops arrive at the castle, where the colonel makes amorous propositions to Fulvia. In response, Julio reveals his true identity to Fulvia, kidnaps her, and forces her to leave with him in his barouche. They find refuge in an old castle, where the owner–who, like Julio, does not like Napoleon–agrees to hide them. However, Vincent arrives at the castle and finds Fulvia, whom he now believes to be a traitor.

In the second act, Fulvia, who has been arrested, is allowed to give a performance to the French armies before she is executed at dawn. Soon Julio and his servant John arrive, and, using a counterfeited document, they are able to convince Vincent to dispatch the French armies to different parts of the country and to free Fulvia. In the third and final act, Vincent and Fulvia are in the woods watching the armies as they leave to wage war elsewhere. Fulvia has decided to marry Vincent, but John arrives to announce Julio's death, which Fulvia suspects may be her fault. As the colonel leaves for a few moments, Julio, who has only pretended to be dead, arrives, and Fulvia realizes that he is the one she loves. They ride away together in a barouche, but they are killed by the bullets of the French army.

Julio is a familiar character in Giono's drama. He is learned in literature and, like Giono's other male protagonists, speaks in a lyrical and imagistic language. Also, he does not kill; rather, he wants the enemy to leave the land because he dislikes war and its accompanying atrocities. During his many exchanges with Vincent, Julio makes his pacifism clear: "Avez-vous vraiment l'espérance, colonel, de construire un monde commun par l'ébranlement concerté de grandes masses d'hommes; quand il y a plus de ressources humaines dans la cervelle d'un enfant que dans les bureaux de tous les ministres d'Europe? . . . C'est parce que je connais la misère du peuple que j'occupe la tranchée face à vous" (Do you really think you can build a common world by the destruction of masses of people when there are more resources in a child's brain than in all offices of European ministers? . . . I know the people's misery, that's why I am against you). According to Ibrahim H. Badr, Julio sees heroism as a "solitary combat motivated by a personal initiative." Badr argues that Julio objects to heroism in the service of nationalism because he sees it as a degrading solitude that takes away the freedom of choice so important to Giono. Julio explains the importance of individuality to Fulvia: an individual is "indivisible" according to etymology, "useless" according to politics. During a discussion with Vincent, Julio emphasizes the power of individuality as Vincent, for whom war is simply a job, reminds him that the army is composed of forty thousand willing men and that he, Julio, is alone: Julio responds by saying, "A vouloir aussi, colonel" (Also willing, colonel). Julio is not only a pacifist but close to nature; he loves the forest and the smell of wet earth. He differs, however, from Giono's characters who are peasants because his goal is to protect the homeland against the enemy instead of cultivating the land. Meanwhile, Fulvia is also a well-developed character who over the course of the play changes her interests from flirtation to love of country.

The most ambitious of Giono's plays, *Le Voyage en calèche* requires six hours to perform in its entirety. The subject of the play is derived from contemporary historical reality, the occupation of France by the Germans. In Smith's opinion, the play proves that Giono never sympathized with the German invaders. It was canceled by German censors during rehearsals and only premiered after World War II, on 21 December 1947, in Paris at the Théâtre du Vieux Colombier. Giono later composed an adaptation of the play titled *La Calèche*, which was first staged in Paris at the Théâtre Sarah Bernhardt on 15 December 1965.

Giono's next play, *Joseph à Dothan* (1952, Joseph in Dothan), is a translation of a tragedy written in 1640 by the famous seventeenth-century Dutch dramatist Joost van Den Vondel. The cultural attaché of the Netherlands had asked for a translation of the play in honor of a visit by the Dutch Queen, Juliana, to France, and Giono accepted the task, although he did not write his adaptation in verse like the original. It premiered in the Provençal city of Orange at the

Title page for Giono's screenplay for a 1959 movie, which featured French comic actor Fernandel (Robert W. Woodruff Library, Emory University)

Théâtre d'Orange on 29 July 1952. The play recounts the story of Genesis 37, the betrayal of Joseph by his jealous brothers. Giono followed the original text but at the end of the play added a monologue by Ruben, the good brother who saved Joseph's life by selling him into slavery. Little has been written about this play. Citron wonders if Joseph represents Giono with his dreams and prophetic mission; Smith underlines the fact that Giono recommended the use of modern clothing for performances of the play in order to "accentuate the universality of this drama of ignominy and jealousy."

In 1953 Giono won the Prix Littéraire de Monaco (The Literature Prize of Monaco), and the following year he was elected to L'Académie Goncourt (The Goncourt Academy), replacing the French writer Colette. Giono's next play, *Domitien* (1964), differs from his earlier dramatic efforts. Written for the radio, it consists of scenes describing the last days of the life of the Roman emperor Domitian. As the play unfolds, Giono describes a popular revolt, the actions of Domitian at court and on the battlefield, and Domitian's awareness that he will be killed by the people he trusts the most. At the end of the play, Domitian appears as a tired man who welcomes death because of the loneliness of his life. Giono gives few directions for the actors or about sound effects, for the most part allowing the dialogue to speak for itself.

During the final fifteen years of his life, Giono continued to write, turning his talents to travel books, prefaces for works by others, and the cinema. In 1959 he wrote the screenplay for, and helped direct, *Crésus,* which starred the well-known French comic actor Fernandel. During these years Giono traveled to England and throughout Italy, but he always returned to the Provençal town where he spent most of his life. Giono died of a heart attack in his native Manosque on the night of 8–9 October 1970.

Jean Giono's theater is significant for the characters it introduced to the French stage. His peasant protagonists are extraordinary, as are both the outlaw hero of *Le Voyage en calèche* and the Emperor Domitian. According to Badr, Giono's characters find themselves isolated in a hostile world. They express sensitivity and idealism in lyrical language that sometimes results in unusually long monologues and dialogues. Hence, Redfern suggests that "It is by his language that, finally, Giono is to be judged . . . Giono is one of the few writers to indulge in a grand style in an age when epics, if written at all, are written small."

Letters:

Correspondance Jean Giono–Lucien Jacques, 2 volumes, edited by Pierre Citron, Cahiers Giono, nos. 1 and 3 (Paris: Gallimard, 1981, 1983)–comprises volume 1: *1922–1929;* and volume 2: *1930–1961;*

Giono and André Gide, *Correspondance 1929–1940,* edited by Roland Bourneuf and Jacques Cotnam (Lyon: Centre d'Etudes Gidiennes, Université de Lyon II, 1983 [i.e., 1984]);

Entretiens avec Jean Amrouche et Taos Amrouche, edited by Henri Godard (Paris: Gallimard, 1990);

Giono and Jean Guéhenno, *Correspondance 1928–1969,* edited by Citron, Collection "Missives" (Paris: Seghers, 1991);

Giono and Jean Paulhan, *Correspondance 1928–1963,* edited by Citron, Cahiers Giono, no. 6 (Paris: Gallimard, 2000).

Bibliography:

Jean Morel, *Bibliographie et médiagraphie des oeuvres de Jean Giono* (Paris & Manosque: Association des amis de Jean Giono/Printemps, 2000).

Biography:

Pierre Citron, *Giono 1895–1970* (Paris: Seuil, 1995).

References:

Serge Added, *Le Théâtre dans les années Vichy, 1940–1944,* preface by Maurice Vaïsse (Paris: Ramsay, 1992);

Ibrahim H. Badr, *Giono et la guerre: Idéologie et imaginaire,* Currents in Comparative Romance Languages and Literatures, no. 77 (New York: Peter Lang, 2000);

Badr, *Jean Giono: L'esthétique de la violence,* Currents in Comparative Romance Languages and Literatures, no. 60 (New York: Peter Lang, 1998);

Pierre Brisson, *Du Meilleur au Pire (à travers le théâtre)* (Paris: Gallimard, 1937);

Françoise Cespedes, Bernard Baritaud, and Véronique Anglard, *L'idée de Bonheur chez Stendhal, Gide, Giono,* Littérature vivante, no. 111 (Paris: Bordas, 1991);

Gérard Diebolt, "Le Théâtre de Jean Giono," dissertation, Université de Strasbourg, 1977);

Henri Fluchère, *Hommage à Jean Giono* (Manosque: Rotary-Club, 1971);

Laurent Fourcault, "Edition critique de deux pièces de Jean Giono: Le Bout de la route et Le Voyage en calèche," dissertation, Université de la Sorbonne Nouvelle, 1985;

Michel Grammain, "La Réception de l'oeuvre de Jean Giono de 1934 à 1944," dissertation, Université de Lilles;

Jean Pierre Grenier, "Giono et le théâtre," *L'arc,* 100 (1986);

Dorothy Knowles, *French Drama of the Inter-War Years: 1918–1939* (London, Toronto, Wellington & Sydney: Harrap, 1967 [i.e., 1968]);

Jean-Marie Leissing, *Découverte du Monde chez C.-F. Ramuz et Jean Giono: Thèse Lettres Zurich* (Zurich: Juris, 1972);

Henri Peyre, *Contemporary French Literature: A Critical Anthology* (New York, Evanston & London: Harper & Row, 1964);

Jacques Pugnet, *Jean Giono,* preface by Paul Morand, Classiques du XXe siècle, no. 21 (Paris: Editions Universitaires, 1955);

W. D. Redfern, *The Private World of Jean Giono* (Durham, N.C.: Duke University Press, 1967);

Jean Ricatte, "Variations sur *La Femme du boulanger,*" *Jean Giono: Les Œuvres de transition 1938–1944: Revue des Lettres Modernes,* 5 (1991): 79–99;

Francis Rouillet-Renouleau, *Théâtralité de Jean Giono,* dissertation, Université de Nantes, 1996;

Maxwell A. Smith, *Jean Giono,* World Authors Series, no. 7 (New York: Twayne, 1966);

Louis Theubet, "Edition critique de deux pièces de Jean Giono: Lanceurs de graines et Domitien," dissertation, Université de Paris IV, 1983.

Papers:

Collections of Jean Giono's papers are held at the Lilly Library, Indiana University, Bloomington, Indiana, and at the Beinecke Rare Book and Manuscript Library, Yale University, New Haven, Connecticut.

Jean Giraudoux
(29 October 1882 – 31 January 1944)

Catharine Savage Brosman
Tulane University

See also the Giraudoux entry in *DLB 65: French Novelists, 1900–1930.*

PLAY PRODUCTIONS: *Siegfried,* Paris, Comédie des Champs-Elysées, 3 May 1928;
Amphitryon 38, Paris, Comédie des Champs-Elysées, 8 November 1929;
Judith, Paris, Théâtre Pigalle, 4 November 1931;
Intermezzo, Paris, Comédie des Champs-Elysées, 1 March 1933;
Tessa, Paris, Théâtre de l'Athénée, 14 November 1934;
La Guerre de Troie n'aura pas lieu, Paris, Théâtre de l'Athénée, 22 November 1935;
Supplément au voyage de Cook, Paris, Théâtre de l'Athénée, 22 November 1935;
Electre, Paris, Théâtre de l'Athénée, 13 May 1937;
L'Impromptu de Paris, Paris, Théâtre de l'Athénée, 4 December 1937;
Cantique des cantiques, Paris, Comédie-Française, 13 October 1938;
Ondine, Paris, Théâtre de l'Athénée, 4 May 1939;
L'Apollon de Marsac, Rio de Janeiro, Municipal Theatre, 16 June 1942; Paris, Théâtre de l'Athénée, 19 April 1947;
Sodome et Gomorrhe, Paris, Théâtre Hébertot, 11 October 1943;
La Folle de Chaillot, Paris, Théâtre de l'Athénée, 22 December 1945;
Pour Lucrèce, Paris, Théâtre Marigny, 6 November 1953.

BOOKS: *Provinciales* (Paris: Grasset, 1909);
L'Ecole des indifférents (Paris: Grasset, 1911);
Retour d'Alsace: Août 1914 (Paris: Emile-Paul, 1916);
Lectures pour une ombre (Paris: Emile-Paul, 1917); translated by Elizabeth S. Sargent as *Campaigns and Intervals* (Boston & New York: Houghton Mifflin, 1918);
Simon le pathétique (Paris: Grasset, 1918; revised, 1926);
Amica America (Paris: Emile-Paul, 1918);
Promenade avec Gabrielle (Paris: Gallimard, 1919);

Jean Giraudoux (© Lipnitzki/Roger-Viollet/Getty Images)

Elpénor (Paris: Emile-Paul, 1919); translated by Richard Howard, with the assistance of Renaud Bruce (New York: Noonday Press, 1958);
Adorable Clio (Paris: Emile-Paul, 1920);
Suzanne et le Pacifique (Paris: Emile-Paul, 1921); translated by Ben Ray Redman as *Suzanne and the Pacific* (New York & London: Putnam, 1923);
Siegfried et le Limousin (Paris: Grasset, 1922); translated by Louis Collier Willcox as *My Friend from Limousin* (New York & London: Harper, 1923);
La Prière sur la Tour Eiffel (Paris: Emile-Paul, 1923);
Juliette au pays des hommes (Paris: Emile-Paul, 1924);
Visite chez le prince (Paris: Emile-Paul, 1924);
Hélène et Touglas; ou, Les Joies de Paris (Paris: Sans Pareil, 1925);
Le Couvent de Bella (Paris: Grasset, 1925);
Premier Rêve signé (Le Dernier Rêve d'Edmond About) (Paris: Emile-Paul, 1925);

Bella (Paris: Grasset, 1926); translated by J. F. Scanlan (New York & London: Knopf, 1927);

Anne chez Simon (Paris: Emile-Paul, 1926);

Les Hommes tigres (Paris: Emile-Paul, 1926);

Le Cerf (Paris: Cité des Livres, 1926);

A la recherche de Bella (Liège: A la Lampe d'Aladin, 1926);

La Première Disparition de Jérôme Bardini (Paris: Sagittaire, 1926); translated as "The First Disappearance of Jérôme Bardini," in *The Best French Short Stories of 1925–1926,* edited by Richard Eaton (Boston: Small, Maynard, 1926), pp. 176–208;

Eglantine (Paris: Grasset, 1927);

Marche vers Clermont (Paris: Cahiers Libres, 1928);

Le Sport (Paris: Hachette, 1928);

Siegfried (Paris: Grasset, 1928); translated by Philip Carr (New York: L. MacVeagh, Dial Press / Toronto: Longmans, Green, 1930);

La Grande Bourgeoise, ou Toute Femme a la vocation (Paris: Kra, 1928);

Amphitryon 38 (Paris: Grasset, 1929); translated by Phyllis La Farge and Peter H. Judd, in *Three Plays* (New York: Hill & Wang, 1964), pp. 79–156;

Le Signe (Paris: Emile-Paul, 1929);

Stéphy (Geneva: Kundig, 1929);

Aventures de Jérôme Bardini (Paris: Emile-Paul, 1930);

Rues et visages de Berlin (Paris: Roseraie, 1930);

Racine (Paris: Grasset, 1930); translated by P. Mansell Jones (Cambridge, U.K.: Fraser, 1938);

Fugues sur Siegfried (Paris: Lapina, 1930);

Judith: Tragédie en trois actes (Paris: Emile-Paul, 1931); translated by Christopher Fry, in *Plays,* volume 1, introduction by Harold Clurman (New York: Oxford University Press, 1963), pp. 10–63;

Je présente Bellita (Paris: Grasset, 1931);

Mirage de Bessines (Paris: Emile-Paul, 1931);

La France sentimentale (Paris: Grasset, 1932);

Berlin (Paris: Emile-Paul, 1932);

Fontranges au Niagara (Paris: Cahiers Libres, 1932);

Intermezzo (Paris: Grasset, 1933); adapted by Maurice Valency as *The Enchanted: A Comedy* (New York: Random House, 1950);

Combat avec l'ange (Paris: Grasset, 1934);

Tessa, ou la nymphe au cœur fidèle, adapted from Margaret Kennedy and Basil Dean's play *The Constant Nymph* (Paris: Grasset, 1934);

Fin de Siegfried (Paris: Grasset, 1934);

La Guerre de Troie n'aura pas lieu (Paris: Grasset, 1935); translated by Fry as *Tiger at the Gates* (London: Methuen, 1955); revised as *The Trojan War Will Not Take Place* (London: Methuen, 1983);

L'Impromptu de Paris (Paris: Grasset, 1937);

Electre (Paris: Grasset, 1937); translated by Winifred Smith as *Electra,* in *From the Modern Repertoire,* second series, edited by Eric Bentley (Denver: University of Denver Press, 1952; London: Indiana University Press, 1952);

Supplément au voyage de Cook (Paris: Grasset, 1937); adapted by Valency as *The Virtuous Island: A Play in One Act–From A Supplement to Cook's Voyage by Jean Giraudoux* (New York: S. French, 1956);

Et moi aussi, j'ai été un petit Meaulnes (Paris: Emile-Paul, 1937);

Les Cinq Tentations de La Fontaine (Paris: Grasset, 1938);

Pour ce onze novembre (Paris: Grasset, 1938);

Cantique des cantiques (Paris: Grasset, 1938); translated by Herma Briffault as *Song of Songs,* in *Makers of the Modern Theater,* edited by Barry Ulanov (New York, Toronto & London: McGraw-Hill, 1961), pp. 468–484;

Alsace et Lorraine (Paris: Gallimard, 1939);

A propos de la rentrée des classes (Paris: François Bernouard, 1939);

Choix des élues (Paris: Grasset, 1939); translated by Henry Russell as *Choice of the Elect* (Evanston, Ill.: Northwestern University Press, 2002);

Ondine (Paris: Grasset, 1939); adapted by Valency as *Ondine: A Romantic Fantasy in Three Acts* (New York: S. French, 1956);

Pleins pouvoirs (Paris: Gallimard, 1939);

Réponse à ceux qui demandent pourquoi nous faisons la guerre et pourquoi nous ne la faisons pas (Allocution prononcée le 14 décembre 1939 par M. Jean Giraudoux, Commissaire général à l'Information, au déjeuner de l'American club, à Paris) (Paris: Dumoulin, 1939); published in English as *Text of the address delivered by M. Jean Giraudoux on December 14th, 1939, at the American Club of Paris* (Paris: Centre d'Informations Documentaires, 1940);

Le Futur Armistice (Paris: Grasset, 1940);

Combat avec l'image (Paris: Emile-Paul, 1941);

Littérature (Paris: Grasset, 1941);

Le Film de la Duchesse de Langeais, d'après la nouvelle de H. de Balzac (Paris: Grasset, 1942);

L'Apollon de Marsac (Rio de Janeiro: supplement to *Don Casmurro,* no. 5 [10 July 1942]);

Sodome et Gomorrhe (Paris: Grasset, 1943); translated by Herma Briffault as *Sodom and Gomorrah,* in *Makers of the Modern Theater,* edited by Barry Ulanov (New York, Toronto & London: McGraw-Hill, 1961), pp. 435–467;

Le Film de Béthanie: Texte de "Les Anges du péché" d'après le scénario de R. L. Bruckberger, Dominicain, Robert Bresson, Jean Giraudoux (Paris: Gallimard, 1944);

Ecrit dans l'ombre (Monaco: Rocher, 1944);

Armistice à Bordeaux (Monaco: Rocher, 1945);

La Folle de Chaillot (Neuchâtel & Paris: Ides et Calendes, 1945); adapted by Valency as *The Madwoman of Chaillot* (New York: Random House, 1947);

Portrait de la Renaissance (Paris: Haumont, 1946);

Sans pouvoirs (Monaco: Rocher, 1946);

L'Apollon de Bellac (Neuchâtel & Paris: Ides et Calendes, 1946); adapted by Valency as *The Apollo of Bellac* (New York: S. French, 1954);

Visitations (Neuchâtel & Paris: Ides et Calendes, 1947);

Pour une politique urbaine (Paris: Arts et Métiers Graphiques, 1947);

De Pleins Pouvoirs à sans pouvoirs (Paris: Gallimard, 1950);

La Française et la France (Paris: Gallimard, 1951);

Les Contes d'un matin (Paris: Gallimard, 1952);

Pour Lucrèce (Paris: Grasset, 1953); translated by Fry as *Duel of Angels* (London: Methuen, 1958);

La Menteuse [fragment], *suivi de Les Gracques* (Paris: Grasset, 1958);

Portugal, suivi de Combat avec l'image (Paris: Grasset, 1958);

Œuvres littéraires diverses (Paris: Grasset, 1958);

Or dans la nuit: Chroniques et préfaces littéraires (1910-1943) (Paris: Grasset, 1969);

La Menteuse (Paris: Grasset, 1969); translated by Howard as *Lying Woman* (New York: Winter House, 1972; London: Gollancz, 1972);

Carnet des Dardanelles (Paris: Le Belier, 1969);

Souvenir de deux existences (Paris: Grasset, 1975).

Editions and Collections: *Théâtre complet de Jean Giraudoux,* 16 volumes (Neuchâtel: Ides et Calendes, 1945-1953);

Œuvre romanesque, 2 volumes (Paris: Grasset, 1955);

Théâtre, 4 volumes (Paris: Grasset, 1959);

Provinciales, edited, with introduction and notes in English, by Robert Gibson (London: Oxford University Press, 1965);

Siegfried, edited, with introduction and notes in English, by Gerald V. Banks (London: Harrap, 1967);

Amphitryon 38, edited, with introduction and notes in English, by R. K. Totton (London: Methuen, 1969);

Intermezzo, edited, with introduction and notes in English, by Ethel E. Tory (London: Harrap, 1970);

Théâtre, 2 volumes (Paris: Grasset, 1971)–comprises volume 1: *Siegfried, Fin de Siegfried, Amphitryon 38, Judith, Intermezzo, Tessa, La guerre de Troie n'aura pas lieu,* and *Electre;* and volume 2: *Supplément au voyage de Cook, L'impromptu de Paris, Cantique des cantiques, Ondine, Sodome et Gomorrhe, L'Apollon de Bellac, La folle de Chaillot, Pour Lucrèce, Les Gracques, Annexes: Et jusqu'à Béthanie* (stage version of the movie *Les anges du péché*), and *La duchesse de Langeais* (stage adaptation of Honoré de Balzac's novella from *L'Histoire des Treize*);

Théâtre complet, edited, with an introduction, by Jacques Body, Bibliothèque de la Pléiade, no. 302 (Paris: Gallimard, 1982);

Oeuvres romanesques complètes, 2 volumes, edited by Body, Bibliothèque de la Pléiade, nos. 368 and 404 (Paris: Gallimard, 1990, 1994);

Théâtre complet, edited by Guy Teissier (Paris: La Pochothèque/Livre de Poche, 1991).

Editions in English: *The Apollo de Bellac,* translated by Ronald Duncan (London, 1957);

Four Plays, adapted, with an introduction, by Maurice Valency (New York: Hill & Wang, 1958)–comprises *The Madwoman of Chaillot, The Apollo of Bellac, The Enchanted,* and *Ondine;*

Plays, 2 volumes, translated by Christopher Fry and Roger Gellert, introduction by Harold Clurman (New York: Oxford University Press, 1963, 1967; London: Methuen, 1963, 1967)–volume 1, translated by Fry, comprises *Judith, Tiger at the Gates,* and *Duel of Angels;* volume 2, translated by Gellert, comprises *Amphitryon 38, Intermezzo,* and *Ondine;*

Three Plays, translated by Phyllis La Farge with Peter H. Judd (New York: Hill & Wang, 1964)–comprises *Siegfried, Amphitryon 38,* and *Electre.*

PRODUCED SCRIPTS: *La Duchesse de Langeais,* motion picture, Films Orange, 1942;

Les Anges du péché, motion picture, by Giraudoux and R. L. Bruckberger, Synops, 1943.

OTHER: "L'Orgueil," in *Les Sept Péchés capitaux,* edited by Jacques de Lacretelle (Paris: Kra, 1927), pp. 1-18;

"Barbe," in *D'Ariadne à Zoé, Alphabet galant et sentimental* (Paris: Librairie de France, 1930);

Alfred de Musset, *Contes et nouvelles,* introduction by Giraudoux (Paris: Cité de Livres, 1931);

Adrienne Thomas, *Catherine Soldat,* preface by Giraudoux (Paris: Stock, 1933);

Annette Kolb, *Mozart,* preface by Giraudoux (Paris: Michel, 1938);

Evelyn Waugh, *Diableries,* preface by Giraudoux (Paris: Grasset, 1938);

"Discours liminaire," in Le Corbusier, *La Charte d'Athènes* (Paris: Plon, 1943); translated by Anthony Eardley in *The Athens Charter* (New York: Grossman, 1973), pp. xv-xix;

Hommage à Marivaux, introduction by Giraudoux (Paris: Sezille, 1944);

Théâtre complet de Marivaux, preface by Giraudoux (Paris: Editions Nationales, 1946).

SELECTED PERIODICAL PUBLICATIONS–
UNCOLLECTED: "Conversations canadiennes," *Idées Modernes*, 1 (February 1909): 323-331;

"L'Olympiade de 1924," *Revue Hebdomadaire*, 9 (1920): 330-333;

"Avant et après les Jeux olympiques," *Annales Politiques et Littéraires* (18 November 1932): 442;

"Le Prix du football," *Annales Politiques et Littéraires* (16 December 1932): 550;

"Amateurs et professionnels," *Annales Politiques et Littéraires* (23 December 1932): 577; (30 December 1932): 605; (6 January 1933): 23;

"La Ligue des droits urbains," *Marianne* (19 April 1933);

"Pour un plus beau Paris (Faculté de Médecine)," *Marianne* (26 April; 3, 10, 17, 31 May; 14 June 1933);

"Les Responsables," *Marianne* (19 July; 6 September 1933);

"La Tragédie: Hier, aujourd'hui," *Conferencia*, 20 (1 October 1933): 385-398;

"Place Saint-Sulpice," *Marianne* (7 February 1934);

"Les Ecrivains, gardiens du domaine national," *Marianne* (16 May 1934);

"La Querelle de la Comédie," *Conferencia*, 24 (1 December 1934): 621-634;

"Les Travaux de France," *Conferencia*, 8 (1 April 1939): 415-432; 9 (15 April 1939): 462-478; 10 (1 May 1939): 537-553; 11 (15 May 1939): 587-604; 12 (1 June 1939): 635-648;

"Une Dictature de l'urbanisme," *Comoedia* (19 February 1944): 1, 2;

"L'Aménagement de la France," *Echo des Etudiants* (31 March 1944).

Although he first distinguished himself in fiction, Jean Giraudoux became famous chiefly through his work in drama, earning a preeminent place among twentieth-century French playwrights. From 1928, when his first play opened, until 1953, when his final drama premiered posthumously, many theatergoers and critics recognized him as a master of both French literature and stagecraft. Literary critic Jacques Body, in his *La Légende et le secret* (1986; translated as *Jean Giraudoux: The Legend and the Secret*, 1991), asserts (with some hyperbole) that Giraudoux was the most famous man of the 1930s, when his work dominated French theater and experienced success abroad in translation. His plays have been revived often, and *La Guerre de Troie n'aura pas lieu* (The Trojan War Will Not Take Place, published and performed 1935; translated as *Tiger at the Gates*, 1955) is said to be the most popular Western play of its period as measured by number of performances, number of translations, and overall book sales.

Among major literary figures who expressed admiration for Giraudoux's work were Paul Claudel, André Gide, Marcel Proust, Paul Valéry, Louis Aragon, and Jean Anouilh. The observation of Colette is apt: "Vertu de la poésie: Giraudoux nous entraîne dans son 'climat' . . . nous y maintient, et nous tenons son lucide oxygène pour notre air natal" (The virtue of poetry: Giraudoux draws us into his "climate," keeps us there, and we take his clear oxygen to be our native air). Giraudoux also had many admirers outside of literary circles. In a 1949 letter to Giraudoux's son (held in the French National Archives), Vincent Auriol, president of the Fourth Republic from 1947 to 1954, expressed esteem for the man and admiration for his work.

Giraudoux's fruitful collaboration with Louis Jouvet at the Comédie des Champs-Elysées, then the Théâtre de l'Athénée, is a model of sympathetic inspiration between artists. Giraudoux's characteristic wit became a recognized style. He was, as an anonymous commentator for *Le Monde* (27 January 2005, The World) put it, Jouvet's "auteur fétiche" (mascot author).

While certain critics–Roger Allard, for instance– have alleged that Giraudoux's style and thinking are not very French, many others have suggested that Giraudoux is a highly Gallic writer whose use of language reveals aspects of the French mind. Hence, in his introduction to Giraudoux's *Théâtre complet* (1991), Guy Teissier speaks of "cet auteur si français" (this author so very French). Rather than dilute his patriotism, Giraudoux's admiration for Germany and the United States, his foreign-service career, and his extensive travel developed his sense of what it meant to be French. Noting Giraudoux's apparent agnosticism, Philippe Dufay describes France as the "objet de sa seule religion" (object of his only religion).

Following Jean Racine, Stendhal, and Proust, Giraudoux was an analyst of love. He identified with great delicacy the feminine principle, or *l'éternel féminin*. Women, he said, were *un phosphore divin* (a divine phosphorus). This sensitivity was complemented by his understanding of men in their relationships with women. However, in contrast to dramatists such as Georges Feydeau–a writer for the *théâtre du boulevard*, commercial theater that often featured bedroom farces– Giraudoux generally treated the subject of sex in a refined or tragic mode, with neither vulgarity nor titillating innuendo.

Giraudoux was less a broadly popular author than one for connoisseurs. His theater, self-consciously literary, depends largely upon the appeal of its style to sensitive spectators and readers. Yet, so many reviewers criticized the style of his drama that he felt compelled to respond in his book *L'Impromptu de Paris* (1937, The Paris Impromptu). Giraudoux's language, called

Photograph of Rosalia "Lilita" Abreu, a wealthy young Cuban woman with Paris connections. Giraudoux fell in love with her in 1909, resulting in a lengthy correspondence, but his love was unrequited (from Lettres à Lilita: 1910-1928, *1989; Thomas Cooper Library, University of South Carolina).*

précieux (refined, elaborate) by Claude-Edmonde Magny and others, is at once lyrical, witty, and searching, often turning on paradox. Such language failed to please critics such as Robert Kemp, who spoke of Giraudoux's *métaphorisme,* his sickness. The playwright also was accused of verbal excesses because, it was averred, words came too easily. A tree, for instance, is "le frère non mobile des hommes" (the nonmobile brother of human beings).

Giraudoux appears elitist, even aristocratic, in contrast to such dramatists as Charles Péguy, Jean-Paul Sartre, and Albert Camus. Fanciful invention dominates his world. As Colette's comment shows, Giraudoux may be considered a poet, but he may also be considered an "Illusioniste" (Illusionist), like one of his characters in *Ondine* (published and performed 1939; adapted, 1956). Jacques Guicharnaud classified Giraudoux's drama under the rubric "Theater of the Supernatural." In fact, in his *Refléxions du comédien* (1938, Reflections of an Actor), Jouvet suggests that his friend's theater depends upon "spells": "A quoi tient le succès de Giraudoux? A la magie incantatoire du verbe dramatique" (What does Giraudoux's success depend on? The incantatory magic of dramatic language). Even when Giraudoux's plays feature common people—waiters, clerks, gardeners—they do not deal straightforwardly with life's blunt facts. Given the historical background against which Giraudoux's plays were produced—economic depression, rearmament, European fascism, class conflict, political disorder, and war—and the development of *littérature engagée* (committed literature, conveying social and political messages), his theater was sometimes dismissed as escapist, denying reality in favor of fantasy and linguistic excess. Marie-Jeanne Durry sees in his work what she calls the incapacity to suffer.

But along with egalitarianism the French love elitism, as French high culture during the reign of Louis XIV demonstrates. Fondness for wordplay, conceits, antitheses, paradoxes, hyperbole, unusual words, and other verbal complications is not foreign to French literature, despite its Cartesian bent and its classicism. Subtle and ornamental language was displayed in the best seventeenth-century salons. When Molière mocked it in *Les Précieuses ridicules* (1659, The Affected Young Ladies), he mocked only its exaggerated affectations, not the spirit of refinement and intellectual conversation, and in the following century it was revived in the form of *marivaudage* in the comedies of Pierre Carlet de Chamblain de Marivaux. Further demonstrating the enduring vein of subtle and ornamental language among the French are Voltaire's wit and love for the *beau détail* (beautiful detail), Victor Hugo's striking hyperboles and antitheses, and Valéry's taste for paradoxes and elegant euphemisms. Not even fantasy is necessarily counter to French tradition. In the seventeenth century Jean de La Fontaine wrote animal fables, and Charles Perrault collected the *Contes de ma mère l'Oye* (1695, Mother Goose Tales). Late-Romantic poets such as Alfred de Musset and Gérard de Nerval exploited dreamy fantasy for their purposes. In fact, Giraudoux published critical pieces on La Fontaine, Marivaux, Musset, and Nerval, showing his awareness of this tradition. Finally, it is difficult to dismiss Giraudoux's work as frivolous: he treated serious topics, often gravely, even tragically.

Hippolyte-Jean Giraudoux was born on 29 October 1882 in Bellac, approximately forty kilometers from Limoges, in the department of Haute-Vienne, part of Limousin before Napoleon's administrative restructuring. Giraudoux was of modest background, his family belonging to the petit bourgeoisie with peasant (farmer) roots. His father, Léger Giraudoux (called Léon), was a minor civil servant, first with the roads and bridges department, then the tax bureau. He was taciturn and often absent. Giraudoux felt closer to his mother, née

Anne Lacoste (called Antoinette), and his older brother, Alexandre, his only sibling, who became a physician. During Giraudoux's childhood the family lived in provincial towns, including Pellevoisin (Berry) and Cerilly (Bourbonnais), where he met Charles-Louis Philippe, a novelist who encouraged his literary activities.

From his earliest school years in Pellevoisin, Giraudoux showed remarkable aptitude. Starting in 1893, he attended the lycée of Châteauroux as a scholarship boarder, studying for the *baccalauréat* (liberal arts degree). The curriculum included Greek, Latin, and French literature and concluded with a year of philosophy, which emphasized the idealism of much nineteenth-century philosophical writing. Giraudoux was a voracious reader, but he was also athletic and enjoyed sports in the gymnasium and outdoors. He returned home seldom, however, and he was often lonely. After taking his *baccalauréat* in 1900, winning the prize for excellence, he moved to the Lycée Lakanal in Sceaux (near Paris) for two years of *khâgne* (further preuniversity studies). At their conclusion he received the Lakanal Prize for excellence, first prize for history and French composition, and, in the national competition, first prize for Greek.

During this time Giraudoux frequented theaters and cafés in the Latin Quarter, where he became acquainted with literary figures. He also continued to distinguish himself with his sporting abilities, placing him among a select group of athletic French writers, including Camus, Saint-Jean Perse (Alexis Leger), and Henri de Montherlant. He never gave up physical exercise, including tennis and swimming. He even wrote about sports and the Olympics, and advocated the development of athletics in France.

In fall 1903, after completing obligatory military service, Giraudoux entered the prestigious Ecole normale supérieure in Paris to study for the *agrégation* (the highest teacher-training degree). The initial step toward this goal, taken in 1904, was to earn his *licence ès lettres* (basic university degree) in French literature at the Sorbonne. His first published texts—sketches and stories—appeared in 1904 and 1906 in publications including *L'Ermitage* (The Hermitage), a respected magazine. Some of these works were included in his first book, titled *Provinciales* (1909, Provincials). In May 1905, having switched to German studies, Giraudoux left for Germany on a fellowship. He spent a year in Munich, where he served as tutor to Paul Morand, whose father, Eugène Morand, was there on a cultural mission. Morand became a writer and diplomat, and a close friend. During this time Giraudoux traveled widely in Germany and central Europe.

When he returned to Paris, Giraudoux did not return to strict academic discipline. He was interested in other things. He obtained his *diplôme d'études supérieures* (1906) but failed the *agrégation* examination (1907). After student teaching at the Lycée Janson-de-Sailly, he had little enthusiasm for a teaching career. Through friends, however, he was appointed as visiting French-language assistant at Harvard University. After a semester there, followed by travels, he returned in March 1908 to Paris and became secretary to the director of a daily, *Le Matin* (The Morning), and co-editor of its literary page, in which he printed some of his own stories pseudonymously. Other stories appeared in the highbrow magazines *Le Mercure de France* (The French Mercury) and *La Nouvelle Revue Française* (The New French Review).

Abandoning his plan to retake the *agrégation* examination, in 1909 he took the foreign-service examinations instead. Failing (by two points) to obtain one of five passes in the "Grand Concours des Ambassades" (grand embassy examination), in 1910 he placed first in the "petit concours des Chancelleries" (little chancellery examination). His active foreign-service career, in which he held many different positions, including chief of press at the Foreign Ministry in the 1920s, lasted until 1941. Like other diplomat-writers, such as Morand, Claudel, and Perse, he was protected by Philippe Berthelot, a high-ranking official. Giraudoux's position allowed for extensive travel, beginning with a journey through central Europe to Constantinople. Over the course of his career he went on many such missions, in addition to personal travels. He is one of the great travelers among twentieth-century French writers, along with Claudel, Gide, Perse, Sartre, and Simone de Beauvoir. However, he avoided almost all foreign assignments, wishing always to return to Paris.

In 1909 Giraudoux fell in love with a wealthy young Cuban woman with Paris connections, Rosalia Abreu, known as Lilita. The love was not, however, returned. The lengthy correspondence between Giraudoux and Abreu reveals his devotion and subsequent heartbreak. Much later she became closely involved with Perse. Another romantic encounter began in 1913, this one with Suzanne Boland, the wife of a military officer named Paul Pineau and mother of two children. Their meeting led to a liaison. Pineau challenged Giraudoux to a duel, which never took place.

When World War I began Giraudoux was called to military service, and in September 1914 he was wounded in the Battle of the Marne. After rehabilitation, he returned to active service. He was promoted from sergeant to second lieutenant, but he was wounded in the Dardanelles. Following convalescence, he returned to government service in the War Ministry, then Foreign Ministry, and published magazine articles and a book of war accounts, *Retour d'Alsace: Août 1914*

Poster for Giraudoux's 1929 play, which he claimed was the thirty-eighth treatment of the Amphitryon myth (<www.nancysteinbockposters.com/entertain-circus/amphitryon38.htm>)

(1916, Return from Alsace: August 1914). Giraudoux was not well, however, having caught virulent dysentery in Turkey. In April 1917 he crossed the Atlantic to help train volunteers for the Allied war effort while resting and undergoing further medical examinations. (He was hospitalized eleven times in connection with war injuries and illness.)

After his return, Giraudoux published *Lectures pour une ombre* (1917; translated as *Campaigns and Intervals*, 1918), then, in 1918, *Amica America* (Friendly America) and the autobiographical novel *Simon le pathétique* (Simon the Sensitive). Twenty-five more works, including *Bella* (1926; translated, 1927) and *Eglantine* (1927), were published before 1930. Giraudoux was one of the principal authors in the catalogue of Bernard Grasset, a young publisher who succeeded by employing new marketing strategies. Emile-Paul also published some of his works.

In December 1919 Suzanne gave birth to Giraudoux's only child, Jean-Pierre. After Suzanne's divorce was pronounced, and after a period of mourning for Léon Giraudoux, recently deceased, Giraudoux and Suzanne were married in February 1921. (Earlier biographers, such as Laurent LeSage and Will L. McLendon, avoided this matter or fabricated a false date for the marriage to protect Giraudoux's reputation.) Suzanne inspired many pages by Giraudoux, notably *Suzanne et le Pacifique* (1921; translated as *Suzanne and the Pacific*, 1923), a fantastic retelling of Daniel Defoe's *Robinson Crusoe* (1719), with a feminine castaway.

Giraudoux was not, however, a faithful husband, and, according to witnesses, his wife was irascible, nervous, and even hysterical. The marriage was marked by domestic storms. In 1925 Giraudoux began an affair with a South American girl, Anita de Madero, which lasted until, against his wishes, she returned to Argentina early in 1936, the year he was named commander in the Legion of Honor. He then began another liaison, this one with Jeanne Loviton, a novelist.

In 1923 Giraudoux proposed to director Jacques Copeau that he adapt for the stage his novel *Siegfried et le Limousin* (1922; translated as *My Friend from Limousin*, 1923), but Copeau's theater closed. Nevertheless, Giraudoux undertook the adaptation, which, like most of his plays, went through many versions, as manuscript evidence shows. Finally, a stageworthy version, titled simply *Siegfried* (performed and published 1928; translated, 1930), was ready for Jouvet early in 1928.

This venture was inspired by Giraudoux's interest in drama, which dated from his school days. He had attended many plays in Paris, and acted in others, including Molière's *Les Précieuses ridicules,* and he had seen the Passion Play in Oberammergau, Germany. Eugène Morand had encouraged him to write for the stage. Giraudoux's admirers were initially apprehensive, supposing that his elaborate language and fantasy, which made him a less popular novelist than, for instance, his contemporary François Mauriac, would not transfer well to the stage. Yet, they soon discovered that his style and approach were ideally suited to the stage, where illusion reigns. In fact, they discovered that the entire theatrical illusion, including elaborate settings and stagecraft, may be complemented by playful or artificial language.

Giraudoux reflected deeply on the cultural meaning and the rationale of organized make-believe. His dramatic corpus comprises fifteen completed plays, one unfinished drama, and fragments from early versions of *Siegfried*. These works range widely in setting and topic. One, *Supplément au voyage de Cook* (performed 1935, published 1937; partially translated as *The Virtuous Island*, 1956), takes place in the South Seas. Three are drawn from Greek mythology: *Amphitryon 38* (performed and published 1929; translated, 1938), *La Guerre de Troie n'aura pas lieu,* and *Electre* (performed and published 1937; translated as *Electra,* 1952). Meanwhile, Hebrew Scripture furnishes the basis for *Judith* (performed and published 1931; translated, 1963), *Cantique des cantiques* (performed and published 1938; translated as *Song of Songs,* 1961), and *Sodome et Gomorrhe* (performed and published 1943; translated as *Sodom and Gomorrah,* 1961). Another play, *Ondine,* takes place in medieval Germany. Others are set in Europe in modern times, although the settings may be fanciful.

Jouvet produced and directed almost all of Giraudoux's plays, and he also took major roles. Exceptions are *Sodome et Gomorrhe,* directed by Douking at the Théâtre Hébertot in 1943, when Jouvet's troupe was in South America, and *Pour Lucrèce* (produced and published 1953; translated as *Duel of Angels,* 1958), produced posthumously at the Théâtre Marigny by the Compagnie Madeleine Renaud and Jean-Louis Barrault. Productions of Giraudoux's texts were aided by other artists, including composers Francis Poulenc and Arthur Honegger, set designer Christian Bérard, and painter Edouard Vuillard. Costumes were provided on occasion by Jeanne Lanvin and Christian Dior. Furthermore, celebrated actors and actresses appeared in many productions of his plays: the one-armed Pierre Renoir, Valentine Tessier, Edwige Feuillère, Marguerite Moreno, Michel Simon, and Gérard Philippe.

Siegfried is not viewed by critics as one of Giraudoux's better plays, being marked by melodramatic imbroglios, but it was nevertheless a resounding stage success, with 243 performances during its first run. The play is designed to exploit tensions between the French and the Germans. As a seasoned diplomat, Giraudoux concluded that, despite friendliness (an optimistic French government had recently made overtures to its Rhenish neighbor) and resemblances between the nations (underlined by rhetorical parallelisms in the play), the Germans and the French were destined to remain antagonistic, as events in the Weimar Republic, with the French occupying the Ruhr region in January 1923 on the pretext of unpaid war reparations, suggested. Translated unfaithfully, *Siegfried* was performed in Germany and Austria as late as 1938, but it was not well received there.

Sartre's essay on Giraudoux, titled "M. Giraudoux et la philosophie d'Aristote" (Mr. Giraudoux and the Philosophy of Aristotle) and published in *Situations 1* (1947), is relevant here: while it concerns Giraudoux's novel *Choix des élues* (1939; translated as *Choice of the Elect,* 2002), his observations apply equally to his drama. Giraudoux's world, Sartre contends, is static and inhabited by essences—"un monde tout fait et qui ne se fait point" (a world which is entirely done and does not *become*). Giraudoux's characters, settings, and props are specimens of fixed types. It is as if he gathers together essential qualities of French people and settings: girl, woman, loving wife, hero, and small village. Such typing may seem reductionist, but it also can be viewed as the proper application of abstract concepts from concrete instances. Hence, Giraudoux can write, in *Siegfried,* referring to Canada, "Comme les mots qui vous viennent d'un pays nouveau et ouvert sont eux-mêmes ouverts, purs!" (How the words that come from a new and open country are themselves open, pure). The result is a highly symbolic world. Among the principal Giralducian types is the adolescent girl, who appears repeatedly, not for her individual psychological or social interest but, according to Jules Roy, as representative of "le type de la jeune fille éternelle" (the type of eternal girlhood).

Examples of stereotyping are abundant throughout Giraudoux's work. For instance, he lays out a dim view of aging in *La Guerre de Troie n'aura pas lieu*: "Quand l'homme adulte touche à ses quarante ans, on lui substitue un vieillard. Lui disparaît. Il n'y a que des rapports d'apparence entre les deux" (When an adult man reaches the age of forty, an old man is substituted for him. He disappears. The connections between them are only apparent). Similarly, in *Judith* he portrays the defeated warrior as the very essence of shame:

> Hideux, tu es hideux! décoloré aussi. Quelle lèpre que la défaite sur un uniforme! . . . Dans les yeux du soldat, y a-t-il deux regards qui se ressemblent plus que celui de la déroute et celui de la lâcheté? . . . Laisse-moi te toucher moi aussi, que je connaisse le froid de la cuirasse en déroute. Et t'embrasser, que j'aie sur mes lèvres le goût de la peau vaincue!

> (Hideous, you are hideous! faded also. What a leprosy defeat is on a uniform! . . . In the soldier's eyes are there two gazes that resemble each other more than those of defeat and cowardice? . . . Let me touch you also, so that I may know the cold of armor in defeat. And kiss you, to have on my lips the taste of conquered skin!)

Because of such passages, Sartre concludes that Giraudoux had reintroduced Aristotelian essences into the twentieth century. Hence, more than one spectator has seen Giraudoux's characters as puppets, lacking individuality and roots in the real.

Alternatively, Giraudoux's types may be viewed as Platonic. Critics who have identified traces of Platonism in Giraudoux's work include René-Marill Albérès and Magny, who writes, "Nous-mêmes, en nous considérant dans l'esprit de Giraudoux, nous ne sommes que l'image déchue de ce que nous aurions pu être: notre amour, notre peur, notre désespoir ne réus-

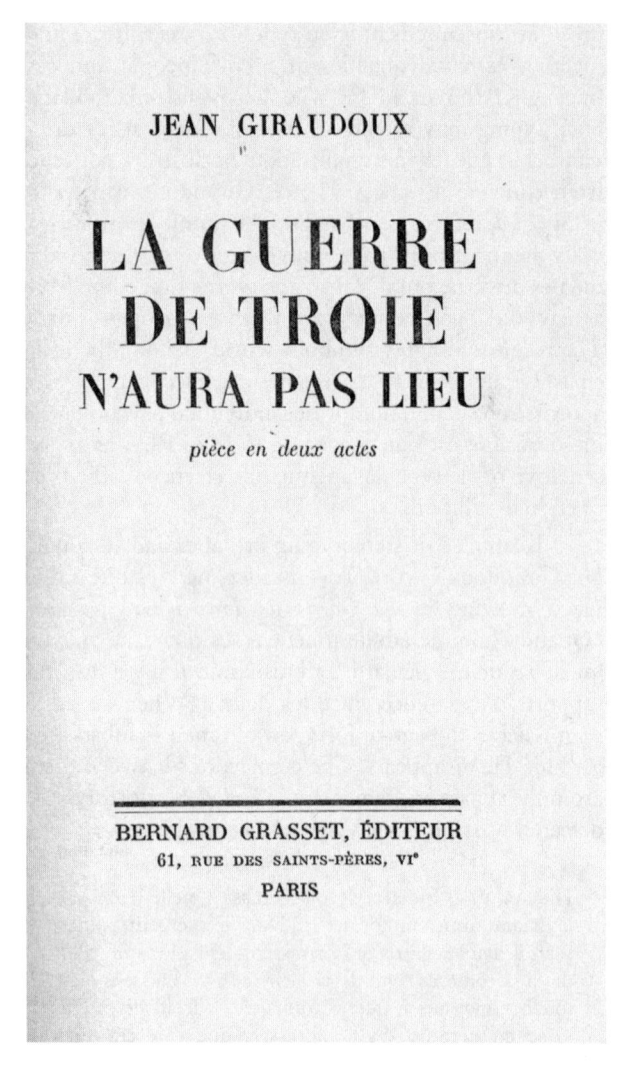

Title page for Giraudoux's 1935 dramatic account of the events leading up to the Trojan War (translated as Tiger at the Gates, *1953, and revised as* The Trojan War Will Not Take Place, *1983), often considered to be the most popular Western play of the period as measured by number of performances, number of translations, and overall book sales (Joyner Library, East Carolina University)*

sissent pas à être pleins et purs; toujours ils demeurent mêlés de leur contraire" (We ourselves, seen in Giraudoux's mind, are only the fallen image of what we could have been: our love, our fear, our despair do not succeed in being full and pure; they always remain mixed with their opposite).

In *Siegfried,* the opposite essences of France and Germany are expressed through representative elements: a postcard-perfect French village; a French philologist who, following tradition, studied in Germany; the consummate Parisian Geneviève; Baron Otto-Wilhelmus von Zelten-Buchenbach; Fontgeloy, a German general of Huguenot ancestry; and heavy German furniture designed by Kohlenschwanzbader. The characters, especially von Zelten and Fontgeloy, are nearly caricatures.

The play concerns a Frenchman, Jacques Forestier, who was wounded in World War I. Found without identification and suffering from amnesia, he was rescued and rehabilitated by Germans and renamed Siegfried, for the national hero. Seven years later, having reached an eminent political position, he plans to launch the sort of rational constitution Germany has always lacked. His idea of rational government is a French ideal, deeply ingrained in him, but he does not recognize its source. His political enemy, von Zelten, is opposed to this progressive movement, in conflict with his understanding of what is essentially German. Having discovered who Siegfried really is, Zelten summons to Germany Siegfried's former fiancée, Geneviève, who had assumed he was dead. Zelten's hopes—that Siegfried's memory will be jarred and he will return home to France—are fulfilled. Siegfried, or Jacques, recognizes his need for a country he has missed, for his French roots. Geneviève tells him:

> Il y a entre les moineaux, les guêpes, les fleurs de ce pays et ceux du tien une différence de nature imperceptible, mais inacceptable pour toi. C'est seulement quand tu retrouveras tes animaux, tes insectes, tes plantes, ces odeurs qui diffèrent pour la même fleur dans chaque pays, que tu pourras vivre heureux.
>
> (Between the sparrows, the wasps, the flowers of this country and yours there is a difference in nature, imperceptible but unacceptable for you. Only when you get back your animals, your insects, your plants, those odors that differ for the same flower in each country, can you live happily.)

The play was not intended as a rejection of Franco-German conciliation, which the author wished to facilitate. It was, rather, an elucidation of fundamental differences.

Giraudoux's next play, *Amphitryon 38,* is so titled because it was, according to the author, the thirty-eighth play on the topic. The claim is unfounded, but there are multiple dramatic versions of the story, including those by Titus Maccius Plautus (*Amphitruo,* late third/early second century B.C.), Molière (*Amphitryon,* produced and published 1668), and Heinrich von Kleist (Amphitryon: *Ein Lustspiel nach Molière* [*Amphitryon:* A Comedy after Molière], 1807). Giraudoux, however, admitted only to reading Molière's. The original production of Giraudoux's play, beginning in 1929, ran to 236 performances, despite the fact that it received little positive attention from critics (André Rouveyre, for instance, gave it an unfavorable review). In German translation, *Amphitryon 38* drew large audiences in Berlin, Vienna,

Prague, and elsewhere. The play was revived in Paris in 1934 to great popular and critical success, and Alfred Lunt and Lynn Fontanne performed in an English translation of the play at the Schubert Theatre in New York in 1937.

Modern adaptations of Greek subject matter were no novelty: Gide, Claudel, and Jean Cocteau, among others, published plays on Greek topics in the early twentieth century. In *Amphitryon 38*, Giraudoux indulges in anachronisms, frequent in his work, but he does not modernize the setting, early Greece, "sur une plantète encore jeune" (on a still-young planet). Giraudoux's play can be approached as a study of destiny and the human condition, a "comédie métaphysique" (metaphysical comedy), according to Jacques Robichez. It can also be approached as a slightly risqué comedy on the age-old topic of the unfaithful woman and the betrayed husband, or as a more idealized study of sexual relationships. The traditional plot is simple: Jupiter seduces the mortal Alcmène, the wife of Amphitryon, and from their union is born Hercules, the demigod destined for great deeds. Giraudoux followed his predecessors in many ways, but he also introduced material of his own. Agreeing apparently with Stendhal's assertion in *De l'amour* (1822, On Love) that the enjoyment of love comes not through force but through seduction, Giraudoux has Jupiter, assisted by Mercure the messenger, try to win Alcmène rather than simply overpower her. She is, however, the embodiment of conjugal happiness and fidelity, and even a god cannot move her. In order to seduce her, Jupiter is obliged to assume the form of Amphitryon, who has left for the war but who, Mercure announces, will come back that night in secret. In this manner is Hercules conceived.

In these events Giraudoux raises the subject of war with transparent contemporary references, such as Amphitryon's statement that "une guerre est toujours la dernière des guerres" (a war is always the last war). Human mortality is likewise treated cleverly. Mercure, testing Jupiter to be sure he really has assumed human form, asks: "Avez-vous l'idée que vous pourrez mourir un jour?" (Do you realize you may die some day?). The answer is convincing: "Non. Que mes amis mourront, pauvres amis, hélas oui! Mais pas moi" (No. That my friends will die, poor friends, alas, yes! But not I).

Jupiter wants a second night with Alcmène, without disguise, so that he may be loved for himself. Mercure, however, is astounded when she refuses. He tries blackmail: unless she agrees, Thebes will be punished by plague and defeat. Alcmène persuades Léda, whom the god already seduced as a swan, to take her place. However, the true Amphitryon arrives, is taken by Alcmène for Jupiter, and is tricked into retiring to his chamber with Léda. Alcmène thus believes, ironically, that she has successfully challenged fatality: "Ruses des hommes, désirs des dieux, ne tiennent pas contre la volonté et l'amour d'une femme fidèle" (Men's tricks, gods' desires do not hold out against the will and love of a faithful wife). Alcmène offers Jupiter not love but friendship, a uniquely human sentiment; as he accepts, he assures the couple that nothing untoward took place. Has he fallen in love with the couple, with their love and their humanity? The gods, Giraudoux seems to suggest, have some reason to envy mortals.

Critics have occasionally mocked the couple's marital happiness, which is highly unusual in Giraudoux's theater, as well as Alcmène's rather bourgeois, unimaginative self-satisfaction that keeps her from aspiring to a higher state. Alternatively, her espousal of the human condition, expressed less tragically than by Friedrich Nietzsche's *amor fati* (love of destiny) and less stoically than by Camus in *Le Mythe de Sisyphe* (1942; translated as "The Myth of Sisyphus," 1955), has been praised by critics. Alcmène's view is practical: "Je ne crains pas la mort. C'est l'enjeu de la vie. Puisque ton Jupiter, à tort ou à raison, a créé la mort sur la terre, je me solidarise avec mon astre. . . . Devenir immortel, c'est trahir, pour un humain" (I do not fear death. It's the stakes of life. Since your Jupiter, wrongly or rightly, created death on the earth, I choose solidarity with my star. . . . To become immortal is betrayal for a human being).

In the late 1920s and early 1930s an undemanding assignment to the commission for evaluating Allied war damages in Turkey afforded Giraudoux considerable free time for writing. In 1934 he was named general inspector of diplomatic and consular posts, a position that led to extensive global travel.

During the 1930s Giraudoux composed five major plays, beginning in 1931 with *Judith,* his only drama labeled a "tragedy." He may have chosen this genre because in 1930 he published *Racine,* a book on Racine's tragedies. Dramatically striking and philosophically dense, *Judith* is perhaps his purest play in terms of theatrical effects. Critic Edmond Jaloux, writing in *L'Intransigeant* (15 November 1931), called it one of the finest contemporary plays. It was, however, the least successful of Giraudoux's dramas, with a first run of only forty-five performances. The story comes from the Book of Judith (Old Testament Apocrypha), dating from A.D. 150 or later, although telling of an earlier time. It had been retold by the nineteenth-century German dramatist Friedrich Hebbel (*Judith,* 1841), among others. After the Hebrews refused to join Nebuchadrezzar, king of the Assyrians, in his wars, he sent his general Holofernes (Holophernes in French) and his troops to punish them. Their water supply was cut off, and their situation was desperate. Then Judith, a devout widow, went to the general's tent as if to assist him, stu-

L'IMPROMPTU
DE PARIS

Pièce en un acte
par
JEAN GIRAUDOUX

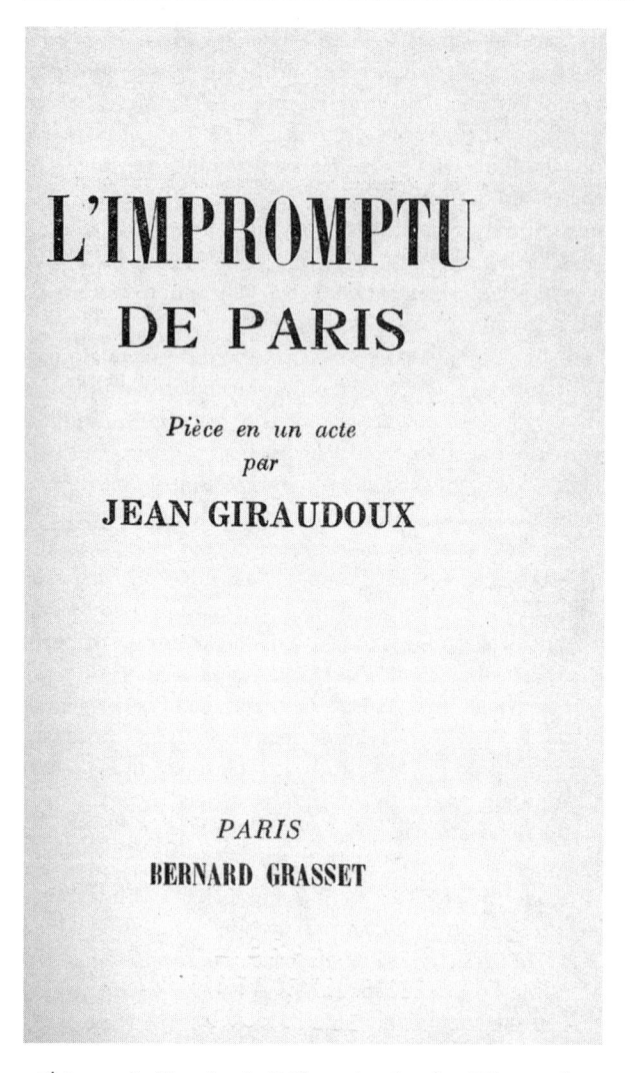

PARIS
BERNARD GRASSET

Title page for Giraudoux's 1937 curtain-raiser, in which actors from Louis Jouvet's troupe play themselves rehearsing and discussing plays, audiences, theater finances, and reviewers (Hodges Library, University of Tennessee)

pified him with liquor, and beheaded him. His troops fled in disarray.

Giraudoux's Judith is a virginal young woman, another of his *jeunes filles*. She is not, however, winsome and innocent, but rather, like Hermione from Racine's *Andromaque* (performed 1667, published 1668) and certain heroines of Pierre Corneille's tragedies, willful, erotic, brutal, proud, and intransigent, demanding in all things supreme fulfillment. Taking liberties with the story, Giraudoux develops slowly the web of desire, envy, charity, fear, and other impulses that lead Judith to recognize her vocation as others try to persuade, dissuade, assist, or trap her. In Holophernes's camp, she is baited and nearly killed, but she arouses his interest as he observes her, unseen. When he reveals himself, she is smitten, and she goes to his alcove as a woman in love, not an assassin. After their night of love, she murders him, not to save her people (whom she despises, she says) but to preserve their love forever, pure and absolute. This motive notwithstanding, her act saves both the Jews and her future image among them.

In *Judith,* Giraudoux's attitude toward the Jews is ambiguous: he suggests admiration for their resistance, but he displays considerable antipathy for them also. Their priests and Jehovah, of whom the heroine speaks with scorn, are portrayed unfavorably. Yet, divine protection is granted Judith, if one interprets the drunken guard as an angel with whom she struggles as she has defied Jehovah. While Claudel denounced the play (in letters quoted in *Théâtre complet* [1982]) as an "immonde ordure" (revolting filth), Gide praised it in his *Journal* (November 1931) as a "pièce d'idées" (play of ideas), saying, "Il a fallu votre art prestigieux pour en doubler le débat abstrait et l'étoffer d'un drame passionnel" (It required your prestigious art to accompany the abstract debate and flesh it out by a drama of passion).

In contrast to *Judith,* the fantasy *Intermezzo* (1933; translated as *The Enchanted,* 1950) is a perennial favorite with audiences, although the initial Paris run was only 116 performances. The title suggests a musical or an Italian motif, and indeed the playwright said that he was initially inspired by the Italian commedia dell'arte, but few traces of such inspiration remain. The play recalls, rather, William Shakespeare's *A Midsummer Night's Dream* (circa 1595) and *As You Like It* (circa 1600), and plays by Musset as well as the German Romantics (Johann Wolfgang von Goethe's *Faust* [1808; translated, 1823] is mentioned).

The title *Intermezzo* fits well Giraudoux's fanciful interlude in the life of a provincial town, where things are topsy-turvy and the real and unreal come together. Transitions in human life form a central motif in the play. Isabelle, the heroine, is on the threshold of adulthood but still girlish: this moment is an intermezzo in her life. Another interlude in the play is the transition between life and death, evoked through the presence of a ghost. In fact, life itself is an intermezzo: "Sa grandeur est d'être brève et pleine entre deux abîmes" (Its grandeur is to be brief and full between two abysses).

The plot turns on the ghost, who appears at twilight. Only Isabelle, the new teacher, has seen him, because, in her pure girlhood, she has the capacity to touch death without fear or harm. She and the ghost form a couple, he enigmatic, she the one who, "près de chaque être, de chaque objet . . . semble la clef destinée à le rendre compréhensible" (near each being, each object . . . seems the key destined to make it comprehensible). A government inspector and various citizens—the mayor, the druggist, the controller of weights and measures, all of whom are sympathetic characters—

investigate the phenomenon. Their investigation is livened by farce, including humorous dialogue between a deaf old woman and her sister. The unimaginative inspector does not believe in the ghost, and he is scandalized by Isabelle's rendezvous with him, as well as her unusual teaching methods (she holds class outdoors). The phantom is real, however: real enough to speak and get shot but not die. At the conclusion of the play, the controller of weights and measures, madly in love with Isabelle and thoroughly alive, asks for her hand. She accepts him and thus chooses life, with its inevitable, radical change into womanhood. Saddened by her betrayal, the ghost, who has been tempted to betrayal himself by refusing death, says farewell.

Half comic pastiche, half tragedy of fate, Giraudoux's play *La Guerre de Troie n'aura pas lieu* opened in 1935 and ran for 195 successive performances. It then was revived for fifty-two more performances in winter 1937–1938. The play was written for learned audiences, but it has proved widely popular. It is loosely based on the *Iliad* and other Greek sources, featuring the kidnapping of Helen by Paris of Troy, the casus belli (cause for war) between Trojans and Greeks, and central Homeric characters. However, the material is handled ingeniously, starting with the historically ironic title. Anachronisms help modernize the story. While no explicit mention is made of contemporary European politics, many allusions reminded audiences of their own time. "Anti-Trojan" music is a clear reference to the dismissal of German music as "non-existent" by the chauvinistic French in 1914, and the depiction of fraternizing between enemy combatants is an allusion to the fraternizing between French and German troops in the no-man's-land areas during 1917. Furthermore, Giraudoux employs the political language of the 1930s, including terms such as "arbitrage" (arbitration), "cas international" (international case), and "pays neutres" (neutral nations), and he makes many references to the horrors of war, which Giraudoux wished for Europe to avoid, even as ominous signs multiplied, with militant regimes in Germany, Italy, and, shortly, Spain.

The play is tightly constructed, with the time of the action almost identical to real theater time. Greek ships have landed, and Ulysse is about to arrive to demand Hélène's return. Priam and other old men wish to keep her, at the risk of war. Meanwhile, Hector sides with his wife, Andromaque, and other women who urge her return. He argues that Greek insults can be reinterpreted as compliments (a diplomatic skill) or simply endured: to him, they are not worth a war. While both Cassandre and Hélène suggest that fate is all-powerful, Hector believes in negotiations. With grandiloquent arguments and in poorly written verse, the old poet Demokos praises war in defense of honor.

Hector's answer—that war and poetry are sisters—suggests that nationalistic rhetoric is dangerous because it increases bellicosity. But the question of wounded honor does not go away. There is, additionally, more than one suggestion that men love war and that it is a source of cultural values.

Multiple incidents show how difficult it is to control events. At Hector's urging, Pâris claims he did not touch Hélène, which causes him to be mocked as impotent; however, sailors from Pâris's ship attest to the contrary. Then, the goddess Iris appears, bringing messages from Aphrodite (love is supreme: Hélène must stay), from Pallas (reason is supreme: Hélène must go back), and from Zeus (Hector and Ulysse must find a way to satisfy both love and reason). The face-to-face encounter of Hector and Ulysse is a reminder of European diplomatic meetings of the interwar period. According to Ulysse, he and Hector cannot prevent war, despite good faith: common soldiers, who see opportunity for plunder, wish to fight, and destiny in the form of Hélène has furnished a pretext. Nevertheless, Ulysse agrees to try to prevent war, but when Hector kills Demokos to end his warmongering, the dying poet accuses the Greek Oiax of the crime. This single false accusation is sufficient to ignite the conflict: war will take place, after all.

La Guerre de Troie n'aura pas lieu is not a simplistic plea for pacifism, although Claudel wrote that "cette apologie de la lâcheté et de la paix à tout prix est répugnante" (this apology of cowardice and peace at any price is repugnant). Instead, it is a commentary on the existence of obscure forces, human or otherwise, and the need to identify and oppose them, that draw nations into war. War seems, if not inevitable, resistant to human opposition. Hector says, "Je gagne chaque combat. Mais de chaque victoire l'enjeu s'envole" (I win each combat. But from each victory the stakes vanish).

In *Electre,* Giraudoux respected the basic story concerning the house of Atreus in works by Aeschylus (*Oresteia,* 458 B.C.), Sophocles (*Electra,* fifth century B.C.), and Euripides (*Electra,* circa 420 B.C.), but he treated the material freely. French precedents include a tragedy by Voltaire (*Oreste,* 1750). Giraudoux's play opened in 1937 and ran for 178 performances. Among Giraudoux's new characters is the *mendiant* (beggar), who acts at first as a chorus, then gradually assumes the characteristics of a prescient god. As in Shakespeare's *Hamlet,* the broad theme of the play is disorder in the state resulting from a royal crime. Electre is another example of purity and intransigence in the tragic mode: she has a pure love of Oreste, a pure hatred of her mother, and a pure desire for revenge after she discovers the fact of her father's murder. Electre proclaims her refusal of complicity and mendacity as a means to civic

Scene from a May 1937 performance of Giraudoux's Electre *at the Théâtre de l'Athénée, Paris, featuring Louis Jouvet, Gabrielle Dorziat, and Renée Devillers (© Lipnitzki/Roger-Viollet/Getty Images)*

order: only rigorous justice is acceptable. Critics' assessments of the play were divided, some judging the text—although not the production—harshly. Some saw political meaning in the outcome, by which individual vengeance (a romantic, individualistic spirit) is preferred to social stability (a conservative position).

Ondine, an audience favorite, ran for sixty-eight performances in spring 1939 and returned to the stage in spring 1940, closing shortly before the German invasion. It was produced in translation in many foreign cities, including at the Forty-Sixth Street Theater in New York in 1954, starring Audrey Hepburn and Mel Ferrer. *Ondine* was part of Jouvet's repertoire in South America, and the production was revived in 1949 in Paris, setting a record as Jouvet's longest-running Giraudoux play (311 performances).

The plot draws on French fairy-tale material, including Nerval's *Sylvie* (1853), and German water-sprite mythology, recorded by the fourteenth century and later popularized in the tale *Undine* (1811) by Frédéric de La Motte-Fouqué, a German Romantic Giraudoux had studied at the Ecole normale supérieure. Giraudoux's earlier works bear traces of his interest in the ageless and soulless nymphs who inhabit the Rhine and other waterways. The play, operatic and including theatrics produced by the Illusioniste (a character responsible for putting on theatricals at a royal castle), has a large cast and is among the most difficult Giralducian works to produce.

As in the German tale, Ondine—another of Giraudoux's pure, innocent feminine figures—falls in love with a mortal, Hans. Although she was adopted by fishermen, she is nevertheless not human, being a type of mermaid. Her fresh, ideal love contrasts with the fickleness of Hans, who was engaged to the princess Bertha but abandons her. The king of the *ondins* (mermen) warns Ondine against marrying a mortal, who will betray her. She agrees Hans must, in that case, die. Here Giraudoux suggests that men, however virtuous in appearance, are not essentially faithful. When the *ondins* first glimpsed Hans, they saw "un bel homme à cheval, la loyauté sur son visage, la sincérité dans la bouche, et alors le mot tromper a couru jusqu'au fond des ondes" (a fine man on horseback, loyalty on his face, sincerity in his mouth, and then the word *deceive* ran to the depths of the waves). Trying to be inhumanly virtuous simply leads to failure. Hans does indeed deceive Ondine, returning to Bertha. His death is followed by her unhappy return to the water. The experiment in becoming human has failed.

Minor works of the 1930s include *Tessa* (1934), adapted from the play *The Constant Nymph* (1926) by Margaret Kennedy and Basil Dean, which is based on Kennedy's novel of the same title (1924), and three one-act plays: *Supplément au voyage de Cook; L'Impromptu de Paris;* and *Cantique des cantiques. Tessa,* named after its heroine, was hailed by Gérard Bauër, in his review in *L'Echo de Paris* (16 November 1934), as a "mélodrame poétique" (poetic melodrama). The 298 performances in the first run testify to how successful Giraudoux was in transforming Kennedy and Dean's English text, treating the story with considerable originality and adding characteristic touches: fantasy, wordplay, and contrasting tones, including gentle irony and disabused melancholy. Multiple couples and other characters, especially girls and young women, offer variations on themes, including youth and adulthood, the desire for purity, love and its suffering, conjugal conflicts, art, and death.

Supplément au voyage de Cook, a satire, appeared on a double bill with *La Guerre de Troie n'aura pas lieu* in 1935–1936. Although not a *pièce à thèse* (thesis play), the topic of the play is serious: the noble savage, a figure that had appeared previously in the works of major French authors such as Michel de Montaigne, Jean-Jacques Rousseau, and Denis Diderot. The 1931 Colonial Exposition had attracted Parisians' attention to the exoticism of the contemporary French colonial empire, including Tahiti. Coincidentally, colonial expansion was in the news in 1935 with Italy's invasion of Ethiopia. Giraudoux already had shown interest in the South Seas in *Suzanne et le Pacifique.* The title, *Supplément au voyage de Cook,* is derived from Diderot's dialogue *Supplément au voyage de Bougainville* (composed 1772, published 1796). Giraudoux borrowed from Diderot and others who wrote on Louis-Antoine de Bougainville and James Cook. Clustered around the central theme of *naturisme,* or living in harmony with nature, are Puritan hypocrisy, economic exploitation, greed, sexual freedom, and happiness.

L'Impromptu de Paris was a curtain-raiser for the revival of *La Guerre de Troie n'aura pas lieu* in which actors from Jouvet's troupe played themselves rehearsing and discussing plays, audiences, theater finances, and reviewers. This piece was written in response to critics, especially those hostile to *Electre*. The principal source is Molière's *L'Impromptu de Versailles* (The Impromptu of Versailles, performed 1663, published 1682), from which a few lines are quoted. Another model is Copeau's Molière-inspired *Impromptu du Vieux-Colombier* (The Impromptu of Vieux-Colombier), first produced in New York in 1917, and a third source is Giraudoux's own article "La Querelle du théâtre" (1931, The Theater Dispute), included in *Littérature* (1941, Literature) as "Discours sur le théâtre" (Discourse on Theater).

L'Impromptu de Paris was not popular and has been revived infrequently, although it is important for offering behind-the-scenes perspectives and a portrait of Jouvet. It is completely realistic. However, the aesthetic irony is that, through presumed reality, the play explores the unreality of theater, including how stage effects are produced, how actors achieve emotional tones, and how acting conveys truth. The play argues that theatrical truth does not consist in didacticism but in aesthetic experience. Answering those who called him too literary, Giraudoux emphasizes the value of refined language and elevated drama. He also argues for the high cultural value of the theater to France and for further state support of theatrical endeavors, saying, "A théâtre carié, nation cariée" (decayed theater, decayed nation). He writes, "Il s'agit de savoir si l'Etat voudra enfin comprendre qu'un peuple n'a une vie réelle grande que s'il a une vie irréelle puissante" (It's a question of finding out whether the State will finally understand that a people has a great real life only if it has a powerful unreal life).

Cantique des cantiques, another curtain-raiser, was produced at the Comédie-Française, a state-subsidized theater. It is a reworking of the biblical text, which is attributed erroneously to Solomon. Its three characters—Solomon, the Shulamite woman he desires, and her beloved, a shepherd—become "Monsieur le Président," Florence, and her fiancé, Jérôme. Monsieur le Président is based on Aristide Briand, who was premier ten times

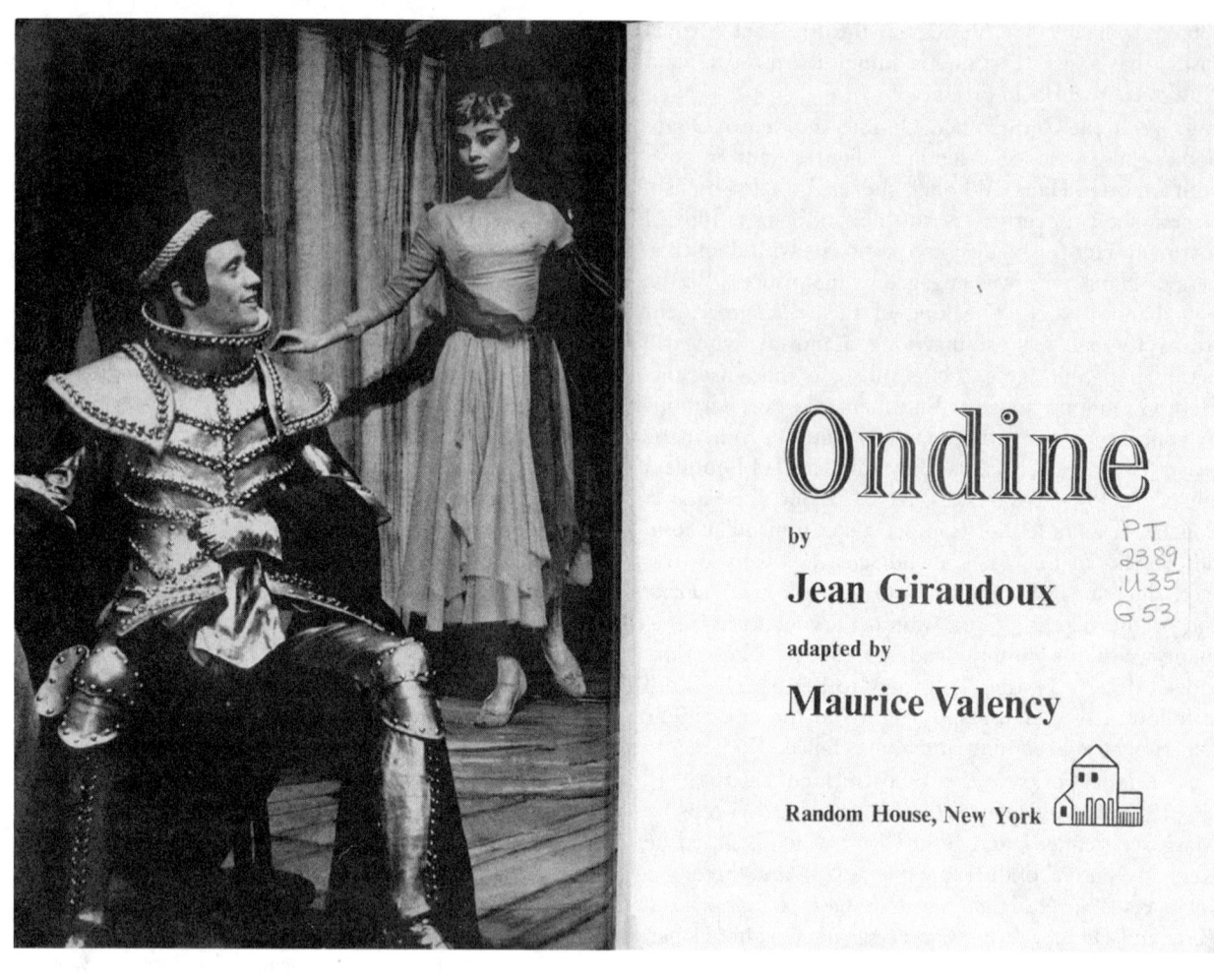

Frontispiece and title page for the 1954 English adaptation of Giraudoux's Ondine *(1939). The frontispiece presents Mel Ferrer and Audrey Hepburn in a scene for the production at the Forty-Sixth Street Theatre, New York (photograph by Milton H. Greene; Thomas Cooper Library, University of South Carolina).*

and strongly supported the League of Nations. The action takes place in a café in the Bois de Boulogne, with the staff serving as a chorus. The situation—a beautiful woman telling her distinguished older lover that, though she adores him, she will marry an ordinary but young man—allows Giraudoux to expound, in witty, elegant language on the theme of love.

Giraudoux's last one-act play, titled *L'Apollon de Bellac* (published 1946; translated as *The Apollo of Bellac*, 1954), was first presented by Jouvet's troupe in Rio de Janeiro in 1942 under the title *L'Apollon de Marsac*. It was revived as such in Paris in 1947, although by then it had been published under the new title, honored in subsequent editions and productions. The "Apollo" of the title is simply an imaginary classical statue, a point of reference for masculine beauty. A light comedy, *L'Apollon de Bellac* has a simple premise: a charming young woman can obtain anything from a man simply by telling him he is handsome. Agnès, the heroine, gets advice about this strategy from "le monsieur de Bellac," who coaches her so well that she wins favor after favor, finally getting a marriage proposal from a crusty gentleman who breaks his engagement to "Chèvredent" (Goat-tooth). Giraudoux's love for beauty—in language, objects, faces, everywhere—shines through the dialogue. The conclusion can, however, be read as dark, since it suggests that the world is so ugly that only mendacity can make it tolerable, and it also suggests that true beauty is illusory.

A difficult period for Giraudoux began in 1939 and continued through the 1940s. The Munich agreements of 1938 had shown that Europe would not avoid general war much longer. Giraudoux had ceased living with Suzanne, their domestic discord having become unbearable; he began living in hotels. That same year he started an affair with a young married journalist, Isabelle Monterou, which lasted until she broke with him in autumn 1943. Giraudoux's son was mobilized in

June 1940, just before France fell, and he subsequently joined the Free French in England. Giraudoux and his son never saw each other again. In summer 1939 Giraudoux was named commissioner of information, a post created to counteract German propaganda. He was criticized for his speeches–critics claimed they were too culturally oriented, lacking in realpolitik, and insufficiently sensitive to fascist threats–just as he was attacked for statements made in *Pleins pouvoirs* (1939, Full Powers) concerning the threat posed to France by political unrest, unwise immigration policies, and general moral and cultural decline. Some people, encouraged by his brief and inconsequential service in the Vichy government and acquaintance with high-placed German cultural figures, even attacked him later as a fascist and collaborationist. However, Giraudoux engaged in no active support of the Nazi regime, which he disliked, and, after brief illusions about Philippe Pétain's leadership, concluded that Vichy was a wrongheaded failure.

Begun in 1938, *Sodome et Gomorrhe,* described by Giraudoux as "une tragédie sur la fin du monde" (a tragedy on the world's end), in a 1941 letter to his son, was completed during winter 1941–1942 under the German occupation and produced in autumn 1943, with music by Honegger. The German censors required one minor cut. Although the play does not amount to a political rallying cry, its pessimism may reflect the war and Occupation. The allusion by the Gardener (a chorus-like character) to the fall of empires recalls French defeat. Conjugal unhappiness also influenced the author. Human beings are portrayed pessimistically. The basis for *Sodome et Gomorrhe* is Genesis 19, which recounts Jehovah's destruction of the wicked Cities of the Plain. A French literary precedent is a poem by Alfred de Vigny (whom Giraudoux mentioned in *Choix des élues*), "La Colère de Samson" (1864, Samson's Wrath), which includes the well-known lines: "La Femme aura Gomorrhe et l'Homme aura Sodome" (Woman will have Gomorrah, and Man will have Sodom).

Giraudoux's principal theme in the play is couples and their inability to love truly and achieve happiness. As the play opens, a few couples–Lia and Jean, Delilah and Samson, Ruth and Jacques–remain, others having separated and fled the burning cities. An archangel announces that if one truly happy couple can be found, God will have mercy. However, what Amphitryon and Alcmène, and Hector and Andromaque, achieve in Giraudoux's earlier plays has become impossible, even with the urging of an angel sent for encouragement. Human beings seek novelty: "Les grands caps de la douceur, les îles de l'entente, les promontoires de la tendresse, on ne peut les revoir qu'avec un nouvel amour" (The great capes of sweetness, the islands of understanding, the promontories of tenderness, one can see them again only with a new love). Furthermore, people feed on conflict. Lia, though filled with hostility, stakes all on Jean, who does not heed her last, unspoken plea. Finally, everything is incinerated. Only the presence of a rose suggests later redemption.

In this somber tragedy Giraudoux displayed dazzling linguistic effects, employing metaphor, paradox, antithesis, hyperbole, reiteration, and other devices. Some critics found his use of these effects excessive and criticized the playwright for creating a pastiche from his earlier works. For example, Claude Jamet, writing for *Notre Combat* (30 October 1943, Our Combat), claimed "Ce ne sont qu'arabesques, broderies et méandres" (It's only arabesques, embroidery and meanders). These effects are not merely ornamental, however, but psychologically expressive, as when Samson says, "Il est une pierre de lune que l'on glisse dans la nuit pour la faire prendre, pour que tout en devienne gel de beauté et de resplendissement: c'est le sommeil de Dalila" (There is a moonstone that one slips into the night to make it "catch," so that everything becomes a frost of beauty and brilliance; it's Delilah's sleep). The play ran for 214 performances.

During this run of *Sodome et Gomorrhe,* Giraudoux, who had long suffered from various health problems as well as wartime privation, died on 31 January 1944 of sudden kidney failure. The hypothesis that he was poisoned was put forth immediately, but political prudence dictated that no autopsy be done. If he was murdered, it may have been because he was at work secretly on papers–a "dossier on France"–and had tried to assemble a modest resistance group intended to contribute to French reconstruction after the German defeat. Although he was released from service, his status as a diplomat made him vulnerable to surveillance by Vichy and German authorities, who perhaps feared his influence.

Giraudoux's last two completed plays were produced posthumously. *La Folle de Chaillot* (performed and published 1945; adapted as *The Madwoman of Chaillot,* 1947), which received a government grant to offset the large production expense, was a tremendous success. General Charles de Gaulle attended the premiere. It had a run of 297 consecutive performances and many productions abroad. The play, which has been compared to Aristophanes' comedies, is chiefly farcical and satirical. Its topic–the tyranny and immorality of high finance (focusing on the "Deux cents familles," or Two Hundred Families, the largest stockholders in the Banque de France)–struck a chord with many Parisians. Artisans and small businesses, threatened by the financial manipulation and uncontrolled international capitalism satirized in the play, traditionally had been honored in France, and the caricatures of robber-baron tycoons recalled German industrial exploitation of French resources. Decades later the play remains

Monique Mélinand, Louis Jouvet, and Marguerite Moreno in Giraudoux's La Folle de Chaillot *(adapted as* The Madwoman of Chaillot*), Théâtre de l'Athénée, Paris, December 1945 (© Lipnitzki/Roger-Viollet/Getty Images)*

timely, with its attacks on venture capitalists and stock-market manipulators whose jargon is designed to fool investors, as well as its attacks on ill-planned urban development, including the destruction of historic neighborhoods and the usurpation of countryside for industrial purposes. From the 1930s Giraudoux had advocated, in lectures and writings, urban planning and prudent environmentalism.

The play is set on a café terrace, where two financiers meet to discuss their project, drilling for petroleum underneath Paris buildings. Whether it is really there is unimportant: the crucial thing is to sell stock to get capital. A large cast of characters from the café and the neighborhood—a dishwasher, street vendors, a juggler, a ragpicker, eccentrics, the madwoman of Chaillot—overhear the plot and, with the madwoman's friends from other neighborhoods, resolve to foil it. They do so by luring the capitalists into her cellar, where they expect to find oil and instead are trapped forever. The madwoman saves from despair a suicidal young victim of the capitalists' blackmail: she makes him see again that life is beautiful, and he falls in love with the charming dishwasher.

The playwright's sympathetic understanding for those on the margins of society, whose lives, modest but authentic, contrast with the capitalists', is visible in his sketches, including their poetic turns of phrase and the fantasy of their world. La Folle and her friends have raised imagination to a powerful level: the dead are present, and objects speak. Their denial of reality does not, however, weaken them, but rather strengthens them, for the world is a "mascarade" (masquerade). Hence, being crazy is being sane. La Folle calls herself "une femme de sens" (a reasonable woman) in contrast to "la folie du monde" (the madness of the world), and the playwright, in a letter to Isabelle Monterou (quoted in *Théâtre complet* [1982]), spoke of his heroine as being "dans sa raison" (in her reason). That is, the brutality of an entirely rationalized existence, where the abstract value of money trumps concrete joys and human beings are merely obstacles to industrial development, can be counteracted only by a sort of folly. Such folly is perfectly at home in the theater, which, as philosopher Gabriel Marcel wrote in connection with the play (*Les Nouvelles Littéraires*, 27 December 1945), "redevient ici une magie, un mode d'incantation" (becomes again here magic and a means of incantation).

The last play Giraudoux completed, *Pour Lucrèce*, starred four outstanding actors: Barrault and Renaud (whose company produced the play), Feuillère, and Jean Servais. It was not particularly successful, although it ran for more than a hundred performances. The title refers to Lucretia, wife of L. Tarquinius Collatinus, whose rape led to the dethronement of Tarquinius Superbus and the establishment of the Roman republic. Dealing in broad strokes with vice and virtue, and consequently melodramatic, *Pour Lucrèce* nevertheless has a tragic, elevated tone, with rigorous construction, long speeches, and, like Racine's tragedies, many *scènes à faire* (confrontations between principals) and much cruelty. Its southern setting (Aix-en-Provence) sets off the powerful passions. Although the play is set during the Second Empire, it recalls eighteenth-century seduction novels such as Pierre-Ambroise-François Choderlos de Laclos's *Les Liaisons dangereuses* (1782; translated as *Dangerous Connections*, 1784), on which Giraudoux wrote a study. There "virtue" is defined in sexual terms only; yet, what matters is chiefly *apparent*, not actual, virtue.

Lucille, married to the public prosecutor, condemns those who do not adhere to her high standards of moral conduct. Led by this intransigence, she informs Armand that his wife, Paola, repeatedly has been unfaithful. Paola arranges, with the local procuress, a revenge by which Lucille, having been drugged, is led to believe that she has been raped by Marcellus, a handsome Don Juan she despises. The psychological consequences are devastating. Lucille shames Marcellus into agreeing to a duel with her new champion, Armand, who kills him; she also informs her husband, whose rage is boundless; and, though she later learns of the hoax, she poisons herself, "for Lucretia" (that is, to maintain women's honor), or because she cannot live with the redefinition of herself and others that the experience has brought about. Words and appearances are crucial: Paola's husband had been satisfied by the illusion of fidelity, as Lucille is shamed by the illusion of infidelity.

Giraudoux's characterization in *Pour Lucrèce* is complicated. He does not paint Lucille in entirely favorable colors. Paola's manipulations seem half-justified by Lucille's betrayal of her sex. Furthermore, Paola has been faithful in her own way by protecting her husband's illusions. The town's easygoing spirit, which tolerated refined sexual dallying, has been destroyed, and civilized relationships between men and women have been replaced by the fatal sexual warfare that characterizes *Sodome et Gomorrhe*. Giraudoux's relentless pessimism often seems to reveal misogyny: in their infidelities, jealousies, and manipulations, women seem despicable. But in this play he is a defender of feminism; he judges men—weak, pompous, unfaithful—severely, and assigns to the procuress the final pronouncement: men should go to eternal damnation. Brilliant insights into the psychology of love and the luminous southern setting cannot offset such a dark picture.

Since Giraudoux's death, many scholarly pieces focusing on his life and works have been published. Although he cherished privacy and published no diary, his manuscripts and correspondence have furnished valuable evidence concerning his private life and his creative process. Scholars have studied the genesis of his plays, assessed his connection to Germany, examined his style, and traced themes through his works. Although he repeatedly expressed hostility to Freudian doctrines, critics interested in psychoanalysis have not neglected him. His narcissistic bent, which he recognized himself, is treated in André Job's psychoanalytical study, which refers to such basic Freudian notions as transfer. Other commentators have attempted to evaluate his work overall. For example, Roy explains that while Giraudoux's novels will be little read because his preciosity is too visible there, his theater will remain "comme une oeuvre représentative de notre temps, d'un temps à la fois illustre par Sartre, qui est l'anti-Giraudoux, et par Giraudoux, qui est l'antiSartre" (as a representative work of our time, a time illustrious both by Sartre, who is the anti-Giraudoux, and by Giraudoux, who is the anti-Sartre).

Perhaps Jean Giraudoux's understanding of theater, expressed in *L'Impromptu de Paris*, offers the best grounds for evaluating his work: "Le théâtre n'est pas un théorème, mais un spectacle, pas une leçon, mais un filtre. . . . Il a moins à entrer dans votre esprit que dans votre imagination et dans vos sens, et c'est pour cela, à mon avis, que le talent de l'écriture lui est indispensable, car c'est le style qui renvoie sur l'âme des spectateurs mille reflets" (Theater is not a theorem but a spectacle, not a lesson, but a filter.... It must enter your mind less than your imagination and your senses, and it's for that reason, in my opinion, that writing talent is indispensable to it, for it's style that sends into the soul of the audience a thousand reflections). While Sartre's theater is accusatory, one may say that Giraudoux's theater, the "lieu d'heureuse lumière, de beau langage, de figures imaginaires" (place of fortunate lighting, fine language, imaginary figures), furnishes a place of redemption for a degraded world.

Letters:

Lettres, edited by Jacques Body (Paris: Klincksieck, 1975);

Correspondance entre Jean Giraudoux et Louis Jouvet, edited by Brett Dawson, Cahiers Jean Giraudoux, no. 9 (Paris: Grasset, 1980), pp. 20–122;

Lettres à Lilita 1910–1928, edited by Mauricette Berne (Paris: Gallimard, 1989).

Interviews:

Frédéric Lefèvre, "Jean Giraudoux," in his *Une heure avec . . . ,* fourth series (Paris: Gallimard, 1924), pp. 141–151;

"De la façon de faire comprendre et goûter les auteurs modernes," *Cahiers de la République des Lettres, des Sciences et des Arts,* 1 (15 April 1926): 70;

A. de Luppé, "Jean Giraudoux," *Le Correspondant,* 311 (25 May 1928): 509–523;

Georges Charensol, *Comment ils écrivent* (Paris: Montaigne, 1932), pp. 103–106;

André Lang, "L'Enchanteur Jean Giraudoux," in his *Tiers de siecle* (Paris: Plon, 1935), pp. 216–221.

Bibliographies:

Laurent LeSage, *L'Œuvre de Jean Giraudoux: Essai de bibliographie chronologique,* 2 volumes (Paris: Nizet / University Park: Pennsylvania University Press, 1956, 1958);

Jacques Body and Brett Dawson, *Supplément à Laurent LeSage, "L'Œuvre de Jean Giraudoux"* (Bellac: Association des Amis de Jean Giraudoux, 1974).

Biographies:

Paul Morand, *Giraudoux: Souvenirs de notre jeunesse* (Geneva: La Palatine, 1948);

Laurent LeSage, *Jean Giraudoux: His Life and Works* (University Park: Pennsylvania State University Press, 1959);

Madeleine Ozeray, *A toujours monsieur Jouvet . . .* (Paris: Buchet-Chastel, 1966);

Jean-Pierre Giraudoux, *Le Fils* (Paris: Grasset, 1967);

Georges Lemaitre, *Giraudoux: The Writer and His Work* (New York: Ungar, 1972);

La Jeunesse de Jean Giraudoux en Berry: Centenaire de Jean Giraudoux (1882–1944) (Châteauroux, 1983);

Philippe Dufay, *Jean Giraudoux: Biographie* (Paris: Julliard, 1993).

References:

René-Marill Albérès, *Esthétique et morale chez Jean Giraudoux* (Paris: Nizet, 1957);

Albérès, *La Genèse du "Siegfried" de Jean Giraudoux* (Paris: Minard, Lettres Modernes, 1963);

Pierre d'Almeida and others, *Analyses et réflexions sur Giraudoux, La Guerre de Troie n'aura pas lieu: L'histoire* (Paris: Ellipses, 1989);

Jacques Body, *Giraudoux et l'Allemagne* (Paris: Didier, 1975);

Body, *La Légende et le secret* (Paris: Presses Universitaires de France, 1986); translated by James Norwood as *Jean Giraudoux: The Legend and the Secret* (Rutherford, N.J.: Fairleigh Dickinson University Press / London & Cranbury, N.J.: Associated University Presses, 1991);

Body, "Nationalisme et cosmopolitanisme dans la pensée de Giraudoux," in *Actes du Congrès de l'Association Internationale de Littérature Comparée* (The Hague & Paris, 1966), pp. 534–540;

Body and Pierre Brunel, eds., *"Electre" de Jean Giraudoux: Regards croisés* (Paris: Klincksieck, 1997);

Arthur C. Buck, *Jean Giraudoux and Oriental Thought: A Study of Affinities* (New York: Peter Lang, 1984);

Cahiers de l'Association Internationale des Etudes Françaises, special Giraudoux issue, 24 (May 1982);

Morton M. Celler, *Giraudoux et la métaphore: Une Etude des images dans ses romans* (The Hague & Paris: Mouton, 1974);

Robert Cohen, *Giraudoux: Three Faces of Destiny* (Chicago: University of Chicago Press, 1968);

Sylvie Coyault and others, eds., *Jean Giraudoux et les mythes* (Clermont-Ferrand: Presses Universitaires Blaise Pascal/Centre de Recherches sur les Littératures Modernes et Contemporaines, 2000);

Aurel David, *Vie et mort de Jean Giraudoux* (Paris: Flammarion, 1967);

Brett Dawson, "De Harvard au Quai d'Orsay (avril 1908–juin 1910)," *Revue d'Histoire Littéraire de la France,* 83 (September–December 1983): 711–724;

Luc Decaunes, "En relisant *Bella,* ou Jean Giraudoux romancier," *Marginales,* 98 (November 1964): 1–10;

Marie-Jeanne Durry, *L'Univers de Giraudoux* (Paris: Mercure de France, 1961);

Esprit Créateur, special Giraudoux issue, 9 (Summer 1969);

"Giraudoux en son temps," *Revue d'Histoire Littéraire de la France,* 83 (September–December 1983): 707–708;

Gunnar Graumann, *"La Guerre de Troie" aura lieu: La préparation de la pièce de Giraudoux,* Etudes romanes de Lund, no. 30 (Lund: Liber Läromedel/ Gleerup, 1979);

Jacques Guicharnaud, *Modern French Theatre from Giraudoux to Beckett* (New Haven: Yale University Press, 1961);

Jacques Houlet, *Le Théâtre de Jean Giraudoux* (Paris: Ardent, 1945);

Donald Percival Inskip, *Jean Giraudoux: The Making of a Dramatist* (London & New York: Oxford University Press, 1958);

André Job, *Giraudoux Narcisse: Genèse d'une écriture romanesque* (Toulouse: Presses Universitaires du Mirail, 1998);

Louis Jouvet, *Réflexions du comédien* (Paris: Nouvelle Revue Critique, 1938);

Victoria B. Korzeniowska, *Giraudoux: "La Guerre de Troie n'aura pas lieu"* (London: Grant & Cutler, 2003);

Korzeniowska, *The Heroine as Social Redeemer in the Plays of Jean Giraudoux,* Modern French Identities, no. 13 (New York: Peter Lang, 2001);

Charles Krance, "Giraudoux's *Suzanne et le Pacifique:* Text, Topoi and Community," *Australian Journal of French Studies,* 14 (May–August 1977): 164–173;

Hubert Laizé, *Premières leçons sur "Electre" de Jean Giraudoux* (Paris: Presses Universitaires de France, 1998);

Laurent LeSage, *Jean Giraudoux, Surrealism, and the German Romantic Ideal* (Urbana: University of Illinois Press, 1952);

Gilbert van de Louw, *La Tragédie grecque dans le théâtre de Giraudoux* (Nancy: Centre Européen Universitaire, 1967);

Claude-Edmonde Magny, *Précieux Giraudoux* (Paris: Seuil, 1968);

Paul A. Mankin, *Precious Irony: The Theatre of Jean Giraudoux* (The Hague: Mouton, 1971);

Charles P. Marie, *Giraudoux aux sources du sens* (Besançon: Editions Austrasie, 1983);

Marie, *La Réalité humaine chez Giraudoux* (Paris: Pensée Universelle, 1975);

Christian Marker, *Giraudoux par lui-méme* (Paris: Editions du Seuil, 1952);

Charles Mauron, *Le Théâtre de Giraudoux: Etude psychocritique* (Paris: Corti, 1971);

Will L. McLendon, "Les 'Antennes' des héros de Giraudoux," *Esprit Créateur,* 9 (Summer 1969): 118–127;

McLendon, "Giraudoux and the Impossible Couple," *PMLA,* 82 (May 1967): 197–205;

McLendon, "Giraudoux and the Split Personality," *PMLA,* 73 (December 1958): 573–584;

McLendon, "Giraudoux, champion de l'urbanisme," *Le Bayou,* 58 (Summer 1954): 69–75;

McLendon, "Un Mutilé de Giraudoux: *Simon le pathétique,*" *French Review,* 31 (December 1957): 99–108;

Marianne Mercier-Campiche, *Le Théâtre de Jean Giraudoux et la condition humaine* (Paris: Domat, 1954);

Paul Morand, *Giraudoux: Souvenirs de notre jeunesse* (Geneva: La Palatine, 1948);

Marie-Christine Moreau, *"Electre" ou l'intransigeance* (Toulouse: Centre Régional de Documentation Pédagogique de Midi-Pyrénées, 1997);

Alain Niederst, *Jean Giraudoux ou l'impossible éternité* (Paris: Nizet, 1994);

Brenda J. Powell, *The Metaphysical Quality of the Tragic: A Study of Sophocles, Giraudoux, and Sartre* (New York: Peter Lang, 1990);

Michel Raimond, *Sur trois pièces de Giraudoux: "La Guerre de Troie n'aura pas lieu," "Electre," "Ondine"* (Paris: Nizet, 1982);

Agnes Raymond, *Jean Giraudoux: The Theatre of Victory and Defeat* (Amherst: University of Massachusetts Press, 1966);

Raymond, "Première ébauche d'un profil stylistique de Giraudoux," *Language and Style,* 6 (Winter 1973): 39–47;

John H. Reilly, *Jean Giraudoux* (Boston: Twayne, 1979);

Revue d'Histoire du Théâtre, special Giraudoux issue, nos. 1–2 (1952);

Jacques Robichez, *Le Théâtre de Giraudoux* (Paris: Société d'Edition d'Enseignement Supérieur, 1976);

Jules Roy, "Les Jeunes Filles dans l'œuvre de Giraudoux et de Montherlant," *Annales Conferencia,* 9 (15 September 1949);

Elisabeth Scheele, *Le "Discours aux morts" de Jean Giraudoux* (New York: Peter Lang, 1997);

Hans Sørensen, *Le Théâtre de Jean Giraudoux: Technique et style* (Aarhus: Universitetsforlaget, 1950).

Papers:

Manuscripts and letters by Jean Giraudoux are at the Fonds Giraudoux and Fonds Louis Jouvet, Bibliothèque Nationale de France; the Fonds Louis Jouvet, Bibliothèque de l'Arsenal; the Fonds Jacques Doucet, Bibliothèque Sainte-Geneviève; the Special Collections Library, Pennsylvania State University; and the Harry Ransom Humanities Research Center, University of Texas at Austin.

Eugène Ionesco

(13 November 1909 – 28 March 1994)

Jeanine Teodorescu-Regier
Elmhurst College

PLAY PRODUCTIONS: *La Cantatrice chauve,* Paris, Théâtre des Noctambules, 11 May 1950;

La Leçon, Paris, Théâtre de Poche, 20 February 1951;

Les Chaises, Paris, Théâtre Lancry, 22 April 1952;

Victimes du devoir, Paris, Théâtre du Quartier Latin, February 1953;

Le Maître, Paris, Théâtre de la Huchette, September 1953;

La Jeune Fille à marier, Paris, Théâtre de la Huchette, 1 September 1953;

Amédée, ou Comment s'en débarasser, Paris, Théâtre de Babylone, 14 April 1954;

Jacques, ou La Soumission, Paris, Théâtre de la Huchette, 15 October 1955;

Le Tableau, Paris, Théâtre de la Huchette, October 1955;

Le Nouveau Locataire, Helsinki, 1955; London, Arts Theatre, 6 November 1956;

L'Impromptu de l'Alma, ou Le Caméléon du berger, Paris, Studio des Champs-Elysées, 20 February 1956;

L'Avenir est dans les œufs, ou Il faut tout pour faire un monde, Paris, Théâtre de la Cité Universitaire, 23 June 1957;

Tueur sans gages, Darmstadt, Germany, Landestheater, 14 April 1958; Paris, Théâtre Récamier, 27 February 1959;

Scène à quatre, Spoleto, Italy, June 1959;

Rhinocéros, Düsseldorf, Schauspielhaus, 6 November 1959; Paris, Théâtre de l'Odéon, 25 January 1960; London, Royal Court Theater, 28 April 1960;

Délire à deux, Paris, Studio des Champs-Elysées, April 1962;

Le Roi se meurt, Paris, Théâtre de l'Alliance Française, 15 December 1962;

Le Piéton de l'air, Paris, Théâtre de l'Odéon, 6 February 1963;

La Soif et la Faim, Paris, Comédie-Française, 28 February 1966;

La Lacune, Paris, Théâtre de l'Odéon, 7 March 1966;

Eugène Ionesco (© Lipnitzki/Roger-Viollet/Getty Images)

Jeux de massacre, Düsseldorf, Schauspielhaus, 24 January 1970;

Macbett, Paris, Théâtre de la Rive Gauche, 27 January 1972;

Ce formidable bordel! Paris, Théâtre Moderne, 10 November 1973;

L'Homme aux valises, Paris, Théâtre de l'Atelier, October 1975;

Voyage chez les morts, New York, Guggenheim Theater, 1980.

BOOKS: *Elegii pentru fiinte mici* (Craiova: Cercul Analelor Române, 1931);

Nu (Bucharest: Vremea, 1934); translated from Romanian into French by Marie-France Ionesco as *Non* (Paris: Gallimard, 1986);

Théâtre, preface by Jacques Lemarchand (Paris: Arcanes, 1953)–includes *La Cantatrice chauve; La Leçon; Jacques, ou La Soumission;* and *Le Salon de l'automobile; La Cantatrice chauve* translated by Donald M. Allen as *The Bald Soprano,* in *Four Plays* (New York: Grove, 1958), pp. 7–42, and by Donald Watson as *The Bald Prima Donna,* in *Plays,* volume 1 (London: Calder, 1958); *La Leçon* translated by Allen as *The Lesson,* in *Four Plays* (New York: Grove, 1958), pp. 43–78, and by Watson as *The Lesson,* in *Plays,* volume 1 (London: Calder, 1958); *Jacques, ou La Soumission* translated by Allen as *Jack, or The Submission,* in *Four Plays* (New York: Grove, 1958), pp. 79–110, and by Watson as *Jacques, or Obedience,* in *Plays,* volume 1 (London: Calder, 1958); *Le Salon de l'automobile* translated by Watson as *The Motor Show,* in *Plays,* volume 5 (London: Calder, 1963);

Théâtre, volume 1 (Paris: Gallimard, 1954)–includes *La Cantatrice chauve; La Leçon; Jacques, ou La Soumission; Les Chaises; Victimes du devoir;* and *Amédée, ou Comment s'en débarrasser; Les Chaises* translated by Allen as *The Chairs,* in *Four Plays* (New York: Grove, 1958), pp. 111–160, and by Watson as *The Chairs,* in *Plays,* volume 1 (London: Calder, 1958); *Victimes du devoir* translated by Watson as *Victims of Duty,* in *Plays,* volume 2 (London: Calder, 1958; New York: Grove, 1958); *Amédée, ou Comment s'en débarrasser* translated by Watson as *Amédée, or How to Get Rid of It,* in *Plays,* volume 2 (London: Calder, 1958; New York: Grove, 1958);

Théâtre, volume 2 (Paris: Gallimard, 1958)–includes *L'Impromptu de l'Alma, ou Le Caméléon du berger; Tueur sans gages; Le Nouveau Locataire; L'Avenir est dans les œufs, ou Il faut tout pour faire un monde; Le Maître;* and *La Jeune Fille à marier; L'Impromptu de l'Alma, ou Le Caméléon du berger* translated by Watson as *Improvisation, or The Shepherd's Chameleon,* in *Plays,* volume 3 (London: Calder, 1960); *Tueur sans gages* translated by Watson as *The Killer,* in *Plays,* volume 3 (London: Calder, 1960); *Le Nouveau Locataire* translated by Watson as *The New Tenant,* in *Plays,* volume 2 (London: Calder 1958; New York: Grove, 1958); *L'Avenir est dans les œufs, ou Il faut tout pour faire un monde,* translated by Derek Prouse as *The Future Is in the Eggs, or It Takes All Sorts to Make a World,* in *Plays,* volume 4 (London: Calder, 1960); *Le Maître* translated by Prouse as *The Leader,* in *Plays,* volume 4 (London: Calder, 1960); and *La Jeune Fille à marier* translated by Watson as *Maid to Marry,* in *Plays,* volume 3 (London: Calder, 1960);

Rhinocéros: Pièce en trois actes et quatre tableaux (Paris: Gallimard, 1959); translated by Prouse as *Rhinoceros,* in *Plays,* volume 4 (London: Calder, 1960);

La Petite Molière, by Jean Anouilh and Roland Laudenbach; *Scènes à quatre: 1 Acte,* by Ionesco (Paris: L'Avant-scène, 1959);

Ionesco, Les rhinocéros au théâtre (Paris: Julliard, 1960);

La Photo du colonel (Paris: Gallimard, 1962); translated by Jean Stewart as *The Colonel's Photograph,* with the exception of "The Stroller in the Air," translated by John Russell (New York: Grove, 1967);

Notes et contre-notes (Paris: Gallimard, 1962); translated by Watson (London: Calder & Boyars, 1964);

Théâtre, volume 3 (Paris: Gallimard, 1963)–includes *Rhinocéros; Le Piéton de l'air; Délire à deux; Le Tableau, Scène à quatre; Les Salutations;* and *La Colère; Le Piéton de l'air* translated by Watson as *A Stroll in the Air,* in *Plays,* volume 6 (London: Calder & Boyars, 1965; New York: Grove, 1968); *Délire à deux* translated by Watson as *Frenzy for Two,* in *Plays,* volume 6 (London: Calder & Boyars, 1965; New York: Grove, 1968); *Les Salutations* translated by Watson as *Salutations,* in *Plays,* volume 7 (London: Calder & Boyars, 1968);

Le Roi se meurt (Paris: Gallimard, 1963); translated by Watson as *Exit the King,* in *Plays,* volume 5 (London: Calder & Boyars, 1963);

Théâtre, volume 4 (Paris: Gallimard, 1966)–includes *Le Roi se meurt; La Soif et la Faim; La Lacune; Le Salon de l'automobile; L'Œuf dur; Pour préparer un œuf dur; Le Jeune Homme à marier;* and *Apprendre à marcher; La Soif et la Faim* translated by Watson as *Hunger and Thirst,* in *Plays,* volume 7 (London: Calder & Boyars, 1968); *La Lacune* translated by Rosette Lamont as *The Gap* (Amherst: University of Massachusetts Press, 1969); *Apprendre à marcher* translated by Watson as *Learning to Walk,* in *Plays,* volume 9 (London: Calder & Boyars, 1973);

Journal en miettes (Paris: Mercure de France, 1967);

Présent passé, passé présent (Paris: Mercure de France, 1968); translated by Helen R. Lane as *Present Past, Past Present: A Personal Memoir* (New York: Grove, 1971; London: Calder & Boyars, 1972); translation republished, with a new introduction by Robert Brustein (New York: Da Capo, 1998);

Story Number 1: For Children Under Three Years of Age, translated by Calvin K. Touwle (New York: Quist, 1968); original French version published as *Conte numéro 1: Pour enfants de moins de trois ans* (Paris: Quist, 1969);

Découvertes, illustrated by Ionesco (Geneva: Skira, 1969);

Mise en train: Première année de français, by Michel Benamou, with original dialogues by Ionesco in collaboration with Monique Callamand (New York: Macmillan / London: Collier-Macmillan, 1969);

Conte numéro 2: Pour enfants de moins de trois ans (Paris: Quist, 1970); translated by Touwle as *Story Number 2: For Children under Three Years of Age* (New York: Quist, 1970);

Discours d'Eugène Ionesco à l'Académie française et réponse de Jean Delay (Paris: Gallimard, 1971);

Conte numéro 3: Pour enfants de plus de trois ans (Paris: Quist, 1971); translated by Ciba Vaughan as *Story Number 3: For Children over Three Years of Age* (New York: Quist, 1971);

Conte numéro 4: Pour enfants de moins de trois ans (Paris: Quist, 1971); translated by Vaughan as *Story Number 4: For Children of Any Age* (New York: Quist, 1973);

Macbett (Paris: Gallimard, 1972); translated by Watson, in *Plays*, volume 9 (London: Calder & Boyars, 1973);

Ce formidable bordel! (Paris: Gallimard, 1973); translated by Helen Gary Bishop as *A Hell of a Mess* (New York: Grove, 1975);

Le Solitaire (Paris: Gallimard, 1973); translated by Richard Seaver as *The Hermit* (New York: Viking, 1974; London: Deutsch, 1975);

Théâtre, volume 5 (Paris: Gallimard, 1974)–includes *Jeux de massacre; Macbett; La Vase;* and *Exercices de conversation et de diction françaises pour étudiants américains; Jeux de massacre* translated by Helen Gary Bishop as *Killing Game* (New York: Grove, 1974);

Théâtre, volume 6 (Paris: Gallimard, 1975)–includes *L'Homme aux valises suivi de Ce formidable bordel!; L'Homme aux valises* adapted by Israel Horovitz, based on the translation by Marie-France Ionesco, as *Man with Bags* (New York: Grove, 1977);

Un homme en question (Paris: Gallimard, 1979);

Pour la culture, contre la politique = Für Kultur, gegen Politik (St. Gall, Switzerland: Erker, 1979);

Théâtre, volume 7 (Paris: Gallimard, 1981)–includes *Voyages chez les morts: Thèmes et variations;* translated by Barbara Wright as *Journeys Among the Dead (Themes and Variations)*, in *Plays*, volume 12 (London: Calder / New York: Riverrun, 1985);

Viata grotesca si tragica a lui Victor Hugo: Hugoliade, translated from Romanian into French by Dragomir Costineanu and Marie-France Ionesco, afterword by Gelu Ionesco (Paris: Gallimard, 1982); translated by Yara Milos as *Hugoliad: The Grotesque and Tragic Life of Victor Hugo* (New York: Grove, 1987);

Le Blanc et le noir (Paris: Gallimard, 1985);

La Main peint: Notes de travail–Die Hand malt: Arbeitsnotizen (St. Gall, Switzerland: Erker, 1987);

La Quête intermittente (Paris: Gallimard, 1987);

Ruptures de silence: Rencontres avec André Coutin (Paris: Mercure de France, 1995);

Littérature roumaine, suivi de Grosse chaleur [Les Grandes Chaleurs] (Saint-Clement-la-Riviere: Fata Morgana, 1998).

Editions and Collections: *Rhinocéros*, edited, with an introduction, by Reuben Y. Ellison and Sowell C. Goding (New York: Holt, Rinehart & Winston, 1961; enlarged, with exercises by Albert Raffanel, 1976);

Three Plays: La Cantatrice chauve; La Leçon; Les chaises, edited, with an introduction and notes in English, by H. F. Brookes and C. E. Fraenkel (London: Heinemann, 1965);

Le Roi se meurt, edited, with an introduction and notes in English, by Robert North (London: Harrap, 1966);

Rhinocéros, edited, with an introduction, by Claude Abastado (Paris: Bordas, 1970);

Le Roi se meurt, edited by Colette Audry (Paris: Larousse, 1972);

Tueur sans gages, edited, with an introduction, by J. H. McCormick (London: University of London Press, 1972);

Victimes du devoir and "Une victime du devoir," edited, with an introduction in English, by Vera Lee (Boston: Houghton Mifflin, 1972)–includes a letter from Ionesco addressed to Lee;

La Cantatrice chauve; La Leçon, edited by Lillian Bulwa and Tamar March (New York: Holt, Rinehart & Winston, 1975);

Le solitaire, edited, with an introduction and notes in English, by Brookes and Fraenkel (London: Heinemann, 1977);

Le Roi se meurt, edited by Christine Géray (Paris: Hatier, 1985);

La Cantatrice chauve et La Leçon, edited by Michel Bigot and Marie-France Savéan (Paris: Gallimard, 1991);

Théâtre complet, edited by Emmanuel Jacquart, Bibliothèque de la Pléiade, no. 372 (Paris: Gallimard, 1991).

Editions in English: *Four Plays: The Bald Soprano; The Lesson; Jack, or the Submission; The Chairs*, translated by Donald M. Allen (New York: Grove, 1958);

Plays, volume 1: *The Lesson, The Chairs, The Bald Prima Donna, Jacques, or Obedience*, translated by Donald Watson (London: Calder, 1958);

Plays, volume 2: *Amédée, or How to Get Rid of It, The New Tenant, Victims of Duty*, translated by Watson (London: Calder, 1958; New York: Grove, 1958);

Plays, volume 3: *The Killer; Improvisation, or the Shepherd's Chameleon; Maid to Marry*, translated by Watson

(London: Calder, 1960); published as *The Killer and Other Plays* (New York: Grove, 1960);

Plays, volume 4: *Rhinoceros; The Leader; The Future is in the Eggs, or It Takes All Sorts to Make a World,* translated by Derek Prouse (London: Calder, 1960); published as *The Rhinocerous and Other Plays* (New York: Grove, 1960);

Plays, volume 5: *Exit the King; Foursome; The Motor Show,* translated by Watson (London: Calder & Boyars, 1963); partially published as *Exit the King* (New York: Grove, 1963);

Plays, volume 6: *A Stroll in the Air; Frenzy for Two,* translated by Watson (London: Calder & Boyars, 1965; New York: Grove, 1968);

Plays, volume 7: *Hunger and Thirst; The Picture; Anger; Salutations,* translated by Watson (London: Calder & Boyars, 1968); published as *Hunger and Thirst and Other Plays* (New York: Grove, 1969);

Plays, volume 8: *Here Comes a Chopper; The Oversight; The Foot of the Wall,* translated by Watson (London: Calder & Boyars, 1971);

Plays, volume 9: *Macbett; The Mire; Learning to Walk,* translated by Watson (London: Calder & Boyars, 1973);

Macbett, translated by Charles Marowitz (New York: Grove, 1973);

A Hell of a Mess, translated by Helen Gary Bishop (New York: Grove, 1975);

Plays, volume 10: *Oh What a Bloody Circus; The Hard-Boiled Egg,* translated by Watson (London: Calder, 1976)–includes Watson's essay "Ionesco and His Early English Critics";

Plays, volume 11: *The Man with the Luggage; The Duel; Double Act; Why Do I Write?* translated by Watson and Clifford Williams (London: Calder, 1979);

Exit the King; The Killer; and Macbett, translated by Marowitz and Watson (New York: Grove, 1985).

PRODUCED SCRIPTS: *Le Salon de l'automobile,* radio, Club d'essai de la radio de Paris, 1952;

Apprendre à marcher, ballet scenario by Ionesco, Théâtre de l'Etoile, April 1960;

Le Jeune homme à marier, script by Ionesco, Télévision Danoise/Eurovision, 2 April 1965;

Maximilien Kolbe, libretto by Ionesco, Festival of Rimini, 28 August 1988.

OTHER: Pavel Dan, *Le Père Urcan,* translated by Ionesco and Gabrielle Gabrin (Marseille: Vigneau, 1945);

Joan Miro, *Quelques fleurs pour des amis, avec un coup d'oeil dur le jardin,* edited by Ionesco (Paris: XXe Siècle, 1964);

Ilarie Voronca, *Onze récits,* preface by Ionesco (Limoges: Rougerie, 1968);

The Niece-Wife, translated by Richard N. Coe, in his *Ionesco: A Study of His Plays* (London: Methuen, 1971), pp. 165–172;

Pierre Alechinsky, *Peintures et écrits,* preface by Ionesco (Paris: Arts et métiers graphiques, 1977).

SELECTED PERIODICAL PUBLICATION–UNCOLLECTED: *Maximilien Kolbe,* translated Rosette C. Lamont, *Performing Arts Journal,* 17 (1982): 32–36;

Scène, translated by Lamont as *Scene, Performing Arts Journal,* 24 (1984): 105–112.

With Samuel Beckett and Arthur Adamov, Eugène Ionesco is widely recognized as the founder of the Theater of the Absurd. His major works, *La Cantatrice chauve* (produced 1950; published 1953; translated as *The Bald Soprano* and *The Bald Prima Donna,* 1958), *La Leçon* (produced 1951; published 1953; translated as *The Lesson,* 1958), *Les Chaises* (produced 1952; published 1954; translated as *The Chairs,* 1958), *Rhinocéros* (published 1959; produced in Germany 1959; original version produced 1960; translated as *Rhinoceros,* 1960), *Le Roi se meurt* (produced 1962; published 1963; translated as *Exit the King,* 1963), and *La Soif et la Faim* (produced 1966; published 1966; translated as *Hunger and Thirst,* 1968), have been translated into most European languages, as well as Chinese, Japanese, and Hebrew, and have been performed all over the world.

Ionesco was a rebellious spirit who portrayed politics satirically, and he denounced any type of fanaticism as symptomatic of humanity's incurable illness. He revolutionized drama with his radical new perspective on language, demonstrating its subversion, banality, and humorous explosions, as well as its domineering power. His works feature nightmarish scenes with sometimes tragic, sometimes ludicrous characters whose surrealistic and grotesque attempts to deal with the absurdity of life fail.

While Ionesco variously subtitled plays "anti-pièce" (antiplay), "drame comique" (comical drama), "comédie naturaliste" (naturalistic drama), "farce tragique" (tragical farce), and "guignolade" (puppet show), he preferred to characterize his dramaturgy as "théâtre de dérision" (theater of derision). This new form of theater, also referred to as "anti-theater," flourished in France in the 1950s. Ionesco was one of its most brilliant practitioners, producing enduring plays that are at once puzzling, hilarious, unsettling, and thought-provoking.

Eugène Ionesco was born Eugen Ionescu in Slatina, Romania, on 13 November 1909. He was the second of Eugen and Marie-Thérèse Ionescu's three children,

Scene from a performance of Ionesco's La Cantatrice chauve *(translated as* The Bald Soprano *and* The Bald Prima Donna, *1958) at the Théâtre Noctambules in Paris, May 1950 (© Lipnitzki/Roger-Viollet/Getty Images)*

although one of the children, a son named Mircea, died at an early age. Eugen Ionescu was a prominent Romanian lawyer who held important positions in government administration. He moved his family to France in 1910 to complete his Juris Doctor in Paris, but he returned to Romania in 1916 to fight in World War I, leaving his wife in Paris to care for their two surviving children, Ionesco and Marilina. Hence, Ionesco spent the turbulent war years shuttling between the Parisian metropolis and the Loire region, at La Chapelle-Anthenaise–a place and time he later fondly recalled as paradisiacal.

The Ionescus' marriage had been fraught with strife, and Ionesco remembered frequent disputes between his parents, as he explains in *Journal en miettes* (1967, Fragments of a Journal) and *Présent passé, passé présent* (1968; translated as *Present Past, Past Present,* 1971). Eugen Ionescu divorced Marie-Thérèse in Romania while she was still in France. When Ionesco was thirteen, however, his mother, unable to provide for her children, returned to Romania and transferred them to their father's custody. Soon after their arrival, Ionesco's stepmother threw Marilina out of the house, forcing her to return to her mother, but Ionesco remained there for the next four years. In his recollections of this period Ionesco refers to persistent disagreements with his tyrannical father, who wanted his son to choose a serious profession in law or engineering. This difficult father-son relationship, as well as Ionesco's disdain for his father's political opportunism and abandonment of his mother, enhanced his negative feelings about his father's country and influenced his decision to remain attached to France and French culture. During these turbulent years Ionesco began writing poetry and reviews in high school.

At the age of seventeen Ionesco left home to live with an aunt, Marilina Marescu. From 1929 to 1933 he attended the University of Bucharest, where he completed a degree in French language and literature. During these years he became famous for his public literary debates with his professor of aesthetics, Mihail Dragomirescu. Ionesco's first publication was a volume of poetry, *Elegii pentru fiinte mici* (Elegies for Miniscule Creatures), published in Romania in 1931. Zaharia Stancu dedicated a few pages to Ionesco in his 1934 *Antologia poetilor tineri* (Anthology of Young Poets).

Ionesco's first volume of essays, *Nu* (No; translated into French as *Non*, 1986), was published in 1934 and incited debate in Romanian literary circles. Ionesco attacked revered Romanian writers of the time–most prominent among them the novelist Camil Petrescu and the poets Tudor Arghezi and Ion Barbu. The humor, self-contradiction, narcissism, and obsessions with death and theatricality that later became hallmarks of Ionesco's theater are present in this first volume, which, together with E. M. Cioran's *Pe culmile disperarii* (1934; translated as *On the Heights of Despair*, 1992), received the Royal Foundation's First Book Award. In his book Ionesco sought an answer to the question: "How can one be Romanian and a literary critic?" He resented the marginality of his birthplace in the geographical and cultural confines of the Balkan Peninsula. In *Nu*, Ionesco portrays himself as a writer and critic limited by the contingencies of his society and doomed by provinciality. In 1936 he composed his third book, a biography titled *Viata grotesca si tragica a lui Victor Hugo: Hugoliade* (1982; translated as *Hugoliad: The Grotesque and Tragic Life of Victor Hugo*, 1987).

After graduating from the University of Bucharest, Ionesco worked as a high-school teacher in the Romanian provinces and in Bucharest. In 1936 he married Rodica Burileanu, a philosophy student who became his lifelong companion. In 1938 Ionesco received a grant from the Institut Français of Bucharest to write a dissertation in Paris on the theme of death in Charles Baudelaire's poetry, a project he never completed. He and his wife returned to Romania in 1940, but he clung to the hope of leaving the country. When offered a diplomatic appointment in 1942, he accepted and relocated with his wife to France, never returning to Romania. Ionesco arrived in France as a representative of the pro-Nazi Antonescu government. Hence, as he explains in *Présent passé, passé présent*, he left profascist Romania "comme un évadé qui s'enfuit dans l'uniforme du gardien" (like an escaped prisoner who flees in the guard's uniform). He accepted the position of cultural secretary at the Romanian consulate in Vichy.

In France, Ionesco wrote articles on Romanian culture and literature, completed translations, and sent to Bucharest chronicles on the cultural and political situation in France that were published in the journal *Viata românească* (Romanian Life). Among the subjects he addressed in these writings was the theory of personalism–endorsing the unique ontological reality, value, and free will of people–developed by Emmanuel Mounier, whom he interviewed.

In 1944 Ionesco's wife Rodica gave birth to their only child, Marie-France, a daughter who became a professor, translator, and writer. She chronicled her father's life in a biography, *Portretul scriitorului în secol: Eugène Ionesco, 1909–1994* (The Writer's Portrait In His Century: Eugène Ionesco, 1909–1994), which was first published in Bucharest in 2003 and then in French translation in 2004. Marie-France also translated some of her father's Romanian works into French.

In 1945–a year after Ion Antonescu's government was toppled, and Romania joined forces with the Soviet Union against Germany–Ionesco submitted to *Viata românească* a sarcastic article castigating Romanian bourgeois nationalism, as well as the army, the police, and the church. His attack on the army caused an uproar, which led to Ionesco's in absentia criminal conviction and sentence of eleven years of prison. In the immediate postwar years, after Ionesco lost his position of cultural attaché at the Romanian consulate, he and his family led a precarious existence. Ionesco worked in a warehouse and then as a juridical and medical proofreader for a few years. He also translated works, including those by Urmuz (Demetru Demetrescu Buzau), a Romanian precursor of Surrealism, from Romanian into French.

In 1949 Ionesco translated into French a play he had originally written in Romanian, *Englezeste fara profesor* (English without a Professor). A friend, Monica Lovinescu, introduced him to Nicolas Bataille, a young director, who produced the play in Paris on 11 May 1950 under the title *La Cantatrice chauve*. The play failed miserably at its premiere, although it was enthusiastically received by prominent Surrealists such as André Breton and Philippe Soupault. The famous critic Jacques Lemarchand of the journal *Le Figaro littéraire* (Literary Figaro) became one of Ionesco's earliest supporters.

La Cantatrice chauve was inspired by Ionesco's attempt to teach himself English using the ASSiMiL method, which is still commonly used in France for teaching oneself foreign languages. The one-act play is filled with banalities gleaned from foreign-language manuals, such as "Le plafond est en haut, le plancher est en bas" (the ceiling is up, the floor is down). In fact, *La Cantatrice chauve* barely has a plot. The main characters are Mr. and Mrs. Smith, Mr. and Mrs. Martin, Mary the Maid, and the Fire Chief. The play opens with Mr. and Mrs. Smith in an English living room. He reads an English newspaper while she darns socks. After a moment of "silence anglais" (English silence), the English clock strikes "dix-sept coups anglais" (seventeen English strokes). Mrs. Smith observes that they and their children have just had a good dinner, having eaten "de la salade anglais" (English soup) and drunk "de l'eau anglais" (English water). Mr. Smith's speech is riddled with clichés and nonsensical remarks. The conversation revolves around several people, both male and female, all named Bobby Watson. Almost every sentence in the dialogue is succeeded by another that contradicts it.

Mary the Maid introduces a new couple: Mr. and Mrs. Martin, who gradually discover, to their astonishment ("Comme c'est bizarre, que c'est curieux, et quelle coïncidence!" [How curious it is, how bizarre, and what a coincidence!]) that they are husband and wife, live at the same address, and have a daughter. But the Maid informs the audience that she is Sherlock Holmes and concludes that the Martins are mistaken. The Fire Chief arrives to see whether there is any fire to extinguish in the house, telling the two couples that his mission is to put out several fires that will ignite at specific times later that afternoon. The characters tell jokes. The clock "a l'esprit de contradiction, elle indique toujours le contraire de l'heure qu'il est" (is contradictory and always indicates the opposite of what the hour really is). The Maid recites an ode to fire in honor of the Fire Chief. In the only reference in the play to the eponymous "Bald Soprano," Mrs. Smith informs the Fire Chief that "elle se coiffe toujours de la meme façon" (she always wears her hair in the same style).

After the Fire Chief's departure, the two couples utter short sentences featuring distorted proverbs that quickly become absurd ("J'aime mieux pondre un oeuf que voler un boeuf" [He who sells an ox today will have an egg tomorrow]) and bizarre observations ("prenez un cercle, carressez-le, il deviendra vicieux!" [Take a circle, caress it, it will turn vicious!]). The pronouncements become increasingly aggressive. At the conclusion of the play, the curtain rises again to reveal the Smiths (the Martins in the British production) seated in the living room and starting the same conversation they had in the opening scene.

La Cantatrice chauve is an attack on bourgeois conformism and a reflection on the impossibility of communication. It remains an example par excellence of the Theater of the Absurd. Along with *La Leçon,* it has been performed every evening at the Théâtre de la Huchette in Paris since 1957 (more than 13,700 performances), a world-record stage run.

Ionesco ventured into acting in 1950, when Bataille offered him the part of Stepan Trofimovich in a staging of Fyodor Dostoevsky's *Besy* (1873; translated as *The Possessed,* 1913), codirected by Bataille and Akakia Viala. Days after this play closed, Ionesco's second one-act play, *La Leçon,* directed by Marcel Cuvelier, opened at the small Parisian Théâtre de Poche. The characters of this play are the Professor, the Pupil, and the Maid. In the opening scene the Maid greets a confident, eighteen-year-old female pupil, who has come to the Professor's house for a one-hour private lesson in preparation for her "doctorat total" (total doctorate). An elderly professor enters the room. He is shy but "de temps à autre, une lueur lubrique dans les yeux" (occasionally a lewd gleam comes into his eyes). A gradual shift in power takes place in the play. Though skilled in addition and multiplication, the Pupil is unable to subtract, so the Professor determines that she is only qualified to work toward the "partial doctorate." During an analysis of the "neo-Spanish languages," the Professor becomes increasingly dictatorial. The Pupil suffers from a toothache, yet the Professor refuses to interrupt the lesson. The Pupil gradually grows weaker, more frightened, and, in the end, entirely passive. In spite of the Maid's warning that "la philologie mène au crime" (philology leads to crime), the Professor takes a knife, and, while explaining its name in various neo-Spanish languages, stabs the Pupil to death. Her legs draped wide over a chair suggest rape. The Maid comes to console the Professor and dispose of the Pupil's body. This Pupil is the Professor's fortieth victim of the day. Explaining that "C'est politique" (it is good politics), the Maid offers the Professor an armband like those worn by Nazis. The play ends with another ring at the door and a new pupil's arrival. The cyclical structure of the play is similar to that of *La Cantatrice chauve.* For Martin Esslin, the play "hinges on the sexual nature of all power and the relationship between language and power as the basis of all human ties."

In *Les Chaises,* a ninety-five-year-old husband and his ninety-four-year-old wife are living in a tower on an island, where they await prominent guests from every walk of life. The Old Man wants to deliver an important message to their guests, but since "j'ai tant de mal à m'exprimer" (I have so much difficulty expressing myself), he hires a professional orator to speak in his name. As the guests arrive one by one, the couple fetches chairs and seats them, but in fact no one appears on stage. The guests' presence is signaled by the chairs and conversations filled with platitudes and memories of childhood, youth and love, often expressed in rueful tones. The chairs take over the stage, making it increasingly difficult for the old couple to move about. When the Emperor arrives and the Orator appears, the Old Man becomes confident that his message will be delivered. He and his wife then commit suicide by jumping from the tower into the waters below. The Orator attempts to speak, but only

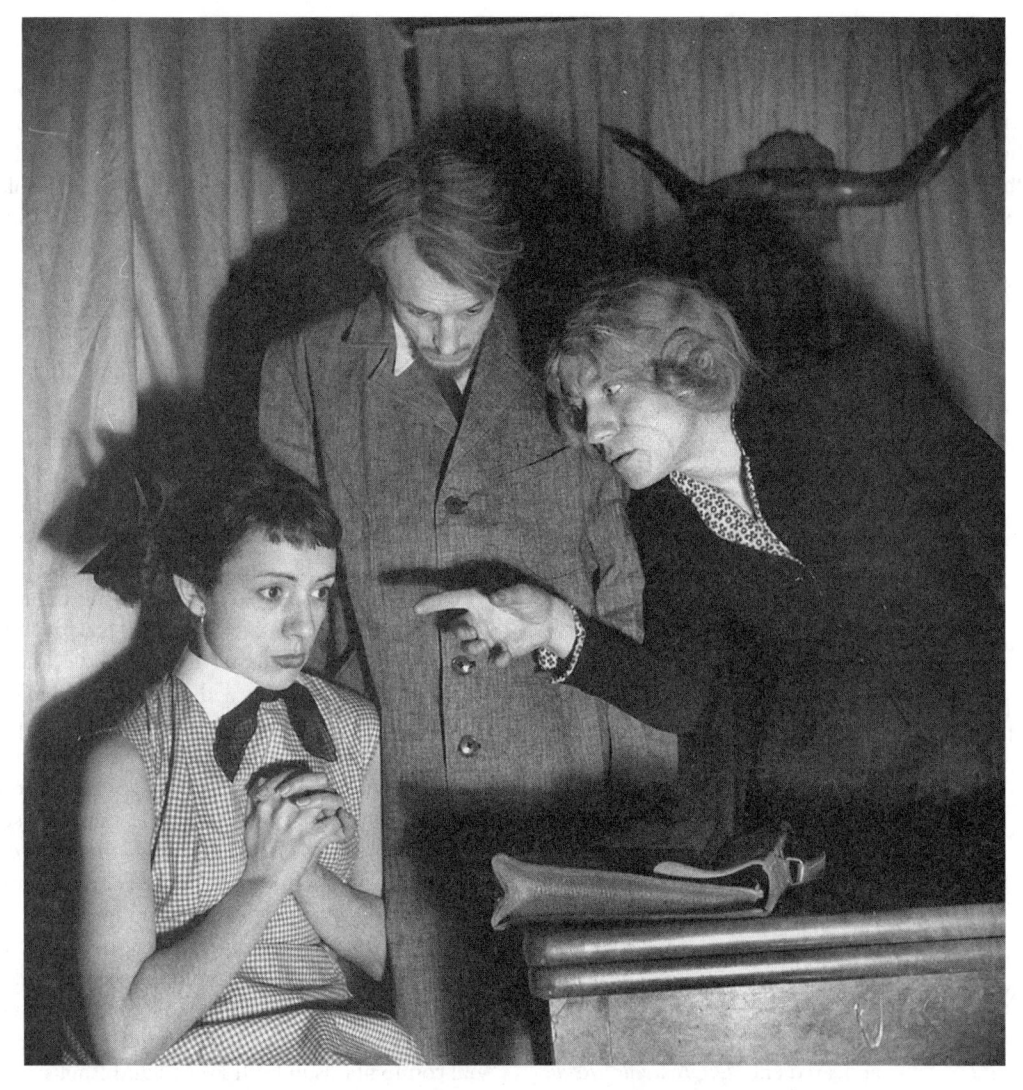

Rosette Zuchelli, Marcel Cuvelier, and Claude Mansard, in Ionesco's La Leçon *(translated as* The Lesson, *1958) at the Théâtre de Poche in Paris, February 1951 (© Lipnitzki/Roger-Viollet/Getty Images)*

inarticulate garble emanates from his mouth. Finally, the Orator scribbles an unintelligible message on the board.

Les Chaises was a failure with the public when it was first produced by Sylvain Dhomme at the Théâtre Lancry. The play achieved success only after a second staging in 1956 by Jacques Mauclair. In an article quoted by Esslin, Jean Anouilh, a prominent French dramatist of the 1940s, judged it "better than Strindberg, because it has its 'black' humor à la Molière, in a manner that is at times terribly funny, because it is horrifying and laughable, poignant and always true."

In 1953 two very short plays, *Le Maître* (published 1958; translated as *The Leader*, 1960) and *La Jeune Fille à marier* (published 1958; translated as *Maid to Marry*, 1960) were produced at the Théâtre de la Huchette in Paris. The first concerns a crowd waiting for the appearance of a headless statesman, and the second features a man and a woman's conversation about Western civilization that is full of platitudes—and the "maiden" of the title is a hirsute man more than eighty years old.

The main characters of Ionesco's next important play, *Victimes du devoir* (produced 1953, published 1954; translated as *Victims of Duty,* 1958), are Choubert and Madeleine, a petit bourgeois couple. The play opens in their apartment, where Choubert is reading the newspaper and Madeleine is darning socks. The Detective arrives to inquire if a former tenant's name, Mallot, ends with a *t* or a *d*. Choubert cannot recall exactly how his neighbor spelled his name, but surmises that it was with a *t*. This answer prompts the Detective (who insists on being addressed as "Chief Inspector") to demand that Choubert probe his own subconscious for facts about Mallot. Instead, Choubert only discovers gaps in his memory. In an attempt to fill them, the Detective forces bread down Choubert's throat. The words "Avalez! Mastiquez!" (Swallow! Chew!) become the refrain of the play. Madeleine cooperates with the Detective and metamorphoses from a middle-aged housewife into a young woman, then back into an older woman, and she later becomes the Detective's mistress. As Choubert delves into his psyche, Madeleine also becomes Choubert's mother. Choubert meets his parents, witnesses disputes between them, becomes a child again, and has a reproachful, yet remorseful, conversation with his father. The elated Choubert begins to rise in the air, but he is brought back to reality by the Detective/psychiatrist and wakes up in a wastebasket.

Near the end of the play, a new character, Nicolas d'Eu ("eu" means "I" in Romanian), appears. He dreams of a new theater, characterizing it as "irrationaliste" (irrationalist): "quand à l'action et la causalité, n'en parlons plus" (plot and motivation, let us not speak of it again) nor "le principe d'identité et de l'unité des caractères" (the principle of identity and unity of character). It is a theater in which "Le tragique se fait comique, le comique est tragique et la vie devient gaie" (the tragic is turning comic, the comic is tragic, and life is becoming more cheerful). Nicolas d'Eu confesses that he sees no need to write because "Nous avons Ionesco et Ionesco, cela suffit!" (We have Ionesco, and that's enough!). In the meantime, Madeleine brings coffee cups into the room at an ever faster pace. As in *Les Chaises*, a proliferation of objects dominates the stage at the conclusion of the play. The themes of the play extend beyond the theory of drama to psychoanalysis, politics, and the misuse of authority.

Ionesco next tranformed a short story, "Oriflamme," which first appeared in *La Nouvelle Revue Française* (The New French Review) in 1954 and was later included in *La Photo du colonel* (1962; translated as *The Colonel's Photograph*, 1967), into a play titled *Amédée, ou Comment s'en débarasser* (produced and published 1954; translated as *Amédée, or How to Get Rid of It*, 1958). The subject of this drama, Ionesco's first three-act play, is a corpse that makes a couple's life unbearable. The corpse, which serves as a metaphor for a dark secret or lost love, swells in "progression géometrique" (geometrical progression), while mushrooms proliferate at the same rate in the apartment. Amédée, a failed playwright, succeeds in taking the corpse out, and in the end he is lifted into the sky by the cadaver-turned-parachute. Critic Leonard Pronko considers the ending unusually positive for Ionesco's work: "For once, the feeling of lightness seems to have won out." For Esslin, the play features one of Ionesco's "most brilliant images. As a stage symbol of tremendous power and immediate impact the growing corpse is sure of its measure of immortality." The play was produced at the Parisian Théâtre de Babylone by the well-known director Jean-Marie Serreau and was revived at the nationally subsidized Odéon-Théâtre de France in 1961.

Only weeks after finishing *Amédée*, Ionesco wrote a one-act play titled *Le Nouveau Locataire* (published 1958; translated as *The New Tenant*, 1958). This play was first performed in Swedish translation in Helsinki in 1955, then in English translation in London in 1956, and not until 1957 in French in Paris. The subject is, again, the proliferation of physical objects, which pour into an apartment, burying the new tenant.

The hero of another of Ionesco's plays from this period, *Jacques, ou La Soumission* (published 1954, produced 1955; translated as *Jack, or The Submission* and *Jack, or Obedience*, 1958), is a young man at home with his family. All of his relatives are named Jack, much like the Bobby Watson characters in *La Cantatrice chauve*. At first Jack's relatives try to humor him, then they resort to threatening and insulting him as they try to bend him to their will. His sister, Jacqueline, reminds him that he is "chronométrable" (subject to time). Jack capitulates to the family's wishes by stating that he likes "les pommes de terre au lard" (potatoes with bacon), and he is introduced to the Roberts, whose daughter Roberta is presented as Jack's potential bride-to-be. Jack rejects Roberta, however, because she has only two noses, so the Roberts immediately introduce their "second fille unique" (second only daughter), who has three. Both Robertas are played by the same actress. Roberta has the talent of bringing to life images of a burning horse running in the desert. The image incites Jack to impersonate the horse. Jack finally succumbs to Roberta's detailed description of her body's "moisture," and the play ends with Roberta and Jack whispering the word "chat," or "pussy," a word with sexual connotations in both French and English. In a play on words involving French terms beginning with *cha-* (as in *charmant, chagrin, chapeau, chalet*), they propose that this one word be uniformly applied to designate all things, thus reducing language to a single word. The final scene depicts Jack and Roberta in an embrace while animal noises can be heard in the background. *Jacques, ou La Soumission* was produced at the Théâtre de la Huchette in October 1955 and starred Jean-Louis Trintignant in the lead role and Reine Courtois as Roberta. It shared billing with a less successful Ionesco play, *Le Tableau* (1963, The Picture), in which a Large Gentleman purchases the portrait of a beautiful woman. He then shoots his sister, the painter, and some other people, and they all metamorphose into beautiful human beings. In the end, the Large Gentleman begs the audience to shoot him, too.

One measure of Ionesco's early success was the publication of his collected plays by the Gallimard publishing house, beginning in 1954. In June 1957 Ionesco's next play, *L'Avenir est dans les œufs, ou Il faut tout pour faire un monde* (published 1958; translated as *The Future Is in the*

Eggs, or It Takes All Sorts to Make a World, 1960), the sequel to *Jacques, ou La Soumission*, was produced at the theater of the Cité Universitaire in Paris. The play begins with Jack and Roberta at home in their living room purring the word *chat*. Both families insist that the couple have many children for the sake of perpetuating the white race. Roberta produces baskets full of eggs, which are then hatched by Jack, who is perched on an incubator. These eggs are to become future officers, bankers, popes, kings, emperors, policemen, opportunists, radicals, Marxists, existentialists, and omelettes. The play ends with the family's unabated insistence on "production" and the fascist slogan "Vive la race blanche!" (Long live the white race!).

L'Impromptu de l'Alma, ou Le Caméléon du berger (performed 1956; published 1958; translated as *Improvisation, or The Shepherd's Chameleon*, 1960) was inspired by Molière's *L'Impromptu de Versailles* (1663, The Impromptu of Versailles). Like Molière, Ionesco makes himself the protagonist of his play. The other characters are three critics called Bartholoméus I, Bartholoméus II, and Bartholoméus III, and a fifth character, the Maid. The dramatic version of Ionesco is trying to write a play about an encounter between a shepherd and a chameleon. One by one, the three critics arrive, each curious about Ionesco's play. The author explains that he does not identify with the chameleon: "Je ne change pas de couleur tous les jours, moi . . . Je ne suis pas à la remorque de la dernière mode" (I do not change color every day . . . I am not being towed along by the latest fashion). Each critic tries to teach Ionesco to write according to the principles of Bertolt Brecht's alienation theory. According to the critics, Ionesco's crime is that he does not write "théâtre engagé" (committed theater) and knows nothing about the latest dramatic theories or the jargon used to express them (terms such as "costumologie" [costumology], "théâtrologie" [theatricology], and "décorologie" [decorology]). The language of the Bartholoméuses becomes aggressive and, although they quarrel among themselves, whenever Ionesco tries to say something, they stop him, explaining that an author who is not in possession of a doctorate is not allowed to have any opinions. Finally, the Maid enters the room and chases the critics away with a broom. Once the Bartholoméuses have left, Ionesco is free to present his own ideas about theater, which, he claims, is for him "la projection sur scène du monde du dedans" (a projection on stage of the world within). However, in his eagerness to explain his own theory in detail, he becomes dogmatic. Hence, Ionesco does not exempt himself from his satire. Finally, the Maid forces Ionesco to come to his senses by throwing one of the Bartholoméuses' robes over his shoulders. Esslin calls this play "Ionesco's most openly polemical play, his most direct attack against his critics . . . The three doctors are purveyors of half-existentialist, half-Brechtian farrago of dramatic theory, with allusions to Adamov, who discovered the Aristotelian principles before Aristotle, [Jean-Paul] Sartre, and, of course, above all, Ionesco's special *bête noire*, Brecht."

Ionesco also defended his ideas about theater in his articles, in his journals, and in speeches delivered at conferences held all over the world. One famous international debate with which Ionesco became involved was the so-called London Controversy. In 1958, after a successful production of *Les Chaises* at the Royal Theater, the powerful British theater critic Kenneth Tynan, who had introduced Ionesco to England, wrote an article for the London *Observer* attacking Ionesco's new plays on political grounds. Tynan charged Ionesco with presenting a world grounded in the fantastic, removed from the social and political realities that found treatment in the works of his contemporaries, including Brecht, Sartre, and Arthur Miller. Ionesco published a defense of his work in the *Observer*. He outlined the tenets of his dramatic theory, clarifying that his theater reflected the psychological aspects of human nature, not reflections of the social and political trends of the time. He explained that he "sought to extend the idiom of the theater" and attempted "to exteriorize, by using objects, the anguish of [his] characters, to make the set speak and the action on the stage more visual, to translate into concrete images terror, regret or remorse, and estrangement, to play with words . . . even perhaps to deform them." Ionesco insisted that "a playwright simply writes plays, in which he can offer only a testimony, not a didactic message," and he critiqued all ideological plays as the "vulgarization of ideology." Tynan responded to this letter, and their dispute inaugurated a public exchange that included contributions from such luminaries as Orson Welles and Philip Toynbee. The *Observer* refused to publish Ionesco's final volley, but the article, "Le Cœur n'est pas sur le main" (Hearts Are Not Worn on the Sleeve), was published in *Cahiers des Saisons* (Notebooks of the Seasons, Winter 1959) and later included in Ionesco's collection of essays *Notes et contre-notes* (1962; translated, 1964).

Ionesco's next play, *Tueur sans gages* (produced and published 1958; translated as *The Killer*, 1960), was inspired by his short story "La Photo du colonel" (1962; translated as "The Colonel's Photograph," 1967). This three-act play was first produced in Darmstadt, Germany, in 1958, and then in Paris at the Théâtre Récamier in February 1959. Bérenger, the main character, visits the paradisiacal Cité Radieuse (radiant city), only to discover the presence of a killer who murders his victims after showing them a mysterious colonel's photograph. In a dramatic expression of his confrontation with mortality, Bérenger reveals his inability to resist the Killer in the monologue that concludes the play. Both Esslin and Jacques Guicharnaud consider *Tueur sans gages* to be one

Jacques Mauclair and Tsilla Chelton in Ionesco's Les Chaises *(translated as* The Chairs, *1958), at the Studio des Champs-Elysées in Paris, February 1956 (© Lipnitzki/Roger-Viollet/Getty Images)*

of Ionesco's most impressive plays because of the simple humanity of the protagonist. It enjoyed a successful run in Paris but was less appreciated in New York in 1960, where it closed after a few performances.

Ionesco's three-act play *Rhinocéros* (produced and published 1959; translated as *Rhinoceros*, 1960), generally considered to be his masterpiece, has been performed to acclaim throughout the world. Adapted for the stage from his 1957 short story of the same title, it premiered in Paris at the state-subsidized Odéon-Théâtre de France under the direction of Jean-Louis Barrault. The English version of the play was directed by Welles and starred Laurence Olivier.

As in *Tueur sans gages,* the protagonist is Bérenger, an ordinary man. He and his friend Jean are seated at a table in a provincial French café. Bérenger arrives late, drinks too much, and feels depressed and alienated. Jean, by contrast, is well kempt, self-righteous, and irritable when contradicted. Jean lectures Bérenger on how to become "civilized" and stay abreast of cultural trends by socializing, reading newspapers, and attending theatrical performances. At a different table, a logician conveys the beauty of logic to an old man by presenting illogical syllogisms, such as "Tous les chats sont mortels. Socrate est mortel. Donc Socrate est un chat" (All cats die. Socrates is dead. Therefore Socrates is a cat). According to him, "Car la justice, c'est la logique" (Logic means Justice). The simultaneous conversations are comically interwoven. Meanwhile, café patrons are astonished to see a rhinoceros running through the street. Before long, another rhinoceros appears. The first act ends with the killing of a woman's cat, the rhinoceroses' first casualty.

Act 2 features two scenes, the first of which is set in a government office where Bérenger works as a proofreader. Law books line the shelves. His colleagues include Dudard, a lawyer; the Deputy Head; Daisy, the secretary; Botard, the Unionist; and their boss, Mr. Papillon, the Chief of Service. The conversation turns to the previous day's event. Like the logician, Botard is more interested in extraneous details about the cat than he is in the event itself. He goes so far as to deny that the killing even occurred, suggesting rather that it represents an "exemple de psychose collective" (example of collective psychosis). However, a rhinoceros appears and demolishes the stairs leading to the second-story office. When a woman named Mrs. Boeuf comes to apologize for her husband's unexplained absences (he has been out of the office for several days), she recognizes traits of her husband in the rampaging rhinoceros and realizes he has become one of them. In a display of unconditional devotion, she leaps through the window, lands on the rhinoceros's back, and rides off with him, indicating that she too has joined the rhinoceroses and will become one of them. Now Botard decries a "plot" and plans to "unmask" the traitors, while the rest of the employees escape through the office window, aided by the fire brigade.

The second scene takes place in Jean's apartment. Bérenger comes to call on Jean, only to discover that his friend is very ill: his voice is hoarse, he becomes more and more agressive, and a horn-like bump protrudes from his forehead. Over the course of their conversation, Jean becomes increasingly dismissive of friendship, morality, and humanism, which—as he says—"est périmé!" (is all washed up!). Before Jean is finally transformed into a rhinoceros, he expresses his admiration for the animal. Bérenger must flee the apartment to keep from being trampled by his friend. To his despair he sees that most of the other tenants have also metamorphosed into rhinoceroses.

Act 3 opens with Bérenger lying on a divan in his room. He has been drinking brandy to appease his anxiety about the rapidly spreading epidemic. The nightmarish roar of rhinoceroses in the streets can be heard in his room. When his colleague Dudard drops by to see him, Bérenger shares his concerns about the growing number of cases of "rhinoceritis," including the logician and the old man from the café. Dudard, an intellectual, is becoming increasingly fascinated with the rhinoceroses, and he also becomes one of them. Bérenger and Daisy, who has also dropped by to see him, are the only two human beings left. Soon Daisy too falls prey to the rhinoceroses' "music." In the end, Bérenger finds himself alone, the last human being. Despite his growing doubts about his own individuality in the face of the collective metamorphosis, he decides not to join the rhinoceroses, but to remain human instead. Besieged by rhinoceroses, he utters his last words: "Je suis le dernier homme, je le resterai jusqu'au bout! Je ne capitule pas!" (I'm the last man left, and I'm staying that way until the end! I am not capitulating!).

Ionesco was appalled by the hateful and violent anti-Semitic outbursts he had witnessed in Romania. He also was disturbed and mystified by the large number of intellectuals who fell prey to fascist ideologies and mass hysteria. Furthermore, *Rhinocéros* was inspired in part by the mass hysteria described by Denis de Rougement in his report on a Nazi rally he attended in 1938 in Nuremberg. In his play Ionesco seeks to represent the process by which human individuals are drawn into collectivities, appearing to undergo transformations so substantial as to strip them of their humanity. The deafening roar of the rhinoceroses in the play represents the overwhelming clamor characteristic of rallies such as the one in Nuremberg. The comical parallel dialogues in the first scene underline the power of rhetoric more than the power of logic. Ultimately, however, Bérenger's refusal to conform in the conclusion suggests the possibility of individual choice despite social pressure.

Death is a recurring theme in Ionesco's journals and plays. Hospitalized for a serious illness, Ionesco read the *Bardo Thodol* (fourteenth century), commonly known as *The Tibetan Book of the Dead*. In his *Journal en miettes,* he states that he wrote *Le Roi se meurt* in order to learn how to die: "Cela devait être une leçon, comme une sorte d'exercice spirituel, une marche progressive, étape par étape, que j'essayais de render accessible vers la fin inéluctable" (It was to be a lesson, a sort of spiritual exercise, a gradual progress, stage by stage, towards the ineluctable end). The play was originally titled *La Cérémonie* (The Ceremony), since it depicts King Bérenger I's ritual of "abdication" from life. Despite its serious subject matter, however, the play features comical and grotesque elements.

The characters of *Le Roi se meurt* are King Bérenger I; Marguerite, his first wife; Marie, his second wife but "the first in his affection"; the Doctor, who is also a surgeon, executioner, bacteriologist, and astrologer; Juliette, the Doctor's housekeeper-nurse; and the Guard, an automaton who echoes the King's medical reports. In order to retain the temporal continuity of the performance, Ionesco did not divide the play into acts or scenes. When the play opens, Marguerite informs the King that he will die at the end of the performance, while the loving and compassionate Marie seeks to protect the King from the reality of his fate. The king's death is foreshadowed by the dilapidation of his palace (the heating is not functioning, and there are cracks in the walls), the state of affairs in his kingdom (the population is aged and dwindling), and by astrological events (the sun has lost its strength, planets are colliding, and comets are dying). With Marguerite's help, Bérenger accepts the truth and gradually learns to detach himself from life, from people, and from memories. In the final scene even the windows and walls slowly disappear, leaving the King alone on stage until he too fades into gray light. Ultimately, the play enacts an initiation ceremony into death in a desacralized world.

In *Le Piéton de l'air* (produced and published 1963; translated as *A Stroll in the Air,* 1965), another protagonist named Bérenger describes apocalyptic visions after his stroll in the air in the Anti-Monde (antiworld). A later drama, *La Lacune* (produced and published 1966; translated as *The Gap,* 1969), presents the story of an academician who fails his *baccalauréat*.

Although dense and long, Ionesco's play *La Soif et la Faim* attracted the attention of Serreau and premiered in 1966 at the bastion of classical French theater in Paris, the Comédie-Française. It was influenced by Ionesco's reading of Zen Buddhist texts and of San Juan de la Cruz. The latter influence is evident in his use of several characters with biblical names: Jean, Marie-Madeleine, Marthe. The play consists of three initial episodes, "La Fuite" (The Flight), "Le Rendez-vous" (The Rendezvous), and "Les Messes noires de la 'Bonne auberge'" (The Black Masses of the Good Inn), to which was added a fourth, "Le Pied du mur" (At the Foot of the Wall). In the first episode, "La Fuite," Jean, the protagonist, is at home in a damp apartment with his wife, Marie-Madeleine, who is tending to their baby daughter. Claustrophobic and plagued by nightmarish visions, Jean decides to leave his family. The second episode, "Le Rendez-vous," depicts Jean's failed rendezvous with an imaginary woman. In the third and longest scene, "Les Messes noires de la 'Bonne auberge,'" Jean, exhausted and aged, arrives at a "monastery-cum-barracks-cum-prison." His host, Father Tarabas, and several other monks try to assuage Jean's insatiable hunger and thirst. In return, he is asked to tell the story of his adventures. Brother Superior, a mute character on stilts and clad in white, supervises the monastery.

The added episode, "Le Pied du mur," was inserted between "Le Rendez-vous" and "Les Messes noires de la 'Bonne Auberge.'" It is a set of dreams, transfigurations of Jean's (and Ionesco's) anxiety and fear of death. Jean arrives at a wall and refuses to go around it in order to continue his journey because he wants to find out what is beyond the wall. Schaeffer—a recurrent protean tyrannical father-figure of Ionesco's dreams—appears with pupils who are singing the Communist Manifesto in Hebrew (demonstrating how he can observe his religion, which is prohibited in his country, under the disguise of totalitarian politics). Shaeffer, now a magician, makes the wall disappear. The episode ends with Jean's encounter with an old woman in rags who is working in a kitchen, perhaps a tragic maternal archetype.

Throughout the play Jean repeats the refrain "Je bois, je mange, je bois, je mange. J'ai encore soif, j'ai encore faim" (the more I eat, the more I am hungry; the more I drink, the more I am thirsty). His crisis of conscience is revealed in the contrast between his repeated claims to have neither seen nor heard anything and the pangs of guilt that nevertheless torment him. The Brothers interrogate Jean then present a play about "education and reeducation" organized by Brother Tarabas for guests at the inn. In this episode, the most overtly political one of the play, "the black masses of the Good Inn" analyze the "entrapment into systems." The play within the play features two characters in cages: Brechtoll, whose name alludes to the German playwright Brecht and whose partisans dress in red to represent Communism, and Tripp, whose partisans are dressed in black to represent their affiliation with religion. Each cage is a trap: in order to receive food, Brechtoll professes belief in God, while Tripp, the believer, acknowledges that he really believes in his soup. Jean realizes that he should not have left his family, but he remains trapped in this place of reeducation, where he must pay off his debt. Although he is a prisoner and unable to return home, Jean is reassured by his wife's and daughter's fidelity.

Beginning in the 1950s and 1960s Ionesco, at the request of Michel Benamou, professor of French at the University of Michigan, wrote humorous dialogues for use in the classroom. These dialogues include *Le Salon de l'automobile* (produced for radio 1952, published 1953; translated as *The Motor Show,* 1963); *Scène à quatre* (Scene for Four; produced 1959, published 1963); *La Jeune Fille à marier; Délire à deux* (produced 1962, published 1963; translated as *Frenzy for Two,* 1965); *Les Salutations* (published 1963; translated as *Salutations,* 1968); *La Colère* (published 1963, translated as *Anger,* 1968); *Pour préparer un œuf dur* (1966, How to Prepare a Hard Boiled Egg); *La Nièce-épouse* (published in English translation as *The Niece-Wife,* 1971); *Le Vicomte* (The Viscount); and *Scène* (translated as *Scene,* 1984), a political sketch written in honor of Václav Havel in the 1980s.

Although Ionesco's principal literary activity in the 1950s and 1960s was drama, he also wrote short stories, including those collected in *La Photo du Colonel,* and several volumes of memoirs (*Notes et contre-notes; Journal en miettes;* and *Présent passé, passé présent*). In 1973 he published a novel, *Le Solitaire* (translated as *The Hermit,* 1974). Around this time he also composed a portion of *Exercices de conversation et de diction françaises pour étudiants américains* (1974, French Conversation and Pronunciation Exercises for American Students), a series of short humorous dialogues reminiscent of the inspiration for *La Cantatrice chauve*. Some of the dialogue published in this book had appeared in Benamov's manual *Mise en train* (1969, Warming-Up). Ionesco also acted, playing the leading role in Heinz von Cramer's *La Vase* (Slime), the 1971 film adaptation of his short story of the same title, published in *La Photo du colonel*.

Daniel Defoe's *A Journal of the Plague Year* (1722) served as Ionesco's inspiration for the play *Jeux de massa-*

Scene from Ionesco's Rhinocéros, *at the Théâtre de l'Odéon, Paris, January 1960. Over the course of the play, characters turn into rhinoceroses one by one, and in the end only the protagonist, Bérenger, is shown desperately clinging to his humanity (© Lipnitzki/Roger-Viollet/Getty Images).*

cre (produced 1970, published 1974; translated as *Killing Game*, 1974). The eighteen episodes depict varieties of death at all levels of society, and death by plague is combined with murders and suicides and ends with an astonishing proliferation of cadavers. During the episodes a Black Monk crosses the stage on stilts. *Jeux de massacre* is among Ionesco's most pessimistic plays.

One of Ionesco's favorite authors was William Shakespeare, whom he considered to have been a precursor of the Theater of the Absurd. Inspired by both Shakespeare and Polish critic Jan Kott's *Szkice o Szekspirze* (1962; translated as *Shakespeare Our Contemporary*, 1964), Ionesco revived Shakespeare's story of deadly ambition in *Macbett* (produced and published 1972; translated, 1973), making his play bleaker than the original. The play is close to Alfred Jarry's *Ubu Roi* (1896; translated, 1951), as Ionesco acknowledged in a 24 January 1972 interview with Claude Cézan in *Les Nouvelles Littéraires* (The Literary News). The comic and grotesque aspects of the play are emphasized not only by the dialogue but also by Ionesco's staging of *Macbett* as a music-hall production, complete with scenes of striptease and singing parts.

Macbett begins with a dialogue between Candor and Glamiss in which each repeats the other's sentences. The two conspire to assassinate Archduke Duncan, for the simple reason that he is "un tyran, un usurpateur, un despote, un dictateur . . . La preuve, c'est qu'il règne" (a tyrant, a usurper, a despot, a dictator . . . The proof is, he's in power). General Macbett appears in the second scene and tells the story of his exploits, mentioning "dozens and dozens," "hundreds and hundreds," "thousands and thousands," and even "millions" of victims and the various ways he has put them to death, concluding by expressing his satisfaction with the events of the day. Banco, Macbett's friend and fellow general, repeats the same story about his own exploits, ending it with the remark: "c'étaient des traîtres. Je n'ai fait qu'obéir aux orders de mon souverain. Service commandé" (they were traitors after all. I obeyed my sovereign's orders. I did my duty).

The Archduke and Lady Duncan are as cruel and bloodthirsty as their generals. Duncan delivers a speech to his troops that is a pastiche of similar speeches made throughout history. Duncan's two enemies, Glamiss and Candor, are imprisoned. In his speech before his execution Candor concludes, "C'est que l'Histoire, dans sa marche, ne l'a pas voulu. C'est l'Histoire qui a raison. . . . Je suis coupable. Notre révolte était cependant nécessaire, pour prouver à quel point j'étais criminel" (History is against me. History is right . . . I am guilty. But our rebellion was necessary, if only to prove that I'm a criminal).

In separate scenes two witches appear to Macbett and Banco, informing Macbett that he will become very powerful, and telling Banco that Macbett will deprive him of his rights but that he will nevertheless be the founder of a thousand-year dynasty of kings. The witches convince Macbett to overthrow Duncan "pour aider les pauvres" (in order to help the poor) and "C'est pour rétablir la paix dans un pays qui a tant souffert" (bring peace to a country which has known such suffering). A striptease scene follows: the witches become beautiful nightclub entertainers, and one of them disguises herself as Lady Duncan and convinces Macbett to kill the Archduke. The macabre mixes with comedy as the triumvirate—Macbett, Banco, and Lady Duncan—kill Duncan while calling each other assassins. Later, Macbett kills Banco, only to be killed by Macol, Duncan's son. Then, instead of providing hope for the restoration of order and harmony, Ionesco's play ends in horror. Against a backdrop of guillotines, Macol warns the crowd about their future during his regime, which will be more atrocious than the previous one: "ma pauvre patrie aura plus de vices qu'auparavant. . . . le noir Macbett semblera pur comme neige . . . en comparant ses actes à mes innombrables méfaits" (My poor country shall have more vices than it had before . . . black Macbett will seem as pure as snow . . . compared with my confineless harm).

Ionesco's next play, *Ce formidable bordel!* (produced and published 1973; translated as *A Hell of a Mess*, 1975), is based on his only novel, *Le Solitaire*, which was inspired by the May 1968 general strike in France. The play presents revolutionaries who advocate a new, just world, yet they behave as unjustly as the bourgeois they criticize. Ionesco interweaves his familiar themes of old age, war, death, and solitude, while he demythologizes the idea of revolution. He was intrigued by the leftist French intelligentsia's attraction to revolutionaries, and he incorporates into the play Marxist clichés used by intellectuals, such as "la lutte des classes" (the struggle of classes), "les sales bourgeois" (the dirty bourgeoisie), "l'exploitation de l'homme par l'homme" (the exploitation of men by men). Here, violence and hypocrisy define the people who are fighting for a "just society." In Ionesco's words, "Toutes les révolutions détruisent les bibliothèques d'Alexandrie" (All revolutions destroy Alexandria's libraries).

Ionesco's late plays are based almost exclusively on oneiric and autobiographical material. *L'Homme aux valises* (produced and published 1975; translated as *Man with Bags*, 1977) represents a series of dreams laced with autobiographical and political recollections, some of which had been mentioned in *Journal en miettes*. In search of his identity, the First Man travels to a country whose language he has forgotten, but he fails to discover his origins because he cannot find the real name of his grandmother's mother. In fact, a clerk at city hall advises the First Man to abandon his search, as it might have serious repercussions for him as a descendant. The clerk hints that the protagonist's maternal ancestor may have been a member of "une catégorie ethnique persécutée . . . une race condamnée" (a persecuted ethnic minority . . . one of the doomed races). The protagonist's two suitcases become heavier and heavier, and he is missing the third and most important piece of luggage, the one containing his manuscript, a detail that underscores the notion of writing as an existential, yet perhaps futile endeavor.

This theme also figures prominently in *Voyages chez les morts: Thèmes et variations* (produced 1980, published 1981; translated as *Journeys Among the Dead (Themes and Variations)*, 1985), which reenacts, as Ionesco explained in a 1984 interview with Arnelle Héliot (quoted by Deborah B. Gaensbauer), a "dreamed autobiography." Here Ionesco depicts a settling of family accounts. The protagonist, Jean, experiences persistent anxiety and remorse because of his failed friendships and literary jealousies. He reflects on the vanity of life and of writing: "Je suis arrivé. Où? J'ai réussi. Quoi? Tout est vain. C'est d'amour que l'on devrait mourir" (I have arrived. But where? I have succeeded—in what? Everything is hollow. What we should die of is love). The play also deals with the father-son relationship in an autobiographical manner. In a nightmarish scene, family quarrels are reenacted, and Jean's mother punishes her tormentors, Jean's father and his new family.

In *Voyage chez les morts*, Ionesco's dramatic oeuvre ends as it began, with the last scene reminiscent of *La Can-*

tatrice chauve. Jean's monologue consists of dislocated sentences and meaningless words, and he acknowledges: "Je n'ai plus mon langage. Plus je dis, moins je parle. Plus je parle, moins je dis" (I've lost my command of language. The more I say, the less I speak. The more I speak, the less I say). As Ionesco revealed in his interview with Héliot, "language is truly tragic the way I wanted it to be. In my first play . . . it was only amusing, or rather laughable. Now even the laughable is surpassed, as well as the derisory character, since he comes to an encounter with absolute nonsense."

In the 1980s Ionesco published a final volume of memoirs, *La Quête intermittente* (1987, The Intermittent Quest), and wrote an unpublished libretto for Dominique Probst's opera *Maximilien Kolbe* (1988). He also took up painting and illustrated several books with his own sketches, including *Le Blanc et le noir* (1985, The White and the Black) and *La Main peint: Notes de travail–Die Hand malt: Arbeitsnotizen* (1987, The Hand Paints: Work Notes).

During this time Ionesco actively participated in conferences in support of human rights, wrote harsh indictments against the Romanian government as well as against other totalitarian regimes, and met and helped dissidents of such countries. As president of the PEN Club, he awarded the Freedom Prize to Havel in 1989. Ionesco signed many petitions for freedom of speech, such as one in defense of Salman Rushdie, and he wrote articles against anti-Semitism and in support of the right to existence of the state of Israel. His ties to Romania became stronger after the 1989 revolution that brought down Nicolae Ceausescu's dictatorship, at which time he acknowledged in interviews that he felt Romanian again. He died on 28 March 1994.

Ionesco was the recipient of many prestigious international awards, including the Jerusalem Prize (1973), the Max Rheinhard Medal (1976), Germany's Order of Merit (1982), the University of Chicago's T. S. Eliot-Ingersoll Prize (1985), the Medal of the City of Paris (1987), and the Molière Prize (1989). In 1970 he was elected to the Académie française; he received the great Austrian Award for European Literature; and he was presented an honorary doctorate by the University of Tel-Aviv. In 1991 he became the first author whose work was published in the prestigious Editions Pléiade while still alive.

Eugène Ionesco's theater evolved during his career. His first plays focus more on language as a means of non-communication, as an expression of automatism and banality, and as a barrier to knowledge of the self and of others. Later, Ionesco became interested in the psychoanalytical aspect of memory and in revealing characters' inner worlds on stage, especially their deep anxieties and obsessions with death. His allusions to politics in the early plays turn into political statements in the later plays. Then, at the very end of his career, Ionesco's plays became highly autobiographical and oneiric.

Ionesco rebelled against traditional French theater. His originality largely consisted of his revolutionary rediscovery of language. He wrote of both the banality of language *(La Cantatrice chauve)* and its destructive power *(La Leçon)*. He depicted language's inadequacy but also its necessity for questioning the world and human beings, their absolutes and their different forms of tyranny *(L'Impromptu de l'Alma; Rhinocéros; Macbett; La Soif et la Faim)*. Ionesco's theatrical language also offers insight into the relationship between the self and others *(L'Homme aux valises; Voyages chez les morts)*. In his later plays, language acquires tragic dimensions by exposing man's ontological anxiety and by demonstrating man's inability to solve metaphysical mysteries *(Tueur sans gages; Le Roi se meurt)*. Ultimately, however, Ionesco relieves the moments of despair and solitude in his plays through humor, his way of coping with the absurd. The features of Ionesco's drama directly and indirectly influenced contemporaries such as Jean Tardieu and Georges Schéhadé, as well as many of the innovative playwrights that emerged in his wake, including Fernando Arrabal, René de Obaldia, Rolland Dubillard, Harold Pinter, and Sam Shepard.

Interviews:

Claude Bonnefoy, *Entretiens avec Eugène Ionesco* (Paris: Belfond, 1966); revised and expanded as *Entre la vie et le rêvue: Entretiens avec Claude Bonnefoy* (Paris: Belfond, 1977); original version translated by Jan Dawson as *Conversations with Eugène Ionesco* (New York: Holt, Rinehart & Winston, 1971);

Claude Abstado, *Eugène Ionesco: Etude suivre d'un entretien avec Eugène Ionesco* (Paris: Bordas, 1971);

Arnelle Héliot, *Le Quotidien de Paris* (28 March 1984).

Biography:

Marie-France Ionesco, *Portretul scriitorului în secol: Eugène Ionesco, 1909–1994* (Bucharest: Humanitas, 2003); translated into French as *Portrait de l'écrivan dans le siècle: Eugène Ionesco, 1909–1994* (Paris: Gallimard, 2004).

References:

Simone Benmussa, *Eugène Ionesco* (Paris: Seghers, 1966);

Jean Claude, "La Mort au théâtre: L'Exemple du *Roi se meurt* de Ionesco," in *La Mort en toutes lettres*, edited by Ernst Gilles (Nancy: Presses Universitaires de Nancy, 1983), pp. 239–252;

Ecaterina Cleynen-Serghiev, *La Jeunesse littéraire d'Eugène Ionesco* (Paris: Presses Universitaires de France, 1993);

Richard Coe, *Ionesco: A Study of His Plays* (Edinburgh: Oliver and Boyd, 1961; revised and enlarged edition, London: Methuen, 1971);

Martin Esslin, *The Theater of the Absurd* (New York: Doubleday, 1961; revised edition, London: Penguin, 1970; New York: Pelican, 1983);

Deborah B. Gaensbauer, *Eugène Ionesco Revisited* (New York: Twayne, 1996; London: Prentice Hall, 1996);

Gaensbauer, *The French Theatre of the Absurd,* Twayne's World Authors Series, no. 822 (Boston: Twayne, 1991);

David I. Grossvogel, *The Blasphemers: The Theatre of Brecht, Ionesco, Beckett, Genet* (Ithaca, N.Y.: Cornell University Press, 1965);

Jacques Guicharnaud, *Modern French Theater from Giraudoux to Genet* (New Haven: Yale University Press, 1967);

Marie-Claude Hubert, *Eugène Ionesco* (Paris: Seuil, 1990);

Hubert, *Langage et corps fantasmé dans le théâtre des années cinquante: Ionesco, Beckett, Adamov* (Paris: Librairie José Corti, 1987);

Gelu Ionescu, *Les débuts littéraires roumains d'Eugène Ionesco: Anatomie d'un échec,* translated by Mirella Nedelco-Patureau. (Heidelberg: Carl Winter Universitätsverlag, 1989);

Emmanuel Jacquart, *Le Théâtre de dérision: Beckett, Ionesco, Adamov* (Paris: Gallimard, 1974);

E. D. Karampetsos, "Ionesco and the Journey of the Shaman," *Journal of Evolutionary Psychology,* 4 (April 1983): 64–77;

Rosette C. Lamont, *Ionesco: A Collection of Critical Essays.* (Englewood Cliffs, N.J.: Prentice Hall, 1973);

Lamont, *Ionesco's Imperatives: The Politics of Culture* (Ann Arbor: University of Michigan Press, 1993);

Romul Munteanu, *Farsa tragica* (Bucharest: Editura Univers, 1970);

Leonard Pronko, *Avant-Garde: The Experimental Theater in France* (Berkeley: University of California Press, 1964);

Geneviève Serreau, *Histoire du "nouveau théâtre"* (Paris: Gallimard, 1966);

Alexandru Tudorica, "Les débuts critiques d'Eugène Ionesco," *International Journal of Rumanian Studies,* 4 (1984–1986): 7–26;

Paul Vernois and Marie-France Ionesco, eds., *Ionesco: Situation et perspectives* (Paris: Belfond, 1980);

George E. Wellwarth, *The Theatre of Protest and Paradox: Developments in the Avant-Garde Drama* (New York University Press, 1964; revised, 1971).

Bernard-Marie Koltès

(9 April 1948 – 15 April 1989)

Martine Antle
University of North Carolina at Chapel Hill

PLAY PRODUCTIONS: *Les Amertumes,* Strasbourg, St. Nicholas Church, May 1970;

La Marche, Strasbourg, Théâtre du Quai, 1971;

Procès ivre, Strasbourg, Théâtre du Quai, 1971;

Récits morts, Strasbourg, Théâtre du Quai, 1973;

La Nuit juste avant les forêts, Avignon, Festival Off d'Avignon, July 1977;

Sallinger, Lyon, Théâtre de l'El Dorado, 1977;

Combat de nègre et de chiens, Paris, Théâtre de l'Odéon, 1981; revised as *Come Dog, Come Night,* New York, La MaMa Experimental Theatre, 1982;

Quai Ouest, Nanterre, Théâtre des Amandiers, April 1986;

Tabataba, Avignon, Théâtre Ouvert, July 1986;

Dans la solitude des champs de coton, Nanterre, Théâtre des Amandiers, 1987;

Le Retour au desert, Nanterre, Théâtre des Amandiers, 1988; Paris, Théâtre de la Ville, 1995;

William Shakespeare, *Le Conte d'hiver,* translated by Koltès, Paris, Théâtre du Rond-Point, September 1988;

Roberto Zucco, Berlin, Schaubühne am Leniner Platz, 1990.

BOOKS: *Combat de nègre et de chiens; La Nuit juste avant les forêts* (Paris: Stock, 1980); *Combat de nègre et de chiens* translated by Matthew Ward as *Struggle of the Dogs and the Black* and *La Nuit juste avant les forêts* translated by Timothy Johns as *Night Just before the Forest,* in *Night Just before the Forest; Struggle of the Dogs and the Black,* Ubu Repertory Theater Publications, no. 2 (New York: Ubu Repertory Theater, 1982);

La Famille des orties: Esquisses et croquis de Bernard-Marie Koltès et François Regnault, autour des Paravents de Jean Genet, by Koltès and François Regnault (Nanterre: Editions Nanterre/Amandiers / Paris: Editions BEBA, 1983);

La Fuite à cheval très loin de la ville (Paris: Editions de Minuit, 1984);

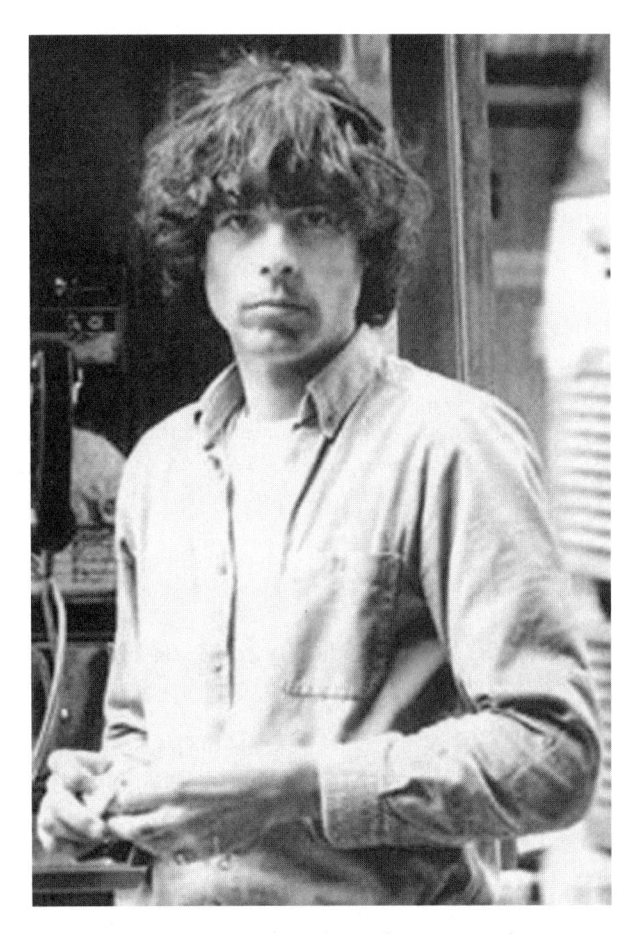

Bernard-Marie Koltès (Mini Teater Ljubljana)

Quai Ouest (Paris: Editions de Minuit, 1985); translated by David Fancy, Alex Johnston, and Joseph Long as *Quay West,* in Koltès, *Plays 2,* edited, with an introduction, by David Bradby and Maria M. Delgado (London: Methuen Drama, 2004);

Dans la solitude des champs de coton (Paris: Editions de Minuit, 1986); translated by Jeffrey Wainwright as *In the Solitude of Cotton Fields* (London: Methuen, 2001);

Le Retour au désert (Paris: Editions de Minuit, 1988); translated by Bradby as *Return to the Desert,* in Koltès, *Plays 1,* edited, with an introduction, by Bradby (London: Methuen Drama, 1997);

Roberto Zucco, suivi de Tabataba (Paris: Editions de Minuit, 1990); *Roberto Zucco* translated by Martin Crimp in Koltès, *Plays 1;*

Prologue, et autres textes (Paris: Editions de Minuit, 1991);

Les Murs: For Two Female Voices (Soprano and Mezzo-Soprano) and Two Trumpets, 1992, music by Robert Zuidam (Amsterdam: Donemus, 1992);

Sallinger (Paris: Editions de Minuit, 1995); translated by Fancy, Johnston, and Long in Koltès, *Plays 2;*

Les Amertumes (Paris: Editions de Minuit, 1998);

L'Héritage (Paris: Editions de Minuit, 1998);

Procès ivre (Paris: Editions de Minuit, 2001);

La Marche (Paris: Editions de Minuit, 2003).

Editions in English: *Plays 1,* edited, with an introduction, by David Bradby (London: Methuen Drama, 1997)–comprises *Black Battles with Dogs,* translated by Bradby and Maria M. Delgado; *Return to the Desert,* translated by Bradby; and *Roberto Zucco,* translated by Martin Crimp;

Plays 2, translated by David Fancy, Alex Johnston, and Joseph Long, edited, with an introduction, by Bradby and Delgado (London: Methuen Drama, 2004)–comprises *Night Just before the Forests, Sallinger, Quay West,* and *In the Solitude of Cotton Fields.*

PRODUCED SCRIPTS: *L'Héritage,* radio, Radio-France Alsace, 1972;

Des Voix sourdes, radio, Radio-France Alsace, 1973;

Combat de nègre et de chiens, radio, France Culture, 1980.

TRANSLATION: William Shakespeare, *Le Conte d'hiver* (Paris: Editions de Minuit, 1988).

Bernard-Marie Koltès emerged as an internationally recognized playwright and stage director in the 1980s. He was the best-known French playwright of his generation and reintroduced the existentialist preoccupations and metaphysical questioning that characterized French theater during the Occupation and the postwar era. He also brought race and gender issues to the French stage. His plays force the audience to confront contemporary social topics such as postcolonialism, racism, and AIDS. In addition, Koltès accorded a renewed importance to dialogue, which had been undervalued by vanguard French playwrights from the 1920s to the 1960s.

Koltès was born on 9 April 1948 in Metz, the capital city of the Moselle region of northeastern France. His father was an officer in the French army who fought in French Indochina and Algeria and was often absent from home as Bernard grew up in the 1950s. Koltès attended the Jesuit school of Saint Clément in Metz, where he obtained his *baccalauréat* to conclude his secondary education. In the late 1960s he became involved in the social and political revolutions that marked the decade, the most important of which, in France, was the general strike of May 1968. Koltès participated actively in the strike that affected students and workers while attending the journalism school of the Université de Strasbourg. At that time he was also considering a career as an organist. A play he attended, however, Seneca's *Medea,* with the actress Maria Casarès in the leading role, changed his life and initiated him into the world of theater.

In 1969, at the age of twenty-one, Koltès wrote his first play, *Les Amertumes* (1998, Bitternesses), adapted from Maksim Gor'ky's 1914 memoir, *My Childhood.* The play was performed in 1970 at the St. Nicholas Church in Strasbourg. The director of the Théâtre National de Strasbourg (TNS, National Theater of Strasbourg), Hubert Gignoux, attended the opening of *Les Amertumes* and became convinced that Koltès was a genius, a true and rare talent. In 1971 Gignoux admitted him to the school of the TNS. That same year, Koltès became increasingly involved in productions at the Théâtre du Quai in Strasbourg, directing his plays *La Marche* (2003, The Walk), an adaptation of the biblical Song of Solomon, and *Procès ivre* (2001, Drunken Trial), based on Fyodor Dostoevsky's *Crime and Punishment* (1866–1867). He directed his *Récits morts* (Dead Narratives), which has not been published, at the Théâtre du Quai in 1973. In addition, Koltès experimented with broadcasts of his works on national French radio. *L'Héritage* (1998, The Inheritance) was broadcast in 1972 and the unpublished *Des Voix sourdes* (Deaf Voices) in 1973.

Koltès traveled around the world from the mid 1970s to the early 1980s. While no accurate record of his travels exists, several interviews indicate that he visited Africa, South America, the United States, Canada, and the Soviet Union. In 1976 he wrote his first dramatic monologue to be published, *La Nuit juste avant les forêts* (1980; translated as *Night Just before the Forest,* 1982), and a play, *Sallinger* (1995; translated, 2004), which was inspired by J. D. Salinger's short stories. *La Nuit juste avant les forêts* is a sixty-page monologue, devoid of punctuation, in which a character on stage struggles against his loneliness and describes the racial tensions of the housing projects where he lives, his brief encounters with prostitutes, and the difficulty of surviving in his world; he speaks to another character who is present on stage but remains silent. David Bradby characterizes this monologue "spoken by an Arab immigrant, destitute, lost and frightened in some French city" as noteworthy for its language, "intense, powerful, carefully worked without departing from the idioms of ordinary speech." *La Nuit juste avant les forêts* premiered at the Festival Off d'Avignon in July 1977. *Sallinger* was also produced the same year in Lyon at the Théâtre de l'El Dorado by Bruno Boeglin.

Koltès's travels to Mali and the Ivory Coast had a great impact on his career and works. His trip to Africa inspired his next play, *Combat de nègre et de chiens* (1980; translated as *Struggle of the Dogs and the Black,* 1982), first performed in 1979 as a *mise en voix* (dramatic reading) at the Centre culturel de la communauté française de Belgique (Cultural Center of the French Community of Belgium) in Paris and then produced as a radio broadcast in 1980. *La Nuit juste avant les forêts* and *Combat de nègre et de chiens* immediately received international recognition and were published by the Paris firm of Stock in 1980, a major achievement because new playwrights in the 1980s faced difficulties in having their works published. The most established firms did not select plays from the contemporary repertoire for publication, and several publishers formerly dedicated to theater discontinued their editions of drama. Owing to financial constraints and the fact that the classical French repertory monopolized the theatrical scene, most playwrights of Koltès's generation could not stage their plays. They opted instead for *mise en voix* performances of their works in small locales and before limited audiences. Koltès stands out among his peers because his plays were performed on stage not only in France but also worldwide. *La Nuit juste avant les forêts* was produced at the Théâtre de l'Odéon in Paris in 1981 and later that year was staged by the most prestigious government-subsidized theater in France, the Comédie-Française in Paris, which was well known for neglecting to stage the works of living authors.

The setting for *Combat de nègre et de chiens* is the construction site of a foreign company in a West African country somewhere between Senegal and Nigeria. All the characters are white except for one, who is black. The play opens as Alboury, the black character, has mysteriously gained entrance to the well-guarded construction site in order to search for the body of his dead brother. The foreman, Horn; a French engineer, Cal; and Horn's fiancée, Léone, newly arrived from France, complete the cast. Horn first tries to convince Alboury to accept compensation for his brother's death, an offer Alboury rejects. In the course of the play it becomes evident that Cal has killed Alboury's brother and thrown the body in the gutter. Much of the action of the play involves the verbal confrontation between the two white men, which Bradby calls "a duel of wills between Horn and Cal. Horn, the boss, is an idealist; . . . With this attitude goes a paternalistic belief in 'co-operation,' that is, the masterminding by Westerners of large engineering

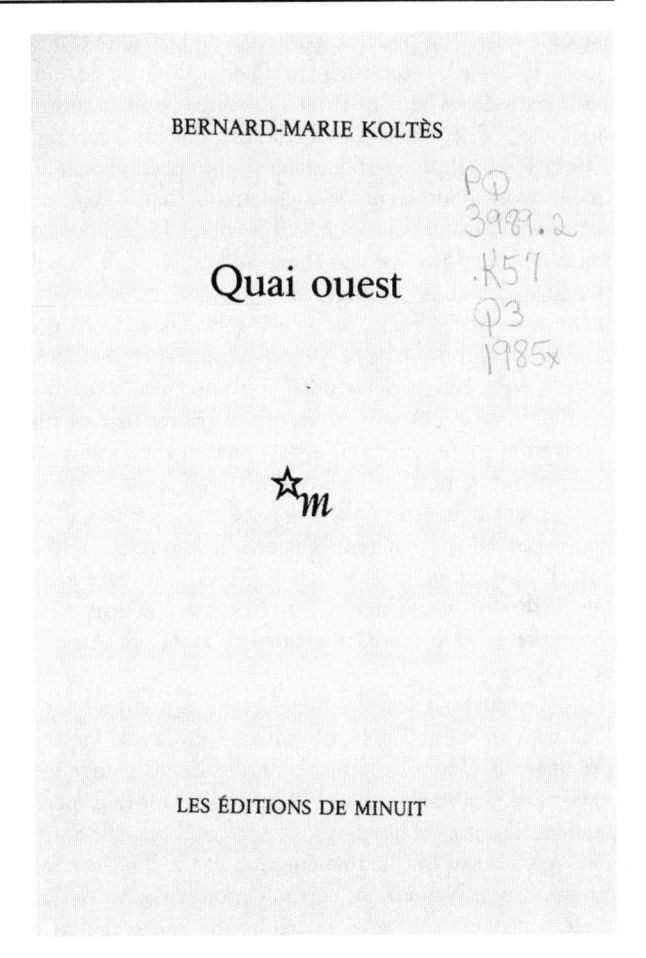

Title page for the 1985 edition of Koltès's play (translated as Quay West, *2004), first performed in 1986, about a group of characters from various backgrounds who meet in an abandoned warehouse on the Hudson River docks in New York (Gorgas Library, University of Alabama)*

schemes for the good of the Third World. Cal, on the other hand, owes allegiance to nothing. His reasons for accepting foreign postings are greed and racism." As the title suggests, dogs, such as Cal's pet and unseen dogs barking in the distance, figure in the play. In Bradby's view, however, the real dogs are the Europeans with whom the Africans must struggle. In the conclusion Cal is shot to death by unseen Africans, and Léone abandons Horn to return to France.

As a Frenchman growing up in the 1960s and involved in demonstrations against the wars in Vietnam and Algeria, Koltès was aware of the role of France in colonization. Cultural and racial tensions pervade *Combat de nègre et de chiens;* yet, Koltès did not write the play to champion Africans over their European colonizers. Rather, as he explained in a 1983 interview in the newspaper *Europe,* "La pièce ne parle pas de l'Afrique et des noirs. Elle parle simplement d'un lieu du monde. On parle parfois des lieux qui sont des sortes de métaphores de la vie" (The play is not about Africa or black people. The play is simply speaking about one specific location in the world. Sometimes, we encounter spaces that are metaphors of life). Throughout his career Koltès consistently affirmed that he was more interested in the interpersonal relations among his characters than in the political or social milieu in which they lived. Both the characters and the plot of *Combat de nègre et de chiens* are developed through dialogue that sometimes takes the form of long speeches in which one character betrays his motivation to the others or argues against their views of society, in a manner reminiscent of *La Nuit juste avant les forêts.* The language of *Combat de nègre et de chiens* is slangy and peppered with vulgarities in an effort to re-create the speech of the kind of men Cal and Horn are based on. Similarly, for verisimilitude, Koltès has Alboury use incomprehensible words that appear to be an African language.

Throughout his life, travel acted as a stimulus to Koltès's career. In 1982 he went to New York for the premiere of *Come Dog, Come Night,* the English-language version of *Combat de nègre et de chiens,* at La MaMa Experimental Theatre. The play was selected in 1983 by Patrice Chéreau for the inauguration of the Théâtre des Amandiers in Nanterre. Chéreau's production was elaborate, with luxurious sets created by the Italian designer Richard Peduzzi, and starred famous French actors of the time, such as Michel Piccoli and Myriam Boyer. This performance became another stepping-stone for Koltès's career and allowed him to live on the proceeds from his writing for the remainder of his life, a privilege he had not had in the past. In addition, this production marked the beginning of a close collaboration between the playwright and Chéreau.

Recognized as the foremost experimental-theater director in France, Chéreau was at his peak in the 1980s. Born in 1944, he had developed his own style, characterized by collaboration with his actors. The French public considered him a visionary who was able to translate images onto the stage. Chéreau also had the ability to stage the works of both classical playwrights, such as Pierre Carlet de Chamblain de Marivaux, and contemporary dramatists. With Koltès, Chéreau was able to pursue his desire for close cooperation between playwright and director that required both to participate actively in the production of a play.

In 1984 Koltès moved to Paris, where he started writing a novel titled *La Fuite à cheval très loin de la ville* (Flight on Horseback Far from the City), published that year by Editions de Minuit, a French *maison d'édition* (publishing house) well known for giving voice to a new generation of novelists and playwrights with the goal of reviving literature and theater. Koltès belongs to what is commonly called the generation of the 1980s and 1990s of Editions de Minuit, which includes Jean-Philippe Toussaint, Jean Echenoz, and Marie Redonnet. As evidence of his importance, Koltès received an entire column in Michel Corvin's *Dictionnaire Encyclopédique du Théâtre* (1991, Encyclopedic Dictionary of Theater).

Because of Koltès's growing success, his plays were published soon after their composition. In 1985 Editions de Minuit published *Quai Ouest* (translated as *Quay West,* 2004). Chéreau directed the play in 1986, with Casarès in the leading role. *Quai Ouest* was written during Koltès's first stay in New York, where he spent much time on the West Pier along the Hudson River in search of inspiration for the locale of his play, finally choosing an abandoned warehouse on the docks of the Hudson. Koltès denied any direct link between the settings of his plays and his characters; for him, the public space functioned as a crossroads where diverse characters from different walks of life could meet, speak, and discover their connections with each other. Among the eight characters in *Quai Ouest* are Abad, a black man who squats in the warehouse and remains silent; a businessman, Koch, who has chosen the warehouse as the ideal place to commit suicide; Monique, Koch's companion; and Charles, who dreams of escaping his marginal place in society. The dialogue includes long statements by individual characters and conversations in which the characters listen and respond to each other. The tone of the play is tragic and speaks of the loss of community as well as of individual identity. Three of the characters die by the end. For Bradby, *Quai Ouest* has a political dimension: "As Koch pursues his ultimately successful quest for annihilation, the tensions set up by the developing action reveal the underlying social and racial stratification of these characters, and through his depiction of these Koltès makes his comments on the state of society under late capitalism." Koltès claimed, however, that the plot and developments in the play were based on nothing more than business and illegal deals.

Dans la solitude des champs de coton (1986; translated as *In the Solitude of Cotton Fields,* 2001), like *Quai Ouest,* was written in the United States; it was produced by Chéreau at the Théâtre des Amandiers in 1987. Being away from France constituted an ideal situation for Koltès's writing process; the geographical distance allowed him to relate to the French language in a new way while being immersed in a different environment. Despite the title of the play, which suggests the rural American South, the setting is an unidentified city at sunrise or sunset. *Dans la solitude des champs de coton* stages a confrontation between two enigmatic main characters, the Dealer and the Client, who engage in a verbal battle. In a brief paragraph that serves as the introduction to the play, Koltès defines the "deal":

> Un *deal* est une transaction commerciale portant sur des valeurs prohibées ou strictement contrôlées, et qui se conclut, dans des espaces neutres, indéfinis, et non prévus à cet usage, entre pourvoyeurs et quémandeurs, par entente tacite, signes conventionnels ou conversations à double sens–dans le but de contourner les risques de trahison et d'escroquerie qu'une telle opération implique–à n'importe quelle heure du jour et de la nuit, indépendamment des heures d'ouverture réglementaires des lieux de commerce homologues, mais plutôt aux heures de fermeture de ceux-ci.
>
> (A *deal* is a commercial transaction of some prohibited or strictly controlled values and which is concluded in neutral, unspecified territory, not set aside for the purpose, between one who purveys and one who has to have, by a tacit understanding, conventional signs or conversations with double meanings–with the goal of bypassing the risks of betrayal and swindle that such an operation implies–at any hour of the day or night, independently of the normal business hours of approved places of business, but rather during the hours when such places are closed.)

Although the exact nature of the "deal" is never revealed, Koltès's description makes clear that it is not commercial; it is effectuated by the words used during an encounter between two people, each of whom wants something from the other or tries to act upon the other through words. Except for the concluding lines, the speeches of each character are long, especially those spoken by the Dealer in his attempt to win over the Client. As the play unfolds, the audience learns that the "deal" is a human interaction and, as such, may become violent. As the Dealer explains, "Deux hommes qui se croisent n'ont pas d'autre choix que de se frapper, avec la violence de l'ennemi ou la douceur de la fraternité" (Two men who cross paths have no other choice but to hit out at each other, with the violence of enmity or the gentleness of fraternity). The concluding words of both the Dealer and the Client evoke weapons and suggest that the characters will turn from verbal to physical combat. In spite of the eloquence with which Koltès's characters speak, their conflict achieves no resolution. Fraternity is not what defines human relations in this play. Human interactions are complex, opaque, and characterized by a lack of emotions that creates a constant tension between the characters.

Tabataba (1990), a short dialogue set in an African village, pits an older sister, Maïmouna, against Petit Aboud, her brother. Maïmouna complains that Aboud wastes his life polishing his Harley Davidson when he could be chasing girls and drinking beer like the other men of the village. Aboud challenges his unmarried sister's right to criticize him and wins the argument. In her final lines Maïmouna joins her brother in motorcycle maintenance. The dialogue is humorous but, like the more serious, concentrates on human relations and the persuasive power of language. *Tabataba* premiered at the Théâtre Ouvert in the Festival d'Avignon in July 1986 as part of a cycle of plays called *Oser aimer* (Dare to Love).

Two additional plays by Koltès were produced before his death in 1989: *Le Retour au désert* (1988; translated as *Return to the Desert*, 1997), first produced by Chéreau in 1988 and later staged by Jacques Nichet in 1995 at the Théâtre de la Ville in Paris; and *Le Conte d'hiver*, a translation of William Shakespeare's *A Winter's Tale* that premiered in September 1988 at the Théâtre du Rond-Point in Paris and ran for 140 performances. Koltès wrote *Le Retour au désert* with French actress Jacqueline Maillan in mind for the main role. In this experiment with the tragicomic form he brings the audience into the life of a bourgeois family living in a French town. Mathilde, who has returned with her adult children from Algeria to live with her brother, Adrien, wants to investigate her family inheritance. The war in Algeria that she has left behind remains present in her mind, and Koltès evokes the connections between France and Algeria by the use of Arabic in Adrien's servant Aziz's conversation with Mathilde and an Arab café owner, as well as by naming later scenes in the play after Muslim prayers and festivities. As in his other plays, Koltès keeps the plot simple but carefully constructs the dialogue to convey a power struggle between the long-separated siblings that easily turns violent. The title is ambiguous; in Bradby's opinion, the desert may be Algeria; the sterile, provincial town where the action takes place; or another, unnamed destination, "where the rich are sufficiently cushioned from the unpleasant realities of life."

Koltès died of AIDS on 15 April 1989, shortly after his forty-first birthday and the completion of his most controversial play, *Roberto Zucco* (1990; translated, 1997), which premiered in Berlin at the Schaubühne am Leniner Platz in 1990. At the time of his death he also left an unfinished play on the French designer Coco Chanel and her female assistant, Consuelo. In *Roberto Zucco*, Koltès followed in the footsteps of playwright Jean Genet, who was fascinated with the social construction of the criminal, by challenging assumptions about criminals in a media-driven culture. The play was inspired by the true story of a killer named Roberto Succo, the *tueur fou* (crazy killer), as he was called in the French press for the series of murders he committed from 1987 to 1988. Succo was also notorious for his participation in multiple assaults, rapes, and robberies. Koltès claimed that the point of departure for his play was a poster of a composite portrait of Succo that he had seen in the subway. The

Although he wrote only a small number of plays, Bernard-Marie Koltès became a major figure in the history of French and European postwar theater. His works have been translated into thirty-six languages and performed throughout the world. He resembles his avant-garde predecessors of the 1950s and 1960s in his evocation of solitude, egocentricity, exclusion, and the difficulty of surrendering to desire and love. Koltès differs, however, from playwrights such as Eugène Ionesco and Samuel Beckett, whose plays demonstrated the absurdity inherent in language or the disintegration of language and communication. Koltès broke away from Antonin Artaud's theories of modern theater that advocated a nonverbal, auditory language on stage, attempting instead to revive the theatrical traditions of seventeenth-century French classicism by reinstating the supremacy of the text. Koltès reintroduced and redefined the dramatic monologue. His characters often do not communicate directly through dialogues but, rather, play the role of silent interlocutors whose silence causes discomfort among the other characters on stage as well as the audience. At the same time, Koltès believed in the role and power of narration. In his plays, characters recount their lives and tell stories, jokes, and anecdotes. They speak in a language that combines familiar speech or argot with argumentation intended to communicate the complexities of human relationships. This insistence on the role and power of language remains Koltès's most important contribution to twentieth-century French theater.

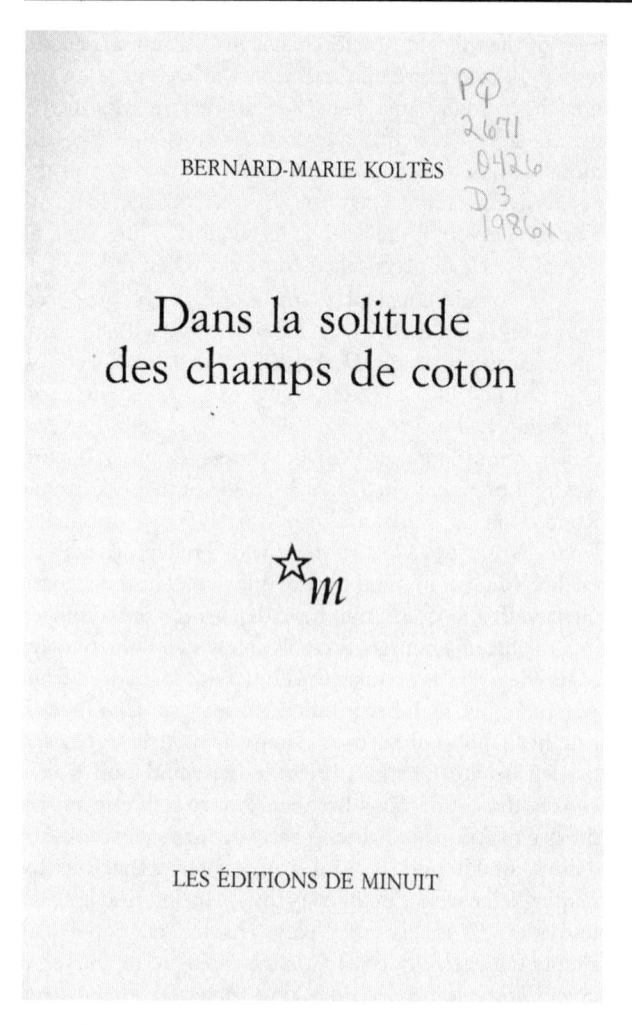

Title page for the 1986 edition of Koltès's play (translated as In the Solitude of Cotton Fields, *2001), first staged in 1987, about two enigmatic characters who negotiate a complex and unexplained deal (Gorgas Library, University of Alabama)*

blurring of fact and fiction is evident in the name of the killer in the play, Zucco, which mimics the name of Succo. Koltès's rendition of Succo's case remains controversial because he did not attempt to explain the cause of the crimes. The play also lacks a resolution. *Roberto Zucco* does not depend on monologues for character development, like Koltès's earlier works. Rather, fifteen scenes present Zucco's life as he moves through different spaces and meets and speaks with more than twenty characters, members of society who are intrigued by him. Zucco is seen only through the eyes of others; his personality remains unreadable and changeable. Koltès does not explore the psychology of the title character, and in newspaper interviews he claimed that he considered the character Zucco normal because anyone was capable of killing.

Interviews:

Une Part de ma vie: Entretiens, 1983–1989 (Paris: Editions de Minuit, 1999).

References:

Christophe Bident, *Bernard-Marie Koltès, généalogies* (Tours: Farrago, 2000);

David Bradby, *Modern French Drama, 1940–1990,* second edition (Cambridge & New York: Cambridge University Press, 1991);

Europe, special Koltès issue, nos. 823–824 (1997);

Roger-François Gauthier, Jean Claude Lallias, and Jean-Jacques Arnaud, *Koltès: Combats avec la scène,* Théâtre aujourd'hui, no. 5 (Paris: Centre national de documentation pédagogique, 1996);

Odéon Théâtre, special Koltès issue, nos. 35–36 (1995);

Marie-Paule Sébastien, *Bernard-Marie Koltès et l'espace Théâtral* (Paris: Harmattan, 2001);

Anne Ubersfeld, *Bernard-Marie Koltès* (Arles: Actes Sud / Paris: Conservatoire national supérieur d'art dramatique, 1999).

Philippe Minyana
(1946 –)

Nicole Simek
Whitman College

PLAY PRODUCTIONS: *Premier Trimestre,* Metz, Comédie de Metz, 1979;

Cartaya, Paris, Centre Georges Pompidou, 1980;

Ariakos, Paris, Théâtre du Quai de la gare, 1983;

Titanic, Avignon, Chapelle des Cordeliers, 1983;

Exposition, Paris, Théâtre Essaïon, 1985;

France et Akim, Avignon, Festival d'Avignon, 1985;

Jojo, music by Georges Aperghis, Strasbourg, Musica, 1990;

Le Prince Constant, by Minyana and Jean-Jacques Préau, adapted from Pedro Calderón de la Barca's *El Principe constante* (1629), Avignon, Festival d'Avignon, 1992;

Murder, Avignon, La Collégiale de Villeneuve-lès-Avignon, 1993;

Purgatoire, Paris, Conservatoire National Supérieur d'Art Dramatique, June 1994;

Commentaires, music by Aperghis, Avignon, Théâtre Benoît XII, 1996;

Reconstitution, Nîmes, 1998;

Monsieur Bild, ou L'Exposition, Florange, Spring 1999;

Portraits, Paris, Théâtre Ouvert, October 1999;

Avenue de la République, St. Denis, Théâtre Gérard Philippe, 1999.

BOOKS: *Laura dans l'olivette: Pièce en vingt-deux tableaux* (Paris: Recherche-Action Théâtre Ouvert, 1980);

Fin d'été à Baccarat (Paris: Edilig, 1984);

Ruines romaines; Quatuor (Paris: Edilig, 1986);

Chambres, Les Guerriers, Volcan (Paris: Edilig, 1988);

Les Petits Aquariums (Arles: Actes Sud, 1989);

Où vas-tu Jérémie? (Paris: Editions Théâtrales, 1989);

Chambres; Inventaires; André (Paris: Editions Théâtrales, 1993);

Drames brefs (Paris: Editions Théâtrales, 1995);

La Maison des morts: Pièce pour acteurs et marionnettes en six mouvements avec prologue et épilogue (Paris: Editions Théâtrales, 1996);

Drames brefs (2) (Paris: Editions Théâtrales, 1997);

Jean Babilée (Paris: Marval, 1998);

Philippe Minyana (photograph by E. Emo; from L'Avant Scène: Théâtre, *1 May 1987; Glenn G. Bartle Library, Binghamton University)*

Anne-Laure et les fantômes, music by Les Trois 8 (Paris: Editions Théâtrales, 1999);

Anne-Marie, suivi de Les Ecritures de Philippe Minyana, avec Robert Cantarella, Roland Fichet, Catherine Hiegel, Fabienne Pascaud (Paris: Théâtre Ouvert, 2000);

Habitations; Pièces (Paris: Editions Théâtrales, 2001); *Habitations* translated by Steve Waters and Christopher Campbell as *Habitats* (London: Oberon, 2002);

Suite 1, Suite 2, Suite 3 (Paris: Editions Théâtrales, 2003);

Le Couloir (Paris: Editions Théâtrales, 2004);

Prologue, entente cordiale, Anne-Marie, by Minyana, Michel Azama, and Frédéric Maragnani (Paris: Théâtre Ouvert, 2004).

PRODUCED SCRIPTS: *Ruines romaines,* radio, France-Culture, 15 October 1981;

Fin d'été à Baccarat, radio, France-Culture, 18 February 1982;

Le Dîner de Lina, radio, France-Culture, 30 June 1982;

Quatuor, radio, France-Culture, 19 April 1984;

Madame Scotto, television, La Sept, 1987;

Inventaires, radio, France-Culture, 26 September 1987;

Inventaires, video, Arcanal, 1990;

Chambres, radio, Radio Suisse Romande, June 1991;

Les Guerriers, radio, France-Culture, 29 June 1991;

André, television, Arte, 1992;

Gang, radio, music by Jean-Marie Sénia, France-Culture, 12 June 1993;

La Maison des morts, radio, France-Culture, 28 October 1995;

Léone, recording, text by Minyana, music by Philippe Mion, Empreintes DIGITALes IMED-9632, 1996;

Papa est monté au ciel, by Minyana and Jacques Renard, television, Arte, October 1998;

Descriptif, radio, France-Culture, 2000.

OTHER: Miguel de Cervantes, *Le Siège de Numance,* translated by Minyana and Jean-Jacques Préau (Arles: Actes Sud, 1992);

Description, in *Théâtre contre l'oubli* (Arles: Actes Sud, 1996);

Histoires, in *Petites pièces d'auteurs* (Paris: Editions Théâtrales, 1998);

Salle des fêtes, in *Petites pièces d'auteurs 2* (Paris: Editions Théâtrales, 2000).

SELECTED PERIODICAL PUBLICATIONS– UNCOLLECTED: *Le Dîner de Lina, L'Avant-scène: Théâtre,* no. 748 (15 April 1984);

Boomerang, ou Le salon rouge, L'Avant-scène: Théâtre, no. 879 (1 December 1990): 3–23;

"Images et langages," *Journal de la SACD,* no. 12 (March 1994): 9;

"Le Petit Corsage blanc," *Les Cahiers de Prospero,* no. 1 (1994): 21–22;

"Café de l'Univers, 11h30, octobre 1994," *Les Cahiers de Prospero,* no. 3 (1 December 1994): 38–39;

"Le Chemin vers une représentation possible," *Les Cahiers de Prospero,* no. 3 (1 December 1994): 26–37;

"La Tour de Montaigne," *Les Cahiers de Prospero,* no. 3 (1 December 1994): 44–46;

Wagon, Du Théâtre: La Revue (1994);

Effigie, Les Cahiers de Prospero, no. 6 (1995);

Gang, music by Jean-Marie Sénia, *L'Avant-scène: Théâtre,* no. 972 (15 June 1995): 3–32;

"Le son, le sens–Ecrire pour un théâtre en chantier," *Puck,* no. 8 (third trimester 1995);

"Tendances de la création théâtrale contemporaine française," *Actes du théâtre,* no. 4 (1 January 1996): 63–81;

"Le Bruit du monde," *Les Cahiers de Prospero,* no. 8 (1 July 1996): 7–73;

"Il faut déposer la parole dans le livre," *La Lettre d'Atlantiques,* 16 (1 February 1997): 2–4.

Philippe Minyana is renowned in France and abroad as a prolific and formally innovative playwright. In addition to being performed on the stage, his works have been interpreted for radio and television. His output includes musical plays, such as *Jojo* (1990); librettos, such as *Léone* (1996); and adaptations of dramas by the Spanish Golden Age writers Miguel de Cervantes and Pedro Calderón de la Barca. Although dominated by concerns for music and the musicality of language, Minyana's plays also draw on the plastic arts, such as painting and photography. Images in the form of slides or photographs are integrated into his works, not simply to set the scene but rather to serve as essential elements of meaning. Suffering, violence, and the body are constant themes in Minyana's works, depicted in a way often described as clinical and with a magnification of detail that critic Michel Corvin has called the "hyperrealism of details" in *Philippe Minyana, ou La parole visible* (2000, Philippe Minyana, or The Visible Word). Minyana's use of logorrhea, or excessive wordiness, and lack of punctuation have fluctuated during his career but are especially evident in his plays of the 1990s. His artistic influences include Anton Chekhov, Thomas Bernhard, Nathalie Sarraute, Herbert Achternbusch, Luc Boltanski, and Peter Handke. Michel Vinaver, a French playwright of the second half of the twentieth century concerned with family conflict and economic issues, ranks as a dominant influence. Minyana's frequently dark humor and sense of horror have also been compared to Samuel Beckett's.

The oldest of three children, Philippe Minyana was born in 1946 in the eastern French city of Besançon. His father worked as a foreman at an automotive factory, while his mother ran a grocery store. Educated in the humanities in Besançon, Minyana moved to Paris in 1980, where he began his theatrical career as both an actor and writer. Later in the same decade, desiring fuller creative independence, he turned his focus to writing alone and composed more than twenty original plays and play adaptations from 1985 to 2004.

Many of Minyana's plays were not published and have not survived. These works include *Premier Trimestre* (1979, First Trimester), *Cartaya* (1980), *Ariakos*

(1983), *Exposition* (1985), *France et Akim* (1985, France and Akim), *Jojo, Murder* (1993), *Purgatoire* (1994, Purgatory), *Commentaires* (1996, Commentaries), *Reconstitution* (1998), *Monsieur Bild, ou L'Exposition* (1999, Mr. Bild, or The Exposition), *Portraits* (1999), and *Avenue de la République* (1999). Many of his published works–including *Laura dans l'olivette: Pièce en vingt-deux tableaux* (1980, Laura in the Olive Grove: Play in Twenty-Two Tableaus), *Le Dîner de Lina* (1984, Lina's Dinner), *Quatuor* (1986, Quartet), *Boomerang, ou Le Salon rouge* (1990, Boomerang, or The Red Salon), *Wagon* (1994), *Effigie* (1995, Effigy), *Gang* (1995), *Description* (1996), *Jean Babilée* (1998), and *Histoires* (1998, Stories)–are not easily available because they were published in anthologies or theater journals, such as *L'Avant-scène: Théâtre,* or by small Parisian presses such as Edilig. Minyana's best-known works are those published by Editions Théâtrales: *Où vas-tu Jérémie?* (1989, Where Are You Going Jeremy?), *Inventaires* (1993, Inventories), *Drames brefs* (1995, Brief Dramas), *La Maison des morts: Pièce pour acteurs et marionnettes en six mouvements avec prologue et épilogue* (1996, The House of the Dead: Play for Actors and Marionettes in Six Movements with Prologue and Epilogue), *Drames brefs (2)* (1997), *Anne-Laure et les fantômes* (1999, Anne-Laura and the Ghosts), *Habitations* (2001; translated as *Habitats,* 2002), *Suite 1, Suite 2, Suite 3* (2003), and *Le Couloir* (2004, The Hallway).

Minyana has given few details of his private life but has spoken often of his art. His artistic development can be described, as he himself has done, as occurring in stages. His first plays served a "therapeutic" function; writing, he said in a 1996 interview with Laurence Cazaux, was closely linked to his relationship with his mother, who committed suicide on 13 August 1980, and he could only begin writing after confronting the difficulties of this relationship. Minyana's earliest plays, *Premier Trimestre, Fin d'été à Baccarat* (1984, End of the Summer at Baccarat), and *Ruines romaines* (1986, Roman Ruins), are set in the eastern France of his youth. *Premier Trimestre* was Minyana's first work and the only one of his early plays produced in the eastern city of Metz. *Fin d'été à Baccarat* takes place, as the title indicates, in the northeastern town famous for its crystal industry, and *Ruines romaines* is set in the thermal spa of Luxeuil-les-Bains, north of Besançon. *Ruines romaines* exemplifies Minyana's early dramatic works. There is no plot or action. Three characters–Vincent, Morin, and Hélène–stand around a coffee machine in their workplace. Hélène complains of her health, and Morin also discusses his health, while Vincent talks about his mother. They occasionally ask questions of each other that go unanswered; more than dialogue, their speeches are revelations of the private obsessions that isolate each character from the others. The *chansons* (songs) inserted

Front cover of the magazine issue that included Minyana's 1987 play about three women in a speaking marathon on a television show (Glenn G. Bartle Library, Binghamton University)

between scenes in *Ruines romaines* (a technique reworked much later in *Le Couloir*) explore the flow and excesses of language, the succession of sounds, and the techniques of monologue, all of which became increasingly significant concerns in Minyana's career.

Minyana's early plays made use of individualized characters (for example, Vincent, Hélène, and Morin in *Ruines romaines*) and dialogue. Beginning in the mid 1980s, however, he moved away from what he saw as a restrictive notion of characterization to focus on language and the actor as a tool for reworking the material that is language. In *Chambres* (Bedrooms, performed 1986, published 1988) there is no dialogue but rather a series of stream-of-consciousness monologues about marital problems and childhood memories. In *Inventaires,* first performed in 1987, three women on a television reality show speak as quickly as possible until a moderator cuts each one off. At times, lighting and noises indicate which woman is to speak. *Chambres* and *Inventaires,* Minyana's two best-known works, as evidenced in part by their addition in 1999 to the *baccalauréat* curriculum studied by all French high-school students, take as a starting point the *fait divers*—the offbeat or miscellaneous news item. The first episode of *Chambres,* for example, gives an account of a young man, Boris Kos, who died with frozen feet in a warehouse in Sochaux, an industrial city near Switzerland. The body and its gestures also play key roles in this work. *Chambres* opens with a long monologue by another character named Kos, in which the dead Boris's ruptured frozen feet figure prominently:

> KOS.– J'avais lu ça que les pieds étaient gelés éclatés! Gelés éclatés j'avais vu dans le dictionnaire que dans le pied il y a le tarse les métatarsiens les orteils et puis je me suis dit aussi que les pieds de Boris c'étaient encore des veines des muscles de la peau alors je me suis dit qu'est-ce qu'on a retrouvé de ses pieds les pieds de Boris Kos le jeune Boris Kos ils écrivent ça dans le journal "le jeune Boris Kos"! Qu'est-ce qu'on a retrouvé des pieds de Boris?

> (KOS.– I'd read that his feet were frozen exploded! Frozen exploded I'd seen in the dictionary that in the foot are the metatarsals the toes and then I also said to myself that in Boris's feet there were also veins muscles skin so I said to myself what did they find of Boris's feet the young Boris Kos they write that in the paper "the young Boris Kos"! What did they find of Boris's feet?)

Minyana seeks to give a voice to the socially marginalized victim of this story. He has expressed, nevertheless, a dislike for lyricism, facile political correctness, sentimentalism, and folklorist writing, all of which he attempts to avoid. In *Inventaires* he places ordinary women in a speaking marathon. His goal is to give the audience an understanding of such people's lives, without reference to their profession or class, by re-creating their anecdotal, everyday speech and the lives they express through this language. As Minyana envisions it, the political dimension of *Chambres* and *Inventaires* resides in the attempt to render, through "stylistic, simply semantic propositions, . . . the reality, duration and limits" of these unexceptional people *(Philippe Minyana, ou La parole visible)*.

In production notes and in public forums, such as those organized by the Théâtre Ouvert in Paris, where many of his plays have been produced, Minyana stresses the transformation that reality undergoes as it is made into art. He has often insisted in interviews that he attempts not simply to reconstruct but rather to poeticize spoken language. Rejecting the notion that writing should seek to reflect reality, he calls into question the function of language as a tool for describing or shaping reality. Minyana emphasizes that language is an object that surpasses or even replaces plot as the main element in theater. Speaking of the interviews with women that served as the raw material for *Inventaires,* he is quoted in *Philippe Minyana, ou La parole visible* as saying, "Il faut tricher, il faut reconstituer cette langue-là. Et c'est cette langue-là qui devient la fiction. C'est pour ça que résumer les pièces je trouve ça épouvantable; ça les appauvrit obligatoirement. Si on résume *Inventaires.* . . . On ne peut pas le résumer. . . . C'est de la parole en fusion, du surgissement de la parole" (You have to cheat, you have to reconstitute that language. And it's that language which becomes fiction. That's why I think it's horrible to summarize plays; it necessarily impoverishes them. If you summarize *Inventaires.* . . . You can't summarize it. . . . It is the fusion of words, the eruption of words).

One of the best-known and most frequently mentioned aspects of *Inventaires* and *Chambres* is their use of logorrhea and monologue. In *Inventaires,* each of the three main characters races to tell a story about herself in relation to an object—a basin, a dress, and a lamp—while *Chambres* consists solely of six monologues. These plays attempt to stage the common human need to speak and confess, but they also raise questions about the use of space, dialogue, and the placement of actors on the stage, technical matters that must be resolved in each new production of the play. Minyana began with an interest in rhythm within long paragraphs or monologues. *Chambres,* for example, is composed of long monologues in which sentences run together with no punctuation. The elimination of punctuation in Minyana's works, at times partial, as in *Les Petits Aquariums* (1989, The Little Aquariums), and at times complete, as in *Chambres,* stems from his desire both to draw attention to the rhythm and sonority of language and to allow for greater interpretative flexibility. He has attributed this stylistic choice to his own experience of freedom as an actor working with Vinaver's unpunctuated texts. Minyana strives to provide a structure like that of a musical composition. He views his plays as scores—that is, highly structured texts that are then brought to life by an actor who, like an instrumentalist, determines the exact phrasing and intensity required by the part.

By the late 1980s Minyana had moved away from his private obsessions to more-universal themes. He has attributed this shift in part to the influence of world events in the late 1980s, such as the wars taking place in Lebanon, Iran, and Iraq, and in part to his discussions with other dramatists at La Chartreuse de Villeneuve-lès-Avignon in 1988. The characters who emerge from this exploration are no longer specific individuals but symbolic figures. Such characters include

Jérémie, in *Où vas-tu Jérémie?*, a lamenting prophet who recalls Jeremiah of the Bible, and "la femme qui saigne" (the bleeding woman) and "les assassins" (the killers) of *Les Petits Aquariums*. In these plays Minyana often combines horror and slapstick in his study of human violence. In *Les Petits Aquariums*, for example, disemboweled men and assassins dressed as butchers appear simultaneously with a comic but grotesque portrayal of strained family relationships set against the rivalry between a child and a chimpanzee. Fear, anxiety, illness, suffering, and revolt are manifested physically in the play through fainting spells, falls, bleeding, and vomiting. Cadavers speak and display open wounds in the second part of *Les Petits Aquariums*, in which Jean-Michel's disemboweled organs appear onstage and the dead José-Garcia carries his lungs for the audience to view. In *Philippe Minyana, ou La parole visible*, Françoise Spiess compares this proliferation of organs and bodily fluids to the author's use of wordiness and names the technique "logorrhée-diarrhée" (logorrhea-diarrhea). In *Les Petits Aquariums*, Minyana uses the body to explore violence, pain, and family tensions—constant themes in his plays—through a humorous treatment of physical suffering. While the body of a chimpanzee lies before them on the stage, a couple debates the events leading to his death. These events include their son's torture of the chimpanzee, the animal's attack and disfigurement of the boy, and the murder of the chimpanzee by police arriving on the scene. After several provocations from the child, who urinates, demands orange juice, and tells his mother he does not love her, the scene ends comically but violently.

Minyana's interest in the musicality of language led him to experiment with musical plays. He collaborated with the composer Georges Aperghis on *Jojo* in 1990 and again in 1996 on *Commentaires*, which was performed at the Avignon summer festival. In 1993 Minyana produced *Gang*, with music by Jean-Marie Sénia, for radio broadcast on France-Culture.

In *Les Guerriers* (The Warriors, published 1988, performed 1991) Minyana explores the emotions associated with traumatic experiences by developing ideas that emerged in conversations with others, including playwrights, actors, and students. *Les Guerriers* was inspired by the journals of Minyana's grandfather, a soldier in World War I, which he found in his mother's attic. In order to gain a better understanding of war and its effect on those who fought it, he visited nursing homes and interviewed retired veterans. The result is a dramatization not only of the hostilities provoked by war and of the individual soldier's experience of war but also of the human propensity for violence and confrontation.

Front cover for the 1988 collection of three of Minyana's plays. The first (Bedrooms, first performed in 1986) consists of six long, unpunctuated monologues; the second (The Warriors, first performed in 1991) was inspired by the journals of his grandfather (Jean and Alexander Heard Library, Vanderbilt University).

Beginning in 1995, Minyana made a shift in focus rather than a change in subject, as he turned his attention to the various experiences and expressions of mourning in *Drames brefs; Drames brefs (2); La Maison des morts; Suite 1, Suite 2, Suite 3;* and *Le Couloir*. Focusing on the figure of the mother (a figure, along with other family members, present in many of Minyana's works), *Drames brefs* strives to operate, Minyana claimed in a 2003 interview with Dominique Mans, on a metaphysical level, presenting stylized characters representative of certain aspects of human emotions and relations to the world. These characters are portrayed without any individualizing traits: they have no physical attributes, profession, class, or personal history. In six tableaux, six characters talk principally about the painful relationships between mothers and sons that come to the fore when sons confront a mother's death, but these characters also mourn the deaths of neighbors and friends. Director Etienne Pommeret considers the ability to bring ordinary people to life through their words Minyana's greatest achievement in *Drames brefs:* "Ces *Drames brefs (1)* sont une variation épique de l'âme ordinaire.... Ces hommes, ces femmes, fréquentent la douleur d'exister" (These *Brief Dramas [1]* are an epic variation of the ordinary soul.... These men, these women, are in close contact with the pain of existence). Short lines are arranged on the page like verse. The repetition of phrases and the breaking down of words into their phonemic units forces the audience to focus on words and their sounds. Pommeret recognized the musicality of this project and proposed working with "acteurs-musiciens-chanteurs" (actor-musicians-singers) in his 2002 production of *Drames brefs* in order to create "une partition de sons, de bruits, d'images" (a score of sounds, of noises, of images).

Minyana is interested in stylization of the body, often recommending to the actors interpreting his roles that their bodies become "abnormally tense" on stage, as he said in the interview with Cazaux. *La Maison des morts* integrates actors and marionettes; the body becomes robotic or wooden in the play as actors appear side by side with dummies or puppets. *La Maison des morts* is also representative of the transformation of language into a musical object. In the opening prologue, which reenacts the murder of a young girl represented by a mannequin, the lines "KI A TUÉ ANNE-CHRISTELLE" (Who killed Anne-Christelle) and "RE-CONS-TI-TU-TION" are intoned by "La voix" (The Voice), "La femme policier" (The Policewoman), and the Mannequin. Other characters named Gros, Car, Sel, and Cagette (fat, for, salt, and tray) act out the variations, consisting of different assassination scenarios, on the mannequin. Orthographic changes mimic the syllabification of spoken language, as in La voix's line "KESKISEPASSE" (What's happening); yet, the attention to rhythm and the visual layout of the lines in verse form create blocks of sonorous poems that cannot be regarded as simple transcriptions of everyday speech:

> GROS.—(*après une série de petits gestes qui marquent son affolement*)
> Car a mis l'cutter al cou d'la
> fifille qui hurla a Car
> a tranchê l'cou d'la fifille qui
> alors gisait
>
> CAR.—(*après une série de petits gestes qui marquent son affolement*)
> A Sel lui a qui a
> mis al cutter au cou d'la
> fifille et ka dit a vai a qui
> tranchê le cou et Gros regardé
> des yeux alors Sel
> a tranchê l'cou d'la fifille qui
> alors gisait
>
> SEL.—(*après une série de petits gestes qui marquent son affolement*)
> Gros a mis
> al cutter a cou d'la fifille
> et Car et Gros
> ensemb avé l'cutter ont tranchê
> al cou d'la fifille et moi suis parti
> é-pou-van-tê
>
> (GROS.—*[after a series of small gestures representing his bewilderment]*
> Car put th'cutter to th'throat a the
> lass who shouted at Car
> slittin th'throat a th' lass who
> was sprawled out then
>
> CAR.—*[after a series of small gestures representing his bewilderment]*
> T' Sel he did who did
> put th'cutter to th'throat a the
> lass an said had to who
> slittin th'throat an Gros looked
> with his eyes so Sel
> slit th'throat a th' lass who
> was sprawled out then
>
> SEL.—*[after a series of small gestures representing his bewilderment]*
> Gros put
> th'cutter to th'throat a th'lass
> an Car an Gros
> together wi th'cutter slit
> th'throat a th' lass an me, left
> ho-ro-fied)

Drames brefs (2) is an exploration of mourning similar to that of *Drames brefs,* as are the pieces in *Suite 1, Suite 2, Suite 3. Anne-Laure et les fantômes* changes themes to evoke a messianic figure drawn from the Judeo-Christian religious tradition through the character Chris. *Le Couloir* again takes up the theme of family tensions as a young man, l'Intrus (The Intruder), returns to his childhood home and siblings after a long absence provoked years before by a conflict. As Minyana notes in the preface to the play, the stage becomes a secular form of "purgatory," exploring guilt, mourning, and the possibility of catharsis.

In addition to words, objects and places also act as organizing components in many of Minyana's works, not only in *Inventaires,* in which the three contestants must describe a basin, a lamp, and a dress, but also in *Drames brefs (2),* in which the characters comment on books, photos, letters, and paintings. In *Habitations,* Minyana questions the ability of an image to represent the body: audience members are confronted with slide projections that characters claim are their likenesses, despite the lack of resemblance between the images onstage and on-screen. *Le Couloir,* the title of which indicates a space between other, more defined spaces, reflects Minyana's conception of the stage as a vacuum or place of limbo. He moved from supplying few indications of place, sometimes limited to scene titles, as in *Ruines romaines,* to writing more-detailed stage directions in later works such as *Le Couloir.* This change took place at the same time that he decided to devote more time to directing in the 1990s. In 2000 Minyana became codirector, with Robert Cantarella, of the Théâtre Dijon-Bourgogne.

Minyana's interest in space extends beyond the stage to the writing process itself, which for him can only take place in certain locations, preferably interior, closed spaces. "Le bureau, la chambre, l'intérieur me conviennent" (The office, the bedroom, the interior suit me), he affirmed in the interview with Mans, describing writing as a way of life that imposes itself on him, in accordance with an internal rhythm, one that is "presque biologique, métabolique" (nearly biological, metabolic). Similarly, he states that the urge to write, the germination of an idea, is felt in the body itself. The act of writing begins by preparing a space on the worktable and the surrounding area; the writing then takes place by hand.

Minyana's shift toward formal concerns requires a different approach to theater on the part of the audience. He is quoted in *Philippe Minyana, ou La parole visible* as saying,

> aujourd'hui, nos théâtres déroutent beaucoup parce que justement, il y a une autre façon de parler qu'on n'a pas encore apprise. . . . Quand je rencontre des enseignants ou des acteurs culturels des Régions, le rapport au texte est toujours identification d'abord, il est toujours moral et sentimental; on s'accroche au fond mais pas à la forme. Or, la forme est peut-être plus important que le fond.

> (today, theater is very disturbing precisely because there is another manner of speaking that hasn't yet been learned. . . . When I meet cultural instructors or actors from the Regions, the relationship to the text is always first one of identification, it's always moral and sentimental; people cling to the content but not the form. Yet, the form is perhaps more important than the content.)

Philippe Minyana's plays build on the formal innovations of the French avant-garde dramatists of the 1950s and 1960s but are more radical in their experiments with language and the body. His texts are difficult for both the audience and the actors confronted with a complex score they must decipher. Minyana is aware of this difficulty; yet, he believes it can be overcome, in part through the actor's careful reading. He views the actor as a collaborator whose work is essential to the creative process, and he has modified or rewritten texts after staging them and observing how actors work with them. The difficulty of this kind of theater resides not so much in understanding the subject of the play, Minyana insists, but rather in understanding what impressions and new forms of sound and movement the play produces.

Front cover for Minyana's play (1989, The Little Aquariums), in which disemboweled men and assassins dressed as butchers appear in conjunction with a comic but grotesque portrayal of strained family relationships (Jean and Alexander Heard Library, Vanderbilt University)

Interviews:

"Ecrire les années 80," *L'Avant-scène: Théâtre,* no. 748 (15 April 1984);

Laurence Cazaux, "Le Théâtre du deuil," *Le Matricule des anges,* no. 15 (20 February 1996): 23;

Dominique Mans, "Philippe Minyana: l'ecriture, la scène," *Bourgogne Côté Livre,* no. 25 (June 2003): 3–7.

References:

Laurence Bailloux, "*Drames brefs (2),*" *Du Théâtre: La Revue,* no. 17 (1 January 1997): 35–39;

David Bradby and Annie Sparks, *Mise en scène: French Theatre Now* (London: Methuen Drama, 1997);

Marie-Pia Bureau, *Chambres/Inventaires: Philippe Minyana* (Paris: Centre National de Documentation Pédagogique, 1999);

"Compagnonnage," *La Chartreuse,* no. 32 (1 September 1995): 6–11;

Jean-Yves Coquelin, "La Douleur au rebond ou Algos et ses saisons," *Théâtre/Public,* no. 133 (1 January 1997): 35–39;

Michel Corvin, "Philippe Minyana," in *Dictionnaire encyclopédique du Théâtre,* third edition (Paris: Larousse, 1998), pp. 1111-1112;

Corvin, ed., *Philippe Minyana, ou La parole visible* (Paris: Editions Théâtrales, 2000);

Gilles Costaz, "Philippe Minyana, la nouvelle Comédie noire," *L'Avant-scène: Théâtre,* no. 879 (1 December 1990);

Joseph Danan and Jean-Pierre Ryngaert, *Eléments pour une histoire du texte de théâtre* (Paris: Dunod, 1997), pp. 175-182;

Jean-Jacques Delfour, "*Drames brefs* de Philippe Minyana," *Du Théâtre: La Revue,* no. 11 (1 December 1996): 18–33;

Daniel Dumas, "Philippe Minyana, Paroles serves et plume libre," *L'Avant-scène: Théâtre,* 972 (15 June 1995);

François Marin, "Les Guerriers," *Scènes Magazine,* no. 127 (1 November 1999): 33–36;

Marie-Madeleine Mervant-Roux, "L'écriture dramatique de Philippe Minyana: des voix travaillées par la scène," in *Ecrire pour le théâtre: les enjeux de l'écriture dramatique,* edited by Marie-Christine Autant-Mathieu (Paris: Centre National de la Recherche Scientifique, 1995);

Anny Milovanoff, "On a transformé les âmes en corps," *Les Cahiers de Prospero,* no. 8 (1 July 1996): 94–97;

Carol Muller, "Rêver le temps: à propos de la création des *Guerriers* de Philippe Minyana," *Du Théâtre: La Revue,* no. 19 (1 January 1998): 21–33;

Fabienne Pascaud, "Philippe Minyana: un 'pilleur de langue,'" *Le Public* (Journal du Théâtre National de la Colline), 6 (1989–1990);

Pascaud, "Vainqueur par chaos," *Télérama* (13 November 1991);

Philippe Minyana, auteur de théâtre, video, CNDP-La Cinquième, 1997;

Etienne Pommeret, "Philippe Minyana, *Drames brefs (1):* Présentation," *Theatre-contemporain.net* (2001) <www.theatre-contemporain.net/spectacles/drames_brefs/presentation.htm>;

Anne Quentin, "Philippe Minyana: Chambre à Part," *Théâtre Magazine,* no. 4 (1 January 2000): 77–79;

Noëlle Renaude, "Le Territoire des bâtisseurs: théâtre en chantier," *Théâtre/Public,* no. 123 (1 April 1995): 23–26;

Corrine Rigaud, "Juste après l'amour, juste avant la mort: la parole obscène (sur le monologue dans le théâtre de Philippe Minyana)," *Alternatives théâtrales,* no. 45 (June 1994);

Irene Sadowska-Guillon, "Le Théâtre-limite de Philippe Minyana," *L'Avant-scène: Théâtre,* no. 809 (1987);

Georges Schlocker, "La Parole affolée: la propension au monologue du théâtre français contemporain," *Jeu,* 72 (1 September 1994): 104–108.

Henry de Montherlant
(21 April 1896 – 21 September 1972)

Henriette Javorck
University of Hamburg

See also the Montherlant entry in DLB 72: French Novelists, 1930–1960.

PLAY PRODUCTIONS: *Pasiphaé,* Paris, Théâtre Pigalle, 6 December 1938;

La Reine morte, Paris, Comédie-Française, 8 December 1942;

Fils de personne, Paris, Théâtre Saint-Georges, 18 December 1943;

Le Maître de Santiago, Paris, Théâtre-Hébertot, 26 January 1948;

Demain il fera jour, Paris, Théâtre-Hébertot, 9 May 1949;

Celles qu'on prend dans ses bras, Paris, Théâtre de la Madeleine, 20 October 1950;

Malatesta, Paris, Théâtre Marigny, 19 December 1950;

Port-Royal, Paris, Théâtre Française, 8 December 1954;

Brocéliande, Paris, Comédie-Française, 1956;

Don Juan, Paris, Théâtre de l'Athénée, 4 November 1958;

Le Cardinal d'Espagne, Paris, Comédie-Française, 1960;

La Guerre civile, Paris, Théâtre de l'Œuvre, 27 January 1965;

La Ville dont le prince est un enfant, Paris, Théâtre Michel, 8 December 1967.

BOOKS: *La Relève du matin* (Paris: Société de France, 1920; revised edition, Paris: Grasset, 1933);

Le Songe (Paris: Grasset, 1922); translated by Terrence Kilmartin as *The Dream* (London: Weidenfeld & Nicolson, 1962; New York: Macmillan, 1963);

Les Olympiques, 2 volumes (Paris: Grasset, 1924)—comprises *Première Olympique: Le Paradis à l'ombre des épées* and *Deuxième Olympique: Les Onze devant la porte dorée;*

Chant funèbre pour les morts de Verdun (Paris: Grasset, 1925);

Les Bestiaires (Paris: Grasset, 1926); translated by Edwin Gile Rich as *The Bullfighters* (New York: Dial, 1927; London: Cape, 1928);

Barrès s'éloigne (Paris: Grasset, 1927);

Aux fontaines du désir (Paris: Grasset, 1927);

Henry de Montherlant, 1937 (© Albin-Guillot/Roger-Viollet/ Getty Images)

Sans remède (Paris: Trémois, 1927);

Un Désir frustré mime l'amour (Paris: Lapina, 1928);

Pages de tendresse (Paris: Grasset, 1928);

Pour le délassement de l'auteur (Paris: Hazan, 1928);

Earinus: Troisième Olympique (Paris: Hazan, 1929);

L'Exil (Paris: Editions du Capitole, 1929);

Le Génie et les fumisteries du divin (Paris: Nouvelle Société, 1929);

Hispano-moresque (Paris: Emile-Paul, 1929);

La Petite Infante de Castille (Paris: Grasset, 1929);

Sous les drapeaux morts (Paris: Editions du Capitole, 1929);

Au petit mutilé (Paris: Editions des Portiques, 1930);

Pour une vierge noire (Paris: Editions du Cadran, 1930);

Mors et vita (Paris: Grasset, 1932);

Les Célibataires (Paris: Grasset, 1934); translated by Thomas McGreevy as *Lament for the Death of an Upper Class* (London: Miles, 1935); republished as *Perish in Their Pride* (New York: Knopf, 1936); translated by Kilmartin as *The Batchelors* (London: Weidenfeld & Nicolson, 1960; New York: Macmillan, 1960);

Encore un instant de bonheur (Paris: Grasset, 1934; enlarged edition, Paris: Editions Rombaldi, 1951);

Il y a encore des paradis. Images d'Alger (Algiers: Soubiron, 1935);

Service inutile (Paris: Grasset, 1935; revised edition, Paris: Gallimard, 1952);

Les Jeunes Filles (Paris: Grasset, 1936); translated as *Young Girls,* in *Pity for Women* (London: Routledge, 1937; New York: Knopf, 1938);

Pasiphaé (Tunis: Editions de Mirages, 1936; Paris: Grasset, 1938);

Pitié pour les femmes (Paris: Grasset, 1936); translated by John Rodker, in *Pity for Women* (London: Routledge, 1937; New York: Knopf, 1938);

Le Démon du bien (Paris: Grasset, 1937); translated by Rodker as *The Demon of Good,* in *Costals and the Hippogriff* (New York: Knopf, 1940);

Flèche du sud (Paris: M. d'Hartoy, 1937);

L'Equinoxe de septembre (Paris: Grasset, 1938);

Les Lépreuses (Paris: Grasset, 1939); translated by Rodker as *The Lepers,* in *Costals and the Hippogriff* (New York: Knopf, 1940); republished as *The Lepers* (London: Routledge, 1949)–comprises *Le Démon du bien* and *Les Lépreuses;*

La Paix dans la guerre (Neuchâtel: Ides et Calendes, 1941);

Le Solstice de juin (Paris: Grasset, 1941);

La Reine morte; ou, Comment on tue les femmes (Paris: Grasset, 1942; revised edition, Paris: Gallimard, 1947); translated by Jonathan Griffin as *Queen After Death,* in *The Master of Santiago, and Four Other Plays* (New York: Knopf, 1951; London: Routledge & Kegan Paul, 1951);

La Vie en forme de proue (Paris: Grasset, 1942);

Fils de personne (Paris: Gallimard, 1944); translated by Griffin as *No Man's Son,* in *The Master of Santiago, and Four Other Plays* (New York: Knopf, 1951; London: Routledge & Kegan Paul, 1951);

Un Incompris (Paris: Gallimard, 1944);

Un Voyageur solitaire est un diable (Paris: Lefebvre, 1945);

Malatesta (Lausanne: Marguerat, 1946; Paris: Gallimard, 1948); translated by Griffin, in *The Master of Santiago, and Four Other Plays* (New York: Knopf, 1951; London: Routledge & Kegan Paul, 1951);

Carnets XXIX à XXXV, du 19 février 1935 au 11 janvier 1939 (Paris: Table Ronde, 1947);

Le Maître de Santiago (Paris: Gallimard, 1947); translated by Griffin as *The Master of Santiago,* in *The Master of Santiago, and Four Other Plays* (New York: Knopf, 1951; London: Routledge & Kegan Paul, 1951);

Pages catholiques (Paris: Plon, 1947);

Carnets XLII et XLIII, du 1 janvier 1942 au 31 décembre 1943 (Paris: Table Ronde, 1948);

Demain il fera jour (Paris: Gallimard, 1949); translated by Griffin as *Tomorrow the Dawn,* in *The Master of Santiago, and Four Other Plays* (New York: Knopf, 1951; London: Routledge & Kegan Paul, 1951);

L'Etoile du soir (Paris: Lefebvre, 1949);

Celles qu'on prend dans ses bras (Paris: Gallimard, 1950);

Coups de soleil, Afrique-Andalousie (Paris: Palatine, 1950);

Notes sur mon théâtre (Paris: Arche, 1950);

Le Théâtre complet, 6 volumes (Neuchâtel & Paris: Ides et Calendes, 1950);

La Cueilleuse de branches (Paris: Horay, 1951);

España sagrada (Paris: Wapler, 1951);

L'Infini est du côté de Malatesta (Paris: Gallimard, 1951);

La Ville dont le prince est un enfant (Paris: Gallimard, 1951); translated by Vivian Cox and Bernard Miles as *The Fire That Consumes* (San Francisco: Ritchie, 1980);

Le Fichier parisien (Paris: Palatine, 1952; enlarged, 1955; revised and enlarged edition, Paris: Gallimard, 1974);

Textes sous une occupation, 1940–1944 (Paris: Gallimard, 1953);

L'Histoire d'amour de "La Rose de sable" (Paris: Plon, 1954); translated by Alec Brown as *Desert Love* (London: Elek, 1957; New York: Noonday Press, 1957);

Port-Royal (Paris: Gallimard, 1954);

Carnets XXII à XXVIII, du 23 avril 1932 au 22 novembre 1934 (Paris: Table Ronde, 1955);

Brocéliande (Paris: Gallimard, 1956);

Carnets XIX à XXI, du 19 septembre 1930 au 26 avril 1932 (Paris: Table Ronde, 1956);

Carnets, années 1930 à 1944 (Paris: Gallimard, 1957);

Don Juan (Paris: Gallimard, 1958); revised and republished as *La Mort qui fait le trottoir* (Paris: Gallimard, 1972);

Romans et œuvres de fiction non théâtrales (Paris: Gallimard, 1959);

Le Cardinal d'Espagne (Paris: Gallimard, 1960);
Le Chaos et la nuit (Paris: Gallimard, 1963); translated by Kilmartin as *Chaos and Night* (London: Weidenfeld & Nicolson, 1964; New York: Macmillan, 1964);
Discours de reception à l'Académie Française (Paris: Gallimard, 1963);
La Guerre civile (Paris: Gallimard, 1965); translated by Griffin as *The Civil War,* in *Theatre of War,* edited by Robert Baldick (Harmondsworth, U.K.: Penguin, 1967);
Va jouer avec cette poussière: Carnets 1958–1964 (Paris: Gallimard, 1966);
La Rose de sable (Paris: Lefebvre, 1967);
Les Garçons (Paris: Gallimard, 1969); translated by Kilmartin as *The Boys* (London: Weidenfeld & Nicolson, 1974);
Le Treizième César (Paris: Gallimard, 1970);
Un Assassin est mon maître (Paris: Gallimard, 1971);
La Tragédie sans masque: Notes de théâtre (Paris: Gallimard, 1972);
Mais aimons-nous ceux que nous aimons? (Paris: Gallimard, 1973);
Tous feux éteints: Carnets 1965, 1966, 1967, carnets sans dates, carnet 1972 (Paris: Gallimard, 1975);
Romans II (Paris: Gallimard, 1982);
Moustique (Paris: Table Ronde, 1986).

Collections: *Théâtre* (Paris: Gallimard, 1955); enlarged as *Théâtre de Montherlant* (Paris: Gallimard, 1968);
Essais (Paris: Gallimard, 1963);
Œuvre Romanesque, 8 volumes (Paris: Editions Lidis, 1963–1964);
Garder tout en composant tout, 1924–1972: carnets inédits, derniers carnets, edited by Jean-Claude Barat and Yasmina Barat ([Paris]: Gallimard, 2001).

Collections in English: *The Master of Santiago, and Four Other Plays,* translated by Jonathan Griffin (New York: Knopf, 1951; London: Routledge & Kegan Paul, 1951)–comprises *La Reine morte; ou, Comment on tue les femmes, Fils de personne, Malatesta, Le Maître de Santiago,* and *Demain il fera jour;*
Selected Essays, translated and edited by John Weightman (London: Weidenfeld & Nicolson, 1960; New York: Macmillan, 1961).

Henry de Montherlant was a nonconformist, and his plays, novels, and essays reflect the controversial themes he encountered during his lifetime. Eager to provoke life as the heroes in his works do, Montherlant questioned the norms of society, and he valued experiences that produced intense emotions. His life and his literature amazed and perplexed twentieth-century society. Montherlant believed in obeying only personal convictions; thus, he disregarded social and political

Montherlant, age eleven, in front of his home (from Jean de Beer, Montherlant, *1963; Thomas Cooper Library, University of South Carolina)*

constraints. His characters–such as Georges Carrion in *Fils de personne* (produced 1943, published 1944; translated as *No Man's Son,* 1951), Bruno in *Un Incompris* (1944, A Misunderstanding), Alvaro Dabo in *Le Maître de Santiago* (published 1947, produced 1948; translated as *The Master of Santiago,* 1951), and the priest de Pradts in *La Ville dont le prince est un enfant* (published 1951, produced 1967; translated as *The Fire That Consumes,* 1980)–all challenge societal law through their actions and beliefs. Montherlant's plays *Malatesta* (published 1946, produced 1950; translated, 1959), *Port-Royal* (published and produced 1954), and *La Guerre civile* (published and produced 1965; translated as *The Civil War,* 1967) deal with rebellion against established institutions and political systems. Montherlant defined himself and found his individual happiness through writing and through sexual contact with young boys. His characters engage in a wide range of practices from misogyny to pedophilia to megalomania to spiritual and sacrificial love. Montherlant acknowledged extreme fear of the sea, the desert, horses, and flying; his heroes battle with human weaknesses in the face of commitment, illness, isolation, and war, whether against a bull, themselves, or a group of people. What prevails as the essence of both Montherlant's life and his literary work is a sense

Scene from Montherlant's La Reine morte *(translated as* Queen after Death, *1951), Comédie-Française, Paris, 1942 (© Collection Roger-Viollet/Getty Images)*

of confidence in individual freedom and personal responsibility for choices made and principles adopted. Montherlant's brilliance lies in the poise and passion with which he faced his life and wrote his many masterpieces.

Montherlant was born on 21 April 1896. He was raised in the countryside at the villa Saint-Ferdinand in Neuilly, on the northwestern edge of Paris, without electricity or central heating–not because his family had no money, but because his father, Joseph Millon de Montherlant, rejected all ideas of modernity and social conformity. His mother, Marguerite, suffered uteral hemorrhaging after giving birth to Henry. She spent most of her time in bed reading, often in the company of her son. Montherlant's parents instilled in him the idea that he was different from his peers. For example, his parents stopped him from singing in a choir because they did not want their son to have to wear a uniform like the other children. Later on, they did not want Henry to take the *baccalauréat,* the French university entrance exams, because they found unacceptable the idea that their son was to be judged by strangers whose merit and background they did not know; Henry, nonetheless, took and passed his *baccalauréat* in philosophy in October 1914. After his father's death in 1914 and his mother's death in 1915, his maternal grandmother, Marguerite de Riancey, became the most significant person in his life. Marguerite de Riancey was religious: she went to mass every day, went to the cathedral of Montmartre at least once a week, and took a pilgrimage to Lourdes every year. She taught Montherlant the significance of having a clear conscience. Moreover, she confirmed in him the idea that a woman's love should be spiritual and unreserved, filled with docility and a sense of subservience before God and man.

Instead of serving as male role models during his upbringing, Montherlant's three uncles provided examples to fight against. His great-uncle, Pietro Riancey, had a disheveled appearance and enjoyed a decadent life that consisted of waking up late, reading, and visiting Parisian cafés. He was an embarrassment to Montherlant. His uncle Henry de Riancey was gifted with his hands, wrote poetry, and took care of the family garden, but he never translated his talents into any lucrative occupation. He also failed to earn Montherlant's esteem. The third uncle, Guy de Courcy, an elegant widower, was the director of the insurance company where Montherlant had his first job, between 1914 and 1916. Montherlant criticized this uncle for having adapted to American capitalism and for showing interest only in financially profitable matters. Though not guiding forces in his childhood, Montherlant's uncles provided the prototypes for the central characters ridiculed in *Les Célibataires* (1934; translated as *Lament for the Death of an Upper Class,* 1935), a novel that traces the downfall of a noble family.

Montherlant's young adulthood was spent in an atmosphere of war. He was wounded in both world wars. In World War I, on 10 November 1918, he received injuries that caused him pain in the lumbar region throughout his life. His first play, *L'Exil* (1929, The Exile), discusses his early desire to join the armed forces in combat. He wrote it at a time when he wanted to join a friend already enlisted in the war, but he was stopped by the worries and pleas of his dying mother. Through the character of Philippe de Presles, the play recounts Montherlant's personal experience and his resentment of women's imprisoning love.

Montherlant waited until the age of forty-two (1938) to have his second play, *Pasiphaé* (published 1936), actually produced at a theater. This play, unlike *L'Exil,* has the professional experience and maturity of an older Montherlant. Referred to as "un poème . . . somptueusement évocateur" (a sumptuously suggestive poem) by Jacques Robichez, the play develops the inner war Pasiphaé faces as she decides to make love to the beautiful white bull, Minos. Pasiphaé deifies herself when she goes against the morals of her Cretan society, accepting all consequences in the name of love. After its premiere on 6 December at the Théâtre Pigalle, *Pasiphaé* also enjoyed success under the direction of Jean Vilar in 1949 at the Avignon Theater Festival.

Montherlant's correspondence with Roger Peyrefitte and the notes in his personal journal, *Carnets,* offer insight into the author's sensual and sexual life. His novel *Les Garçons* (1969; translated as *The Boys,* 1974) summarizes the essence of his sexual views and experiences. Montherlant came into conflict because of his sexual orientation at age sixteen when he was discharged from Saint-Croix boys' school for suspected homosexual activities. Later in life, he walked the streets of Paris, particularly the boulevard Bonne-Nouvelle and the boulevard Rochechouart, looking for young boys to buy. He often had young boy companions or servants, both in France and abroad in Algeria, Morocco, Spain, and Italy. His novel *Moustique* (Mosquito), published posthumously in 1986, recounts Montherlant's relationship with his *garçonnet* (young male attendant) during his travels between 1925 and 1930. Moustique's presence exasperates the author because of the youth's awkwardness and stupidity at the same time as it saves him from loneliness and fills him with paternal and altruistic love. The author feels a moral responsibility to educate and protect the youth.

Thus, he keeps the young man in his service for five years and turns him into a scout. Montherlant always tried to educate and help the boys he had loved.

As his biographer Pierre Sipriot explains, Montherlant believed the only difference between homosexual and heterosexual love was the possibility to procreate. Otherwise, love was an intensification of life and therefore, by nature, positive. Though he was vain (he had had wrinkles under his eyes operated on by his mid fifties), Montherlant wanted to maintain a masculine appearance. He was embarrassed, for example, by André Gide's flamboyantly homosexual manners and clothing. However, Montherlant was not attracted to men with masculine features, preferring instead young boys at the time when they still had their androgynous side and were searching for their sexuality. Montherlant saw the friendship between the adolescent and the adult as constructive, one through which the adolescent could benefit from the wisdom of the elder, and the adult could enjoy giving unconditional love while enjoying the innocence of the yet uncorrupted youth. Montherlant also believed homosexuality should be socially accepted, but as a personal secret, not to be lived out or flaunted in public.

More than for his pedophilia or homosexuality, Montherlant was condemned for his supposed misogyny. Between 1936 and 1939 he published a series of four books that became his most read and most controversial works: *Les Jeunes Filles* (1936; translated as *Young Girls,* 1937), *Pitié pour les femmes* (1936; translated as *Pity for Women,* 1937), *Le Démon du bien* (1937; translated as *The Demon of Good,* 1940), and *Les Lépreuses* (1939; translated as *The Lepers,* 1940). In these novels, the central character, Pierre Costals, a successful writer modeled after Montherlant, finds traditional couples horrifying because they lead to boredom, inevitably limit personal freedom, and end in a slow and torturous death. Women are, to both Costals and Montherlant, manipulative, silly, and insincere beings, physically and intellectually inferior to men. However, Costals, unlike Montherlant, does not reject relationships with women and even accepts the idea of marriage with a woman who could give him children and act as a secretary, thus facilitating his work. In her *Le deuxième sexe* (1949, The Second Sex), Simone de Beauvoir writes that for Montherlant, "La femme idéale est parfaitement stupide et parfaitement soumise; elle est toujours prête à accueillir l'homme, et ne lui demande jamais rien" (The ideal woman is perfectly stupid and obedient; she is always ready to serve a man without ever asking for anything in return). Solange Dandelliot meets the requirement of such a female spouse, but her interfering mother ruins her chances of matrimony with Costals. Though Montherlant's novels may appear relentlessly

Annie Ducaux and Andrée de Chauveron in Montherlant's Port-Royal, *Comédie-Française, Paris, December 1954 (© Lipnitzki/Roger-Viollet/Getty Images)*

antifeminist to contemporary readers, his ideas complied with the attitude toward women in the early 1900s. In fact, Beauvoir suggests that Montherlant actually provoked women to speak up for themselves and thus initiated a feminist movement. She writes, "Si Montherlant avait véritablement dégonflé le mythe de l'éternel féminin, il faudrait l'en féliciter: c'est en niant la Femme qu'on peut aider les femmes à s'assumer comme êtres humains" (We should congratulate Montherlant for demystifying the eternal woman, because it is by rejecting the idea of womanhood that women can finally assert themselves as human beings).

Montherlant's closest and most familial relationship in the early 1940s was with Mme N.'s two sons, Roland and Edouard. Between 1940 and 1941, Montherlant lived with the family in Nice, providing full financial support and taking care of the children. Every morning he boxed with Edouard, and in the evening he helped Robert with his homework. The children's tenderness and gratitude filled him with sensual energy. Montherlant's sexual relationships with young boys did not always translate into acts, and if so, Montherlant insisted that the adolescent in question was always in charge of what occurred and to what degree.

Montherlant took part in World War II as an unofficial war correspondent for the magazine *Marianne* and was again wounded, this time in four places, by the flying remnants from the explosion of a nearby bomb. He also took part in civic duties; for example, in February 1941 he arranged for the release from prison of Marguerite Lauze, a young mother and teacher who had been arrested simply for stating in class that Philippe Pétain (general, marshal of France, premier of Vichy France) was old. Nevertheless, after World War II, though not charged for collaboration with the Germans or the Vichy government, Montherlant appeared in various newspapers on lists of traitors that included such writers as Louis-Ferdinand Céline, Robert Brasillach, Marcel Jouhandeau, and Jean Giono. Despite such treatment, Montherlant's patriotism subsisted through the Algerian War. In spring 1932 Montherlant completed *La Rose de sable* (1967, The Rose of Sand), a novel that offers a critical view of French colonization told through a love story between a French officer, Lucien Auligny, and a young Arab girl named Ram. Montherlant did not publish *La Rose de sable* until after the Algerian War, in order to make sure his novel would not create propaganda for those who wanted to attack France.

The majority of Montherlant's plays were written between 1942 and 1965 (nine plays in this period compared to only four novels), mainly because paper was not readily available during times of war. In 1942 Jean-Louis Vaudoyer, from the Comédie-Française, asked Montherlant to adapt an historical story already developed by Luis Velez de Guevara in *Reinar después de morir* (To Reign after Death). Montherlant, unmotivated and cold in a Paris threatened by the gestapo and exposed to the first bombings raids, went to Grasse in Southern France, where the landscape and countryside inspired him to create his characters. The resulting play, *La Reine morte* (published and produced 1942; translated as *Queen After Death*, 1951) tells the story of how young Prince Don Pedro marries Inès to spite his father, the King of Ferrante. When the King of Ferrante finds out that Inès is already pregnant, he has her assassinated in a desperate reaction. However, the King of Ferrante is killed in return, and Don Pedro places the queenly crown upon the head of his murdered bride. *La Reine morte* made a statement against intolerance and, presented in December 1942 in the midst of bombing blackouts, suggested that Benito Mussolini and Adolf Hitler, just as the King of Ferrante, had run out of resources and could only resort to desperate and heartless acts that would return to haunt them. The play was an enormous success, continued to be produced throughout France for the duration of the war, and was made popular again in 1948, 1954, and 1966.

Montherlant's subsequent theatrical contribution began as a two-hundred-page novel that discusses the author's time spent in Nice with Mme N. and her two sons, Edouard and Roland. The play *Fils de personne* disguises the autobiographical elements of the original text: Georges Carrion, a famous lawyer, enjoys having brief, undemanding affairs with women. Marie, one of his mistresses, pregnant with his child, is abandoned by him, only to be rediscovered thirteen years later during the war. Though he possesses the power to make substantial changes in the political situation of the time, such as to generate an armistice or prevent the occupation, Georges cowers from his social obligations and decides to focus his ambitions and frustrations on his son, Gillou, who, having been educated by a woman, reads comic strips, watches silly movies, pays into the national lottery, and subscribes to commonplace societal distractions. Instead of learning from his father's lessons and corrections, however, Gillou only dives deeper into his world of trashy magazines and undignified music shows on the radio. Georges soon gives up on Gillou and abandons him again. Lost in the quarrels and personal conflicts of his parents, Gillou is nobody's son. Through *Fils de personne*, Montherlant demonstrated the ability to write with humility and engage in self-criticism. At the same time, he expanded on his critical view of women and of popular, mainstream culture. *Fils de personne* was first produced on 18 December 1943 at the Théâtre Saint-Georges under the direction of Henri Rollan. Because of the concise length of the play, a one-act comedy often accompanied the production. *Un Incompris* comically parallels Georges Carrion's conduct toward Gillou through the character of Bruno, a man who separates from the love of his life, Rosette, on a matter of principle–because the latter cannot show up for their rendezvous on time.

Before he continued the story of *Fils de personne* in *Demain il fera jour* (produced and published 1949; translated as *Tomorrow the Dawn*, 1951), Montherlant developed another family drama with a political twist. In *Le Maître de Santiago,* Alvaro Dabo leads the frugal and quiet life of a middle-aged father, though as a chevalier he earlier fought in the Order of Santiago to drive out the Moors and reestablish Christianity in Spain. His daughter, Mariana, plots to involve her father in a profitable crusade to America that would ensure her a substantial dowry and the chance to marry Don Jacinto. In accordance with Montherlant's idea that only personal motives should drive one to commit to a public cause, Alvaro decides to leave his simple life and reengage in a crusade to please his daughter, whom he also knights at the end of the play.

Controversy followed Montherlant through *Celles qu'on prend dans ses bras* (produced and published 1950;

Those We Take in Our Arms), though the play avoids political issues and focuses on the difference between spiritual and physical love. The love triangle formed by the fifty-eight-year-old antiques dealer Ravier, his sixty-year-old assistant, Mlle Andriot, and eighteen-year-old Christine Villancy, who sells her arts and crafts to make ends meet, presents a spectrum of emotions that ranges from love to lust. The most interesting development of the play stems from the change of emotions experienced by Ravier, who loves Christine in her innocence but worships her when she gives herself to him.

Writing during and in the aftermath of World War II, Montherlant probed the theme of political engagement. He remained well informed about political and military conflicts throughout his life. His experiences led him to conclude, however, that voicing personal opinions publicly was frivolous and useless, because times always changed, as did systems and beliefs. With time, his military fervor diminished. Political convictions were worth fighting for and dying for only if they somehow directly reached into a person's private sphere, a principle also observed by the unconventional hero of the play *Malatesta*. With the character of Malatesta, a nobleman from Rimini, Montherlant presents the type of hero he wanted to be: honest and sensitive, philanthropic and brave, yet confident in his right to exercise his free will and engage in all the vices to his liking. His wife, Isotta, represents the epitome of a woman's love, full of patience and tolerance, modeled after the love Montherlant received from his mother and grandmother. Malatesta's thirteen-year-old mistress, Vannela, is an example of the androgynous sex object so highly esteemed by Montherlant. Nevertheless, Robichez says the play is "mal construite" (badly constructed) and that the public "s'y est ennuyé . . . parce qu'elle est apparue comme une série de scenes sans nécessité et parce que l'action . . . piétine à partir du troisième et se perd jusqu'à la mort du héros" (was bored by the succession of actionless scenes that dawdle on from act 3 to the hero's death).

The essence of religious conviction preoccupied Montherlant's next project, *Port-Royal,* first presented at the Théâtre Française on 8 December 1954 by director Jean Meyer. The play takes place in summer 1664 at the time when the nuns at Port-Royal were accused of Jansenism and asked to sign the *Formulaire* that denounced this overly rigorous and heretical practice of Catholicism. The play debates the true duty of the nuns and the value of religion by asking the question: Is it more important to pray and devote oneself to God or to stand up to human accusations and defend an institution? Three central characters answer the question differently. Sister Flavie abandons her religious obligations in an ambitious effort to become abbess, but her terrestrial aspirations meet with no success. Sister Angélique fights relentlessly, but, having entered a human battle, has to accept a human outcome and stand by as eighteen of the nuns accused of being particularly rebellious are removed from the convent. Finally, Sister Françoise, who tries to fulfill her function as God's devout servant through rigorous prayer and meditation, only attains peace of mind and spiritual strength when she finally decides to engage in earthly battle and defend Port-Royal. Montherlant exposed again a controversial debate, considering all sides and allowing the public to draw their own conclusions.

La Ville dont le prince est un enfant is set in a Catholic boys' school. Written in three days in 1929, played in parts on the radio in 1941, and published in 1951 by Gallimard, the play had its theatrical debut in 1967 because Montherlant would not authorize its release, afraid that it might damage the reputation of religious schools. An autobiographical account, *La Ville dont le prince est un enfant* retells the events surrounding Montherlant's dismissal from the boys' school he attended in Neuilly in 1912. André Sevrais (Montherlant), sixteen years old, unites his open veins in an expression of love with those of Serge Sandrier, fourteen years old (known after 1958 as Serge Souplier). The priest de Pradts surprises the boys in their act and declares that such a special friendship could prove detrimental to the younger child's education. Montherlant thus reinforces his belief that special friendships, while acceptable, should be enjoyed in secret. The priest de Pradts, also in love with Serge, professes acting in the youth's best interest; he sends André away, but only to keep Serge unattached and close by. In this work, Montherlant ridicules his own philosophy toward his young lovers, whom he allegedly wanted to educate and protect with his love. As André leaves, cynically remarking that he only regrets having studied for his exams and not being allowed to play Pyrrhus in the school production, Montherlant attempts to redress the distress and embarrassment caused to him by his dismissal from school at age sixteen. The controversy the play generated also guaranteed its success.

With *Brocéliande* (produced and published 1956), Montherlant broaches the sensitive topic of nobility. Selling titles has a long history in France. Louis XIV initiated the idea to finance his wars. Napoleon III also authorized it. The practice was adapted by the Fourth Republic and continued all the way to 1947. Though not allowed to intermarry with true nobles, *la personne anoblie* (the person raised to the ranks of nobility) was accepted into salons and fashionable society, provided of course, that he or she still had considerable money. The Montherlants bought their title, and Montherlant's

Paul Guers and Didier Haudepin in a December 1967 performance, at the Théâtre Michel in Paris, of Montherlant's
La ville dont le prince est un enfant *(published 1951, translated as* The Fire That Consumes, *1980)*
(© Lipnitzki/Roger-Viollet/Getty Images)

mother took great pleasure in signing her son's school report cards as the Comtesse de Montherlant. Montherlant used the title of *comte* (Count) until 1925, when he decided to give it up. *Brocéliande* exposes this French preoccupation with nobility, at the expense of Persilès, an aging, ordinary office worker who is told (by the genealogist Bonnet de la Bonnetière) that he descends from Saint Louis. When Persilès discovers that Saint Louis engendered some fifteen thousand descendants, he kills himself.

Two years later, Montherlant's ideals of manliness surface with a truly modern and original *Don Juan* (produced and published 1958), presented for the first time by Georges Vitaly on 4 November at the Théâtre de l'Athénée. Sixty-six years old in Sevilla during the 1630s, Don Juan has a son, Alcacer, and lives his life as a *libertin* (libertine). Respected and charming, he explains his theories of life to the Commander de Ulloa, the father of one of his conquests, and convinces the latter to engage in a clandestine love affair. Women, including the Countess de Ulloa, condemn and pursue Don Juan, but the hero rides away at the end of the play, still a noncompromised *libertin,* not at all punished by divine retribution, and in search of new adventures.

Montherlant faced perhaps the most open controversy concerning one of his works on 19 March 1961, when, during a performance of his *Le Cardinal d'Espagne* (produced and published 1960; The Cardinal of Spain) at the Comédie-Française, a group of students set off stink bombs and screamed insults at the actors and the author. Forty-seven arrests were made, and the show went on to enjoy enormous success and earn the congratulations of the minister of culture, André Malraux. Through an historical piece that takes the coming to power of Charles Quint as center focus, the play restates Montherlant's belief that human agitation amounts to nothing. Before the action of the play begins, Jeanne La Folle marries Philippe I, prince of the Netherlands, and watches her husband die, poisoned for the crown by her own father, Ferdinand II. The play takes place during three days in 1517, when, after Ferdinand II's death, the Cardinal Cisneros elects to the crown Jeanne and Philippe's son, the future Charles Quint. The Spanish noblemen disapprove of Charles because of his youth and his Flemish origins, and the old Cardinal finds himself besieged by the struggle. Montherlant's moral is delivered by a woman, Jeanne La Folle, considered crazy and imprisoned in the tower of Tordesillas. Jeanne explains to the Cardinal that despite his earthly battles, every man is buried with nothing but his bones at the end of his life.

John Batchelor explains how Montherlant classified the political developments of the 1950s and 1960s in Germany, Indochina, Cuba, and Algeria as an attestation that the world had learned nothing from the two world wars and had surrendered to a life of violence and unrest. What bothered Montherlant most was that these world quarrels continued to victimize young people by forcing them to participate in and fall victim to conflicts they neither understood nor cared about. Batchelor elucidates how Montherlant found wasteful the sacrifice of human lives for wars that ultimately revolved around power and money, rather than human values or differences.

Finding in Roman history a microcosm for his own time, Montherlant broached this subject with his *La Guerre civile*. In Julius Caesar's camp in 48 B.C., the troops divided as a result of the antagonism between Pompée and Caesar. Act 1 explores why the troops divided and concludes that the cause was a preoccupation with power and money. Act 2 discusses the loneliness of Cato, the humanitarian, in the face of a war in which he does not wish to participate. He does not wish to cower, but he does not want to lose his individuality by taking sides with any particular group. Cato's sentiments express Montherlant's position on any social conflict throughout his lifetime. Cato senses, and the audience knows from history, that Pompée will not prosper and will lose his life in the attack against Caesar. In a senseless conflict, Cato decides he can only take the side of the unlikely winner. Act 3, subtitled *Perdita tempora*, or wasted time, allows civil war, personified, to speak out and say that all who participate are guilty, that no one can be certain of being on the right side, because a hero could at any time become a traitor, depending on the outcome of the conflict. The character of Laetorius, who unites against Caesar and even kills one hundred of his own soldiers fallen into Caesar's captivity, embodies violence.

The Chorus ties the three acts together and represents the voice of truth. Obeying the seventeenth-century rules of *bienséance* (propriety), the play ends before any violence occurs on stage, right as Pompée's troops set out for battle.

By 1968 Montherlant only mocked the May student demonstrations in Paris. In his opinion, they amounted to nothing but the frustrated and futile buzzing of the masses, the only outcome to be expected by any rebellion or war.

Montherlant wrote one last play in his lifetime. *Mais aimons-nous ceux que nous aimons?* (1973, But Do We Love Those We Love?) recounts the author's encounter in a hotel room with Dominique and throws a critical look at young virgins. As Montherlant believed, the play explains that if a young girl is truly innocent, she is not familiar with the necessary precautions that make sex safe and enjoyable. On the other hand, if a young girl seems eager for the act, she is a fraudulent virgin. As the play attests, Montherlant's dislike of young girls accompanied him into the last year of his life.

Montherlant spent most of his adult life at 25, quai Voltaire, in a first-floor apartment overlooking the Seine and the Louvre. He lived to write, either in his office, filled with statues (ancient busts), or sitting on a bench somewhere outside. In his *Montherlant par lui-même* (1953), Pierre Sipriot explains that writing equaled life for Montherlant. Sipriot writes, "Ecrire, c'est, ici, l'acte plénier de vivre: la passion réglée par une volonté et un choix en vue de l'oeuvre d'art" (In his [Montherlant's] case, writing is the essential expression of life). In 1934 Montherlant received the Grand Prix of literature from the Académie française and his *Théâtre* was published in 1955 and again in 1968 by Gallimard. He continued to write to the end of his life. He decided to commit suicide because he felt he could no longer work. For the last ten years of his life, he suffered from dizzy spells and blurry vision. In 1968 he had an accident that injured his head and caused him to lose his left eye. The doctors told him if he tired his remaining eye by reading and writing, he might go blind. He kept writing and editing his texts. His strength and his eyesight continued to diminish, and he was frequently hospitalized. In 1971 he completed his *Un Assassin est mon maître* (An Assassin Is My Master), a novel about life in hospitals and how different people experience their deaths. Shortly thereafter, on 21 September 1972, he took cyanide and shot himself. He was seventy-six years old. His ashes were buried in the temple of the Forum in Rome in 1973.

In the more than one hundred years since his birth, many have criticized Henry de Montherlant for both his lifestyle and his literature. Still others, including the Académie française, have praised him and admired him. Readers continue to buy his books, and his plays continue to attract audiences to the theater. Montherlant's works are filled with the richness and energy of a no-nonsense author's account of timeless conflicts: war, sex, and individuality in the face of pressure from the masses. Montherlant wrote about what he believed and what he lived, and he stood behind his freedom and nonconformity uncompromisingly, to the last moments of his life.

Letters:

Henry de Montherlant / Roger Peyrefitte: Correspondance [1938–1941] (Paris: Laffont, 1983).

Biographies:

Pierre Sipriot, *Montherlant sans masque: l'enfant prodigue 1895–1932* (Paris: Laffont, 1982);

Sipriot, *Montherlant sans masque: écris avec ton sang 1932–1972* (Paris: Laffont, 1990).

References:

John Batchelor, *Existence and Imagination: The Theater of Henry de Montherlant* (Queensland, Australia: St. Lucia University of Queensland Press, 1967);

Simone de Beauvoir, *Le deuxième sexe,* volume 1 (Paris: Gallimard, 1949);

Lucille Becker, *Henry de Montherlant* (Carbondale: Southern Illinois University Press / London: Feffer & Simmons, 1970);

John Cruikshank, *Montherlant* (Edinburgh: Oliver & Boyd, 1964);

Robert B. Johnson, *Henry de Montherlant* (New York: Twayne, 1968);

Michel Raimond, *Les Romans de Montherlant* (Paris: Société d'édition d'enseignement supérieur, 1982);

Jacques Robichez, *Le Théâtre de Montherlant* (Paris: Société d'edition d'enseignement supérieur, 1973);

Pierre Sipriot, *Montherlant par lui-même* (Paris: Editions du Seuil, 1953);

John Weightman, "Incomplete Attachments," *TLS: The Times Literary Supplement,* 5 September 1986, p. 979.

Marcel Pagnol

(28 February 1895 – 18 April 1974)

Brett Bowles
Iowa State University

PLAY PRODUCTIONS: *Tonton, ou Joseph veut rester pur,* by Pagnol and Paul Nivoix, Marseille, Théâtre des Variétés, 10 August 1923;

Les Marchands de gloire, by Pagnol and Nivoix, Paris, Théâtre de la Madeleine, 15 April 1925;

Un Direct au coeur, by Pagnol and Nivoix, Lille, Théâtre de l'Alhambra, 12 March 1926;

Jazz, Monte Carlo, Grand Théâtre, 9 December 1926; Paris, Théâtre des Arts, 21 December 1926;

Topaze, Paris, Théâtre des Variétés, 9 October 1928;

Marius, Paris, Théâtre de Paris, 9 March 1929;

Fanny, Paris, Théâtre de Paris, 5 December 1931;

César, Paris, Théâtre des Variétés, 18 December 1946;

Judas, Paris, Théâtre de Paris, 6 October 1955;

Fabien, Paris, Théâtre des Bouffes-Parisiens, 28 September 1956.

BOOKS: *Topaze: Pièce en quatre actes* (Paris: Fasquelle, 1930); translated by Renée Waldinger as *Topaze* (Great Neck, N.Y.: Barron's Educational Series, 1958);

Marius: Pièce en quatre actes et six tableaux (Paris: Fasquelle, 1931);

Fanny: Pièce en trois actes et quatre tableaux (Paris: Fasquelle, 1932);

Pirouettes (Paris: Fasquelle, 1932);

Merlusse; Cigalon (Paris: Fasquelle, 1936);

César (Paris: Fasquelle, 1937);

Regain (Paris: Editions Marcel Pagnol, 1937);

La Femme du boulanger (Paris: Editions Marcel Pagnol, 1938);

Le Schpountz (Paris: Editions Marcel Pagnol, 1938);

La Fille du puisatier (Paris: Fasquelle, 1941);

Cantini (Marseille: Perrin, 1946);

Le Premier Amour (Romans-sur-Isère: J.-A. Domergue, 1946);

Discours de réception à l'Académie Française (Paris: Fasquelle, 1947);

Notes sur le rire (Paris: Nagel, 1947);

La Belle Meunière: Scénario et dialogues sur des mélodies de Franz Schubert (Paris: Editions Self, 1948);

Marcel Pagnol, 1946 (© Roger-Viollet/Getty Images)

Critique des critiques (Pairs: Nagel, 1949);

Angèle (Paris: Fasquelle, 1953);

Jazz: Comédie dramatique en quatre actes (Paris: Fasquelle, 1954);

Trois Lettres de mon moulin (Paris: Flammarion, 1954); revised and enlarged as *Quatre Lettres de mon moulin* (Monte Carlo: Pastorelly, 1979);

Judas (Monte Carlo: Pastorelly, 1955);

Rapport de M. Marcel Pagnol, directeur de l'Académie, sur les prix de vertu: Institut de France, Académie Française, séance publique annuelle du jeudi 20 décembre 1956 (Paris: Firmin-Didot, 1956);

Souvenirs d'enfance, 4 volumes (Monte Carlo: Pastorelly, 1957–1960; Paris: Julliard, 1977)—comprises volume 1, *La Gloire de mon père* (1957); volume 2, *Le*

Château de ma mère (1958); volume 3, *Le Temps des secrets* (1960); and volume 4, *Le Temps des amours* (1977); volumes 1 and 2 translated by Rita Barisse as *The Days Were Too Short* (London: Hamilton, 1960; Garden City, N.Y.: Doubleday, 1960); volume 3 translated by Barisse as *The Time of Secrets* (London: Hamilton, 1962; Garden City, N.Y.: Doubleday, 1962); volume 4 translated by Eileen Ellenbogen as *The Time of Love* (London: Hamilton, 1979);

Réponse au Discours de réception de Marcel Achard à l'Académie Française (Paris: Firmin-Didot, 1959);

Ambrogiani (Paris: Presses Artistiques, 1961);

L'Eau des collines, 2 volumes (Paris: Editions de Provence, 1962)—comprises *Jean de Florette* and *Manon des Sources;* translated by W. E. van Heyningen as *The Water of the Hills: Jean de Florette and Manon of the Springs* (London: Deutsch / Berkeley, Cal.: North Point Press, 1988);

Oeuvres complètes, 6 volumes (Paris: Editions de Provence, 1964–1973)—comprises volume 1, *Les marchands de gloire,* by Pagnol and Paul Nivoix, and *Topaze* (1964); volume 2, *Marius* and *Fanny* (1966); volume 3, *La Cinématurgie, César,* and *Merlusse* (1967); volume 4, *Judas, Fabien,* and *Jofroi* (1968); volume 5, *La Gloire de mon père, Pirouettes,* and *Discours d'inauguration du Lyceé Marcel Pagnol* (1973); and volume 6, *La femme du boulanger, Regain,* and *Critique des critiques* (1973);

Le Masque de fer (Paris: Editions de Provence, 1965); revised as *Le Secret du masque de fer* (Paris: Editions de Provence, 1973);

Oeuvres complètes, 12 volumes (Paris: Club de l'Honnête Homme, 1970–1971)—comprises volume 1, *Marius, Fanny,* and *César;* volume 2, *Les Marchands de gloire, Judas,* and *Phaéton;* volume 3, *Topaze, Fabien,* and *Catulle;* volume 4, *Jofroi, Merlusse, Cigalon, Regain,* and *Naïs;* volume 5, *Le Schpountz, La Femme du boulanger, La Fille du puisatier,* and *Le Rosier de Mme. Husson;* volume 6, *La Belle Meunière, Angèle, Trois Lettres de mon moulin,* and *La Prière aux étoiles;* volume 7, *Jean de Florette* and *Manon des sources;* volume 8, *Hamlet, Les Bucoliques,* and *Le Songe d'une nuit d'été;* volume 9, *Cinématurgie de Paris, Critique des critiques, Notes sur le rire,* and *Discours;* volume 10, *Pirouettes, Le Premier Amour,* and *Le Masque de fer;* volume 11, *La Gloire de mon père* and *Le Château de ma mère;* and volume 12, *Le Temps des secrets* and *Poèmes;*

Confidences (Paris: Julliard, 1981);

Notes sur le rire; Critique des critiques; La Petite Fille aux yeux sombres; L'Infâme truc (Monte Carlo: Pastorelly, 1982);

Manon des sources: Dialogue du film réalisé en 1952 (Monte Carlo: Pastorelly, 1984);

Inédits, edited by Jacqueline Pagnol and Frédéric Pagnol (Paris: Vertige du Nord/Carrère, 1986; revised and enlarged edition, Monte Carlo: Pastorelly, 1992).

Collections: *Oeuvres dramatiques: Théâtre et cinéma* (Paris: Gallimard, 1954);

Les Sermons de Marcel Pagnol, edited by Norbert Calmels (Revest-Saint-Martin: R. Morel, 1967);

La Trilogie marseillaise, 3 volumes (Paris: Fallois, 1992)—comprises volume 1, *Marius;* volume 2, *Fanny;* and volume 3, *César;*

Oeuvres complètes, 3 volumes (Paris: Fallois, 1995)—comprises volume 1, *Théâtre;* volume 2, *Cinéma;* and volume 3, *Souvenirs et romans.*

PRODUCED SCRIPTS: *Marius,* motion picture, Paramount Pictures, 1931;

Direct au coeur, by Pagnol and Paul Nivoix, motion picture, Europa Films/Films P. J. de Venloo, 1932;

Fanny, motion picture, Les Films Marcel Pagnol/Les Etablissements Braunberger-Richebé, 1932;

L'Agonie des aigles, motion picture, Pagnol/Roger Richebé, 1933;

Le Gendre de Monsieur Poirier, motion picture, Les Auteurs Associés, 1933;

Jofroi, motion picture, Les Auteurs Associés, 1933;

Topaze, motion picture, Paramount Pictures, 1933;

Angèle, motion picture, Les Films Marcel Pagnol, 1934;

L'Article 330, motion picture, Les Auteurs Associés, 1934;

Tartarin de Tarascon, motion picture, Pathé Cinéma, 1934;

Cigalon, motion picture, Les Films Marcel Pagnol, 1935;

Merlusse, motion picture, Les Films Marcel Pagnol, 1935;

César, motion picture, Les Films Marcel Pagnol, 1936;

Topaze, motion picture, Les Films Marcel Pagnol, 1936;

Regain, motion picture, Les Films Marcel Pagnol, 1937;

La Femme du boulanger, motion picture, Les Films Marcel Pagnol, 1938;

Le Schpountz, motion picture, Les Films Marcel Pagnol, 1938;

Monsieur Brotonneau, motion picture, Les Films Marcel Pagnol, 1939;

La Fille du puisatier, motion picture, Les Films Marcel Pagnol, 1940;

Arlette et l'amour, motion picture, Société Nouvelle des Etablissements Gaumont, 1943;

Naïs, motion picture, Société Nouvelle des Films Marcel Pagnol, 1945;

La Belle Meunière, motion picture, Société Nouvelle des Films Marcel Pagnol, 1948;

Le Rosier de Madame Husson, motion picture, Eminente Films/Les Films Agiman, 1950;

Topaze, motion picture, Les Films Marcel Pagnol, 1951;

Manon des sources, motion picture, Les Films Marcel Pagnol, 1952;

Carnaval, motion picture, Société Nouvelle des Films Marcel Pagnol, 1953;

Les Lettres de mon moulin, motion picture, Compagnie Méditerranéenne de Films, 1954;

Le Curé de Cucugnan, television, Compagnie Méditerranéenne de Films, November 1954;

La Dame aux camélias, television, 31 March 1962.

OTHER: William Shakespeare, *Hamlet,* translated, with a preface, by Pagnol (Paris: Nagel, 1947);

Virgil, *Les Bucoliques,* translated, with a preface and notes, by Pagnol (Paris: Grasset, 1958);

Georges Colomb, *La Famille Fenouillard,* preface by Pagnol (Paris: Librairie Armand Colin, 1965);

Shakespeare, *Le Songe d'une nuit d'été,* translated, with a preface, by Pagnol, in *Oeuvres complètes,* volume 8 (Paris: Club de l'Honnête Homme, 1971).

SELECTED PERIODICAL PUBLICATIONS–UNCOLLECTED: "Le film parlant offre à l'écrivain des ressources nouvelles," *Le Journal,* 17 May 1930;

"Le cinéma parlant, théâtre de demain," *Interview* (18 October 1932);

"Je n'ai pas changé de métier," *Cinémonde* (17 August 1933);

"Non, je n'ai pas trahi l'art dramatique," *Paris-Soir* (6 January 1934);

"Je ne fais que du théâtre," *Le Jour,* 17 May 1935.

Marcel Pagnol was one of the most popular and versatile writers of twentieth-century France. Although now remembered primarily as a screenwriter and motion-picture director, he was also a successful playwright, essayist, and novelist. His career began in the theater, which always remained his first love and served as a model for his subsequent creative endeavors. The plays that initially established Pagnol's reputation–*Topaze* (1928), *Marius* (1929), and *Fanny* (1931)– remain his most enduring contributions to French literature, followed closely by his four-volume autobiography, *Souvenirs d'enfance* (1957–1977, Memories of Childhood).

Marcel Paul Pagnol was born on 28 February 1895 in Aubagne, a small town in southeastern France located twelve miles from Marseille. The oldest child of Joseph Pagnol, a public-school teacher dedicated to promoting the secular values of the Third Republic, and his wife, Augustine Lansot Pagnol, a seamstress and devout Catholic who had her son secretly baptized, Marcel enjoyed a happy and uneventful childhood. He had three siblings: Paul (born in 1898), Germaine (1902), and René (1909). Although the Pagnols relocated often to accommodate Joseph's changing teaching assignments, they never strayed from Marseille after initially moving there in 1897. Beginning in 1904, the family divided its time between the city and a tranquil vacation house in the Marcellin valley between Marseille and Aubagne. The experience, recounted with lyrical nostalgia in *Souvenirs d'enfance,* instilled a strong sense of regional identity in Pagnol and underscored the contrast between rural and urban culture, which later became a central theme in his movies.

To the consternation of his father, Pagnol was an underachiever as a student, described by his teachers as "intelligent," "distracted," and "not especially hardworking." His class rank in science and mathematics remained consistently mediocre throughout middle and high school, but in languages he improved gradually after being forced to repeat a grade in 1907. His mother's untimely death in 1910 and his father's marriage two years later to a much younger woman appear not to have affected Pagnol adversely, for he won composition awards in Latin, English, and German on the way to receiving his baccalaureate in 1913. At the same time he also began publishing bucolic poems in a local literary magazine, *Massilia,* drawing inspiration from Virgil, the nineteenth-century Provençal poet Frédéric Mistral, and his own summer adventures exploring the countryside with a childhood friend, David Magnan.

Pagnol's first publications sparked in him an irrepressible ambition to achieve fame and an entrepreneurial spirit that were to define his career. Working with a team of classmates, he founded two short-lived literary magazines while finishing high school. The first, titled *Le Bohème* (The Bohemian), folded after only two issues for lack of funding; the second, *Fortunio* (The Lucky, or Wealthy, One), fared somewhat better, but the outbreak of World War I in August 1914 interrupted the publication of the journal. Drafted shortly thereafter, Pagnol was assigned to the supply section of an infantry unit, for which he maintained oil lamps. He served less than six months in all, receiving a medical discharge in May 1915 after a series of five examinations. The explanation for Pagnol's condition, officially listed as an irregular heartbeat, probably lies in his inhaling of sulfur fumes from the matches used to light the lamps. Whether his incapacitation was accidental or intentional, as was suggested by neighborhood friends, Pagnol escaped the murderous combat that killed almost 1.5 million Frenchmen, including his friend Magnan and a cousin, André Pagnol.

Pagnol spent the remainder of the war pursuing a teaching career and honing his writing skills. While completing teaching internships at middle schools in Tarascon and Digne, he worked toward a *license-ès-lettres* (equivalent to a B.A. degree) from the University of Montpellier and wrote a three-act verse play titled *Le Droit d'aimer* (The Right to Love), an historical melodrama set in the sixteenth century that recounts forbidden love between two aristocratic teenagers from rival families. In early 1916 Pagnol received his university degree and married his sweetheart, Simonne Colin, after a brief but passionate courtship. Initially assigned to Pamiers in southwestern France, in 1919 he was subsequently named professor of English at high schools in Aix-en-Provence and then Marseille.

The homecoming allowed Pagnol, whose literary ambitions remained undiminished, to resurrect *Fortunio* with the assistance of several former classmates. Edited by Pagnol and Jean Ballard, the journal began on shaky financial ground but secured several advertising sponsors and gradually gained momentum, reaching a monthly print run of more than a thousand copies by the end of 1922. While working on a pair of plays modeled after classical Greek theater, *Ulysse chez les Phéaciens* (Ulysses amid the Phocaeans) and *Catulle* (1922, Catullus), Pagnol also wrote his first novella, *La Petite Fille aux yeux sombres* (The Little Girl with Dark Eyes). Published in *Fortunio* in 1921, it is a semi-autobiographical story of the author's high-school adventures and first taste of lost love.

In mid 1922 an unexpected transfer to the Lycée Condorcet in Paris, one of the most prestigious high schools in France, afforded Pagnol his long-awaited chance to enter the Parisian literary world. As his letters to his friends make clear, the move strained the young couple financially and emotionally; both suffered from the dreary weather and experienced intense homesickness. Despite eye problems and recurring migraines caused by poor diet and stress, Pagnol worked tirelessly to make a name for himself. At first he attempted to repackage *Fortunio* for a Parisian audience, but bitter quarrels with his collaborators over the focus and scope of the magazine soon prompted him to abandon journalism for theater.

Thanks to Paul Nivoix, a fellow Marseillais who was working as a columnist for the high-profile arts newspaper *Comoedia*, Pagnol realized that classically inspired tragedies held little appeal for popular audiences, who relished melodrama and satire. To capitalize on that trend, Nivoix and Pagnol co-authored a vaudevillian farce titled *Tonton, ou Joseph veut rester pur* (1923, Uncle, or Joseph Wants to Remain Pure), about a woman who desperately attempts to become pregnant immediately after the death of her rich husband so that

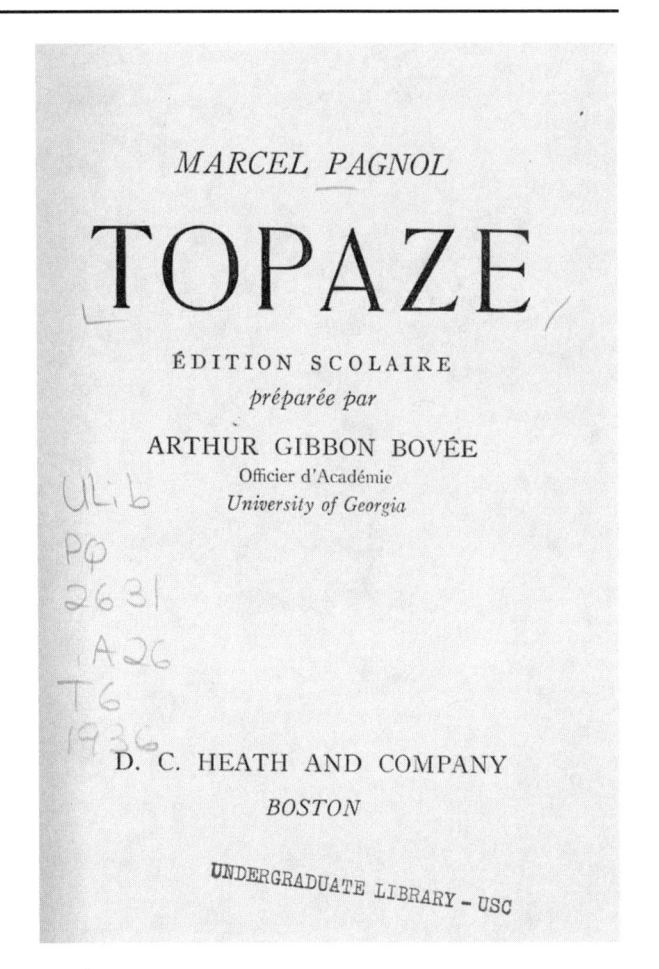

Title page for the 1936 American edition of Pagnol's 1928 play about a schoolteacher who comes to realize the futility of adhering to high ethical standards (Thomas Cooper Library, University of South Carolina)

she may tap the fortune denied her by a prenuptial agreement. The play was unanimously turned down in Paris but was accepted in August 1923 for a weeklong, end-of-season production at the Théâtre des Variétés in Marseille. By industry standards it was a flop, both critically and at the box office; yet, Pagnol viewed the experience as a success, for it netted him an instant profit of Fr 700, roughly a fourth of his annual teaching salary.

Pagnol redoubled his writing efforts the following year, drafting with Nivoix a pair of bitingly satirical plays based on current events. The first, *Les Marchands de gloire* (1925, The Merchants of Glory), published in the 6 February 1926 issue of *La Petite Illustration*, targeted the political manipulation of collective mourning over World War I. After the war France was faced with the difficult task of commemorating its fallen soldiers without retroactively justifying a needless and egregiously mismanaged conflict that had decimated an entire generation of young men and irreparably dam-

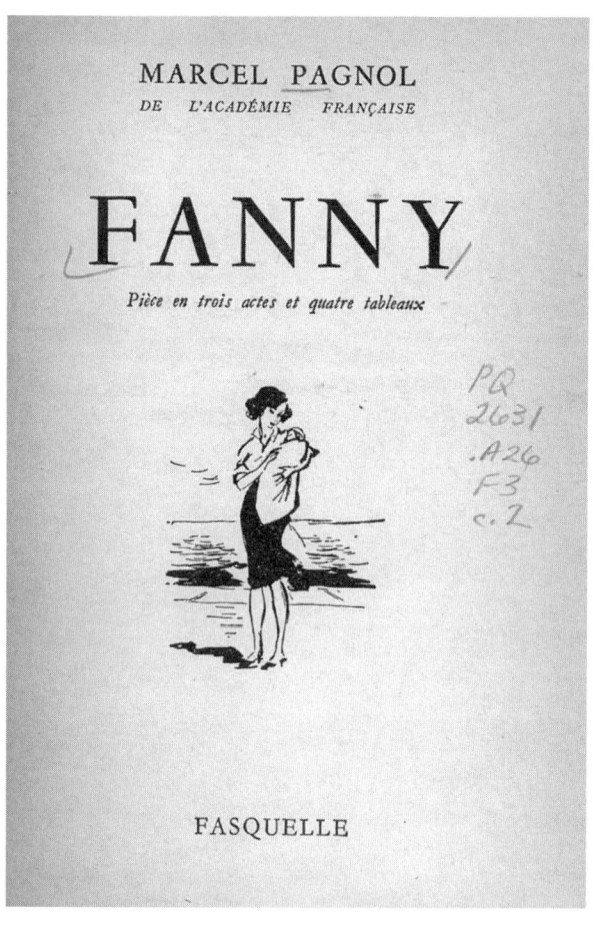

Title page for the 1946 edition of Pagnol's 1931 play, first published in 1932, the second part of the Marseille Trilogy, about César and Marius Olivier, a father and son living in the Old Port district of Marseille, and Marius's relationship with Fanny, a seafood vendor (Thomas Cooper Library, University of South Carolina)

aged the demographic and economic health of the nation. Public debate about the issue was intense and found expression in a wide variety of artistic forms, including Abel Gance's pacifist movie *J'Accuse!* (1919, I Accuse!), the construction of war memorials in virtually every French village, the inauguration of the Tombeau du Soldat Inconnu (Tomb of the Unknown Soldier) in Paris on 11 November 1923, and a host of literary works, many written by veterans.

Les Marchands de gloire was inspired in part by Paul Raynal's controversial play *Le Tombeau sous l'Arc de Triomphe* (The Tomb beneath the Arc de Triomphe), produced at the Comédie-Française in early 1924, as well as Pagnol's observation of his uncle Adolphe, whose son André died in 1919 from mustard-gas inhalation. Prior to the war Adolphe had been a staunch pacifist, but he proudly accepted André's posthumous military decorations and remembered him as a patriotic hero. Building on that premise, the play tells the story of Edouard Bachelet, an honest bureaucrat from a small provincial town whose only son, Henri, is reported dead in the Battle of Verdun. Overcome with grief and dedicated to preserving Henri's memory, he becomes the president of a national philanthropic association for parents who lost children in the war.

A group of corrupt businessmen intent on exploiting Edouard Bachelet's notoriety to further their own interests convinces him to lead a newly created right-wing party in the upcoming parliamentary elections. The day before the vote Henri unexpectedly returns home, having spent the last eight years in a military hospital recovering from shell shock and amnesia. Bachelet, acting under the influence of his cronies, agrees to hide his son until after the election, which yields a landslide victory for the fictitious Radical-Nationalist-Christian ticket. He begins to regret the ruse after being named minister of pensions and wants to reveal the truth. Yet, Henri, motivated by a desire to protect his father's career and by his own material self-interest, follows the counsel of a political adviser, who suggests that he assume a new identity in exchange for a lavish villa in Corsica and a substantial monthly stipend drawn from party funds. The cynically ironic message of *Les Marchands de gloire,* encapsulated in the adviser's quip that "la première qualité d'un héros, c'est d'être mort et enterré" (the primary attribute of a hero is to be dead and buried), culminates in the final scene, in which Bachelet, standing before an idealized portrait of Henri in uniform, makes a tearful speech expressing his unshakeable love of country and the hope that one day his son might return alive. Upon hearing these words, Henri removes his hat and bows his head respectfully, commenting to a reporter that "je l'ai beaucoup connu" (I knew the deceased well).

Les Marchands de gloire premiered in Paris at the Théâtre de la Madeleine on 15 April 1925 and drew virtually unanimous praise from critics, who described it as "remarkable," "captivating," "original," and "powerful." André Rivoire, noted theater columnist for the daily newspaper *Le Temps,* compared Nivoix and Pagnol's "masterful debut" to the mordant work of nineteenth-century dramatist Henry Becque and concluded, "I would be very surprised if at least one of the authors did not become a great name in French theater." Despite such acclaim, *Les Marchands de gloire* did not do well at the box office and ran for only thirteen performances—a failure probably linked to the sensitive subject matter and excessive pessimism of the play.

In their next collaboration, *Un Direct au coeur* (1926, A Jab to the Heart), Pagnol and Nivoix lightened the tone of their satire by taking aim at the box-

Raimu (stage name of Jules Muraire) as César Olivier and Pierre Fresnay as Marius Olivier in the 1936 motion picture César, *the final part of Pagnol's Marseille Trilogy, which he adapted for the stage in 1946 (© Roger-Viollet/Getty Images)*

ing industry. Based loosely on the scandalous Georges Carpentier–Louis Fal championship fight of September 1922, in which Fal ignored arrangements to throw the match and knocked out his opponent, the play focuses on Kid Marc, a kindhearted, idealistic pugilist whose corrupt manager procures him a championship by fixing a series of bouts. Blinded by his instant celebrity, Kid spurns his virtuous sweetheart, Clairette, in favor of an egotistical, decadent actress interested in furthering her own fame. When Kid is knocked out in a legitimate rematch, his manager, new girlfriend, and fans all abandon him. In the end, however, Clairette takes Kid back, and he happily decides to give up boxing to pursue a university degree. *Un Direct au coeur* premiered in Lille on 12 March 1926 and featured several nationally known actors in the lead roles. Despite positive reviews and the kind of happy ending that audiences typically appreciated, the production folded after a week.

Although only moderate successes, *Les Marchands de gloire* and *Un Direct au coeur* convinced Pagnol that he could make a living as a playwright. After resigning from *Fortunio* in early 1925, he took a permanent leave of absence from the Lycée Condorcet to concentrate fully on his new career. At the same time his personal life was also changing rapidly. Since moving to Paris, he had spent less and less time with Simonne while pursuing his teaching duties and working on multiple writing projects. In 1924 he began seeing a stage actress named Orane Demazis, who was to remain his companion for the next thirteen years. Simonne refused her husband's request for a divorce on religious grounds, opting instead for a permanent separation. She expressed her deep sense of betrayal by publishing a three-act play titled *Scrupules, ou la parole donnée* (1934, Scruples, or Promises Made), in which an ambitious author leaves his wife shortly after achieving success. Pagnol and Simonne remained legally married until 1941. In the meantime he fathered three children: Jacques (born in 1930), with British stage actress Kitty Murphy; and Jean-Pierre (1933) and Francine (1935), both with Demazis.

Cover for the DVD of the 1986 movie based on Pagnol's 1962 novel of the same title (Richland County Public Library)

The tangled nexus of morality, career advancement, and love that Pagnol experienced in his own life was central to his next two plays, *Jazz* (1926) and *Topaze*. In *Jazz*, first published in the 2 April 1927 issue of *La Petite Illustration*, a high-school teacher named Jean Blaise discovers what he believes to be an unknown dialogue by Plato and dedicates the next twenty years of his life to reconstructing and annotating the fragmentary text. He attains international renown and a prestigious nomination to the Sorbonne but renounces everything else in his single-minded pursuit of knowledge—family, friends, and romance. When a rival scholar finds a complete version of the same text and proves definitively that it is only a pastiche of Plato by a minor grammarian from the first century A.D., Blaise resigns from the university and bitterly repudiates all intellectual pursuits as worthless.

At the urging of a seemingly benevolent, ghost-like incarnation of his younger self, the fifty-six-year-old Blaise vows to make up for lost time by brusquely proposing to Cécile, an attractive student in his class. She initially accepts out of pity but in the end cannot bring herself to marry him and departs with a suitor her own age. Blaise's younger self tries to tempt his double into a life of debauchery by opening a magical portal to a Montmartre jazz club filled with grotesque hookers, erotic dancing, and flowing champagne. The horrified Blaise pulls a revolver from his desk and attempts to kill his tormentor, who diabolically proclaims his desire to avenge a lifetime of sensual deprivation. The young man shoots Blaise in the ensuing struggle and disappears as the portal closes, leaving the professor's lifeless body alone amid a collection of scholarly tomes scattered symbolically across the floor.

First performed in Monte Carlo, Monaco, and then in Paris at the end of 1926, *Jazz* was an immediate hit with critics, who praised Pagnol's innovative staging techniques and mixture of parody with pathos to create a "philosophical morality tale" that simultaneously entertained spectators and suggested that a balance between the cerebral and corporeal life was crucial to happiness. Apart from the obviously autobiographical content, *Jazz* also draws on several classics of modern literature that Pagnol knew well: Johann Wolfgang von Goethe's *Faust* (1808, 1832), Oscar Wilde's *The Picture of Dorian Gray* (1891), and Charles Dickens's *A Christmas Carol* (1843). With strong performances by Harry Baur as Blaise and Demazis as Cécile, *Jazz* did well at the box office, having a ten-week run that ended only because Baur had to fulfill other contractual obligations.

With *Topaze*, first performed in 1928 and published in 1930, Pagnol finally achieved the fame and wealth that he had pursued tenaciously since adolescence. The play reproduces the themes and characters of his previous works by using the moral corruption of a naive protagonist to mock social injustice. The main character is an idealistic schoolteacher, Albert Topaze, whose selfless devotion to his social and intellectual mission is absolute. He corrects the papers of a fellow teacher, the headmaster's lazy daughter; tutors weak pupils at no charge and on his own time; and warns students against greed and deceit. After the venal headmaster fires Topaze for refusing to change the failing grades of a student from a rich, influential family, the teacher is tricked by a city-council member, Régis Castel-Bénac, and his mistress, Suzy Courtois, into serving as a front man for their illegal business activities and trafficking in political influence.

When Topaze realizes the truth, he is at first paralyzed with guilt and refuses to spend the substantial commissions he receives on all transactions. A visit from the headmaster, who now treats his former colleague with respect instead of condescension, changes Topaze's attitude by making him realize the futility of adhering to high ethical standards. As Topaze puts it,

Si je veux une maison moderne, une fausse dent invisible, la permission de faire gras le vendredi, mon éloge dans les journaux ou une femme dans mon lit, l'obtiendrai-je par des prières, le dévouement, ou la vertu? Il ne faut qu'entr'ouvrir son coffre et dire un petit mot: "Combien?" . . . Malgré les rêveurs, malgré les poètes et peut-être malgré mon coeur, j'ai appris la grande leçon: les hommes ne sont pas bons. C'est la force qui gouverne le monde, et ces petits rectangles de papier bruissant, voilà la forme moderne de la force.

(If I want a modern house, permission to sleep late on Fridays, praise in the newspapers, or a woman in my bed, will I get any of them through prayer, loyalty, or virtue? It suffices to open one's wallet and speak the words "how much?" . . . Despite the dreamers, despite the poets, and perhaps despite my own heart, I have learned the grand lesson of life: men are not good. It is power that governs the world, and those little rustling paper rectangles are the modern form of power.)

Committed to avenging the injustice he suffered as a result of his past morality, Topaze quickly transforms himself into a Machiavellian crime boss, ousting Castel-Bénac from power and taking Suzy for himself.

Topaze thus combines the cynicism and social satire of *Les Marchands de gloire* with the plot structure of *Jazz;* however, whereas the two earlier plays end on a tragic note, *Topaze* paradoxically presents the embrace of vice as a tool of social justice. In so doing, Pagnol denounces corrupt political and social institutions while simultaneously celebrating the wily individual who revolts against the system from within by turning its corruption in his favor. As a modern-day bandit-hero, Topaze personifies the trickster character prevalent in French folklore and popular theater since the medieval period. In the preface to the play Pagnol notes that in a more direct sense, Topaze was inspired by his father, who dedicated himself to teaching "avec un dévouement, une abnégation d'apôtre. . . . Si mon père n'avait pas été paralysé par son idéal, par ses principes, par son respect des autres, il aurait pu réussir aussi bien que tous les hommes d'affaires, les courtiers, les politiciens, et les 'agents immobiliers' dont les procédés n'étaient pas tout à fait catholiques" (with the devotion and abnegation of an apostle. . . . If my father had not been paralyzed by his principles, by his respect for others, he could have succeeded just as well as any of the businessmen, the courtiers, the politicians, and the "real estate agents" whose methods were not entirely scrupulous).

Topaze premiered at the Théâtre des Variétés in Paris on 9 October 1928 and immediately made Pagnol famous, creating a frenzy of popular enthusiasm unseen in the theater world since Edmond Rostand's *Cyrano de Bergerac* (1897). In little more than a year, the box-office receipts for *Topaze* and the run of continuous performances shattered all existing records. By early 1930 the play had been translated into ten foreign languages and staged four thousand times, grossing an estimated Fr 20,000,000 in France and Fr 80,000,000 abroad. Though some critics chided Pagnol for his "vaudevillian" use of caricature and "facile" exploitation of popular antigovernment sentiment, most hailed the play as a masterpiece. In *Le Journal*, Gaston de Pawloski described *Topaze* as "a true human comedy worthy of our great Molière and our immense Rabelais." Louis Schneider of *Le Gaulois* added that "the scenes are often bitter and Mr. Pagnol does not spare his contemporaries the harsh truth about our society. He reprimands us while making us laugh; therein lies the true mark of great comedy."

The strongest dissenting opinion came from Elisabeth Sauvy, an internationally known novelist and reporter, who deplored Pagnol's "apology for immorality" and his negative representation of women. "The two female characters"–Suzy and Ernestine Muche, the headmaster's daughter–"are false," she wrote. "Both are simply dolls who manipulate men in their own interest, dramatic marionettes into which the author did not know how to breathe life." Sauvy concluded that Pagnol's stereotypical view of women was "immature" and "naive," even challenging him to write a sequel recounting Topaze's affair with Suzy. Given Sauvy's extensive connections in the literary world, her critique was perhaps motivated in part by knowledge of Pagnol's marital infidelity and his separation from Simonne.

Following the unprecedented success of *Topaze,* Pagnol had no difficulty placing his next play, *Marius,* which assured his place in the history of French theater. *Marius,* first performed in 1929 and published in 1931, abandons sociopolitical commentary and the cosmopolitan business world in favor of family melodrama leavened with regional type characters. Set in the Old Port section of Marseille, *Marius* is built around the themes of father-son conflict and familial duty versus personal ambition. Marius, the twenty-two-year-old son of widower César Olivier, dreams of becoming a sailor and traveling the world but feels obligated to help his father run the family bar. The irascible César is incapable of expressing his affection for Marius and still treats him like a child. Marius attempts to resign himself to a mundane, petty bourgeois life in Marseille and begins seeing a neighborhood seafood vendor named Fanny, with whom he falls in love. The two make plans to marry, but the lure of adventure at sea continues to torment Marius. When he has the opportunity to leave aboard a three-masted schooner bound for the Indian Ocean, Fanny selflessly urges him to go. He does so without

Cover for the DVD of the 1986 sequel to Jean de Florette
(Richland County Public Library)

telling César, who in the closing scene of the play joyfully tells the devastated Fanny how much he is looking forward to the upcoming wedding.

Throughout *Marius,* Pagnol lightens the pathos of the plot with light comedy based on local color. Several characters personifying regional stereotypes join the action: Escartefigue, a dull-witted, cuckolded ferry captain; Panisse, a complacent, wealthy bourgeois; Honorine, a rotund, voluble seafood vendor; and Piquoiseau, a worldly, vagabond sailor. They personify in caricature the cultural traits traditionally associated with Marseille: a desire to enjoy life that often borders on laziness, a quick temper, a penchant for exaggeration, chauvinistic pride in their city, and a charming naiveté regarding life elsewhere. The resulting combination of heartfelt drama and vaudevillian mirth gave *Marius* a unique appeal that made it an overnight classic following its premiere on 9 March 1929.

The critical and financial success of *Marius* rivaled that of *Topaze,* elevating the cast to instant stardom. Lead actors Raimu (the stage name of Jules Muraire, who played César), Pierre Fresnay (Marius), Demazis (Fanny), and Fernand Charpin (Panisse) all enjoyed successful theater and cinema careers thanks to the publicity surrounding *Marius.* Shortly after the debut of the play, Pagnol began writing a sequel, *Fanny,* in which the heroine discovers that she is pregnant by the departed Marius and marries Panisse in order to save her family's honor. A year later Marius returns from his voyage and attempts to win back Fanny, but César convinces him to accept the status quo for the good of Fanny and the baby. The eagerly awaited second part of what later became known as the Marseille Trilogy opened to sold-out theaters on 5 December 1931 but was overshadowed somewhat by Pagnol's rapidly developing movie career. *Fanny* was published in 1932.

The possibility of adapting his works for the cinema occurred to Pagnol in May 1930, after he first saw a talkie in London. At that time, members of the silent-movie establishment and other performing artists were uneasy about the new sound technology. For the former group it constituted a lamentable vulgarization of the so-called seventh art; for the latter it represented an unwelcome competitor to music halls and boulevard theater. Pagnol's position as a star playwright put him in an ideal position to denounce talkies, but instead he viewed the ability to record images with dialogue as a means of enhancing the power of theater. In "Le film parlant offre à l'écrivain des ressources nouvelles" (The Talking Film Offers New Resources to the Writer), an article published by the Parisian newspaper *Le Journal* (17 May 1930) to honor the six hundredth consecutive performance of *Topaze,* Pagnol claimed that sound cinema would allow stage directors "d'isoler un centre comique ou dramatique" (to isolate comic and dramatic effect) by focusing on the subtlest nuances of speech and physical expression—details that might be overshadowed or overlooked in the context of a live play. This focus, he contended, would in turn eliminate the need for unrealistic exaggeration on the part of actors, making their performances more natural and evocative for the audience. In addition, movies could standardize the viewing experience, thereby ensuring that each spectator saw the play exactly as the director and actors intended it. Pagnol concluded enthusiastically that sound cinema would soon render all other forms of dramatic expression obsolete, using a destructive metaphor to make his point: "Voilà ce que nous apporte la merveilleuse découverte; nous sauterons la rampe, nous tournerons tout autour de la scène, nous ferons éclater tous les murs du théâtre, nous mettrons en morceaux le décor ou l'acteur. Pour la première fois, des auteurs dramatiques pourront réaliser des oeuvres que ni Molière, ni Shakespeare n'ont eu les moyens de tenter" (Here is what this marvelous discovery offers us: we will blow up the footlights, we will film all around the stage, we will explode the theater's walls, we will dissect the scenery and the actors. For the first time dramatic authors will be able to create works of art that neither Molière nor Shakespeare had the means to attempt."

These remarks sparked a national scandal and drew virtually unanimous vilification from Pagnol's peers in the theater world; yet, he thrived on the controversy and began looking for a way to put his ideas into practice. Shortly after his article was published, he met Robert Kane, executive director of a studio complex that Paramount Pictures had just finished building outside Paris. Kane proposed bringing *Marius* and *Topaze* to the screen, and Pagnol accepted immediately. Directed by Alexander Korda and Louis Gasnier, respectively, the adaptations allowed Pagnol to learn the basics of moviemaking, highlighted the efficiency of a centralized studio system, and confirmed his intuition regarding the commercial potential of talkies. The motion-picture versions of *Marius*, released in October 1931, and *Topaze*, released in January 1933, set box-office records, prompting Pagnol to give up theater and devote himself full-time to making movies. Marc Allégret's successful movie adaptation of *Fanny* in mid 1932, a project on which Pagnol served as producer, served as the final stage in his cinematic apprenticeship.

Pagnol used the proceeds from his trio of "canned theater" movies to found his own production company, Les Films Marcel Pagnol, and to build a small but well-equipped complex in Marseille that included studios and a film-developing laboratory. To publicize his new business and his unorthodox approach to cinema, he also launched a magazine titled *Les Cahiers du film* (1933–1934, Film Notebooks). The inaugural issue included a provocative article by Pagnol "Cinématurgie de Paris," announcing the economic demise of silent movies and theater: "Lorsque j'écris que le muet est mort et que le théâtre est à l'agonie, je veux dire que le commerce qui nourrissait le muet est mort, que le commerce du théâtre est près de la faillite. A la place de ces deux commerces, est né le commerce du film parlant, qui a dévoré les deux autres: la prospérité de ce nouveau commerce nourrit abondamment un nouvel art, et prouve que ce nouvel art a conquis l'intérêt du public" (When I write that silent cinema is dead and that theater is dying, I mean that the business which fed silent film is dead and that the theater business is on the verge of bankruptcy. The business of talking film has displaced and devoured the other two; the prosperity of this new commerce is already richly supporting a new art and proves that this new art has won over the public).

This willful embrace of cinema as a mass-market entertainment product rather than as a form of art redoubled the attacks against Pagnol by defenders of theater and silent cinema, but the unprecedented financial success of his movies both nationally and internationally soon made him the pride of the French motion-picture industry. From 1933 to 1954 Pagnol directed seventeen movies, including the hits *Angèle* (1934), *César* (1936, the third part of the Marseille Trilogy), *Regain* (1937, Harvest), *Le Schpountz* (1938, The Groupie), *La Femme du boulanger* (1938, The Baker's Wife), *La Fille du puisatier* (1940, The Well Digger's Daughter), and *Manon des sources* (1952, Manon of the Spring). In 1945 he married the actress Jacqueline Bouvier, with whom he had two children: Frédéric, born the following year, and Estelle, who was born in 1951 but died three years later.

Apart from the stage production of *César* in 1946, the year he was elected to the Académie Française (French Academy), Pagnol did not write any plays during his moviemaking career, returning to the theater only in 1955 with *Judas,* a reinterpretation of the circumstances surrounding the Passion of Christ. Pagnol rejects the quintessential image of Judas as a greedy traitor, portraying him instead as a devoted martyr who at Jesus' request agrees to commit the ultimate transgression in order to make possible the salvation of mankind. As Judas says in a last prayer before hanging himself, "Mon souvenir sera maudit dans les siècles des siècles, les meilleurs me refuseront une prière, plus jamais un petit enfant ne sera baptisé de mon nom. Cette amertume, je l'accepte. Tu m'as choisi d'incarner la laideur des hommes, que Ta Volonté soit faite" (My memory will be damned for all eternity, the best of men will refuse to pray for me; nevermore will a little child be baptized in my name. I accept this bitter fate. You chose me to incarnate mankind's ugliness. May Your Will be done). The play met with a tepid response from critics and audiences. Several prominent Catholic and Jewish leaders dismissed Pagnol's revisionist theology as unfounded speculation that bordered on blasphemy. During the twelfth performance of *Judas,* Raymond Pellegrin, the actor interpreting the title role, suffered a heart attack onstage and blacked out; two days later his replacement, Roger Rudel, was struck with acute appendicitis. Rumors of divine intervention began to spread, and the director of the Théâtre de Paris shut down the production soon afterward.

The bitterness and misanthropy that Pagnol took away from the experience showed up the following year in *Fabien,* which premiered at the Théâtre des Bouffes-Parisiens in Paris on 28 September 1956 and was first published in the December 1956 *Paris-Théâtre*. The play is a cynical vaudeville about an indolent, lecherous photographer whose kindhearted, obese wife, Milly, indulges his every whim and believes him to be a great artist. When Milly's attractive younger sister comes to live with the couple, Fabien persuades her to pose nude for postcard photos and then seduces her. Milly blames her sister for the affair and drives her away, even agreeing to help Fabien find another model for his postcards. *Fabien* was an utter disaster critically and commercially, prompting Pagnol to abandon theater definitively and turn to prose as an outlet for his storytelling talents.

The third and final stage of Pagnol's literary career restored his fame and ensured the popularity of his works with a new generation of readers. *La Gloire de mon père* (1957, My Father's Glory) and *Le Château de ma mère* (1958, My Mother's Castle), the first two volumes of *Souvenirs d'enfance*, became overnight best-sellers. They provided an embellished, thickly nostalgic remembrance of the summers Pagnol spent with family and friends in the countryside near Marseille. The single-volume English translation of the two books, *The Days Were Too Short*, was published in 1960. The third installment of the autobiography, *Le Temps des secrets* (1960; translated as *The Time of Secrets*, 1962), was equally successful. In 1962 Pagnol published *Jean de Florette* and *Manon des sources*, a pair of acclaimed novels with the collective title *L'Eau des collines* (translated as *The Water of the Hills: Jean de Florette and Manon of the Springs*, 1988), based on his screenplay for the 1952 movie *Manon des sources*. He spent the final decade of his life working on *Le Masque de fer* (1965, The Iron Mask; revised as *Le Secret du masque de fer*, 1973), an historical essay regarding the identity of the notorious man in the iron mask (whom Pagnol claimed was Louis XIV's twin brother), and *Le Temps des amours* (1977; translated as *The Time of Love*, 1979), the posthumously published fourth installment of *Souvenirs d'enfance*. He also enjoyed family life with his second wife, Jacqueline, and youngest son, Frédéric. Pagnol died in Paris on 18 April 1974 and was buried in the village of La Treille near Aubagne beneath a memorial that reads "Fontes, amicos, uxorem dilexit" (He cherished springs, friends, and his wife).

Since his death the popularity of Marcel Pagnol's works has continued to grow as an expression of collective nostalgia for traditional French culture and concerns regarding the dehumanizing effects of globalization. The thorny socio-economic problems that have plagued the country since the mid 1970s—including a consistently high unemployment rate, difficulties integrating Muslim immigrants into the secular republic, and growing sympathy for extreme right-wing political parties such as the Front National (National Front)—have amplified the appeal of Pagnol's biting social satires and idealized representation of early-twentieth-century France. Since 1977 the first two volumes of his autobiography, *La Gloire de mon père* and *Le Château de ma mère*, have been required reading in all French middle schools, thereby perpetuating his status as a national icon among a new generation of readers.

The 1986 motion-picture adaptations of *Jean de Florette* and *Manon des sources* were critically acclaimed box-office successes. Four years later the movie versions of *La Gloire de mon père* and *Le Château de ma mère* were equally successful. The filmed adaptations of Pagnol's plays from the 1930s continue to sell briskly on video and are the only black-and-white productions still shown during prime time on French network television. His ongoing celebrity also feeds a thriving commercial industry. In February 1995 Aubagne welcomed more than one hundred thousand visitors to celebrate the centenary of Pagnol's birth. In addition to taking guided tours of the sites featured in his novels and movies, tourists who visit the town can admire Le Petit Monde de Marcel Pagnol (The Little World of Marcel Pagnol), an expansive display of painted figurines immortalizing Pagnol's best-loved characters in action. Handmade by local craftspeople using a traditional method that dates back to the seventeenth century, these *santons* (from *santoun*, "little saint" in the Provençal language) are expensive and collectible artifacts of Provençal culture. The cult surrounding Pagnol shows no signs of diminishing. His plays and prose will likely remain a symbolic anchor for French collective memory and national identity for many years to come.

Biographies:

Georges Berni, *Marcel Pagnol: Sa vie, son oeuvre* (Aubagne: Editions Côte d'Azur, 1980);

Raymond Castans, *Marcel Pagnol: Biographie* (Paris: J. C. Lattès, 1987);

Jean-Baptiste Luppi, *De Pagnol Marcel à Marcel Pagnol: Voyage aux sources de sa gloire* (Marseille: P. Tacussel, 1995).

References:

Jacques Bens, *Pagnol* (Paris: Seuil, 1994);

Georges Berni, *Dans les pas de Marcel Pagnol: Toute sa Provence dans un fauteuil* (Aubagne: Office du Tourisme, 1995);

Claude Beylie, *Marcel Pagnol, ou Le Cinéma en liberté*, revised and enlarged edition (Paris: Fallois, 1995);

C. E. J. Caldicott, *Marcel Pagnol* (Boston: Twayne, 1977);

Isabelle Cavallo and Christelle Weingarten, *Marcel Pagnol*, CD-ROM (Boulogne-Billancourt: Compagnie Méditerranéenne de Films / Aubagne: Université de Provence/Ville d'Aubagne, 1996);

Jean-Jacques Jélot-Blanc and Guy Morel, *Pagnol inconnu*, preface by Jacqueline Pagnol (Paris: M. Lafon/ Editions de La Treille, 1998);

Marcel Pagnol–Site Officiel <www.marcel-pagnol.com> [accessed 25 August 2005].

Papers:

Eighty-two letters that Marcel Pagnol wrote to Jean Ballard from 1922 to 1969 are in the *Cahiers du sud* archive at the Bibliothèque Municipale de Marseille.

Henri Pichette
(24 January 1924 – 30 October 2000)

Jason Owens
South Dakota State University

PLAY PRODUCTIONS: *Les Epiphanies,* Paris, Théâtre des Noctambules, 3 December 1947;
Nucléa, Paris, Théâtre Nationale Populaire, 3 May 1952.

BOOKS: *Quatre poèmes/Quatre dessins,* illustrated by Roger Mandel (Marseille: Self-produced facsimiles [2 copies], 1944);
Xylophonie contre la grande presse et son petit public, with Antonin Artaud (Paris: Davy, 1946);
Apoèmes (Paris: Fontaine, 1947);
Les Epiphanies: mystère profane (Paris: K, 1948; revised edition, Paris: Gallimard, 1969; revised and enlarged, 1997);
Rond point, Joyce au participe futur, Pages pour Chaplin (Paris: Mercure de France, 1950);
Le Point vélique (Paris: Mercure de France, 1950);
Lettres arc-en-ciel (Paris: L'Arche, 1950)—comprises *Lettre rouge avec la réponse de Max-Pol Fouchet* and *lettre orangée à André Breton;*
Nucléa (Paris: L'Arche, 1952);
Les Revendications: Apoèmes. Les armes de justice. Evolution de la révolution, illustrated by Jean Bazaine, Jacques Villon, Edouard Pignon, Antoni Clavé, Aristide Caillaud, Pablo Picasso, Marcel Gromaire, Felix de Boeck, and others (Paris: Mercure de France, 1958);
Dents de lait dents de loup (Paris: P. de Tartas, 1959; revised and enlarged edition, Paris: Gallimard, 1962);
Odes à chacun (Paris: Gallimard, 1961; revised, 1988);
Tombeau de Gérard Philipe (Paris: Gallimard, 1961);
Odes à la neige (N.p.: Le Livre contemporain et les Bibliophiles franco-suisses, 1967);
[Les] ditelis du rougegorge (Paris: Gallimard, 2005).
Collections: *Apoèmes* with *Lambeaux d'un Manuscrit d'Amour* and fragments of *"Sélénite"* (Paris: Gallimard, 1995);
Dents de lait dents de loup (Paris: Gallimard, 2005).

OTHER: *Appel où il est fait état des principes de la République et l'honneur de la France* (Paris: Esprit, 1960);
Guerre et poésie; spectacle récital, mise en scène de Jean-louis Barrult. A collaboration of Carlos Vilardebo (cinema), Maurice Roche (music), Pichette (scenic slides), and Juliette Caputo (visual elements) (Paris, 1961).

Henri Pichette (from the cover for Henri Pichette 1924, *1978; Harlan Hatcher Graduate Library, University of Michigan)*

Although Henri Pichette wrote only two stage productions, the attention and controversy generated by *Les Epiphanies* (performed 1947, published 1948; The Epiphanies) eclipses the fame he gained for his decades of work as a poet and agitator. Jacques G. Benay wrote in *The French Review* in 1966:

> L'expérience de Pichette, peu connue en dehors des historiens de ce théâtre, Vauthier, Adamov, Beckett, Ionesco la reprennent sous une forme ou une autre parce qu'elle répond à l'un de leurs buts essentiels qui est de provoquer *le spectateur.*

(The experience of Pichette, little known beyond historians of this theater, has been taken up by Vauthier, Adamov, Beckett, and Ionesco in one form or another because it responds to one of their essential goals, which is provoking *the viewer*.)

Benay sums up Pichette's connection to more-famous absurdists, but while their work featured action and passages where silence spoke, the *puissance du verbe* (the power of the word) was the center, if not the whole, of Pichette's productions.

Pichette was born on 24 January 1924 in Châteauroux, a large industrial city in north-central France, to a mother from Nîmes and a father whose family had moved from Quebec to the United States to France. The poet used his birth name, Harry Paul Pichette, until changing it to the French form, Henri, in 1945. He lived in several households in several regions of France during his childhood.

World War II began for Pichette with a bombardment in May 1940 that profoundly affected him and ended as he deserted the *chantiers de la jeunesse* (roadwork program for youth), a construction program created by the Vichy government. He followed French forces into Alsace and Germany, first as a soldier and then as a war correspondent. Pichette married in 1945 and fathered his first child, Christine. The marriage ended in divorce in 1950, and he fathered another daughter named Clotilde with his second wife in 1953.

Pichette's first attempts to find a public for his poems led to his joining forces with his friend Antonin Artaud, whose work had been rejected—as had Pichette's—by the review *Arts et lettres*. The two published *Xylophonie contre la grande presse et son petit public* (Xylophony against the Big Press and Its Little Public) in 1946; it consisted of a piece by Artaud and Pichette's *Apoème* (Apoem) later numbered *Apoème 5*. Fifty-three copies were printed.

Pichette's work reflects an obsession with war. Only two years after the end of World War II, he achieved his greatest success with *Les Epiphanies*. The play features war, along with love, as a central theme, yet is without the dramatic conflict one would expect, given such subject matter.

Les Epiphanies is divided into *La Genèse*, *L'Amour*, *La Guerre*, *Le Délire*, and *L'accomplissement* (Genesis, Love, War, Delirium, Achievement), each part showing biblical parallels. The strongest section is the second, in which the protagonist, *le poète*, and his lover, *l'amoureuse*, speak in a series of *I* statements in which the verbs are all neologisms, nouns from which Pichette has formed verbs:

le poète: je te vertige
l'amoureuse: et tu me recommences . . .
le poète: te chaise, te table . . . te havre, te cèdre . . . te diphtongue, te syllabe . . . te septembre octobre novembre décembre et le temps qu'il faudra

(I vertigo you
and you restart me . . .
I chair you, table you . . . harbor you, cedar you . . . diphthong you, syllable you . . . September October November December you and all of the time that it will take.)

Such freedom in forming one part of speech from another is taken for granted in the Anglo-Saxon world; yet, in France, Pichette feels obliged to justify his action over several pages in a supplement to the printed edition, pointing to a propensity in Middle and Old French to coin such terms, to their continued use among rustics in France, and to their constant invention in Quebec.

The lovers' Eden-like joy is interrupted by the arrival of Monsieur Diable (Mr. Devil) and a voice crying "éditon spéciale! . . . mobilisation générale" (extra!, extra! . . . general mobilization!), thus foreshadowing act 3, *"La guerre."* The fourth act shows M. Diable ignoring the poet's entreaties and ordering him executed. In *"L'état"* (the civil state), the devil figure establishes his dominion on Earth, and the poet continues to speak, although the state into which he has been resurrected is unclear.

To detail a story line in either of Pichette's plays is not actually crucial, since Pichette strives for neither action nor character development. Roger Shattuck called the works "plotless," adding that "Pichette and his fellow poets want to write poetry to be seen and heard. The great risk they run is that of lacking a sure dramatic sense, for the theatre cannot content itself with mere declamation of resonant lines."

The controversy around the play, subtitled *mystère profane* (A Profane Mystery), began before opening night (3 December 1947), with the original venue's owner backing out of the staging after reading the script, forcing the play to debut in a much smaller house, the Théâtre des Noctambules. Soon, however, it moved to a larger stage.

Widely held suspicions that Pichette was a poet who used the theater to ensure that his poems were heard are buttressed by the attention he put into *Les Epiphanies* when it was published. Unable to rely on theatrical giants such as director Georges Vitaly for a commanding presentation, he instead employed a plethora of typefaces, including pages of white words on a black background for a passage in which heavy bombers arrive, as well as words appearing to drip down the page. Furthermore, most of his references are so obscure that a later edition included a glossary running three dozen pages, in which, for example, he explains his spelling of *"drapot,"* which combines the French words *drapeau* (flag) and *pot de chambre* (chamber pot). Such devices do not lend themselves to reproduction on stage.

Pichette lets a letter or symbol stand for each character, and, although the printed work is dedicated to Gérard Philipe, the actors of the stage production (Philipe, Jeanne Moreau, Maria Casarès, Michel Michalon, and Roger Blin—all famous actors of the French stage and screen) are nowhere mentioned in the volume. Leonard Cabell Pronko wrote that as a play it "probably would have been intolerable without the talents of Philipe, Blin, and Casarès, who made of it a brilliant poetic recital, for the verbal brilliance and invention is undeniable." He speaks of the "irony of such a unique voice, so egotistical yet best voiced by friends."

Pichette's first widely distributed writings, *Apoèmes,* written in 1945, were published in a review, *Fontaine,* a few weeks after the opening of *Les Epiphanies.* Pichette quickly sought to establish himself on the literary scene, speaking about political concerns and publishing his opinions on art—addressing, for example, his *Lettre Orange* (Orange Letter) on Surrealism to André Breton, who had congratulated him backstage upon seeing *Les Epiphanies.*

Five years after *Les Epiphanies,* the up-and-coming Jean Vilar chose Pichette's new work, *Nucléa* (1952, Nuclea) as one of the first plays, along with pieces by Bertolt Brecht and Molière, that he staged as the first director of the Théâtre National Populaire, a vast hall formerly used by the United Nations. The production, which premiered on 3 May 1952, featured Alexander Calder's sets and the first major use in France of stereo sound with audiotape in theater for the recorded voices accompanying the score by Maurice Jarre.

Part 1 of the play is a *cauchemar* (nightmare) titled *"Les infernales"* (The Infernals). The action commences with many voices repeating lines in Latin and French, including cries of *"les tanks";* tanks are mentioned at the beginning of *"La guerre,"* the war section of *Les Epiphanies,* as well. However, the weightiness of the subject matter does not impede Pichette from the wordplay nor the repetition and sonic effects that characterize all of his work, with such lines as "bohème poème bohème" (Bohemia poem Bohemia).

The figure Gladior, played by Vilar, symbolizes war (as had Monsieur Diable in the previous piece). He states, as circus music plays, "j'ai recordé ma leçon entre la grosse Bertha et la Bombe atomique, et que dès

Gérard Philipe in the original production of Pichette's best-known work, Les Epiphanies *(The Epiphanies), Théâtre des Noctambules, 1947 (© Lipnitzki/Roger-Viollet/Getty Images)*

que je fus en âge de donner la réplique j'ai fait partie de l'Intelligence Service" (I memorized my lesson between Big Bertha and the atomic Bomb and since I was of the age to give a reply I have been part of the Intelligence Service). But just as the references to World War II are opaque in *Les Epiphanies,* the East-West conflict of the period is seldom referred to concretely in *Nucléa,* although Philipe's character is named Tellur. *Tellure* (tellurium in English), an element used in making bombs, resembles the name of Edward Teller, "father" of the hydrogen bomb, which also debuted in 1952. Pichette compares science to religion in a passage in which *Le Deuxième Capitaine* (the Second Captain) evokes "Tous les seigneurs en puissance qui étudiaient, analysaient et compulsaient la Bible ou l'Encyclopédie" (All of the lords in power who have studied, analyzed and inspected the Bible or the Encyclopedia). His line is taken up by "a voice":

> selon que nous appliquerons le théorème de Mars à une unité h . . . dans l'ordre somathématique suivant: á lyrique, â psychique, ã conscienciel, ä religieux, etc. . . , nous obtiendrons des résultats parfaitement contradictoires.

Front cover for the 1998 publication of Pichette's play about love and war, which was first performed in 1947 and published in 1948 (Jean and Alexander Heard Library, Vanderbilt University)

(according to which we apply the theorem of Mars in one unit h . . . in the following somatic/mathematical order: *á* lyric, *â* psychic, *ã* conscious, *ä* religious, etc. . . , we will obtain perfectly contradictory results.)

The second part of the piece, *"Le ciel humain"* (Human Heaven), described not as a nightmare but simply as a dream, is literally and literarily of a different tone. Perhaps to reflect the order that is impossible to achieve in wartime, this half is in Alexandrines, the traditional twelve-syllable French meter, reminiscent not of avant-garde theater but rather of the theater of the age of Molière written in verse. The text of *Nucléa* again features the repetition of lines, the strings of verbs or nouns found in its predecessor, *Les Épiphanies*.

Many critics found the high-profile play overblown yet underwhelming, but audiences showed more enthusiasm. Still, more than one critic uses the simple word "failure" to describe in retrospect Pichette's second and last stage production. The lack of conflict that resulted from relegating heaven and hell to different halves of the work practically precluded traditional dramatic conflict.

Pichette collaborated with the review *Esprit* beginning in 1954 with three *Poèmes offerts* (Offered Poems). In 1958 *Les Revendications* (Claims) appeared with illustrations by ten artists, including Pablo Picasso. This collection included the older *Apoèmes*, from which Shattuck generalized about Pichette's brilliance and his limitations:

> The spirited variety of Pichette's language, his rudimentary and often drifting composition, his unstinting use of the simple series as a poetic technique—all these aspects of his work give it the quality of a conglomeration. He dazzles and disturbs, often without making us precisely aware of what he is driving at. And yet the basic style in all his works is that of hortatory monologue. *"J'écris des mots qui boxent"* (I write words that box), he writes in *Apoèmes,* and everything conspires to this end.

In 1961 he published *Tombeau de Gérard Philipe* (Tomb of Gérard Philipe), his eulogy for the comic actor to whom many give credit for sustaining Pichette's plays. Philipe had died at age thirty-seven in 1959. The closest Pichette came later to another theatrical production was *Guerre et poésie; spectacle-récital* (War and Poetry, a performance-recital) with Carlos Vilardebo, Maurice Roche, Juliette Caputo, and James Pichette (his brother, who was a painter).

Pichette had visited his father's home, Quebec, in 1960 but had difficulty entering the United States because of his erstwhile communist sympathies. A petition circulated among American academics and artists led to his subsequently being able to give lectures in the United States. Pichette spent much of 1962–1964 in Quebec, fascinated by the French spoken there. He thus was not in France at the time of the death of his father, who had arrived in France with the Expeditionary Corps, a unit of troops charged with a military mission, in 1917, during World War I. Returning to France, Pichette undertook the "word by word" revision of his already published works so fervently that the revolts of May 1968 passed him by. This omission occurred despite his having written,

> Faire fondamentalement de la politique, c'est être poète.
> Transformer le monde,
> œuvrer à l'embellir,
> participer de la création une et indivisible.
>
> (To be a poet is to be involved fundamentally in politics,
> to transform the world,

> to work to beautify,
>
> to partake of creation one and indivisible.)

Pichette later spoke out against celebrating the bicentennial of the bloody French Revolution.

An exposition at the Bibliothèque Municipale (municipal library) of Pau (December 1978–January 1979) was titled "Henri Pichette 1924?" perhaps an allusion to assumptions that the seldom-heard-from poet had died. Between 1968 and 1981, Pichette published only two poems, both of which he had written in the 1940s. Pichette explains in the catalogue of the exposition: "Peu après la brusque mort de Gérard Philipe, je pris le chemin intérieur qui devait longuement me conduire à une intime retraite" (Shortly after the unexpected death of Gérard Philipe, I took an interior path that slowly drove me to an intimate retirement). His teenage daughter by his second marriage had died a few months before the exhibit opened. A few months after the exhibit in Pau closed, a solo reading in Paris of his definitively revised *Epiphanies* reportedly attracted an audience of four.

In 1984 Pichette refused the Ordre des Arts et des Lettres (The Order of Arts and Letters) from the French Ministry of Culture. Besides revising his earlier published works over decades, Pichette devoted years to writing about the *rougegorge familier* (the common robin), a bird he saw as a symbol of the linguistic diversity of France. Birds appear throughout his oeuvre. His last poem, written shortly before he was hospitalized, speaks of a sensitive bird recognizing Christ. As his appreciation for classic forms of verse grew, so did his opinion of the Catholic Church. Gabriel Marcel included Pichette in his list of authors bringing about a "resacralisation du théâtre" (resacrilization of the theater) through their treatment of religious themes.

Pichette had been considered a fellow traveler of the Communists before the Soviet crackdown in Hungary in 1956. Subsequent events, including the Soviet censoring of his *Revendications*, provoked him during a trip to read *Guerre et Poésie* at the Exposition Française in Moscow. This recital, in turn, led him later to call himself a "poète et anticommuniste déclaré" (a poet and declared anti-Communist). His name was taken off a petition in favor of independence for Quebec in 1980 when he insisted that this phrase follow his signature in *Le Monde*. In 1982 Pichette published a revised *Poèmes offerts,* and in 1988 he published a revision of *Odes à chacun* (Odes to Everybody).

Pichette died of cancer 30 October 2000 in Paris. His obituary in *Le Monde,* like most comments on his career, centered on his *Epiphanies,* "qui a marqué la poésie française de la deuxième moitié du siècle" (which left its mark on French poetry of the last half of the century). This obituary bears witness once again to the primacy of poetry over drama in all of his work. The influence of James Joyce, Arthur Rimbaud, and François Rabelais on Pichette were also often mentioned.

Most critics grant Henri Pichette his superior strengths as a poet while denigrating his reach for exceeding his grasp in the theatrical productions that eclipsed the renown of his work on the printed page. Pronko writes,

> About midway between the poles of Babel and Eden [his terms for the new and old theatres] stand three writers, Henri Pichette, Michel de Ghelderode, and Jacques Audiberti. The first two, strictly speaking, perhaps do not belong to the dramatic avant-garde of the 1950s. Pichette, because he is first of all a poet and his two incursions into the theatrical field have only shown up his shortcomings as a dramatist.

Georges Nepveu and other critics called Pichette's theater *A-Théâtre*—in contrast to the antitheater of Eugène Ionesco—in part for the extent to which "action becomes lost in words and the show vanishes into flights of lyricism." Kenneth S. White called Pichette "richly poetic but too difficult for widespread acceptance." Henri Pichette is better known for his first flash of success as a playwright at age twenty-three than for the half century he spent far from the stage as a lone poetic voice.

References:

Jacques G. Benay, "Le Classicisme du théâtre d'avant-garde," *French Review,* 39 (May 1966): 875–886;

Compagnie de la Irrépressable, Paris <http://irrepressible.free.fr>;

J. S. Doubrovsky, "Ionesco and the Comic of Absurdity," *Yale French Studies,* 23 (1959): 3–10;

Leonard Cabell Pronko, *Avant-Garde: The Experimental Theater in France* (Berkeley: University of California Press, 1962);

Oreste F. Pucciani, "The French Theatre," *French Review,* 29 (May 1956): 449–456;

Roger Shattuck, "A Poet's Progress: Henri Pichette," *French Review,* 32 (December 1958): 111–119;

Kenneth S. White, "Le Théâtre en France depuis la libération," *Modern Language Notes,* 76 (April 1961): 371–375.

Roger Planchon
(12 September 1931 -)

Francine Heather Conley
College of St. Catherine

PLAY PRODUCTIONS: William Shakespeare, *La Nuit des Rois,* adapted by Planchon and Théâtre de la Cité, Lyon, Parc de la Tête d'or, 1952;

Burlesque-digest, adapted by Planchon and Théâtre de la Cité from Jean Tardieu's *Pas d'orchidée pour Miss Blandish* and *Terreur en Oklahoma,* Lyon, Théâtre de la Comédie, 1953;

Cartouche, Lyon, Théâtre de la Comédie, 1953;

Oklahoma, Lyon, Théâtre de la Comédie, 1953;

Christopher Marlowe, *Edward II,* adapted by Planchon and Arthur Adamov, translated by Adamov, Lyon, Festival de Comédie, 1954;

Alexandre Dumas *père, Les Trois Mousquetaires,* adapted by Planchon and Théâtre de la Cité, Villeurbanne, Théâtre de la Cité, 1958;

Molière, *George Dandin,* adapted by Planchon and Théâtre de la Cité, Villeurbanne, Théâtre de la Cité, 1960;

La Remise, Villeurbanne, Théâtre de la Cité, 1962;

Armand Gatti, *La Vie imaginaire de l'éboueur Auguste G.,* adapted by Planchon and Théâtre de la Cité, Villeurbanne, Théâtre de la Cité, 1962;

O M'man Chicago, by Planchon and Jacques Rosner, Villeurbanne, Théâtre de la Cité, 1963;

Carlo Goldoni, *La Villégiature,* adapted by Planchon and Michel Arnaud, Villeurbanne, Théâtre de la Cité, 1963;

Shakespeare, *Falstaff,* adapted by Planchon from *Henry IV,* part 2, Villeurbanne, Théâtre de la Cité, 1965;

Patte blanche, Villeurbanne, Théâtre de la Cité, 1965;

Récital Maupassant, adapted by Planchon and Gérard Guillamat from Guy de Maupassant, Villeurbanne, Théâtre de la Cité, 1965;

Sean O'Casey, *Poussière pourpre,* adapted by Planchon, translated by Jacqueline Autrusseau and Maurice Goldring, Villeurbanne, Théâtre de la Cité, 1966;

Bleus, blancs, rouges, ou Les Libertins, Villeurbanne, Théâtre de la Cité, 1967; translated by John Burgess as *Blues, Whites, and Reds,* Birmingham, Repertory Theater, 1974;

John Arden, *Le dernier Adieu d'Armstrong,* adapted by Planchon, Villeurbanne, Théâtre de la Cité, 1967;

Récital Dickens, adapted by Planchon and Guillamat from Charles Dickens, Villeurbanne, Théâtre de la Cité, 1967;

Roger Vitrac, *Le Coup de Trafalgar,* adapted by Planchon and Vitrac, Villeurbanne, Théâtre de la Cité, 1968;

Dans le Vent . . . Grrr . . . , Villeurbanne, Théâtre de la Cité, 1968;

La Contestation et la mise en pièces de la plus illustre des tragédies françaises, "Le Cid," de Pierre Corneille, suivie d'une "cruelle" mise à mort de l'auteur dramatique et d'une distribution gracieuse de diverses conserves culturelles, Villeurbanne, Théâtre de la Cité, 1969;

L'Infâme, Villeurbanne, Théâtre de la Cité, 1969;

Homme pour Homme, Villeurbanne, Théâtre de la Cité, 1970;

La Langue au Chat, Villeurbanne, Théâtre de la Cité, 1972;

Marlowe, *The Massacre at Paris,* adapted by Planchon and Jean Vauthier, Villeurbanne, Théâtre National Populaire, 1972;

Le Cochon noir, Villeurbanne, Théâtre de la Cité, 11 December 1973; Paris, Théâtre de la Porte Saint-Martin, 1974;

Arthur Adamov, *A.A. Théâtres d'Arthur Adamov,* adapted by Planchon and Théâtre National Populaire, Villeurbanne, Théâtre National Populaire, 1975; Paris, Palais de Chaillot, 1976;

Edward Bond, *Lear,* adapted by Planchon, Villeurbanne, Théâtre National Populaire, 1975;

Gilles de Rais, Villeurbanne, Théâtre National Populaire, 1976;

Alice par d'obscurs chemins, Lyon, Théâtre National Populaire, 1983.

BOOKS: *Le Cochon noir; La Remise* (Paris: Gallimard, 1973);

Gilles de Rais; L'Infâme (Paris: Gallimard, 1975);

Roger Planchon (photograph by A.I.G.L.E.S.; from Yvette Daoust, Roger Planchon: Director and Playwright, *1981; Thomas Cooper Library, University of South Carolina)*

Alice par d'obscurs chemins (Paris: Editions l'Un dans l'Autre, 1986);

Les Libertins: Des Bleus, des Blancs, des Rouges, janvier 1788 – juin 1800: Une comédie (Villeurbanne: Théâtre National Populaire, 1996);

Le Radeau de la "Méduse," ou Gustave et Théo (Villeurbanne: Théâtre National Populaire, 1997);

Le vieil Hiver (Villeurbanne: Théâtre National Populaire, 1997);

Lautrec, by Planchon and Danièle Devynck (Paris: Plume, 1998);

Apprentissages: Mémoires (Paris: Plon, 2004).

PRODUCED SCRIPTS: *Dandin,* motion picture, Les Films du Losange, 1987;

Louis, enfant roi, motion picture, Les Films du Losange, 1993;

Lautrec, motion picture, Les Films du Losange, 1998.

OTHER: William Shakespeare, *King Henry IV, Part One,* introduction by Planchon (London: Folio Society, 1965);

Rajak Ohanian: Exposition, preface by Planchon (Oyonnax: Centre Culturel Louis Aragon, 1983);

Molière, *L'Avare: Comédie, 1668,* preface by Planchon (Paris: Librairie Générale Français, 1986);

Molière, *George Dandin, ou, Le mari confondu: Comédie, 1668, suivi de La Jalousie du Barbouille,* preface by Planchon (Paris: Librairie Générale Française, 1987).

SELECTED PERIODICAL PUBLICATIONS–UNCOLLECTED: "Propos sur Bertolt Brecht," *Théâtre Populaire,* no. 11 (1955): 65–67;

"Notes pour Dandin," *Théâtre Populaire,* no. 34 (1959): 47–50;

"Orthodoxies," *Théâtre Populaire,* no. 46 (1962): 117–134;

"La Mise en scène du 'Tartuffe,'" *Art et Education,* no. 21 (1969): 16–18;

Untitled text on Arthur Adamov, *Les Lettres Françaises,* 25 (March 1970): 5;

"Creating a Theatre of Real Life," *Theatre Quarterly,* 2, no. 5 (1972): 46–55;

"Un théâtre qui mobilise," *Preuves,* new series no. 18 (1974): 47–51;

"'Blues, Whites and Reds': The Humours of a History Play," translated by John Burgess, *Theatre Quarterly,* no. 15 (1974): 27–31;

"Le Sens de la marche d'Arthur Adamov par lui-même," *La Nouvelle Critique,* no. 100 (1977): 34–38;

"Taking on the TNP: Theatre as Social and Artistic Adventure," translated by Burgess, *Theatre Quarterly,* no. 25 (Spring 1977): 25–33;

"D'Artaud à Racine," *Etudes* (August 1977): 217–234.

Roger Planchon is one of the most prolific and remarkable artists to emerge in France during the 1950s. He has earned an international reputation for his work as a theater director, writer, moviemaker, and actor. He has played a key part in redefining the role of the director, he has made a significant contribution to the movement to decentralize French culture, and he has drawn critical attention to the provinces as a place of rich cultural and artistic activity.

Born on 12 September 1931 to a working-class family in Saint-Chamond, located in the department of the Loire, Planchon moved to the industrial city of Lyon at an early age with his parents, Emile Planchon and Augusta Nogier Planchon. His mother died when he was young, and he moved to the Ardèche region to live with his grandfather, where, until he was fourteen, he spent most of his time herding cattle. His working-class and provincial childhood left an indelible impression on him and his art. As a teenager Roger went to a private Jesuit school, but he never liked it and dropped out early. He was illiterate until a mentor took an interest in him and encouraged him to study painting, literature, philosophy, and cinema. Shortly thereafter, Planchon frequented the literary cafés of Lyon, where he spent time reciting the avant-garde poetry of Jean-Nicolas-Arthur Rimbaud and Henri Michaux and discussing the Surrealist works of Antonin Artaud, Georges Bataille, and Jean Genet. Planchon eventually completed his education by taking occasional courses and teaching himself. He worked as a bank clerk from 1947 to 1949. In 1948 he completed a theater internship with Henri Cordreaux and Hubert Gignoux in Lyon, where he also met Isabelle Sadoyan, a future collaborator. By the age of eighteen, he had decided to pursue a career in theater.

Besides being a voracious reader, Planchon had an early interest in American movies, especially silent pictures and 1940s Hollywood musicals. His fascination for the cinema developed into an intellectual and artistic pursuit. He became an avid reader of *Les Cahiers du Cinéma*, which began publication in 1951; well before he began to make his first serious movies in the 1970s, he adopted cinematic concepts from the journal to refine his own directing habits in the theater. Planchon married Colette Dompietrini in 1958; they have two sons.

Planchon's dramatic oeuvre does not fit into a single category. It includes his own works and plays he did not write but adapted for his productions. Besides his own plays, he has directed more than sixty works by playwrights such as William Shakespeare, Molière, Jean Racine, Pierre Carlet de Chamblain de Marivaux, Bertolt Brecht, Arthur Adamov, Michel Vinaver, Roland Dubillard, and Eugène Ionesco. Planchon is best known as a stage director, although he has received critical acclaim for his acting and for contributing new ideas to the changing social climate of the 1960s. Like other artists of his generation, he brought sociohistorical and class issues to the forefront in France, and he questioned the limits of art and, in particular, theater. Starting in the 1950s, he made a conscious effort to experiment and blend diverse forms of stagecraft from every possible source, including Elizabethan theater, American burlesque, gangster movies, Brecht, Adamov, Aristotle, and his own contemporary Jean Vilar. What sets Planchon apart from his peers is that he produced some of the first plays set specifically in the provincial regions of France. He was also one of the few directors to popularize theater aggressively by going door-to-door to invite spectators and producing publications and exhibitions so as to make theater available to an audience of everyday workers. In his dramatic works he rendered palpable the controversies and difficult sociopolitical realities of provincial working-class life.

Planchon's theatrical career began in 1949, when he and a group of friends—Claude Lochy, Robert Gilbert, Sadoyan, and Georges Barrier—formed an amateur theater company. They first performed a play by Lochy, *Les Chemins clos* (1949, Closed Roads), in a small theater in Lyon. The group experimented with a range of comic traditions, mixing styles that included slapstick from American movies; French mime from the tradition of Jacques Lecoq, Marcel Marceau, and Jean-Louis Barrault; and the Surrealist humor of Alfred Jarry and Roger Vitrac.

Planchon's earliest role models were the Surrealist poets and avant-garde dramatists such as Artaud and Brecht. In 1950 he made his debut as a director, winning a regional prize for his unconventional direction of Georges Courteline's *Bottines et collets montés* in Mâcon. The prize of Fr 25,000 enabled the troupe to establish itself as a semiprofessional company called Le Théâtre de la Comédie (TCV), a name that became official in 1952. Planchon and the TCV continued to improvise with burlesque in their adaptations of many plays, such as *Les Aventures de Rocambole* (1952, The Adventures of Rocambole), by Lucien Dabril, and *Burlesque-digest* (1953), an adaptation of works by Jean Tardieu.

After the burlesque series TCV adapted several Elizabethan classics. Their adaptation of Shakespeare's *Twelfth Night* (1601) as *La Nuit des Rois* (Night of Kings) for a 1952 municipal festival in Lyon attracted the notice of international groups, who invited the troupe to perform outside of the city, thus helping the company to establish a wider reputation. From 1951 to 1952 TCV developed a repertoire of classic and Surrealist plays, including Christopher Marlowe's *Dr. Faustus* (1594), Shakespeare's *Twelfth Night* and *The Merry Wives of Windsor* (1600), René Char's *Claire* (1952), and *La Vie est un songe,* an adaptation of Pedro Calderón de la

Planchon as Duverger and Jean Bouise as Célestin in the 1969 production at the Théâtre Montparnasse, Paris, of Planchon's L'Infâme *(1969, The Villain), based on the true story of a priest who murdered his pregnant mistress (photograph by Bernand; from Yvette Daoust,* Roger Planchon: Director and Playwright, *1981; Thomas Cooper Library, University of South Carolina)*

Barca's *La Vida es sueño* (1635, Life Is a Dream). In 1952 TCV found an abandoned printing plant in Lyon and, despite the substandard acoustics of the building, converted it into the company's own theater space.

Planchon's career took a significant turn when Brecht and the Berliner Ensemble visited Paris to perform Brecht's *Mutter Courage und ihre Kinder* (1941; translated as *Mother Courage and Her Children,* 1966) in 1954. Planchon did not see the production because his own troupe was performing Brecht's *Der gute Mensch von Sezuan* (1943; translated as *The Good Woman of Setzuan,* 1948) at the same time, but he met the playwright when the Berliner Ensemble returned in 1955 to perform Brecht's *Der kaukasische Kreidekreis* (1948; translated as *The Caucasian Chalk Circle,* 1948). After a transforming conversation, Planchon became convinced of the need to research Brecht's concept of epic theater. Brecht taught him that a director should produce plays in which the visual, or dramatic, and written, or scenic, components share an equal responsibility onstage. Each play produced should have a specific social context and seem relevant to the contemporary viewer.

Planchon adopted Brechtian techniques in his own works while TCV produced several avant-garde plays, including Adamov's *Le Sens de la marche* (1953, The Meaning of the March) and *Le Professeur Taranne* (1953, Professor Taranne). Adamov and Planchon became friends and collaborators out of their shared interest in Artaud and the Elizabethan tradition. In 1954 Adamov adapted Heinrich Von Kleist's *Der zerbrochne Krug* (1811; translated as *The Broken Jug,* 1939) and a burlesque version of Marlowe's *Edward II* (1592) for TCV. During this same period Planchon also directed Vitrac's vaudeville show *Victor, ou les enfants au pouvoir* (1928, Victor, or the Children in Power) and Ionesco's *Amédée ou comment s'en débarasser* (1954; translated as *Amédée or How to Get Rid of It,* 1958), about the difficulties of distinguishing reality from illusion.

In 1956 Planchon met Vinaver after the latter sent him the script of his *Aujourd'hui, ou Les Coréens* (1956, Today, or The Koreans). Their common interest in Brechtian alienation techniques led to friendship and collaboration. From 1957 to 1961 Planchon produced some of Brecht's plays that best exemplify epic theater as the art of estrangement, including an adaptation of *Der gute Mensch von Sezuan* as *La Bonne Âme de Sé-Tchouan*; *Grand-peur et misère du Troisième Reich*, originally *Furcht und Elend des III. Reich* (1938, Fear and Misery of the Third Reich; translated as *The Private Life of the Master Race*, 1944); and *Schweyk dans la deuxième guerre mondiale*, originally *Schweyk im zweiten Weltkrieg* (1957; translated as *Schweyk in the Second World War*, 1967). Critics viewed these productions as "imitations" of the author's style. In 1957 Planchon adopted Brecht's alienation techniques in a production of Adamov's *Paolo Paoli* (1957), which critics hailed as one of Planchon's and Adamov's finest plays in the Brechtian mode. During the production, Brecht-inspired projections appeared on the walls, interrupting the flow of the narrative so as to remind the audience of the historical veracity of the context of the play. The images gave the impression of a documentary, and painted backdrops with slogans and logos helped to draw comparisons between past and contemporary social ills.

By the end of 1957, TCV had achieved a new level of professionalism. The members agreed to sacrifice themselves for the benefit of the company and perform all week in addition to working their daytime jobs. That same year, Planchon publicly expressed his desire to decentralize and make theater a form of public service. Theater, he argued, should be for the people and reflect the sociopolitical concerns of the time. To this end, TCV distributed questionnaires among the people of the provincial town of Villeurbanne, near Lyon, asking which plays they wanted to see. By popular request, Planchon staged Shakespeare's *Henry IV* (circa 1596–1597), with part 1 titled *Le Prince* and part 2 titled *Falstaff*, but in productions quite different from those done in Paris at the Théâtre National Populaire (TNP). Planchon's interpretation of *Henry IV* combined two styles: heightened, Brechtian theatricality and classical realism. Set against a backdrop of massive shifting maps that situated the plays in a real historical setting, the productions made the implicit conflicts explicit.

Following *Henry IV*, Planchon directed Lochy's adaptation of Alexandre Dumas *père*'s romantic comedy *Les Trois Mousquetaires* (1844; translated as *The Three Musketeers*, 1846) in 1958. Planchon and Lochy edited the script into a series of thematic indications, leaving the actors room to improvise. Planchon's interpretation mocked Dumas's romantic vision by the insertion of indications of the social world not obvious in the text, such as a romantic scene between Buckingham and the queen set against the backdrop of a worker standing on a ladder dusting off a chandelier.

In 1958, with the help of Jacques Rosner, Planchon wrote his own play, *O M'man Chicago*, which was staged in 1963. In preparation for writing it, he researched the legend of the American gangster Al Capone. The play explores Capone's life, the distorted facts of his career, and the realities of the Prohibition era. Written in the underworld slang of the period, the script is divided into nineteen tableaux that are punctuated with Lochy's song-and-dance creations, reminiscent of classical *comédie-ballets* (comedies with music and dancing). The TCV's production of *O M'man Chicago* explored the dispute between Capone's Sicilian criminals and their Irish competitors in the illegal business of alcohol trade. When Capone decides to "come clean," he realizes his own dependence on crime because he needs capital to create a new business. He continues bootlegging and other criminal activities to build his savings, and just as he achieves prosperity, the 1929 stock-market crash ruins him. Also depicted is the famous trial in which he is convicted for income-tax evasion. Capone's character is presented through the words of three dream figures, M'man Chicago (representing Capone's mother and the city of Chicago), Food Daddy's Fog (a metaphor for the Windy City), and Pottawattomie (a crippled Indian and sole survivor of a tribe otherwise exterminated by white men). The dream figures act as projections of Capone's imagination and show the private world of a lawbreaker. Despite the extensive research Planchon did for *O M'man Chicago*, the French public was not aware enough of the cultural importance of Capone to understand the critical depiction of an American society that allows gangsters to come to power. Instead, the play was seen as entertainment.

In 1959 André Malraux—then the French minister of culture—joined efforts to decentralize state-subsidized theaters in France. These theaters were divided into three categories: the lowest paid, or *troupe permanente* (permanent company); the middle category, or *centre dramatique* (dramatic center); and the highest paid, *maison de culture* (cultural center). In 1959 TCV became the first subsidized *troupe permanente* to be located in the provinces rather than in Paris, and by 1963 the company had been promoted to the highest status of subsidized theater, *maison de culture*. Planchon accepted the offer because the municipal TCV theater was dilapidated. The group made Villeurbanne, where they had already won a local following, the new national dramatic center of provincial France.

As director of the new Théâtre Municipal de Villeurbanne, Planchon's artistic reputation expanded,

Roger Blin as the Hermit in the 1974 production at the Théâtre de la Porte Saint-Martin, Paris, of Planchon's Le Cochon noir *(1973, The Black Pig), a play set at the time of the Paris Commune that explores the conflict between old and new values in a village (photograph by Rajak Ohanian; from Yvette Daoust,* Roger Planchon: Director and Playwright, *1981; Thomas Cooper Library, University of South Carolina)*

and his creative vision attracted attention. Shortly after 1964 he gave many interviews in which he stated that a play finds its meaning only off the page and that the director alone has the power to choose the appropriate *langage scénique* (scenic language), a concept rendering the power of the script and the playwright equal to a director's visual and auditory interpretative powers. Planchon intimated that any script—whether contemporary or classical—is only as meaningful as a director's choices and the production elements (costumes, set design, actors, lighting, and music) make the text look and sound.

With Planchon as director and with the status of a *maison de culture,* TCV-Villeurbanne took the liberty of experimenting with the French classics, especially those considered immutable texts, such as Marivaux's *La Seconde Surprise de l'amour* (1727, The Second Surprise of Love), Molière's *Le Tartuffe* (1669), and Racine's *Bérénice* (1670). Unlike classical interpretations, which focused on bringing the psychology of the characters to the forefront, these plays as directed by Planchon shifted the audience's attention to the larger historical context of the period in which they were written, thus creating a dialogue between contemporary social attitudes and those of the past.

In 1960 Planchon produced Molière's *George Dandin* (1668), a production for which he became famous. (He later directed and wrote the screenplay for the 1987 motion-picture adaptation, *Dandin.*) Once again straying from traditional interpretations, with designer René Allio he sought to create a contemporary version of a classic that compared the social attitudes of the seventeenth century with those of 1960s France. Whereas in Molière's original version Dandin, a rich peasant who tries to escape his class by marrying a rich demoiselle, is the object of ridicule, Planchon's production examined the social contradictions and background that manipulated Dandin's destiny. The set—a realistic farmyard with mud and hay—re-created the atmosphere of seventeenth-century peasant life in the provinces. TCV continued to perform the play through 1970.

In 1961 Planchon wrote the first of his "provincial" plays, *La Remise* (1962). The others, *L'Infâme* (1969, The Villain), *Le Cochon noir* (1973, The Black

Pig), and *Gilles de Rais* (1975), were produced during a long period of cultural turmoil in France. On one hand, these plays are closer to late-nineteenth-century naturalism in their portrayal of the material conditions of lower-class life than to the critical realism that Planchon claimed to admire in Brecht's plays. On the other hand, Planchon's staging of these plays added a degree of antinaturalism to their look and feel. They are classified as "provincial" because they expose the realities and hardships of peasant life and the rural communities that survive in the provinces. Largely influenced by the works of the American writers William Faulkner, Herman Melville, and J. D. Salinger, the plays dramatize questions about the human condition in the context of peasant life. They are also filled with visual details reminiscent of Planchon's childhood surroundings.

La Remise underwent a series of revisions before being published in 1973. The title refers to many ideas but primarily to the act of resetting something in its place, or to a storage space or shed. The published version covers the time period from the end of World War I in 1918 until the fall of Dien Bien Phu in 1954. The story develops from a police investigation into the murder of Emile Chausson, the grandfather of Paul Chausson. The murder brings Paul back to the village of Borée, where, to his surprise, he rediscovers the origins of his own father, Célestin. In the opening scene of the play, Célestin lies dying in a city hospital with Paul at his side. The plot focuses on the psychological journey of Paul, the protagonist and outsider.

In the second version of *La Remise*, Planchon omitted the narrator present in the first version and followed the Aristotelian model, wherein each inquiry leading up to the grandfather's murder has a presentation, climax, and outcome. Unlike the naturalistic facade and classical structure of the plot, the inquiries are played out simultaneously before an antinatural, Brecht-inspired fragmented stage design, otherwise known as a *décor explosé* (exploded set). Multiple stages allow different scenes, times, and perceptions of reality to interconnect. The dying father, for example, is visible on stage, as is the *remise* (shed) in Borée where each inquiry is recounted. All the events leading up to the murder are told from various points of view–those of the police, a country doctor, a witness, and characters who fought in World War I. As a result, the reasons for Emile's murder are not easily explained, and the play is far from being didactic. Instead, *La Remise* sets up a personal dilemma that reflects–at least symbolically–an historical one. The events in the story are linked to a larger and more complex web of international politics and ideological, spiritual, and social problems. The effects of the outer world slowly take their toll on the dynamic provincial village of Borée. Economic and industrial changes, the exodus of country youth to urban centers, and a mountainside reforestation project cause major shifts in the landscape and in the relations among members of the Chausson family. In the reconstruction of events, Paul, Emile, Gabriel, and other characters struggle to find their place and function in a changing world. Each faces the responsibility of making a choice. In order to survive, they invent new values in a world where a man's worth was once inextricably linked to the land on which generations before him had depended, an idea that Planchon's other provincial plays develop further.

In 1967 Planchon looked back at another defining moment in French history with *Bleus, blancs, rouges, ou Les Libertins* (Blues, Whites, Reds, or The Libertines), a dramatization of the French Revolution. The play has gone through a series of revisions and was published in 1996. It was one of Planchon's first works to be produced abroad by the British directors John Burgess and Michael Simpson, whose company, the Birmingham Repertory Theater, staged it in 1974 as *Blues, Whites, and Reds*. Sometimes criticized for being too intellectual, *Bleus, blancs, rouges* presents the French Revolution in the years 1789 and 1800 in a series of nonlinear tableaux. The title refers to the different political camps into which France was divided at the time: white, for the aristocrats; blue, for the common people; and red, for the revolutionaries. The play is set in various places: France, émigré routes, Florence, and Milan. It is also told through multiple but unpredictably interconnected points of view.

Bleus, blancs, rouges questions the human and moral dilemmas that result from participating in or being a victim of the revolution. The plot follows the adventures of a wide range of characters, and in doing so, it explores the long-term effects of the revolution on different classes, as well as the desire to escape history unscathed. The play specifically treats the moral dilemmas faced by characters who emigrate together: Aubier d'Arbonne, the libertine aristocrat leader who refuses to marry Maurille, a young bourgeoise; Aubier's brother, a homosexual archbishop, and his associates; Mme Renoir, the mother of Maurille, and her old companion, Mlle Mignot; and Edouard Thierry, Maurille's lover, who also happens to be the archbishop's favorite. In the end, Mme Renoir's servants stay behind to join different revolutionary camps, and she herself is guillotined. Thierry is killed fighting for the royalist cause, and the archbishop survives by begging his friends in other countries to save him. Aubier, Maurille, and Mlle Mignot survive but become impoverished and depend on theft, arms trafficking, and prostitution to survive.

The first version of the play, set in the provinces and in Paris, focused on a tortured love affair between

Fanny Reman, Nelly Borgeaud, Patrick Messe, Colette Dompietrini, Gérard Guillaumat, Anne Cariel, and Guy Tréjan in a scene from Planchon's 1976 production in Villeurbanne of Molière's Le Tartuffe *(1669), which he first directed in 1962 (photograph by Etienne George; from* L'Avant Scène: Théâtre, *1977; Thomas Cooper Library, University of South Carolina)*

Aubier and Maurille. The second version, which Planchon produced in 1971, was more politicized, and *Les Libertins* was dropped from the title, although it was reinstated for the 1996 published text. Set in the provinces of France and Italy, the second version suggests that the revolution left the provinces with little more than dreams deferred. Power passed not from the hands of aristocrats to the commoners who actually fought in the revolution but to the hands of the bourgeoisie. Those who survived the events—libertines, aristocrats, clergymen, and revolutionaries—overcame obstacles because they lived by and for an ideology, however flawed. Even the morally inconsistent characters who believe in a cause become respectable citizens in Napoleon's empire, whereas the passive, uncritical characters are killed, hurt, or impoverished.

After *La Remise* the sociocultural revolution of May 1968 helped Planchon to occupy a more prominent place in the French theatrical scene. Like his contemporaries Barrault, who directed the Théâtre de l'Odéon in Paris, and Ariane Mnouchkine and her troupe, the Théâtre du Soleil (Theater of the Sun), Planchon and TCV joined discussions about how theater could participate in the changing social context and progressive rhetoric of the times. He became an activist who believed that theater could mobilize people to act against social injustice and could change cultural attitudes toward privilege and class. Planchon's powerful public statements about theater, the responsibility of the director, and mise-en-scène (staging) transformed critical perceptions about the director's role in France after 1968.

The events of 1968 inspired Planchon and TCV to attempt *la création collective* (collective creation), a new dramatic genre with Marxist political undertones. *Créations collectives* were scripts and productions composed by a company as a group effort. French companies producing them tended to live as well as work together in a communal environment. They refused hierarchies among actors, directors, and writers, choosing instead to create texts together through improvisation. Collective creations rendered the notions of "author" and "director" obsolete.

At the same time, TCV was drawn to *le théâtre populaire* (popular theater), a highly politicized experiment in 1960s France. After 1968, many artists agreed to make theater more intellectually accessible and financially affordable to a wider, popular public, especially by selling tickets at low cost. Planchon and his troupe had been working collectively since the 1950s; contrary to the contemporary trend of renouncing the director in favor of the collective, after 1968 Planchon became known as the director and author of his troupe's productions. Nonetheless, he and TCV participated actively in redetermining artistic standards to attract a wider range of people to the theater. In 1968 Planchon also opened a new cinema, the Cinéma National Populaire, in Lyon, with the goal of offering quality movies to the provincial public at an accessible price.

In 1969, soon after Planchon had read Bataille's *Le Procès de Gilles de Rais* (1959, The Trial of Gilles de Rais), he wrote his second provincial play, *L'Infâme*, first published in 1970 in the journal *Travail Théâtral* and published in book form in 1975. The play is based on the true account of a parish priest, l'Abbé Desnoyers, from the village of Uruffe in Lorraine. Desnoyers murdered his mistress, a local girl nine months pregnant with his child. He cut out the fetus and christened and killed it, disfiguring it so that it would not be recognized as his. This incident shocked the country, and the controversial trial inspired several plays, movies, novels, and studies.

Planchon was eager to adapt the story of Desnoyers because he felt that the effects of the incident permeated all French social classes and raised questions about the Catholic identity of the nation. In *L'Infâme* the real-life characters and places are renamed (the priest is Duverger, and the village is Lauzun, in the Ardèche region), and the incident itself is not presented. Rather, the play investigates the response of the community to the event after it has happened and implicitly questions the ecclesiastical hierarchy and principles by showing how church members react to what happened after the crime. *L'Infâme* points out a variety of moral dilemmas brought to light by the crime and seems to adopt a compassionate view of Duverger. Everyone is guilty in the end. The peasants are prisoners of a limited vocabulary in the same way that the priests are prisoners isolated by the principles of their faith. The audience is left to decide if Duverger was driven to the act by shame and the pressures of the Church. The play ends with the arrest of the priest.

In 1969 Planchon and TCV reflected on the events of 1968 by attacking seventeenth-century playwright Pierre Corneille in a collective creation called *La Mise en pièces du "Cid."* The witty title refers to the project TCV had in mind: it means both a tearing to pieces and a staging of multiple versions of *Le Cid* (1637), one of Corneille's best-known tragedies. The original full title expressed this goal in a more satirical fashion: *La Contestation et la mise en pièces de la plus illustre des tragédies françaises, "Le Cid," de Pierre Corneille, suivie d'une "cruelle" mise à mort de l'auteur dramatique et d'une distribution gracieuse de diverses conserves culturelles* (The Contestation and Tearing to Pieces of the Most Illustrious of French Tragedies, "Le Cid," by Pierre Corneille, Followed by a "Cruel" Putting to Death of the Playwright and a Gracious Distribution of Diverse Cultural Preserves). Not only did the play mock Corneille, it also satirized German playwright Peter Weiss's 1964 play with an equally long title: *Die Verfolgung und Ermordung Jean-Paul Marats, dargestellt durch die Schauspielgruppe des Hospizes zu Charenton unter Anleitung des Herrn de Sade* (translated as *The Persecution and Assassination of Jean-Paul Marat as Performed by the Inmates of the Asylum of Charenton under the Direction of the Marquis de Sade*, 1965).

TCV's play was a farce and dealt with what the troupe considered to be the "impasse" of theater in the 1960s, when it seemed that drama had become stifled by tradition. The French government subsidized, or at least considered "appropriate" theater, only the texts of the "greats," such as Shakespeare, Corneille, and Racine. In reaction to this trend, *La Mise en pièces du "Cid"* begins with the question "What is theater?" The play concludes with an open-ended answer: theater can be anything as long as it is dramatic. *La Mise en pièces du "Cid"* is a satirical collage of diverse theatrical styles, from lighthearted slapstick to academic theater. It mocks revolutionary and academic approaches to theater; it makes light of anything too serious, such as censorship and the predictable styles of well-known directors. The play goes so far as to critique TCV's own predictability and the limits of its persistently radical repertoire. Besides being self-reflexive, the play is above all a reflection on the problematic relationship between French theater companies and the government that subsidizes them. It asks how artists can be free to create when the government has the final say on what is deemed an appropriate repertoire for the public. *La Mise en pièces du "Cid"* ends with Corneille stuffed into a dustbin and a statement that suggests the events of 1968 will become their own myth.

In the early 1970s Planchon was invited by Jacques Duhamel, the French minister of cultural affairs, to replace Vilar as director of the Théâtre National Populaire, located in the Palais de Chaillot in Paris. The TNP's influence and reputation had waned since Vilar's resignation following the events of May 1968. Planchon accepted, on condition that the company stay close to the audience it had cultivated in Villeurbanne. He renamed the already existing TCV the Théâtre National Populaire-Villeurbanne. This change brought new success to the company and introduced new directors Gilbert and Patrice Chéreau. (Chéreau later became famous.) With this newly subsidized company Planchon toured France and the rest of Europe.

In 1972 Planchon, sensing the effects of television on French society, created the musical comedy *La Langue au Chat* (The Cat's Tale). The play, which is organized into a collage of television programs, examines the disease of mass deception. The world Planchon depicts is governed by televised images, where the notion of anything "natural" is deformed and where individualism and ideology cease to exist. Inspired by Ben Jonson's 1610 play *The Alchemist* (and, it seems, by Brecht's *Schweyk im zweiten Weltkrieg*), Planchon set *La Langue au Chat* in France in the year 2000, after a civil war in which half of the French population has been exterminated. The government decides to save the remaining survivors, devoid of hope, from committing suicide by assigning them a new, spiritually visionary leader, Le Chat (The Cat), a television personality (played by Planchon in the 1975 production). As the new minister of culture and information, Le Chat promises to inaugurate a new era. Working with designer Max Schoendorff, Planchon created a set consisting of an industrialized, claustrophobic underground studio with nothing natural, only bulky machinery and steely props. As a character Le Chat is an ambiguous imposter who neither collaborates with nor completely resists the authorities. He tells the people they are being "fooled," but he also realizes the power he has over his television viewers. Eventually, Le Chat is denounced as a delirious fraud, but the audience is left wondering about the future of this self-annihilating civilization.

In 1973 Planchon wrote and produced his third peasant play, *Le Cochon noir,* with the TNP-Villeurbanne, for which he won the Ibsen Prize in 1974. The play is set in 1871 during *la semaine sanglante* (the bloody week) of the Paris Commune, when the Communards were executed. For Planchon the Paris Commune represented a turning point in French history, an event during which the proletariat took control and social order was challenged. Planchon sets the play in a provincial region resembling the Ardèche of his childhood.

Le Cochon noir tells the story of village inhabitants who, far from the events taking place in Paris, feel the effects of the Commune. Unlike *La Remise* and *L'Infâme,* which reenact an inquiry into the past, this play takes place in the present. As in Planchon's other provincial plays, the opening depicts a critical event. A village thug named Gédéon rapes a young woman, Violette, on her wedding day. Violette is terrified to admit the truth to anybody, and as a result the community sends her into isolation because they believe she is possessed by the devil. A character known as the Hermit (he is also the village sorcerer) intervenes and subsequently competes with the local parish priest for spiritual control of the villagers. The parish priest, portrayed as a lecherous old womanizer, denounces the Hermit on his deathbed. To prove the priest and villagers wrong, the Hermit cures Violette by performing a pagan-Christian exorcism, after which she disappears and commits suicide.

Le Cochon noir shows the complex relationship between a late-nineteenth-century provincial community's pagan beliefs and the events of the Paris Commune, along with the modern values of the industrial age that the city represents. The village and its rituals seem backward and abnormal, but Planchon suggests that villagers at that time were physically isolated from the capital and therefore lived by moral codes quite different from those of the Communards. The effects of the Commune are felt in the provinces, despite physical isolation. This idea is best illustrated through Violette's bridegroom, Toin, who returns from Paris wounded and using a cane. At the wedding feast the sense of loss is also noticeable in the greater attendance of women than men. In addition, the influence of the city on the country is made clear by a stage design in which the events of Paris are placed in the background while those in the village are placed in the foreground. The underlying questions about community and the moral codes one lives by are explored by the staging of Violette's suicide at the same time as the massacre of the innocent Communards. The end of the play suggests that life will go on after these events. While the community is at fault, it cannot resolve the moral hypocrisies that history has made possible.

In 1974 Planchon was deeply affected by the death of his friend and collaborator Adamov. To honor Adamov, he and the TNP-Villeurbanne created *A.A. Théâtres d'Arthur Adamov* (A.A. Plays of Arthur Adamov), a collage of excerpts from Adamov's plays, memoirs, and other writings in five tableaux, which was first staged in 1975. Planchon and the troupe did not alter Adamov's plays as much as reveal, through the scenes they chose, recurring motifs in the playwright's work: a repressive family background and a fear of women that resulted in psychological impotence. The production also illustrated the tension between Adamov's desire to become involved with others and his overpowering feeling of isolation caused by the pressures of modern life. *A.A. Théâtres d'Arthur Adamov* also examined Adamov's lifelong hesitancy toward political commitment, a theme the writer himself tried to illustrate in *Paolo Paoli*. In Planchon's view, Adamov's plays were imperfect and for that reason among the most flexible and

Planchon as Gilles and Michel Beaune as Jean Blouyn in the 1976 Théâtre National Populaire production in Paris of Planchon's Gilles de Rais *(1975), about a fifteenth-century knight who fought along with Joan of Arc and was named field marshal of France but was later executed amid allegations of heresy and child murder (photograph by Etienne George; from Yvette Daoust,* Roger Planchon: Director and Playwright, *1981; Thomas Cooper Library, University of South Carolina)*

important for young directors. For Planchon, Adamov played a critical role in encouraging innovation among young directors such as Vilar, Roger Blin, Mnouchkine, Jacques Mauclair, and Jean-Marie Serreau, all of whom were Planchon's contemporaries and had engaged in the movement to decentralize French theater in the 1960s.

Planchon's fourth peasant play, *Gilles de Rais,* to some extent resembles *L'Infâme*. Published in 1975 and first produced in 1976, the play fictionalizes the life of Gilles de Rais, the insane *maréchal de France* (field marshal of France) and knight, who was Joan of Arc's comrade in arms. A lover of spectacle, in 1435 he reconstructed the 1429 Battle of Orléans so he could play his own role as heroic knight again; he even planned his own funeral. In 1440, charged with the practice of alchemy and the sexual abuse, torture, and murder of more than a hundred children, he was condemned for heresy by an ecclesiastical court and sentenced to death by a civil court for murder. (Although in the play and in other popular accounts he is sentenced to burn at the stake, he was actually hanged.)

Like many of Planchon's characters, Gilles de Rais embodies the contradictions of a ruined hero.

Unlike the three other peasant plays that are specifically about peasant characters, *Gilles de Rais* resembles more nearly a medieval morality play that examines the religious and pagan beliefs of medieval society. As the play explores the life of Gilles de Rais, it questions his eccentricities, position, and reception in a prescientific, superstitious society. It asks why he was considered a criminal and how burning him at the stake could be justified. The first half of the play exposes Gilles de Rais's contradictions. The second half stages his trial, juxtaposing the inner workings of his ruined mind with the community's self-righteous condemnation and execution of a madman it believes possessed by evil spirits.

In the 1980s Planchon turned some of his attention to directing and acting in movies, leaving his duties at the TNP-Villeurbanne. His departure resulted in the eventual breakup of the company in 1995. Planchon's best-known motion pictures show traces of his affinity for mixing drama and realism, as well as his tendency to portray different historical periods and social climates. The movies he acted in include *Molière* (1978), *Le Retour de Martin Guerre* (1982, The Return of Martin Guerre), *Danton* (1983), *Camille Claudel* (1988), and *Leclerc, un rêve d'Indochine* (2003, Leclerc, a Dream of Indochina). He directed and wrote the screenplays for *Dandin*, the 1987 adaptation of Molière's *George Dandin*; *Louis, enfant roi* (1993, Louis, Child King); and *Lautrec* (1998). Planchon's movies have achieved some critical success for their original style, but his greatest accomplishment was the popular and collective theater he produced with the TCV in the 1950s and 1960s.

Planchon continued writing, acting, and producing plays in the 1980s. His later plays, such as *Alice par d'obscurs chemins* (1983, Alice along Obscure Paths), underscore his persistent obsession with inquiry into the past. In this case the story opens through Alice, a French student, who meets F. Scott Fitzgerald in a reverie while she is researching his life with Zelda Fitzgerald. Other late plays include *Le vieil Hiver* (Old Winter), *Fragile Forêt* (Fragile Forest), and *Les Voyages Extraordinaires* (Extraordinary Voyages), all published in *Collections Théâtres* in 1987. Planchon has been honored in France with the Prix Georges Lherminier du Syndicat de la critique dramatique (1986), the Chevalier des Arts et des Lettres, the croix de guerre, and the Chevalier Légion d'honneur (all in 1998).

Even after Planchon joined the movements to popularize theater and compose collective creations, he remained the primary decision maker in his theater. He made the final choices for each production, even if he collaborated with the actors and set and costume designers. Without the artistic contributions of his company members, Planchon could not have realized the productions for which he remains famous. Nevertheless, critics argue that his insistence on the director's authority created the potential for directors to neglect the collaborative value of theater and instead view themselves as all-powerful in deciding the final form of a play.

Roger Planchon has made repeated attempts to reinterpret the notion of "traditional" theater. He represents a significant contribution to twentieth-century drama for many reasons but especially for his curious and bold creative drive and for his ability to reinterpret classics in fresh ways. His dedication to popular theater and movies, his desire to reach audiences beyond the middle class, and his experimentation with new ideas and dramatic forms—despite the quarrels over government subsidies such experiments provoked—have made him a vigorous participant in discussions about the possibilities of art. The plays Planchon wrote are historically grounded and can be read as contributions to the analysis of a basic human dilemma: people are both creators of and created by history and the societies to which they belong.

Interviews:

"Conversation avec Planchon: Le Living et Grotowski," *Art et Education*, no. 21 (1969): 42–48;

"Journée débat avec Roger Planchon," *Art et Education*, nos. 22–23 (1969): 15–95;

"Marx, les fruits et la speculation: A propos de Par-dessus bord," interview with Michel Vinaver, Emile Breton, and François Hincker, *La Nouvelle Critique*, no. 85 (1975): 34–37;

"Un théâtre qui tient compte de l'histoire: Après 'Le Tartuffe' et 'Le Cochon noir,'" interview with Annie Ubersfeld, Antoine Casanova, Jean-Pierre Léonardini, and Michel Bataillon, *La Nouvelle Critique*, no. 85 (1975): 21–29;

"Entretien de Michel Bataillon avec Roger Planchon," *La Nouvelle Critique*, no. 100 (1977): 34–38;

"I'm a Museum Guard," interview with Rosette Lamont, *Performing Arts Journal*, 16, no. 6 (1981): 97–109.

References:

David Bradby, *Modern French Drama, 1940–1980* (Cambridge & New York: Cambridge University Press, 1984);

Bradby, *The Theatre of Roger Planchon* (Cambridge & Teaneck, N.J.: Chadwyck-Healy/Consortium for Drama and Media in Higher Education, 1984);

John Burgess, "Roger Planchon's 'The Black Pig' at Villeurbanne," *Theatre Quarterly*, no. 14 (1974): 56–86;

Dan M. Church, "Roger Planchon," in *Theatrical Directors: A Biographical Dictionary,* edited by John W. Frick and Stephen M. Vallillo (Westport, Conn.: Greenwood Press, 1994), pp. 314–316;

Gilles Colpart, "Dandin," *La Revue du cinema*, no. 435 (1988): 29–31;

Emile Copfermann, *Roger Planchon* (Lausanne: Editions l'Age d'Homme, 1969);

Copfermann, *Théâtres de Roger Planchon* (Paris: Union Générale d'Editions, 1977);

Yvette Daoust, *Roger Planchon, Director and Playwright* (Cambridge & New York: Cambridge University Press, 1981);

Jean Duvignaud and others, *Itinéraire de Roger Planchon, 1953–1964* (Paris: L'Arche, 1970);

Phyllis Hartnoll, "Roger Planchon," in *The Oxford Companion to the Theatre,* edited by Hartnoll, fourth edition (Oxford: Oxford University Press, 1983), pp. 644–645;

Michael Kustow, "Roger Planchon: Actor, Director, Playwright," *Theatre Quarterly*, no. 5 (1972): 42–57.

Yasmina Reza

(1 May 1959 –)

Inas Messiha
Pennsylvania State University

PLAY PRODUCTIONS: *Conversations après un enterrement,* Paris, Théâtre-Villette, 15 January 1986;

La Traversée de l'hiver, Orléans, Centre Dramatique d'Orléans, 6 October 1989;

Art, Berlin, 1994; Paris, Comédie des Champs-Elysées, 28 October 1994; London, Royal Shakespeare Company at the Barbican, 1998;

L'Homme du hasard, Paris, Théâtre Hébertot, 19 September 1995;

Trois versions de la vie, Paris, Théâtre Antoine, 7 November 2000;

Une Pièce espagnole: théâtre, Paris, Théâtre de la Madeleine, January 2004.

BOOKS: *Conversations après un enterrement* (Arles: Actes Sud / Paris: Papiers, 1986); translated by Christopher Hampton as *Conversations after a Burial* (London: Faber & Faber, 2000);

La Traversée de l'hiver (Arles: Actes Sud, 1989);

Art (Arles: Actes Sud, 1994); translated by Hampton as *Art* (London: Faber & Faber, 1996);

L'Homme du hasard (Arles: Actes-Sud, 1995); translated by Hampton as *The Unexpected Man* (London & Boston: Faber & Faber, 1998);

Hammerklavier: récit (Paris: Michel, 1997); translated by Carol Gosman (London: Faber & Faber, 2000; New York: G. Braziller, 2000);

Une Désolation: roman (Paris: Michel, 1999); translated by Carol Brown Janeway as *Desolation* (London: Hamilton, 2002; New York: Knopf, 2002);

Le Pique-nique de Lulu Kreutz (Paris: Michel, 1999);

Trois versions de la vie (Paris: Michel, 2000); translated by Hampton as *Life x 3* (London: Faber & Faber, 2000);

Adam Haberberg: roman (Paris: Michel, 2002);

Une Pièce espagnole: théâtre (Paris: Michel, 2004).

Collection: *Théâtre* (Paris: Michel, 1997)–comprises *Conversations après un enterrement, La Traversée de l'hiver,* and *Art;* enlarged, 1999–includes *L'Homme du hasard.*

Yasmina Reza, 6 June 1998, in New York with the Tony Award for Best Play, Art, *first performed and published 1994*
(© Getty Images)

PRODUCED SCRIPT: *Le Pique-nique de Lulu Kreutz: un film de Didier Martiny,* motion picture, Polydor international GmbH, 2000.

Yasmina Reza gained fame at the age of twenty-three with her first play, *Conversations après un enterrement* (produced and published, 1986; translated as *Conversa-*

tions after a Burial, 2000). Her plays have been translated into thirty-five languages and shown throughout the world—in Paris, Berlin, London, Tokyo, Bombay, Johannesburg, Buenos Aires, Cairo, Bratislava, Vienna, Athens, New York, Stockholm, and Israel. Critics have judged her work alternately as intelligent, elegant, and intriguing as well as bitter, nihilistic, trivial, and hollow. The presence of comic elements does not lessen the gravity of her themes, such as the fear of aging and the effect of time on dreams and desires. She writes about the concerns of the middle class, especially social status, modernism, art, and relationships. Most of her characters are bewildered but highly conscious of their lives, which they view, often bitterly, as failures.

Reza was born 1 May 1959 in Paris, the daughter of a Hungarian violinist mother and a Russian-Iranian father. Reza's maternal grandparents had moved from Hungary to New York when the Iron Curtain fell, but her musician mother decided to settle in Paris. Her father, a businessman, came from a Russian Jewish family of Spanish and Persian ancestry. (Their name was Gedaliah until the nineteenth century, and the part of Reza's family that immigrated to Israel took back that name. Like many Persian Jews, her grandparents had taken a common Persian name to avoid persecution.) Reza's grandfather was a traveling salesman living in Moscow when her father was born in 1918 during the middle of the Russian Revolution. Fleeing Bolshevism, her grandfather moved his family once again to safety, this time to Paris. With her parents, Reza spoke English mixed with other languages. She had a cosmopolitan experience during her childhood in this well-off, artistic, music-loving, open-minded family, whose friends came from many countries. She spent her vacations in Switzerland or Austria witnessing the lifestyle of the last generation of cosmopolitan Central Europeans.

Reza started writing at age seven. She received her *baccalauréat* (high-school degree) at age sixteen and, in her early twenties, her *license* (B.A.) in sociology and theater studies at the University of Paris X in Nanterre, a suburb to the north of Paris. After her academic training in Nanterre, she attended the Jacques Lecoq International Drama School in Paris, a school designed not only to train actors in movement but also to form authors and teachers of theater. She began working as an actress in Paris in the mid 1980s and appeared in many plays by contemporary authors, as well as plays by the French classical writers Molière and Pierre Carlet de Chamblain de Marivaux and early-twentieth-century author and humorist Sacha Guitry. Reza failed to gain admittance to the Paris Music Conservatory, a refusal she considered an injustice to her musical abilities, which she inherited from both her mother and her father, an amateur pianist. Ludwig van Beethoven, whose portrait hung in her parents' house and, later, above her own piano, represented her ideal of masculinity. It is the somber, yet imposing, image of a man who was strong, but disappointed by people. The picture left a great impression on Reza.

Reza's first attempt at writing for the stage was *Conversations après un enterrement.* The play is set on a family property in the Loiret, a *département* (French state) to the south of Paris. The main characters—Nathan, Edith, and Alex—are siblings, single and in their forties, who have just buried their father according to his wish, in the garden of his own house, and not next to his wife, Lila, who had died about twenty-three years earlier. Present are Pierre, sixty-five, the maternal uncle; his wife of two years, Julienne, sixty-four; and Elisa, thirty-five, Alex's former mistress. The family members attempt to come to terms with the death of this unlikable man who was nonetheless loved. The characters must also come to an understanding of each other, make sense of repressed feelings, find closure to old conflicts, and set a new direction for the future. Love affairs are revealed; parent-child relationships are analyzed; and tensions arise and die down while the protagonists gather around the kitchen table to eat a pot-au-feu, a simple meal of boiled beef and vegetables. The conclusion of the play focuses upon the loves of two of the siblings, Nathan and Edith. Nathan and his brother's former mistress, Elisa, come together in the conclusion. Edith announces that her lover is also coming. This first play establishes the themes that Reza returns to in later plays: social class, family relations, and love. For *Conversations après un enterrement,* Reza won the prestigious Molière Award (the French equivalent of the American Antoinette Perry ["Tony"] Award) for best author. After its premiere in Paris at the Théâtre-Villette, the play was produced in translation throughout Europe and in South America.

In 1988, Reza gave birth to her first child, a girl. Her son was born five years later. Also in 1988 she translated an adaptation of Franz Kafka's novella *The Metamorphosis* (1915) for performance by Roman Polanski and was nominated for the Molière Award for translation. Her second play also won a Molière for the best *théâtre alternatif* (fringe production) of 1990. *La Traversée de l'hiver* (1989, Winter Crossing) is set in the gardens of a resort hotel situated in the isolated but serene mountains of Switzerland. The interactions among six people staying at the same hotel for a few days constitute the focus of this play. Emma, sixty, lives in Paris and has never married. Her brother, Avner, a divorcé who lives in Buenos Aires, enjoys regular stays in the Swiss mountains where he can escape his two unsuccessful adult sons and a boring business that gives him both riches and worries. In the course of the play, Emma and Avner reveal that they were forced to escape Romania in 1940 at the onset of World War II and later traveled the world with their

Front cover for the 2000 translated paperback edition of Reza's first play, Conversations après un enterrement, *1986 (Bruccoli Clark Layman Archives)*

parents. Emma is nostalgic for her past and the joy and innocence of a younger age, while Avner feels guilty for having lived a luxurious and carefree life during the war at a time when many children were dying. Suzanne, fifty-five, has been married twice and lives in Lausanne. She is accompanied by her adult daughter, Ariane, who is often moody and inconsiderate. Two more men complete the gathering. Kurt Blensk is present without his wife and seems too clumsy and unrefined to please the ladies. Balint is a writer struggling to produce works that will allow him to create a sense of identity. As the characters engage in typical activities associated with life in resorts—such as mountain walks, card games, and concerts—love connections form and dissolve among them in spite of age differences and sometimes contrary to expectations: Blensk courts the older woman, Emma; Ariane favors the older men, Blensk and Avner, over the younger Balint. In spite of a buildup of tension as the characters interact, an air of friendship and harmony arises during the conclusion when the group goes to a concert and dinner. Comforting words are spoken, and the future appears hopeful. *La Traversée de l'hiver* is an example of what critic Ben Brantley describes as Reza's contribution to French theater: "But if the world that Ms. Reza describes is filled with snarled ambiguities, her plays are as orderly as an obsessive-compulsive's sock drawer.... They are plays that suggest reassuringly that human depths can, after all, be measured by a slide rule" (*The New York Times*, 4 January 2004). This play has not been translated into English and premiered in Orléans rather than Paris.

Art (produced and published, 1994; translated as *Art*, 1996) is Reza's third theatrical production and the one that brought her international fame. This play about culture and friendship won the author ten awards, including Molières for the best play, best production, and best author. Three friends from the educated upper class disagree on the meaning and value of art. Serge buys a painting for a great deal of money (Fr 200,000). This painting consists of a white canvas with fine white diagonal scars. He believes the painting is a great purchase because an art gallery would buy it from him for a higher price and because a famous painter named Antrios created it. Marc, Serge's friend, accuses Serge of becoming a pretentious and snobbish intellectual. Serge, in turn, accuses Marc of being narrow-minded. Serge is deeply offended and seems to need Marc's approval. Yvan, their other friend, does not want to offend anyone and tries to remain neutral. This conflict over the meaning of art also includes a study of male friendship and of the French upper class. Serge is an always-exhausted dermatologist who works long hours, is divorced, and sees his children once a week. Marc is an aeronautical engineer who has a girlfriend and considers himself a mentor to the other men. Yvan is a failed businessman who is getting married and has to resolve a family disagreement about whose name should appear on the wedding invitations. A final gesture of goodwill reconciles the friends but leaves the issues unresolved. The play premiered in Berlin in 1994 and had a successful opening in Paris in October of the same year. Later important productions include the London production by the Royal Shakespeare Company (1998) and the New York production starring Alan Alda as Marc. Both the French and English versions of the play enjoyed runs of several years. *Art* won the Tony Award for best play in 1998, and in 1996 it won the British Olivier Award for best comedy.

Only a year after *Art*, Reza composed her fourth dramatic work, *L'Homme du hasard* (produced and published, 1995; translated as *The Unexpected Man*, 1998). In this play for two characters, a man and a woman share the same train compartment as they travel from Paris to

Frankfurt. Paul Parsky, a writer, and Martha, an admirer of Parsky who carries his latest novel in her bag, take turns reflecting on their lives. This reflection takes the form of alternating interior monologues; no exchange occurs between the protagonists until the end of the play. This play, as is *Art,* is more about human relationships than art. "Bitter" is the word Parsky repeatedly uses to describe his feelings toward his life. Aging and dissatisfied, he wonders if any reader is capable of understanding his latest, and last, book, *The Unexpected Man.* He meditates over his different relationships and finds them all lacking and degenerated. His daughter, Nathalie; his son, Jean; his friend Maurice; his secretary, Mrs. Cerda; and his friend Elie—all contribute to a failed and incoherent life. On the train, Martha admires this elegant novelist whose books offered her hundreds of moments of eternity. An attractive woman and the mother of two children, Martha misses her friend Serge, who died recently. She wants to speak with Parsky, to whom she feels connected through the books he has written and she has read. When she finally finds the courage to take her book out, Parsky is delighted, and some laughter finds its way into their conversation. Considering its lack of action, *L'Homme du hasard* is more difficult to stage than Reza's earlier plays; however, it had a successful run in Paris, where it premiered in 1995, and later in London.

Hammerklavier: récit (1997; translated, 2000) is Reza's first novel. It is a collection of forty-four biographical anecdotes, focusing on Reza's close family and friends and preoccupied with the passing of time, which the author describes as her intimate enemy, along with aging, becoming ill, and dying. The title story is a memory of her ailing father trying to play the Beethoven adagio for the hammerklavier. A second novel, *Une Désolation: roman* (1999; translated as *Desolation,* 2002), is an extended monologue in which a character named Samuel Perlman meditates upon his life, especially his family relationships. He concludes that happiness equals mediocrity and idiocy.

In 2000, Reza returned to playwriting with *Trois versions de la vie* (translated as *Life x 3,* 2000), her most critically acclaimed play. In three acts, the same scene is replayed three times with few variations. Henri and Sonia, a married couple, are trying to put their son, Arnaud, six years old, to bed. Sonia is a lawyer, and Henri is a physicist about to publish a paper on the flatness of galaxy halos. This paper is vital to the advancement of Henri's career and has him in a state of anxiety. Suddenly, Hubert Finidori, Henri's superior, and his wife, Inès, arrive for dinner, a day earlier than expected. Henri and Sonia are not prepared to entertain and can only offer snacks and alcoholic beverages. An awkward evening ensues filled with observations, sometimes embarrassing and cruel, on each character. Minor changes in each act result in different outcomes in the dynamics of the relationships among the main characters, as well as the protagonists' outlooks on life. As with painting and literature in her earlier plays, science in this play is less important in itself than as a means of bringing different personalities together. Philippe Tesson, in his review of the play for *Le Figaro Magazine* (2 December 2000), suggested that *Trois versions de la vie* "s'articule autour de deux propositions essentielles, clairement exprimées. La première: vivre dans les sommets de la pensée ne confère pas une particulière hauteur de vue. La second, corollaire: les mots les plus insignifiants engagent l'être" (is structured according to two essential ideas that are clearly expressed. The first: the highest activities of the intellect do not bring with them a particularly lofty understanding [of life]. The second, a corollary: even the most insignificant words engage our being). For Tesson, this play demonstrates that Reza is not simply a portrayer of the contemporary French upper classes in comedy but a dramatist of the human psyche: "*Trois versions de la vie . . .* est davantage qu'une comédie de moeurs et va par là même plus loin qu'*Art*. La pièce esquisse, à défaut de la développer, une vision de la vie d'une belle lucidité" (*Life x 3 . . .* is more than a comedy of manners and thus goes further than *Art*. The play sketches, instead of developing, a vision of life, and does so with beautiful lucidity). Jean-Louis Pinte of *Figaroscope* (22 November 2000) also underlined the power of the language of the play, noting that Reza "montre ainsi la force des mots, leur violence, leur pouvoir de destruction sur un individu" (thus shows the force of words, their violence, their power of destruction on an individual) and comparing her ability to create drama from everyday situations to that of the celebrated novelist and dramatist Nathalie Sarraute. The play premiered simultaneously in Vienna, Paris, and Athens in the autumn of 2000. In the Parisian production, Reza played one of the female roles, to the surprise and favorable reception of the audience.

Reza wrote the dialogue for *Le Pique-nique de Lulu Kreutz: un film de Didier Martiny* (1999, Lulu Kreutz's Picnic), a movie directed by her companion Didier Martiny. This work is a love story between Anna, a married woman and mother of a small child, and Jascha Steg, a well-known cellist. Anna's husband, Primo, is a scientist who loves his wife but is occupied with his work in which he finds beauty and purpose. The screenplay explores the blurred line between maturity and desperate old age. It also examines the tender relationship between a father and his son, the dynamics within the family, Jewish identity, the dread of aging, and the unattainable meaning of life.

Adam Haberberg: roman (2002, Adam Haberberg), Reza's third novel, takes as its subject an unhappily married writer filled with doubts about his work and trying to discover the connection between literature and life. After

Front cover for the 2000 British edition of Reza's play Trois versions de la vie *(2000), three versions of a scene in which a couple have unexpected company for dinner, the husband's boss and his wife (Bruccoli Clark Layman Archives)*

meeting an old school friend who invites him to her house, Adam realizes how dear his family is to him. Without resolving any of the distressing issues in his life, Adam, in the last scene, is looking forward to seeing his family and pursuing his quest for answers.

Une Pièce espagnole: théâtre (produced and published 2004, A Spanish Play), which premiered at Paris's Théâtre de la Madeleine in January 2004, returns to an exploration of family relations and art–the theater. The structure of the play is complicated and confusing. Twenty-eight short segments alternate between real life and scenes from a play. Characters in the real-life segments are also the actors in the play. The play segments are all titled "Spanish play," while the real-life segments all include the word "imaginary" in their titles. The constant oscillation between the real and the imaginary leads to a confusion between the two. The main characters are two sisters, Nuria and Aurelia, and their mother. Sibling rivalry governs the relationship between famous movie star Nuria and struggling theater actress Aurelia. The mother-daughter relationships also suffer from misunderstandings and bitterness. At the same time, the support and love between Aurelia and her husband is diminishing. The actors, the well known and the less well known alike, constantly reevaluate their worth and the meaning of their profession. The conclusion is typical of Reza's theater: while the problems of art and human relationships are not resolved, the future holds promise.

Having first been trained as an actress, Yasmina Reza writes plays with acting and staging in mind. Her works have attracted French actors and, thanks to her translator Christopher Hampton, important American and British actors, too, such as Albert Finney, Alda, Stacey Keach, and Helen Hunt. Reza has been criticized for the lack of profundity in her themes–the family, the couple, work, ordinary life. For Simon Hattenstone, "Yasmina Reza is not so much a writer as a cultural phenomenon. . . . Maybe her creations have a peculiar resonance in the post-political age. Her characters . . . are self-obsessed, desperately ambitious for achievement, whatever form that achievement takes. They reek of futility but lack the desperate humanity of Beckett's existential no-hopers" (*The Guardian*, 1 January 2001). Brantley has gone so far as to call her plays "slender sitcoms, elegantly streaked with troubling shadows and shaped with Cartesian symmetry" (*The New York Times*, 1 April 2003), and Sheridan Morley has termed Reza "intellectual theatre lite" (*The Spectator*, 6 January 2001). Morley goes on to explain, however, Reza's success: " . . . she has plugged in to an entire generation of disaffected playgoers, those who found serious dramas too long and often boring, and light comedies too trivial to occupy their busy schedules." Her plays appeal to a growing society of professionals, indifferent to classical plays, that sees itself portrayed onstage in her works. While addressing serious themes, Reza's theater provides witty, as well as relevant, entertainment.

References:

Olivier Schmitt, "Yasmina Reza, Auteur Made in France a Success," *Le Monde*, 10 (November 2000);

Richard Zoglin, "Broadway and Beyond: Three Shows that Probably Won't Save the Great White Way," *Time*, 5 (April 2003).

Jules Romains
(Louis Farigoule)
(26 August 1885 – 14 August 1972)

Susan McCready
University of South Alabama

See also the Romains entry in *DLB 65: French Novelists, 1900–1930.*

PLAY PRODUCTIONS: *L'Armée dans la ville,* Paris, Théâtre de l'Odéon, 4 March 1911;

Cromedeyre-le-vieil, Paris, Théâtre du Vieux-Colombier, 26 May 1920;

Monsieur Le Trouhadec saisi par la débauche, Paris, Comédie des Champs-Elysées, 13 March 1923;

Amédée et les messieurs en rang, Paris, Comédie des Champs-Elysées, 15 December 1923;

Knock, ou Le Triomphe de la médecine, Paris, Comédie des Champs-Elysées, 15 December 1923;

La Scintillante, Paris, Comédie des Champs-Elysées, 7 October 1924;

Le Mariage de Le Trouhadec, Paris, Comédie des Champs-Elysées, 31 January 1925;

Le Dictateur, Paris, Comédie des Champs-Elysées, 5 October 1926;

Démétrios, Paris, Comédie des Champs-Elysées, 9 October 1926;

Jean le Maufranc, Paris, Théâtre des Arts, 1 December 1926;

Volpone, Paris, Théâtre de l'Atelier, 23 November 1928;

Le Déjeuner marocain, Paris, Théâtre Saint-Georges, 9 February 1929;

Musse, ou l'école de l'hypocrisie, Paris, Théâtre de l'Atelier, 21 November 1930;

Boën, ou la posession des biens, Paris, Théâtre de l'Odéon, 4 December 1930;

Donogoo, ou Les Mystères de la science, Paris, Théâtre Pigalle, 19 December 1931;

L'An Mil, Paris, Théâtre Sarah Bernhardt, 13 March 1947.

BOOKS: *Le Bourg régénéré, petite légende* (Paris: L. Vanier, 1906);

La Vie unanime (Paris: L'Abbaye, 1908);

Un Etre en marche (Paris: Mercure de France, 1910);

Jules Romains, 1947 (© Lipnitzki/Roger-Viollet/Getty Images)

Manuel de déification (Paris: E. Sansot, 1910);

L'Armée dans la ville (Paris: Mercure de France, 1911);

Mort de quelqu'un (Paris: E. Figuière, 1911); translated by Desmond MacCarthy and Sidney Waterlow as *The Death of a Nobody* (London: Latimer, 1914; New York: Huebsch, 1914);

Puissances de Paris (Paris: E. Figuière, 1911);

Les Copains (Paris: E. Figuière, 1913); translated by Jacques Le Clerq as *The Boys in the Back Room* (New York: McBride, 1937);

Odes et prières (Paris: Mercure de France, 1913);

Sur les quais de la Villette (Paris: E. Figuière, 1914); republished as *Le Vin blanc de la Villette* (Paris: Gallimard, 1923);

Europe (Paris: Gallimard, 1916);

Cromedeyre-le-vieil (Paris: Gallimard, 1920);

Donogoo-Tonka, ou Les Miracles de la science (Paris: Gallimard, 1920); translated and adapted by Gilbert Seldes as *Donogoo* (New York: Federal Theatre Project, 1937);

La Vision extra-rétinienne et le sens paroptique, as Louis Farigoule (Paris: Gallimard, 1920; expanded, 1921); translated by C. K. Ogden as *Eyeless Sight: A Study of Extra-retinal Vision and the Paroptic Sense* (London & New York: Putnam, 1924);

Le Voyage des amants (Paris: Editions de la Nouvelle Revue Française, 1920);

Amour couleur de Paris (Paris: Editions de la Nouvelle Revue Française, 1921);

Monsieur Le Trouhadec saisi par la débauche (Paris: Editions de la Nouvelle Revue Française, 1921);

Psyché, 3 volumes: *Lucienne, Le Dieu des corps, Quand le navire...* (Paris: Gallimard, 1922–1929); *Lucienne* translated by Waldo Frank (New York: Boni & Liveright, 1925); all three volumes translated by John Rodker as *The Body's Rapture* (Oxford: Boriswood, 1933; New York: Liveright, 1933);

Petit Traité de versification, by Romains and Georges Chennevière (Paris: Nouvelle Revue Française, 1923);

Théâtre de Jules Romains, 7 volumes (Paris: Nouvelle Revue Française, 1924–1935)–comprises volume 1, 1924: *Knock, Monsieur le Trouhade saisi par la débauche,* translated by Hanley Granville-Barker as *Doctor Knock* (London: Benn, 1925; New York: S. French, 1925); volume 2, 1925: *Le Mariage de le Trouhadec, La Scintillante; La Scintillante* translated by Virginia Vernon and Frank Vernon as *The Peach,* in *Modern One-act Plays from the French* (New York & Los Angeles: S. French / London: S. French, 1933); volume 3, 1926: *Cromedeyre-le-vieil, Amédée et les messieurs en rang;* volume 4, 1926: *Le Dictateur, Démétrios;* volume 5, 1929: *Volpone,* with Stefan Zweig; Ben Jonson, *Le Déjeuner marocain;* volume 6, 1929: *Jean le Maufranc, Musse ou l'école de l'hypocrisie;* and volume 7, 1935: *Boën ou la posession des biens, Donogoo;*

Chants des dix années (Paris: Gallimard, 1928);

Pièces en un acte: La Scintillante; Amédée et les messieurs en rang; Démétrios; Le Déjeuner marocain (Paris: Gallimard, 1930);

Problèmes d'aujourd'hui (Paris: Editions KRA, 1931); revised as *Problèmes européens* (Paris: Flammarion, 1933);

Les Hommes de bonne volonté, 27 volumes (Paris: Flammarion, 1932–1946)–comprises *Le 6 octobre, Crime de Quinette, Les Amours enfantines, Eros de Paris, Les Superbes, Les Humbles, Recherche d'une église, Province, Montée des périls, Les Pouvoirs, Recours à l'abîme, Les Créateurs, Mission à Rome, Le Drapeau noir, Prélude à Verdun, Verdun, Vorge contre Quinette, La Douceur de la vie, Cette Grande Lueur à l'est, Le Monde est ton aventure, Journée dans la montagne, Les Travaux et les joies, Naissance de la bande, Comparutions, Le Tapis magique, Françoise, Le 7 octobre;* translated by W. B. Wells and Gerard Hopkins as *Men of Good Will,* 14 volumes (New York: Knopf, 1933–1946; London & Toronto: Dickson, 1933–1946);

Le Couple France-Allemagne (Paris: Flammarion, 1934);

Visite aux Américains (Paris: Flammarion, 1936);

L'Homme blanc (Paris: Flammarion, 1937);

Cela dépend de vous (Paris: Flammarion, 1939);

Sept Mystères du destin de l'Europe (New York: Editions de la Maison Française, 1940); translated by Germaine Brée as *Seven Mysteries of Europe* (New York: Knopf, 1940; London & Melbourne: Hutchinson, 1941);

Salsette découvre l'Amérique (New York: Editions de la Maison Française, 1940); translated by Lewis Galantière as *Salsette Discovers America* (New York: Knopf, 1942);

Grâce encore pour la terre! (New York: Editions de la Maison Française, 1941);

Nomentanus le réfugié (New York: Editions de la Maison Française, 1943; Paris: Table Ronde, 1945);

Bertrand de Ganges (New York: Editions de la Maison Française, 1944); republished in *Bertrand de Ganges, suivi de Nomentanus le réfugié* (Paris: Flammarion, 1947);

Retrouver la foi (New York: Editions de la Maison Française, 1944; Paris: Flammarion, 1945);

Académie française. Réception de M. Jules Romains, le 7 novembre 1946. Discours de M. Jules Romains. Discours de M. Georges Duhamel (Paris: Editions du Monde, 1946);

L'An mil (Paris: Editions de l'Odéon, 1947);

Le Problème numéro un (Paris: Plon, 1947);

Pierres levées (Paris: Flammarion, 1948);

Le Moulin et l'hospice (Paris: Flammarion, 1949);

Docteur Knock. Fragments de la doctrine secrète recueillis par Jules Romains (Paris: M. Bruker, 1949);

Salsette découvre l'Amérique, suivi de Lettres de Salsette (Paris: Flammarion, 1950);

Violation de frontières (Paris: Flammarion, 1951); translated by Gerard Hopkins as *Tussles with Time* (London: Sidgwick & Jackson, 1952);

Interviews avec Dieu, as John W. Hicks (Paris: Flammarion, 1952);

Saints de notre calendrier: Goethe, Balzac, Hugo, Baudelaire, Gobineau, Zola, Strindberg, France, Zweig, Gide, Chennevière, Fargue (Paris: Flammarion, 1952);

Maisons (Paris: Seghers, 1953);

Confidences d'un auteur dramatique (Paris: Editions Estienne, 1953);

Examen de conscience des français (Paris: Flammarion, 1954); translated by Cornelia Schaeffer as *A Frenchman Examines his Conscience* (London: Deutsch, 1955);

Passagers de cette planète, où allons-nous? (Paris: Grasset, 1955);

Le Fils de Jerphanion (Paris: Flammarion, 1956);

Le Roman des douze, by Romains and others (Paris: R. Julliard, 1957);

Une Femme singulière (Paris: Flammarion, 1957); translated by Arnold Pomerans as *The Adventuress* (London: Muller, 1958);

Situation de la terre (Paris: Flammarion, 1958); translated by Richard Howard as *As It Is on Earth* (New York: Macmillan, 1962);

Souvenirs et confidences d'un écrivain (Paris: Fayard, 1958);

Le Besoin de voir clair: Deuxième rapport Antonelli (Paris: Flammarion, 1958);

Hommes, médecins, machines (Paris: Flammarion, 1959);

Mémoires de Madame Chauverel, 2 volumes (Paris: Flammarion, 1959, 1960);

Les Hauts et les bas de la liberté (Paris: Flammarion, 1960);

Pour raison garder, 3 volumes (Paris: Flammarion, 1960–1967);

Un Grand Honnête Homme (Paris: Flammarion, 1961);

Portraits d'inconnus (Paris: Flammarion, 1962);

Ai-je fait ce que j'ai voulu? (Paris: Wesmael-Charlier, 1964);

Lettres à un ami, 2 volumes (Paris: Flammarion, 1964, 1965);

Lettre ouverte contre une vaste conspiration (Paris: A. Michel, 1966); translated by Harold J. Salemson as *Open Letter Against a Vast Conspiracy* (New York: J. H. Heinemann, 1968);

Marc-Aurèle, ou L'Empereur de bonne volonté (Paris: Flammarion, 1968);

Amitiés et rencontres (Paris: Flammarion, 1970).

PRODUCED SCRIPTS: *Das Bildnis,* 1923;
Knock, ou le triomphe de la médecine, 1925;
Knock, ou le triomphe de la médecine, 1933;
Donogoo Tonka, 1936;
Volpone, 1941;
Knock, ou le triomphe de la médecine, 1950.

SELECTED PERIODICAL PUBLICATIONS–UNCOLLECTED: "Ode génoise," *Nouvelle Revue Française,* 22 (1 May 1924): 517–537;

Title page for the 1950 edition of Romains's 1920 play in which the character Le Trouhadec, hero of several more plays, first appears. Seemingly dull-witted, Le Trouhadec always outsmarts everyone else (Thomas Cooper Library, University of South Carolina).

"Ce Siècle avait dix ans: Une jeunesse littéraire," *Conférencia,* 38 (15 December 1949): 483–498.

Jules Romains is considered one of the most important authors of the interwar period in France. He began his literary career before World War I as a poet but is known principally for his twenty-seven volume *roman fleuve* (saga), *Les Hommes de bonne volonté,* which appeared between 1932 and 1946 (translated as *Men of Good Will,* 1933–1946). Although he is remembered principally as a playwright, thanks to the commercial and critical success of the comedy *Knock, ou Le Triomphe de la médecine* (1923; translated as *Doctor Knock,* 1925),

Romains exercised an important influence on the development of the theatrical aesthetic between the wars. His plays were produced by such leading directors of the day as André Antoine, Jacques Copeau, Charles Dullin, Louis Jouvet, and Georges Pitoëff. Moreover, Romains shared in Copeau's experimental work as the director of his Ecole du Vieux-Colombier (Vieux-Colombier Theater School) from 1921 through 1923. A pacifist and advocate for international cooperation, Romains spent World War II in the United States and Mexico. He was elected to the Académie Française in 1946, soon after his return to France. Romains wrote one last play in 1947 and then devoted himself to the novel and increasingly to essays.

The only son of Henri Farigoule and Marie Richier, Jules Romains was born Louis-Henri-Jean Farigoule on 26 August 1885. He grew up in Paris, where his father taught in the public schools. A gifted student, Romains earned his *baccalauréat classique* in 1900 and a second *baccalauréat* in philosophy in 1902, the same year in which he published his first literary work, "Le Chef-d'œuvre" (The Masterpiece), a poem, in *La Revue jeune*. Already for this first publication, Romains adopted his pen name, which he claimed to have chosen because it was simple, easy to pronounce, and expressed a certain "sympathie pour Rome" (love of Rome). Romains continued to publish poetry and to gain some recognition as a writer as he prepared to enter the Ecole Normale Supérieure (ENS). He was accepted in 1905 but entered the elite institution only after completing his military service in 1906.

During this period, Romains was developing his philosophy of *unanisme*, or unanism, which he defined as the expression of "la vie unanime et collective" (unanimous, collective life). In memoirs and interviews, Romains often spoke of his discovery of unanism in 1903: walking along the streets of Paris, he had an intuition of the interconnectedness of all people. Romains believed that groups possess a sort of collective soul, generated by the disparate individuals who make up the group. In his unanimist writing, he sought to illustrate the relationship between the group and its individual members. He went on to develop this idea further through his association with the Abbaye poets (a name coined in 1905 by Charles Vildrac, who dreamed of founding a Rabelaisian abbey)—for example, Vildrac and Georges Duhamel. The Abbaye press published Romains's first volume of poetry, *La Vie unanime*, in 1908.

As he completed his studies, Romains continued to publish poetry and prose and made his first foray into the theater in 1911 with the verse play *L'Armée dans la ville* (The Army in the City). The play deals with some of Romains's early unanimist ideas, as it explores the relationship between the citizens of a town and the army occupying it. The townspeople work collectively to overthrow the army, and although they succeed in killing all of the soldiers, their rebellion is finally put down by reinforcements from the outside. The Théâtre de l'Odéon, where *L'Armée dans la ville* was produced, occupied a singular position in the French theater scene at that time: it was an official, national stage, one of only two state-supported theaters. (The other was the Comédie Française.) At the same time, the Théâtre de l'Odéon was seen as an innovative, if not experimental, theatrical venue, thanks to the work of its director, Antoine, who had revitalized the French stage at his independent Théâtre Libre in the late nineteenth century. The premiere of *L'Armée dans la ville* at the Odéon was something of a theatrical event, but ultimately the play was a disappointment and closed shortly after it opened.

In 1912 Romains married his first wife, Gabrielle Gaffé. While he continued to teach, he pursued his literary career, publishing both poetry—*Puissances de Paris* (1911, Powers of Paris); *Odes et prières* (1913, Odes and Prayers);—and prose works—*Mort de quelqu'un* (1911; translated as The Death of a Nobody, 1914); *Les Copains* (1913; translated as The Boys in the Backroom, 1937); and *Sur les quais de la Villette* (1914, On the Quays of la Vilette). Because of medical problems, Romains served in a clerical capacity during World War I and was discharged in 1915. He taught in Paris for a year and then took a post in Nice, where he met writer Maurice-Polydore-Marie-Bernard Maeterlinck and artist Henri-Emile-Benoît Matisse. Like most of his contemporaries, Romains was profoundly affected by the war. His optimistic credo of unanism turned more cynical in the years after the war, and although he continued to explore the relationships of individuals and groups, he remained aware of the dangers of the interconnectedness he had lauded in his more primitive unanism.

In 1919, confident that he could make a living as a writer, Romains resigned his teaching post and moved back to Paris. Once there, he continued his literary career but also engaged in the scientific research that yielded his only publication under the name Louis Farigoule, *La Vision extra-rétinienne et le sens paroptique* (1920; translated as *Eyeless Sight: A Study of Extra-retinal Vision and the Paroptic Sense*, 1924). Romains had hoped to prove the scientific merits of the theory of "eyeless sight," but was bitterly disappointed when the scientific community ridiculed his work. Although he continued to believe in the value of scientific progress, Romains, stung by rejection, went on to satirize the scientific and medical professions in several of his plays.

Romains had stayed away from the theater for nearly ten years after *L'Armée dans la ville*, and not until Copeau produced *Cromedeyre-le-vieil* in 1920 did Romains's career onstage begin in earnest. In this "modern tragedy," Romains explores once again the relationship between the individual and the collective, this time focusing, as in *Le Dictateur* (1926, The Dictator), on the group's leader, Emmanuel Hélier, and the moral dilemmas he faces. Although this play was the only one by Romains produced by Copeau, Romains acted as the director of the Ecole du Vieux-Colombier (the theatrical school founded by Copeau as an adjunct to his Théâtre du Vieux-Colombier) from 1921 to 1923. *Cromedeyre-le-vieil* earned critical praise, but it was not Romains's breakthrough as a playwright.

Artistic differences with Copeau over his next play led Romains to the most important professional relationship of his career in the theater, that with director and actor Jouvet. A former student of Copeau's and an innovative director in his own right, Jouvet produced Romains's five-act comedy *Monsieur Le Trouhadec saisi par la débauche* (Monsieur le Trouhadec in the Throes of Debauchery) at the Comédie des Champs-Elysées in March 1923. The play was a popular and critical success and earned praise from Romains's first director, Antoine, who had by then turned theatrical critic. The hero of the play, Monsieur Le Trouhadec, is a hapless academic always on the verge of being swindled, who falls in love with an actress in Monte Carlo. The character had appeared in a 1920 motion-picture treatment, *Donogoo-Tonka, ou Les Miracles de la science* (Donogoo-Tonka, or The Miracles of Science), which later was adapted and staged again in 1931; he also appears in *Le Mariage de Le Trouhadec* (The Marriage of Le Trouhadec), staged by Jouvet in 1925.

An unlikely hero, Le Trouhadec seems at first to be the perfect patsy, but in all of the plays in which he is featured, he eventually outwits those who try to outwit him. Romains said of his hero, "Le Trouhadec est une bête; mais c'est aussi un malin" (Le Trouhadec may be stupid, but he is also sly). As *Donogoo* opens, Le Trouhadec's discovery of the golden city of Donogoo is about to be revealed as a fraud. With the help of Bénin, an amiable huckster, who is another recurring character in the Le Trouhadec plays and in the novel *Les Copains*, the hero hatches a scheme to found the mysterious city he claims to have already discovered. His sleight of hand succeeds; the newly founded Donogoo is taken for the recently discovered Donogoo, and Le Trouhadec's academic reputation is assured. The prosperous inhabitants of Donogoo go on to establish their own religion: "Le Culte de l'Erreur Scientifique" (The Cult of Scientific Error). All of the Le Trouhadec plays deal with two themes to which Romains repeatedly returns in his plays: fraud and scientific progress. His treatment of these themes is, however, not always a straightforward satire: in *Donogoo*, for example, the hero's fraudulent actions are crowned with success; and modern science, though parodied in the "Cult of Scientific Error," in fact makes possible the prosperity and happiness of the citizens of the utopian Donogoo. Romains was at once optimistic and skeptical with respect to science, and he harbored a subtle admiration for the fast-talking con artists who were often his heroes, as in *Démétrios* (1926), *Volpone* (1928), *Le Déjeuner marocain* (1929, The Moroccan Luncheon), and *Knock*.

After the success of *Monsieur Le Trouhadec saisi par la débauche*, Romains paired a second time with Jouvet in 1923 to produce the most successful play of either's career–*Knock, ou Le Triomphe de la médecine*. Docteur Knock, the eponymous hero of the play, follows a trajectory similar to that of Le Trouhadec: the first scene makes clear that the savvy Docteur Parpalaid has taken advantage of his inexperienced colleague in the sale of his practice. By the end of the play, however, Knock, using his new medical method, has assured his financial success by making everyone in his small town a permanent patient. Like most of Romains's mature plays, *Knock* explores in part the problems of the individual faced with the complications of modern life. Romains himself saw the play as a sort of comedic case study, staging what happens when modern medical discourse is introduced into an isolated community. "Nous assistons," he writes, "à la propagation d'une foi dans une collectivité" (We are witnesses to the propagation of a faith within a collective). According to Docteur Knock, everybody is by definition sick and in need of medical care. The inhabitants of the village, seduced by an initial free visit and the subsequent interest Knock takes in their affairs, are only too happy to see themselves as fascinating medical cases and to produce new symptoms for Knock to address, and filling Knock's coffers in the process. The play leaves open to interpretation whether Knock is a thoroughly adept grifter or a slightly mad disciple of the new cult of medicine; the doubt underscores Romains's ambivalent admiration for both con men and men of science. *Knock* is by far Romains's best-known play and the one most often read and produced. In fact, *Knock* was such a reliable draw that Jouvet confessed to staging it any time he needed money–six times at the Champs-Elysées between 1924 and 1933 and seven more times at the Théâtre de l'Athénée between 1935 and 1949. The play has spawned three movie adaptations, the first one a silent film in 1925 and then two versions starring Jouvet in 1933 and 1950.

Nowhere does Romains address the promise and problems of modern life more directly than in *Jean le*

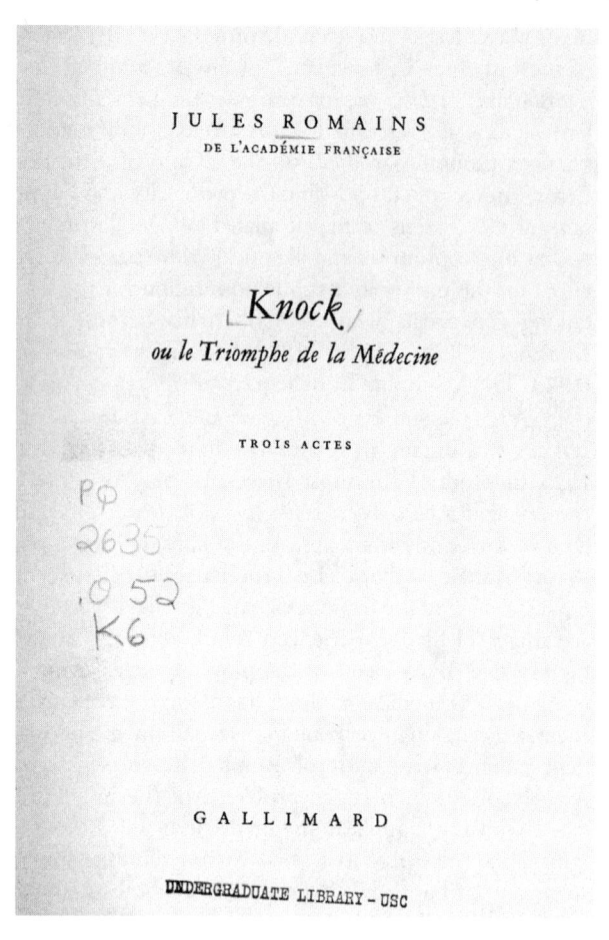

Title page for Romains's critically and commercially successful 1923 play (translated as Doctor Knock, *1949), a comedy about a small-town doctor who becomes successful by assuming that everyone is sick (Thomas Cooper Library, University of South Carolina)*

Maufranc, produced in 1926 by Pitoëff at the Théâtre des Arts and the later version of this same play, *Musse, ou l'école de l'hypocrisie* (Musse or the School for Hypocrisy), produced by Dullin at the Théâtre de l'Atelier in 1930. Both plays present a hero who feels enslaved by modern life and particularly by the well-meaning ideologues who seek to control human behavior. In both versions of the play, the hero's ire is turned against the "Ligue internationale pour la protection de l'homme moderne" (International League for the Protection of Modern Man), an organization whose goal is to protect modern man, essentially by making all of his decisions for him. In the first version, the hero escapes their control by remaking himself and leading a double life: he appears to be the perfect, obedient modern subject, but under an assumed identity he remains free. In *Musse,* on the other hand, the hero denounces the hypocritical leaders of the Protection League, striking a blow for the individual against the machine of modern society.

Jean le Maufranc, judged too long and heavy-handed by audiences and critics, closed quickly, but the 1930 version was more successful, cementing Romains's relationship with Dullin, who also produced Romains's last play, in 1947. The two had previously collaborated on *Volpone,* an adaptation of Ben Jonson's play, which was the first production at Dullin's struggling theater to reach a truly broad audience, widening the appeal of the small art-house theater to a more mainstream group of theatergoers. Romains wrote *Volpone* after seeing Stéfan Zweig's adaptation of the play in Berlin in 1926, and Zweig is sometimes credited as co-author of the play. In this play, too, Romains explores the theme of chicanery and the relationship of the charming con man to his hapless (if not altogether undeserving) victims. As in his other plays about swindlers, Romains operates his own sleight-of-hand in the conclusion, as Volpone is swindled by his assistant, Mosca, of his ill-gotten gains. *Volpone* struck a nerve with French audiences in the late 1920s, as a series of financial scandals rocked the government and the banking industry. According to Dullin, audiences made cynical by the various scandals and by their own victimization at the hands of the wealthy and powerful, were delighted by Romains's satire of the rich in which everyone is recognizable; no one is likable; and nearly everyone is punished.

While Romains's plays are (with two notable exceptions) not overtly political, clearly his plays reflect concerns shared by his contemporaries about the individual's place in a world in which power and wealth are increasingly concentrated in the hands of a few. Several of his plays treat the theme of class, including the two one-act plays that opened for *Knock–Amédée et les messieurs en rang* (1923, Amédée and the Gentleman in a Row) and *La Scintillante* (1924; translated as The Peach, 1933). *Amédée* in particular addresses the dehumanizing nature of modern life and the devaluation of work. *Boën, ou la possession des biens* (1930, Boen, or the Possession of Goods) addresses the question of class from the point of view of the capitalist, but the conclusion is similar: modern life, modern work, and even modern wealth are isolating. *Boën* was not well-liked by critics and had only a short run at the Théâtre de l'Odéon in December of 1930.

In his 1926 play *Le Dictateur* (The Dictator) and in *Grâce encore pour la terre!* (1941, Mercy for the Earth Once More!) Romains takes on contemporary political topics directly. *Le Dictateur* stages the dilemma of a radical political leader who must choose to compromise the revolutionary movement that brought him to power in order to maintain his power. In this play Romains deals with the contemporary question of the rise of fascism, but his overriding agenda remains the exploration of the relationship of the individual (and in particular of the leader) to the group. *Grâce encore pour la terre!* on the other hand, is an unabashed antiwar polemic, in which God holds a cabinet meeting to decide the fate of the earth. In this rather heavy satire, Romains critiques the way in which leaders use patriotism to manipulate the average citizen and pleads for individuals to work toward peace. The play was to have been produced at the Comédie Française but was canceled after the outbreak of the war.

The 1920s were Jules Romains's heyday in the theater, with fourteen of his plays produced by some of the most influential directors of the decade. His successes, such as *Knock* and *Volpone*, by far outweighed his failures, and his popularity as a playwright was still strong even as he began to turn increasingly toward the novel. In the 1930s Romains began his most ambitious literary project, the largest *roman fleuve* in French, *Les Hommes de bonne volonté*, which appeared between 1932 and 1946. The novel, the twenty-seven volumes of which are organized around the principle of unanism (focusing on groups, rather than on individual recurrent characters), spans the period from 1908 to 1933. World War I is at the center of the work, and the novel reflects contemporary concerns about the rise of fascism, the place of the individual, and the role of technology in modern life.

During this period, Romains also became increasingly political, actively promoting peace between France and Germany. Prose works from this period, *Problèmes d'aujourd'hui* (1931, Problems of Today) and *Le Couple France-Allemagne* (1934, The France-German Couple), attest to his growing commitment to politics and in particular to pan-European cooperation. After separating from his first wife in 1934 and divorcing in 1936, Romains married Lise Dreyfus on 18 December 1936. Elected president of the international PEN club in 1936, Romains traveled extensively in the late 1930s, including a trip to the United States, which he treats in *Visite aux Américains* (1936, Visit to the Americans).

During the Occupation, Romains and his wife fled to the United States, where Romains lectured at Middlebury College in Vermont. Their apartment in Paris was ransacked by the Gestapo in 1943, and many of Romains's papers were lost. The couple later traveled south to Mexico, where they founded the Petit Théâtre Français. Jouvet's troupe performed *Knock* and *Monsieur Le Trouhadec saisi par la débauche* there in 1943.

When he returned to France, Romains continued to speak and write about the theater in *Confidences d'un auteur dramatique* (1953, Confidences of a Dramatic Author) and *Ai-je fait ce que j'ai voulu?* (1964, Have I Done What I meant to Do?) but made only one attempt at writing for the theater, with the millenarian play *L'An mil* (The Year One Thousand), produced by Dullin at the Théâtre Sarah Bernhardt in 1947. The play was a failure and an inauspicious ending to an august career in the theater. Romains later said that this failure, along with a lack of interest among directors in producing the unpublished play "Barbazouk," which he had written in Mexico in 1945, definitively turned him away from the theater. With the deaths of Dullin in 1949 and Jouvet in 1951, Romains no longer felt connected to the theatrical world and chose to devote himself entirely to fiction and essays. Romains died 14 August 1972.

Whether as poet, novelist, essayist, or playwright, Jules Romains was a writer profoundly committed to addressing contemporary problems in his work. In the theater, satire was his weapon of choice, but his wit is always tempered with real compassion for the plight of the individual faced with the challenges and absurdities of modern life. Although much more critical attention has been focused on Jean Giraudoux and Paul Claudel, Romains is still among the most important playwrights of the interwar period, and he was certainly the most successful in commercial terms.

Testifying to a profound ambivalence about modernity and the promises of science and technology, Romains's theatrical oeuvre occupies a respected place in the grand tradition of satirical French literature, and his plays remain an invaluable document of their time. In a 1966 address given in honor of the tricentennial of the *Misanthrope* of Molière, he spoke in Molière's voice: "J'aurai atteint mon but, lorsque j'aurai fait rire toute une salle aussi franchement qu'au spectacle d'une farce, mais avec un arrière-goût de réflexion morale ou philosophique" (I will have achieved my goal, when I have made a whole theater laugh as frankly as at a farce, but with an after-taste of moral or philosophical reflection). In attributing this aim to the most admired French playwright, the author of *Knock* might well have been speaking for himself.

Letters:

Correspondance André Gide–Jules Romains: l'individu et l'unanime (Paris: Flammarion, 1976);

Correspondance Jacques Copeau–Jules Romains: deux êtres en marche [1913-1946] (Paris: Flammarion, 1978);

Correspondance André Gide–Jules Romains, edited by Claude Martin (Lyon: Publications du Centre d'Etudes Gidiennes, 1979);

Correspondance Jules Romains–Guillaume Apollinaire, edited by Martin (Paris: J.-M. Place, 1994).

References:

Douglas W. Alden, "The News on October 6," *Romance Notes*, 12 (Spring 1971): 235-243;

Alden, "Quinette, Landru, and Raskolnikoff," *French Review*, 43 (December 1969): 215–226;

Harry Bergholz, "Jules Romains and his 'Men of Good Will,'" *Modern Language Journal*, 35 (April 1951): 303–309;

Madeleine Berry, *Jules Romains: sa vie, son œuvre* (Paris: Editions du conquistador, 1953);

Berry, "L'Œuvre poétique et romanesque de Jules Romains," *Cahiers de la Compagnie Madeleine Renaud-Jean-Louis Barrault*, 3, no. 9 (1955): 27–34;

Denis Boak, *Jules Romains* (New York: Twayne, 1974);

André Bourin, *Connaissance de Jules Romains, discutée par Jules Romains: essai de géographie littéraire* (Paris: Flammarion, 1961);

Germaine Brée and Margaret Guiton, "Georges Duhamel and Jules Romains: Men of Good Will," in their *An Age of Fiction* (New Brunswick, N.J.: Rutgers University Press, 1957);

Cahiers Jules Romains (Paris: Flammarion, 1976–1982);

John Cocking, "Jules Romains and Unanimism," *World Review*, new series 27 (May 1951): 33–37;

Wallace Fowlie, "The Novel of Jules Romains," *Southern Review*, 7 (Spring 1942): 880–892;

Philippe Jolivet, "Le Comique dans le théâtre de Jules Romains," *Orbis Litterarum*, 11 (1956): 229–236;

Jolivet, "*Les Hommes de bonne volonté* de Jules Romains, technique et style," *Nottingham French Studies*, 1 (May 1962): 39–49;

Jolivet, "Le Théâtre poétique de Jules Romains," *Orbis Litterarum*, 9 (1954): 120–128;

Lise Jules-Romains, *Les Vies inimitables: souvenirs* (Paris: Flammarion, 1985);

Berthold Mahn, *Souvenirs du Vieux-Colombier, 55 dessins originaux précédés d'un texte de Jules Romains* (Paris: C. Aveline, 1926);

Dominique Memmi, *Jules Romains ou la passion de parvenir* (Paris: La Dispute, 1998);

P. J. Norrish, *The Drama of the Group: A Study of Unanimism in the Plays of Jules Romains* (Cambridge: Cambridge University Press, 1958);

Norrish, "Romains and 'L'Abbaye,'" *Modern Language Review*, 52 (October 1957): 518–525;

Aaron Schaffer, "Jules Romains Despairs of Men of Good Will," *American Scholar*, 17 (Spring 1948): 191–200;

Ben Stoltzfus, "Unanimism Revisited," *Modern Language Quarterly*, 21 (September 1960): 239–245;

François Stupp, *Jules Romains de la Chapuze à la Coupole* (Saint-Julien-Chapteuil: Editions du Roure, 2001);

Leland Thielemann, "The Problem of Unity and Individualism in Romains' Social Philosophy," *Modern Language Quarterly*, 2 (1941): 249–262;

Harold H. Watts, "Jules Romains: The Quinette Beneath the Skin," *Rocky Mountain Review*, 10 (Spring 1946): 125–135;

Clotilde Wilson, "Sartre's Graveyard of Chimeras: *La Nausée* and *Mort de quelqu'un*," *French Review*, 38 (1965): 744–753.

Armand Salacrou
(9 August 1899 – 23 November 1989)

Rosemary Plater-Zyberk Clark

PLAY PRODUCTIONS: *Tour à terre,* Paris, Maison de l'Oeuvre, 24 December 1925;

Le Pont de l'Europe, Paris, Théâtre national de l'Odéon, 30 November 1927;

Patchouli, Paris, Théâtre de l'Atelier, 22 January 1930;

Atlas–Hôtel, Paris, Théâtre de l'Atelier, 15 April 1931;

La Vie en rose, Paris, Théâtre du Vieux-Colombier, 3 December 1931;

Une Femme libre, Paris, Théâtre de l'Oeuvre, 4 October 1934;

Les Frénétiques, Paris, Théâtre Daunou, 5 December 1934;

L'Inconnue d'Arras, Paris, La Comédie des Champs-Elysées, 22 November 1935;

Un Homme comme les autres, Paris, Théâtre de l'Oeuvre, 24 November 1936;

La Terre est ronde, Paris, Théâtre de l'Atelier, 7 November 1938;

Histoire de rire, Paris, Théâtre de la Madeleine, 22 December 1939;

La Marguerite, Paris, Théâtre Pigalle, 28 October 1944;

Les Fiancés du Havre, Paris, La Comédie-Française, 10 December 1944;

Le Soldat et la sorcière, Paris, Théâtre Sarah-Bernhardt, 5 December 1945;

Les Nuits de la colère, Paris, Théâtre Marigny, 12 December 1946;

L'Archipel Lenoir, Paris, Théâtre Montparnasse, 8 November 1947;

Pourquoi pas moi? and *Poof,* Brussels, Théâtre du Rideau, 24 September 1948; Paris, Théâtre-Edouard VII, 26 October 1950;

La Beauté du diable, une tragi-comédie, by Salacrou and René Clair, Paris, Théâtre national de l'Opéra, 16 March 1950;

Dieu le savait, Paris, Théâtre Saint-Georges, 2 December 1950;

Sens interdit, Paris, Théâtre du Quartier-Latin, 6 January 1953;

Les Invités du bon Dieu, Brussels, Théâtre du Parc, 11 September 1953;

Armand Salacrou (from the front cover for Annie Ubersfeld, Armand Salacrou, *1970; Thomas Cooper Library, University of South Carolina)*

Le Casseur d'assiettes, Leiden, 7 April 1954;

Le Miroir, Paris, Théâtre des Ambassadeurs, 21 September 1956;

Une Femme trop honnête, Paris, Théâtre-Edouard VII, 1 December 1956;

Un Homme comme les autres, Paris, La Comédie-Française, 8 October 1959;

Boulevard Durand, Le Havre, Centre Dramatique du Nord, 19 September 1961;

Comme les chardons, Paris, La Comédie-Française, 26 October 1964.

BOOKS: *Le Casseur d'assiettes* (Paris: Simon, 1925);

Tour à terre, Le Pont de l'Europe (Paris: Ramlot, 1928);

Patchouli (Paris: Gallimard, 1930);

Atlas-Hôtel: pièce en trois actes (Paris: Les Cahiers de "Bravo," 1931);

Une femme libre. Atlas-Hôtel (Paris: Gallimard, 1934); *Atlas-Hôtel* revised as *Atlas-Hôtel (version définitive), pièce en 3 actes* (Paris: L'Illustration, 1937);

L'Inconnue d'Arras, pièce en 3 actes. Les Frénétiques, pièce en 5 tableaux (Paris: Gallimard, 1936);

La Vie en rose, impromptu en un acte (Marseille: Mistral, 1936);

La Terre est ronde. Précédé de Un homme comme les autres (Paris: Gallimard, 1938); *La Terre est ronde* translated by Norman Stokle as *The World Is Round*, in *Three Plays by Armand Salacrou* (Minneapolis: University of Minnesota Press, 1967); definitive edition of *Un homme comme les autres* (1974);

Histoire de rire. Farce dramatique en trois actes (N.p., 1940); translated by Stokle as *When the Music Stops*, in *Three Plays by Armand Salacrou* (Minneapolis: University of Minnesota Press, 1967);

Histoire de rire, suivi de Le casseur d'assiettes, de La Marguerite (Paris: Gallimard, 1941); *La Marguerite* translated by Stokle as *Marguerite*, in *Three Plays by Armand Salacrou* (Minneapolis: University of Minnesota Press, 1967);

Théâtre, volume 3 (Paris: Gallimard, 1942)–comprises *Une femme libre*, *L'Inconnue d'Arras*, and *Un homme comme les autres*;

Théâtre, volume 1 (Paris: Gallimard, 1943)–comprises *Le Casseur d'assiettes*, *Tour à terre*, *Le Pont de l'Europe*, and *Patchouli*;

Théâtre, volume 2 (Paris: Gallimard, 1944)–comprises *Atlas-Hôtel*, *Les Frénétiques*, and *La Vie en rose*;

Les Fiancés du Havre, pièce en trois actes (Paris: Gallimard, 1944);

Théâtre, volume 4 (Paris: Gallimard, 1945)–comprises *La Terre est ronde*, *Histoire de rire*, and *La Marguerite*;

Théâtre, volume 5 (Paris: Gallimard, 1947)–comprises *Les Nuits de la colère*, *Les Fiancés du Havre*, and *Le Soldat et la sorcière*;

Théâtre, volume 5 (Paris: Gallimard, 1947)–comprises *Patchouli*, *Le Casseur d'assiettes*, *Tour à terre*, and *Le Pont de l'Europe*;

L'Archipel Lenoir, ou Il ne faut pas toucher aux choses immobiles, pièce en 2 parties (Paris: Gallimard, 1948);

Pourquoi pas moi? pièce en un acte, suivi de Poof, comédie-ballet (Paris: Bordas, 1948);

La Beauté du diable, une tragi-comédie, by Salacrou and René Clair (Paris: Bobigny, 1950);

L'Archipel Lenoir (Paris: Gallimard, 1950);

Dieu le savait, ou la vie n'est pas sérieuse suivi de Pourquoi pas moi? (Paris: Gallimard, 1951);

Dieu le savait! ou la Vie n'est pas sérieuse, pièce en 3 actes (Paris: Bobigny, 1951);

Sens interdit, text by Salacrou, illustrations by André Beaudin (Paris: Gallimard, 1952);

Les Invités du Bon Dieu, vaudeville en trois actes (Paris: Gallimard, 1953);

Théâtre, volume 6 (Paris: Gallimard, 1954)–comprises *L'Archipel Lenoir*, *Poof*, *Dieu le savait*, *La vie et la mort de Charles Dullin*, and *Mes certitudes et incertitudes morales et politiques*;

Théâtre, volume 7 (Paris: Gallimard, 1956)–comprises *Pourquoi pas moi? Sens interdit*, *Les Invités du bon Dieu*, and *Le Miroir*;

Une Femme trop honnête, pièce en 3 actes (Paris: Gallimard, 1956);

Le Miroir, pièce en 4 actes (Paris: Femina-théâtre, 1956);

La Boule de verre (Paris: Ecole Estienne, 1958);

La Beauté du diable, movie script written by Salacrou and Clair, in Clair, *Comédies et commentaires* (Paris: Gallimard, 1959);

Boulevard Durand, chronique d'un procès oublié drame en deux parties (Paris: Gallimard, 1960);

Les Idées de la nuit (Paris: Fayard, 1960);

Comme les chardons, pièce sans entracte (Paris: Gallimard, 1964);

Théâtre, volume 8 (Paris: Gallimard, 1966)–comprises *Une Femme trop honnête*, *Boulevard Durand*, and *Comme les chardons*;

La Rue noire: pièce en deux parties (Paris: Gallimard, 1967);

Dans la salle des pas perdus, 2 volumes (Paris: Gallimard, 1974, 1976);

Théâtre, volume 1, definitive edition (Paris: Gallimard, 1977)–comprises *Le Casseur d'assiettes*, *Tour à terre*, *Note du 19 mars 1929 et lettre aux critiques*, *Le Pont de l'Europe*, *La Boule de verre*, and *Pièces à lire(s)*.

Armand Salacrou's career as a playwright extended from 1925 to 1972. His work includes twenty-five plays performed and published, three *pièces à lire* (plays for reading), which were not staged, two more plays performed in radio broadcasts, and one movie scenario on which he collaborated with René Clair, who produced the movie. In addition, Salacrou wrote several volumes of memoirs and commentaries on his own theater and on drama in general. In the 1930s, Salacrou's plays became among the most often performed in France during that time, and his plays continued to be performed into the 1970s. His works were staged throughout Europe and on other continents. In 1935, *L'Inconnue d'Arras* (The Unknown Woman of Arras; first published 1942) was performed at the Comédie des Champs-Elysées in Paris and demonstrated his originality as a dramatist through the use of the flashback technique.

Armand Salacrou was born on 9 August 1899, in Rouen, France, to a family of modest means, but he did not allow this circumstance to prevent him from acquiring an extensive education. At age twelve, Armand entered the lycée in Le Havre, where his family had moved when he was two years old. While there, he became friends with Georges Limbour, who became a Surrealist poet, and Jean Dubuffet, who became a well-known artist. Salacrou also took music lessons from Léon Dufy, brother of Raoul Dufy, another future well-known artist.

After successfully completing the *baccalauréat* examination at the end of high school, Salacrou began medical studies in Paris. These studies included working in several hospitals, where his close contact with sickness and death made a profound impression on him. He did not complete his medical studies, having discovered that he preferred literature, especially poetry. He decided to study philosophy, and in 1921 he received a *Diplôme d'études supérieures* in philosophy. A year later, he married a young woman from Le Havre; their long marriage was happy. For a short time, Salacrou worked as a journalist to earn a living. During this period, he met André Masson, a Surrealist artist, and through Masson, Salacrou widened his circle of artist and writer friends to include Juan Gris, Joan Miro, Michel Leiris, Tristan Tzara, and Antonin Artaud.

Two years later (1924), when Salacrou received a law degree, he was already writing plays that incorporated Surrealist elements, such as imagery drawn from dreams and settings in imaginary locations. These early efforts, which he called *pièces à lire* (plays for reading), were never staged. In 1925, however, several important events in his life occurred. Two of his *pièces à lire* were published in a Belgian journal; his first child, Camille, was born; and he began working for a movie company. Feeling the strain of supporting his family, Salacrou left the cinema to enter the advertising business. This venture quickly became highly successful and allowed him to leave his time-consuming job in movie production to concentrate on his writing.

Between 1924 and 1931, six of his plays were performed, with little success. In 1934, however, *Une Femme libre* (A Woman of Freedom) was performed and was a hit. The play concerns a young woman, Lucie, and her escape from marriage and conventional life. Both her Aunt Adrienne, a proponent of bourgeois morality, and her fiancé, Jacques, a fatalist who has constructed a miniature solar system in his home to remind him that the cosmos is a fixed and closed system, contrast with Lucie and her quest for freedom. According to Jacques Guicharnaud in *Modern French Theater from Giraudoux to Genet, 1918–1939* (1975), in this play Salacrou stresses that "all man's unhappiness comes from time's irreversibility.... Salacrou adds a sharp awareness of man's solitude in the cosmos." *Une Femme libre* was staged by Paulette Pax, a notable director of the time, who, according to Salacrou in volume three of *Théâtre* (1970), said to him during the applause at the end of the first performance, "Un tel triomphe, on ne le connaît qu'une fois dans une vie d'auteur" (Such a triumph is enjoyed only once in the life of an author).

Salacrou is credited with being the first French playwright to use the flashback technique extensively in his work. This commonplace technique of the cinema was a daring innovation in the theater of the 1930s. Salacrou's first use of the flashback is found in his next play, *Les Frénétiques* (The Frenzied Ones; published 1936), the story of a domineering movie executive, which premiered in December 1934. Scenes 3 and 4 of the Third Tableau return two characters to ten years before through stage lighting, costumes, and scenery. Salacrou employs this technique to underscore the inexorable nature of the influence of the past on the characters' present lives. In *Les Frénétiques,* the lives of the four main characters have become disordered, just as chronological time is "disordered" onstage. The flashback technique reflects materially the dislocation that has occurred in the lives of these characters.

L'Inconnue d'Arras takes this technique even further. The play opens with a gunshot heard on a darkened stage: the suicide of the protagonist occurs as the curtain rises. After the first fifteen seconds of highly dramatic action, the entire play is presented as a flashback that ostensibly takes place in Ulysse's memory. One particular incident from his recent past that impels Ulysse to seek absolute freedom is that he wants to escape from the knowledge that his wife has been unfaithful to him. He also wants to be free from the suffocating mediocrity of his life. The suicide and the notion that a dying person sees his life flash before him in the final seconds before death provide a structure that allows Salacrou to illustrate a constant theme of his theater–the irrevocability of the past.

In the performance of *L'Inconnue d'Arras,* Ulysse's memories crowd onto the stage, as if they are actually flashing before his eyes. The *aventure* (adventure), as Nicolas, Ulysse's manservant, calls it, begins with an outpouring of all the words Ulysse has uttered or heard during his lifetime. A motley crowd of characters representing his memories presses forward, demanding to be heard and to live in his memory. They include a young woman who has no name–"l'inconnue" of the title. As more characters crowd onstage, the audience sees the different layers of the protagonist's past intermingled. Different moments of Ulysse's life appear simultaneously. Salacrou includes many complex flashbacks within the larger structure of the play, itself one long flashback. The public's and the critics' initial reactions to the performance were mixed. However, *L'Inconnue*

Pierre Renoir and Sophie Desmaret in Salacrou's Le Soldat et la Sorcière *(The Soldier and the Witch), Théâtre Sarah-Bernhardt, Paris, 1945 (© Lipnitzki/Roger-Viollet/Getty Images; from Annie Ubersfeld,* Armand Salacrou, *1970; Thomas Cooper Library, University of South Carolina)*

d'Arras, along with *Les Nuits de la colère* (Nights of Wrath; produced 1946, published 1947), are the author's two plays that have had the greatest success in terms of how many performances have been given and how many places throughout the world they have been staged.

Three more of Salacrou's plays were produced in the 1930s. In November 1936, *Un Homme comme les autres* (An Ordinary Man; published 1938) opened at the Théâtre de l'Oeuvre in Paris. One of Salacrou's darkest dramas, it portrays mankind as trapped in deceit and degradation in a godless universe. According to Guicharnaud, this story of infidelity and sexual obsession follows the traditions of late-nineteenth-century naturalist theater: "a complete psychological structure, details that are somewhat caricatural or typical, and manners in tune with their environment or social origins." Despite its pessimistic atmosphere, this play was a popular success and drew critical acclaim; it had several revivals—in 1944, 1947, and 1958.

Two years after this play opened, Salacrou's first play based on historical events or characters, *La Terre est ronde* (published 1938; translated as *The World Is Round*, 1967), was performed at the Théâtre de l'Atelier on 7 November 1938. Set in Renaissance Florence between 1492 and 1498, the play re-creates the rise to power of the Dominican monk Girolamo Savonarola and his subsequent downfall, as well as the effect his beliefs had on the citizens of Florence. Salacrou evokes two historical events as background for the play: the first is Savonarola's aid to the French under Charles VIII, which resulted in the expulsion of the Medicis from Florence; the other, the conflict between the new liberal humanism interested in science and exploration, as evidenced by the character Silvio and his excitement at learning that the world is not flat but round, and medieval ideas represented by Savonarola's attempts to maintain God at the center of the Florentine universe. This attitude is seen in the monk's orders to burn the city's "vanités" (vanities—secular books and works of art). The old world and the old morality are disintegrating, making way for the new ideas burgeoning at the time, but Savonarola and his followers struggle against them.

In 1938 French theater audiences saw in *La Terre est ronde* an attack on Adolf Hitler and fascism. The violence, cruelty, and excesses provoked by Savonarola's orders in the play could easily be seen as references to what was happening in Europe at the time. According to Annie Ubersfeld in *Armand Salacrou* (1970), ". . . les représentations, avec Dullin dans le rôle de Savonarola, and Barrault dans celui de Silvio, furent parmi les grands événements théâtraux d'avant-guerre" (the performances, with Charles Dullin as Savonarola and Jean-Louis Barrault as Silvio, were among the most important theatrical occasions of the period before World War II). Salacrou states in volume four of his *Théâtre* (1945) that the theater public had misunderstood his play: " . . . le public déforma la pièce. Ses préoccupations l'emportèrent sur les miennes. . . . Je dois reconnaître que le succès de *La Terre est ronde* fut le résultat d'un malentendu indiscutable" (. . . the theater public changed the meaning of the play. Its preoccupations prevailed over mine. . . . I must recognize that the success of *La Terre est ronde* was the result of an unquestionable misunderstanding). In this same volume, Salacrou states that the critic M. Talladoire judged that the play expressed an eternal problem—the struggle between the flesh and the spirit, between God and sin.

In 1940, Salacrou was called for military service. After the fall of France, he was imprisoned in Brest but managed to escape on the same day as his capture. Several months later, he was demobilized. In 1942 he joined the Front National, a resistance movement, and worked in the clandestine press, editing and broadcasting the news, as well as continuing to write plays.

In 1943, 1944, and 1945, the prestigious French publishing house Gallimard printed volumes one, two, and three of his *Théâtre*. In March 1944, Salacrou joined the "Forces Françaises Libres," General Charles de Gaulle's troops that fought alongside the Allies.

Later that year, after the liberation of the capital, two of his plays were produced in Paris: *La Marguerite* (published 1941; translated as *Marguerite*, 1967) and *Les Fiancés du Havre* (The Fiancés of Le Havre; published 1944). Both were staged for the first time in Paris, the first at the Théâtre Pigalle on 28 October 1944 and the second at the Comédie-Française on 10 December 1944. The subject of both plays is family life. In *La Marguerite*, a young widow who cares for her dying father-in-law and seeks comfort in the affections of the family doctor realizes that she still loves her deceased husband when a hungry stranger approaches the family for a handout. The blind father-in-law forces the stranger to assume the role of his lost son and dies contentedly in his "son's" arms. After struggling against her father-in-law's illusion that his son is not dead, Marguerite is converted to the illusion in the final lines of the play and dismisses her lover. In the introduction to *Three Plays by Armand Salacrou*, Stephen Porter judges this one-act play a successful blend of melodrama and improbable events: "the impossible can carry conviction when acted naturalistically in the familiar style of domestic drama." *Les Fiancés du Havre* presents the caustic side of Salacrou's work. It recounts the disintegration of two families after they discover that their two sons were exchanged at birth and each brought up by the wrong set of parents.

After the war, Salacrou was offered two administrative positions in the French government, first as director of Radio-France in 1946 and then as administrator of the Comédie-Française, France's premier theater company, in 1947. He turned down both positions, preferring to devote his time to his writing. In 1946 he was made an officer of the Légion d'Honneur in recognition of his military service. On 12 December of the same year, his play about the French Resistance, *Les Nuits de la colère*, opened in Paris at the Théâtre Marigny under the direction of Barrault and was an immediate success, in part because of the stellar cast: besides Barrault in the leading role of Jean Cordeau, Marie-Hélène Dasté acted the part of his wife, Louise; Madeleine Renaud performed the role of Pierrette Bazire; Jean Desailly played her husband, Bernard Bazire; and Pierre Renoir acted the part of Dédé, one of Jean's colleagues in the Resistance. In May 1947, the Piccolo Teatro in Milan, Italy, opened its season with the play, directed by Giorgio Strehler. The play was performed in seventeen countries outside of France—from London to Tel Aviv to Osaka. In 1962, the Compagnie Renauld-Barrault performed the play in the Union of Soviet Socialist Republics (U.S.S.R.).

The setting for *Les Nuits de la colère* is Chartres, in April 1944, when France continued to suffer under the Nazi occupation. The plot deals with an incident involving members of the French Resistance and their attempt to sabotage the Nazi transportation system by derailing a German fuel train. Salacrou renders this dramatic incident more vivid by dislocating chronological time and space through flashbacks and "flash-forwards." The author had already used the flashback technique in earlier plays, notably in *Les Frénétiques* and in *L'Inconnue d'Arras*, but the technical aspects of the disarrangement of time are more complex and more thoroughly elaborated in *Les Nuits de la colère*.

The play has eight characters—Jean Cordeau, Rivoire, Dédé, and Lecoq, all members of the Resistance; Jean's wife, Louise; another couple, Pierrette and Bernard Bazire, who have been close friends of Jean and Louise since before the war; and Pisançon, who turns out to be a collaborator who works for the Gestapo in Chartres. Jean, an engineer, has the job of placing and setting off explosives on a train track. The curtain rises on a scene of violence: machine-gun fire and shouting are heard. Three characters are shot down onstage before the spectators' eyes: Rivoire has just gunned down Bernard, who collapses to the floor and dies. Pisançon enters, and Rivoire guns him down also. Pisançon, however, does not die immediately but is able to shoot before he expires and send Rivoire to his death also, along with Bernard, whom Rivoire had come to shoot for his role in betraying Jean to the Gestapo. In the course of the play, Salacrou resurrects some of the dead characters, and, in part 1, scene 3, Pierrette Bazire, who is not dead, joins in the conversation with two dead men. This meeting between characters alive and dead allows the author to build the suspense concerning what has really happened to Jean Cordeau. The audience gradually discovers who Jean is, what he did to be injured, and his relationship to Bernard and Pierrette Bazire.

Throughout his career, Salacrou wrote plays in the tradition of the Boulevard Theater—that is, plays on farcical or salacious subjects that served as after-dinner entertainment. Three of his most popular dramas in this category of light drama were written and staged during and immediately after World War II: *Histoire de rire* (produced 1939, published 1940; translated as *When the Music Stops*, 1967), *Le Soldat et la sorcière* (The Soldier and the Witch; produced 1945, published 1947), and *L'Archipel Lenoir* (The Lenoir Archipelago; produced 1947, published 1948). *Histoire de rire* moves from a comic treatment of cuckoldry to pathos. *Le Soldat et la sorcière*, in spite of being designated a *divertissement historique* (historical entertainment), also concerns sexual mores. It was staged at the Théâtre Sarah-Bernhardt, well known for Boulevard Theater productions. *L'Archipel Lenoir* tells the story of a family that ultimately asks a profligate grandfather to commit suicide in order to preserve the family's honor. Dorothy Knowles, in *French Drama of the Inter-War Years* (1967), says that she believes that the interest of this last play resides in its dialogue and the mixture of realism and improbability: "The dialogue is brilliant; it is completely and deliberately unrealistic when taken as a whole, though each single response rings true. This adds to the comic element already present in the situation."

In 1947 Salacrou collaborated with Clair, the movie director, on a motion-picture version of the Faust legend: *La Beauté du diable* (The Devil's Charm; produced and published 1950). *Poof,* a play about the advertising industry, was produced in Brussels in 1948. That same year Salacrou traveled to New York City to give several lectures about *Les Nuits de la colère,* which was playing there. In 1949 he was elected to membership in the Académie Goncourt, a group of ten writers that annually chooses the recipient of the Goncourt literary prize, the most coveted in France.

During the 1950s, Salacrou continued to write new plays, which were produced, while revivals of his previous plays were performed in France and other countries. His new works–*Dieu le savait* (God Knew It; produced 1950, published 1951); *Sens interdit* (One-way; published 1952, produced 1953); *Les Invités du bon Dieu* (The Good God's Guests; produced 1953, published 1956); *Une Femme trop honnête* (A Too Honest Woman; produced and published 1956); and *Le Miroir* (The Mirror; produced and published 1956)–are "much closer to the tradition of the Boulevard theater," in Knowles's opinion.

In 1961, *Boulevard Durand* (1960, Durand Boulevard) opened in Le Havre and later in Paris. Salacrou called the play a "Chronique d'un procès oublié" (Chronicle of a forgotten trial), indicating that the events portrayed in the drama actually took place. Salacrou recounts in dramatic form a miscarriage of justice that occurred in Le Havre in 1910 and that the author witnessed as a child. Salacrou dedicated *Boulevard Durand* to the memory of Jules Durand, a dockworker in Le Havre who became active in the coalworkers' union in order to combat, as Salacrou said in volume eight of *Théâtre,* "la brutalité de la misère" (the brutality of extreme poverty), which trapped workers.

Ubersfeld writes of this play: "*Boulevard Durand* est une oeuvre capitale, non seulement dans la carrière de Salacrou, mais aussi dans l'histoire du théâtre contemporain" (*Boulevard Durand* is a major work, not only in Salacrou's career, but also in the history of contemporary theater). For Knowles, *Boulevard Durand* is Salacrou's " . . . contribution to the struggle against future injustice" and, like *Les Nuits de la colère,* highly successful. After its opening in Le Havre, it played in Paris, where it was so popular that seats were difficult to obtain. For two years afterward, it played throughout France to sold-out houses (148 performances in fifty cities, with almost ninety-four thousand spectators). It was also performed in Liverpool and Ankara. In 1968 it aired on French television to commemorate the twentieth anniversary of the International Declaration of the Rights of Man; and in 1970, it went on tour again, playing in seventeen cities in France.

Fifteen years after the opening of *Les Nuits de la colère,* Salacrou created another character who sought to live honorably in the face of oppression, this time caused by the tyranny of poverty, not by political tyranny. Jules Durand is a dockworker who loads coal onto the ships of Le Havre. In an effort to improve the conditions of his fellow workers, he becomes the secretary of a dockworkers' union and speaks out against the company's injustices. The lack of response to the union's requests leads the union to call a strike that paralyzes the port. Jules's father loses his job because of his son's activity in the union; Jules is offered a manager's position with the firm if he agrees to end the strike; and strikebreakers are employed. An altercation between one of the strikebreakers and four striking workers results in the death of the strikebreaker. Durand is accused of instigating the strikers to crime, then arrested and imprisoned. At his trial he is defended by René Coty (president of France, 1954–1959), who is unable to persuade the judges that his client has been falsely accused. The judges, in fact, rarely allow the lawyer to finish his sentences and are not interested in the truth. The jury condemns Durand to death, but protests by French labor unions and even the widow of the murdered strikebreaker save him from the guillotine. After seven years of imprisonment, Durand's sentence is commuted, but he leaves prison insane. His release leads to a new incarceration in a mental asylum, where he dies eight years later.

The setting of *Boulevard Durand* is realistic. The play opens in a café frequented by the dockworkers in the port of Le Havre. Salacrou insists upon their apathy, induced by alcohol and fatigue and encouraged by the company's policy of allowing bars to operate on the workplace, by having four workers collapse, inebriated, in the rain-drenched street. Guns are shot onstage during the fight between strikers and strikebreakers. Through secondary characters and contrasting scenes, Salacrou also incorporates his protagonist's story into the economic and social history of early-twentieth-century France. Luc Siemens represents the shipping-company owners who will be forced into bankruptcy by the strike. Scenes 2 and 3 oppose Siemens's seaside villa,

Charles Dullin and Pierre Bertin in Salacrou's L'Archipel Lenoir *(The Lenoir Archipelago), Théâtre Montparnasse, Paris, November 1947 (© Lipnitzki/Roger-Viollet/Getty Images)*

empty except for his wife, with the spare Durand home, where an extended family lives and works together. In the episodes following Jules's condemnation, Salacrou juxtaposes three scenes: newspaper headlines announcing the suicide of Jules's father are projected on a screen, below which the stage is divided between a scene of Jules in prison and a scene of union workers protesting his imprisonment. This juxtaposition suggests the far-reaching consequences of the Durand case. In addition, contrasts of light and darkness dramatize the episodes of Jules's sentencing and the prison years, during which the real Jules Durand's eyesight weakened.

The following year (1962) Salacrou traveled to Russia with the renowned Barrault-Renaud theater company to see their production of *Les Nuits de la colère*. In 1964, *Comme les chardons* (Like the Thistles; published 1966) was performed at the Comédie-Française, the author's fifth play to be staged there. In this play, Salacrou returns to the use of the flashback to evoke an older woman's remembrance of a past love. His last play, *La Rue noire* (The Dark Street), published in 1967, was never staged, although it was performed on French radio in 1971 and 1972.

Salacrou and his wife, Lucienne, left Paris in 1970 to move back to Le Havre, where he worked on his memoirs. Two volumes of *Dans la salle des pas perdus* (In the Waiting Room) were published in 1974 and 1976. Salacrou's active and full life ended on 23 November 1989. He was ninety years old.

Armand Salacrou was not only prolific but varied in his dramatic production. This variety makes his oeuvre difficult to classify. Porter, in his introduction to the English versions of *La Terre est ronde, Histoire de rire,* and *Marguerite,* observes that "Salacrou may be hard to get a hold of at first reading . . . the large historical epic, the brittle sex comedy, and the moralizing domestic drama seem to come from different writers with totally different techniques and intents." Guicharnaud best sums up Salacrou's achievement as the formulation of "a theater of man. . . . the spectacle he creates shows man at grips with himself, aware of transcendency, but a transcendency represented by others, by the mystery of passing time, and by the physical cosmos, infinite and incomprehensible."

References:

Philippe Bébon, *Salacrou* (Paris: Editions Universitaires, 1971);

David Bradby, *Modern French Drama 1940–1980* (Cambridge: Cambridge University Press, 1984), pp. 50–52;

Jacques Fauve, "A Drama of Essence: Salacrou and Others," *Yale French Studies,* 14 (1954–1955): 30–40;

Fiorenza di Franco, *Le Théâtre de Salacrou* (Paris: Gallimard, 1970);

Jacques Guicharnaud, *Modern French Theater from Giraudoux to Genet, 1918–1939* (New Haven: Yale University Press, 1975), pp. 87–97;

Dorothy Knowles, *French Drama of the Inter-War Years* (London: Harrap, 1967), pp. 143–158;

David Looseley, *A Search for Commitment: The Theater of Armand Salacrou* (Exeter: University of Exeter Press, 1985);

Paul-Louis Mignon, *Salacrou* (Paris: Gallimard, 1960);

Pierrette Portron, Marie-Françoise Rose, and Yolande Simon, *Hommage à Armand Salacrou* (Le Havre: Isoète, 1990);

Serge Radine, *Anouilh, Lenormand, Salacrou. Trois Dramaturges à la recherche de leur vérité* (Geneva: Editions des Trois Collines, 1951), pp. 99–140;

Juris Silenieks, *Themes and Dramatic Forms in the Plays of Armand Salacrou* (Lincoln: University of Nebraska, 1967);

Pierre-Henri Simon, *Théâtre et destin. La Signification de la renaissance dramatique en France au XXe siècle* (Paris: Colin, 1966), pp. 119–141;

Annie Ubersfeld, *Armand Salacrou* (Paris: Seghers, 1970);

Jose Van Den Esch, *Armand Salacrou, dramaturge de l'angoisse* (Paris: Editions du Temps Présent, 1947).

Papers:

Armand Salacrou's manuscripts are located at the Bibliothèque Municipale Armand Salacrou, Le Havre, France.

Nathalie Sarraute

(18 July 1900 – 19 October 1999)

Sarah Hurlburt
Whitman College

See also the Sarraute entry in *DLB 83: French Novelists Since 1960.*

PLAY PRODUCTIONS: *Le Silence* and *Le Mensonge,* Paris, Petit Odéon, 10 January 1967;

BB, Paris, Espace Pierre Cardin, 5 February 1973; adapted into sign language, Limoges, France, Festival des théâtres francophones, 2001;

Elle est là, Paris, Centre Georges Pompidou, Autumn 1978;

Pour un oui ou pour un non, Paris, Petit Théâtre du Rond-Point, 17 February 1986.

BOOKS: *Tropismes* (Paris: Denoël, 1939; revised and enlarged edition, Paris: Editions de Minuit, 1957); translated by Maria Jolas as *Tropisms,* in *Tropisms, and The Age of Suspicion* (London: Calder, 1963); republished as *Tropisms* (New York: Braziller, 1963);

Portrait d'un inconnu, preface by Jean-Paul Sartre (Paris: R. Marin, 1948); translated by Jolas as *Portrait of a Man Unknown* (New York: Braziller, 1958; London: Calder, 1959);

Martereau (Paris: Gallimard, 1953); translated by Jolas (New York: Braziller, 1959; London: Calder, 1964);

L'Ere du soupçon: Essais sur le roman (Paris: Gallimard, 1956)–comprises "De Dostoïevsky à Kafka," "L'Ere du soupçon," "Conversation et sous-conversation," and "Ce que voient les oiseaux"; translated by Jolas as *The Age of Suspicion,* in *Tropisms, and The Age of Suspicion;* republished as *The Age of Suspicion: Essays on the Novel* (New York: Braziller, 1963); *L'Ere du soupçon* republished, with a preface by Sarraute (Paris: Gallimard, 1964);

Le Planétarium (Paris: Gallimard, 1959); translated by Jolas as *The Planetarium* (New York: Braziller, 1960; London: Calder, 1961);

Les Fruits d'or (Paris: Gallimard, 1963); translated by Jolas as *The Golden Fruits* (New York: Braziller, 1964; London: Calder, 1965);

Nathalie Sarraute, 1964 (AP Wide World)

Le Silence, suivi de Le Mensonge (Paris: Gallimard, 1967); translated by Jolas as *Silence, and The Lie* (London: Calder & Boyars, 1969);

Entre la vie et la mort (Paris: Gallimard, 1968); translated by Jolas as *Between Life and Death* (New York: Braziller, 1969; London: Calder & Boyars, 1970);

Isma, ou Ce qui s'appelle rien, suivi de Le Silence et Le Mensonge (Paris: Gallimard, 1970); *Isma* translated by Jolas and Barbara Wright as *Izzum,* in *Collected Plays* (1980);

325

Vous les entendez? (Paris: Gallimard, 1972); translated by Jolas as *Do You Hear Them?* (New York: Braziller, 1973; London: Calder & Boyars, 1975);

"*Disent les imbéciles*" (Paris: Gallimard, 1976); translated by Jolas as "*Fools Say*" (New York: Braziller, 1977; London: Calder, 1977);

Théâtre (Paris: Gallimard, 1978)–comprises *Elle est là, C'est beau, Isma, Le Mensonge,* and *Le Silence;* translated by Jolas and Wright as *Collected Plays* (London: Calder, 1980; New York: Braziller, 1981)–comprises *It Is There, It's Beautiful, Izzum, The Lie,* and *Silence; Théâtre* enlarged to include *Pour un oui ou pour un non* (Paris: Gallimard, 1993);

L'Usage de la parole (Paris: Gallimard, 1980); translated by Wright as *The Use of Speech* (New York: Braziller, 1983; London: Calder, 1983);

Pour un oui ou pour un non (Paris: Gallimard, 1982);

Enfance (Paris: Gallimard 1983); translated by Wright as *Childhood* (New York: Braziller, 1984; London: Calder, 1984);

Paul Valéry et l'enfant d'éléphant; Flaubert le précurseur (Paris: Gallimard, 1986);

Tu ne t'aimes pas (Paris: Gallimard, 1989); translated by Wright as *You Don't Love Yourself* (New York: Braziller, 1990);

Ici (Paris: Gallimard, 1995); translated by Wright as *Here* (New York: Braziller, 1997);

Ouvrez (Paris: Gallimard, 1997).

Editions and Collection: *Enfance,* edited by Marie-France Savéan, Collection Folio Plus, no. 4 (Paris: Gallimard, 1995);

Oeuvres complètes, edited by Jean-Yves Tadié and others, Bibliothèque de la Pléiade, no. 432 (Paris: Gallimard, 1996);

C'est beau, edited by Arnaud Rykner, Collection Folio/Théâtre, no. 63 (Paris: Gallimard, 2000).

PRODUCED SCRIPTS: *Le Silence,* radio, translated by Elmar Tophoven, Süddeutscher Rundfunk, 1 April 1964;

Le Mensonge, radio, France-Culture/Radio-Télévision Belge; translated by Tophoven, Süddeutscher Rundfunk, 2 March 1966;

Isma, ou Ce qui s'appelle rien, radio, in German, Süddeutscher Rundfunk, 7 January 1970; in French, France-Culture, 28 June 1970;

C'est beau, radio, France-Culture, 16 October 1972;

Elle est là, radio, Süddeutscher Rundfunk, 1979;

Pour un oui ou pour un non, radio, Radio France, 13 December 1981.

RECORDINGS: *Tropismes, et L'Usage de la parole,* read by Sarraute and Madeleine Renaud, Des Femmes, 1980;

Enfance, read by Sarraute, Auvidis AD 804, 1986;

Nathalie Sarraute lit Entre la vie et la mort, Des Femmes, 1987;

Les Fruits d'or, read by Sarraute, Auvidis AD 805, 1987;

Nathalie Sarraute lit Ici, Des Femmes, 1995.

SELECTED PERIODICAL PUBLICATION–UNCOLLECTED: "Nathalie Sarraute a réponse à tous," *Le Figaro,* 4 February 1972, pp. 13, 15.

Nathalie Sarraute's status as a novelist has overshadowed her theatrical production, in part because she wrote far fewer plays than novels. Yet, her theater is dense, subtly constructed, and deceptively accessible. It has been performed throughout the Western world, on stages in Belgium, Canada, and the United States, as well as in France. Actors and directors are drawn to the complexity of Sarraute's texts, with their precise language and intonation, and intrigued by the complete lack of staging instructions and the accompanying freedom entailed by the absence of such directions.

Sarraute was born Natalie Tcherniak in Ivanova-Voznessensk, Russia, on 18 July 1900. Her mother, Pauline Chatounovsky Tcherniak, was an author who wrote under the pseudonym N. Vikhrovski, and her father, Ilya Tcherniak, was a chemist and, briefly, a political activist. Her parents divorced when she was two years old and remarried other partners, living in Paris, Russia, Budapest, and Switzerland throughout Nathalie's childhood. Although most of her primary education took place in France, until the age of nine she traveled back and forth between parents and countries, speaking French, Russian, German, and, eventually, English. After 1909 she lived with her father in Paris, receiving infrequent, long visits from her mother. Sarraute did not visit Russia again until 1935.

Sarraute grew up in Paris surrounded by Russian and French intellectuals, arguing about books with her father and supported by him in her educational goals. She studied history at Oxford University in 1921 and history and sociology in Berlin in 1922 before returning to Paris to attend law school. There she met her future husband, Raymond Sarraute, in 1923; they married in 1925, and both practiced law. Their first daughter, Claude, was born in 1927. Her legal career was short-lived, however, and in 1932, one year before the birth of her third daughter, Dominique, she ceased practicing law entirely and began to write. Her first book, *Tropismes* (translated as *Tropisms,* 1963), was published in 1939. Over the course of the next sixty years she wrote eleven novels, six plays, an autobiography, and several critical works.

World War II was a difficult time for the Sarraute family. Raymond was mobilized, and Nathalie and her father registered as Jews. She was disbarred in 1940 under the Vichy regime because of her Jewish heritage. When it appeared that her husband would be disbarred as well because of their relationship, they divorced immediately. Denounced in 1942 by the baker of the village in which they were staying, she barely escaped arrest. She spent the rest of the war separated from her family but staying nearby, at one point using the pseudonym Nicole Sauvage and posing as her daughters' governess. She and her husband remarried in 1956 and remained together until his death in 1985. Raymond was her first reader and staunchest supporter, often traveling with her to her conferences.

The title of *Tropismes,* a biological term for the involuntary attraction or repulsion of an organism to a given stimulus (for example, plants turning toward light), describes the constant and uncontrollable undertow of sensation that Sarraute believed governed all human interaction. She explained tropisms as those indefinable movements that slide along the outer edges of consciousness but motivate every gesture and emotion. Sarraute's tropisms should not be confused with the traditional *monologue intérieur* (interior monologue, or stream of consciousness), which presents a character's thoughts or feelings directly. Rather, she examines each fleeting, involuntary sensation, communicating it through imagery and the rhythm of her sentences, while the dialogue in her novels remains anodyne. These tropisms, as she defines them in her first book, form the basis of all of her subsequent writings.

Sarraute gave dozens of interviews and attended conferences about her works in the latter half of her life, traveling throughout Europe and the United States to speak. Most of this material is concerned primarily with her novels. Only one of her critical essays deals directly with her drama: "Le gant retourné" (The Inside-Out Glove), first presented in 1974 as a lecture in Madison, Wisconsin, published in *Cahiers Renaud Barrault* in 1975, and collected in *Oeuvres complètes* (1996, Complete Works). In this relatively short essay Sarraute explains that what constitutes the *sous-conversation* (subconversation) in her novels—communicated to the reader through imagery and rhythm—becomes the action itself in her plays; hence, her initial reluctance to write for the theater, since the actual dialogue in her novels conveys none of the meaning. As a solution, Sarraute "turned the glove," as she puts it in the essay, eliminating the surface dialogue of her novels and moving the predialogue—the tropisms explored through the narrative voice—to center stage. Instead of attempting to have the actors convey unspoken emotions through physical expression while speaking ordinary dialogue, she put each silent impulse or enthusiasm into words.

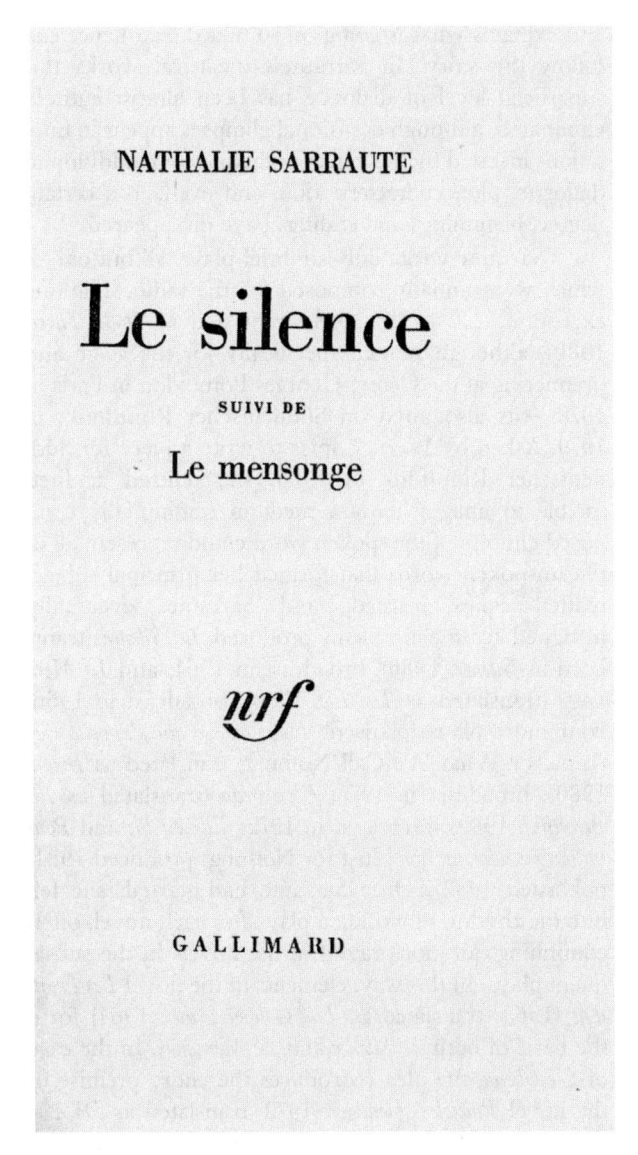

Title page for the 1967 edition of Sarraute's first two plays (translated as Silence *and* The Lie, *1980), which were initially broadcast on radio in 1964 and 1966, respectively (Thomas Cooper Library, University of South Carolina)*

This transition marks the essential difference between Sarraute's works for the theater and her novels. In the latter the dialogue represents only a small portion of the entire text. In her plays normal dialogue—everything that would be in quotation marks in her novels—disappears entirely, and everything that would not be in quotation marks in the novels becomes the dialogue. As a result, in Sarraute's drama, action in the traditional sense has been effaced. In traditional theater much of the dialogue describes the action of the play and explains what is going on so that the audience can follow the story. In Sarraute's theatrical works this superficial level of dialogue has been almost entirely eliminated, although occasional glimpses appear in quotations inserted by the voices in the plays. In addition to dialogue, plot, characterization, and even, to a certain degree, beginnings and endings have disappeared.

Sarraute wrote only six brief plays, all but one of which were initially composed for the radio. The one exception, *Elle est là* (1978; translated as *It Is There,* 1980), although written specifically for the stage and premiering at the Centre Georges Pompidou in Paris in 1978, was also aired on Süddeutscher Rundfunk, in 1979. Asked by Werner Spies to write a piece for Süddeutscher Rundfunk in 1963, she refused at first, unable to imagine how a medium traditionally composed entirely of the spoken word could represent all of the unspoken words that formed her principal subject matter. Spies insisted, and Sarraute, eventually intrigued by the problem, produced *Le Silence* (translated as *Silence,* 1980), broadcast in 1964, and *Le Mensonge* (translated as *The Lie,* 1980), broadcast in 1966. Four more plays followed: *Isma, ou Ce qui s'appelle rien* (Isma, or What We Call Nothing; translated as *Izzum,* 1980), broadcast in 1970; *C'est beau* (translated as *It's Beautiful,* 1980), broadcast in 1972; *Elle est là;* and *Pour un oui ou pour un non* (Just for Nothing; produced 1981, published 1982). Once Sarraute had started, she fell into the rhythm of writing a play after each novel, often continuing questions raised in the novels in the subsequent plays. In this way, elements of the novel *Les Fruits d'or* (1963; translated as *The Golden Fruits,* 1964) form the basis of both *Le Silence* and *Le Mensonge.* In the case of *C'est beau,* the play reproduces the entire premise of the novel *Vous les entendez?* (1972; translated as *Do You Hear Them?* 1973) but with a different sort of conclusion.

The elimination of action in Sarraute's theatrical works is consistent with the near absence of physical stage directions. When the plays are read on radio, the few stage directions seem logical since almost all of them indicate specific vocal inflections, such as "*horrifié*" (horrified), "*voix terrible*" (terrifying voice), and "*De plus en plus rageur*" (more and more enraged). There are no scenic directions because there is no one location or even a time in which the plays are set. Sarraute claimed that as she worked, she never imagined specific actions or scenes for her *sous-conversations,* leaving that work entirely to the director. Only her last two plays include actual, though still minimal, physical stage instructions, indicating, for example, that F. "*se tourne vers la salle*" (turns toward the audience) or that "*F. entre, s'occupe à une table, range des papiers*" (F. enters, works at a table, straightens papers).

The absence of the physical world of the stage in Sarraute's plays also corresponds with a similar minimalism in her characters. Many of them do not have names and are designated only by letters and numbers, such as H1, F1, and F2. The anonymity, or perhaps the universality, of these characters goes beyond their lack of traditional names. The characters in *Le Silence,* the first and perhaps the most abstract of Sarraute's plays, lack not only names but also separate, distinct identities. F1 declares that she would never be able to remain silent the way Jean-Pierre seems to do—a statement that seems to demarcate clearly individual characteristics—only to declare a few lines later that she would be capable of keeping quiet until the end of time. Sarraute is not playing with the distinction between a true and a false expression. Each of these statements is equally true, sincerely felt, and possible for anyone. Nor does she establish separate identities for her characters through dialogue. By her own admission, Sarraute was not interested in the physical appearance, social class, motivations, individual psychology, or even the gender of her characters. She believed that all of these elements belonged to a superficial level of detail that had little relevance for the truths of her subterranean world. She claimed that in her plays the designation of masculine or feminine characters was simply a necessary convenience, a way to vary tonalities and avoid monotony in the voices. In *Le Silence,* for example, the placement of certain phrases and not others in the mouth of F1 is as arbitrary as the distinction between F1 and H1.

Questions of gender and individual identity continue to infiltrate critical discussions about Sarraute's drama, however, frequently in the context of her peculiarly anonymous naming convention. She was confronted by actors attempting to interpret the role of gender in her plays. When Emmanuelle Laborit spoke with her about using women to play H1 and H2—two roles that, until that time, had been exclusively interpreted by men—in a sign-language adaptation of *Pour un oui ou pour un non,* Sarraute apparently laughed and claimed that the *H* stood for *humain* (human) and not *homme* (man), as was the common assumption.

Sarraute described her drama as real but not realistic, an awkward moment magnified a thousand times and examined from all sides. Despite the discomfort produced by these awkward moments, the results are sometimes quite funny. In a 1974 interview with Simone Benmussa she said, "L'humour vient du grossissement. C'est toujours humoristique quand on grossit une chose infime. C'est comique. Moi, quand j'écris je m'amuse, c'est à la fois terrible et comique" (The humor comes from the magnification. It's always humorous when a tiny thing is hugely magnified. It's funny. When I write I have fun, and it's simultaneously horrible and funny). Reviews of performances of Sarraute's plays consistently mention the dark hilarity of her work and the spontaneous laughter provoked by the unbearable.

These brief plays with no physical action and no traditional plot are cataclysmic, despite their humor. In each one Sarraute examines how a small word, an inflection even, can threaten to destroy the world. Her tropisms consist of these small, strained moments in conversation. In *Le Silence* one character's refusal to speak provokes a crisis state in those around him, and their internal preoccupations brought to the surface by this stimulus form the principal action of the play. In *Le Mensonge* the exposure of an inconsequential lie threatens the foundation of social discourse. In *Isma, ou Ce qui s'appelle rien* a group of characters desperately seeks to identify what it is that irritates them about another couple, eventually concluding that it is the way they pronounce words ending in *ism*. *C'est beau* explores a couple's inability to express enthusiasm or appreciation in front of their son. *Elle est là* examines the extraordinary discomfort produced by the knowledge that another person has an irrevocably different idea from one's own. In *Pour un oui ou pour un non,* the title of which may also be translated as "Constantly" or "For No Good Reason," an unfortunate pause in one friend's expression of appreciation, his way of saying "C'est bien, ça" (That's fine), causes an irreparable rupture between the two characters. In each case, the characters are trapped between their simultaneous desire and their inability to put a name to their problem, falling back repeatedly on a word used in the subtitle of *Isma, rien* (nothing).

The real point of rupture in Sarraute's plays is not silence, a lie, or a certain way of pronouncing a word, but a different character's sudden inability to pretend or overlook. The various problems presented at the beginning of each play already exist—in fact, may have existed for some time. In *Pour un oui ou pour un non,* for example, the fatal "C'est bien, ça" was pronounced at an unspecified time in the past, but far enough in the past for an estrangement already to be in place. The action is thus not this moment of pronunciation but rather the moment when another character, H2 in this case, can no longer tolerate the situation. *Le Silence* begins with H1's inability while telling a story to put up further with Jean-Pierre's mutism, which, until this point, the other characters have managed to ignore. In *Le Mensonge* this moment of loss of control has already taken place before the start of the play, which opens with the other characters' discussing how they felt when Pierre exposed an acquaintance of theirs in the process of telling a lie, a lie of no consequence to anyone except Pierre, with his heightened sensibilities.

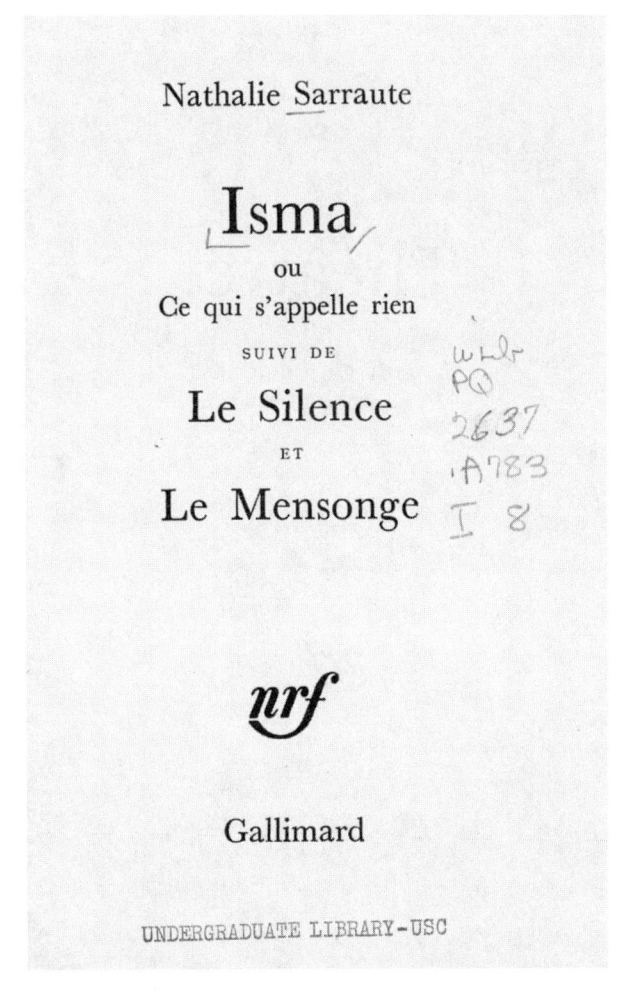

Title page for Sarraute's play (Isma, or What We Call Nothing; translated as Izzum, *1980) about a group of characters irritated by a speech tic of their neighbors, which was first performed as a radio play in 1970 and was published that same year along with her first two plays (Thomas Cooper Library, University of South Carolina)*

At the same time, just as Sarraute's plays begin with a character who can no longer tolerate a particular inflection or situation, they frequently end with this same character capitulating in some way in an awkward retreat from the stand taken at the beginning. In his commentary in the drama section in Sarraute's *Oeuvres complètes,* Arnaud Rykner points out that only when H1 resumes his story at the end of *Le Silence* does Jean-Pierre finally speak, as though the entire play were a parenthetical expression, a cataclysmic blink of an eye in a larger scene—as though, indeed, it never took place at all. Similarly, at the end of *Le Mensonge,* Pierre finally obtains the confession from Simone that he fought to extract: that she was joking. The idea that there is such

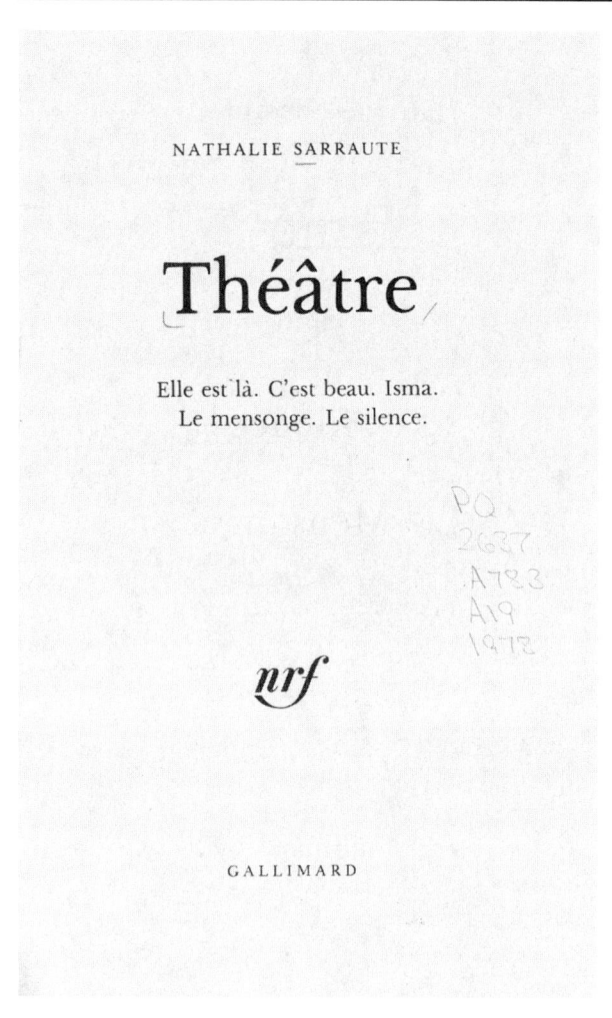

Title page for the 1978 edition of Sarraute's collected dramas, which was enlarged in 1993 to include a sixth play, Pour un oui ou pour un non *(Constantly), initially published in 1982 and first performed in 1986, about two friends who become estranged over a minor misunderstanding (Thomas Cooper Library, University of South Carolina)*

a thing as truth and that this truth can be expressed in words evaporates in the face of words that have no meaning or, worse, potentially have every meaning.

Plot summaries of Sarraute's plays are thus inadequate to describe the action because the tropism is the sole action. In *Isma, ou Ce qui s'appelle rien,* for example, the whole play turns on the need to put a name to that which by its nature has no name–the tropism, or, in this case, "ce qui s'appelle rien." The action, or, as Rykner calls it in *Théâtres du nouveau roman: Sarraute, Pinget, Duras* (1988), the *logodrame* (logodrama) of the play, centers on this difficulty with naming. Through naming, the characters seek to categorize their feeling of malaise, thereby appropriating the authority of language to their cause. The problem is that the feelings these characters are attempting to pinpoint belong to the subterranean world of Sarraute's tropisms, whereas names necessarily belong to the superficial world of everyday dialogue:

> ELLE: Un vrai crime. Ça, c'est une chance. Un crime. Quelque chose d'énorme. Quelque chose de prévu par toutes les lois. Mais nous . . . vous voyez . . . Isma . . . n'aboutirait jamais à des choses comme ça. . . .
>
> LUI: Isma . . . quand on le suit jusqu'à sa source . . . ça nous conduit. . . .
>
> ELLE, tout bas: À l'indicible. Qui n'a pas de nom. Qui n'est prévu nulle part. Que rien n'interdit.
>
> LUI: Quelque chose de glissant . . . qui vous file entre les doigts. . . .
>
> (HER: A true crime. Oh, that would be great luck. A crime. Something huge. Something foreseen by all the laws. But we . . . well . . . Isma . . . will never come to such a thing. . . .
>
> HIM: Isma . . . when you follow all the way to its source . . . it takes you. . . .
>
> HER, softly: To the unspeakable. That which has no name. Which isn't accounted for anywhere. Which nothing forbids.
>
> HIM: Something slippery . . . that slides between your fingers. . . .)

"Isma" is the term the characters use to refer to a speech tic of their neighbors, the Dubuits, who overemphasize the last syllable of words ending in *ism*. The intensity of their revulsion for this habit is completely out of proportion with the "crime" itself. This reaction is the tropism, "what we call nothing"–the powerful, indefinable sensation that has no name and cannot have a name. At the end of the play the characters are no farther advanced than at the beginning, their attempts at naming the problem with the Dubuits coming to nothing.

Beginning with *Isma,* Sarraute introduced the complication of preexisting relationships. The precise relationships among the voices in *Le Silence* and *Le Mensonge* are unclear. In *Isma,* Sarraute explores for the first time how the relationships among the characters determine the intensity of their reaction to the tropism. In *C'est beau* the relationship between parents and children defines the arena, since an inability to express enthusiasm in front of a mere acquaintance, for example, would not register as a serious problem. The fact that their son cannot express enthusiasm before them makes this particular tropism a source of acute anguish for Lui and Elle. *Elle est là* explores a different kind of relationship, that of the workplace, with its constant contact and sense of hierarchy. In *Pour un oui ou pour un non* the characters openly discuss their relationship, the history of a friendship dating back to their childhood. In each case Sarraute explores the destructive power of a negative tropism in the context of a strong social bond. If the negative urge is not controlled in some way, named, and explained, it threatens to destroy the structure of the relationship, whether it occurs in society in general, as in *Le Silence* and *Le Mensonge,* or in specific subsets of society, as in the four later plays.

C'est beau marks another transition point in Sarraute's theater, characterized in part by a net reduction in the number of characters. Whereas *Le Silence, Le Mensonge,* and *Isma* have from six to nine characters, *C'est beau* has only three; *Elle est là* and *Pour un oui ou pour un non* both have only four. Not only are there fewer characters in the last three plays, but the characters themselves are much more distinct from one another, a consequence of Sarraute's introduction of specific social contexts to these plays. These characters cannot be described as individual personalities but rather as representing specific—and different—positions, each one the embodiment of a particular impulse. As a result, a sequential reading leaves the impression of decreased abstraction over the course of the six plays.

Sarraute's last three plays introduce a new character, the audience. Only *Elle est là* incorporates the audience into the action of the play, as each of the characters at various points addresses the audience directly. Sarraute places the audience in the role of the silent, anonymous, plural judge, in this case the judge who does not speak, although the characters claim to know what it would say if it were to do so. A small ball of paper with the word "intolérance" written on it, supposedly thrown out of the dark onto the stage, stands in for the voice of the jury. The audience takes on the judicial function of the "Voix" (Voice) in *C'est beau* and of the neighbors summoned to judge in *Pour un oui ou pour un non,* in which a neutral third party is used to judge the scene.

Nathalie Sarraute herself was her own best critic. The many conference lectures and interviews she gave over the last thirty years of her life are an invaluable resource for those seeking to understand the mechanics of her endeavor and a caution against certain kinds of criticism. She systematically rejected critical attempts to interpret her books through biography (for example, the idea that she was the product of a broken home), genre (the *nouveau roman,* or new novel), and gender. Sarraute resisted critical categories in the same way that her characters resist names. In her life, her novels, and her plays, she strongly believed in one common human condition. She felt that, at the most profound level, the inner world of all people is experienced in much the same way. By the time of her death on 19 October 1999, she had spent more than sixty years exploring this vision. If she had not succeeded in this enterprise in some fundamental way, her theatrical works would not be so touching and funny—nor would they be so uncomfortable to watch.

Interviews:

"Conversation avec François Bondy," in *Nathalie Sarraute,* by Mimica Cranaki and Yvon Belaval (Paris: Gallimard, 1965);

Bettina L. Knapp, "Interview with Nathalie Sarraute," *Kentucky Romance Quarterly,* 14, no. 3 (1967): 283–295;

Germaine Brée, "Nathalie Sarraute," *Contemporary Literature,* 14 (1973): 137–146;

Gretchen Rous Besser, "Colloque avec Nathalie Sarraute: 22 avril 1976," *French Review,* 50 (December 1976): 284–289;

Jean-Louis de Rambures, "Nathalie Sarraute: Une Table dans un coin de bistro," in his *Comment travaillent les écrivains* (Paris: Flammarion, 1978), pp. 149–154;

Claudde Régy, "Les Faits divers de la parole," *Les Nouvelles Littéraires,* no. 2719 (10–17 January 1980);

Alison Finch and David Kelley, "Propos sur la technique du roman," *French Studies,* 39 (July 1985): 305–315;

André Rollin, *Ils écrivent: Où? Quand? Comment?* (Paris: Mazarine/France-Culture, 1986);

Simone Benmussa, *Nathalie Sarraute* (Lyon: La Manufacture, 1987);

Jason Weiss, "Nathalie Sarraute," in his *Writing at Risk: Interviews in Paris with Uncommon Writers* (Iowa City: University of Iowa Press, 1991), pp. 145–166;

Isabelle Huppert, "Rencontre avec Nathalie Sarraute," *Cahiers du Cinéma,* no. 477 (March 1994): 7–14;

Un siècle d'écrivains: Nathalie Sarraute, video, Institut National de l'Audiovisuel, 1995.

Bibliography:

Sheila M. Bell, *Nathalie Sarraute: A Bibliography* (London: Grant & Cutler, 1982).

References:

André Allemand, *L'oeuvre romanesque de Nathalie Sarraute* (Neuchâtel: Baconnière, 1980);

Annie Angremy, *Nathalie Sarraute: Portrait d'un écrivain* (Paris: Bibliothèque nationale de France, 1995);

Arc, special Sarraute issue, no. 95 (1984);

Françoise Asso, *Nathalie Sarraute: Une écriture de l'effraction* (Paris: Presses universitaires de France, 1995);

Sheila M. Bell, "The Conjurer's Hat: Sarraute Criticism since 1980," *Romance Studies,* 23 (Spring 1994): 85–103;

Gretchen Rous Besser, *Nathalie Sarraute* (Boston: Twayne, 1979);

Besser, "Nathalie Sarraute: *Pour un oui ou pour un non*," *French Review,* 56 (April 1983): 791–792;

Michelle E. Bloom, "Les Silences de Maeterlinck et Sarraute," in *Les Propos spectacle: Etudes de pragmatique théâtrale,* edited by Sanda Golopentia (New York: Peter Lang, 1996), pp. 209–229;

Huguette Bouchardeau, *Nathalie Sarraute* (Paris: Flammarion, 2003);

Rachel Boué, *Nathalie Sarraute: La sensation en quête de parole* (Paris: L'Harmattan, 1997);

H. A. Bouraoui, "Silence ou mensonge: Dilemme du nouveau romancier dans le théâtre de Nathalie Sarraute," in *Studies on the French Theater,* edited by William Goode (Baltimore: American Association of Teachers of French, 1972), p. 136;

Maurice Cagnon, "Les Pieces de Nathalie Sarraute: Voix et contrevoix," *Bulletin des Jeunes Romanistes,* no. 20 (1974): 97–102;

Françoise Calin, *La vie retrouvée: Etude de l'oeuvre romanesque de Nathalie Sarraute* (Paris: Lettres modernes, 1976);

C'est beau de Nathalie Sarraute, video, Films for the Humanities, 1980;

Isabelle Chave, ed., *Nathalie Sarraute, ou L'Usage de l'écriture,* Critique: Revue générale des publications françaises et étrangères, nos. 656–657 (Paris: Seuil, 2002);

Alan J. Clayton and Bernard Alazet, eds., *Nathalie Sarraute,* Revue des sciences humaines, no. 217 (Lille: Université de Lille III, 1990);

Michael de Cock, "La Parole et ce qu'elle cache: Etude de deux pièces de Nathalie Sarraute," *Revue Romane,* 30, no. 1 (1995): 81–90;

Ann Cothran, "Nathalie Sarraute," in *French Women Writers: A Bio-Bibliographical Source Book,* edited by Eva Martin Sartori and Dorothy Wynne Zimmerman (New York: Greenwood Press, 1991), pp. 412–422;

Mimica Cranaki and Yvon Belaval, *Nathalie Sarraute* (Paris: Gallimard, 1965);

Dominique Denes, "Intériorité et théâtralité chez Nathalie Sarraute et Marguerite Duras ou comment montrer le lieu d'où parle le texte," in *Texte et théâtralité,* edited by Raymonde Robert (Nancy: Presses Universitaires de Nancy, 2000), pp. 195–201;

Eric Eigenmann, *La parole empruntée: Sarraute, Pinget, Vinaver: Théâtres du dialogisme* (Paris: L'Arche, 1996);

Elisabeth Eliez-Rüegg, *La Conscience d'autrui et la conscience des objets dans l'oeuvre de Nathalie Sarraute* (Berne: Herbert Lang / Frankfurt am Main: Peter Lang, 1972);

Serge Fauchereau, ed., *Aujourd'hui Nathalie Sarraute,* Digraphe, no. 32 (Paris: Temps actuels, 1984);

Wilfried Floeck, "Nathalie Sarraute, dramaturge, à la recherche des pulsions intérieures de l'âme," *Revue d'Histoire du Théâtre,* 44, no. 4 (October–December 1992): 295–304;

Denise Goitein, "A propos d'*Isma*: Reflexions sur le théâtre de Nathalie Sarraute," *French Studies,* 30, no. 1 (1976): 43–56;

Goitein, "Nathalie Sarraute as Dramatist," *Yale French Studies,* 46 (1971): 102–112;

Olga Gomez, "Fleshing Out the Text: Lassalle's Production of Sarraute's *Pour un oui ou pour un non* at 'Le Petit Théâtre,' Le Théâtre National de la Colline," *French Studies Bulletin: A Quarterly Supplement,* 70 (Spring 1999): 14–15;

Janice Berkowitz Gross, "Women Writing across Purposes: The Theater of Marguerite Duras and Nathalie Sarraute," *Modern Drama,* 32 (March 1989): 39–47;

Liza Henderson, "Sarraute's Silences," *Theater,* 20 (Winter 1988): 22–24;

Jean-Luc Jaccard, *Nathalie Sarraute* (Zurich: Juris, 1967);

Steen Jansen, *Analyse de la forme dramatique du Mensonge de Nathalie Sarraute, précédée de Nathalie Sarraute, Le Mensonge,* Etudes romanes de l'Université de Copenhague, no. 9 (Copenhagen: Akademisk Forlag, 1976);

Bettina Leibowitz Knapp, *Nathalie Sarraute* (Amsterdam & Atlanta: Rodopi, 1994);

Lise Leibacher-Ouvrard and Monique Wittig, eds., "Nathalie Sarraute ou le texte du for intérieur," *L'Esprit Createur,* 36 (Summer 1996);

Francine de Martinoir, "A la naissance même du drame," *La Quinzaine littéraire,* no. 367 (16–31 March 1982): 35–36;

Le Métier d'écrire, part 2, video, Institut national de l'audiovisuel, 1993;

René Micha, *Nathalie Sarraute* (Paris: Editions Universitaires, 1966);

Judith G. Miller, "Nathalie Sarraute: How to Do Mean Things with Words," *Modern Drama,* 34 (March 1991): 118–127;

Valerie Minogue, "Nathalie Sarraute (1900-1999): A Tribute," *Romance Studies,* 17 (December 1999): 3–6;

Minogue, "'N'est-on pas tous pareils?' Nathalie Sarraute and the Question of Gender," *Theatre Research International,* 23 (Autumn 1998): 267–274;

Minogue, "Voices, Virtualities and Ventriloquism: Nathalie Sarraute's *Pour un oui ou pour un non*," *French Studies,* 49 (April 1995): 164–177;

Minogue and Sabine Raffy, eds., *Autour de Nathalie Sarraute: Actes du colloque international de Cerisy-la-Salle des 9 au 19 juillet 1989* (Paris: Diffusion les Belles Lettres, 1995);

A. S. Newman, *Une Poésie des discours: Essai sur les romans de Nathalie Sarraute* (Geneva: Droz, 1976);

Patrice Pavis, *Le théâtre contemporain: Analyse des textes, de Sarraute à Vinaver* (Paris: Nathan, 2002);

John Phillips, "Language on Trial: Nathalie Sarraute's *Pour un oui ou pour un non*," *La Chouette*, no. 19 (1987): 43–53;

Phillips, "The Repressed Feminine: Nathalie Sarraute's *Elle est là*," *Theatre Research International*, 23 (Autumn 1998): 277–282;

Phillips, "Sarraute's *Pour un oui ou pour un non:* 'Un gaz hilarant dans un gant retourné,'" *French Studies Bulletin: A Quarterly Supplement*, 43 (Summer 1992): 16–17;

Phillips, "Le Théâtre de Nathalie Sarraute: Un verbe devenu chair? *Le Silence, Elle est là* au Théâtre du Vieux Colombier, Paris (du 7 avril au 13 juin, 1993)," *French Studies Bulletin: A Quarterly Supplement*, 49 (Winter 1993): 19–21;

Evelyn Pieiller, "Nathalie Sarraute et le tremblement des certitudes," *La Quinzaine Litteraire*, no. 318 (February 1980): 27;

Jean Pierrot, *Nathalie Sarraute* (Paris: J. Corti, 1990);

Bernard Pingaud, "Le Personnage dans l'oeuvre de Nathalie Sarraute," *Preuves*, no. 154 (December 1963): 19–34;

Jérôme Prieur, "Nathalie Sarraute: *C'est beau*," *Les Cahiers du Chemin*, no. 26 (15 January 1976): 179–181;

Marta Prunes, "Sobre el teatro de Nathalie Sarraute: Por que la obra dramatica de Sarraute es tan indispensable como su narrativa," *Quimera*, no. 190 (2000): 10–17;

Claude Régy, "Nathalie Sarraute: Un Théâtre d'action; *C'est beau:* Théâtre de la violence; Divagations de mise en scène," *Cahiers Renaud Barrault*, no. 89 (1975): 80–89;

John Rothenberg, "Gender in Question in the Theatre of Nathalie Sarraute," *Forum for Modern Language Studies*, 35 (July 1999): 311–320;

Rothenberg, "The Hunter Hunted: Social Strategies in Sarraute's Theatre," *Nottingham French Studies*, 34 (Autumn 1995): 22–30;

Rothenberg, "Imagery in Sarraute's *Pour un oui ou pour un non*," *French Studies Bulletin: A Quarterly Supplement*, 41 (Winter 1991–1992): 15–17;

Rothenberg, "Imagery in the Theater of Nathalie Sarraute," *Neophilologus*, 82 (July 1998): 385–392;

Rothenberg, "More on Sarraute's Theater," *French Studies Bulletin: A Quarterly Supplement*, 44 (Autumn 1992): 20;

Rothenberg, "The Problem of Character in the Theatre of Nathalie Sarraute," *Nottingham French Studies*, 40 (Autumn 2001): 37–45;

Rothenberg, "Structures of the Unspoken: The Theatre of Nathalie Sarraute," *Orbis Litterarum: International Review of Literary Studies*, 58, no. 3 (2003): 189–201;

Arnaud Rykner, "Théâtre et exorcisme: Les Ecorchés de la parole," *Poétique: Revue de Théorie et d'Analyse Litteraires*, 26 (April 1995): 153–162;

Rykner, *Théâtres du nouveau roman: Sarraute, Pinget, Duras* (Paris: J. Corti, 1988), pp. 33–80;

Rykner, ed., *Nathalie Sarraute* (Paris: Seuil, 1991);

Roger Shattuck, "The Voice of Nathalie Sarraute," *French Review*, 68 (May 1995): 955–963;

Benjamin Suhl, "Nathalie Sarraute's Latest Play: *C'est beau*," *Romance Notes*, 20 (Winter 1979–1980): 178–181;

Ruth Z. Temple, *Nathalie Sarraute* (New York: Columbia University Press, 1968);

Alexandre Terneuil, "Violence et révolte des femmes dans le théâtre de Marguerite Yourcenar, Nathalie Sarraute et Marguerite Duras," *Theatre Research International*, 23 (Autumn 1998): 261–266;

Micheline Tison-Braun, *Nathalie Sarraute, ou, La Recherche de l'authenticité* (Paris: Gallimard, 1971);

Pierre Verdrager, *Le Sens critique: La Réception de Nathalie Sarraute par la presse* (Paris: L'Harmattan, 2001);

Michel Vinaver, "*Pour un oui ou pour un non*," in *Ecritures dramatiques: Essais d'analyse de textes de théâtre*, edited by Vinaver (Arles: Actes Sud, 1993), pp. 15–45;

Julius Wilhelm, *Nouveau roman und anti-théâtre: Robbe-Grillet, Butor, Sarraute, C. Simon, Beckett, Ionesco, Adamov, Genet: Eine Einführung* (Stuttgart: Kohlhammer, 1972);

Gerda Zeltner, "Nathalie Sarraute et l'impossible réalisme," *Mercure de France*, no. 345 (August 1962): 593–608.

Jean-Paul Sartre

(21 June 1905 – 15 April 1980)

John Ireland
University of Illinois at Chicago

See also the Sartre entries in *DLB 72: French Novelists, 1930–1960* and *DLB 296: Twentieth-Century European Cultural Theorists, Second Series.*

PLAY PRODUCTIONS: *Bariona, ou Le Fils du tonnerre,* Trier, Stalag XII-D, 24 December 1940;

Les Mouches, Paris, Théâtre de la Cité, 3 June 1943;

Huis clos, Paris, Théâtre du Vieux-Colombier, 27 May 1944;

Morts sans sépulture, Paris, Théâtre Antoine, 8 November 1946;

La Putain respectueuse, Paris, Théâtre Antoine, 8 November 1946;

Les Mains sales, Paris, Théâtre Antoine, 2 April 1948;

Le Diable et le Bon Dieu, Paris, Théâtre Antoine, 7 June 1951;

Kean, Paris, Théâtre Sarah-Bernhardt, 14 November 1953;

Nekrassov, Paris, Théâtre Antoine, 8 June 1955;

Les Séquestrés d'Altona, Paris, Théâtre de la Renaissance, 23 September 1959;

Les Troyennes, Paris, Théâtre National Populaire, 10 March 1965.

BOOKS: *L'Imagination* (Paris: Alcan, 1936); translated by Forrest Williams as *Imagination: A Psychological Critique* (Ann Arbor: University of Michigan Press, 1962);

La Nausée (Paris: Gallimard, 1938); translated by Lloyd Alexander as *Nausea* (Norfolk, Conn.: New Directions, 1949); republished as *The Diary of Antoine Roquentin* (London: Lehmann, 1949);

Esquisse d'une théorie des emotions (Paris: Hermann, 1939); translated by Bernard Frechtman as *The Emotions: Outline of a Theory* (New York: Philosophical Library, 1948);

Le Mur (Paris: Gallimard, 1939); translated by Alexander as *The Wall, and Other Stories* (New York: New Directions, 1948); republished as *Intimacy, and Other Stories* (New York: New Directions, 1948; London: P. Nevill, 1949);

Jean-Paul Sartre, circa 1947 (Hulton/Getty Images)

L'Imaginaire: Psychologie phénoménologique de l'imagination (Paris: Gallimard, 1940); translated by Frechtman as *The Psychology of Imagination* (New York: Philosophical Library, 1948);

L'Etre et le néant: Essai d'ontologie phénoménologique (Paris: Gallimard, 1943); translated in part by Hazel E. Barnes as *Existential Psychoanalysis* (New York: Philosophical Library, 1953); translated in full by Barnes as *Being and Nothingness: An Essay on Phenomenological Ontology* (New York: Philosophical

334

Library, 1956; London: Methuen, 1957); part 1, chapter 2, of *L'Etre et le néant* republished as *La Mauvaise Foi*, edited by Marc Wetzel (Paris: Hatier, 1985);

Les Mouches (Paris: Gallimard, 1943); translated by Stuart Gilbert as *The Flies*, in *The Flies and In Camera* (London: Hamilton, 1946); republished as *No Exit (Huis clos), a Play in One Act, and The Flies (Les Mouches), a Play in Three Acts* (New York: Knopf, 1947);

L'Age de raison, volume 1 of *Les Chemins de la liberté* (Paris: Gallimard, 1945; revised, 1960); translated by Eric Sutton as *The Age of Reason* (New York: Knopf, 1947; London: Hamilton, 1947);

Huis clos (Paris: Gallimard, 1945); translated by Gilbert as *In Camera*, in *The Flies and In Camera;* and as *No Exit*, in *No Exit (Huis clos), a Play in One Act, and The Flies (Les Mouches), a Play in Three Acts;*

Le Sursis, volume 2 of *Les Chemins de la liberté* (Paris: Gallimard, 1945); translated by Sutton as *The Reprieve* (New York: Knopf, 1947; London: Hamilton, 1947);

L'Existentialisme est un humanisme (Paris: Nagel, 1946); translated by Frechtman as *Existentialism* (New York: Philosophical Library, 1947) and by Philip Mairet as *Existentialism and Humanism* (London: Methuen, 1948);

Explication de L'étranger (Paris: Aux dépens du Palimugre, 1946);

Morts sans sépulture (Lausanne: Marguerat, 1946); translated by Lionel Abel as *The Victors*, in *Three Plays* (New York: Knopf, 1949), and by Kitty Black as *Men without Shadows*, in *Three Plays* (London: Hamilton, 1949);

La Putain respectueuse (Paris: Nagel, 1946); translated by Abel as *The Respectful Prostitute*, in *Three Plays* (New York: Knopf, 1949), and by Black as *The Respectable Prostitute*, in *Three Plays* (London: Hamilton, 1949);

Réflexions sur la question juive (Paris: Morihien, 1946); translated by George J. Becker as *Anti-Semite and Jew* (New York: Schocken, 1948) and by Erik de Mauny as *Portrait of the Anti-Semite* (London: Secker & Warburg, 1948);

Baudelaire, précédé d'une note de Michel Leiris (Paris: Gallimard, 1947); translated by Martin Turnell as *Baudelaire* (London: Horizon, 1949; Norfolk, Conn.: New Directions, 1950);

L'Homme et les choses (Paris: Seghers, 1947);

Les Jeux sont faits (Paris: Nagel, 1947); translated by Louise Varèse as *The Chips Are Down* (New York: Lear, 1948; London & New York: Rider, 1951);

Situations, I (Paris: Gallimard, 1947); translated in part by Annette Michelson in *Literary and Philosophical Essays* (New York: Criterion, 1955; London: Rider, 1955); republished as *Literary Essays* (New York: Philosophical Library, 1957);

L'Engrenage (Paris: Nagel, 1948); translated by Mervyn Savill as *In the Mesh: A Scenario* (London: Dakers, 1954);

Les Mains sales (Paris: Gallimard, 1948); translated by Abel as *Dirty Hands*, in *Three Plays* (New York: Knopf, 1949), and by Black as *Crime Passionnel*, in *Three Plays* (London: Hamilton, 1949);

Situations, II: Qu'est-ce que la littérature? (Paris: Gallimard, 1948); translated in part by Frechtman as *What is Literature?* (New York: Philosophical Library, 1949; London: Methuen, 1950); republished as *Literature and Existentialism* (New York: Citadel, 1962);

Visages, précédé de Portraits officiels (Paris: Seghers, 1948);

Entretiens sur la politique, by Sartre, David Rousset, and Gérard Rosenthal (Paris: Gallimard, 1949);

La Mort dans l'âme, volume 3 of *Les Chemins de la liberté* (Paris: Gallimard, 1949); translated by Gerard Hopkins as *Iron in the Soul* (London: Hamilton, 1950); republished as *Troubled Sleep* (New York: Knopf, 1951);

Nourritures, suivi d'extraits de La Nausée (Paris: Damase, 1949);

Situations, III (Paris: Gallimard, 1949); translated in part by Michelson in *Literary and Philosophical Essays;*

Le Diable et le Bon Dieu (Paris: Gallimard, 1951); translated by Black as *Lucifer and the Lord* (London: Hamilton, 1952); republished as *The Devil and the Good Lord*, in *The Devil and the Good Lord, and Two Other Plays* (New York: Knopf, 1960);

Saint Genet, comédien et martyr (Paris: Gallimard, 1952); translated by Frechtman as *Saint Genet, Actor and Martyr* (New York: Braziller, 1963; London: W. H. Allen, 1964);

Kean, adapted from *Kean, ou Désordre et génie* (1836), by Alexandre Dumas *père* (Paris: Gallimard, 1954); translated by Black as *Kean; or, Disorder and Genius* (London: Hamilton, 1954); republished in *The Devil and the Good Lord, and Two Other Plays;*

Nekrassov (Paris: Gallimard, 1956); translated by Sylvia and George Leeson as *Nekrassov, a Farce* (London: Hamilton, 1956); republished in *The Devil and the Good Lord, and Two Other Plays;*

The Transcendence of the Ego: An Existentialist Theory of Consciousness, edited and translated by Williams and Robert Kirkpatrick (New York: Noonday Press, 1957); original version published as *La Transcendance de L'égo: Esquisse d'une description phénoménologique* (Paris: Vrin, 1965);

Critique de la raison dialectique, volume 1: *Théorie des ensembles pratiques* (Paris: Gallimard, 1960)–includes

"Question de méthode," translated by Barnes as *Search for a Method* (New York: Knopf, 1963); *Théorie des ensembles pratiques* translated by Alan Sheridan-Smith as *Critique of Dialectical Reason: Theory of Practical Ensembles,* edited by Jonathan Rée (London: NLB / Atlantic Highlands, N.J.: Humanities Press, 1976);

Les Séquestrés d'Altona (Paris: Gallimard, 1960); translated by Sylvia and George Leeson as *Loser Wins* (London: Hamilton, 1960); republished as *The Condemned of Altona* (New York: Knopf, 1961);

Bariona, ou Le Fils du tonnerre (Paris: Anjou-Copies, 1962);

Marxisme et existentialisme: Controverse sur la dialectique, by Sartre and others (Paris: Plon, 1962);

Il Filosofo e la politica, translated by Luciana Trentin and Romano Ledda (Rome: Riuniti, 1964);

Les Mots (Paris: Gallimard, 1964); translated by Frechtman as *The Words* (New York: Braziller, 1964) and by Irene Clephane as *Words* (London: Hamilton, 1964);

Situations, IV: Portraits (Paris: Gallimard, 1964); translated by Benita Eisler as *Situations* (New York: Braziller, 1965; London: Hamilton, 1965);

Situations, V: Colonialisme et néo-colonialisme (Paris: Gallimard, 1964); translated by Azzedine Haddour, Steve Brewer, and Terry McWilliams as *Colonialism and Neocolonialism* (London & New York: Routledge, 2001);

Situations, VI: Problèmes du marxisme, I (Paris: Gallimard, 1964)–includes "Les communistes et la paix," translated by Martha H. Fletcher and John R. Kleinschmidt in *The Communists and Peace, with a Reply to Claude Lefort* (New York: Braziller, 1968) and by Clephane in *The Communists and Peace, with an Answer to Claude Lefort* (London: Hamilton, 1969);

Situations, VII: Problèmes du marxisme, II (Paris: Gallimard, 1965)–includes "Réponse à Claude Lefort," translated by Fletcher and Kleinschmidt in *The Communists and Peace, with a Reply to Claude Lefort* and by Clephane in *The Communists and Peace, with an Answer to Claude Lefort;* and "Le Fantome de Staline," translated by Fletcher and Kleinschmidt as *The Ghost of Stalin* (New York: Braziller, 1968);

Les Troyennes, adapted from *Trojan Women* (415 B.C.), by Euripides (Paris: Gallimard, 1965); translated by Ronald Duncan as *The Trojan Women* (New York: Knopf, 1967; London: Hamilton, 1967);

On Genocide, and A Summary of the Evidence and the Judgments of the International War Crimes Tribunal, by Sartre and Arlette Elkaïm-Sartre (Boston: Beacon, 1968);

Les Communistes ont peur de la révolution (Paris: Didier, 1969); translated by Elaine P. Halperin as "Communists are Afraid of Revolution: Two Interviews," *Midway: A Magazine of Discovery in the Arts and Sciences,* 10, no. 1 (1969): 41–61;

L'Idiot de la famille: Gustave Flaubert de 1821-1857, 3 volumes (Paris: Gallimard, 1971-1972); translated by Carol Cosman as *The Family Idiot: Gustave Flaubert, 1821-1857,* 5 volumes (Chicago: University of Chicago Press, 1981-1993);

Plaidoyer pour les intellectuels (Paris: Gallimard, 1972);

Situations, VIII: Autour de 68 (Paris: Gallimard, 1972); translated in part by John Matthews in *Between Existentialism and Marxism* (London: NLB, 1974; New York: Pantheon, 1975);

Situations, IX: Mélanges (Paris: Gallimard, 1972); translated in part by Matthews in *Between Existentialism and Marxism;*

Un Théâtre de situations, edited by Michel Contat and Michel Rybalka (Paris: Gallimard, 1973; revised and enlarged, Paris: Gallimard, 1992); translated by Frank Jellinek as *Sartre on Theater* (London: Quartet, 1976; New York: Pantheon, 1976);

On a raison de se révolter: Discussions, by Sartre, Philippe Gavi, and Pierre Victor (Paris: Gallimard, 1974);

Situations, X: Politique et autobiographie (Paris: Gallimard, 1976); translated by Paul Auster and Lydia Davis as *Life/Situations: Essays Written and Spoken* (New York: Pantheon, 1977);

Oeuvres romanesques, edited by Contat and Rybalka (Paris: Gallimard, 1981)–comprises *La Nausée; Le Mur; Les Chemins de la liberté: L'Age de raison, Le Sursis,* and *La Mort dans l'âme; Drôle d'amitié; Dépaysement;* and *La Dernière chance;*

Cahiers pour une morale (Paris: Gallimard, 1983); translated by David Pellauer as *Notebooks for an Ethics* (Chicago: University of Chicago Press, 1992);

Les Carnets de la drôle de guerre: Novembre 1939 – mars 1940 (Paris: Gallimard, 1983); translated by Quintin Hoare as *War Diaries of Jean-Paul Sartre: November 1939 – March 1940* (New York: Pantheon, 1984); republished as *War Diaries: Notebooks from a Phoney War, November 1939 – March 1940* (London: Verso, 1984);

Le Scénario Freud (Paris: Gallimard, 1984); translated by Hoare as *The Freud Scenario,* edited by J. B. Pontalis (Chicago: University of Chicago Press, 1985; London: Verso, 1985);

Critique de la raison dialectique, volume 2: *L'Intelligibilité de l'histoire,* edited by Elkaïm-Sartre (Paris: Gallimard, 1985); translated by Hoare as *Critique of Dialectical Reason,* volume 2: *The Intelligibility of History* (London & New York: Verso, 1991);

Mallarmé: La Lucidité et sa face d'ombre, edited by Elkaïm-Sartre (Paris: Gallimard, 1986);

Vérité et existence, edited by Elkaïm-Sartre (Paris: Gallimard, 1989); translated by Adrian van den Hoven as *Truth and Existence,* edited by Ronald Aronson (Chicago: University of Chicago Press, 1992).

Collections: *Théâtre* (Paris: Gallimard, 1947)–comprises *Les Mouches, Huis clos, Morts sans sépulture,* and *La Putain respectueuse;* enlarged to include *Les Mains sales, Le Diable et le Bon Dieu, Kean, Nekrassov,* and *Les Séquestrés d'Altona* (Paris: Gallimard, 1962);

Théâtre complet, edited by Michel Contat and others (Paris: Gallimard, 2005)–comprises *Les Mouches, Huis clos, Morts sans sépulture, La Putain respectueuse, Les Mains sales, Le Diable et le Bon Dieu, Kean, Nekrassov, Les Séquestrés d'Altona,* and *Les Troyennes.*

Editions in English: *Sartre on Cuba* (New York: Ballantine, 1961);

Politics and Literature, translated by J. A. Underwood and John Calder (London: Calder & Boyers, 1973).

PRODUCED SCRIPTS: *Les Jeux sont faits,* motion picture, by Sartre, Jacques-Laurent Bost, and Jean Delannoy, Les Films Gibé, 1947;

Les Mains sales, motion picture, dialogue by Sartre, Les Films Fernand Rivers, 1951;

La Putain respectueuse, motion picture, Artès Films/Les Films Agiman, 1952;

Les Sorcières de Salem, motion picture, adapted from Arthur Miller's *The Crucible* (1953), Compagnie Industrielle et Commerciale Cinématographique/Deutsche Film AG/Films Borderie, 1957;

Freud, motion picture, by Sartre (uncredited), Charles Kaufman, and Wolfgang Reinhardt, Universal International Pictures, 1962;

Le Mur, motion picture, dialogue by Sartre, Les Films Niepce/Procinex, 1967.

OTHER: Francis Jeanson, *Le Problème moral et la pensée de Sartre,* preface by Sartre (Paris: Editions du Myrte, 1947); translated by Robert V. Stone as *Sartre and the Problem of Morality* (Bloomington: Indiana University Press, 1980);

"Orphée noir," in *Anthologie de la nouvelle poésie nègre et malgache de langue française,* edited by Léopold Sédar Senghor (Paris: Presses Universitaires de France, 1948); translated by S. W. Allen as *Black Orpheus* (Paris: Gallimard, 1963);

Hervé Bazin and others, *L'Affaire Henri Martin,* commentary by Sartre (Paris: Gallimard, 1953);

Henri Cartier-Bresson, *D'Une Chine à l'autre,* preface by Sartre (Paris: Delpire, 1954); translated by Edward Hyams as *China in Transition: A Moment in History* (London: Thames & Hudson, 1956);

"Une Victoire," in *La Question,* by Henri Alleg (Lausanne: La Cité, 1958), pp. 72–88; translated by John Calder as "A Victory," in *The Question* (London: Calder, 1958), pp. 13–36;

Roger Garaudy, *Perspectives de l'homme: Existentialism, pensée catholique, marxisme,* letter by Sartre (Paris: Presses Universitaires de France, 1959);

"Doigts et non-doigts," in *Wols en personne: Aquarelles et dessins,* by Wols (Paris: Delpire, 1963); translated by Norbert Guterman as "Fingers and Non-Fingers," in *Watercolors, Drawings, Writings* (New York: Abrams, 1965);

Ronald D. Laing and David G. Cooper, *Reason and Violence: A Decade of Sartre's Philosophy, 1950–1960,* foreword by Sartre (London: Tavistock, 1964);

Que peut la littérature? by Sartre and others (Paris: Union Générale d'Editions, 1965);

Roberto Sebastián Matta Echaurren, *Un Soleil, un Viêt-nam,* text by Sartre (Paris: Comité Viet-Nam National, 1967);

Georges Michel, *La Promenade du dimanche,* preface by Sartre (Paris: Gallimard, 1967);

Tribunal Russell: Le Jugement de Stockholm, opening speech and other texts by Sartre (Paris: Gallimard, 1967); translated as *Against the Crime of Silence: Proceedings of the Russell International War Crimes Tribunal, Stockholm, Copenhagen* (New York: Bertrand Russell Peace Foundation, 1968);

Roger Pic, *Au coeur du Vietnam,* preface by Sartre (Paris: Maspero, 1968);

Le Procès Régis Debray, text by Sartre (Paris: Maspero, 1968);

"Le Socialisme qui venait du froid," in *Trois Générations: Entretiens sur le phénomène culturel tchécoslovaque,* edited by Antonin Liehm (Paris: Gallimard, 1970); translated by Helen R. Lane as "The Socialism That Came In from the Cold," *Evergreen Review,* 14 (November 1970): 27–32, 65–73;

"Textes retrouvés de J.-P. Sartre," in *Les Ecrits de Sartre,* edited by Michel Contat and Michel Rybalka (Paris: Gallimard, 1970), pp. 501–745; translated by Richard C. McCleary as *Selected Prose,* volume 2 of *The Writings of Jean-Paul Sartre* (Evanston, Ill.: Northwestern University Press, 1974);

Gisèle Halimi, *Le Procès de Burgos,* preface by Sartre (Paris: Gallimard, 1971);

Michèle Manceaux, *Les Maos en France,* foreword by Sartre (Paris: Gallimard, 1972).

The best known of Jean-Paul Sartre's eleven plays are probably the most popular part of his entire literary corpus. The sheer volume of publications and produc-

Front page of the underground Resistance newspaper that began appearing openly after the Liberation in August 1944, with an article by Sartre, writing as a special correspondent in the United States, comparing the conditions of French and American workers (© Collection Roger-Viollet/Getty Images)

tions of his major plays makes him an important figure of the twentieth-century French stage. Yet, there are several indications that in his own eyes, Sartre considered his status as a dramatist to be only of secondary importance. Although he had dreamed of being a great writer since childhood, for a long time Sartre equated writing with narrative prose; in his eyes, literary success meant achieving greatness primarily as a novelist. Later, when he had completed his studies in philosophy at the elite Ecole Normale Supérieure in Paris, his drive for literary fame became coupled with a determination to make his mark as a philosopher.

Sartre's earliest masterpiece, the novel *La Nausée* (1938; translated as *Nausea* and as *The Diary of Antoine Roquentin*, 1949), in which the central character establishes a fictional context for a series of philosophical discoveries about existence, represents a fusion of the two disciplines of literature and philosophy. The following year, pursuing a more clearly literary vein, Sartre published a collection of short stories, *Le Mur* (1939; translated as *The Wall, and Other Stories* and as *Intimacy, and Other Stories*, 1948), which attracted significant critical attention. Later, during World War II, when he was deployed as a private attached to a meteorological section of the infantry, he began work on the three novels that make up the trilogy *Les Chemins de la liberté* (1945–1949, Roads to Freedom), the first two volumes of which, *L'Age de raison* (translated as *The Age of Reason*, 1947) and *Le Sursis* (translated as *The Reprieve*, 1947), were published in 1945. By that year Sartre had also published several volumes on philosophy, including *L'Imaginaire: Psychologie phénoménologique de l'imagination* (1940; translated as *The Psychology of Imagination*, 1948), an important contribution to understanding the phenomenology of the image and the relationship of imagination to perception. After his return to Paris from a prisoner-of-war camp in early 1941, Sartre began work on *L'Etre et le néant: Essai d'ontologie phénoménologique* (translated as *Being and Nothingness: An Essay on Phenomenological Ontology*, 1956), which was published in 1943, the year his play *Les Mouches* (translated as *The Flies*, 1946) was produced in Paris. From the onset of Sartre's fame in the years following the liberation of France in 1945 until his death in 1980, he was asked to write articles and give lectures and interviews on many different subjects ranging from literature and art to music, current events, and politics; he was also asked to contribute prefaces to other writers' works. He also received invitations to write about and comment on theater, not only in France and the rest of Europe but also in the United States. In the ten volumes of *Situations* published from 1947 to 1976 in which his literary, cultural, and political writings were collected, there is no trace of Sartre's interviews, lectures, and other writings concerning theater, another indication that drama was not a primary concern for him. Michel Contat and Michel Rybalka tracked down what they could find of his theater lectures and interviews and published them as *Un Théâtre de situations* (1973; translated as *Sartre on Theater*, 1976). It was the only collection of Sartre's writings published in French during his lifetime that he had not compiled himself.

Jean-Paul Charles-Aymard Sartre was born in Paris on 21 June 1905, the only child of Jean-Baptiste Sartre (who died when Sartre was still an infant) and Anne-Marie Schweitzer Sartre, a first cousin of Albert Schweitzer. Sartre provides an account of his childhood in his 1964 memoir, *Les Mots* (translated as *The Words*, 1964). Although playacting is an important metaphor in *Les Mots,* he makes little mention of the role of theater as such in his apprenticeship as a writer. Not until the posthumous publication of *Les Carnets de la drôle de guerre: Novembre 1939 – mars 1940* (1983; translated as *War Diaries of Jean-Paul Sartre: November 1939 – March 1940* and as *War Diaries: Notebooks from a Phoney War, November 1939 – March 1940,* 1984) did readers learn the extent to which Sartre's first "literary" triumphs were in fact theatrical. As a child of six or seven he had been given a set of finger puppets, which he would take to the Jardin du Luxembourg (Luxembourg Gardens) near his family's apartment. There, using the back of a park chair as a frame for his shows, Poulou, as the young Sartre was called, made up short puppet plays that regularly attracted an audience of young playmates. Later, after his mother's remarriage and the family's temporary move to La Rochelle on the French coast, the adolescent Sartre enjoyed accompanying his mother to watch operettas at the municipal theater. He also began experimenting with playwriting. Back in Paris and attending the Lycée Henri IV, Sartre apparently wrote a play inspired by Alfred Jarry, featuring a depiction of Auguste Rodin's sculpture *The Thinker* (1879–1900) as a kind of Père Ubu, the title character of Jarry's 1896 play *Ubu Roi* (King Ubu). Sartre was also an enthusiastic performer. At the Ecole Normale Supérieure he gained a reputation as a satirist and comic actor in the comic revues staged by students at the end of each academic year. Shortly after graduation he wrote two more plays: "Epiméthée," about Epimetheus, the brother of Prometheus, and "J'aurai un bel enterrement" (I Will Have a Fine Funeral), inspired by Luigi Pirandello. None of the manuscripts associated with these early plays seems to have survived.

In 1932, during Sartre's difficult years as a high-school teacher in Le Havre, Simone Jollivet, a former girlfriend and aspiring actress (she was also the model for Anny in *La Nausée*), introduced him to the stage director Charles Dullin, whose mistress she had become. This meeting with one of the founding members of the legendary Cartel, a group of directors seeking to revitalize French theater, proved a seminal encounter for Sartre's later development as a dramatist. Throughout his life he insisted that everything he knew about theater and playwriting he had learned from Dullin. For the first time Sartre and Simone de Beauvoir, his lifelong companion, were able to watch a great actor, director, and theatrical mentor work with a professional company. Watching from the wings of the Atelier, Dullin's experimental theater, Sartre was also able to gain a backstage perspective on theatrical production. Later, when he embarked on his first serious attempts at playwriting, Dullin's precepts guided him. Dullin's help was not limited to questions of style or technique, however. When Sartre returned to occupied Paris from the prisoner-of-war camp in which he was interned in 1940, Dullin asked him if he would like to teach a course on the history of theater to the students at the Atelier, leaving the choice of curriculum to his discretion. Shortly after negotiations with Jean-Louis Barrault to direct *Les Mouches* fell through in 1943, Dullin stepped into the breach at considerable personal and financial risk to stage Sartre's first major play.

Although Sartre for many years pretended otherwise, *Les Mouches* was in fact his second produced play. He wrote the earliest of his plays for which a manuscript still exists while a prisoner of war in Germany in 1940, but, because he claimed not to like the result, *Bariona, ou Le Fils du tonnerre* (1962, Bariona, or The Son of Thunder) was not published until more than twenty years later, and then only in a limited edition. Sartre also never allowed the play to be professionally produced. The staging of the quickly written drama in a prisoner-of-war camp also presented many practical difficulties. Nevertheless, eyewitness accounts of the three performances suggest that the result was more positive than Sartre would have his readers believe.

After the collapse of France in June 1940, Sartre was captured with other men from his unit; following a brief period of internment in France, they were transported by train to Stalag XII-D, a prisoner-of-war camp outside Trier, in Germany. Despite the deprivations and discomforts of incarceration, Sartre insisted that his experience as a prisoner of war marked an essential and positive moment in his personal evolution. In the camp he encountered a group of priests, as hostile to Nazi ideology as himself, with whom he discussed both philosophy and theology. As winter approached, the question of the coming Christmas celebration arose, and a suggestion was made (according to some accounts, by Sartre himself) that the camp put on a Nativity play. Whether or not he initiated the project, Sartre did volunteer to write and direct the play (taking on, in addition, the role of Balthazar, one of the Three Magi). Three weeks later a rough draft was ready, and rehearsals began. *Bariona, ou Le Fils du tonnerre* presented Sartre with quite a challenge since his ambition was to write a play that would appeal to believers and nonbelievers alike. Sartre himself was an atheist, and the play weaves into the retelling of the birth of Jesus a drama that proclaims the absolute nature of human freedom, even as it issues a call to arms against occupation and oppression, a message full of political resonances thinly concealed beneath the biblical elements that provided enough cover for the play to be passed by the prison censor.

In Sartre's idiosyncratic retelling of the Christmas story, the birth of Christ is overshadowed by the drama of a Judean village suffering under Roman occupation and the village leader's decision that, in their hopeless circumstances, all procreation must cease. The village leader, Bariona, is a resistance fighter who has just asked his wife, Sarah, to abort their unborn child. Initially hostile to the idea of an infant Messiah, he finally accepts the birth of Jesus as a symbol of hope. When, at the end of the play, Bariona sacrifices himself and his men so that Mary, Joseph, and Jesus can escape capture by the Romans, his only conversion is to a new but still secular understanding of human freedom that his reprieved child will have to confront in his turn.

Bariona, ou Le Fils du tonnerre was staged on 24, 25, and 26 December 1940, each performance drawing an audience of close to two thousand prisoners. After the first performance a Christmas mass was celebrated. The play was enthusiastically received, and even Sartre, who subsequently judged the play harshly, wrote to Beauvoir of his emotion as he contemplated the audience of silent men, absorbed in the story unfolding in front of them. The letter ends with Sartre's firm declaration that he will write more plays. *Bariona, ou Le Fils du tonnerre* thus crystallized a crucial moment in his personal and intellectual development. After the individualism of his prewar years—reflected in *La Nausée*, the short stories of *Le Mur*, and his philosophical writings—the months Sartre spent in the camp provided the transforming experience that set him on the path to socialism. In addition to bringing about his political conversion, Sartre's involvement with *Bariona, ou Le Fils du tonnerre* introduced him to a corresponding creative forum that emphasized collective rather than individual concerns. By revealing the power of theater to galvanize an audience, the play gave Sartre the idea of committed theater that he developed in conjunction with his theories of "littérature engagée" (committed literature) after the war.

Freed from the prisoner-of-war camp and allowed to return to Paris in early 1941, Sartre, notes Beauvoir in *La Force de l'âge* (1960; translated as *The Prime of Life*, 1962), was a changed man, anxious to become active politically, which, in the context of occupied France, meant activity in the Resistance. Rebuffed by various

Habib Benglia and Héléna Bossis (stage name of Henriette Berriau) in the 1946 Théâtre Antoine, Paris, production of Sartre's La Putain respectueuse *(translated as* The Respectful Prostitute *and as* The Respectable Prostitute, *1949), based on the 1931 Scottsboro Boys rape case (© Lipnitzki/Roger-Viollet/Getty Images)*

Resistance groups that were skeptical of his motives and had little use for literary intellectuals, Sartre tried over the course of several months to put together his own network but dissolved it when he realized that the risks exceeded the potential effectiveness of the group. In 1942, still at work on *L'Etre et le néant* and the first two volumes of *Les Chemins de la liberté,* Sartre began to think of another play, inspired in part by the example of *Bariona, ou Le Fils du tonnerre*. It too was to carry a message of freedom and resistance, this time under the protective cover of a Greek myth. Initially, Barrault had agreed to stage the new play, *Les Mouches,* but Sartre, sensing the director's reluctance after months of inactivity, approached Dullin, who in a controversial move had assumed the direction of the Théâtre de la Cité, which had recently been "Aryanized" (placed under German administrative control). Dullin agreed, rehearsals began, and *Les Mouches* premiered at the theater on 3 June 1943.

Adapting Aeschylus's *Oresteia* (458 B.C.), Sartre set out to undercut the classical notion of tragic destiny, making the decision of Orestes (Oreste in *Les Mouches*) to avenge his father and kill both Clytemnestra (Clytemnestre) and Aegisthus (Egisthe), the principal indicator of his freedom. Arriving incognito in Argos, Oreste finds his city dominated by the ideology of culpability and remorse that Egisthe, in tandem with Jupiter, has instituted. Sartre's innovation was to situate the conflict of the play not between Oreste and Egisthe, as in the original, but between Oreste and Jupiter, the god whose metaphysical ideology of expiation and remorse for his human subjects has been translated into political terms by his accomplice, Egisthe. Instead of succumbing to madness after the double murder, as in the classical myth, Oreste defends his conduct with passion and eloquence, fully accepting the consequences of his act. Confronting the angry citizens of Argos, who have been liberated by the murders but are frightened by their sudden freedom, Oreste leaves the city, taking with him both the swarms of flies, symbols of guilt that tormented Argos, and the Furies, the vengeful spirits who also figure in the Orestes legend. Left to themselves, the people of Argos will have to decide what they can make of their newly liberated state.

In presenting his adaptation, Sartre was constrained by the censorship that forced him to hide any message of resistance and revolt behind the well-known Greek myth. As a result, in interviews that accompanied the premiere, he declared that his play sought to demonstrate the absolute nature of human freedom, linking his discussion of freedom to the theoretical elaborations he had developed in *L'Etre et le néant*. After the war he proposed a different type of commentary, reminding his audience that the Occupation had precluded any possibility of talking directly about the political message of *Les Mouches* and confirming that his depiction of Argos, with its cult of remorse and expiation, was an obvious if veiled reference to the Vichy government, just as the alliance between Jupiter and Egisthe was intended as a symbol of the collusion between Henri Pétain and the Catholic Church. In the same vein, Sartre stated that his portrayal of Oreste was designed to offer moral support to Resistance fighters who worried about the inevitable reprisals that direct military action against the Germans provoked.

Although a political reading of *Les Mouches* now seems obvious, it is clear from the different reactions to Dullin's production that Sartre's message of resistance was perceptible to only a small number of initiates. There had been a revival of adaptations from Greek classical theater during the Occupation years; many critics viewed Sartre's play as another concession to the current neoclassical vogue without taking into account his considerable amendments and innovations. Dullin's production, a bold staging that featured modernist sculptures and masks, added to the critics' confusion. Caught up in denouncing the "cubist, dadaist bric-à-brac" onstage and deploring the lack of stage sense deployed by both playwright and director, reviewers such as Alain Laubreaux in *Le Petit Parisien* (5 June 1943) criticized *Les Mouches* on aesthetic grounds, its message misunderstood or ignored. Six months after the premiere, however, critic Michel Leiris both praised the play and indicated the political stakes of Sartre's adaptation in the underground journal *Les Lettres françaises*. In general, not until after the Liberation did productions of the play help to establish Sartre's reputation as a playwright. Only then could the population respond to declarations such as Oreste's pronouncement "la vie humaine commence de l'autre côté du désespoir" (human life begins on the other side of despair).

Many critics consider Sartre's next play, *Huis clos* (translated as *In Camera,* 1946, and as *No Exit,* 1947), to be his best, although it was not his favorite dramatic work. It is his most ingeniously theatrical play, and although the initial critical reception following the premiere on 27 May 1944 was not more positive than that for *Les Mouches,* almost every critic remarked on the obvious theatrical talent of the author. *Huis clos* was roundly condemned for immorality.

Sartre had written *Les Mouches* in part to help launch the career of Olga Kosakiewicz, a former student of Beauvoir, who played the role of Electra, Oreste's sister. Subsequently, Marc Barbezat, a businessman and publisher of the journal *L'Arbalète* (which later published works by Jean Genet), suggested that Sartre write a short play with only two or three characters and a single set that could easily be taken on tour. The new play was also to launch two more aspiring actresses: Wanda Kosakiewicz, Olga's sister, and Barbezat's wife, Olga. After thinking initially of another form of sequestration—a cellar during an air raid—Sartre came up with the idea of three characters condemned to hell for all eternity. In that setting the three characters would all remain onstage for the duration of the play and have equally important roles. Although neither Wanda nor Olga Barbezat (who was subsequently arrested by the Germans) finally played the roles originally intended for them, Wanda, under her stage name, Marie Olivier, later became the actress most closely associated with Sartre's female roles, many of which were explicitly written with her in mind.

Sartre wrote *Huis clos,* initially titled "Les Autres" (The Others), in a matter of days. He originally intended it to tour in the Zone Sud (Southern Zone, unoccupied France), thinking there was little chance that any Parisian theater would welcome his next play after the failure of *Les Mouches.* He nevertheless reached an agreement with the director of the Parisian Théâtre du Vieux-Colombier, Paul Annet Badel, even though Annet Badel had reservations about Sartre's proposed director, Albert Camus, who was also slated to play the character Garcin in *Huis clos.* Sartre had met Camus some months previously, and the two had begun a friendship that flourished until politics separated them in 1952. Although Camus had been active in theater as an amateur, Annet Badel persuaded Sartre that a more experienced hand was needed, and the production was entrusted to Raymond Rouleau. Camus, stripped of his directing role, left the project altogether and was replaced by Michel Vitold. Sartre and Annet Badel argued over who should play the role of Estelle, finally choosing Gaby Sylvia, Annet Badel's wife, over Wanda Kosakiewicz. The role of Inès was awarded to Rouleau's former wife, Tania Balachova. Sartre later admitted that the final cast was so good that he could never subsequently separate his own conception of the characters of *Huis clos* from the extraordinary performances of these actors.

Sartre offered little commentary on *Huis clos* other than to try much later to correct some of the sweeping interpretations of the most famous line in the play: "l'enfer, c'est les Autres" (hell is other people). It is obviously linked to some of the central ideas of *L'Etre et le néant*, which had been published the year before the premiere of the play in 1944. In putting onstage a deserter, a lesbian, and an infanticide, each of whom seeks a degree of collusion with one of the two others—a complicity that is systematically thwarted by the third character, acting as the "bourreau" (tormentor) of the other two—Sartre created a radical illustration of the section of *L'Etre et le néant* titled "Les Relations concrètes avec autrui" (Concrete Relations with Others), in which he demonstrates that the most basic relationship between individuals is conflict. If individual consciousness is free, that freedom is constrained when placed in the field of another human consciousness: each will struggle to assert its freedom over the other by transforming the other into an object. The theatrical structure of *Huis clos* complicates the philosophical model by combining the comic and sentimental elements of the popular boulevard theater of the 1910s and 1920s with the realistic and pessimistic themes of fin de siècle naturalist theater. In *Huis clos* the conventions of both types of theater become targets for parody. In a subversion of boulevard farce, the attempts by two of the three characters to pair off while excluding the intrusive third party degenerate into a series of sadomasochistic confrontations fueled by jealousy and hate. Unlike "living" individuals who are free to change themselves through defining acts, these "dead" characters cannot act to change themselves. All human relationships are not similarly doomed, Sartre insisted later, although it took him many years and considerable intellectual effort to formulate a philosophical model that superseded his early ontological pessimism.

Sartre's setting and choice of characters for his exploration of interpersonal relationships constituted a multifaceted attack on the social and religious underpinnings of Catholic Vichy France. This attack on Christian morality caught the attention of reviewers. Sartre's depiction of hell as an endless succession of hotel rooms ridicules Christian metaphysics: "Comment pouvez-vous croire ces âneries?" (Really, sir, how could you believe such cock-and-bull stories?) scoffs the valet in Garcin's face at the beginning of the play. *Huis clos* also mocks the traditions of religious theater that the Vichy state had attempted to revive and celebrate with evangelistic playwrights such as Henri Ghéon. Beyond questions of religious faith, Sartre's characters, especially Estelle, a bourgeois socialite, undermine the ideals and conven-

Tania Balachova, Michel Vitold, and Michèle Alfa in the 1946 Théâtre de la Potinière, Paris, production of Sartre's Huis clos *(1944; translated as* In Camera, *1946, and as* No Exit, *1947), about three people condemned to hell in the form of an exitless room where each must endure the company of the other two for eternity (© Lipnitzki/Roger-Viollet/Getty Images)*

tions of polite society, exposing the inconsistencies and hypocrisies of Vichy ideology. As the thin veneer of social niceties is stripped away and her euphemisms and evasions become more disturbingly hollow, the crudest forms of sexual desire replace the redemptive qualities of true love and self-sacrifice that Estelle parades. In its derisive parody of Christian myth, *Huis clos* replaces the terror of eternal damnation with a scathing depiction of bourgeois hypocrisy and a corrosive aesthetics of extreme embarrassment.

Many of the reviews that followed the premiere of *Huis clos* focused on the monstrous immorality of Sartre's degenerate characters. References to "rutting monsters" and Sartre's predilection for degradation ran rife in the collaborationist and Catholic press. Sartre's philosophical message was obscured by the more immediately striking features of the play. Many reviewers saw *Huis clos* as just a strangely perverse ménage à trois, a grotesque version of the boulevard tradition. After the Liberation, as productions began again at the Théâtre du Vieux-Colombier, Sartre's courage in opposing the values of collaborationist Vichy won him more support than the play itself, which was judged too dark and pessimistic to help revitalize the spirit of France after the traumatic war years. Nevertheless, *Huis clos* was commercially successful; as it was steadily revived throughout the late 1940s and

1950s, the critical reputation of the play grew to match its popular appeal. Though initially it owed much of its success to the scandal provoked by the deviant characters, the play evolved into a staple of the French postwar repertoire before becoming a classic of modern theater on stages worldwide.

In 1944, however, Sartre felt that the circumstances created by the Liberation demanded a new kind of drama; in the immediate postwar years he began to formulate a vision of theater that was closely tied to his conception of *engagement* (commitment). Turning away from the nineteenth century and the psychological theater of "caractères" (personalities), he sought to create what he called "un théâtre de situations" (a theater of situations). In a lecture titled "Forger des mythes" (translated as "Forgers of Myths," 1976), given during his second tour of the United States in 1946, Sartre offered a famous summary of what became in effect a theatrical manifesto: "l'homme libre dans les limites de sa propre situation, l'homme qui choisit, qu'il le veuille ou non, pour tous les autres quand il choisit pour lui-même–voilà le sujet de nos pièces" (the man who is free within the limits of his own situation, who chooses, whether he wishes to or not, for everyone else when he chooses for himself–that is the subject of our plays). In opposition to a bourgeois tradition that he saw as obsessed with psychology and human nature, Sartre wanted his theater audience to reflect on the choices made by individuals in certain concrete and crucial situations, choices objectified by acts that defined those individuals and affirmed their values.

In the immediate postwar years one such situation was the Resistance. In the aftermath of the Liberation, all of France had witnessed the painful process of *épuration* (purification), as French citizens suspected of collaboration with the Germans were tried both in the courts and in the realm of public opinion. The Resistance was a counterweight to this difficult and depressing process and was duly celebrated. For Parisian theaters freed from the constraints of censorship, the Resistance was an attractive and timely subject to bring to the stage. The first productions were hagiographic, bolstering the attractive myth that France had strongly resisted the Germans and that the Resistance had played a central role in defeating the Occupation forces. In his first play after the Liberation, *Morts sans sépulture* (1946; translated as *The Victors* and as *Men without Shadows*, 1949), Sartre offered a much less comforting assessment of both collaboration and the Resistance.

Morts sans sépulture is set in mid July 1944, after the Allied landing and with the outcome of the war no longer in doubt. A group of *maquisards* (Resistance fighters) is arrested after a failed operation in the Vercors region that has cost them and a group of villagers about three hundred lives. Three men–Canoris, a communist of Greek origin; Henri; and Sorbier–as well as a woman, Lucie, are held together with Lucie's fifteen-year-old brother, François, by a group of Vichy *miliciens* (paramilitaries) who are intent on finding the whereabouts of the Resistance fighters' leader and will use torture to obtain the information they want. None in the group knows where the leader, Jean, is hidden. Suddenly, the door is unlocked, and Jean is pushed into the room. He has been picked up by a patrol, but the *miliciens* are unaware of his identity, and he has a good cover story. He is later released and is thus able to warn another group of Resistance fighters and prevent them from walking into a trap. For now, the prisoners have reason to remain silent. After Henri and Sorbier are tortured and Sorbier kills himself to avoid betraying Jean, the survivors realize that the boy, François, will not be able to resist interrogation. In order to save Jean and the sixty other *maquisards*, Lucie, who is also Jean's lover, accepts that her brother must be silenced, and he is strangled by his comrades. Jean gains his release and, before leaving, tells Canoris that more suffering is unnecessary. He suggests that they feed the *miliciens* false information and negotiate for their lives. The others finally agree, but are double-crossed by the *miliciens*, who have them executed anyway.

Sartre had difficulty finding a theater willing to accept a play in which characters were tortured onstage. After weeks of refusals, Simone Berriau, who had recently taken over the administration of a Right Bank theater, the Théâtre Antoine, more used to boulevard plays than to committed political theater, accepted *Morts sans sépulture*. Sartre agreed to write a second play–given the brevity of *Morts sans sépulture*–to complete the program: *La Putain respectueuse* (1946; translated as *The Respectful Prostitute* and as *The Respectable Prostitute*, 1949). Subsequently, Berriau and the Théâtre Antoine put on almost all of Sartre's plays.

Morts sans sépulture provoked outrage. The depiction of the Resistance fighters as bunglers and victims and the apparently gratuitous and horrific episodes of Grand Guignol violence (as many reviewers termed them), which turned the playgoers into shocked voyeurs, precipitated a storm of protest. Women in the audience fainted, and the screams of the men tortured onstage had many spectators running for the exits. Sartre sharply reduced the visible violence after the opening night, but, beyond the immediate discomfort he had caused members of the audience, he also forced them to think about the horrific aspects of the Occupation that they most wanted to forget. Significantly, in *Morts sans sépulture* there is not a German in sight. The only torturers are Frenchmen.

Despite mostly negative reviews, *Morts sans sépulture* was a commercial success, with an initial run of more than 150 performances. Sartre, however, declared that the play was a failure, maintaining that he had been wrong to create a situation in which all the characters were doomed from the outset. In general, he felt that the Resistance was a subject that offered more possibilities for the screen than for the stage.

La Putain respectueuse, which Sartre wrote quickly on his return from America to be performed in conjunction with *Morts sans sépulture,* received better notices and a better reception from the audience than its companion piece. Julien Bertheau's staging was admired, and Héléna Bossis (Berriau's daughter, whose real name was Henriette Berriau), who played the title role, created a sensation. The play was inspired by the 1931 Scottsboro, Alabama, case in which two young white women testified that they had been raped by nine black men on a train. After the first trial (later ruled a mistrial), in which eight of the nine Negroes were condemned to death, one of the accusers, Ruby Bates, sought refuge with a minister and later recanted. Sartre gleaned the basic events of the case from a book by Vladimir Pozner, *Les Etats-Désunis* (1938, The Divided States), which had been a best-seller in France. However accurate Pozner's version (Sartre had met Pozner in Los Angeles in 1945, during his first American tour), Sartre decided to adapt the basic outline but made several significant alterations. The title character is even more starkly marginalized by her profession as a prostitute. Instead of a virtuous minister to help Lizzie (the character based on Bates) reconcile with her conscience and tell the truth, Sartre introduces a corrupt senator who induces her false testimony, just as his son, Fred, prevents her from recanting at the end of the play.

Although *La Putain respectueuse* was generally a critical success as well as a box-office hit, it was also considered scandalous and sparked arguments and loud protests in the theater. The scandal focused on two issues that were abundantly covered by the press. The first concerned charges of obscenity brought against Sartre, an issue highlighted by the title of the play, which became famous in the mutilated form in which it appeared on the walls of the Paris Métro: *La P. . . Respectueuse.* Métro administrators would not countenance the complete word *putain* in any form of advertisement and thereby inadvertently created a neologism, "une respectueuse." This term became for a time an accepted euphemism for *prostitute,* particularly since new laws had been adopted in France regulating prostitution in March 1946, creating a further connection between Sartre's play and current events.

The second issue raised by *La Putain respectueuse* concerned what some critics saw as Sartre's evident anti-Americanism. One member of the Paris municipal council, Edouard Frédéric-Dupont, attempted to have the Préfecture ban the play on the grounds that it was insulting to the liberators of France. Sartre insisted, however, that he had no intention of insulting America. He was, on the contrary, simply joining a debate in which many American writers were themselves active. In addition, offers were said to have been made by theatrical producers in New York to have Bossis re-create the principal role in a new production there, and attempts to halt the play because of its anti-American stance soon melted away. When the English-language adaptation, *The Respectful Prostitute,* opened in New York in 1948 (with toned-down dialogue), it was a hit, moving from a small Bleecker Street theater to the Cort Theatre on Broadway, where it ran for more than three hundred performances. Sartre's later political positions and the notable successes of the play in socialist countries, however, revived the early charges of anti-Americanism.

Since the premiere of *La Putain respectueuse* the play has done well, with productions all over the world. It also inspired a 1952 motion-picture adaptation, directed by Marcel Pagliero and Charles Brabant, featuring Barbara Laage in the title role. The movie, while not a critical or commercial success, is significant in that Sartre, who wrote the screenplay, was persuaded by Pagliero to modify the play and particularly to change the ending. In the final scene of the movie, Lizzie refuses Fred's offer and agrees to testify for the Negro. Sartre's willingness to write a new ending for motion-picture audiences also made it easier for him to accept the same modification to his play when it was staged in Moscow. With this much more optimistic ending (from the perspective of social justice and race relations), *La Putain respectueuse* became hugely successful not only in the Soviet Union but also in communist countries generally, in large part because of its negative vision of the United States. When Sartre and Beauvoir visited Cuba in 1960, they were invited by Fidel Castro to a production of the play at the National Theater in Havana that received extensive coverage by the Cuban press.

Although the political dimension of Sartre's drama had been a central feature of his playwriting since *Bariona, ou Le Fils du tonnerre* and his conversion to socialism, not until the Cold War and the hardening of the divide between the NATO and Warsaw Pact countries in the late 1940s did politics really take center stage in his plays, to the exclusion of virtually all other considerations. Sartre, however, insisted that his next theatrical work, *Les Mains sales* (1948; translated as *Dirty Hands* and as *Crime Passionnel,* 1949), was not a political play but a play about politics, since it contrasted idealistic and pragmatic perspectives of political strategy within a revolutionary left-wing party. As the title suggests, the play concerns the possibility of engaging in revolutionary politics without getting one's hands dirty–in other words, without compromising one's political ideals. A feature of this

Sartre and writer André Gide in the southeastern French village of Cabris, circa 1950 (© Harlingue/Roger Viollet/Getty Images)

debate is the question of violence—more specifically, the question of political assassination, which is a central feature of the play. Beauvoir notes that the plot was inspired in large part by the example of Leon Trotsky's murder in Mexico. *Les Mains sales* was also a personal play, with elements taken from discussions with many of Sartre's personal friends (Camus in particular, but also Maurice Merleau-Ponty and Arthur Koestler). The protagonist, Hugo, is in many ways a transposed portrait of Sartre's friend Paul Nizan, killed in 1940, whose memory was subsequently vilified by his communist comrades because he renounced the party in the wake of the Hitler-Stalin Pact. The play is also a reflection of Sartre's own political evolution, on the eve of the period in which he was to declare himself a fellow traveler of the Communist Party.

According to Beauvoir, Sartre began work on *Les Mains sales* during the Christmas vacation of 1947, a period in which he was about to engage in a more overt form of political action. In February 1948 Sartre, together with David Rousset, Bernard Lefort, Georges Altman, and others, announced the founding of a new political party, the Rassemblement Démocratique Révolutionnaire (RDR, Revolutionary Democratic Assembly), committed to forging a *troisième voie* (third way) between the antagonistic superpowers of the Cold War that would allow Europe to become an agent for peace and an unaligned socialist federation—a democratic alternative to Stalinism. The collapse of the RDR a year later, under ferocious attacks both from the Right and the Left, ultimately forced Sartre to ally himself more closely with the Communists until the invasion of Hungary in 1956.

Les Mains sales was a great success because it made the theoretical debate between the young bourgeois idealist, Hugo, and the older, pragmatic working-class party leader, Hoederer, dramatically compelling. Hugo, a party journalist who yearns for direct action, volunteers to kill Hoederer, a party boss who in the name of realpolitik is maneuvering to drag the party into a political alliance that will corrupt its revolutionary ideals. Emotionally complex, since Hugo comes to love the man he does in fact kill, the play also employs irony, as the party subsequently adopts the political strategy for which it had previously condemned Hoederer. Because Hugo insists on holding firmly to his political idealism, he is also killed by party members at the end of the play. Staged at the

Théâtre Antoine and using actors trained in the boulevard tradition, with André Luguet and François Périer in the lead roles, *Les Mains sales* was the theatrical event of 1948. Little by little, however, the great success of the play was marred in Sartre's eyes by a political controversy he had not anticipated. In interviews accompanying the premiere, Sartre was asked whether he was more supportive of Hugo or Hoederer. He refused to take sides, maintaining that a dramatist should pose the problem without imposing a solution. In the absence of any authoritative response from the author, reviewers made up their own minds. Since the mainstream press lauded the play, it was bitterly attacked by the communist press, which viewed it as anticommunist propaganda. Sartre belatedly declared that his personal sympathies had always been on the side of Hoederer.

In December 1948 the Soviet Union pressured authorities in Helsinki to ban a production of *Les Mains sales* as "propaganda hostile to the U.S.S.R." In New York in 1949, Sartre disavowed a Broadway adaptation, titled *Red Gloves* (with Charles Boyer as Hoederer), which had taken considerable liberties with the play and transformed the two protagonists. Sartre also dissociated himself from a 1951 movie adaptation directed by Fernand Rivers and Berriau, with Pierre Brasseur as Hoederer, which was also denounced for its anticommunist bias. Finally, Sartre decided to intervene directly and declared that, henceforth, productions of the play would be allowed only with the express consent of the communist party of the country in which it was being staged. This decision gave subsequent productions added meaning, particularly in the late 1950s and the 1960s. *Les Mains sales* proved popular in countries in which communists were debating and contesting the legacy of Stalinism, such as Italy—where Sartre was often supported by the Communist Party, which he found enlightened and congenial, as demonstrated by his detailed discussion of the play with Paolo Caruso in 1964—and Yugoslavia and Czechoslovakia, two states that were seeking to distance themselves from the Soviet model of communism.

As *Les Mains sales* clearly demonstrated, the whole question of media coverage became a two-edged sword for Sartre, the most famous European intellectual in the postwar years. In 1951 a press campaign initiated by journalists and devoted to his next play, *Le Diable et le Bon Dieu* (translated as *Lucifer and the Lord*, 1952, and as *The Devil and the Good Lord*, 1960), was launched before the play was even written, six months before the opening night of 7 June 1951. Before the premiere a combination of rumors and reports from the theater kept up a debate about the impending event. Several factors contributed to the sense of anticipation surrounding *Le Diable et le Bon Dieu*. The title, given Sartre's well-publicized atheism, was provocative. Backstage at the Théâtre Antoine, it was said that he was writing "Le Soulier de Satan" (Satan's Slipper), an underhand reference to Paul Claudel's *Le Soulier de satin* (1928–1929; translated as *The Satin Slipper*, 1955), a play completely unlike Sartre's drama. In addition to speculation that *Le Diable et le Bon Dieu* was a theatrical manifesto for atheism, other rumors maintained that the play was to serve as a prelude to a treatise demonstrating that good and evil had no fixed, definitive meaning.

As rehearsals progressed, rumors continued, with constant reports and updates on the most eagerly awaited theatrical event of the season. Interest was also fueled by the all-star cast, which was to include Brasseur and his costar from Marcel Carné's celebrated 1945 movie *Les Enfants du paradis* (Children of Paradise), Maria Casarès, as well as Jean Vilar, who later left the cast to take charge of the newly founded Théâtre National Populaire. The director of the play, Louis Jouvet, was a legend of the theater, and his association with the project was made more poignant by the fact that he was terminally ill and died later that summer, on 16 August 1951. As the opening night approached, rumors of dissension circulated. The play was said to be too long, lasting more than four hours, and still unfinished. The cost of the production was reported to be prohibitive. Rehearsals were chaotic and contentious. Many of these rumors were well-founded: Jouvet and Sartre saw both life and the theater differently and did not get along personally. Brasseur was unhappy in the title role and joined Jouvet and Berriau in begging Sartre to make cuts. The playwright responded with additional scenes. Finally, as pressure mounted, he agreed to eliminate certain sequences and to reduce Brasseur's role slightly.

In the final week before *Le Diable et le Bon Dieu* opened, Sartre gave a series of interviews in an attempt to forestall misunderstandings. Despite the historical setting and the protagonist, a folk hero and literary icon in Germany—Goetz von Berlichingen was the title character of a 1773 play by Johann Wolfgang von Goethe—Sartre maintained that he did not intend *Le Diable et le Bon Dieu* to be an historical play. The idea had been suggested to him some years before by Barrault, who had described for him a play by Miguel de Cervantes, *El rufián dichoso* (1615, The Happy Ruffian), in which a bandit, tired of doing evil, decides that his future conduct will depend on a roll of the dice. As a clap of thunder sounds above, he rolls the dice, loses, and converts to a life of virtue, which entails expiating the sins of others before he dies a virtual saint. Sartre was careful to stress, however, that his Goetz cheats when he rolls the dice. Although he has not yet broken with God, he chooses his own course of action, not divine providence. But Goetz's conversion to a life of Christian virtue in no way lessens the suffering around him, so he makes a more radical choice: he decides that God does not exist and that man alone is the measure of all ethical human conduct. Embracing a new relative ethics that admits the painful necessity of violence, Goetz decides at the end of the play to lead the peasant army in its war against the barons.

Sartre's decision to situate his characters in sixteenth-century Lutheran Germany meant that they all existed naturally in a religious atmosphere where there were no clear distinctions between theological, philosophical, and political issues. As a result, the question of good and evil on which the play is built moves seamlessly from a theological to a political plane. As for Goetz's discovery that God does not exist, Sartre said that his point was only to show that in an environment where the question of good and evil depends on religious absolutes, mankind always suffers.

Although as a rule Sartre wrote his plays spontaneously and quickly, he had been thinking about *Le Diable et le Bon Dieu* for almost two years before writing it and had amassed extensive documentation on the period. Portions of the dialogue between Goetz and Nasty are culled from documented pronouncements made by Martin Luther and Thomas Münzer, an Anabaptist radical. The play also explores the contemporary Sartrean themes of violence, bastardy, and engagement. Sartre later said that *Le Diable et le Bon Dieu* was his most personal play, the one in which he had invested himself most heavily. Despite all the conflict and controversy that accompanied the creation of the play, he insisted to the end of his life that of all his theatrical works, it remained his favorite.

Le Diable et le Bon Dieu was not a great critical success. The right-wing and Catholic press were naturally hostile—the Bishop of Liège instructed his congregation that seeing the play would be a "faute grave" (grave error)—but even influential critics on the Left, such as Elsa Triolet, felt that Sartre had failed in his attempt to create a relevant analogy between conflicts in the play and the contemporary political situation in France. Nevertheless, *Le Diable et le Bon Dieu* was a great commercial success, with more than two hundred performances during its initial Paris run. It then toured widely around France, as well as in Switzerland, England, and North Africa. In particular, the play won Brasseur great acclaim, in part because of the sheer physical demands of the central role. Pierre Morin, asked to fill in when Brasseur was briefly indisposed, lost his voice after his second performance.

Although their relationship did not ripen into friendship, this first triumphant theatrical collaboration between Sartre and Brasseur led to Sartre's next play two years later: the adaptation of a drama by Alexandre Dumas *père*, an unexpected departure at this stage of Sartre's career, when he was otherwise consumed by Cold War politics. During the rehearsals for *Le Diable et le Bon Dieu*, Brasseur had mentioned to Sartre an idea for a play first suggested to him by Dullin in the late 1930s. At the height of the French Romantic period, Dumas had been approached by Frédérick Lemaître, the first great French Shakespearian actor, requesting that he write a play about the English actor Edmund Kean, a legend of the stage who late in his career had come to France and performed *Othello* in Paris during a celebrated tour of 1827–1828. *Kean, ou Désordre et génie* (1836, Kean, or Disorder and Genius) was the result, a fanciful portrait of the life and times of the great English Romantic actor, an impoverished street player who transformed English theater with his innovative and iconoclastic interpretations of William Shakespeare's works. In Dumas's play, Kean's extraordinary performances with the Drury Lane theater company have propelled him into fashionable society, where he is adopted by the Prince of Wales, even as he is snubbed by other court aristocrats who are disdainful of his lowly origins. Dumas's play was a huge success. Lemaître triumphed in the title role, which includes a famous "play within the play" sequence in which Kean, onstage, steps out of his role to insult the Prince of Wales (seated in the audience), who has sacrificed their friendship to pursue a countess whom Kean is also courting. At the end of the play the two friends are reconciled, and Kean leaves London to tour the United States.

In the summer of 1953 Sartre wrote *Kean* (translated as *Kean; or, Disorder and Genius,* 1954), his adaptation of Dumas's play. Brasseur, who had already played the role of Lemaître in *Les Enfants du paradis,* both starred in and directed *Kean* at the Théâtre Sarah-Bernhardt in November of that year. In interviews accompanying the opening night, Sartre insisted that his play was only an adaptation and that *Kean,* published in February 1954 with Dumas's text as an appendix, did not really belong in his dramatic corpus; he stated in the 1953 theater program that he had only "ôté la rouille et quelques moisissures" (cleaned up the rust and some mould) in the original. Despite the almost identical plots, the focus of the two plays is, however, quite different. Dumas's Kean is torn by the impossibility of reconciling his poor but honest origins as a *saltimbanque* (traveling street player) with his desire for acceptance in the brilliant but corrupt circles of court society that his talent and apparent friendship with the Prince of Wales have provisionally opened up for him. In comparison, Sartre's Kean is less concerned with the precariousness of his social situation; he is, however, consumed by the ontological paradoxes of his condition as an actor. Sartre saw in *Kean* an opportunity to develop the inquiry into imagination that he had initiated in his first investigations as a philosopher. In Sartre's play Kean is preoccupied with the dramatic roles that usurp but at the same time validate his existence,

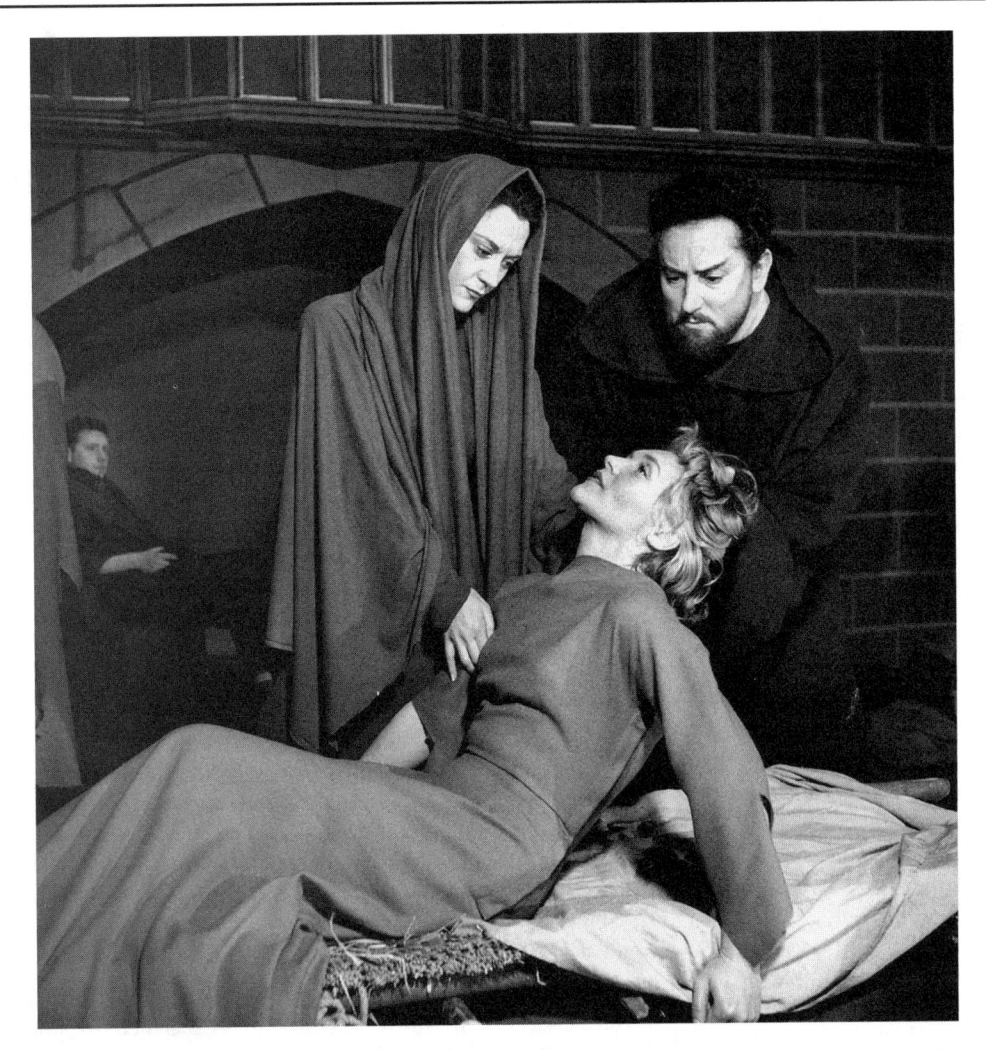

Maria Casarès, Marie Olivier (stage name of Wanda Kosakiewicz), and Pierre Brasseur in the 1951 Théâtre Antoine, Paris, production of Sartre's Le Diable et le Bon Dieu *(translated as* Lucifer and the Lord, *1952, and as* The Devil and the Good Lord, *1960), about a sixteenth-century German folk hero who leads a peasant revolt after discovering that a life of Christian virtue does nothing to ease the suffering around him (© Lipnitzki/Roger-Viollet/Getty Images)*

and he wonders if he will always be possessed by imaginary beings and attitudes that condition his responses. Like many Sartrean heroes, the historical Kean was an illegitimate child, which made him both self-reliant from an early age and sensitive to social hypocrisy. Like Sartre, Kean was physically small, unprepossessing, and a rebellious artist.

Critical reviews of *Kean* were mixed; some critics regretted that Sartre had undermined the conventions of Dumas's Romantic drama in favor of a didactic philosophical exercise, while others welcomed his innovations. Brasseur's performance, however, won accolades from every quarter, and the play was commercially successful. After a full season in Paris, the production went on an extensive tour. *Kean* inspired a 1956 movie adaptation in Italy and was staged all over Europe in productions that were favorably received. The play was successfully revived in 1987 at the Théâtre Marigny in Paris, with Jean-Paul Belmondo in the title role.

Part of the success of *Kean* was linked to lighthearted, comic elements that are rare in Sartre's plays. An exception is *Nekrassov* (1955; translated as *Nekrassov, a Farce*, 1956), the only purely comic farce in Sartre's dramatic corpus. *Nekrassov* is simultaneously Sartre's most amusing play, with several wildly funny scenes, and his least successful, because of its uneven composition and uncompromising and didactic pro-Soviet stance. Inspired by real-life cases in which Soviet defectors to the West were exploited for anti-Communist propaganda, Sartre chose as his central character a destitute con man, Georges de Valera, who decides to impersonate a Soviet defector named Nekrassov and is paid for his revelations about the failures of socialism by an opportunistic anti-Communist newspaper, *Soir à Paris*. Little by little, the false defector becomes further involved in anti-Communist politics until he is saved, personally and professionally, by a virtuous and enlightened left-wing female journalist.

The commercial prospects of *Nekrassov* were probably not helped by the comic scorn Sartre directed against the same press that he needed to publicize the play. *Soir à Paris* was an obvious reference to the most widely read Parisian evening paper, *France-soir,* and Sartre's description of the unscrupulous director of the paper (originally slated to be played by Louis de Funès) closely matched Pierre Lazareff, the press baron who ran *France-soir* and was also a close friend of Berriau, whose Théâtre Antoine staged the play. Nor was Lazareff the only recognizable target. Several writers and political figures, including Koestler and André Malraux, were lampooned in *Nekrassov*, which was obviously a *pièce à clef*, despite Sartre's repeated denials.

Nekrassov closed after only sixty performances, and Sartre later declared it a failed play, although under the title *Georges de Valera* it was a huge hit in Moscow six months later. Sartre felt that he had been wrong to build the whole play around a confidence trickster, although it is tempting to establish parallels between Georges the con man and Sartre's theory of the actor, incarnated in Kean. Both are professionally linked to the illusions they create and manipulate; unlike those around them, they know that the world really is a stage. History had the final word: the optimistic assessment of Communist societies in the play was irreparably damaged only months later when Soviet tanks rolled into Hungary.

The memory of the failure of *Nekrassov*—Sartre's only real commercial flop since *Les Mouches*—contributed to a series of problems that made *Les Séquestrés d'Altona* (produced 1959, published 1960; translated as *Loser Wins*, 1960, and as *The Condemned of Altona*, 1961) his greatest challenge as a playwright. Many years of overwork fueled by amphetamine abuse had precipitated a crisis in Sartre's health, from which he recovered only slowly. He was having trouble finishing the *Critique de la raison dialectique* (1960, 1985; translated as *Critique of Dialectical Reason*, 1976, 1991), his contribution to Marxist theory, only the first volume of which was published during his lifetime. The political tragedy of Hungary in 1956 had forced him to reevaluate his relationship to Soviet Marxism, while, closer to home, the intensification of the Algerian War and the French elections of 1958 had deeply demoralized the French Left. In this climate the task of conceiving and realizing his most ambitious play—a play that was to take on the systematic torture of Algerians by French soldiers, present an indictment of modern capitalism, and offer a pessimistic portrait of a century still gripped by the atrocities of Nazi Germany, Stalinist Russia, and colonial injustice—was for many months more than Sartre could manage.

Faced once again with the problem of government censorship as the Algerian War grew more brutal, Sartre decided to situate *Les Séquestrés d'Altona* in contemporary Germany and use the legacy of Nazi war crimes as a cover for his immediate concerns. The play opens in a Hamburg suburb, Altona, where Frantz, the scion of an important industrialist family, has sequestered himself in an upstairs room of the family mansion for thirteen years, since returning home with the last remnants of the defeated German army from the Russian front. He admits no one except Leni, his sister, who brings him food and, from time to time, sleeps with him. His father, dying of cancer, wants a final meeting. From this dramatic starting point, in which a recluse effectively holds the whole family hostage, the conflicts that result implicate a whole nation, if not, as the final monologue suggests, all of humanity. Prevented from saving a Jewish rabbi from a concentration camp built on land his father leased to the Nazis, Frantz reveals that he later tortured prisoners on the Russian front. In the years since the defeat of Germany, the father's shipbuilding empire has grown more powerful, despite his dealings with Nazis and Americans—all in the name of realpolitik. Ostensibly in hiding so as not to witness the final destruction of Germany, the tormented and hallucinating Frantz actually cannot bear to contemplate the prosperity of the nation. Human actions and intentions in the play have been subverted by what Sartre calls *contre-finalité* (counter-finality) in *Critique de la raison dialectique*, the theft of man's praxis by his technological and social environment. At the end of the play, Frantz and his father are united in a double suicide. The last words of the drama, a plea for understanding addressed to the future, are spoken by a tape recorder with no one onstage.

Despite the subject matter of *Les Séquestrés d'Altona* and the fact that it took more than four hours to perform, the play was a commercial success, running uninterruptedly at the Théâtre de la Renaissance in Paris for the entire 1959–1960 season. It was also a critical success, with Serge Reggiani acclaimed in the role of Frantz. A new production by François Périer at the Théâtre de l'Athénée in 1965 was also successful, a claim that cannot be made for *I Sequestrati di Altona* (1963), a motion-picture adaptation directed by Vittorio de Sica, despite an all-star cast featuring Maximilian Schell as Frantz, Fredric March as the father, and Sophia Loren. Sartre dissociated himself entirely from the movie.

Sartre wrote only one more work for the stage, an adaptation of Euripides' *Trojan Women* (415 B.C.) as *Les Troyennes* (1965; translated as *The Trojan Women*, 1967), which premiered on 10 March 1965 at the Théâtre National Populaire and was directed by Michael Cacoyannis, director of the movie *Zorba the Greek* (1964). Unlike *Kean,* this adaptation was faithful to the original–Sartre even used a verse form of dialogue–although his denunciation of war brought up the issue of contemporary colonial wars. *Les Troyennes* ends with Poseidon addressing the audience: "Faites la guerre, mortels imbéciles. . . . Vous en crèverez. Tous" (Wage war, foolish mortals. . . . It will kill you. All of you). At the time the play opened, the first contingents of American troops were arriving in Vietnam, a decade after defeated French troops had left Indochina. One year later, Sartre accepted an invitation to join the Russell International War Crimes Tribunal, formed by Bertrand Russell to investigate American war crimes.

Les Troyennes remains the only published testimonial to Sartre's activity as a playwright after 1959; however, a theater project provisionally titled "Le Pari" (The Wager) preoccupied him for some time both before and after that date. In his last interview on theater, given to Bernard Dort only months before his death on 15 April 1980, Sartre provided a vivid account of the play. Like *Bariona,* "Le Pari" was to have focused on an impending birth and was to have been staged as a mystery play, in which an expectant mother is shown by supernatural means the life that her son, a revolutionary activist, will lead. It is a terrible existence of suffering and deprivation, leading finally to his execution. But the son's sacrifice will not be in vain: with his death comes the triumph of the revolution, and so the mother agrees to give birth, wagering that her son, even if he cannot change the terrible events she has seen, will somehow transform his life of struggle and illustrate the meaning of human freedom.

The outline of "Le Pari" features an opposition found in all of Sartre's politically committed plays: his attraction to socialism and egalitarianism on the one hand and to messianic heroes on the other. Pulled back and forth between these contradictory poles, Sartre's drama suggests that his conversion from the individualism of his young adulthood to socialism and committed political activism was never as complete or as stable as he claimed. In addition to his activism, however, there are many reasons for Sartre's investment in theater. He wrote his plays out of ideological conviction, but he also wrote them for money, which he desperately needed to support the members of his extended "family" (including the Kosakiewicz sisters and various friends and mistresses), many of whom had no reliable source of income. He also needed to supply work for actresses, such as Olivier, with whom he had been intimate and whose careers depended on his continued support. At times Sartre found the practical details and compromises vexing. Ideologically, he welcomed the collective creative process, but privately, he was often irritated by his dealings with theater directors and actors whose sense of his plays often clashed with his own. Temperamentally, Sartre did not like depending on others in matters of artistic creation.

Formally, unlike Bertolt Brecht and Samuel Beckett, Jean-Paul Sartre was not an innovator of the stage or of dramatic language, nor was he a great theorist of theatrical practice. His plays remain popular in large part because of the fascination that Sartre, the multifaceted intellectual, continues to exert. Will they one day be staged as classics of the French stage? More-recent productions by directors such as Daniel Mesguich suggest that Sartre's plays are not as firmly tied to their historical moment as many critics once feared and that future generations may well see these plays in a quite different light, separating them from Sartre's own overwhelming aura.

Letters:

Simone de Beauvoir, ed., *Lettres au Castor et à quelques autres,* 2 volumes (Paris: Gallimard, 1983); translated in part by Matthew Ward, Irene Ilton, and Marilyn Myatt as *Thoughtful Passions: Jean-Paul Sartre's Intimate Letters to Simone de Beauvoir, 1926–1939* (New York: Macmillan, 1987).

Interviews:

Yvon Novy, "Ce que nous dit Jean-Paul Sartre de sa première pièce," *Comoedia,* 24 April 1943;

Paul Carrière, "*Les Jeux sont faits?* Tout le contraire d'une pièce existentialiste," *Figaro,* 29 April 1947, p. 4;

René Guilly, "Dans *Les Mains sales,* Jean-Paul Sartre pose le problème de la fin et des moyens," *Combat,* 31 March 1948;

Marcel Péju, "Le Diable et le Bon Dieu, nous dit Sartre, c'est la même chose . . . moi je choisis l'homme," *Samedi-Soir* (2–8 June 1951);

Jean Duché, "Jean-Paul Sartre répond à la critique dramatique et offre un guide au spectateur pour suivre *Le Diable et le Bon Dieu,*" *Le Figaro littéraire* (30 June 1951);

Renée Saurel, "La véritable figure de Kean," *Les Lettres Françaises* (12–19 November 1953);

Henri Magnan, "Avant la création de *Nekrassov* au Théâtre Antoine, Sartre nous dit . . . ," *Le Monde,* 1 June 1955, p. 9; translated by Rima Drell Reck as "Said Jean-Paul Sartre," *Yale French Studies,* 16 (Winter 1955–1956): 3, 7;

Bernard Dort, "*Les Séquéstrés d'Altona* nous concernent tous," *Théâtre populaire,* 6, no. 4 (1959): 1–13;

"L'Ecrivain doit refuser de se laisser transformer en institution," *Le Monde,* 24 October 1964, p. 14; translated by Richard Howard as "Sartre on the

Nobel Prize," *New York Review of Books,* 17 December 1964, pp. 5–6;

Bernard Pingaud, "*Les Troyennes,* Jean-Paul Sartre s'explique," *Bref,* no. 83 (February 1965);

Dort, "Au Théâtre, l'imaginaire doit être pur dans sa manière même de se donner au réel: Entretien avec Jean-Paul Sartre par Bernard Dort," *Travail théâtral,* nos. 32–33 (1980).

Bibliographies:

Allen J. Belkind, *Jean-Paul Sartre: Sartre and Existentialism in English: A Bibliographical Guide* (Kent, Ohio: Kent State University Press, 1970);

Michel Contat and Michel Rybalka, eds., *Les Ecrits de Sartre* (Paris: Gallimard, 1970), pp. 47–482; translated by Richard C. McCleary as *A Bibliographical Life,* volume 1 of *The Writings of Jean-Paul Sartre* (Evanston, Ill.: Northwestern University Press, 1974);

Robert Wilcocks, *Jean-Paul Sartre: A Bibliography of International Criticism* (Edmonton: University of Alberta Press, 1975);

François and Claire Lapointe, *Jean-Paul Sartre and His Critics: An International Bibliography (1938–1980),* revised edition (Bowling Green, Ohio: Philosophy Documentation Center/Bowling Green State University, 1981).

Biographies:

Kenneth Thompson and Margaret Thompson, *Sartre, Life and Works* (New York & Bicester, U.K.: Facts on File, 1984);

Annie Cohen-Solal, *Sartre: 1905–1980* (Paris: Gallimard, 1985); translated by Anna Cancogni as *Sartre: A Life,* edited by Norman MacAfee (New York: Pantheon, 1987);

Ronald Hayman, *Sartre: A Life* (New York: Simon & Schuster, 1987);

Denis Bertholet, *Sartre* (Paris: Plon, 2000).

References:

Françoise Bagot and Michel Kail, *Jean-Paul Sartre: Les Mains sales* (Paris: Presses Universitaires de France, 1985);

Thomas Bishop, *Huis clos de Jean-Paul Sartre* (Paris: Hachette, 1975);

Marc Buffat, *Les Mains sales de Jean-Paul Sartre* (Paris: Gallimard, 1991);

Michel Contat, *Explication des Séquestrés d'Altona de Jean-Paul Sartre* (Paris: Minard, 1968);

Mireille Cornud-Peyron, *Les Mouches, Huis clos* (Paris: Nathan, 1991);

Ted Freeman, *Theatres of War: French Committed Theatre from the Second World War to the Cold War* (Exeter: University of Exeter Press, 1998);

Ingrid Galster, *Le Théâtre de Jean-Paul Sartre devant ses premiers critiques,* second edition (Paris: L'Harmattan, 2001);

Lucien Goldmann, *Structures mentales et création culturelle* (Paris: Anthropos, 1970);

Keith Gore, *Sartre: La Nausée and Les Mouches* (London: Arnold, 1970);

John Ireland, *Sartre, un art déloyal: Théâtralité et engagement* (Paris: J.-M. Place, 1994);

Jean-Louis Jeannelle, *Jean-Paul Sartre: Les Mouches* (Rosny-sous-Bois: Bréal, 1998);

Francis Jeanson, *Sartre par lui-même* (Paris: Seuil, 1955);

Frank Laraque, *La Révolte dans le théâtre de Sartre vu par un homme du Tiers monde* (Paris: J.-P. Delarge, 1976);

Claude Launay, *Le Diable et le Bon Dieu, Sarte: Analyse critique* (Paris: Hatier, 1970);

Bernard Lecherbonnier, *Huis clos, Sartre: Analyse critique* (Paris: Hatier, 1972);

Robert Lorris, *Sartre dramaturge* (Paris: Nizet, 1975);

Jean-François Louette, *Sartre contra Nietzsche (Les Mouches, Huis clos, Les Mots)* (Grenoble: Presses Universitaires de Grenoble, 1996);

Dorothy McCall, *The Theatre of Jean-Paul Sartre* (New York: Columbia University Press, 1969);

François Noudelmann, *Huis clos et Les Mouches de Jean-Paul Sartre* (Paris: Gallimard, 1993);

Peter Royle, *Sartre, l'enfer et le liberté: Etude de Huis clos et des Mouches* (Quebec: Presses de l'Université Laval, 1973);

Luciano Verona, *Le Théâtre de Jean-Paul Sartre,* second edition (Milan: Cisalpino, 1994);

Pierre Verstraeten, *Violence et éthique: Esquisse d'une critique de la morale dialectique à partir du théâtre politique de Sartre* (Paris: Gallimard, 1972).

Papers:

The Bibliothèque nationale de France in Paris has manuscripts of several of Jean-Paul Sartre's plays, although few have been classified to date. Others are either lost or in private hands.

Georges Schéhadé

(2 November 1905 – 17 January 1989)

Kristin M. Vining-Stauffer
Whitman College

PLAY PRODUCTIONS: *Monsieur Bob'le,* Paris, Théâtre de la Huchette, 30 January 1951;

La Soirée des proverbes, Paris, Petit Théâtre Marigny, 30 January 1954;

Histoire de Vasco, Zurich, Switzerland, Schauspielhaus, 15 October 1956; Paris, Théâtre Sarah-Bernhardt, 1 October 1957;

Les Violettes, Bochum, Germany, Schauspielhaus, 21 September 1960; Chalon-sur-Saône, France, Théâtre de Bourgogne, 23 September 1966;

Le Voyage, Paris, Théâtre de France (Odéon), 17 February 1961;

L'Emigré de Brisbane, Munich, Residenztheater, 12 January 1965.

BOOKS: *Etincelles* (Paris: Editions de la Pensée Latine, 1928);

Poésies (Paris: GLM, 1938);

Rodogune Sinne (Paris: GLM, 1947);

Poésies II (Paris: GLM, 1948);

Poésies III (Paris: GLM, 1949);

Poésie Zéro, ou L'Ecolier sultan (Paris: GLM, 1950);

Si tu rencontres un ramier (Paris: Editions L'Arche, 1951);

Monsieur Bob'le (Paris: Gallimard, 1951);

Les Poésies (Paris: Gallimard, 1952);

La Soirée des proverbes (Paris: Gallimard, 1954);

Histoire de Vasco (Paris: Julliard, 1956); translated by Robert Baldick as *Vasco,* in *Theatre of War,* edited by Baldick (Harmondsworth, U.K.: Penguin, 1967);

Les Violettes (Paris: Gallimard, 1960);

Le Voyage (Paris: Gallimard, 1961);

L'Emigré de Brisbane (Paris: Gallimard, 1965);

Les Poésies, suivi de Portrait de Jules et de Recit de l'An Zero (Paris: Gallimard, 1969);

L'Habit fait le prince (Paris: Gallimard, 1973);

L'Ecolier sultan suivi de Rodogune Sinne (Paris: Gallimard, 1973);

Anthologie du vers unique (Paris: Ramsay, 1977);

Le Nageur d'un seul amour (Paris: Gallimard, 1985);

Georges Schéhadé, 1961 (© Lipnitzki/Roger-Viollet/Getty Images)

Poésies VII: derniers poèmes, dessins inédits (Beirut: Editions Dar an-Nahar, 1998);

Chagrin d'amour (Beirut: Editions Dar An-Nahar, 1999).

Collections: *Les Œuvres poétiques complètes,* edited by Nadia Tuéni and Jad Hatem (Beirut: Editions Dar An-Nahar, 1986);

Œuvre complète: La Poésie, edited by Gaëtan Picon, Jean-Claude Morin, and Joseph Issa (Beirut: Editions Dar An-Nahar, 1998);

Œuvre complète: Le Théâtre, 2 volumes, edited by Danielle Baglione and Albert Dichy (Beirut: Editions Dar An-Nahar, 1998).

PRODUCED SCRIPT: *Goya,* motion picture, Films Franco-Africains, 1957.

Georges Schéhadé owes his reputation as a dramatist to six plays written and produced principally in Paris in the 1950s and 1960s. Martin Esslin in *The Theater of the Absurd* (1961) calls Schéhadé a member of the "poetic avant-garde," who, along with Henri Pichette and Jean Vauthier, constituted a trend in French theater of the postwar period that ran parallel to, but was distinct from, the absurdist avant-garde of Samuel Beckett, Eugène Ionesco, Arthur Adamov, and Jean Genet. According to Esslin, this poetic avant-garde "is more lyrical, and far less violent and grotesque [than the Theater of the Absurd]. Even more important is its different attitude toward language . . . it aspires to plays that are in effect poems, images composed of a rich web of verbal associations." At a time when absurdist playwrights parodied and criticized language, Schéhadé wrote dramatic works that relied on the evocative power of words, an accomplishment all the more interesting considering that his native tongue was not French but Arabic.

Georges Elias Schéhadé was born in Alexandria, Egypt, on 2 November 1905 to a Greek Orthodox family from Lebanon. The few details of his early life he revealed in interviews indicate that the family lived an international life. As a youth, Schéhadé traveled a great deal, moving back and forth between Beirut, Lebanon, and Paris. Schéhadé claimed throughout his life that he felt homesick for Beirut when in Paris and for Paris when in Beirut.

Schéhadé began his literary career as a poet in Paris. By the mid 1920s he had attracted the admiration of established poets Léon-Paul Fargue and Valéry Larbaud; Paul Eluard introduced him to the Surrealists. Schéhadé published his first volume of verse, *Etincelles* (Sparks), in 1928, followed by *Poésies* (1938, Poetry) and five other collections between 1938 and his death, all in French. He also composed a one-act impromptu play, *Le Chagrin d'amour* (The Heart Ache), in 1938 as an entertainment for a French military officers' ball and published it in *Le Jour* (3 July 1938) and again in *Les Cahiers de la Comédie Française* (Winter 1994); it was published in book form in Lebanon in 1999.

During World War II, Schéhadé lived in Lebanon. On his return trip to France in 1946, he met a young Frenchwoman, Brigitte Collerais, whom he married in 1951. Their only son, Elie-Philippe, was born in Beirut at the end of this same year. From 1949 until 1960 Schéhadé worked for the United Nations Educational, Scientific and Cultural Organization (UNESCO) in Paris while remaining active in literary circles. He counted among his acquaintances poets Pierre-Jean Jouve, Eluard, and René Char; painter Marc Chagall; and playwrights Beckett and Ionesco. By 1951 Schéhadé had turned his attention from poetry to drama, or, more accurately, to a type of theater that incorporated poetry.

Schéhadé's first play in three acts, *Monsieur Bob'le* (Mr. Bob'le), premiered on 30 January 1951 at the Théâtre de la Huchette in Paris, directed by Georges Vitaly and performed by the Compagnie Georges Vitaly. According to Wallace Fowlie, the Parisian press was so hostile to the production of the strange *Monsieur Bob'le* that they tried to close it down. The play, however, was publicly supported by the poets André Breton and Char, playwright Pichette, and actor Gérard Philipe. The controversy over the play came to be known as "la bataille de *Monsieur Bob'le*" (the battle of *Monsieur Bob'le*)–an allusion to "la bataille d'*Hernani*" (the battle of *Hernani*) of 1830, the controversy over Victor Hugo's play that pitted the young Romantics against the older generation. It begins with preparations for the departure of Monsieur Bob'le, beloved leader and father figure of the imaginary village of Paola Scala. Bob'le leaves on a quest for fortune, although he disdains wealth. His people often quote from a book that includes Bob'le's wisdom; *Le Trémandour* records such comments as "Celui qui porte un chapeau doit être plus juste que les autres, car, à priori, il pèche contre la lune et le soleil . . ." (He who wears a hat must be more just than other men, because, a priori, he sins against the moon and the sun . . .) and "Le sommeil n'est pas seulement un répit, et pour notre corps un pâturage, le sommeil, c'est la perfection de la vie, parce qu'il est plein de songes . . . et sans âge!" (Sleep is not only a respite, and fodder for our bodies, sleep is the perfection of life, because it is full of dreams . . . and ageless!). The departure of Monsieur Bob'le upsets the community of Paola Scala. As his valet, Arnold, says, "ce qui distingue Paola Scala des autres contrées, des autres villages, malgré leur récoltes et leurs nids, c'est la présence de Monsieur Bob'le" (what distinguishes Paola Scala from other countries, from other villages, in spite of their harvests and their nests, is the presence of Monsieur Bob'le).

The main event of act 2 is the arrival of José Marco, a colorful character sent by Monsieur Bob'le to give the people of Paola Scala news concerning Bob'le's well-being. José Marco speaks at length of the work that currently preoccupies Bob'le, after which Marco inexplicably disappears. Act 3 concerns Bob'le's death. Two characters, Alexandre and Soubise, who attend him on his deathbed, explain that Bob'le was on his return sea voyage when he fell ill. Bob'le's presence affected the crew and passengers, as well as the ship itself, which refuses to continue sailing without him. On his deathbed, Bob'le invites Alexandre to find a home in Paola Scala, teaches him from *Le Trémandour,* and names him in a prophetic manner "Alexandre de Paola Scala."

Arnold reads with Bob'le from *Le Trémandour* the line "Celui qui rêve se mélange à l'air" (He who dreams mixes himself with the air); then Arnold also disappears. Finally, Monsieur Bob'le dies, apparently leaving the world to join the air by way of his dreams. Alexandre sets out for Paola Scala to finish Bob'le's journey. Schéhadé's first complete play includes features common to all his plays: lyrical language, a confusion between dream and reality, the alternation of comic and serious elements, and an ambiguous conclusion.

Schéhadé's next play, *La Soirée des proverbes* (The Evening of Proverbs), was first performed on 30 January 1954 at the Petit Théâtre Marigny in Paris by the Compagnie Madeleine Renaud–Jean-Louis Barrault under the direction of Jean-Louis Barrault. It was published by Gallimard the same year. Schéhadé was fortunate to attract the attention of Barrault, the director who popularized Paul Claudel's verse dramas and who eventually became the director of the government-subsidized Théâtre de France. According to David Bradby, Barrault considered Schéhadé's poetic drama compatible with his notion of "total theater," which "experiment[ed] with mime, dance and other expressive means." *La Soirée des proverbes* was the first of many collaborations between the writer and the director.

La Soirée des proverbes opens with an offstage speech before the curtain rises; it introduces the central preoccupations of childhood and the play–fantasy and dream: "Si la mélodie peut survivre dans l'âme d'un enfant, si tout ce qui fut esprit demeure, je vais raconter l'historie d'une nuit merveilleuse" (If melody can survive in the soul of a child, if everything that was spirit remains, I am going to tell the story of a marvelous night). In act 1 several characters have stopped at the "Auberge du Cygne Blanc" (The Inn of the White Swan) to pick up a lantern before making a nighttime journey to the soirée of the *Quatre Diamants* (Four Diamonds), an evening described by one attendee, Le Président Domino, as the moment of intellectual and spiritual revelation: "Cette soirée devait réunir, dans un site élevé, des hommes remarquables, des spécialistes de la connaissance, des astronomes de l'âme, des abbés; pour discuter des problèmes les plus compliqués" (This soirée was supposed to bring together, in an elevated place, remarkable men, specialists of knowledge, astronomers of the soul, priests; to discuss the most complicated problems). The protagonist, Argengeorge, a poet, resists the temptation of Domino's description, declaring he has no intention of participating in the evening. The remarks of L'Ecolière Follète (Follette the Schoolgirl), however, renew his interest in the event. She appears to dream out loud, revealing that the evening will be, for her, the scene of a tryst: "Je ne suis pas abandonnée; j'attends quelqu'un. Il va sûrement venir.

Front cover for the 1951 first edition of Schéhadé's play about a village father-figure and leader who leaves to seek his fortune, although he does not believe in wealth (Thomas Cooper Library, University of South Carolina)

(Après un temps.) Je vais à la soirée" (I am not abandoned; I am waiting for someone. He will surely come. [After a pause] I am going to the ball). Argengeorge's resistence begins to break down. At the end of act 1, Argengeorge's beloved, Hélène, arrives at the inn to embark upon a romantic journey with him but is unable to dissuade him from leaving her for the experience of the *Quatre Diamants*. A rejected Hélène asks before she exits, "Le rêve est donc plus fort que l'amour?" (Dreams are thus stronger than love?). Argengeorge has already called the soirée "Et ce qui existe" (And what exists), demonstrating that the possibility of fulfilling a dream exercises a greater attraction than ordinary human sentiment.

Act 2 is set in the woods outside of the *Quatre Diamants*. Not all of the characters appearing in act 1 have received permission to enter the house where the soirée takes place. They stand on the outside of the festivities, attentive, nevertheless, to the activities from which they have been barred. Argengeorge arrives at the height of anticipation. His monologue resembles poetry through its repetition of the phrase, "O belle nuit!" (O beautiful night!). He eventually gains entrance, but as he walks into the house, the characters remaining outside express their worry over Argengeorge's security. Act 2 ends with their cries to him to flee to safety.

Act 3 is the soirée of the *Quatre Diamants,* where all dreams are deflated. Argengeorge must confront old age and death. This particular soirée is a restaging of an earlier soirée but is a failure, since the glory of the earlier event cannot be re-created. Argengeorge discovers an older double, *le Chasseur Alexis* (Alexis the Hunter), who is also present and who embodies what Argengeorge will be in the future, a man disappointed by his inability to realize his dream of enlightenment. Rather than live to this disappointing end, Argengeorge chooses to be killed by his future self, thus preserving his youthful ambitions. Leonard Pronko remarks that "the dramatic quality of Schéhadé's plays largely lies in their appeal to our inborn desire to imitate what we once did instinctively."

Histoire de Vasco (translated as *Vasco,* 1967) premiered on 15 October 1956 at the Schauspielhaus in Zurich by the Compagnie Madeleine Renaud–Jean-Louis Barrault under Barrault's direction; it was published in the same year. Schéhadé changes from the format of three acts to a story in six tableaux. In program notes from the Théâtre Sarah-Bernhardt, the prominent Parisian theater where *Histoire de Vasco* was restaged successfully in 1957, Schéhadé wrote that *Histoire de Vasco* is a book of images or a dream inspired by looking at his son's toy soldiers, which began to take on a life of their own:

> Dans mon esprit, comme vous le voyez, cette *Histoire de Vasco,* inspirée par des jouets, devait finir bien. Rien à faire! les petits soldats de mon fils tuèrent Vasco. Et je me suis demandé s'il n'y a pas des choses maudites jusque dans leurs représentations et leurs apparences les plus charmantes. Je parle bien sûr des petits soldats de plomb de mon fils.

> (In my mind, as you see, this Story of Vasco, inspired by toys, had to turn out well. I couldn't help it! my son's little soldiers killed Vasco. And I asked myself if there don't exist damnable things even in their most charming representations and appearances. I am speaking of course of my son's tin soldiers.)

Set around 1850, the first tableau introduces Lieutenant Septembre and two of the main characters, Marguerite and her father, César. Schéhadé describes the father as "le roi de la fantaisie. Très humain . . . Une sorte de poète-prophète-bohème" (the king of fantasy. Very human . . . A sort of poet-prophet-Bohemian) and the daughter as "Très belle. Compagne idéale des 'fantaisies' de son père. Pleine de rêve et en même temps de vie" (Very beautiful. The ideal companion of her father's "fantaisies." Full of dream and life at the same time). Marguerite and César point Lieutenant Septembre in the right direction for finding Vasco, the object of his search. Marguerite then dreams of falling in love and being engaged to a barber.

Vasco, a barber who does not want to go to war, is also a dreamer who daily pretends to cut the hair of imaginary customers in his shop. When Lieutenant Septembre finds Vasco and reads a letter from General Le Mirador enlisting Vasco to perform a secret mission, Vasco, believing that he is being enlisted for his hair-cutting and styling skills, accepts. Marguerite and César discover the town with Vasco's shop. When Marguerite reads the sign, *Vasco Coiffeur* (Vasco, Barber), she immediately connects the barber of her dreams with Vasco and sets out to find him.

Le Mirador has chosen Vasco because of his innocence rather than his bravery; the dangerous mission is to deliver a message to the enemy: "Vasco accomplira sa mission parce qu'il a peur! . . . Je n'aime pas les héros. Ils sont rarement utiles et toujours encombrants! Un homme qui a peur est efficace et dangereux, si l'on sait s'en servir"(Vasco will accomplish his mission because he is afraid! . . . I don't like heroes. They are seldom useful and always burdensome! A man who is frightened is efficacious and dangerous, if one knows how to use him). Marguerite and César arrive at the military camp just as Vasco, who has taken the alias "Joachim the idiot" to protect his identity on his mission, departs for the enemy camp. Unaware that she speaks to the barber Vasco, Marguerite speaks to "Joachim" of her sought-after fiancé.

Vasco is captured by enemy soldiers on the lookout for Le Mirador's messenger. During the interrogation by the enemy lieutenant Barberis, Vasco realizes that he is the barber Marguerite seeks. This discovery gives him the courage to risk his life for his compatriots. The ending tableau presents Marguerite's grieving for Vasco in fulfillment of the prophecy of widows spoken in the introduction of the play: "Et les jeunes filles seront veuves, même en rêve!" (And young children will be widows, even in their dreams!). The final word is given to Lieutenant Septembre, the man seeking Vasco in the opening tableau: "Victoire!" (Victory!). As in *La Soirée des proverbes* and *Monsieur Bob'le,* the hero's death serves to preserve his innocence and purity.

In addition to theater, Schéhadé wrote the screenplay *Goya* (1957) for which he won the Prix international de la critique at the Cannes Film Festival that year. He continued to divide his time between France and Lebanon and began working at the French Embassy in Lebanon in 1960. During the next decade Schéhadé turned again to the composition of poetry, publishing *Si tu rencontres un ramier* (1951, If You Find a Branch) and *Les Poésies* (1952 and 1969, Poems), as well as three plays: *Les Violettes* (1960, Violets), *Le Voyage* (1961, The Trip), and *L'Emigré de Brisbane* (1965, The Emigré from Brisbane).

Les Violettes is a comedy in eleven tableaux with "chansonnettes," or lighthearted songs. Published by Gallimard in 1960, its first production was a German translation by Karl-Günther Simon, directed by Hans Schalla, performed at the Schauspielhaus in Bochum, Germany, on 21 September 1960. It was first performed in France on 23 September 1966 for the third Festival de Chalon-sur-Saône by the Théâtre de Bourgogne, directed by Roland Monod, rather than on the Parisian stage, where Schéhadé had achieved his earlier successes. *Les Violettes* is set in a boardinghouse inhabited by astonishing characters. Madame Borrommée runs the boardinghouse and believes she has a gift for numbers, but her mathematical equations are impossible and ridiculous. Mademoiselle Justini, her daughter, wishes to marry three men at once and courts them simultaneously. Zanzi is constantly seasick from reading a book about a stormy sea. When Aristote, who works in the boardinghouse, tries to repair the clock that is malfunctioning, the Baron Fernagut, one of the residents, believes Aristote is being too rough with the clock and sings a verse from a chansonnette: "Aristote / Aristote / Un peu plus de courtoisie / Et de philosophie / Envers les objets / Dits inanimés / Je vous en prie!" (Aristote /Aristote / A little more courtesy / And philosophy / Towards objects / Called inanimate / I beg you!). Characters remain contented until Professeur Kufman, a devil-like figure, arrives with a diabolical scheme to use violets for global mass destruction. Ultimately, he runs off with Mademoiselle Justini as the members of the boardinghouse continue his cataclysmic experimentation. Schéhadé relieves the violence of this conclusion through his characters, more fantastic than real, and the comical songs that are performed periodically in the tableaux.

Le Voyage, published in 1961 by Gallimard, was first produced during the same year on 17 February at the Théâtre de France (Odéon) in Paris under the direction of Barrault. Barrault had taken over the direction of this national, state-subsidized theater in 1959 and immediately set out to introduce contempo-

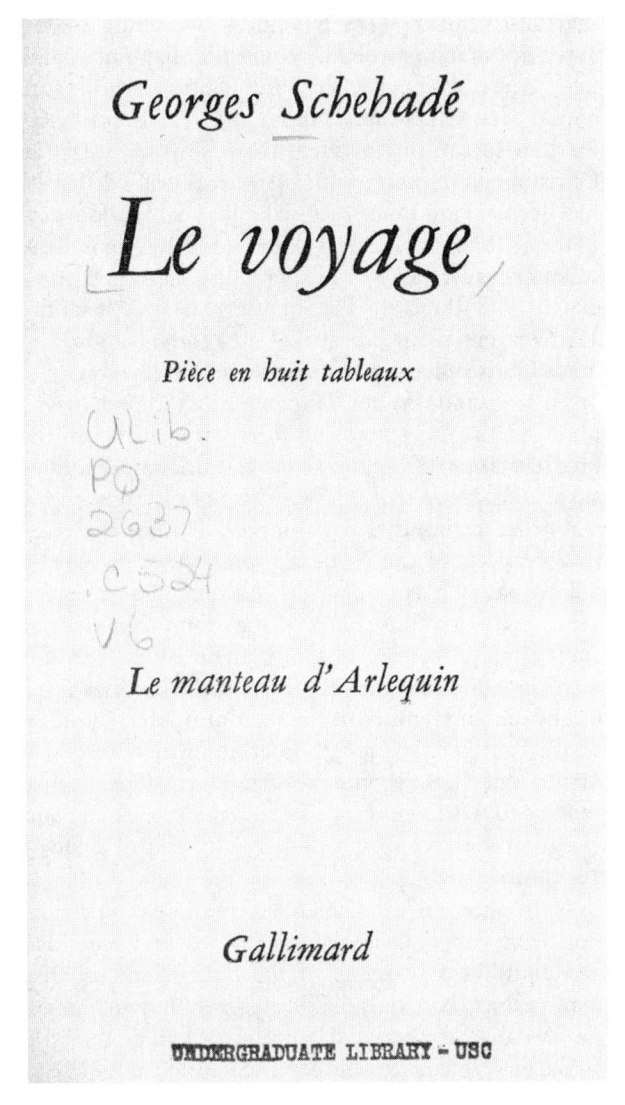

Title page for Schéhadé's play (1961, The Trip), about a button-shop worker who longs to take a sea voyage but who is set up by a murderer (Thomas Cooper Library, University of South Carolina)

rary works into the standard program of classical French drama. Schéhadé's fifth play was one of Barrault's first choices for performance, and the Odéon production helped spread Schéhadé's reputation as a playwright.

The protagonist of *Le Voyage* is another dreamer. Christopher works in a button shop in Bristol, where he gazes at the sea in hopes of going on a sea voyage. The owner of the shop is Monsieur Strawberry, an eccentric and comical man who believes that buttons "sont les auxiliaires de la vertu . . . sans les boutons, qu'est-ce qu'on n'aurait pas vu!" (are the auxiliaries of virtue . . . without buttons, imagine what you would have seen!). A coworker, Georgia, is saddened that Christopher seeks happiness by sailing to faraway destinations when he could find happiness with her. Matelot Jim enters the button shop and approaches Christopher about the real opportunity for him to sail on the Help-Horn ship to Australia. Christopher responds with interest, revealing that he has been saving money to make his real sea journey. Later, Christopher enters a brasserie frequented by sailors because he likes to spend time near men associated with the sea. The quartermaster, Alexandre Wittiker, enters the bar, strikes up a conversation, and lends Christopher his uniform so he can imagine himself a real sailor. When Madame Edda finds Christopher in his borrowed uniform, she suspects the quartermaster of impure motives. Madame Edda's suspicions prove true, and Christopher is arrested for a murder committed by Wittiker. During the trial, two versions of the crime are presented; in both, a talking parrot plays a key role. Although he has never been to the exotic seaport of the story, Christopher spins such a convincing tale that he is set free, but with the condition that he pay with his savings for a tombstone in memory of the man murdered by Alexandre Wittiker. His judges later admit that they will divide this money among themselves. Christopher returns to work, giving up his intention to travel and choosing the love of the shop girl instead of a life of adventure.

In addition to Schéhadé's common preoccupation with voyages, dreams, and love, *Le Voyage* also accomplishes a blending of the human and nonhuman realms. Not only talking parrots but inanimate forces, such as the wind, appear as living, thinking characters "plein de pensées et la forme mobile des anges . . . suspendu à rien" (full of thoughts and the mobile form of angels . . . suspended from nothingness). Barrault praised Schéhadé's ability to create poetic descriptions for the stage that transformed simple landscapes into "civilized, elegant, and noble visions."

L'Emigré de Brisbane (published 1965, The Emigré of Brisbane), a play in nine tableaux, premiered on 12 January 1965 in a German translation for the Residenztheater of Munich, directed by Kurt Meisel. One night, in or around the year 1925, a silent stranger is driven to a Sicilian village by a coachman who is constantly chattering at his horse, Coco. The stranger descends from the carriage and looks slowly around the town. He is found dead the next morning by the villagers with a picture of himself as a young man in his pocket and money in his possession. The mayor's secretary publicly announces the death of the stranger and puts his picture on a tree, hoping to trigger any memories associated with the dead stranger. It is suspected that a village woman was once involved with the stranger and secretly bore his child, who would now be the recipient of the dead man's considerable fortune. The wives (Rosa, Laura, and Maria) of three friends (Picaluga, Scaramella, and Barbi) are the prime suspects. The three couples are thrown into a stressful situation as the husbands and wives discuss the possibilities of a link with the stranger. One character predicts, "c'est le commencement d'une grande tragédie" (it's the beginning of a big tragedy). Anna, a girl from the village, sees the picture on the tree and falls asleep beneath it to dream. That night, one of the husbands, Barbi, decides that whether or not his wife Maria knew the man, they will say, in order to claim the fortune, that she was the one who had had the love affair. The wife refuses to go along with the plan, and as the argument intensifies, Barbi murders Maria, unaware that his friend Picaluga had overheard the argument. The following morning, Barbi lies about the murder, claiming that Maria had confessed to having a romance with the stranger; thus, the murder is perceived as honorable and just by the villagers. As Barbi leaves for a nearby town to turn himself in to the authorities, Picaluga loads his rifle and follows Barbi into the forest. In the conclusion of the play, the same coachman with Coco the horse brings another mysterious stranger to the same Sicilian village. When the passenger asks why he has been brought to a different destination than the one he requested, the coachman responds, "pour l'amour de l'esthéthique!" (for the love of the aesthetic!) and reveals that this village is where he brings all of his passengers, regardless of where they wish to go.

Schéhadé's last published theatrical work is the pantomime *L'Habit fait le prince* (1973, Clothes Make the Prince). The main character, Armen, inherits a princely outfit when the tailor who employs him closes shop. Armen is unintentionally mistaken for a prince, acquires a coachman, receives great respect, and falls in love with a young lady named Mirabelle. Melchior, a malevolent character, discovers that Armen is not a prince and plots to unmask him. In the end, when the truth is revealed, Armen still wins the hand of the beautiful girl with the blessing of her father, and the couple lives happily ever after. If the plot is simple, the scenes are elaborate, with mischievous stars interacting with humans, musicians silently playing their instruments, and sound effects, such as violent sneezes, that are seen, but not heard. When one particular "sound effect" is actually audible, a performer dressed as a mechanic enters the scene to remind the mimes, "Arrêtez-ça ne va pas. . . . Dans la pantomime on ne fait pas de bruit!" (Stop–that's no good. . . . In pantomime you don't make any noise!). The only other spoken dialogue in the play within the play occurs when the villain attempts to unmask the innocent hero.

Schéhadé achieved international recognition in 1986 when he became the first recipient of the Grand prix de la francophonie, a prize awarded by the French Academy to authors who write in French by choice rather than because they were born in France. In 1987 he received an official invitation from the Société Royale of Canada to attend the Francophone summit in Quebec. Schéhadé moved to Paris after his mother's death in 1978 and remained active as a poet but wrote no more plays. The civil wars in the Middle East, in his native Lebanon in the 1980s, marred his final years before his death on 17 January 1989.

Barrault, the director who brought Georges Schéhadé's plays to the attention of the French public, in the introduction to *Œuvre complète: Le Théâtre* (1998, Complete Works: The Theater) called Schéhadé "un des plus précieux poètes de notre Nation spirituelle" (one of the most precious poets of our spiritual nation). Schéhadé's dramatic works—celebrating youth, love, and fantasy in imagistic and lyrical language—also offered an alternative to the absurdist theater emerging during the same decade that insisted upon the uselessness and incomprehensibility of the human condition. Schéhadé's theater, as Bradby has pointed out, was popular in the 1950s, especially in the small, independent "art" theaters of Paris, because critics and theatergoers of the time found the "verbal pyrotechnics and poetic force" of such plays more familiar and more acceptable than "the bleak, colourless worlds created by Adamov, Ionesco and Beckett."

References:

David Bradby, *Modern French Drama 1940–1990* (Cambridge: Cambridge University Press, 1991), pp. 170, 188, 230;

Martin Esslin, *The Theater of the Absurd* (Garden City, N.Y.: Doubleday, 1961);

Wallace Fowlie, *Dionysus in Paris: A Guide to Contemporary French Theater* (New York: Meridan Press, 1960);

Jacques Guicharnaud, *Modern French Theater from Giraudoux to Genet* (New Haven: Yale University Press, 1967), pp. 162–164;

Diah Saba Jazzar, *Introduction au Théâtre de Georges Schéhadé* (Beirut: Dar An-Nahar, 1998);

Leonard Pronko, *Avant-Garde: The Experimental Theater in France* (Berkeley: University of California Press, 1964), pp. 188–196.

Jean Tardieu
(1 November 1903 – 27 January 1995)

Patricia Lancaster
Rollins College

PLAY PRODUCTIONS: *Qui est là?* Anvers, Théâtre du foyer, 20 May 1949;

Un Mot pour un autre, Paris, Théâtre Agnès-Capri, February 1950;

La Politesse inutile, Brussels, Ari et Youri Demeure, 1950; Paris, Théâtre de la Huchette, June 1955;

Ce que parler veut dire, ou Le Patois des familles, Paris, Théâtre du Quartier Latin, April 1951;

Oswald et Zénaïde, ou Les Apartés, Paris, Théâtre du Quartier Latin, April 1951;

Faust et Yorick, Paris, Théâtre du Quartier Latin, October 1951;

Il y avait foule au manoir, Paris, Théâtre du Quartier Latin, October 1951;

Un Geste pour un autre, Paris, Théâtre du Quartier Latin, October 1951; Paris, Théâtre de la Huchette, 10 June 1955;

Conversation-Sinfonietta, Paris, Théâtre du Quartier Latin, October 1951;

Les Amants du Métro, Paris, Théâtre Lancry, 22 April 1952;

Eux seuls le savent, Paris, Spectacle de Michel de Ré, November 1952;

Le Meuble, Bienne, Compagnie Jean Ber, 14 September 1954; Paris, Théâtre de la Huchette, 10 June 1955;

La Serrure, Paris, Théâtre de la Huchette, 10 June 1955;

La Société Apollon, ou Comment parler des arts, Paris, Théâtre de la Huchette, 10 June 1955;

La Sonate et les trois messieurs, ou Comment parler musique, Paris, Théâtre de la Huchette, 10 June 1955;

Les Temps du verbe, Paris, Théâtre de la Huchette, 10 February 1956;

Une Voix sans personne, Paris, Théâtre de la Huchette, 10 February 1956;

L'A.B.C. de notre vie, Paris, Théâtre de l'Alliance Française, 30 May 1959;

Rythme à trois temps, ou Le Temple de Ségeste, Paris, Théâtre de l'Alliance Française, 30 May 1959;

L'Ile des vifs et l'île des lents, Betz-le-Château, 8 February 1976;

Jean Tardieu (photograph by André Bonin; from the cover of Emilie Noulet, Jean Tardieu, *1964; Thomas Cooper Library, University of South Carolina)*

Le Style enfantin, Betz-le-Château, 8 February 1976;

Une Soirée en Provence, Brussels, Théâtre du Rideau, 5 March 1976; Paris, Théâtre du Rond-Point, February 1987;

Une Consultation, Brussels, Théâtre du Rideau, 5 March 1976;

Des Arbres et des hommes, Fougères, May 1979;

Le Rite du premier soir, Paris, Théâtre Essaion, 26 October 1983;

Malédictions d'une Furie, Saint-Denis, Théâtre du Centre culturel Jean Vilar, 1 June 1984;

La Cité sans sommeil, translated as *The Sleepless City,* New York, La MaMa Experimental Theatre, April 1987; original version, Paris, Théâtre de l'Ecole normale supérieure, April 1989;

Le Professeur Froeppel, Montreuil, Théâtre de Montreuil, 29 February 1988;

Pénombre et chuchotements, Turin, Centre culturel, 29 April 1988.

BOOKS: *Le Fleuve caché* (Paris: La Pléiade, 1933);

Accents (Paris: Gallimard, 1939);

Le Témoin invisible (Paris: Gallimard, 1943);

Figures (Paris: Gallimard, 1944); revised and enlarged as *Les Portes de toile* (Paris: Gallimard, 1969);

Poèmes (Paris: Editions du Seuil, 1944);

"Lapicque," in *Bazaine, Estève, Lapicque,* by Tardieu, André Frénaud, and Jean Lescure (Paris: Carré, 1945);

Le Démon de l'irréalité (Neuchâtel: Ides & Calendes, 1946);

Les Dieux étouffés (Paris: Seghers, 1946);

Il était une fois, deux fois, trois fois . . . , ou La Table de multiplication en vers (Paris: Gallimard, 1947);

Jours pétrifiés, 1943–1944: Poèmes (Paris: Nouvelle Revue Française, 1947); revised and enlarged as *Jours pétrifiés, 1942–1944: Poèmes* (Paris: Gallimard, 1948);

Monsieur, Monsieur: Poèmes (Paris: Gallimard, 1951);

Un Mot pour un autre (Paris: Gallimard, 1951); title play translated by George E. Wellwarth as *One Word for Another,* in *Modern French Theatre: The Avant-garde, Dada, and Surrealism,* edited by Wellwarth and Michael Benedikt (New York: Dutton, 1966); *Un Mot pour un autre* revised and enlarged as *Le Professeur Froeppel* (Paris: Gallimard, 1978);

La première personne du singulier (Paris: Gallimard, 1952);

"Madrépores, ou L'Architecte imaginaire," in *Farouche à quatre feuilles,* by Tardieu, André Breton, Lise Deharme, and Julien Gracq (Paris: Grasset, 1954);

Une Voix sans personne (Paris: Gallimard, 1954);

Théâtre de chambre (Paris: Gallimard, 1955)—comprises *Qui est là?; La Politesse inutile; Le Sacre de la nuit; Le Meuble; La Serrure; Le Guichet; Monsieur Moi; Faust et Yorick; La Sonate et les trois messieurs, ou Comment parler musique; La Société Apollon, ou Comment parler des arts; Oswald et Zénaïde, ou Les Apartés; Ce que parler veut dire, ou Le Patois des familles; Il y avait foule au manoir; Eux seuls le savent; Un Geste pour un autre;* and *Conversation-Sinfonietta;* revised and enlarged to include *Un Mot pour un autre* (Paris: Gallimard, 1966);

L'Espace et la flûte: Variations sur douze dessins de Picasso, illustrations by Pablo Picasso (Paris: Gallimard, 1958);

De la peinture que l'on dit abstraite (Lausanne: Mermod, 1960);

Poèmes à jouer (Paris: Gallimard, 1960)—comprises *L'A.B.C. de notre vie; Rythme à trois temps, ou Le Temple de Ségeste; Une Voix sans personne; Les Temps du verbe; Les Amants du Métro;* and *Tonnerre sans orage, ou Les Dieux inutiles;* revised and enlarged to include *Des Arbres et des hommes, Trois personnes entrées dans des tableaux,* and *Malédictions d'une Furie* (Paris: Gallimard, 1969);

Choix de poèmes (1924–1954) (Paris: Gallimard, 1961);

Histoires obscures (Paris: Gallimard, 1961);

Hollande, text by Tardieu, illustrations by Jean Bazaine (Paris: Maeght, 1962);

Conversation-Sinfonietta: Essai d'orchestration typographique par Massin, réalisé avec la collaboration du studio Hollenstein (Paris: Gallimard, 1966);

Pages d'écriture (Paris: Gallimard, 1967);

Grandeurs et faiblesses de la radio: Essai sur l'évolution, le rôle créateur et la portée culturelle de l'art radiophonique dans la société contemporaine, by Tardieu and others (Paris: UNESCO, 1969);

Le Souper: Opéra pour un personnage en un acte, libretto by Tardieu, music by Marius Constant (Paris: Amphion, 1969);

Un clavier pour un autre: Opéra-bouffe en un acte, libretto by Tardieu, music by Claude Arrieu (Paris: Amphion, 1971);

La Part de l'ombre, suivi de La première personne du singulier et de Retour sans fin, preface by Yvon Belaval (Paris: Gallimard, 1972);

C'est-à-dire, illustrations by Fernand Dubuis (Paris: Richar, 1973);

Le parquet se soulève, illustrations by Max Ernst (Vaduz, Liechtenstein: Brunidor, 1973);

Obscurité du jour (Geneva: Skira, 1974);

Bazaine, by Tardieu, Jean-Claude Schneider, and Viveca Bosson (Paris: Maeght, 1975);

Une Soirée en Provence, ou Le Mot et le cri: Pièces radiophoniques et livrets d'opéras de chambre (Paris: Gallimard, 1975);

Dix variations sur une ligne, l'oeuvre plastique du Prof. Froeppel (La Louvière, Belgium: Daily-Bul, 1976);

Formeries (Paris: Gallimard, 1976); translated by Gail Graham and Sylvie Mathé (Ann Arbor: Translation Press/Ardis, 1983);

L'Ombre, la branche, illustrations by Bazaine (Paris: Maeght, 1977);

Comme ceci, comme cela (Paris: Gallimard, 1979);

Jean Tardieu, un poète, edited by Jean-Marie Le Sidaner (Paris: Gallimard, 1981);

Les Tours de Trébizonde, et autres textes (Paris: Gallimard, 1983);

La Cité sans sommeil et autres pièces (Paris: Gallimard, 1984);

Des Idées et des ombres (Saint-Michel-sur-Orge: RLD, 1984);

Frénaud, Tardieu, by Tardieu and Frénaud (Marseille: Sud, 1984);

Margeries: Poèmes inédits, 1910–1985 (Paris: Gallimard, 1986);

Les Figures du Mouvement (Paris: Grenelle, 1987);

Un Lot de joyeuses affiches, suivi de Cinq petites annonces (Paris: RLD, 1987);

Poèmes à voir, illustrations by Pierre Alechinsky (Paris: RLD, 1987);

Causeries devant la fenêtre (Lausanne: Pingoud, 1988);

Les Phénomènes de la Nature, illustrations by Jean Cortot (Paris: Maeght, 1988);

On vient chercher Monsieur Jean (Paris: Gallimard, 1990);

Je m'amuse en rimant (Paris: Gallimard, 1991);

Petit bestiare de la dévoration (Paris: Maeght, 1991);

Le Miroir Ebloui: Poèmes traduits des arts (1927–1992) (Paris: Gallimard, 1993);

Da Capo: Poèmes (Paris: Gallimard, 1995);

Finissez vos phrases! (Paris: Gallimard, 2000);

L'Amateur de théâtre, edited by Paul-Louis Mignon and Delphine Hautois, preface by Mignon (Paris: Gallimard, 2003).

Collections: *Le Fleuve caché: Poésies, 1938–1961,* preface by G. E. Clancier (Paris: Gallimard, 1968)—comprises *Accents; Le Témoin invisible; Jours pétrifiés; Monsieur, Monsieur; Une Voix sans personne;* and *Histoires obscures;*

L'Accent grave et l'accent aigu (Paris: Gallimard, 1986)—comprises *Formeries; Comme ceci, comme cela;* and *Les Tours de Trébizonde;*

La Comédie du langage, suivi de La triple mort du Client (Paris: Gallimard, 1987);

La Comédie de la comédie, suivi de La Comédie des arts et de Poèmes à jouer (Paris: Gallimard, 1990);

La Comédie du drame (Paris: Gallimard, 1993);

Oeuvres, edited by Jean-Yves Debreuille, Alix Turolla-Tardieu, and Delphine Hautois, preface by Gérard Macé (Paris: Gallimard, 2003).

Editions in English: *The Underground Lovers, and Other Experimental Plays,* translated, with an introduction, by Colin Duckworth (London: Allen & Unwin, 1968)—comprises *The Underground Lovers, Who Goes There? Courtesy Doesn't Pay, The Contraption, The Enquiry Office, Mr. Me (Dialogue with a Brilliant Partner), Faust and Yorick, The Sonata and the Three Gentlemen, or How to Speak Music, The Apollo Society, or How to Talk about the Arts, The Crowd up at the Manor, They Alone Know,* and *Conversation-Sinfonietta;*

The River Underground: Selected Poems and Prose, translated by David Kelley (Newcastle upon Tyne: Bloodaxe, 1991);

Going–Going–Gone! or, The Client Dies Thrice, translated by Kelley (Cambridge: Black Apollo Press, 1999)—comprises *The Contraption, The Keyhole,* and *The Enquiry Office.*

OTHER: Johann Wolfgang von Goethe, *Iphigénie en Tauride,* translated by Tardieu, in Goethe, *Théâtre,* introduction by André Gide (Paris: Gallimard, 1942);

Charles d'Orléans, *Choix de rondeaux,* edited, with a preface, by Tardieu (Paris: Egloff, 1947);

Jacques Villon, *Cent tableaux de Jacques Villon,* preface by Tardieu (Paris: Galerie Charpentier, 1961);

Hans Hartung, *Hans Hartung,* text by Tardieu (Paris: Hazan, 1962);

Fernand Dubuis, *Dubuis,* preface by Tardieu (Paris: Galerie Jacques Massol, 1968);

Charles d'Orléans, *Poésies,* preface by Tardieu (Paris: Club Français du Livre, 1970);

Hartung, *Un Monde ignoré,* text by Tardieu (Geneva: Skira, 1974);

Pierre Alechinsky, *Carta Canta,* text by Tardieu (Paris: RLD, 1987);

Guy Bardone, *Bardone: Aquarelles et lithographies,* text by Tardieu (Paris: Bouquinerie de l'Institut, 1992);

Goethe, *Elégie de Marienbad, et autres poèmes,* translated, with a preface, by Tardieu (Paris: Gallimard, 1993).

SELECTED PERIODICAL PUBLICATION– UNCOLLECTED: "The Club d'essai," translated by K. Skude, *BBC Quarterly,* 7, no. 4 (1952): 227–234.

Jean Tardieu was a prolific author of poetry and short prose works, but his international reputation rests primarily on two small collections of short plays that earned him a place among the avant-garde dramatists of the mid twentieth century. In *Théâtre de chambre* (1955, Chamber Theater) and *Poèmes à jouer* (1960, Poems to Be Played), Tardieu satirizes conventional forms of expression and experiments with a wide range of innovative dramatic techniques. The first title implies that the plays, like chamber music, require few performers and are to be enjoyed in an intimate setting. The second title is a pun in that most of the poems are to be played not only in the dramatic sense but also in a style resembling musical performance. Tardieu fulfills the promise of these titles by exhibiting a remarkable ability to organize language so that it imitates the sonor-

Scene from the April 1952 production at the Théâtre Lancry in Paris of Les Amants du Métro *(translated as* The Underground Lovers, *1968), which Tardieu called "a comic ballet with dance or music," about two lovers who quarrel at a subway station but reconcile during their ride (© Lipnitzki/Roger-Viollet/Getty Images)*

ities, rhythms, and formal patterns of various musical forms. He often described his dramatic work as a "well-tempered clavichord of dramaturgy," modeled after Johann Sebastian Bach's experimentation with keyboard techniques in *The Well-Tempered Clavier* (1722, 1742).

The only child of Victor Tardieu and Caroline Luigini Tardieu, Jean Tardieu was born on 1 November 1903 at the home of a relative in Saint-Germain de Joux, in the Jura Mountains. By 1905 the Tardieu family was back in Paris, where Caroline Tardieu, whose father and grandfather were orchestra conductors, gave harp lessons. Her husband, a postimpressionist artist, had a studio on the top floor of their apartment. The young Jean was profoundly influenced by the sound of his mother's music and by his father's love of painting and poetry. In a journal begun at age seven, he wrote that his first movements and thoughts were cadenced to his mother's playing and that poetry never seemed more beautiful than when accompanied by the sound of the harp.

The Tardieu family's peaceful life was disrupted by the outbreak of World War I. Victor Tardieu enlisted in 1914 and was demobilized in 1918. While home on leave, he took his son to a production of Molière's *Le Malade imaginaire* (1673, The Imaginary Invalid). The boy developed an admiration for Molière's comedies and wrote his first play, "L'Inspecteur, ou Le Magister malgré lui" (The Inspector, or The Unwilling Magister), at the age of fifteen. Emilie Noulet, a poet and close friend of Tardieu, describes this unpublished parody of a literature class as amusing and well crafted. By age seventeen Tardieu had added two more short comedies to his journal, which he edited and recopied under the title "Jeux Puérils" (Childish Games). He studied at the Lycée Condorcet and passed his first *baccalauréat* in Latin and Greek in 1919.

Tardieu began studying philosophy at the Sorbonne in 1920, the year that his father left for a six-month stay in Hanoi. The position became permanent, and Victor Tardieu later founded the School of Fine Arts of Indochina. He remained in Hanoi until his death in 1937, keeping in close touch with his family through letters. In early 1921 Jean Tardieu suffered an attack of mental and nervous exhaustion that prevented his taking the *baccalauréat* in philosophy. In various autobiographical essays and notes he describes experiencing a sudden panic when he looked into his shaving mirror one April morning and suddenly became afraid of his "double" and aware of the strangeness of existence. Several months of rest allowed Tardieu to pass the philosophy exam in October, but his doctor advised him to discontinue his studies for another year. "Consoler" (To Console), an unpublished play from this period of recuperation, seems to reflect that moment of crisis before the mirror, for the protagonist, Pierre, suffers from a similar perception of the great gulf between the exterior world and the inner man. He says at one point, "Il me semble que tout ce qui m'entoure est affaibli, assourdi, comme s'il y avait entre les objets et moi une brume épaisse" (It seems that everything around me is weakened, muffled, as though between objects and me there were a thick fog).

To assuage his sense of disorientation and uncertainty, Tardieu wrote prose and poetry. The act of artistic creation provided a momentary sense of accomplishment, a means of defining himself and determining his own destiny. In the summer of 1922 his inclination toward literature was encouraged by an invitation to attend a literary seminar at the abbey of Pontigny in Burgundy. Organized by the distinguished professor of Greek Paul Desjardins, the seminar brought Tardieu into contact with many influential writers and critics, including André Gide, Roger Martin du Gard, Ernst-Robert Curtius, and Lytton Strachey. For the young student the experience was "beneficial and unforgettable." By 1924 he had changed his course of study from law to literature. Until he finished his *license ès lettres* (equivalent to a B.A. degree) in 1927, Tardieu continued to attend the summer seminars and to spend time in Paris with noted authors such as Jean Paulhan, Charles du Bos, and Léon Chestov (Lev Shestov). He became close friends with the poet Francis Ponge and met some of the greatest writers of the twentieth century, including Georges Bataille, André Malraux, Paul Valéry, and Miguel de Unamuno.

After finishing his *license,* Tardieu showed some poems to Gide, who forwarded them to Paulhan, editor of *La Nouvelle Revue Française*. Of the three poems published in the September 1927 issue of the review, "L'Etranger" (The Stranger) is particularly significant, for it poses a question that appears repeatedly in Tardieu's poetry and drama: "De moi à moi, quelle est cette distance?" (From me to me, what is this distance?). The poem explores the oscillation between that which changes and that which endures and between presence and absence. This oscillation takes over the poet's soul, which sometimes affirms and sometimes denies its own existence. The disoriented soul, aware of a growing polarity, tries desperately to define itself but is incapable of surmounting its double finality in the conclusion: "Tu ne seras jamais que l'ombre folle / D'un inconnu qui garde ses secrets" (You will never be more than the foolish shadow / Of an unknown who keeps his secrets).

Like variations on a theme, many of Tardieu's poems and plays express the inner turmoil described in "L'Etranger." In the preface to *Accents* (1939) he describes intolerable moments when the world seems too encumbered with physical objects and one wishes to escape into some region outside space, where these objects, along with the spectator himself, would be reduced to nothingness. Yet, this state in turn becomes unbearable, and one needs the reassuring presence of familiar objects. The act of writing provides a means of easing this cyclical anguish. Tardieu says that in his writing he seeks to conquer a nameless fear by forcing himself to imitate the "voice of the Enemy." He devotes himself to the pursuit of a certain accent, and, when he thinks that he has closed in on it, his anxiety dissipates. At that moment, according to Tardieu, "C'est moi qui parle: IL est volé" (I am the one speaking: HE has flown away). The existence of these two voices, or accents, led Tardieu from poetry to poetic dialogue and then to drama.

From 1927 to 1930 Tardieu lived in Indochina, having obtained authorization to fulfill his military service in Hanoi. He worked in an office at headquarters and lived with his father. Tardieu met a young scientist, Marie-Laure Blot, who was working as the director of a laboratory in the hospital of Hanoi. After their return to Paris they were married in 1932. Marie-Laure began working at the Muséum National d'Histoire Naturelle (National Museum of Natural History), and Tardieu took a job in the administration of the national museums. Their daughter, Alix, was born in 1936. Tardieu's museum work and his sophisticated appreciation of art led him to write prose poems that attempt to translate the essence of a given painting into words, an aspiration that appeared later in the plays *Rythme à trois temps, ou Le Temple de Ségeste* (Rhythm in Triple Meter, or The Temple of Segesta; produced 1959, published 1960) and *Trois personnes entrées dans des tableaux* (Three Persons Entered into Paintings; produced 1964; published 1969).

In the 1930s Tardieu completed "L'Archipel" (The Archipelago), a translation of Friedrich Hölderlin's "Der Archipelagus" (1800), and brought out two volumes of his own poetry, *Le Fleuve caché* (1933, The Hidden River) and *Accents,* which included

"L'Archipel." He was employed by the publishing firm Hachette and collaborated with Tatiana Doudkine-Chestov on the publication of a weekly newspaper called *Toute l'Edition,* an enterprise that continued until he was recalled to military service in 1939.

During the German Occupation, Tardieu participated in the clandestine literary activity of the Resistance. He was released from military service in 1940 and was hired, along with other unemployed intellectuals, by the library of the Ministère de la Marine (Ministry of the Navy). Working in the archives served as camouflage for several writers of the Resistance. The war years brought Tardieu into close contact with the authors Paul Eluard, Jean Lescure, Raymond Queneau, Pierre Seghers, Max-Pol Fouchet, and André Frénaud, who became a close friend. In 1943 Tardieu published *Le Témoin invisible* (The Invisible Witness), a poetry collection that includes some allusions to life in Paris during the Occupation. His prose poems based on works of art were published as *Figures* (1944), which was later revised and enlarged as *Les Portes de toile* (1969, Gates of Canvas).

After the liberation of Paris in August 1944, Tardieu began to publish dramatic criticism in *France-Soir* and in a weekly newspaper, *Action.* In *La Dramaturgie poétique de Jean Tardieu* (1981, The Poetic Dramaturgy of Jean Tardieu) Paul Vernois notes that Tardieu's reviews were not merely commentary but rather a critique of the theater of the period and a call for the revitalization of the French stage. Tardieu complained that Parisian theaters offered too many revivals and plays based on well-known themes. Disappointed that innovation in drama lagged behind the new trends in painting and music, he called for a theater with more imagination and mystery, less realism, new approaches to language, and more-exciting scenography.

In 1946 Tardieu joined Radiodiffusion Française (French Radio) as head of the dramatic service and was soon charged with creating the Club d'essai, an experimental workshop of Radiodiffusion-Télévision Française (French Radio-Television), the successor to Radiodiffusion Française. Exploring radio as an art form, Tardieu brought to the airwaves some of the greatest authors of the twentieth century–Paul Claudel, Gide, Albert Camus, Jules Supervielle, Colette, and François Mauriac–as well as radio versions of major novels, including Gustave Flaubert's *Madame Bovary* (1857) and Gide's *La Porte étroite* (1909; translated as *Strait Is the Gate,* 1924). The club was concerned with gaining technical mastery of the possibilities of radio as well as providing high-quality programs. In "The Club d'essai," written for the *BBC Quarterly* in 1952 and published in English translation, Tardieu states the philosophy of the workshop:

> In seeking always the best, the most difficult, and the newest approach, it attaches more importance to the future than to the immediate present. It may exceed its aims but never fall short of them–as in all artistic evolution: what today seems strange, unusual, obscure, and appreciable only by the few may tomorrow become the new form of expression and thought which is acceptable to and adopted by all.

Equally interesting is Tardieu's statement of policy: "Needless to say, none of the artistic research carried out by the *Club d'essai* was, strictly speaking, exclusive. . . . It has, however, always been a rule that the *Club d'essai* should relinquish a particular branch of research as soon as the main radio programmes begin to use the formula on a larger scale."

Tardieu's first published plays date from the same period as his drama criticism and his experimentation in radio. His work as a playwright followed the tenets of the Club d'essai. Inventive and experimental, he explored a broad range of topics and tried out new theatrical techniques, going on to something new once other playwrights began to "use the formula on a larger scale."

In the mid 1940s Tardieu wrote three quite different plays: *Tonnerre sans orage, ou Les Dieux inutiles* (1960, Thunder without Storm, or The Useless Gods), *Qui est là?* (Who Goes There?, produced 1949, published 1955), and *Un Mot pour un autre* (produced 1950, published 1951; translated as *One Word for Another,* 1966). These plays are the prototypes of Tardieu's primary dramatic forms. The first is a poetic dialogue, the second a dark comedy (a "lyrical nightmare," in the author's words), and the third a whimsical parody of everyday language and customs.

Tonnerre sans orage, written in 1944, is a one-act play based on the myth of Prometheus. It provides an understanding of Tardieu's concept of art as well as his vision of the human condition. His reinterpretation of the Prometheus myth bears the unmistakable stamp of existentialist philosophy. The play explores two contrasting reactions to the sudden revelation that the gods do not exist and that the universe is not coherent and ordered. It is, instead, the absurd place described in Camus's *Le Mythe de Sisyphe* (1942; translated as *The Myth of Sisyphus,* 1955) as a "universe suddenly deprived of illusions and light," in which there is a "divorce between man and his life, the actor and his setting."

Deucalion and his father, Prometheus, experience a sudden rupture in their world when Asia, Prometheus's mother, reveals that she invented the Olympian gods and their superhuman exploits in order to help control her willful son. The style and structure of this early play indicate Tardieu's ability to harmonize form and content. Although written in free verse, the dialogue has a majestic rhythm and serious dramatic

Jacques Polieri and Lucie Arnold in Tardieu's La Société Apollon, ou Comment parler des arts *(translated as* The Apollo Society, or How to Talk about the Arts, *1968), a spoof of art-appreciation groups, staged in June 1955 at the Théâtre de la Huchette in Paris (© Lipnitzki/Roger-Viollet/Getty Images)*

tone reminiscent of the twelve-syllable verse of the classical French alexandrine. Tardieu's verses tend toward long, often complex accumulations of clauses into a sort of verbal crescendo and decrescendo. The stage directions advise the actors to speak slowly, chanting in a strong voice with a minimum of dramatic effects.

The use of free verse allowed Tardieu to adapt meter and rhythm to the emotions of the characters, from the lyrical duets of Asia and Deucalion to the thundering final monologue of Prometheus. Instead of a traditional stage set, the play provides each character with a personal decor—a red glow for Prometheus, a sea-green color for Asia, and a brown sail and blue sky motif that follows Deucalion. To avoid realism, the sound of thunder is produced by percussion instruments. The actors are instructed to stand facing the audience and to use slow, studied gestures. Tardieu was thus moving in the direction that he, as well as dramatic theorists Jacques Copeau and Gordon Craig, advocated: a less realistic and more "theatrical" approach to drama.

Prometheus voices the human desire to discover and understand the nature of things. He demands rational, scientific explanations and uses his own reason and science to steal the gods' fire. The knowledge that they never existed makes him furious. His struggles, always directed against them, now seem ridiculous. If the gods do not exist, his own life loses its meaning. In contrast, Deucalion feels only intense sadness, for he always sensed the existence of the gods in the beauty of the world around him. He lived in harmony with the world and saw only the love of the gods in the universe. Deucalion laments that the world will henceforth guard its secret language and that he will be silent in a world that seems to speak all the time but responds to no one.

Deucalion finally comes to terms with the nonexistence of the gods and sails forth, as he says, "cherchant dans le reflet des deux abîmes une alliance avec mon nouveau dieu–le néant" (seeking in the reflection of the two abysses an alliance with my new god–nothingness). His search for wisdom is a quest for unity and peace, an alliance with the truth. The embodiment of intuitive knowledge and poetic sensibility, Deucalion will try to live in the same harmony with nothingness that he did in a world supposedly filled with benevolent gods. Prometheus, in contrast, sets humankind on a course of folly and murder by unleashing fire on the world. The result evokes the horrors of World War II–"lifeless smoking ashes," "deep craters," "acrid smoke," and "charred skeletons." In stealing fire from the fictitious gods and in struggling to master the universe, Prometheus brings mankind not enlightenment but death and destruction.

Tonnerre sans orage demonstrates that Tardieu understood existentialist philosophy and was interested in its implications. His main concern in the play, however, is the position of the artist in an absurd universe. He seems to despair of any real change in most people, who, like Prometheus, will continue their struggle toward whatever horror awaits them. But artists, such as Deucalion and Tardieu himself, must accept the absurdity of life and seek alliance with "le néant," constantly and patiently striving to learn its language in order to capture this new reality of the human condition through their art.

Qui est là?, written in 1946, deals with the psychological reality of the threat of violence. Tardieu states that "the actors must give the impression–well known to psychologists–that all this must already have happened somewhere." The events echo the hopes and fears that take the form of dreams or, sometimes, nightmares. Over dinner a father questions his wife and son about the events of the day. Since he already knows the answers to his routine questions, he supplies them himself. "What did you do this morning? I went to school. And you? I went to market." A mysterious black-robed woman appears and warns of some impending danger. Then a man enters, strangles the father, throws the corpse over his shoulder, and leaves the house. In the light of dawn the father arises from a field littered with bodies and returns to his family. His attitude, however, has the dignity of death. To his wife's observation that he used to be alive, he responds, "In each one of us, Man is dead. He is no more, is not, or is not yet." The earlier comfortable monotony of family life stands in stark contrast with his new understanding. He perceives that he was not alive in the truest sense of the word, for Man, or human dignity, is either dead or not yet alive.

He suggests that they search together, for "one day, in our midst . . . he will be." Less nihilistic than many modern plays, *Qui est là?* expresses hope for the renewal of human dignity in the father's imperative, "Cherchons ensemble" (Let's look together).

In a similarly disturbing play, *La Politesse inutile* (produced 1950; published 1955; translated as *Courtesy Doesn't Pay*, 1968), a mysterious stranger inflicts a cruel surprise on a self-important professor. The professor is reduced from an authority figure to a helpless victim when the visitor slaps him violently several times. As in *Qui est là?*, the unexpected brutality of the stranger seems to imply unthinking obedience to an order rather than any personal enmity toward the victim. The stranger is merely an instrument of some authority, come to administer a warning to an overly complacent professor whose misguided teaching may be as dangerous in its own way as the brute force of the visitor.

Similar themes and staging are present in three of Tardieu's plays from the late 1940s and early 1950s. In each the main character is the Client, who comes to a violent end. In *Le Meuble* (produced 1954, published 1955; translated as *The Contraption*, 1968), *Le Guichet* (1955; translated as *The Enquiry Office*, 1968), and *La Serrure* (1955; translated as *The Keyhole*, 1999), the Client functions, according to Tardieu, as a pathetic symbol of the little man, the ordinary citizen. In each case he is victim, whether it be of technology, bureaucracy, or misguided idealism, and he is brought face-to-face with the greatest enemy, death. Like *Qui est là?*, these plays experiment with dramatic techniques that became the hallmarks of avant-garde drama. Tardieu uses a dream-like atmosphere, character types, simple staging, stylized gestures, unexpected violence, and a strong element of parody to convey meaning through an immediate, visceral impact rather than through rational argument.

Tardieu takes a much lighter approach to the subject of modern society in the 1951 volume *Un Mot pour un autre*, which was revised in 1978 as *Le Professeur Froeppel*. The book purports to be the diary and posthumously published works of Professor Froeppel, a scholar whose research is devoted to nonsense words, body language, the problem of meaning, and the use of baby talk within the family unit. Froeppel is Deucalion wearing a comic mask. Like Deucalion, the professor senses that there is a kind of universal language; he even sets out to write a "Dictionnaire de la signification universelle" (Dictionary of Universal Meaning). Regrettably, he succumbs to a cold that he caught while trying to communicate with a small tree, and the dictionary remains unfinished.

Among Froeppel's works is the play *Un Mot pour un autre*, written to illustrate "la grandeur et la fragilité du langage humain" (the grandeur and fragility of the human language). The premise is that a strange epidemic causes people to mistake one word for another, as if they were grabbing words at random out of a hat. The result is a comical commentary on social conventions and clichés, demonstrating that most teatime conversation is mere repetition of stock phrases and gestures, perfectly comprehensible even when the wrong nouns and verbs are used. For example, the hostess coos politely, "Chère, tres chère peluche! Depuis combien de trous, depuis combien de galets n'avais-je pas eu le mitron de vous sucrée!" (Dear, very dear plush! It's been so many holes, so many pebbles since I've had the cowl to sugar you!). The sentence is amusing but not puzzling because it follows an expected pattern. When the guest responds, ". . . j'étais moi-même très très vitreuse! Mes trois plus jeunes tourteaux ont eu la citronnade, l'un après l'autre" (. . . I was very vitreous myself! My three youngest crabs have had the lemonade, one after the other), the audience can guess that her children have been ill.

The subject of *Un Mot pour un autre,* the guest's suspicion that her husband is having an affair with the hostess, is as trite as the conversation and equally easy to follow. Tardieu demonstrates that audiences hear what they expect to hear and that actors in conventional scenes convey as much by gesture and tone as by words. Believing that words had lost their impact in traditional theater, he sought to restore the power of language and to shake the audience from its complacent acceptance of trite situations onstage. His efforts in this direction include three plays: *Oswald et Zénaïde, ou Les Apartés* (Oswald and Zenaide, or Asides; produced 1951, published 1955), *Il y avait foule au manoir* (produced 1951, published 1955; translated as *The Crowd up at the Manor,* 1968), and *Eux seuls le savent* (produced 1952, published 1955; translated as *They Alone Know,* 1968). The first is a study of asides, the second of dramatic monologues, and the third of peripeties (abrupt changes in action). These humorous exaggerations of timeworn plots and stage conventions display Tardieu's versatility and wry sense of humor to good advantage.

Several of Tardieu's plays from the early 1950s take up themes that appeared in the research attributed to the fictional Froeppel. In *Un Geste pour un autre* (One Gesture for Another; produced 1951, published 1955), Tardieu parodies a fashionable soirée by depicting a typical party in a faraway land called the Nameless Archipelago. Guests use feathers to tickle each other's noses, cough loudly to express appreciation during a poetry reading, and become somewhat embarrassed when they need to ask the location of the kitchen—eating is a private activity.

Ce que parler veut dire, ou Le Patois des familles (What Talking Means, or The Patois of Families; produced 1951, published 1955) takes aim at learned discourse. It features Froeppel speaking authoritatively on the "meaning" of nonsense words and the use of baby talk by otherwise normal married couples. In a comical ending, he concludes, "Nous avons vu partout l'à-peu-près se substituer au mot propre, le geste remplir les vides béants du vocabulaire et le galimatias enfantin envahir le langage des adultes! . . . Et maint'nant, au dodo!" (Everywhere we have seen approximation substituted for the exact word, gesture used to fill yawning gaps in vocabulary and baby talk invading the language of adults! . . . An' wight now, I go night-night!).

Tardieu pokes fun at art appreciation lessons in *La Société Apollon, ou Comment parler des arts* (1955; translated as *The Apollo Society, or How to Talk about the Arts,* 1968). He spoofs a weekly meeting of some enthusiastic but uninformed art lovers whose teacher knows how to talk about art, if not how to recognize it. On a visit to an artist's studio, she gives an abstruse lecture on a metal object, assuming that it is a modern sculpture. The artist, proud of his creation, describes its features at length to the admiring crowd. He then shocks them with the news that it is a vegetable chopper that he intends to display at the next Salon of Bourgeois Cuisine.

In all of his comedies Tardieu combines a comment on human fears or foibles with some form of dramatic experimentation. *Une Voix sans personne* (A Voice without Anyone; published 1954, produced 1956), written in 1950, is Tardieu's most audacious departure from conventional drama. The title has a double meaning: an indication that there are no actors and a reference to the voice that Tardieu evokes so often in his poetry. Set in the living room of a country villa, the only visible action comes from changes and movement of stage lighting. It is a play without characters; the text is read either over a loudspeaker or by an actor standing in the shadows with his back to the stage.

Tardieu gives precise directions for the lighting, sound effects, and vocal interpretation of *Une Voix sans personne* in order to dramatize a real and intimate poetic experience. If a poem is merely a voice with no one there, the play is an attempt to control that voice and to give it physical reality. As the anonymous voice speaks, the stage shows what should take place in the imagination of a person reading the text. It is a way of saying that poetry is not merely words but a total sensory experience. The play is an experiment with a different kind of language, integrating words, objects, light, shadow, sound, and silence.

In *The Theatre of the Absurd* (1961) Martin Esslin calls *Une Voix sans personne* an interesting and ingenious experiment but observes that it merely proves that lighting and decor have a part to play in creating poetry on the stage. "But," he says, "this has never been in need of proof." Noulet calls the play an "alliance intime du chant et de la scène, de la poésie et du théâtre" (an

Roger Montsoret, Lucien Guervil, and Georges Aubert in the June 1955 Théâtre de la Huchette production of
La Sonate et les trois messieurs, ou Comment parler musique *(translated as* The Sonata and
the Three Gentlemen, or How to Speak Music, *1968), in which the verbal interplay among the
three characters resembles the flow of music in a sonata (© Lipnitzki/Roger-Viollet/Getty Images)*

intimate marriage of song and stage, of poetry and theater). Upon reading *Une Voix sans personne* in the journal *La Table ronde* in August 1952, Martin du Gard wrote to Tardieu that he liked the play. He praised its perfection and originality, calling it "un pur petit chef d'oeuvre" (a pure small masterpiece).

Tardieu's quest for a new dramatic style led him to substitute musical structure for traditional dramatic action as an organizing principle in *Conversation-Sinfonietta* (produced 1951; published 1955; translated, 1968), *Les Amants du Métro* (produced 1952; published 1960; translated as *The Underground Lovers,* 1968), and *La Sonate et les trois messieurs, ou Comment parler musique* (1955; translated as *The Sonata and the Three Gentlemen, or How to Speak Music,* 1968). Aside from a desire to give formal strength and structural unity to his poetic dialogues, Tardieu was also motivated by a love of music and the ambition to use words in the way that a composer uses notes.

Conversation-Sinfonietta is an experiment in speech composition that imitates a performance by a chamber group. The setting is a radio station and the six characters, like musicians, are seated around a microphone. Divided into three movements, the dialogue is little more than a banal conversation about romance, but it is written with such careful attention to rhythm that a sense of musical tempo emerges. It ends with the players repeating "et tout et tout et tout" (and all and all and all) in a parody of what Tardieu calls "certain interminable conclusions in classical music."

La Sonate et les trois messieurs is less comical and comes close to a kind of verbal music in which sound, meaning, and rhythm blend harmoniously. The text captures the feeling of the three movements of a sonata and even suggests changes of key by using certain combinations of vowel sounds. The three men of the title discuss an undefined "something" that they have heard, possibly a musical composition.

Tardieu adds the element of choreography in *Les Amants du Métro,* which he called "a comic ballet with dance or music." This two-act play brings together several themes previously developed in shorter sketches, blending elements from his abstract plays and nonsense plays with a statement about the common man's sense of isolation and alienation from society. The characters are a couple, Lui and Elle, and twenty-three subway passengers, played by five or six actors. In the first act the lovers quarrel in the subway station. In the second act Lui must successively change places with six passengers (one of them a mannequin) in order to move closer to Elle. The six symbolize isolation in that they separate the lovers and are lost in the kind of anonymity that people assume in public places. Lui overcomes each obstacle, often by means of strange, nonsensical exchanges. At last he is reunited with Elle, and the play ends with a love duo spoken in waltz time.

In *Les Amants du Métro,* Tardieu's progress as a playwright is evident. The play is longer, more complex in its thematic elements, and more satisfying as a dramatic spectacle than many of his earlier works. It prepared the way for one of Tardieu's longest and most intricate works, *L'A.B.C. de notre vie* (The A.B.C. of Our Life; produced 1959; published 1960). The play imitates the concerto form, with a Protagonist taking the part of the solo instrument and the other actors forming the orchestral accompaniment. It is presented either without scenery or with an abstract suggestion of the atmosphere of a large city. The Protagonist, a young office worker on his day off, seeks to define himself but is forced to come to terms with the incessant noise of humanity that impinges upon the silence of his thoughts and dreams. The structure of the play derives not from plot but from the association, opposition, and blending of three themes: the illusion of individuality, the power of love, and humanity's perpetual commentary upon itself. Critic Robert Champigny compares Tardieu's achievement in *L'A.B.C. de notre vie* to that of William Shakespeare, in that the poetic aspects of drama serve to suggest what lies beyond the dramatic sphere of existence. Champigny writes that the play "fills the dual mission which can be assigned to the theater: exposure of the theatrical in human beings and suggestion of what lies beyond the theatrical."

Most of the plays in *Théâtre de chambre* and *Poèmes à jouer* were produced in Paris between 1949 and 1959. Presented in groups or included on the same bill with works by contemporary playwrights such as Eugène Ionesco, Tardieu's plays were well received by critics and the public. He continued to write for the radio and to publish poetry and prose in the following decade, but he did not publish any more plays until after he retired from Radiodiffusion-Télévision Française in 1969. Among his most lasting accomplishments was the popular program *France-Musique,* which he started with composer Marius Constant. In retirement Tardieu continued to publish collections of poetry and prose, to collaborate with visual artists, and to publish dramatic works for both radio and stage. He and his wife, Marie-Laure, were both successful in their chosen work. She published many scientific books and articles on tropical plants and retired as director of the laboratory at the Ecole des hautes études (School of Advanced Studies) in 1972. Their daughter, Alix, an accomplished singer, married Giuseppe Baudo, an Italian engineer, in 1963 and gave birth to a son, Nicolas, in 1969. Alix was divorced and married Giovanni Turola, a lawyer from Milan, in 1975. Her second son, Giacomo, was born in 1976.

Tardieu's third volume of plays, *Une Soirée en Provence, ou Le Mot et le cri: Pièces radiophoniques et livrets d'opéras de chambre* (1975, An Evening in Provence, or The Word and the Cry: Radio Plays and Chamber Opera Librettos), comprises five radio plays, an adaptation of Voltaire's *Candide* (1759) for radio, three librettos for comic operas, and the synopsis of a libretto that composer Paul Hindemith intended to set to music. Tardieu and Hindemith had agreed upon the text, but the latter's death in 1963 prevented the realization of the project. Although initially written for radio, several of the plays were adapted for the stage, most notably the title work, which Tardieu called a dialogue in four movements. The dialogue between Monsieur A and Monsieur B concerns the question of language. The former seeks peace of mind and wishes to free himself from external reality by ridding his thoughts of all signification; the latter expresses his rebellion against the human condition through cries of despair and horror. By different paths they arrive at the same realization of the ambiguity and emptiness of language, ending their conversation with words called out at random.

La Cité sans sommeil et autres pièces (1984, The Sleepless City and Other Plays), Tardieu's last volume of plays, comprises four short plays and three farces. The title play was first produced (in translation as *The Sleepless City*) by La MaMa Experimental Theatre in New York in 1987. It is Tardieu's last major theatrical work and one that brings together several of his recurring themes: the misuse of authority, the importance of dreams, the power of language, and the healing influence of love and beauty. The premise is that a despot, identified as The Promoter, is using a serum to prevent the citizens of his town from sleeping. He wants them to be constantly awake and productive, so the police are instructed to arrest anyone found sleeping. Terrible silent monsters, nightmares that have been too long denied access, begin to invade the town. A graceful young couple, Paola and Mario, help to bring about the end of the crisis. In the town square Mario announces, "La parole est l'arme la plus forte. Il ne faut pas se taire. Il faut braver les menaces, toutes les menaces" (The word is the strongest weapon. We must not keep silent. We must confront the menaces, all the menaces).

Publications from the last decade of Tardieu's life brought to light previously unpublished poems, essays, and autobiographical notes. He also published three paperback volumes of his plays, this time grouping them by genre: *La Comédie du langage, suivi de La triple mort du Client* (1987, The Comedy of Language, followed by The Triple Death of the Client), *La Comédie de la comédie, suivi de La Comédie des arts et de Poèmes à jouer* (1990, The Comedy of Comedy, followed by The Comedy of Arts and Poems to Be Played), and *La comédie du drame* (1993, The Comedy of Drama). In France he divided his time between Paris and his homes in Gerberoy and Villiers-sous-Grès. He also acquired a place in San Felice, Italy, in order to spend time near his daughter and her family.

During his lifetime Tardieu's plays were translated and performed in Europe, the United States, and Asia. He was recognized as one of the great innovators of the theater and a consummate master of the French language. His contributions to French literature and radio were honored by many awards, including the Grand Prix de Poésie de l'Académie Française (1972, Grand Poetry Prize of the French Academy), the Prix du Théâtre de la Société des Auteurs et Compositeurs Dramatiques (1979, the Theater Prize of the Society of Dramatic Authors and Composers), and the Prix de la Société des Gens de Lettres (1983, 1986, Prize of the Society of Writers). On his ninetieth birthday Tardieu was honored with the Grand Prix National des Lettres (National Grand Prize for Literature) at a ceremony in the Louvre. He died at age ninety-one on 27 January 1995 in the hospital at Créteil.

In a 1991 interview with Christian Cottet-Emard, Tardieu gave a new twist to his lifelong sense of the duality of existence. Cottet-Emard commented, "Il y a un double personnage chez vous . . ." (There is a double character in you . . .). Tardieu replied, "En effet un enfant qui serait aussi un vieillard, un vieillard qui serait aussi un enfant!" (Indeed a child who might also be an old man, an old man who might also be a child!). Jean Tardieu never lost the ability to approach life with child-like wonder and creativity even though the adult in him acknowledged its potential for disappointment and danger. His plays reflect the questions and discoveries of an inquisitive and inventive mind. They trace his quest for meaning in life and his abiding concern with aesthetics. The result is a portrait of human beings as thinking, feeling individuals capable of formulating and expressing ideas and thereby capable of creating a sense of order in a silent and disquieting universe.

Letters:

Lettre de Hanoï à Roger Martin du Gard (Paris: Gallimard, 1997);

Tardieu and Roger Martin du Gard, *Lettres croisées: 1923–1958,* edited by Claude Debon and André Daspre (Paris: Gallimard, 2003);

Tardieu and Jacques Heurgon, *Le Ciel a eu le temps de changer: Correspondance, 1922–1944,* edited by Delphine Hautois (Paris: Institut Mémoires de l'Edition Contemporaine, 2004).

References:

Robert Champigny, "Satire and Poetry in Two Plays by Jean Tardieu," *American Legion of Honor Magazine,* 35, no. 2 (1964);

G. E. Clancier, "Une voix et des personnes," *Mercure de France,* 3 (May 1963): 131–142;

Christian Cottet-Emard, *Jean Tardieu, un passant, un passeur: Essai* (Charlieu: La Bartavelle, 1997);

Jean-Yves Debreuille, *Lire Tardieu* (Lyon: Presses Universitaires de Lyon, 1988);

Martin Esslin, *The Theatre of the Absurd* (Garden City, N.Y.: Doubleday, 1961);

Laurent Flieder, *Jean Tardieu, ou La Présence absente* (Paris: Nizet, 1993);

Edmond Kinds, *Jean Tardieu, ou L'Enigme d'exister* (Brussels: Editions de Université de Bruxelles, 1973);

Christophe Lagier, *Le Théâtre de la parole-spectacle: Jacques Audiberti, René de Obaldia et Jean Tardieu* (Birmingham, Ala.: Summa, 2000);

Emilie Noulet, *Jean Tardieu: Choix de textes, bibliographie, portraits, fac-similés,* Poètes d'aujourd'hui, no. 109 (Paris: Seghers, 1964);

Jean Onimus, *Jean Tardieu: Un Rire inquiet* (Seyssel: Champ Vallon, 1985);

Leonard Pronko, *Avant-Garde: The Experimental Theater in France* (Berkeley: University of California Press, 1962);

Jacques Réda, "Jean Tardieu," *Nouvelle Revue Française,* 16 (October 1968): 494–501;

Constantin Tacou and Françoise Dax-Boyer, eds., *Jean Tardieu,* L'Herne, no. 59 (Paris: Editions de l'Herne, 1991);

Paul Vernois, *La Dramaturgie poétique de Jean Tardieu,* preface by Tardieu (Paris: Klincksieck, 1981).

Boris Vian

(10 March 1920 – 23 June 1959)

Alexander Hertich
Bradley University

See also the Vian entry in *DLB 72: French Novelists, 1930–1960.*

PLAY PRODUCTIONS: *J'irai cracher sur vos tombes,* Paris, Théâtre Verlaine, 22 April 1948;

L'Equarrissage pour tous, Paris, Théâtre des Noctambules, 11 April 1950;

Les Bâtisseurs d'empire, Paris, Théâtre Récamier, 22 December 1959;

Le Dernier des métiers, Paris, Café-Théâtre de la Grande Sévérine, October 1964;

Le Goûter des généraux, Paris, Théâtre de la Gaîté-Montparnasse, 18 September 1965;

Série blême, Nantes, Maison de la Culture de Nantes, 24 October 1973;

Tête de Méduse, Abidjan, 29 January 1974;

Le Chasseur français, Paris, Théâtre Présent de La Villette, December 1975.

BOOKS: *J'irai cracher sur vos tombes,* as Vernon Sullivan (Paris: Scorpion, 1946); translated by Vian and Milton Rosenthal as *I Shall Spit on Your Graves* (Paris: Vendôme Press, 1948);

Vercoquin et le plancton (Paris: Gallimard, 1946);

L'Ecume des jours (Paris: Gallimard, 1947); translated by Stanley Chapman as *Froth on the Daydream* (London: Rapp & Carroll, 1967); translated by John Sturrock as *Mood Indigo* (New York: Grove, 1968);

L'Automne à Pékin (Paris: Scorpion, 1947; revised edition, Paris: de Minuit, 1956);

Les Morts ont tous la même peau (Paris: J. d'Halluin, 1947);

Barnum's Digest (Paris: Deux Menteurs, 1948);

Et on tuera tous les affreux, as Sullivan (Paris: Scorpion, 1948);

Les Fourmis (Paris: Scorpion, 1949);

Cantilènes en gelée (Limoges: Rougerie, 1950);

Elles se rendent pas compte, as Sullivan (Paris: J. d'Halluin, 1950);

L'Equarrissage pour tous; Le Dernier des métiers (Paris: Toutain, 1950); translated by Marc Estrin as

Boris Vian, 1948 (© Lipnitzki/Roger-Viollet/Getty Images)

Knackery for All, in *Plays for a New Theater* (New York: New Directions, 1966); translated by Simon Watson Taylor as *A Knacker's ABC* (New York: Grove, 1968);

L'Herbe Rouge (Paris: Toutain, 1950);

L'Arrache-cœur (Paris: Vrille, 1953); translated by Chapman as *Heartsnatcher* (London: Rapp & Whiting, 1968);

En avant la zizique . . . et par ici les gros sous (Paris: Livre Contemporain, 1958);

Fiesta (Paris: Editions Heugel, 1958);

Les Bâtisseurs d'empire; ou, Le Schmürz (Paris: L'Arche, 1959); translated by Taylor as *The Empire Builders*

(New York: Grove, 1967; London: Methuen, 1971);

Le Goûter des généraux (Paris: Collège de 'Pataphysique, 1962); translated by Taylor as *The General's Tea Party* (New York: Grove, 1967);

Je ne voudrais pas crever (Paris: Jean-Jacques Pauvert, 1962);

L'Arrache-cœur, L'Herbe Rouge; romans. Les Lurettes fourrées; nouvelles inédites, presented by Pierre Kast and François Caradec (Paris: Jean-Jacques Pauvert, 1962);

Textes et chansons (Paris: Julliard, 1966);

Trouble dans les Andains (Paris: Editions de la Jeune Parque, 1966);

Chroniques de jazz, edited by Lucien Malson (Paris: Editions de la Jeune Parque, 1967);

Cantilènes en gelée; Barnum's Digest; Vingt poèmes inédits (Paris: Union Générale d'Editions, 1970);

Théâtre inédit (Paris: Jean-Jacques Pauvert, 1970);

Le Loup-garou, suivi de douze autres nouvelles, edited by Noël Arnaud (Paris: C. Bourgois, 1970);

Les Morts ont tous la même peau: suivi de Et on tuera tous les affreux (Paris: Loisirs, 1973);

Manuel de Saint-Germain-des-Près, edited by Arnaud (Paris: Chene, 1974);

Chroniques du menteur, edited by Arnaud (Paris: C. Bourgois, 1974);

Le Chevalier de Neige (Paris: C. Bourgois, 1974);

Petits Spectacles (Paris: C. Bourgois, 1977);

Les Morts ont tous la même peau (Paris: Union Générale d'Editions, 1977);

Traité de civisme, edited by Guy Laforet (Paris: C. Bourgois, 1979);

Ecrits pornographiques, edited by Arnaud (Paris: C. Bourgois, 1980);

Le ratichon baigneur et autres nouvelles inédites, edited by Arnaud (Paris: C. Bourgois, 1981);

Autres écrits sur le jazz, edited by Claude Rameil (Paris: C. Bourgois, 1981);

La Belle époque, edited by Rameil (Paris: C. Bourgois, 1982);

Opéras, edited by Arnaud (Paris: C. Bourgois, 1982);

Rue des ravissantes et dix-huit autres scénarios cinématographiques, edited by Arnaud (Paris: C. Bourgois, 1989);

Boris Vian en verve, edited by Arnaud (Paris: Horay, 2002);

Blues pour un chat noir: et autres nouvelles, edited and annotated by Marc Lapprand (Paris: Librairie générale française, 2002);

Titre Cent sonnets, edited by Arnaud (Paris: C. Bourgois, 2005).

Collections: *Théâtre* (Paris: Jean-Jacques Pauvert, 1965)–comprises *Les Bâtisseurs d'empire, Le Goûter des généraux,* and *L'Equarrissage pour tous;*

Théâtre, volume 2, edited by Noël Arnaud (Paris: Union Générale d' Editions, 1991)–comprises *Tête de Méduse, Le Chasseur français,* and *Série blême;*

Œuvres, 15 volumes (Paris: Fayard, 1999–2003).

TRANSLATIONS: Omar N. Bradley, *Histoire d'un soldat* (Paris: Gallimard, 1952);

August Strindberg, *Mademoiselle Julie* (Paris: Arche, 1952);

A. E. van Vogt, *Le Monde des A* (Paris: Gallimard, 1953);

Nelsen Algren, *L'Homme au bras d'or* (Paris: Gallimard, 1956).

SELECTED PERIODICAL PUBLICATION–UNCOLLECTED: "Approche indirecte de l'objet," *Dossiers Acénonètes du Collège de 'Pataphysique,* 12 (1960).

Engineer, jazz musician, jazz critic, songwriter, scriptwriter, actor, translator, pataphysician, novelist, and playwright, Boris Vian pursued a "full life," as the title of a well-known biography states. Although Vian only lived to age thirty-nine, he produced a stunning quantity of texts. His complete works comprise more than eleven thousand pages. Yet, during his short lifetime Vian's works remained relatively obscure; they were poorly distributed and often difficult to obtain. In fact, no scholarly articles were written about Vian before 1965, and only after his death in 1959 did his works begin to receive attention. During his life, he was primarily known as the "prince" of the Saint-Germain-des-Près nightclub scene, a jazz aficionado, and the "translator" of a scandalous novel, *J'irai cracher sur vos tombes* (1946; translated as *I Shall Spit on Your Graves,* 1948).

Boris Vian was born on 10 March 1920 in Ville-d'Avray, Paris, France. He was one of four children of Paul and Yvonne (Ravenez) Vian, a wealthy bourgeois couple. In 1932 Vian was diagnosed with rheumatic fever, which affected his heart, a problem that plagued him until his death. Also during the 1930s the Vian family fortunes started a long downhill slide. This change in fortune forced Boris's father to seek gainful employment, which he despised. Paul Vian also openly mocked other common bourgeois social values. Liberal and unquestionably apolitical, he was antimilitary and virulently anticlerical. These themes that marked Vian's youth–the frailty of life, economic hardship, antimilitarism, and anticlericalism–also recur throughout his plays and other literary works.

Although Vian began his studies in philosophy, he soon changed to mathematics and eventually matriculated in 1939 at the Ecole Centrale, a well-respected French engineering school. In 1941 he married Michelle Léglise and began writing to entertain her. (In 1942, the couple had a son, Patrick, and in 1948, a daughter, Carole.) Because of his continuing poor health, Vian was not drafted into service during World War II and was able to graduate from the Ecole Centrale in 1942. He went on to hold a variety of engineering positions while simultaneously playing in an amateur jazz band with his brother and writing prolifically.

Primarily known as a novelist, Vian wrote ten plays as well as many short skits and scenarios. During his lifetime his works for the stage remained unpopular. Only two of his plays—*L'Equarrissage pour tous* (produced and published 1950; translated as *Knackery for All*, 1966 and *A Knacker's ABC*, 1968) and a 1948 stage adaptation of *J'irai cracher sur vos tombes*—were produced before his death, and only three were published. Yet, the plays remain integral to Vian's corpus. Vian was drawn to the theater in part because it allowed him to impart a distillation of his social views, presented directly to the audience, while highlighting the plasticity and potential playfulness of language.

Like the works of many of his contemporaries during the post–World War II theatrical renaissance, Vian's theater is frequently categorized as absurdist, marked by Surrealism, humor, wordplay, and nonsense. Yet, while his plays unquestionably demonstrate a debt to Alfred Jarry, author of *Ubu roi* (1896, Ubu the King), Vian's theater is more realistic, frequently examining social questions of the period. Vian's plays provide a biting critique of society and bourgeois social values through the use of satire and the absurd; they appear humorous while simultaneously possessing a serious subtext. His theater often appears destructive—nothing is sacred—yet, one should not always interpret it literally. Using non-Aristotelian logic, burlesque, and open endings, his plays should not be labeled as didactic or intellectual. Rather, Vian's works allow space for multiple approaches while simultaneously underlining human stupidity and the absurdity of life.

Just after the publication of his first novel, *Vercoquin et le plancton* (1946, Vinegrub and the Plankton), and while still working at a newspaper office and regularly playing trumpet, Vian started *L'Equarrissage pour tous*, his first play, in February 1947, finishing it in April of the same year. Because of the extremely controversial subject matter as well as other production problems, the play was neither staged nor published in its complete form until three years later. It premiered on 11 April 1950 at the Théâtre des Noctambules in Paris. However, the play was not popular and was replaced one month later by Eugène Ionesco's *La Cantatrice Chauve* (1954; translated as *The Bald Soprano*, 1965), which remains in production today.

Dedicated to Vian's "close enemy" Charlemagne, *L'Equarrissage pour tous*, a "paramilitary vaudeville," takes place in Arromanches during the morning of 6 June 1944, when American troops landed on the Normandy beaches to liberate France from German occupation. The setting is the living room of a knacker and his family, complete with a pit for horse rendering. A military unit has landed at the knacker's house, and a fierce battle is being waged outside; yet, the family seems concerned only with the marriage of their daughter Marie to Heinz Schittermach, a German soldier whom she loves and with whom she has been sleeping for the past four years. The family attempts to finalize the details of the wedding as soldiers from different armies—German, Japanese, French, and American—parade through the living room, leave weapons, use the restroom, and play strip poker, exchanging uniforms. This constant passage of stereotypical characters, in addition to the fact that Marie's mother and sister have the same name, lends the play its broad comedic base.

The family also invites two siblings who no longer live at home, Jacques, a paratrooper with the American army, and Catherine, a "pinup" paratrooper in red boots and miniskirt in the Soviet army. Heinz's commander, Captain Künsterlich, does not wish Heinz to marry, for he is the only living soldier in his unit. If Heinz leaves, the captain will no longer have anyone to command. To aid their daughter, the family knocks out Künsterlich and lets him fall into the pit. The family then sits down to a celebratory meal. But Catherine and Jacques, like typical siblings, begin to argue, and soon the celebration turns into a brawl, with nearly everyone falling into the pit. Two French officers finally arrive to inform the family that they have been liberated and that their home is the only one still standing. Nevertheless, it must be razed because it is "out of line" with the "Plan of the Future." The house is destroyed. The French lieutenant, the only survivor, exclaims, "Vive la France" as the "Marseillaise" blares out.

In a preface to *L'Equarrissage pour tous*, Vian proclaimed that for him war inspired "ni réflexes patriotiques . . . ni piété soudaine . . . rien qu'une colère désespérée" (neither patriotic reflexes. . . nor sudden piety . . . nothing but desperate anger). As the "tous" (all) of the title indicates, no single army or nation is marked for derision. Although the Germans and Japanese are lampooned, so are the French, Americans, and English: the knacker's pit is open to all. Anyone's life can end at any moment. Moreover, Vian's pit of ridicule also engulfs such entrenched values as family,

Scene from Vian's L'Equarrissage pour tous *(Knackery for All), Paris, Théâtre des Noctambules, April 1950 (© Lipnitzki/Roger-Viollet/Getty Images)*

homeland, work, politics, military, and morality. This complete lack of reverence was extremely controversial, considering that this play was staged so soon after the end of World War II. While a few critics such as Jean Cocteau praised *L'Equarrissage pour tous,* most wrote scathing reviews. The French daily *Le Figaro* called the play a "gâchés" (waste) of actors' talent and stated that while Vian might have wished his satire to be "provoquant" (provocative), it was nothing but "haïssable" (detestable) (17 April 1950).

Vian's second foray into the theater, an adaptation of his novel *J'irai cracher sur vos tombes,* was nearly as controversial as his first. Started on a bet and completed in more than two weeks, the novel is an American-style hard-boiled thriller, supposedly written by an American, Vernon Sullivan, with Vian as translator. The novel tells of Lee Anderson, an African American whose skin is so light he can pass as Caucasian, and his desire for murderous revenge after his brother is lynched for dating a white woman. Because it included many graphic scenes of sex and sadistic violence, the novel was called pornographic by many, a designation that may have helped lead to its great popular success.

In the fall of 1947, one year after the novel had appeared, Vian signed a contract to create a theatrical adaptation, which premiered 22 April 1948. This gap between the start of the project and its staging, in addition to the continuing popularity of the novel, led to a media frenzy, with some journalists spreading rumors that such famed actors as Juliette Gréco and Yves Montand would play leading roles, while others denounced the play before seeing the production or reading the script.

Although it was billed by the Verlaine Theater as "the most audacious play of the season" and the city of Paris outlawed subway advertisements that included its title, *J'irai cracher sur vos tombes* opened to poor reviews and closed fewer than three months later. While the theme of racism was popular at the time, as witnessed by the popularity of Jean-Paul Sartre's *La Putain respectueuse* (1947; translated as *The Respectful Prostitute,* 1955), Vian's play remained unsuccessful. This lack of popularity resulted in large part from Vian's adaptation. Fearing censorship and wishing to show that he was not simply a pornographic writer, he altered the focus of the stage production from the debauchery and wild parties of the novel to racial problems; nearly all eroticism was expurgated and so was any violence offstage. Eliminating the multiple locations of the novel, Vian sets the play in Anderson's bedroom and juxtaposes dialogue with long tirades during which Anderson decries racism to Jérémie, a mute African American custodian who was not in the original novel and who serves here as Anderson's confidant. This verbosity and lack of action engender the feeling of a staged reading. The dynamic quality found in Vian's later plays is nonexistent.

Vian composed his third play, *Le Dernier des métiers* (The Lowest Occupation; published 1950, performed 1964), in the spring of 1950 during the preproduction of *L'Equarrissage pour tous*. During rehearsals for *L'Equarrissage pour tous,* the theater company realized that it was too short to last for a full evening. Vian then wrote the short, comedic work *Le dernier des métiers* as a supplement. Although the company director approved, the theater director was "shocked by the extremely profane tone" of the play. It was not staged until October 1964.

Le dernier des métiers, a biting satire of what today would be televangelism, offers a prime example of Vian's anticlericalism at its most virulent. During the late 1940s and early 1950s some members of the clergy modernized and, using radio and other means of mass communication, became media stars. The play takes place in the "intimate and sordid" chambers of the reverend Father Saureilles, which closely resemble a theatrical dressing room, complete with makeup table, autographed photos, posters, and assistants, including a sexton and several boy scouts. A radio reporter wishes to interview the priest during the intermission of Saureilles's latest production. Occasionally interrupted by the boisterous scouts or the delivery of flowers, including a bouquet from his "pal" Paul Quelaudel–another jab by Vian against established theater (that is, the theater of Paul Claudel) and religion–Father Saureilles acts like a jaded movie star, speaking of previous productions and his love for the stage. Filled with exaggerated characters and vain dialogue, this playlet underlines the disparity between Saureilles's words and his actions. It satirizes those who preach simplicity, yet seem not to follow their own tenets.

Vian also wrote the short play *Un Radical barbu* (2003, A Bearded Radical) in 1950. Set in a "training room" just outside the parliamentary meeting hall, *Un Radical barbu* satirizes the uncertain political climate in post–World War II France. The Fourth Republic, founded in January 1947, was designed to bring stability to the country. Yet, trauma and uncertainty remained and led to a lack of consensus, many political parties, and constantly changing cabinets. In Vian's play, politicians have become pugilists, and the house of parliament a boxing ring. The representatives still argue their opinions, but in an abbreviated manner. They then fight, literally, with those who do not agree. As the play opens, Alexandre, the bearded radical and member of parliament, is scheduled to speak. He is nervous. His trainer, Jack, tries to buoy his spirits and prepare him for the confrontation. In the course of a heated discussion outside the chambers, Alexandre is knocked out. Since he is incapacitated and unable to go before parliament, the trainer enters in his place. Although the action takes place offstage, several characters offer updates of Jack's uproarious success: he has been elected president. Alexandre awakes. Learning of the quick political upheaval, he exclaims, "That's not parliamentary!"

Several other works by Vian were published in 1950, including *L'Herbe Rouge* (Red Grass) and *Elles se rendent pas compte* (They Don't Realize); however, like Vian's theatrical productions, they were complete failures. Because of the poor sales of these works as well as Vian's extremely active social life, he was forced to seek income from other sources, primarily through translation. At this time he translated General Omar N. Bradley's *A Soldier's Story* (1951) as *Histoire d'un soldat* (1952). Bradley's vanity appalled the already antimilitaristic writer. Vian felt that many of the general's actions during World War II resulted not from a wish to defeat the enemy, but rather from his egocentrism and desire to outperform and vex the English general Bernard Montgomery. This disgust inspired Vian in 1951 to write *Le Goûter des généraux* (published 1962, performed 1965; translated as *The General's Tea Party,* 1967).

Le Goûter des généraux, like other Vian plays, uses satire to denounce the insanity of war, while also mocking the military, politicians, and the clergy. James Audubon Wilson, a childish general who still lives with his overbearing mother, is told by Léon Plantin, president of the French council, that he must go to war. The French economy is faltering because of overproduction, and Plantin sees the military as the solution, since it is the most efficient consumer. As Plantin explains, "c'est le consommateur qui paie l'armée, Audubon, et c'est l'armée qui consomme" (consumers pay for the military, and the military consumes). Audubon invites several other generals to his home for tea and convinces them to declare war. They soon realize, however, that while they are willing to fight, they have no enemy.

Plantin tries, at the beginning of act 2, to convince either the Americans, the Russians, or the Chinese to do battle, but none are willing. They finally decide to declare war on Morocco and Algeria. When the third act opens, two years later, French central command has moved to Sweden. The French generals, along with the American, Russian, and Chinese generals from act 2 and a collusive priest named Tapecul, start to drink, sing, and play Russian roulette. The generals kill themselves one by one to the uproarious cheers of the survivors. Audubon finally has his turn, and after several failed attempts, shoots himself, crying, "I won!" As in *L'Equarrissage pour tous,* the "Marseillaise" is played, and a lone general in full regalia walks across the stage towing a cannon behind him.

Because of its strong antimilitary tone, as well as its allusions to Pétain and his collaborationist Vichy government, no one would produce the polemical play. Aware of the political and theatrical climate, Vian seems to have anticipated this reaction, as a second version of the play illustrates. This alternate work opens with a young playwright, Jean, and his wife, Francine, waiting in a producer's office. The couple soon learns that Bataillard, the producer, has not read the manuscript. They begin to describe the work, which becomes a complete, staged version of the play. The producer remains unimpressed, saying that the subject of war is "worn out" and that the play is unstageable. Livid and vituperative, Jean denounces the state of contemporary theater, berating audiences, directors, and producers. At the conclusion of the play he is about to leave when an assistant rushes on the scene holding a newspaper: France has just declared war on Africa.

A decade after the inception of the play, the political climate had changed in France. After an unsuccessful debut at the Statstheater in Braunschweig, Germany, in November 1964, *Le Goûter des généraux* opened at the Gaîté-Montparnasse Theater in September 1965 to great success. The play ran for nearly a year, with 309 performances. This work helped solidify Vian's reputation as a master of satire, albeit after his death. The popularity of the play continues; it has been reprised many times, including a musical version, *Drôle de goûter* (An Odd Tea Party), presented in 1990.

Moving away from political satire and its endemic controversy, Vian's next works for the stage were much lighter. *Tête de Méduse* (Medusa's Head; published in *Théâtre inédit,* 1970, performed 1974) maintains the burlesque qualities of his previous plays while transposing them to a more traditional setting, a one-act vaudevillian farce in the style of Georges Feydeau. Vian again found inspiration in a popular phenomenon–plastic surgery. Antoine and Lucie Bonneau have an unusual arrangement. Lucie has been unfaithful for sixteen years. But according to their rules, she may only have an affair with an individual for six months; then she must find someone new. This system is dually beneficial. Lucie receives satisfaction, which Antoine is unable to provide. Antoine, jealous of Lucie's affairs, is inspired to write, yet does not feel threatened because of the short duration of the affairs. The problem, however, is that Lucie has been seeing the same gentleman, Francis, for the last sixteen years. Every six months he has had plastic surgery so that his appearance changes, and Antoine remains duped. Yet, the many surgeries have altered the structure of his skull, and a horn has started to grow. At the conclusion of the play, Lucie decides to leave with Claude, Francis's friend. Francis's horn now has a purpose. Devastated, the two cuckolds solace one another as Antoine starts writing his next masterpiece.

Conceived in 1952, *Série blême* (Pale Serial; performed 1973, published 1991) follows the less polemical tone of *Tête de Méduse,* albeit with a more lugubrious subject. An allusion to the popular "série noire" (black series) thrillers published by Gallimard (itself a short-lived companion series), *Série blême,* like *J'irai cracher sur vos tombes,* was inspired by the hard-boiled fiction of American writers such as Dashiell Hammett and Raymond Chandler. Like its predecessor, *Série blême* is a farce that also explores the difficulties of writing. When the play opens, James Monroe, Marilyn's younger brother, is reveling in the solitude of his mountain chalet, which permits him to write. However, a plane crashes, and he is soon inundated with many unwelcome guests. This commotion disrupts Monroe's work. Using his "Petit traité du parfait criminel" (Short Treatise on Criminal Perfection), he proceeds to kill each interloper in a different way. In the final scene, two soldiers on a training mission arrive and tell Monroe that they and the other members of their unit will need to stay at his chalet.

The interest of the play lies primarily in its language and form. The entire work is written in alexandrines, a poetic constraint that contrasts starkly with the subject matter of the text. This juxtaposition is further underlined by Monroe's language. He speaks only in an esoteric, yet authentic, slang. These features have limited the appeal of the play, however, for the majority of French people cannot completely comprehend the difficult (and now dated) language.

After 1950 Vian's interests in the stage diversified. Although he continued to write plays, he also began composing musicals, ballets, operas, and other stage works. Moreover, while Vian's health limited his ability to perform–in fact, his doctors forbade him from playing the trumpet–it did not extinguish his interest in music. He began to compose lyrics and in the following

H. Viriojeux, D. Saval, M. Cheminat, A. Navarre, and I. Alvarez in Vian's Les Bâtisseurs d'empire *(The Empire Builders), Théâtre Récamier, Paris, December 1959 (© Lipnitzki/Roger-Viollet/Getty Images)*

five years wrote five hundred songs, nearly three hundred of which were recorded. On 8 February 1954 Vian married Ursula Kubler. (He and his first wife had divorced in 1952.) In October 1955 he became an artistic director with Philips Recording Company, a position he held until 1959, producing approximately sixty albums.

Le Chasseur français (The French Hunter; performed 1975, published 1991), a musical play written in 1955, spans the gap between these worlds. It exemplifies Vian's fascination with America, for it combines two of his areas of interest, thrillers and music. American musicals were popular in France during the 1950s, and with *Le Chasseur français,* Vian wished to create his own version. The play derives its title from a French hunting magazine of the same name. The magazine was extremely popular after World War II, in large part because of its many personal ads. Vian combined many of his favorite elements—hard-boiled fiction, the difficulty of writing, slang, infidelity, popular culture, and criticisms of bourgeois family values—to create a musical comedy with a traditional happy ending.

However, he only wrote the book for *Le Chasseur français.* Not until 1975 did Stéphane Varegues, with Ursula Vian, compose a score for the nineteen songs of the musical. Reaction to the production was mixed. While some enjoyed the light humor of the work, others, echoing criticisms leveled against *Tête de Méduse* and *Série blême,* found it simplistic and dated.

In 1956 Vian composed another short, twisted, vaudevillian work, *Chambre de célibataire* (2003, Bachelor Pad, published in *Oeuvres*). It is a wide farce, but the cuckold is a hopeful lover, not a husband. Jacques borrows his friend's apartment in order to seduce Denise.

But just as they lie down by the hearth, they notice that the fire is out of control and are forced to call the fire department. The fire chief asks Denise to help him search for a chimney-sweeping certificate. Jacques, the jilted lover, hears their moans of pleasure coming through the chimney.

Vian's health was failing rapidly at this time. During the summer of 1956 and again in the fall of 1957 he suffered severe bouts of pulmonary edema. Vian told his wife, "I shall not reach my fortieth birthday . . . don't depend on me too much." Yet, he continued to work. Over the period of a few days in July 1957 he wrote his last major work, one that helped create his reputation as both a dramatist and a writer. *Les Bâtisseurs d'empire* (performed and published 1959; translated as *The Empire Builders*, 1967) marks Vian's return to serious theater. The influence of Alfred Korzybsky's theories is strong in the play, for much of the intrigue results from a tension between reality and the language used to describe it. Vian returns to themes found in *L'Equarrissage pour tous* and *Le Goûter des généraux*, but without their slapstick humor. Vian no longer merely asks the audience to laugh at the absurdity of war, but rather to examine the mind-set that makes it possible. This sobering focus makes *Les Bâtisseurs d'empire* perhaps Vian's most deeply political work for the stage.

Although the title evokes colonialism and capitalism, the play does not take place in contemporary France. Rather, the Dupont family lives in an absurd, almost postapocalyptic universe, similar to those found in Samuel Beckett's works. In addition to the family, the cast includes a perspicacious maid who, scandalized by the family's languor, eventually leaves, and the *schmürz*, a mute creature wrapped in tattered bandages. The *schmürz*, whose neologistic name is based on the German "schmerz" (pain) and Jarry's "merdre," remains one of Vian's best known and most powerful characters. Originally conceived as an Arab in an early version of the work, it acts as a scapegoat, underscoring crumbling bourgeois morals. Whenever the father becomes flustered under his daughter's questioning, he walks over to the *schmürz*, whose presence he refuses to recognize, and beats it.

The Duponts are haunted by a harrowing, inexplicable noise that compels them repeatedly to vacate their dwelling. Each time, they move to the floor above, leaving many of their possessions behind. Each apartment is smaller and more poorly appointed than its predecessor. Yet, only Zénobie, the daughter, notices this gradual deterioration. The mother and father cannot, or will not, recall their past. Rapt by fear, the father eventually leaves his wife and daughter behind in an effort, he believes, to save himself. At the conclusion, the father, in a tiny attic room, is left to confront his own guilt as the *schmürz* silently watches. Vian offered two possible endings to the play. In one version, the noise again resounds as the scene fades to black, while in an alternative version "et peut-être que la porte s'ouvre et qu'il entre, vagues silhouettes dans le noir, de schmürz" (perhaps schmürzes enter, vague outlines in the dark).

Although the play was published during his lifetime, Vian did not live to see its production. He died of a heart attack on 23 June 1959 during a screening of a movie adaptation of his novel *J'irai cracher sur vos tombes*, nearly six months to the day before the premiere of the play on 22 December. Continuing until March 1960, the production was extremely popular, attracting nearly twenty thousand spectators during its first run. The work was soon translated and became a success in many European countries.

Les Bâtisseurs d'empire marked a turning point for Vian's literary standing. Critics no longer equated Vian's work with simple scandalmongering. Meanwhile, as memories of the war faded, the public's conceptions of patriotism and the military changed. Works that had been judged as indecorous and controversial were now seen as original and thought provoking. Old texts were reprinted and unpublished works were released.

Boris Vian's importance and legacy were soon understood. A prolific and diverse dramatist and writer, Vian combined inventive and humorous wordplay with provocation. Even his lightest works for stage include themes found in his more polemical plays. Bourgeois family values are constantly questioned, and with them the political and military power structures that enable this hegemony. Vian gave alienation and nonconformism a poetic form, pushing readers to question the status quo and imagine their own freedom.

Bibliographies:

François Caradec, "Pour une bibliographie de Boris Vian," *Dossiers Acénonètes du Collége de 'Pataphysique*, 12 (1960): 111–138; supplemented in *Dossiers Acénonètes du Collège de 'Pataphysique*, 18–19 (1962): 123–127;

Yves Gindrat, *Par mots épars: Vian: Boris le demystificateur aurait 75 ans: catalogue commenté de 1,567 items de et sur Vian* (Lausanne: Bibliothèque Municipale, 1995).

Biographies:

Henri Baudin, *Boris Vian: La poursuite de la vie totale* (Paris: Editions du Centurion, 1966);

Michel Fauré, *Les Vies posthumes de Boris Vian* (Paris: Union Générale d'Editions, 1975);

Noël Arnaud, *Les Vies parallèles de Boris Vian,* fifth edition (Paris: C. Bourgois, 1981);

Geneviève Beauvarlet, *Boris Vian: 1920–1959: Portrait d'un bricoleur* (Paris: Hachette, 1982);

Philippe Boggio, *Boris Vian* (Paris: Flammarion, 1993).

References:

Noël Arnaud, *Les Dossiers de l'affaire "J'irai cracher sur vos tombes"* (Paris: C. Bourgois, 1974);

Jacques Bens, *Boris Vian* (Paris: Bordas, 1976);

Bizarre, special combined Vian issue, nos. 39–40 (February 1966);

Boris Vian: Colloque du Centre Culturel International de Cerisy-la-Salle, 23 juillet au 2 août 1976, edited by Arnaud and Henri Baudin (Paris: Union Générale d'Editions, 1977);

Pierre Christin, "Gloire posthume et consommation de masse: Boris Vian dans la société française," *Esprit Créateur,* 7 (Summer 1967): 135–143;

Alfred Cismaru, *Boris Vian* (New York: Twayne, 1974);

Jean Clouzet, *Boris Vian* (Paris: Seghers, 1966);

Alain Costes, *Lecture plurielle de "L'Ecume des jours"* (Paris: Union Générale d'Editions, 1979);

Dossiers Acénonètes du Collége de 'Pataphysique, 12 (1960): 18–19;

Michel Gauthier, *"L'Ecume des jours," analyse critique* (Paris: Hatier, 1973);

Daniel Grojnowski, "L'Univers de Boris Vian," *Critique* (January 1965): 17–28;

Marc Lapprand, *Boris Vian: La vie contre: biographie critique* (Ottawa: Presses de l'université d'Ottawa / Paris: Nizet, 1993);

David Noakes, *Boris Vian* (Paris: Editions Universitaires, 1964);

Obliques, special combined Vian issue, 8–9 (1976);

Gilbert Pestureau, *Dictionnaire des personnages de Vian* (Paris: C. Bourgois, 1985);

Laurence M. Porter, "Family Values: Decoding Boris Vian's *Les Bâtisseurs d'empire*," *Studies in Twentieth Century Literature,* 21 (Summer 1997): 399–415;

Michel Rybalka, *Boris Vian: Essai d'interprétation et de documentation* (Paris: Lettres Modernes Minard, 1969);

Vian, Queneau, Prévert: Trois fous du language, Actes du colloque Vian-Queneau-Prévert, [12–13–14 mars], Université de Victoria (Canada), 1992, edited by Lapprand (Nancy: Presses Universitaires de Nancy, 1993).

Michel Vinaver
(Michel Grinberg)
(1927 -)

Kevin Elstob
California State University, Sacramento

PLAY PRODUCTIONS: *Aujourd'hui ou Les Coréens,* Lyon, Théâtre de la Comédie, 24 October 1956;
La Fête du Cordonnier, translation of Thomas Dekker's *The Shoemaker's Holiday,* Paris, Palais de Chaillot, 5 March 1959;
La Demande d'emploi, Paris, Théâtre 347, 29 March 1973;
Par-dessus bord, Paris, Odéon-Théâtre de l'Europe (Pierre Dux), 27 May 1974; complete version, La Chaux-de-Fonds, Switzerland, Théâtre Populaire Romand, 3 June 1983;
Iphigénie Hôtel, Paris, Centre Georges Pompidou, 2 March 1977;
Dissident, il va sans dire, Paris, Théâtre de l'Est Parisien, 14 February 1978;
Nina, c'est autre chose, Paris, Théâtre de l'Est Parisien, 14 February 1978;
Les Travaux et les jours, Annecy, Théâtre éclaté d'Annecy, 8 January 1980;
Les Huissiers, Lyon, Théâtre Les Ateliers, 22 April 1980;
A la renverse, Paris, Théâtre National de Chaillot, 25 November 1980;
L'Ordinaire, Paris, Théâtre Gémier, 10 March 1983;
Le Suicidé, Paris, La Comédie Française au Théâtre National de l'Odéon, 26 April 1984;
Les Estivants, Paris, La Comédie Française, 15 May 1986;
Les Voisins, Paris, Le Jardin d'Hiver, Théâtre Ouvert, 17 October 1986;
L'Emission de télévision, Paris, La Comédie Française au Théâtre National de l'Odéon, 6 March 1990;
Jules César, translation of William Shakespeare's *Julius Caesar,* Geneva, Switzerland, La Comédie de Genève, 19 October 1990;
Le Temps et la chambre, translation of Botho Strauss's *Die Zeit und das Zimmer,* Paris, Théâtre National de l'Odéon, 4 October 1991;
Le Dernier Sursaut, Rungis, Théâtre de Rungis, 28 September 1993;

Michel Vinaver (from <www.latrappe-theatre.com>)

King, Paris, Théâtre National de la Colline, 11 March 1999;
La Visite du chanceller autrichien en Suisse, Paris, Théâtre National de la Colline, 22 January 2001.

BOOKS: *Lataume* (Paris: Gallimard, 1950);
L'Objecteur (Paris: Gallimard, 1951);
Les Coréens (Paris: Gallimard, 1956);
Les Huissiers (Paris: Théâtre populaire, 1958);

Iphigénie Hôtel (Paris: L'Arche, 1960);

Par-dessus bord (Paris: L'Arche, 1972);

La Demande d'emploi (Paris: L'Arche, 1973);

Théâtre de Chambre (Dissident, il va sans dire, Nina, c'est autre chose) (Paris: L'Arche, 1978);

Les Travaux et les jours (Paris: L'Arche, 1979);

A la renverse (Lausanne: L'Aire, 1980);

Les Histoires de Rosalie (Paris: Flammarion, 1980);

Ecrits sur le théâtre (Lausanne: L'Aire, 1982); enlarged as *Ecrits sur le théâtre,* 2 volumes (Paris: L'Arche, 1998);

Lapiaz: anatomie d'un paysage, by Vinaver and Michel Séméniako (Paris: Passage, 1982);

L'Ordinaire (Lausanne: L'Aire, 1982);

Les Français vus par les Français, as Guy Nevers (Paris: Barrault, 1985);

Théâtre complet, 2 volumes (Arles: Actes Sud / Lausanne: L'Aire, 1986)–volume 2 includes *Portrait d'une femme;*

Les Voisins (Paris: L'Avant-Scène, 1986);

Le Compte rendu d'Avignon (Arles: Actes Sud, 1987);

Le Dernier Sursaut (Arles: Actes Sud / Paris: Papiers, 1989);

L'Emission de télévision (Arles: Actes Sud / Paris: Papiers, 1989);

Ecritures dramatiques, 2 volumes (Arles: L'Arche, 1993);

King; suivi de Les huissiers: nouvelle version (Arles: Actes Sud / Montreal: Leméac, 1998);

La Visite du chancelier autrichien en Suisse (Paris: L'Arche, 2000);

Théâtre d'Aujourd'hui, numéro 8 (Paris: Services Culture Editions Ressources pour l'Education National, 2000);

L'Objecteur (Paris: L'Arche, 2001);

11 septembre 2001 / 11 September 2001 (Paris: L'Arche, 2002);

L'Objecteur; 11 septembre 2001; Les Troyennes (Paris: L'Arche, 2003).

Collection: *Théâtre complet* (Paris: L'Arche, 2002–).

TRANSLATIONS: Henry Green, *Amour* (Paris: Gallimard, 1954);

Thomas Dekker, *La Fête du Cordonnier* (Paris: L'Arche, 1959);

Maksim Gor'ky, *Les Estivants* (Paris: Comédie française, 1983);

T. S. Eliot, *La Terre Vague,* in *Poésie,* no. 31 (1984);

Nikolai Erdman, *Le Suicidé* (Arles: Actes Sud / Lausanne: L'Aire, 1986);

William Shakespeare, *Jules César* (Arles: Actes Sud / Paris: Papiers, 1989);

Botho Strauss, *Le Temps et le chambre* (Paris: L'Arche, 1989).

Michel Vinaver has been writing plays in France since 1955 and has become increasingly respected and his plays widely produced. He published two novels with Gallimard in 1950 and 1951. In 1953 Gillette, a large American multinational company that was expanding in Europe, hired him. Vinaver climbed the corporate ladder at Gillette, becoming a managing director there in the mid 1960s. Although he resigned from management in 1979, he retained an advisory role. He wrote his first play, *Les Coréens* (The Koreans; produced and published 1956), in 1955, and thus began his career as a dramatist. He has taught theater studies at the University of Paris III (1982–1988), then at the University of Paris 8 (since 1988), and has organized and participated in many workshops and *journées d'études* (days of study) on theater and creative writing. His plays have reached a wide public through productions by important directors–including, most notably, Roger Planchon. All his plays have been produced in France, and some have been performed in other European countries, the United States, and Canada. These plays cover a wide range of topics–from war to corporate management and from family strife to the power of the media. The common theme of all his dramas is the role of *l'économique* (economics). His professional activities with Gillette have given Vinaver an unusually broad perspective on the workings of large corporations and the power of economics, which he sees as the crucial element in people's lives. His definition of economics as set forth in *Ecrits sur le théâtre* (1982, Writings on the Theater) is expansive, not focused solely on the business world:

C'est de plus en plus par l'économique–et non plus comme autrefois, par le divin, ou même par le social qui continue de se désagréger–que les gens tissent leur lien au monde. Ils veulent participer complètement de l'ordre économique; en même temps, ils sont dans l'angoisse d'être rejetés hors de cet ordre. C'est de cette dialectique dans notre quotidien que naissent les situations comiques: nous agissons, pensons en tant que producteurs-consommateurs à part entière; nous sommes simultanément consommés, anéantis.

(More and more it is through economics–not the divine, as in the past, or even the social, which continues to disintegrate–that people weave their connection to the world. They want to participate fully in the economic order; at the same time they are wracked by the anxiety of rejection from this order. Through this dialectic of daily lives comic situations are born: we act, think completely as producers and consumers; we are simultaneously consumed, annihilated.)

Vinaver characterizes his writing style as *laisser venir*–wait and see. He lets subjects come to him and allows his ideas to sort themselves out gradually. He surprises his spectators by presenting them with familiar situations, characters, and words that provoke questions. His work deals with the contemporary world through unconventional writing. From the beginnings of his association with theater, Vinaver was drawn to the capacity of the theater to offer multiple possibilities of investigation and revelation. Although Vinaver is reticent about linking the biographical information of his life and his theater, his personal background has given him multiple perspectives: Russian, American, and French; classical Greek and Elizabethan drama; modernist theater and poetry; left-wing politics; and a professional career at the heart of capitalist expansion.

Of Russian Jewish parents, Vinaver was born Michel Grinberg in Paris in 1927. During the Soviet Revolution, his father, Leon Grinberg, left Russia for Paris, where he first worked in his uncle's antique shop, "A la Vieille Russie" (In Old Russia), and then set up his own antique business. Later, he set up another store in New York when the family fled from the Nazi occupation of France. Sophie Vinaver, Michel's mother, also left Russia during the revolution. She met Leon Grinberg in Paris, where they married in 1925. Like her father, she was a lawyer. After World War II, she became head of the women's rights section of the Human Rights Department of the United Nations in New York.

Vinaver finished elementary school in Paris but had to complete his secondary education at the Lycée Français of New York. After his *baccalauréat* (diploma giving one access to higher education) in June 1944, he went to Wesleyan University, Middletown, Connecticut, for a summer. In the fall of 1944 he volunteered for the Free French Forces as part of his military service. He did not see any active duty, since the chaotic direction of the French army kept many units from participating in the final stage of the war. After the war, he returned to Wesleyan, graduating in 1947 with a bachelor's degree in English and American literature. He then moved to England, where he stayed with his uncle, a professor of language and literature at the University of Manchester.

Vinaver's interest in writing grew out of problems he was having with his undergraduate thesis on Franz Kafka. His adviser suggested that he submit a collection of short stories in lieu of a thesis. During Albert Camus's visit to the United States in 1946, Vinaver, who had taken his mother's maiden name, approached Camus in the vestibule of a New York hotel and asked the well-known writer to read his short stories. Camus encouraged the young student to send him a novel when he had completed one. With

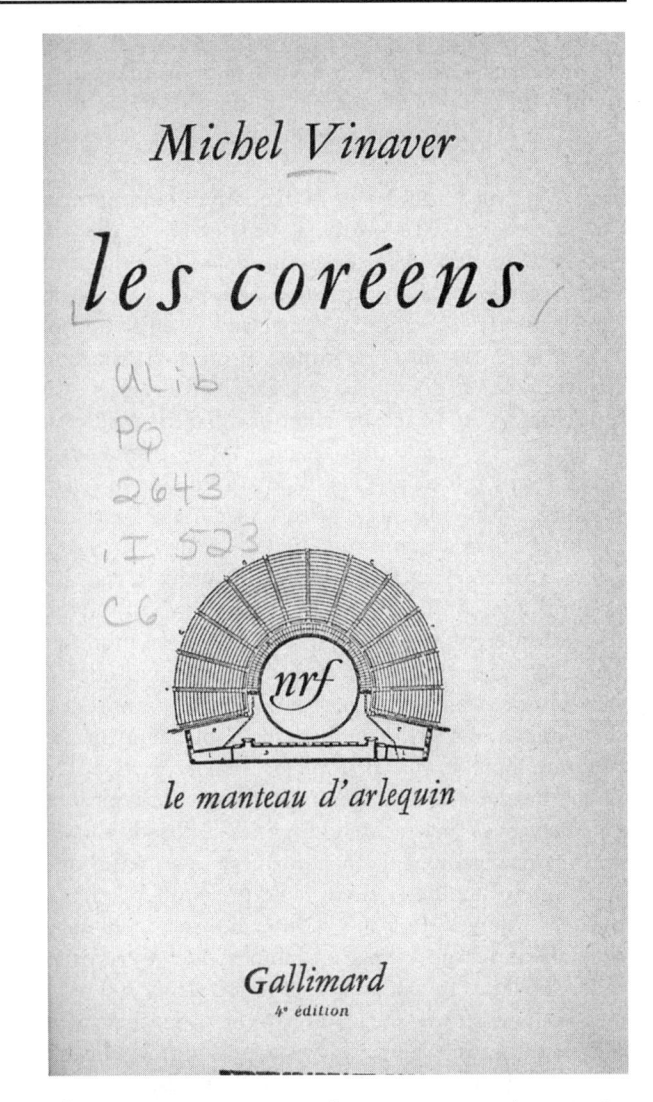

Title page for Vinaver's first play (1956, The Koreans*), which takes place during the Korean War (Thomas Cooper Library, University of South Carolina)*

Camus's support, Vinaver published *Lataume* with the Gallimard press in 1950.

Whether writing a novel or a drama, Vinaver's compositional method resembles that of T. S. Eliot. As a student Vinaver discovered Eliot's *The Waste Land* (1922), which he translated into French as *La Terre Vague* in 1947 (published 1984). This translation was the first of several Vinaver undertook during his career; others were Henry Green's novel *Loving* (1945), William Shakespeare's *Julius Caesar* (circa 1599), and plays by Maksim Gor'ky, Nikolai Erdman, Thomas Dekker, and Botho Strauss. Vinaver calls his encounter with Eliot's poetry the foundation of his work. Eliot's rhythms, his counterpoint of different styles and idioms, resonate in all of Vinaver's writing: echoes of

Dante, for example, are juxtaposed with banal conversations. Vinaver presents the features of ordinary life–home, business, and commerce–but he also often brings in mythical figures and stories of the everyday world.

Vinaver's attraction to Greek myth, and particularly to ancient Greek drama, began with a class at Wesleyan dedicated to the anthropological origins of Greek theater. Vinaver wrote a series of articles on Greek myths in *Critique* and reviewed a translation of Hesiod's works by his former professor, Norman Brown, who had inspired his classical interests. An attraction to the Greeks was not unusual for writers in France of the 1930s, 1940s, and 1950s. Jean Giraudoux, Jean-Paul Sartre, Camus, Jean Anouilh, and Jean Cocteau, for instance, used allegorical parallels between ancient myth and modern reality to create provocative interpretations of contemporary social and political life. What made Vinaver's use of Greek drama different was his exploration of its dramatic function rather than of its stories. Vinaver considered that Greek drama changed the spectators' attitudes, their points of view, and their states of being. In the program note to his first play, Vinaver wrote that Greek theater acts as a kind of initiation rite typical of tribal societies in which children pass into adulthood, seasons change, and the participants move "from one situation to another." In his interpretation of Greek theater, Vinaver does not group tales into a literary unit about heroic events as Homer did. Vinaver is more similar to Hesiod, whose *Theogony* (circa 700 B.C.) and *Works and Days* (circa 700 B.C.) are assemblages of digression, counterpoint, and juxtaposition. Myths are mixed with advice on farming techniques; mistakes and misadventures rival with lessons on seafaring.

Vinaver creates gaps between elements in his plays that the audience is encouraged to fill in. Vinaver likens this approach to that of Georges Braque, who felt that the meaning of his paintings was not in what the paintings represent, say an apple and a plate, but in what lies "entre-deux" (between the two). As he states in *Ecrits sur le théâtre,* Vinaver applies this approach to theater: "attacher moins d'importance aux personnages et aux événements présentés, davantage à ce qui les sépare et les relie; moins à ce qui est dit, davantage au fait que ce qui est dit est dit–dit à tel instant, en tel endroit, avec tel geste et tel accent" (attach less importance to the characters and the events, and more to that which separates and links them together; less to what is said and more to the fact that what is said is said–said at that time in that place, with that gesture or with that accent).

In 1950, he wrote a second novel, *L'Objecteur* (The Objector), published by Gallimard in 1951; it received the prix Fénéon. He finished a *licence* (B.A.) in French at the Sorbonne and moved to his maternal grandfather's house in Annecy, near the French-Swiss border. Gillette answered a "job wanted" ad he placed in the *International Herald Tribune*. Thinking that Vinaver had a legal background, Gillette made him head of administration in their new offices in Annecy. His first task was to help Gillette promote its Toni "home perm" by bringing pressure on the French government to repeal a law, passed in 1949 thanks to the national association of hairdressers' lobby, that forbade the sale of an acid ingredient essential to the kits. The campaign came to nothing–Gillette abandoned its idea–but the intertwining of political, economic, and private motivations had a strong influence on Vinaver.

In Annecy, he became interested in a summer festival for theater students and amateurs conducted by Gabriel Monnet. He took particular interest in their production of Shakespeare's *Hamlet* (1603–1605). Roland Barthes, a literary theorist who had been his friend since 1947, asked Vinaver to submit an article on the production for the newly created journal *Théâtre Populaire*. Vinaver articulated his views of theater (later published in *Ecrits sur le théâtre*) as an art form that does not demonstrate a point, but rather lays out the facts; the object of theater is not "de démontrer comment est fait le monde mais de donner le monde immédiatement" (to demonstrate how the world is made, but to give the world in its immediacy).

A year later, in 1955, Vinaver's appreciation for theater became more pronounced as he followed the rehearsals and performance of Alfred Jarry's *Ubu Roi* (Ubu the King, published 1896) at the Annecy summer workshop. Monnet asked Vinaver to write a play for the next summer. Vinaver wrote "Aujourd'hui," which subsequently became *Aujourd'hui ou Les Coréens* (Today or The Koreans, produced and published 1956) and finally *Les Coréens*. The play, set in Korea during the Korean War, presents the friendship between a French soldier and a pro-Communist Korean peasant girl, as well as the reactions of the soldier's platoon to war in the Korean jungle. It challenges the image of the army–any army–as an embodiment of the will of the nation. This demystification of the wars of "liberation" earned Vinaver the mantle of "the French Brecht" for encouraging the audience to question their socio-economic and sociopolitical environment.

Ideology, however, was not central to Vinaver. Barthes characterized Vinaver's work as creating a pre-ideological territory where, without acting irresponsibly, characters are not fully aware of how or where they fit. Vinaver leaves to the audience imagining the characters' path to consciousness. His discontinuous dramatic method has something in common with Bertolt Brecht's epic theater; however, Vinaver's work does not seek to clarify a set of contradictions but to open theater to an array of viewpoints. Planchon directed the first production of *Les Coréens* in October 1956 in Lyon. Jean-Marie Serreau produced the play in Paris in February 1957. These productions received critical acclaim.

Over the next two years, Vinaver wrote *Les Huissiers* (The Ushers; published 1958; produced 1980) and *Iphigénie Hôtel* (Iphigénie Hotel; published 1960, produced 1977). The first, set in 1957, stages the French government's ineffective response to the Algerian War. One of the major elements is the central role of normally marginal *huissiers*—the employees in government offices who control the comings and goings of people. The second play presents the attempted military coup by the French army in Algeria through the eyes of a group of French tourists marooned in a hotel in Greece. Neither play was performed immediately. Gilles Chavassieux put on *Les Huissiers* in Lyon in 1980, and Antoine Vitez produced *Iphigénie Hôtel* in Paris in 1977.

In 1958, at the request of Jean Vilar, artistic director of the Théâtre National Populaire in Paris, Vinaver adapted *The Shoemaker's Holiday* (1600), an Elizabethan play by Thomas Dekker in which love, money, and war are seen through the everyday activities of a group of villagers. He liked the lack of a clear denouement in the play: the audience does not feel the security of having the outcome told to them but has to search through the characters' everyday reality to arrive at a conclusion. The play was produced under unsatisfactory circumstances as Vilar lost interest and had Georges Wilson direct the production.

Between 1960 and 1966, Vinaver was promoted to chief executive officer (CEO) of Gillette in Belgium, in Italy, and finally in France. Because of his positions, he moved to Belgium and then to Italy. Although he remained connected to the theater through his reviews and articles for theater journals, he was unable to write any more theater until 1967, when he began work on *Par-dessus bord* (Overboard; published 1972, produced 1974). While writing the play in Annecy, to which he had returned, he was involved in implementing Gillette's new "creative marketing" and led the negotiations for Gillette to acquire a controlling interest in S. T. Dupont, an old family firm from Annecy that manufactured luxury goods. In Annecy, he ran a factory that experienced no work stoppage during the strikes and political upheaval of May and June 1968. The plant was highly automated and the workers well paid.

He completed *Par-dessus bord* in 1969. With sixty characters, twenty-five sets, and a requirement of

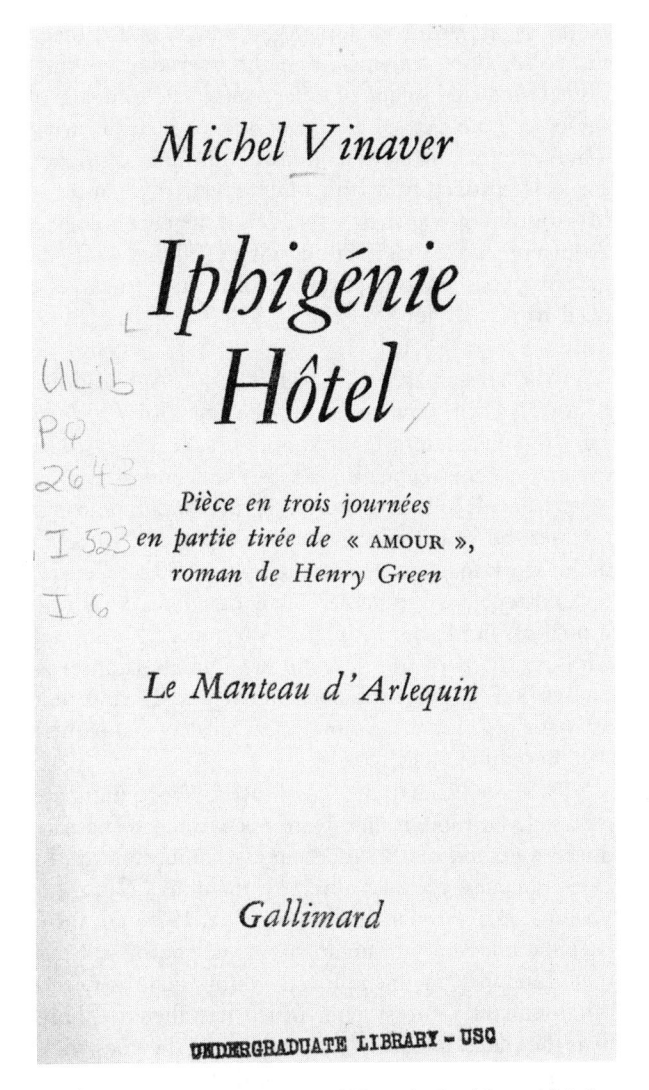

Title page for the 1963 edition of Vinaver's play (first published 1960, produced 1977), set in Algeria during an attempted military coup by the French army (Thomas Cooper Library, University of South Carolina)

between seven and nine hours for staging, the play had to be shortened for its premiere, directed by Planchon in 1974. Charles Joris directed a complete version in Switzerland in 1983. The play intertwines Vinaver's twin occupations of theater and business so that they comment upon one another. Ravoire et Dehaze, a toilet-paper manufacturing company, has to face the competition of Softies, a new brand of toilet roll from United Paper Company, an American business. Scenes of marketing campaigns, involving pop-star endorsements and press conferences in visually appealing locations, are juxtaposed with scenes in a nightclub, where beatniks stage spontaneous performances. Other scenes present a classroom in which a professor lectures on

Norse sagas; ordinary family gatherings; board meetings; shop-floor activities; and the everyday making, distributing, and selling of toilet paper. The montage of these separate yet simultaneous scenes disrupts what Vinaver terms the natural authority of capitalism. Each scene is distinct from the others; yet, the pause or blackout follows at such a speed that the chronological arrangement of time is undermined, along with the generally accepted importance of certain ideas—the need to have a job and the "freedom" of free enterprise.

La Demande d'emploi (1973, The Job Application), Vinaver's next play, continues the focus of *Par-dessus bord*, but in a more concise and practical way. The drama presents capitalism as a fixed entity around which people's lives revolve. A personnel manager assesses the values of prospective employees, while an out-of-work manager seeks employment. His wife tries to hold together the home. Their daughter, a radical, browbeats her father with leftist sloganeering, goes out with an African, and refuses to have an abortion even though she is pregnant and unmarried. Despite her activism and left-wing views, she fails to sympathize with her father's plight.

Vinaver's next two plays were short, intimate pieces. Even though they were not written to be produced together, many saw them as chamber pieces. In 1978, Jacques Lassalle directed them as *Théâtre de Chambre*. *Dissident* (Dissident; published 1978) encapsulates the ambiguity of unemployment, youth, and dissent. Philippe, an unemployed youth, silently rejects the dominant value system, which has alienated him; he is the silent dissident, "il va sans dire" (he goes without saying). *Nina, c'est autre chose* (Nina Is Something Else; published 1978) presents an array of political attitudes through the discussions of three apartment mates, two men and a woman. Nina is apolitical; she does not feel that taking her sexual-harassment complaint to an industrial tribunal is necessary. Philippe encourages her to plead her case. He is a Communist activist, but his political persuasion does not stop his being promoted to foreman and intervening on behalf of management to fire Tahar, an Algerian worker. Charles, the third apartment mate, seems conservative in his views, but he hits his boss in a conflict over the boss's treatment of his female staff. Vinaver thus outlines rebellion and acceptance of the social order as part of a complex social picture. Silence can be employed as a form of resistance, but it can also signify defeat.

Also in 1978, the industrial plant Vinaver was managing at Faberges (near Annecy) went on strike, and workers occupied the factory. Inspired by the industrial action, Vinaver wrote *Les Travaux et les jours* (Works and Days; published 1979, produced 1980). This play uncovers personal and political issues facing employees and management in the after-sales department of a small French coffee grinder company being bought out by a large European firm. *À la renverse* (Backwards; published and produced 1980), written in 1979, is about cosmetics, advertising, and the way the media feeds on popular anxieties. It includes televised sequences, which reflect upon the role of television in society.

At the end of 1979, Vinaver resigned from Gillette to take up writing full time. In 1980, he adapted Nikolai Erdman's *The Suicide* (1975), working from his father's literal translation from the Russian. The production of *Les Travaux et le jours* by Alain Françon that same year and the productions of three of his other plays in 1980 showed how well Vinaver had been received as a dramatist. Between 1973 and 1980, eight of his plays were performed.

In 1981, he wrote the ambiguously titled *L'Ordinaire* (The Ordinary; published 1982, produced 1983). The play is loosely based on the story of a group of Uruguayan rugby players who survived a plane crash in the Andes. They stayed alive for more than forty days in the snow-covered mountains by drinking melted snow and eating the bodies of the dead passengers. In Vinaver's adaptation of Piers Paul Read's account of the rugby players' ordeal in *Alive* (1975), a group of businessmen and their associates try to survive in the Andes after their plane crashes.

The first part of the play focuses on the last leg of a business trip to Brazil, Argentina, and Chile aboard the private jet of Robert Lamb, chairman and managing director of Housies. The company makes easy-to-assemble house-building kits, which will help the president-generals get rid of the untidy shantytowns surrounding the suburbs of many of their cities. Protected by the dictatorial rule of leaders such as Augusto Pinochet, Housies can take full advantage of the new markets offered by the poverty-stricken nations, and the executives and their staffs can make the most of the restaurants, streets, and the overall ambience of Rio, Lima, and Buenos Aires; for the Housies executives the private jet opens up Latin America as an exotic vacation land. The play thus makes the domination of the business rationale into something physical. Since policy decisions are made in the plane, high above the earth, the audience sees how companies subordinate technology and science to their goals.

In the second act, the play traces the group's attempts to survive after the crash. The life-and-death situation elevates the ordinary, everyday need for food to the extraordinary. The dangerous circumstance makes an imperative of maintaining the commonplace activities of eating, drinking, sleeping, and communicating. Some of the passengers, however, remain anchored in their "ordinary" lives from before the accident. The political content grows out of the confrontation between these types of ordinary experience.

Far from revealing an anticapitalist revolution at work, Vinaver's play allows the crisscrossing conversations atop the mountain to chip away at the power of the multinational corporation. The play seizes the biting reality of the all-encompassing political economy. The spectator is offered bits and pieces of dialogue: family, business, adventure, and personal disappointments. Together, the snatches of conversation reveal the mixtures of ideas, hopes, and fears that subvert the capitalist stability of the early part of the play. The conversations bring up disparate visions of life in the corporate world.

Vinaver's passion for the workings of the business world is tempered by his interest in the human condition. In 1980, *Les Histoires de Rosalie* (Rosalie's Stories), a children's book, was published. In 1982, the Comédie Française commissioned Vinaver to write an adaptation of Maksim Gor'ky's *Summerfolk* (1975) for a guest production by Jacques Lassalle. Vinaver also began teaching at the University of Paris III. His collected writings on theater were published as *Ecrits sur le théâtre* by L'Aire Théâtrale in Lausanne. In 1998, L'Arche publishing house in Paris re-edited *Ecrits sur le théâtre* as *Ecrits sur le théâtre,* volume one, since they had collected a second volume of his writings, *Ecrits sur le théâtre,* volume two.

In 1984, Vinaver finished two plays, *Les Voisins* (The Neighbors; produced and published 1986) and *Portrait d'une femme* (Portrait of a Lady; published 1986). *Les Voisins* describes the fused lives of two neighboring families in adjoining houses. It explores the private domain of family and home in which the two families attempt to resuscitate the traditional bourgeois power base of close family loyalties and careful marriages. The success of *Les Voisins,* which won the Ibsen prize for the best production of the year in 1986, lies in the subversive nature of a seemingly banal bourgeois play. For thirty years, Blason and Laheu had been neighbors, but now the impending marriage of their two children brings together the two households, fractured by the loss of mothers. The conversations of the four characters show how firmly property and business values are embedded in the lifestyles of Blason and Laheu. They talk incessantly about economic philosophy and the affairs of their respective companies. Moreover, they judge their children according to their relative business sense. These two twentieth-century families reaffirm nineteenth-century French bourgeois attitudes.

Solid though these values may be, Vinaver invites the audience to consider the cracks in the stability of the French bourgeois doctrine. When the four family members find themselves out of work, the fathers create a small antique-restoration business, and the children, Alice and Ulysse, dream of opening a restaurant in a small run-down farm that they plan to renovate. Having found Fr 38,000 worth of gold in an antique sideboard they were about to restore, the fathers imagine using the money to build a much bigger company in which they would be corporate heads. This dream of re-creating the rules of the system they have left, however, precipitates Ulysse's suicide attempt. The boy's self-inflicted injuries suggest his rejection of the social norms embraced by the fathers. What is more, his suicide attempt is an unexpected action for a placid "good son" who does his best to adhere to the prerogatives of capitalism. *Les Voisins* reveals French bourgeois society clinging to its principles but so wrapped up in trade and capitalist production that it detaches itself from its central foundation—the family.

Portrait d'une femme, by contrast, is based on the newspaper reports of the trial of a woman who murdered her lover. As the title of the play suggests, the politics of this play concern viewpoint; the protagonist of the play, the murderer Sophie, and the politics of the judicial system are perceived in a different way.

In *L'Emission de télévision* (The Television Program; published 1989, produced 1990), Vinaver created a comedy that, in an era of increasing *télé-réalité* (reality television) programs, gives an ironic view of television, industrial relations, and the job market. With the issue of long-term unemployment as its backdrop, the play asks pertinent questions about the power of television to render industrial problems, particularly unemployment, palatable.

Referred to as Vinaver's most Moliéresque play, *L'Emission de télévision* shows the producers of a successful human-interest, magazine-style program planning a show about the effects of unemployment on older workers. Seeking a balanced view, the producers want to show some long-term unemployed fifty-year-olds and someone in that age group who has found another job. They come upon a couple of middle-aged neighbors who, after a long layoff, have other jobs. The format of the show only requires one of them, so each aspirant has to convince the program host of the value of his story in order to be chosen for the show.

In their attempts to give an impartial version of events, the show presenters first offer a variety of sad perspectives on unemployment, with its destructive effects on family life and the psychological scars it leaves on the inner self. Then comes the "happy story"

- 1 -

U N

(L'intérieur de la cabine de l'avion. Bess, Bob, Dick et Joe, autour d'une table, jouent aux cartes. Pat, à une autre table, tape à la machine. Sur une couchette, Ed dort. Sur une autre couchette, Sue, allongée, lit un magazine, la tête sur les genoux de Jack, assis dans l'angle. Nan se fait les ongles des pieds. Jim, par intermittence, va et vient entre la cabine et le poste de pilotage.)

① L'ÉTAT DES CHOSES

Sue   C'est fini Jack
       C'est la fin de notre histoire

Jack   Mais Santiago est une ville sinistre

Sue   J'aimerais que tu ne reviennes pas encore une fois là-dessus
       Dans le fond/toi aussi/
       Tu sais que c'est fini

Jack   Tu ne m'aimes plus ?

Sue   Non
       Toi non plus
       On a conclu tout ça avant de partir
       C'était bien
       Maintenant tu essaies de tout réouvrir

Jack   Santiago est une ville où il n'y a rien
       Je ne peux pas t'abandonner à Santiago
       Je te ramène à Seattle de Seattle tu iras où tu voudras je te paierai le voyage pour où tu voudras en attendant tu réfléchiras

Two pages of the typescript for Vinaver's 1983 play L'Ordinaire, *with his notations indicating slight pause* (légère pause); *break* (détacher); *link or run in* (enchaîner); *emphasis* (accent, intensité); *rhyme or assonance* (rime, assonance); *and similar inflection* (analogie) *(courtesy of Michel Vinaver; from David Bradby,* The Theater of Michel Vinaver, *1993; Thomas Cooper Library, University of South Carolina)*

```
Sue     Tu ne m'abandonnes pas
        C'est moi qui me taille mais pour que tu te mettes ça dans la tête

Jack    Il n'y a rien absolument rien à Santiago tu aurais dû rester à Rio  [LP]
        J'oublie que tu n'as pas aimé Rio
        Tu es la première personne que je connaisse qui n'ait pas été
              happée par le charme de Rio

Sue     Je ne cherche pas les beautés touristiques

Jack    Tu aurais pu rester à Buenos Aires
        A Buenos Aires il se passe des choses

Sue     Je veux un endroit quelconque Jack où tu ne seras pas
```

Notations

- [LP] légère pause
- | détacher
- ⌡   enchaîner
- ∧   accent, intensité
- •   rime, assonance
- —   analogie

Scene from a production of Vinaver's Portrait of a Woman, *at the Florida State University School of Theatre, Tallahassee, November 1992 (from <www.scottscenic.com/Portrait_of_a_Woman_ProductionPhotos.htm>)*

of a man who managed to find work. The television professionals weave into their articulate version of unemployment the half sentences and fragmented remarks of the unemployed, giving that necessary element of gritty reality that will attract viewers. They create an enthralling view of social problems, but this well-choreographed exposition of politics does not change the situation, since the presenters have a tendency to see the rosier side of issues. Spectators find comfort in these oases of salvation.

Vinaver's theater surprises by offering the spectator something that on the surface seems familiar, even ordinary. However, his position is not that of the observing anthropologist. On the contrary, as he says in *Ecrits sur le théâtre,* he does not try to chronicle the everyday but to find it: "elle n'est pas donnée, il s'agit de la capter, de la faire émettre" (it is not a given, you have to pick up its signal and broadcast it). His point of view is not from outside but from inside. Vinaver's work is an assembly, a montage, or a weaving of elements that may at first seem void of any particular interest. The unusual juxtaposition of disparate elements produces miniphenomena that Vinaver calls "décharges ironiques" (ironic discharges). The irony is in the gap that appears between what is expected and what is produced.

Vinaver does not have a specific political agenda, but he aims to provoke a liberating sensation in his spectators. This feeling overcomes their natural aversion to critical views of themselves. Once these psychological barriers have come down, the audience is free to recognize onstage what they seek to avoid in everyday experience. In evoking daily life, Vinaver reflects upon the human sense of belonging—the need to retain a place in society in order to function well; the frequent need to sacrifice something precious in order to maintain status, job, and family.

While composing plays, Vinaver continued to write critical articles on theater. In *Le Compte rendu d'Avignon* (1987, The Account of Avignon), he presented the difficulties facing the dramatist as writer, since most of the theatrical world seemed to revolve around the work of the director. As part of his work as teacher, he has promoted the reading of plays with his students and worked on a method for teaching theater. Similarly, between 1982 and 1987 he helped create and was chairman of the drama committee of the Centre National des Lettres. In 1986, he attained a milestone when Actes Sud published all of his plays in a two-volume *Théâtre complet*. The same publishing house began re-editing his complete plays in 2002. Actes Sud has projected an eight-volume *Théâtre complet*.

Following the publication of *L'Emission de télévision,* Vitez commissioned Vinaver to write an impromptu for the annual Molière celebration at the Comédie Française. Vinaver wrote *Le Dernier Sursaut* (The Last Surprise; published 1989, produced 1993), a satirical farce about a group of moviemakers and actors who make a motion picture about Molière. Their version does not suit the official perception of Molière held by the Théâtre Français, official guardian of Molière's memory. Vinaver's pastiche was inspired by the troubles that surrounded the opening in France of Martin Scorsese's *The Last Temptation of Christ* (1988).

In 1988, Vinaver translated Shakespeare's *Julius Caesar* (translated as *Jules César;* published 1989; produced 1990). Patrice Chéreau commissioned Vinaver to translate Botho Strauss's *Die Zeit und das Zimmer* (1988) as *Le temps et la chambre* (Time and the Bedroom; published 1989, produced 1991), which Chéreau directed at the Odéon Theater in Paris. Vinaver also expanded his work with the pedagogical side of theater. With the Inspecteur Général des Lettres, Vinaver oversaw and worked on critical editions of plays based on his own teaching. The editions were divided into four parts—the complete text, followed by three sections: *fragment,* a line-by-line textual analysis that uncovers the dramatic workings of the play; *mise en pratique,* ideas for collective exercises such as *mise en voix, mise en espace, mise en jeu; contexte,* writings by other writers and the author put together with and against historical and biographical indications in order to get a sense of the play's context. One of the volumes by Vinaver includes twenty-eight fragments with analyses ranging from Shakespeare and Jean Racine to Marguerite Duras, Bernard-Marie Koltès, and Rainer Werner Fassbinder.

In 1997 Vinaver wrote *King* (published 1998, produced 1999), a biographical play about King C. Gillette, the founder of Gillette, the company for which Vinaver had worked for many years. *King* was given its world premiere at the Théâtre National de la Colline under the direction of Françon. During the same season, Françon also directed Vinaver's *Les Huissiers.*

Vinaver took a more interventionist political stance at the turn of the millennium. He did not like the warm reception given by Swiss leaders to the Austrian chancellor, a Nazi sympathizer, during a visit to Switzerland. In *La Visite du chancelier autrichien en Suisse* (The Austrian Chancellor's Visit to Switzerland; published 2000, produced 2001) Vinaver wrote an open letter denouncing the visit. The text of *La Visite du chancelier autrichien en Suisse* focuses on Austria, but it also brings up French politics. Vinaver returned to the theme of objecting in 2001 by rewriting his novel *L'Objecteur* as a play published in 2001. Obeying a structure based on simultaneity, interweaving, and polyphony, the work invites the audience to see things from different points of view in a continuity that is repeatedly broken. Vinaver investigates the theme of resistance in his adaptation of Euripides' *The Trojan Women* as *Les Troyennes* (The Trojans; published 2003). Though beaten and forced into slavery by the conquering Greeks, the Trojans Hecuba, Cassandra, and Andromaque await their fates, but do not concede defeat.

On 11 September 2001, terrorists attacked New York's Twin Towers and the Pentagon in Washington, D.C. In the days that followed the attacks, Vinaver wrote a work, *11 septembre 2001* (11 September 2001; published 2002), that functions like an ancient Greek chorus. The voices are those of passengers on planes, pilots, air traffic controllers, office workers in the Twin Towers, George Bush, and Osama bin Laden. Their words create an incredulous swell in which disbelief at the awesome power of those attacks reveals the world as less stable, more vulnerable than many had thought.

In all of his work, Michel Vinaver pursues the everyday aspect of existence in an attempt to see how it fits or does not fit within larger historical story lines. In his plays he stages many worlds—the soldier's, the family's, the television executives', the youth's, and that of business and commerce, a world he knows from the inside, having been an executive with Gillette for so many years. He employs a fragmented structure owing much to the poetics of Eliot, as well as his own views of displacement and disjuncture. Rejecting the romantic view of the artist as a man with a mission, Vinaver's drama provokes cracks in the established order. Through ironic humor or juxtaposition, he uncovers the world in an unexpected light. His achievement is to have abandoned a theater of stories for a theater of possibilities that goes beyond the failure of the linear plotline. In the 1960s, writers such as Arthur Adamov and Armand Gatti had already pointed toward this theater of possibilities. Gatti, for example, had invoked the need for different, parallel realities to be shown simultaneously onstage. Vinaver's plays represent a further refinement of similar ideas, suggesting that if to make sense of life as a linear sequence is possible, then one must go back to each separate situation and try out its possible combinations. In this way a new form of epic theater is created, in which the modernist aesthetic of the tableau is viewed like a kaleidoscope from different but intersecting viewpoints. These ideas are the pioneering visions that explain the place occupied by Vinaver in the French theater today.

References:

David Bradby, *Modern French Drama: 1940–1990* (Cambridge: Cambridge University Press, 1991);

Bradby, *The Theater of Michel Vinaver* (Ann Arbor: University of Michigan Press, 1993);

Kevin Elstob, *The Plays of Michel Vinaver: Political Theatre in France* (New York: Peter Lang, 1992);

Anne Ubersfeld, *Vinaver dramaturge* (Paris: Librairie Théâtrale, 1989).

Roger Vitrac

(17 November 1899 – 22 January 1952)

Alexander Hertich
Bradley University

PLAY PRODUCTIONS: *Les Mystères de l'amour*, Paris, Théâtre de Grenelle, 1 June 1927;

Victor, ou Les Enfants au pouvoir, Paris, Comédie des Champs-Elysées, 24 December 1928;

Le Coup de Trafalgar, Paris, Théâtre de l'Atelier, 8 June 1934;

Le Camelot, Paris, Théâtre de l'Atelier, 12 October 1936;

Les Demoiselles du large, Paris, Théâtre de l'Oeuvre, 20 April 1938;

Le Loup-garou, Paris, Théâtre des Noctambules, 27 February 1940;

Le Sabre de mon père, Paris, Théâtre de Paris, 17 February 1951;

Médor, Paris, Théâtre du Studio des Champs-Elysées, 10 December 1966;

Entrée libre, Vincennes, Théâtre Daniel-Sorano, 8 February 1967;

Le Peintre, Turin, Teatro delle Dieci, December 1967.

BOOKS: *Le Faune noir* (Paris: Lhen, 1919);

Les Mystères de l'amour: Drame en trois actes précédés d'un prologue (Paris: Gallimard, 1924); translated by Ralph J. Gladstone as *The Mysteries of Love*, in *Modern French Theater: The Avant-Garde, Dada, and Surrealism*, edited by Michael Benedikt and George E. Wellwarth (New York: Dutton, 1964), pp. 227–267;

Connaissance de la mort (Paris: Gallimard, 1926);

Cruautés de la nuit (Marseille: Cahiers du Sud, 1927);

Humorisitiques (Paris: Gallimard, 1927);

Victor, ou Les Enfants au pouvoir: Drame bourgeois en trois actes (Paris: Denoël, 1929);

Le Théâtre Alfred Jarry et l'hostilité publique, by Vitrac and Antonin Artaud (Paris, 1930);

Le Coup de Trafalgar (Paris: Gallimard, 1935);

Théâtre, 4 volumes (Paris: Gallimard, 1946–1964)—comprises volume 1, *Victor, ou Les Enfants au pouvoir; Le Coup de Trafalgar;* and *Le Camelot* (1946); volume 2, *Les Mystères de l'amour, Les Demoiselles du large,* and *Le Loup-garou* (1948); volume 3, *Le Peintre*, translated by M. Josephson as *The Painter*, in *Broom*, 3, no. 3 (October 1922): 223–226; *Mademoiselle Piège; Entrée libre*, translated by Nahma Sandrow as *Free Entry*, in *Surrealism: Theater, Arts, Ideas* (New York: Harper & Row, 1972), pp. 103–112; *Poison*, translated by Malcolm Cowley in *Broom*, 5, no. 4 (November 1923): 226–228; *L'Ephémère; La Bagarre;* and *Médor* (1964); and volume 4, *La Croisière oubliée, Le Sabre de mon père,* and *Le Condamné* (1964);

Dés-Lyre: Poésies complètes, edited by Henri Béhar (Paris: Gallimard, 1964);

Le Voyage oublié, preface by Jean-Pierre Han (Limoges: Rougerie, 1974);

Champ de bataille, preface by Han (Mortemart: Rougerie, 1975);

Roger Vitrac, 1936 (© Lipnitzki/Roger-Viollet/Getty Images)

Re-tour de manivelle, preface by Han (Mortemart: Rougerie, 1976);

Le Destin change de chevaux, preface by Han (Mortemart: Rougerie, 1980);

Le premier bal de Cécile, edited by Han (Mortemart: Rougerie, 1984);

L'Enlèvement des Sabines, edited by Han (Paris: Deyrolle, 1990).

PRODUCED SCRIPTS: *Pattes de mouches,* motion picture, by Vitrac and Jean Grémillon, L'Alliance Française Européenne, 1936;

L'Homme de nulle part, motion picture, dialogue by Vitrac, General Productions, 1937;

Alerte en Méditerranée, motion picture, by Vitrac, Léo Joannon, and T. H. Robert, Compagnie Commerciale Française Cinématographique/Société des Films Vega, 1938;

Le Joueur d'échecs, motion picture, by Vitrac and others, Société des Films Vega, 1938;

Sixième étage, motion picture, Compagnie Industrielle et Commerciale Cinématographique, 1940;

L'Assassin a peur la nuit, motion picture, by Vitrac and Jean Delannoy, DisCina, 1942;

Feu sacré, motion picture, by Vitrac, Maurice Cloche, and Pierre Rocher, Production Artistique et Cinématographique, 1942;

Macao, l'enfer du jeu, motion picture, by Vitrac and Pierre-Gilles Veber, Demofilm, 1942;

Le Mort ne reçoit plus, motion picture, dialogue by Vitrac, Cinématographique Méditerranéenne de Production/Union Française de Production Cinématographique, 1944;

Bethsabée, motion picture, by Vitrac and Jacques Rémy, Compagnie Industrielle et Commerciale Cinématographique/Les Films Corona, 1947;

Si ça peut vous faire plaisir, motion picture, dialogue by Vitrac, Jacques Daniel-Norman, and Jean Manse, Pathé Consortium Cinéma, 1948.

OTHER: *Georges de Chirico: Vingt-neuf reproductions de peintures,* critical essay by Vitrac (Paris: Gallimard, 1928);

Jacques Lipchitz, *Jacques Lipchitz: Vingt-neuf reproductions de ses oeuvres précédées d'une étude critique,* critical essay by Vitrac (Paris: Gallimard, 1929);

"Moralement puer," in *Un Cadavre* (Paris, 1930), p. 2.

SELECTED PERIODICAL PUBLICATIONS–UNCOLLECTED: *Monument, Littérature,* new series 2 (1 April 1922): 22–33;

"Dormir," *Les Hommes du jour* (28 April 1923): 6;

"Note sur l'Ombilic des limbes," *Nouvelle Revue Française,* no. 147 (1 December 1925): 755.

Although he wrote a vast number of plays of various styles, Roger Vitrac is almost exclusively known for an early work, *Victor, ou Les Enfants au pouvoir* (Victor, or The Children Are in Power; produced, 1928; published, 1929). One of the first members of the Surrealist movement, Vitrac went on to cofound the highly experimental Théâtre Alfred Jarry with Antonin Artaud in the late 1920s. After the theater group disbanded, Vitrac turned to semi-autobiographical plays and accessible bourgeois comedies. This abrupt change confounded many critics, as these works seemed antithetical to his early, avant-garde drama. These contradictions, along with the esoteric nature of his early works, his difficulty in finishing texts, his quiet life away from scandal and headlines, his alcoholism, and his eventual poor health, led to Vitrac's relative obscurity in the canon of twentieth-century theater. Yet, since his death in 1952, many critics have argued that his works, through their sharp questioning of language, bourgeois values, and logic, as well as their markedly oneiric qualities, adumbrate the absurdist theater of the 1950s.

Vitrac's works for the stage resist convention and categorization. Not only his early, Surrealist plays but also his later, more traditional plays were arguably subversive, for they often lacked the strong plot, rhythm, and characters that typify traditional theater. Furthermore, dialogue frequently proceeds through alliterative associations and puns, not logic. Vitrac also resisted theory. Except for the pamphlet *Le Théâtre Alfred Jarry et l'hostilité publique* (1930, The Alfred Jarry Theater and Public Hostility) and short essays on other dramatists, he wrote no theoretical texts. Throughout his career Vitrac stressed that a theatrical work should explain itself; he transcribed "la vie comme elle est" (life as it is). Any play that needed a theoretical introduction or explanation was, in his view, unfinished.

At the same time, Vitrac's works are steeped in psychology and Freudian theory. Like many of his fellow Surrealists, he was fascinated by Sigmund Freud's theories on dreams and tried to incorporate their unique logic in his plays. In *Le Camelot* (The Hawker; produced, 1936; published, 1946) the title character proclaims: "La vie imite le rêve" (Life imitates dreams), an apt description of the reality portrayed in many of Vitrac's plays. Freudian slips and repression of childhood traumas frequently serve as linchpins in his dramas. Yet, these Freudian themes often remain tacit. Although the ideas are central, no character explains why events might be important in the characters' development.

Roger Eugène Simon Vitrac was born on 17 November 1899 in Pinsac, a small village in the Midi-Pyrénées region of southwestern France. Attracted to the stage from a young age, he enjoyed attending performances by traveling theater and marionette troupes. Although the first few years of his childhood were happy, his youth was generally painful. After the family moved to nearby Souillac, Vitrac's parents began to argue increasingly frequently. His father, Jules Vitrac, would spend hours in the local café, occasionally with his son, where Vitrac was exposed to many elements of the social sphere, as well as to his father's vices. A philanderer and chronic gambler, his father lost nearly all of the family money, including his wife's dowry. These events marked the young boy, and Vitrac eventually dramatized them in *Le Sabre de mon père* (My Father's Sabre), first performed in 1951 and published that same year in the journal *France Illustration*.

In 1910 a brother, Patrice Vitrac, was born, but he died two years later. Vitrac was deeply affected, believing that his brother's premature death was unjust. This remorse manifests itself in his drama, in which the name Patrice recurs and children, often with special but fragile powers, play central roles. The family moved to Paris in 1911, opening a new world for Vitrac's imagination. After an unremarkable education, he enlisted for national military service in October 1920. Here he was introduced to Dadaism and to the personalities who were later to become members of the Surrealist movement.

After World War I a strong drive for pacifism existed in France. This desire manifested itself in the "Lettres et droit" (Humanities and Law) unit of the 104th Infantry, whose members were both soldiers and students. Somehow Vitrac managed to join this regiment, even though he was not enrolled in an academic institution. Among these "student officers," Vitrac cultivated a circle of friends who were also interested in contemporary literature and art, and they soon started a small theater troupe. During this period Vitrac wrote and produced his first play, *La Fenêtre vorace* (The Voracious Window), which has been lost. According to Michel Sanouillet, the work demonstrated a "Dadaic character," criticizing traditional morals and questioning language and logic.

Vitrac married his first cousin, Gérardine Vitrac, in October 1920, but the marriage lasted only six months. While Gérardine longed for the south of France, Vitrac was interested in Paris and its literary scene. On 14 April 1921 he attended the famed Dada demonstration at the Saint-Julien-le-Pauvre Church. Here he became better acquainted with many of the most important voices in the movement, including Louis Aragon, who introduced him to many progressive writers of the Parisian literary scene. Aragon strongly supported Vitrac, and in 1924 he wrote the most famous and enduring proclamation about the young playwright: "Magic has no secrets from Roger Vitrac, who is preparing a Theater of Conflagration in which people die as in a wood."

Enamored of *Littérature*, an avant-garde literary publication, Vitrac and his friends started a journal, *Aventure* (Adventure). Only three issues were published, from November 1921 to January 1922. In addition to serving unofficially as editor, Vitrac also contributed to the periodical. The final issue included his *Le Peintre* (translated as *The Painter*, 1922). This one-act play introduced many of the themes that continued to appear in his works, including adultery, the place of the child in an adult world, the meaninglessness of language, and the question of identity.

Starting from the core of a traditional vaudevillian farce with a lovers' triangle, misunderstandings, and disguises, *Le Peintre* twists theatrical convention. The painter constantly says and does the opposite of others, changing his identity and reasoning until the logic of the play has turned back upon itself and a new "reality" is created. As the play opens, he is painting a door red but proclaims it green; he also claims to have murdered Mr. Parchemin, a name that he lifted from a young boy. Mrs. Parchemin arrives onstage and soon agrees, declaring the door green and the painter a murderer before calling him Mr. Parchemin. A constant battle between words and actions, the play continues with puns and parallel monologues accumulating until these verbal high jinks completely flummox the audience. A striking example of Vitrac's disdain for traditional theater, *Le Peintre* ultimately asks what identity and reality are. Just as a red door might be green if everyone agrees, the husband can also be the lover, or the thief a police officer.

Over the course of the next several months, Vitrac published five other works, some of which appeared in *Littérature*. The April 1922 issue included the short text *Monument*. Only three pages long, it features a striking juxtaposition of styles and includes a scene on the back of a bus, an interrogation, and readings of a letter and a press clipping. Like *La Fenêtre vorace*, it shows the influence of Dada. There is no single answer or interpretation of how the different sections interrelate, if they do. The perplexing mixture of genres questions the sharp divisions among prose, poetry, and theater found in traditional literature.

In October 1922 *Mademoiselle Piège* (Miss Trap), a "fragment," appeared in *Littérature*. In a technique common to modernist literature, the spectators are forced to participate in the spectacle. They must construct their own plot, since no background or explanation is given for the characters' words or actions. While the hotel setting may seem mundane, the potential banality is contrasted with striking images of blood and death, a juxtaposition that figures frequently in Vitrac's drama.

Vitrac's output from the early 1920s shows a progression from works marked by Dadaism to plays that he and others labeled as Surrealist. While initially attracted to Dada, Vitrac, like many others, felt that its ideas were becoming stale. A movement that proposed to destroy tradition had itself become almost traditional. During this period Vitrac became friendly with André Breton, whose ideas and personality had a profound impact on his drama and his life. With Paul Eluard and Jean-André Boiffard, Vitrac also helped to edit the first issue of *La Révolution surréaliste* (The Surrealist Revolution), which appeared in December 1924. Recognizing Vitrac's contribution, Breton in his first *Manifeste du surréalisme* (1924; translated in *Manifestoes of Surrealism*, 1969) characterized the playwright as someone who had "shown ABSOLUTE SURREALISM."

Vitrac deplored the French theatrical climate of the early 1920s. "N'allez pas au spectacle. Couchez-vous" (Don't go to the show. Go to bed), he exhorted theatergoers in the article "Dormir" (1923, To Sleep). Following Breton's proclamation "lâchez tout" (leave everything), as well as the Surrealist goal of fusing dream and reality, Vitrac's works became increasingly dream-like. *Entrée libre* (translated as *Free Entry*, 1972), written in 1922 but not published until 1964 and not staged until 1967, marked his first attempt to transcribe dreams into a theatrical setting. Using oneiric techniques such as ellipsis and metamorphosis, each of the three main characters in the play has two dreams, with a middle tableau comprising "tout le drame" (the entire drama). Tinged with violence and angst, *Entrée libre* employs dreams to recast the psychological drama of a lovers' triangle.

Vitrac's next work for the stage, *Poison* (translated, 1923), first published in *Littérature* in January 1923, also shows evidence of the forthcoming Surrealist revolution. In addition to dedicating the work to Breton, Vitrac categorized the play as Surrealist in his 1944 outline for an unwritten preface, "Le Théâtre de l'Incendie" (Theater of Conflagration), a title borrowed from Aragon. Although some critics agree with this classification, others argue that *Poison* is not a strictly Surrealist text.

Inspired partially by silent movies, *Poison* again defies traditional language. Using only sounds and images, this "drame sans paroles" (drama without words) is made up of twelve tableaux. The first six offer a variety of fantastic scenes, including one in which a painter smashes open a wall and starts to pull a cable, eventually dragging a steamship through the wall and onto the stage. The third scene is the recitation of a poem, which begins "Entre l'amour et l'orthographe / Il y a une plume pour penser . . ." (Between love and spelling / There is a pen for thinking . . .). While exemplifying the Surrealist desire to record the fleeting and uncategorizable ideas of the mind, the poem also underlines the central theme of *Poison*: words are inadequate. The conclusion of the play further highlights this motif. The seventh through eleventh tableaux offer different settings but the same action: a character holds a sign with the number of the scene written on it. The play concludes with a haunting image, "une bouche qui fait le simulacre de parler" (a mouth that simulates speaking).

Vitrac's next play, *Les Mystères de l'amour* (1924; translated as *The Mysteries of Love*, 1964), tells of the relationship between two lovers, Patrice and Léa. Not only was it Vitrac's first work to be staged in a theater, premiering in 1927, he also considered it his "première pièce" (first play). He later described it as "Une oeuvre ironique qui concrétisait à la scène l'inquiétude, la double solitude, les arrière-pensées criminelles et l'érotisme des amants. Pour la première fois un *rêve réel* fut réalisé sur le théâtre" (An ironic work that renders concrete on stage the disquiet, double solitude, hidden criminal

The French singer Georgius (stage name of Georges Guibourg) in Vitrac's Le Camelot *(The Hawker) during the first production of the play in October 1936 at the Théâtre de l'Atelier in Paris (© Lipnitzki/Roger-Viollet/ Getty Images)*

thoughts, and eroticism of lovers. For the first time, a *real dream* was realized on stage). This "drame surréaliste" (Surrealist drama), as Vitrac subtitled the play in volume 2 of *Théâtre* (1948), takes the themes of his earlier works and develops them further. It juxtaposes the unconscious, apparent reality, and drama to create a bold new work. As Vitrac wrote, in the author's note to the play in *Théâtre,* the characters "vivre comme on rêve" (live as one dreams) and "rêver comme on vit" (dream as one lives). By putting various characters' thoughts and desires directly onstage without any introductory context, Vitrac again places a great burden on the spectators. The traditionally accepted divisions between reality and fiction, author and text, and actor and audience member are constantly drawn into question.

Instead of taking place onstage, the first act of *Les Mystères de l'amour* begins in a stage box with the curtain down and the house lights illuminated. Suddenly the distance between spectator and spectacle dissolves; the "fourth wall" begins to crumble. Patrice, at Léa's feet, offers her flowers. They appear to talk to one another, but in a disconnected dialogue, in which questions and replies seem to have no correlation. In loud asides, the two then tell the audience how dearly they love one other. Soon, however, members of the audience (played by actors) respond, asking "why?" Other voices join in until shots are fired and everything goes black. When the lights come back on, Patrice is fighting his rival, Dovic. From behind the footlights, a brief scene follows that seems to have no relation to anything that precedes or follows. The curtain falls. Several members of the audience begin to complain, and the theater director appears. He tells the audience that the performance is over and that the author, Théophile Mouchet, has just committed suicide. Cries of "Author" begin. The curtain rises and an actor playing the author appears, covered in blood and roaring with laughter. Two curtains suddenly fall.

The second tableau in act 1 is violent. It appears to be Léa's nightmare, although some critics disagree. Unlike *Entrée libre,* in which each character's dream is introduced, in *Les Mystères de l'amour* there is no context. After a brief scene in which Patrice drops Léa's baby (a doll) into the Seine, there are several dismembered bodies as well as a dinner with Léa's dead father and David Lloyd George, played by Dovic.

The second act opens with Léa lying on a bed. As she and Patrice talk, her hand begins to smoke, but neither seems upset by this. A butcher enters and reprimands Léa, informing her that he will not return for such a pittance of bone. Léa and Patrice continue with their nonsensical dialogue. Then, while she is offstage giving birth to a son, Patrice, Madame Morin (Léa's mother), and Dovic call for the author because Patrice is uncertain about the direction of the play. But the playwright offers no answers. Patrice proceeds to bludgeon Madame Morin and Dovic until the stage is "éclaboussée de sang" (sprayed with blood). Léa returns with her son, and Patrice places him on a pedestal. The child falls off and dies, again highlighting the fragility of children.

After a brief fourth tableau, a scene fraught with parataxis in which Patrice appears as Benito Mussolini, the final act of *Les Mystères de l'amour* opens with Léa in the custody of two policemen because she has destroyed her hotel room. Léa magically summons Patrice, who appears and frightens the officers. After Patrice has an illogical discussion with several children, the author reappears onstage. He offers Patrice a revolver–"c'est nécessaire" (it's necessary), he notes–and Patrice fires upon him. This action has no effect on the author, who tells Patrice that the firearm is necessary for the conclusion and that he should "faites-le dans l'intérêt du drame" (do it in the interest of the drama). The author then hands a second revolver to Léa. As the play closes, Léa fires, and Patrice cries out: "Qu'as-tu fait, Léa? Qu'as-tu fait? Tu viens de tuer un spectateur" (What have you done Léa? What have you done? You just killed a spectator). Just as words and reality can come under attack, so may members of the audience. The security of a traditional story and production are no longer possible.

Vitrac met Artaud in 1924, the same year that *Les Mystères de l'amour* was published. Learning that they had similar ideas about theater, they soon became close friends, and in 1925 each published an article in *La Nouvelle Revue Française* lauding the other. At the same time, Vitrac was falling out of favor with Breton. According to a letter by Artaud, by September 1925 Breton had asked him to disassociate himself from Vitrac. Ultimately, Vitrac, along with many other members of the Surrealist group, including Artaud, were officially excommunicated in Breton's *Second Manifeste du surréalisme* (1930; translated in *Manifestoes of Surrealism*). While there is no irrefutable evidence as to why Vitrac was banished, there are several possible reasons, some philosophical and others personal. He was committed to pursuing literary goals and embraced the theater, which Breton criticized because of its implicit adherence to old values. Breton believed that theater was inherently false and that a Surrealist theater was impossible. Vitrac also refused to commit himself politically; he did not join the Communist Party, as Breton urged him to do. Finally, while he did attend some gatherings, Vitrac did not follow Breton's orders to the letter, which the dictatorial leader demanded. Regardless of the precise reason, Vitrac's expulsion had a great effect on him; according to some of his acquaintances, he was deeply depressed.

In late September 1926 Vitrac, Artaud, and Robert Aron founded the Théâtre Alfred Jarry. The trio chose Jarry's name to signify the direction of their endeavor. Like the iconoclastic author of *Ubu Roi* (1896, King Ubu), they wished "de contribuer à la ruine du théâtre tel qu'il existe actuellement en France" (to contribute to the ruin of the theater such as it presently exists in France), as Vitrac wrote. The Théâtre Alfred Jarry disdained the trite realism that predominated in the 1920s. They wanted "pour arriver à ce que [*sic*] tout ce qu'il y a d'obscur dans l'esprit, d'enfoui. . . . Tout ce qui appartient à l'illisibilité et à la fascination magnétique des rêves . . . ces couches sombres de la conscience . . . sont tout ce qui nous préoccupe dans l'esprit" (to reach all that is obscure in the mind, that is buried. . . . All that belongs to the unreadable and to the magnetic fascination of dreams . . . these dark layers of the conscious . . . are all that concerns our minds . . .). While the group staged only four productions, which were generally ignored by the public, the Théâtre Alfred Jarry had a profound effect on the theater of the second half of the twentieth century.

Given the proclamation of the Théâtre Alfred Jarry that "Ce n'est pas à l'esprit ou aux sens des spectateurs que nous nous addressons, mais à toute leur existence" (It is not at the spectators' minds nor at their senses that we aim, but at their entire existence), it is not surprising that *Les Mystères de l'amour* was the troupe's first production. The premiere was originally scheduled for 15 January 1927. Owing to a lack of funds, however, it was postponed until 1 June of that year, when the first three acts were presented at the Théâtre de Grenelle in Paris. Although the critical reaction was limited, in part because of the obscurity of the troupe and the play, it was generally favorable. The audience did not, however, react as Artaud had hoped. They were not incited to action but remained passive in their seats.

After *Les Mystères de l'amour,* which left the Théâtre Alfred Jarry more than Fr 6,000 in debt, the company's next production was an excerpt from Paul Claudel's play *Partage de midi* (1906; translated as *Break of Noon,* 1960) and a screening of Vsevolod Pudovkin's 1926 motion picture *Mother* on 14 January 1928. Illustrating the theater company's claim that they "do not serve authors" but rather "use them," the play was produced against Claudel's wishes, and the movie was illegally imported. Giving no title in the program, Artaud presented the play as a farce. Breton, who was in the audience, soon recognized the work and told the uncertain audience that it was merely a play by Claudel, which greatly upset Artaud. Owing to continuing tensions between the Surrealists and Vitrac and Artaud, the next production of the Théâtre Alfred Jarry, August Strindberg's *A Dream Play* (1902), was also disrupted.

The final production of the Théâtre Alfred Jarry was also its most famous, Vitrac's *Victor, ou Les Enfants au pouvoir,* a work considered by many to be a masterpiece of Surrealist theater. Although Vitrac had written several collections of poetry and an autobiographical work, *Connaissance de la mort* (1926, Knowledge of Death), in the preceding years, *Victor, ou Les Enfants au pouvoir* marked his first return to the stage since *Les Mystères de l'amour*. Vitrac had finished most of the play a year before its debut, but because of continuing financial difficulties, as well as problems associated with the previous productions of the Théâtre Alfred Jarry, the premiere was delayed until 24 December 1928.

Unlike Vitrac's previous plays, *Victor, ou Les Enfants au pouvoir* is precisely situated, both physically and temporally, based on newspaper clippings from the period depicted. The action of the play takes place on 12 September 1909, from eight in the evening until midnight, in the apartment of the bourgeois Paumelle family. For the first edition of the play, published in 1929, Vitrac provided the subtitle *Drame bourgeois en trois actes* (Bourgeois Drama in Three Acts). Because the play was based on the conventions of traditional bourgeois theater, audiences quickly recognized the world portrayed onstage. Yet, the characters constantly question what is commonly accepted. Vitrac later described the work as "tantôt lyrique, tantôt ironique, tantôt direct . . . dirigé contre la famille bourgeoise, avec comme discriminants: l'adultère, l'inceste, la scatologie, la colère, la poésie surréaliste, le patriotisme, la folie, la honte et la mort" (sometimes lyrical, sometimes ironic, sometimes direct . . . aimed against the bourgeois family, whose discriminants are: adultery, incest, scatology, anger, surrealist poetry, patriotism, madness, shame and death). The play offers the audience both a twisted vaudevillian farce and a Surrealist drama filled with dreams, wordplay, and scandal.

Victor, a giant and "terriblement intelligent" nine-year-old who also prophesies his own death, is celebrating his birthday. He utters the first line of the play: ". . . Et le fruit de votre entaille est béni" (. . . And blessed be the fruit of your gash), to which Lili, the maid, responds: "D'abord, c'est le fruit de vos entrailles, qu'il faut dire" (First off, you should say the fruit of your womb). This perversion of liturgical language immediately alerts the audience that speech is unsure and that no institution is safe from the pointed criticism of the play.

Family friends, the Magneaus, arrive for the birthday party, and Victor gleans from their daughter, Esther, evidence corroborating his suspicions about his

Juliette Gréco and Yvan Peuck in the second production of Vitrac's Victor, ou Les Enfants au pouvoir *(1928, Victor, or The Children Are in Power), staged at Paris's Théâtre Agnès-Capri in November 1946 (© Lipnitzki/ Roger-Viollet/Getty Images)*

father's affair with Thérèse Magneau, Esther's mother. Victor reveals his suspicions to the two adulterers through word games and veiled allusions. He then begins to antagonize Antoine, Esther's mentally unstable father, who flies into tirades when certain words or names are mentioned. After the final guest, General Longségur, arrives, the group sits down to an awkward dinner. Victor reads a poem, the Surreal qualities of which completely escape the other guests. Antoine proclaims that he is a cuckold, and Victor and Esther play "papa et maman" (daddy and momma), reenacting a scene they had witnessed between Thérèse and Charles Paumelle, Victor's father. This *Hamlet*-like farce upsets the dinner guests, and Antoine leaves. In an effort to reanimate the evening, the general tells Victor that since it is his birthday, he may have anything he wants. Victor replies that he wants to "jouer à dada" (ride horsey) on the general, who acquiesces.

As the second act opens, Thérèse and Charles are discussing what action to take since their relationship has been revealed. Victor overhears that Esther is not Antoine's child but rather his own father's. Tension mounts as others enter the living room. Charles notes that it would take a "miracle" to save the ruined evening, and a miracle seemingly arrives: Ida Mortemart, Emilie Paumelle's long-lost childhood friend, who suffers from uncontrollable flatulence. Again turning theatrical illusion on itself, Charles remarks that if a dramatist had used this trick, the audience would have complained of "l'invraisemblance" (implausibility). Ida's arrival, however, does not bring a miracle; rather, as her last name announces, she brings death.

Charles and Emilie have retired to their bedroom at the beginning of the third act. Although Charles tries to reconcile, his wife is still upset and attacks him with a hammer. They eventually retire to bed, but Victor soon enters, complaining of a stomachache. He notes that, given his parents' incessant arguing and the revolver next to their bed, something terrible will happen. His mental anguish has somatically transformed itself into physical pain. The joys of childhood freedom have been destroyed by bourgeois hypocrisy.

The Paumelles' rest is further interrupted by an array of interlopers—Lili, Thérèse, and finally the Magneaus' maid, who brings a suicide note from Antoine. Victor announces that he is dying but that he has also found the secret to the "Uniquat." After briefly leaving, Charles returns with both a doctor and a gun. The doctor can find nothing wrong, but Victor knows he is dying "de la mort" (from death). The curtain falls and shots are fired. When the curtain rises, Emilie and Charles are dead next to Victor's bed, a smoking revolver between them. The maid enters and cries, "Mais c'est un drame!" (It's a drama!).

Although the subject matter of *Victor, ou Les Enfants au pouvoir* was audacious—Artaud claimed that the title alone illustrated "a basic disrespect for all established values"—the production did not cause much controversy, nor was it a success. The first production had a run of three performances. This brief run was owing in part to popular opinion, for many thought that the Théâtre Alfred Jarry was a student group unworthy of concern. The limited critical reactions were mixed. While some believed the play a prank designed to shock the audience, others, such as François Vitry, saw "an acute criticism of bourgeois life."

In 1946 *Victor, ou Les Enfants au pouvoir* was produced by the Compagnie du Thyase, under the direction of Michel de Ré. Although unsuccessful, it did have a profound effect on Jean Anouilh, whom Vitrac had befriended in 1938. Anouilh was so taken by the play that he directed it in 1962. This third production was a triumph, with critics such as Gilles Sandier from the *Arts* claiming in a 10 October 1962 review that Vitrac's play was as profound as Jean Genet's *Les Nègres* (1958; translated as *The Blacks,*

1960). After this production Vitrac's name entered the pantheon of twentieth-century French theater. Ten years after his death, Vitrac was finally a success. *Victor, ou Les Enfants au pouvoir* has since had several successful reprises, including a 1982 production at the Comédie-Française.

In 1929 Vitrac wrote *L'Ephémère* (Ephemera), published the following year in the journal *Variétés*. This short, impossible-to-stage "Phantasmagoria," dedicated to the Surrealist painter André Masson, presents a continuing metamorphosis of scenes, including a giant eye and a lake that floats above a dining room. Vitrac later labeled the play "scientific"; yet, he does not seem to be interested in concrete knowledge but rather in that which cannot be comprehended.

L'Ephémère was Vitrac's last truly experimental play, marking an end to "Le Théâtre de l'Incendie." He now turned to more patently autobiographical subjects and more-traditional dramaturgy. Yet, these new works did not fit precisely into the mold of traditional theater. Often wordy and lacking the pacing and intrigue found in popular works for the stage, Vitrac's plays from the 1930s until his death in 1952, like those from the 1920s, remained unpopular and were primarily ignored.

These changes in Vitrac's approach to theater, as well as the continued financial problems of the Théâtre Alfred Jarry, placed a strain on his professional relationship with Artaud. By the time *Le Théâtre Alfred Jarry et l'hostilité publique* was published in 1930, their friendship was nearly finished. Nevertheless, Artaud insisted on directing Vitrac's next drama, *Le Coup de Trafalgar* (1935, The Unforeseen Incident). For this play, written over the course of several years, Vitrac drew heavily on memories of his neighbors during his adolescence in Paris. Spanning several years, *Le Coup de Trafalgar* follows the interweaving stories of several residents of a Parisian apartment building. Arcade Lemercier apparently tries to swindle his neighbors out of money in order to invest in a phony Egyptian treasure hunt, while others attempt to have him framed. Later, the audience learns that his evidence was not fabricated. Throughout the many subplots one question persists: why did Flore Médard shave half of her head? In the end, no answer is given; nor are the various plotlines resolved. The play shows "life as it is."

The lack of coherence in *Le Coup de Trafalgar*, both in the plot and the characters, troubled Artaud, and he asked Vitrac to revise the play, which further clouded their friendship. Artaud was never able to secure financing for a production, and Vitrac, intent on seeing his work performed, looked elsewhere. The play finally premiered on 8 June 1934 at the Théâtre de l'Atelier in Paris, under the direction of Marcel Herrand. It received generally negative reviews, one of which came

Jean Anouilh and Vitrac at a rehearsal for the 1946 production of Victor, ou Les Enfants en pouvoir, *which impressed Anouilh so much that he directed the play himself in 1962 (© Lipnitzki/Roger-Viollet/Getty Images)*

from Artaud. After this rebuke Vitrac and Artaud ceased to speak to one another. Even twelve years later, at the highly publicized revival of *Victor, ou Les Enfants au pouvoir,* they refused to talk.

In his next play, *Les Demoiselles du large* (Maidens of the Sea), Vitrac seems to have abandoned the comic and subversive elements that exemplified his dramaturgy. Written in the summer of 1933 and first published in the monthly *Les Oeuvres libres* in 1938, this serious play tells a story of love, death, and psychological pain. Pierre Delrieu arrives on a Breton island where two sisters, Marie and Anna de Bressac, live. Pierre soon falls in love with the younger, less-sophisticated sister, Marie. Charles, their brother, arrives home after a tour with the navy. He tells Pierre of his lover, Dora, who has also been Pierre's girlfriend. She committed suicide, and Charles is certain that it is his own fault. After chiding her for an incident with a local when they were in Greece, he forgot to take her with him on the navy vessel, and she killed herself. At the conclusion of the play, Anna, feeling unloved, also commits suicide. Charles blames the death on Pierre, who has been sleeping with Marie. Charles returns to the navy, and the remaining couple abandons Marie's family home. While many of the characters' actions can be understood in terms of Freudian psychoanalysis, their motivations are not made clear. In a 1938 interview in *Ce Soir,* Vitrac himself said that *Les Demoiselles du large* was "essentiellement une pièce d'emotion psychologique, traitée par son côté le plus intérieur" (essentially a play of psychological emotion, handled from its most interior angle). This opaque abstractness limited the appeal of the play, and the 1938 premiere received mixed reviews.

Vitrac's personal life became increasingly troubled in the 1930s. Unable to earn a living as a playwright, he began to work in cinema, adapting novels for the screen. This work, along with his continuing depression and problems with alcohol, further limited his literary production. He frequently started works but had great difficulty finishing them. A summer at a detoxification clinic in 1934 did inspire him, however, to write his next work, *Le Loup-garou* (The Werewolf), first published in *Les Oeuvres libres* in 1946. Borrowing from a traditional story of a loup-garou who, if he does not visit a church every night, will not return to his human form, Vitrac created a werewolf named André Camo Dumont, a man cursed to sleep with a different woman every night. As soon as one resists his charms, he will be cured. The loup-garou seeks treatment at a private clinic filled with quirky characters based on Vitrac's acquaintances. This comedic work, filled with vaudevillian situations, wordplay, and larger-than-life characters, also includes psychoanalytical elements. It was first staged in February 1940 but, because of World War II, had a limited run of approximately twenty shows.

Rapidly written in March 1936, *Le Camelot* returns to the illusions of *Le Coup de Trafalgar*. Based on the unbridled possibilities and scandals of the 1920s, the play recounts the rise of Louis-Toussaint Lacassagne, a hawker who rises from petty schemer to media magnate to government official. First performed in October 1936 at the Théâtre de l'Atelier, *Le Camelot* received generally negative reviews. As with many of Vitrac's other productions, critics were unsure of the meaning of the play, its politics, and the intended audience. The critic for *Candide* (29 October 1936) wrote that Vitrac had succeeded only "in making everything vague, muddy, indiscernible."

These mounting failures gravely limited Vitrac's appeal. Only one more of his plays was produced during his lifetime. Yet, he continued to write. In 1938 he finished *La Bagarre* (1964, The Brawl), a love story about a failing writer based in part on an incident involving one of his friends. *Médor* (published, 1964; produced, 1966), written in 1939, parodies a typical lovers' triangle. Both members of an unhappy couple are considering an affair and leaving the other on the night of their anniversary. The maid, however, brings home Médor, a St. Bernard dog. Intrigued, the couple remains at home. In their dreams Médor, played by a human, teaches them that they still love one another.

Just before the outbreak of the war, Vitrac returned to the south of France. He first worked with Radiodiffusion Française (French Radio) in the Bordeaux region and then in 1941 moved to Nice, where he did more work for the movie industry. These years were difficult for Vitrac. Although he wished to remain productive, his writing had virtually stopped. He continued to abuse alcohol, eventually developing hypertension and vision problems. Attempting to end this artistic slump, he started the plays "Au Monomotapa" (At Monomotapa) and *Le Destin change de chevaux* (Destiny Changes Horses), but he never finished either one, although the latter was published in its incomplete state in 1980.

After the war Vitrac completed several other plays, including *Le Condamné* (1964, The Condemned Man), begun in 1946 but not completed until 1951, a short comedy about a man who believes he is dying and wishes to make love with his best friend's wife; and *La Croisière oubliée* (1964, The Forgotten Cruise), written in 1949, a comedic radio drama about two married people who have a brief fling on a Mediterranean cruise.

With *Le Sabre de mon père,* Vitrac returned to the pains of his childhood in Pinsac. Begun in 1945, the play was not completed until 1950, when, according to Vitrac, "le refoulement" (the repression) that had been hindering him finally gave way, aided perhaps by his father's death. Other events also encouraged Vitrac. After the publication of the first two volumes of *Théâtre,* his collected theater works, in 1946 and 1948, he was awarded the Légion d'honneur (Legion of Honor) on 4 March 1950, and in August of that year he remarried.

Le Sabre de mon père features the return of the Dujardin family, who originally appeared in *Le Coup de Trafalgar*. Based almost directly on Vitrac's father, Mr. Dujardin is a compulsive gambler who spends long hours at the local café losing money, while his wife considers taking a lover. The Dujardins' son, Simon (Vitrac's middle name), witnesses his father's many humiliations. Eventually the family, who is disliked by the entire community, sells their few remaining belongings and moves to Paris. These events lead Simon to become a writer, just as Vitrac did. The play premiered on 17 February 1951 at the Théâtre de Paris. Like Vitrac's other works, it received mixed reviews, and it closed after thirty performances. Critics found that the play lacked direction and were unsure of whether Vitrac wished to provide a nostalgic look at provincial life at the beginning of the twentieth century or a psychological family study. At this time his health was rapidly declining; he suffered several bouts of paralysis and died on 22 January 1952. He was buried in his hometown of Pinsac.

Roger Vitrac's drama is quite varied, ranging from the experimental Dadaist and Surrealist works of the 1920s to the vaudevillian comedies and autobiographical works of the 1930s and 1940s. This multifarious style led in part to his obscurity during his lifetime. As Renée Saurel wrote in *Combat* (19 February 1951) after the opening of *Le Sabre de mon père*, "it is hard to believe that the author of *Sabre* is the same Vitrac who from 1927–1929 directed with Artaud the Théâtre Alfred Jarry and in whose works one finds a bit of Ubu's verve."

"Ubu's verve" is unquestionably present in texts from Vitrac's "Théâtre de l'Incendie," including *Les Mystères de l'amour* and his most famous work, *Victor, ou Les Enfants au pouvoir*. Filled with oneiric imagery, wordplay, and irreverence, Vitrac's iconoclastic plays opened the door to modern theater.

Letters:

Alain Virmaux and Odette Virmaux, eds., *Lettres à Jean Peyaubert* (Mortemart: Rougerie, 1991).

Biography:

Henri Béhar, *Roger Vitrac: Un Réprouvé du surréalisme* (Paris: Nizet, 1966).

References:

Martine Antle, *Théâtre et poésie surrealistes: Vitrac et la scène virtuelle* (Birmingham, Ala.: Summa, 1988);

Michele Bacholle, "Roger Vitrac: Victor ou le chevalier messianique," *Romantic Review*, 88, no. 2 (1997): 305–313;

François Baron, *Les Frontières du bonheur* (Paris: Gallimard, 1954);

Henri Béhar, *Etude sur le théâtre dada et surréaliste* (Paris: Gallimard, 1967);

Béhar, *Vitrac: Théâtre ouvert sur le rêve* (Paris: F. Nathan / Brussels: Labor, 1980);

Sven Åke Heed, *Le Coco du dada: Victor, ou Les enfants au pouvoir de Roger Vitrac* (Lund, Sweden: CWK Gleerup, 1983);

Annette Shandler Levitt, "The Domestic Tragedies of Roger Vitrac," *Modern Drama*, 30 (December 1987): 514–527;

J. H. Matthews, *Theatre in Dada and Surrealism* (Syracuse, N.Y.: Syracuse University Press, 1974);

Nahma Sandrow, *Surrealism: Theater, Arts, Ideas* (New York: Harper & Row, 1972);

Michel Sanouillet, *Dada à Paris* (Paris: Pauvert, 1965).

Papers:

Some of Rogert Vitrac's papers are in the Bibliothèque littéraire Jacques Doucet in Paris.

Jean-Paul Wenzel
(13 July 1947 -   )

Christine E. B. Moritz
University of Northern Colorado

PLAY PRODUCTIONS: *Loin d'Hagondange,* Théatre Ouvert, "Mise en espace" Festival d'Avignon, 22 July 1975; translated as *Far from Harrisburg,* New York, La Mama Theatre, 1978;

Marianne attend le mariage, by Wenzel and Claudine Fiévet; Paris, Théâtre Ouvert–Beaubourg, 1977;

Dorénavant I, Paris, Théâtre de l'Est Parisien, 1977;

Les Incertains, Paris, Théatre Ouvert–Petit Odéon Théâtre, 1978;

Simple retour, Hérisson, Théâtre Ouvert, 1980;

Honte à l'Humanité, by Wenzel, Olivier Perrier, and Jean-Louis Hourdin, Montluçon, Centre Dramatique National, 1980;

Doublages, Saint-Denis, Théâtre Gérard Philippe, 1981;

Vater Land, le pays de nos pères, by Wenzel and Bernard Bloch, Hérisson, Théâtre de l'Aquarium, 1983;

L'Homme de main, Montluçon, Centre Dramatique National, 1988;

La Fin des monstres, Montluçon, Centre Dramatique National, 1993;

Faire bleu, Montluçon, Centre Dramatique National, 1999.

BOOKS: *Loin d'Hagondange,* by Wenzel, with *Marianne attend le mariage,* by Wenzel and Claudine Fiévet (Louise Doutreligne) (Paris: Stock, 1975); translated by Françoise Kourilsky and Nicholas Kepros as *Far from Hagondange* with *Vater Land, the Country of Our Fathers* (New York: UBU Repertory Theatre, 1984);

Les Incertains (Paris: Tapuscrit/Théâtre Ouvert, 1978);

Doublages (Paris: Albin Michel, 1981);

Vater Land, le pays de nos pères, by Wenzel and Bernard Bloch (Paris: Tapuscrit, 1983); translated by Timothy Johns as *Vater Land, the Country of Our Fathers* with *Far from Hagondange* (New York: UBU Repertory Theatre, 1984);

Mado and *Boucherie de nuit,* in *Cinq Auteurs,* edited by Evelyne Pieller (Paris: Revue Autrement, 1986);

Jean-Paul Wenzel (from <http://www.theatre-contemporain.net/auteurs/wenzel/pdgjpw.htm>)

Faire bleu (Besançon, France: Les Solitaires Intempestifs, 2000); translated by Lin Coghlan as *Rising Blue* (London: Oberon, 2002).

SELECTED PERIODICAL PUBLICATION–UNCOLLECTED: "Virus," *Théâtre public,* 74 (1987): 16–17.

OTHER: *La Fin des monstres; suivi de Boucherie de nuit; et de Mado* (Paris: L'Avant-Scène, 1995).

A versatile actor, director, and playwright, Jean-Paul Wenzel has been identified by modern critics as one of the founders of the "New Realism," or *Théâtre du quotidien* (Workaday, or Everyday, Theatre), in France. This new style of dramaturgy turns away from the abstract *Théâtre de l'absurde* (Theater of the Absurd), focusing instead on the social and psychological realities of ordinary people in ordinary situations, thus exposing the flaws of modern society and personal relationships. Yet, while his works effectively convey the underlying, despairing realities of real people, the techniques Wenzel uses are a mix of heightened realism and nonrealistic theater. The settings of his plays are sparse, but authentic; topics are genuine and believable–for example, the loneliness and confusion of retirement following a lifetime dedicated to work, a spurned lover, a pregnant girl fearful of her parents' reaction, and a group of itinerant circus performers facing imminent dissolution. Moreover, the dialogues are fractured, and lengthy silences in Wenzel's plays are interspersed with long, chatty monologues, often about banal topics. At the same time, Wenzel's disjointed, nonchronological story lines, alternating between reality and illusion, create a sense of malaise and confusion of identity in the characters. Wenzel is noted for his use of an innovative verbal technique labeled "polylogue" by Jean-Pierre Sarrazac (according to Bettina L. Knapp in *French Theatre since 1968* [1995]), in which one or more characters seemingly talk to one another without ever hearing what the other is saying. However, as Wenzel states in the preface to his play *Doublages* (1981, Dubbings), the characters may actually incorporate elements of each other's monologue into their own, thus creating a kind of third dialogue, that of the play itself: "Aucun lien apparent entre ces deux 'histoires.' Pourtant le frôlement, l'interférence, les croisements de leurs récits créent une relation, un dialogue, un troisième temps, celui de la représentation" (No apparent link between these two "stories." Yet the brief convergences, interferences, and crisscrossings of their narratives create a relationship, a dialogue, a third moment in time, that of the performance).

Little has been written about events and circumstances that have influenced Wenzel's work. He was born 13 July 1947 in Saint-Etienne, a modest working-class city in eastern France widely renowned for its coal-mining and metallurgical industries (especially armaments) and considered by some to be the birthplace of the industrial revolution in France. Occupied by the Germans during the Vichy period, Saint-Etienne was repeatedly bombed by Allied forces in 1944; the bombings resulted in the deaths of nearly a thousand people and the destruction of more than 1,100 buildings. Following the war, Saint-Etienne also experienced the decline of its mining industry and the typical financial and social difficulties that accompany such upheavals in the fiscal base of a city. Wenzel's childhood and adolescence in this environment greatly influenced his dramatic work, in which abandonment (by institutions as well as by individuals) is a prevalent theme, as are questions of identity and hopelessness. Wenzel personally experienced abandonment in 1953 when his father left his family and disappeared with no explanation. Nearly thirty years later, with his friend and colleague Bernard Bloch, Wenzel made a series of trips to Germany in order to discover and understand his father's homeland (and indirectly, himself), with an ultimate goal of creating a play based on these experiences.

Wenzel originally trained for a career in metallurgy. His friend and colleague Claude Duneton tells the story of how he ran into the young Wenzel, following the final examinations for the latter's metalworking diploma. Wenzel explained to his friend that in a moment of lucid panic, surrounded by the screaming milling machines of the factory, he had envisioned his future as a metallurgist and knew it was not for him. In that moment, one swift movement resulted in a broken machine and a life change. He left the workshop without a word and told his friend, less than an hour later, that he had decided to become an actor. "C'est ça ou rien" (It's either that or nothing), Wenzel said, according to Duneton in the preface to *Cinq Auteurs* (1986, Five Authors). And so, in 1966 at the age of nineteen, Wenzel enrolled in the Ecole Supérieure d'Art Dramatique du Théatre National de Strasbourg (School of Advanced Dramatic Arts of the National Theatre of Strasbourg), which he attended until 1969. While a student there, he made the acquaintance of actor/director André Steiger and of director Robert Gironès, two talented men whom Wenzel, according to a 1979 *Théâtre public* article by Y. Davis, credits as playing a significant role in his own development as a playwright. When he finished his formal studies, Wenzel procured a position for the opening of the theater Les Bouffles du Nord, in Paris, where he acted in a variety of plays, including William Shakespeare's *Timon of Athens* (1623) in 1974, directed by Peter Brook, former co-director of the Royal Shakespeare Company and founder of the Centre international de création théâtrale (International Center for Theater Creation), an intercultural (British/French) theater project. During the production of *Timon of Athens*, Wenzel met two other aspiring actor/writers, Olivier Perrier and Jean-Louis Hourdin, who became important collaborators in many of his later enterprises.

Despite his success as an actor, Wenzel derived increasingly "less pleasure from playing in stories of princes who did not interest him," as he explains on the Théâtre de Hérisson website. He felt a need to fill a void he had identified in the theater repertoire. He wished to give a voice to the little people–he counted himself as part of this group–and at the same time, to create a theater experience that would appeal to average people, as well as to sophisticated bourgeois theatergoers in Paris. To begin to achieve these goals, in 1975 Wenzel undertook two endeavors that distinguished him as an important new figure in French theater. First, he founded his own experimental acting group, Le Théâtre du quotidien, a name soon applied by critics to an entire school of playwriting that, in addition to Wenzel, included Georges Michel, Réné Kalisky, and Michel Deutsch. Then Wenzel seized the opportunity to *mettre en espace* (space-set) his first play, *Loin d'Hagondange* (published 1975; translated as *Far from Hagondange*, 1984), at the summer Theater Festival in Avignon in 1975. A "space setting" is a kind of "super reading"—a performance of a briefly rehearsed play by actors on an empty stage, with no costumes or lighting, followed by a discussion among the actors, director, and audience, according to E. M. Donnachie. Critics said that Wenzel's play "scored a bull's-eye" (Théâtre de Hérisson website), and was produced the following year at the Comédie de Caen (Caen Theatre), for which it received the Prix de la critique (Critics Prize) for the category of Meilleure Création Française (Best French Production). To date, *Loin d'Hagondange* has been translated into eighteen languages and has been performed in twenty countries. The American translation, originally called *Far from Harrisburg* and now titled *Far from Hagondange*, was translated by Françoise Kourilsky and Nicholas Kepros and directed by Kourilsky in New York's La Mama Theatre in 1978.

Loin d'Hagondange, which has been widely acclaimed and extensively discussed, tells the story of a newly retired couple, George and Marie, who spent their entire working lives in the industrial town of Hagondange, he laboring in the steelworks and she dutifully raising their family. According to the expectations of society, they saved for retirement and finally earned their reward—a quiet life in the countryside. Not having given much thought to what retirement might entail beyond moving to their dream house, they find themselves profoundly unhappy and confused in their new circumstances. Their sense of identity and purpose in life is now missing; they do not know what to do with themselves, or with each other. George tries to recreate his former routine in the steel mills, leaving the house in the morning to spend his days in his workshop, fixing the rain gutters, making a pipe rack, and building an iron table, while Marie constantly cleans her spotless house. Their conversations are full of banalities and complaints, and of course, resonant with silences. As Wenzel notes in an interview with N. Collet for the journal *Théâtre public,* "Ce qui importe, c'est le non-dit" (What is important is what is not said). Wenzel's use of silence is notable—long pauses do not in fact conceal a vast mine of profound thoughts and feelings that go unsaid. Instead, they represent an utter lack of meaning in the couple's lives. Nothing is said because there is nothing to say. They have lived their lives as society expects, and at the end of their working (useful) days, they find themselves abandoned and forgotten by the society that used them up. As a preface to the play, Wenzel quotes Jean-Paul Sartre, who said, "What makes people grow old is, on the one hand, of course, the slow disintegration of the body, and on the other, the way people are treated in our society, in terms of their labor power and nothing else. Basically, society arranges from the beginning to treat a worker as an old person later on. It is interested in productive power and nothing beyond that" (from *Far from Hagondange*). When he was a student in Strasbourg, Wenzel himself lived the events of May 1968, the student protest that began in Paris but soon led to a general strike that paralyzed France for an entire month; this experience, as well as his keen awareness of the lives of working people in Saint-Etienne, influenced the writing of *Loin d'Hagondange* as well as his later plays. In describing his goals for *Loin d'Hagondange,* and for workaday theater in general, Wenzel asserts that he does not try to show "une tranche de vie car les personnages sont tout le temps dans une position de crise, à un moment décisif de leur vie où ils peuvent basculer d'un côté ou de l'autre, soit arriver à analyser et comprendre la réalité, soit être à nouveau ressaisis et étouffés par l'oppression" (a slice of life, because the characters are in a constant state of crisis, in a decisive time of their lives, when they could topple from one side to the other, either to end up analyzing and comprehending reality, or to find themselves again seized by and suffocated by oppression).

Following the success of *Loin d'Hagondange,* Wenzel continued his multiple roles in the theater—acting, directing, and writing. In 1976, together with his colleagues Perrier and Hourdin, he founded the theater troupe known as Les Fédérés (The Federated Players) in Hérisson, a tiny medieval town just twenty kilometers north of the city of Montluçon, and about three hundred kilometers south of Paris. The choice of this small Auvergne community was significant. The three friends, according to the website for the Théâtre de Hérisson, felt that far from the riches of the capital, they would be seen as "les derniers représentants d'un théâtre populaire qui n'est pas populiste" (the latest representatives of a popular theater which was not also populist). Moreover, they would be able to continue to question themselves and their work in a way they might not have, had they stayed to work in Paris. Since its inception, Les Fédérés has become a prolific and popular institution in the Auvergne region, hosting an annual summer theater festival—Les Rencontres théâtrales de Hérisson (Theatrical Encounters of Hérisson), as well as a two-week writers' workshop—Avril des Auteurs (Authors' April) every spring. Les Fédérés received the recognition of the Ministry of Culture in

1981 and inaugurated its own theater in a former factory in 1985. In 1993, with the support of the Ministry of Culture, the company became the Centre Dramatique National de la Région Auvergne (National Drama Center of the Auvergne Region).

Wenzel's second play, *Marianne attend le mariage* (Marianne Saves Herself for Marriage; published 1975, performed 1977), written in collaboration with Claudine Fiévet, was apparently based on a "fait divers" (short news item) in the newspaper. The play is the story of Marianne, oldest daughter in a working-class family, who labors with her father and sister in a local garment factory. She is engaged and knows that marrying would allow her to leave her tedious job, but she cannot bring herself to set a date for the wedding, even though she has just discovered that she is pregnant. All around her, everyone wonders what she is waiting for. Marianne seems to have a vague idea that she must leave her narrowly defined life in order to find happiness, but she does not have any idea how to break out of the mold. As with *Loin d'Hagondange,* the family members' inability to communicate, or even to know their own minds, is represented by awkward, disjointed conversations and uncomfortable silences. At the slightest suggestion of a difficult topic, Marianne's mother suggests either turning on the television or just not thinking about it.

In describing his first play, David Bradby quotes Wenzel as saying that he "felt that the sentimentality of *Loin d'Hagondange* reassured and comforted too many people, that it veiled the violence of daily life that is contained in the play." This issue is addressed in *Marianne attend le mariage* by the concerns of the parents about the family's reputation, which overshadow their attitudes toward their children. Consequently, when each daughter faces a private tragedy, discussions center on what is "correct" and what people will think rather than on the feelings and lives at stake; the results are disastrous. This notion of the potential for violence that rests just below the surface of human interactions is a theme to which Wenzel returns with increasing explicitness in subsequent plays. Other themes addressed in *Marianne attend le mariage* include worker unrest at a factory and the idea of replaceable daughters, in contrast with the one good son, who comes home at last to take care of his parents. Following its production by the Théâtre Ouvert in 1977, *Marianne attend le mariage* received the Prix de la SACD pour Talent Nouveau (Society of Dramatic Authors and Composers Prize for New Talent). Also in 1977, Wenzel wrote and produced *Dorénavant I* (Henceforth I) at the fall drama festival of the Théâtre de l'Est Parisien (East Paris Theatre). This play, however, was never published, and nothing has been written about it.

Front cover for the 1995 edition of Wenzel's first play (1975; translated as Far from Hagondange, *1979) (from <http://www.amazon.com>)*

In 1978 Wenzel wrote and directed his fourth play, *Les Incertains* (The Uncertain Ones), a sparsely set play–composed of a series of fifteen brief scenes–that relates the dysfunctional relationship between Pierre, a painter, and his girlfriend, Anne, a writer. The striking differences between the two characters are at the root of their inability to communicate with each other. Pierre, shown always standing, is a free spirit, wanting to discover the world, interested in experiencing life, with a seemingly unfathomable sense of optimism, while Anne, shown always lying horizontal in her bed, is pessimistic, afraid to go outside, distrustful of everything and everyone, and especially of Pierre's blissful naiveté. Little happens in the first two-thirds of the play. The characters talk to each other in confusing, nonsensical dialogue, but communicate little. Gradually, though, each begins to view the world through the other's eyes, and their dialogues become more communicative. Anne discovers some hope in her life, while Pierre begins to lose his positive outlook. Finally, Pierre comes home after burning all of his paintings and announces to Anne that he no longer loves her and is leaving. Anne, relieved, finds the change gives her a new energy. She feels able to stand, clean her apartment, and go out. She is ready to experience life and to write again. This play was directed at the Petit Odéon Theatre by Alain Mergnant.

In 1980 Wenzel wrote *Simple retour* (Simple Return), the story of a man who returns to his hometown after an absence of seven years only to find the town and its inhabitants in the midst of economic and psychological decline. Although never published, this play was given a reading at the Théâtre Ouvert in Hérisson. Also in 1980, Wenzel collaborated with his friends Perrier and Hourdin to write *Honte à l'Humanité* (Shame on Humanity), which became one of fourteen "spectacles avec bestiaux" (plays with beasts), primarily written by Perrier, and featuring–depending on the production–draft horses, cows, pigs, and sheep. Wenzel directed the production of this play at the Centre Dramatique National in Montluçon.

In 1981 Wenzel wrote and directed *Doublages*, which was presented both at Hérisson and at the Théâtre Gérard Philippe in Saint-Denis. Standing in the midst of a sparse and bleak winter landscape, a mother, age sixty, tells the dismal, intimate story of her life, while her daughter, thirty years younger, recounts in painful detail the story of the night her husband/lover abandoned her. *Doublages* is probably the best example of Wenzel's innovative technique of the "polylogue." Each character tells her story in bits and pieces, alternating with the bits and pieces of the other's narrative. Though they are onstage together and seem to be talking to each other (as one might expect a mother and daughter to do), they only rarely acknowledge the other's story, absorbed as each is in her own misery. The breaks in the stories have been calculated to match at certain points, and once in a while each character seems to respond to something the other says. The intersection of the stories creates, in effect, a third dialogue, as Wenzel calls it, the story of the play itself. As with his previous plays, *Doublages* addresses the themes of abandonment and identity as well as the notion that violence always lies just beneath the expression of human emotions. The play uses musical terms to announce the different scenes. The first scene is called the overture, and program notes indicate cello and saxophone themes for the mother and daughter, respectively. At the end of the overture, the two instruments play together. Next comes the first movement (Night, the dream), then the second movement (Dawn, reality), and finally the third movement (Day, illusion).

In 1981 Wenzel decided, along with his friend Bloch, to travel to Germany to learn more about the country from which both their fathers had come, in the hopes of creating a play about postwar Germany. Bloch's father, according to Knapp, was a German Jew who left Germany in 1934, married an Alsatian, enlisted in the Foreign Legion, and fought against the Nazis. Wenzel knew only that his own father had been a member of the Wehrmacht (German military forces) occupying Saint-Etienne during World War II and had married his mother after deserting the German army. For their research, the two made several trips to Germany in 1982, during which time Wenzel also held a teaching post at the Comédie de Saint-Etienne (Saint-Etienne Theatre Company). On one of those trips by chance Wenzel located and reconnected with his father. He wrote in his travel journal about his harsh first meeting with his father and included an account of the meeting at the beginning of the published play.

The first publication of *Vater Land, le pays de nos pères* (1983; translated as *Vater Land, the Country of Our Fathers,* 1984) includes information about the origin of the play, including a description of the inception of the idea, several travel-diary entries of both Wenzel and Bloch, detailed narrative monologues of all the main characters, a discussion by an observer of how Wenzel and Bloch with a group of ten actors improvised a series of scenes based on the individual narratives, and then how Wenzel was able to sit down and write the play. The play itself takes up only 57 pages of a 180-page publication. *Vater Land, le pays de nos pères* is the story of Wilhelm Klutz, a German army officer who deserts his unit in occupied Saint-Etienne in 1944. Following a night of heavy drinking, he accidentally kills a French acquaintance and sees his own salvation in his friend's death. Taking the Frenchman's identity papers, he leaves his own papers (and his uniform) on his dead comrade, and becomes "a new person." Under his new identity, he makes a life for himself in Saint-Etienne, marrying the woman he loves and setting up a successful business with his father-in-law. But, when the Frenchman's brother, Henri, comes back from a German prison camp, looking for his brother, Klutz realizes he can no longer play his charade, and he disappears, returning to his homeland, but not to his former life. All of this information is actually only background to the core of the play, which deals with Henri's search for his brother's killer and the search by Klutz's son, Jean, to find his father.

Vater Land, le pays de nos pères, like *Doublages,* makes extensive use of the "polylogue" technique, which, coupled with the nonchronological plot, serves to disorient the reader/viewer in a way that reflects the confusion expressed by the characters themselves. Jean as a grown man is looking for his father perhaps fifteen to twenty years after Klutz disappeared, while Henri begins searching for his father mere months after his father's disappearance, starting in 1945. Jean's quest serves as a kind of broken narration of Henri's search, and all the characters narrate their own stories, surrounded by the others, who neither see nor hear them. And yet, the various characters often echo something that another has said previously, creating an impression of fragile continuity between the stories, while at the same time highlighting the sense of alienation each portrays. Following Henri's journey chasing Klutz from Baden-Baden to Frankfurt, to Wuppertal, and finally to Hamburg, over the course of four years, the reader/viewer encounters much of the devastation of postwar Germany, both physical and social, including bombed-out buildings, the black market, couples fornicating in caves, and an utter lack of trust under any circumstances. Wenzel effectively portrays the postwar period through gritty detailed scenes and sparse dialogue bringing to the fore the raw cynicism that developed in the German population at that time. Yet, he does not offer any solutions. The scene in which Jean finally finds his father is rife with suspicion, as Wilhelm Klutz says to his son, "Si tu n'es pas Jean, je te tue" (If you're not Jean, I'll kill you). *Vater Land, le pays de nos pères* was performed by Bloch's Scarface Ensemble in 1983 and received the Prix de la Critique (Critic's Prize) for the "best French production" in 1984.

Following the success of *Vater Land, le pays de nos pères,* Wenzel wrote two plays in 1984, *Boucherie de nuit* (1986, Night Butchery) and *Mado* (1986). These two plays depart from Wenzel's previous works in that the violence previously implied in his characters' lives is brought closer to the surface. *Boucherie de nuit* tells the story of Alain, a young butcher's apprentice spurned by his fiancée, who calls him a coward because he avoided his military service on the grounds of a slight physical problem. She also tells him that he smells bad and that she does not want to live the life of a butcher's wife. Confused and angry in the face of this callous rejection, Alain quickly progresses to irrational rantings and finds a way to "make war" to impress his girlfriend, with predictably disastrous results. Long rambling monologues, unheard by other characters, interspersed with empty silences, heighten Alain's sense of alienation and the audience's sense of impending tragedy. *Mado,* published as the companion piece to *Boucherie de nuit,* is extremely short—only four pages—and yet implies an even more violent solution to the problem of abandonment. In brief, *Mado* is the story of a young woman whose husband, or perhaps boyfriend, has abandoned her along with their two young children. To take revenge on the children's father, in her despair she turns on her own children, who try to avoid her rage by telling her fairy tales, in a ploy reminiscent of Scherezade. The effects of the "polylogue" technique are more grievous in *Mado* than in any of Wenzel's previous plays, because in it, the children do hear and understand their mother's plans, while the mother is oblivious to anything they say. The violence in both *Mado* and *Boucherie de nuit* is not graphic, but it is all the more disturbing because of its unambiguous nature.

Between 1984 and 1994, Wenzel devoted the majority of his energies to his directing career, producing twelve different plays, including one of his own, *L'Homme de main* (Man of the Hand), written in 1987 and produced in 1988 by Les Fédérés. This play was not published. In 1993, Wenzel wrote and produced *La Fin des monstres* (The End of the Monsters), which is the story of a group of itinerant Hungarian circus performers, grounded for lack of a travel permit and trying to live and work together in order to make something of their art. Narrated primarily by the Fat Lady, *La Fin des monstres* is dark and confusing, and the latent violence in Wenzel's previous plays is more overtly expressed in this play, when, in a practice session, the young knife thrower sends a blade into his own father's open mouth, killing him instantly. The situation is ambiguous, however: was it an accident, did the son murder his father for some previous breach of their relationship, or did he respond to a desperate appeal in his father's eyes to help him end his wretched life? In spite of all the troubles the troupe experiences, they manage to hold things together until the fateful day when their mascot, a lively dog named Catzouro, is poisoned and dies. With him die all their dreams of ever reviving their circus. They split up and go their own ways, with the two most talented performers finding success in the American performance circuit. *La Fin des monstres* differs in many ways from Wenzel's other plays. While it depicts ostensibly real people in believable situations, it also strays from Wenzel's pattern of portraying people that the audience might recognize and identify with. Also, dialogues are somewhat more direct; instances of characters talking but not hearing each other are fewer.

In 1995 Wenzel was named director of the Ecole de Théâtre du Théâtre National de Bretagne (Theatre School of the National Theatre of Brittany) in Rennes, a position he held until 1999. Also in 1999, Wenzel wrote and produced *Faire bleu* (performed 1999; published 2000; translated as *Rising Blue,* 2002), a piece he termed an echo to his first play, *Loin d'Hagondange. Faire Bleu* takes another look at the story of retired steelworkers, only this time, twenty-five years later, the retirees are Lucie, the daughter of the characters from *Loin d'Hagondange,* and her husband, André, who have inherited the country house from Lucie's parents. Whereas his father-in-law tried to inject meaning in his life by spending long days tinkering in his workshop,

Monique Brun and Olivier Perrier in Wenzel's Faire bleu *(translated as* Rising Blue, *2002), Centre Dramatique National, Montluçon, 1999 (from <http://www.theatre-contemporain.net/spectacles/fairbleu/photo/hag2.jpg>)*

André fills the void of his now purposeless life trying to better himself, by constantly watching video documentaries and studying astronomy. Whereas her mother filled the void by constantly cleaning, Lucie occupies herself with a constant acquisition of new household appliances and decorations for their home. And while George and Marie reminisced fondly about their lives in Hagondange and wondered about their children, still working in the factory, André and Lucie have no more steelworks to imagine: the plant has been torn down, and a theme park has been built on its grounds. In fact, their own children are now making their living working in the amusement park, dressing up as Schtroumpfs, Smurf-like blue cartoon characters. The soberness of *Loin d'Hagondange* is replaced in *Faire bleu* by a kind of absurd grotesqueness. George was depressed without his work routine; André progresses in his depression to a state of near hysteria, contemplating the mysteries of the universe and the lack of meaning in life. The consumerism of the end of the twentieth century is represented in their constant spending on appliances and videos, which for André sometimes include pornography. Society's attitude toward the people at the bottom seems to be even more cynical—use them up and throw them away without a second thought. *Faire bleu* and *Loin d'Hagondange* were produced for several months "en dyptique" (in tandem) to give audiences a chance to experience the transformation.

Wenzel continues to work in many aspects of the theater, most notably as a director and teacher, supporting new dramatists in French theater. He also has acted in several movies, including *Un Médecin des lumières* (Doctor of Light) in 1987, directed by René Allio; *Nuits noires* (Black Nights) in 1989, directed by Gisèle Cavali; *La Vie de Bohême* (Bohemian Life) in 1991, directed by Aki Kaurismäki; and *Jo et Marie* (Jo and Marie) in 1993, directed by Tania Stöcklin.

Jean-Paul Wenzel has drawn attention to the drama found in everyday life and played a central role in developing the school of drama now known as *Théâtre du quotidien* (Everyday Theater). His plays are a somber, often authentic reflection of the turbulent world he perceives, and he makes no apology for their cynical quality. In a short piece published in the journal *Théâtre public* in 1987, Wenzel explains, "A ceux qui trouvent mes pièces et mon univers trop pessimistes, je voudrais leur donner la réponse que m'a faite Heiner Müller pendant une conversation: 'Non, je ne suis pas un auteur pessimiste, car je crois qu'il y aura non seulement une troisième guerre mondiale mais aussi une quatrième'" (To those who find my plays and my universe too pessimistic, I would like to give them the response made to me by Heiner Müller during a conversation: "No, I am not a pessimistic author, for I believe that not only will there be a third world war, but also a fourth"). He is also noteworthy for his innovative technique, "polylogue." As he recounts in an interview published in 1979, one evening, there was a guy in the corner of the theater, who jokingly said to him, "'Ce que vous faites, c'est du vent!' En effet, nous revendiquons de faire du vent! Une société où le vent ne souffle plus est une société dangereuse!" ("What you are doing is just wind [hot air]!" In effect, we want to make wind [fan the flames]! A society where the wind no longer blows is a dangerous society!).

Interviews:

N. Collet, "Loin d'Hagondange. Entretien avec Jean-Paul Wenzel," *Théâtre public*, 5–6 (1975): 21–22;

Y. Davis, "Ce que vous faites, c'est du vent. Entretien avec Jean-Louis Hourdin, Olivier Perrier, et Jean-Paul Wenzel," *Théâtre public*, 28–29 (1979): 3–8.

References:

T. Bishop, "Theater and the Everyday in France: Le *Théâtre du Quotidien*," in *The Art of the Everyday: The Quotidien in Postwar French Culture*, edited by L. Gumpert (New York: New York University Press, 1997), pp. 65–78;

David Bradby, *Modern French Drama 1940–1990* (Cambridge, Mass.: Cambridge University Press, 1991), pp. 241–246;

E. M. Donnachie, "Serge Rezvani and France's Théâtre Ouvert: Clash between Dramatist and Producer," *Modern Drama*, 22, no. 1 (1979): 67–77;

Colette Godard and France Mugler, "Théâtre Ouvert and Drama Creation in France," *Sub-Stance: A Review of Theory and Criticism*, nos. 18–19 (1977): 73–80;

"Jean-Paul Wenzel" <http://www.theatre-contemporain.net/avrildesauteurs/loin.htm>;

David Jeffery, "Théâtre Ouvert," *Theatre Research International*, 9 (Spring 1984): 59–73;

Bettina L. Knapp, *French Theatre since 1968* (New York: Twayne / London: Prentice Hall, 1995).

Checklist of Further Readings

Artaud, Antonin. *The Theatre and Its Double,* translated by Mary Caroline Richards. New York: Grove, 1958.

Béhar, Henri. "Alfred Jarry et le théâtre français à la fin du XIXe siècle," in *1894: European Theatre in Turmoil—Meaning and Significance of the Theatre a Hundred Years Ago,* edited by Hub Hermans, Wessel Krul, and Hans van Maanen. Amsterdam: Rodopi, 1996, pp. 41–54.

Bishop, Tom. *From the Left Bank: Reflections on the Modern French Theatre and Novel.* New York: New York University Press, 1997.

Bishop. "Theater and the Everyday in France: Le Théâtre du Quotidien," in *The Art of the Everyday: The Quotidian in Postwar French Culture.* New York: New York University Press, 1997, pp. 65–77.

Bradby, David. *Modern French Drama 1940–1990,* revised and updated edition. Cambridge: Cambridge University Press, 1991.

Calleran, Jeanne, and Jenny S. Spencer, eds. *Staging Resistance: Essays on Political Theatre.* Ann Arbor: University of Michigan Press, 1998.

Cohn, Ruby. "Ariane Mnouchkine: Playwright of a Collective," in *Feminine Focus: The New Women Playwrights,* edited by Enoch Brater. Oxford: Oxford University Press, 1989, pp. 53–63.

Cohn. *Currents in Contemporary Drama.* Bloomington: Indiana University Press, 1969.

Conley, Francine Heather. "La Création d'un espace: The Politics of Space in the Early Works of the Théâtre du Soleil." Dissertation, University of Wisconsin, 1998.

Daniels, May. *The French Drama of the Unspoken.* Westport, Conn.: Greenwood Press, 1977.

Donahue, Thomas J. "Mnouchkine, Vilar, and Copeau: Popular Theatre and Paradox," *Modern Language Studies,* 21, no. 4 (Fall 1991): 31–42.

Epstein, Lisa Jo. "Identity in the Making: Ariane Mnouchkine and the Théâtre du Soleil." Dissertation, University of Texas, 1998.

Esslin, Martin. *The Theatre of the Absurd.* Garden City, N.Y.: Doubleday, 1969.

Finter, Helga. "Antonin Artaud and the Impossible Theatre: The Legacy of the Theatre of Cruelty," translated by Matthew Griffin, *The Drama Review: A Journal of Performance Studies,* 41, no. 4 (Winter 1997): 15–40.

Fletcher, John, ed. *Forces in Modern French Drama.* London: University of London Press, 1972.

Fowlie, Wallace. *Dionysus in Paris: A Guide to Contemporary French Theater.* New York: Meridian, 1960.

From Stage to Street, Yale French Studies, 46 (1971).

Gaensbauer, Deborah B. *French Theatre of the Absurd.* Boston: Twayne, 1991.

Guicharnaud, Jacques. *Modern French Theatre from Giraudoux to Genet.* New Haven: Yale University Press, 1967.

Hand, Richard J., and Michael Wilson. "The Grand Guignol: Aspects of Theory and Practice," *Theatre Research International,* 25, no. 3 (Autumn 2000): 266–275.

Hollier, Denis, ed. *A New History of French Literature.* Cambridge, Mass.: Harvard University Press, 1989.

Ionesco, Eugène. *Notes and Counternotes: Writings on the Theatre,* translated by Donald Watson. New York: Grove, 1964.

Kiernander, Adrian. "The Role of Ariane Mnouchkine at the Théâtre du Soleil," *Modern Drama*, 33, no. 3 (September 1990): 322–331.

Knapp, Bettina. *French Theatre Since 1968*. New York: Twayne, 1995.

Knapp. "The Reign of the Theatrical Director: Antoine and Lugné-Poë," *The French Review: Journal of the American Association of Teachers of French*, 61, no. 6 (May 1988): 866–877.

Knowles, Dorothy. *French Drama of the Interwar Years, 1918–1939*. London: Harrap, 1967.

Lagarde, André, and Laurent Michard. *XXe siècle: Les Grands auteurs français*. Paris: Bordas, 1962.

The Modern Theatre and Its Background, Yale French Studies, 3, no. 1 (1950).

Motley: Today's French Theatre, Yale French Studies, 14 (Winter 1954–1955).

Ogden, Phillip. "Le Théâtre Libre," *Modern Language Notes*, 12, no. 5 (May 1897): 146–154.

Pronko, Leonard. *Avant-Garde: The Experimental Theater in France*. Berkeley: University of California Press, 1962.

Richardson, Helen Elizabeth. "The Théâtre du Soleil and the Quest for Popular Theatre in the Twentieth Century." Dissertation, University of California, Berkeley, 1991.

Roberts, Ann T. "Brecht and Artaud: Their Impact on American Theatre of the 1960s and 1970s," in *Myths and Realities of Contemporary French Theatre: Comparative Views*, edited by Patricia Hopkins and Wendell Aycock. Lubbock: Texas Tech Press, 1985, pp. 85–98.

Stafford, Andy. "Constructing a Radical Popular Theatre: Roland Barthes, Brecht and Théâtre populaire," *French Cultural Studies*, 7, no. 1 (February 1996): 33–48.

Stafford. "'Un Théâtre grand et civique': Shakespeare and Popular Theatre in Post-War France," *Actes de Langue Française et de Linguistique/Symposium on French Language and Linguistics*, 10–11 (1997–1998): 145–153.

Whitton, David. "Whatever Happened to Théâtre Populaire?: The Unfinished History of People's Theatre in France," *European Studies: A Journal of European Culture, History, and Politics*, 17 (2001): 53–71.

Contributors

Elizabeth M. Anthony .... Wake Forest University
Martine Antle .... University of North Carolina at Chapel Hill
Brett Bowles .... Iowa State University
Catharine Savage Brosman .... Tulane University
Culley Jane Carson .... Austin Peay State University
Rosemary Plater-Zyberk Clark ....
Francine Heather Conley .... College of St. Catherine
Dale Cosper... Whitman College
Jerry L. Curtis .... Ohio State University–Newark
Kevin Elstob .... California State University, Sacramento
Klaus Engelhardt... Lewis and Clark College
Meredith Goldsmith .... Whitman College
Alexander Hertich.. Bradley University
Sarah Hurlburt .... Whitman College
Guy F. Imhoff .... Saint Bonaventure University
John Ireland... University of Illinois at Chicago
Henriette Javorek .... University of Hamburg
Drew Jones .... Queens College, The City University of New York
Kristy Clark Koth ....
Christophe Lagier .... California State University, Los Angeles
Patricia Lancaster .... Rollins College
Susan McCready.. University of South Alabama
Inas Messiha .... Pennsylvania State University
Christine E. B. Moritz.. University of Northern Colorado
Madhuri Mukherjee .... William Paterson University
Mary Anne O'Neil .... Whitman College
Jason Owens .... South Dakota State University
Michel Rocchi .... University of Puget Sound
Nicole Simek .... Whitman College
Jeanine Teodorescu-Regier .... Elmhurst College
Kristin M. Vining-Stauffer.. Whitman College

Cumulative Index

Dictionary of Literary Biography, Volumes 1-321
Dictionary of Literary Biography Yearbook, 1980-2002
Dictionary of Literary Biography Documentary Series, Volumes 1-19
Concise Dictionary of American Literary Biography, Volumes 1-7
Concise Dictionary of British Literary Biography, Volumes 1-8
Concise Dictionary of World Literary Biography, Volumes 1-4

Cumulative Index

DLB before number: *Dictionary of Literary Biography,* Volumes 1-321
Y before number: *Dictionary of Literary Biography Yearbook,* 1980-2002
DS before number: *Dictionary of Literary Biography Documentary Series,* Volumes 1-19
CDALB before number: *Concise Dictionary of American Literary Biography,* Volumes 1-7
CDBLB before number: *Concise Dictionary of British Literary Biography,* Volumes 1-8
CDWLB before number: *Concise Dictionary of World Literary Biography,* Volumes 1-4

A

Aakjær, Jeppe 1866-1930 ... DLB-214
Aarestrup, Emil 1800-1856 ... DLB-300
Abbey, Edward 1927-1989 ... DLB-256, 275
Abbey, Edwin Austin 1852-1911 ... DLB-188
Abbey, Maj. J. R. 1894-1969 ... DLB-201
Abbey Press ... DLB-49
The Abbey Theatre and Irish Drama, 1900-1945 ... DLB-10
Abbot, Willis J. 1863-1934 ... DLB-29
Abbott, Edwin A. 1838-1926 ... DLB-178
Abbott, Jacob 1803-1879 ... DLB-1, 42, 243
Abbott, Lee K. 1947- ... DLB-130
Abbott, Lyman 1835-1922 ... DLB-79
Abbott, Robert S. 1868-1940 ... DLB-29, 91
'Abd al-Hamid al-Katib circa 689-750 ... DLB-311
Abe Kōbō 1924-1993 ... DLB-182
Abelaira, Augusto 1926- ... DLB-287
Abelard, Peter circa 1079-1142? ... DLB-115, 208
Abelard-Schuman ... DLB-46
Abell, Arunah S. 1806-1888 ... DLB-43
Abell, Kjeld 1901-1961 ... DLB-214
Abercrombie, Lascelles 1881-1938 ... DLB-19
The Friends of the Dymock Poets ... Y-00
Aberdeen University Press Limited ... DLB-106
Abish, Walter 1931- ... DLB-130, 227
Ablesimov, Aleksandr Onisimovich 1742-1783 ... DLB-150
Abraham à Sancta Clara 1644-1709 ... DLB-168
Abrahams, Peter 1919- ... DLB-117, 225; CDWLB-3
Abramov, Fedor Aleksandrovich 1920-1983 ... DLB-302
Abrams, M. H. 1912- ... DLB-67
Abramson, Jesse 1904-1979 ... DLB-241
Abrogans circa 790-800 ... DLB-148
Abschatz, Hans Aßmann von 1646-1699 ... DLB-168
Abse, Dannie 1923- ... DLB-27, 245
Abu al-'Atahiyah 748-825? ... DLB-311

Abu Nuwas circa 757-814 or 815 ... DLB-311
Abu Tammam circa 805-845 ... DLB-311
Abutsu-ni 1221-1283 ... DLB-203
Academy Chicago Publishers ... DLB-46
Accius circa 170 B.C.-circa 80 B.C. ... DLB-211
"An account of the death of the Chevalier de La Barre," Voltaire ... DLB-314
Accrocca, Elio Filippo 1923-1996 ... DLB-128
Ace Books ... DLB-46
Achebe, Chinua 1930- ... DLB-117; CDWLB-3
Achtenberg, Herbert 1938- ... DLB-124
Ackerman, Diane 1948- ... DLB-120
Ackroyd, Peter 1949- ... DLB-155, 231
Acorn, Milton 1923-1986 ... DLB-53
Acosta, José de 1540-1600 ... DLB-318
Acosta, Oscar Zeta 1935?-1974? ... DLB-82
Acosta Torres, José 1925- ... DLB-209
Actors Theatre of Louisville ... DLB-7
Adair, Gilbert 1944- ... DLB-194
Adair, James 1709?-1783? ... DLB-30
Aðalsteinn Kristmundsson (see Steinn Steinarr)
Adam, Graeme Mercer 1839-1912 ... DLB-99
Adam, Robert Borthwick, II 1863-1940 ... DLB-187
Adame, Leonard 1947- ... DLB-82
Adameşteanu, Gabriel 1942- ... DLB-232
Adamic, Louis 1898-1951 ... DLB-9
Adamov, Arthur Surenovitch 1908-1970 ... DLB-321
Adamovich, Georgii 1894-1972 ... DLB-317
Adams, Abigail 1744-1818 ... DLB-183, 200
Adams, Alice 1926-1999 ... DLB-234; Y-86
Adams, Bertha Leith (Mrs. Leith Adams, Mrs. R. S. de Courcy Laffan) 1837?-1912 ... DLB-240
Adams, Brooks 1848-1927 ... DLB-47
Adams, Charles Francis, Jr. 1835-1915 ... DLB-47
Adams, Douglas 1952-2001 ... DLB-261; Y-83
Adams, Franklin P. 1881-1960 ... DLB-29
Adams, Hannah 1755-1832 ... DLB-200
Adams, Henry 1838-1918 ... DLB-12, 47, 189
Adams, Herbert Baxter 1850-1901 ... DLB-47

Adams, James Truslow 1878-1949 ... DLB-17; DS-17
Adams, John 1735-1826 ... DLB-31, 183
Adams, John Quincy 1767-1848 ... DLB-37
Adams, Léonie 1899-1988 ... DLB-48
Adams, Levi 1802-1832 ... DLB-99
Adams, Richard 1920- ... DLB-261
Adams, Samuel 1722-1803 ... DLB-31, 43
Adams, Sarah Fuller Flower 1805-1848 ... DLB-199
Adams, Thomas 1582/1583-1652 ... DLB-151
Adams, William Taylor 1822-1897 ... DLB-42
J. S. and C. Adams [publishing house] ... DLB-49
Adamson, Harold 1906-1980 ... DLB-265
Adamson, Sir John 1867-1950 ... DLB-98
Adamson, Robert 1943- ... DLB-289
Adcock, Arthur St. John 1864-1930 ... DLB-135
Adcock, Betty 1938- ... DLB-105
"Certain Gifts" ... DLB-105
Tribute to James Dickey ... Y-97
Adcock, Fleur 1934- ... DLB-40
Addams, Jane 1860-1935 ... DLB-303
Addison, Joseph 1672-1719 ... DLB-101; CDBLB-2
Ade, George 1866-1944 ... DLB-11, 25
Adeler, Max (see Clark, Charles Heber)
Adlard, Mark 1932- ... DLB-261
Adler, Richard 1921- ... DLB-265
Adonias Filho (Adonias Aguiar Filho) 1915-1990 ... DLB-145, 307
Adorno, Theodor W. 1903-1969 ... DLB-242
Adoum, Jorge Enrique 1926- ... DLB-283
Advance Publishing Company ... DLB-49
Ady, Endre 1877-1919 ... DLB-215; CDWLB-4
AE 1867-1935 ... DLB-19; CDBLB-5
Ælfric circa 955-circa 1010 ... DLB-146
Aeschines circa 390 B.C.-circa 320 B.C. ... DLB-176
Aeschylus 525-524 B.C.-456-455 B.C. ... DLB-176; CDWLB-1
Aesthetic Papers ... DLB-1

Aesthetics
   Eighteenth-Century Aesthetic
      Theories DLB-31

African Literature
   Letter from Khartoum Y-90

African American
   Afro-American Literary Critics:
      An Introduction DLB-33

   The Black Aesthetic: Background DS-8

   The Black Arts Movement,
      by Larry Neal DLB-38

   Black Theaters and Theater Organizations
      in America, 1961-1982:
      A Research List DLB-38

   Black Theatre: A Forum [excerpts] . . . DLB-38

   Callaloo [journal] Y-87

   Community and Commentators:
      Black Theatre and Its Critics DLB-38

   The Emergence of Black
      Women Writers DS-8

   The Hatch-Billops Collection DLB-76

   A Look at the Contemporary Black
      Theatre Movement DLB-38

   The Moorland-Spingarn Research
      Center DLB-76

   "The Negro as a Writer," by
      G. M. McClellan DLB-50

   "Negro Poets and Their Poetry," by
      Wallace Thurman DLB-50

   Olaudah Equiano and Unfinished Journeys:
      The Slave-Narrative Tradition and
      Twentieth-Century Continuities, by
      Paul Edwards and Pauline T.
      Wangman DLB-117

   PHYLON (Fourth Quarter, 1950),
      The Negro in Literature:
      The Current Scene DLB-76

   The Schomburg Center for Research
      in Black Culture DLB-76

   Three Documents [poets], by John
      Edward Bruce DLB-50

After Dinner Opera Company Y-92

Agassiz, Elizabeth Cary 1822-1907 . . . . . . DLB-189

Agassiz, Louis 1807-1873 . . . . DLB-1, 235

Agee, James
   1909-1955 . . . . DLB-2, 26, 152; CDALB-1

   The Agee Legacy: A Conference at
      the University of Tennessee
      at Knoxville Y-89

Aguilera Malta, Demetrio 1909-1981 . . . . DLB-145

Aguirre, Isidora 1919- DLB-305

Agustini, Delmira 1886-1914 . . . . DLB-290

Ahlin, Lars 1915-1997 . . . . DLB-257

Ai 1947- DLB-120

Aichinger, Ilse 1921- DLB-85, 299

Aickman, Robert 1914-1981 . . . . DLB-261

Aidoo, Ama Ata 1942- DLB-117; CDWLB-3

Aiken, Conrad
   1889-1973 . . . . DLB-9, 45, 102; CDALB-5

Aiken, Joan 1924-2004 . . . . DLB-161

Aikin, Lucy 1781-1864 . . . . DLB-144, 163

Ainsworth, William Harrison
   1805-1882 . . . . DLB-21

Aïssé, Charlotte-Elizabeth 1694?-1733 . . . DLB-313

Aistis, Jonas 1904-1973 . . . . . DLB-220; CDWLB-4

Aitken, George A. 1860-1917 . . . . DLB-149

Robert Aitken [publishing house] DLB-49

Aitmatov, Chingiz 1928- DLB-302

Akenside, Mark 1721-1770 . . . . DLB-109

Akhmatova, Anna Andreevna
   1889-1966 . . . . DLB-295

Akins, Zoë 1886-1958 . . . . DLB-26

Aksakov, Ivan Sergeevich 1823-1826 . . . . . DLB-277

Aksakov, Sergei Timofeevich
   1791-1859 . . . . DLB-198

Aksyonov, Vassily 1932- DLB-302

Akunin, Boris (Grigorii Shalvovich
   Chkhartishvili) 1956- DLB-285

Akutagawa Ryūnosuke 1892-1927 . . . . . . DLB-180

Alabaster, William 1568-1640 . . . . DLB-132

Alain de Lille circa 1116-1202/1203 . . . . DLB-208

Alain-Fournier 1886-1914 . . . . DLB-65

Alanus de Insulis (see Alain de Lille)

Alarcón, Francisco X. 1954- DLB-122

Alarcón, Justo S. 1930- DLB-209

Alba, Nanina 1915-1968 . . . . DLB-41

Albee, Edward 1928- . . . DLB-7, 266; CDALB-1

Albert, Octavia 1853-ca. 1889 . . . . DLB-221

Albert the Great circa 1200-1280 . . . . . . DLB-115

Alberti, Rafael 1902-1999 . . . . DLB-108

Albertinus, Aegidius circa 1560-1620 . . . . DLB-164

Alcaeus born circa 620 B.C. DLB-176

Alcoforado, Mariana, the Portuguese Nun
   1640-1723 . . . . DLB-287

Alcott, Amos Bronson
   1799-1888 . . . . DLB-1, 223; DS-5

Alcott, Louisa May 1832-1888
   . . . DLB-1, 42, 79, 223, 239; DS-14; CDALB-3

Alcott, William Andrus 1798-1859 . . . . DLB-1, 243

Alcuin circa 732-804 . . . . DLB-148

Aldana, Francisco de 1537-1578 . . . . DLB-318

Aldanov, Mark (Mark Landau)
   1886-1957 . . . . DLB-317

Alden, Henry Mills 1836-1919 . . . . DLB-79

Alden, Isabella 1841-1930 . . . . DLB-42

John B. Alden [publishing house] DLB-49

Alden, Beardsley, and Company DLB-49

Aldington, Richard
   1892-1962 . . . . DLB-20, 36, 100, 149

Aldis, Dorothy 1896-1966 . . . . DLB-22

Aldis, H. G. 1863-1919 . . . . DLB-184

Aldiss, Brian W. 1925- DLB-14, 261, 271

Aldrich, Thomas Bailey
   1836-1907 . . . . DLB-42, 71, 74, 79

Alegría, Ciro 1909-1967 . . . . DLB-113

Alegría, Claribel 1924- DLB-145, 283

Aleixandre, Vicente 1898-1984 . . . . DLB-108

Aleksandravičius, Jonas (see Aistis, Jonas)

Aleksandrov, Aleksandr Andreevich
   (see Durova, Nadezhda Andreevna)

Alekseeva, Marina Anatol'evna
   (see Marinina, Aleksandra)

d'Alembert, Jean Le Rond 1717-1783 . . . . DLB-313

Alencar, José de 1829-1877 . . . . DLB-307

Aleramo, Sibilla (Rena Pierangeli Faccio)
   1876-1960 . . . . DLB-114, 264

Aleshkovsky, Petr Markovich 1957- DLB-285

Aleshkovsky, Yuz 1929- DLB-317

Alexander, Cecil Frances 1818-1895 . . . . DLB-199

Alexander, Charles 1868-1923 . . . . DLB-91

Charles Wesley Alexander
   [publishing house] DLB-49

Alexander, James 1691-1756 . . . . DLB-24

Alexander, Lloyd 1924- DLB-52

Alexander, Sir William, Earl of Stirling
   1577?-1640 . . . . DLB-121

Alexie, Sherman 1966- DLB-175, 206, 278

Alexis, Willibald 1798-1871 . . . . DLB-133

Alf laylah wa laylah
   ninth century onward DLB-311

Alfred, King 849-899 . . . . DLB-146

Alger, Horatio, Jr. 1832-1899 . . . . DLB-42

Algonquin Books of Chapel Hill DLB-46

Algren, Nelson
   1909-1981 . . . . DLB-9; Y-81, 82; CDALB-1

   Nelson Algren: An International
      Symposium Y-00

'Ali ibn Abi Talib circa 600-661 . . . . DLB-311

Aljamiado Literature DLB-286

Allan, Andrew 1907-1974 . . . . DLB-88

Allan, Ted 1916-1995 . . . . DLB-68

Allbeury, Ted 1917- DLB-87

Alldritt, Keith 1935- DLB-14

Allen, Dick 1939- DLB-282

Allen, Ethan 1738-1789 . . . . DLB-31

Allen, Frederick Lewis 1890-1954 . . . . DLB-137

Allen, Gay Wilson 1903-1995 . . . . . DLB-103; Y-95

Allen, George 1808-1876 . . . . DLB-59

Allen, Grant 1848-1899 . . . . DLB-70, 92, 178

Allen, Henry W. 1912-1991 . . . . Y-85

Allen, Hervey 1889-1949 . . . . DLB-9, 45, 316

Allen, James 1739-1808 . . . . DLB-31

Allen, James Lane 1849-1925 . . . . DLB-71

Allen, Jay Presson 1922- DLB-26

John Allen and Company DLB-49

Allen, Paula Gunn 1939- DLB-175

Allen, Samuel W. 1917- DLB-41

Allen, Woody 1935- DLB-44

George Allen [publishing house] DLB-106

George Allen and Unwin Limited DLB-112

Allende, Isabel 1942- DLB-145; CDWLB-3

Alline, Henry 1748-1784 . . . . DLB-99

Allingham, Margery 1904-1966 . . . . DLB-77

   The Margery Allingham Society Y-98

Allingham, William 1824-1889 . . . . DLB-35

W. L. Allison [publishing house] DLB-49

The *Alliterative Morte Arthure and the Stanzaic Morte Arthur* circa 1350-1400 ....DLB-146

Allott, Kenneth 1912-1973 ....DLB-20

Allston, Washington 1779-1843 ....DLB-1, 235

Almeida, Manuel Antônio de 1831-1861 ....DLB-307

John Almon [publishing house] DLB-154

Alonzo, Dámaso 1898-1990...........DLB-108

Alsop, George 1636-post 1673 ....DLB-24

Alsop, Richard 1761-1815 ....DLB-37

Henry Altemus and Company..........DLB-49

Altenberg, Peter 1885-1919 ....DLB-81

Althusser, Louis 1918-1990 ....DLB-242

Altolaguirre, Manuel 1905-1959 ....DLB-108

Aluko, T. M. 1918- DLB-117

Alurista 1947- DLB-82

Alvarez, A. 1929- DLB-14, 40

Alvarez, Julia 1950- DLB-282

Alvaro, Corrado 1895-1956............DLB-264

Alver, Betti 1906-1989 ......DLB-220; CDWLB-4

Amadi, Elechi 1934- DLB-117

Amado, Jorge 1912-2001 ....DLB-113

Amalrik, Andrei 1938-1980 ....DLB-302

Ambler, Eric 1909-1998................DLB-77

The Library of America.................DLB-46

The Library of America: An Assessment After Two Decades Y-02

America: or, A Poem on the Settlement of the British Colonies, by Timothy Dwight DLB-37

American Bible Society Department of Library, Archives, and Institutional Research Y-97

American Conservatory Theatre DLB-7

American Culture American Proletarian Culture: The Twenties and Thirties........DS-11

Studies in American Jewish Literature.......Y-02

The American Library in Paris Y-93

American Literature The Literary Scene and Situation and... (Who Besides Oprah) Really Runs American Literature? Y-99

Who Owns American Literature, by Henry Taylor Y-94

Who Runs American Literature? Y-94

American News Company...............DLB-49

A Century of Poetry, a Lifetime of Collecting: J. M. Edelstein's Collection of Twentieth-Century American Poetry Y-02

The American Poets' Corner: The First Three Years (1983-1986)...............Y-86

American Publishing Company..........DLB-49

American Spectator [Editorial] Rationale From the Initial Issue of the American Spectator (November 1932)................DLB-137

American Stationers' Company..........DLB-49

The American Studies Association of Norway......................Y-00

American Sunday-School Union DLB-49

American Temperance Union DLB-49

American Tract Society DLB-49

The American Trust for the British Library ..Y-96

American Writers' Congress 25-27 April 1935 ....DLB-303

American Writers Congress The American Writers Congress (9-12 October 1981) Y-81

The American Writers Congress: A Report on Continuing Business Y-81

Ames, Fisher 1758-1808.................DLB-37

Ames, Mary Clemmer 1831-1884 ....DLB-23

Ames, William 1576-1633 ....DLB-281

Amfiteatrov, Aleksandr 1862-1938 ......DLB-317

Amiel, Henri-Frédéric 1821-1881........DLB-217

Amini, Johari M. 1935- DLB-41

Amis, Kingsley 1922-1995 ......DLB-15, 27, 100, 139, Y-96; CDBLB-7

Amis, Martin 1949- DLB-14, 194

Ammianus Marcellinus circa A.D. 330-A.D. 395 ....DLB-211

Ammons, A. R. 1926-2001 ....DLB-5, 165

Amory, Thomas 1691?-1788 ....DLB-39

Anania, Michael 1939- DLB-193

Anaya, Rudolfo A. 1937- DLB-82, 206, 278

Ancrene Riwle circa 1200-1225 ....DLB-146

Andersch, Alfred 1914-1980 ....DLB-69

Andersen, Benny 1929- DLB-214

Andersen, Hans Christian 1805-1875 ....DLB-300

Anderson, Alexander 1775-1870 ....DLB-188

Anderson, David 1929- DLB-241

Anderson, Frederick Irving 1877-1947....DLB-202

Anderson, Margaret 1886-1973 ....DLB-4, 91

Anderson, Maxwell 1888-1959 ....DLB-7, 228

Anderson, Patrick 1915-1979............DLB-68

Anderson, Paul Y. 1893-1938 ....DLB-29

Anderson, Poul 1926-2001 ....DLB-8

Tribute to Isaac Asimov Y-92

Anderson, Robert 1750-1830...........DLB-142

Anderson, Robert 1917- DLB-7

Anderson, Sherwood 1876-1941 .....DLB-4, 9, 86; DS-1; CDALB-4

Andrade, Jorge (Aluísio Jorge Andrade Franco) 1922-1984 ....DLB-307

Andrade, Mario de 1893-1945..........DLB-307

Andrade, Oswald de (José Oswald de Sousa Andrade) 1890-1954 ....DLB-307

Andreae, Johann Valentin 1586-1654 ....DLB-164

Andreas Capellanus fl. circa 1185 ....DLB-208

Andreas-Salomé, Lou 1861-1937 ....DLB-66

Andreev, Leonid Nikolaevich 1871-1919 ....DLB-295

Andres, Stefan 1906-1970 ....DLB-69

Andresen, Sophia de Mello Breyner 1919- DLB-287

Andreu, Blanca 1959- DLB-134

Andrewes, Lancelot 1555-1626 .....DLB-151, 172

Andrews, Charles M. 1863-1943.........DLB-17

Andrews, Miles Peter ?-1814 ....DLB-89

Andrews, Stephen Pearl 1812-1886......DLB-250

Andrian, Leopold von 1875-1951 ....DLB-81

Andrić, Ivo 1892-1975 ......DLB-147; CDWLB-4

Andrieux, Louis (see Aragon, Louis)

Andrus, Silas, and Son..................DLB-49

Andrzejewski, Jerzy 1909-1983 ....DLB-215

Angell, James Burrill 1829-1916 ....DLB-64

Angell, Roger 1920- DLB-171, 185

Angelou, Maya 1928- DLB-38; CDALB-7

Tribute to Julian Mayfield.............Y-84

Anger, Jane fl. 1589 ....DLB-136

Angers, Félicité (see Conan, Laure)

The *Anglo-Saxon Chronicle* circa 890-1154 ....DLB-146

Angus and Robertson (UK) Limited DLB-112

Anhalt, Edward 1914-2000 ....DLB-26

Anissimov, Myriam 1943- DLB-299

Anker, Nini Roll 1873-1942............DLB-297

Annenkov, Pavel Vasil'evich 1813?-1887 ....DLB-277

Annensky, Innokentii Fedorovich 1855-1909 ....DLB-295

Henry F. Anners [publishing house] DLB-49

Annolied between 1077 and 1081.........DLB-148

Anouilh, Jean 1910-1987 ....DLB-321

Anscombe, G. E. M. 1919-2001.........DLB-262

Anselm of Canterbury 1033-1109 ....DLB-115

Anstey, F. 1856-1934..............DLB-141, 178

'Antarah ('Antar ibn Shaddad al-'Absi) ?-early seventh century? DLB-311

Anthologizing New Formalism DLB-282

Anthony, Michael 1932- DLB-125

Anthony, Piers 1934- DLB-8

Anthony, Susanna 1726-1791...........DLB-200

Antin, David 1932- DLB-169

Antin, Mary 1881-1949 ....DLB-221; Y-84

Anton Ulrich, Duke of Brunswick-Lüneburg 1633-1714 ....DLB-168

Antschel, Paul (see Celan, Paul)

Antunes, António Lobo 1942- DLB-287

Anyidoho, Kofi 1947- DLB-157

Anzaldúa, Gloria 1942- DLB-122

Anzengruber, Ludwig 1839-1889 ....DLB-129

Apess, William 1798-1839 ....DLB-175, 243

Apodaca, Rudy S. 1939- DLB-82

Apollinaire, Guillaume 1880-1918...DLB-258, 321

Apollonius Rhodius third century B.C. DLB-176

Apple, Max 1941- DLB-130

Appelfeld, Aḥaron 1932- DLB-299

D. Appleton and Company DLB-49

Appleton-Century-Crofts DLB-46	Armitage, G. E. (Robert Edric) 1956- . . DLB-267	Asimov, Isaac 1920-1992 . . . . DLB-8; Y-92
Applewhite, James 1935- DLB-105	Armstrong, Martin Donisthorpe 1882-1974 . . . . DLB-197	Tribute to John Ciardi Y-86
Tribute to James Dickey Y-97	Armstrong, Richard 1903-1986 . . . . DLB-160	Askew, Anne circa 1521-1546 . . . . DLB-136
Apple-wood Books DLB-46	Armstrong, Terence Ian Fytton (see Gawsworth, John)	Aspazija 1865-1943 . . . . DLB-220; CDWLB-4
April, Jean-Pierre 1948- DLB-251	Arnauld, Antoine 1612-1694 . . . . DLB-268	Asselin, Olivar 1874-1937 . . . . DLB-92
Apukhtin, Aleksei Nikolaevich 1840-1893 . . . . DLB-277	Arndt, Ernst Moritz 1769-1860 . . . . DLB-90	The Association of American Publishers Y-99
Apuleius circa A.D. 125-post A.D. 164 . . . . DLB-211; CDWLB-1	Arnim, Achim von 1781-1831 . . . . DLB-90	The Association for Documentary Editing Y-00
Aquin, Hubert 1929-1977 . . . . DLB-53	Arnim, Bettina von 1785-1859 . . . . DLB-90	The Association for the Study of Literature and Environment (ASLE) Y-99
Aquinas, Thomas 1224/1225-1274 . . . . . . DLB-115	Arnim, Elizabeth von (Countess Mary Annette Beauchamp Russell) 1866-1941 . . . . DLB-197	Astell, Mary 1666-1731 . . . . DLB-252
Aragon, Louis 1897-1982 . . . . DLB-72, 258	Arno Press DLB-46	Astley, Thea 1925- DLB-289
Aragon, Vernacular Translations in the Crowns of Castile and 1352-1515 . . . DLB-286	Arnold, Edwin 1832-1904 . . . . DLB-35	Astley, William (see Warung, Price)
Aralica, Ivan 1930- DLB-181	Arnold, Edwin L. 1857-1935 . . . . DLB-178	Asturias, Miguel Ángel 1899-1974 . . . . DLB-113, 290; CDWLB-3
Aratus of Soli circa 315 B.C.-circa 239 B.C. DLB-176	Arnold, Matthew 1822-1888 . . . . DLB-32, 57; CDBLB-4	Atava, S. (see Terpigorev, Sergei Nikolaevich)
Arbasino, Alberto 1930- DLB-196	Preface to *Poems* (1853) DLB-32	Atheneum Publishers DLB-46
Arbor House Publishing Company DLB-46	Arnold, Thomas 1795-1842 . . . . DLB-55	Atherton, Gertrude 1857-1948 . . . . . DLB-9, 78, 186
Arbuthnot, John 1667-1735 . . . . DLB-101	Edward Arnold [publishing house] DLB-112	Athlone Press DLB-112
Arcadia House DLB-46	Arnott, Peter 1962- DLB-233	Atkins, Josiah circa 1755-1781 . . . . DLB-31
Arce, Julio G. (see Ulica, Jorge)	Arnow, Harriette Simpson 1908-1986 . . . . . DLB-6	Atkins, Russell 1926- DLB-41
Archer, William 1856-1924 . . . . DLB-10	Arp, Bill (see Smith, Charles Henry)	Atkinson, Kate 1951- DLB-267
Archilochhus mid seventh century B.C.E. DLB-176	Arpino, Giovanni 1927-1987 . . . . DLB-177	Atkinson, Louisa 1834-1872 . . . . DLB-230
The Archpoet circa 1130?-? DLB-148	Arrabal, Fernando 1932- DLB-321	The Atlantic Monthly Press DLB-46
Archpriest Avvakum (Petrovich) 1620?-1682 . . . . DLB-150	Arrebo, Anders 1587-1637 . . . . DLB-300	Attaway, William 1911-1986 . . . . DLB-76
Arden, John 1930- DLB-13, 245	Arreola, Juan José 1918-2001 . . . . DLB-113	Atwood, Margaret 1939- DLB-53, 251
Arden of Faversham DLB-62	Arrian circa 89-circa 155 . . . . DLB-176	Aubert, Alvin 1930- DLB-41
Ardis Publishers Y-89	J. W. Arrowsmith [publishing house] DLB-106	Aubert de Gaspé, Phillipe-Ignace-François 1814-1841 . . . . DLB-99
Ardizzone, Edward 1900-1979 . . . . DLB-160	Arrufat, Antón 1935- DLB-305	Aubert de Gaspé, Phillipe-Joseph 1786-1871 . . . . DLB-99
Arellano, Juan Estevan 1947- DLB-122	Art	
The Arena Publishing Company DLB-49	John Dos Passos: Artist Y-99	Aubin, Napoléon 1812-1890 . . . . DLB-99
Arena Stage DLB-7	The First Post-Impressionist Exhibition DS-5	Aubin, Penelope 1685-circa 1731 . . . . DLB-39
Arenas, Reinaldo 1943-1990 . . . . DLB-145	The Omega Workshops DS-10	Preface to *The Life of Charlotta du Pont* (1723) DLB-39
Arendt, Hannah 1906-1975 . . . . DLB-242	The Second Post-Impressionist Exhibition DS-5	Aubrey-Fletcher, Henry Lancelot (see Wade, Henry)
Arensberg, Ann 1937- Y-82	Artaud, Antonin 1896-1948 . . . . DLB-258, 321	Auchincloss, Louis 1917- DLB-2, 244; Y-80
Arghezi, Tudor 1880-1967 . . . . DLB-220; CDWLB-4	Artel, Jorge 1909-1994 . . . . DLB-283	Auden, W. H. 1907-1973 . . . . DLB-10, 20; CDBLB-6
Arguedas, José María 1911-1969 . . . . DLB-113	Arthur, Timothy Shay 1809-1885 . . . . DLB-3, 42, 79, 250; DS-13	Audiberti, Jacques 1899-1965 . . . . DLB-321
Argüelles, Hugo 1932-2003 . . . . DLB-305	Artmann, H. C. 1921-2000 . . . . DLB-85	Audio Art in America: A Personal Memoir . . . Y-85
Argueta, Manlio 1936- DLB-145	Artsybashev, Mikhail Petrovich 1878-1927 . . . . DLB-295	Audubon, John James 1785-1851 . . . . DLB-248
'Arib al-Ma'muniyah 797-890 . . . . DLB-311	Arvin, Newton 1900-1963 . . . . DLB-103	Audubon, John Woodhouse 1812-1862 . . . . DLB-183
Arias, Ron 1941- DLB-82	Asch, Nathan 1902-1964 . . . . DLB-4, 28	Auerbach, Berthold 1812-1882 . . . . DLB-133
Arishima Takeo 1878-1923 . . . . DLB-180	Nathan Asch Remembers Ford Madox Ford, Sam Roth, and Hart Crane Y-02	Auernheimer, Raoul 1876-1948 . . . . DLB-81
Aristophanes circa 446 B.C.-circa 386 B.C. DLB-176; CDWLB-1	Ascham, Roger 1515/1516-1568 . . . . DLB-236	Augier, Emile 1820-1889 . . . . DLB-192
Aristotle 384 B.C.-322 B.C. DLB-176; CDWLB-1	Aseev, Nikolai Nikolaevich 1889-1963 . . . . DLB-295	Augustine 354-430 . . . . DLB-115
Ariyoshi Sawako 1931-1984 . . . . DLB-182	Ash, John 1948- DLB-40	Aulnoy, Marie-Catherine Le Jumel de Barneville, comtesse d' 1650/1651-1705 . . . . DLB-268
Arland, Marcel 1899-1986 . . . . DLB-72	Ashbery, John 1927- DLB-5, 165; Y-81	Aulus Gellius circa A.D. 125-circa A.D. 180? DLB-211
Arlen, Michael 1895-1956 . . . . DLB-36, 77, 162	Ashbridge, Elizabeth 1713-1755 . . . . DLB-200	
Arlt, Roberto 1900-1942 . . . . DLB-305	Ashburnham, Bertram Lord 1797-1878 . . . . DLB-184	Austen, Jane 1775-1817 . . . . . . DLB-116; CDBLB-3
Armah, Ayi Kwei 1939- . . . DLB-117; CDWLB-3	Ashendene Press DLB-112	Auster, Paul 1947- DLB-227
Armantrout, Rae 1947- DLB-193	Asher, Sandy 1942- Y-83	Austin, Alfred 1835-1913 . . . . DLB-35
Der arme Hartmann ?-after 1150 . . . . DLB-148	Ashton, Winifred (see Dane, Clemence)	Austin, J. L. 1911-1960 . . . . DLB-262
Armed Services Editions DLB-46		Austin, Jane Goodwin 1831-1894 . . . . DLB-202

Austin, John 1790-1859 ....DLB-262
Austin, Mary Hunter
    1868-1934 .... DLB-9, 78, 206, 221, 275
Austin, William 1778-1841..............DLB-74
Australie (Emily Manning)
    1845-1890 ....DLB-230
Authors and Newspapers Association DLB-46
Authors' Publishing Company...........DLB-49
Avallone, Michael 1924-1999......DLB-306; Y-99
    Tribute to John D. MacDonald......... Y-86
    Tribute to Kenneth Millar............. Y-83
    Tribute to Raymond Chandler......... Y-88
Avalon Books........................DLB-46
Avancini, Nicolaus 1611-1686 ....DLB-164
Avendaño, Fausto 1941- DLB-82
Averroës 1126-1198..................DLB-115
Avery, Gillian 1926- DLB-161
Avicenna 980-1037...................DLB-115
Ávila Jiménez, Antonio 1898-1965.......DLB-283
Avison, Margaret 1918-1987 ....DLB-53
Avon Books DLB-46
Avyžius, Jonas 1922-1999 ....DLB-220
Awdry, Wilbert Vere 1911-1997 ....DLB-160
Awoonor, Kofi 1935- DLB-117
Ayckbourn, Alan 1939- DLB-13, 245
Ayer, A. J. 1910-1989.................DLB-262
Aymé, Marcel 1902-1967...............DLB-72
Aytoun, Sir Robert 1570-1638 ....DLB-121
Aytoun, William Edmondstoune
    1813-1865 ....DLB-32, 159
Azevedo, Aluísio 1857-1913............DLB-307
Azevedo, Manuel Antônio Álvares de
    1831-1852 ....DLB-307

B

B.V. (see Thomson, James)
Babbitt, Irving 1865-1933 ....DLB-63
Babbitt, Natalie 1932- DLB-52
John Babcock [publishing house]........DLB-49
Babel, Isaak Emmanuilovich
    1894-1940 ....DLB-272
Babits, Mihály 1883-1941 ...DLB-215; CDWLB-4
Babrius circa 150-200..................DLB-176
Babson, Marian 1929- DLB-276
Baca, Jimmy Santiago 1952- DLB-122
Bacchelli, Riccardo 1891-1985..........DLB-264
Bache, Benjamin Franklin 1769-1798 ....DLB-43
Bachelard, Gaston 1884-1962 ....DLB-296
Bacheller, Irving 1859-1950............DLB-202
Bachmann, Ingeborg 1926-1973..........DLB-85
Bačinskaitė-Bučienė, Salomėja (see Nėris, Salomėja)
Bacon, Delia 1811-1859 ....DLB-1, 243
Bacon, Francis
    1561-1626 ....DLB-151, 236, 252; CDBLB-1
Bacon, Sir Nicholas circa 1510-1579 ....DLB-132
Bacon, Roger circa 1214/1220-1292 ....DLB-115

Bacon, Thomas circa 1700-1768.........DLB-31
Bacovia, George
    1881-1957 ....DLB-220; CDWLB-4
Richard G. Badger and Company........DLB-49
Bagaduce Music Lending Library Y-00
Bage, Robert 1728-1801................DLB-39
Bagehot, Walter 1826-1877 ....DLB-55
Baggesen, Jens 1764-1826 ....DLB-300
Bagley, Desmond 1923-1983 ....DLB-87
Bagley, Sarah G. 1806-1848?............DLB-239
Bagnold, Enid 1889-1981 ..DLB-13, 160, 191, 245
Bagryana, Elisaveta
    1893-1991 ....DLB-147; CDWLB-4
Bahr, Hermann 1863-1934 ....DLB-81, 118
Bailey, Abigail Abbot
    1746-1815 ....DLB-200
Bailey, Alfred Goldsworthy 1905-1997 ....DLB-68
Bailey, H. C. 1878-1961................DLB-77
Bailey, Jacob 1731-1808................DLB-99
Bailey, Paul 1937- DLB-14, 271
Bailey, Philip James 1816-1902 ....DLB-32
Francis Bailey [publishing house]........DLB-49
Baillargeon, Pierre 1916-1967 ....DLB-88
Baillie, Hugh 1890-1966 ....DLB-29
Baillie, Joanna 1762-1851 ....DLB-93
Bailyn, Bernard 1922- DLB-17
Bain, Alexander
    English Composition and Rhetoric (1866)
    [excerpt] DLB-57
Bainbridge, Beryl 1933- DLB-14, 231
Baird, Irene 1901-1981 ....DLB-68
Baker, Augustine 1575-1641 ....DLB-151
Baker, Carlos 1909-1987 ....DLB-103
Baker, David 1954- DLB-120
Baker, George Pierce 1866-1935 ....DLB-266
Baker, Herschel C. 1914-1990..........DLB-111
Baker, Houston A., Jr. 1943- DLB-67
Baker, Howard
    Tribute to Caroline Gordon Y-81
    Tribute to Katherine Anne Porter....... Y-80
Baker, Nicholson 1957- DLB-227; Y-00
    Review of Nicholson Baker's Double Fold:
      Libraries and the Assault on Paper Y-00
Baker, Samuel White 1821-1893 ....DLB-166
Baker, Thomas 1656-1740.............DLB-213
Walter H. Baker Company
    ("Baker's Plays") DLB-49
The Baker and Taylor Company DLB-49
Bakhtin, Mikhail Mikhailovich
    1895-1975 ....DLB-242
Bakunin, Mikhail Aleksandrovich
    1814-1876 ....DLB-277
Balaban, John 1943- DLB-120
Bald, Wambly 1902-1990 ....DLB-4
Balde, Jacob 1604-1668 ....DLB-164
Balderston, John 1889-1954............DLB-26
Baldwin, James 1924-1987
    .....DLB-2, 7, 33, 249, 278; Y-87; CDALB-1

Baldwin, Joseph Glover
    1815-1864 ....DLB-3, 11, 248
Baldwin, Louisa (Mrs. Alfred Baldwin)
    1845-1925 ....DLB-240
Baldwin, William circa 1515-1563.......DLB-132
Richard and Anne Baldwin
    [publishing house]................DLB-170
Bale, John 1495-1563 ....DLB-132
Balestrini, Nanni 1935- DLB-128, 196
Balfour, Sir Andrew 1630-1694.........DLB-213
Balfour, Arthur James 1848-1930 ......DLB-190
Balfour, Sir James 1600-1657...........DLB-213
Ballantine Books DLB-46
Ballantyne, R. M. 1825-1894 ....DLB-163
Ballard, J. G. 1930- DLB-14, 207, 261, 319
Ballard, Martha Moore 1735-1812.......DLB-200
Ballerini, Luigi 1940- DLB-128
Ballou, Maturin Murray (Lieutenant Murray)
    1820-1895 ....DLB-79, 189
Robert O. Ballou [publishing house] DLB-46
Bal'mont, Konstantin Dmitrievich
    1867-1942....................DLB-295
Balzac, Guez de 1597?-1654 ....DLB-268
Balzac, Honoré de 1799-1855 ....DLB-119
Bambara, Toni Cade
    1939-1995 ....DLB-38, 218; CDALB-7
Bamford, Samuel 1788-1872 ....DLB-190
A. L. Bancroft and Company DLB-49
Bancroft, George 1800-1891 ...DLB-1, 30, 59, 243
Bancroft, Hubert Howe 1832-1918 ...DLB-47, 140
Bandeira, Manuel 1886-1968............DLB-307
Bandelier, Adolph F. 1840-1914 ....DLB-186
Bang, Herman 1857-1912 ....DLB-300
Bangs, John Kendrick 1862-1922 .....DLB-11, 79
Banim, John 1798-1842 ....DLB-116, 158, 159
Banim, Michael 1796-1874..........DLB-158, 159
Banks, Iain (M.) 1954- DLB-194, 261
Banks, John circa 1653-1706 ....DLB-80
Banks, Russell 1940- DLB-130, 278
Bannerman, Helen 1862-1946...........DLB-141
Bantam Books DLB-46
Banti, Anna 1895-1985 ....DLB-177
Banville, John 1945- DLB-14, 271
Banville, Théodore de 1823-1891 ....DLB-217
Baraka, Amiri
    1934- DLB-5, 7, 16, 38; DS-8; CDALB-1
Barańczak, Stanisław 1946- DLB-232
Baranskaia, Natal'ia Vladimirovna
    1908- DLB-302
Baratynsky, Evgenii Abramovich
    1800-1844 ....DLB-205
Barba-Jacob, Porfirio 1883-1942 ....DLB-283
Barbauld, Anna Laetitia
    1743-1825 ....DLB-107, 109, 142, 158
Barbeau, Marius 1883-1969..............DLB-92
Barber, John Warner 1798-1885 ....DLB-30
Bàrberi Squarotti, Giorgio 1929- DLB-128

Barbey d'Aurevilly, Jules-Amédée
    1808-1889 .... DLB-119
Barbier, Auguste 1805-1882 .... DLB-217
Barbilian, Dan (see Barbu, Ion)
Barbour, John circa 1316-1395 .... DLB-146
Barbour, Ralph Henry 1870-1944 .... DLB-22
Barbu, Ion 1895-1961 ...... DLB-220; CDWLB-4
Barbusse, Henri 1873-1935 .... DLB-65
Barclay, Alexander circa 1475-1552 ..... DLB-132
E. E. Barclay and Company DLB-49
C. W. Bardeen [publishing house] DLB-49
Barham, Richard Harris 1788-1845 ..... DLB-159
Barich, Bill 1943- DLB-185
Baring, Maurice 1874-1945 .... DLB-34
Baring-Gould, Sabine 1834-1924 ... DLB-156, 190
Barker, A. L. 1918-2002 .... DLB-14, 139
Barker, Clive 1952- DLB-261
Barker, Dudley (see Black, Lionel)
Barker, George 1913-1991 .... DLB-20
Barker, Harley Granville 1877-1946 ...... DLB-10
Barker, Howard 1946- DLB-13, 233
Barker, James Nelson 1784-1858 .... DLB-37
Barker, Jane 1652-1727 .... DLB-39, 131
Barker, Lady Mary Anne 1831-1911 .... DLB-166
Barker, Pat 1943- DLB-271
Barker, William circa 1520-after 1576 ... DLB-132
Arthur Barker Limited DLB-112
Barkov, Ivan Semenovich 1732-1768 .... DLB-150
Barks, Coleman 1937- DLB-5
Barlach, Ernst 1870-1938 .... DLB-56, 118
Barlow, Joel 1754-1812 .... DLB-37
    The Prospect of Peace (1778) DLB-37
Barnard, John 1681-1770 .... DLB-24
Barnard, Marjorie (M. Barnard Eldershaw)
    1897-1987 .... DLB-260
Barnard, Robert 1936- DLB-276
Barne, Kitty (Mary Catherine Barne)
    1883-1957 .... DLB-160
Barnes, Barnabe 1571-1609 .... DLB-132
Barnes, Djuna 1892-1982 .... DLB-4, 9, 45; DS-15
Barnes, Jim 1933- DLB-175
Barnes, Julian 1946- DLB-194; Y-93
    Notes for a Checklist of Publications Y-01
Barnes, Margaret Ayer 1886-1967 .... DLB-9
Barnes, Peter 1931- DLB-13, 233
Barnes, William 1801-1886 .... DLB-32
A. S. Barnes and Company DLB-49
Barnes and Noble Books DLB-46
Barnet, Miguel 1940- DLB-145
Barney, Natalie 1876-1972 .... DLB-4; DS-15
Barnfield, Richard 1574-1627 ....DLB-172
Richard W. Baron [publishing house] DLB-46
Barr, Amelia Edith Huddleston
    1831-1919 .... DLB-202, 221
Barr, Robert 1850-1912 .... DLB-70, 92

Barral, Carlos 1928-1989 .... DLB-134
Barrax, Gerald William 1933- DLB-41, 120
Barrès, Maurice 1862-1923 .... DLB-123
Barreno, Maria Isabel (see The Three Marias:
    A Landmark Case in Portuguese
    Literary History)
Barrett, Eaton Stannard 1786-1820 ...... DLB-116
Barrie, J. M.
    1860-1937 ...... DLB-10, 141, 156; CDBLB-5
Barrie and Jenkins DLB-112
Barrio, Raymond 1921- DLB-82
Barrios, Gregg 1945- DLB-122
Barry, Philip 1896-1949 .... DLB-7, 228
Barry, Robertine (see Françoise)
Barry, Sebastian 1955- DLB-245
Barse and Hopkins DLB-46
Barstow, Stan 1928- DLB-14, 139, 207
    Tribute to John Braine Y-86
Barth, John 1930- DLB-2, 227
Barthelme, Donald
    1931-1989 ....DLB-2, 234; Y-80, 89
Barthelme, Frederick 1943- DLB-244; Y-85
Barthes, Roland 1915-1980 .... DLB-296
Bartholomew, Frank 1898-1985 .... DLB-127
Bartlett, John 1820-1905 .... DLB-1, 235
Bartol, Cyrus Augustus 1813-1900 .... DLB-1, 235
Barton, Bernard 1784-1849 .... DLB-96
Barton, John ca. 1610-1675 .... DLB-236
Barton, Thomas Pennant 1803-1869 .... DLB-140
Bartram, John 1699-1777 .... DLB-31
Bartram, William 1739-1823 .... DLB-37
Barykova, Anna Pavlovna 1839-1893 ....DLB-277
Bashshar ibn Burd circa 714-circa 784 ... DLB-311
Basic Books DLB-46
Basille, Theodore (see Becon, Thomas)
Bass, Rick 1958- DLB-212, 275
Bass, T. J. 1932- Y-81
Bassani, Giorgio 1916-2000 .... DLB-128, 177, 299
Basse, William circa 1583-1653 .... DLB-121
Bassett, John Spencer 1867-1928 .... DLB-17
Bassler, Thomas Joseph (see Bass, T. J.)
Bate, Walter Jackson 1918-1999 ......DLB-67, 103
Bateman, Stephen circa 1510-1584 ...... DLB-136
Christopher Bateman
    [publishing house] DLB-170
Bates, H. E. 1905-1974 .... DLB-162, 191
Bates, Katharine Lee 1859-1929 .... DLB-71
Batiushkov, Konstantin Nikolaevich
    1787-1855 .... DLB-205
B. T. Batsford [publishing house] DLB-106
Batteux, Charles 1713-1780 .... DLB-313
Battiscombe, Georgina 1905- DLB-155
The Battle of Maldon circa 1000 .... DLB-146
Baudelaire, Charles 1821-1867 .... DLB-217
Baudrillard, Jean 1929- DLB-296
Bauer, Bruno 1809-1882 .... DLB-133

Bauer, Wolfgang 1941- DLB-124
Baum, L. Frank 1856-1919 .... DLB-22
Baum, Vicki 1888-1960 .... DLB-85
Baumbach, Jonathan 1933- Y-80
Bausch, Richard 1945- DLB-130
    Tribute to James Dickey Y-97
    Tribute to Peter Taylor Y-94
Bausch, Robert 1945- DLB-218
Bawden, Nina 1925- DLB-14, 161, 207
Bax, Clifford 1886-1962 ....DLB-10, 100
Baxter, Charles 1947- DLB-130
Bayer, Eleanor (see Perry, Eleanor)
Bayer, Konrad 1932-1964 .... DLB-85
Bayle, Pierre 1647-1706 ....DLB-268, 313
Bayley, Barrington J. 1937- DLB-261
Baynes, Pauline 1922- DLB-160
Baynton, Barbara 1857-1929 .... DLB-230
Bazin, Hervé (Jean Pierre Marie Hervé-Bazin)
    1911-1996 .... DLB-83
The BBC Four Samuel Johnson Prize
    for Non fiction Y-02
Beach, Sylvia
    1887-1962 .... DLB-4; DS-15
Beacon Press DLB-49
Beadle and Adams DLB-49
Beagle, Peter S. 1939- Y-80
Beal, M. F. 1937- Y-81
Beale, Howard K. 1899-1959 .... DLB-17
Beard, Charles A. 1874-1948 .... DLB-17
Beat Generation (Beats)
    As I See It, by Carolyn Cassady DLB-16
    A Beat Chronology: The First Twenty-five
        Years, 1944-1969 .... DLB-16
    The Commercialization of the Image
        of Revolt, by Kenneth Rexroth ... DLB-16
    Four Essays on the Beat Generation .. DLB-16
    in New York City DLB-237
    in the West DLB-237
    Outlaw Days DLB-16
    Periodicals of DLB-16
Beattie, Ann 1947- DLB-218, 278; Y-82
Beattie, James 1735-1803 .... DLB-109
Beatty, Chester 1875-1968 .... DLB-201
Beauchemin, Nérée 1850-1931 .... DLB-92
Beauchemin, Yves 1941- DLB-60
Beaugrand, Honoré 1848-1906 .... DLB-99
Beaulieu, Victor-Lévy 1945- DLB-53
Beaumarchais, Pierre-Augustin Caron de
    1732-1799 .... DLB-313
Beaumer, Mme de ?-1766 .... DLB-313
Beaumont, Francis circa 1584-1616
    and Fletcher, John
    1579-1625 .... DLB-58; CDBLB-1
Beaumont, Sir John 1583?-1627 .... DLB-121
Beaumont, Joseph 1616-1699 .... DLB-126
Beauvoir, Simone de 1908-1986 ....DLB-72; Y-86
    Personal Tribute to Simone de Beauvoir ... Y-86

Beaver, Bruce 1928- DLB-289
Becher, Ulrich 1910-1990 ....DLB-69
Becker, Carl 1873-1945 ....DLB-17
Becker, Jurek 1937-1997...........DLB-75, 299
Becker, Jurgen 1932- DLB-75
Beckett, Mary 1926- DLB-319
Beckett, Samuel 1906-1989
  ..DLB-13, 15, 233, 319, 321; Y-90; CDBLB-7
Beckford, William 1760-1844........DLB-39, 213
Beckham, Barry 1944- DLB-33
Bećković, Matija 1939- DLB-181
Becon, Thomas circa 1512-1567 ....DLB-136
Becque, Henry 1837-1899 ....DLB-192
Beddoes, Thomas 1760-1808...........DLB-158
Beddoes, Thomas Lovell 1803-1849 .....DLB-96
Bede circa 673-735..................DLB-146
Bedford-Jones, H. 1887-1949 ....DLB-251
Bedregal, Yolanda 1913-1999 ....DLB-283
Beebe, William 1877-1962 ....DLB-275
Beecher, Catharine Esther
  1800-1878 ....DLB-1, 243
Beecher, Henry Ward
  1813-1887 ....DLB-3, 43, 250
Beer, George L. 1872-1920 ....DLB-47
Beer, Johann 1655-1700...............DLB-168
Beer, Patricia 1919-1999 ....DLB-40
Beerbohm, Max 1872-1956 ....DLB-34, 100
Beer-Hofmann, Richard 1866-1945......DLB-81
Beers, Henry A. 1847-1926 ....DLB-71
S. O. Beeton [publishing house].........DLB-106
Begley, Louis 1933- DLB-299
Bégon, Elisabeth 1696-1755 ....DLB-99
Behan, Brendan
  1923-1964 ....DLB-13, 233; CDBLB-7
Behn, Aphra 1640?-1689........DLB-39, 80, 131
Behn, Harry 1898-1973 ....DLB-61
Behrman, S. N. 1893-1973 ....DLB-7, 44
Beklemishev, Iurii Solomonvich
  (see Krymov, Iurii Solomonovich)
Belaney, Archibald Stansfeld (see Grey Owl)
Belasco, David 1853-1931 ....DLB-7
Clarke Belford and Company DLB-49
Belgian Luxembourg American Studies
  Association Y-01
Belinsky, Vissarion Grigor'evich
  1811-1848 ....DLB-198
Belitt, Ben 1911-2003.................DLB-5
Belknap, Jeremy 1744-1798 ....DLB-30, 37
Bell, Adrian 1901-1980 ....DLB-191
Bell, Clive 1881-1964................. DS-10
Bell, Daniel 1919- DLB-246
Bell, Gertrude Margaret Lowthian
  1868-1926 ....DLB-174
Bell, James Madison 1826-1902 ....DLB-50
Bell, Madison Smartt 1957- DLB-218, 278
  Tribute to Andrew Nelson Lytle........ Y-95
  Tribute to Peter Taylor............. Y-94

Bell, Marvin 1937- DLB-5
Bell, Millicent 1919- DLB-111
Bell, Quentin 1910-1996 ....DLB-155
Bell, Vanessa 1879-1961 .... DS-10
George Bell and Sons.................DLB-106
Robert Bell [publishing house]..........DLB-49
Bellamy, Edward 1850-1898 ....DLB-12
Bellamy, Joseph 1719-1790.............DLB-31
John Bellamy [publishing house] DLB-170
La Belle Assemblée 1806-1837 ....DLB-110
Bellezza, Dario 1944-1996 ....DLB-128
Belli, Carlos Germán 1927- DLB-290
Belli, Gioconda 1948- DLB-290
Belloc, Hilaire 1870-1953 .... DLB-19, 100, 141, 174
Belloc, Madame (see Parkes, Bessie Rayner)
Bellonci, Maria 1902-1986.............DLB-196
Bellow, Saul 1915-2005 .... DLB-2, 28, 299; Y-82;
                                    DS-3; CDALB-1
  Tribute to Isaac Bashevis Singer Y-91
Belmont Productions DLB-46
Belov, Vasilii Ivanovich 1932- DLB-302
Bels, Alberts 1938- DLB-232
Belševica, Vizma 1931- DLB-232; CDWLB-4
Bely, Andrei 1880-1934................DLB-295
Bemelmans, Ludwig 1898-1962..........DLB-22
Bemis, Samuel Flagg 1891-1973..........DLB-17
William Bemrose [publishing house].....DLB-106
Ben no Naishi 1228?-1271?.............DLB-203
Benchley, Robert 1889-1945 ....DLB-11
Bencúr, Matej (see Kukučin, Martin)
Benedetti, Mario 1920- DLB-113
Benedict, Pinckney 1964- DLB-244
Benedict, Ruth 1887-1948 ....DLB-246
Benedictus, David 1938- DLB-14
Benedikt Gröndal 1826-1907...........DLB-293
Benedikt, Michael 1935- DLB-5
Benediktov, Vladimir Grigor'evich
  1807-1873....................DLB-205
Benét, Stephen Vincent
  1898-1943 ....DLB-4, 48, 102, 249
  Stephen Vincent Benét Centenary Y-97
Benét, William Rose 1886-1950 ....DLB-45
Benford, Gregory 1941- Y-82
Benítez, Sandra 1941- DLB-292
Benjamin, Park 1809-1864.....DLB-3, 59, 73, 250
Benjamin, Peter (see Cunningham, Peter)
Benjamin, S. G. W. 1837-1914..........DLB-189
Benjamin, Walter 1892-1940 ....DLB-242
Benlowes, Edward 1602-1676 ....DLB-126
Benn, Gottfried 1886-1956 ....DLB-56
Benn Brothers Limited................DLB-106
Bennett, Alan 1934- DLB-310
Bennett, Arnold
  1867-1931 ....DLB-10, 34, 98, 135; CDBLB-5
  The Arnold Bennett Society Y-98

Bennett, Charles 1899-1995............DLB-44
Bennett, Emerson 1822-1905...........DLB-202
Bennett, Gwendolyn 1902-1981 ....DLB-51
Bennett, Hal 1930- DLB-33
Bennett, James Gordon 1795-1872........DLB-43
Bennett, James Gordon, Jr. 1841-1918.....DLB-23
Bennett, John 1865-1956 ....DLB-42
Bennett, Louise 1919- DLB-117; CDWLB-3
Benni, Stefano 1947- DLB-196
Benoist, Françoise-Albine Puzin de
  La Martinière 1731-1809...........DLB-313
Benoit, Jacques 1941- DLB-60
Benson, A. C. 1862-1925................DLB-98
Benson, E. F. 1867-1940...........DLB-135, 153
  The E. F. Benson Society Y-98
  The Tilling Society Y-98
Benson, Jackson J. 1930- DLB-111
Benson, Robert Hugh 1871-1914........DLB-153
Benson, Stella 1892-1933...........DLB-36, 162
Bent, James Theodore 1852-1897 ....DLB-174
Bent, Mabel Virginia Anna ?-? DLB-174
Bentham, Jeremy 1748-1832 ... DLB-107, 158, 252
Bentley, E. C. 1875-1956 ....DLB-70
Bentley, Phyllis 1894-1977.............DLB-191
Bentley, Richard 1662-1742............DLB-252
Richard Bentley [publishing house]......DLB-106
Benton, Robert 1932- DLB-44
Benziger Brothers DLB-49
Beowulf circa 900-1000 or 790-825
  ....DLB-146; CDBLB-1
Berberova, Nina 1901-1993............DLB-317
Berent, Wacław 1873-1940 ....DLB-215
Beresford, Anne 1929- DLB-40
Beresford, John Davys
  1873-1947 ....DLB-162, 178, 197
  "Experiment in the Novel" (1929)
  [excerpt] DLB-36
Beresford-Howe, Constance 1922- DLB-88
R. G. Berford Company DLB-49
Berg, Elizabeth 1948- DLB-292
Berg, Stephen 1934- DLB-5
Bergengruen, Werner 1892-1964 ....DLB-56
Berger, John 1926- DLB-14, 207, 319
Berger, Meyer 1898-1959 ....DLB-29
Berger, Thomas 1924- DLB-2; Y-80
  A Statement by Thomas Berger Y-80
Bergman, Hjalmar 1883-1931 ....DLB-259
Bergman, Ingmar 1918- DLB-257
Berkeley, Anthony 1893-1971 ....DLB-77
Berkeley, George 1685-1753 .... DLB-31, 101, 252
The Berkley Publishing Corporation......DLB-46
Berkman, Alexander 1870-1936.........DLB-303
Berlin, Irving 1888-1989 ....DLB-265
Berlin, Lucia 1936- DLB-130
Berman, Marshall 1940- DLB-246

Berman, Sabina 1955- DLB-305	Beyle, Marie-Henri (see Stendhal)	"The New Biography," by Virginia Woolf, *New York Herald Tribune*, 30 October 1927 . . . . DLB-149
Bernal, Vicente J. 1888-1915 . . . . DLB-82	Białoszewski, Miron 1922-1983 . . . . DLB-232	
Bernanos, Georges 1888-1948 . . . . DLB-72	Bianco, Margery Williams 1881-1944 . . . DLB-160	"The Practice of Biography," in *The English Sense of Humour and Other Essays*, by Harold Nicolson DLB-149
Bernard, Catherine 1663?-1712. . . . . DLB-268	Bibaud, Adèle 1854-1941 . . . . DLB-92	
Bernard, Harry 1898-1979 . . . . DLB-92	Bibaud, Michel 1782-1857 . . . . DLB-99	
Bernard, John 1756-1828 . . . . DLB-37	Bibliography	"Principles of Biography," in *Elizabethan and Other Essays*, by Sidney Lee . . DLB-149
Bernard of Chartres circa 1060-1124? . . . DLB-115	Bibliographical and Textual Scholarship Since World War II Y-89	
Bernard of Clairvaux 1090-1153 . . . . DLB-208		Remarks at the Opening of "The Biographical Part of Literature" Exhibition, by William R. Cagle. Y-98
Bernard, Richard 1568-1641/1642 . . . . . . DLB-281	Center for Bibliographical Studies and Research at the University of California, Riverside Y-91	
Bernard Silvestris fl. circa 1130-1160 . . . . DLB-208		Survey of Literary Biographies Y-00
	The Great Bibliographers Series Y-93	A Transit of Poets and Others: American Biography in 1982. . . . . Y-82
Bernardin de Saint-Pierre 1737-1814. . . . . DLB-313	Primary Bibliography: A Retrospective . . . Y-95	
Bernari, Carlo 1909-1992. . . . . .DLB-177	Bichsel, Peter 1935- DLB-75	The Year in Literary Biography Y-83–01
Bernhard, Thomas 1931-1989 . . . . DLB-85, 124; CDWLB-2	Bickerstaff, Isaac John 1733-circa 1808. . . . DLB-89	
Berniéres, Louis de 1954- DLB-271	Drexel Biddle [publishing house] DLB-49	Biography, The Practice of: An Interview with B. L. Reid. Y-83
Bernstein, Charles 1950- DLB-169	Bidermann, Jacob 1577 or 1578-1639 . . . . DLB-164	An Interview with David Herbert Donald . . Y-87
Berriault, Gina 1926-1999 . . . . DLB-130		An Interview with Humphrey Carpenter. . . .Y-84
Berrigan, Daniel 1921- DLB-5	Bidwell, Walter Hilliard 1798-1881 . . . . . . DLB-79	An Interview with Joan Mellen Y-94
Berrigan, Ted 1934-1983 . . . . DLB-5, 169	Biehl, Charlotta Dorothea 1731-1788 . . . . DLB-300	An Interview with John Caldwell Guilds Y-92
Berry, Wendell 1934- DLB-5, 6, 234, 275	Bienek, Horst 1930-1990 . . . . DLB-75	An Interview with William Manchester. . . Y-85
Berryman, John 1914-1972 . . . . DLB-48; CDALB-1	Bierbaum, Otto Julius 1865-1910 . . . . DLB-66	John Bioren [publishing house]. DLB-49
Bersianik, Louky 1930- DLB-60	Bierce, Ambrose 1842-1914? DLB-11, 12, 23, 71, 74, 186; CDALB-3	Bioy Casares, Adolfo 1914-1999 . . . . DLB-113
Berssenbrugge, Mei-mei 1947- DLB-312		Bird, Isabella Lucy 1831-1904 . . . . DLB-166
Thomas Berthelet [publishing house] DLB-170	Bigelow, William F. 1879-1966. . . . . DLB-91	Bird, Robert Montgomery 1806-1854 . . . DLB-202
Berto, Giuseppe 1914-1978. . . . . .DLB-177	Biggers, Earl Derr 1884-1933 . . . . DLB-306	Bird, William 1888-1963 . . . . DLB-4; DS-15
Bertocci, Peter Anthony 1910-1989 . . . . . .DLB-279	Biggle, Lloyd, Jr. 1923-2002 . . . . DLB-8	The Cost of the *Cantos:* William Bird to Ezra Pound Y-01
Bertolucci, Attilio 1911-2000. . . . . DLB-128	Bigiaretti, Libero 1905-1993 . . . . .DLB-177	
Berton, Pierre 1920-2004 . . . . DLB-68	Bigland, Eileen 1898-1970. . . . . DLB-195	Birken, Sigmund von 1626-1681 . . . . . . DLB-164
Bertrand, Louis "Aloysius" 1807-1841 . . . DLB-217	Biglow, Hosea (see Lowell, James Russell)	Birney, Earle 1904-1995. . . . . DLB-88
Besant, Sir Walter 1836-1901 . . . . . . DLB-135, 190	Bigongiari, Piero 1914-1997 . . . . DLB-128	Birrell, Augustine 1850-1933 . . . . DLB-98
Bessa-Luís, Agustina 1922- DLB-287	Bilac, Olavo 1865-1918 . . . . DLB-307	Bisher, Furman 1918- DLB-171
Bessette, Gerard 1920- DLB-53	Bilenchi, Romano 1909-1989 . . . . DLB-264	Bishop, Elizabeth 1911-1979. . . . . DLB-5, 169; CDALB-6
Bessie, Alvah 1904-1985. . . . . DLB-26	Billinger, Richard 1890-1965 . . . . DLB-124	
Bester, Alfred 1913-1987. . . . . DLB-8	Billings, Hammatt 1818-1874 . . . . DLB-188	The Elizabeth Bishop Society. Y-01
Besterman, Theodore 1904-1976 . . . . . . DLB-201	Billings, John Shaw 1898-1975 . . . . DLB-137	Bishop, John Peale 1892-1944 . . . . . . DLB-4, 9, 45
Beston, Henry (Henry Beston Sheahan) 1888-1968 .DLB-275	Billings, Josh (see Shaw, Henry Wheeler)	Bismarck, Otto von 1815-1898. . . . . DLB-129
	Binchy, Maeve 1940- DLB-319	Bisset, Robert 1759-1805 . . . . DLB-142
Best-Seller Lists An Assessment. Y-84	Binding, Rudolf G. 1867-1938 . . . . DLB-66	Bissett, Bill 1939- DLB-53
	Bingay, Malcolm 1884-1953. . . . . DLB-241	Bitov, Andrei Georgievich 1937- DLB-302
What's Really Wrong With Bestseller Lists Y-84	Bingham, Caleb 1757-1817 . . . . DLB-42	Bitzius, Albert (see Gotthelf, Jeremias)
	Bingham, George Barry 1906-1988 . . . . . DLB-127	Bjørnboe, Jens 1920-1976 . . . . DLB-297
Bestuzhev, Aleksandr Aleksandrovich (Marlinsky) 1797-1837 . . . . DLB-198	Bingham, Sallie 1937- DLB-234	Bjørnvig, Thorkild 1918- DLB-214
Bestuzhev, Nikolai Aleksandrovich 1791-1855. DLB-198	William Bingley [publishing house] DLB-154	Black, David (D. M.) 1941- DLB-40
	Binyon, Laurence 1869-1943 . . . . DLB-19	Black, Gavin (Oswald Morris Wynd) 1913-1998 .DLB-276
Betham-Edwards, Matilda Barbara (see Edwards, Matilda Barbara Betham-)	*Biographia Brittanica* DLB-142	
	Biography	Black, Lionel (Dudley Barker) 1910-1980 .DLB-276
Betjeman, John 1906-1984 . . . . DLB-20; Y-84; CDBLB-7	Biographical Documents Y-84, 85	
	A Celebration of Literary Biography Y-98	Black, Winifred 1863-1936. . . . . DLB-25
Betocchi, Carlo 1899-1986 . . . . DLB-128	Conference on Modern Biography Y-85	Walter J. Black [publishing house] DLB-46
Bettarini, Mariella 1942- DLB-128	The Cult of Biography Excerpts from the Second Folio Debate: "Biographies are generally a disease of English Literature" Y-86	Blackamore, Arthur 1679-? DLB-24, 39
Betts, Doris 1932- DLB-218; Y-82		Blackburn, Alexander L. 1929- Y-85
Beveridge, Albert J. 1862-1927 . . . . DLB-17		Blackburn, John 1923-1993 . . . . DLB-261
Beverley, Robert circa 1673-1722 . . . . . DLB-24, 30		Blackburn, Paul 1926-1971 . . . . .DLB-16; Y-81
Bevilacqua, Alberto 1934- DLB-196	New Approaches to Biography: Challenges from Critical Theory, USC Conference on Literary Studies, 1990 . . . . Y-90	Blackburn, Thomas 1916-1977. . . . . DLB-27
Bevington, Louisa Sarah 1845-1895 . . . . . DLB-199		Blacker, Terence 1948- DLB-271
		Blackmore, R. D. 1825-1900 . . . . DLB-18

Blackmore, Sir Richard 1654-1729....... DLB-131

Blackmur, R. P. 1904-1965 .... DLB-63

Blackwell, Alice Stone 1857-1950........ DLB-303

Basil Blackwell, Publisher DLB-106

Blackwood, Algernon Henry
    1869-1951 .... DLB-153, 156, 178

Blackwood, Caroline 1931-1996 ..... DLB-14, 207

William Blackwood and Sons, Ltd....... DLB-154

Blackwood's Edinburgh Magazine
    1817-1980 .... DLB-110

Blades, William 1824-1890 .... DLB-184

Blaga, Lucian 1895-1961 .... DLB-220

Blagden, Isabella 1817?-1873 .... DLB-199

Blair, Eric Arthur (see Orwell, George)

Blair, Francis Preston 1791-1876 .... DLB-43

Blair, Hugh
    Lectures on Rhetoric and Belles Lettres (1783),
    [excerpts]..................... DLB-31

Blair, James circa 1655-1743............ DLB-24

Blair, John Durburrow 1759-1823 .... DLB-37

Blais, Marie-Claire 1939- DLB-53

Blaise, Clark 1940- DLB-53

Blake, George 1893-1961............... DLB-191

Blake, Lillie Devereux 1833-1913 .... DLB-202, 221

Blake, Nicholas (C. Day Lewis)
    1904-1972 .... DLB-77

Blake, William
    1757-1827....... DLB-93, 154, 163; CDBLB-3

The Blakiston Company DLB-49

Blanchard, Stephen 1950- DLB-267

Blanchot, Maurice 1907-2003........ DLB-72, 296

Blanckenburg, Christian Friedrich von
    1744-1796...................... DLB-94

Blandiana, Ana 1942- DLB-232; CDWLB-4

Blanshard, Brand 1892-1987 .... DLB-279

Blaser, Robin 1925- DLB-165

Blaumanis, Rūdolfs 1863-1908 .... DLB-220

Bleasdale, Alan 1946- DLB-245

Bledsoe, Albert Taylor
    1809-1877 .... DLB-3, 79, 248

Bleecker, Ann Eliza 1752-1783 .... DLB-200

Blelock and Company DLB-49

Blennerhassett, Margaret Agnew
    1773-1842 .... DLB-99

Geoffrey Bles [publishing house] DLB-112

Blessington, Marguerite, Countess of
    1789-1849 .... DLB-166

Blew, Mary Clearman 1939- DLB-256

Blicher, Steen Steensen 1782-1848....... DLB-300

The Blickling Homilies circa 971 .... DLB-146

Blind, Mathilde 1841-1896 .... DLB-199

Blish, James 1921-1975.................. DLB-8

E. Bliss and E. White
    [publishing house] DLB-49

Bliven, Bruce 1889-1977 .... DLB-137

Blixen, Karen 1885-1962 .... DLB-214

Bloch, Ernst 1885-1977 .... DLB-296

Bloch, Robert 1917-1994 .... DLB-44
    Tribute to John D. MacDonald......... Y-86

Block, Lawrence 1938- DLB-226

Block, Rudolph (see Lessing, Bruno)

Blok, Aleksandr Aleksandrovich
    1880-1921 .... DLB-295

Blondal, Patricia 1926-1959............. DLB-88

Bloom, Harold 1930- DLB-67

Bloomer, Amelia 1818-1894 .... DLB-79

Bloomfield, Robert 1766-1823 .... DLB-93

Bloomsbury Group DS-10
    The *Dreannought* Hoax................ DS-10

Bloor, Ella Reeve 1862-1951 .... DLB-303

Blotner, Joseph 1923- DLB-111

Blount, Thomas 1618?-1679 .... DLB-236

Bloy, Léon 1846-1917 .... DLB-123

Blume, Judy 1938- DLB-52
    Tribute to Theodor Seuss Geisel Y-91

Blunck, Hans Friedrich 1888-1961 .... DLB-66

Blunden, Edmund 1896-1974 ... DLB-20, 100, 155

Blundeville, Thomas 1522?-1606 .... DLB-236

Blunt, Lady Anne Isabella Noel
    1837-1917 .... DLB-174

Blunt, Wilfrid Scawen 1840-1922 .... DLB-19, 174

Bly, Nellie (see Cochrane, Elizabeth)

Bly, Robert 1926- DLB-5

Blyton, Enid 1897-1968 .... DLB-160

Boaden, James 1762-1839 .... DLB-89

Boal, Augusto 1931- DLB-307

Boas, Frederick S. 1862-1957 .... DLB-149

The Bobbs-Merrill Company DLB-46, 291
    The Bobbs-Merrill Archive at the
    Lilly Library, Indiana University Y-90

Boborykin, Petr Dmitrievich
    1836-1921 .... DLB-238

Bobrov, Semen Sergeevich
    1763?-1810 .... DLB-150

Bobrowski, Johannes 1917-1965 .... DLB-75

Bocage, Manuel Maria Barbosa du
    1765-1805 .... DLB-287

Bodenheim, Maxwell 1892-1954....... DLB-9, 45

Bodenstedt, Friedrich von 1819-1892 .... DLB-129

Bodini, Vittorio 1914-1970............. DLB-128

Bodkin, M. McDonnell 1850-1933 .... DLB-70

Bodley, Sir Thomas 1545-1613 .... DLB-213

Bodley Head DLB-112

Bodmer, Johann Jakob 1698-1783 .... DLB-97

Bodmershof, Imma von 1895-1982 ...... DLB-85

Bodsworth, Fred 1918- DLB-68

Böðvar Guðmundsson 1939- DLB-293

Boehm, Sydney 1908-1990 .... DLB-44

Boer, Charles 1939- DLB-5

Boethius circa 480-circa 524 .... DLB-115

Boethius of Dacia circa 1240-?......... DLB-115

Bogan, Louise 1897-1970 .... DLB-45, 169

Bogarde, Dirk 1921-1999 .... DLB-14

Bogdanov, Aleksandr Aleksandrovich
    1873-1928 .... DLB-295

Bogdanovich, Ippolit Fedorovich
    circa 1743-1803 .... DLB-150

David Bogue [publishing house] DLB-106

Bohjalian, Chris 1960- DLB-292

Böhme, Jakob 1575-1624 .... DLB-164

H. G. Bohn [publishing house] DLB-106

Bohse, August 1661-1742................ DLB-168

Boie, Heinrich Christian 1744-1806....... DLB-94

Boileau-Despréaux, Nicolas 1636-1711 .... DLB-268

Bojunga, Lygia 1932- DLB-307

Bok, Edward W. 1863-1930 ...... DLB-91; DS-16

Boland, Eavan 1944- DLB-40

Boldrewood, Rolf (Thomas Alexander Browne)
    1826?-1915 .... DLB-230

Bolingbroke, Henry St. John, Viscount
    1678-1751 .... DLB-101

Böll, Heinrich
    1917-1985 .... DLB-69; Y-85; CDWLB-2

Bolling, Robert 1738-1775 .... DLB-31

Bolotov, Andrei Timofeevich
    1738-1833 .... DLB-150

Bolt, Carol 1941- DLB-60

Bolt, Robert 1924-1995 .... DLB-13, 233

Bolton, Herbert E. 1870-1953 .... DLB-17

Bonaventura DLB-90

Bonaventure circa 1217-1274 .... DLB-115

Bonaviri, Giuseppe 1924- DLB-177

Bond, Edward 1934- DLB-13, 310

Bond, Michael 1926- DLB-161

Bondarev, Iurii Vasil'evich 1924- DLB-302

Albert and Charles Boni
    [publishing house]................ DLB-46

Boni and Liveright.................... DLB-46

Bonnefoy, Yves 1923- DLB-258

Bonner, Marita 1899-1971 .... DLB-228

Bonner, Paul Hyde 1893-1968............ DS-17

Bonner, Sherwood (see McDowell, Katharine
    Sherwood Bonner)

Robert Bonner's Sons DLB-49

Bonnin, Gertrude Simmons (see Zitkala-Ša)

Bonsanti, Alessandro 1904-1984 .... DLB-177

Bontempelli, Massimo 1878-1960 ...... DLB-264

Bontemps, Arna 1902-1973 .... DLB-48, 51

The Book Buyer (1867-1880, 1884-1918,
    1935-1938 .... DS-13

The Book League of America DLB-46

Book Reviewing
    The American Book Review: A Sketch .. Y-92
    Book Reviewing and the
    Literary Scene................. Y-96, 97
    Book Reviewing in America Y-87–94
    Book Reviewing in America and the
    Literary Scene..................... Y-95
    Book Reviewing in Texas Y-94
    Book Reviews in Glossy Magazines Y-95

Do They or Don't They?
  Writers Reading Book Reviews Y-01
The Most Powerful Book Review
  in America [*New York Times
  Book Review*] Y-82
Some Surprises and Universal Truths Y-92
The Year in Book Reviewing and the
  Literary Situation Y-98
Book Supply Company DLB-49
The Book Trade History Group Y-93
The Booker Prize Y-96–98
  Address by Anthony Thwaite,
    Chairman of the Booker Prize Judges
    Comments from Former Booker
    Prize Winners Y-86
Boorde, Andrew circa 1490-1549 ..... DLB-136
Boorstin, Daniel J. 1914- DLB-17
  Tribute to Archibald MacLeish Y-82
  Tribute to Charles Scribner Jr. Y-95
Booth, Franklin 1874-1948 .... DLB-188
Booth, Mary L. 1831-1889 .... DLB-79
Booth, Philip 1925- Y-82
Booth, Wayne C. 1921- DLB-67
Booth, William 1829-1912 .... DLB-190
Bor, Josef 1906-1979 .... DLB-299
Borchardt, Rudolf 1877-1945 .... DLB-66
Borchert, Wolfgang 1921-1947 ..... DLB-69, 124
Bording, Anders 1619-1677 .... DLB-300
Borel, Pétrus 1809-1859 .... DLB-119
Borgen, Johan 1902-1979 .... DLB-297
Borges, Jorge Luis
  1899-1986 ... DLB-113, 283; Y-86; CDWLB-3
  The Poetry of Jorge Luis Borges Y-86
  A Personal Tribute Y-86
Borgese, Giuseppe Antonio 1882-1952 ... DLB-264
Börne, Ludwig 1786-1837 .... DLB-90
Bornstein, Miriam 1950- DLB-209
Borowski, Tadeusz
  1922-1951 .... DLB-215; CDWLB-4
Borrow, George 1803-1881 ..... DLB-21, 55, 166
Bosanquet, Bernard 1848-1923 .... DLB-262
Boscán, Juan circa 1490-1542 .... DLB-318
Bosch, Juan 1909-2001 .... DLB-145
Bosco, Henri 1888-1976 .... DLB-72
Bosco, Monique 1927- DLB-53
Bosman, Herman Charles 1905-1951 .... DLB-225
Bossuet, Jacques-Bénigne 1627-1704 .... DLB-268
Bostic, Joe 1908-1988 .... DLB-241
Boston, Lucy M. 1892-1990 .... DLB-161
Boston Quarterly Review DLB-1
Boston University
  Editorial Institute at Boston University ... Y-00
  Special Collections at Boston University .. Y-99
Boswell, James
  1740-1795 .... DLB-104, 142; CDBLB-2
Boswell, Robert 1953- DLB-234
Bosworth, David Y-82

Excerpt from "Excerpts from a Report
  of the Commission," in *The Death
  of Descartes* Y-82
Bote, Hermann circa 1460-circa 1520 ... DLB-179
Botev, Khristo 1847-1876 .... DLB-147
Botkin, Vasilii Petrovich 1811-1869 ..... DLB-277
Botta, Anne C. Lynch 1815-1891 ..... DLB-3, 250
Botto, Ján (see Krasko, Ivan)
Bottome, Phyllis 1882-1963 .... DLB-197
Bottomley, Gordon 1874-1948 .... DLB-10
Bottoms, David 1949- DLB-120; Y-83
  Tribute to James Dickey Y-97
Bottrall, Ronald 1906-1959 .... DLB-20
Bouchardy, Joseph 1810-1870 .... DLB-192
Boucher, Anthony 1911-1968 .... DLB-8
Boucher, Jonathan 1738-1804 .... DLB-31
Boucher de Boucherville, Georges
  1814-1894 .... DLB-99
Boudreau, Daniel (see Coste, Donat)
Bouhours, Dominique 1628-1702 ...... DLB-268
Bourassa, Napoléon 1827-1916 .... DLB-99
Bourget, Paul 1852-1935 .... DLB-123
Bourinot, John George 1837-1902 ..... DLB-99
Bourjaily, Vance 1922- DLB-2, 143
Bourne, Edward Gaylord 1860-1908 .... DLB-47
Bourne, Randolph 1886-1918 .... DLB-63
Bousoño, Carlos 1923- DLB-108
Bousquet, Joë 1897-1950 .... DLB-72
Bova, Ben 1932- Y-81
Bovard, Oliver K. 1872-1945 .... DLB-25
Bove, Emmanuel 1898-1945 .... DLB-72
Bowen, Elizabeth
  1899-1973 .... DLB-15, 162; CDBLB-7
Bowen, Francis 1811-1890 .... DLB-1, 59, 235
Bowen, John 1924- DLB-13
Bowen, Marjorie 1886-1952 .... DLB-153
Bowen-Merrill Company DLB-49
Bowering, George 1935- DLB-53
Bowers, Bathsheba 1671-1718 .... DLB-200
Bowers, Claude G. 1878-1958 .... DLB-17
Bowers, Edgar 1924-2000 .... DLB-5
Bowers, Fredson Thayer
  1905-1991 .... DLB-140; Y-91
  The Editorial Style of Fredson Bowers ... Y-91
  Fredson Bowers and
    Studies in Bibliography Y-91
  Fredson Bowers and the Cambridge
    Beaumont and Fletcher Y-91
  Fredson Bowers as Critic of Renaissance
    Dramatic Literature Y-91
  Fredson Bowers as Music Critic Y-91
  Fredson Bowers, Master Teacher Y-91
  An Interview [on Nabokov] Y-80
  Working with Fredson Bowers Y-91
Bowles, Paul 1910-1999 ...... DLB-5, 6, 218; Y-99
Bowles, Samuel, III 1826-1878 .... DLB-43

Bowles, William Lisle 1762-1850 .... DLB-93
Bowman, Louise Morey 1882-1944 ..... DLB-68
Bowne, Borden Parker 1847-1919 ...... DLB-270
Boyd, James 1888-1944 .... DLB-9; DS-16
Boyd, John 1912-2002 .... DLB-310
Boyd, John 1919- DLB-8
Boyd, Martin 1893-1972 .... DLB-260
Boyd, Thomas 1898-1935 .... DLB-9, 316; DS-16
Boyd, William 1952- DLB-231
Boye, Karin 1900-1941 .... DLB-259
Boyesen, Hjalmar Hjorth
  1848-1895 .... DLB-12, 71; DS-13
Boylan, Clare 1948- DLB-267
Boyle, Kay 1902-1992   DLB-4, 9, 48, 86; DS-15;
  .... Y-93
Boyle, Roger, Earl of Orrery 1621-1679 ... DLB-80
Boyle, T. Coraghessan
  1948- DLB-218, 278; Y-86
Božić, Mirko 1919- DLB-181
Brackenbury, Alison 1953- DLB-40
Brackenridge, Hugh Henry
  1748-1816 .... DLB-11, 37
  The Rising Glory of America DLB-37
Brackett, Charles 1892-1969 .... DLB-26
Brackett, Leigh 1915-1978 .... DLB-8, 26
John Bradburn [publishing house] DLB-49
Bradbury, Malcolm 1932-2000 ...... DLB-14, 207
Bradbury, Ray 1920- DLB-2, 8; CDALB-6
Bradbury and Evans DLB-106
Braddon, Mary Elizabeth
  1835-1915 .... DLB-18, 70, 156
Bradford, Andrew 1686-1742 .... DLB-43, 73
Bradford, Gamaliel 1863-1932 .... DLB-17
Bradford, John 1749-1830 .... DLB-43
Bradford, Roark 1896-1948 .... DLB-86
Bradford, William 1590-1657 .... DLB-24, 30
Bradford, William, III 1719-1791 .... DLB-43, 73
Bradlaugh, Charles 1833-1891 .... DLB-57
Bradley, David 1950- DLB-33
Bradley, F. H. 1846-1924 .... DLB-262
Bradley, Katherine Harris (see Field, Michael)
Bradley, Marion Zimmer 1930-1999 ... DLB-8
Bradley, William Aspenwall 1878-1939 ... DLB-4
Ira Bradley and Company DLB-49
J. W. Bradley and Company DLB-49
Bradshaw, Henry 1831-1886 .... DLB-184
Bradstreet, Anne
  1612 or 1613-1672 .... DLB-24; CDALB-2
Bradūnas, Kazys 1917- DLB-220
Bradwardine, Thomas circa 1295-1349 .. DLB-115
Brady, Frank 1924-1986 .... DLB-111
Frederic A. Brady [publishing house] DLB-49
Braga, Rubem 1913-1990 .... DLB-307
Bragg, Melvyn 1939- DLB-14, 271
Brahe, Tycho 1546-1601 .... DLB-300
Charles H. Brainard [publishing house] ... DLB-49

Braine, John
1922-1986 ....DLB-15; Y-86; CDBLB-7

Braithwait, Richard 1588-1673 ....DLB-151

Braithwaite, William Stanley
1878-1962 ....DLB-50, 54

Bräker, Ulrich 1735-1798............DLB-94

Bramah, Ernest 1868-1942 ....DLB-70

Branagan, Thomas 1774-1843 ....DLB-37

Brancati, Vitaliano 1907-1954 ....DLB-264

Branch, William Blackwell 1927- DLB-76

Brand, Christianna 1907-1988 ....DLB-276

Brand, Max (see Faust, Frederick Schiller)

Brandão, Raul 1867-1930..............DLB-287

Branden Press DLB-46

Brandes, Georg 1842-1927..............DLB-300

Branner, H.C. 1903-1966 ....DLB-214

Brant, Sebastian 1457-1521 ....DLB-179

Brassey, Lady Annie (Allnutt)
1839-1887 ....DLB-166

Brathwaite, Edward Kamau
1930- DLB-125; CDWLB-3

Brault, Jacques 1933- DLB-53

Braun, Matt 1932- DLB-212

Braun, Volker 1939- DLB-75, 124

Brautigan, Richard
1935-1984 ....DLB-2, 5, 206; Y-80, 84

Braxton, Joanne M. 1950- DLB-41

Bray, Anne Eliza 1790-1883............DLB-116

Bray, Thomas 1656-1730................DLB-24

Brazdžionis, Bernardas 1907-2002 ......DLB-220

George Braziller [publishing house].......DLB-46

The Bread Loaf Writers' Conference 1983 ... Y-84

Breasted, James Henry 1865-1935........DLB-47

Brecht, Bertolt
1898-1956 ....DLB-56, 124; CDWLB-2

Bredel, Willi 1901-1964................DLB-56

Bregendahl, Marie 1867-1940 ....DLB-214

Breitinger, Johann Jakob 1701-1776 ....DLB-97

Brekke, Paal 1923-1993 ....DLB-297

Bremser, Bonnie 1939- DLB-16

Bremser, Ray 1934-1998 ....DLB-16

Brennan, Christopher 1870-1932........DLB-230

Brentano, Bernard von 1901-1964........DLB-56

Brentano, Clemens 1778-1842 ....DLB-90

Brentano, Franz 1838-1917 ....DLB-296

Brentano's DLB-49

Brenton, Howard 1942- DLB-13

Breslin, Jimmy 1929-1996 ....DLB-185

Breton, André 1896-1966 ....DLB-65, 258

Breton, Nicholas circa 1555-circa 1626 ...DLB-136

The Breton Lays
1300-early fifteenth century.........DLB-146

Brett, Simon 1945- DLB-276

Brewer, Gil 1922-1983................DLB-306

Brewer, Luther A. 1858-1933 ....DLB-187

Brewer, Warren and Putnam............DLB-46

Brewster, Elizabeth 1922- DLB-60

Breytenbach, Breyten 1939- DLB-225

Bridge, Ann (Lady Mary Dolling Sanders
O'Malley) 1889-1974................DLB-191

Bridge, Horatio 1806-1893 ....DLB-183

Bridgers, Sue Ellen 1942- DLB-52

Bridges, Robert
1844-1930 ....DLB-19, 98; CDBLB-5

The Bridgewater Library..............DLB-213

Bridie, James 1888-1951 ....DLB-10

Brieux, Eugene 1858-1932.............DLB-192

Brigadere, Anna
1861-1933 ....DLB-220; CDWLB-4

Briggs, Charles Frederick
1804-1877 ....DLB-3, 250

Brighouse, Harold 1882-1958 ....DLB-10

Bright, Mary Chavelita Dunne
(see Egerton, George)

Brightman, Edgar Sheffield 1884-1953 ... DLB-270

B. J. Brimmer Company DLB-46

Brines, Francisco 1932- DLB-134

Brink, André 1935- DLB-225

Brinley, George, Jr. 1817-1875 ....DLB-140

Brinnin, John Malcolm 1916-1998........DLB-48

Brisbane, Albert 1809-1890 ....DLB-3, 250

Brisbane, Arthur 1864-1936 ....DLB-25

British Academy DLB-112

The British Critic 1793-1843 ....DLB-110

British Library
The American Trust for the
British Library Y-96

The British Library and the Regular
Readers' Group Y-91

Building the New British Library
at St Pancras....................Y-94

British Literary Prizes DLB-207; Y-98

British Literature
The "Angry Young Men"...........DLB-15

Author-Printers, 1476-1599 ....DLB-167

The Comic Tradition Continued DLB-15

Documents on Sixteenth-Century
Literature DLB-167, 172

Eikon Basilike 1649 ....DLB-151

Letter from London Y-96

A Mirror for Magistrates DLB-167

"Modern English Prose" (1876),
by George Saintsbury...........DLB-57

Sex, Class, Politics, and Religion [in the
British Novel, 1930-1959]........DLB-15

Victorians on Rhetoric and Prose
Style DLB-57

The Year in British Fiction Y-99–01

"You've Never Had It So Good," Gusted
by "Winds of Change": British
Fiction in the 1950s, 1960s,
and After.....................DLB-14

British Literature, Old and Middle English
Anglo-Norman Literature in the
Development of Middle English
Literature DLB-146

The Alliterative Morte Arthure and the
Stanzaic Morte Arthur
circa 1350-1400................DLB-146

Ancrene Riwle circa 1200-1225 ......DLB-146

The Anglo-Saxon Chronicle circa
890-1154.....................DLB-146

The Battle of Maldon circa 1000......DLB-146

Beowulf circa 900-1000 or
790-825............DLB-146; CDBLB-1

The Blickling Homilies circa 971.....DLB-146

The Breton Lays
1300-early fifteenth century DLB-146

The Castle of Perseverance
circa 1400-1425................DLB-146

The Celtic Background to Medieval
English Literature.............DLB-146

The Chester Plays circa 1505-1532;
revisions until 1575............DLB-146

Cursor Mundi circa 1300 ....DLB-146

The English Language: 410
to 1500 ....DLB-146

The Germanic Epic and Old English
Heroic Poetry: Widsith, Waldere,
and The Fight at Finnsburg DLB-146

Judith circa 930 ....DLB-146

The Matter of England 1240-1400 ... DLB-146

The Matter of Rome early twelfth to
late fifteenth centuries..........DLB-146

Middle English Literature:
An Introduction DLB-146

The Middle English Lyric..........DLB-146

Morality Plays: Mankind circa 1450-1500
and Everyman circa 1500 ....DLB-146

N-Town Plays circa 1468 to early
sixteenth century DLB-146

Old English Literature:
An Introduction DLB-146

Old English Riddles
eighth to tenth centuries........DLB-146

The Owl and the Nightingale
circa 1189-1199...............DLB-146

The Paston Letters 1422-1509.........DLB-146

The Seafarer circa 970 ....DLB-146

The South English Legendary circa
thirteenth to fifteenth centuries DLB-146

The British Review and London Critical
Journal 1811-1825................DLB-110

Brito, Aristeo 1942- DLB-122

Brittain, Vera 1893-1970 ....DLB-191

Briusov, Valerii Iakovlevich
1873-1924 ....DLB-295

Brizeux, Auguste 1803-1858 ....DLB-217

Broadway Publishing Company DLB-46

Broch, Hermann
1886-1951 ....DLB-85, 124; CDWLB-2

Brochu, André 1942- DLB-53

Brock, Edwin 1927-1997 ....DLB-40

Brockes, Barthold Heinrich 1680-1747 ...DLB-168

Brod, Max 1884-1968 ....DLB-81

Brodber, Erna 1940- DLB-157

Brodhead, John R. 1814-1873 ....DLB-30

Brodkey, Harold 1930-1996..........DLB-130

Brodsky, Joseph (Iosif Aleksandrovich
    Brodsky) 1940-1996.........DLB-285; Y-87

    Nobel Lecture 1987................Y-87

Brodsky, Michael 1948-...........DLB-244

Broeg, Bob 1918-................DLB-171

Brøgger, Suzanne 1944-...........DLB-214

Brome, Richard circa 1590-1652........DLB-58

Brome, Vincent 1910-2004...........DLB-155

Bromfield, Louis 1896-1956........DLB-4, 9, 86

Bromige, David 1933-..............DLB-193

Broner, E. M. 1930-................DLB-28

    Tribute to Bernard Malamud..........Y-86

Bronk, William 1918-1999............DLB-165

Bronnen, Arnolt 1895-1959...........DLB-124

Brontë, Anne 1820-1849..........DLB-21, 199

Brontë, Charlotte
    1816-1855......DLB-21, 159, 199; CDBLB-4

Brontë, Emily
    1818-1848.......DLB-21, 32, 199; CDBLB-4

The Brontë Society..................Y-98

Brook, Stephen 1947-..............DLB-204

Brook Farm 1841-1847........DLB-1; 223; DS-5

Brooke, Frances 1724-1789..........DLB-39, 99

Brooke, Henry 1703?-1783...........DLB-39

Brooke, L. Leslie 1862-1940........DLB-141

Brooke, Margaret, Ranee of Sarawak
    1849-1936......................DLB-174

Brooke, Rupert
    1887-1915..........DLB-19, 216; CDBLB-6

    The Friends of the Dymock Poets........Y-00

Brooker, Bertram 1888-1955..........DLB-88

Brooke-Rose, Christine 1923-.....DLB-14, 231

Brookner, Anita 1928-..........DLB-194; Y-87

Brooks, Charles Timothy 1813-1883..DLB-1, 243

Brooks, Cleanth 1906-1994.......DLB-63; Y-94

    Tribute to Katherine Anne Porter.......Y-80

    Tribute to Walker Percy............Y-90

Brooks, Gwendolyn
    1917-2000........DLB-5, 76, 165; CDALB-1

    Tribute to Julian Mayfield............Y-84

Brooks, Jeremy 1926-1994.............DLB-14

Brooks, Mel 1926-..................DLB-26

Brooks, Noah 1830-1903........DLB-42; DS-13

Brooks, Richard 1912-1992............DLB-44

Brooks, Van Wyck 1886-1963...DLB-45, 63, 103

Brophy, Brigid 1929-1995.......DLB-14, 70, 271

Brophy, John 1899-1965.............DLB-191

Brorson, Hans Adolph 1694-1764......DLB-300

Brossard, Chandler 1922-1993.........DLB-16

Brossard, Nicole 1943-...............DLB-53

Broster, Dorothy Kathleen 1877-1950....DLB-160

Brother Antoninus (see Everson, William)

Brotherton, Lord 1856-1930..........DLB-184

Brougham, John 1810-1880............DLB-11

Brougham and Vaux, Henry Peter
    Brougham, Baron 1778-1868....DLB-110, 158

Broughton, James 1913-1999...........DLB-5

Broughton, Rhoda 1840-1920..........DLB-18

Broun, Heywood 1888-1939........DLB-29, 171

Browder, Earl 1891-1973............DLB-303

Brown, Alice 1856-1948..............DLB-78

Brown, Bob 1886-1959........DLB-4, 45; DS-15

Brown, Cecil 1943-.................DLB-33

Brown, Charles Brockden
    1771-1810.........DLB-37, 59, 73; CDALB-2

Brown, Christy 1932-1981............DLB-14

Brown, Dee 1908-2002.................Y-80

Brown, Frank London 1927-1962.......DLB-76

Brown, Fredric 1906-1972.............DLB-8

Brown, George Mackay
    1921-1996............DLB-14, 27, 139, 271

Brown, Harry 1917-1986..............DLB-26

Brown, Ian 1945-..................DLB-310

Brown, Larry 1951-...........DLB-234, 292

Brown, Lew 1893-1958...............DLB-265

Brown, Marcia 1918-................DLB-61

Brown, Margaret Wise 1910-1952......DLB-22

Brown, Morna Doris (see Ferrars, Elizabeth)

Brown, Oliver Madox 1855-1874.......DLB-21

Brown, Sterling 1901-1989......DLB-48, 51, 63

Brown, T. E. 1830-1897..............DLB-35

Brown, Thomas Alexander (see Boldrewood, Rolf)

Brown, Warren 1894-1978............DLB-241

Brown, William Hill 1765-1793........DLB-37

Brown, William Wells
    1815-1884............DLB-3, 50, 183, 248

Brown University
    The Festival of Vanguard Narrative.....Y-93

Browne, Charles Farrar 1834-1867......DLB-11

Browne, Frances 1816-1879..........DLB-199

Browne, Francis Fisher 1843-1913.....DLB-79

Browne, Howard 1908-1999..........DLB-226

Browne, J. Ross 1821-1875...........DLB-202

Browne, Michael Dennis 1940-........DLB-40

Browne, Sir Thomas 1605-1682........DLB-151

Browne, William, of Tavistock
    1590-1645......................DLB-121

Browne, Wynyard 1911-1964......DLB-13, 233

Browne and Nolan..................DLB-106

Brownell, W. C. 1851-1928...........DLB-71

Browning, Elizabeth Barrett
    1806-1861..........DLB-32, 199; CDBLB-4

Browning, Robert
    1812-1889.........DLB-32, 163; CDBLB-4

    Essay on Chatterton................DLB-32

    Introductory Essay: *Letters of Percy*
    Bysshe Shelley (1852)............DLB-32

    "The Novel in [Robert Browning's]
    'The Ring and the Book'" (1912),
    by Henry James................DLB-32

Brownjohn, Allan 1931-..............DLB-40

    Tribute to John Betjeman............Y-84

Brownson, Orestes Augustus
    1803-1876..........DLB-1, 59, 73, 243; DS-5

Bruccoli, Matthew J. 1931-..........DLB-103

    Joseph [Heller] and George [V. Higgins]...Y-99

    Response [to Busch on Fitzgerald].......Y-96

    Tribute to Albert Erskine.............Y-93

    Tribute to Charles E. Feinberg........Y-88

    Working with Fredson Bowers.........Y-91

Bruce, Charles 1906-1971............DLB-68

Bruce, John Edward 1856-1924

    Three Documents [African American
    poets].......................DLB-50

Bruce, Leo 1903-1979................DLB-77

Bruce, Mary Grant 1878-1958........DLB-230

Bruce, Philip Alexander 1856-1933......DLB-47

Bruce-Novoa, Juan 1944-............DLB-82

Bruckman, Clyde 1894-1955...........DLB-26

Bruckner, Ferdinand 1891-1958.......DLB-118

Brundage, John Herbert (see Herbert, John)

Brunner, John 1934-1995............DLB-261

    Tribute to Theodore Sturgeon.........Y-85

Brutus, Dennis
    1924-..........DLB-117, 225; CDWLB-3

Bryan, C. D. B. 1936-..............DLB-185

Bryan, William Jennings 1860-1925.....DLB-303

Bryant, Arthur 1899-1985...........DLB-149

Bryant, William Cullen 1794-1878
    ....DLB-3, 43, 59, 189, 250; CDALB-2

Bryce, James 1838-1922.........DLB-166, 190

Bryce Echenique, Alfredo
    1939-..............DLB-145; CDWLB-3

Bryden, Bill 1942-.................DLB-233

Brydges, Sir Samuel Egerton
    1762-1837..................DLB-107, 142

Bryskett, Lodowick 1546?-1612........DLB-167

Buchan, John 1875-1940.........DLB-34, 70, 156

Buchanan, George 1506-1582..........DLB-132

Buchanan, Robert 1841-1901........DLB-18, 35

    "The Fleshly School of Poetry and
    Other Phenomena of the Day"
    (1872).......................DLB-35

    "The Fleshly School of Poetry:
    Mr. D. G. Rossetti" (1871),
    by Thomas Maitland...........DLB-35

Buchler, Justus 1914-1991...........DLB-279

Buchman, Sidney 1902-1975...........DLB-26

Buchner, Augustus 1591-1661........DLB-164

Büchner, Georg
    1813-1837..............DLB-133; CDWLB-2

Bucholtz, Andreas Heinrich 1607-1671....DLB-168

Buck, Pearl S. 1892-1973..DLB-9, 102; CDALB-7

Bucke, Charles 1781-1846...........DLB-110

Bucke, Richard Maurice 1837-1902......DLB-99

Buckingham, Edwin 1810-1833.........DLB-73

Buckingham, Joseph Tinker 1779-1861...DLB-73

Buckler, Ernest 1908-1984...........DLB-68

Buckley, Vincent 1925-1988..........DLB-289

Buckley, William F., Jr. 1925-....DLB-137; Y-80

Publisher's Statement From the
    Initial Issue of *National Review*
    (19 November 1955)..........DLB-137

Buckminster, Joseph Stevens
    1784-1812......................DLB-37

Buckner, Robert 1906-1989............DLB-26

Budd, Thomas ?-1698..................DLB-24

Budrys, A. J. 1931-....................DLB-8

Buechner, Frederick 1926-............Y-80

Buell, John 1927-.....................DLB-53

Buenaventura, Enrique 1925-2003......DLB-305

Bufalino, Gesualdo 1920-1996.........DLB-196

Buffon, Georges-Louis Leclerc de
    1707-1788....................DLB-313

    "Le Discours sur le style".......DLB-314

Job Buffum [publishing house].........DLB-49

Bugnet, Georges 1879-1981............DLB-92

al-Buhturi 821-897....................DLB-311

Buies, Arthur 1840-1901..............DLB-99

Bukiet, Melvin Jules 1953-............DLB-299

Bukowski, Charles 1920-1994....DLB-5, 130, 169

Bulatović, Miodrag
    1930-1991............DLB-181; CDWLB-4

Bulgakov, Mikhail Afanas'evich
    1891-1940....................DLB-272

Bulgarin, Faddei Venediktovich
    1789-1859....................DLB-198

Bulger, Bozeman 1877-1932............DLB-171

Bull, Olaf 1883-1933..................DLB-297

Bullein, William
    between 1520 and 1530-1576.......DLB-167

Bullins, Ed 1935-.............DLB-7, 38, 249

Bulosan, Carlos 1911-1956............DLB-312

Bulwer, John 1606-1656................DLB-236

Bulwer-Lytton, Edward (also Edward
    Bulwer) 1803-1873..............DLB-21

    "On Art in Fiction" (1838).........DLB-21

Bumpus, Jerry 1937-....................Y-81

Bunce and Brother....................DLB-49

Bunin, Ivan 1870-1953................DLB-317

Bunner, H. C. 1855-1896............DLB-78, 79

Bunting, Basil 1900-1985..............DLB-20

Buntline, Ned (Edward Zane Carroll
    Judson) 1821-1886..............DLB-186

Bunyan, John 1628-1688.....DLB-39; CDBLB-2

    The Author's Apology for
    His Book....................DLB-39

Burch, Robert 1925-...................DLB-52

Burciaga, José Antonio 1940-..........DLB-82

Burdekin, Katharine (Murray Constantine)
    1896-1963....................DLB-255

Bürger, Gottfried August 1747-1794....DLB-94

Burgess, Anthony (John Anthony Burgess Wilson)
    1917-1993......DLB-14, 194, 261; CDBLB-8

    The Anthony Burgess Archive at
    the Harry Ransom Humanities
    Research Center................Y-98

    Anthony Burgess's *99 Novels:*
    An Opinion Poll................Y-84

Burgess, Gelett 1866-1951.............DLB-11

Burgess, John W. 1844-1931............DLB-47

Burgess, Thornton W. 1874-1965........DLB-22

Burgess, Stringer and Company.........DLB-49

Burgos, Julia de 1914-1953............DLB-290

Burick, Si 1909-1986..................DLB-171

Burk, John Daly circa 1772-1808.......DLB-37

Burk, Ronnie 1955-....................DLB-209

Burke, Edmund 1729?-1797........DLB-104, 252

Burke, James Lee 1936-................DLB-226

Burke, Johnny 1908-1964...............DLB-265

Burke, Kenneth 1897-1993..........DLB-45, 63

Burke, Thomas 1886-1945...............DLB-197

Burley, Dan 1907-1962.................DLB-241

Burley, W. J. 1914-...................DLB-276

Burlingame, Edward Livermore
    1848-1922....................DLB-79

Burliuk, David 1882-1967..............DLB-317

Burman, Carina 1960-..................DLB-257

Burnet, Gilbert 1643-1715.............DLB-101

Burnett, Frances Hodgson
    1849-1924..........DLB-42, 141; DS-13, 14

Burnett, W. R. 1899-1982...........DLB-9, 226

Burnett, Whit 1899-1973...............DLB-137

Burney, Fanny 1752-1840...............DLB-39

    Dedication, *The Wanderer* (1814)...DLB-39

    Preface to *Evelina* (1778)........DLB-39

Burns, Alan 1929-..................DLB-14, 194

Burns, Joanne 1945-...................DLB-289

Burns, John Horne 1916-1953...........Y-85

Burns, Robert 1759-1796......DLB-109; CDBLB-3

Burns and Oates.......................DLB-106

Burnshaw, Stanley 1906-.........DLB-48; Y-97

    James Dickey and Stanley Burnshaw
    Correspondence..................Y-02

    Review of Stanley Burnshaw: The
    Collected Poems and Selected
    Prose..........................Y-02

    Tribute to Robert Penn Warren......Y-89

Burr, C. Chauncey 1815?-1883..........DLB-79

Burr, Esther Edwards 1732-1758........DLB-200

Burroughs, Edgar Rice 1875-1950........DLB-8

    The Burroughs Bibliophiles.........Y-98

Burroughs, John 1837-1921..........DLB-64, 275

Burroughs, Margaret T. G. 1917-.......DLB-41

Burroughs, William S., Jr. 1947-1981...DLB-16

Burroughs, William Seward 1914-1997
    ....DLB-2, 8, 16, 152, 237; Y-81, 97

Burroway, Janet 1936-..................DLB-6

Burt, Maxwell Struthers
    1882-1954................DLB-86; DS-16

A. L. Burt and Company...............DLB-49

Burton, Hester 1913-2000..............DLB-161

Burton, Isabel Arundell 1831-1896.....DLB-166

Burton, Miles (see Rhode, John)

Burton, Richard Francis
    1821-1890.................DLB-55, 166, 184

Burton, Robert 1577-1640..............DLB-151

Burton, Virginia Lee 1909-1968........DLB-22

Burton, William Evans 1804-1860.......DLB-73

Burwell, Adam Hood 1790-1849..........DLB-99

Bury, Lady Charlotte 1775-1861........DLB-116

Busch, Frederick 1941-.............DLB-6, 218

    Excerpts from Frederick Busch's USC
    Remarks [on F. Scott Fitzgerald].....Y-96

    Tribute to James Laughlin..........Y-97

    Tribute to Raymond Carver..........Y-88

Busch, Niven 1903-1991................DLB-44

Bushnell, Horace
    1802-1876.....................DS-13

Business & Literature
    The Claims of Business and Literature:
    An Undergraduate Essay by
    Maxwell Perkins................Y-01

Bussières, Arthur de 1877-1913........DLB-92

Butler, Charles circa 1560-1647.......DLB-236

Butler, Guy 1918-.....................DLB-225

Butler, Joseph 1692-1752..............DLB-252

Butler, Josephine Elizabeth
    1828-1906...................DLB-190

Butler, Juan 1942-1981................DLB-53

Butler, Judith 1956-..................DLB-246

Butler, Octavia E. 1947-..............DLB-33

Butler, Pierce 1884-1953..............DLB-187

Butler, Robert Olen 1945-.............DLB-173

Butler, Samuel 1613-1680..........DLB-101, 126

Butler, Samuel
    1835-1902........DLB-18, 57, 174; CDBLB-5

Butler, William Francis 1838-1910.....DLB-166

E. H. Butler and Company..............DLB-49

Butor, Michel 1926-...................DLB-83

Nathaniel Butter [publishing house]...DLB-170

Butterworth, Hezekiah 1839-1905.......DLB-42

Buttitta, Ignazio 1899-1997...........DLB-114

Butts, Mary 1890-1937.................DLB-240

Buzo, Alex 1944-......................DLB-289

Buzzati, Dino 1906-1972...............DLB-177

Byars, Betsy 1928-....................DLB-52

Byatt, A. S. 1936-...........DLB-14, 194, 319

Byles, Mather 1707-1788...............DLB-24

Henry Bynneman [publishing house]....DLB-170

Bynner, Witter 1881-1968..............DLB-54

Byrd, William circa 1543-1623.........DLB-172

Byrd, William, II 1674-1744.......DLB-24, 140

Byrne, John Keyes (see Leonard, Hugh)

Byron, George Gordon, Lord
    1788-1824..........DLB-96, 110; CDBLB-3

    The Byron Society of America......Y-00

Byron, Robert 1905-1941...............DLB-195

Byzantine Novel, The Spanish..........DLB-318

C

Caballero Bonald, José Manuel
    1926-........................DLB-108

Cumulative Index

Cabañero, Eladio 1930- DLB-134

Cabell, James Branch 1879-1958 .... DLB-9, 78

Cabeza de Baca, Manuel 1853-1915 ..... DLB-122

Cabeza de Baca Gilbert, Fabiola
 1898-1993 .... DLB-122

Cable, George Washington
 1844-1925 .... .DLB-12, 74; DS-13

Cable, Mildred 1878-1952 .... DLB-195

Cabral, Manuel del 1907-1999 .... DLB-283

Cabral de Melo Neto, João
 1920-1999 .... DLB-307

Cabrera, Lydia 1900-1991 .... DLB-145

Cabrera Infante, Guillermo
 1929- DLB-113; CDWLB-3

Cabrujas, José Ignacio 1937-1995 .... DLB-305

Cadell [publishing house] DLB-154

Cady, Edwin H. 1917- DLB-103

Caedmon fl. 658-680 .... DLB-146

Caedmon School circa 660-899 .... DLB-146

Caesar, Irving 1895-1996 .... DLB-265

Cafés, Brasseries, and Bistros DS-15

Cage, John 1912-1992 .... DLB-193

Cahan, Abraham 1860-1951 .... DLB-9, 25, 28

Cahn, Sammy 1913-1993 .... DLB-265

Cain, George 1943- DLB-33

Cain, James M. 1892-1977 .... DLB-226

Cain, Paul (Peter Ruric, George Sims)
 1902-1966 .... DLB-306

Caird, Edward 1835-1908 .... DLB-262

Caird, Mona 1854-1932 .... DLB-197

Čaks, Aleksandrs
 1901-1950 .... DLB-220; CDWLB-4

Caldecott, Randolph 1846-1886 .... DLB-163

John Calder Limited
 [Publishing house] DLB-112

Calderón de la Barca, Fanny
 1804-1882 .... DLB-183

Caldwell, Ben 1937- DLB-38

Caldwell, Erskine 1903-1987 .... DLB-9, 86

H. M. Caldwell Company DLB-49

Caldwell, Taylor 1900-1985 ....DS-17

Calhoun, John C. 1782-1850 .... DLB-3, 248

Călinescu, George 1899-1965 .... DLB-220

Calisher, Hortense 1911- DLB-2, 218

Calkins, Mary Whiton 1863-1930 ......DLB-270

Callaghan, Mary Rose 1944- DLB-207

Callaghan, Morley 1903-1990 .... DLB-68; DS-15

Callahan, S. Alice 1868-1894 ......DLB-175, 221

Callaloo [journal] Y-87

Callimachus circa 305 B.C.-240 B.C. DLB-176

Calmer, Edgar 1907-1986 .... DLB-4

Calverley, C. S. 1831-1884 .... DLB-35

Calvert, George Henry
 1803-1889 .... DLB-1, 64, 248

Calverton, V. F. (George Goetz)
 1900-1940 .... DLB-303

Calvino, Italo 1923-1985 .... DLB-196

Cambridge, Ada 1844-1926 .... DLB-230

Cambridge Press DLB-49

Cambridge Songs (Carmina Cantabrigensia)
 circa 1050 .... DLB-148

Cambridge University
 Cambridge and the Apostles DS-5

Cambridge University Press DLB-170

Camden, William 1551-1623 ....DLB-172

Camden House: An Interview with
 James Hardin Y-92

Cameron, Eleanor 1912-2000 .... DLB-52

Cameron, George Frederick
 1854-1885 .... DLB-99

Cameron, Lucy Lyttelton 1781-1858 .... DLB-163

Cameron, Peter 1959- DLB-234

Cameron, William Bleasdell 1862-1951 ... DLB-99

Camm, John 1718-1778 .... DLB-31

Camões, Luís de 1524-1580 .... DLB-287

Camon, Ferdinando 1935- DLB-196

Camp, Walter 1859-1925 .... DLB-241

Campana, Dino 1885-1932 .... DLB-114

Campbell, Bebe Moore 1950- DLB-227

Campbell, David 1915-1979 .... DLB-260

Campbell, Gabrielle Margaret Vere
 (see Shearing, Joseph, and Bowen, Marjorie)

Campbell, James Dykes 1838-1895 ..... DLB-144

Campbell, James Edwin 1867-1896 .... DLB-50

Campbell, John 1653-1728 .... DLB-43

Campbell, John W., Jr. 1910-1971 .... DLB-8

Campbell, Ramsey 1946- DLB-261

Campbell, Robert 1927-2000 .... DLB-306

Campbell, Roy 1901-1957 .... DLB-20, 225

Campbell, Thomas 1777-1844 ..... DLB-93, 144

Campbell, William Edward (see March, William)

Campbell, William Wilfred 1858-1918 ... DLB-92

Campion, Edmund 1539-1581 .... DLB-167

Campion, Thomas
 1567-1620 .... DLB-58, 172; CDBLB-1

Campo, Rafael 1964- DLB-282

Campton, David 1924- DLB-245

Camus, Albert 1913-1960 .... DLB-72, 321

Camus, Jean-Pierre 1584-1652 ....DLB-268

The Canadian Publishers' Records Database .. Y-96

Canby, Henry Seidel 1878-1961 .... DLB-91

Cancioneros DLB-286

Candelaria, Cordelia 1943- DLB-82

Candelaria, Nash 1928- DLB-82

Candide, Voltaire DLB-314

Canetti, Elias
 1905-1994 .... DLB-85, 124; CDWLB-2

Canham, Erwin Dain 1904-1982 .... DLB-127

Canitz, Friedrich Rudolph Ludwig von
 1654-1699 .... DLB-168

Cankar, Ivan 1876-1918 .....DLB-147; CDWLB-4

Cannan, Gilbert 1884-1955 ....DLB-10, 197

Cannan, Joanna 1896-1961 .... DLB-191

Cannell, Kathleen 1891-1974 .... DLB-4

Cannell, Skipwith 1887-1957 .... DLB-45

Canning, George 1770-1827 .... DLB-158

Cannon, Jimmy 1910-1973 ....DLB-171

Cano, Daniel 1947- DLB-209

Old Dogs / New Tricks? New
 Technologies, the Canon, and the
 Structure of the Profession Y-02

Cantú, Norma Elia 1947- DLB-209

Cantwell, Robert 1908-1978 .... DLB-9

Jonathan Cape and Harrison Smith
 [publishing house] DLB-46

Jonathan Cape Limited DLB-112

Čapek, Karel 1890-1938 ..... DLB-215; CDWLB-4

Capen, Joseph 1658-1725 .... DLB-24

Capes, Bernard 1854-1918 .... DLB-156

Capote, Truman 1924-1984
 .... DLB-2, 185, 227; Y-80, 84; CDALB-1

Capps, Benjamin 1922- DLB-256

Caproni, Giorgio 1912-1990 .... DLB-128

Caragiale, Mateiu Ioan 1885-1936 ...... DLB-220

Carballido, Emilio 1925- DLB-305

Cardarelli, Vincenzo 1887-1959 .... DLB-114

Cardenal, Ernesto 1925- DLB-290

Cárdenas, Reyes 1948- DLB-122

Cardinal, Marie 1929-2001 .... DLB-83

Cardoza y Aragón, Luis 1901-1992 ..... DLB-290

Carew, Jan 1920- DLB-157

Carew, Thomas 1594 or 1595-1640 .... DLB-126

Carey, Henry circa 1687-1689-1743 ...... DLB-84

Carey, Mathew 1760-1839 ....DLB-37, 73

M. Carey and Company DLB-49

Carey, Peter 1943- DLB-289

Carey and Hart DLB-49

Carlell, Lodowick 1602-1675 .... DLB-58

Carleton, William 1794-1869 .... DLB-159

G. W. Carleton [publishing house] DLB-49

Carlile, Richard 1790-1843 ....DLB-110, 158

Carlson, Ron 1947- DLB-244

Carlyle, Jane Welsh 1801-1866 .... DLB-55

Carlyle, Thomas
 1795-1881 .... DLB-55, 144; CDBLB-3

 "The Hero as Man of Letters:
  Johnson, Rousseau, Burns"
  (1841) [excerpt] DLB-57

 The Hero as Poet. Dante; Shakspeare
  (1841) DLB-32

Carman, Bliss 1861-1929 .... DLB-92

Carmina Burana circa 1230 .... DLB-138

Carnap, Rudolf 1891-1970 ....DLB-270

Carnero, Guillermo 1947- DLB-108

Carossa, Hans 1878-1956 .... DLB-66

Carpenter, Humphrey
 1946-2005 ....DLB-155; Y-84, 99

Carpenter, Stephen Cullen ?-1820? DLB-73

Carpentier, Alejo
 1904-1980 ....DLB-113; CDWLB-3

Carr, Emily 1871-1945 .... DLB-68

Carr, John Dickson 1906-1977.........DLB-306	Casey, Juanita 1925- DLB-14	Cela, Camilo José 1916-2002.............. Y-89
Carr, Marina 1964- DLB-245	Casey, Michael 1947- DLB-5	Nobel Lecture 1989................. Y-89
Carr, Virginia Spencer 1929-......DLB-111; Y-00	Cassady, Carolyn 1923- DLB-16	Celan, Paul 1920-1970.......DLB-69; CDWLB-2
Carrera Andrade, Jorge 1903-1978 ......DLB-283	"As I See It"....................DLB-16	Celati, Gianni 1937- DLB-196
Carrier, Roch 1937- DLB-53	Cassady, Neal 1926-1968 ....DLB-16, 237	Celaya, Gabriel 1911-1991 ....DLB-108
Carrillo, Adolfo 1855-1926 ....DLB-122	Cassell and Company DLB-106	Céline, Louis-Ferdinand 1894-1961.......DLB-72
Carroll, Gladys Hasty 1904-1999 ....DLB-9	Cassell Publishing Company............DLB-49	Celtis, Conrad 1459-1508 ....DLB-179
Carroll, John 1735-1815................DLB-37	Cassill, R. V. 1919-2002 ....DLB-6, 218; Y-02	Cendrars, Blaise 1887-1961 ....DLB-258
Carroll, John 1809-1884 ....DLB-99	Tribute to James Dickey Y-97	The Steinbeck Centennial Y-02
Carroll, Lewis 1832-1898......DLB-18, 163, 178; CDBLB-4	Cassity, Turner 1929- DLB-105; Y-02	Censorship
The Lewis Carroll Centenary......... Y-98	Cassius Dio circa 155/164-post 229 ......DLB-176	The Island Trees Case: A Symposium on School Library Censorship......... Y-82
The Lewis Carroll Society of North America Y-00	Cassola, Carlo 1917-1987..............DLB-177	Center for Bibliographical Studies and Research at the University of California, Riverside................. Y-91
Carroll, Paul 1927-1996 ....DLB-16	Castellano, Olivia 1944- DLB-122	Center for Book Research................. Y-84
Carroll, Paul Vincent 1900-1968.........DLB-10	Castellanos, Rosario 1925-1974 ......DLB-113, 290; CDWLB-3	The Center for the Book in the Library of Congress.................. Y-93
Carroll and Graf Publishers DLB-46	Castelo Branco, Camilo 1825-1890......DLB-287	A New Voice: The Center for the Book's First Five Years............. Y-83
Carruth, Hayden 1921- DLB-5, 165	Castile, Protest Poetry in DLB-286	Centlivre, Susanna 1669?-1723 ....DLB-84
Tribute to James Dickey Y-97	Castile and Aragon, Vernacular Translations in Crowns of 1352-1515 ....DLB-286	The Centre for Writing, Publishing and Printing History at the University of Reading........................ Y-00
Tribute to Raymond Carver........... Y-88	Castillejo, Cristóbal de 1490?-1550 ......DLB-318	
Carryl, Charles E. 1841-1920 ....DLB-42	Castillo, Ana 1953- DLB-122, 227	The Century Company................DLB-49
Carson, Anne 1950- DLB-193	Castillo, Rafael C. 1950- DLB-209	A Century of Poetry, a Lifetime of Collecting: J. M. Edelstein's Collection of Twentieth-Century American Poetry Y-02
Carson, Rachel 1907-1964 ....DLB-275	*The Castle of Perseverance* circa 1400-1425...................DLB-146	
Carswell, Catherine 1879-1946 ....DLB-36	Castlemon, Harry (see Fosdick, Charles Austin)	Cernuda, Luis 1902-1963 ....DLB-134
Cartagena, Alfonso de ca. 1384-1456 ....DLB-286	Castro, Consuelo de 1946- DLB-307	Cerruto, Oscar 1912-1981..............DLB-283
Cartagena, Teresa de 1425?-? DLB-286	Castro Alves, Antônio de 1847-1871 .....DLB-307	Cervantes, Lorna Dee 1954- DLB-82
Cărtărescu, Mirea 1956- DLB-232	Čašule, Kole 1921- DLB-181	Césaire, Aimé 1913- DLB-321
Carter, Angela 1940-1992 .... DLB-14, 207, 261, 319	Caswall, Edward 1814-1878.............DLB-32	de Céspedes, Alba 1911-1997 ....DLB-264
Carter, Elizabeth 1717-1806 ....DLB-109	Catacalos, Rosemary 1944- DLB-122	Cetina, Gutierre de 1514-17?-1556 ......DLB-318
Carter, Henry (see Leslie, Frank)	Cather, Willa 1873-1947 ....DLB-9, 54, 78, 256; DS-1; CDALB-3	Ch., T. (see Marchenko, Anastasiia Iakovlevna)
Carter, Hodding, Jr. 1907-1972 ....DLB-127		Cha, Theresa Hak Kyung 1951-1982 ....DLB-312
Carter, Jared 1939- DLB-282	The Willa Cather Pioneer Memorial and Education Foundation Y-00	Chaadaev, Petr Iakovlevich 1794-1856 ....DLB-198
Carter, John 1905-1975 ....DLB-201	Catherine II (Ekaterina Alekseevna), "The Great," Empress of Russia 1729-1796 ....DLB-150	Chabon, Michael 1963- DLB-278
Carter, Landon 1710-1778 ....DLB-31		Chacel, Rosa 1898-1994 ....DLB-134
Carter, Lin 1930-1988 .... Y-81	Catherwood, Mary Hartwell 1847-1902 ...DLB-78	Chacón, Eusebio 1869-1948 ....DLB-82
Carter, Martin 1927-1997 ....DLB-117; CDWLB-3	Catledge, Turner 1901-1983 ....DLB-127	Chacón, Felipe Maximiliano 1873-?.......DLB-82
Carter, Robert, and Brothers............DLB-49	Catlin, George 1796-1872..........DLB-186, 189	Chadwick, Henry 1824-1908...........DLB-241
Carter and Hendee DLB-49	Cato the Elder 234 B.C.-149 B.C.........DLB-211	Chadwyck-Healey's Full-Text Literary Databases: Editing Commercial Databases of Primary Literary Texts................ Y-95
Cartwright, Jim 1958- DLB-245	Cattafi, Bartolo 1922-1979 ....DLB-128	
Cartwright, John 1740-1824............DLB-158	Catton, Bruce 1899-1978 ....DLB-17	Challans, Eileen Mary (see Renault, Mary)
Cartwright, William circa 1611-1643.....DLB-126	Catullus circa 84 B.C.-54 B.C. DLB-211; CDWLB-1	Chalmers, George 1742-1825............DLB-30
Caruthers, William Alexander 1802-1846....................DLB-3, 248		Chaloner, Sir Thomas 1520-1565 ....DLB-167
	Causley, Charles 1917-2003 ....DLB-27	Chamberlain, Samuel S. 1851-1916.......DLB-25
Carver, Jonathan 1710-1780.............DLB-31	Caute, David 1936- DLB-14, 231	Chamberland, Paul 1939- DLB-60
Carver, Raymond 1938-1988 .. DLB-130; Y-83,88	Cavendish, Duchess of Newcastle, Margaret Lucas 1623?-1673 ....DLB-131, 252, 281	Chamberlin, William Henry 1897-1969....DLB-29
First Strauss "Livings" Awarded to Cynthia Ozick and Raymond Carver An Interview with Raymond Carver ... Y-83		Chambers, Charles Haddon 1860-1921 ...DLB-10
	Cawein, Madison 1865-1914............DLB-54	Chambers, María Cristina (see Mena, María Cristina)
Carvic, Heron 1917?-1980..............DLB-276	William Caxton [publishing house]......DLB-170	Chambers, Robert W. 1865-1933........DLB-202
Cary, Alice 1820-1871 ....DLB-202	The Caxton Printers, Limited DLB-46	W. and R. Chambers [publishing house]................DLB-106
Cary, Joyce 1888-1957....DLB-15, 100; CDBLB-6	Caylor, O. P. 1849-1897 ....DLB-241	
Cary, Patrick 1623?-1657..............DLB-131	Caylus, Marthe-Marguerite de 1671-1729 ....DLB-313	
Casal, Julián del 1863-1893 ....DLB-283		
Case, John 1540-1600 ....DLB-281	Cayrol, Jean 1911-2005 ....DLB-83	
Casey, Gavin 1907-1964 ....DLB-260	Cecil, Lord David 1902-1986 ....DLB-155	Chambers, Whittaker 1901-1961 ....DLB-303

Chamfort, Sébastien-Roch Nicolas de
1740?-1794 . . . . DLB-313
Chamisso, Adelbert von 1781-1838 . . . . . . DLB-90
Champfleury 1821-1889 . . . . DLB-119
Chan, Jeffery Paul 1942- DLB-312
Chandler, Harry 1864-1944 . . . . DLB-29
Chandler, Norman 1899-1973 . . . . DLB-127
Chandler, Otis 1927- DLB-127
Chandler, Raymond
1888-1959 . . . DLB-226, 253; DS-6; CDALB-5
Raymond Chandler Centenary Y-88
Chang, Diana 1934- DLB-312
Channing, Edward 1856-1931 . . . . DLB-17
Channing, Edward Tyrrell
1790-1856 . . . . DLB-1, 59, 235
Channing, William Ellery
1780-1842 . . . . DLB-1, 59, 235
Channing, William Ellery, II
1817-1901 . . . . DLB-1, 223
Channing, William Henry
1810-1884 . . . . DLB-1, 59, 243
Chapelain, Jean 1595-1674 . . . . DLB-268
Chaplin, Charlie 1889-1977 . . . . DLB-44
Chapman, George
1559 or 1560-1634 . . . . DLB-62, 121
Chapman, Olive Murray 1892-1977 . . . . . DLB-195
Chapman, R. W. 1881-1960 . . . . DLB-201
Chapman, William 1850-1917 . . . . DLB-99
John Chapman [publishing house] DLB-106
Chapman and Hall [publishing house] . . . DLB-106
Chappell, Fred 1936- DLB-6, 105
"A Detail in a Poem" DLB-105
Tribute to Peter Taylor Y-94
Chappell, William 1582-1649 . . . . DLB-236
Char, René 1907-1988 . . . . DLB-258
Charbonneau, Jean 1875-1960 . . . . DLB-92
Charbonneau, Robert 1911-1967 . . . . DLB-68
Charles, Gerda 1914-1996 . . . . DLB-14
William Charles [publishing house] DLB-49
Charles d'Orléans 1394-1465 . . . . DLB-208
Charley (see Mann, Charles)
Charrière, Isabelle de 1740-1805 . . . . DLB-313
Charskaia, Lidiia 1875-1937 . . . . DLB-295
Charteris, Leslie 1907-1993 . . . . DLB-77
Chartier, Alain circa 1385-1430 . . . . DLB-208
Charyn, Jerome 1937- Y-83
Chase, Borden 1900-1971 . . . . DLB-26
Chase, Edna Woolman 1877-1957 . . . . DLB-91
Chase, James Hadley (René Raymond)
1906-1985 . . . . DLB-276
Chase, Mary Coyle 1907-1981 . . . . DLB-228
Chase-Riboud, Barbara 1936- DLB-33
Chateaubriand, François-René de
1768-1848 . . . . DLB-119
Châtelet, Gabrielle-Emilie Du
1706-1749 . . . . DLB-313
Chatterton, Thomas 1752-1770 . . . . DLB-109

Essay on Chatterton (1842), by
Robert Browning DLB-32
Chatto and Windus DLB-106
Chatwin, Bruce 1940-1989 . . . . DLB-194, 204
Chaucer, Geoffrey
1340?-1400 . . . . DLB-146; CDBLB-1
New Chaucer Society Y-00
Chaudhuri, Amit 1962- DLB-267
Chauncy, Charles 1705-1787 . . . . DLB-24
Chauveau, Pierre-Joseph-Olivier
1820-1890 . . . . DLB-99
Chávez, Denise 1948- DLB-122
Chávez, Fray Angélico 1910-1996 . . . . DLB-82
Chayefsky, Paddy 1923-1981 . . . . . DLB-7, 44; Y-81
Cheesman, Evelyn 1881-1969 . . . . DLB-195
Cheever, Ezekiel 1615-1708 . . . . DLB-24
Cheever, George Barrell 1807-1890 . . . . . . DLB-59
Cheever, John 1912-1982
. . . . DLB-2, 102, 227; Y-80, 82; CDALB-1
Cheever, Susan 1943- Y-82
Cheke, Sir John 1514-1557 . . . . DLB-132
Chekhov, Anton Pavlovich 1860-1904 . . . . DLB-277
Chelsea House DLB-46
Chênedollé, Charles de 1769-1833 . . . . . . DLB-217
Cheney, Brainard
Tribute to Caroline Gordon Y-81
Cheney, Ednah Dow 1824-1904 . . . . . DLB-1, 223
Cheney, Harriet Vaughan 1796-1889 . . . . . DLB-99
Chénier, Marie-Joseph 1764-1811 . . . . DLB-192
Cherny, Sasha 1880-1932 . . . . DLB-317
Chernyshevsky, Nikolai Gavrilovich
1828-1889 . . . . DLB-238
Cherry, Kelly 1940- Y-83
Cherryh, C. J. 1942- Y-80
Chesebro', Caroline 1825-1873 . . . . DLB-202
Chesney, Sir George Tomkyns
1830-1895 . . . . DLB-190
Chesnut, Mary Boykin 1823-1886 . . . . DLB-239
Chesnutt, Charles Waddell
1858-1932 . . . . DLB-12, 50, 78
Chesson, Mrs. Nora (see Hopper, Nora)
Chester, Alfred 1928-1971 . . . . DLB-130
Chester, George Randolph 1869-1924 . . . . DLB-78
The Chester Plays circa 1505-1532;
revisions until 1575 . . . . DLB-146
Chesterfield, Philip Dormer Stanhope,
Fourth Earl of 1694-1773 . . . . DLB-104
Chesterton, G. K. 1874-1936
. . . DLB-10, 19, 34, 70, 98, 149, 178; CDBLB-6
"The Ethics of Elfland" (1908) DLB-178
Chettle, Henry
circa 1560-circa 1607 . . . . DLB-136
Cheuse, Alan 1940- DLB-244
Chew, Ada Nield 1870-1945 . . . . DLB-135
Cheyney, Edward P. 1861-1947 . . . . DLB-47
Chiang Yee 1903-1977 . . . . DLB-312
Chiara, Piero 1913-1986 . . . . DLB-177

Chicanos
Chicano History DLB-82
Chicano Language DLB-82
Chicano Literature: A Bibliography . . DLB-209
A Contemporary Flourescence of Chicano
Literature Y-84
Literatura Chicanesca: The View From
Without DLB-82
Child, Francis James 1825-1896 . . . DLB-1, 64, 235
Child, Lydia Maria 1802-1880 . . . . . DLB-1, 74, 243
Child, Philip 1898-1978 . . . . DLB-68
Childers, Erskine 1870-1922 . . . . DLB-70
Children's Literature
Afterword: Propaganda, Namby-Pamby,
and Some Books of Distinction . . . DLB-52
Children's Book Awards and Prizes . . . DLB-61
Children's Book Illustration in the
Twentieth Century DLB-61
Children's Illustrators, 1800-1880 . . . DLB-163
The Harry Potter Phenomenon Y-99
Pony Stories, Omnibus
Essay on DLB-160
The Reality of One Woman's Dream:
The de Grummond Children's
Literature Collection Y-99
School Stories, 1914-1960 . . . . DLB-160
The Year in Children's
Books Y-92–96, 98–01
The Year in Children's Literature Y-97
Childress, Alice 1916-1994 . . . . DLB-7, 38, 249
Childress, Mark 1957- DLB-292
Childs, George W. 1829-1894 . . . . DLB-23
Chilton Book Company DLB-46
Chin, Frank 1940- DLB-206, 312
Chin, Justin 1969- DLB-312
Chin, Marilyn 1955- DLB-312
Chinweizu 1943- DLB-157
Chinnov, Igor' 1909-1996 . . . . DLB-317
Chitham, Edward 1932- DLB-155
Chittenden, Hiram Martin 1858-1917 . . . . DLB-47
Chivers, Thomas Holley 1809-1858 . . DLB-3, 248
Chkhartishvili, Grigorii Shalvovich
(see Akunin, Boris)
Chocano, José Santos 1875-1934 . . . . DLB-290
Cholmondeley, Mary 1859-1925 . . . . DLB-197
Chomsky, Noam 1928- DLB-246
Chopin, Kate 1850-1904 . . . DLB-12, 78; CDALB-3
Chopin, René 1885-1953 . . . . DLB-92
Choquette, Adrienne 1915-1973 . . . . DLB-68
Choquette, Robert 1905-1991 . . . . DLB-68
Choyce, Lesley 1951- DLB-251
Chrétien de Troyes
circa 1140-circa 1190 . . . . DLB-208
Christensen, Inger 1935- DLB-214
Christensen, Lars Saabye 1953- DLB-297
The Christian Examiner DLB-1
The Christian Publishing Company DLB-49

Christie, Agatha
1890-1976 . . . . DLB-13, 77, 245; CDBLB-6
Christine de Pizan
circa 1365-circa 1431. . . . . .DLB-208
Christopher, John (Sam Youd) 1922- . . .DLB-255
Christus und die Samariterin circa 950 . . . . . .DLB-148
Christy, Howard Chandler 1873-1952 . . .DLB-188
Chu, Louis 1915-1970 . . . . .DLB-312
Chukovskaia, Lidiia 1907-1996 . . . . .DLB-302
Chulkov, Mikhail Dmitrievich
1743?-1792. . . . . .DLB-150
Church, Benjamin 1734-1778. . . . . .DLB-31
Church, Francis Pharcellus 1839-1906 . . . .DLB-79
Church, Peggy Pond 1903-1986 . . . . .DLB-212
Church, Richard 1893-1972. . . . . .DLB-191
Church, William Conant 1836-1917 . . . . . .DLB-79
Churchill, Caryl 1938- DLB-13, 310
Churchill, Charles 1731-1764. . . . . .DLB-109
Churchill, Winston 1871-1947. . . . . .DLB-202
Churchill, Sir Winston
1874-1965 . . . . . . .DLB-100; DS-16; CDBLB-5
Churchyard, Thomas 1520?-1604. . . . . . . .DLB-132
E. Churton and Company. DLB-106
Chute, Marchette 1909-1994 . . . . .DLB-103
Ciardi, John 1916-1986 . . . . .DLB-5; Y-86
Cibber, Colley 1671-1757. . . . . .DLB-84
Cicero 106 B.C.-43 B.C. DLB-211, CDWLB-1
Cima, Annalisa 1941- DLB-128
Čingo, Živko 1935-1987 . . . . .DLB-181
Cioran, E. M. 1911-1995. . . . . .DLB-220
Čipkus, Alfonsas (see Nyka-Niliūnas, Alfonsas)
Cirese, Eugenio 1884-1955 . . . . .DLB-114
Cīrulis, Jānis (see Bels, Alberts)
Cisneros, Antonio 1942- DLB-290
Cisneros, Sandra 1954- DLB-122, 152
City Lights Books DLB-46
Civil War (1861–1865)
  Battles and Leaders of the Civil War . . .DLB-47
  Official Records of the Rebellion DLB-47
  Recording the Civil War. DLB-47
Cixous, Hélène 1937- DLB-83, 242
Claire d'Albe, Sophie Cottin. DLB-314
Clampitt, Amy 1920-1994 . . . . .DLB-105
  Tribute to Alfred A. Knopf. Y-84
Clancy, Tom 1947- DLB-227
Clapper, Raymond 1892-1944. . . . . .DLB-29
Clare, John 1793-1864 . . . . .DLB-55, 96
Clarendon, Edward Hyde, Earl of
1609-1674 .DLB-101
Clark, Alfred Alexander Gordon
(see Hare, Cyril)
Clark, Ann Nolan 1896-1995 . . . . .DLB-52
Clark, C. E. Frazer, Jr. 1925-2001 . . DLB-187; Y-01
  C. E. Frazer Clark Jr. and
  Hawthorne Bibliography DLB-269
  The Publications of C. E. Frazer
  Clark Jr. DLB-269

Clark, Catherine Anthony 1892-1977 . . . . .DLB-68
Clark, Charles Heber 1841-1915. . . . . .DLB-11
Clark, Davis Wasgatt 1812-1871 . . . . .DLB-79
Clark, Douglas 1919-1993 . . . . .DLB-276
Clark, Eleanor 1913-1996 . . . . .DLB-6
Clark, J. P. 1935- DLB-117; CDWLB-3
Clark, Lewis Gaylord
1808-1873 . . . . .DLB-3, 64, 73, 250
Clark, Mary Higgins 1929- DLB-306
Clark, Walter Van Tilburg
1909-1971 . . . . .DLB-9, 206
Clark, William 1770-1838 . . . . . .DLB-183, 186
Clark, William Andrews, Jr.
1877-1934 .DLB-187
C. M. Clark Publishing Company. DLB-46
Clarke, Sir Arthur C. 1917- DLB-261
  Tribute to Theodore Sturgeon Y-85
Clarke, Austin 1896-1974. . . . . .DLB-10, 20
Clarke, Austin C. 1934- DLB-53, 125
Clarke, Gillian 1937- DLB-40
Clarke, James Freeman
1810-1888 . . . . .DLB-1, 59, 235; DS-5
Clarke, John circa 1596-1658. . . . . .DLB-281
Clarke, Lindsay 1939- DLB-231
Clarke, Marcus 1846-1881 . . . . .DLB-230
Clarke, Pauline 1921- DLB-161
Clarke, Rebecca Sophia 1833-1906 . . . . . .DLB-42
Clarke, Samuel 1675-1729 . . . . .DLB-252
Robert Clarke and Company DLB-49
Clarkson, Thomas 1760-1846 . . . . .DLB-158
Claudel, Paul 1868-1955 . . . . . .DLB-192, 258, 321
Claudius, Matthias 1740-1815 . . . . .DLB-97
Clausen, Andy 1943- DLB-16
Claussen, Sophus 1865-1931 . . . . .DLB-300
Clawson, John L. 1865-1933 . . . . .DLB-187
Claxton, Remsen and Haffelfinger DLB-49
Clay, Cassius Marcellus 1810-1903. . . . . . .DLB-43
Clayton, Richard (see Haggard, William)
Cleage, Pearl 1948- DLB-228
Cleary, Beverly 1916- DLB-52
Cleary, Kate McPhelim 1863-1905 . . . . . .DLB-221
Cleaver, Vera 1919-1992 and
  Cleaver, Bill 1920-1981. . . . . .DLB-52
Cleeve, Brian 1921-2003 . . . . .DLB-276
Cleland, John 1710-1789 . . . . .DLB-39
Clemens, Samuel Langhorne (Mark Twain)
1835-1910 . . . . .DLB-11, 12, 23, 64, 74,
186, 189; CDALB-3
  Comments From Authors and Scholars on
  their First Reading of *Huck Finn*. Y-85
  Huck at 100: How Old Is
  Huckleberry Finn? Y-85
  Mark Twain on Perpetual Copyright Y-92
  A New Edition of *Huck Finn* Y-85
Clement, Hal 1922-2003 . . . . .DLB-8
Clemo, Jack 1916-1994 . . . . .DLB-27
Clephane, Elizabeth Cecilia 1830-1869 . . .DLB-199

Cleveland, John 1613-1658 . . . . .DLB-126
Cliff, Michelle 1946- DLB-157; CDWLB-3
Clifford, Lady Anne 1590-1676. . . . . .DLB-151
Clifford, James L. 1901-1978 . . . . .DLB-103
Clifford, Lucy 1853?-1929. . . . .DLB-135, 141, 197
Clift, Charmian 1923-1969 . . . . .DLB-260
Clifton, Lucille 1936- DLB-5, 41
Clines, Francis X. 1938- DLB-185
Clive, Caroline (V) 1801-1873. . . . . .DLB-199
Edward J. Clode [publishing house] DLB-46
Clough, Arthur Hugh 1819-1861 . . . . .DLB-32
Cloutier, Cécile 1930- DLB-60
Clouts, Sidney 1926-1982 . . . . .DLB-225
Clutton-Brock, Arthur 1868-1924 . . . . . . .DLB-98
Coates, Robert M.
1897-1973 . . . . .DLB-4, 9, 102; DS-15
Coatsworth, Elizabeth 1893-1986 . . . . .DLB-22
Cobb, Charles E., Jr. 1943- DLB-41
Cobb, Frank I. 1869-1923 . . . . .DLB-25
Cobb, Irvin S. 1876-1944. . . . . . . .DLB-11, 25, 86
Cobbe, Frances Power 1822-1904 . . . . . . .DLB-190
Cobbett, William 1763-1835 . . . .DLB-43, 107, 158
Cobbledick, Gordon 1898-1969 . . . . .DLB-171
Cochran, Thomas C. 1902-1999 . . . . .DLB-17
Cochrane, Elizabeth 1867-1922 . . . . . .DLB-25, 189
Cockerell, Sir Sydney 1867-1962. . . . . . . .DLB-201
Cockerill, John A. 1845-1896 . . . . .DLB-23
Cocteau, Jean 1889-1963 . . . . . . .DLB-65, 258, 321
Coderre, Emile (see Jean Narrache)
Cody, Liza 1944- DLB-276
Coe, Jonathan 1961- DLB-231
Coetzee, J. M. 1940- DLB-225
Coffee, Lenore J. 1900?-1984 . . . . .DLB-44
Coffin, Robert P. Tristram 1892-1955. . . . .DLB-45
Coghill, Mrs. Harry (see Walker, Anna Louisa)
Cogswell, Fred 1917- DLB-60
Cogswell, Mason Fitch 1761-1830 . . . . . . .DLB-37
Cohan, George M. 1878-1942 . . . . .DLB-249
Cohen, Arthur A. 1928-1986. . . . . .DLB-28
Cohen, Leonard 1934- DLB-53
Cohen, Matt 1942- DLB-53
Cohen, Morris Raphael 1880-1947 . . . . . .DLB-270
Colasanti, Marina 1937- DLB-307
Colbeck, Norman 1903-1987. . . . . .DLB-201
Colden, Cadwallader
1688-1776 . . . . .DLB-24, 30, 270
Colden, Jane 1724-1766 . . . . .DLB-200
Cole, Barry 1936- DLB-14
Cole, George Watson 1850-1939 . . . . . . .DLB-140
Colegate, Isabel 1931- DLB-14, 231
Coleman, Emily Holmes 1899-1974 . . . . . . .DLB-4
Coleman, Wanda 1946- DLB-130
Coleridge, Hartley 1796-1849 . . . . .DLB-96
Coleridge, Mary 1861-1907. . . . . .DLB-19, 98

Coleridge, Samuel Taylor 1772-1834 ....DLB-93, 107; CDBLB-3	Commynes, Philippe de circa 1447-1511................DLB-208	Conway, Moncure Daniel 1832-1907 ....DLB-1, 223
Coleridge, Sara 1802-1852 ....DLB-199	Compton, D. G. 1930- DLB-261	Cook, Ebenezer circa 1667-circa 1732.....DLB-24
Colet, John 1467-1519.................DLB-132	Compton-Burnett, Ivy 1884?-1969.......DLB-36	Cook, Edward Tyas 1857-1919 ....DLB-149
Colette 1873-1954....................DLB-65	Conan, Laure (Félicité Angers) 1845-1924 ....DLB-99	Cook, Eliza 1818-1889.................DLB-199
Colette, Sidonie Gabrielle (see Colette)	Concord, Massachusetts Concord History and Life.........DLB-223	Cook, George Cram 1873-1924.........DLB-266
Colinas, Antonio 1946- DLB-134	Concord: Literary History of a Town DLB-223	Cook, Michael 1933-1994 ....DLB-53
Coll, Joseph Clement 1881-1921 ....DLB-188	The Old Manse, by Hawthorne.....DLB-223	David C. Cook Publishing Company DLB-49
A Century of Poetry, a Lifetime of Collecting: J. M. Edelstein's Collection of Twentieth-Century American Poetry Y-02	The Thoreauvian Pilgrimage: The Structure of an American Cult ..DLB-223	Cooke, George Willis 1848-1923.........DLB-71
Collier, John 1901-1980 ....DLB-77, 255	Concrete Poetry DLB-307	Cooke, John Esten 1830-1886 ....DLB-3, 248
Collier, John Payne 1789-1883 ....DLB-184	Conde, Carmen 1901-1996 ....DLB-108	Cooke, Philip Pendleton 1816-1850 ....DLB-3, 59, 248
Collier, Mary 1690-1762.................DLB-95	Condillac, Etienne Bonnot de 1714-1780 ....DLB-313	Cooke, Rose Terry 1827-1892 ....DLB-12, 74
Collier, Robert J. 1876-1918 ....DLB-91	Condorcet, Marie-Jean-Antoine-Nicolas Caritat, marquis de 1743-1794...............DLB-313	Increase Cooke and Company..........DLB-49
P. F. Collier [publishing house].........DLB-49	"The Tenth Stage"................DLB-314	Cook-Lynn, Elizabeth 1930- DLB-175
Collin and Small.....................DLB-49	Congreve, William 1670-1729 ....DLB-39, 84; CDBLB-2	Coolbrith, Ina 1841-1928.........DLB-54, 186
Collingwood, R. G. 1889-1943.........DLB-262	Preface to *Incognita* (1692)...........DLB-39	Cooley, Peter 1940- DLB-105
Collingwood, W. G. 1854-1932.........DLB-149	W. B. Conkey Company DLB-49	"Into the Mirror" DLB-105
Collins, An florist circa 1653 ....DLB-131	Conlon, Evelyn 1952- DLB-319	Coolidge, Clark 1939- DLB-193
Collins, Anthony 1676-1729 ....DLB-252	Conn, Stewart 1936- DLB-233	Coolidge, Susan (see Woolsey, Sarah Chauncy)
Collins, Merle 1950- DLB-157	Connell, Evan S., Jr. 1924- DLB-2; Y-81	George Coolidge [publishing house]......DLB-49
Collins, Michael 1964- DLB-267	Connelly, Marc 1890-1980..........DLB-7; Y-80	Cooper, Anna Julia 1858-1964.........DLB-221
Collins, Michael (see Lynds, Dennis)	Connolly, Cyril 1903-1974 ....DLB-98	Cooper, Edith Emma 1862-1913 ....DLB-240
Collins, Mortimer 1827-1876 ....DLB-21, 35	Connolly, James B. 1868-1957 ....DLB-78	Cooper, Giles 1918-1966 ....DLB-13
Collins, Tom (see Furphy, Joseph)	Connor, Ralph (Charles William Gordon) 1860-1937...................DLB-92	Cooper, J. California 19??- DLB-212
Collins, Wilkie 1824-1889 ......DLB-18, 70, 159; CDBLB-4	Connor, Tony 1930- DLB-40	Cooper, James Fenimore 1789-1851........DLB-3, 183, 250; CDALB-2
"The Unknown Public" (1858) [excerpt]......................DLB-57	Conquest, Robert 1917- DLB-27	The Bicentennial of James Fenimore Cooper: An International Celebration........Y-89
The Wilkie Collins Society Y-98	Conrad, Joseph 1857-1924....DLB-10, 34, 98, 156; CDBLB-5	The James Fenimore Cooper Society.....Y-01
Collins, William 1721-1759.............DLB-109	John Conrad and Company............DLB-49	Cooper, Kent 1880-1965 ....DLB-29
Isaac Collins [publishing house] DLB-49	Conroy, Jack 1899-1990................Y-81	Cooper, Susan 1935- DLB-161, 261
William Collins, Sons and Company DLB-154	A Tribute [to Nelson Algren]...........Y-81	Cooper, Susan Fenimore 1813-1894.....DLB-239
Collis, Maurice 1889-1973 ....DLB-195	Conroy, Pat 1945- DLB-6	William Cooper [publishing house] DLB-170
Collyer, Mary 1716?-1763?.............DLB-39	Considine, Bob 1906-1975 ....DLB-241	J. Coote [publishing house]............DLB-154
Colman, Benjamin 1673-1747 ....DLB-24	Consolo, Vincenzo 1933- DLB-196	Coover, Robert 1932- DLB-2, 227; Y-81
Colman, George, the Elder 1732-1794 ....DLB-89	Constable, Henry 1562-1613 ....DLB-136	Tribute to Donald Barthelme........Y-89
Colman, George, the Younger 1762-1836......................DLB-89	Archibald Constable and Company.....DLB-154	Tribute to Theodor Seuss Geisel Y-91
S. Colman [publishing house]..........DLB-49	Constable and Company Limited DLB-112	Copeland and Day....................DLB-49
Colombo, John Robert 1936- DLB-53	Constant, Benjamin 1767-1830 ....DLB-119	Ćopić, Branko 1915-1984.............DLB-181
Colonial Literature DLB-307	Constant de Rebecque, Henri-Benjamin de (see Constant, Benjamin)	Copland, Robert 1470?-1548 ....DLB-136
Colquhoun, Patrick 1745-1820 ....DLB-158	Constantine, David 1944- DLB-40	Coppard, A. E. 1878-1957 ....DLB-162
Colter, Cyrus 1910-2002 ....DLB-33	Constantine, Murray (see Burdekin, Katharine)	Coppée, François 1842-1908 ....DLB-217
Colum, Padraic 1881-1972 ....DLB-19	Constantin-Weyer, Maurice 1881-1964 ...DLB-92	Coppel, Alfred 1921-2004 ....Y-83
The Columbia History of the American Novel A Symposium on Y-92	*Contempo* (magazine) Contempo Caravan: Kites in a Windstorm Y-85	Tribute to Jessamyn West Y-84
Columbus, Christopher 1451-1506 .....DLB-318	The Continental Publishing Company....DLB-49	Coppola, Francis Ford 1939- DLB-44
Columella fl. first century A.D. DLB-211	A Conversation between William Riggan and Janette Turner Hospital Y-02	Copway, George (Kah-ge-ga-gah-bowh) 1818-1869 ....DLB-175, 183
Colvin, Sir Sidney 1845-1927 ....DLB-149	Conversations with Editors Y-95	Copyright The Development of the Author's Copyright in Britain DLB-154
Colwin, Laurie 1944-1992 ....DLB-218; Y-80	Conway, Anne 1631-1679 ....DLB-252	The Digital Millennium Copyright Act: Expanding Copyright Protection in Cyberspace and Beyond Y-98
Comden, Betty 1915- and Green, Adolph 1918-2002 ......DLB-44, 265		Editorial: The Extension of Copyright ...Y-02
Comi, Girolamo 1890-1968 ....DLB-114		Mark Twain on Perpetual Copyright Y-92
Comisso, Giovanni 1895-1969 ....DLB-264		
Commager, Henry Steele 1902-1998 .....DLB-17		

Public Domain and the Violation
   of Texts Y-97

The Question of American Copyright
   in the Nineteenth Century
   Preface, by George Haven Putnam
   The Evolution of Copyright, by
      Brander Matthews
   Summary of Copyright Legislation in
      the United States, by R. R. Bowker
   Analysis of the Provisions of the
      Copyright Law of 1891, by
      George Haven Putnam
   The Contest for International Copyright,
      by George Haven Putnam
   Cheap Books and Good Books,
      by Brander Matthews DLB-49

Writers and Their Copyright Holders:
   the WATCH Project Y-94

Corazzini, Sergio 1886-1907 .... DLB-114
Corbett, Richard 1582-1635 .... DLB-121
Corbière, Tristan 1845-1875 .... DLB-217
Corcoran, Barbara 1911- DLB-52
Cordelli, Franco 1943- DLB-196
Corelli, Marie 1855-1924.......... DLB-34, 156
Corle, Edwin 1906-1956 .... Y-85
Corman, Cid 1924-2004 .... DLB-5, 193
Cormier, Robert 1925-2000.... DLB-52; CDALB-6
   Tribute to Theodor Seuss Geisel........ Y-91
Corn, Alfred 1943- DLB-120, 282; Y-80
Corneille, Pierre 1606-1684.............. DLB-268
Cornford, Frances 1886-1960 .... DLB-240
Cornish, Sam 1935- DLB-41
Cornish, William
   circa 1465-circa 1524............. DLB-132
Cornwall, Barry (see Procter, Bryan Waller)
Cornwallis, Sir William, the Younger
   circa 1579-1614 .... DLB-151
Cornwell, David John Moore (see le Carré, John)
Cornwell, Patricia 1956- DLB-306
Coronel Urtecho, José 1906-1994 .... DLB-290
Corpi, Lucha 1945- DLB-82
Corrington, John William
   1932-1988 .... DLB-6, 244
Corriveau, Monique 1927-1976 .... DLB-251
Corrothers, James D. 1869-1917 .... DLB-50
Corso, Gregory 1930-2001 .... DLB-5, 16, 237
Cortázar, Julio 1914-1984 ... DLB-113; CDWLB-3
Cortéz, Carlos 1923-2005 .... DLB-209
Cortez, Jayne 1936- DLB-41
Corvinus, Gottlieb Siegmund
   1677-1746..................... DLB-168
Corvo, Baron (see Rolfe, Frederick William)
Cory, Annie Sophie (see Cross, Victoria)
Cory, Desmond (Shaun Lloyd McCarthy)
   1928- DLB-276
Cory, William Johnson 1823-1892 .... DLB-35
Coryate, Thomas 1577?-1617 ...... DLB-151, 172
Ćosić, Dobrica 1921- DLB-181; CDWLB-4
Cosin, John 1595-1672............ DLB-151, 213
Cosmopolitan Book Corporation DLB-46
Cossa, Roberto 1934- DLB-305

Costa, Maria Velho da (see The Three Marias:
   A Landmark Case in Portuguese
   Literary History)
Costain, Thomas B. 1885-1965 .... DLB-9
Coste, Donat (Daniel Boudreau)
   1912-1957 .... DLB-88
Costello, Louisa Stuart 1799-1870 .... DLB-166
Cota-Cárdenas, Margarita 1941- DLB-122
Côté, Denis 1954- DLB-251
Cotten, Bruce 1873-1954 .... DLB-187
Cotter, Joseph Seamon, Jr. 1895-1919 ..... DLB-50
Cotter, Joseph Seamon, Sr. 1861-1949 ..... DLB-50
Cottin, Sophie 1770-1807 .... DLB-313
   Claire d'Albe DLB-314
Joseph Cottle [publishing house] DLB-154
Cotton, Charles 1630-1687 .... DLB-131
Cotton, John 1584-1652................ DLB-24
Cotton, Sir Robert Bruce 1571-1631 ..... DLB-213
Coulter, John 1888-1980 .... DLB-68
Cournos, John 1881-1966 .... DLB-54
Courteline, Georges 1858-1929 .... DLB-192
Cousins, Margaret 1905-1996 .... DLB-137
Cousins, Norman 1915-1990........... DLB-137
Couvreur, Jessie (see Tasma)
Coventry, Francis 1725-1754 .... DLB-39
   Dedication, *The History of Pompey
   the Little* (1751).................. DLB-39
Coverdale, Miles 1487 or 1488-1569..... DLB-167
N. Coverly [publishing house].......... DLB-49
Covici-Friede DLB-46
Cowan, Peter 1914-2002 .... DLB-260
Coward, Noel
   1899-1973 .... DLB-10, 245; CDBLB-6
Coward, McCann and Geoghegan DLB-46
Cowles, Gardner 1861-1946 .... DLB-29
Cowles, Gardner "Mike", Jr.
   1903-1985 .... DLB-127, 137
Cowley, Abraham 1618-1667 ...... DLB-131, 151
Cowley, Hannah 1743-1809 .... DLB-89
Cowley, Malcolm
   1898-1989 .... DLB-4, 48; DS-15; Y-81, 89
Cowper, Richard (John Middleton Murry Jr.)
   1926-2002 .... DLB-261
Cowper, William 1731-1800 .... DLB-104, 109
Cox, A. B. (see Berkeley, Anthony)
Cox, James McMahon 1903-1974 .... DLB-127
Cox, James Middleton 1870-1957 ...... DLB-127
Cox, Leonard circa 1495-circa 1550 ..... DLB-281
Cox, Palmer 1840-1924................ DLB-42
Coxe, Louis 1918-1993 .... DLB-5
Coxe, Tench 1755-1824................ DLB-37
Cozzens, Frederick S. 1818-1869 .... DLB-202
Cozzens, James Gould 1903-1978 ....
   .... DLB-9, 294; Y-84; DS-2; CDALB-1
   Cozzens's *Michael Scarlett* Y-97
   Ernest Hemingway's Reaction to
      James Gould Cozzens Y-98

James Gould Cozzens–A View
   from Afar Y-97
James Gould Cozzens: How to
   Read Him..................... Y-97
James Gould Cozzens Symposium and
   Exhibition at the University of
   South Carolina, Columbia Y-00
Mens Rea (or Something) Y-97
Novels for Grown-Ups Y-97
Crabbe, George 1754-1832 .... DLB-93
Crace, Jim 1946- DLB-231
Crackanthorpe, Hubert 1870-1896 ...... DLB-135
Craddock, Charles Egbert (see Murfree, Mary N.)
Cradock, Thomas 1718-1770 .... DLB-31
Craig, Daniel H. 1811-1895............. DLB-43
Craik, Dinah Maria 1826-1887 ..... DLB-35, 163
Cramer, Richard Ben 1950- DLB-185
Cranch, Christopher Pearse
   1813-1892 .... DLB-1, 42, 243; DS-5
Crane, Hart 1899-1932 ..... DLB-4, 48; CDALB-4
   Nathan Asch Remembers Ford Madox
   Ford, Sam Roth, and Hart Crane.... Y-02
Crane, R. S. 1886-1967 .... DLB-63
Crane, Stephen
   1871-1900 .... DLB-12, 54, 78; CDALB-3
   Stephen Crane: A Revaluation, Virginia
      Tech Conference, 1989 .... Y-89
   The Stephen Crane Society......... Y-98, 01
Crane, Walter 1845-1915 .... DLB-163
Cranmer, Thomas 1489-1556 ...... DLB-132, 213
Crapsey, Adelaide 1878-1914............ DLB-54
Crashaw, Richard 1612/1613-1649 ...... DLB-126
Craven, Avery 1885-1980 .... DLB-17
Crawford, Charles 1752-circa 1815 .... DLB-31
Crawford, F. Marion 1854-1909 .... DLB-71
Crawford, Isabel Valancy 1850-1887 ..... DLB-92
Crawley, Alan 1887-1975 .... DLB-68
Crayon, Geoffrey (see Irving, Washington)
Crayon, Porte (see Strother, David Hunter)
Creamer, Robert W. 1922- DLB-171
Creasey, John 1908-1973............... DLB-77
Creative Age Press.................... DLB-46
Creative Nonfiction Y-02
Crébillon, Claude-Prosper Jolyot de *fils*
   1707-1777 .... DLB-313
Crébillon, Claude-Prosper Jolyot de *père*
   1674-1762 .... DLB-313
William Creech [publishing house] DLB-154
Thomas Creede [publishing house] DLB-170
Creel, George 1876-1953 .... DLB-25
Creeley, Robert 1926-2005
   .... DLB-5, 16, 169; DS-17
Creelman, James
   1859-1915 .... DLB-23
Cregan, David 1931- DLB-13
Creighton, Donald 1902-1979 .... DLB-88
Crémazie, Octave 1827-1879 .... DLB-99
Crémer, Victoriano 1909?- DLB-108

Cumulative Index

Crescas, Hasdai circa 1340-1412?....... DLB-115
Crespo, Angel 1926-1995 .... DLB-134
Cresset Press...................... DLB-112
Cresswell, Helen 1934- DLB-161
Crèvecoeur, Michel Guillaume Jean de
  1735-1813..................... DLB-37
Crewe, Candida 1964- DLB-207
Crews, Harry 1935- DLB-6, 143, 185
Crichton, Michael (John Lange, Jeffrey Hudson,
  Michael Douglas) 1942- DLB-292; Y-81
Crispin, Edmund (Robert Bruce Montgomery)
  1921-1978..................... DLB-87
Cristofer, Michael 1946- DLB-7
Criticism
  Afro-American Literary Critics:
    An Introduction.............. DLB-33
  The Consolidation of Opinion: Critical
    Responses to the Modernists..... DLB-36
  "Criticism in Relation to Novels"
    (1863), by G. H. Lewes........ DLB-21
  The Limits of Pluralism DLB-67
  Modern Critical Terms, Schools, and
    Movements DLB-67
  "Panic Among the Philistines":
    A Postscript, An Interview
    with Bryan Griffin................Y-81
  The Recovery of Literature: Criticism
    in the 1990s: A Symposium......... Y-91
  The Stealthy School of Criticism (1871),
    by Dante Gabriel Rossetti DLB-35
Crnjanski, Miloš
  1893-1977............DLB-147; CDWLB-4
Crocker, Hannah Mather 1752-1829 .... DLB-200
Crockett, David (Davy)
  1786-1836............ DLB-3, 11, 183, 248
Croft-Cooke, Rupert (see Bruce, Leo)
Crofts, Freeman Wills 1879-1957 .... DLB-77
Croker, John Wilson 1780-1857 .... DLB-110
Croly, George 1780-1860 .... DLB-159
Croly, Herbert 1869-1930 .... DLB-91
Croly, Jane Cunningham 1829-1901 ..... DLB-23
Crompton, Richmal 1890-1969 .... DLB-160
Cronin, A. J. 1896-1981 .... DLB-191
Cros, Charles 1842-1888 .... DLB-217
Crosby, Caresse 1892-1970 and
  Crosby, Harry 1898-1929 and ...DLB-4; DS-15
Crosby, Harry 1898-1929 .... DLB-48
Crosland, Camilla Toulmin (Mrs. Newton
  Crosland) 1812-1895 .... DLB-240
Cross, Amanda (Carolyn G. Heilbrun)
  1926-2003 .... DLB-306
Cross, Gillian 1945- DLB-161
Cross, Victoria 1868-1952 ....DLB-135, 197
Crossley-Holland, Kevin 1941- DLB-40, 161
Crothers, Rachel 1870-1958 ....DLB-7, 266
Thomas Y. Crowell Company DLB-49
Crowley, John 1942- Y-82
Crowley, Mart 1935- DLB-7, 266
Crown Publishers.................... DLB-46
Crowne, John 1641-1712 .... DLB-80

Crowninshield, Edward Augustus
  1817-1859 .... DLB-140
Crowninshield, Frank 1872-1947 .... DLB-91
Croy, Homer 1883-1965 .... DLB-4
Crumley, James 1939- DLB-226; Y-84
Cruse, Mary Anne 1825?-1910 .... DLB-239
Cruz, Migdalia 1958- DLB-249
Cruz, Sor Juana Inés de la 1651-1695.... DLB-305
Cruz, Victor Hernández 1949- DLB-41
Cruz e Sousa, João 1861-1898 .... DLB-307
Csokor, Franz Theodor 1885-1969 ...... DLB-81
Csoóri, Sándor 1930- DLB-232; CDWLB-4
Cuadra, Pablo Antonio 1912-2002..... DLB-290
Cuala Press...................... DLB-112
Cudworth, Ralph 1617-1688........... DLB-252
Cueva, Juan de la 1543-1612 .... DLB-318
Cugoano, Quobna Ottabah 1797-?.......... Y-02
Cullen, Countee
  1903-1946 .... DLB-4, 48, 51; CDALB-4
Culler, Jonathan D. 1944- DLB-67, 246
Cullinan, Elizabeth 1933- DLB-234
Culverwel, Nathaniel 1619?-1651?...... DLB-252
Cumberland, Richard 1732-1811 .... DLB-89
Cummings, Constance Gordon
  1837-1924.....................DLB-174
Cummings, E. E.
  1894-1962 .... DLB-4, 48; CDALB-5
  The E. E. Cummings Society........... Y-01
Cummings, Ray 1887-1957............... DLB-8
Cummings and Hilliard DLB-49
Cummins, Maria Susanna 1827-1866..... DLB-42
Cumpián, Carlos 1953- DLB-209
Cunard, Nancy 1896-1965 .... DLB-240
Joseph Cundall [publishing house] DLB-106
Cuney, Waring 1906-1976 .... DLB-51
Cuney-Hare, Maude 1874-1936 .... DLB-52
Cunha, Euclides da 1866-1909......... DLB-307
Cunningham, Allan
  1784-1842.................. DLB-116, 144
Cunningham, J. V. 1911-1985 .... DLB-5
Cunningham, Michael 1952- DLB-292
Cunningham, Peter (Peter Lauder, Peter
  Benjamin) 1947- DLB-267
Peter F. Cunningham
  [publishing house] DLB-49
Cunqueiro, Alvaro 1911-1981 .... DLB-134
Cuomo, George 1929- Y-80
Cupples, Upham and Company......... DLB-49
Cupples and Leon DLB-46
Cuppy, Will 1884-1949 .... DLB-11
Curiel, Barbara Brinson 1956- DLB-209
Edmund Curll [publishing house]....... DLB-154
Currie, James 1756-1805............. DLB-142
Currie, Mary Montgomerie Lamb Singleton,
  Lady Currie (see Fane, Violet)
Cursor Mundi circa 1300................ DLB-146
Curti, Merle E. 1897-1996 .... DLB-17

Curtis, Anthony 1926- DLB-155
Curtis, Cyrus H. K. 1850-1933 .... DLB-91
Curtis, George William
  1824-1892 .... DLB-1, 43, 223
Curzon, Robert 1810-1873 .... DLB-166
Curzon, Sarah Anne 1833-1898......... DLB-99
Cusack, Dymphna 1902-1981 .... DLB-260
Cushing, Eliza Lanesford
  1794-1886..................... DLB-99
Cushing, Harvey 1869-1939 ....DLB-187
Custance, Olive (Lady Alfred Douglas)
  1874-1944.................... DLB-240
Cynewulf circa 770-840 .... DLB-146
Cyrano de Bergerac, Savinien de
  1619-1655 ....DLB-268
Czepko, Daniel 1605-1660 .... DLB-164
Czerniawski, Adam 1934- DLB-232

D

Dabit, Eugène 1898-1936.............. DLB-65
Daborne, Robert circa 1580-1628........ DLB-58
Dąbrowska, Maria
  1889-1965 ....DLB-215; CDWLB-4
Dacey, Philip 1939- DLB-105
  "Eyes Across Centuries:
    Contemporary Poetry and 'That
    Vision Thing,'" DLB-105
Dach, Simon 1605-1659 .... DLB-164
Dacier, Anne Le Fèvre 1647-1720....... DLB-313
Dagerman, Stig 1923-1954 .... DLB-259
Daggett, Rollin M. 1831-1901 .... DLB-79
D'Aguiar, Fred 1960- DLB-157
Dahl, Roald 1916-1990......... DLB-139, 255
  Tribute to Alfred A. Knopf Y-84
Dahlberg, Edward 1900-1977 .... DLB-48
Dahn, Felix 1834-1912 .... DLB-129
The Daily Worker DLB-303
Dal', Vladimir Ivanovich (Kazak Vladimir
  Lugansky) 1801-1872............. DLB-198
Dale, Peter 1938- DLB-40
Daley, Arthur 1904-1974 ....DLB-171
Dall, Caroline Healey 1822-1912..... DLB-1, 235
Dallas, E. S. 1828-1879 .... DLB-55
  The Gay Science [excerpt](1866) DLB-21
The Dallas Theater Center............. DLB-7
D'Alton, Louis 1900-1951 .... DLB-10
Dalton, Roque 1935-1975 .... DLB-283
Daly, Carroll John 1889-1958 .... DLB-226
Daly, T. A. 1871-1948 .... DLB-11
Damon, S. Foster 1893-1971 .... DLB-45
William S. Damrell [publishing house].... DLB-49
Dana, Charles A. 1819-1897...... DLB-3, 23, 250
Dana, Richard Henry, Jr.
  1815-1882 .... DLB-1, 183, 235
Dandridge, Ray Garfield 1882-1930 ..... DLB-51
Dane, Clemence 1887-1965 ....DLB-10, 197
Danforth, John 1660-1730 .... DLB-24

Danforth, Samuel, I 1626-1674 . . . . DLB-24

Danforth, Samuel, II 1666-1727 . . . . DLB-24

Dangerous Acquaintances, Pierre-Ambroise-François Choderlos de Laclos DLB-314

Daniel, John M. 1825-1865 . . . . DLB-43

Daniel, Samuel 1562 or 1563-1619 . . . . DLB-62

Daniel Press DLB-106

Daniel', Iulii 1925-1988 . . . . DLB-302

Daniells, Roy 1902-1979 . . . . DLB-68

Daniels, Jim 1956- DLB-120

Daniels, Jonathan 1902-1981 . . . . DLB-127

Daniels, Josephus 1862-1948 . . . . DLB-29

Daniels, Sarah 1957- DLB-245

Danilevsky, Grigorii Petrovich 1829-1890 . . . . DLB-238

Dannay, Frederic 1905-1982 . . . . DLB-137

Danner, Margaret Esse 1915- DLB-41

John Danter [publishing house] DLB-170

Dantin, Louis (Eugene Seers) 1865-1945 . . . . DLB-92

Danto, Arthur C. 1924- DLB-279

Danzig, Allison 1898-1987 . . . . DLB-171

D'Arcy, Ella circa 1857-1937 . . . . DLB-135

Darío, Rubén 1867-1916 . . . . DLB-290

Dark, Eleanor 1901-1985 . . . . DLB-260

Darke, Nick 1948- DLB-233

Darley, Felix Octavious Carr 1822-1888 . . . . DLB-188

Darley, George 1795-1846 . . . . DLB-96

Darmesteter, Madame James (see Robinson, A. Mary F.)

Darrow, Clarence 1857-1938 . . . . DLB-303

Darwin, Charles 1809-1882 . . . . . DLB-57, 166

Darwin, Erasmus 1731-1802 . . . . DLB-93

Daryush, Elizabeth 1887-1977 . . . . DLB-20

Dashkova, Ekaterina Romanovna (née Vorontsova) 1743-1810 . . . . DLB-150

Dashwood, Edmée Elizabeth Monica de la Pasture (see Delafield, E. M.)

Daudet, Alphonse 1840-1897 . . . . DLB-123

d'Aulaire, Edgar Parin 1898-1986 and d'Aulaire, Ingri 1904-1980 . . . . DLB-22

Davenant, Sir William 1606-1668 . . . . DLB-58, 126

Davenport, Guy 1927-2005 . . . . DLB-130

Tribute to John Gardner Y-82

Davenport, Marcia 1903-1996 . . . . DS-17

Davenport, Robert circa 17th century DLB-58

Daves, Delmer 1904-1977 . . . . DLB-26

Davey, Frank 1940- DLB-53

Davidson, Avram 1923-1993 . . . . DLB-8

Davidson, Donald 1893-1968 . . . . DLB-45

Davidson, Donald 1917-2003 . . . . DLB-279

Davidson, John 1857-1909 . . . . DLB-19

Davidson, Lionel 1922- DLB-14, 276

Davidson, Robyn 1950- DLB-204

Davidson, Sara 1943- DLB-185

Davið Stefánsson frá Fagraskógi 1895-1964 . . . . DLB-293

Davie, Donald 1922-1995 . . . . DLB-27

Davie, Elspeth 1919-1995 . . . . DLB-139

Davies, Sir John 1569-1626 . . . . DLB-172

Davies, John, of Hereford 1565?-1618. . . . DLB-121

Davies, Rhys 1901-1978. . . . . DLB-139, 191

Davies, Robertson 1913-1995 . . . . DLB-68

Davies, Samuel 1723-1761 . . . . DLB-31

Davies, Thomas 1712?-1785 . . . . . . DLB-142, 154

Davies, W. H. 1871-1940. . . . . DLB-19, 174

Peter Davies Limited DLB-112

Davin, Nicholas Flood 1840?-1901 . . . . . . DLB-99

Daviot, Gordon 1896?-1952 . . . . DLB-10
(see also Tey, Josephine)

Davis, Arthur Hoey (see Rudd, Steele)

Davis, Benjamin J. 1903-1964 . . . . DLB-303

Davis, Charles A. (Major J. Downing) 1795-1867 . . . . DLB-11

Davis, Clyde Brion 1894-1962 . . . . DLB-9

Davis, Dick 1945- DLB-40, 282

Davis, Frank Marshall 1905-1987 . . . . DLB-51

Davis, H. L. 1894-1960 . . . . DLB-9, 206

Davis, John 1774-1854 . . . . DLB-37

Davis, Lydia 1947- DLB-130

Davis, Margaret Thomson 1926- DLB-14

Davis, Ossie 1917-2005 . . . . DLB-7, 38, 249

Davis, Owen 1874-1956. . . . . DLB-249

Davis, Paxton 1925-1994 . . . . Y-89

Davis, Rebecca Harding 1831-1910 . . . . DLB-74, 239

Davis, Richard Harding 1864-1916 . . . . DLB-12, 23, 78, 79, 189; DS-13

Davis, Samuel Cole 1764-1809 . . . . DLB-37

Davis, Samuel Post 1850-1918 . . . . DLB-202

Davison, Frank Dalby 1893-1970 . . . . DLB-260

Davison, Peter 1928- DLB-5

Davydov, Denis Vasil'evich 1784-1839 . . . . DLB-205

Davys, Mary 1674-1732 . . . . DLB-39

Preface to *The Works of Mrs. Davys* (1725) DLB-39

DAW Books DLB-46

Dawe, Bruce 1930- DLB-289

Dawson, Ernest 1882-1947 . . . . . . DLB-140; Y-02

Dawson, Fielding 1930- DLB-130

Dawson, Sarah Morgan 1842-1909 . . . . . . DLB-239

Dawson, William 1704-1752 . . . . DLB-31

Day, Angel fl. 1583-1599 . . . . DLB-167, 236

Day, Benjamin Henry 1810-1889 . . . . DLB-43

Day, Clarence 1874-1935. . . . . DLB-11

Day, Dorothy 1897-1980 . . . . DLB-29

Day, Frank Parker 1881-1950 . . . . DLB-92

Day, John circa 1574-circa 1640 . . . . DLB-62

Day, Thomas 1748-1789 . . . . DLB-39

John Day [publishing house] DLB-170

The John Day Company DLB-46

Mahlon Day [publishing house] DLB-49

Day Lewis, C. (see Blake, Nicholas)

Dazai Osamu 1909-1948 . . . . DLB-182

Deacon, William Arthur 1890-1977 . . . . . . DLB-68

Deal, Borden 1922-1985 . . . . DLB-6

de Angeli, Marguerite 1889-1987 . . . . DLB-22

De Angelis, Milo 1951- DLB-128

Debord, Guy 1931-1994 . . . . DLB-296

De Bow, J. D. B. 1820-1867 . . . . . . DLB-3, 79, 248

Debs, Eugene V. 1855-1926 . . . . DLB-303

de Bruyn, Günter 1926- DLB-75

de Camp, L. Sprague 1907-2000 . . . . DLB-8

De Carlo, Andrea 1952- DLB-196

De Casas, Celso A. 1944- DLB-209

Dechert, Robert 1895-1975 . . . . DLB-187

Declaration of the Rights of Man and of the Citizen DLB-314

Declaration of the Rights of Woman, Olympe de Gouges DLB-314

Dedications, Inscriptions, and Annotations Y-01–02

Dee, John 1527-1608 or 1609 . . . . . . DLB-136, 213

Deeping, George Warwick 1877-1950 . . . . DLB-153

Deffand, Marie de Vichy-Chamrond, marquise Du 1696-1780 . . . . DLB-313

Defoe, Daniel 1660-1731 . . . . . . DLB-39, 95, 101; CDBLB-2

Preface to *Colonel Jack* (1722) DLB-39

Preface to *The Farther Adventures of Robinson Crusoe* (1719) DLB-39

Preface to *Moll Flanders* (1722) DLB-39

Preface to *Robinson Crusoe* (1719) DLB-39

Preface to *Roxana* (1724) DLB-39

de Fontaine, Felix Gregory 1834-1896 . . . . . DLB-43

De Forest, John William 1826-1906 . . . . DLB-12, 189

DeFrees, Madeline 1919- DLB-105

"The Poet's Kaleidoscope: The Element of Surprise in the Making of the Poem" DLB-105

DeGolyer, Everette Lee 1886-1956 . . . . . . DLB-187

de Graff, Robert 1895-1981 . . . . Y-81

de Graft, Joe 1924-1978 . . . . DLB-117

De Heinrico circa 980? DLB-148

Deighton, Len 1929- DLB-87; CDBLB-8

DeJong, Meindert 1906-1991 . . . . DLB-52

Dekker, Thomas circa 1572-1632 . . . . . . DLB-62, 172; CDBLB-1

Delacorte, George T., Jr. 1894-1991 . . . . . . DLB-91

Delafield, E. M. 1890-1943 . . . . DLB-34

Delahaye, Guy (Guillaume Lahaise) 1888-1969 . . . . DLB-92

de la Mare, Walter 1873-1956 . . . . . DLB-19, 153, 162, 255; CDBLB-6

Deland, Margaret 1857-1945 . . . . DLB-78

Delaney, Shelagh 1939- DLB-13; CDBLB-8

Delano, Amasa 1763-1823 . . . . DLB-183

Delany, Martin Robinson 1812-1885 ..... DLB-50
Delany, Samuel R. 1942- DLB-8, 33
de la Roche, Mazo 1879-1961 .... DLB-68
Delavigne, Jean François Casimir
  1793-1843 .... DLB-192
Delbanco, Nicholas 1942- DLB-6, 234
Delblanc, Sven 1931-1992 .... DLB-257
Del Castillo, Ramón 1949- DLB-209
Deledda, Grazia 1871-1936 .... DLB-264
De León, Nephtal 1945- DLB-82
Deleuze, Gilles 1925-1995 .... DLB-296
Delfini, Antonio 1907-1963 .... DLB-264
Delgado, Abelardo Barrientos 1931- DLB-82
Del Giudice, Daniele 1949- DLB-196
De Libero, Libero 1906-1981 .... DLB-114
Delicado, Francisco
  circa 1475-circa 1540? DLB-318
DeLillo, Don 1936- DLB-6, 173
de Lint, Charles 1951- DLB-251
de Lisser H. G. 1878-1944 .... DLB-117
Dell, Floyd 1887-1969 .... DLB-9
Dell Publishing Company DLB-46
delle Grazie, Marie Eugene 1864-1931 .... DLB-81
Deloney, Thomas died 1600 .... DLB-167
Deloria, Ella C. 1889-1971 .... DLB-175
Deloria, Vine, Jr. 1933- DLB-175
del Rey, Lester 1915-1993 .... DLB-8
Del Vecchio, John M. 1947- DS-9
Del'vig, Anton Antonovich 1798-1831 ... DLB-205
de Man, Paul 1919-1983 .... DLB-67
DeMarinis, Rick 1934- DLB-218
Demby, William 1922- DLB-33
De Mille, James 1833-1880 .... DLB-99, 251
de Mille, William 1878-1955 .... DLB-266
Deming, Philander 1829-1915 .... DLB-74
Deml, Jakub 1878-1961 .... DLB-215
Demorest, William Jennings 1822-1895 ... DLB-79
De Morgan, William 1839-1917 .... DLB-153
Demosthenes 384 B.C.-322 B.C. DLB-176
Henry Denham [publishing house] DLB-170
Denham, Sir John 1615-1669 .... DLB-58, 126
Denison, Merrill 1893-1975 .... DLB-92
T. S. Denison and Company DLB-49
Dennery, Adolphe Philippe 1811-1899 ... DLB-192
Dennie, Joseph 1768-1812 ..... DLB-37, 43, 59, 73
Dennis, C. J. 1876-1938 .... DLB-260
Dennis, John 1658-1734 .... DLB-101
Dennis, Nigel 1912-1989 .... DLB-13, 15, 233
Denslow, W. W. 1856-1915 .... DLB-188
Dent, J. M., and Sons DLB-112
Dent, Lester 1904-1959 .... DLB-306
Dent, Tom 1932-1998 .... DLB-38
Denton, Daniel circa 1626-1703 .... DLB-24
DePaola, Tomie 1934- DLB-61
De Quille, Dan 1829-1898 .... DLB-186

De Quincey, Thomas
  1785-1859 .... DLB-110, 144; CDBLB-3
  "Rhetoric" (1828; revised, 1859)
    [excerpt] DLB-57
  "Style" (1840; revised, 1859)
    [excerpt] DLB-57
Derby, George Horatio 1823-1861 .... DLB-11
J. C. Derby and Company DLB-49
Derby and Miller DLB-49
De Ricci, Seymour 1881-1942 .... DLB-201
Derleth, August 1909-1971 .... DLB-9; DS-17
Derrida, Jacques 1930-2004 .... DLB-242
The Derrydale Press DLB-46
Derzhavin, Gavriil Romanovich
  1743-1816 .... DLB-150
Desai, Anita 1937- DLB-271
Desaulniers, Gonzalve 1863-1934 .... DLB-92
Desbordes-Valmore, Marceline
  1786-1859 .... DLB-217
Descartes, René 1596-1650 .... DLB-268
Deschamps, Emile 1791-1871 .... DLB-217
Deschamps, Eustache 1340?-1404 ...... DLB-208
Desbiens, Jean-Paul 1927- DLB-53
des Forêts, Louis-Rene 1918-2001 ...... DLB-83
Desiato, Luca 1941- DLB-196
Desjardins, Marie-Catherine
  (see Villedieu, Madame de)
Desnica, Vladan 1905-1967 .... DLB-181
Desnos, Robert 1900-1945 .... DLB-258
DesRochers, Alfred 1901-1978 .... DLB-68
Desrosiers, Léo-Paul 1896-1967 .... DLB-68
Dessaulles, Louis-Antoine 1819-1895 .... DLB-99
Dessi, Giuseppe 1909-1977 .... DLB-177
Destouches, Louis-Ferdinand
  (see Céline, Louis-Ferdinand)
Desvignes, Lucette 1926- DLB-321
DeSylva, Buddy 1895-1950 .... DLB-265
De Tabley, Lord 1835-1895 .... DLB-35
Deutsch, Babette 1895-1982 .... DLB-45
Deutsch, Niklaus Manuel
  (see Manuel, Niklaus)
André Deutsch Limited DLB-112
Devanny, Jean 1894-1962 .... DLB-260
Deveaux, Alexis 1948- DLB-38
De Vere, Aubrey 1814-1902 .... DLB-35
Devereux, second Earl of Essex, Robert
  1565-1601 .... DLB-136
The Devin-Adair Company DLB-46
De Vinne, Theodore Low
  1828-1914 .... DLB-187
Devlin, Anne 1951- DLB-245
DeVoto, Bernard 1897-1955 .... DLB-9, 256
De Vries, Peter 1910-1993 .... DLB-6; Y-82
  Tribute to Albert Erskine Y-93
Dewart, Edward Hartley 1828-1903 ..... DLB-99
Dewdney, Christopher 1951- DLB-60
Dewdney, Selwyn 1909-1979 .... DLB-68

Dewey, John 1859-1952 .... DLB-246, 270
Dewey, Orville 1794-1882 .... DLB-243
Dewey, Thomas B. 1915-1981 .... DLB-226
DeWitt, Robert M., Publisher DLB-49
DeWolfe, Fiske and Company DLB-49
Dexter, Colin 1930- DLB-87
de Young, M. H. 1849-1925 .... DLB-25
Dhlomo, H. I. E. 1903-1956 .... DLB-157, 225
Dhu al-Rummah (Abu al-Harith Ghaylan ibn 'Uqbah)
  circa 696-circa 735 .... DLB-311
Dhuoda circa 803-after 843 .... DLB-148
The Dial 1840-1844 .... DLB-223
The Dial Press DLB-46
"Dialogue entre un prêtre et un moribond,"
  Marquis de Sade DLB-314
Diamond, I. A. L. 1920-1988 .... DLB-26
Dias Gomes, Alfredo 1922-1999 .... DLB-307
Díaz del Castillo, Bernal
  circa 1496-1584 .... DLB-318
Dibble, L. Grace 1902-1998 .... DLB-204
Dibdin, Thomas Frognall
  1776-1847 .... DLB-184
Di Cicco, Pier Giorgio 1949- DLB-60
Dick, Philip K. 1928-1982 .... DLB-8
Dick and Fitzgerald DLB-49
Dickens, Charles 1812-1870
  .... DLB-21, 55, 70, 159,
  166; DS-5; CDBLB-4
Dickey, Eric Jerome 1961- DLB-292
Dickey, James 1923-1997 .... DLB-5, 193;
  Y-82, 93, 96, 97; DS-7, 19; CDALB-6
  James Dickey and Stanley Burnshaw
    Correspondence Y-02
  James Dickey at Seventy–A Tribute Y-93
  James Dickey, American Poet Y-96
  The James Dickey Society Y-99
  The Life of James Dickey: A Lecture to
    the Friends of the Emory Libraries,
    by Henry Hart Y-98
  Tribute to Archibald MacLeish Y-82
  Tribute to Malcolm Cowley Y-89
  Tribute to Truman Capote Y-84
  Tributes [to Dickey] Y-97
Dickey, William
  1928-1994 .... DLB-5
Dickinson, Emily
  1830-1886 .... DLB-1, 243; CDALB-3
Dickinson, John 1732-1808 .... DLB-31
Dickinson, Jonathan 1688-1747 .... DLB-24
Dickinson, Patric 1914-1994 .... DLB-27
Dickinson, Peter 1927- DLB-87, 161, 276
John Dicks [publishing house] DLB-106
Dickson, Gordon R.
  1923-2001 .... DLB-8
Dictionary of Literary Biography
  Annual Awards for *Dictionary of
  Literary Biography* Editors and
  Contributors Y-98–02
Dictionary of Literary Biography
  Yearbook Awards Y-92–93, 97–02

438

The Dictionary of National Biography........DLB-144

Diderot, Denis 1713-1784..............DLB-313

"The Encyclopedia"..............DLB-314

Didion, Joan 1934-
......DLB-2, 173, 185; Y-81, 86; CDALB-6

Di Donato, Pietro 1911-1992..............DLB-9

Die Fürstliche Bibliothek Corvey..........Y-96

Diego, Gerardo 1896-1987..............DLB-134

Dietz, Howard 1896-1983..............DLB-265

Digby, Everard 1550?-1605..............DLB-281

Digges, Thomas circa 1546-1595........DLB-136

The Digital Millennium Copyright Act: Expanding Copyright Protection in Cyberspace and Beyond..............Y-98

Diktonius, Elmer 1896-1961..............DLB-259

Dillard, Annie 1945-......DLB-275, 278; Y-80

Dillard, R. H. W. 1937-..........DLB-5, 244

Charles T. Dillingham Company........DLB-49

G. W. Dillingham Company..............DLB-49

Edward and Charles Dilly [publishing house]..............DLB-154

Dilthey, Wilhelm 1833-1911..............DLB-129

Dimitrova, Blaga 1922-...DLB-181; CDWLB-4

Dimov, Dimitr 1909-1966..............DLB-181

Dimsdale, Thomas J. 1831?-1866..........DLB-186

Dinescu, Mircea 1950-..............DLB-232

Dinesen, Isak (see Blixen, Karen)

Dingelstedt, Franz von 1814-1881........DLB-133

Dinis, Júlio (Joaquim Guilherme Gomes Coelho) 1839-1871..........DLB-287

Dintenfass, Mark 1941-..............Y-84

Diogenes, Jr. (see Brougham, John)

Diogenes Laertius circa 200..............DLB-176

DiPrima, Diane 1934-..........DLB-5, 16

Disch, Thomas M. 1940-..........DLB-8, 282

"Le Discours sur le style," Georges-Louis Leclerc de Buffon..............DLB-314

Diski, Jenny 1947-..............DLB-271

Disney, Walt 1901-1966..............DLB-22

Disraeli, Benjamin 1804-1881........DLB-21, 55

D'Israeli, Isaac 1766-1848..............DLB-107

DLB Award for Distinguished Literary Criticism..............Y-02

Ditlevsen, Tove 1917-1976..............DLB-214

Ditzen, Rudolf (see Fallada, Hans)

Dix, Dorothea Lynde 1802-1887......DLB-1, 235

Dix, Dorothy (see Gilmer, Elizabeth Meriwether)

Dix, Edwards and Company..............DLB-49

Dix, Gertrude circa 1874-?..............DLB-197

Dixie, Florence Douglas 1857-1905......DLB-174

Dixon, Ella Hepworth 1855 or 1857-1932..............DLB-197

Dixon, Paige (see Corcoran, Barbara)

Dixon, Richard Watson 1833-1900........DLB-19

Dixon, Stephen 1936-..............DLB-130

DLB Award for Distinguished Literary Criticism..............Y-02

Dmitriev, Andrei Viktorovich 1956-...DLB-285

Dmitriev, Ivan Ivanovich 1760-1837.....DLB-150

Dobell, Bertram 1842-1914..............DLB-184

Dobell, Sydney 1824-1874..............DLB-32

Dobie, J. Frank 1888-1964..............DLB-212

Dobles Yzaguirre, Julieta 1943-........DLB-283

Döblin, Alfred 1878-1957.....DLB-66; CDWLB-2

Dobroliubov, Nikolai Aleksandrovich 1836-1861..............DLB-277

Dobson, Austin 1840-1921.........DLB-35, 144

Dobson, Rosemary 1920-..............DLB-260

Doctorow, E. L. 1931-.....DLB-2, 28, 173; Y-80; CDALB-6

Dodd, Susan M. 1946-..............DLB-244

Dodd, William E. 1869-1940..............DLB-17

Anne Dodd [publishing house]........DLB-154

Dodd, Mead and Company..............DLB-49

Doderer, Heimito von 1896-1966........DLB-85

B. W. Dodge and Company..............DLB-46

Dodge, Mary Abigail 1833-1896........DLB-221

Dodge, Mary Mapes 1831?-1905..........DLB-42, 79; DS-13

Dodge Publishing Company..............DLB-49

Dodgson, Charles Lutwidge (see Carroll, Lewis)

Dodsley, Robert 1703-1764..............DLB-95

R. Dodsley [publishing house]..........DLB-154

Dodson, Owen 1914-1983..............DLB-76

Dodwell, Christina 1951-..............DLB-204

Doesticks, Q. K. Philander, P. B. (see Thomson, Mortimer)

Doheny, Carrie Estelle 1875-1958.......DLB-140

Doherty, John 1798?-1854..............DLB-190

Doig, Ivan 1939-..............DLB-206

Doinaş, Ştefan Augustin 1922-..........DLB-232

Domínguez, Sylvia Maida 1935-..........DLB-122

Donaghy, Michael 1954-..............DLB-282

Patrick Donahoe [publishing house]......DLB-49

Donald, David H. 1920-........DLB-17; Y-87

Donaldson, Scott 1928-..............DLB-111

Doni, Rodolfo 1919-..............DLB-177

Donleavy, J. P. 1926-..........DLB-6, 173

Donnadieu, Marguerite (see Duras, Marguerite)

Donne, John 1572-1631..........DLB-121, 151; CDBLB-1

Donnelly, Ignatius 1831-1901..............DLB-12

R. R. Donnelley and Sons Company......DLB-49

Donoghue, Emma 1969-..............DLB-267

Donohue and Henneberry..............DLB-49

Donoso, José 1924-1996 ....DLB-113; CDWLB-3

M. Doolady [publishing house]..........DLB-49

Dooley, Ebon (see Ebon)

Doolittle, Hilda 1886-1961.....DLB-4, 45; DS-15

Doplicher, Fabio 1938-..............DLB-128

Dor, Milo 1923-..............DLB-85

George H. Doran Company..............DLB-46

Dorcey, Mary 1950-..............DLB-319

Dorgelès, Roland 1886-1973..............DLB-65

Dorn, Edward 1929-1999..............DLB-5

Dorr, Rheta Childe 1866-1948..........DLB-25

Dorris, Michael 1945-1997..............DLB-175

Dorset and Middlesex, Charles Sackville, Lord Buckhurst, Earl of 1643-1706....DLB-131

Dorsey, Candas Jane 1952-..........DLB-251

Dorst, Tankred 1925-..........DLB-75, 124

Dos Passos, John 1896-1970
........DLB-4, 9, 316; DS-1, 15; CDALB-5

John Dos Passos: A Centennial Commemoration..............Y-96

John Dos Passos: Artist..............Y-99

John Dos Passos Newsletter..........Y-00

U.S.A. (Documentary)..............DLB-274

Dostoevsky, Fyodor 1821-1881........DLB-238

Doubleday and Company..............DLB-49

Doubrovsky, Serge 1928-..............DLB-299

Dougall, Lily 1858-1923..............DLB-92

Doughty, Charles M. 1843-1926..............DLB-19, 57, 174

Douglas, Lady Alfred (see Custance, Olive)

Douglas, Ellen (Josephine Ayres Haxton) 1921-..............DLB-292

Douglas, Gavin 1476-1522..............DLB-132

Douglas, Keith 1920-1944..............DLB-27

Douglas, Norman 1868-1952........DLB-34, 195

Douglass, Frederick 1817-1895
........DLB-1, 43, 50, 79, 243; CDALB-2

Frederick Douglass Creative Arts Center Y-01

Douglass, William circa 1691-1752.......DLB-24

Dourado, Autran 1926-........DLB-145, 307

Dove, Arthur G. 1880-1946..............DLB-188

Dove, Rita 1952-..........DLB-120; CDALB-7

Dover Publications..............DLB-46

Doves Press..............DLB-112

Dovlatov, Sergei Donatovich 1941-1990..............DLB-285

Dowden, Edward 1843-1913........DLB-35, 149

Dowell, Coleman 1925-1985..............DLB-130

Dowland, John 1563-1626..............DLB-172

Downes, Gwladys 1915-..............DLB-88

Downing, J., Major (see Davis, Charles A.)

Downing, Major Jack (see Smith, Seba)

Dowriche, Anne before 1560-after 1613..............DLB-172

Dowson, Ernest 1867-1900........DLB-19, 135

William Doxey [publishing house].......DLB-49

Doyle, Sir Arthur Conan 1859-1930...DLB-18, 70, 156, 178; CDBLB-5

The Priory Scholars of New York......Y-99

Doyle, Kirby 1932-..............DLB-16

Doyle, Roddy 1958-..............DLB-194

Drabble, Margaret 1939-........DLB-14, 155, 231; CDBLB-8

Tribute to Graham Greene............Y-91

Drach, Albert 1902-1995..............DLB-85

439

Cumulative Index

Drachmann, Holger 1846-1908 .... DLB-300
Dracula (Documentary) DLB-304
Dragojević, Danijel 1934- DLB-181
Dragún, Osvaldo 1929-1999 .... DLB-305
Drake, Samuel Gardner 1798-1875...... DLB-187
Drama (*See* Theater)
The Dramatic Publishing Company...... DLB-49
Dramatists Play Service DLB-46
Drant, Thomas
   early 1540s?-1578................. DLB-167
Draper, John W. 1811-1882............ DLB-30
Draper, Lyman C. 1815-1891........... DLB-30
Drayton, Michael 1563-1631 .... DLB-121
Dreiser, Theodore 1871-1945
   ....DLB-9, 12, 102, 137; DS-1; CDALB-3
   The International Theodore Dreiser
     Society....................... Y-01
   Notes from the Underground
     of *Sister Carrie*................ Y-01
Dresser, Davis 1904-1977 .... DLB-226
Drew, Elizabeth A.
   "A Note on Technique" [excerpt]
   (1926) DLB-36
Drewitz, Ingeborg 1923-1986 .... DLB-75
Drieu La Rochelle, Pierre 1893-1945 ..... DLB-72
Drinker, Elizabeth 1735-1807 .... DLB-200
Drinkwater, John 1882-1937......DLB-10, 19, 149
   The Friends of the Dymock Poets Y-00
Droste-Hülshoff, Annette von
   1797-1848 .... DLB-133; CDWLB-2
The Drue Heinz Literature Prize
   Excerpt from "Excerpts from a Report
   of the Commission," in David
   Bosworth's *The Death of Descartes*
   An Interview with David Bosworth...... Y-82
Drummond, William, of Hawthornden
   1585-1649 .... DLB-121, 213
Drummond, William Henry 1854-1907... DLB-92
Drummond de Andrade, Carlos
   1902-1987..................... DLB-307
Druzhinin, Aleksandr Vasil'evich
   1824-1864 .... DLB-238
Druzhnikov, Yuri 1933- DLB-317
Dryden, Charles 1860?-1931 ....DLB-171
Dryden, John
   1631-1700...... DLB-80, 101, 131; CDBLB-2
Držić, Marin
   circa 1508-1567 ....DLB-147; CDWLB-4
Duane, William 1760-1835............ DLB-43
Dubé, Marcel 1930- DLB-53
Dubé, Rodolphe (see Hertel, François)
Dubie, Norman 1945- DLB-120
Dubin, Al 1891-1945 .... DLB-265
Du Boccage, Anne-Marie 1710-1802..... DLB-313
Dubois, Silvia 1788 or 1789?-1889 ...... DLB-239
Du Bois, W. E. B.
   1868-1963 ....DLB-47, 50, 91, 246; CDALB-3
Du Bois, William Pène 1916-1993 ..... DLB-61
Dubrovina, Ekaterina Oskarovna
   1846-1913..................... DLB-238

Dubus, Andre 1936-1999 .... DLB-130
   Tribute to Michael M. Rea Y-97
Dubus, Andre, III 1959- DLB-292
Ducange, Victor 1783-1833 .... DLB-192
Du Chaillu, Paul Belloni 1831?-1903.... DLB-189
Ducharme, Réjean 1941- DLB-60
Dučić, Jovan 1871-1943 .....DLB-147; CDWLB-4
Duck, Stephen 1705?-1756 .... DLB-95
Gerald Duckworth and Company
   Limited...................... DLB-112
Duclaux, Madame Mary (see Robinson, A. Mary F.)
Dudek, Louis 1918-2001 .... DLB-88
Dudintsev, Vladimir Dmitrievich
   1918-1998 .... DLB-302
Dudley-Smith, Trevor (see Hall, Adam)
Duell, Sloan and Pearce DLB-46
Duerer, Albrecht 1471-1528 ....DLB-179
Duff Gordon, Lucie 1821-1869 .... DLB-166
Dufferin, Helen Lady, Countess of Gifford
   1807-1867 .... DLB-199
Duffield and Green................. DLB-46
Duffy, Maureen 1933- DLB-14, 310
Dufief, Nicholas Gouin 1776-1834 ...... DLB-187
Dufresne, John 1948- DLB-292
Dugan, Alan 1923-2003 .... DLB-5
Dugard, William 1606-1662........DLB-170, 281
William Dugard [publishing house] DLB-170
Dugas, Marcel 1883-1947 .... DLB-92
William Dugdale [publishing house]..... DLB-106
Duhamel, Georges 1884-1966 .... DLB-65
Dujardin, Edouard 1861-1949 .... DLB-123
Dukes, Ashley 1885-1959 .... DLB-10
Dumas, Alexandre *fils* 1824-1895 .... DLB-192
Dumas, Alexandre *père* 1802-1870..... DLB-119, 192
Dumas, Henry 1934-1968 .... DLB-41
du Maurier, Daphne 1907-1989 .... DLB-191
Du Maurier, George 1834-1896 .....DLB-153, 178
Dummett, Michael 1925- DLB-262
Dunbar, Paul Laurence
   1872-1906............DLB-50, 54, 78; CDALB-3
   Introduction to *Lyrics of Lowly Life* (1896),
   by William Dean Howells........ DLB-50
Dunbar, William
   circa 1460-circa 1522 .... DLB-132, 146
Duncan, Dave 1933- DLB-251
Duncan, David James 1952- DLB-256
Duncan, Norman 1871-1916........... DLB-92
Duncan, Quince 1940- DLB-145
Duncan, Robert 1919-1988 ...... DLB-5, 16, 193
Duncan, Ronald 1914-1982 .... DLB-13
Duncan, Sara Jeannette 1861-1922 ..... DLB-92
Dunigan, Edward, and Brother DLB-49
Dunlap, John 1747-1812 .... DLB-43
Dunlap, William 1766-1839 ......DLB-30, 37, 59
Dunlop, William "Tiger" 1792-1848 ..... DLB-99
Dunmore, Helen 1952- DLB-267

Dunn, Douglas 1942- DLB-40
Dunn, Harvey Thomas 1884-1952 ..... DLB-188
Dunn, Stephen 1939- DLB-105
   "The Good, The Not So Good" DLB-105
Dunne, Dominick 1925- DLB-306
Dunne, Finley Peter 1867-1936........ DLB-11, 23
Dunne, John Gregory 1932- Y-80
Dunne, Philip 1908-1992 .... DLB-26
Dunning, Ralph Cheever 1878-1930 ...... DLB-4
Dunning, William A. 1857-1922..........DLB-17
Duns Scotus, John circa 1266-1308 ..... DLB-115
Dunsany, Lord (Edward John Moreton
   Drax Plunkett, Baron Dunsany)
   1878-1957......... DLB-10, 77, 153, 156, 255
Dunton, W. Herbert 1878-1936........ DLB-188
John Dunton [publishing house].........DLB-170
Dupin, Amantine-Aurore-Lucile (see Sand, George)
Du Pont de Nemours, Pierre Samuel
   1739-1817..................... DLB-313
Dupuy, Eliza Ann 1814-1880 .... DLB-248
Durack, Mary 1913-1994 .... DLB-260
Durand, Lucile (see Bersianik, Louky)
Duranti, Francesca 1935- DLB-196
Duranty, Walter 1884-1957 .... DLB-29
Duras, Marguerite (Marguerite Donnadieu)
   1914-1996 .... DLB-83, 321
Durfey, Thomas 1653-1723 .... DLB-80
Durova, Nadezhda Andreevna
   (Aleksandr Andreevich Aleksandrov)
   1783-1866 .... DLB-198
Durrell, Lawrence 1912-1990
   ....DLB-15, 27, 204; Y-90; CDBLB-7
William Durrell [publishing house] DLB-49
Dürrenmatt, Friedrich
   1921-1990 ....DLB-69, 124; CDWLB-2
Duston, Hannah 1657-1737............ DLB-200
Dutt, Toru 1856-1877................ DLB-240
E. P. Dutton and Company DLB-49
Duun, Olav 1876-1939................ DLB-297
Duvoisin, Roger 1904-1980 .... DLB-61
Duyckinck, Evert Augustus
   1816-1878 .... DLB-3, 64, 250
Duyckinck, George L.
   1823-1863 .... DLB-3, 250
Duyckinck and Company DLB-49
Dwight, John Sullivan 1813-1893..... DLB-1, 235
Dwight, Timothy 1752-1817............ DLB-37
   *America: or, A Poem on the Settlement
   of the British Colonies*, by
   Timothy Dwight................ DLB-37
Dybek, Stuart 1942- DLB-130
   Tribute to Michael M. Rea Y-97
Dyer, Charles 1928- DLB-13
Dyer, Sir Edward 1543-1607 .... DLB-136
Dyer, George 1755-1841................ DLB-93
Dyer, John 1699-1757 .... DLB-95
Dyk, Viktor 1877-1931 .... DLB-215
Dylan, Bob 1941- DLB-16

E

Eager, Edward 1911-1964 . . . . DLB-22

Eagleton, Terry 1943- DLB-242

Eames, Wilberforce
1855-1937 . . . . DLB-140

Earle, Alice Morse
1853-1911 . . . . DLB-221

Earle, John 1600 or 1601-1665 . . . . DLB-151

James H. Earle and Company DLB-49

East Europe
Independence and Destruction,
1918-1941 . . . . DLB-220

Social Theory and Ethnography:
Language and Ethnicity in
Western versus Eastern Man DLB-220

Eastlake, William 1917-1997 . . . . DLB-6, 206

Eastman, Carol ?- DLB-44

Eastman, Charles A. (Ohiyesa)
1858-1939 . . . . DLB-175

Eastman, Max 1883-1969 . . . . DLB-91

Eaton, Daniel Isaac 1753-1814 . . . . DLB-158

Eaton, Edith Maude 1865-1914 . . . . . DLB-221, 312

Eaton, Winnifred 1875-1954 . . . . DLB-221, 312

Eberhart, Richard 1904-2005 . . . DLB-48; CDALB-1

Tribute to Robert Penn Warren Y-89

Ebner, Jeannie 1918-2004 . . . . DLB-85

Ebner-Eschenbach, Marie von
1830-1916 . . . . DLB-81

Ebon 1942- DLB-41

E-Books' Second Act in Libraries Y-02

Ecbasis Captivi circa 1045 . . . . DLB-148

Ecco Press DLB-46

Eckhart, Meister circa 1260-circa 1328 . . . DLB-115

The Eclectic Review 1805-1868 . . . . DLB-110

Eco, Umberto 1932- DLB-196, 242

Eddison, E. R. 1882-1945 . . . . DLB-255

Edel, Leon 1907-1997 . . . . DLB-103

Edelfeldt, Inger 1956- DLB-257

J. M. Edelstein's Collection of Twentieth-
Century American Poetry (A Century of Poetry,
a Lifetime of Collecting) Y-02

Edes, Benjamin 1732-1803 . . . . DLB-43

Edgar, David 1948- DLB-13, 233

Viewpoint: Politics and
Performance DLB-13

Edgerton, Clyde 1944- DLB-278

Edgeworth, Maria
1768-1849 . . . . DLB-116, 159, 163

The Edinburgh Review 1802-1929 . . . . DLB-110

Edinburgh University Press DLB-112

Editing
Conversations with Editors Y-95

Editorial Statements DLB-137

The Editorial Style of Fredson Bowers . . . Y-91

Editorial: The Extension of Copyright . . . Y-02

We See the Editor at Work Y-97

Whose Ulysses? The Function of Editing . . Y-97

The Editor Publishing Company DLB-49

Editorial Institute at Boston University Y-00

Edmonds, Helen Woods Ferguson
(see Kavan, Anna)

Edmonds, Randolph 1900-1983 . . . . DLB-51

Edmonds, Walter D. 1903-1998 . . . . DLB-9

Edric, Robert (see Armitage, G. E.)

Edschmid, Kasimir 1890-1966 . . . . DLB-56

Edson, Margaret 1961- DLB-266

Edson, Russell 1935- DLB-244

Edwards, Amelia Anne Blandford
1831-1892 . . . . DLB-174

Edwards, Dic 1953- DLB-245

Edwards, Edward 1812-1886 . . . . DLB-184

Edwards, Jonathan 1703-1758 . . . . . . DLB-24, 270

Edwards, Jonathan, Jr. 1745-1801 . . . . DLB-37

Edwards, Junius 1929- DLB-33

Edwards, Matilda Barbara Betham
1836-1919 . . . . DLB-174

Edwards, Richard 1524-1566 . . . . DLB-62

Edwards, Sarah Pierpont 1710-1758 . . . . . DLB-200

James Edwards [publishing house] DLB-154

Effinger, George Alec 1947- DLB-8

Egerton, George 1859-1945 . . . . DLB-135

Eggleston, Edward 1837-1902 . . . . DLB-12

Eggleston, Wilfred 1901-1986 . . . . DLB-92

Eglītis, Anšlavs 1906-1993 . . . . DLB-220

Eguren, José María 1874-1942 . . . . DLB-290

Ehrenreich, Barbara 1941- DLB-246

Ehrenstein, Albert 1886-1950 . . . . DLB-81

Ehrhart, W. D. 1948- DS-9

Ehrlich, Gretel 1946- DLB-212, 275

Eich, Günter 1907-1972 . . . . DLB-69, 124

Eichendorff, Joseph Freiherr von
1788-1857 . . . . DLB-90

Eifukumon'in 1271-1342 . . . . DLB-203

Eigner, Larry 1926-1996 . . . . DLB-5, 193

Eikon Basilike 1649 . . . . DLB-151

Eilhart von Oberge
circa 1140-circa 1195 . . . . DLB-148

Einar Benediktsson 1864-1940 . . . . DLB-293

Einar Kárason 1955- DLB-293

Einar Már Guðmundsson 1954- DLB-293

Einhard circa 770-840 . . . . DLB-148

Eiseley, Loren 1907-1977 . . . . DLB-275, DS-17

Eisenberg, Deborah 1945- DLB-244

Eisenreich, Herbert 1925-1986 . . . . DLB-85

Eisner, Kurt 1867-1919 . . . . DLB-66

Ekelöf, Gunnar 1907-1968 . . . . DLB-259

Eklund, Gordon 1945- Y-83

Ekman, Kerstin 1933- DLB-257

Ekwensi, Cyprian 1921- . . . DLB-117; CDWLB-3

Elaw, Zilpha circa 1790-? DLB-239

George Eld [publishing house] DLB-170

Elder, Lonne, III 1931- DLB-7, 38, 44

Paul Elder and Company DLB-49

Eldershaw, Flora (M. Barnard Eldershaw)
1897-1956 . . . . DLB-260

Eldershaw, M. Barnard (see Barnard, Marjorie and
Eldershaw, Flora)

The Electronic Text Center and the Electronic
Archive of Early American Fiction at the
University of Virginia Library Y-98

Eliade, Mircea 1907-1986 . . . . DLB-220; CDWLB-4

Elie, Robert 1915-1973 . . . . DLB-88

Elin Pelin 1877-1949 . . . . DLB-147; CDWLB-4

Eliot, George
1819-1880 . . . . DLB-21, 35, 55; CDBLB-4

The George Eliot Fellowship Y-99

Eliot, John 1604-1690 . . . . DLB-24

Eliot, T. S. 1888-1965
. . . . DLB-7, 10, 45, 63, 245; CDALB-5

T. S. Eliot Centennial: The Return
of the Old Possum Y-88

The T. S. Eliot Society: Celebration and
Scholarship, 1980-1999 . . . . Y-99

Eliot's Court Press DLB-170

Elizabeth I 1533-1603 . . . . DLB-136

Elizabeth von Nassau-Saarbrücken
after 1393-1456 . . . . DLB-179

Elizondo, Salvador 1932- DLB-145

Elizondo, Sergio 1930- DLB-82

Elkin, Stanley
1930-1995 . . . . DLB-2, 28, 218, 278; Y-80

Elles, Dora Amy (see Wentworth, Patricia)

Ellet, Elizabeth F. 1818?-1877 . . . . DLB-30

Elliot, Ebenezer 1781-1849 . . . . DLB-96, 190

Elliot, Frances Minto (Dickinson)
1820-1898 . . . . DLB-166

Elliott, Charlotte 1789-1871 . . . . DLB-199

Elliott, George 1923- DLB-68

Elliott, George P. 1918-1980 . . . . DLB-244

Elliott, Janice 1931-1995 . . . . DLB-14

Elliott, Sarah Barnwell 1848-1928 . . . . DLB-221

Elliott, Sumner Locke 1917-1991 . . . . DLB-289

Elliott, Thomes and Talbot DLB-49

Elliott, William, III 1788-1863 . . . . DLB-3, 248

Ellin, Stanley 1916-1986 . . . . DLB-306

Ellis, Alice Thomas (Anna Margaret Haycraft)
1932- DLB-194

Ellis, Bret Easton 1964- DLB-292

Ellis, Edward S. 1840-1916 . . . . DLB-42

Frederick Staridge Ellis
[publishing house] DLB-106

Ellis, George E.
"The New Controversy Concerning
Miracles DS-5

The George H. Ellis Company DLB-49

Ellis, Havelock 1859-1939 . . . . DLB-190

Ellison, Harlan 1934- DLB-8

Tribute to Isaac Asimov Y-92

Ellison, Ralph
1914-1994 . . . DLB-2, 76, 227; Y-94; CDALB-1

Ellmann, Richard 1918-1987 . . . . . . DLB-103; Y-87

Ellroy, James 1948- DLB-226; Y-91

Cumulative Index

Tribute to John D. MacDonald Y-86
Tribute to Raymond Chandler Y-88
Eluard, Paul 1895-1952 . . . . DLB-258
Elyot, Thomas 1490?-1546. . . . . DLB-136
Emanuel, James Andrew 1921- DLB-41
Emecheta, Buchi 1944- DLB-117; CDWLB-3
Emerson, Ralph Waldo
 1803-1882 . . . . . DLB-1, 59, 73, 183, 223, 270;
  DS-5; CDALB-2
 Ralph Waldo Emerson in 1982 . . . . Y-82
 The Ralph Waldo Emerson Society. Y-99
Emerson, William 1769-1811 . . . . DLB-37
Emerson, William R. 1923-1997. . . . . Y-97
Emin, Fedor Aleksandrovich
 circa 1735-1770. . . . . DLB-150
Emmanuel, Pierre 1916-1984 . . . . DLB-258
Empedocles fifth century B.C. DLB-176
Empson, William 1906-1984 . . . . DLB-20
Enchi Fumiko 1905-1986 . . . . DLB-182
"The Encyclopedia," Denis Diderot. DLB-314
Ende, Michael 1929-1995. . . . . DLB-75
Endō Shūsaku 1923-1996 . . . . DLB-182
Engel, Marian 1933-1985 . . . . DLB-53
Engel'gardt, Sof'ia Vladimirovna
 1828-1894 .DLB-277
Engels, Friedrich 1820-1895 . . . . DLB-129
Engle, Paul 1908-1991 . . . . DLB-48
 Tribute to Robert Penn Warren Y-89
English, Thomas Dunn 1819-1902. . . . . . DLB-202
Ennius 239 B.C.-169 B.C. DLB-211
Enquist, Per Olov 1934- DLB-257
Enright, Anne 1962- DLB-267
Enright, D. J. 1920-2002. . . . . DLB-27
Enright, Elizabeth 1909-1968 . . . . DLB-22
Epic, The Sixteenth-Century Spanish. . . . DLB-318
Epictetus circa 55-circa 125-130 . . . . .DLB-176
Epicurus 342/341 B.C.-271/270 B.C. DLB-176
d'Epinay, Louise (Louise-Florence-Pétronille Tardieu
 d'Esclavelles, marquise d'Epinay)
 1726-1783 . . . . DLB-313
Epps, Bernard 1936- DLB-53
Epshtein, Mikhail Naumovich 1950- . . DLB-285
Epstein, Julius 1909-2000 and
 Epstein, Philip 1909-1952. . . . . DLB-26
Epstein, Leslie 1938- DLB-299
Editors, Conversations with Y-95
Equiano, Olaudah
 circa 1745-1797 . . . . . . .DLB-37, 50; CDWLB-3
 Olaudah Equiano and Unfinished
  Journeys: The Slave-Narrative
  Tradition and Twentieth-Century
  Continuities. DLB-117
Eragny Press. DLB-112
Erasmus, Desiderius 1467-1536 . . . . DLB-136
Erba, Luciano 1922- DLB-128
Erdman, Nikolai Robertovich
 1900-1970. DLB-272
Erdrich, Louise
 1954- DLB-152, 175, 206; CDALB-7

Erenburg, Il'ia Grigor'evich 1891-1967 . . .DLB-272
Erichsen-Brown, Gwethalyn Graham
 (see Graham, Gwethalyn)
Eriugena, John Scottus circa 810-877 . . . . DLB-115
Ernst, Paul 1866-1933 . . . . DLB-66, 118
Erofeev, Venedikt Vasil'evich
 1938-1990 . . . . DLB-285
Erofeev, Viktor Vladimirovich 1947- . . . DLB-285
Ershov, Petr Pavlovich 1815-1869 . . . . . . DLB-205
Erskine, Albert 1911-1993 . . . . Y-93
 At Home with Albert Erskine Y-00
Erskine, John 1879-1951 . . . . DLB-9, 102
Erskine, Mrs. Steuart ?-1948 . . . . DLB-195
Ertel', Aleksandr Ivanovich
 1855-1908 . . . . DLB-238
Ervine, St. John Greer 1883-1971 . . . . DLB-10
Eschenburg, Johann Joachim
 1743-1820. . . . . DLB-97
Escofet, Cristina 1945- DLB-305
Escoto, Julio 1944- DLB-145
Esdaile, Arundell 1880-1956. . . . . DLB-201
Esenin, Sergei Aleksandrovich
 1895-1925 . . . . DLB-295
Eshleman, Clayton 1935- DLB-5
Espaillat, Rhina P. 1932- DLB-282
Espanca, Florbela 1894-1930 . . . . DLB-287
Espriu, Salvador 1913-1985 . . . . DLB-134
Ess Ess Publishing Company DLB-49
Essex House Press DLB-112
Esson, Louis 1878-1943 . . . . DLB-260
Essop, Ahmed 1931- DLB-225
Esterházy, Péter 1950- . . . DLB-232; CDWLB-4
Estes, Eleanor 1906-1988 . . . . DLB-22
Estes and Lauriat DLB-49
Estleman, Loren D. 1952- DLB-226
Eszterhas, Joe 1944- DLB-185
Etherege, George 1636-circa 1692 . . . . . . DLB-80
Ethridge, Mark, Sr. 1896-1981 . . . . DLB-127
Ets, Marie Hall 1893-1984 . . . . DLB-22
Etter, David 1928- DLB-105
Ettner, Johann Christoph
 1654-1724. DLB-168
Eudora Welty Remembered in
 Two Exhibits Y-02
Eugene Gant's Projected Works. Y-01
Eupolemius fl. circa 1095 . . . . DLB-148
Euripides circa 484 B.C.-407/406 B.C.
 .DLB-176; CDWLB-1
Evans, Augusta Jane 1835-1909 . . . . DLB-239
Evans, Caradoc 1878-1945 . . . . DLB-162
Evans, Charles 1850-1935 . . . . DLB-187
Evans, Donald 1884-1921. . . . . DLB-54
Evans, George Henry 1805-1856 . . . . DLB-43
Evans, Hubert 1892-1986. . . . . DLB-92
Evans, Mari 1923- DLB-41
Evans, Mary Ann (see Eliot, George)
Evans, Nathaniel 1742-1767 . . . . DLB-31

Evans, Sebastian 1830-1909 . . . . DLB-35
Evans, Ray 1915- DLB-265
M. Evans and Company. DLB-46
Evaristi, Marcella 1953- DLB-233
Everett, Alexander Hill 1790-1847 . . . . . . DLB-59
Everett, Edward 1794-1865 . . . . . . DLB-1, 59, 235
Everson, R. G. 1903- DLB-88
Everson, William 1912-1994 . . . . . . DLB-5, 16, 212
Evreinov, Nikolai 1879-1953 . . . . DLB-317
Ewald, Johannes 1743-1781. . . . . DLB-300
Ewart, Gavin 1916-1995. . . . . DLB-40
Ewing, Juliana Horatia
 1841-1885 . . . . DLB-21, 163
The Examiner 1808-1881 . . . . DLB-110
Exley, Frederick 1929-1992 . . . . . . .DLB-143; Y-81
Editorial: The Extension of Copyright. Y-02
von Eyb, Albrecht 1420-1475 . . . . .DLB-179
Eyre and Spottiswoode. DLB-106
Ezera, Regīna 1930- DLB-232
Ezzo ?-after 1065 . . . . DLB-148

F

Faber, Frederick William 1814-1863 . . . . . DLB-32
Faber and Faber Limited. DLB-112
Faccio, Rena (see Aleramo, Sibilla)
Facsimiles
 The Uses of Facsimile: A Symposium Y-90
Fadeev, Aleksandr Aleksandrovich
 1901-1956 . . . . .DLB-272
Fagundo, Ana María 1938- DLB-134
Fainzil'berg, Il'ia Arnol'dovich
 (see Il'f, Il'ia and Petrov, Evgenii)
Fair, Ronald L. 1932- DLB-33
Fairfax, Beatrice (see Manning, Marie)
Fairlie, Gerard 1899-1983. . . . . DLB-77
Faldbakken, Knut 1941- DLB-297
Falkberget, Johan (Johan Petter Lillebakken)
 1879-1967. . . . . DLB-297
Fallada, Hans 1893-1947 . . . . DLB-56
Fancher, Betsy 1928- Y-83
Fane, Violet 1843-1905. . . . . DLB-35
Fanfrolico Press DLB-112
Fanning, Katherine 1927- DLB-127
Fanon, Frantz 1925-1961 . . . . DLB-296
Fanshawe, Sir Richard 1608-1666 . . . . . . DLB-126
Fantasy Press Publishers. DLB-46
Fante, John 1909-1983 . . . . .DLB-130; Y-83
Al-Farabi circa 870-950 . . . . DLB-115
Farabough, Laura 1949- DLB-228
Farah, Nuruddin 1945- DLB-125; CDWLB-3
Farber, Norma 1909-1984 . . . . DLB-61
A Farewell to Arms (Documentary) DLB-308
Fargue, Léon-Paul 1876-1947 . . . . DLB-258
Farigoule, Louis (see Romains, Jules)
Farjeon, Eleanor 1881-1965 . . . . DLB-160
Farley, Harriet 1812-1907 . . . . DLB-239

Farley, Walter 1920-1989 ....DLB-22
Farmborough, Florence 1887-1978.......DLB-204
Farmer, Penelope 1939- DLB-161
Farmer, Philip José 1918- DLB-8
Farnaby, Thomas 1575?-1647 ....DLB-236
Farningham, Marianne (see Hearn, Mary Anne)
Farquhar, George circa 1677-1707 ....DLB-84
Farquharson, Martha (see Finley, Martha)
Farrar, Frederic William 1831-1903.......DLB-163
Farrar, Straus and Giroux DLB-46
Farrar and Rinehart................DLB-46
Farrell, J. G. 1935-1979 ....DLB-14, 271
Farrell, James T. 1904-1979 ....DLB-4, 9, 86; DS-2
Fast, Howard 1914-2003 ....DLB-9
Faulkner, William 1897-1962................
    DLB-9, 11, 44, 102, 316; DS-2; Y-86; CDALB-5
    Faulkner and Yoknapatawpha
        Conference, Oxford, Mississippi Y-97
    Faulkner Centennial Addresses Y-97
    "Faulkner 100–Celebrating the Work,"
        University of South Carolina,
        Columbia Y-97
    Impressions of William Faulkner Y-97
    William Faulkner and the People-to-People
        Program Y-86
    William Faulkner Centenary
        Celebrations Y-97
    The William Faulkner Society......... Y-99
George Faulkner [publishing house] DLB-154
Faulks, Sebastian 1953- DLB-207
Fauset, Jessie Redmon 1882-1961 ....DLB-51
Faust, Frederick Schiller (Max Brand)
    1892-1944....................DLB-256
Faust, Irvin
    1924- DLB-2, 28, 218, 278; Y-80, 00
    I Wake Up Screaming [Response to
        Ken Auletta] Y-97
    Tribute to Bernard Malamud Y-86
    Tribute to Isaac Bashevis Singer Y-91
    Tribute to Meyer Levin Y-81
Fawcett, Edgar 1847-1904 ....DLB-202
Fawcett, Millicent Garrett 1847-1929.....DLB-190
Fawcett Books DLB-46
Fay, Theodore Sedgwick 1807-1898 ....DLB-202
Fearing, Kenneth 1902-1961 ....DLB-9
Federal Writers' Project DLB-46
Federman, Raymond 1928- Y-80
Fedin, Konstantin Aleksandrovich
    1892-1977....................DLB-272
Fedorov, Innokentii Vasil'evich
    (see Omulevsky, Innokentii Vasil'evich)
Feiffer, Jules 1929- DLB-7, 44
Feinberg, Charles E. 1899-1988.... DLB-187; Y-88
Feind, Barthold 1678-1721.............DLB-168
Feinstein, Elaine 1930- DLB-14, 40
Feirstein, Frederick 1940- DLB-282
Feiss, Paul Louis 1875-1952 ....DLB-187
Feldman, Irving 1928- DLB-169

Felipe, Carlos 1911-1975 ....DLB-305
Felipe, Léon 1884-1968 ....DLB-108
Fell, Frederick, Publishers DLB-46
Fellowship of Southern Writers Y-98
Felltham, Owen 1602?-1668 ....DLB-126, 151
Felman, Shoshana 1942- DLB-246
Fels, Ludwig 1946- DLB-75
Felton, Cornelius Conway
    1807-1862 ....DLB-1, 235
Fel'zen, Iurii (Nikolai Berngardovich Freidenshtein)
    1894?-1943 ....DLB-317
Mothe-Fénelon, François de Salignac de la
    1651-1715 ....DLB-268
Fenn, Harry 1837-1911 ....DLB-188
Fennario, David 1947- DLB-60
Fenner, Dudley 1558?-1587? DLB-236
Fenno, Jenny 1765?-1803............DLB-200
Fenno, John 1751-1798................DLB-43
R. F. Fenno and Company..............DLB-49
Fenoglio, Beppe 1922-1963 ....DLB-177
Fenton, Geoffrey 1539?-1608.........DLB-136
Fenton, James 1949- DLB-40
The Hemingway/Fenton
    Correspondence Y-02
Ferber, Edna 1885-1968.......DLB-9, 28, 86, 266
Ferdinand, Vallery, III (see Salaam, Kalamu ya)
Ferguson, Sir Samuel 1810-1886 ....DLB-32
Ferguson, William Scott 1875-1954 ....DLB-47
Fergusson, Robert 1750-1774 ....DLB-109
Ferland, Albert 1872-1943 ....DLB-92
Ferlinghetti, Lawrence
    1919- DLB-5, 16; CDALB-1
    Tribute to Kenneth Rexroth Y-82
Fermor, Patrick Leigh 1915- DLB-204
Fern, Fanny (see Parton, Sara Payson Willis)
Ferrars, Elizabeth (Morna Doris Brown)
    1907-1995 ....DLB-87
Ferré, Rosario 1942- DLB-145
Ferreira, Vergílio 1916-1996 ....DLB-287
E. Ferret and Company DLB-49
Ferrier, Susan 1782-1854 ....DLB-116
Ferril, Thomas Hornsby 1896-1988 .....DLB-206
Ferrini, Vincent 1913- DLB-48
Ferron, Jacques 1921-1985..............DLB-60
Ferron, Madeleine 1922- DLB-53
Ferrucci, Franco 1936- DLB-196
Fet, Afanasii Afanas'evich
    1820?-1892 ....DLB-277
Fetridge and Company DLB-49
Feuchtersleben, Ernst Freiherr von
    1806-1849 ....DLB-133
Feuchtwanger, Lion 1884-1958 ....DLB-66
Feuerbach, Ludwig 1804-1872 ....DLB-133
Feuillet, Octave 1821-1890............DLB-192
Feydeau, Georges 1862-1921.........DLB-192
Fibiger, Mathilde 1830-1872 ....DLB-300
Fichte, Johann Gottlieb 1762-1814........DLB-90

Ficke, Arthur Davison 1883-1945 ....DLB-54
Fiction
    American Fiction and the 1930s DLB-9
    Fiction Best-Sellers, 1910-1945 ....DLB-9
    Postmodern Holocaust Fiction DLB-299
    The Year in Fiction........Y-84, 86, 89, 94–99
    The Year in Fiction: A Biased View Y-83
    The Year in U.S. Fiction Y-00, 01
    The Year's Work in Fiction: A Survey... Y-82
Fiedler, Leslie A. 1917-2003..........DLB-28, 67
    Tribute to Bernard Malamud Y-86
    Tribute to James Dickey Y-97
Field, Barron 1789-1846................DLB-230
Field, Edward 1924- DLB-105
Field, Eugene 1850-1895 .. DLB-23, 42, 140; DS-13
Field, John 1545?-1588 ....DLB-167
Field, Joseph M. 1810-1856 ....DLB-248
Field, Marshall, III 1893-1956............DLB-127
Field, Marshall, IV 1916-1965............DLB-127
Field, Marshall, V 1941- DLB-127
Field, Michael (Katherine Harris Bradley)
    1846-1914 ....DLB-240
    "The Poetry File" DLB-105
Field, Nathan 1587-1619 or 1620.........DLB-58
Field, Rachel 1894-1942..............DLB-9, 22
Fielding, Helen 1958- DLB-231
Fielding, Henry
    1707-1754........DLB-39, 84, 101; CDBLB-2
    "Defense of Amelia" (1752)...........DLB-39
    The History of the Adventures of Joseph Andrews
        [excerpt] (1742)................DLB-39
    Letter to [Samuel] Richardson on Clarissa
        (1748) DLB-39
    Preface to Joseph Andrews (1742) DLB-39
    Preface to Sarah Fielding's Familiar
        Letters (1747) [excerpt]..........DLB-39
    Preface to Sarah Fielding's The
        Adventures of David Simple (1744) ...DLB-39
    Review of Clarissa (1748) DLB-39
    Tom Jones (1749) [excerpt] DLB-39
Fielding, Sarah 1710-1768................DLB-39
    Preface to The Cry (1754) DLB-39
Fields, Annie Adams 1834-1915 ....DLB-221
Fields, Dorothy 1905-1974..............DLB-265
Fields, James T. 1817-1881.........DLB-1, 235
Fields, Julia 1938- DLB-41
Fields, Osgood and Company DLB-49
Fields, W. C. 1880-1946 ....DLB-44
Fierstein, Harvey 1954- DLB-266
Figes, Eva 1932- DLB-14, 271
Figuera, Angela 1902-1984 ....DLB-108
Filmer, Sir Robert 1586-1653 ....DLB-151
Filson, John circa 1753-1788................DLB-37
Finch, Anne, Countess of Winchilsea
    1661-1720 ....DLB-95
Finch, Annie 1956- DLB-282
Finch, Robert 1900- DLB-88

443

Cumulative Index

Findley, Timothy 1930-2002 .... DLB-53
Finlay, Ian Hamilton 1925- DLB-40
Finley, Martha 1828-1909 .... DLB-42
Finn, Elizabeth Anne (McCaul)
   1825-1921 .... DLB-166
Finnegan, Seamus 1949- DLB-245
Finney, Jack 1911-1995 .... DLB-8
Finney, Walter Braden (see Finney, Jack)
Firbank, Ronald 1886-1926 .... DLB-36
Firmin, Giles 1615-1697 .... DLB-24
First Edition Library/Collectors'
   Reprints, Inc. Y-91
Fischart, Johann
   1546 or 1547-1590 or 1591 .... DLB-179
Fischer, Karoline Auguste Fernandine
   1764-1842 .... DLB-94
Fischer, Tibor 1959- DLB-231
Fish, Stanley 1938- DLB-67
Fishacre, Richard 1205-1248 .... DLB-115
Fisher, Clay (see Allen, Henry W.)
Fisher, Dorothy Canfield 1879-1958 ... DLB-9, 102
Fisher, Leonard Everett 1924- DLB-61
Fisher, Roy 1930- DLB-40
Fisher, Rudolph 1897-1934 .... DLB-51, 102
Fisher, Steve 1913-1980 .... DLB-226
Fisher, Sydney George 1856-1927 ..... DLB-47
Fisher, Vardis 1895-1968 .... DLB-9, 206
Fiske, John 1608-1677 .... DLB-24
Fiske, John 1842-1901 .... DLB-47, 64
Fitch, Thomas circa 1700-1774 .... DLB-31
Fitch, William Clyde 1865-1909 .... DLB-7
FitzGerald, Edward 1809-1883 .... DLB-32
Fitzgerald, F. Scott 1896-1940
   ...... DLB-4, 9, 86; Y-81, 92;
   DS-1, 15, 16; CDALB-4
  F. Scott Fitzgerald: A Descriptive
   Bibliography, Supplement (2001) Y-01
  F. Scott Fitzgerald Centenary
   Celebrations Y-96
  F. Scott Fitzgerald Inducted into the
   American Poets' Corner at St. John
   the Divine; Ezra Pound Banned Y-99
  "F. Scott Fitzgerald: St. Paul's Native Son
   and Distinguished American Writer":
   University of Minnesota Conference,
   29-31 October 1982 .... Y-82
  First International F. Scott Fitzgerald
   Conference Y-92
  The Great Gatsby (Documentary) DLB-219
  Tender Is the Night (Documentary) ... DLB-273
Fitzgerald, Penelope 1916-2000 ..... DLB-14, 194
Fitzgerald, Robert 1910-1985 .... Y-80
FitzGerald, Robert D. 1902-1987 ..... DLB-260
Fitzgerald, Thomas 1819-1891 .... DLB-23
Fitzgerald, Zelda Sayre 1900-1948 .... Y-84
Fitzhugh, Louise 1928-1974 .... DLB-52
Fitzhugh, William circa 1651-1701 ..... DLB-24
Flagg, James Montgomery 1877-1960 .... DLB-188
Flanagan, Thomas 1923-2002 .... Y-80

Flanner, Hildegarde 1899-1987 .... DLB-48
Flanner, Janet 1892-1978 .... DLB-4; DS-15
Flannery, Peter 1951- DLB-233
Flaubert, Gustave 1821-1880 ...... DLB-119, 301
Flavin, Martin 1883-1967 .... DLB-9
Fleck, Konrad (fl. circa 1220) DLB-138
Flecker, James Elroy 1884-1915 ...... DLB-10, 19
Fleeson, Doris 1901-1970 .... DLB-29
Fleißer, Marieluise 1901-1974 ...... DLB-56, 124
Fleischer, Nat 1887-1972 .... DLB-241
Fleming, Abraham 1552?-1607 .... DLB-236
Fleming, Ian 1908-1964 ... DLB-87, 201; CDBLB-7
Fleming, Joan 1908-1980 .... DLB-276
Fleming, May Agnes 1840-1880 .... DLB-99
Fleming, Paul 1609-1640 .... DLB-164
Fleming, Peter 1907-1971 .... DLB-195
Fletcher, Giles, the Elder 1546-1611 .... DLB-136
Fletcher, Giles, the Younger
   1585 or 1586-1623 .... DLB-121
Fletcher, J. S. 1863-1935 .... DLB-70
Fletcher, John 1579-1625 .... DLB-58
Fletcher, John Gould 1886-1950 ...... DLB-4, 45
Fletcher, Phineas 1582-1650 .... DLB-121
Flieg, Helmut (see Heym, Stefan)
Flint, F. S. 1885-1960 .... DLB-19
Flint, Timothy 1780-1840 .... DLB-73, 186
Fløgstad, Kjartan 1944- DLB-297
Florensky, Pavel Aleksandrovich
   1882-1937 .... DLB-295
Flores, Juan de fl. 1470-1500 .... DLB-286
Flores-Williams, Jason 1969- DLB-209
Florio, John 1553?-1625 .... DLB-172
Fludd, Robert 1574-1637 .... DLB-281
Flynn, Elizabeth Gurley 1890-1964 ..... DLB-303
Fo, Dario 1926- Y-97
  Nobel Lecture 1997: Contra Jogulatores
   Obloquentes Y-97
Foden, Giles 1967- DLB-267
Fofanov, Konstantin Mikhailovich
   1862-1911 .... DLB-277
Foix, J. V. 1893-1987 .... DLB-134
Foley, Martha 1897-1977 .... DLB-137
Folger, Henry Clay 1857-1930 .... DLB-140
Folio Society DLB-112
Follain, Jean 1903-1971 .... DLB-258
Follen, Charles 1796-1840 .... DLB-235
Follen, Eliza Lee (Cabot) 1787-1860 ... DLB-1, 235
Follett, Ken 1949- DLB-87; Y-81
Follett Publishing Company DLB-46
John West Folsom [publishing house] DLB-49
Folz, Hans
   between 1435 and 1440-1513 .... DLB-179
Fonseca, Manuel da 1911-1993 .... DLB-287
Fonseca, Rubem 1925- DLB-307
Fontane, Theodor
   1819-1898 .... DLB-129; CDWLB-2

Fontenelle, Bernard Le Bovier de
   1657-1757 .... DLB-268, 313
Fontes, Montserrat 1940- DLB-209
Fonvisin, Denis Ivanovich
   1744 or 1745-1792 .... DLB-150
Foote, Horton 1916- DLB-26, 266
Foote, Mary Hallock
   1847-1938 .... DLB-186, 188, 202, 221
Foote, Samuel 1721-1777 .... DLB-89
Foote, Shelby 1916-2005 .... DLB-2, 17
Forbes, Calvin 1945- DLB-41
Forbes, Ester 1891-1967 .... DLB-22
Forbes, Rosita 1893?-1967 .... DLB-195
Forbes and Company DLB-49
Force, Peter 1790-1868 .... DLB-30
Forché, Carolyn 1950- DLB-5, 193
Ford, Charles Henri 1913-2002 ...... DLB-4, 48
Ford, Corey 1902-1969 .... DLB-11
Ford, Ford Madox
   1873-1939 ...... DLB-34, 98, 162; CDBLB-6
  Nathan Asch Remembers Ford Madox
   Ford, Sam Roth, and Hart Crane Y-02
J. B. Ford and Company DLB-49
Ford, Jesse Hill 1928-1996 .... DLB-6
Ford, John 1586-? DLB-58; CDBLB-1
Ford, R. A. D. 1915-1998 .... DLB-88
Ford, Richard 1944- DLB-227
Ford, Worthington C. 1858-1941 .... DLB-47
Fords, Howard, and Hulbert DLB-49
Foreman, Carl 1914-1984 .... DLB-26
Forester, C. S. 1899-1966 .... DLB-191
  The C. S. Forester Society Y-00
Forester, Frank (see Herbert, Henry William)
Formalism, New
  Anthologizing New Formalism DLB-282
   The Little Magazines of the
   New Formalism DLB-282
   The New Narrative Poetry DLB-282
   Presses of the New Formalism and
   the New Narrative DLB-282
   The Prosody of the New Formalism . DLB-282
   Younger Women Poets of the
   New Formalism DLB-282
Forman, Harry Buxton 1842-1917 ...... DLB-184
Fornés, María Irene 1930- DLB-7
Forrest, Leon 1937-1997 .... DLB-33
Forsh, Ol'ga Dmitrievna 1873-1961 .... DLB-272
Forster, E. M. 1879-1970
  ..DLB-34, 98, 162, 178, 195; DS-10; CDBLB-6
  "Fantasy," from *Aspects of the Novel*
   (1927) DLB-178
Forster, Georg 1754-1794 .... DLB-94
Forster, John 1812-1876 .... DLB-144
Forster, Margaret 1938- DLB-155, 271
Forsyth, Frederick 1938- DLB-87
Forsyth, William
   "Literary Style" (1857) [excerpt] DLB-57
Forten, Charlotte L. 1837-1914 ..... DLB-50, 239

Pages from Her Diary............DLB-50
Fortini, Franco 1917-1994..............DLB-128
Fortune, Mary ca. 1833-ca. 1910........DLB-230
Fortune, T. Thomas 1856-1928..........DLB-23
Fosdick, Charles Austin 1842-1915......DLB-42
Fosse, Jon 1959- DLB-297
Foster, David 1944- DLB-289
Foster, Genevieve 1893-1979...........DLB-61
Foster, Hannah Webster
    1758-1840....................DLB-37, 200
Foster, John 1648-1681................DLB-24
Foster, Michael 1904-1956..............DLB-9
Foster, Myles Birket 1825-1899........DLB-184
Foster, William Z. 1881-1961..........DLB-303
Foucault, Michel 1926-1984............DLB-242
Robert and Andrew Foulis
    [publishing house]..............DLB-154
Fouqué, Caroline de la Motte 1774-1831....DLB-90
Fouqué, Friedrich de la Motte
    1777-1843.........................DLB-90
Four Seas Company.....................DLB-46
Four Winds Press......................DLB-46
Fournier, Henri Alban (see Alain-Fournier)
Fowler, Christopher 1953- DLB-267
Fowler, Connie May 1958- DLB-292
Fowler and Wells Company DLB-49
Fowles, John
    1926- DLB-14, 139, 207; CDBLB-8
Fox, John 1939- DLB-245
Fox, John, Jr. 1862 or 1863-1919....DLB-9; DS-13
Fox, Paula 1923- DLB-52
Fox, Richard Kyle 1846-1922...........DLB-79
Fox, William Price 1926- DLB-2; Y-81
    Remembering Joe Heller.............Y-99
Richard K. Fox [publishing house].......DLB-49
Foxe, John 1517-1587..................DLB-132
Fraenkel, Michael 1896-1957............DLB-4
Frame, Ronald 1953- DLB-319
France, Anatole 1844-1924.............DLB-123
France, Richard 1938- DLB-7
Francis, Convers 1795-1863.........DLB-1, 235
Francis, Dick 1920- DLB-87; CDBLB-8
Francis, Sir Frank 1901-1988..........DLB-201
Francis, Jeffrey, Lord 1773-1850......DLB-107
C. S. Francis [publishing house].......DLB-49
Franck, Sebastian 1499-1542...........DLB-179
Francke, Kuno 1855-1930...............DLB-71
Françoise (Robertine Barry) 1863-1910....DLB-92
François, Louise von 1817-1893........DLB-129
Frank, Bruno 1887-1945................DLB-118
Frank, Leonhard 1882-1961..........DLB-56, 118
Frank, Melvin 1913-1988...............DLB-26
Frank, Waldo 1889-1967.............DLB-9, 63
Franken, Rose 1895?-1988 ......DLB-228, Y-84
Franklin, Benjamin
    1706-1790.....DLB-24, 43, 73, 183; CDALB-2

Franklin, James 1697-1735 ....DLB-43
Franklin, John 1786-1847..............DLB-99
Franklin, Miles 1879-1954 ....DLB-230
Franklin Library DLB-46
Frantz, Ralph Jules 1902-1979 ....DLB-4
Franzos, Karl Emil 1848-1904 ....DLB-129
Fraser, Antonia 1932- DLB-276
Fraser, G. S. 1915-1980 ....DLB-27
Fraser, Kathleen 1935- DLB-169
Frattini, Alberto 1922- DLB-128
Frau Ava ?-1127.......................DLB-148
Fraunce, Abraham 1558?-1592 or 1593...DLB-236
Frayn, Michael 1933- DLB-13, 14, 194, 245
Frazier, Charles 1950- DLB-292
Fréchette, Louis-Honoré 1839-1908.......DLB-99
Frederic, Harold 1856-1898....DLB-12, 23; DS-13
Freed, Arthur 1894-1973 ....DLB-265
Freeling, Nicolas 1927-2003 ....DLB-87
    Tribute to Georges Simenon...........Y-89
Freeman, Douglas Southall
    1886-1953.................DLB-17; DS-17
Freeman, Joseph 1897-1965 ....DLB-303
Freeman, Judith 1946- DLB-256
Freeman, Legh Richmond 1842-1915.....DLB-23
Freeman, Mary E. Wilkins
    1852-1930 ....DLB-12, 78, 221
Freeman, R. Austin 1862-1943 ....DLB-70
Freidank circa 1170-circa 1233........DLB-138
Freiligrath, Ferdinand 1810-1876 ......DLB-133
Fremlin, Celia 1914- DLB-276
Frémont, Jessie Benton 1834-1902.....DLB-183
Frémont, John Charles
    1813-1890..................DLB-183, 186
French, Alice 1850-1934 ....DLB-74; DS-13
French, David 1939- DLB-53
French, Evangeline 1869-1960..........DLB-195
French, Francesca 1871-1960 ....DLB-195
James French [publishing house] DLB-49
Samuel French [publishing house] DLB-49
Samuel French, Limited................DLB-106
French Literature
    Georges-Louis Leclerc de Buffon, "Le Discours
        sur le style".................DLB-314
    Marie-Jean-Antoine-Nicolas Caritat, marquis de
        Condorcet, "The Tenth Stage"..DLB-314
    Sophie Cottin, Claire d'Albe DLB-314
    Declaration of the Rights of Man and of
        the Citizen DLB-314
    Denis Diderot, "The Encyclopedia" ..DLB-314
    Epic and Beast Epic...............DLB-208
    French Arthurian Literature DLB-208
    Olympe de Gouges, Declaration of the Rights
        of Woman....................DLB-314
    Françoise d'Issembourg de Graffigny, Letters from
        a Peruvian Woman..............DLB-314
    Claude-Adrien Helvétius, The Spirit of
        Laws DLB-314

Paul Henri Thiry, baron d'Holbach (writing as
    Jean-Baptiste de Mirabaud), The System
    of Nature DLB-314
Pierre-Ambroise-François Choderlos de Laclos,
    Dangerous Acquaintances.........DLB-314
Lyric Poetry DLB-268
Louis-Sébastien Mercier, Le Tableau
    de Paris DLB-314
Charles-Louis de Secondat, baron de
    Montesquieu, The Spirit of Laws...DLB-314
Other Poets.....................DLB-217
Poetry in Nineteenth-Century France:
    Cultural Background and Critical
    Commentary DLB-217
Roman de la Rose: Guillaume de Lorris
    1200 to 1205-circa 1230, Jean de
    Meun 1235/1240-circa 1305.....DLB-208
Jean-Jacques Rousseau, The Social
    Contract DLB-314
Marquis de Sade, "Dialogue entre un prêtre et
    un moribond"..................DLB-314
Saints' Lives DLB-208
Troubadours, Trobaíritz, and
    Trouvères DLB-208
Anne-Robert-Jacques Turgot, baron de l'Aulne,
    "Memorandum on Local
    Government" DLB-314
Voltaire, "An account of the death of the cheva-
    lier de La Barre"..............DLB-314
Voltaire, Candide DLB-314
Voltaire, Philosophical Dictionary.......DLB-314
French Theater
    Medieval French Drama DLB-208
    Parisian Theater, Fall 1984: Toward
        a New Baroque................Y-85
Freneau, Philip 1752-1832 ....DLB-37, 43
    The Rising Glory of America DLB-37
Freni, Melo 1934- DLB-128
Fréron, Elie Catherine 1718-1776........DLB-313
Freshfield, Douglas W. 1845-1934 ......DLB-174
Freud, Sigmund 1856-1939 ....DLB-296
Freytag, Gustav 1816-1895 ....DLB-129
Fríða Á. Sigurðardóttir 1940- DLB-293
Fridegård, Jan 1897-1968..............DLB-259
Fried, Erich 1921-1988 ....DLB-85
Friedan, Betty 1921- DLB-246
Friedman, Bruce Jay 1930- DLB-2, 28, 244
Friedman, Carl 1952- DLB-299
Friedman, Kinky 1944- DLB-292
Friedrich von Hausen circa 1171-1190....DLB-138
Friel, Brian 1929- DLB-13, 319
Friend, Krebs 1895?-1967? DLB-4
Fries, Fritz Rudolf 1935- DLB-75
Frisch, Max
    1911-1991 ....DLB-69, 124; CDWLB-2
Frischlin, Nicodemus 1547-1590 ....DLB-179
Frischmuth, Barbara 1941- DLB-85
Fritz, Jean 1915- DLB-52
Froissart, Jean circa 1337-circa 1404.......DLB-208
Fromm, Erich 1900-1980...............DLB-296

Fromentin, Eugene 1820-1876 .... DLB-123
Frontinus circa A.D. 35-A.D. 103/104..... DLB-211
Frost, A. B. 1851-1928 .... DLB-188; DS-13
Frost, Robert
    1874-1963......... DLB-54; DS-7; CDALB-4
    The Friends of the Dymock Poets Y-00
Frostenson, Katarina 1953- DLB-257
Frothingham, Octavius Brooks
    1822-1895 .... DLB-1, 243
Froude, James Anthony
    1818-1894................DLB-18, 57, 144
Fruitlands 1843-1844 .... DLB-1, 223; DS-5
Fry, Christopher 1907-2005 .... DLB-13
    Tribute to John Betjeman............. Y-84
Fry, Roger 1866-1934.................DS-10
Fry, Stephen 1957- DLB-207
Frye, Northrop 1912-1991 .... DLB-67, 68, 246
Fuchs, Daniel 1909-1993 .....DLB-9, 26, 28; Y-93
    Tribute to Isaac Bashevis Singer Y-91
Fuentes, Carlos 1928- DLB-113; CDWLB-3
Fuertes, Gloria 1918-1998............. DLB-108
Fugard, Athol 1932- DLB-225
The Fugitives and the Agrarians:
    The First Exhibition................. Y-85
Fujiwara no Shunzei 1114-1204 .... DLB-203
Fujiwara no Tameaki 1230s?-1290s? DLB-203
Fujiwara no Tameie 1198-1275......... DLB-203
Fujiwara no Teika 1162-1241 .... DLB-203
Fuks, Ladislav 1923-1994............. DLB-299
Fulbecke, William 1560-1603? DLB-172
Fuller, Charles 1939- DLB-38, 266
Fuller, Henry Blake 1857-1929 .... DLB-12
Fuller, John 1937- DLB-40
Fuller, Margaret (see Fuller, Sarah)
Fuller, Roy 1912-1991 .... DLB-15, 20
    Tribute to Christopher Isherwood....... Y-86
Fuller, Samuel 1912-1997 .... DLB-26
Fuller, Sarah 1810-1850 .... DLB-1, 59, 73,
    183, 223, 239; DS-5; CDALB-2
Fuller, Thomas 1608-1661 .... DLB-151
Fullerton, Hugh 1873-1945.............DLB-171
Fullwood, William fl. 1568 .... DLB-236
Fulton, Alice 1952- DLB-193
Fulton, Len 1934- Y-86
Fulton, Robin 1937- DLB-40
Furbank, P. N. 1920- DLB-155
Furetière, Antoine 1619-1688 .... DLB-268
Furman, Laura 1945- Y-86
Furmanov, Dmitrii Andreevich
    1891-1926 .... DLB-272
Furness, Horace Howard 1833-1912 ..... DLB-64
Furness, William Henry
    1802-1896 .... DLB-1, 235
Furnivall, Frederick James 1825-1910.... DLB-184
Furphy, Joseph (Tom Collins)
    1843-1912..................... DLB-230
Furthman, Jules 1888-1966............ DLB-26

    Shakespeare and Montaigne: A
        Symposium by Jules Furthman Y-02
Furui Yoshikichi 1937- DLB-182
Fushimi, Emperor 1265-1317 .... DLB-203
Futabatei Shimei (Hasegawa Tatsunosuke)
    1864-1909 .... DLB-180
Fyleman, Rose 1877-1957 .... DLB-160

G

Gaarder, Jostein 1952- DLB-297
Gadallah, Leslie 1939- DLB-251
Gadamer, Hans-Georg 1900-2002 ..... DLB-296
Gadda, Carlo Emilio 1893-1973........DLB-177
Gaddis, William 1922-1998 ....DLB-2, 278
    William Gaddis: A Tribute Y-99
Gág, Wanda 1893-1946 .... DLB-22
Gagarin, Ivan Sergeevich 1814-1882 .... DLB-198
Gagnon, Madeleine 1938- DLB-60
Gaiman, Neil 1960- DLB-261
Gaine, Hugh 1726-1807 .... DLB-43
Hugh Gaine [publishing house] DLB-49
Gaines, Ernest J.
    1933- DLB-2, 33, 152; Y-80; CDALB-6
Gaiser, Gerd 1908-1976 .... DLB-69
Gaitskill, Mary 1954- DLB-244
Galarza, Ernesto 1905-1984 .... DLB-122
Galaxy Science Fiction Novels DLB-46
Galbraith, Robert (or Caubraith)
    circa 1483-1544 .... DLB-281
Gale, Zona 1874-1938...........DLB-9, 228, 78
Galen of Pergamon 129-after 210........DLB-176
Gales, Winifred Marshall 1761-1839 .... DLB-200
Galich, Aleksandr 1918-1977 .... DLB-317
Medieval Galician-Portuguese Poetry.... DLB-287
Gall, Louise von 1815-1855 .... DLB-133
Gallagher, Tess 1943- DLB-120, 212, 244
Gallagher, Wes 1911-1997 .... DLB-127
Gallagher, William Davis 1808-1894 ..... DLB-73
Gallant, Mavis 1922- DLB-53
Gallegos, María Magdalena 1935- DLB-209
Gallico, Paul 1897-1976..............DLB-9, 171
Gallop, Jane 1952- DLB-246
Galloway, Grace Growden 1727-1782.... DLB-200
Galloway, Janice 1956- DLB-319
Gallup, Donald 1913-2000 .... DLB-187
Galsworthy, John 1867-1933
    ...... DLB-10, 34, 98, 162; DS-16; CDBLB-5
Galt, John 1779-1839 ....DLB-99, 116, 159
Galton, Sir Francis 1822-1911 .... DLB-166
Galvin, Brendan 1938- DLB-5
Gambaro, Griselda 1928- DLB-305
Gambit.................... DLB-46
Gamboa, Reymundo 1948- DLB-122
Gammer Gurton's Needle................ DLB-62
Gan, Elena Andreevna (Zeneida R-va)
    1814-1842 .... DLB-198

Gandlevsky, Sergei Markovich
    1952- DLB-285
Gannett, Frank E. 1876-1957 .... DLB-29
Gant, Eugene: Projected Works............Y-01
Gao Xingjian 1940- Y-00
    Nobel Lecture 2000: "The Case for
        Literature"...................... Y-00
Gaos, Vicente 1919-1980 .... DLB-134
García, Andrew 1854?-1943........... DLB-209
García, Cristina 1958- DLB-292
García, Lionel G. 1935- DLB-82
García, Richard 1941- DLB-209
García, Santiago 1928- DLB-305
García Márquez, Gabriel
    1928- DLB-113; Y-82; CDWLB-3
    The Magical World of Macondo........ Y-82
    Nobel Lecture 1982: The Solitude of
        Latin America Y-82
    A Tribute to Gabriel García Márquez Y-82
García Marruz, Fina 1923- DLB-283
García-Camarillo, Cecilio 1943- DLB-209
Garcilaso de la Vega circa 1503-1536.... DLB-318
Garcilaso de la Vega, Inca 1539-1616 ... DLB-318
Gardam, Jane 1928- DLB-14, 161, 231
Gardell, Jonas 1963- DLB-257
Garden, Alexander circa 1685-1756 ...... DLB-31
Gardiner, John Rolfe 1936- DLB-244
Gardiner, Margaret Power Farmer
    (see Blessington, Marguerite, Countess of)
Gardner, John
    1933-1982 .... DLB-2; Y-82; CDALB-7
Garfield, Leon 1921-1996............. DLB-161
Garis, Howard R. 1873-1962 .... DLB-22
Garland, Hamlin 1860-1940...DLB-12, 71, 78, 186
    The Hamlin Garland Society........... Y-01
Garneau, François-Xavier 1809-1866..... DLB-99
Garneau, Hector de Saint-Denys
    1912-1943 .... DLB-88
Garneau, Michel 1939- DLB-53
Garner, Alan 1934- DLB-161, 261
Garner, Hugh 1913-1979 .... DLB-68
Garnett, David 1892-1981 .... DLB-34
Garnett, Eve 1900-1991 .... DLB-160
Garnett, Richard 1835-1906........... DLB-184
Garrard, Lewis H. 1829-1887.......... DLB-186
Garraty, John A. 1920- DLB-17
Garrett, Almeida (João Baptista da Silva
    Leitão de Almeida Garrett)
    1799-1854..................... DLB-287
Garrett, George
    1929- DLB-2, 5, 130, 152; Y-83
    Literary Prizes Y-00
    My Summer Reading Orgy: Reading
        for Fun and Games: One Reader's
        Report on the Summer of 2001...... Y-01
    A Summing Up at Century's End Y-99
    Tribute to James Dickey Y-97
    Tribute to Michael M. Rea Y-97

Tribute to Paxton Davis Y-94	Gelb, Arthur 1924- DLB-103	*Ecbasis Captivi* circa 1045 . . . . DLB-148
Tribute to Peter Taylor Y-94	Gelb, Barbara 1926- DLB-103	*Georgslied* 896? DLB-148
Tribute to William Goyen Y-83	Gelber, Jack 1932- DLB-7, 228	German Literature and Culture from Charlemagne to the Early Courtly Period DLB-148; CDWLB-2
A Writer Talking: A Collage Y-00	Gélinas, Gratien 1909-1999 . . . . DLB-88	
Garrett, John Work 1872-1942 . . . . DLB-187	Gellert, Christian Fuerchtegott 1715-1769 . . . . DLB-97	The Germanic Epic and Old English Heroic Poetry: *Widsith, Waldere,* and *The Fight at Finnsburg* DLB-146
Garrick, David 1717-1779 . . . . DLB-84, 213		
Garrison, William Lloyd 1805-1879 . . . . DLB-1, 43, 235; CDALB-2	Gellhorn, Martha 1908-1998 . . . . Y-82, 98	
	Gems, Pam 1925- DLB-13	Graf Rudolf between circa 1170 and circa 1185 . . . . DLB-148
Garro, Elena 1920-1998 . . . . DLB-145	Genet, Jean 1910-1986 . . . . DLB-72, 321; Y-86	
Garshin, Vsevolod Mikhailovich 1855-1888 . . . . DLB-277	Genette, Gérard 1930- DLB-242	*Heliand* circa 850 . . . . DLB-148
	Genevoix, Maurice 1890-1980 . . . . DLB-65	*Das Hildebrandslied* circa 820 . . . . DLB-148; CDWLB-2
Garth, Samuel 1661-1719 . . . . DLB-95	Genis, Aleksandr Aleksandrovich 1953- DLB-285	
Garve, Andrew 1908-2001 . . . . DLB-87		*Kaiserchronik* circa 1147 . . . . DLB-148
Gary, Romain 1914-1980 . . . . DLB-83, 299	Genlis, Stéphanie-Félicité Ducrest, comtesse de 1746-1830 . . . . DLB-313	The Legends of the Saints and a Medieval Christian Worldview DLB-148
Gascoigne, George 1539?-1577 . . . . DLB-136		
Gascoyne, David 1916-2001 . . . . DLB-20	Genovese, Eugene D. 1930- DLB-17	
Gash, Jonathan (John Grant) 1933- DLB-276	Gent, Peter 1942- Y-82	*Ludus de Antichristo* circa 1160 . . . . DLB-148
Gaskell, Elizabeth Cleghorn 1810-1865 . . . . . . DLB-21, 144, 159; CDBLB-4	Geoffrey of Monmouth circa 1100-1155 . . . . DLB-146	*Ludwigslied* 881 or 882 . . . . DLB-148
		Muspilli circa 790-circa 850 . . . . DLB-148
The Gaskell Society Y-98	George, Elizabeth 1949- DLB-306	*Old German Genesis* and *Old German Exodus* circa 1050-circa 1130 . . . . . DLB-148
Gaskell, Jane 1941- DLB-261	George, Henry 1839-1897 . . . . DLB-23	
Gaspey, Thomas 1788-1871 . . . . DLB-116	George, Jean Craighead 1919- DLB-52	Old High German Charms and Blessings DLB-148; CDWLB-2
Gass, William H. 1924- DLB-2, 227	George, W. L. 1882-1926 . . . . DLB-197	
Gates, Doris 1901-1987 . . . . DLB-22	George III, King of Great Britain and Ireland 1738-1820 . . . . DLB-213	The *Old High German Isidor* circa 790-800 . . . . DLB-148
Gates, Henry Louis, Jr. 1950- DLB-67		
Gates, Lewis E. 1860-1924 . . . . DLB-71	*Georgslied* 896? DLB-148	*Petruslied* circa 854? DLB-148
Gatto, Alfonso 1909-1976 . . . . DLB-114	Gerber, Merrill Joan 1938- DLB-218	*Physiologus* circa 1070-circa 1150 . . . . . . DLB-148
Gault, William Campbell 1910-1995 . . . . . DLB-226	Gerhardie, William 1895-1977 . . . . DLB-36	*Ruodlieb* circa 1050-1075 . . . . DLB-148
Tribute to Kenneth Millar Y-83	Gerhardt, Paul 1607-1676 . . . . DLB-164	"Spielmannsepen" (circa 1152 circa 1500) DLB-148
Gaunt, Mary 1861-1942 . . . . DLB-174, 230	Gérin, Winifred 1901-1981 . . . . DLB-155	
Gautier, Théophile 1811-1872 . . . . DLB-119	Gérin-Lajoie, Antoine 1824-1882 . . . . DLB-99	The Strasbourg Oaths 842 . . . . DLB-148
Gautreaux, Tim 1947- DLB-292	German Literature A Call to Letters and an Invitation to the Electric Chair DLB-75	*Tatian* circa 830 . . . . DLB-148
Gauvreau, Claude 1925-1971 . . . . DLB-88		*Waltharius* circa 825 . . . . DLB-148
The *Gawain*-Poet fl. circa 1350-1400 . . . . DLB-146		*Wessobrunner Gebet* circa 787-815 . . . . . . DLB-148
	The Conversion of an Unpolitical Man DLB-66	German Theater German Drama 800-1280 . . . . DLB-138
Gawsworth, John (Terence Ian Fytton Armstrong) 1912-1970 . . . . DLB-255	The German Radio Play DLB-124	
	The German Transformation from the Baroque to the Enlightenment DLB-97	German Drama from Naturalism to Fascism: 1889-1933 . . . . DLB-118
Gay, Ebenezer 1696-1787 . . . . DLB-24		
Gay, John 1685-1732 . . . . DLB-84, 95	Germanophilism DLB-66	Gernsback, Hugo 1884-1967 . . . . DLB-8, 137
Gayarré, Charles E. A. 1805-1895 . . . . DLB-30	A Letter from a New Germany Y-90	Gerould, Katharine Fullerton 1879-1944 . . . . DLB-78
Charles Gaylord [publishing house] DLB-49	The Making of a People DLB-66	
Gaylord, Edward King 1873-1974 . . . . DLB-127	The Novel of Impressionism DLB-66	Samuel Gerrish [publishing house] DLB-49
Gaylord, Edward Lewis 1919-2003 . . . . . . DLB-127	Pattern and Paradigm: History as Design DLB-75	Gerrold, David 1944- DLB-8
Gazdanov, Gaito 1903-1971 . . . . DLB-317		Gersão, Teolinda 1940- DLB-287
Gébler, Carlo 1954- DLB-271	Premisses Y-90	Gershon, Karen 1923-1993 . . . . DLB-299
Geda, Sigitas 1943- DLB-232	The 'Twenties and Berlin DLB-66	Gershwin, Ira 1896-1983 . . . . DLB-265
Geddes, Gary 1940- DLB-60	Wolfram von Eschenbach's *Parzival:* Prologue and Book 3 . . . . DLB-138	The Ira Gershwin Centenary Y-96
Geddes, Virgil 1897-1989 . . . . DLB-4		Gerson, Jean 1363-1429 . . . . DLB-208
Gedeon (Georgii Andreevich Krinovsky) circa 1730-1763 . . . . DLB-150	Writers and Politics: 1871-1918 . . . . . . DLB-66	Gersonides 1288-1344 . . . . DLB-115
	German Literature, Middle Ages *Abrogans* circa 790-800 . . . . DLB-148	Gerstäcker, Friedrich 1816-1872 . . . . DLB-129
Gee, Maggie 1948- DLB-207		Gertsen, Aleksandr Ivanovich (see Herzen, Alexander)
Gee, Shirley 1932- DLB-245	*Annolied* between 1077 and 1081 . . . . . DLB-148	
Geibel, Emanuel 1815-1884 . . . . DLB-129	The Arthurian Tradition and Its European Context DLB-138	Gerstenberg, Heinrich Wilhelm von 1737-1823 . . . . DLB-97
Geiogamah, Hanay 1945- DLB-175		
Geis, Bernard, Associates DLB-46	*Cambridge Songs (Carmina Cantabrigensia)* circa 1050 . . . . DLB-148	Gervinus, Georg Gottfried 1805-1871 . . . . DLB-133
Geisel, Theodor Seuss 1904-1991 . . . DLB-61; Y-91		
	Christus und die Samariterin circa 950 . . . DLB-148	Gery, John 1953- DLB-282
	De Heinrico circa 980? DLB-148	Geßner, Solomon 1730-1788 . . . . DLB-97
		Geston, Mark S. 1946- DLB-8

447

Al-Ghazali 1058-1111 .... DLB-115	Gimferrer, Pere (Pedro) 1945- DLB-134	Glover, Keith 1966- DLB-249
Ghelderode, Michel de (Adolphe-Adhémar Martens) 1898-1962 .... DLB-321	Ginger, Aleksandr S. 1897-1965 .... DLB-317	Glover, Richard 1712-1785............. DLB-95
Gibbings, Robert 1889-1958........... DLB-195	Gingrich, Arnold 1903-1976........... DLB-137	Glover, Sue 1943- DLB-310
Gibbon, Edward 1737-1794........... DLB-104	Prospectus From the Initial Issue of *Esquire* (Autumn 1933)......... DLB-137	Glück, Louise 1943- DLB-5
Gibbon, John Murray 1875-1952 .... DLB-92	"With the Editorial Ken," Prospectus From the Initial Issue of *Ken* (7 April 1938) DLB-137	Glyn, Elinor 1864-1943 .... DLB-153
Gibbon, Lewis Grassic (see Mitchell, James Leslie)		Gnedich, Nikolai Ivanovich 1784-1833... DLB-205
Gibbons, Floyd 1887-1939 .... DLB-25	Ginsberg, Allen 1926-1997.... DLB-5, 16, 169, 237; CDALB-1	Gobineau, Joseph-Arthur de 1816-1882 .... DLB-123
Gibbons, Kaye 1960- DLB-292		Godber, John 1956- DLB-233
Gibbons, Reginald 1947- DLB-120	Ginzburg, Evgeniia 1904-1977.................. DLB-302	Godbout, Jacques 1933- DLB-53
Gibbons, William eighteenth century..... DLB-73	Ginzburg, Lidiia Iakovlevna 1902-1990 .... DLB-302	Goddard, Morrill 1865-1937 .... DLB-25
Gibson, Charles Dana 1867-1944................ DLB-188; DS-13	Ginzburg, Natalia 1916-1991 ....DLB-177	Goddard, William 1740-1817 .... DLB-43
Gibson, Graeme 1934- DLB-53	Ginzkey, Franz Karl 1871-1963 .... DLB-81	Godden, Rumer 1907-1998............ DLB-161
Gibson, Margaret 1944- DLB-120	Gioia, Dana 1950- DLB-120, 282	Godey, Louis A. 1804-1878 .... DLB-73
Gibson, Margaret Dunlop 1843-1920.....DLB-174	Giono, Jean 1895-1970 .... DLB-72, 321	Godey and McMichael................ DLB-49
Gibson, Wilfrid 1878-1962 .... DLB-19	Giotti, Virgilio 1885-1957 .... DLB-114	Godfrey, Dave 1938- DLB-60
The Friends of the Dymock Poets Y-00	Giovanni, Nikki 1943- ... DLB-5, 41; CDALB-7	Godfrey, Thomas 1736-1763 .... DLB-31
Gibson, William 1914- DLB-7	Giovannitti, Arturo 1884-1959......... DLB-303	Godine, David R., Publisher DLB-46
Gibson, William 1948- DLB-251	Gipson, Lawrence Henry 1880-1971 ..... DLB-17	Godkin, E. L. 1831-1902 .... DLB-79
Gide, André 1869-1951 .... DLB-65, 321	Girard, Rodolphe 1879-1956 .... DLB-92	Godolphin, Sidney 1610-1643 .... DLB-126
Giguère, Diane 1937- DLB-53	Giraudoux, Jean 1882-1944 .... DLB-65, 321	Godwin, Gail 1937- DLB-6, 234
Giguère, Roland 1929- DLB-60	Girondo, Oliverio 1891-1967 .... DLB-283	M. J. Godwin and Company DLB-154
Gil de Biedma, Jaime 1929-1990........ DLB-108	Gissing, George 1857-1903......DLB-18, 135, 184	Godwin, Mary Jane Clairmont 1766-1841.................... DLB-163
Gil-Albert, Juan 1906-1994............ DLB-134	The Place of Realism in Fiction (1895)...DLB-18	Godwin, Parke 1816-1904 .... DLB-3, 64, 250
Gilbert, Anthony 1899-1973........... DLB-77	Giudici, Giovanni 1924- DLB-128	Godwin, William 1756-1836 .... DLB-39, 104, 142, 158, 163, 262; CDBLB-3
Gilbert, Elizabeth 1969- DLB-292	Giuliani, Alfredo 1924- DLB-128	
Gilbert, Sir Humphrey 1537-1583....... DLB-136	Gjellerup, Karl 1857-1919 .... DLB-300	Preface to *St. Leon* (1799) DLB-39
Gilbert, Michael 1912- DLB-87	Glackens, William J. 1870-1938 .... DLB-188	Goering, Reinhard 1887-1936......... DLB-118
Gilbert, Sandra M. 1936- DLB-120, 246	Gladilin, Anatolii Tikhonovich 1935- DLB-302	Goes, Albrecht 1908- DLB-69
Gilchrist, Alexander 1828-1861 .... DLB-144		Goethe, Johann Wolfgang von 1749-1832............. DLB-94; CDWLB-2
Gilchrist, Ellen 1935- DLB-130	Gladkov, Fedor Vasil'evich 1883-1958....DLB-272	
Gilder, Jeannette L. 1849-1916.......... DLB-79	Gladstone, William Ewart 1809-1898 ....DLB-57, 184	Goetz, Curt 1888-1960............... DLB-124
Gilder, Richard Watson 1844-1909 ... DLB-64, 79		Goffe, Thomas circa 1592-1629......... DLB-58
Gildersleeve, Basil 1831-1924........... DLB-71	Glaeser, Ernst 1902-1963 .... DLB-69	Goffstein, M. B. 1940- DLB-61
Giles, Henry 1809-1882 .... DLB-64	Glancy, Diane 1941- DLB-175	Gogarty, Oliver St. John 1878-1957 ... DLB-15, 19
Giles of Rome circa 1243-1316......... DLB-115	Glanvill, Joseph 1636-1680............ DLB-252	Gogol, Nikolai Vasil'evich 1809-1852 ... DLB-198
Gilfillan, George 1813-1878 .... DLB-144	Glanville, Brian 1931- DLB-15, 139	Goines, Donald 1937-1974 .... DLB-33
Gill, Eric 1882-1940 .... DLB-98	Glapthorne, Henry 1610-1643?........ DLB-58	Gold, Herbert 1924- DLB-2; Y-81
Gill, Sarah Prince 1728-1771 .... DLB-200	Glasgow, Ellen 1873-1945 .... DLB-9, 12	Tribute to William Saroyan............ Y-81
William F. Gill Company DLB-49	The Ellen Glasgow Society Y-01	Gold, Michael 1893-1967 .... DLB-9, 28
Gillespie, A. Lincoln, Jr. 1895-1950 ...... DLB-4	Glasier, Katharine Bruce 1867-1950 ..... DLB-190	Goldbarth, Albert 1948- DLB-120
Gillespie, Haven 1883-1975 .... DLB-265	Glaspell, Susan 1876-1948 ....DLB-7, 9, 78, 228	Goldberg, Dick 1947- DLB-7
Gilliam, Florence fl. twentieth century DLB-4	Glass, Montague 1877-1934 .... DLB-11	Golden Cockerel Press............... DLB-112
Gilliatt, Penelope 1932-1993............ DLB-14	Glassco, John 1909-1981 .... DLB-68	Golding, Arthur 1536-1606 .... DLB-136
Gillott, Jacky 1939-1980............... DLB-14	Glauser, Friedrich 1896-1938 .... DLB-56	Golding, Louis 1895-1958 .... DLB-195
Gilman, Caroline H. 1794-1888 .... DLB-3, 73	Glavin, Anthony 1946- DLB-319	Golding, William 1911-1993 ....DLB-15, 100, 255; Y-83; CDBLB-7
Gilman, Charlotte Perkins 1860-1935 ... DLB-221	F. Gleason's Publishing Hall............ DLB-49	
The Charlotte Perkins Gilman Society ... Y-99	Gleim, Johann Wilhelm Ludwig 1719-1803.................... DLB-97	Nobel Lecture 1993 .... Y-83
W. and J. Gilman [publishing house] DLB-49		The Stature of William Golding Y-83
Gilmer, Elizabeth Meriwether 1861-1951 .... DLB-29	Glendinning, Robin 1938- DLB-310	Goldman, Emma 1869-1940 .... DLB-221
	Glendinning, Victoria 1937- DLB-155	Goldman, William 1931- DLB-44
Gilmer, Francis Walker 1790-1826....... DLB-37	Glidden, Frederick Dilley (Luke Short) 1908-1975.................. DLB-256	Goldring, Douglas 1887-1960...........DLB-197
Gilmore, Mary 1865-1962 .... DLB-260		Goldschmidt, Meïr Aron 1819-1887..... DLB-300
Gilroy, Frank D. 1925- DLB-7	Glinka, Fedor Nikolaevich 1786-1880.... DLB-205	Goldsmith, Oliver 1730?-1774 .... DLB-39, 89, 104, 109, 142; CDBLB-2

Goldsmith, Oliver 1794-1861............DLB-99
Goldsmith Publishing Company.........DLB-46
Goldstein, Richard 1944- DLB-185
Gollancz, Sir Israel 1864-1930.........DLB-201
Victor Gollancz Limited...............DLB-112
Gomberville, Marin Le Roy, sieur de
 1600?-1674......................DLB-268
Gombrowicz, Witold
 1904-1969...........DLB-215; CDWLB-4
Gomez, Madeleine-Angélique Poisson de
 1684-1770......................DLB-313
Gómez de Ciudad Real, Alvar (Alvar Gómez
 de Guadalajara) 1488-1538.........DLB-318
Gómez-Quiñones, Juan 1942- DLB-122
Laurence James Gomme
 [publishing house].................DLB-46
Gompers, Samuel 1850-1924..........DLB-303
Gonçalves Dias, Antônio 1823-1864.....DLB-307
Goncharov, Ivan Aleksandrovich
 1812-1891......................DLB-238
Goncourt, Edmond de 1822-1896.......DLB-123
Goncourt, Jules de 1830-1870........DLB-123
Gonzales, Rodolfo "Corky" 1928- DLB-122
Gonzales-Berry, Erlinda 1942- DLB-209
 "Chicano Language"...............DLB-82
González, Angel 1925- DLB-108
Gonzalez, Genaro 1949- DLB-122
Gonzalez, N. V. M. 1915-1999.........DLB-312
González, Otto-Raúl 1921- DLB-290
Gonzalez, Ray 1952- DLB-122
González de Mireles, Jovita
 1899-1983......................DLB-122
González Martínez, Enrique 1871-1952...DLB-290
González-T., César A. 1931- DLB-82
Goodis, David 1917-1967.............DLB-226
Goodison, Lorna 1947- DLB-157
Goodman, Allegra 1967- DLB-244
Goodman, Nelson 1906-1998 ....DLB-279
Goodman, Paul 1911-1972.........DLB-130, 246
The Goodman Theatre DLB-7
Goodrich, Frances 1891-1984 and
 Hackett, Albert 1900-1995 ....DLB-26
Goodrich, Samuel Griswold
 1793-1860..............DLB-1, 42, 73, 243
S. G. Goodrich [publishing house].......DLB-49
C. E. Goodspeed and Company DLB-49
Goodwin, Stephen 1943- Y-82
Googe, Barnabe 1540-1594...........DLB-132
Gookin, Daniel 1612-1687.............DLB-24
Goran, Lester 1928- DLB-244
Gordimer, Nadine 1923- DLB-225; Y-91
 Nobel Lecture 1991.................Y-91
Gordon, Adam Lindsay 1833-1870......DLB-230
Gordon, Caroline
 1895-1981.......DLB-4, 9, 102; DS-17; Y-81
Gordon, Charles F. (see OyamO)
Gordon, Charles William (see Connor, Ralph)

Gordon, Giles 1940- DLB-14, 139, 207
Gordon, Helen Cameron, Lady Russell
 1867-1949.....................DLB-195
Gordon, Lyndall 1941- DLB-155
Gordon, Mack 1904-1959 ....DLB-265
Gordon, Mary 1949- DLB-6; Y-81
Gordone, Charles 1925-1995............DLB-7
Gore, Catherine 1800-1861...........DLB-116
Gore-Booth, Eva 1870-1926...........DLB-240
Gores, Joe 1931- DLB-226; Y-02
 Tribute to Kenneth Millar.............Y-83
 Tribute to Raymond Chandler.........Y-88
Gorey, Edward 1925-2000..............DLB-61
Gorgias of Leontini
 circa 485 B.C.-376 B.C. DLB-176
Gor'ky, Maksim 1868-1936............DLB-295
Gorodetsky, Sergei Mitrofanovich
 1884-1967......................DLB-295
Gorostiza, José 1901-1979 ....DLB-290
Görres, Joseph 1776-1848 ....DLB-90
Gosse, Edmund 1849-1928 ..... DLB-57, 144, 184
Gosson, Stephen 1554-1624............DLB-172
 The Schoole of Abuse (1579) DLB-172
Gotanda, Philip Kan 1951- DLB-266
Gotlieb, Phyllis 1926- DLB-88, 251
Go-Toba 1180-1239..................DLB-203
Gottfried von Straßburg
 died before 1230 ....DLB-138; CDWLB-2
Gotthelf, Jeremias 1797-1854 ....DLB-133
Gottschalk circa 804/808-869..........DLB-148
Gottsched, Johann Christoph
 1700-1766......................DLB-97
Götz, Johann Nikolaus 1721-1781 ......DLB-97
Goudge, Elizabeth 1900-1984 ....DLB-191
Gouges, Olympe de 1748-1793 ....DLB-313
 Declaration of the Rights of Woman......DLB-314
Gough, John B. 1817-1886............DLB-243
Gould, Wallace 1882-1940 ....DLB-54
Govoni, Corrado 1884-1965 ....DLB-114
Govrin, Michal 1950- DLB-299
Gower, John circa 1330-1408 ....DLB-146
Goyen, William 1915-1983 ..... DLB-2, 218; Y-83
Goytisolo, José Agustín 1928- DLB-134
Gozzano, Guido 1883-1916 ....DLB-114
Grabbe, Christian Dietrich 1801-1836....DLB-133
Gracq, Julien (Louis Poirier) 1910- DLB-83
Grady, Henry W. 1850-1889 ....DLB-23
Graf, Oskar Maria 1894-1967 ....DLB-56
Graf Rudolf between circa 1170 and
 circa 1185 ....DLB-148
Graff, Gerald 1937- DLB-246
Graffigny, Françoise d'Issembourg de
 1695-1758......................DLB-313
 Letters from a Peruvian Woman DLB-314
Richard Grafton [publishing house]......DLB-170
Grafton, Sue 1940- DLB-226

Graham, Frank 1893-1965............DLB-241
Graham, George Rex 1813-1894.........DLB-73
Graham, Gwethalyn (Gwethalyn Graham
 Erichsen-Brown) 1913-1965 ....DLB-88
Graham, Jorie 1951- DLB-120
Graham, Katharine 1917-2001..........DLB-127
Graham, Lorenz 1902-1989............DLB-76
Graham, Philip 1915-1963............DLB-127
Graham, R. B. Cunninghame
 1852-1936................DLB-98, 135, 174
Graham, Shirley 1896-1977............DLB-76
Graham, Stephen 1884-1975 ....DLB-195
Graham, W. S. 1918-1986............DLB-20
William H. Graham [publishing house]....DLB-49
Graham, Winston 1910-2003 ....DLB-77
Grahame, Kenneth 1859-1932... DLB-34, 141, 178
Grainger, Martin Allerdale 1874-1941.....DLB-92
Gramatky, Hardie 1907-1979 ....DLB-22
Gramcko, Ida 1924-1994 ....DLB-290
Gramsci, Antonio 1891-1937...........DLB-296
Granada, Fray Luis de 1504-1588.......DLB-318
Grand, Sarah 1854-1943 ....DLB-135, 197
Grandbois, Alain 1900-1975 ....DLB-92
Grandson, Oton de circa 1345-1397 .....DLB-208
Grange, John circa 1556-? DLB-136
Granger, Thomas 1578-1627 ....DLB-281
Granich, Irwin (see Gold, Michael)
Granin, Daniil 1918- DLB-302
Granovsky, Timofei Nikolaevich
 1813-1855......................DLB-198
Grant, Anne MacVicar 1755-1838.......DLB-200
Grant, Duncan 1885-1978 ....DS-10
Grant, George 1918-1988 ....DLB-88
Grant, George Monro 1835-1902 ....DLB-99
Grant, Harry J. 1881-1963.............DLB-29
Grant, James Edward 1905-1966........DLB-26
Grant, John (see Gash, Jonathan)
 War of the Words (and Pictures): The Creation
 of a Graphic Novel...............Y-02
Grass, Günter 1927- ... DLB-75, 124; CDWLB-2
 Nobel Lecture 1999:
 "To Be Continued . . ." Y-99
 Tribute to Helen Wolff...............Y-94
Grasty, Charles H. 1863-1924...........DLB-25
Grau, Shirley Ann 1929- DLB-2, 218
Graves, John 1920- Y-83
Graves, Richard 1715-1804............DLB-39
Graves, Robert 1895-1985
 . . . DLB-20, 100, 191; DS-18; Y-85; CDBLB-6
 The St. John's College
 Robert Graves Trust Y-96
Gray, Alasdair 1934- DLB-194, 261, 319
Gray, Asa 1810-1888..............DLB-1, 235
Gray, David 1838-1861...............DLB-32
Gray, Simon 1936- DLB-13
Gray, Thomas 1716-1771.....DLB-109; CDBLB-2

Cumulative Index

Grayson, Richard 1951- DLB-234
Grayson, William J. 1788-1863.... DLB-3, 64, 248
The Great Bibliographers Series............ Y-93
The Great Gatsby (Documentary) DLB-219
"The Greatness of Southern Literature":
  League of the South Institute for the
  Study of Southern Culture and History
  .... Y-02
Grech, Nikolai Ivanovich 1787-1867..... DLB-198
Greeley, Horace 1811-1872 .. DLB-3, 43, 189, 250
Green, Adolph 1915-2002 .... DLB-44, 265
Green, Anna Katharine
  1846-1935 .... DLB-202, 221
Green, Duff 1791-1875 .... DLB-43
Green, Elizabeth Shippen 1871-1954 .... DLB-188
Green, Gerald 1922- DLB-28
Green, Henry 1905-1973 .... DLB-15
Green, Jonas 1712-1767................ DLB-31
Green, Joseph 1706-1780............... DLB-31
Green, Julien 1900-1998 .... DLB-4, 72
Green, Paul 1894-1981....... DLB-7, 9, 249; Y-81
Green, T. H. 1836-1882........ DLB-190, 262
Green, Terence M. 1947- DLB-251
T. and S. Green [publishing house] DLB-49
Green Tiger Press..................... DLB-46
Timothy Green [publishing house]....... DLB-49
Greenaway, Kate 1846-1901.......... DLB-141
Greenberg: Publisher DLB-46
Greene, Asa 1789-1838................. DLB-11
Greene, Belle da Costa 1883-1950 ...... DLB-187
Greene, Graham 1904-1991
  .... DLB-13, 15, 77, 100, 162, 201, 204;
  Y-85, 91; CDBLB-7
  Tribute to Christopher Isherwood....... Y-86
Greene, Robert 1558-1592 .... DLB-62, 167
Greene, Robert Bernard (Bob), Jr.
  1947- DLB-185
Benjamin H Greene [publishing house] ... DLB-49
Greenfield, George 1917-2000........... Y-91, 00
  Derek Robinson's Review of George
  Greenfield's *Rich Dust*............. Y-02
Greenhow, Robert 1800-1854 .... DLB-30
Greenlee, William B. 1872-1953........ DLB-187
Greenough, Horatio 1805-1852 ...... DLB-1, 235
Greenwell, Dora 1821-1882 .... DLB-35, 199
Greenwillow Books DLB-46
Greenwood, Grace (see Lippincott, Sara Jane Clarke)
Greenwood, Walter 1903-1974...... DLB-10, 191
Greer, Ben 1948- DLB-6
Greflinger, Georg 1620?-1677......... DLB-164
Greg, W. R. 1809-1881 .... DLB-55
Greg, W. W. 1875-1959 .... DLB-201
Gregg, Josiah 1806-1850.......... DLB-183, 186
Gregg Press......................... DLB-46
Gregory, Horace 1898-1982 .... DLB-48
Gregory, Isabella Augusta Persse, Lady
  1852-1932 .... DLB-10

Gregory of Rimini circa 1300-1358 ..... DLB-115
Gregynog Press DLB-112
Greiff, León de 1895-1976 .... DLB-283
Greiffenberg, Catharina Regina von
  1633-1694 .... DLB-168
Greig, Noël 1944- DLB-245
Grekova, Irina (Elena Sergeevna Venttsel')
  1907-2002..................... DLB-302
Grenfell, Wilfred Thomason
  1865-1940..................... DLB-92
Gress, Elsa 1919-1988 .... DLB-214
Greve, Felix Paul (see Grove, Frederick Philip)
Greville, Fulke, First Lord Brooke
  1554-1628 .... DLB-62, 172
Grey, Sir George, K.C.B. 1812-1898 .... DLB-184
Grey, Lady Jane 1537-1554 .... DLB-132
Grey, Zane 1872-1939 .... DLB-9, 212
  Zane Grey's West Society Y-00
Grey Owl (Archibald Stansfeld Belaney)
  1888-1938 .... DLB-92; DS-17
Grey Walls Press DLB-112
Griboedov, Aleksandr Sergeevich
  1795?-1829.................... DLB-205
Grice, Paul 1913-1988 .... DLB-279
Grier, Eldon 1917- DLB-88
Grieve, C. M. (see MacDiarmid, Hugh)
Griffin, Bartholomew fl. 1596........... DLB-172
Griffin, Bryan
  "Panic Among the Philistines":
  A Postscript, An Interview
  with Bryan Griffin................ Y-81
Griffin, Gerald 1803-1840 .... DLB-159
The Griffin Poetry Prize................ Y-00
Griffith, Elizabeth 1727?-1793........ DLB-39, 89
  Preface to *The Delicate Distress* (1769) .. DLB-39
Griffith, George 1857-1906............ DLB-178
Ralph Griffiths [publishing house] DLB-154
Griffiths, Trevor 1935- DLB-13, 245
S. C. Griggs and Company DLB-49
Griggs, Sutton Elbert 1872-1930......... DLB-50
Grignon, Claude-Henri 1894-1976....... DLB-68
Grigor'ev, Apollon Aleksandrovich
  1822-1864 .... DLB-277
Grigorovich, Dmitrii Vasil'evich
  1822-1899 .... DLB-238
Grigson, Geoffrey 1905-1985 .... DLB-27
Grillparzer, Franz
  1791-1872............ DLB-133; CDWLB-2
Grimald, Nicholas
  circa 1519-circa 1562 .... DLB-136
Grimké, Angelina Weld 1880-1958 ... DLB-50, 54
Grimké, Sarah Moore 1792-1873 .... DLB-239
Grimm, Frédéric Melchior 1723-1807.... DLB-313
Grimm, Hans 1875-1959 .... DLB-66
Grimm, Jacob 1785-1863 .... DLB-90
Grimm, Wilhelm
  1786-1859............ DLB-90; CDWLB-2
Grimmelshausen, Johann Jacob Christoffel von
  1621 or 1622-1676 ..... DLB-168; CDWLB-2

Grimshaw, Beatrice Ethel 1871-1953 .....DLB-174
Grímur Thomsen 1820-1896 .... DLB-293
Grin, Aleksandr Stepanovich
  1880-1932 .... DLB-272
Grindal, Edmund 1519 or 1520-1583 ... DLB-132
Gripe, Maria (Kristina) 1923- DLB-257
Griswold, Rufus Wilmot
  1815-1857................ DLB-3, 59, 250
Gronlund, Laurence 1846-1899........ DLB-303
Grosart, Alexander Balloch 1827-1899... DLB-184
Grosholz, Emily 1950- DLB-282
Gross, Milt 1895-1953 .... DLB-11
Grosset and Dunlap DLB-49
Grosseteste, Robert circa 1160-1253..... DLB-115
Grossman, Allen 1932- DLB-193
Grossman, David 1954- DLB-299
Grossman, Vasilii Semenovich
  1905-1964 .... DLB-272
Grossman Publishers DLB-46
Grosvenor, Gilbert H. 1875-1966....... DLB-91
Groth, Klaus 1819-1899 .... DLB-129
Groulx, Lionel 1878-1967............. DLB-68
Grove, Frederick Philip (Felix Paul Greve)
  1879-1948..................... DLB-92
Grove Press DLB-46
Groys, Boris Efimovich 1947- DLB-285
Grubb, Davis 1919-1980 .... DLB-6
Gruelle, Johnny 1880-1938........... DLB-22
von Grumbach, Argula
  1492-after 1563?.................DLB-179
Grundtvig, N. F. S. 1783-1872 .... DLB-300
Grymeston, Elizabeth
  before 1563-before 1604 .... DLB-136
Grynberg, Henryk 1936- DLB-299
Gryphius, Andreas
  1616-1664 .... DLB-164; CDWLB-2
Gryphius, Christian 1649-1706 .... DLB-168
Guare, John 1938- DLB-7, 249
Guarnieri, Gianfrancesco 1934- DLB-307
Guberman, Igor Mironovich 1936- ... DLB-285
Guðbergur Bergsson 1932- DLB-293
Guðmundur Böðvarsson 1904-1974..... DLB-293
Guðmundur Gíslason Hagalín
  1898-1985 .... DLB-293
Guðmundur Magnússon (see Jón Trausti)
Guerra, Tonino 1920- DLB-128
Guest, Barbara 1920- DLB-5, 193
Guevara, Fray Antonio de 1480?-1545 .. DLB-318
Guèvremont, Germaine 1893-1968 ...... DLB-68
Guglielminetti, Amalia 1881-1941 ...... DLB-264
Guidacci, Margherita 1921-1992 .... DLB-128
Guillén, Jorge 1893-1984 .... DLB-108
Guillén, Nicolás 1902-1989 .... DLB-283
Guilloux, Louis 1899-1980............. DLB-72
Guilpin, Everard
  circa 1572-after 1608? DLB-136
Guiney, Louise Imogen 1861-1920 ...... DLB-54

Guiterman, Arthur 1871-1943 . . . . .DLB-11

Gul', Roman 1896-1986. . . . . .DLB-317

Gumilev, Nikolai Stepanovich
1886-1921 . . . . .DLB-295

Günderrode, Caroline von
1780-1806 . . . . .DLB-90

Gundulić, Ivan 1589-1638 . . . DLB-147; CDWLB-4

Gunesekera, Romesh 1954- DLB-267

Gunn, Bill 1934-1989. . . . . .DLB-38

Gunn, James E. 1923- DLB-8

Gunn, Neil M. 1891-1973 . . . . .DLB-15

Gunn, Thom 1929- DLB-27; CDBLB-8

Gunnar Gunnarsson 1889-1975. . . . . . . .DLB-293

Gunnars, Kristjana 1948- DLB-60

Günther, Johann Christian 1695-1723 . . . .DLB-168

Gurik, Robert 1932- DLB-60

Gurney, A. R. 1930- DLB-266

Gurney, Ivor 1890-1937. . . . . Y-02

The Ivor Gurney Society Y-98

Guro, Elena Genrikhovna 1877-1913. . . . .DLB-295

Gustafson, Ralph 1909-1995 . . . . .DLB-88

Gustafsson, Lars 1936- DLB-257

Gütersloh, Albert Paris 1887-1973 . . . . .DLB-81

Guterson, David 1956- DLB-292

Guthrie, A. B., Jr. 1901-1991 . . . . .DLB-6, 212

Guthrie, Ramon 1896-1973 . . . . .DLB-4

Guthrie, Thomas Anstey (see Anstey, FC)

Guthrie, Woody 1912-1967. . . . . .DLB-303

The Guthrie Theater DLB-7

Gutiérrez Nájera, Manuel 1859-1895. . . . .DLB-290

Guttormur J. Guttormsson 1878-1966 . . . .DLB-293

Gutzkow, Karl 1811-1878 . . . . .DLB-133

Guy, Ray 1939- DLB-60

Guy, Rosa 1925- DLB-33

Guyot, Arnold 1807-1884 . . . . DS-13

Gwynn, R. S. 1948- DLB-282

Gwynne, Erskine 1898-1948 . . . . .DLB-4

Gyles, John 1680-1755 . . . . .DLB-99

Gyllembourg, Thomasine 1773-1856. . . . .DLB-300

Gyllensten, Lars 1921- DLB-257

Gyrðir Elíasson 1961- DLB-293

Gysin, Brion 1916-1986. . . . . .DLB-16

H

H.D. (see Doolittle, Hilda)

Habermas, Jürgen 1929- DLB-242

Habington, William 1605-1654 . . . . .DLB-126

Hacker, Marilyn 1942- DLB-120, 282

Hackett, Albert 1900-1995. . . . . .DLB-26

Hacks, Peter 1928- DLB-124

Hadas, Rachel 1948- DLB-120, 282

Hadden, Briton 1898-1929 . . . . .DLB-91

Hagedorn, Friedrich von 1708-1754. . . . . .DLB-168

Hagedorn, Jessica Tarahata 1949- DLB-312

Hagelstange, Rudolf 1912-1984. . . . . .DLB-69

Hagerup, Inger 1905-1985. . . . . .DLB-297

Haggard, H. Rider
1856-1925 . . . . .DLB-70, 156, 174, 178

Haggard, William (Richard Clayton)
1907-1993 . . . . DLB-276; Y-93

Hagy, Alyson 1960- DLB-244

Hahn-Hahn, Ida Gräfin von 1805-1880 . .DLB-133

Haig-Brown, Roderick 1908-1976 . . . . .DLB-88

Haight, Gordon S. 1901-1985 . . . . .DLB-103

Hailey, Arthur 1920-2004 . . . . .DLB-88; Y-82

Haines, John 1924- DLB-5, 212

Hake, Edward fl. 1566-1604 . . . . .DLB-136

Hake, Thomas Gordon 1809-1895 . . . . . . .DLB-32

Hakluyt, Richard 1552?-1616 . . . . .DLB-136

Halas, František 1901-1949 . . . . .DLB-215

Halbe, Max 1865-1944 . . . . .DLB-118

Halberstam, David 1934- DLB-241

Haldane, Charlotte 1894-1969. . . . . .DLB-191

Haldane, J. B. S. 1892-1964 . . . . .DLB-160

Haldeman, Joe 1943- DLB-8

Haldeman-Julius Company DLB-46

Hale, E. J., and Son DLB-49

Hale, Edward Everett
1822-1909 . . . . .DLB-1, 42, 74, 235

Hale, Janet Campbell 1946- DLB-175

Hale, Kathleen 1898-2000 . . . . .DLB-160

Hale, Leo Thomas (see Ebon)

Hale, Lucretia Peabody 1820-1900 . . . . . . .DLB-42

Hale, Nancy
1908-1988 . . . . DLB-86; DS-17; Y-80, 88

Hale, Sarah Josepha (Buell)
1788-1879 . . . . .DLB-1, 42, 73, 243

Hale, Susan 1833-1910 . . . . .DLB-221

Hales, John 1584-1656. . . . . .DLB-151

Halévy, Ludovic 1834-1908 . . . . .DLB-192

Haley, Alex 1921-1992 . . . . . . .DLB-38; CDALB-7

Haliburton, Thomas Chandler
1796-1865 .DLB-11, 99

Hall, Adam (Trevor Dudley-Smith)
1920-1995 . . . . .DLB-276

Hall, Anna Maria 1800-1881 . . . . .DLB-159

Hall, Donald 1928- DLB-5

Hall, Edward 1497-1547. . . . . .DLB-132

Hall, Halsey 1898-1977 . . . . .DLB-241

Hall, James 1793-1868 . . . . .DLB-73, 74

Hall, Joseph 1574-1656 . . . . .DLB-121, 151

Hall, Radclyffe 1880-1943 . . . . .DLB-191

Hall, Rodney 1935- DLB-289

Hall, Sarah Ewing 1761-1830 . . . . .DLB-200

Hall, Stuart 1932- DLB-242

Samuel Hall [publishing house] DLB-49

al-Hallaj 857-922 . . . . .DLB-311

Hallam, Arthur Henry 1811-1833 . . . . .DLB-32

On Some of the Characteristics of
Modern Poetry and On the
Lyrical Poems of Alfred
Tennyson (1831) DLB-32

Halldór Laxness (Halldór Guðjónsson)
1902-1998 . . . . .DLB-293

Halleck, Fitz-Greene 1790-1867 . . . . . . .DLB-3, 250

Haller, Albrecht von 1708-1777 . . . . .DLB-168

Halliday, Brett (see Dresser, Davis)

Halliwell-Phillipps, James Orchard
1820-1889 . . . . .DLB-184

Hallmann, Johann Christian
1640-1704 or 1716? DLB-168

Hallmark Editions DLB-46

Halper, Albert 1904-1984 . . . . .DLB-9

Halperin, John William 1941- DLB-111

Halstead, Murat 1829-1908. . . . . .DLB-23

Hamann, Johann Georg 1730-1788 . . . . . .DLB-97

Hamburger, Michael 1924- DLB-27

Hamilton, Alexander 1712-1756. . . . . .DLB-31

Hamilton, Alexander 1755?-1804 . . . . .DLB-37

Hamilton, Cicely 1872-1952 . . . . .DLB-10, 197

Hamilton, Edmond 1904-1977. . . . . .DLB-8

Hamilton, Elizabeth 1758-1816 . . . . .DLB-116, 158

Hamilton, Gail (see Corcoran, Barbara)

Hamilton, Gail (see Dodge, Mary Abigail)

Hamish Hamilton Limited. DLB-112

Hamilton, Hugo 1953- DLB-267

Hamilton, Ian 1938-2001. . . . . .DLB-40, 155

Hamilton, Janet 1795-1873. . . . . .DLB-199

Hamilton, Mary Agnes 1884-1962 . . . . . .DLB-197

Hamilton, Patrick 1904-1962. . . . . .DLB-10, 191

Hamilton, Virginia 1936-2002 . . . DLB-33, 52; Y-01

Hamilton, Sir William 1788-1856 . . . . . . .DLB-262

Hamilton-Paterson, James 1941- DLB-267

Hammerstein, Oscar, 2nd 1895-1960 . . . DLB-265

Hammett, Dashiell
1894-1961 . . . . .DLB-226; DS-6; CDALB-5

An Appeal in TAC. Y-91

The Glass Key and Other Dashiell
Hammett Mysteries Y-96

Knopf to Hammett: The Editoral
Correspondence Y-00

The Maltese Falcon (Documentary) DLB-280

Hammon, Jupiter 1711-died between
1790 and 1806. . . . . .DLB-31, 50

Hammond, John ?-1663. . . . . .DLB-24

Hamner, Earl 1923- DLB-6

Hampson, John 1901-1955 . . . . .DLB-191

Hampton, Christopher 1946- DLB-13

Hamsun, Knut 1859-1952 . . . . .DLB-297

Handel-Mazzetti, Enrica von 1871-1955 . . .DLB-81

Handke, Peter 1942- DLB-85, 124

Handlin, Oscar 1915- DLB-17

Hankin, St. John 1869-1909. . . . . .DLB-10

Hanley, Clifford 1922- DLB-14

Hanley, James 1901-1985 . . . . .DLB-191

Hannah, Barry 1942- DLB-6, 234

Hannay, James 1827-1873 . . . . .DLB-21

Hannes Hafstein 1861-1922. . . . . .DLB-293

Hano, Arnold 1922- DLB-241
Hanrahan, Barbara 1939-1991 ....DLB-289
Hansberry, Lorraine
   1930-1965 ....DLB-7, 38; CDALB-1
Hansen, Joseph 1923-2004 ....DLB-226
Hansen, Martin A. 1909-1955 ....DLB-214
Hansen, Thorkild 1927-1989 ....DLB-214
Hanson, Elizabeth 1684-1737 ....DLB-200
Hapgood, Norman 1868-1937 ....DLB-91
Happel, Eberhard Werner 1647-1690....DLB-168
Harbach, Otto 1873-1963.............DLB-265
The Harbinger 1845-1849 ....DLB-1, 223
Harburg, E. Y. "Yip" 1896-1981 ....DLB-265
Harcourt Brace Jovanovich DLB-46
Hardenberg, Friedrich von (see Novalis)
Harding, Walter 1917-1996 ....DLB-111
Hardwick, Elizabeth 1916- DLB-6
Hardy, Alexandre 1572?-1632 ....DLB-268
Hardy, Frank 1917-1994..............DLB-260
Hardy, Thomas
   1840-1928 ......DLB-18, 19, 135; CDBLB-5
   "Candour in English Fiction" (1890)....DLB-18
Hare, Cyril 1900-1958 ....DLB-77
Hare, David 1947- DLB-13, 310
Hare, R. M. 1919-2002..............DLB-262
Hargrove, Marion 1919-2003..........DLB-11
Häring, Georg Wilhelm Heinrich
   (see Alexis, Willibald)
Harington, Donald 1935- DLB-152
Harington, Sir John 1560-1612........DLB-136
Harjo, Joy 1951- DLB-120, 175
Harkness, Margaret (John Law)
   1854-1923 ....DLB-197
Harley, Edward, second Earl of Oxford
   1689-1741....................DLB-213
Harley, Robert, first Earl of Oxford
   1661-1724....................DLB-213
Harlow, Robert 1923- DLB-60
Harman, Thomas fl. 1566-1573 ....DLB-136
Harness, Charles L. 1915- DLB-8
Harnett, Cynthia 1893-1981...........DLB-161
Harnick, Sheldon 1924- DLB-265
   Tribute to Ira Gershwin..............Y-96
   Tribute to Lorenz Hart Y-95
Harper, Edith Alice Mary (see Wickham, Anna)
Harper, Fletcher 1806-1877 ....DLB-79
Harper, Frances Ellen Watkins
   1825-1911....................DLB-50, 221
Harper, Michael S. 1938- DLB-41
Harper and Brothers................DLB-49
Harpur, Charles 1813-1868 ....DLB-230
Harraden, Beatrice 1864-1943 ....DLB-153
George G. Harrap and Company
   Limited.......................DLB-112
Harriot, Thomas 1560-1621 ....DLB-136
Harris, Alexander 1805-1874 ....DLB-230
Harris, Benjamin ?-circa 1720 ....DLB-42, 43

Harris, Christie 1907-2002 ....DLB-88
Harris, Errol E. 1908- DLB-279
Harris, Frank 1856-1931 ....DLB-156, 197
Harris, George Washington
   1814-1869 ....DLB-3, 11, 248
Harris, Joanne 1964- DLB-271
Harris, Joel Chandler
   1848-1908 ....DLB-11, 23, 42, 78, 91
   The Joel Chandler Harris Association....Y-99
Harris, Mark 1922- DLB-2; Y-80
   Tribute to Frederick A. Pottle Y-87
Harris, William Torrey 1835-1909......DLB-270
Harris, Wilson 1921- DLB-117; CDWLB-3
Harrison, Mrs. Burton
   (see Harrison, Constance Cary)
Harrison, Charles Yale 1898-1954 ....DLB-68
Harrison, Constance Cary 1843-1920 ...DLB-221
Harrison, Frederic 1831-1923........DLB-57, 190
   "On Style in English Prose" (1898) ... DLB-57
Harrison, Harry 1925- DLB-8
James P. Harrison Company DLB-49
Harrison, Jim 1937- Y-82
Harrison, M. John 1945- DLB-261
Harrison, Mary St. Leger Kingsley
   (see Malet, Lucas)
Harrison, Paul Carter 1936- DLB-38
Harrison, Susan Frances 1859-1935 .....DLB-99
Harrison, Tony 1937- DLB-40, 245
Harrison, William 1535-1593 ....DLB-136
Harrison, William 1933- DLB-234
Harrisse, Henry 1829-1910 ....DLB-47
The Harry Ransom Humanities Research Center
   at the University of Texas at Austin......Y-00
Harryman, Carla 1952- DLB-193
Harsdörffer, Georg Philipp 1607-1658 ... DLB-164
Harsent, David 1942- DLB-40
Hart, Albert Bushnell 1854-1943 ....DLB-17
Hart, Anne 1768-1834 ....DLB-200
Hart, Elizabeth 1771-1833............DLB-200
Hart, Julia Catherine 1796-1867 ....DLB-99
Hart, Lorenz 1895-1943 ....DLB-265
   Larry Hart: Still an Influence.........Y-95
   Lorenz Hart: An American Lyricist......Y-95
   The Lorenz Hart Centenary Y-95
Hart, Moss 1904-1961 ....DLB-7, 266
Hart, Oliver 1723-1795...............DLB-31
Rupert Hart-Davis Limited............DLB-112
Harte, Bret 1836-1902
   ....DLB-12, 64, 74, 79, 186; CDALB-3
Harte, Edward Holmead 1922- DLB-127
Harte, Houston Harriman 1927- DLB-127
Harte, Jack 1944- DLB-319
Hartlaub, Felix 1913-1945 ....DLB-56
Hartlebon, Otto Erich 1864-1905.......DLB-118
Hartley, David 1705-1757 ....DLB-252
Hartley, L. P. 1895-1972............DLB-15, 139

Hartley, Marsden 1877-1943...........DLB-54
Hartling, Peter 1933- DLB-75
Hartman, Geoffrey H. 1929- DLB-67
Hartmann, Sadakichi 1867-1944.........DLB-54
Hartmann von Aue
   circa 1160-circa 1205 ....DLB-138; CDWLB-2
Hartshorne, Charles 1897-2000 ....DLB-270
Haruf, Kent 1943- DLB-292
Harvey, Gabriel 1550?-1631 ... DLB-167, 213, 281
Harvey, Jack (see Rankin, Ian)
Harvey, Jean-Charles 1891-1967 ....DLB-88
Harvill Press Limited DLB-112
Harwood, Gwen 1920-1995 ....DLB-289
Harwood, Lee 1939- DLB-40
Harwood, Ronald 1934- DLB-13
al-Hasan al-Basri 642-728..............DLB-311
Hašek, Jaroslav 1883-1923 ...DLB-215; CDWLB-4
Haskins, Charles Homer 1870-1937 ......DLB-47
Haslam, Gerald 1937- DLB-212
Hass, Robert 1941- DLB-105, 206
Hasselstrom, Linda M. 1943- DLB-256
Hastings, Michael 1938- DLB-233
Hatar, Győző 1914- DLB-215
The Hatch-Billops Collection DLB-76
Hathaway, William 1944- DLB-120
Hatherly, Ana 1929- DLB-287
Hauch, Carsten 1790-1872 ....DLB-300
Hauff, Wilhelm 1802-1827.............DLB-90
Hauge, Olav H. 1908-1994 ....DLB-297
Haugen, Paal-Helge 1945- DLB-297
Haugwitz, August Adolph von
   1647-1706....................DLB-168
Hauptmann, Carl 1858-1921 ....DLB-66, 118
Hauptmann, Gerhart
   1862-1946 ....DLB-66, 118; CDWLB-2
Hauser, Marianne 1910- Y-83
Havel, Václav 1936- DLB-232; CDWLB-4
Haven, Alice B. Neal 1827-1863........DLB-250
Havergal, Frances Ridley 1836-1879 ....DLB-199
Hawes, Stephen 1475?-before 1529 .....DLB-132
Hawker, Robert Stephen 1803-1875......DLB-32
Hawkes, John
   1925-1998 ....DLB-2, 7, 227; Y-80, Y-98
   John Hawkes: A Tribute Y-98
   Tribute to Donald Barthelme...........Y-89
Hawkesworth, John 1720-1773 ....DLB-142
Hawkins, Sir Anthony Hope (see Hope, Anthony)
Hawkins, Sir John 1719-1789 ....DLB-104, 142
Hawkins, Walter Everette 1883-? DLB-50
Hawthorne, Nathaniel 1804-1864
   ...DLB-1, 74, 183, 223, 269; DS-5; CDALB-2
   The Nathaniel Hawthorne Society.......Y-00
   The Old Manse DLB-223
Hawthorne, Sophia Peabody
   1809-1871..................DLB-183, 239
Hay, John 1835-1905 ....DLB-12, 47, 189

Hay, John 1915- DLB-275
Hayashi Fumiko 1903-1951............DLB-180
Haycox, Ernest 1899-1950............DLB-206
Haycraft, Anna Margaret (see Ellis, Alice Thomas)
Hayden, Robert
  1913-1980 ....DLB-5, 76; CDALB-1
Haydon, Benjamin Robert 1786-1846....DLB-110
Hayes, John Michael 1919- DLB-26
Hayley, William 1745-1820 ....DLB-93, 142
Haym, Rudolf 1821-1901 ....DLB-129
Hayman, Robert 1575-1629............DLB-99
Hayman, Ronald 1932- DLB-155
Hayne, Paul Hamilton
  1830-1886 ....DLB-3, 64, 79, 248
Hays, Mary 1760-1843............DLB-142, 158
Hayslip, Le Ly 1949- DLB-312
Hayward, John 1905-1965.............DLB-201
Haywood, Eliza 1693?-1756............DLB-39
  Dedication of *Lasselia* [excerpt]
    (1723) DLB-39
  Preface to *The Disguis'd Prince*
    [excerpt] (1723)................DLB-39
  The Tea-Table [excerpt]...............DLB-39
Haywood, William D. 1869-1928 ....DLB-303
Willis P. Hazard [publishing house].......DLB-49
Hazlitt, William 1778-1830.........DLB-110, 158
Hazzard, Shirley 1931- DLB-289; Y-82
Head, Bessie
  1937-1986 ....DLB-117, 225; CDWLB-3
Headley, Joel T. 1813-1897 ...DLB-30, 183; DS-13
Heaney, Seamus 1939-...DLB-40; Y-95; CDBLB-8
  Nobel Lecture 1994: Crediting Poetry ...Y-95
Heard, Nathan C. 1936- DLB-33
Hearn, Lafcadio 1850-1904 ......DLB-12, 78, 189
Hearn, Mary Anne (Marianne Farningham,
  Eva Hope) 1834-1909 ....DLB-240
Hearne, John 1926- DLB-117
Hearne, Samuel 1745-1792.............DLB-99
Hearne, Thomas 1678?-1735..........DLB-213
Hearst, William Randolph 1863-1951.....DLB-25
Hearst, William Randolph, Jr.
  1908-1993 ....DLB-127
Heartman, Charles Frederick
  1883-1953 ....DLB-187
Heath, Catherine 1924- DLB-14
Heath, James Ewell 1792-1862.........DLB-248
Heath, Roy A. K. 1926- DLB-117
Heath-Stubbs, John 1918- DLB-27
Heavysege, Charles 1816-1876 ....DLB-99
Hebbel, Friedrich
  1813-1863 ....DLB-129; CDWLB-2
Hebel, Johann Peter 1760-1826 ....DLB-90
Heber, Richard 1774-1833.............DLB-184
Hébert, Anne 1916-2000 ....DLB-68
Hébert, Jacques 1923- DLB-53
Hebreo, León circa 1460-1520..........DLB-318

Hecht, Anthony 1923- DLB-5, 169
Hecht, Ben 1894-1964....DLB-7, 9, 25, 26, 28, 86
Hecker, Isaac Thomas 1819-1888.....DLB-1, 243
Hedge, Frederic Henry
  1805-1890 ....DLB-1, 59, 243; DS-5
Hefner, Hugh M. 1926- DLB-137
Hegel, Georg Wilhelm Friedrich
  1770-1831 ....DLB-90
Heiberg, Johan Ludvig 1791-1860.......DLB-300
Heiberg, Johanne Luise 1812-1890 ......DLB-300
Heide, Robert 1939- DLB-249
Heidegger, Martin 1889-1976 ....DLB-296
Heidish, Marcy 1947- Y-82
Heißenbüttel, Helmut 1921-1996 ....DLB-75
Heike monogatari DLB-203
Hein, Christoph 1944- DLB-124; CDWLB-2
Hein, Piet 1905-1996..................DLB-214
Heine, Heinrich 1797-1856....DLB-90; CDWLB-2
Heinemann, Larry 1944- DS-9
William Heinemann Limited...........DLB-112
Heinesen, William 1900-1991 ....DLB-214
Heinlein, Robert A. 1907-1988...........DLB-8
Heinrich, Willi 1920- DLB-75
Heinrich Julius of Brunswick
  1564-1613 ....DLB-164
Heinrich von dem Türlîn
  fl. circa 1230 ....DLB-138
Heinrich von Melk
  fl. after 1160 ....DLB-148
Heinrich von Veldeke
  circa 1145-circa 1190..............DLB-138
Heinse, Wilhelm 1746-1803.............DLB-94
Heinz, W. C. 1915- DLB-171
Heiskell, John 1872-1972 ....DLB-127
Hejinian, Lyn 1941- DLB-165
Helder, Herberto 1930- DLB-287
Heliand circa 850 ....DLB-148
Heller, Joseph
  1923-1999 ......DLB-2, 28, 227; Y-80, 99, 02
  Excerpts from Joseph Heller's
    USC Address, "The Literature
    of Despair"......................Y-96
  Remembering Joe Heller, by William
    Price Fox........................Y-99
  A Tribute to Joseph Heller Y-99
Heller, Michael 1937- DLB-165
Hellman, Lillian 1906-1984 .....DLB-7, 228; Y-84
Hellwig, Johann 1609-1674 ....DLB-164
Helprin, Mark 1947- Y-85; CDALB-7
Helvétius, Claude-Adrien 1715-1771 .....DLB-313
  The Spirit of Laws DLB-314
Helwig, David 1938- DLB-60
Hemans, Felicia 1793-1835.............DLB-96
Hemenway, Abby Maria 1828-1890 .....DLB-243
Hemingway, Ernest 1899-1961...DLB-4, 9, 102,
  210, 316; Y-81, 87, 99; DS-1, 15, 16; CDALB-4
  A Centennial Celebration Y-99
  Come to Papa Y-99

The Ernest Hemingway Collection at
  the John F. Kennedy Library Y-99
Ernest Hemingway Declines to
  Introduce *War and Peace* Y-01
Ernest Hemingway's Reaction to
  James Gould Cozzens..............Y-98
Ernest Hemingway's Toronto Journalism
  Revisited: With Three Previously
  Unrecorded Stories................Y-92
Falsifying Hemingway.................Y-96
A Farewell to Arms (Documentary) DLB-308
Hemingway Centenary Celebration
  at the JFK Library Y-99
The Hemingway/Fenton
  Correspondence Y-02
Hemingway in the JFK Y-99
The Hemingway Letters Project
  Finds an Editor..................Y-02
Hemingway Salesmen's Dummies Y-00
Hemingway: Twenty-Five Years Later ...Y-85
A Literary Archaeologist Digs On:
  A Brief Interview with Michael
  Reynolds........................Y-99
Not Immediately Discernible . . . but
  Eventually Quite Clear: The *First
  Light* and *Final Years* of
  Hemingway's Centenary Y-99
Packaging Papa: *The Garden of Eden*......Y-86
Second International Hemingway
  Colloquium: Cuba Y-98
Hémon, Louis 1880-1913 ....DLB-92
Hempel, Amy 1951- DLB-218
Hempel, Carl G. 1905-1997............DLB-279
Hemphill, Paul 1936- Y-87
Hénault, Gilles 1920-1996..............DLB-88
Henchman, Daniel 1689-1761 ....DLB-24
Henderson, Alice Corbin 1881-1949 .....DLB-54
Henderson, Archibald 1877-1963........DLB-103
Henderson, David 1942- DLB-41
Henderson, George Wylie 1904-1965.....DLB-51
Henderson, Zenna 1917-1983 ....DLB-8
Henighan, Tom 1934- DLB-251
Henisch, Peter 1943- DLB-85
Henley, Beth 1952- Y-86
Henley, William Ernest 1849-1903.......DLB-19
Henniker, Florence 1855-1923..........DLB-135
Henning, Rachel 1826-1914 ....DLB-230
Henningsen, Agnes 1868-1962 ....DLB-214
Henry, Alexander 1739-1824............DLB-99
Henry, Buck 1930- DLB-26
Henry, Marguerite 1902-1997 ....DLB-22
Henry, O. (see Porter, William Sydney)
Henry, Robert Selph 1889-1970..........DLB-17
Henry, Will (see Allen, Henry W.)
Henry VIII of England 1491-1547 ......DLB-132
Henry of Ghent
  circa 1217-1229 - 1293..............DLB-115
Henryson, Robert
  1420s or 1430s-circa 1505..........DLB-146

Henschke, Alfred (see Klabund)

Hensher, Philip 1965- DLB-267

Hensley, Sophie Almon 1866-1946. ...... DLB-99

Henson, Lance 1944- DLB-175

Henty, G. A. 1832-1902 .... DLB-18, 141

    The Henty Society Y-98

Hentz, Caroline Lee 1800-1856 ...... DLB-3, 248

Heraclitus
    fl. circa 500 B.C. DLB-176

Herbert, Agnes circa 1880-1960 .... DLB-174

Herbert, Alan Patrick 1890-1971 ... DLB-10, 191

Herbert, Edward, Lord, of Cherbury
    1582-1648 .... DLB-121, 151, 252

Herbert, Frank 1920-1986 ..... DLB-8; CDALB-7

Herbert, George 1593-1633 .. DLB-126; CDBLB-1

Herbert, Henry William 1807-1858 .... DLB-3, 73

Herbert, John 1926-2001 .... DLB-53

Herbert, Mary Sidney, Countess of Pembroke (see Sidney, Mary)

Herbert, Xavier 1901-1984............ DLB-260

Herbert, Zbigniew
    1924-1998 .... DLB-232; CDWLB-4

Herbst, Josephine 1892-1969 .... DLB-9

Herburger, Gunter 1932- DLB-75, 124

Herculano, Alexandre 1810-1877 ...... DLB-287

Hercules, Frank E. M. 1917-1996 .... DLB-33

Herder, Johann Gottfried 1744-1803 ..... DLB-97

B. Herder Book Company DLB-49

Heredia, José-María de 1842-1905 ...... DLB-217

Herford, Charles Harold 1853-1931 .... DLB-149

Hergesheimer, Joseph 1880-1954 ..... DLB-9, 102

Heritage Press...................... DLB-46

Hermann the Lame 1013-1054......... DLB-148

Hermes, Johann Timotheu 1738-1821 .... DLB-97

Hermlin, Stephan 1915-1997 .... DLB-69

Hernández, Alfonso C. 1938- DLB-122

Hernández, Inés 1947- DLB-122

Hernández, Miguel 1910-1942 .... DLB-134

Hernton, Calvin C. 1932- DLB-38

Herodotus circa 484 B.C.-circa 420 B.C.
    ....DLB-176; CDWLB-1

Heron, Robert 1764-1807 .... DLB-142

Herr, Michael 1940- DLB-185

Herrera, Darío 1870-1914............. DLB-290

Herrera, Fernando de 1534?-1597 ...... DLB-318

Herrera, Juan Felipe 1948- DLB-122

E. R. Herrick and Company DLB-49

Herrick, Robert 1591-1674............ DLB-126

Herrick, Robert 1868-1938.........DLB-9, 12, 78

Herrick, William 1915-2004.............. Y-83

Herrmann, John 1900-1959 .... DLB-4

Hersey, John
    1914-1993....DLB-6, 185, 278, 299; CDALB-7

Hertel, François 1905-1985............. DLB-68

Hervé-Bazin, Jean Pierre Marie (see Bazin, Hervé)

Hervey, John, Lord 1696-1743 .... DLB-101

Herwig, Georg 1817-1875............ DLB-133

Herzen, Alexander (Aleksandr Ivanovich
    Gersten) 1812-1870 ....DLB-277

Herzog, Emile Salomon Wilhelm
    (see Maurois, André)

Hesiod eighth century B.C. DLB-176

Hesse, Hermann
    1877-1962 .... DLB-66; CDWLB-2

Hessus, Eobanus 1488-1540............DLB-179

Heureka! (see Kertész, Imre and Nobel Prize
    in Literature: 2002) Y-02

Hewat, Alexander circa 1743-circa 1824... DLB-30

Hewett, Dorothy 1923-2002.......... DLB-289

Hewitt, John 1907-1987................ DLB-27

Hewlett, Maurice 1861-1923 .... DLB-34, 156

Heyen, William 1940- DLB-5

Heyer, Georgette 1902-1974..........DLB-77, 191

Heym, Stefan 1913-2001 .... DLB-69

Heyse, Paul 1830-1914................ DLB-129

Heytesbury, William
    circa 1310-1372 or 1373 .... DLB-115

Heyward, Dorothy 1890-1961 ....DLB-7, 249

Heyward, DuBose 1885-1940 ...DLB-7, 9, 45, 249

Heywood, John 1497?-1580?.......... DLB-136

Heywood, Thomas 1573 or 1574-1641.... DLB-62

Hiaasen, Carl 1953- DLB-292

Hibberd, Jack 1940- DLB-289

Hibbs, Ben 1901-1975................ DLB-137

    "The Saturday Evening Post reaffirms
    a policy," Ben Hibb's Statement
    in *The Saturday Evening Post*
    (16 May 1942)................ DLB-137

Hichens, Robert S. 1864-1950 .... DLB-153

Hickey, Emily 1845-1924............. DLB-199

Hickman, William Albert 1877-1957...... DLB-92

Hicks, Granville 1901-1982 .... DLB-246

Hidalgo, José Luis 1919-1947 .... DLB-108

Hiebert, Paul 1892-1987............... DLB-68

Hieng, Andrej 1925- DLB-181

Hierro, José 1922-2002................ DLB-108

Higgins, Aidan 1927- DLB-14

Higgins, Colin 1941-1988............. DLB-26

Higgins, George V.
    1939-1999 ....DLB-2; Y-81, 98–99

    Afterword [in response to Cozzen's
    Mens Rea (or Something)]........... Y-97

    At End of Day: The Last George V.
    Higgins Novel Y-99

    The Books of George V. Higgins:
    A Checklist of Editions
    and Printings Y-00

    George V. Higgins in Class Y-02

    Tribute to Alfred A. Knopf Y-84

    Tributes to George V. Higgins Y-99

    "What You Lose on the Swings You Make
    Up on the Merry-Go-Round" ... Y-99

Higginson, Thomas Wentworth
    1823-1911 .... DLB-1, 64, 243

Highsmith, Patricia 1921-1995 .... DLB-306

Highwater, Jamake 1942?- DLB-52; Y-85

Hijuelos, Oscar 1951- DLB-145

Hildegard von Bingen 1098-1179....... DLB-148

Das Hildesbrandslied
    circa 820............. DLB-148; CDWLB-2

Hildesheimer, Wolfgang 1916-1991... DLB-69, 124

Hildreth, Richard 1807-1865 .. DLB-1, 30, 59, 235

Hill, Aaron 1685-1750 .... DLB-84

Hill, Geoffrey 1932- DLB-40; CDBLB-8

George M. Hill Company DLB-49

Hill, "Sir" John 1714?-1775............. DLB-39

Lawrence Hill and Company,
    Publishers...................... DLB-46

Hill, Joe 1879-1915 .... DLB-303

Hill, Leslie 1880-1960................ DLB-51

Hill, Reginald 1936- DLB-276

Hill, Susan 1942- DLB-14, 139

Hill, Walter 1942- DLB-44

Hill and Wang DLB-46

Hillberry, Conrad 1928- DLB-120

Hillerman, Tony 1925- DLB-206, 306

Hilliard, Gray and Company DLB-49

Hills, Lee 1906-2000..................DLB-127

Hillyer, Robert 1895-1961 .... DLB-54

Hilsenrath, Edgar 1926- DLB-299

Hilton, James 1900-1954 ....DLB-34, 77

Hilton, Walter died 1396 .... DLB-146

Hilton and Company DLB-49

Himes, Chester 1909-1984....DLB-2, 76, 143, 226

Joseph Hindmarsh [publishing house] DLB-170

Hine, Daryl 1936- DLB-60

Hingley, Ronald 1920- DLB-155

Hinojosa-Smith, Rolando 1929- DLB-82

Hinton, S. E. 1948- CDALB-7

Hippel, Theodor Gottlieb von
    1741-1796 .... DLB-97

Hippius, Zinaida Nikolaevna
    1869-1945 .... DLB-295

Hippocrates of Cos fl. circa
    425 B.C. DLB-176; CDWLB-1

Hirabayashi Taiko 1905-1972 .... DLB-180

Hirsch, E. D., Jr. 1928- DLB-67

Hirsch, Edward 1950- DLB-120

"Historical Novel," The Holocaust DLB-299

Hoagland, Edward 1932- DLB-6

Hoagland, Everett H., III 1942- DLB-41

Hoban, Russell 1925- DLB-52; Y-90

Hobbes, Thomas 1588-1679... DLB-151, 252, 281

Hobby, Oveta 1905-1995..............DLB-127

Hobby, William 1878-1964 ....DLB-127

Hobsbaum, Philip 1932- DLB-40

Hobsbawm, Eric (Francis Newton)
    1917- DLB-296

Hobson, Laura Z. 1900-1986........... DLB-28

Hobson, Sarah 1947- DLB-204

Hoby, Thomas 1530-1566 .... DLB-132

Hoccleve, Thomas
  circa 1368-circa 1437............DLB-146
Hoch, Edward D. 1930- DLB-306
Hochhuth, Rolf 1931- DLB-124
Hochman, Sandra 1936- DLB-5
Hocken, Thomas Morland 1836-1910....DLB-184
Hocking, William Ernest 1873-1966.....DLB-270
Hodder and Stoughton, Limited........DLB-106
Hodgins, Jack 1938- DLB-60
Hodgman, Helen 1945- DLB-14
Hodgskin, Thomas 1787-1869..........DLB-158
Hodgson, Ralph 1871-1962............DLB-19
Hodgson, William Hope
  1877-1918............ DLB-70, 153, 156, 178
Hoe, Robert, III 1839-1909..........DLB-187
Hoeg, Peter 1957- DLB-214
Hoel, Sigurd 1890-1960..............DLB-297
Hoem, Edvard 1949- DLB-297
Hoffenstein, Samuel 1890-1947........DLB-11
Hoffman, Alice 1952- DLB-292
Hoffman, Charles Fenno 1806-1884...DLB-3, 250
Hoffman, Daniel 1923- DLB-5
  Tribute to Robert Graves Y-85
Hoffmann, E. T. A.
  1776-1822............. DLB-90; CDWLB-2
Hoffman, Frank B. 1888-1958.........DLB-188
Hoffman, William 1925- DLB-234
  Tribute to Paxton Davis Y-94
Hoffmanswaldau, Christian Hoffman von
  1616-1679 ....DLB-168
Hofmann, Michael 1957- DLB-40
Hofmannsthal, Hugo von
  1874-1929......... DLB-81, 118; CDWLB-2
Hofmo, Gunvor 1921-1995.............DLB-297
Hofstadter, Richard 1916-1970 .... DLB-17, 246
Hogan, Desmond 1950- DLB-14, 319
Hogan, Linda 1947- DLB-175
Hogan and Thompson..................DLB-49
Hogarth Press DLB-112; DS-10
Hogg, James 1770-1835 .... DLB-93, 116, 159
Hohberg, Wolfgang Helmhard Freiherr von
  1612-1688 ....DLB-168
von Hohenheim, Philippus Aureolus
  Theophrastus Bombastus (see Paracelsus)
Hohl, Ludwig 1904-1980...............DLB-56
Højholt, Per 1928- DLB-214
Holan, Vladimir 1905-1980...........DLB-215
d'Holbach, Paul Henri Thiry, baron
  1723-1789 ....DLB-313
  The System of Nature (as Jean-Baptiste de
    Mirabaud)...................DLB-314
Holberg, Ludvig 1684-1754...........DLB-300
Holbrook, David 1923- DLB-14, 40
Holcroft, Thomas 1745-1809....DLB-39, 89, 158
  Preface to *Alwyn* (1780).............DLB-39
Holden, Jonathan 1941- DLB-105
  "Contemporary Verse Story-telling"...DLB-105

Holden, Molly 1927-1981 ....DLB-40
Hölderlin, Friedrich
  1770-1843 ....DLB-90; CDWLB-2
Holdstock, Robert 1948- DLB-261
Holiday House....................DLB-46
Holinshed, Raphael died 1580..........DLB-167
Holland, J. G. 1819-1881................ DS-13
Holland, Norman N. 1927- DLB-67
Hollander, John 1929- DLB-5
Holley, Marietta 1836-1926...........DLB-11
Hollinghurst, Alan 1954- DLB-207
Hollingsworth, Margaret 1940- DLB-60
Hollo, Anselm 1934- DLB-40
Holloway, Emory 1885-1977...........DLB-103
Holloway, John 1920- DLB-27
Holloway House Publishing Company....DLB-46
Holme, Constance 1880-1955...........DLB-34
Holmes, Abraham S. 1821?-1908 ....DLB-99
Holmes, John Clellon 1926-1988.....DLB-16, 237
  "Four Essays on the Beat
    Generation" DLB-16
Holmes, Mary Jane 1825-1907 .....DLB-202, 221
Holmes, Oliver Wendell
  1809-1894........DLB-1, 189, 235; CDALB-2
Holmes, Richard 1945- DLB-155
Holmes, Thomas James 1874-1959 ......DLB-187
The Holocaust "Historical Novel".......DLB-299
Holocaust Fiction, Postmodern DLB-299
Holocaust Novel, The "Second-Generation"
  ....DLB-299
Holroyd, Michael 1935- DLB-155; Y-99
Holst, Hermann E. von 1841-1904 ....DLB-47
Holt, John 1721-1784..................DLB-43
Henry Holt and Company DLB-49, 284
Holt, Rinehart and Winston DLB-46
Holtby, Winifred 1898-1935 ....DLB-191
Holthusen, Hans Egon 1913-1997........DLB-69
Hölty, Ludwig Christoph Heinrich
  1748-1776.....................DLB-94
Holub, Miroslav
  1923-1998...........DLB-232; CDWLB-4
Holz, Arno 1863-1929................DLB-118
Home, Henry, Lord Kames
  (see Kames, Henry Home, Lord)
Home, John 1722-1808 ....DLB-84
Home, William Douglas 1912-1992 ......DLB-13
Home Publishing Company DLB-49
Homer circa eighth-seventh centuries B.C.
  ....DLB-176; CDWLB-1
Homer, Winslow 1836-1910 ....DLB-188
Homes, Geoffrey (see Mainwaring, Daniel)
Honan, Park 1928- DLB-111
Hone, William 1780-1842 .... DLB-110, 158
Hongo, Garrett Kaoru 1951- DLB-120, 312
Honig, Edwin 1919- DLB-5
Hood, Hugh 1928-2000.................DLB-53
Hood, Mary 1946- DLB-234

Hood, Thomas 1799-1845..............DLB-96
Hook, Sidney 1902-1989..............DLB-279
Hook, Theodore 1788-1841............DLB-116
Hooker, Jeremy 1941- DLB-40
Hooker, Richard 1554-1600 ....DLB-132
Hooker, Thomas 1586-1647 ....DLB-24
hooks, bell 1952- DLB-246
Hooper, Johnson Jones
  1815-1862 ....DLB-3, 11, 248
Hope, A. D. 1907-2000 ....DLB-289
Hope, Anthony 1863-1933 .... DLB-153, 156
Hope, Christopher 1944- DLB-225
Hope, Eva (see Hearn, Mary Anne)
Hope, Laurence (Adela Florence
  Cory Nicolson) 1865-1904 ....DLB-240
Hopkins, Ellice 1836-1904...........DLB-190
Hopkins, Gerard Manley
  1844-1889...........DLB-35, 57; CDBLB-5
Hopkins, John ?-1570..................DLB-132
Hopkins, John H., and Son DLB-46
Hopkins, Lemuel 1750-1801 ....DLB-37
Hopkins, Pauline Elizabeth 1859-1930 ....DLB-50
Hopkins, Samuel 1721-1803 ....DLB-31
Hopkinson, Francis 1737-1791 ....DLB-31
Hopkinson, Nalo 1960- DLB-251
Hopper, Nora (Mrs. Nora Chesson)
  1871-1906 ....DLB-240
Hoppin, Augustus 1828-1896 ....DLB-188
Hora, Josef 1891-1945......DLB-215; CDWLB-4
Horace 65 B.C.-8 B.C.........DLB-211; CDWLB-1
Horgan, Paul 1903-1995 ..... DLB-102, 212; Y-85
  Tribute to Alfred A. Knopf............ Y-84
Horizon Press DLB-46
Horkheimer, Max 1895-1973...........DLB-296
Hornby, C. H. St. John 1867-1946......DLB-201
Hornby, Nick 1957- DLB-207
Horne, Frank 1899-1974 ....DLB-51
Horne, Richard Henry (Hengist)
  1802 or 1803-1884 ....DLB-32
Horne, Thomas 1608-1654 ....DLB-281
Horney, Karen 1885-1952.............DLB-246
Hornung, E. W. 1866-1921..............DLB-70
Horovitz, Israel 1939- DLB-7
Horta, Maria Teresa (see The Three Marias:
  A Landmark Case in Portuguese
  Literary History)
Horton, George Moses 1797?-1883? DLB-50
  George Moses Horton Society Y-99
Horváth, Ödön von 1901-1938......DLB-85, 124
Horwood, Harold 1923- DLB-60
E. and E. Hosford [publishing house] DLB-49
Hoskens, Jane Fenn 1693-1770?..........DLB-200
Hoskyns, John circa 1566-1638.....DLB-121, 281
Hosokawa Yūsai 1535-1610 ....DLB-203
Hospers, John 1918- DLB-279
Hostovský, Egon 1908-1973 ....DLB-215

Hotchkiss and Company DLB-49

Hough, Emerson 1857-1923 . . . . DLB-9, 212

Houghton, Stanley 1881-1913 . . . . DLB-10

Houghton Mifflin Company. DLB-49

Hours at Home DS-13

Household, Geoffrey 1900-1988. . . . . DLB-87

Housman, A. E. 1859-1936 . . . DLB-19; CDBLB-5

Housman, Laurence 1865-1959 . . . . DLB-10

Houston, Pam 1962- DLB-244

Houwald, Ernst von 1778-1845 . . . . DLB-90

Hovey, Richard 1864-1900. . . . . DLB-54

Howard, Donald R. 1927-1987 . . . . DLB-111

Howard, Maureen 1930- Y-83

Howard, Richard 1929- DLB-5

Howard, Roy W. 1883-1964 . . . . DLB-29

Howard, Sidney 1891-1939 . . . . DLB-7, 26, 249

Howard, Thomas, second Earl of Arundel
  1585-1646 . . . . DLB-213

Howe, E. W. 1853-1937 . . . . DLB-12, 25

Howe, Henry 1816-1893 . . . . DLB-30

Howe, Irving 1920-1993. . . . . DLB-67

Howe, Joseph 1804-1873 . . . . DLB-99

Howe, Julia Ward 1819-1910 . . . . DLB-1, 189, 235

Howe, Percival Presland 1886-1944. . . . . DLB-149

Howe, Susan 1937- DLB-120

Howell, Clark, Sr. 1863-1936. . . . . DLB-25

Howell, Evan P. 1839-1905 . . . . DLB-23

Howell, James 1594?-1666 . . . . DLB-151

Howell, Soskin and Company DLB-46

Howell, Warren Richardson
  1912-1984. . . . . DLB-140

Howells, William Dean 1837-1920
  . . . . .DLB-12, 64, 74, 79, 189; CDALB-3

  Introduction to Paul Laurence
    Dunbar's *Lyrics of Lowly Life*
    (1896) DLB-50

  The William Dean Howells Society. Y-01

Howitt, Mary 1799-1888. . . . . DLB-110, 199

Howitt, William 1792-1879. . . . . DLB-110

Hoyem, Andrew 1935- DLB-5

Hoyers, Anna Ovena 1584-1655 . . . . DLB-164

Hoyle, Fred 1915-2001 . . . . DLB-261

Hoyos, Angela de 1940- DLB-82

Henry Hoyt [publishing house] DLB-49

Hoyt, Palmer 1897-1979 . . . . DLB-127

Hrabal, Bohumil 1914-1997 . . . . DLB-232

Hrabanus Maurus 776?-856 . . . . DLB-148

Hronský, Josef Cíger 1896-1960 . . . . DLB-215

Hrotsvit of Gandersheim
  circa 935-circa 1000 . . . . DLB-148

Hubbard, Elbert 1856-1915 . . . . DLB-91

Hubbard, Kin 1868-1930 . . . . DLB-11

Hubbard, William circa 1621-1704. . . . . . DLB-24

Huber, Therese 1764-1829 . . . . DLB-90

Huch, Friedrich 1873-1913 . . . . DLB-66

Huch, Ricarda 1864-1947 . . . . DLB-66

Huddle, David 1942- DLB-130

Hudgins, Andrew 1951- DLB-120, 282

Hudson, Henry Norman 1814-1886 . . . . . DLB-64

Hudson, Stephen 1868?-1944. . . . . DLB-197

Hudson, W. H. 1841-1922. . . . . .DLB-98, 153, 174

Hudson and Goodwin DLB-49

Huebsch, B. W., oral history Y-99

B. W. Huebsch [publishing house]. DLB-46

Hueffer, Oliver Madox 1876-1931 . . . . . DLB-197

Huet, Pierre Daniel
  Preface to *The History of Romances*
  (1715) DLB-39

Hugh of St. Victor circa 1096-1141 . . . . DLB-208

Hughes, David 1930- DLB-14

Hughes, Dusty 1947- DLB-233

Hughes, Hatcher 1881-1945. . . . . DLB-249

Hughes, John 1677-1720 . . . . DLB-84

Hughes, Langston 1902-1967 . . . . . DLB-4, 7, 48,
  51, 86, 228, 315; DS-15; CDALB-5

Hughes, Richard 1900-1976 . . . . DLB-15, 161

Hughes, Ted 1930-1998 . . . . DLB-40, 161

Hughes, Thomas 1822-1896 . . . . DLB-18, 163

Hugo, Richard 1923-1982 . . . . DLB-5, 206

Hugo, Victor 1802-1885. . . . . . DLB-119, 192, 217

Hugo Awards and Nebula Awards DLB-8

Huidobro, Vicente 1893-1948 . . . . DLB-283

Hull, Richard 1896-1973. . . . . DLB-77

Hulda (Unnur Benediktsdóttir Bjarklind)
  1881-1946 . . . . DLB-293

Hulme, T. E. 1883-1917 . . . . DLB-19

Hulton, Anne ?-1779?. DLB-200

Humanism, Sixteenth-Century
  Spanish. DLB-318

Humboldt, Alexander von 1769-1859 . . . . DLB-90

Humboldt, Wilhelm von 1767-1835 . . . . . DLB-90

Hume, David 1711-1776 . . . . DLB-104, 252

Hume, Fergus 1859-1932 . . . . DLB-70

Hume, Sophia 1702-1774 . . . . DLB-200

Hume-Rothery, Mary Catherine
  1824-1885 . . . . DLB-240

Humishuma
  (see Mourning Dove)

Hummer, T. R. 1950- DLB-120

Humor
  American Humor: A Historical
    Survey DLB-11

  American Humor Studies Association Y-99

  The Comic Tradition Continued
    [in the British Novel] DLB-15

  Humorous Book Illustration DLB-11

  International Society for Humor Studies . . Y-99

  Newspaper Syndication of American
    Humor. DLB-11

  Selected Humorous Magazines
    (1820-1950) DLB-11

Bruce Humphries [publishing house] DLB-46

Humphrey, Duke of Gloucester
  1391-1447. DLB-213

Humphrey, William
  1924-1997 . . . . .DLB-6, 212, 234, 278

Humphreys, David 1752-1818 . . . . DLB-37

Humphreys, Emyr 1919- DLB-15

Humphreys, Josephine 1945- DLB-292

Hunayn ibn Ishaq 809-873 or 877 . . . . . DLB-311

Huncke, Herbert 1915-1996. . . . . DLB-16

Huneker, James Gibbons
  1857-1921. . . . . DLB-71

Hunold, Christian Friedrich
  1681-1721. DLB-168

Hunt, Irene 1907- DLB-52

Hunt, Leigh 1784-1859. . . . . .DLB-96, 110, 144

Hunt, Violet 1862-1942 . . . . .DLB-162, 197

Hunt, William Gibbes 1791-1833 . . . . . . DLB-73

Hunter, Evan (Ed McBain)
  1926-2005 . . . . .DLB-306; Y-82

  Tribute to John D. MacDonald Y-86

Hunter, Jim 1939- DLB-14

Hunter, Kristin 1931- DLB-33

  Tribute to Julian Mayfield Y-84

Hunter, Mollie 1922- DLB-161

Hunter, N. C. 1908-1971 . . . . DLB-10

Hunter-Duvar, John 1821-1899 . . . . DLB-99

Huntington, Henry E. 1850-1927. . . . . . DLB-140

  The Henry E. Huntington Library Y-92

Huntington, Susan Mansfield
  1791-1823. DLB-200

Hurd and Houghton DLB-49

Hurst, Fannie 1889-1968 . . . . DLB-86

Hurst and Blackett DLB-106

Hurst and Company DLB-49

Hurston, Zora Neale
  1901?-1960. . . . . .DLB-51, 86; CDALB-7

Husserl, Edmund 1859-1938 . . . . DLB-296

Husson, Jules-François-Félix (see Champfleury)

Huston, John 1906-1987. . . . . DLB-26

Hutcheson, Francis 1694-1746 . . . . . DLB-31, 252

Hutchinson, Ron 1947- DLB-245

Hutchinson, R. C. 1907-1975 . . . . DLB-191

Hutchinson, Thomas 1711-1780. . . . . DLB-30, 31

Hutchinson and Company
  (Publishers) Limited. DLB-112

Huth, Angela 1938- DLB-271

Hutton, Richard Holt
  1826-1897 . . . . DLB-57

von Hutten, Ulrich 1488-1523 . . . . .DLB-179

Huxley, Aldous 1894-1963
  . . . . . DLB-36, 100, 162, 195, 255; CDBLB-6

Huxley, Elspeth Josceline
  1907-1997 . . . . .DLB-77, 204

Huxley, T. H. 1825-1895. . . . . DLB-57

Huyghue, Douglas Smith 1816-1891 . . . . DLB-99

Huysmans, Joris-Karl 1848-1907 . . . . . . DLB-123

Hwang, David Henry
  1957- DLB-212, 228, 312

Hyde, Donald 1909-1966. . . . . .DLB-187

Hyde, Mary 1912-2003 . . . . .DLB-187

Hyman, Trina Schart 1939- DLB-61

I

Iavorsky, Stefan 1658-1722 ....DLB-150
Iazykov, Nikolai Mikhailovich
  1803-1846 ....DLB-205
Ibáñez, Armando P. 1949- DLB-209
Ibáñez, Sara de 1909-1971 ....DLB-290
Ibarbourou, Juana de 1892-1979 ....DLB-290
Ibn Abi Tahir Tayfur 820-893..........DLB-311
Ibn Qutaybah 828-889................DLB-311
Ibn al-Rumi 836-896 ....DLB-311
Ibn Sa'd 784-845 ....DLB-311
Ibrahim al-Mawsili 742 or 743-803 or 804.DLB-311
Ibn Bajja circa 1077-1138 ....DLB-115
Ibn Gabirol, Solomon
  circa 1021-circa 1058..............DLB-115
Ibn al-Muqaffa' circa 723-759..........DLB-311
Ibn al-Mu'tazz 861-908 ....DLB-311
Ibuse Masuji 1898-1993..............DLB-180
Ichijō Kanera
  (see Ichijō Kaneyoshi)
Ichijō Kaneyoshi (Ichijō Kanera)
  1402-1481 ....DLB-203
Iffland, August Wilhelm
  1759-1814 ....DLB-94
Iggulden, John 1917- DLB-289
Ignatieff, Michael 1947- DLB-267
Ignatow, David 1914-1997............DLB-5
Ike, Chukwuemeka 1931- DLB-157
Ikkyū Sōjun 1394-1481 ....DLB-203
Iles, Francis
  (see Berkeley, Anthony)
Il'f, Il'ia (Il'ia Arnol'dovich Fainzil'berg)
  1897-1937 ....DLB-272
Illich, Ivan 1926-2002 ....DLB-242
Illustration
  Children's Book Illustration in the
    Twentieth Century............DLB-61
  Children's Illustrators, 1800-1880....DLB-163
  Early American Book Illustration DLB-49
  The Iconography of Science-Fiction
    Art DLB-8
  The Illustration of Early German
    Literary Manuscripts, circa
    1150-circa 1300...............DLB-148
  Minor Illustrators, 1880-1914 ....DLB-141
Illyés, Gyula 1902-1983 ..... DLB-215; CDWLB-4
Imbs, Bravig 1904-1946............DLB-4; DS-15
Imbuga, Francis D. 1947- DLB-157
Immermann, Karl 1796-1840..........DLB-133
Imru' al-Qays circa 526-circa 565 ....DLB-311
Inchbald, Elizabeth 1753-1821 ....DLB-39, 89
Indiana University Press Y-02
Ingamells, Rex 1913-1955 ....DLB-260
Inge, William 1913-1973 ...DLB-7, 249; CDALB-1
Ingelow, Jean 1820-1897 ....DLB-35, 163
Ingemann, B. S. 1789-1862 ....DLB-300

Ingersoll, Ralph 1900-1985 ....DLB-127
The Ingersoll Prizes...................Y-84
Ingoldsby, Thomas (see Barham, Richard Harris)
Ingraham, Joseph Holt 1809-1860.....DLB-3, 248
Inman, John 1805-1850 ....DLB-73
Innerhofer, Franz 1944- DLB-85
Innes, Michael (J. I. M. Stewart)
  1906-1994 ....DLB-276
Innis, Harold Adams 1894-1952 ....DLB-88
Innis, Mary Quayle 1899-1972 ....DLB-88
Inō Sōgi 1421-1502 ....DLB-203
Inoue Yasushi 1907-1991 ....DLB-182
"The Greatness of Southern Literature":
  League of the South Institute for the
  Study of Southern Culture and History
  ....Y-02
International Publishers Company DLB-46
Internet (publishing and commerce)
  Author Websites..................Y-97
  The Book Trade and the Internet.......Y-00
  E-Books Turn the Corner..............Y-98
  The E-Researcher: Possibilities
    and Pitfalls Y-00
  Interviews on E-publishing Y-00
  John Updike on the Internet Y-97
  LitCheck Website Y-01
  Virtual Books and Enemies of Books Y-00
Interviews
  Adoff, Arnold Y-01
  Aldridge, John W..................Y-91
  Anastas, Benjamin.................Y-98
  Baker, Nicholson..................Y-00
  Bank, Melissa Y-98
  Bass, T. J. Y-80
  Bernstein, Harriet Y-82
  Betts, Doris Y-82
  Bosworth, David..................Y-82
  Bottoms, David Y-83
  Bowers, Fredson Y-80
  Burnshaw, Stanley.................Y-97
  Carpenter, Humphrey...........Y-84, 99
  Carr, Virginia Spencer Y-00
  Carver, Raymond Y-83
  Cherry, Kelly Y-83
  Conroy, Jack Y-81
  Coppel, Alfred....................Y-83
  Cowley, Malcolm Y-81
  Davis, Paxton Y-89
  Devito, Carlo Y-94
  De Vries, Peter Y-82
  Dickey, James Y-82
  Donald, David Herbert.............Y-87
  Editors, Conversations with Y-95
  Ellroy, James Y-91
  Fancher, Betsy....................Y-83
  Faust, Irvin Y-00

Fulton, Len Y-86
Furst, Alan........................Y-01
Garrett, George....................Y-83
Gelfman, Jane Y-93
Goldwater, Walter Y-93
Gores, Joe Y-02
Greenfield, George Y-91
Griffin, Bryan Y-81
Groom, Winston...................Y-01
Guilds, John Caldwell..............Y-92
Hamilton, Virginia Y-01
Hardin, James Y-92
Harris, Mark.....................Y-80
Harrison, Jim.....................Y-82
Hazzard, Shirley Y-82
Herrick, William..................Y-01
Higgins, George V.................Y-98
Hoban, Russell Y-90
Holroyd, Michael Y-99
Horowitz, Glen Y-90
Iggulden, John Y-01
Jakes, John......................Y-83
Jenkinson, Edward B...............Y-82
Jenks, Tom Y-86
Kaplan, Justin Y-86
King, Florence....................Y-85
Klopfer, Donald S. Y-97
Krug, Judith Y-82
Lamm, Donald Y-95
Laughlin, James..................Y-96
Lawrence, Starling................Y-95
Lindsay, Jack....................Y-84
Mailer, Norman Y-97
Manchester, William Y-85
Max, D. T. Y-94
McCormack, Thomas...............Y-98
McNamara, Katherine..............Y-97
Mellen, Joan Y-94
Menaker, Daniel..................Y-97
Mooneyham, Lamarr Y-82
Murray, Les Y-01
Nosworth, David Y-82
O'Connor, Patrick Y-84, 99
Ozick, Cynthia Y-83
Penner, Jonathan Y-83
Pennington, Lee Y-82
Penzler, Otto Y-96
Plimpton, George Y-99
Potok, Chaim Y-84
Powell, Padgett Y-01
Prescott, Peter S. Y-86
Rabe, David Y-91
Rechy, John.....................Y-82
Reid, B. L. Y-83

Reynolds, Michael Y-95, 99
Robinson, Derek Y-02
Rollyson, Carl Y-97
Rosset, Barney Y-02
Schlafly, Phyllis Y-82
Schroeder, Patricia Y-99
Schulberg, Budd Y-81, 01
Scribner, Charles, III Y-94
Sipper, Ralph Y-94
Smith, Cork Y-95
Staley, Thomas F. Y-00
Styron, William Y-80
Talese, Nan Y-94
Thornton, John Y-94
Toth, Susan Allen Y-86
Tyler, Anne Y-82
Vaughan, Samuel Y-97
Von Ogtrop, Kristin Y-92
Wallenstein, Barry Y-92
Weintraub, Stanley Y-82
Williams, J. Chamberlain Y-84
Into the Past: William Jovanovich's
  Reflections in Publishing Y-02
Ionesco, Eugène 1909-1994 . . . . DLB-321
Ireland, David 1927- DLB-289
The National Library of Ireland's
  New James Joyce Manuscripts Y-02
Irigaray, Luce 1930- DLB-296
Irving, John 1942- DLB-6, 278; Y-82
Irving, Washington 1783-1859
  . . . . DLB-3, 11, 30, 59, 73, 74,
                       183, 186, 250; CDALB-2
Irwin, Grace 1907- DLB-68
Irwin, Will 1873-1948 . . . . DLB-25
Isaksson, Ulla 1916-2000 . . . . DLB-257
Iser, Wolfgang 1926- DLB-242
Isherwood, Christopher
  1904-1986 . . . . DLB-15, 195; Y-86
  The Christopher Isherwood Archive,
    The Huntington Library Y-99
Ishiguro, Kazuo 1954- DLB-194
Ishikawa Jun 1899-1987 . . . . DLB-182
Iskander, Fazil' Abdulevich 1929- DLB-302
The Island Trees Case: A Symposium on
  School Library Censorship
    An Interview with Judith Krug
    An Interview with Phyllis Schlafly
    An Interview with Edward B. Jenkinson
    An Interview with Lamarr Mooneyham
    An Interview with Harriet Bernstein Y-82
Islas, Arturo
  1938-1991 . . . . DLB-122
Issit, Debbie 1966- DLB-233
Ivanišević, Drago 1907-1981 . . . . DLB-181
Ivanov, Georgii 1894-1954 . . . . DLB-317
Ivanov, Viacheslav Ivanovich
  1866-1949 . . . . DLB-295
Ivanov, Vsevolod Viacheslavovich
  1895-1963 . . . . DLB-272

Ivask, Yuri 1907-1986 . . . . DLB-317
Ivaska, Astrīde 1926- DLB-232
M. J. Ivers and Company DLB-49
Iwaniuk, Wacław 1915-2001 . . . . DLB-215
Iwano Hōmei 1873-1920 . . . . DLB-180
Iwaszkiewicz, Jarosław 1894-1980 . . . . . DLB-215
Iyayi, Festus 1947- DLB-157
Izumi Kyōka 1873-1939 . . . . DLB-180

J

Jackmon, Marvin E. (see Marvin X)
Jacks, L. P. 1860-1955 . . . . DLB-135
Jackson, Angela 1951- DLB-41
Jackson, Charles 1903-1968 . . . . DLB-234
Jackson, Helen Hunt
  1830-1885 . . . . DLB-42, 47, 186, 189
Jackson, Holbrook 1874-1948 . . . . DLB-98
Jackson, Laura Riding 1901-1991 . . . . . DLB-48
Jackson, Shirley
  1916-1965 . . . . DLB-6, 234; CDALB-1
Jacob, Max 1876-1944 . . . . DLB-258
Jacob, Naomi 1884?-1964 . . . . DLB-191
Jacob, Piers Anthony Dillingham
  (see Anthony, Piers)
Jacob, Violet 1863-1946 . . . . DLB-240
Jacobi, Friedrich Heinrich 1743-1819 . . . . DLB-94
Jacobi, Johann Georg 1740-1841 . . . . DLB-97
George W. Jacobs and Company DLB-49
Jacobs, Harriet 1813-1897 . . . . DLB-239
Jacobs, Joseph 1854-1916 . . . . DLB-141
Jacobs, W. W. 1863-1943 . . . . DLB-135
  The W. W. Jacobs Appreciation Society . . Y-98
Jacobsen, J. P. 1847-1885 . . . . DLB-300
Jacobsen, Jørgen-Frantz 1900-1938 . . . . DLB-214
Jacobsen, Josephine 1908- DLB-244
Jacobsen, Rolf 1907-1994 . . . . DLB-297
Jacobson, Dan 1929- DLB-14, 207, 225, 319
Jacobson, Howard 1942- DLB-207
Jacques de Vitry circa 1160/1170-1240 . . . DLB-208
Jæger, Frank 1926-1977 . . . . DLB-214
Ja'far al-Sadiq circa 702-765 . . . . DLB-311
William Jaggard [publishing house] DLB-170
Jahier, Piero 1884-1966 . . . . DLB-114, 264
al-Jahiz circa 776-868 or 869 . . . . DLB-311
Jahnn, Hans Henny 1894-1959 . . . . . DLB-56, 124
Jaimes, Freyre, Ricardo 1866?-1933 . . . . DLB-283
Jakes, John 1932- DLB-278; Y-83
  Tribute to John Gardner Y-82
  Tribute to John D. MacDonald Y-86
Jakobína Johnson (Jakobína Sigurbjarnardóttir)
  1883-1977 . . . . DLB-293
Jakobson, Roman 1896-1982 . . . . DLB-242
James, Alice 1848-1892 . . . . DLB-221
James, C. L. R. 1901-1989 . . . . DLB-125
James, George P. R. 1801-1860 . . . . DLB-116

James, Henry 1843-1916
  . . . . DLB-12, 71, 74, 189; DS-13; CDALB-3
  "The Future of the Novel" (1899) DLB-18
  "The Novel in [Robert Browning's]
    'The Ring and the Book'"
    (1912) DLB-32
James, John circa 1633-1729 . . . . DLB-24
James, M. R. 1862-1936 . . . . DLB-156, 201
James, Naomi 1949- DLB-204
James, P. D. (Phyllis Dorothy James White)
  1920- DLB-87, 276; DS-17; CDBLB-8
  Tribute to Charles Scribner Jr. Y-95
James, Thomas 1572?-1629 . . . . DLB-213
U. P. James [publishing house] DLB-49
James, Will 1892-1942 . . . . DS-16
James, William 1842-1910 . . . . DLB-270
James VI of Scotland, I of England
  1566-1625 . . . . DLB-151, 172
  Ane Schort Treatise Conteining Some Revlis
    and Cautelis to Be Obseruit and
    Eschewit in Scottis Poesi (1584) DLB-172
Jameson, Anna 1794-1860 . . . . DLB-99, 166
Jameson, Fredric 1934- DLB-67
Jameson, J. Franklin 1859-1937 . . . . DLB-17
Jameson, Storm 1891-1986 . . . . DLB-36
Jančar, Drago 1948- DLB-181
Janés, Clara 1940- DLB-134
Janevski, Slavko 1920-2000 . . DLB-181; CDWLB-4
Janowitz, Tama 1957- DLB-292
Jansson, Tove 1914-2001 . . . . DLB-257
Janvier, Thomas 1849-1913 . . . . DLB-202
Japan
  "The Development of Meiji Japan" . . DLB-180
  "Encounter with the West" DLB-180
Japanese Literature
  Letter from Japan Y-94, 98
  Medieval Travel Diaries DLB-203
  Surveys: 1987-1995 . . . . DLB-182
Jaramillo, Cleofas M. 1878-1956 . . . . DLB-122
Jaramillo Levi, Enrique 1944- DLB-290
Jarir after 650-circa 730 . . . . DLB-311
Jarman, Mark 1952- DLB-120, 282
Jarrell, Randall
  1914-1965 . . . . DLB-48, 52; CDALB-1
Jarrold and Sons DLB-106
Jarry, Alfred 1873-1907 . . . . DLB-192, 258
Jarves, James Jackson 1818-1888 . . . . . . DLB-189
Jasmin, Claude 1930- DLB-60
Jaunsudrabiņš, Jānis 1877-1962 . . . . DLB-220
Jay, John 1745-1829 . . . . DLB-31
Jean de Garlande (see John of Garland)
Jefferies, Richard 1848-1887 . . . . DLB-98, 141
  The Richard Jefferies Society Y-98
Jeffers, Lance 1919-1985 . . . . DLB-41
Jeffers, Robinson
  1887-1962 . . . . DLB-45, 212; CDALB-4
Jefferson, Thomas
  1743-1826 . . . . DLB-31, 183; CDALB-2

Jégé 1866-1940...................DLB-215
Jelinek, Elfriede 1946- DLB-85
Jellicoe, Ann 1927- DLB-13, 233
Jemison, Mary circa 1742-1833........DLB-239
Jen, Gish 1955- DLB-312
Jenkins, Dan 1929- DLB-241
Jenkins, Elizabeth 1905- DLB-155
Jenkins, Robin 1912-2005 ....DLB-14, 271
Jenkins, William Fitzgerald (see Leinster, Murray)
Herbert Jenkins Limited...............DLB-112
Jennings, Elizabeth 1926- DLB-27
Jens, Walter 1923- DLB-69
Jensen, Axel 1932-2003 ....DLB-297
Jensen, Johannes V. 1873-1950 ....DLB-214
Jensen, Merrill 1905-1980 ....DLB-17
Jensen, Thit 1876-1957................DLB-214
Jephson, Robert 1736-1803 ....DLB-89
Jerome, Jerome K. 1859-1927 .... DLB-10, 34, 135
   The Jerome K. Jerome Society Y-98
Jerome, Judson 1927-1991 ....DLB-105
   "Reflections: After a Tornado" DLB-105
Jerrold, Douglas 1803-1857 ....DLB-158, 159
Jersild, Per Christian 1935- DLB-257
Jesse, F. Tennyson 1888-1958 ....DLB-77
Jewel, John 1522-1571 ....DLB-236
John P. Jewett and Company............DLB-49
Jewett, Sarah Orne 1849-1909 .... DLB-12, 74, 221
The Jewish Publication Society DLB-49
Studies in American Jewish Literature....... Y-02
Jewitt, John Rodgers 1783-1821..........DLB-99
Jewsbury, Geraldine 1812-1880..........DLB-21
Jewsbury, Maria Jane 1800-1833 ....DLB-199
Jhabvala, Ruth Prawer 1927- DLB-139, 194
Jiménez, Juan Ramón 1881-1958.........DLB-134
Jin, Ha 1956- DLB-244, 292
Joans, Ted 1928-2003 ....DLB-16, 41
Jōha 1525-1602 ....DLB-203
Jóhann Sigurjónsson 1880-1919.........DLB-293
Jóhannes úr Kötlum 1899-1972.........DLB-293
Johannis de Garlandia (see John of Garland)
John, Errol 1924-1988 ....DLB-233
John, Eugenie (see Marlitt, E.)
John of Dumbleton
   circa 1310-circa 1349..............DLB-115
John of Garland (Jean de Garlande,
   Johannis de Garlandia)
   circa 1195-circa 1272..............DLB-208
The John Reed Clubs DLB-303
Johns, Captain W. E. 1893-1968.........DLB-160
Johnson, Mrs. A. E. ca. 1858-1922 ......DLB-221
Johnson, Amelia (see Johnson, Mrs. A. E.)
Johnson, B. S. 1933-1973 ....DLB-14, 40
Johnson, Charles 1679-1748............DLB-84
Johnson, Charles 1948- DLB-33, 278
Johnson, Charles S. 1893-1956 ....DLB-51, 91

Johnson, Colin (Mudrooroo) 1938- DLB-289
Johnson, Denis 1949- DLB-120
Johnson, Diane 1934- Y-80
Johnson, Dorothy M. 1905–1984 ......DLB-206
Johnson, E. Pauline (Tekahionwake)
   1861-1913.....................DLB-175
Johnson, Edgar 1901-1995.............DLB-103
Johnson, Edward 1598-1672 ....DLB-24
Johnson, Eyvind 1900-1976...........DLB-259
Johnson, Fenton 1888-1958 ....DLB-45, 50
Johnson, Georgia Douglas
   1877?-1966 ....DLB-51, 249
Johnson, Gerald W. 1890-1980 ....DLB-29
Johnson, Greg 1953- DLB-234
Johnson, Helene 1907-1995 ....DLB-51
Jacob Johnson and Company DLB-49
Johnson, James Weldon
   1871-1938 ....DLB-51; CDALB-4
Johnson, John H. 1918- DLB-137
   "Backstage," Statement From the
   Initial Issue of Ebony
   (November 1945................DLB-137
Johnson, Joseph [publishing house] DLB-154
Johnson, Linton Kwesi 1952- DLB-157
Johnson, Lionel 1867-1902..............DLB-19
Johnson, Nunnally 1897-1977 ....DLB-26
Johnson, Owen 1878-1952................ Y-87
Johnson, Pamela Hansford 1912-1981.....DLB-15
Johnson, Pauline 1861-1913.............DLB-92
Johnson, Ronald 1935-1998...........DLB-169
Johnson, Samuel 1696-1772... DLB-24; CDBLB-2
Johnson, Samuel
   1709-1784 .... DLB-39, 95, 104, 142, 213
   Rambler, no. 4 (1750) [excerpt]........DLB-39
The BBC Four Samuel Johnson Prize
   for Non-fiction..................... Y-02
Johnson, Samuel 1822-1882..........DLB-1, 243
Johnson, Susanna 1730-1810 ....DLB-200
Johnson, Terry 1955- DLB-233
Johnson, Uwe 1934-1984..... DLB-75; CDWLB-2
Benjamin Johnson [publishing house] DLB-49
Benjamin, Jacob, and Robert Johnson
   [publishing house].................DLB-49
Johnston, Annie Fellows 1863-1931......DLB-42
Johnston, Basil H. 1929- DLB-60
Johnston, David Claypole 1798?-1865....DLB-188
Johnston, Denis 1901-1984 ....DLB-10
Johnston, Ellen 1835-1873 ....DLB-199
Johnston, George 1912-1970 ....DLB-260
Johnston, George 1913-1970 ....DLB-88
Johnston, Sir Harry 1858-1927 ....DLB-174
Johnston, Jennifer 1930- DLB-14
Johnston, Mary 1870-1936...............DLB-9
Johnston, Richard Malcolm 1822-1898 ....DLB-74
Johnstone, Charles 1719?-1800? DLB-39
Johst, Hanns 1890-1978................DLB-124
Jökull Jakobsson 1933-1978 ....DLB-293

Jolas, Eugene 1894-1952 ....DLB-4, 45
Jón Stefán Sveinsson or Svensson (see Nonni)
Jón Trausti (Guðmundur Magnússon)
   1873-1918 ....DLB-293
Jón úr Vör (Jón Jónsson) 1917-2000.....DLB-293
Jónas Hallgrímsson 1807-1845..........DLB-293
Jones, Alice C. 1853-1933 ....DLB-92
Jones, Charles C., Jr. 1831-1893 ....DLB-30
Jones, D. G. 1929- DLB-53
Jones, David
   1895-1974 ....DLB-20, 100; CDBLB-7
Jones, Diana Wynne 1934- DLB-161
Jones, Ebenezer 1820-1860 ....DLB-32
Jones, Ernest 1819-1868................DLB-32
Jones, Gayl 1949- DLB-33, 278
Jones, George 1800-1870 ....DLB-183
Jones, Glyn 1905-1995..................DLB-15
Jones, Gwyn 1907- DLB-15, 139
Jones, Henry Arthur 1851-1929 ....DLB-10
Jones, Hugh circa 1692-1760 ....DLB-24
Jones, James 1921-1977 .... DLB-2, 143; DS-17
   James Jones Papers in the Handy
   Writers' Colony Collection at
   the University of Illinois at
   Springfield Y-98
   The James Jones Society Y-92
Jones, Jenkin Lloyd 1911-2004 ....DLB-127
Jones, John Beauchamp 1810-1866 ......DLB-202
Jones, Joseph, Major
   (see Thompson, William Tappan)
Jones, LeRoi (see Baraka, Amiri)
Jones, Lewis 1897-1939 ....DLB-15
Jones, Madison 1925- DLB-152
Jones, Marie 1951- DLB-233
Jones, Preston 1936-1979 ....DLB-7
Jones, Rodney 1950- DLB-120
Jones, Thom 1945- DLB-244
Jones, Sir William 1746-1794 ....DLB-109
Jones, William Alfred 1817-1900 ....DLB-59
Jones's Publishing House...............DLB-49
Jong, Erica 1942- DLB-2, 5, 28, 152
Jonke, Gert F. 1946- DLB-85
Jonson, Ben
   1572?-1637 ....DLB-62, 121; CDBLB-1
Jonsson, Tor 1916-1951................DLB-297
Jordan, June 1936- DLB-38
Jorgensen, Johannes 1866-1956.........DLB-300
Joseph, Jenny 1932- DLB-40
Joseph and George..................... Y-99
Michael Joseph Limited DLB-112
Josephson, Matthew 1899-1978 ....DLB-4
Josephus, Flavius 37-100................DLB-176
Josephy, Alvin M., Jr.
   Tribute to Alfred A. Knopf............. Y-84
Josiah Allen's Wife (see Holley, Marietta)
Josipovici, Gabriel 1940- DLB-14, 319
Josselyn, John ?-1675 ....DLB-24

Cumulative Index

Joudry, Patricia 1921-2000 . . . . DLB-88
Jouve, Pierre Jean 1887-1976. . . . . DLB-258
Jovanovich, William 1920-2001 . . . . Y-01
   Into the Past: William Jovanovich's
      Reflections on Publishing Y-02
   [Response to Ken Auletta] Y-97
   The Temper of the West: William
      Jovanovich. Y-02
   Tribute to Charles Scribner Jr. Y-95
Jovine, Francesco 1902-1950 . . . . DLB-264
Jovine, Giuseppe 1922- DLB-128
Joyaux, Philippe (see Sollers, Philippe)
Joyce, Adrien (see Eastman, Carol)
Joyce, James 1882-1941
    . . . . DLB-10, 19, 36, 162, 247; CDBLB-6
   Danis Rose and the Rendering of *Ulysses*. . . Y-97
   James Joyce Centenary: Dublin, 1982 . . . . Y-82
   James Joyce Conference. Y-85
   A Joyce (Con)Text: Danis Rose and the
      Remaking of *Ulysses*. Y-97
   The National Library of Ireland's
      New James Joyce Manuscripts. Y-02
   The New *Ulysses*. Y-84
   Public Domain and the Violation of
      Texts Y-97
   The Quinn Draft of James Joyce's
      Circe Manuscript. Y-00
   Stephen Joyce's Letter to the Editor of
      The Irish Times Y-97
   Ulysses, Reader's Edition: First Reactions . . Y-97
   We See the Editor at Work Y-97
   Whose *Ulysses?* The Function of Editing . . Y-97
Jozsef, Attila 1905-1937. . . . . DLB-215; CDWLB-4
San Juan de la Cruz 1542-1591. . . . . DLB-318
Juarroz, Roberto 1925-1995 . . . . DLB-283
Orange Judd Publishing Company. DLB-49
Judd, Sylvester 1813-1853 . . . . DLB-1, 243
Judith circa 930 . . . . DLB-146
Juel-Hansen, Erna 1845-1922 . . . . DLB-300
Julian of Norwich 1342-circa 1420 . . . . . DLB-1146
Julius Caesar
   100 B.C.-44 B.C. DLB-211; CDWLB-1
June, Jennie
   (see Croly, Jane Cunningham)
Jung, Carl Gustav 1875-1961 . . . . DLB-296
Jung, Franz 1888-1963 . . . . DLB-118
Jünger, Ernst 1895-1998 . . . . . DLB-56; CDWLB-2
Der jüngere Titurel circa 1275 . . . . DLB-138
Jung-Stilling, Johann Heinrich
   1740-1817 . . . . DLB-94
Junqueiro, Abílio Manuel Guerra
   1850-1923 . . . . DLB-287
Justice, Donald 1925- Y-83
Juvenal circa A.D. 60-circa A.D. 130
   . . . . DLB-211; CDWLB-1
The Juvenile Library
   (see M. J. Godwin and Company)

K

Kacew, Romain (see Gary, Romain)
Kafka, Franz 1883-1924 . . . . . DLB-81; CDWLB-2
Kahn, Gus 1886-1941. . . . . DLB-265
Kahn, Roger 1927- DLB-171
Kaikō Takeshi 1939-1989. . . . . DLB-182
Káinn (Kristján Níels Jónsson/Kristjan
   Niels Julius) 1860-1936 . . . . DLB-293
Kaiser, Georg 1878-1945 . . . DLB-124; CDWLB-2
Kaiserchronik circa 1147 . . . . DLB-148
Kaleb, Vjekoslav 1905- DLB-181
Kalechofsky, Roberta 1931- DLB-28
Kaler, James Otis 1848-1912. . . . . DLB-12, 42
Kalmar, Bert 1884-1947 . . . . DLB-265
Kamensky, Vasilii Vasil'evich
   1884-1961 . . . . DLB-295
Kames, Henry Home, Lord
   1696-1782. . . . . DLB-31, 104
Kamo no Chōmei (Kamo no Nagaakira)
   1153 or 1155-1216 . . . . DLB-203
Kamo no Nagaakira (see Kamo no Chōmei)
Kampmann, Christian 1939-1988. . . . . . DLB-214
Kandel, Lenore 1932- DLB-16
Kane, Sarah 1971-1999 . . . . DLB-310
Kaneko, Lonny 1939- DLB-312
Kang, Younghill 1903-1972 . . . . DLB-312
Kanin, Garson 1912-1999. . . . . DLB-7
   A Tribute (to Marc Connelly) Y-80
Kaniuk, Yoram 1930- DLB-299
Kant, Hermann 1926- DLB-75
Kant, Immanuel 1724-1804. . . . . DLB-94
Kantemir, Antiokh Dmitrievich
   1708-1744 . . . . DLB-150
Kantor, MacKinlay 1904-1977 . . . . . . DLB-9, 102
Kanze Kōjirō Nobumitsu 1435-1516 . . . DLB-203
Kanze Motokiyo (see Zeimi)
Kaplan, Fred 1937- DLB-111
Kaplan, Johanna 1942- DLB-28
Kaplan, Justin 1925- DLB-111; Y-86
Kaplinski, Jaan 1941- DLB-232
Kapnist, Vasilii Vasilevich 1758?-1823 . . . DLB-150
Karadžić, Vuk Stefanović
   1787-1864 . . . . .DLB-147; CDWLB-4
Karamzin, Nikolai Mikhailovich
   1766-1826. DLB-150
Karinthy, Frigyes 1887-1938. . . . . DLB-215
Karmel, Ilona 1925-2000 . . . . DLB-299
Karsch, Anna Louisa 1722-1791 . . . . DLB-97
Kasack, Hermann 1896-1966 . . . . DLB-69
Kasai Zenzō 1887-1927 . . . . DLB-180
Kaschnitz, Marie Luise 1901-1974 . . . . . . DLB-69
Kassák, Lajos 1887-1967 . . . . DLB-215
Kaštelan, Jure 1919-1990 . . . . DLB-147
Kästner, Erich 1899-1974 . . . . DLB-56
Kataev, Evgenii Petrovich
   (see Il'f, Il'ia and Petrov, Evgenii)

Kataev, Valentin Petrovich 1897-1986 . . . .DLB-272
Katenin, Pavel Aleksandrovich
   1792-1853. DLB-205
Kattan, Naim 1928- DLB-53
Katz, Steve 1935- Y-83
Ka-Tzetnik 135633 (Yehiel Dinur)
   1909-2001 . . . . DLB-299
Kauffman, Janet 1945- DLB-218; Y-86
Kauffmann, Samuel 1898-1971. . . . . . . .DLB-127
Kaufman, Bob 1925-1986. . . . . DLB-16, 41
Kaufman, George S. 1889-1961 . . . . DLB-7
Kaufmann, Walter 1921-1980 . . . . .DLB-279
Kavan, Anna (Helen Woods Ferguson
   Edmonds) 1901-1968. . . . . DLB-255
Kavanagh, P. J. 1931- DLB-40
Kavanagh, Patrick 1904-1967 . . . . DLB-15, 20
Kaverin, Veniamin Aleksandrovich
   (Veniamin Aleksandrovich Zil'ber)
   1902-1989 .DLB-272
Kawabata Yasunari 1899-1972 . . . . DLB-180
Kay, Guy Gavriel 1954- DLB-251
Kaye-Smith, Sheila 1887-1956. . . . . DLB-36
Kazakov, Iurii Pavlovich 1927-1982 . . . . DLB-302
Kazin, Alfred 1915-1998 . . . . DLB-67
Keane, John B. 1928-2002 . . . . DLB-13
Keary, Annie 1825-1879 . . . . DLB-163
Keary, Eliza 1827-1918 . . . . DLB-240
Keating, H. R. F. 1926- DLB-87
Keatley, Charlotte 1960- DLB-245
Keats, Ezra Jack 1916-1983 . . . . DLB-61
Keats, John 1795-1821 . . . DLB-96, 110; CDBLB-3
Keble, John 1792-1866 . . . . DLB-32, 55
Keckley, Elizabeth 1818?-1907 . . . . DLB-239
Keeble, John 1944- Y-83
Keeffe, Barrie 1945- DLB-13, 245
Keeley, James 1867-1934 . . . . DLB-25
W. B. Keen, Cooke and Company DLB-49
The Mystery of Carolyn Keene Y-02
Kefala, Antigone 1935- DLB-289
Keillor, Garrison 1942- Y-87
Keith, Marian (Mary Esther MacGregor)
   1874?-1961 . . . . DLB-92
Keller, Gary D. 1943- DLB-82
Keller, Gottfried
   1819-1890 . . . . .DLB-129; CDWLB-2
Keller, Helen 1880-1968. . . . . DLB-303
Kelley, Edith Summers 1884-1956 . . . . . . DLB-9
Kelley, Emma Dunham ?-?. DLB-221
Kelley, Florence 1859-1932 . . . . DLB-303
Kelley, William Melvin 1937- DLB-33
Kellogg, Ansel Nash 1832-1886 . . . . DLB-23
Kellogg, Steven 1941- DLB-61
Kelly, George E. 1887-1974. . . . . .DLB-7, 249
Kelly, Hugh 1739-1777 . . . . DLB-89
Kelly, Piet and Company DLB-49
Kelly, Robert 1935- DLB-5, 130, 165

460

Kelman, James 1946- DLB-194, 319
Kelmscott Press DLB-112
Kelton, Elmer 1926- DLB-256
Kemble, E. W. 1861-1933 ....DLB-188
Kemble, Fanny 1809-1893 ....DLB-32
Kemelman, Harry 1908-1996 ....DLB-28
Kempe, Margery circa 1373-1438 .....DLB-146
Kempinski, Tom 1938- DLB-310
Kempner, Friederike 1836-1904 ......DLB-129
Kempowski, Walter 1929- DLB-75
Kenan, Randall 1963- DLB-292
Claude Kendall [publishing company].....DLB-46
Kendall, Henry 1839-1882............DLB-230
Kendall, May 1861-1943..............DLB-240
Kendell, George 1809-1867 ....DLB-43
Keneally, Thomas 1935- DLB-289, 299
Kenedy, P. J., and Sons DLB-49
Kenkō circa 1283-circa 1352 ....DLB-203
Kenna, Peter 1930-1987..............DLB-289
Kennan, George 1845-1924............DLB-189
Kennedy, A. L. 1965- DLB-271
Kennedy, Adrienne 1931- DLB-38
Kennedy, John Pendleton 1795-1870...DLB-3, 248
Kennedy, Leo 1907-2000..............DLB-88
Kennedy, Margaret 1896-1967 ....DLB-36
Kennedy, Patrick 1801-1873 ....DLB-159
Kennedy, Richard S. 1920- DLB-111; Y-02
Kennedy, William 1928- DLB-143; Y-85
Kennedy, X. J. 1929- DLB-5
    Tribute to John Ciardi Y-86
Kennelly, Brendan 1936- DLB-40
Kenner, Hugh 1923-2003 ....DLB-67
    Tribute to Cleanth Brooks Y-80
Mitchell Kennerley [publishing house].....DLB-46
Kenny, Maurice 1929- DLB-175
Kent, Frank R. 1877-1958 ....DLB-29
Kenyon, Jane 1947-1995..............DLB-120
Kenzheev, Bakhyt Shkurullaevich
    1950- DLB-285
Keough, Hugh Edmund 1864-1912......DLB-171
Keppler and Schwartzmann............DLB-49
Ker, John, third Duke of Roxburghe
    1740-1804 ....DLB-213
Ker, N. R. 1908-1982................DLB-201
Keralio-Robert, Louise-Félicité de
    1758-1822 ....DLB-313
Kerlan, Irvin 1912-1963.............DLB-187
Kermode, Frank 1919- DLB-242
Kern, Jerome 1885-1945 ....DLB-187
Kernaghan, Eileen 1939- DLB-251
Kerner, Justinus 1786-1862 ....DLB-90
Kerouac, Jack
    1922-1969...DLB-2, 16, 237; DS-3; CDALB-1
    Auction of Jack Kerouac's
        On the Road Scroll Y-01
    The Jack Kerouac Revival............ Y-95

"Re-meeting of Old Friends":
    The Jack Kerouac Conference Y-82
Statement of Correction to "The Jack
    Kerouac Revival" Y-96
Kerouac, Jan 1952-1996..............DLB-16
Charles H. Kerr and Company DLB-49
Kerr, Orpheus C. (see Newell, Robert Henry)
Kersh, Gerald 1911-1968.............DLB-255
Kertész, Imre DLB-299; Y-02
Kesey, Ken
    1935-2001 ....DLB-2, 16, 206; CDALB-6
Kessel, Joseph 1898-1979..............DLB-72
Kessel, Martin 1901-1990.............DLB-56
Kesten, Hermann 1900-1996...........DLB-56
Keun, Irmgard 1905-1982.............DLB-69
Key, Ellen 1849-1926................DLB-259
Key and Biddle DLB-49
Keynes, Sir Geoffrey 1887-1982......DLB-201
Keynes, John Maynard 1883-1946 .... DS-10
Keyserling, Eduard von 1855-1918.....DLB-66
al-Khalil ibn Ahmad circa 718-791 ...DLB-311
Khan, Ismith 1925-2002 ....DLB-125
al-Khansa' fl. late sixth-mid
    seventh centuries DLB-311
Kharitonov, Evgenii Vladimirovich
    1941-1981 ....DLB-285
Kharitonov, Mark Sergeevich 1937- ...DLB-285
Khaytov, Nikolay 1919- DLB-181
Khemnitser, Ivan Ivanovich
    1745-1784 ....DLB-150
Kheraskov, Mikhail Matveevich
    1733-1807 ....DLB-150
Khlebnikov, Velimir 1885-1922 ......DLB-295
Khodasevich, Vladislav 1886-1939 ...DLB-317
Khomiakov, Aleksei Stepanovich
    1804-1860 ....DLB-205
Khristov, Boris 1945- DLB-181
Khvoshchinskaia, Nadezhda Dmitrievna
    1824-1889 ....DLB-238
Khvostov, Dmitrii Ivanovich
    1757-1835 ....DLB-150
Kibirov, Timur Iur'evich (Timur
    Iur'evich Zapoev) 1955- DLB-285
Kidd, Adam 1802?-1831 ....DLB-99
William Kidd [publishing house].....DLB-106
Kidde, Harald 1878-1918.............DLB-300
Kidder, Tracy 1945- DLB-185
Kiely, Benedict 1919- DLB-15, 319
Kieran, John 1892-1981..............DLB-171
Kierkegaard, Søren 1813-1855 ....DLB-300
Kies, Marietta 1853-1899............DLB-270
Kiggins and Kellogg..................DLB-49
Kiley, Jed 1889-1962 ....DLB-4
Kilgore, Bernard 1908-1967..........DLB-127
Kilian, Crawford 1941- DLB-251
Killens, John Oliver 1916-1987 ......DLB-33
    Tribute to Julian Mayfield............ Y-84
Killigrew, Anne 1660-1685...........DLB-131

Killigrew, Thomas 1612-1683 ....DLB-58
Kilmer, Joyce 1886-1918 ....DLB-45
Kilroy, Thomas 1934- DLB-233
Kilwardby, Robert circa 1215-1279 ......DLB-115
Kilworth, Garry 1941- DLB-261
Kim, Anatolii Andreevich 1939- DLB-285
Kimball, Richard Burleigh 1816-1892....DLB-202
Kincaid, Jamaica 1949-
    ....DLB-157, 227; CDALB-7; CDWLB-3
Kinck, Hans Ernst 1865-1926 ....DLB-297
King, Charles 1844-1933 ....DLB-186
King, Clarence 1842-1901 ....DLB-12
King, Florence 1936- Y-85
King, Francis 1923- DLB-15, 139
King, Grace 1852-1932 ....DLB-12, 78
King, Harriet Hamilton 1840-1920 ...DLB-199
King, Henry 1592-1669 ....DLB-126
Solomon King [publishing house] DLB-49
King, Stephen 1947- DLB-143; Y-80
King, Susan Petigru 1824-1875 ......DLB-239
King, Thomas 1943- DLB-175
King, Woodie, Jr. 1937- DLB-38
Kinglake, Alexander William
    1809-1891 ....DLB-55, 166
Kingo, Thomas 1634-1703.............DLB-300
Kingsbury, Donald 1929- DLB-251
Kingsley, Charles
    1819-1875 ....DLB-21, 32, 163, 178, 190
Kingsley, Henry 1830-1876 ......DLB-21, 230
Kingsley, Mary Henrietta 1862-1900.....DLB-174
Kingsley, Sidney 1906-1995..............DLB-7
Kingsmill, Hugh 1889-1949............DLB-149
Kingsolver, Barbara
    1955- DLB-206; CDALB-7
Kingston, Maxine Hong
    1940- ..DLB-173, 212, 312; Y-80; CDALB-7
Kingston, William Henry Giles
    1814-1880 ....DLB-163
Kinnan, Mary Lewis 1763-1848........DLB-200
Kinnell, Galway 1927- DLB-5; Y-87
Kinsella, Thomas 1928- DLB-27
Kipling, Rudyard 1865-1936
    ....DLB-19, 34, 141, 156; CDBLB-5
Kipphardt, Heinar 1922-1982 ....DLB-124
Kirby, William 1817-1906 ....DLB-99
Kircher, Athanasius 1602-1680 ......DLB-164
Kireevsky, Ivan Vasil'evich 1806-1856 ...DLB-198
Kireevsky, Petr Vasil'evich 1808-1856 ...DLB-205
Kirk, Hans 1898-1962 ....DLB-214
Kirk, John Foster 1824-1904 ....DLB-79
Kirkconnell, Watson 1895-1977 ....DLB-68
Kirkland, Caroline M.
    1801-1864 ....DLB-3, 73, 74, 250; DS-13
Kirkland, Joseph 1830-1893...........DLB-12
Francis Kirkman [publishing house] DLB-170
Kirkpatrick, Clayton 1915-2004 .....DLB-127
Kirkup, James 1918- DLB-27

Cumulative Index

Kirouac, Conrad (see Marie-Victorin, Frère)

Kirsch, Sarah 1935- DLB-75

Kirst, Hans Hellmut 1914-1989 .... DLB-69

Kiš, Danilo 1935-1989 ..... DLB-181; CDWLB-4

Kita Morio 1927- DLB-182

Kitcat, Mabel Greenhow 1859-1922..... DLB-135

Kitchin, C. H. B. 1895-1967 .... DLB-77

Kittredge, William 1932- DLB-212, 244

Kiukhel'beker, Vil'gel'm Karlovich
1797-1846 .... DLB-205

Kizer, Carolyn 1925- DLB-5, 169

Kjaerstad, Jan 1953- DLB-297

Klabund 1890-1928 .... DLB-66

Klaj, Johann 1616-1656 .... DLB-164

Klappert, Peter 1942- DLB-5

Klass, Philip (see Tenn, William)

Klein, A. M. 1909-1972 .... DLB-68

Kleist, Ewald von 1715-1759 .... DLB-97

Kleist, Heinrich von
1777-1811 .... DLB-90; CDWLB-2

Klíma, Ivan 1931- DLB-232; CDWLB-4

Klimentev, Andrei Platonovic
(see Platonov, Andrei Platonovich)

Klinger, Friedrich Maximilian
1752-1831 .... DLB-94

Kliuev, Nikolai Alekseevich 1884-1937 .. DLB-295

Kliushnikov, Viktor Petrovich
1841-1892 .... DLB-238

Klopfer, Donald S.
Impressions of William Faulkner Y-97

    Oral History Interview with Donald
    S. Klopfer. Y-97

    Tribute to Alfred A. Knopf Y-84

Klopstock, Friedrich Gottlieb
1724-1803 .... DLB-97

Klopstock, Meta 1728-1758 .... DLB-97

Kluge, Alexander 1932- DLB-75

Kluge, P. F. 1942- Y-02

Knapp, Joseph Palmer 1864-1951 ...... DLB-91

Knapp, Samuel Lorenzo 1783-1838 ...... DLB-59

J. J. and P. Knapton [publishing house] .. DLB-154

Kniazhnin, Iakov Borisovich
1740-1791 .... DLB-150

Knickerbocker, Diedrich (see Irving, Washington)

Knigge, Adolph Franz Friedrich Ludwig,
Freiherr von 1752-1796 .... DLB-94

Charles Knight and Company DLB-106

Knight, Damon 1922-2002 .... DLB-8

Knight, Etheridge 1931-1992 .... DLB-41

Knight, John S. 1894-1981 .... DLB-29

Knight, Sarah Kemble 1666-1727 .... DLB-24, 200

Knight-Bruce, G. W. H. 1852-1896 .....DLB-174

Knister, Raymond 1899-1932 .... DLB-68

Knoblock, Edward 1874-1945 .... DLB-10

Knopf, Alfred A. 1892-1984 .... Y-84

    Knopf to Hammett: The Editoral
    Correspondence Y-00

Alfred A. Knopf [publishing house] DLB-46

Knorr von Rosenroth, Christian
1636-1689 .... DLB-168

Knowles, John 1926-2001...... DLB-6; CDALB-6

Knox, Frank 1874-1944 .... DLB-29

Knox, John circa 1514-1572 .... DLB-132

Knox, John Armoy 1850-1906 .... DLB-23

Knox, Lucy 1845-1884 .... DLB-240

Knox, Ronald Arbuthnott 1888-1957..... DLB-77

Knox, Thomas Wallace 1835-1896 ..... DLB-189

Knudsen, Jakob 1858-1917 .... DLB-300

Knut, Dovid 1900-1955 .... DLB-317

Kobayashi Takiji 1903-1933........... DLB-180

Kober, Arthur 1900-1975 .... DLB-11

Kobiakova, Aleksandra Petrovna
1823-1892 .... DLB-238

Kocbek, Edvard 1904-1981 ...DLB-147; CDWLB-4

Koch, C. J. 1932- DLB-289

Koch, Howard 1902-1995 .... DLB-26

Koch, Kenneth 1925-2002 .... DLB-5

Kōda Rohan 1867-1947 .... DLB-180

Koehler, Ted 1894 1973 .... DLB-265

Koenigsberg, Moses 1879-1945 .... DLB-25

Koeppen, Wolfgang 1906-1996 .... DLB-69

Koertge, Ronald 1940- DLB-105

Koestler, Arthur 1905-1983 ...... Y-83; CDBLB-7

Kohn, John S. Van E. 1906-1976 .... DLB-187

Kokhanovskaia
(see Sokhanskaia, Nadezhda Stepanova)

Kokoschka, Oskar 1886-1980 .... DLB-124

Kolb, Annette 1870-1967 .... DLB-66

Kolbenheyer, Erwin Guido
1878-1962 .... DLB-66, 124

Kolleritsch, Alfred 1931- DLB-85

Kolodny, Annette 1941- DLB-67

Koltès, Bernard-Marie 1948-1989....... DLB-321

Kol'tsov, Aleksei Vasil'evich
1809-1842 .... DLB-205

Komarov, Matvei circa 1730-1812 ...... DLB-150

Komroff, Manuel 1890-1974............ DLB-4

Komunyakaa, Yusef 1947- DLB-120

Kondoleon, Harry 1955-1994 .... DLB-266

Koneski, Blaže 1921-1993 ... DLB-181; CDWLB-4

Konigsburg, E. L. 1930- DLB-52

Konparu Zenchiku 1405-1468? DLB-203

Konrád, György 1933- DLB-232; CDWLB-4

Konrad von Würzburg
circa 1230-1287 .... DLB-138

Konstantinov, Aleko 1863-1897 .... DLB-147

Konwicki, Tadeusz 1926- DLB-232

Koontz, Dean 1945- DLB-292

Kooser, Ted 1939- DLB-105

Kopit, Arthur 1937- DLB-7

Kops, Bernard 1926?- DLB-13

Kornbluth, C. M. 1923-1958 .... DLB-8

Körner, Theodor 1791-1813........... DLB-90

Kornfeld, Paul 1889-1942 .... DLB-118

Korolenko, Vladimir Galaktionovich
1853-1921 ....DLB-277

Kosinski, Jerzy 1933-1991 ......DLB-2, 299; Y-82

Kosmač, Ciril 1910-1980 .... DLB-181

Kosovel, Srečko 1904-1926 ....DLB-147

Kostrov, Ermil Ivanovich 1755-1796 .... DLB-150

Kotzebue, August von 1761-1819 .... DLB-94

Kotzwinkle, William 1938- DLB-173

Kovačić, Ante 1854-1889 ....DLB-147

Kovalevskaia, Sof'ia Vasil'evna
1850-1891 ....DLB-277

Kovič, Kajetan 1931- DLB-181

Kozlov, Ivan Ivanovich 1779-1840 ..... DLB-205

Kracauer, Siegfried 1889-1966 .... DLB-296

Kraf, Elaine 1946- Y-81

Kramer, Jane 1938- DLB-185

Kramer, Larry 1935- DLB-249

Kramer, Mark 1944- DLB-185

Kranjčević, Silvije Strahimir 1865-1908 ...DLB-147

Krasko, Ivan 1876-1958 .... DLB-215

Krasna, Norman 1909-1984 .... DLB-26

Kraus, Hans Peter 1907-1988 ....DLB-187

Kraus, Karl 1874-1936 .... DLB-118

Krause, Herbert 1905-1976 .... DLB-256

Krauss, Ruth 1911-1993 .... DLB-52

Kreisel, Henry 1922-1991 .... DLB-88

Krestovsky V.
(see Khvoshchinskaia, Nadezhda Dmitrievna)

Krestovsky, Vsevolod Vladimirovich
1839-1895 .... DLB-238

Kreuder, Ernst 1903-1972 .... DLB-69

Krėvė-Mickevičius, Vincas 1882-1954 ... DLB-220

Kreymborg, Alfred 1883-1966 .... DLB-4, 54

Krieger, Murray 1923-2000 .... DLB-67

Krim, Seymour 1922-1989 .... DLB-16

Kripke, Saul 1940- DLB-279

Kristensen, Tom 1893-1974 .... DLB-214

Kristeva, Julia 1941- DLB-242

Kristján Níels Jónsson/Kristjan Niels Julius
(see Káinn)

Kritzer, Hyman W. 1918-2002........... Y-02

Krivulin, Viktor Borisovich 1944-2001 .. DLB-285

Krleža, Miroslav
1893-1981 ....DLB-147; CDWLB-4

Krock, Arthur 1886-1974 .... DLB-29

Kroetsch, Robert 1927- DLB-53

Kropotkin, Petr Alekseevich 1842-1921 ...DLB-277

Kross, Jaan 1920- DLB-232

Kruchenykh, Aleksei Eliseevich
1886-1968 .... DLB-295

Krúdy, Gyula 1878-1933 .... DLB-215

Krutch, Joseph Wood
1893-1970 ....DLB-63, 206, 275

Krylov, Ivan Andreevich 1769-1844..... DLB-150

Krymov, Iurii Solomonovich
(Iurii Solomonovich Beklemishev)
1908-1941 ....DLB-272

Kubin, Alfred 1877-1959 ....DLB-81	La Chaussée, Pierre-Claude Nivelle de 1692-1754 ....DLB-313	L'Amour, Louis 1908-1988........DLB-206; Y-80
Kubrick, Stanley 1928-1999............DLB-26	Laclos, Pierre-Ambroise-François Choderlos de 1741-1803 ....DLB-313	Lampman, Archibald 1861-1899........DLB-92
Kudrun circa 1230-1240 ....DLB-138		Lamson, Wolffe and Company.........DLB-49
Kuffstein, Hans Ludwig von 1582-1656 ..DLB-164	*Dangerous Acquaintances* DLB-314	Lancer Books......................DLB-46
Kuhlmann, Quirinus 1651-1689 ....DLB-168	Lacombe, Patrice (see Trullier-Lacombe, Joseph Patrice)	Lanchester, John 1962- DLB-267
Kuhn, Thomas S. 1922-1996..........DLB-279	Lacretelle, Jacques de 1888-1985.........DLB-65	Lander, Peter (see Cunningham, Peter)
Kuhnau, Johann 1660-1722 ....DLB-168	Lacy, Ed 1911-1968................DLB-226	Landesman, Jay 1919- and Landesman, Fran 1927-...............DLB-16
Kukol'nik, Nestor Vasil'evich 1809-1868......................DLB-205	Lacy, Sam 1903- DLB-171	Landolfi, Tommaso 1908-1979 ....DLB-177
Kukučín, Martin 1860-1928...........DLB-215; CDWLB-4	Ladd, Joseph Brown 1764-1786.........DLB-37	Landon, Letitia Elizabeth 1802-1838......DLB-96
	La Farge, Oliver 1901-1963..............DLB-9	Landor, Walter Savage 1775-1864....DLB-93, 107
Kumin, Maxine 1925- DLB-5	Lafayette, Marie-Madeleine, comtesse de 1634-1693 ....DLB-268	Landry, Napoléon-P. 1884-1956 ....DLB-92
Kuncewicz, Maria 1895-1989..........DLB-215		Landvik, Lorna 1954- DLB-292
Kundera, Milan 1929- DLB-232; CDWLB-4	Laffan, Mrs. R. S. de Courcy (see Adams, Bertha Leith)	Lane, Charles 1800-1870 ....DLB-1, 223; DS-5
Kunene, Mazisi 1930- DLB-117	Lafferty, R. A. 1914-2002 ....DLB-8	Lane, F. C. 1885-1984...............DLB-241
Kunikida Doppo 1869-1908 ....DLB-180	La Flesche, Francis 1857-1932 ....DLB-175	Lane, Laurence W. 1890-1967 ....DLB-91
Kunitz, Stanley 1905- DLB-48	La Fontaine, Jean de 1621-1695........DLB-268	Lane, M. Travis 1934- DLB-60
Kunjufu, Johari M. (see Amini, Johari M.)	Laforge, Jules 1860-1887 ....DLB-217	Lane, Patrick 1939- DLB-53
Kunnert, Gunter 1929- DLB-75	Lagerkvist, Pär 1891-1974 ....DLB-259	Lane, Pinkie Gordon 1923- DLB-41
Kunze, Reiner 1933- DLB-75	Lagerlöf, Selma 1858-1940......................DLB-259	John Lane Company DLB-49
Kuo, Helena 1911-1999..............DLB-312		Laney, Al 1896-1988............. DLB-4, 171
Kupferberg, Tuli 1923- DLB-16	Lagorio, Gina 1922- DLB-196	Lang, Andrew 1844-1912 ......DLB-98, 141, 184
Kuprin, Aleksandr Ivanovich 1870-1938 ....DLB-295	La Guma, Alex 1925-1985........ DLB-117, 225; CDWLB-3	Langer, Susanne K. 1895-1985 ....DLB-270
		Langevin, André 1927- DLB-60
Kuraev, Mikhail Nikolaevich 1939- DLB-285	Lahaise, Guillaume (see Delahaye, Guy)	Langford, David 1953- DLB-261
Kurahashi Yumiko 1935- DLB-182	La Harpe, Jean-François de 1739-1803.....DLB-313	Langgässer, Elisabeth 1899-1950.........DLB-69
Kureishi, Hanif 1954- DLB-194, 245	Lahontan, Louis-Armand de Lom d'Arce, Baron de 1666-1715?................DLB-99	Langhorne, John 1735-1779 ....DLB-109
Kürnberger, Ferdinand 1821-1879.......DLB-129		Langland, William circa 1330-circa 1400. .DLB-146
Kurz, Isolde 1853-1944 ....DLB-66	Laing, Kojo 1946- DLB-157	Langton, Anna 1804-1893...............DLB-99
Kusenberg, Kurt 1904-1983............DLB-69	Laird, Carobeth 1895-1983 .... Y-82	Lanham, Edwin 1904-1979 ....DLB-4
Kushchevsky, Ivan Afanas'evich 1847-1876......................DLB-238	Laird and Lee DLB-49	Lanier, Sidney 1842-1881 ....DLB-64; DS-13
	Lake, Paul 1951- DLB-282	Lanyer, Aemilia 1569-1645 ....DLB-121
Kushner, Tony 1956- DLB-228	Lalić, Ivan V. 1931-1996 ....DLB-181	Lapointe, Gatien 1931-1983 ....DLB-88
Kuttner, Henry 1915-1958...............DLB-8	Lalić, Mihailo 1914-1992..............DLB-181	Lapointe, Paul-Marie 1929- DLB-88
Kuzmin, Mikhail Alekseevich 1872-1936 ....DLB-295	Lalonde, Michèle 1937- DLB-60	Larcom, Lucy 1824-1893..........DLB-221, 243
	Lamantia, Philip 1927- DLB-16	Lardner, John 1912-1960..............DLB-171
Kuznetsov, Anatoli 1929-1979 ....DLB-299, 302	Lamartine, Alphonse de 1790-1869 ....DLB-217	Lardner, Ring 1885-1933 ...... DLB-11, 25, 86, 171; DS-16; CDALB-4
Kyd, Thomas 1558-1594...............DLB-62	Lamb, Lady Caroline 1785-1828 ....DLB-116	Lardner 100: Ring Lardner Centennial Symposium............ Y-85
Kyffin, Maurice circa 1560?-1598 ....DLB-136		
Kyger, Joanne 1934- DLB-16	Lamb, Charles 1775-1834 ......DLB-93, 107, 163; CDBLB-3	Lardner, Ring, Jr. 1915-2000....... DLB-26, Y-00
Kyne, Peter B. 1880-1957 ....DLB-78		Larkin, Philip 1922-1985......DLB-27; CDBLB-8
Kyōgoku Tamekane 1254-1332.........DLB-203	Lamb, Mary 1764-1874 ....DLB-163	The Philip Larkin Society Y-99
Kyrklund, Willy 1921- DLB-257	Lambert, Angela 1940- DLB-271	La Roche, Sophie von 1730-1807.........DLB-94
	Lambert, Anne-Thérèse de (Anne-Thérèse de Marguenat de Courcelles, marquise de Lambert) 1647-1733.......................DLB-313	La Rochefoucauld, François duc de 1613-1680 ....DLB-268
L		
	Lambert, Betty 1933-1983 ....DLB-60	La Rocque, Gilbert 1943-1984..........DLB-60
L. E. L. (see Landon, Letitia Elizabeth)	La Mettrie, Julien Offroy de 1709-1751 ....DLB-313	Laroque de Roquebrune, Robert (see Roquebrune, Robert de)
Laberge, Albert 1871-1960..............DLB-68		
Laberge, Marie 1950- DLB-60	Lamm, Donald Goodbye, Gutenberg? A Lecture at the New York Public Library, 18 April 1995 .... Y-95	Larrick, Nancy 1910-2004 ....DLB-61
Labiche, Eugène 1815-1888...........DLB-192		Lars, Claudia 1899-1974 ....DLB-283
Labrunie, Gerard (see Nerval, Gerard de)		Larsen, Nella 1893-1964 ....DLB-51
La Bruyère, Jean de 1645-1696.........DLB-268	Lamming, George 1927- DLB-125; CDWLB-3	Larsen, Thøger 1875-1928............DLB-300
La Calprenède 1609?-1663 ....DLB-268		Larson, Clinton F. 1919-1994 ....DLB-256
Lacan, Jacques 1901-1981 ....DLB-296	La Mothe Le Vayer, François de 1588-1672 ....DLB-268	La Sale, Antoine de circa 1386-1460/1467 ....DLB-208
La Capria, Raffaele 1922- DLB-196		

Cumulative Index

Las Casas, Fray Bartolomé de
1474-1566.................... DLB-318

Lasch, Christopher 1932-1994 .... DLB-246

Lasdun, James 1958- DLB-319

Lasker-Schüler, Else 1869-1945 ..... DLB-66, 124

Lasnier, Rina 1915-1997............... DLB-88

Lassalle, Ferdinand 1825-1864 .... DLB-129

Late-Medieval Castilian Theater DLB-286

Latham, Robert 1912-1995............ DLB-201

Lathan, Emma (Mary Jane Latsis [1927-1997] and Martha Henissart [1929-]) DLB-306

Lathrop, Dorothy P. 1891-1980 .... DLB-22

Lathrop, George Parsons 1851-1898 ..... DLB-71

Lathrop, John, Jr. 1772-1820............ DLB-37

Latimer, Hugh 1492?-1555............ DLB-136

Latimore, Jewel Christine McLawler (see Amini, Johari M.)

Latin Literature, The Uniqueness of DLB-211

La Tour du Pin, Patrice de 1911-1975 ... DLB-258

Latymer, William 1498-1583 .... DLB-132

Laube, Heinrich 1806-1884 .... DLB-133

Laud, William 1573-1645............ DLB-213

Laughlin, James 1914-1997......DLB-48; Y-96, 97

    A Tribute [to Henry Miller]............ Y-80

    Tribute to Albert Erskine............. Y-93

    Tribute to Kenneth Rexroth Y-82

    Tribute to Malcolm Cowley Y-89

Laumer, Keith 1925-1993................ DLB-8

Lauremberg, Johann 1590-1658 .... DLB-164

Laurence, Margaret 1926-1987.......... DLB-53

Laurentius von Schnüffis 1633-1702..... DLB-168

Laurents, Arthur 1918- DLB-26

Laurie, Annie (see Black, Winifred)

Laut, Agnes Christiana 1871-1936 .... DLB-92

Lauterbach, Ann 1942- DLB-193

Lautréamont, Isidore Lucien Ducasse, Comte de 1846-1870 .... DLB-217

Lavater, Johann Kaspar 1741-1801....... DLB-97

Lavin, Mary 1912-1996 .... DLB-15, 319

Law, John (see Harkness, Margaret)

Lawes, Henry 1596-1662 .... DLB-126

Lawler, Ray 1922- DLB-289

Lawless, Anthony (see MacDonald, Philip)

Lawless, Emily (The Hon. Emily Lawless) 1845-1913.................... DLB-240

Lawrence, D. H. 1885-1930
..... DLB-10, 19, 36, 98, 162, 195; CDBLB-6

    The D. H. Lawrence Society of North America................... Y-00

Lawrence, David 1888-1973........... DLB-29

Lawrence, Jerome 1915-2004 .... DLB-228

Lawrence, Seymour 1926-1994 .... Y-94

    Tribute to Richard Yates Y-92

Lawrence, T. E. 1888-1935 .... DLB-195

    The T. E. Lawrence Society........... Y-98

Lawson, George 1598-1678 .... DLB-213

Lawson, Henry 1867-1922 .... DLB-230

Lawson, John ?-1711................. DLB-24

Lawson, John Howard 1894-1977 ...... DLB-228

Lawson, Louisa Albury 1848-1920...... DLB-230

Lawson, Robert 1892-1957............. DLB-22

Lawson, Victor F. 1850-1925 .... DLB-25

Layard, Austen Henry 1817-1894....... DLB-166

Layton, Irving 1912- DLB-88

LaZamon fl. circa 1200............... DLB-146

Lazarević, Laza K. 1851-1890.......... DLB-147

Lazarus, George 1904-1997 .... DLB-201

Lazhechnikov, Ivan Ivanovich 1792-1869..................... DLB-198

Lea, Henry Charles 1825-1909 .... DLB-47

Lea, Sydney 1942- DLB-120, 282

Lea, Tom 1907-2001................... DLB-6

Leacock, John 1729-1802 .... DLB-31

Leacock, Stephen 1869-1944 .... DLB-92

Lead, Jane Ward 1623-1704 .... DLB-131

Leadenhall Press.................... DLB-106

"The Greatness of Southern Literature": League of the South Institute for the Study of Southern Culture and History Y-02

Leakey, Caroline Woolmer 1827-1881.... DLB-230

Leapor, Mary 1722-1746............... DLB-109

Lear, Edward 1812-1888 ...... DLB-32, 163, 166

Leary, Timothy 1920-1996............ DLB-16

W. A. Leary and Company DLB-49

Léautaud, Paul 1872-1956 .... DLB-65

Leavis, F. R. 1895-1978................ DLB-242

Leavitt, David 1961- DLB-130

Leavitt and Allen DLB-49

Le Blond, Mrs. Aubrey 1861-1934........DLB-174

le Carré, John (David John Moore Cornwell) 1931- DLB-87; CDBLB-8

    Tribute to Graham Greene Y-91

    Tribute to George Greenfield Y-00

Lécavelé, Roland (see Dorgeles, Roland)

Lechlitner, Ruth 1901- DLB-48

Leclerc, Félix 1914-1988................ DLB-60

Le Clézio, J. M. G. 1940- DLB-83

Leder, Rudolf (see Hermlin, Stephan)

Lederer, Charles 1910-1976 .... DLB-26

Ledwidge, Francis 1887-1917 .... DLB-20

Lee, Chang-rae 1965- DLB-312

Lee, Cherylene 1953- DLB-312

Lee, Dennis 1939- DLB-53

Lee, Don L. (see Madhubuti, Haki R.)

Lee, George W. 1894-1976............ DLB-51

Lee, Gus 1946- DLB-312

Lee, Harper 1926- DLB-6; CDALB-1

Lee, Harriet 1757-1851 and Lee, Sophia 1750-1824 .... DLB-39

Lee, Laurie 1914-1997 .... DLB-27

Lee, Leslie 1935- DLB-266

Lee, Li-Young 1957- DLB-165, 312

Lee, Manfred B. 1905-1971 ....DLB-137

Lee, Nathaniel circa 1645-1692 .... DLB-80

Lee, Robert E. 1918-1994.............. DLB-228

Lee, Sir Sidney 1859-1926 .... DLB-149, 184

    "Principles of Biography," in *Elizabethan and Other Essays* DLB-149

Lee, Tanith 1947- DLB-261

Lee, Vernon 1856-1935 ....DLB-57, 153, 156, 174, 178

Lee and Shepard..................... DLB-49

Le Fanu, Joseph Sheridan 1814-1873............. DLB-21, 70, 159, 178

Leffland, Ella 1931- Y-84

le Fort, Gertrud von 1876-1971......... DLB-66

Le Gallienne, Richard 1866-1947......... DLB-4

Legaré, Hugh Swinton 1797-1843.................DLB-3, 59, 73, 248

Legaré, James Mathewes 1823-1859.... DLB-3, 248

Léger, Antoine J. 1880-1950............ DLB-88

Leggett, William 1801-1839 .... DLB-250

Le Guin, Ursula K. 1929- DLB-8, 52, 256, 275; CDALB-6

Lehman, Ernest 1920- DLB-44

Lehmann, John 1907-1989 .... DLB-27, 100

John Lehmann Limited................ DLB-112

Lehmann, Rosamond 1901-1990 .... DLB-15

Lehmann, Wilhelm 1882-1968.......... DLB-56

Leiber, Fritz 1910-1992................. DLB-8

Leibniz, Gottfried Wilhelm 1646-1716 ... DLB-168

Leicester University Press DLB-112

Leigh, Carolyn 1926-1983 .... DLB-265

Leigh, W. R. 1866-1955................ DLB-188

Leinster, Murray 1896-1975 .... DLB-8

Leiser, Bill 1898-1965................. DLB-241

Leisewitz, Johann Anton 1752-1806...... DLB-94

Leitch, Maurice 1933- DLB-14

Leithauser, Brad 1943- DLB-120, 282

Leland, Charles G. 1824-1903 .... DLB-11

Leland, John 1503?-1552 .... DLB-136

Lemay, Pamphile 1837-1918............ DLB-99

Lemelin, Roger 1919-1992 .... DLB-88

Lemercier, Louis-Jean-Népomucène 1771-1840..................... DLB-192

Le Moine, James MacPherson 1825-1912 . DLB-99

Lemon, Mark 1809-1870 .... DLB-163

Le Moyne, Jean 1913-1996............. DLB-88

Lemperly, Paul 1858-1939 ....DLB-187

Leñero, Vicente 1933- DLB-305

L'Engle, Madeleine 1918- DLB-52

Lennart, Isobel 1915-1971 .... DLB-44

Lennox, Charlotte 1729 or 1730-1804 .... DLB-39

Lenox, James 1800-1880............... DLB-140

Lenski, Lois 1893-1974................ DLB-22

Lentricchia, Frank 1940- DLB-246

Lenz, Hermann 1913-1998............. DLB-69

Lenz, J. M. R. 1751-1792 .... DLB-94
Lenz, Siegfried 1926- DLB-75
León, Fray Luis de 1527-1591 .... DLB-318
Leonard, Elmore 1925- DLB-173, 226
Leonard, Hugh 1926- DLB-13
Leonard, William Ellery 1876-1944 .... DLB-54
Leong, Russell C. 1950- DLB-312
Leonov, Leonid Maksimovich
  1899-1994 .... DLB-272
Leonowens, Anna 1834-1914 .... DLB-99, 166
Leont'ev, Konstantin Nikolaevich
  1831-1891 .... DLB-277
Leopold, Aldo 1887-1948 .... DLB-275
LePan, Douglas 1914-1998 .... DLB-88
Lepik, Kalju 1920-1999 .... DLB-232
Leprohon, Rosanna Eleanor 1829-1879 ... DLB-99
Le Queux, William 1864-1927 .... DLB-70
Lermontov, Mikhail Iur'evich
  1814-1841 .... DLB-205
Lerner, Alan Jay 1918-1986 .... DLB-265
Lerner, Max 1902-1992 .... DLB-29
Lernet-Holenia, Alexander 1897-1976 ..... DLB-85
Le Rossignol, James 1866-1969 .... DLB-92
Lesage, Alain-René 1668-1747 .... DLB-313
Lescarbot, Marc circa 1570-1642 .... DLB-99
LeSeur, William Dawson 1840-1917 ..... DLB-92
LeSieg, Theo. (see Geisel, Theodor Seuss)
Leskov, Nikolai Semenovich
  1831-1895 .... DLB-238
Leslie, Doris before 1902-1982 .... DLB-191
Leslie, Eliza 1787-1858 .... DLB-202
Leslie, Frank (Henry Carter)
  1821-1880 .... DLB-43, 79
Frank Leslie [publishing house] DLB-49
Leśmian, Bolesław 1878-1937 .... DLB-215
Lesperance, John 1835?-1891 .... DLB-99
Lespinasse, Julie de 1732-1776 .... DLB-313
Lessing, Bruno 1870-1940 .... DLB-28
Lessing, Doris
  1919- DLB-15, 139; Y-85; CDBLB-8
Lessing, Gotthold Ephraim
  1729-1781 .... DLB-97; CDWLB-2
  The Lessing Society Y-00
Le Sueur, Meridel 1900-1996 .... DLB-303
Lettau, Reinhard 1929-1996 .... DLB-75
Letters from a Peruvian Woman, Françoise d'Issembourg
  de Graffigny DLB-314
The Hemingway Letters Project Finds
  an Editor Y-02
Lever, Charles 1806-1872 .... DLB-21
Lever, Ralph ca. 1527-1585 .... DLB-236
Leverson, Ada 1862-1933 .... DLB-153
Levertov, Denise
  1923-1997 .... DLB-5, 165; CDALB-7
Levi, Peter 1931-2000 .... DLB-40
Levi, Primo 1919-1987 .... DLB-177, 299
Levien, Sonya 1888-1960 .... DLB-44

Levin, Meyer 1905-1981 .... DLB-9, 28; Y-81
Levin, Phillis 1954- DLB-282
Lévinas, Emmanuel 1906-1995 .... DLB-296
Levine, Norman 1923- DLB-88
Levine, Philip 1928- DLB-5
Levis, Larry 1946- DLB-120
Lévi-Strauss, Claude 1908- DLB-242
Levitov, Aleksandr Ivanovich
  1835?-1877 .... DLB-277
Levy, Amy 1861-1889 .... DLB-156, 240
Levy, Benn Wolfe 1900-1973 ...... DLB-13; Y-81
Levy, Deborah 1959- DLB-310
Lewald, Fanny 1811-1889 .... DLB-129
Lewes, George Henry 1817-1878 ..... DLB-55, 144
  "Criticism in Relation to Novels"
    (1863) DLB-21
  The Principles of Success in Literature
    (1865) [excerpt] DLB-57
Lewis, Agnes Smith 1843-1926 .... DLB-174
Lewis, Alfred H. 1857-1914 .... DLB-25, 186
Lewis, Alun 1915-1944 .... DLB-20, 162
Lewis, C. Day (see Day Lewis, C.)
Lewis, C. I. 1883-1964 .... DLB-270
Lewis, C. S. 1898-1963
  .... DLB-15, 100, 160, 255; CDBLB-7
  The New York C. S. Lewis Society Y-99
Lewis, Charles B. 1842-1924 .... DLB-11
Lewis, David 1941-2001 .... DLB-279
Lewis, Henry Clay 1825-1850 .... DLB-3, 248
Lewis, Janet 1899-1999 .... Y-87
  Tribute to Katherine Anne Porter Y-80
Lewis, Matthew Gregory
  1775-1818 .... DLB-39, 158, 178
Lewis, Meriwether 1774-1809 ..... DLB-183, 186
Lewis, Norman 1908-2003 .... DLB-204
Lewis, R. W. B. 1917-2002 .... DLB-111
Lewis, Richard circa 1700-1734 .... DLB-24
Lewis, Saunders 1893-1985 .... DLB-310
Lewis, Sinclair
  1885-1951 ..... DLB-9, 102; DS-1; CDALB-4
  Sinclair Lewis Centennial Conference Y-85
  The Sinclair Lewis Society Y-99
Lewis, Wilmarth Sheldon 1895-1979 ..... DLB-140
Lewis, Wyndham 1882-1957 .... DLB-15
  Time and Western Man
    [excerpt] (1927) DLB-36
Lewisohn, Ludwig 1882-1955 ... DLB-4, 9, 28, 102
Leyendecker, J. C. 1874-1951 .... DLB-188
Leyner, Mark 1956- DLB-292
Lezama Lima, José 1910-1976 ...... DLB-113, 283
Lézardière, Marie-Charlotte-Pauline Robert de
  1754-1835 .... DLB-313
L'Heureux, John 1934- DLB-244
Libbey, Laura Jean 1862-1924 .... DLB-221
Libedinsky, Iurii Nikolaevich
  1898-1959 .... DLB-272
The Liberator DLB-303

Library History Group Y-01
E-Books' Second Act in Libraries Y-02
The Library of America DLB-46
The Library of America: An Assessment
  After Two Decades Y-02
Licensing Act of 1737 .... DLB-84
Leonard Lichfield I [publishing house] ... DLB-170
Lichtenberg, Georg Christoph
  1742-1799 .... DLB-94
The Liddle Collection Y-97
Lidman, Sara 1923-2004 .... DLB-257
Lieb, Fred 1888-1980 .... DLB-171
Liebling, A. J. 1904-1963 .... DLB-4, 171
Lieutenant Murray (see Ballou, Maturin Murray)
Lighthall, William Douw 1857-1954 ...... DLB-92
Lihn, Enrique 1929-1988 .... DLB-283
Lilar, Françoise (see Mallet-Joris, Françoise)
Lili'uokalani, Queen 1838-1917 .... DLB-221
Lillo, George 1691-1739 .... DLB-84
Lilly, J. K., Jr. 1893-1966 .... DLB-140
Lilly, Wait and Company DLB-49
Lily, William circa 1468-1522 .... DLB-132
Lim, Shirley Geok-lin 1944- DLB-312
Lima, Jorge de 1893-1953 .... DLB-307
Lima Barreto, Afonso Henriques de
  1881-1922 .... DLB-307
Limited Editions Club DLB-46
Limón, Graciela 1938- DLB-209
Limonov, Eduard 1943- DLB-317
Lincoln and Edmands DLB-49
Lind, Jakov 1927- DLB-299
Linda Vilhjálmsdóttir 1958- DLB-293
Lindesay, Ethel Forence
  (see Richardson, Henry Handel)
Lindgren, Astrid 1907-2002 .... DLB-257
Lindgren, Torgny 1938- DLB-257
Lindsay, Alexander William, Twenty-fifth
  Earl of Crawford 1812-1880 .... DLB-184
Lindsay, Sir David circa 1485-1555 ..... DLB-132
Lindsay, David 1878-1945 .... DLB-255
Lindsay, Jack 1900-1990 .... Y-84
Lindsay, Lady (Caroline Blanche
  Elizabeth Fitzroy Lindsay)
  1844-1912 .... DLB-199
Lindsay, Norman 1879-1969 .... DLB-260
Lindsay, Vachel
  1879-1931 .... DLB-54; CDALB-3
Linebarger, Paul Myron Anthony
  (see Smith, Cordwainer)
Link, Arthur S. 1920-1998 .... DLB-17
Linn, Ed 1922-2000 .... DLB-241
Linn, John Blair 1777-1804 .... DLB-37
Lins, Osman 1924-1978 .... DLB-145, 307
Linton, Eliza Lynn 1822-1898 .... DLB-18
Linton, William James 1812-1897 .... DLB-32
Barnaby Bernard Lintot
  [publishing house] DLB-170

Lion Books DLB-46	The Humanities Research Center, University of Texas. Y-82	The Nathaniel Hawthorne Society. Y-00
Lionni, Leo 1910-1999 . . . . DLB-61	The John Carter Brown Library Y-85	The [George Alfred] Henty Society Y-98
Lippard, George 1822-1854 . . . . DLB-202	Kent State Special Collections Y-86	George Moses Horton Society. Y-99
Lippincott, Sara Jane Clarke 1823-1904 . . . . DLB-43	The Lilly Library. Y-84	The William Dean Howells Society. Y-01
J. B. Lippincott Company. DLB-49	The Modern Literary Manuscripts Collection in the Special Collections of the Washington University Libraries Y-87	WW2 HMSO Paperbacks Society. Y-98
Lippmann, Walter 1889-1974. . . . . DLB-29		American Humor Studies Association Y-99
Lipton, Lawrence 1898-1975 . . . . DLB-16		International Society for Humor Studies . . . Y-99
Lisboa, Irene 1892-1958. . . . . DLB-287	A Publisher's Archives: G. P. Putnam Y-92	The W. W. Jacobs Appreciation Society . . Y-98
Liscow, Christian Ludwig 1701-1760 . . . . DLB-97	Special Collections at Boston University Y-99	The Richard Jefferies Society. Y-98
Lish, Gordon 1934- DLB-130	The University of Virginia Libraries Y-91	The Jerome K. Jerome Society. Y-98
Tribute to Donald Barthelme. Y-89	The William Charvat American Fiction Collection at the Ohio State University Libraries Y-92	The D. H. Lawrence Society of North America Y-00
Tribute to James Dickey Y-97		The T. E. Lawrence Society Y-98
Lisle, Charles-Marie-René Leconte de 1818-1894. . . . . DLB-217	Literary Societies Y-98–02	The [Gotthold] Lessing Society Y-00
Lispector, Clarice 1925?-1977 . . . . DLB-113, 307; CDWLB-3	The Margery Allingham Society Y-98	The New York C. S. Lewis Society Y-99
	The American Studies Association of Norway Y-00	The Sinclair Lewis Society Y-99
LitCheck Website. Y-01		The Jack London Research Center Y-00
Literary Awards and Honors Y-81–02	The Arnold Bennett Society. Y-98	The Jack London Society. Y-99
Booker Prize. Y-86, 96–98	The Association for the Study of Literature and Environment (ASLE) Y-99	The Cormac McCarthy Society. Y-99
The Drue Heinz Literature Prize Y-82		The Melville Society Y-01
The Elmer Holmes Bobst Awards in Arts and Letters. Y-87		The Arthur Miller Society Y-01
	Belgian Luxembourg American Studies Association Y-01	The Milton Society of America Y-00
The Griffin Poetry Prize Y-00		International Marianne Moore Society . . . Y-98
Literary Prizes [British] DLB-15, 207	The E. F. Benson Society. Y-98	International Nabokov Society. Y-99
National Book Critics Circle Awards. Y-00–01	The Elizabeth Bishop Society. Y-01	The Vladimir Nabokov Society. Y-01
	The [Edgar Rice] Burroughs Bibliophiles Y-98	The Flannery O'Connor Society Y-99
The National Jewish Book Awards. Y-85		The Wilfred Owen Association Y-98
	The Byron Society of America. Y-00	Penguin Collectors' Society Y-98
Nobel Prize. Y-80–02	The Lewis Carroll Society of North America Y-00	The [E. A.] Poe Studies Association. Y-99
Winning an Edgar Y-98		The Katherine Anne Porter Society. Y-01
The Literary Chronicle and Weekly Review 1819-1828 . . . . DLB-110	The Willa Cather Pioneer Memorial and Education Foundation Y-00	The Beatrix Potter Society. Y-98
	New Chaucer Society. Y-00	The Ezra Pound Society Y-01
Literary Periodicals:	The Wilkie Collins Society Y-98	The Powys Society. Y-98
Callaloo Y-87	The James Fenimore Cooper Society Y-01	Proust Society of America Y-00
Expatriates in Paris DS-15	The Stephen Crane Society Y-98, 01	The Dorothy L. Sayers Society Y-98
New Literary Periodicals: A Report for 1987 . . . . Y-87	The E. E. Cummings Society. Y-01	The Bernard Shaw Society. Y-99
	The James Dickey Society Y-99	The Society for the Study of Southern Literature Y-00
A Report for 1988 . . . . DLB-88	John Dos Passos Newsletter. Y-00	
A Report for 1989 . . . . Y-89	The Priory Scholars [Sir Arthur Conan Doyle] of New York Y-99	The Wallace Stevens Society Y-99
A Report for 1990 . . . . Y-90		The Harriet Beecher Stowe Center Y-00
A Report for 1991 . . . . Y-91	The International Theodore Dreiser Society. Y-01	The R. S. Surtees Society. Y-98
A Report for 1992 . . . . Y-92		The Thoreau Society Y-99
A Report for 1993 . . . . Y-93	The Friends of the Dymock Poets Y-00	The Tilling [E. F. Benson] Society Y-98
Literary Research Archives	The George Eliot Fellowship Y-99	The Trollope Societies. Y-00
The Anthony Burgess Archive at the Harry Ransom Humanities Research Center Y-98	The T. S. Eliot Society: Celebration and Scholarship, 1980-1999 . . . . Y-99	H. G. Wells Society Y-98
		The Western Literature Association Y-99
Archives of Charles Scribner's Sons. DS-17	The Ralph Waldo Emerson Society Y-99	The William Carlos Williams Society Y-99
Berg Collection of English and American Literature of the New York Public Library Y-83	The William Faulkner Society Y-99	The Henry Williamson Society Y-98
	The C. S. Forester Society Y-00	The [Nero] Wolfe Pack Y-99
	The Hamlin Garland Society. Y-01	The Thomas Wolfe Society. Y-99
The Bobbs-Merrill Archive at the Lilly Library, Indiana University Y-90	The [Elizabeth] Gaskell Society Y-98	Worldwide Wodehouse Societies Y-98
	The Charlotte Perkins Gilman Society . . . Y-99	The W. B. Yeats Society of N.Y. Y-99
Die Fürstliche Bibliothek Corvey. Y-96	The Ellen Glasgow Society Y-01	The Charlotte M. Yonge Fellowship Y-98
Guide to the Archives of Publishers, Journals, and Literary Agents in North American Libraries Y-93	Zane Grey's West Society Y-00	Literary Theory
	The Ivor Gurney Society Y-98	The Year in Literary Theory. Y-92–Y-93
The Henry E. Huntington Library Y-92	The Joel Chandler Harris Association Y-99	

Literature at Nurse, or Circulating Morals (1885),
  by George Moore DLB-18
Litt, Toby 1968- DLB-267, 319
Littell, Eliakim 1797-1870 ....DLB-79
Littell, Robert S. 1831-1896.............DLB-79
Little, Brown and Company DLB-49
Little Magazines and Newspapers DS-15
  Selected English-Language Little
    Magazines and Newspapers
    [France, 1920-1939] DLB-4
The Little Magazines of the
  New Formalism..................DLB-282
The Little Review 1914-1929 .... DS-15
Littlewood, Joan 1914-2002.............DLB-13
Liu, Aimee E. 1953- DLB-312
Lively, Penelope 1933- DLB-14, 161, 207
Liverpool University Press DLB-112
The Lives of the Poets (1753) DLB-142
Livesay, Dorothy 1909-1996 ....DLB-68
Livesay, Florence Randal 1874-1953 ......DLB-92
Livings, Henry 1929-1998...............DLB-13
Livingston, Anne Howe 1763-1841 ... DLB-37, 200
Livingston, Jay 1915-2001 ....DLB-265
Livingston, Myra Cohn 1926-1996 ....DLB-61
Livingston, William 1723-1790 ....DLB-31
Livingstone, David 1813-1873 ....DLB-166
Livingstone, Douglas 1932-1996 ....DLB-225
Livshits, Benedikt Konstantinovich
  1886-1938 or 1939 ....DLB-295
Livy 59 B.C.-A.D. 17 .... DLB-211; CDWLB-1
Liyong, Taban lo (see Taban lo Liyong)
Lizárraga, Sylvia S. 1925- DLB-82
Llewellyn, Richard 1906-1983...........DLB-15
Lloréns Torres, Luis 1876-1944..........DLB-290
Edward Lloyd [publishing house] DLB-106
Lobato, José Bento Monteiro
  1882-1948 ....DLB-307
Lobel, Arnold 1933- DLB-61
Lochhead, Liz 1947- DLB-310
Lochridge, Betsy Hopkins (see Fancher, Betsy)
Locke, Alain 1886-1954................DLB-51
Locke, David Ross 1833-1888........DLB-11, 23
Locke, John 1632-1704.....DLB-31, 101, 213, 252
Locke, Richard Adams 1800-1871 ....DLB-43
Locker-Lampson, Frederick
  1821-1895 ....DLB-35, 184
Lockhart, John Gibson
  1794-1854 .... DLB-110, 116 144
Lockridge, Francis 1896-1963 ....DLB-306
Lockridge, Richard 1898-1982............DLB-306
Lockridge, Ross, Jr. 1914-1948 .... DLB-143; Y-80
Locrine and Selimus....................DLB-62
Lodge, David 1935- DLB-14, 194
Lodge, George Cabot 1873-1909 ....DLB-54
Lodge, Henry Cabot 1850-1924 ....DLB-47
Lodge, Thomas 1558-1625 ....DLB-172
  Defence of Poetry (1579) [excerpt] DLB-172

Loeb, Harold 1891-1974 ....DLB-4; DS-15
Loeb, William 1905-1981 ....DLB-127
Loesser, Frank 1910-1969 ....DLB-265
Lofting, Hugh 1886-1947.............DLB-160
Logan, Deborah Norris 1761-1839 ......DLB-200
Logan, James 1674-1751............DLB-24, 140
Logan, John 1923-1987 ....DLB-5
Logan, Martha Daniell 1704?-1779 ......DLB-200
Logan, William 1950- DLB-120
Logau, Friedrich von 1605-1655 ....DLB-164
Logue, Christopher 1926- DLB-27
Lohenstein, Daniel Casper von
  1635-1683 ....DLB-168
Lo-Johansson, Ivar 1901-1990 ....DLB-259
Lokert, George (or Lockhart)
  circa 1485-1547 ....DLB-281
Lomonosov, Mikhail Vasil'evich
  1711-1765.....................DLB-150
London, Jack
  1876-1916 .....DLB-8, 12, 78, 212; CDALB-3
  The Jack London Research Center...... Y-00
  The Jack London Society Y-99
The London Magazine 1820-1829 ....DLB-110
Long, David 1948- DLB-244
Long, H., and Brother DLB-49
Long, Haniel 1888-1956 ....DLB-45
Long, Ray 1878-1935.................DLB-137
Longfellow, Henry Wadsworth
  1807-1882 ....DLB-1, 59, 235; CDALB-2
Longfellow, Samuel 1819-1892 ....DLB-1
Longford, Elizabeth 1906-2002 ....DLB-155
  Tribute to Alfred A. Knopf............ Y-84
Longinus circa first century DLB-176
Longley, Michael 1939- DLB-40
T. Longman [publishing house].........DLB-154
Longmans, Green and Company DLB-49
Longmore, George 1793?-1867 ....DLB-99
Longstreet, Augustus Baldwin
  1790-1870 .... DLB-3, 11, 74, 248
D. Longworth [publishing house] DLB-49
Lønn, Øystein 1936- DLB-297
Lonsdale, Frederick 1881-1954 ....DLB-10
Loos, Anita 1893-1981..... DLB-11, 26, 228; Y-81
Lopate, Phillip 1943- Y-80
Lope de Rueda 1510?-1565? DLB-318
Lopes, Fernão 1380/1390?-1460?........DLB-287
Lopez, Barry 1945- DLB-256, 275
López, Diana (see Isabella, Ríos)
López, Josefina 1969- DLB-209
López de Mendoza, Íñigo
  (see Santillana, Marqués de)
López Velarde, Ramón 1888-1921 ......DLB-290
Loranger, Jean-Aubert 1896-1942 ....DLB-92
Lorca, Federico García 1898-1936.......DLB-108
Lord, John Keast 1818-1872 ....DLB-99
Lorde, Audre 1934-1992 ....DLB-41

Lorimer, George Horace 1867-1937.......DLB-91
A. K. Loring [publishing house]..........DLB-49
Loring and Mussey DLB-46
Lorris, Guillaume de (see *Roman de la Rose*)
Lossing, Benson J. 1813-1891 ....DLB-30
Lothar, Ernst 1890-1974 ....DLB-81
D. Lothrop and Company..............DLB-49
Lothrop, Harriet M. 1844-1924..........DLB-42
Loti, Pierre 1850-1923................DLB-123
Lotichius Secundus, Petrus 1528-1560 ... DLB-179
Lott, Emmeline fl. nineteenth century DLB-166
Louisiana State University Press Y-97
Lounsbury, Thomas R. 1838-1915 ....DLB-71
Louÿs, Pierre 1870-1925 ....DLB-123
Løveid, Cecile 1951- DLB-297
Lovejoy, Arthur O. 1873-1962 ....DLB-270
Lovelace, Earl 1935- DLB-125; CDWLB-3
Lovelace, Richard 1618-1657...........DLB-131
John W. Lovell Company DLB-49
Lovell, Coryell and Company...........DLB-49
Lover, Samuel 1797-1868..........DLB-159, 190
Lovesey, Peter 1936- DLB-87
  Tribute to Georges Simenon........... Y-89
Lovinescu, Eugen
  1881-1943 .... DLB-220; CDWLB-4
Lovingood, Sut
  (see Harris, George Washington)
Low, Samuel 1765-? DLB-37
Lowell, Amy 1874-1925..............DLB-54, 140
Lowell, James Russell 1819-1891
  ...... DLB-1, 11, 64, 79, 189, 235; CDALB-2
Lowell, Robert
  1917-1977.............DLB-5, 169; CDALB-7
Lowenfels, Walter 1897-1976.............DLB-4
Lowndes, Marie Belloc 1868-1947........DLB-70
Lowndes, William Thomas 1798-1843 ... DLB-184
Humphrey Lownes [publishing house] ... DLB-170
Lowry, Lois 1937- DLB-52
Lowry, Malcolm 1909-1957....DLB-15; CDBLB-7
Lowther, Pat 1935-1975...............DLB-53
Loy, Mina 1882-1966.................DLB-4, 54
Loynaz, Dulce María 1902-1997 ....DLB-283
Lozeau, Albert 1878-1924 ....DLB-92
Lubbock, Percy 1879-1965 ....DLB-149
Lucan A.D. 39-A.D. 65 ....DLB-211
Lucas, E. V. 1868-1938 .... DLB-98, 149, 153
Fielding Lucas Jr. [publishing house] DLB-49
Luce, Clare Booth 1903-1987 ....DLB-228
Luce, Henry R. 1898-1967 ....DLB-91
John W. Luce and Company............DLB-46
Lucena, Juan de ca. 1430-1501 ....DLB-286
Lucian circa 120-180 ....DLB-176
Lucie-Smith, Edward 1933- DLB-40
Lucilius circa 180 B.C.-102/101 B.C.......DLB-211
Lucini, Gian Pietro 1867-1914 ....DLB-114

Cumulative Index

Luco Cruchaga, Germán 1894-1936 .... DLB-305
Lucretius circa 94 B.C.-circa 49 B.C.
.... DLB-211; CDWLB-1
Luder, Peter circa 1415-1472 .... DLB-179
Ludlam, Charles 1943-1987 .... DLB-266
Ludlum, Robert 1927-2001............. Y-82
Ludus de Antichristo circa 1160 .... DLB-148
Ludvigson, Susan 1942- DLB-120
Ludwig, Jack 1922- DLB-60
Ludwig, Otto 1813-1865............... DLB-129
Ludwigslied 881 or 882............... DLB-148
Luera, Yolanda 1953- DLB-122
Luft, Lya 1938- DLB-145
Lugansky, Kazak Vladimir
 (see Dal', Vladimir Ivanovich)
Lugn, Kristina 1948- DLB-257
Lugones, Leopoldo 1874-1938 .... DLB-283
Luhan, Mabel Dodge 1879-1962 .... DLB-303
Lukács, Georg (see Lukács, György)
Lukács, György
 1885-1971....... DLB-215, 242; CDWLB-4
Luke, Peter 1919-1995 .... DLB-13
Lummis, Charles F. 1859-1928.......... DLB-186
Lundkvist, Artur 1906-1991 .... DLB-259
Lunts, Lev Natanovich
 1901-1924 .... DLB-272
F. M. Lupton Company DLB-49
Lupus of Ferrières
 circa 805-circa 862 .... DLB-148
Lurie, Alison 1926- DLB-2
Lussu, Emilio 1890-1975............... DLB-264
Lustig, Arnošt 1926- DLB-232, 299
Luther, Martin
 1483-1546 .... DLB-179; CDWLB-2
Luzi, Mario 1914-2005 .... DLB-128
L'vov, Nikolai Aleksandrovich
 1751-1803 .... DLB-150
Lyall, Gavin 1932-2003 .... DLB-87
Lydgate, John circa 1370-1450 .... DLB-146
Lyly, John circa 1554-1606.......... DLB-62, 167
Lynch, Martin 1950- DLB-310
Lynch, Patricia 1898-1972 .... DLB-160
Lynch, Richard fl. 1596-1601 .... DLB-172
Lynd, Robert 1879-1949.............. DLB-98
Lynds, Dennis (Michael Collins)
 1924- DLB-306
 Tribute to John D. MacDonald Y-86
 Tribute to Kenneth Millar Y-83
 Why I Write Mysteries: Night and Day .. Y-85
Lyon, Matthew 1749-1822 .... DLB-43
Lyotard, Jean-François 1924-1998 ...... DLB-242
Lyricists
 Additional Lyricists: 1920-1960..... DLB-265
Lysias circa 459 B.C.-circa 380 B.C........DLB-176
Lytle, Andrew 1902-1995 ..... DLB-6; Y-95
 Tribute to Caroline Gordon Y-81
 Tribute to Katherine Anne Porter Y-80

Lytton, Edward
 (see Bulwer-Lytton, Edward)
Lytton, Edward Robert Bulwer
 1831-1891 .... DLB-32

M

Maass, Joachim 1901-1972 .... DLB-69
Mabie, Hamilton Wright 1845-1916 ..... DLB-71
Mac A'Ghobhainn, Iain (see Smith, Iain Crichton)
MacArthur, Charles 1895-1956 .....DLB-7, 25, 44
Macaulay, Catherine 1731-1791 .... DLB-104
Macaulay, David 1945- DLB-61
Macaulay, Rose 1881-1958............ DLB-36
Macaulay, Thomas Babington
 1800-1859 .... DLB-32, 55; CDBLB-4
Macaulay Company.................. DLB-46
MacBeth, George 1932-1992 .... DLB-40
Macbeth, Madge 1880-1965............ DLB-92
MacCaig, Norman 1910-1996 .... DLB-27
MacDiarmid, Hugh
 1892-1978............... DLB-20; CDBLB-7
MacDonald, Cynthia 1928- DLB-105
MacDonald, George 1824-1905.... DLB-18, 163, 178
MacDonald, John D.
 1916-1986 ....DLB-8, 306; Y-86
MacDonald, Philip 1899?-1980 .... DLB-77
Macdonald, Ross (see Millar, Kenneth)
Macdonald, Sharman 1951- DLB-245
MacDonald, Wilson 1880-1967 .... DLB-92
Macdonald and Company (Publishers) .. DLB-112
MacEwen, Gwendolyn 1941-1987 ... DLB-53, 251
Macfadden, Bernarr 1868-1955 ...... DLB-25, 91
MacGregor, John 1825-1892 .... DLB-166
MacGregor, Mary Esther (see Keith, Marian)
Macherey, Pierre 1938- DLB-296
Machado, Antonio 1875-1939.......... DLB-108
Machado, Manuel 1874-1947 .... DLB-108
Machado de Assis, Joaquim Maria
 1839-1908 .... DLB-307
Machar, Agnes Maule 1837-1927 .... DLB-92
Machaut, Guillaume de
 circa 1300-1377 .... DLB-208
Machen, Arthur Llewelyn Jones
 1863-1947................DLB-36, 156, 178
MacIlmaine, Roland fl. 1574............ DLB-281
MacInnes, Colin 1914-1976 .... DLB-14
MacInnes, Helen 1907-1985 .... DLB-87
Mac Intyre, Tom 1931- DLB-245
Mačiulis, Jonas (see Maironis, Jonas)
Mack, Maynard 1909-2001 .... DLB-111
Mackall, Leonard L. 1879-1937 .... DLB-140
MacKay, Isabel Ecclestone 1875-1928 .... DLB-92
Mackay, Shena 1944- DLB-231, 319
MacKaye, Percy 1875-1956 .... DLB-54
Macken, Walter 1915-1967 .... DLB-13
MacKenna, John 1952- DLB-319
Mackenzie, Alexander 1763-1820 .... DLB-99

Mackenzie, Alexander Slidell
 1803-1848 .... DLB-183
Mackenzie, Compton 1883-1972 .....DLB-34, 100
Mackenzie, Henry 1745-1831.......... DLB-39
 The Lounger, no. 20 (1785) DLB-39
Mackenzie, Kenneth (Seaforth Mackenzie)
 1913-1955 .... DLB-260
Mackenzie, William 1758-1828.........DLB-187
Mackey, Nathaniel 1947- DLB-169
Mackey, William Wellington 1937- DLB-38
Mackintosh, Elizabeth (see Tey, Josephine)
Mackintosh, Sir James 1765-1832 ...... DLB-158
Macklin, Charles 1699-1797 .... DLB-89
Maclaren, Ian (see Watson, John)
Maclaren-Ross, Julian 1912-1964 .... DLB-319
MacLaverty, Bernard 1942- DLB-267
MacLean, Alistair 1922-1987 ....DLB-276
MacLean, Katherine Anne 1925- DLB-8
Maclean, Norman 1902-1990.......... DLB-206
MacLeish, Archibald 1892-1982
 ....DLB-4, 7, 45; Y-82; DS-15; CDALB-7
MacLennan, Hugh 1907-1990 .... DLB-68
MacLeod, Alistair 1936- DLB-60
Macleod, Fiona (see Sharp, William)
Macleod, Norman 1906-1985 .... DLB-4
Mac Low, Jackson 1922-2004.......... DLB-193
MacMahon, Bryan 1909-1998 .... DLB-319
Macmillan and Company............ DLB-106
The Macmillan Company DLB-49
Macmillan's English Men of Letters,
 First Series (1878-1892) DLB-144
MacNamara, Brinsley 1890-1963........ DLB-10
MacNeice, Louis 1907-1963 .... DLB-10, 20
Macphail, Andrew 1864-1938 .... DLB-92
Macpherson, James 1736-1796 .... DLB-109
Macpherson, Jay 1931- DLB-53
Macpherson, Jeanie 1884-1946.......... DLB-44
Macrae Smith Company............. DLB-46
MacRaye, Lucy Betty (see Webling, Lucy)
John Macrone [publishing house] DLB-106
MacShane, Frank 1927-1999........... DLB-111
Macy-Masius DLB-46
Madden, David 1933- DLB-6
Madden, Sir Frederic 1801-1873........ DLB-184
Maddow, Ben 1909-1992 .... DLB-44
Maddux, Rachel 1912-1983 ....DLB-234; Y-93
Madgett, Naomi Long 1923- DLB-76
Madhubuti, Haki R. 1942- DLB-5, 41; DS-8
Madison, James 1751-1836............. DLB-37
Madsen, Svend Åge 1939- DLB-214
Madrigal, Alfonso Fernández de (El Tostado)
 ca. 1405-1455................... DLB-286
Maeterlinck, Maurice 1862-1949 .... DLB-192
Mafūz, Najīb 1911- Y-88
 Nobel Lecture 1988 .... Y-88

The Little Magazines of the
    New Formalism..................DLB-282
Magee, David 1905-1977..............DLB-187
Maginn, William 1794-1842.......DLB-110, 159
Magoffin, Susan Shelby 1827-1855......DLB-239
Mahan, Alfred Thayer 1840-1914........DLB-47
Maheux-Forcier, Louise 1929-.........DLB-60
Mahin, John Lee 1902-1984............DLB-44
Mahon, Derek 1941-...................DLB-40
Maiakovsky, Vladimir Vladimirovich
    1893-1930........................DLB-295
Maikov, Apollon Nikolaevich
    1821-1897........................DLB-277
Maikov, Vasilii Ivanovich 1728-1778.....DLB-150
Mailer, Norman 1923-
    ......DLB-2, 16, 28, 185, 278; Y-80, 83, 97;
    DS-3; CDALB-6
    Tribute to Isaac Bashevis Singer........Y-91
    Tribute to Meyer Levin..............Y-81
Maillart, Ella 1903-1997.............DLB-195
Maillet, Adrienne 1885-1963..........DLB-68
Maillet, Antonine 1929-.............DLB-60
Maillu, David G. 1939-..............DLB-157
Maimonides, Moses 1138-1204.........DLB-115
Main Selections of the Book-of-the-Month
    Club, 1926-1945....................DLB-9
Mainwaring, Daniel 1902-1977.........DLB-44
Mair, Charles 1838-1927..............DLB-99
Mair, John circa 1467-1550...........DLB-281
Maironis, Jonas 1862-1932..DLB-220; CDWLB-4
Mais, Roger 1905-1955.....DLB-125; CDWLB-3
Maitland, Sara 1950-................DLB-271
Major, Andre 1942-..................DLB-60
Major, Charles 1856-1913............DLB-202
Major, Clarence 1936-...............DLB-33
Major, Kevin 1949-..................DLB-60
Major Books.........................DLB-46
Makanin, Vladimir Semenovich
    1937-............................DLB-285
Makarenko, Anton Semenovich
    1888-1939........................DLB-272
Makemie, Francis circa 1658-1708.....DLB-24
The Making of Americans Contract.........Y-98
Makovsky, Sergei 1877-1962..........DLB-317
Maksimov, Vladimir Emel'ianovich
    1930-1995........................DLB-302
Maksimović, Desanka
    1898-1993...........DLB-147; CDWLB-4
Malamud, Bernard 1914-1986
    ....DLB-2, 28, 152; Y-80, 86; CDALB-1
    Bernard Malamud Archive at the
        Harry Ransom Humanities
        Research Center..............Y-00
Mălăncioiu, Ileana 1940-............DLB-232
Malaparte, Curzio
    (Kurt Erich Suckert) 1898-1957.....DLB-264
Malerba, Luigi 1927-................DLB-196
Malet, Lucas 1852-1931..............DLB-153
Mallarmé, Stéphane 1842-1898........DLB-217

Malleson, Lucy Beatrice (see Gilbert, Anthony)
Mallet-Joris, Françoise (Françoise Lilar)
    1930-.............................DLB-83
Mallock, W. H. 1849-1923.........DLB-18, 57
    "Every Man His Own Poet; or,
        The Inspired Singer's Recipe
        Book" (1877)..................DLB-35
    "Le Style c'est l'homme" (1892)......DLB-57
    Memoirs of Life and Literature (1920),
        [excerpt].....................DLB-57
Malone, Dumas 1892-1986............DLB-17
Malone, Edmond 1741-1812..........DLB-142
Malory, Sir Thomas
    circa 1400-1410 - 1471....DLB-146; CDBLB-1
Malouf, David 1934-.................DLB-289
Malpede, Karen 1945-................DLB-249
Malraux, André 1901-1976............DLB-72
The Maltese Falcon (Documentary)........DLB-280
Malthus, Thomas Robert
    1766-1834...................DLB-107, 158
Maltz, Albert 1908-1985.............DLB-102
Malzberg, Barry N. 1939-............DLB-8
Mamet, David 1947-..................DLB-7
Mamin, Dmitrii Narkisovich
    1852-1912........................DLB-238
Manaka, Matsemela 1956-............DLB-157
Manchester University Press.........DLB-112
Mandel, Eli 1922-1992................DLB-53
Mandel'shtam, Nadezhda Iakovlevna
    1899-1980........................DLB-302
Mandel'shtam, Osip Emil'evich
    1891-1938........................DLB-295
Mandeville, Bernard 1670-1733.......DLB-101
Mandeville, Sir John
    mid fourteenth century...........DLB-146
Mandiargues, André Pieyre de
    1909-1991.........................DLB-83
Manea, Norman 1936-................DLB-232
Manfred, Frederick 1912-1994....DLB-6, 212, 227
Manfredi, Gianfranco 1948-..........DLB-196
Mangan, Sherry 1904-1961............DLB-4
Manganelli, Giorgio 1922-1990.......DLB-196
Manilius fl. first century A.D........DLB-211
Mankiewicz, Herman 1897-1953........DLB-26
Mankiewicz, Joseph L. 1909-1993.....DLB-44
Mankowitz, Wolf 1924-1998...........DLB-15
Manley, Delarivière 1672?-1724......DLB-39, 80
    Preface to *The Secret History, of Queen
        Zarah, and the Zarazians* (1705).....DLB-39
Mann, Abby 1927-....................DLB-44
Mann, Charles 1929-1998..............Y-98
Mann, Emily 1952-...................DLB-266
Mann, Heinrich 1871-1950........DLB-66, 118
Mann, Horace 1796-1859............DLB-1, 235
Mann, Klaus 1906-1949...............DLB-56
Mann, Mary Peabody 1806-1887......DLB-239
Mann, Thomas 1875-1955....DLB-66; CDWLB-2
Mann, William D'Alton 1839-1920.....DLB-137

Mannin, Ethel 1900-1984.........DLB-191, 195
Manning, Emily (see Australie)
Manning, Frederic 1882-1935.........DLB-260
Manning, Laurence 1899-1972.........DLB-251
Manning, Marie 1873?-1945............DLB-29
Manning and Loring..................DLB-49
Mannyng, Robert fl.
    1303-1338........................DLB-146
Mano, D. Keith 1942-.................DLB-6
Manor Books........................DLB-46
Manrique, Gómez 1412?-1490.........DLB-286
Manrique, Jorge ca. 1440-1479......DLB-286
Mansfield, Katherine 1888-1923......DLB-162
Mantel, Hilary 1952-................DLB-271
Manuel, Niklaus circa 1484-1530.....DLB-179
Manzini, Gianna 1896-1974...........DLB-177
Mapanje, Jack 1944-.................DLB-157
Maraini, Dacia 1936-................DLB-196
Maraise, Marie-Catherine-Renée Darcel de
    1737-1822........................DLB-314
Maramzin, Vladimir Rafailovich
    1934-............................DLB-302
March, William (William Edward Campbell)
    1893-1954..............DLB-9, 86, 316
Marchand, Leslie A. 1900-1999.......DLB-103
Marchant, Bessie 1862-1941..........DLB-160
Marchant, Tony 1959-................DLB-245
Marchenko, Anastasiia Iakovlevna
    1830-1880........................DLB-238
Marchessault, Jovette 1938-.........DLB-60
Marcinkevičius, Justinas 1930-.......DLB-232
Marcos, Plínio (Plínio Marcos de Barros)
    1935-1999........................DLB-307
Marcus, Frank 1928-.................DLB-13
Marcuse, Herbert 1898-1979..........DLB-242
Marden, Orison Swett 1850-1924......DLB-137
Marechera, Dambudzo 1952-1987......DLB-157
Marek, Richard, Books...............DLB-46
Mares, E. A. 1938-..................DLB-122
Margulies, Donald 1954-.............DLB-228
Mariana, Juan de 1535 or 1536-1624....DLB-318
Mariani, Paul 1940-.................DLB-111
Marie de France fl. 1160-1178.......DLB-208
Marie-Victorin, Frère (Conrad Kirouac)
    1885-1944.........................DLB-92
Marin, Biagio 1891-1985.............DLB-128
Marinetti, Filippo Tommaso
    1876-1944.....................DLB-114, 264
Marinina, Aleksandra (Marina Anatol'evna
    Alekseeva) 1957-................DLB-285
Marinković, Ranko
    1913-2001............DLB-147; CDWLB-4
Marion, Frances 1886-1973...........DLB-44
Marius, Richard C. 1933-1999.........Y-85
Marivaux, Pierre Carlet de Chamblain de
    1688-1763........................DLB-314
Markevich, Boleslav Mikhailovich
    1822-1884........................DLB-238

Markfield, Wallace 1926-2002 . . . . DLB-2, 28
Markham, E. A. 1939- DLB-319
Markham, Edwin 1852-1940 . . . . DLB-54, 186
Markish, David 1938- DLB-317
Markle, Fletcher 1921-1991 . . . . DLB-68; Y-91
Marlatt, Daphne 1942- DLB-60
Marlitt, E. 1825-1887 . . . . DLB-129
Marlowe, Christopher
  1564-1593 . . . . DLB-62; CDBLB-1
Marlyn, John 1912-1985 . . . . DLB-88
Marmion, Shakerley 1603-1639 . . . . DLB-58
Marmontel, Jean-François 1723-1799 . . . . DLB-314
Der Marner before 1230-circa 1287 . . . . . DLB-138
Marnham, Patrick 1943- DLB-204
The *Marprelate Tracts* 1588-1589 . . . . DLB-132
Marquand, John P. 1893-1960 . . . . DLB-9, 102
Marques, Helena 1935- DLB-287
Marqués, René 1919-1979 . . . . DLB-113, 305
Marquis, Don 1878-1937 . . . . DLB-11, 25
Marriott, Anne 1913-1997 . . . . DLB-68
Marryat, Frederick 1792-1848 . . . . DLB-21, 163
Marsh, Capen, Lyon and Webb DLB-49
Marsh, George Perkins
  1801-1882 . . . . DLB-1, 64, 243
Marsh, James 1794-1842 . . . . DLB-1, 59
Marsh, Narcissus 1638-1713 . . . . DLB-213
Marsh, Ngaio 1899-1982 . . . . DLB-77
Marshall, Alan 1902-1984 . . . . DLB-260
Marshall, Edison 1894-1967 . . . . DLB-102
Marshall, Edward 1932- DLB-16
Marshall, Emma 1828-1899 . . . . DLB-163
Marshall, James 1942-1992 . . . . DLB-61
Marshall, Joyce 1913- DLB-88
Marshall, Paule 1929- DLB-33, 157, 227
Marshall, Tom 1938-1993 . . . . DLB-60
Marsilius of Padua
  circa 1275-circa 1342 . . . . DLB-115
Mars-Jones, Adam 1954- DLB-207, 319
Marson, Una 1905-1965 . . . . DLB-157
Marston, John 1576-1634 . . . . DLB-58, 172
Marston, Philip Bourke 1850-1887 . . . . . . DLB-35
Martens, Kurt 1870-1945 . . . . DLB-66
Martí, José 1853-1895 . . . . DLB-290
Martial circa A.D. 40-circa A.D. 103
  . . . . DLB-211; CDWLB-1
William S. Martien [publishing house] DLB-49
Martin, Abe (see Hubbard, Kin)
Martin, Catherine ca. 1847-1937 . . . . DLB-230
Martin, Charles 1942- DLB-120, 282
Martin, Claire 1914- DLB-60
Martin, David 1915-1997 . . . . DLB-260
Martin, Jay 1935- DLB-111
Martin, Johann (see Laurentius von Schnüffis)
Martin, Thomas 1696-1771 . . . . DLB-213
Martin, Violet Florence (see Ross, Martin)

Martin du Gard, Roger 1881-1958 . . . . DLB-65
Martineau, Harriet
  1802-1876 . . . . . DLB-21, 55, 159, 163, 166, 190
Martínez, Demetria 1960- DLB-209
Martínez de Toledo, Alfonso
  1398?-1468 . . . . DLB-286
Martínez, Eliud 1935- DLB-122
Martínez, Max 1943- DLB-82
Martínez, Rubén 1962- DLB-209
Martinson, Harry 1904-1978 . . . . DLB-259
Martinson, Moa 1890-1964 . . . . DLB-259
Martone, Michael 1955- DLB-218
Martyn, Edward 1859-1923 . . . . DLB-10
Marvell, Andrew
  1621-1678 . . . . DLB-131; CDBLB-2
Marvin X 1944- DLB-38
Marx, Karl 1818-1883 . . . . DLB-129
Marzials, Theo 1850-1920 . . . . DLB-35
Masefield, John 1878-1967
  . . . . DLB-10, 19, 153, 160; CDBLB-5
Masham, Damaris Cudworth, Lady
  1659-1708 . . . . DLB-252
Masino, Paola 1908-1989 . . . . DLB-264
Mason, A. E. W. 1865-1948 . . . . DLB-70
Mason, Bobbie Ann
  1940- DLB-173; Y-87; CDALB-7
Mason, F. van Wyck (Geoffrey Coffin, Frank W.
  Mason, Ward Weaver) 1901-1978 . . . DLB-306
Mason, William 1725-1797 . . . . DLB-142
Mason Brothers DLB-49
The *Massachusetts Quarterly Review*
  1847-1850 . . . . DLB-1
The *Masses* DLB-303
Massey, Gerald 1828-1907 . . . . DLB-32
Massey, Linton R. 1900-1974 . . . . DLB-187
Massie, Allan 1938- DLB-271
Massinger, Philip 1583-1640 . . . . DLB-58
Masson, David 1822-1907 . . . . DLB-144
Masters, Edgar Lee
  1868-1950 . . . . DLB-54; CDALB-3
Masters, Hilary 1928- DLB-244
Mastronardi, Lucio 1930-1979 . . . . DLB-177
Mat' Maria (Elizaveta Kuz'mina-Karavdeva
  Skobtsova, née Pilenko) 1891-1945 . . . . DLB-317
Matevski, Mateja 1929- . . . DLB-181; CDWLB-4
Mather, Cotton
  1663-1728 . . . . DLB-24, 30, 140; CDALB-2
Mather, Increase 1639-1723 . . . . DLB-24
Mather, Richard 1596-1669 . . . . DLB-24
Matheson, Annie 1853-1924 . . . . DLB-240
Matheson, Richard 1926- DLB-8, 44
Matheus, John F. 1887-1986 . . . . DLB-51
Mathews, Aidan 1956- DLB-319
Mathews, Cornelius 1817?-1889 . . . DLB-3, 64, 250
Elkin Mathews [publishing house] DLB-112
Mathews, John Joseph 1894-1979 . . . . DLB-175
Mathias, Roland 1915- DLB-27
Mathis, June 1892-1927 . . . . DLB-44

Mathis, Sharon Bell 1937- DLB-33
Matković, Marijan 1915-1985 . . . . DLB-181
Matoš, Antun Gustav 1873-1914 . . . . DLB-147
Matos Paoli, Francisco 1915-2000 . . . . . . DLB-290
Matsumoto Seichō 1909-1992 . . . . DLB-182
The Matter of England 1240-1400 . . . . . . DLB-146
The Matter of Rome early twelfth to late
  fifteenth century DLB-146
Matthew of Vendôme
  circa 1130-circa 1200 . . . . DLB-208
Matthews, Brander 1852-1929 . . DLB-71, 78; DS-13
Matthews, Jack 1925- DLB-6
Matthews, Victoria Earle 1861-1907 . . . . DLB-221
Matthews, William 1942-1997 . . . . DLB-5
Matthías Jochumsson 1835-1920 . . . . DLB-293
Matthías Johannessen 1930- DLB-293
Matthiessen, F. O. 1902-1950 . . . . DLB-63
Matthiessen, Peter 1927- DLB-6, 173, 275
Maturin, Charles Robert 1780-1824 . . . . . DLB-178
Maugham, W. Somerset 1874-1965
  . . . . . DLB-10, 36, 77, 100, 162, 195; CDBLB-6
Maupassant, Guy de 1850-1893 . . . . DLB-123
Maupertuis, Pierre-Louis Moreau de
  1698-1759 . . . . DLB-314
Maupin, Armistead 1944- DLB-278
Mauriac, Claude 1914-1996 . . . . DLB-83
Mauriac, François 1885-1970 . . . . DLB-65
Maurice, Frederick Denison 1805-1872 . . . DLB-55
Maurois, André 1885-1967 . . . . DLB-65
Maury, James 1718-1769 . . . . DLB-31
Mavor, Elizabeth 1927- DLB-14
Mavor, Osborne Henry (see Bridie, James)
Maxwell, Gavin 1914-1969 . . . . DLB-204
Maxwell, William
  1908-2000 . . . . DLB-218, 278; Y-80
  Tribute to Nancy Hale Y-88
H. Maxwell [publishing house] DLB-49
John Maxwell [publishing house] DLB-106
May, Elaine 1932- DLB-44
May, Karl 1842-1912 . . . . DLB-129
May, Thomas 1595/1596-1650 . . . . DLB-58
Mayer, Bernadette 1945- DLB-165
Mayer, Mercer 1943- DLB-61
Mayer, O. B. 1818-1891 . . . . DLB-3, 248
Mayes, Herbert R. 1900-1987 . . . . DLB-137
Mayes, Wendell 1919-1992 . . . . DLB-26
Mayfield, Julian 1928-1984 . . . . DLB-33; Y-84
Mayhew, Henry 1812-1887 . . . . DLB-18, 55, 190
Mayhew, Jonathan 1720-1766 . . . . DLB-31
Mayne, Ethel Colburn 1865-1941 . . . . . . DLB-197
Mayne, Jasper 1604-1672 . . . . DLB-126
Mayne, Seymour 1944- DLB-60
Mayor, Flora Macdonald 1872-1932 . . . . . DLB-36
Mayröcker, Friederike 1924- DLB-85
Mazrui, Ali A. 1933- DLB-125
Mažuranić, Ivan 1814-1890 . . . . DLB-147

Mazursky, Paul 1930- DLB-44
McAlmon, Robert 1896-1956 ...DLB-4, 45; DS-15
    "A Night at Bricktop's" Y-01
McArthur, Peter 1866-1924..............DLB-92
McAuley, James 1917-1976................DLB-260
Robert M. McBride and Company DLB-46
McCabe, Patrick 1955- DLB-194
McCafferty, Owen 1961- DLB-310
McCaffrey, Anne 1926- DLB-8
McCann, Colum 1965- DLB-267
McCarthy, Cormac 1933- DLB-6, 143, 256
    The Cormac McCarthy Society Y-99
McCarthy, Mary 1912-1989 ....DLB-2; Y-81
McCarthy, Shaun Lloyd (see Cory, Desmond)
McCay, Winsor 1871-1934 ....DLB-22
McClane, Albert Jules 1922-1991 ....DLB-171
McClatchy, C. K. 1858-1936..............DLB-25
McClellan, George Marion 1860-1934 ....DLB-50
    "The Negro as a Writer"............DLB-50
McCloskey, Robert 1914-2003 ....DLB-22
McCloy, Helen 1904-1992................DLB-306
McClung, Nellie Letitia 1873-1951 ....DLB-92
McClure, James 1939- DLB-276
McClure, Joanna 1930- DLB-16
McClure, Michael 1932- DLB-16
McClure, Phillips and Company DLB-46
McClure, S. S. 1857-1949.................DLB-91
A. C. McClurg and Company............DLB-49
McCluskey, John A., Jr. 1944- DLB-33
McCollum, Michael A. 1946- Y-87
McConnell, William C. 1917- DLB-88
McCord, David 1897-1997................DLB-61
McCord, Louisa S. 1810-1879 ....DLB-248
McCorkle, Jill 1958- DLB-234; Y-87
McCorkle, Samuel Eusebius 1746-1811....DLB-37
McCormick, Anne O'Hare 1880-1954 ....DLB-29
McCormick, Kenneth Dale 1906-1997 ...... Y-97
McCormick, Robert R. 1880-1955 ....DLB-29
McCourt, Edward 1907-1972.............DLB-88
McCoy, Horace 1897-1955 ....DLB-9
McCrae, Hugh 1876-1958 ....DLB-260
McCrae, John 1872-1918 ....DLB-92
McCrumb, Sharyn 1948- DLB-306
McCullagh, Joseph B. 1842-1896.........DLB-23
McCullers, Carson
    1917-1967 ..... DLB-2, 7, 173, 228; CDALB-1
McCulloch, Thomas 1776-1843 ....DLB-99
McCunn, Ruthanne Lum 1946- DLB-312
McDermott, Alice 1953- DLB-292
McDonald, Forrest 1927- DLB-17
McDonald, Walter 1934- DLB-105, DS-9
    "Getting Started: Accepting the
    Regions You Own—or Which
    Own You" DLB-105
    Tribute to James Dickey Y-97

McDougall, Colin 1917-1984............DLB-68
McDowell, Katharine Sherwood Bonner
    1849-1883 ....DLB-202, 239
Obolensky McDowell
    [publishing house] DLB-46
McEwan, Ian 1948- DLB-14, 194, 319
McFadden, David 1940- DLB-60
McFall, Frances Elizabeth Clarke
    (see Grand, Sarah)
McFarland, Ron 1942- DLB-256
McFarlane, Leslie 1902-1977 ....DLB-88
McFee, William 1881-1966 ....DLB-153
McGahern, John 1934- DLB-14, 231, 319
McGee, Thomas D'Arcy 1825-1868 ......DLB-99
McGeehan, W. O. 1879-1933 ...... DLB-25, 171
McGill, Ralph 1898-1969................DLB-29
McGinley, Phyllis 1905-1978 ....DLB-11, 48
McGinniss, Joe 1942- DLB-185
McGirt, James E. 1874-1930 ....DLB-50
McGlashan and Gill.................DLB-106
McGough, Roger 1937- DLB-40
McGrath, John 1935- DLB-233
McGrath, Patrick 1950- DLB-231
McGraw-Hill.....................DLB-46
McGuane, Thomas 1939- DLB-2, 212; Y-80
    Tribute to Seymour Lawrence Y-94
McGuckian, Medbh 1950- DLB-40
McGuffey, William Holmes 1800-1873 ....DLB-42
McGuinness, Frank 1953- DLB-245
McHenry, James 1785-1845 ....DLB-202
McIlvanney, William 1936- DLB-14, 207
McIlwraith, Jean Newton 1859-1938......DLB-92
McInerney, Jay 1955- DLB-292
McInerny, Ralph 1929- DLB-306
McIntosh, Maria Jane 1803-1878....DLB-239, 248
McIntyre, James 1827-1906 ....DLB-99
McIntyre, O. O. 1884-1938 ....DLB-25
McKay, Claude 1889-1948 .... DLB-4, 45, 51, 117
The David McKay Company DLB-49
McKean, William V. 1820-1903 ....DLB-23
McKenna, Stephen 1888-1967..........DLB-197
The McKenzie Trust.................. Y-96
McKerrow, R. B. 1872-1940 ....DLB-201
McKinley, Robin 1952- DLB-52
McKnight, Reginald 1956- DLB-234
McLachlan, Alexander 1818-1896........DLB-99
McLaren, Floris Clark 1904-1978 ....DLB-68
McLaverty, Michael 1907-1992 ....DLB-15
McLean, Duncan 1964- DLB-267
McLean, John R. 1848-1916 ....DLB-23
McLean, William L. 1852-1931 ....DLB-25
McLennan, William 1856-1904 ....DLB-92
McLoughlin Brothers..................DLB-49
McLuhan, Marshall 1911-1980 ....DLB-88
McMaster, John Bach 1852-1932.........DLB-47

McMillan, Terri 1951- DLB-292
McMurtry, Larry 1936-
    .... DLB-2, 143, 256; Y-80, 87; CDALB-6
McNally, Terrence 1939- DLB-7, 249
McNeil, Florence 1937- DLB-60
McNeile, Herman Cyril 1888-1937 ....DLB-77
McNickle, D'Arcy 1904-1977 ...... DLB-175, 212
McPhee, John 1931- DLB-185, 275
McPherson, James Alan 1943- DLB-38, 244
McPherson, Sandra 1943- Y-86
McTaggart, J. M. E. 1866-1925.........DLB-262
McWhirter, George 1939- DLB-60
McWilliam, Candia 1955- DLB-267
McWilliams, Carey 1905-1980 ....DLB-137
    "*The Nation's* Future," Carey
    McWilliams's Editorial Policy
    in *Nation* DLB-137
Mda, Zakes 1948- DLB-225
Mead, George Herbert 1863-1931.......DLB-270
Mead, L. T. 1844-1914 ....DLB-141
Mead, Matthew 1924- DLB-40
Mead, Taylor circa 1931- DLB-16
Meany, Tom 1903-1964 ....DLB-171
Mechthild von Magdeburg
    circa 1207-circa 1282 ....DLB-138
Medieval Galician-Portuguese Poetry DLB-287
Medill, Joseph 1823-1899 ....DLB-43
Medoff, Mark 1940- DLB-7
Meek, Alexander Beaufort
    1814-1865 ....DLB-3, 248
Meeke, Mary ?-1816 ....DLB-116
Mei, Lev Aleksandrovich 1822-1862.....DLB-277
Meinke, Peter 1932- DLB-5
Meireles, Cecília 1901-1964............DLB-307
Mejía, Pedro 1497-1551 ....DLB-318
Mejia Vallejo, Manuel 1923- DLB-113
Melanchthon, Philipp 1497-1560 ....DLB-179
Melançon, Robert 1947- DLB-60
Mell, Max 1882-1971................DLB-81, 124
Mellow, James R. 1926-1997 ....DLB-111
Mel'nikov, Pavel Ivanovich 1818-1883 ...DLB-238
Meltzer, David 1937- DLB-16
Meltzer, Milton 1915- DLB-61
Melville, Elizabeth, Lady Culross
    circa 1585-1640 ....DLB-172
Melville, Herman
    1819-1891 ....DLB-3, 74, 250; CDALB-2
    The Melville Society Y-01
Melville, James
    (Roy Peter Martin) 1931- DLB-276
"Memorandum on Local Government," Anne-
    Robert-Jacques Turgot, bacon de
    l'Aulne........................DLB-314
Mena, Juan de 1411-1456 ....DLB-286
Mena, María Cristina 1893-1965....DLB-209, 221
Menander 342-341 B.C.-circa 292-291 B.C.
    .... DLB-176; CDWLB-1
Menantes (see Hunold, Christian Friedrich)

Cumulative Index

Mencke, Johann Burckhard 1674-1732... DLB-168
Mencken, H. L. 1880-1956
........DLB-11, 29, 63, 137, 222; CDALB-4
"Berlin, February, 1917" Y-00
From the Initial Issue of *American Mercury* (January 1924) DLB-137
Mencken and Nietzsche: An Unpublished Excerpt from H. L. Mencken's *My Life as Author and Editor* Y-93
Mendelssohn, Moses 1729-1786 .... DLB-97
Mendes, Catulle 1841-1909 .... DLB-217
Méndez M., Miguel 1930- DLB-82
Mendoza, Diego Hurtado de 1504-1575................... DLB-318
The Mercantile Library of New York Y-96
Mercer, Cecil William (see Yates, Dornford)
Mercer, David 1928-1980......... DLB-13, 310
Mercer, John 1704-1768 .... DLB-31
Mercer, Johnny 1909-1976 .... DLB-265
Mercier, Louis-Sébastien 1740-1814 ..... DLB-314
Le Tableau de Paris............... DLB-314
Meredith, George 1828-1909 ....DLB-18, 35, 57, 159; CDBLB-4
Meredith, Louisa Anne 1812-1895 .. DLB-166, 230
Meredith, Owen (see Lytton, Edward Robert Bulwer)
Meredith, William 1919- DLB-5
Meres, Francis
Palladis Tamia, Wits Treasurie (1598) [excerpt].................DLB-172
Merezhkovsky, Dmitrii Sergeevich 1865-1941 .... DLB-295
Mergerle, Johann Ulrich (see Abraham ä Sancta Clara)
Mérimée, Prosper 1803-1870 ...... DLB-119, 192
Merivale, John Herman 1779-1844....... DLB-96
Meriwether, Louise 1923- DLB-33
Merleau-Ponty, Maurice 1908-1961 ..... DLB-296
Merlin Press DLB-112
Merriam, Eve 1916-1992 .... DLB-61
The Merriam Company............... DLB-49
Merril, Judith 1923-1997............. DLB-251
Tribute to Theodore Sturgeon Y-85
Merrill, James 1926-1995 ....DLB-5, 165; Y-85
Merrill and Baker DLB-49
The Mershon Company.............. DLB-49
Merton, Thomas 1915-1968....... DLB-48; Y-81
Merwin, W. S. 1927- DLB-5, 169
Julian Messner [publishing house] DLB-46
Mészöly, Miklós 1921- DLB-232
J. Metcalf [publishing house]........... DLB-49
Metcalf, John 1938- DLB-60
The Methodist Book Concern DLB-49
Methuen and Company.............. DLB-112
Meun, Jean de (see *Roman de la Rose*)
Mew, Charlotte 1869-1928......... DLB-19, 135
Mewshaw, Michael 1943- Y-80

Tribute to Albert Erskine.............. Y-93
Meyer, Conrad Ferdinand 1825-1898 ... DLB-129
Meyer, E. Y. 1946- DLB-75
Meyer, Eugene 1875-1959 .... DLB-29
Meyer, Michael 1921-2000........... DLB-155
Meyers, Jeffrey 1939- DLB-111
Meynell, Alice 1847-1922 .... DLB-19, 98
Meynell, Viola 1885-1956 .... DLB-153
Meyrink, Gustav 1868-1932.......... DLB-81
Mézières, Philipe de circa 1327-1405 .... DLB-208
Michael, Ib 1945- DLB-214
Michael, Livi 1960- DLB-267
Michaëlis, Karen 1872-1950 .... DLB-214
Michaels, Anne 1958- DLB-299
Michaels, Leonard 1933-2003 .... DLB-130
Michaux, Henri 1899-1984........... DLB-258
Micheaux, Oscar 1884-1951.......... DLB-50
Michel of Northgate, Dan circa 1265-circa 1340 .... DLB-146
Micheline, Jack 1929-1998 .... DLB-16
Michener, James A. 1907?-1997 .... DLB-6
Micklejohn, George circa 1717-1818...... DLB-31
Middle Hill Press DLB-106
Middleton, Christopher 1926- DLB-40
Middleton, Richard 1882-1911........ DLB-156
Middleton, Stanley 1919- DLB-14
Middleton, Thomas 1580-1627 .... DLB-58
Miegel, Agnes 1879-1964 .... DLB-56
Mieželaitis, Eduardas 1919-1997 .... DLB-220
Miguéis, José Rodrigues 1901-1980 ..... DLB-287
Mihailović, Dragoslav 1930- DLB-181
Mihalić, Slavko 1928- DLB-181
Mikhailov, A. (see Sheller, Aleksandr Konstantinovich)
Mikhailov, Mikhail Larionovich 1829-1865 .... DLB-238
Mikhailovsky, Nikolai Konstantinovich 1842-1904 ....DLB-277
Miles, Josephine 1911-1985 .... DLB-48
Miles, Susan (Ursula Wyllie Roberts) 1888-1975................... DLB-240
Miliković, Branko 1934-1961 .... DLB-181
Milius, John 1944- DLB-44
Mill, James 1773-1836.........DLB-107, 158, 262
Mill, John Stuart 1806-1873......DLB-55, 190, 262; CDBLB-4
Thoughts on Poetry and Its Varieties (1833) DLB-32
Andrew Millar [publishing house] DLB-154
Millar, Kenneth 1915-1983 ....DLB-2, 226; Y-83; DS-6
Millay, Edna St. Vincent 1892-1950 .... DLB-45, 249; CDALB-4
Millen, Sarah Gertrude 1888-1968...... DLB-225
Miller, Andrew 1960- DLB-267
Miller, Arthur 1915-2005 .. DLB-7, 266; CDALB-1
The Arthur Miller Society Y-01

Miller, Caroline 1903-1992 .... DLB-9
Miller, Eugene Ethelbert 1950- DLB-41
Tribute to Julian Mayfield Y-84
Miller, Heather Ross 1939- DLB-120
Miller, Henry 1891-1980 .... DLB-4, 9; Y-80; CDALB-5
Miller, Hugh 1802-1856.............. DLB-190
Miller, J. Hillis 1928- DLB-67
Miller, Jason 1939- DLB-7
Miller, Joaquin 1839-1913 .... DLB-186
Miller, May 1899-1995............... DLB-41
Miller, Paul 1906-1991.............. DLB-127
Miller, Perry 1905-1963 ....DLB-17, 63
Miller, Sue 1943- DLB-143
Miller, Vassar 1924-1998 .... DLB-105
Miller, Walter M., Jr. 1923-1996 .... DLB-8
Miller, Webb 1892-1940 .... DLB-29
James Miller [publishing house] DLB-49
Millett, Kate 1934- DLB-246
Millhauser, Steven 1943- DLB-2
Millican, Arthenia J. Bates 1920- DLB-38
Milligan, Alice 1866-1953............. DLB-240
Mills, Magnus 1954- DLB-267
Mills and Boon..................... DLB-112
Milman, Henry Hart 1796-1868......... DLB-96
Milne, A. A. 1882-1956 ..... DLB-10, 77, 100, 160
Milner, Ron 1938- DLB-38
William Milner [publishing house]...... DLB-106
Milnes, Richard Monckton (Lord Houghton) 1809-1885 .... DLB-32, 184
Milton, John 1608-1674..... DLB-131, 151, 281; CDBLB-2
The Milton Society of America Y-00
Miłosz, Czesław 1911-2004 ....DLB-215; CDWLB-4
Minakami Tsutomu 1919- DLB-182
Minamoto no Sanetomo 1192-1219 ..... DLB-203
Minco, Marga 1920- DLB-299
The Minerva Press................... DLB-154
Minnesang circa 1150-1280.............. DLB-138
The Music of *Minnesang* DLB-138
Minns, Susan 1839-1938 .... DLB-140
Minsky, Nikolai 1855-1937 ....DLB-317
Minton, Balch and Company.......... DLB-46
Minyana, Philippe 1946- DLB-321
Mirbeau, Octave 1848-1917 .... DLB-123, 192
Mirikitani, Janice 1941- DLB-312
Mirk, John died after 1414?........... DLB-146
Miró, Ricardo 1883-1940 .... DLB-290
Miron, Gaston 1928-1996 .... DLB-60
A Mirror for Magistrates.................. DLB-167
Mirsky, D. S. 1890-1939................DLB-317
Mishima Yukio 1925-1970 .... DLB-182
Mistral, Gabriela 1889-1957 .... DLB-283
Mitchel, Jonathan 1624-1668 .... DLB-24

Mitchell, Adrian 1932- DLB-40
Mitchell, Donald Grant
    1822-1908 ....DLB-1, 243; DS-13
Mitchell, Gladys 1901-1983..............DLB-77
Mitchell, James Leslie 1901-1935.........DLB-15
Mitchell, John (see Slater, Patrick)
Mitchell, John Ames 1845-1918..........DLB-79
Mitchell, Joseph 1908-1996 ....DLB-185; Y-96
Mitchell, Julian 1935- DLB-14
Mitchell, Ken 1940- DLB-60
Mitchell, Langdon 1862-1935 ....DLB-7
Mitchell, Loften 1919-2001 ....DLB-38
Mitchell, Margaret 1900-1949 ...DLB-9; CDALB-7
Mitchell, S. Weir 1829-1914 ....DLB-202
Mitchell, W. J. T. 1942- DLB-246
Mitchell, W. O. 1914-1998 ....DLB-88
Mitchison, Naomi Margaret (Haldane)
    1897-1999 ....DLB-160, 191, 255, 319
Mitford, Mary Russell 1787-1855....DLB-110, 116
Mitford, Nancy 1904-1973............DLB-191
Mittelholzer, Edgar
    1909-1965 ....DLB-117; CDWLB-3
Mitterer, Erika 1906-2001 ....DLB-85
Mitterer, Felix 1948- DLB-124
Mitternacht, Johann Sebastian
    1613-1679 ....DLB-168
Miyamoto Yuriko 1899-1951...........DLB-180
Mizener, Arthur 1907-1988 ....DLB-103
Mo, Timothy 1950- DLB-194
Moberg, Vilhelm 1898-1973 ....DLB-259
Modern Age Books DLB-46
Modern Language Association of America
    The Modern Language Association of
    America Celebrates Its Centennial .. Y-84
The Modern Library DLB-46
Modiano, Patrick 1945- DLB-83, 299
Moffat, Yard and Company DLB-46
Moffet, Thomas 1553-1604 ....DLB-136
Mofolo, Thomas 1876-1948............DLB-225
Mohr, Nicholasa 1938- DLB-145
Moix, Ana María 1947- DLB-134
Molesworth, Louisa 1839-1921 ....DLB-135
Molière (Jean-Baptiste Poquelin)
    1622-1673 ....DLB-268
Møller, Poul Martin 1794-1838 ....DLB-300
Möllhausen, Balduin 1825-1905 ....DLB-129
Molnár, Ferenc 1878-1952 ...DLB-215; CDWLB-4
Molnár, Miklós (see Mészöly, Miklós)
Momaday, N. Scott
    1934- DLB-143, 175, 256; CDALB-7
Monkhouse, Allan 1858-1936 ....DLB-10
Monro, Harold 1879-1932.............DLB-19
Monroe, Harriet 1860-1936.........DLB-54, 91
Monsarrat, Nicholas 1910-1979 ....DLB-15
Montagu, Lady Mary Wortley
    1689-1762 ....DLB-95, 101
Montague, C. E. 1867-1928 ....DLB-197

Montague, John 1929- DLB-40
Montale, Eugenio 1896-1981...........DLB-114
Montalvo, Garci Rodríguez de
    ca. 1450?-before 1505 ....DLB-286
Montalvo, José 1946-1994.............DLB-209
Montemayor, Jorge de 1521?-1561? DLB-318
Monterroso, Augusto 1921-2003........DLB-145
Montesquieu, Charles-Louis de Secondat, baron de
    1689-1755 ....DLB-314
    The Spirit of Laws DLB-314
Montesquiou, Robert de 1855-1921 .....DLB-217
Montgomerie, Alexander
    circa 1550?-1598 ....DLB-167
Montgomery, James 1771-1854 ......DLB-93, 158
Montgomery, John 1919- DLB-16
Montgomery, Lucy Maud
    1874-1942 ....DLB-92; DS-14
Montgomery, Marion 1925- DLB-6
Montgomery, Robert Bruce (see Crispin, Edmund)
Montherlant, Henry de 1896-1972 ...DLB-72, 321
The Monthly Review 1749-1844..........DLB-110
Monti, Ricardo 1944- DLB-305
Montigny, Louvigny de 1876-1955 ....DLB-92
Montoya, José 1932- DLB-122
Moodie, John Wedderburn Dunbar
    1797-1869.....................DLB-99
Moodie, Susanna 1803-1885 ....DLB-99
Moody, Joshua circa 1633-1697..........DLB-24
Moody, William Vaughn 1869-1910.... DLB-7, 54
Moorcock, Michael 1939-   DLB-14, 231, 261, 319
Moore, Alan 1953- DLB-261
Moore, Brian 1921-1999 ....DLB-251
Moore, Catherine L. 1911-1987..........DLB-8
Moore, Clement Clarke 1779-1863 ....DLB-42
Moore, Dora Mavor 1888-1979 ....DLB-92
Moore, G. E. 1873-1958 ....DLB-262
Moore, George 1852-1933.... DLB-10, 18, 57, 135
    Literature at Nurse, or Circulating Morals
        (1885) DLB-18
Moore, Lorrie 1957- DLB-234
Moore, Marianne
    1887-1972.........DLB-45; DS-7; CDALB-5
    International Marianne Moore Society ... Y-98
Moore, Mavor 1919- DLB-88
Moore, Richard 1927- DLB-105
    "The No Self, the Little Self, and
        the Poets" DLB-105
Moore, T. Sturge 1870-1944 ....DLB-19
Moore, Thomas 1779-1852 ....DLB-96, 144
Moore, Ward 1903-1978 ....DLB-8
Moore, Wilstach, Keys and Company DLB-49
Moorehead, Alan 1901-1983 ....DLB-204
Moorhouse, Frank 1938- DLB-289
Moorhouse, Geoffrey 1931- DLB-204
Moorish Novel of the Sixteenth
    Century, The DLB-318

The Moorland-Spingarn Research
    Center.......................DLB-76
Moorman, Mary C. 1905-1994 ....DLB-155
Mora, Pat 1942- DLB-209
Moraes, Vinicius de 1913-1980.........DLB-307
Moraga, Cherríe 1952- DLB-82, 249
Morales, Alejandro 1944- DLB-82
Morales, Mario Roberto 1947- DLB-145
Morales, Rafael 1919- DLB-108
Morality Plays: Mankind circa 1450-1500
    and Everyman circa 1500 ....DLB-146
Morand, Paul (1888-1976)..............DLB-65
Morante, Elsa 1912-1985 ....DLB-177
Morata, Olympia Fulvia 1526-1555......DLB-179
Moravia, Alberto 1907-1990 ....DLB-177
Mordaunt, Elinor 1872-1942 ....DLB-174
Mordovtsev, Daniil Lukich 1830-1905 ...DLB-238
More, Hannah
    1745-1833 ....DLB-107, 109, 116, 158
More, Henry 1614-1687 ....DLB-126, 252
More, Sir Thomas
    1477/1478-1535 ....DLB-136, 281
Morejón, Nancy 1944- DLB-283
Morellet, André 1727-1819.............DLB-314
Morency, Pierre 1942- DLB-60
Moreno, Dorinda 1939- DLB-122
Moretti, Marino 1885-1979 ....DLB-114, 264
Morgan, Berry 1919-2002 ....DLB-6
Morgan, Charles 1894-1958 ....DLB-34, 100
Morgan, Edmund S. 1916- DLB-17
Morgan, Edwin 1920- DLB-27
Morgan, John Pierpont 1837-1913.......DLB-140
Morgan, John Pierpont, Jr. 1867-1943 ....DLB-140
Morgan, Robert 1944- DLB-120, 292
Morgan, Sydney Owenson, Lady
    1776?-1859 ....DLB-116, 158
Morgner, Irmtraud 1933-1990............DLB-75
Morhof, Daniel Georg 1639-1691 ....DLB-164
Mori, Kyoko 1957- DLB-312
Mori Ōgai 1862-1922 ....DLB-180
Mori, Toshio 1910-1980 ....DLB-312
Móricz, Zsigmond 1879-1942 ....DLB-215
Morier, James Justinian
    1782 or 1783?-1849 ....DLB-116
Mörike, Eduard 1804-1875 ....DLB-133
Morin, Paul 1889-1963 ....DLB-92
Morison, Richard 1514?-1556..........DLB-136
Morison, Samuel Eliot 1887-1976.........DLB-17
Morison, Stanley 1889-1967 ....DLB-201
Moritz, Karl Philipp 1756-1793 ....DLB-94
Moriz von Craûn circa 1220-1230........DLB-138
Morley, Christopher 1890-1957 ....DLB-9
Morley, John 1838-1923 .... DLB-57, 144, 190
Moro, César 1903-1956................DLB-290
Morris, George Pope 1802-1864 ....DLB-73
Morris, James Humphrey (see Morris, Jan)

Morris, Jan 1926- DLB-204

Morris, Lewis 1833-1907 .... DLB-35

Morris, Margaret 1737-1816 .... DLB-200

Morris, Mary McGarry 1943- DLB-292

Morris, Richard B. 1904-1989 .... DLB-17

Morris, William 1834-1896
..... DLB-18, 35, 57, 156, 178, 184; CDBLB-4

Morris, Willie 1934-1999 .... Y-80

    Tribute to Irwin Shaw Y-84

    Tribute to James Dickey Y-97

Morris, Wright
    1910-1998............DLB-2, 206, 218; Y-81

Morrison, Arthur 1863-1945 ....DLB-70, 135, 197

Morrison, Charles Clayton 1874-1966 .... DLB-91

Morrison, John 1904-1998 .... DLB-260

Morrison, Toni 1931-
    .... DLB-6, 33, 143; Y-81, 93; CDALB-6

    Nobel Lecture 1993 .... Y-93

Morrissy, Mary 1957- DLB-267

William Morrow and Company......... DLB-46

Morse, James Herbert 1841-1923 .... DLB-71

Morse, Jedidiah 1761-1826 .... DLB-37

Morse, John T., Jr. 1840-1937 .... DLB-47

Morselli, Guido 1912-1973 ....DLB-177

Morte Arthure, the *Alliterative* and the
    Stanzaic circa 1350-1400 .... DLB-146

Mortimer, Favell Lee 1802-1878........ DLB-163

Mortimer, John
    1923- DLB-13, 245, 271; CDBLB-8

Morton, Carlos 1942- DLB-122

Morton, H. V. 1892-1979............. DLB-195

John P. Morton and Company......... DLB-49

Morton, Nathaniel 1613-1685 .... DLB-24

Morton, Sarah Wentworth 1759-1846 .... DLB-37

Morton, Thomas circa 1579-circa 1647 ... DLB-24

Moscherosch, Johann Michael
    1601-1669 .... DLB-164

Humphrey Moseley
    [publishing house] DLB-170

Möser, Justus 1720-1794 .... DLB-97

Mosley, Nicholas 1923- DLB-14, 207

Mosley, Walter 1952- DLB-306

Moss, Arthur 1889-1969................ DLB-4

Moss, Howard 1922-1987............... DLB-5

Moss, Thylias 1954- DLB-120

Motion, Andrew 1952- DLB-40

Motley, John Lothrop
    1814-1877................ DLB-1, 30, 59, 235

Motley, Willard 1909-1965 .... DLB-76, 143

Mott, Lucretia 1793-1880 .... DLB-239

Benjamin Motte Jr.
    [publishing house] DLB-154

Motteux, Peter Anthony 1663-1718 ...... DLB-80

Mottram, R. H. 1883-1971 .... DLB-36

Mount, Ferdinand 1939- DLB-231

Mouré, Erin 1955- DLB-60

Mourning Dove (Humishuma) between
    1882 and 1888?-1936..........DLB-175, 221

Movies
    Fiction into Film, 1928-1975: A List
    of Movies Based on the Works
    of Authors in British Novelists,
    1930-1959 .... DLB-15

    Movies from Books, 1920-1974 .... DLB-9

Mowat, Farley 1921- DLB-68

A. R. Mowbray and Company,
    Limited..................... DLB-106

Mowrer, Edgar Ansel 1892-1977 .... DLB-29

Mowrer, Paul Scott 1887-1971 .... DLB-29

Edward Moxon [publishing house] DLB-106

Joseph Moxon [publishing house]........DLB-170

Moyes, Patricia 1923-2000 ....DLB-276

Mphahlele, Es'kia (Ezekiel)
    1919- DLB-125, 225; CDWLB-3

Mrożek, Sławomir 1930- .. DLB-232; CDWLB-4

Mtshali, Oswald Mbuyiseni
    1940- DLB-125, 225

al-Mubarrad 826-898 or 899 .... DLB-311

Mucedorus........................ DLB-62

Mudford, William 1782-1848.......... DLB-159

Mudrooroo (see Johnson, Colin)

Mueller, Lisel 1924- DLB-105

Muhajir, El (see Marvin X)

Muhajir, Nazzam Al Fitnah (see Marvin X)

Muhammad the Prophet circa 570-632... DLB-311

Mühlbach, Luise 1814-1873 .... DLB-133

Muir, Edwin 1887-1959 ....DLB-20, 100, 191

Muir, Helen 1937- DLB-14

Muir, John 1838-1914.............DLB-186, 275

Muir, Percy 1894-1979 .... DLB-201

Mujū Ichien 1226-1312.............. DLB-203

Mukherjee, Bharati 1940- DLB-60, 218

Mulcaster, Richard 1531 or 1532-1611 .. DLB-167

Muldoon, Paul 1951- DLB-40

Mulisch, Harry 1927- DLB-299

Mulkerns, Val 1925- DLB-319

Müller, Friedrich (see Müller, Maler)

Müller, Heiner 1929-1995 .... DLB-124

Müller, Maler 1749-1825 .... DLB-94

Muller, Marcia 1944- DLB-226

Müller, Wilhelm 1794-1827 .... DLB-90

Mumford, Lewis 1895-1990............ DLB-63

Munby, A. N. L. 1913-1974 .... DLB-201

Munby, Arthur Joseph 1828-1910 .... DLB-35

Munday, Anthony 1560-1633 ....DLB-62, 172

Mundt, Clara (see Mühlbach, Luise)

Mundt, Theodore 1808-1861 .... DLB-133

Munford, Robert circa 1737-1783 .... DLB-31

Mungoshi, Charles 1947- DLB-157

Munk, Kaj 1898-1944................ DLB-214

Munonye, John 1929- DLB-117

Munro, Alice 1931- DLB-53

George Munro [publishing house] DLB-49

Munro, H. H.
    1870-1916.......... DLB-34, 162; CDBLB-5

Munro, Neil 1864-1930 .... DLB-156

Norman L. Munro [publishing house] DLB-49

Munroe, Kirk 1850-1930 .... DLB-42

Munroe and Francis DLB-49

James Munroe and Company.......... DLB-49

Joel Munsell [publishing house] DLB-49

Munsey, Frank A. 1854-1925......... DLB-25, 91

Frank A. Munsey and Company DLB-49

Mura, David 1952- DLB-312

Murakami Haruki 1949- DLB-182

Muratov, Pavel 1881-1950.............DLB-317

Murayama, Milton 1923- DLB-312

Murav'ev, Mikhail Nikitich 1757-1807 ... DLB-150

Murdoch, Iris 1919-1999
    .... DLB-14, 194, 233; CDBLB-8

Murdock, James
    From *Sketches of Modern Philosophy* DS-5

Murdock, Rupert 1931- DLB-127

Murfree, Mary N. 1850-1922.........DLB-12, 74

Murger, Henry 1822-1861 .... DLB-119

Murger, Louis-Henri (see Murger, Henry)

Murnane, Gerald 1939- DLB-289

Murner, Thomas 1475-1537.............DLB-179

Muro, Amado 1915-1971 .... DLB-82

Murphy, Arthur 1727-1805......... DLB-89, 142

Murphy, Beatrice M. 1908-1992 .... DLB-76

Murphy, Dervla 1931- DLB-204

Murphy, Emily 1868-1933 .... DLB-99

Murphy, Jack 1923-1980 .... DLB-241

John Murphy and Company DLB-49

Murphy, John H., III 1916- DLB-127

Murphy, Richard 1927-1993 .... DLB-40

Murphy, Tom 1935- DLB-310

Murray, Albert L. 1916- DLB-38

Murray, Gilbert 1866-1957............. DLB-10

Murray, Jim 1919-1998 .... DLB-241

John Murray [publishing house]........ DLB-154

Murray, Judith Sargent 1751-1820 ....DLB-37, 200

Murray, Les 1938- DLB-289

Murray, Pauli 1910-1985 .... DLB-41

Murry, John Middleton 1889-1957...... DLB-149

    "The Break-Up of the Novel"
    (1922) DLB-36

Murry, John Middleton, Jr. (see Cowper, Richard)

Musäus, Johann Karl August 1735-1787 ... DLB-97

Muschg, Adolf 1934- DLB-75

Musil, Robert
    1880-1942 ....DLB-81, 124; CDWLB-2

Muspilli circa 790-circa 850 .... DLB-148

Musset, Alfred de 1810-1857 ....DLB-192, 217

Benjamin B. Mussey
    and Company DLB-49

Muste, A. J. 1885-1967................ DLB-303

Mutafchieva, Vera 1929- DLB-181

Mutis, Alvaro 1923- DLB-283
Mwangi, Meja 1948- DLB-125
Myers, Frederic W. H. 1843-1901 ....DLB-190
Myers, Gustavus 1872-1942..........DLB-47
Myers, L. H. 1881-1944................DLB-15
Myers, Walter Dean 1937- DLB-33
Myerson, Julie 1960- DLB-267
Mykle, Agnar 1915-1994............DLB-297
Mykolaitis-Putinas, Vincas 1893-1967 ....DLB-220
Myles, Eileen 1949- DLB-193
Myrdal, Jan 1927- DLB-257
Mystery
   1985: The Year of the Mystery: A Symposium Y-85
   Comments from Other Writers Y-85
   The Second Annual New York Festival of Mystery Y-00
   Why I Read Mysteries Y-85
   Why I Write Mysteries: Night and Day, by Michael Collins Y-85

N

Na Prous Boneta circa 1296-1328 ....DLB-208
Nabl, Franz 1883-1974.................DLB-81
Nabokov, Véra 1902-1991................Y-91
Nabokov, Vladimir 1899-1977 ...... DLB-2, 244, 278, 317; Y-80, 91; DS-3; CDALB-1
   International Nabokov Society Y-99
   An Interview [On Nabokov], by Fredson Bowers Y-80
   Nabokov Festival at Cornell Y-83
   The Vladimir Nabokov Archive in the Berg Collection of the New York Public Library: An Overview Y-91
   The Vladimir Nabokov Society Y-01
Nádaši, Ladislav (see Jégé)
Naden, Constance 1858-1889 ....DLB-199
Nadezhdin, Nikolai Ivanovich 1804-1856 ....DLB-198
Nadson, Semen Iakovlevich 1862-1887 ...DLB-277
Naevius circa 265 B.C.-201 B.C..........DLB-211
Nafis and Cornish DLB-49
Nagai Kafū 1879-1959 ....DLB-180
Nagel, Ernest 1901-1985 ....DLB-279
Nagibin, Iurii Markovich 1920-1994 .....DLB-302
Nagrodskaia, Evdokiia Apollonovna 1866-1930 ....DLB-295
Naipaul, Shiva 1945-1985 .... DLB-157; Y-85
Naipaul, V. S. 1932- DLB-125, 204, 207; Y-85, Y-01; CDBLB-8; CDWLB-3
   Nobel Lecture 2001: "Two Worlds"..... Y-01
Nakagami Kenji 1946-1992 ....DLB-182
Nakano-in Masatada no Musume (see Nijō, Lady)
Nałkowska, Zofia 1884-1954...........DLB-215
Namora, Fernando 1919-1989 ....DLB-287
Joseph Nancrede [publishing house] DLB-49
Naranjo, Carmen 1930- DLB-145

Narbikova, Valeriia Spartakovna 1958- DLB-285
Narezhny, Vasilii Trofimovich 1780-1825 ....DLB-198
Narrache, Jean (Emile Coderre) 1893-1970 ....DLB-92
Nasby, Petroleum Vesuvius (see Locke, David Ross)
Eveleigh Nash [publishing house] DLB-112
Nash, Ogden 1902-1971..............DLB-11
Nashe, Thomas 1567-1601?...........DLB-167
Nason, Jerry 1910-1986 ....DLB-241
Nasr, Seyyed Hossein 1933- DLB-279
Nast, Condé 1873-1942 ....DLB-91
Nast, Thomas 1840-1902.............DLB-188
Nastasijević, Momčilo 1894-1938 ....DLB-147
Nathan, George Jean 1882-1958 ....DLB-137
Nathan, Robert 1894-1985 ....DLB-9
Nation, Carry A. 1846-1911 ....DLB-303
National Book Critics Circle Awards..... Y-00–01
The National Jewish Book Awards Y-85
Natsume Sōseki 1867-1916............DLB-180
Naughton, Bill 1910-1992 ....DLB-13
Nava, Michael 1954- DLB-306
Navarro, Joe 1953- DLB-209
Naylor, Gloria 1950- DLB-173
Nazor, Vladimir 1876-1949 ....DLB-147
Ndebele, Njabulo 1948- DLB-157, 225
Neagoe, Peter 1881-1960................DLB-4
Neal, John 1793-1876...........DLB-1, 59, 243
Neal, Joseph C. 1807-1847............DLB-11
Neal, Larry 1937-1981 ....DLB-38
The Neale Publishing Company DLB-49
Nearing, Scott 1883-1983............DLB-303
Nebel, Frederick 1903-1967..........DLB-226
Nebrija, Antonio de 1442 or 1444-1522 ..DLB-286
Nedreaas, Torborg 1906-1987.........DLB-297
F. Tennyson Neely [publishing house].....DLB-49
Negoițescu, Ion 1921-1993 ....DLB-220
Negri, Ada 1870-1945 ....DLB-114
Neihardt, John G. 1881-1973 ..... DLB-9, 54, 256
Neidhart von Reuental circa 1185-circa 1240...............DLB-138
Neilson, John Shaw 1872-1942 ....DLB-230
Nekrasov, Nikolai Alekseevich 1821-1877 .... DLB-277
Nekrasov, Viktor Platonovich 1911-1987 ....DLB-302
Neledinsky-Meletsky, Iurii Aleksandrovich 1752-1828 ....DLB-150
Nelligan, Emile 1879-1941 ....DLB-92
Nelson, Alice Moore Dunbar 1875-1935 ...DLB-50
Nelson, Antonya 1961- DLB-244
Nelson, Kent 1943- DLB-234
Nelson, Richard K. 1941- DLB-275
Nelson, Thomas, and Sons [U.K.]......DLB-106
Nelson, Thomas, and Sons [U.S.] DLB-49

Nelson, William 1908-1978 ....DLB-103
Nelson, William Rockhill 1841-1915......DLB-23
Nemerov, Howard 1920-1991..... DLB-5, 6; Y-83
Németh, László 1901-1975............DLB-215
Nepos circa 100 B.C.-post 27 B.C........DLB-211
Nėris, Salomėja 1904-1945 ..DLB-220; CDWLB-4
Neruda, Pablo 1904-1973 ....DLB-283
Nerval, Gérard de 1808-1855 ....DLB-217
Nervo, Amado 1870-1919 ....DLB-290
Nesbit, E. 1858-1924 .... DLB-141, 153, 178
Ness, Evaline 1911-1986 ....DLB-61
Nestroy, Johann 1801-1862............DLB-133
Nettleship, R. L. 1846-1892............DLB-262
Neugeboren, Jay 1938- DLB-28
Neukirch, Benjamin 1655-1729 ....DLB-168
Neumann, Alfred 1895-1952 ....DLB-56
Neumann, Ferenc (see Molnár, Ferenc)
Neumark, Georg 1621-1681 ....DLB-164
Neumeister, Erdmann 1671-1756...........DLB-168
Nevins, Allan 1890-1971 .... DLB-17; DS-17
Nevinson, Henry Woodd 1856-1941 ....DLB-135
The New American Library DLB-46
New Directions Publishing Corporation ...DLB-46
The New Monthly Magazine 1814-1884.....DLB-110
New York Times Book Review Y-82
John Newbery [publishing house] DLB-154
Newbolt, Henry 1862-1938.............DLB-19
Newbound, Bernard Slade (see Slade, Bernard)
Newby, Eric 1919- DLB-204
Newby, P. H. 1918-1997 ....DLB-15
Thomas Cautley Newby [publishing house].................DLB-106
Newcomb, Charles King 1820-1894 ...DLB-1, 223
Newell, Peter 1862-1924 ....DLB-42
Newell, Robert Henry 1836-1901 ....DLB-11
Newhouse, Samuel I. 1895-1979 ....DLB-127
Newman, Cecil Earl 1903-1976 ....DLB-127
Newman, David 1937- DLB-44
Newman, Frances 1883-1928.............. Y-80
Newman, Francis William 1805-1897 ....DLB-190
Newman, G. F. 1946- DLB-310
Newman, John Henry 1801-1890 ....DLB-18, 32, 55
Mark Newman [publishing house]........DLB-49
Newmarch, Rosa Harriet 1857-1940 .....DLB-240
George Newnes Limited DLB-112
Newsome, Effie Lee 1885-1979 ....DLB-76
Newton, A. Edward 1864-1940.........DLB-140
Newton, Sir Isaac 1642-1727 ....DLB-252
Nexø, Martin Andersen 1869-1954......DLB-214
Nezval, Vítěslav 1900-1958............DLB-215; CDWLB-4
Ngugi wa Thiong'o 1938- DLB-125; CDWLB-3
Niatum, Duane 1938- DLB-175

Cumulative Index

The *Nibelungenlied* and the *Klage*
circa 1200....................DLB-138
Nichol, B. P. 1944-1988..............DLB-53
Nicholas of Cusa 1401-1464..........DLB-115
Nichols, Ann 1891?-1966............DLB-249
Nichols, Beverly 1898-1983.........DLB-191
Nichols, Dudley 1895-1960..........DLB-26
Nichols, Grace 1950-................DLB-157
Nichols, John 1940-.................Y-82
Nichols, Mary Sargeant (Neal) Gove
1810-1884....................DLB-1, 243
Nichols, Peter 1927-............DLB-13, 245
Nichols, Roy F. 1896-1973............DLB-17
Nichols, Ruth 1948-.................DLB-60
Nicholson, Edward Williams Byron
1849-1912....................DLB-184
Nicholson, Geoff 1953-.............DLB-271
Nicholson, Norman 1914-1987.........DLB-27
Nicholson, William 1872-1949.......DLB-141
Ní Chuilleanáin, Eiléan 1942-........DLB-40
Nicol, Eric 1919-...................DLB-68
Nicolai, Friedrich 1733-1811.........DLB-97
Nicolas de Clamanges circa 1363-1437...DLB-208
Nicolay, John G. 1832-1901 and
Hay, John 1838-1905..............DLB-47
Nicole, Pierre 1625-1695............DLB-268
Nicolson, Adela Florence Cory (see Hope, Laurence)
Nicolson, Harold 1886-1968......DLB-100, 149
"The Practice of Biography," in
*The English Sense of Humour and
Other Essays*.................DLB-149
Nicolson, Nigel 1917-2004...........DLB-155
Ní Dhuibhne, Éilís 1954-............DLB-319
Niebuhr, Reinhold 1892-1971......DLB-17; DS-17
Niedecker, Lorine 1903-1970..........DLB-48
Nieman, Lucius W. 1857-1935..........DLB-25
Nietzsche, Friedrich
1844-1900............DLB-129; CDWLB-2
Mencken and Nietzsche: An Unpublished
Excerpt from H. L. Mencken's *My Life
as Author and Editor*..............Y-93
Nievo, Stanislao 1928-..............DLB-196
Niggli, Josefina 1910-1983............Y-80
Nightingale, Florence 1820-1910.....DLB-166
Nijō, Lady (Nakano-in Masatada no Musume)
1258-after 1306................DLB-203
Nijō Yoshimoto 1320-1388............DLB-203
Nikitin, Ivan Savvich 1824-1861.....DLB-277
Nikitin, Nikolai Nikolaevich 1895-1963..DLB-272
Nikolev, Nikolai Petrovich 1758-1815...DLB-150
Niles, Hezekiah 1777-1839............DLB-43
Nims, John Frederick 1913-1999.......DLB-5
Tribute to Nancy Hale...............Y-88
Nin, Anaïs 1903-1977...........DLB-2, 4, 152
Nína Björk Árnadóttir 1941-2000.....DLB-293
Niño, Raúl 1961-...................DLB-209
Nissenson, Hugh 1933-...............DLB-28

Niven, Frederick John 1878-1944.....DLB-92
Niven, Larry 1938-...................DLB-8
Nixon, Howard M. 1909-1983.........DLB-201
Nizan, Paul 1905-1940...............DLB-72
Njegoš, Petar II Petrović
1813-1851..............DLB-147; CDWLB-4
Nkosi, Lewis 1936-.............DLB-157, 225
Noah, Mordecai M. 1785-1851........DLB-250
Noailles, Anna de 1876-1933........DLB-258
Nobel Peace Prize
The Nobel Prize and Literary Politics....Y-88
Elie Wiesel......................Y-86
Nobel Prize in Literature
Joseph Brodsky...................Y-87
Camilo José Cela.................Y-89
Dario Fo........................Y-97
Gabriel García Márquez...........Y-82
William Golding..................Y-83
Nadine Gordimer..................Y-91
Günter Grass....................Y-99
Seamus Heaney...................Y-95
Imre Kertész....................Y-02
Najīb Mahfūz....................Y-88
Toni Morrison...................Y-93
V. S. Naipaul...................Y-01
Kenzaburō Ōe....................Y-94
Octavio Paz.....................Y-90
José Saramago...................Y-98
Jaroslav Seifert................Y-84
Claude Simon....................Y-85
Wole Soyinka....................Y-86
Wisława Szymborska..............Y-96
Derek Walcott...................Y-92
Gao Xingjian....................Y-00
Nobre, António 1867-1900...........DLB-287
Nodier, Charles 1780-1844..........DLB-119
Noël, Marie (Marie Mélanie Rouget)
1883-1967....................DLB-258
Noel, Roden 1834-1894..............DLB-35
Nogami Yaeko 1885-1985.............DLB-180
Nogo, Rajko Petrov 1945-...........DLB-181
Nolan, William F. 1928-.............DLB-8
Tribute to Raymond Chandler........Y-88
Noland, C. F. M. 1810?-1858........DLB-11
Noma Hiroshi 1915-1991.............DLB-182
Nonesuch Press.....................DLB-112
Creative Nonfiction.................Y-02
Nonni (Jón Stefán Sveinsson or Svensson)
1857-1944....................DLB-293
Noon, Jeff 1957-...................DLB-267
Noonan, Robert Phillipe (see Tressell, Robert)
Noonday Press......................DLB-46
Noone, John 1936-...................DLB-14
Nora, Eugenio de 1923-.............DLB-134
Nordan, Lewis 1939-................DLB-234

Nordbrandt, Henrik 1945-...........DLB-214
Nordhoff, Charles 1887-1947.........DLB-9
Norén, Lars 1944-..................DLB-257
Norfolk, Lawrence 1963-............DLB-267
Norman, Charles 1904-1996..........DLB-111
Norman, Marsha 1947-..........DLB-266; Y-84
Norris, Charles G. 1881-1945........DLB-9
Norris, Frank
1870-1902.......DLB-12, 71, 186; CDALB-3
Norris, Helen 1916-................DLB-292
Norris, John 1657-1712.............DLB-252
Norris, Leslie 1921-............DLB-27, 256
Norse, Harold 1916-.................DLB-16
Norte, Marisela 1955-..............DLB-209
North, Marianne 1830-1890..........DLB-174
North Point Press...................DLB-46
Nortje, Arthur 1942-1970.......DLB-125, 225
Norton, Alice Mary (see Norton, Andre)
Norton, Andre 1912-2005.........DLB-8, 52
Norton, Andrews 1786-1853...DLB-1, 235; DS-5
Norton, Caroline 1808-1877....DLB-21, 159, 199
Norton, Charles Eliot
1827-1908................DLB-1, 64, 235
Norton, John 1606-1663..............DLB-24
Norton, Mary 1903-1992.............DLB-160
Norton, Thomas 1532-1584............DLB-62
W. W. Norton and Company...........DLB-46
Norwood, Robert 1874-1932...........DLB-92
Nosaka Akiyuki 1930-...............DLB-182
Nossack, Hans Erich 1901-1977.......DLB-69
Notker Balbulus circa 840-912......DLB-148
Notker III of Saint Gall
circa 950-1022...................DLB-148
Notker von Zweifalten ?-1095.......DLB-148
Nourse, Alan E. 1928-1992...........DLB-8
Novak, Slobodan 1924-..............DLB-181
Novak, Vjenceslav 1859-1905........DLB-147
Novakovich, Josip 1956-............DLB-244
Novalis 1772-1801...........DLB-90; CDWLB-2
Novaro, Mario 1868-1944............DLB-114
Novás Calvo, Lino 1903-1983........DLB-145
Novelists
Library Journal Statements and
Questionnaires from First Novelists....Y-87
Novels
The Columbia History of the American Novel
A Symposium on..................Y-92
The Great Modern Library Scam......Y-98
Novels for Grown-Ups...............Y-97
The Proletarian Novel..............DLB-9
Novel, The "Second-Generation" Holocaust
...............................DLB-299
The Year in the Novel......Y-87–88, Y-90–93
Novels, British
"The Break-Up of the Novel" (1922),
by John Middleton Murry.......DLB-36
The Consolidation of Opinion: Critical
Responses to the Modernists.....DLB-36

"Criticism in Relation to Novels"
(1863), by G. H. Lewes DLB-21

"Experiment in the Novel" (1929)
[excerpt], by John D. Beresford . . . DLB-36

"The Future of the Novel" (1899), by
Henry James DLB-18

The Gay Science (1866), by E. S. Dallas
[excerpt] DLB-21

A Haughty and Proud Generation
(1922), by Ford Madox Hueffer . . . DLB-36

Literary Effects of World War II DLB-15

"Modern Novelists –Great and Small"
(1855), by Margaret Oliphant. DLB-21

The Modernists (1932),
by Joseph Warren Beach DLB-36

A Note on Technique (1926), by
Elizabeth A. Drew [excerpts] DLB-36

Novel-Reading: *The Works of Charles
Dickens; The Works of W. Makepeace
Thackeray* (1879),
by Anthony Trollope DLB-21

Novels with a Purpose (1864), by
Justin M'Carthy DLB-21

"On Art in Fiction" (1838),
by Edward Bulwer DLB-21

The Present State of the English Novel
(1892), by George Saintsbury DLB-18

Representative Men and Women:
A Historical Perspective on
the British Novel, 1930-1960 . . . . . DLB-15

"The Revolt" (1937), by Mary Colum
[excerpts] DLB-36

"Sensation Novels" (1863), by
H. L. Manse DLB-21

Sex, Class, Politics, and Religion [in
the British Novel, 1930-1959] DLB-15

Time and Western Man (1927),
by Wyndham Lewis [excerpts] DLB-36

Noventa, Giacomo 1898-1960 . . . . DLB-114

Novikov, Nikolai Ivanovich
1744-1818 . . . . DLB-150

Novomeský, Laco 1904-1976 . . . . DLB-215

Nowlan, Alden 1933-1983 . . . . DLB-53

Noyes, Alfred 1880-1958 . . . . DLB-20

Noyes, Crosby S. 1825-1908 . . . . DLB-23

Noyes, Nicholas 1647-1717 . . . . DLB-24

Noyes, Theodore W. 1858-1946 . . . . DLB-29

Nozick, Robert 1938-2002 . . . . DLB-279

N-Town Plays circa 1468 to early
sixteenth century DLB-146

Nugent, Frank 1908-1965 . . . . DLB-44

Núñez, Sigrid 1951- DLB-312

Nušić, Branislav
1864-1938 . . . . DLB-147; CDWLB-4

David Nutt [publishing house] DLB-106

Nwapa, Flora
1931-1993 . . . . DLB-125; CDWLB-3

Nye, Edgar Wilson (Bill)
1850-1896 . . . . DLB-11, 23, 186

Nye, Naomi Shihab 1952- DLB-120

Nye, Robert 1939- DLB-14, 271

Nyka-Niliūnas, Alfonsas 1919- DLB-220

O

Oakes, Urian circa 1631-1681 . . . . DLB-24

Oakes Smith, Elizabeth
1806-1893 . . . . DLB-1, 239, 243

Oakley, Violet 1874-1961 . . . . DLB-188

Oates, Joyce Carol 1938-
. . . . DLB-2, 5, 130; Y-81; CDALB-6

Tribute to Michael M. Rea Y-97

Ōba Minako 1930- DLB-182

Ober, Frederick Albion 1849-1913 . . . . . DLB-189

Ober, William 1920-1993 . . . . Y-93

Oberholtzer, Ellis Paxson 1868-1936 . . . . DLB-47

The Obituary as Literary Form Y-02

Obradović, Dositej 1740?-1811 . . . . DLB-147

O'Brien, Charlotte Grace 1845-1909 . . . . DLB-240

O'Brien, Edna 1932- DLB-14, 231, 319; CDBLB-8

O'Brien, Fitz-James 1828-1862 . . . . DLB-74

O'Brien, Flann (see O'Nolan, Brian)

O'Brien, Kate 1897-1974 . . . . DLB-15

O'Brien, Tim
1946- DLB-152; Y-80; DS-9; CDALB-7

Ó Cadhain, Máirtín 1905-1970 . . . . DLB-319

O'Casey, Sean 1880-1964 . . . . DLB-10; CDBLB-6

Occom, Samson 1723-1792 . . . . DLB-175

Occomy, Marita Bonner 1899-1971 . . . . . DLB-51

Ochs, Adolph S. 1858-1935 . . . . DLB-25

Ochs-Oakes, George Washington
1861-1931 . . . . DLB-137

O'Connor, Flannery 1925-1964
. . . . DLB-2, 152; Y-80; DS-12; CDALB-1

The Flannery O'Connor Society Y-99

O'Connor, Frank 1903-1966 . . . . DLB-162

O'Connor, Joseph 1963- DLB-267

Octopus Publishing Group DLB-112

Oda Sakunosuke 1913-1947 . . . . DLB-182

Odell, Jonathan 1737-1818 . . . . DLB-31, 99

O'Dell, Scott 1903-1989 . . . . DLB-52

Odets, Clifford 1906-1963 . . . . DLB-7, 26

Odhams Press Limited DLB-112

Odio, Eunice 1922-1974 . . . . DLB-283

Odoevsky, Aleksandr Ivanovich
1802-1839 . . . . DLB-205

Odoevsky, Vladimir Fedorovich
1804 or 1803-1869 . . . . DLB-198

Odoevtseva, Irina 1895-1990 . . . . DLB-317

O'Donnell, Peter 1920- DLB-87

O'Donovan, Michael (see O'Connor, Frank)

O'Dowd, Bernard 1866-1953 . . . . DLB-230

Ōe, Kenzaburō 1935- DLB-182; Y-94

Nobel Lecture 1994: Japan, the
Ambiguous, and Myself Y-94

Oehlenschläger, Adam 1779-1850 . . . . . . DLB-300

O'Faolain, Julia 1932- DLB-14, 231, 319

O'Faolain, Sean 1900-1991 . . . . DLB-15, 162

Off-Loop Theatres DLB-7

Offord, Carl Ruthven 1910-1990 . . . . DLB-76

O'Flaherty, Liam 1896-1984 . . . DLB-36, 162; Y-84

Ogarev, Nikolai Platonovich 1813-1877 . . DLB-277

J. S. Ogilvie and Company DLB-49

Ogilvy, Eliza 1822-1912 . . . . DLB-199

Ogot, Grace 1930- DLB-125

O'Grady, Desmond 1935- DLB-40

Ogunyemi, Wale 1939- DLB-157

O'Hagan, Howard 1902-1982 . . . . DLB-68

O'Hara, Frank 1926-1966 . . . . DLB-5, 16, 193

O'Hara, John
1905-1970 . . . . DLB-9, 86; DS-2; CDALB-5

John O'Hara's Pottsville Journalism Y-88

O'Hare, Kate Richards 1876-1948 . . . . . . DLB-303

O'Hegarty, P. S. 1879-1955 . . . . DLB-201

Ohio State University
The William Charvat American Fiction
Collection at the Ohio State
University Libraries Y-92

Okada, John 1923-1971 . . . . DLB-312

Okara, Gabriel 1921- DLB-125; CDWLB-3

O'Keeffe, John 1747-1833 . . . . DLB-89

Nicholas Okes [publishing house] DLB-170

Okigbo, Christopher
1930-1967 . . . . DLB-125; CDWLB-3

Okot p'Bitek 1931-1982 . . . . . DLB-125; CDWLB-3

Okpewho, Isidore 1941- DLB-157

Okri, Ben 1959- DLB-157, 231, 319

Ólafur Jóhann Sigurðsson 1918-1988 . . . . DLB-293

Old Dogs / New Tricks? New Technologies,
the Canon, and the Structure of
the Profession Y-02

Old Franklin Publishing House DLB-49

Old German Genesis and *Old German Exodus*
circa 1050-circa 1130 . . . . DLB-148

The *Old High German Isidor*
circa 790-800 . . . . DLB-148

Older, Fremont 1856-1935 . . . . DLB-25

Oldham, John 1653-1683 . . . . DLB-131

Oldman, C. B. 1894-1969 . . . . DLB-201

Olds, Sharon 1942- DLB-120

Olearius, Adam 1599-1671 . . . . DLB-164

O'Leary, Ellen 1831-1889 . . . . DLB-240

O'Leary, Juan E. 1879-1969 . . . . DLB-290

Olesha, Iurii Karlovich 1899-1960 . . . . . . DLB-272

Oliphant, Laurence 1829?-1888 . . . . . . DLB-18, 166

Oliphant, Margaret 1828-1897 . . . DLB-18, 159, 190

"Modern Novelists–Great and Small"
(1855) DLB-21

Oliveira, Carlos de 1921-1981 . . . . DLB-287

Oliver, Chad 1928-1993 . . . . DLB-8

Oliver, Mary 1935- DLB-5, 193

Ollier, Claude 1922- DLB-83

Olsen, Tillie 1912/1913-
. . . . DLB-28, 206; Y-80; CDALB-7

Olson, Charles 1910-1970 . . . . DLB-5, 16, 193

Olson, Elder 1909-1992 . . . . DLB-48, 63

Olson, Sigurd F. 1899-1982 . . . . DLB-275

The Omega Workshops DS-10

Cumulative Index

Omotoso, Kole 1943- DLB-125
Omulevsky, Innokentii Vasil'evich
    1836 [or 1837]-1883 .... DLB-238
Ondaatje, Michael 1943- DLB-60
O'Neill, Eugene 1888-1953..... DLB-7; CDALB-5
    Eugene O'Neill Memorial Theater
        Center DLB-7
    Eugene O'Neill's Letters: A Review...... Y-88
Onetti, Juan Carlos
    1909-1994 .... DLB-113; CDWLB-3
Onions, George Oliver 1872-1961 ...... DLB-153
Onofri, Arturo 1885-1928 .... DLB-114
O'Nolan, Brian 1911-1966 .... DLB-231
Oodgeroo of the Tribe Noonuccal
    (Kath Walker) 1920-1993 .... DLB-289
Opie, Amelia 1769-1853 .... DLB-116, 159
Opitz, Martin 1597-1639............... DLB-164
Oppen, George 1908-1984 .... DLB-5, 165
Oppenheim, E. Phillips 1866-1946 .... DLB-70
Oppenheim, James 1882-1932 .... DLB-28
Oppenheimer, Joel 1930-1988 .... DLB-5, 193
Optic, Oliver (see Adams, William Taylor)
Orczy, Emma, Baroness 1865-1947 ...... DLB-70
Oregon Shakespeare Festival Y-00
Origo, Iris 1902-1988 .... DLB-155
O'Riordan, Kate 1960- DLB-267
Orlovitz, Gil 1918-1973 .... DLB-2, 5
Orlovsky, Peter 1933- DLB-16
Ormond, John 1923- DLB-27
Ornitz, Samuel 1890-1957 .... DLB-28, 44
O'Rourke, P. J. 1947- DLB-185
Orozco, Olga 1920-1999............... DLB-283
Orten, Jiří 1919-1941 .... DLB-215
Ortese, Anna Maria 1914- DLB-177
Ortiz, Simon J. 1941- DLB-120, 175, 256
Ortnit and *Wolfdietrich* circa 1225-1250.... DLB-138
Orton, Joe 1933-1967 .... DLB-13, 310; CDBLB-8
Orwell, George (Eric Arthur Blair)
    1903-1950 .. DLB-15, 98, 195, 255; CDBLB-7
    The Orwell Year Y-84
    (Re-)Publishing Orwell................ Y-86
Ory, Carlos Edmundo de 1923- DLB-134
Osbey, Brenda Marie 1957- DLB-120
Osbon, B. S. 1827-1912................ DLB-43
Osborn, Sarah 1714-1796 .... DLB-200
Osborne, John 1929-1994..... DLB-13; CDBLB-7
Osgood, Frances Sargent 1811-1850..... DLB-250
Osgood, Herbert L. 1855-1918.......... DLB-47
James R. Osgood and Company DLB-49
Osgood, McIlvaine and Company...... DLB-112
O'Shaughnessy, Arthur 1844-1881...... DLB-35
Patrick O'Shea [publishing house] DLB-49
Osipov, Nikolai Petrovich 1751-1799 .... DLB-150
Oskison, John Milton 1879-1947........DLB-175
Osler, Sir William 1849-1919 .... DLB-184
Osofisan, Femi 1946- DLB-125; CDWLB-3

Ostenso, Martha 1900-1963 .... DLB-92
Ostrauskas, Kostas 1926- DLB-232
Ostriker, Alicia 1937- DLB-120
Ostrovsky, Aleksandr Nikolaevich
    1823-1886 ....DLB-277
Ostrovsky, Nikolai Alekseevich
    1904-1936 ....DLB-272
Osundare, Niyi 1947- DLB-157; CDWLB-3
Oswald, Eleazer 1755-1795 .... DLB-43
Oswald von Wolkenstein
    1376 or 1377-1445 ....DLB-179
Otero, Blas de 1916-1979 .... DLB-134
Otero, Miguel Antonio 1859-1944 ...... DLB-82
Otero, Nina 1881-1965................ DLB-209
Otero Silva, Miguel 1908-1985......... DLB-145
Otfried von Weißenburg
    circa 800-circa 875? DLB-148
Otis, Broaders and Company........... DLB-49
Otis, James (see Kaler, James Otis)
Otis, James, Jr. 1725-1783............... DLB-31
Otsup, Nikolai 1894-1958.............. DLB-317
Ottaway, James 1911-2000............. DLB-127
Ottendorfer, Oswald 1826-1900 .... DLB-23
Ottieri, Ottiero 1924-2002 ....DLB-177
Otto-Peters, Louise 1819-1895 .... DLB-129
Otway, Thomas 1652-1685 .... DLB-80
Ouellette, Fernand 1930- DLB-60
Ouida 1839-1908 .... DLB-18, 156
Outing Publishing Company DLB-46
Overbury, Sir Thomas
    circa 1581-1613 .... DLB-151
The Overlook Press DLB-46
Ovid 43 B.C.-A.D. 17 .... DLB-211; CDWLB-1
Oviedo, Gonzalo Fernández de
    1478-1557..................... DLB-318
Owen, Guy 1925-1981................. DLB-5
Owen, John 1564-1622................ DLB-121
John Owen [publishing house] DLB-49
Peter Owen Limited DLB-112
Owen, Robert 1771-1858 ....DLB-107, 158
Owen, Wilfred
    1893-1918 .... DLB-20; DS-18; CDBLB-6
    A Centenary Celebration............. Y-93
    The Wilfred Owen Association Y-98
The Owl and the Nightingale
    circa 1189-1199 .... DLB-146
Owsley, Frank L. 1890-1956 .... DLB-17
Oxford, Seventeenth Earl of, Edward
    de Vere 1550-1604................DLB-172
OyamO (Charles F. Gordon)
    1943- DLB-266
Ozerov, Vladislav Aleksandrovich
    1769-1816 .... DLB-150
Ozick, Cynthia 1928- ...DLB-28, 152, 299; Y-82
    First Strauss "Livings" Awarded
        to Cynthia Ozick and
        Raymond Carver
        An Interview with Cynthia Ozick Y-83
    Tribute to Michael M. Rea Y-97

P

Pace, Richard 1482?-1536 .... DLB-167
Pacey, Desmond 1917-1975 .... DLB-88
Pacheco, José Emilio 1939- DLB-290
Pack, Robert 1929- DLB-5
Padell Publishing Company DLB-46
Padgett, Ron 1942- DLB-5
Padilla, Ernesto Chávez 1944- DLB-122
L. C. Page and Company.............. DLB-49
Page, Louise 1955- DLB-233
Page, P. K. 1916- DLB-68
Page, Thomas Nelson
    1853-1922 ....DLB-12, 78; DS-13
Page, Walter Hines 1855-1918........DLB-71, 91
Paget, Francis Edward 1806-1882 ...... DLB-163
Paget, Violet (see Lee, Vernon)
Pagliarani, Elio 1927- DLB-128
Pagnol, Marcel 1895-1974 .... DLB-321
Pain, Barry 1864-1928 ....DLB-135, 197
Pain, Philip ?-circa 1666............... DLB-24
Paine, Robert Treat, Jr. 1773-1811 .... DLB-37
Paine, Thomas
    1737-1809 .... DLB-31, 43, 73, 158; CDALB-2
Painter, George D. 1914- DLB-155
Painter, William 1540?-1594 .... DLB-136
Palazzeschi, Aldo 1885-1974...... DLB-114, 264
Palei, Marina Anatol'evna 1955- DLB-285
Palencia, Alfonso de 1424-1492 .... DLB-286
Palés Matos, Luis 1898-1959 .... DLB-290
Paley, Grace 1922- DLB-28, 218
Paley, William 1743-1805.............. DLB-252
Palfrey, John Gorham
    1796-1881................. DLB-1, 30, 235
Palgrave, Francis Turner 1824-1897...... DLB-35
Palmer, Joe H. 1904-1952..............DLB-171
Palmer, Michael 1943- DLB-169
Palmer, Nettie 1885-1964 .... DLB-260
Palmer, Vance 1885-1959 .... DLB-260
Paltock, Robert 1697-1767 .... DLB-39
Paludan, Jacob 1896-1975............. DLB-214
Paludin-Müller, Frederik 1809-1876..... DLB-300
Pan Books Limited.................. DLB-112
Panaev, Ivan Ivanovich 1812-1862...... DLB-198
Panaeva, Avdot'ia Iakovlevna
    1820-1893 .... DLB-238
Panama, Norman 1914-2003 and
    Frank, Melvin 1913-1988........... DLB-26
Pancake, Breece D'J 1952-1979......... DLB-130
Panduro, Leif 1923-1977 .... DLB-214
Panero, Leopoldo 1909-1962 .... DLB-108
Pangborn, Edgar 1909-1976 .... DLB-8
Panizzi, Sir Anthony 1797-1879......... DLB-184
Panneton, Philippe (see Ringuet)
Panova, Vera Fedorovna 1905-1973..... DLB-302
Panshin, Alexei 1940- DLB-8

Pansy (see Alden, Isabella)
Pantheon Books...................DLB-46
Papadat-Bengescu, Hortensia
 1876-1955 ....DLB-220
Papantonio, Michael 1907-1976 ....DLB-187
Paperback Library...................DLB-46
Paperback Science Fiction DLB-8
Papini, Giovanni 1881-1956 ....DLB-264
Paquet, Alfons 1881-1944 ....DLB-66
Paracelsus 1493-1541.................DLB-179
Paradis, Suzanne 1936- DLB-53
Páral, Vladimír, 1932- DLB-232
Pardoe, Julia 1804-1862................DLB-166
Paredes, Américo 1915-1999 ....DLB-209
Pareja Diezcanseco, Alfredo 1908-1993...DLB-145
Parents' Magazine Press................DLB-46
Paretsky, Sara 1947- DLB-306
Parfit, Derek 1942- DLB-262
Parise, Goffredo 1929-1986 ....DLB-177
Parish, Mitchell 1900-1993 ....DLB-265
Parizeau, Alice 1930-1990 ....DLB-60
Park, Ruth 1923?- DLB-260
Parke, John 1754-1789 ....DLB-31
Parker, Dan 1893-1967 ....DLB-241
Parker, Dorothy 1893-1967........DLB-11, 45, 86
Parker, Gilbert 1860-1932 ....DLB-99
Parker, James 1714-1770.................DLB-43
Parker, John [publishing house].........DLB-106
Parker, Matthew 1504-1575.............DLB-213
Parker, Robert B. 1932- DLB-306
Parker, Stewart 1941-1988..............DLB-245
Parker, Theodore 1810-1860....DLB-1, 235; DS-5
Parker, William Riley 1906-1968 ....DLB-103
J. H. Parker [publishing house] DLB-106
Parkes, Bessie Rayner (Madame Belloc)
 1829-1925.....................DLB-240
Parkman, Francis
 1823-1893.........DLB-1, 30, 183, 186, 235
Parks, Gordon 1912- DLB-33
Parks, Tim 1954- DLB-231
Parks, William 1698-1750 ....DLB-43
William Parks [publishing house] DLB-49
Parley, Peter (see Goodrich, Samuel Griswold)
Parmenides late sixth-fifth century B.C.....DLB-176
Parnell, Thomas 1679-1718 ....DLB-95
Parnicki, Teodor 1908-1988 ....DLB-215
Parnok, Sofiia Iakovlevna (Parnokh)
 1885-1933......................DLB-295
Parr, Catherine 1513?-1548...............DLB-136
Parra, Nicanor 1914- DLB-283
Parrington, Vernon L. 1871-1929 .....DLB-17, 63
Parrish, Maxfield 1870-1966 ....DLB-188
Parronchi, Alessandro 1914-............DLB-128
Parshchikov, Aleksei Maksimovich
 (Raiderman) 1954- DLB-285
Partisan Review DLB-303

Parton, James 1822-1891...............DLB-30
Parton, Sara Payson Willis
 1811-1872 ....DLB-43, 74, 239
S. W. Partridge and Company DLB-106
Parun, Vesna 1922- DLB-181; CDWLB-4
Pascal, Blaise 1623-1662................DLB-268
Pasinetti, Pier Maria 1913- DLB-177
 Tribute to Albert Erskine Y-93
Pasolini, Pier Paolo 1922-1975......DLB-128, 177
Pastan, Linda 1932- DLB-5
Pasternak, Boris
 1890-1960....................DLB-302
Paston, George (Emily Morse Symonds)
 1860-1936 ....DLB-149, 197
The Paston Letters 1422-1509 ....DLB-146
Pastoral Novel of the Sixteenth
 Century, The DLB-318
Pastorius, Francis Daniel
 1651-circa 1720.................DLB-24
Patchen, Kenneth 1911-1972 ....DLB-16, 48
Pater, Walter 1839-1894 ..DLB-57, 156; CDBLB-4
 Aesthetic Poetry (1873) DLB-35
 "Style" (1888) [excerpt] DLB-57
Paterson, A. B. "Banjo" 1864-1941 ......DLB-230
Paterson, Katherine 1932- DLB-52
Patmore, Coventry 1823-1896.........DLB-35, 98
Paton, Alan 1903-1988 ....DLB-225; DS-17
Paton, Joseph Noel 1821-1901............DLB-35
Paton Walsh, Jill 1937- DLB-161
Patrick, Edwin Hill ("Ted") 1901-1964 ...DLB-137
Patrick, John 1906-1995..................DLB-7
Pattee, Fred Lewis 1863-1950 ....DLB-71
Patterson, Alicia 1906-1963 ....DLB-127
Patterson, Eleanor Medill 1881-1948......DLB-29
Patterson, Eugene 1923- DLB-127
Patterson, Joseph Medill 1879-1946.......DLB-29
Pattillo, Henry 1726-1801 ....DLB-37
Paul, Elliot 1891-1958 ....DLB-4; DS-15
Paul, Jean (see Richter, Johann Paul Friedrich)
Paul, Kegan, Trench, Trubner and
 Company Limited................DLB-106
Peter Paul Book Company DLB-49
Stanley Paul and Company Limited DLB-112
Paulding, James Kirke
 1778-1860 ....DLB-3, 59, 74, 250
Paulin, Tom 1949- DLB-40
Pauper, Peter, Press...................DLB-46
Paustovsky, Konstantin Georgievich
 1892-1968 ....DLB-272
Pavese, Cesare 1908-1950 ....DLB-128, 177
Pavić, Milorad 1929- DLB-181; CDWLB-4
Pavlov, Konstantin 1933- DLB-181
Pavlov, Nikolai Filippovich 1803-1864......DLB-198
Pavlova, Karolina Karlovna 1807-1893 ....DLB-205
Pavlović, Miodrag
 1928- DLB-181; CDWLB-4
Pavlovsky, Eduardo 1933- DLB-305

Paxton, John 1911-1985................DLB-44
Payn, James 1830-1898 ....DLB-18
Payne, John 1842-1916 ....DLB-35
Payne, John Howard 1791-1852 ....DLB-37
Payson and Clarke DLB-46
Paz, Octavio 1914-1998..........DLB-290; Y-90, 98
 Nobel Lecture 1990..................Y-90
Pazzi, Roberto 1946- DLB-196
Pea, Enrico 1881-1958.................DLB-264
Peabody, Elizabeth Palmer
 1804-1894.....................DLB-1, 223
 Preface to *Record of a School:
 Exemplifying the General Principles
 of Spiritual Culture*..................DS-5
Elizabeth Palmer Peabody
 [publishing house]..................DLB-49
Peabody, Josephine Preston 1874-1922 ...DLB-249
Peabody, Oliver William Bourn
 1799-1848......................DLB-59
Peace, Roger 1899-1968 ....DLB-127
Peacham, Henry 1578-1644?...........DLB-151
Peacham, Henry, the Elder
 1547-1634 ....DLB-172, 236
Peachtree Publishers, Limited DLB-46
Peacock, Molly 1947- DLB-120
Peacock, Thomas Love 1785-1866 ...DLB-96, 116
Pead, Deuel ?-1727....................DLB-24
Peake, Mervyn 1911-1968......DLB-15, 160, 255
Peale, Rembrandt 1778-1860 ....DLB-183
Pear Tree Press DLB-112
Pearce, Philippa 1920- DLB-161
H. B. Pearson [publishing house].........DLB-49
Pearson, Hesketh 1887-1964 ....DLB-149
Peattie, Donald Culross 1898-1964 ......DLB-275
Pechersky, Andrei (see Mel'nikov, Pavel Ivanovich)
Peck, George W. 1840-1916 ....DLB-23, 42
H. C. Peck and Theo. Bliss
 [publishing house]..................DLB-49
Peck, Harry Thurston 1856-1914 .....DLB-71, 91
Peden, William 1913-1999...............DLB-234
 Tribute to William Goyen Y-83
Peele, George 1556-1596...........DLB-62, 167
Pegler, Westbrook 1894-1969 ....DLB-171
Péguy, Charles 1873-1914 ....DLB-258
Peirce, Charles Sanders 1839-1914 ......DLB-270
Pekić, Borislav 1930-1992 ...DLB-181; CDWLB-4
Pelecanos, George P. 1957- DLB-306
Pelevin, Viktor Olegovich 1962- DLB-285
Pellegrini and Cudahy.................DLB-46
Pelletier, Aimé (see Vac, Bertrand)
Pelletier, Francine 1959- DLB-251
Pellicer, Carlos 1897?-1977.............DLB-290
Pemberton, Sir Max 1863-1950.........DLB-70
de la Peña, Terri 1947- DLB-209
Penfield, Edward 1866-1925 ....DLB-188
Penguin Books [U.K.] DLB-112

Fifty Penguin Years Y-85	Peters, Lenrie 1932- DLB-117	Phillips, Ulrich B. 1877-1934. . . . . .DLB-17
Penguin Collectors' Society Y-98	Peters, Robert 1924- DLB-105	Phillips, Wendell 1811-1884. . . . . DLB-235
Penguin Books [U.S.] DLB-46	"Foreword to *Ludwig of Baviria*" DLB-105	Phillips, Willard 1784-1873. . . . . DLB-59
Penn, William 1644-1718 . . . . DLB-24	Petersham, Maud 1889-1971 and Petersham, Miska 1888-1960. . . . . DLB-22	Phillips, William 1907-2002 . . . . .DLB-137
Penn Publishing Company. DLB-49		Phillips, Sampson and Company DLB-49
Penna, Sandro 1906-1977 . . . . DLB-114	Peterson, Charles Jacobs 1819-1887. . . . . . DLB-79	Phillpotts, Adelaide Eden (Adelaide Ross) 1896-1993 . . . . DLB-191
Pennell, Joseph 1857-1926. . . . . DLB-188	Peterson, Len 1917- DLB-88	
Penner, Jonathan 1940- Y-83	Peterson, Levi S. 1933- DLB-206	Phillpotts, Eden 1862-1960. . .DLB-10, 70, 135, 153
Pennington, Lee 1939- Y-82	Peterson, Louis 1922-1998 . . . . DLB-76	Philo circa 20-15 B.C.-circa A.D. 50 . . . . . . .DLB-176
Penton, Brian 1904-1951 . . . . DLB-260	Peterson, T. B., and Brothers DLB-49	*Philosophical Dictionary*, Voltaire DLB-314
Pepper, Stephen C. 1891-1972 . . . . .DLB-270	Petitclair, Pierre 1813-1860. . . . . DLB-99	Philosophical Library DLB-46
Pepys, Samuel 1633-1703. . . . . DLB-101, 213; CDBLB-2	Petrescu, Camil 1894-1957 . . . . DLB-220	Philosophy Eighteenth-Century Philosophical Background DLB-31
	Petronius circa A.D. 20-A.D. 66 . . . . DLB-211; CDWLB-1	
Percy, Thomas 1729-1811 . . . . DLB-104		Philosophic Thought in Boston DLB-235
Percy, Walker 1916-1990. . . . . . .DLB-2; Y-80, 90	Petrov, Aleksandar 1938- DLB-181	Translators of the Twelfth Century: Literary Issues Raised and Impact Created DLB-115
Tribute to Caroline Gordon Y-81	Petrov, Evgenii (Evgenii Petrovich Kataev) 1903-1942 .DLB-272	
Percy, William 1575-1648. . . . . .DLB-172		
Perec, Georges 1936-1982 . . . . DLB-83, 299	Petrov, Gavriil 1730-1801. . . . . DLB-150	Elihu Phinney [publishing house]. DLB-49
Perelman, Bob 1947- DLB-193	Petrov, Valeri 1920- DLB-181	Phoenix, John (see Derby, George Horatio)
Perelman, S. J. 1904-1979 . . . . DLB-11, 44	Petrov, Vasilii Petrovich 1736-1799 . . . . . DLB-150	PHYLON (Fourth Quarter, 1950), The Negro in Literature: The Current Scene. DLB-76
Pérez de Guzmán, Fernán ca. 1377-ca. 1460. . . . . DLB-286	Petrović, Rastko 1898-1949 . . . . .DLB-147; CDWLB-4	
Perez, Raymundo "Tigre" 1946- DLB-122	Petrushevskaia, Liudmila Stefanovna 1938- DLB-285	*Physiologus* circa 1070-circa 1150 . . . . DLB-148
		Piccolo, Lucio 1903-1969 . . . . DLB-114
Peri Rossi, Cristina 1941- DLB-145, 290	*Petruslied* circa 854?. DLB-148	Pichette, Henri 1924-2000 . . . . DLB-321
Perkins, Eugene 1932- DLB-41	Petry, Ann 1908-1997. . . . . DLB-76	Pickard, Tom 1946- DLB-40
Perkins, Maxwell The Claims of Business and Literature: An Undergraduate Essay Y-01	Pettie, George circa 1548-1589 . . . . DLB-136	William Pickering [publishing house]. . . . DLB-106
	Pétur Gunnarsson 1947- DLB-293	Pickthall, Marjorie 1883-1922 . . . . DLB-92
	Peyton, K. M. 1929- DLB-161	Picoult, Jodi 1966- DLB-292
Perkins, William 1558-1602 . . . . DLB-281	Pfaffe Konrad fl. circa 1172 . . . . DLB-148	Pictorial Printing Company DLB-49
Perkoff, Stuart Z. 1930-1974. . . . . DLB-16	Pfaffe Lamprecht fl. circa 1150 . . . . DLB-148	Piel, Gerard 1915-2004. . . . . .DLB-137
Perley, Moses Henry 1804-1862 . . . . DLB-99	Pfeiffer, Emily 1827-1890 . . . . DLB-199	"An Announcement to Our Readers," Gerard Piel's Statement in *Scientific American* (April 1948) DLB-137
Permabooks DLB-46	Pforzheimer, Carl H. 1879-1957 . . . . DLB-140	
Perovsky, Aleksei Alekseevich (Antonii Pogorel'sky) 1787-1836. . . . . DLB-198	Phaedrus circa 18 B.C.-circa A.D. 50 . . . . . DLB-211	
	Phaer, Thomas 1510?-1560 . . . . DLB-167	Pielmeier, John 1949- DLB-266
Perrault, Charles 1628-1703 . . . . DLB-268	Phaidon Press Limited DLB-112	Piercy, Marge 1936- DLB-120, 227
Perri, Henry 1561-1617 . . . . DLB-236	Pharr, Robert Deane 1916-1992. . . . . DLB-33	Pierro, Albino 1916-1995 . . . . DLB-128
Perrin, Alice 1867-1934. . . . . DLB-156	Phelps, Elizabeth Stuart 1815-1852. . . . . . DLB-202	Pignotti, Lamberto 1926- DLB-128
Perry, Anne 1938- DLB-276	Phelps, Elizabeth Stuart 1844-1911. . . DLB-74, 221	Pike, Albert 1809-1891. . . . . .DLB-74
Perry, Bliss 1860-1954 . . . . DLB-71	Philander von der Linde (see Mencke, Johann Burckhard)	Pike, Zebulon Montgomery 1779-1813. . . DLB-183
Perry, Eleanor 1915-1981. . . . . DLB-44		Pillat, Ion 1891-1945 . . . . DLB-220
Perry, Henry (see Perri, Henry)	Philby, H. St. John B. 1885-1960 . . . . DLB-195	Pil'niak, Boris Andreevich (Boris Andreevich Vogau) 1894-1938 . . . . .DLB-272
Perry, Matthew 1794-1858 . . . . DLB-183	Philip, Marlene Nourbese 1947- DLB-157	
Perry, Sampson 1747-1823 . . . . DLB-158	Philippe, Charles-Louis 1874-1909 . . . . . . DLB-65	Pilon, Jean-Guy 1930- DLB-60
Perse, Saint-John 1887-1975 . . . . DLB-258	Philips, John 1676-1708. . . . . DLB-95	Pinar, Florencia fl. ca. late fifteenth century. DLB-286
Persius A.D. 34-A.D. 62 . . . . DLB-211	Philips, Katherine 1632-1664 . . . . DLB-131	
Perutz, Leo 1882-1957 . . . . DLB-81	Phillipps, Sir Thomas 1792-1872 . . . . DLB-184	Pinckney, Eliza Lucas 1722-1793 . . . . DLB-200
Pesetsky, Bette 1932- DLB-130	Phillips, Caryl 1958- DLB-157	Pinckney, Josephine 1895-1957 . . . . DLB-6
Pessanha, Camilo 1867-1926 . . . . DLB-287	Phillips, David Graham 1867-1911 . . . . DLB-9, 12, 303	Pindar circa 518 B.C.-circa 438 B.C. .DLB-176; CDWLB-1
Pessoa, Fernando 1888-1935 . . . . DLB-287		
Pestalozzi, Johann Heinrich 1746-1827 . . . . DLB-94	Phillips, Jayne Anne 1952- DLB-292; Y-80	Pindar, Peter (see Wolcot, John)
Peter, Laurence J. 1919-1990 . . . . DLB-53	Tribute to Seymour Lawrence. Y-94	Pineda, Cecile 1942- DLB-209
Peter of Spain circa 1205-1277 . . . . DLB-115	Phillips, Robert 1938- DLB-105	Pinero, Arthur Wing 1855-1934. . . . . DLB-10
Peterkin, Julia 1880-1961 . . . . DLB-9	"Finding, Losing, Reclaiming: A Note on My Poems" DLB-105	Piñero, Miguel 1946-1988 . . . . DLB-266
Peters, Ellis (Edith Pargeter) 1913-1995. .DLB-276		Pinget, Robert 1919-1997 . . . . DLB-83
	Tribute to William Goyen. Y-83	Pinkney, Edward Coote 1802-1828 . . . . . DLB-248
	Phillips, Stephen 1864-1915 . . . . DLB-10	Pinnacle Books DLB-46

Piñon, Nélida 1935- DLB-145, 307
Pinsky, Robert 1940- Y-82
    Reappointed Poet Laureate............Y-98
Pinter, Harold 1930- ...DLB-13, 310; CDBLB-8
    Writing for the Theatre.............DLB-13
Pinto, Fernão Mendes 1509/1511?-1583 ..DLB-287
Piontek, Heinz 1925- DLB-75
Piozzi, Hester Lynch [Thrale]
    1741-1821 ....DLB-104, 142
Piper, H. Beam 1904-1964................DLB-8
Piper, Watty DLB-22
Pirandello, Luigi 1867-1936.............DLB-264
Pirckheimer, Caritas 1467-1532........DLB-179
Pirckheimer, Willibald 1470-1530 ....DLB-179
Pires, José Cardoso 1925-1998 ....DLB-287
Pisar, Samuel 1929- Y-83
Pisarev, Dmitrii Ivanovich 1840-1868 ....DLB-277
Pisemsky, Aleksei Feofilaktovich
    1821-1881 ....DLB-238
Pitkin, Timothy 1766-1847 ....DLB-30
Pitter, Ruth 1897-1992................DLB-20
Pix, Mary 1666-1709 ....DLB-80
Pixerécourt, René Charles Guilbert de
    1773-1844 ....DLB-192
Pizarnik, Alejandra 1936-1972 ....DLB-283
Plá, Josefina 1909-1999 ....DLB-290
Plaatje, Sol T. 1876-1932 ....DLB-125, 225
Planchon, Roger 1931- DLB-321
Plante, David 1940- Y-83
Platen, August von 1796-1835 ....DLB-90
Plantinga, Alvin 1932- DLB-279
Plath, Sylvia
    1932-1963 ....DLB-5, 6, 152; CDALB-1
Plato circa 428 B.C.-348-347 B.C.
    ....DLB-176; CDWLB-1
Plato, Ann 1824-? DLB-239
Platon 1737-1812 ....DLB-150
Platonov, Andrei Platonovich (Andrei
    Platonovich Klimentev)
    1899-1951 ....DLB-272
Platt, Charles 1945- DLB-261
Platt and Munk Company..............DLB-46
Plautus circa 254 B.C.-184 B.C.
    ....DLB-211; CDWLB-1
Playboy Press.......................DLB-46
John Playford [publishing house].......DLB-170
Der Pleier fl. circa 1250 ....DLB-138
Pleijel, Agneta 1940- DLB-257
Plenzdorf, Ulrich 1934- DLB-75
Pleshcheev, Aleksei Nikolaevich
    1825?-1893 ....DLB-277
Plessen, Elizabeth 1944- DLB-75
Pletnev, Petr Aleksandrovich
    1792-1865 ....DLB-205
Pliekšāne, Elza Rozenberga (see Aspazija)
Pliekšāns, Jānis (see Rainis, Jānis)
Plievier, Theodor 1892-1955 ....DLB-69

Plimpton, George 1927-2003 . . DLB-185, 241; Y-99
Pliny the Elder A.D. 23/24-A.D. 79 ....DLB-211
Pliny the Younger
    circa A.D. 61-A.D. 112 ....DLB-211
Plomer, William
    1903-1973 ....DLB-20, 162, 191, 225
Plotinus 204-270............DLB-176; CDWLB-1
Plowright, Teresa 1952- DLB-251
Plume, Thomas 1630-1704 ....DLB-213
Plumly, Stanley 1939- DLB-5, 193
Plumpp, Sterling D. 1940- DLB-41
Plunkett, James 1920-2003.............DLB-14
Plutarch
    circa 46-circa 120......DLB-176; CDWLB-1
Plymell, Charles 1935- DLB-16
Pocket Books.......................DLB-46
Podestá, José J. 1858-1937 ....DLB-305
Poe, Edgar Allan 1809-1849
    ....DLB-3, 59, 73, 74, 248; CDALB-2
    The Poe Studies Association...........Y-99
Poe, James 1921-1980 ....DLB-44
The Poet Laureate of the United States......Y-86
    Statements from Former Consultants
        in Poetry......................Y-86
Poetry
    Aesthetic Poetry (1873) DLB-35
    A Century of Poetry, a Lifetime of
        Collecting: J. M. Edelstein's
        Collection of Twentieth-
        Century American Poetry Y-02
    "Certain Gifts," by Betty Adcock DLB-105
    Concrete Poetry DLB-307
    Contempo Caravan: Kites in a
        Windstorm....................Y-85
    "Contemporary Verse Story-telling,"
        by Jonathan Holden DLB-105
    "A Detail in a Poem," by Fred
        Chappell.....................DLB-105
    "The English Renaissance of Art"
        (1908), by Oscar Wilde DLB-35
    "Every Man His Own Poet; or,
        The Inspired Singer's Recipe
        Book" (1877), by
        H. W. Mallock................DLB-35
    "Eyes Across Centuries: Contemporary
        Poetry and 'That Vision Thing,'"
        by Philip Dacey DLB-105
    A Field Guide to Recent Schools
        of American Poetry..............Y-86
    "Finding, Losing, Reclaiming:
        A Note on My Poems,
        by Robert Phillips"...........DLB-105
    "The Fleshly School of Poetry and Other
        Phenomena of the Day" (1872) ...DLB-35
    "The Fleshly School of Poetry:
        Mr. D. G. Rossetti" (1871) DLB-35
    The G. Ross Roy Scottish Poetry Collection
        at the University of South Carolina ..Y-89
    "Getting Started: Accepting the Regions
        You Own—or Which Own You,"
        by Walter McDonald DLB-105
    "The Good, The Not So Good," by
        Stephen Dunn................DLB-105

    The Griffin Poetry Prize Y-00
    The Hero as Poet. Dante; Shakspeare
        (1841), by Thomas Carlyle DLB-32
    "Images and 'Images,'" by Charles
        Simic.......................DLB-105
    "Into the Mirror," by Peter Cooley...DLB-105
    "Knots into Webs: Some Autobiographical
        Sources," by Dabney Stuart DLB-105
    "L'Envoi" (1882), by Oscar Wilde DLB-35
    "Living in Ruin," by Gerald Stern ...DLB-105
    Looking for the Golden Mountain:
        Poetry Reviewing................Y-89
    Lyric Poetry (French)...............DLB-268
    Medieval Galician-Portuguese
        Poetry.......................DLB-287
    "The No Self, the Little Self, and the
        Poets," by Richard Moore DLB-105
    On Some of the Characteristics of Modern
        Poetry and On the Lyrical Poems of
        Alfred Tennyson (1831).........DLB-32
    The Pitt Poetry Series: Poetry Publishing
        Today........................Y-85
    "The Poetry File," by Edward
        Field DLB-105
    Poetry in Nineteenth-Century France:
        Cultural Background and Critical
        Commentary DLB-217
    The Poetry of Jorge Luis Borges........Y-86
    "The Poet's Kaleidoscope: The Element
        of Surprise in the Making of the
        Poem" by Madeline DeFrees DLB-105
    The Pre-Raphaelite Controversy DLB-35
    Protest Poetry in Castile DLB-286
    "Reflections: After a Tornado,"
        by Judson Jerome DLB-105
    Statements from Former Consultants
        in Poetry......................Y-86
    Statements on the Art of Poetry DLB-54
    The Study of Poetry (1880), by
        Matthew Arnold................DLB-35
    A Survey of Poetry Anthologies,
        1879-1960 ....DLB-54
    Thoughts on Poetry and Its Varieties
        (1833), by John Stuart Mill.......DLB-32
    Under the Microscope (1872), by
        A. C. Swinburne...............DLB-35
    The Unterberg Poetry Center of the
        92nd Street Y Y-98
    Victorian Poetry: Five Critical
        Views DLBV-35
    Year in Poetry Y-83-92, 94–01
    Year's Work in American Poetry Y-82
Poets
    The Lives of the Poets (1753) DLB-142
    Minor Poets of the Earlier
        Seventeenth Century DLB-121
    Other British Poets Who Fell
        in the Great War DLB-216
    Other Poets [French]...............DLB-217
    Second-Generation Minor Poets of
        the Seventeenth Century DLB-126
    Third-Generation Minor Poets of
        the Seventeenth Century DLB-131

Pogodin, Mikhail Petrovich 1800-1875... DLB-198
Pogorel'sky, Antonii
  (see Perovsky, Aleksei Alekseevich)
Pohl, Frederik 1919- DLB-8
   Tribute to Isaac Asimov............... Y-92
   Tribute to Theodore Sturgeon......... Y-85
Poirier, Louis (see Gracq, Julien)
Poláček, Karel 1892-1945... DLB-215; CDWLB-4
Polanyi, Michael 1891-1976 .... DLB-100
Pole, Reginald 1500-1558............. DLB-132
Polevoi, Nikolai Alekseevich 1796-1846.. DLB-198
Polezhaev, Aleksandr Ivanovich
  1804-1838 .... DLB-205
Poliakoff, Stephen 1952- DLB-13
Polidori, John William 1795-1821....... DLB-116
Polite, Carlene Hatcher 1932- DLB-33
Pollard, Alfred W. 1859-1944.......... DLB-201
Pollard, Edward A. 1832-1872 .... DLB-30
Pollard, Graham 1903-1976 .... DLB-201
Pollard, Percival 1869-1911 .... DLB-71
Pollard and Moss DLB-49
Pollock, Sharon 1936- DLB-60
Polonsky, Abraham 1910-1999......... DLB-26
Polonsky, Iakov Petrovich 1819-1898 ... DLB-277
Polotsky, Simeon 1629-1680 .... DLB-150
Polybius circa 200 B.C.-118 B.C. DLB-176
Pomialovsky, Nikolai Gerasimovich
  1835-1863 .... DLB-238
Pomilio, Mario 1921-1990 ....DLB-177
Pompéia, Raul (Raul d'Avila Pompéia)
  1863-1895 .... DLB-307
Ponce, Mary Helen 1938- DLB-122
Ponce-Montoya, Juanita 1949- DLB-122
Ponet, John 1516?-1556 .... DLB-132
Ponge, Francis 1899-1988........ DLB-258; Y-02
Poniatowska, Elena
  1933- DLB-113; CDWLB-3
Ponsard, François 1814-1867 .... DLB-192
William Ponsonby [publishing house] DLB-170
Pontiggia, Giuseppe 1934- DLB-196
Pontoppidan, Henrik 1857-1943........ DLB-300
Pony Stories, Omnibus Essay on DLB-160
Poole, Ernest 1880-1950............... DLB-9
Poole, Sophia 1804-1891 .... DLB-166
Poore, Benjamin Perley 1820-1887....... DLB-23
Popa, Vasko 1922-1991 .... DLB-181; CDWLB-4
Pope, Abbie Hanscom 1858-1894....... DLB-140
Pope, Alexander
  1688-1744...... DLB-95, 101, 213; CDBLB-2
Poplavsky, Boris 1903-1935 .... DLB-317
Popov, Aleksandr Serafimovich
  (see Serafimovich, Aleksandr Serafimovich)
Popov, Evgenii Anatol'evich 1946- DLB-285
Popov, Mikhail Ivanovich
  1742-circa 1790................. DLB-150
Popović, Aleksandar 1929-1996 .... DLB-181
Popper, Karl 1902-1994 .... DLB-262

Popular Culture Association/
  American Culture Association Y-99
Popular Library DLB-46
Poquelin, Jean-Baptiste (see Molière)
Porete, Marguerite ?-1310 .... DLB-208
Porlock, Martin (see MacDonald, Philip)
Porpoise Press..................... DLB-112
Porta, Antonio 1935-1989 .... DLB-128
Porter, Anna Maria 1780-1832..... DLB-116, 159
Porter, Cole 1891-1964 .... DLB-265
Porter, David 1780-1843............. DLB-183
Porter, Eleanor H. 1868-1920........... DLB-9
Porter, Gene Stratton (see Stratton-Porter, Gene)
Porter, Hal 1911-1984 .... DLB-260
Porter, Henry circa sixteenth century..... DLB-62
Porter, Jane 1776-1850 .... DLB-116, 159
Porter, Katherine Anne 1890-1980
  ....DLB-4, 9, 102; Y-80; DS-12; CDALB-7
  The Katherine Anne Porter Society...... Y-01
Porter, Peter 1929- DLB-40, 289
Porter, William Sydney (O. Henry)
  1862-1910 ....DLB-12, 78, 79; CDALB-3
Porter, William T. 1809-1858 .... DLB-3, 43, 250
Porter and Coates.................... DLB-49
Portillo Trambley, Estela 1927-1998..... DLB-209
Portis, Charles 1933- DLB-6
Medieval Galician-Portuguese Poetry.... DLB-287
Posey, Alexander 1873-1908...........DLB-175
Postans, Marianne circa 1810-1865 ..... DLB-166
Postgate, Raymond 1896-1971 ....DLB-276
Postl, Carl (see Sealsfield, Carl)
Postmodern Holocaust Fiction DLB-299
Poston, Ted 1906-1974............. DLB-51
Potekhin, Aleksei Antipovich
  1829-1908 .... DLB-238
Potok, Chaim 1929-2002 .... DLB-28, 152
  A Conversation with Chaim Potok Y-84
  Tribute to Bernard Malamud Y-86
Potter, Beatrix 1866-1943............. DLB-141
  The Beatrix Potter Society............ Y-98
Potter, David M. 1910-1971 .... DLB-17
Potter, Dennis 1935-1994 .... DLB-233
John E. Potter and Company DLB-49
Pottle, Frederick A. 1897-1987 .....DLB-103; Y-87
Poulin, Jacques 1937- DLB-60
Pound, Ezra 1885-1972
  .... DLB-4, 45, 63; DS-15; CDALB-4
  The Cost of the Cantos: William Bird
    to Ezra Pound Y-01
  The Ezra Pound Society Y-01
Poverman, C. E. 1944- DLB-234
Povey, Meic 1950- DLB-310
Povich, Shirley 1905-1998 ....DLB-171
Powell, Anthony 1905-2000... DLB-15; CDBLB-7
  The Anthony Powell Society: Powell and
    the First Biennial Conference Y-01

Powell, Dawn 1897-1965
  Dawn Powell, Where Have You Been
    All Our Lives?................... Y-97
Powell, John Wesley 1834-1902........ DLB-186
Powell, Padgett 1952- DLB-234
Powers, J. F. 1917-1999............. DLB-130
Powers, Jimmy 1903-1995 .... DLB-241
Pownall, David 1938- DLB-14
Powys, John Cowper 1872-1963..... DLB-15, 255
Powys, Llewelyn 1884-1939........... DLB-98
Powys, T. F. 1875-1953 .... DLB-36, 162
  The Powys Society.................. Y-98
Poynter, Nelson 1903-1978...........DLB-127
Prado, Adélia 1935- DLB-307
Prado, Pedro 1886-1952............ DLB-283
Prados, Emilio 1899-1962 .... DLB-134
Praed, Mrs. Caroline (see Praed, Rosa)
Praed, Rosa (Mrs. Caroline Praed)
  1851-1935 .... DLB-230
Praed, Winthrop Mackworth 1802-1839 .. DLB-96
Praeger Publishers DLB-46
Praetorius, Johannes 1630-1680 .... DLB-168
Pratolini, Vasco 1913-1991...........DLB-177
Pratt, E. J. 1882-1964 .... DLB-92
Pratt, Samuel Jackson 1749-1814 .... DLB-39
Preciado Martin, Patricia 1939- DLB-209
Préfontaine, Yves 1937- DLB-53
Prelutsky, Jack 1940- DLB-61
Prentice, George D. 1802-1870.......... DLB-43
Prentice-Hall....................... DLB-46
Prescott, Orville 1906-1996 .... Y-96
Prescott, William Hickling
  1796-1859......... DLB-1, 30, 59, 235
Prešeren, Francè
  1800-1849 ....DLB-147; CDWLB-4
Presses (See also Publishing)
  Small Presses in Great Britain and
    Ireland, 1960-1985 .... DLB-40
  Small Presses I: Jargon Society.......... Y-84
  Small Presses II: The Spirit That Moves
    Us Press Y-85
  Small Presses III: Pushcart Press Y-87
Preston, Margaret Junkin
  1820-1897 .... DLB-239, 248
Preston, May Wilson 1873-1949 ...... DLB-188
Preston, Thomas 1537-1598........... DLB-62
Prévert, Jacques 1900-1977 .... DLB-258
Prévost d'Exiles, Antoine François
  1697-1763...................... DLB-314
Price, Anthony 1928- DLB-276
Price, Reynolds 1933- DLB-2, 218, 278
Price, Richard 1723-1791 .... DLB-158
Price, Richard 1949- Y-81
Prichard, Katharine Susannah
  1883-1969 .... DLB-260
Prideaux, John 1578-1650............. DLB-236
Priest, Christopher 1943- DLB-14, 207, 261

Priestley, J. B. 1894-1984
. . . DLB-10, 34, 77, 100, 139; Y-84; CDBLB-6

Priestley, Joseph 1733-1804 . . . . DLB-252

Prigov, Dmitrii Aleksandrovich 1940- . . DLB-285

Prime, Benjamin Young 1733-1791 . . . . DLB-31

Primrose, Diana floruit circa 1630. . . . . . . DLB-126

Prince, F. T. 1912-2003 . . . . DLB-20

Prince, Nancy Gardner
1799-circa 1856 . . . . DLB-239

Prince, Thomas 1687-1758 . . . . DLB-24, 140

Pringle, Thomas 1789-1834 . . . . DLB-225

Printz, Wolfgang Casper 1641-1717 . . . . . . DLB-168

Prior, Matthew 1664-1721 . . . . DLB-95

Prisco, Michele 1920-2003 . . . . DLB-177

Prishvin, Mikhail Mikhailovich
1873-1954 . . . . DLB-272

Pritchard, William H. 1932- DLB-111

Pritchett, V. S. 1900-1997 . . . . DLB-15, 139

Probyn, May 1856 or 1857-1909 . . . . DLB-199

Procter, Adelaide Anne 1825-1864 . . . DLB-32, 199

Procter, Bryan Waller 1787-1874 . . . . . DLB-96, 144

Proctor, Robert 1868-1903 . . . . DLB-184

Prokopovich, Feofan 1681?-1736 . . . . DLB-150

Prokosch, Frederic 1906-1989 . . . . DLB-48

Pronzini, Bill 1943- DLB-226

Propertius circa 50 B.C.-post 16 B.C.
. . . . DLB-211; CDWLB-1

Propper, Dan 1937- DLB-16

Prose, Francine 1947- DLB-234

Protagoras circa 490 B.C.-420 B.C. DLB-176

Protest Poetry in Castile
ca. 1445-ca. 1506 . . . . DLB-286

Proud, Robert 1728-1813 . . . . DLB-30

Proust, Marcel 1871-1922 . . . . DLB-65

Marcel Proust at 129 and the Proust
Society of America Y-00

Marcel Proust's *Remembrance of Things Past*:
The Rediscovered Galley Proofs Y-00

Prutkov, Koz'ma Petrovich
1803-1863 . . . . DLB-277

Prynne, J. H. 1936- DLB-40

Przybyszewski, Stanislaw 1868-1927 . . . . . . DLB-66

Pseudo-Dionysius the Areopagite floruit
circa 500 . . . . DLB-115

Public Lending Right in America
PLR and the Meaning of Literary
Property Y-83

Statement by Sen. Charles
McC. Mathias, Jr. PLR. Y-83

Statements on PLR by American Writers . . . Y-83

Public Lending Right in the United Kingdom
The First Year in the United Kingdom . . . Y-83

Publishers [listed by individual names]
Publishers, Conversations with:
An Interview with Charles Scribner III . . Y-94

An Interview with Donald Lamm Y-95

An Interview with James Laughlin Y-96

An Interview with Patrick O'Connor Y-84

Publishing
The Art and Mystery of Publishing:
Interviews Y-97

Book Publishing Accounting: Some Basic
Concepts Y-98

1873 Publishers' Catalogues DLB-49

The Literary Scene 2002: Publishing, Book
Reviewing, and Literary Journalism . . Y-02

Main Trends in Twentieth-Century
Book Clubs DLB-46

Overview of U.S. Book Publishing,
1910-1945 . . . . DLB-9

The Pitt Poetry Series: Poetry Publishing
Today Y-85

Publishing Fiction at LSU Press Y-87

The Publishing Industry in 1998:
Sturm-und-drang.com Y-98

The Publishing Industry in 1999 . . . . Y-99

Publishers and Agents: The Columbia
Connection Y-87

Responses to Ken Auletta Y-97

Southern Writers Between the Wars . . . DLB-9

The State of Publishing. Y-97

Trends in Twentieth-Century
Mass Market Publishing DLB-46

The Year in Book Publishing Y-86

Pückler-Muskau, Hermann von
1785-1871 . . . . DLB-133

Pufendorf, Samuel von 1632-1694 . . . . DLB-168

Pugh, Edwin William 1874-1930 . . . . DLB-135

Pugin, A. Welby 1812-1852 . . . . DLB-55

Puig, Manuel 1932-1990 . . . . DLB-113; CDWLB-3

Puisieux, Madeleine d'Arsant de
1720-1798 . . . . DLB-314

Pulgar, Hernando del (Fernando del Pulgar)
ca. 1436-ca. 1492 . . . . DLB-286

Pulitzer, Joseph 1847-1911 . . . . DLB-23

Pulitzer, Joseph, Jr. 1885-1955 . . . . DLB-29

Pulitzer Prizes for the Novel, 1917-1945 . . . . DLB-9

Pulliam, Eugene 1889-1975 . . . . DLB-127

Purcell, Deirdre 1945- DLB-267

Purchas, Samuel 1577?-1626 . . . . DLB-151

Purdy, Al 1918-2000 . . . . DLB-88

Purdy, James 1923- DLB-2, 218

Purdy, Ken W. 1913-1972 . . . . DLB-137

Pusey, Edward Bouverie 1800-1882 . . . . . . DLB-55

Pushkin, Aleksandr Sergeevich
1799-1837 . . . . DLB-205

Pushkin, Vasilii L'vovich
1766-1830 . . . . DLB-205

Putnam, George Palmer
1814-1872 . . . . DLB-3, 79, 250, 254

G. P. Putnam [publishing house] DLB-254

G. P. Putnam's Sons [U.K.] DLB-106

G. P. Putnam's Sons [U.S.] DLB-49

A Publisher's Archives: G. P. Putnam . . . Y-92

Putnam, Hilary 1926- DLB-279

Putnam, Samuel 1892-1950 . . . . DLB-4; DS-15

Puttenham, George 1529?-1590 . . . . DLB-281

Puzo, Mario 1920-1999 . . . . DLB-6

Pyle, Ernie 1900-1945 . . . . DLB-29

Pyle, Howard
1853-1911 . . . . DLB-42, 188; DS-13

Pyle, Robert Michael 1947- DLB-275

Pym, Barbara 1913-1980 . . . . . . DLB-14, 207; Y-87

Pynchon, Thomas 1937- DLB-2, 173

Pyramid Books DLB-46

Pyrnelle, Louise-Clarke 1850-1907 . . . . DLB-42

Pythagoras circa 570 B.C.-? DLB-176

Q

Qays ibn al-Mulawwah circa 680-710 . . . . DLB-311

Quad, M. (see Lewis, Charles B.)

Quaritch, Bernard 1819-1899 . . . . DLB-184

Quarles, Francis 1592-1644 . . . . DLB-126

The Quarterly Review 1809-1967 . . . . DLB-110

Quasimodo, Salvatore 1901-1968 . . . . DLB-114

Queen, Ellery (see Dannay, Frederic, and
Manfred B. Lee)

Queen, Frank 1822-1882 . . . . DLB-241

The Queen City Publishing House DLB-49

Queirós, Eça de 1845-1900 . . . . DLB-287

Queneau, Raymond 1903-1976 . . . . . . DLB-72, 258

Quennell, Peter 1905-1993 . . . . DLB-155, 195

Quental, Antero de
1842-1891 . . . . DLB-287

Quesada, José Luis 1948- DLB-290

Quesnel, Joseph 1746-1809 . . . . DLB-99

Quiller-Couch, Sir Arthur Thomas
1863-1944 . . . . DLB-135, 153, 190

Quin, Ann 1936-1973 . . . . DLB-14, 231

Quinault, Philippe 1635-1688 . . . . DLB-268

Quincy, Samuel, of Georgia
fl. eighteenth century DLB-31

Quincy, Samuel, of Massachusetts
1734-1789 . . . . DLB-31

Quindlen, Anna 1952- DLB-292

Quine, W. V. 1908-2000 . . . . DLB-279

Quinn, Anthony 1915-2001 . . . . DLB-122

Quinn, John 1870-1924 . . . . DLB-187

Quiñónez, Naomi 1951- DLB-209

Quintana, Leroy V. 1944- DLB-82

Quintana, Miguel de 1671-1748
A Forerunner of Chicano
Literature DLB-122

Quintilian
circa A.D. 40-circa A.D. 96 . . . . DLB-211

Quintus Curtius Rufus
fl. A.D. 35. . . . . DLB-211

Harlin Quist Books DLB-46

Quoirez, Françoise (see Sagan, Françoise)

R

Raabe, Wilhelm 1831-1910 . . . . DLB-129

Raban, Jonathan 1942- DLB-204

Rabe, David 1940- DLB-7, 228; Y-91

Cumulative Index

Rabi'ah al-'Adawiyyah circa 720-801 .... DLB-311
Raboni, Giovanni 1932- DLB-128
Rachilde 1860-1953 .... DLB-123, 192
Racin, Kočo 1908-1943 .... DLB-147
Racine, Jean 1639-1699 .... DLB-268
Rackham, Arthur 1867-1939.......... DLB-141
Raczymow, Henri 1948- DLB-299
Radauskas, Henrikas
  1910-1970............ DLB-220; CDWLB-4
Radcliffe, Ann 1764-1823 ....DLB-39, 178
Raddall, Thomas 1903-1994 .... DLB-68
Radford, Dollie 1858-1920............ DLB-240
Radichkov, Yordan 1929-2004........ DLB-181
Radiguet, Raymond 1903-1923 .... DLB-65
Radishchev, Aleksandr Nikolaevich
  1749-1802..................... DLB-150
Radnóti, Miklós
  1909-1944 .... DLB-215; CDWLB-4
Radrigán, Juan 1937- DLB-305
Radványi, Netty Reiling (see Seghers, Anna)
Rahv, Philip 1908-1973............. DLB-137
Raich, Semen Egorovich 1792-1855 ..... DLB-205
Raičković, Stevan 1928- DLB-181
Raiderman (see Parshchikov, Aleksei Maksimovich)
Raimund, Ferdinand Jakob 1790-1836 .... DLB-90
Raine, Craig 1944- DLB-40
Raine, Kathleen 1908-2003............ DLB-20
Rainis, Jānis 1865-1929..... DLB-220; CDWLB-4
Rainolde, Richard
  circa 1530-1606 .... DLB-136, 236
Rainolds, John 1549-1607............. DLB-281
Rakić, Milan 1876-1938 .....DLB-147; CDWLB-4
Rakosi, Carl 1903-2004 .... DLB-193
Ralegh, Sir Walter
  1554?-1618............ DLB-172; CDBLB-1
Raleigh, Walter
  Style (1897) [excerpt]............... DLB-57
Ralin, Radoy 1923-2004.............. DLB-181
Ralph, Julian 1853-1903 .... DLB-23
Ramat, Silvio 1939- DLB-128
Ramée, Marie Louise de la (see Ouida)
Ramírez, Sergío 1942- DLB-145
Ramke, Bin 1947- DLB-120
Ramler, Karl Wilhelm 1725-1798 .... DLB-97
Ramon Ribeyro, Julio 1929-1994 .... DLB-145
Ramos, Graciliano 1892-1953 .... DLB-307
Ramos, Manuel 1948- DLB-209
Ramos Sucre, José Antonio 1890-1930... DLB-290
Ramous, Mario 1924- DLB-128
Rampersad, Arnold 1941- DLB-111
Ramsay, Allan 1684 or 1685-1758 .... DLB-95
Ramsay, David 1749-1815 .... DLB-30
Ramsay, Martha Laurens 1759-1811 .... DLB-200
Ramsey, Frank P. 1903-1930 .... DLB-262
Ranch, Hieronimus Justesen
  1539-1607..................... DLB-300

Ranck, Katherine Quintana 1942- DLB-122
Rand, Avery and Company DLB-49
Rand, Ayn 1905-1982.... DLB-227, 279; CDALB-7
Rand McNally and Company DLB-49
Randall, David Anton 1905-1975....... DLB-140
Randall, Dudley 1914-2000 .... DLB-41
Randall, Henry S. 1811-1876 .... DLB-30
Randall, James G. 1881-1953 .... DLB-17
  The Randall Jarrell Symposium: A Small
    Collection of Randall Jarrells......... Y-86
  Excerpts From Papers Delivered at the
    Randall Jarrel Symposium.......... Y-86
Randall, John Herman, Jr. 1899-1980 ....DLB-279
Randolph, A. Philip 1889-1979......... DLB-91
Anson D. F. Randolph
  [publishing house] DLB-49
Randolph, Thomas 1605-1635...... DLB-58, 126
Random House DLB-46
Rankin, Ian (Jack Harvey) 1960- DLB-267
Henry Ranlet [publishing house] DLB-49
Ransom, Harry 1908-1976 .... DLB-187
Ransom, John Crowe
  1888-1974.......... DLB-45, 63; CDALB-7
Ransome, Arthur 1884-1967 .... DLB-160
Raphael, Frederic 1931- DLB-14, 319
Raphaelson, Samson 1896-1983........ DLB-44
Rare Book Dealers
  Bertram Rota and His Bookshop........ Y-91
  An Interview with Glenn Horowitz....... Y-90
  An Interview with Otto Penzler......... Y-96
  An Interview with Ralph Sipper........ Y-94
  New York City Bookshops in the
    1930s and 1940s: The Recollections
    of Walter Goldwater............... Y-93
Rare Books
  Research in the American Antiquarian
    Book Trade.................... Y-97
  Two Hundred Years of Rare Books and
    Literary Collections at the
    University of South Carolina Y-00
Rascón Banda, Víctor Hugo 1948- DLB-305
Rashi circa 1040-1105................ DLB-208
Raskin, Ellen 1928-1984............... DLB-52
Rasputin, Valentin Grigor'evich
  1937- DLB-302
Rastell, John 1475?-1536..........DLB-136, 170
Rattigan, Terence
  1911-1977............. DLB-13; CDBLB-7
Raven, Simon 1927-2001 ....DLB-271
Ravenhill, Mark 1966- DLB-310
Ravnkilde, Adda 1862-1883 .... DLB-300
Rawicz, Piotr 1919-1982............. DLB-299
Rawlings, Marjorie Kinnan 1896-1953
  .... DLB-9, 22, 102; DS-17; CDALB-7
Rawlinson, Richard 1690-1755......... DLB-213
Rawlinson, Thomas 1681-1725 .... DLB-213
Rawls, John 1921-2002................DLB-279
Raworth, Tom 1938- DLB-40
Ray, David 1932- DLB-5

Ray, Gordon Norton 1915-1986 ....DLB-103, 140
Ray, Henrietta Cordelia 1849-1916 ...... DLB-50
Raymond, Ernest 1888-1974 .... DLB-191
Raymond, Henry J. 1820-1869........DLB-43, 79
Raymond, René (see Chase, James Hadley)
Razaf, Andy 1895-1973 .... DLB-265
al-Razi 865?-925?..................... DLB-311
Rea, Michael 1927-1996................. Y-97
  Michael M. Rea and the Rea Award for
    the Short Story Y-97
Reach, Angus 1821-1856 .... DLB-70
Read, Herbert 1893-1968.......... DLB-20, 149
Read, Martha Meredith
  fl. nineteenth century............. DLB-200
Read, Opie 1852-1939 .... DLB-23
Read, Piers Paul 1941- DLB-14
Reade, Charles 1814-1884 .... DLB-21
Reader's Digest Condensed Books....... DLB-46
Readers Ulysses Symposium Y-97
Reading, Peter 1946- DLB-40
Reading Series in New York City.......... Y-96
Reaney, James 1926- DLB-68
Rebhun, Paul 1500?-1546..............DLB-179
Rèbora, Clemente 1885-1957.......... DLB-114
Rebreanu, Liviu 1885-1944 .... DLB-220
Rechy, John 1934- DLB-122, 278; Y-82
Redding, J. Saunders 1906-1988........DLB-63, 76
J. S. Redfield [publishing house] DLB-49
Redgrove, Peter 1932-2003 .... DLB-40
Redmon, Anne 1943- Y-86
Redmond, Eugene B. 1937- DLB-41
Redol, Alves 1911-1969 .... DLB-287
James Redpath [publishing house] DLB-49
Reed, Henry 1808-1854 .... DLB-59
Reed, Henry 1914-1986 .... DLB-27
Reed, Ishmael
  1938- DLB-2, 5, 33, 169, 227; DS-8
Reed, Rex 1938- DLB-185
Reed, Sampson 1800-1880 .... DLB-1, 235
Reed, Talbot Baines 1852-1893 .... DLB-141
Reedy, William Marion 1862-1920 ...... DLB-91
Reese, Lizette Woodworth 1856-1935 .... DLB-54
Reese, Thomas 1742-1796 .... DLB-37
Reeve, Clara 1729-1807 .... DLB-39
  Preface to *The Old English Baron*
    (1778).......................... DLB-39
  The Progress of Romance (1785)
    [excerpt]...................... DLB-39
Reeves, James 1909-1978 .... DLB-161
Reeves, John 1926- DLB-88
Reeves-Stevens, Garfield 1953- DLB-251
Régio, José (José Maria dos Reis Pereira)
  1901-1969 .... DLB-287
Henry Regnery Company DLB-46
Rêgo, José Lins do 1901-1957 .... DLB-307
Rehberg, Hans 1901-1963 .... DLB-124

Rehfisch, Hans José 1891-1960 . . . . DLB-124

Reich, Ebbe Kløvedal 1940- DLB-214

Reid, Alastair 1926- DLB-27

Reid, B. L. 1918-1990 . . . . DLB-111

Reid, Christopher 1949- DLB-40

Reid, Forrest 1875-1947 . . . . DLB-153

Reid, Helen Rogers 1882-1970 . . . . DLB-29

Reid, James fl. eighteenth century DLB-31

Reid, Mayne 1818-1883 . . . . DLB-21, 163

Reid, Thomas 1710-1796 . . . . DLB-31, 252

Reid, V. S. (Vic) 1913-1987 . . . . DLB-125

Reid, Whitelaw 1837-1912 . . . . DLB-23

Reilly and Lee Publishing Company DLB-46

Reimann, Brigitte 1933-1973 . . . . DLB-75

Reinmar der Alte circa 1165-circa 1205 . . . DLB-138

Reinmar von Zweter
   circa 1200-circa 1250 . . . . DLB-138

Reisch, Walter 1903-1983 . . . . DLB-44

Reizei Family DLB-203

Religion
   A Crisis of Culture: The Changing
      Role of Religion in the
      New Republic DLB-37

Remarque, Erich Maria
   1898-1970 . . . . DLB-56; CDWLB-2

Remington, Frederic
   1861-1909 . . . . DLB-12, 186, 188

Remizov, Aleksei Mikhailovich
   1877-1957 . . . . DLB-295

Renaud, Jacques 1943- DLB-60

Renault, Mary 1905-1983 . . . . Y-83

Rendell, Ruth (Barbara Vine)
   1930- DLB-87, 276

Rensselaer, Maria van Cortlandt van
   1645-1689 . . . . DLB-200

Repplier, Agnes 1855-1950 . . . . DLB-221

Reshetnikov, Fedor Mikhailovich
   1841-1871 . . . . DLB-238

Restif (Rétif) de La Bretonne, Nicolas-Edme
   1734-1806 . . . . DLB-314

Rettenbacher, Simon 1634-1706 . . . . DLB-168

Retz, Jean-François-Paul de Gondi,
   cardinal de 1613-1679 . . . . DLB-268

Reuchlin, Johannes 1455-1522 . . . . DLB-179

Reuter, Christian 1665-after 1712 . . . . DLB-168

Fleming H. Revell Company DLB-49

Reverdy, Pierre 1889-1960 . . . . DLB-258

Reuter, Fritz 1810-1874 . . . . DLB-129

Reuter, Gabriele 1859-1941 . . . . DLB-66

Reventlow, Franziska Gräfin zu
   1871-1918 . . . . DLB-66

Review of Reviews Office DLB-112

Rexroth, Kenneth 1905-1982
   . . . . . . DLB-16, 48, 165, 212; Y-82; CDALB-1

   The Commercialization of the Image
      of Revolt DLB-16

Rey, H. A. 1898-1977 . . . . DLB-22

Reyes, Carlos José 1941- DLB-305

Reynal and Hitchcock DLB-46

Reynolds, G. W. M. 1814-1879 . . . . DLB-21

Reynolds, John Hamilton
   1794-1852 . . . . DLB-96

Reynolds, Sir Joshua 1723-1792 . . . . DLB-104

Reynolds, Mack 1917-1983 . . . . DLB-8

Reza, Yazmina 1959- DLB-321

Reznikoff, Charles 1894-1976 . . . . DLB-28, 45

Rhetoric
   Continental European Rhetoricians,
      1400-1600, and Their Influence
      in Reaissance England DLB-236
   A Finding Guide to Key Works on
      Microfilm DLB-236
   Glossary of Terms and Definitions of
      Rhetoic and Logic DLB-236

Rhett, Robert Barnwell 1800-1876 . . . . DLB-43

Rhode, John 1884-1964 . . . . DLB-77

Rhodes, Eugene Manlove 1869-1934 . . . . DLB-256

Rhodes, James Ford 1848-1927 . . . . DLB-47

Rhodes, Richard 1937- DLB-185

Rhys, Jean 1890-1979
   . . . . DLB-36, 117, 162; CDBLB-7; CDWLB-3

Ribeiro, Bernadim
   fl. ca. 1475/1482-1526/1544 . . . . DLB-287

Ricardo, David 1772-1823 . . . . DLB-107, 158

Ricardou, Jean 1932- DLB-83

Riccoboni, Marie-Jeanne (Marie-Jeanne de
   Heurles Laboras de Mézières Riccoboni)
   1713-1792 . . . . DLB-314

Rice, Anne (A. N. Roquelare, Anne Rampling)
   1941- DLB-292

Rice, Christopher 1978- DLB-292

Rice, Elmer 1892-1967 . . . . DLB-4, 7

Rice, Grantland 1880-1954 . . . . DLB-29, 171

Rich, Adrienne 1929- DLB-5, 67; CDALB-7

Richard, Mark 1955- DLB-234

Richard de Fournival
   1201-1259 or 1260 . . . . DLB-208

Richards, David Adams 1950- DLB-53

Richards, George circa 1760-1814 . . . . DLB-37

Richards, I. A. 1893-1979 . . . . DLB-27

Richards, Laura E. 1850-1943 . . . . DLB-42

Richards, William Carey 1818-1892 . . . . . DLB-73

Grant Richards [publishing house] DLB-112

Richardson, Charles F. 1851-1913 . . . . DLB-71

Richardson, Dorothy M. 1873-1957 . . . . . . DLB-36

   The Novels of Dorothy Richardson
      (1918), by May Sinclair DLB-36

Richardson, Henry Handel
   (Ethel Florence Lindesay Robertson)
   1870-1946 . . . . DLB-197, 230

Richardson, Jack 1935- DLB-7

Richardson, John 1796-1852 . . . . DLB-99

Richardson, Samuel
   1689-1761 . . . . DLB-39, 154; CDBLB-2

   Introductory Letters from the Second
      Edition of Pamela (1741) DLB-39

   Postscript to [the Third Edition of]
      Clarissa (1751) DLB-39

   Preface to the First Edition of
      Pamela (1740) DLB-39

   Preface to the Third Edition of
      Clarissa (1751) [excerpt] DLB-39

   Preface to Volume 1 of Clarissa
      (1747) DLB-39

   Preface to Volume 3 of Clarissa
      (1748) DLB-39

Richardson, Willis 1889-1977 . . . . DLB-51

Riche, Barnabe 1542-1617 . . . . DLB-136

Richepin, Jean 1849-1926 . . . . DLB-192

Richler, Mordecai 1931-2001 . . . . DLB-53

Richter, Conrad 1890-1968 . . . . DLB-9, 212

Richter, Hans Werner 1908-1993 . . . . DLB-69

Richter, Johann Paul Friedrich
   1763-1825 . . . . DLB-94; CDWLB-2

Joseph Rickerby [publishing house] DLB-106

Rickword, Edgell 1898-1982 . . . . DLB-20

Riddell, Charlotte 1832-1906 . . . . DLB-156

Riddell, John (see Ford, Corey)

Ridge, John Rollin 1827-1867 . . . . DLB-175

Ridge, Lola 1873-1941 . . . . DLB-54

Ridge, William Pett 1859-1930 . . . . DLB-135

Riding, Laura (see Jackson, Laura Riding)

Ridler, Anne 1912-2001 . . . . DLB-27

Ridruego, Dionisio 1912-1975 . . . . DLB-108

Riel, Louis 1844-1885 . . . . DLB-99

Riemer, Johannes 1648-1714 . . . . DLB-168

Rifbjerg, Klaus 1931- DLB-214

Riffaterre, Michael 1924- DLB-67

A Conversation between William Riggan
   and Janette Turner Hospital Y-02

Riggs, Lynn 1899-1954 . . . . DLB-175

Riis, Jacob 1849-1914 . . . . DLB-23

John C. Riker [publishing house] DLB-49

Riley, James 1777-1840 . . . . DLB-183

Riley, John 1938-1978 . . . . DLB-40

Rilke, Rainer Maria
   1875-1926 . . . . DLB-81; CDWLB-2

Rimanelli, Giose 1926- DLB-177

Rimbaud, Jean-Nicolas-Arthur
   1854-1891 . . . . DLB-217

Rinehart and Company DLB-46

Ringuet 1895-1960 . . . . DLB-68

Ringwood, Gwen Pharis 1910-1984 . . . . . . DLB-88

Rinser, Luise 1911-2002 . . . . DLB-69

Ríos, Alberto 1952- DLB-122

Ríos, Isabella 1948- DLB-82

Ripley, Arthur 1895-1961 . . . . DLB-44

Ripley, George 1802-1880 . . . . . DLB-1, 64, 73, 235

The Rising Glory of America:
   Three Poems DLB-37

The Rising Glory of America: Written in 1771
   (1786), by Hugh Henry Brackenridge
   and Philip Freneau DLB-37

Riskin, Robert 1897-1955 . . . . DLB-26

Risse, Heinz 1898-1989 . . . . DLB-69

Rist, Johann 1607-1667 . . . . DLB-164

Cumulative Index

Ristikivi, Karl 1912-1977..............DLB-220

Ritchie, Anna Mowatt 1819-1870.....DLB-3, 250

Ritchie, Anne Thackeray 1837-1919......DLB-18

Ritchie, Thomas 1778-1854..............DLB-43

The Ritz Paris Hemingway Award..........Y-85

    Mario Varga Llosa's Acceptance Speech..Y-85

Rivard, Adjutor 1868-1945..............DLB-92

Rive, Richard 1931-1989.........DLB-125, 225

Rivera, José 1955-.....................DLB-249

Rivera, Marina 1942-...................DLB-122

Rivera, Tomás 1935-1984................DLB-82

Rivers, Conrad Kent 1933-1968..........DLB-41

Riverside Press........................DLB-49

Rivington, James circa 1724-1802.......DLB-43

Charles Rivington [publishing house]...DLB-154

Rivkin, Allen 1903-1990................DLB-26

Roa Bastos, Augusto 1917-2005..........DLB-113

Robbe-Grillet, Alain 1922-..............DLB-83

Robbins, Tom 1936-......................Y-80

Roberts, Charles G. D. 1860-1943.......DLB-92

Roberts, Dorothy 1906-1993..............DLB-88

Roberts, Elizabeth Madox
    1881-1941................DLB-9, 54, 102

Roberts, John (see Swynnerton, Thomas)

Roberts, Kate 1891-1985................DLB-319

Roberts, Keith 1935-2000...............DLB-261

Roberts, Kenneth 1885-1957..............DLB-9

Roberts, Michèle 1949-.................DLB-231

Roberts, Theodore Goodridge
    1877-1953..........................DLB-92

Roberts, Ursula Wyllie (see Miles, Susan)

Roberts, William 1767-1849.............DLB-142

James Roberts [publishing house].......DLB-154

Roberts Brothers.......................DLB-49

A. M. Robertson and Company............DLB-49

Robertson, Ethel Florence Lindesay
    (see Richardson, Henry Handel)

Robertson, William 1721-1793...........DLB-104

Robin, Leo 1895-1984...................DLB-265

Robins, Elizabeth 1862-1952............DLB-197

Robinson, A. Mary F. (Madame James
    Darmesteter, Madame Mary
    Duclaux) 1857-1944.................DLB-240

Robinson, Casey 1903-1979..............DLB-44

Robinson, Derek 1932-...................Y-02

Robinson, Edwin Arlington
    1869-1935..............DLB-54; CDALB-3

    Review by Derek Robinson of George
    Greenfield's *Rich Dust*..............Y-02

Robinson, Henry Crabb 1775-1867.......DLB-107

Robinson, James Harvey 1863-1936......DLB-47

Robinson, Lennox 1886-1958.............DLB-10

Robinson, Mabel Louise 1874-1962.......DLB-22

Robinson, Marilynne 1943-..............DLB-206

Robinson, Mary 1758-1800...............DLB-158

Robinson, Richard circa 1545-1607......DLB-167

Robinson, Therese 1797-1870........DLB-59, 133

Robison, Mary 1949-...................DLB-130

Roblès, Emmanuel 1914-1995.............DLB-83

Roccatagliata Ceccardi, Ceccardo
    1871-1919.........................DLB-114

Rocha, Adolfo Correira da (see Torga, Miguel)

Roche, Billy 1949-.....................DLB-233

Rochester, John Wilmot, Earl of
    1647-1680.........................DLB-131

Rochon, Esther 1948-...................DLB-251

Rock, Howard 1911-1976.................DLB-127

Rockwell, Norman Perceval 1894-1978..DLB-188

Rodgers, Carolyn M. 1945-..............DLB-41

Rodgers, W. R. 1909-1969...............DLB-20

Rodney, Lester 1911-...................DLB-241

Rodrigues, Nelson 1912-1980...........DLB-307

Rodríguez, Claudio 1934-1999..........DLB-134

Rodríguez, Joe D. 1943-................DLB-209

Rodríguez, Luis J. 1954-...............DLB-209

Rodriguez, Richard 1944-..........DLB-82, 256

Rodríguez Julia, Edgardo 1946-........DLB-145

Roe, E. P. 1838-1888...................DLB-202

Roethke, Theodore
    1908-1963...........DLB-5, 206; CDALB-1

Rogers, Jane 1952-.....................DLB-194

Rogers, Pattiann 1940-.................DLB-105

Rogers, Samuel 1763-1855...............DLB-93

Rogers, Will 1879-1935.................DLB-11

Rohmer, Sax 1883-1959..................DLB-70

Roiphe, Anne 1935-......................Y-80

Rojas, Arnold R. 1896-1988.............DLB-82

Rojas, Fernando de ca. 1475-1541......DLB-286

Roland de la Platière, Marie-Jeanne
    (Madame Roland) 1754-1793.........DLB-314

Rolfe, Edwin (Solomon Fishman)
    1909-1954.........................DLB-303

Rolfe, Frederick William
    1860-1913......................DLB-34, 156

Rolland, Romain 1866-1944..............DLB-65

Rolle, Richard circa 1290-1300 - 1349...DLB-146

Rölvaag, O. E. 1876-1931............DLB-9, 212

Romains, Jules 1885-1972...........DLB-65, 321

A. Roman and Company...................DLB-49

Roman de la Rose: Guillaume de Lorris
    1200/1205-circa 1230, Jean de
    Meun 1235-1240-circa 1305........DLB-208

Romano, Lalla 1906-2001................DLB-177

Romano, Octavio 1923-..................DLB-122

Rome, Harold 1908-1993.................DLB-265

Romero, Leo 1950-......................DLB-122

Romero, Lin 1947-......................DLB-122

Romero, Orlando 1945-..................DLB-82

Rook, Clarence 1863-1915...............DLB-135

Roosevelt, Theodore
    1858-1919....................DLB-47, 186, 275

Root, Waverley 1903-1982...............DLB-4

Root, William Pitt 1941-...............DLB-120

Roquebrune, Robert de 1889-1978........DLB-68

Rorty, Richard 1931-................DLB-246, 279

Rosa, João Guimarães 1908-1967...DLB-113, 307

Rosales, Luis 1910-1992................DLB-134

Roscoe, William 1753-1831..............DLB-163

Rose, Dilys 1954-......................DLB-319

Rose, Reginald 1920-2002...............DLB-26

Rose, Wendy 1948-......................DLB-175

Rosegger, Peter 1843-1918..............DLB-129

Rosei, Peter 1946-.....................DLB-85

Rosen, Norma 1925-.....................DLB-28

Rosenbach, A. S. W. 1876-1952..........DLB-140

Rosenbaum, Ron 1946-...................DLB-185

Rosenbaum, Thane 1960-.................DLB-299

Rosenberg, Isaac 1890-1918.........DLB-20, 216

Rosenfeld, Isaac 1918-1956.............DLB-28

Rosenthal, Harold 1914-1999............DLB-241

    Jimmy, Red, and Others: Harold
    Rosenthal Remembers the Stars of
    the Press Box......................Y-01

Rosenthal, M. L. 1917-1996..............DLB-5

Rosenwald, Lessing J. 1891-1979........DLB-187

Ross, Alexander 1591-1654..............DLB-151

Ross, Harold 1892-1951.................DLB-137

Ross, Jerry 1926-1955..................DLB-265

Ross, Leonard Q. (see Rosten, Leo)

Ross, Lillian 1927-....................DLB-185

Ross, Martin 1862-1915.................DLB-135

Ross, Sinclair 1908-1996...............DLB-88

Ross, W. W. E. 1894-1966...............DLB-88

Rosselli, Amelia 1930-1996.............DLB-128

Rossen, Robert 1908-1966...............DLB-26

Rosset, Barney 1922-....................Y-02

Rossetti, Christina 1830-1894...DLB-35, 163, 240

Rossetti, Dante Gabriel
    1828-1882..................DLB-35; CDBLB-4

    The Stealthy School of
    Criticism (1871)...................DLB-35

Rossner, Judith 1935-...................DLB-6

Rostand, Edmond 1868-1918..............DLB-192

Rosten, Leo 1908-1997..................DLB-11

Rostenberg, Leona 1908-2005............DLB-140

Rostopchina, Evdokiia Petrovna
    1811-1858.........................DLB-205

Rostovsky, Dimitrii 1651-1709..........DLB-150

Rota, Bertram 1903-1966................DLB-201

    Bertram Rota and His Bookshop.......Y-91

Roth, Gerhard 1942-................DLB-85, 124

Roth, Henry 1906?-1995.................DLB-28

Roth, Joseph 1894-1939.................DLB-85

Roth, Philip
    1933-.......DLB-2, 28, 173; Y-82; CDALB-6

Rothenberg, Jerome 1931-............DLB-5, 193

Rothschild Family......................DLB-184

Rotimi, Ola 1938-......................DLB-125

Rotrou, Jean 1609-1650.................DLB-268

Rousseau, Jean-Jacques 1712-1778 . . . . . . .DLB-314
   The Social Contract DLB-314
Routhier, Adolphe-Basile 1839-1920 . . . . . .DLB-99
Routier, Simone 1901-1987 . . . . .DLB-88
George Routledge and Sons DLB-106
Roversi, Roberto 1923- DLB-128
Rowe, Elizabeth Singer 1674-1737 . . . . .DLB-39, 95
Rowe, Nicholas 1674-1718 . . . . .DLB-84
Rowlands, Ian 1964- DLB-310
Rowlands, Samuel circa 1570-1630 . . . . . .DLB-121
Rowlandson, Mary
   circa 1637-circa 1711 . . . . .DLB-24, 200
Rowley, William circa 1585-1626 . . . . . . .DLB-58
Rowling, J. K.
   The Harry Potter Phenomenon Y-99
Rowse, A. L. 1903-1997 . . . . .DLB-155
Rowson, Susanna Haswell
   circa 1762-1824 . . . . DLB-37, 200
Roy, Camille 1870-1943 . . . . .DLB-92
The G. Ross Roy Scottish Poetry Collection
   at the University of South Carolina Y-89
Roy, Gabrielle 1909-1983 . . . . .DLB-68
Roy, Jules 1907-2000 . . . . .DLB-83
The Royal Court Theatre and the English
   Stage Company DLB-13
The Royal Court Theatre and the New
   Drama DLB-10
The Royal Shakespeare Company
   at the Swan Y-88
Royall, Anne Newport 1769-1854 . . . .DLB-43, 248
Royce, Josiah 1855-1916 . . . . .DLB-270
The Roycroft Printing Shop DLB-49
Royde-Smith, Naomi 1875-1964 . . . . .DLB-191
Royster, Vermont 1914-1996 . . . . .DLB-127
Richard Royston [publishing house] DLB-170
Rozanov, Vasilii Vasil'evich
   1856-1919 . . . . .DLB-295
Różewicz, Tadeusz 1921- DLB-232
Ruark, Gibbons 1941- DLB-120
Ruban, Vasilii Grigorevich 1742-1795 . . . .DLB-150
Rubens, Bernice 1928-2004 . . . . .DLB-14, 207
Rubião, Murilo 1916-1991 . . . . .DLB-307
Rubina, Dina Il'inichna 1953- DLB-285
Rubinshtein, Lev Semenovich 1947- . . .DLB-285
Rudd and Carleton DLB-49
Rudd, Steele (Arthur Hoey Davis) DLB-230
Rudkin, David 1936- DLB-13
Rudnick, Paul 1957- DLB-266
Rudnicki, Adolf 1909-1990 . . . . .DLB-299
Rudolf von Ems circa 1200-circa 1254 . . .DLB-138
Ruffin, Josephine St. Pierre 1842-1924 . . . .DLB-79
Rufo, Juan Gutiérrez 1547?-1620? DLB-318
Ruganda, John 1941- DLB-157
Ruggles, Henry Joseph 1813-1906 . . . . . . .DLB-64
Ruiz de Burton, María Amparo
   1832-1895 . . . . .DLB-209, 221
Rukeyser, Muriel 1913-1980 . . . . .DLB-48

Rule, Jane 1931- DLB-60
Rulfo, Juan 1918-1986 . . . . . .DLB-113; CDWLB-3
Rumaker, Michael 1932- DLB-16
Rumens, Carol 1944- DLB-40
Rummo, Paul-Eerik 1942- DLB-232
Runyon, Damon
   1880-1946 . . . . .DLB-11, 86, 171
Ruodlieb circa 1050-1075 . . . . .DLB-148
Rush, Benjamin 1746-1813 . . . . .DLB-37
Rush, Rebecca 1779-? DLB-200
Rushdie, Salman 1947- DLB-194
Rusk, Ralph L. 1888-1962 . . . . .DLB-103
Ruskin, John
   1819-1900 . . . . . .DLB-55, 163, 190; CDBLB-4
Russ, Joanna 1937- DLB-8
Russell, Benjamin 1761-1845 . . . . .DLB-43
Russell, Bertrand 1872-1970 . . . . . . .DLB-100, 262
Russell, Charles Edward 1860-1941 . . . . . .DLB-25
Russell, Charles M. 1864-1926 . . . . .DLB-188
Russell, Eric Frank 1905-1978 . . . . .DLB-255
Russell, Fred 1906-2003 . . . . .DLB-241
Russell, George William (see AE)
Russell, Countess Mary Annette Beauchamp
   (see Arnim, Elizabeth von)
Russell, Willy 1947- DLB-233
B. B. Russell and Company DLB-49
R. H. Russell and Son DLB-49
Rutebeuf fl.1249-1277 . . . . .DLB-208
Rutherford, Mark 1831-1913 . . . . .DLB-18
Ruxton, George Frederick
   1821-1848 . . . . .DLB-186
R-va, Zeneida (see Gan, Elena Andreevna)
Ryan, James 1952- DLB-267
Ryan, Michael 1946- Y-82
Ryan, Oscar 1904- DLB-68
Rybakov, Anatolii Naumovich
   1911-1994 . . . . .DLB-302
Ryder, Jack 1871-1936 . . . . .DLB-241
Ryga, George 1932-1987 . . . . .DLB-60
Rylands, Enriqueta Augustina Tennant
   1843-1908 . . . . .DLB-184
Rylands, John 1801-1888 . . . . .DLB-184
Ryle, Gilbert 1900-1976 . . . . .DLB-262
Ryleev, Kondratii Fedorovich
   1795-1826 . . . . .DLB-205
Rymer, Thomas 1643?-1713 . . . . .DLB-101
Ryskind, Morrie 1895-1985 . . . . .DLB-26
Rzhevsky, Aleksei Andreevich
   1737-1804 . . . . .DLB-150

S

The Saalfield Publishing Company DLB-46
Saba, Umberto 1883-1957 . . . . .DLB-114
Sábato, Ernesto 1911- DLB-145; CDWLB-3
Saberhagen, Fred 1930- DLB-8
Sabin, Joseph 1821-1881 . . . . .DLB-187

Sabino, Fernando (Fernando Tavares Sabino)
   1923-2004 . . . . .DLB-307
Sacer, Gottfried Wilhelm 1635-1699 . . . . .DLB-168
Sachs, Hans 1494-1576 . . . . . DLB-179; CDWLB-2
Sá-Carneiro, Mário de 1890-1916 . . . . . . .DLB-287
Sack, John 1930-2004 . . . . .DLB-185
Sackler, Howard 1929-1982 . . . . .DLB-7
Sackville, Lady Margaret 1881-1963 . . . . .DLB-240
Sackville, Thomas 1536-1608 and
   Norton, Thomas 1532-1584 . . . . .DLB-62
Sackville, Thomas 1536-1608 . . . . .DLB-132
Sackville-West, Edward 1901-1965 . . . . . .DLB-191
Sackville-West, Vita 1892-1962 . . . . . .DLB-34, 195
Sá de Miranda, Francisco de
   1481-1588? DLB-287
Sade, Marquis de (Donatien-Alphonse-François,
   comte de Sade) 1740-1814 . . . . . . .DLB-314
   "Dialogue entre un prêtre et un
   moribond" DLB-314
Sadlier, Mary Anne 1820-1903 . . . . .DLB-99
D. and J. Sadlier and Company DLB-49
Sadoff, Ira 1945- DLB-120
Sadoveanu, Mihail 1880-1961 . . . . .DLB-220
Sadur, Nina Nikolaevna 1950- DLB-285
Sáenz, Benjamin Alire 1954- DLB-209
Saenz, Jaime 1921-1986 . . . . .DLB-145, 283
Saffin, John circa 1626-1710 . . . . .DLB-24
Sagan, Françoise 1935- DLB-83
Sage, Robert 1899-1962 . . . . .DLB-4
Sagel, Jim 1947- .DLB-82
Sagendorph, Robb Hansell 1900-1970 . . . .DLB-137
Sahagún, Carlos 1938- DLB-108
Sahkomaapii, Piitai (see Highwater, Jamake)
Sahl, Hans 1902-1993 . . . . .DLB-69
Said, Edward W. 1935- DLB-67
Saigyō 1118-1190 . . . . .DLB-203
Saijo, Albert 1926- DLB-312
Saiko, George 1892-1962 . . . . .DLB-85
Sainte-Beuve, Charles-Augustin
   1804-1869 . . . . .DLB-217
Saint-Exupéry, Antoine de 1900-1944 . . . . .DLB-72
St. John, J. Allen 1872-1957 . . . . .DLB-188
St John, Madeleine 1942- DLB-267
St. Johns, Adela Rogers 1894-1988 . . . . . . .DLB-29
St. Omer, Garth 1931- DLB-117
Saint Pierre, Michel de 1916-1987 . . . . . . .DLB-83
Saintsbury, George 1845-1933 . . . . . . DLB-57, 149
   "Modern English Prose" (1876) DLB-57
   The Present State of the English
   Novel (1892), ...DLB-18
Saint-Simon, Louis de Rouvroy, duc de
   1675-1755 . . . . .DLB-314
St. Dominic's Press DLB-112
The St. John's College Robert Graves Trust . . Y-96
St. Martin's Press .DLB-46
St. Nicholas 1873-1881 . . . . DS-13
Saiokuken Sōchō 1448-1532 . . . . .DLB-203

Saki (see Munro, H. H.)
Salaam, Kalamu ya 1947- DLB-38
Salacrou, Armand 1899-1989 .... DLB-321
Šalamun, Tomaž 1941- ... DLB-181; CDWLB-4
Salas, Floyd 1931- DLB-82
Sálaz-Marquez, Rubén 1935- DLB-122
Salcedo, Hugo 1964- DLB-305
Salemson, Harold J. 1910-1988. .... DLB-4
Salesbury, William 1520?-1584?. DLB-281
Salinas, Luis Omar 1937- DLB-82
Salinas, Pedro 1891-1951 .... DLB-134
Salinger, J. D.
 1919- DLB-2, 102, 173; CDALB-1
Salkey, Andrew 1928-1995 .... DLB-125
Sallust circa 86 B.C.-35 B.C.
 .... DLB-211; CDWLB-1
Salt, Waldo 1914-1987 .... DLB-44
Salter, James 1925- DLB-130
Salter, Mary Jo 1954- DLB-120
Saltus, Edgar 1855-1921 .... DLB-202
Saltykov, Mikhail Evgrafovich
 1826-1889 .... DLB-238
Salustri, Carlo Alberto (see Trilussa)
Salverson, Laura Goodman 1890-1970. ... DLB-92
Samain, Albert 1858-1900. .... DLB-217
Sampson, Richard Henry (see Hull, Richard)
Samuels, Ernest 1903-1996. .... DLB-111
Sanborn, Franklin Benjamin
 1831-1917. .... DLB-1, 223
Sánchez, Florencio 1875-1910 .... DLB-305
Sánchez, Luis Rafael 1936- DLB-145, 305
Sánchez, Philomeno "Phil" 1917- DLB-122
Sánchez, Ricardo 1941-1995. .... DLB-82
Sánchez, Saúl 1943- DLB-209
Sanchez, Sonia 1934- DLB-41; DS-8
Sánchez de Arévalo, Rodrigo
 1404-1470. .... DLB-286
Sánchez de Badajoz, Diego ?-1552? DLB-318
Sand, George 1804-1876 .... DLB-119, 192
Sandburg, Carl
 1878-1967. .... DLB-17, 54; CDALB-3
Sandel, Cora (Sara Fabricius)
 1880-1974. .... DLB-297
Sandemose, Aksel 1899-1965 .... DLB-297
Sanders, Edward 1939- DLB-16, 244
Sanderson, Robert 1587-1663 .... DLB-281
Sandoz, Mari 1896-1966. .... DLB-9, 212
Sandwell, B. K. 1876-1954 .... DLB-92
Sandy, Stephen 1934- DLB-165
Sandys, George 1578-1644 .... DLB-24, 121
Sangster, Charles 1822-1893 .... DLB-99
Sanguineti, Edoardo 1930- DLB-128
Sanjōnishi Sanetaka 1455-1537. .... DLB-203
San Pedro, Diego de fl. ca. 1492. ..... DLB-286
Sansay, Leonora ?-after 1823 .... DLB-200
Sansom, William 1912-1976 .... DLB-139

Sant'Anna, Affonso Romano de
 1937- DLB-307
Santayana, George
 1863-1952 ......DLB-54, 71, 246, 270; DS-13
Santiago, Danny 1911-1988 .... DLB-122
Santillana, Marqués de (Íñigo López de Mendoza)
 1398-1458 .... DLB-286
Santmyer, Helen Hooven 1895-1986 .... Y-84
Santos, Bienvenido 1911-1996 .... DLB-312
Sanvitale, Francesca 1928- DLB-196
Sapidus, Joannes 1490-1561 ....DLB-179
Sapir, Edward 1884-1939 .... DLB-92
Sapper (see McNeile, Herman Cyril)
Sappho circa 620 B.C.-circa 550 B.C.
 .... DLB-176; CDWLB-1
Saramago, José 1922- DLB-287; Y-98
 Nobel Lecture 1998: How Characters
 Became the Masters and the Author
 Their Apprentice Y-98
Sarban (John W. Wall) 1910-1989. ..... DLB-255
Sardou, Victorien 1831-1908 .... DLB-192
Sarduy, Severo 1937-1993. .... DLB-113
Sargent, Pamela 1948- DLB-8
Saro-Wiwa, Ken 1941- DLB-157
Saroyan, Aram
 Rites of Passage [on William Saroyan]. ... Y-83
Saroyan, William
 1908-1981 .....DLB-7, 9, 86; Y-81; CDALB-7
Sarraute, Nathalie 1900-1999 .... DLB-83, 321
Sarrazin, Albertine 1937-1967 .... DLB-83
Sarris, Greg 1952- DLB-175
Sarton, May 1912-1995 ....DLB-48; Y-81
Sartre, Jean-Paul 1905-1980 .... DLB-72, 296, 321
Sassoon, Siegfried
 1886-1967 .... DLB-20, 191; DS-18
 A Centenary Essay Y-86
 Tributes from Vivien F. Clarke and
 Michael Thorpe. Y-86
Sata Ineko 1904-1998 .... DLB-180
Saturday Review Press DLB-46
Saunders, James 1925-2004 .... DLB-13
Saunders, John Monk 1897-1940 ...... DLB-26
Saunders, Margaret Marshall
 1861-1947. .... DLB-92
Saunders and Otley DLB-106
Saussure, Ferdinand de 1857-1913 ...... DLB-242
Savage, James 1784-1873. .... DLB-30
Savage, Marmion W. 1803?-1872. .... DLB-21
Savage, Richard 1697?-1743 .... DLB-95
Savard, Félix-Antoine 1896-1982 .... DLB-68
Savery, Henry 1791-1842 .... DLB-230
Saville, (Leonard) Malcolm 1901-1982. .. DLB-160
Savinio, Alberto 1891-1952 .... DLB-264
Sawyer, Robert J. 1960- DLB-251
Sawyer, Ruth 1880-1970 .... DLB-22
Sayers, Dorothy L.
 1893-1957. .... DLB-10, 36, 77, 100; CDBLB-6
 The Dorothy L. Sayers Society Y-98

Sayle, Charles Edward 1864-1924 ...... DLB-184
Sayles, John Thomas 1950- DLB-44
Sbarbaro, Camillo 1888-1967 .... DLB-114
Scalapino, Leslie 1947- DLB-193
Scannell, Vernon 1922- DLB-27
Scarry, Richard 1919-1994 .... DLB-61
Schack, Hans Egede 1820-1859 .... DLB-300
Schaefer, Jack 1907-1991 .... DLB-212
Schaeffer, Albrecht 1885-1950 .... DLB-66
Schaeffer, Susan Fromberg 1941- .. DLB-28, 299
Schaff, Philip 1819-1893 ....DS-13
Schaper, Edzard 1908-1984 .... DLB-69
Scharf, J. Thomas 1843-1898 .... DLB-47
Schede, Paul Melissus 1539-1602 ....DLB-179
Scheffel, Joseph Viktor von 1826-1886. .. DLB-129
Scheffler, Johann 1624-1677 .... DLB-164
Schéhadé, Georges 1905-1999 .... DLB-321
Schelling, Friedrich Wilhelm Joseph von
 1775-1854 .... DLB-90
Scherer, Wilhelm 1841-1886 .... DLB-129
Scherfig, Hans 1905-1979 .... DLB-214
Schickele, René 1883-1940 .... DLB-66
Schiff, Dorothy 1903-1989 ....DLB-127
Schiller, Friedrich
 1759-1805. .... DLB-94; CDWLB-2
Schirmer, David 1623-1687 .... DLB-164
Schlaf, Johannes 1862-1941 .... DLB-118
Schlegel, August Wilhelm 1767-1845 ..... DLB-94
Schlegel, Dorothea 1763-1839. .... DLB-90
Schlegel, Friedrich 1772-1829 .... DLB-90
Schleiermacher, Friedrich 1768-1834 ..... DLB-90
Schlesinger, Arthur M., Jr. 1917- DLB-17
Schlumberger, Jean 1877-1968 .... DLB-65
Schmid, Eduard Hermann Wilhelm
 (see Edschmid, Kasimir)
Schmidt, Arno 1914-1979 .... DLB-69
Schmidt, Johann Kaspar (see Stirner, Max)
Schmidt, Michael 1947- DLB-40
Schmidtbonn, Wilhelm August
 1876-1952. .... DLB-118
Schmitz, Aron Hector (see Svevo, Italo)
Schmitz, James H. 1911-1981 .... DLB-8
Schnabel, Johann Gottfried 1692-1760 ... DLB-168
Schnackenberg, Gjertrud 1953- DLB-120
Schnitzler, Arthur
 1862-1931 ....DLB-81, 118; CDWLB-2
Schnurre, Wolfdietrich 1920-1989 ...... DLB-69
Schocken Books DLB-46
Scholartis Press DLB-112
Scholderer, Victor 1880-1971 .... DLB-201
The Schomburg Center for Research
 in Black Culture. DLB-76
Schönbeck, Virgilio (see Giotti, Virgilio)
Schönherr, Karl 1867-1943 .... DLB-118
Schoolcraft, Jane Johnston 1800-1841. .....DLB-175
School Stories, 1914-1960. .... DLB-160

Schopenhauer, Arthur 1788-1860 . . . . .DLB-90
Schopenhauer, Johanna 1766-1838 . . . . . . .DLB-90
Schorer, Mark 1908-1977. . . . . .DLB-103
Schottelius, Justus Georg 1612-1676 . . . . .DLB-164
Schouler, James 1839-1920 . . . . .DLB-47
Schoultz, Solveig von 1907-1996 . . . . . . .DLB-259
Schrader, Paul 1946- DLB-44
Schreiner, Olive
  1855-1920 . . . . DLB-18, 156, 190, 225
Schroeder, Andreas 1946- DLB-53
Schubart, Christian Friedrich Daniel
  1739-1791 . . . . .DLB-97
Schubert, Gotthilf Heinrich 1780-1860 . . . .DLB-90
Schücking, Levin 1814-1883 . . . . .DLB-133
Schulberg, Budd 1914- DLB-6, 26, 28; Y-81
  Excerpts from USC Presentation
    [on F. Scott Fitzgerald] Y-96
F. J. Schulte and Company. DLB-49
Schulz, Bruno 1892-1942 . . . . DLB-215; CDWLB-4
Schulze, Hans (see Praetorius, Johannes)
Schupp, Johann Balthasar 1610-1661. . . . .DLB-164
Schurz, Carl 1829-1906 . . . . .DLB-23
Schuyler, George S. 1895-1977 . . . . DLB-29, 51
Schuyler, James 1923-1991 . . . . DLB-5, 169
Schwartz, Delmore 1913-1966 . . . . DLB-28, 48
Schwartz, Jonathan 1938- Y-82
Schwartz, Lynne Sharon 1939- DLB-218
Schwarz, Sibylle 1621-1638 . . . . .DLB-164
Schwarz-Bart, Andre 1928- DLB-299
Schwerner, Armand 1927-1999 . . . . .DLB-165
Schwob, Marcel 1867-1905 . . . . .DLB-123
Sciascia, Leonardo 1921-1989 . . . . .DLB-177
Science Fiction and Fantasy
  Documents in British Fantasy and
    Science Fiction DLB-178
  Hugo Awards and Nebula Awards DLB-8
  The Iconography of Science-Fiction
    Art DLB-8
  The New Wave. DLB-8
  Paperback Science Fiction DLB-8
  Science Fantasy DLB-8
  Science-Fiction Fandom and
    Conventions DLB-8
  Science-Fiction Fanzines: The Time
    Binders DLB-8
  Science-Fiction Films DLB-8
  Science Fiction Writers of America
    and the Nebula Award DLB-8
  Selected Science-Fiction Magazines and
    Anthologies. DLB-8
  A World Chronology of Important Science
    Fiction Works (1818-1979) DLB-8
  The Year in Science Fiction
    and Fantasy. Y-00, 01
Scot, Reginald circa 1538-1599 . . . . .DLB-136
Scotellaro, Rocco 1923-1953 . . . . .DLB-128
Scott, Alicia Anne (Lady John Scott)
  1810-1900 . . . . .DLB-240

Scott, Catharine Amy Dawson
  1865-1934 . . . . .DLB-240
Scott, Dennis 1939-1991 . . . . .DLB-125
Scott, Dixon 1881-1915 . . . . .DLB-98
Scott, Duncan Campbell 1862-1947. . . . . . .DLB-92
Scott, Evelyn 1893-1963 . . . . DLB-9, 48
Scott, F. R. 1899-1985 . . . . .DLB-88
Scott, Frederick George 1861-1944 . . . . . . .DLB-92
Scott, Geoffrey 1884-1929 . . . . .DLB-149
Scott, Harvey W. 1838-1910 . . . . .DLB-23
Scott, Lady Jane (see Scott, Alicia Anne)
Scott, Paul 1920-1978. . . . . DLB-14, 207
Scott, Sarah 1723-1795 . . . . .DLB-39
Scott, Tom 1918-1995 . . . . .DLB-27
Scott, Sir Walter 1771-1832
  . . . . . DLB-93, 107, 116, 144, 159; CDBLB-3
Scott, William Bell 1811-1890 . . . . .DLB-32
Walter Scott Publishing Company
  Limited DLB-112
William R. Scott [publishing house]. DLB-46
Scott-Heron, Gil 1949- DLB-41
Scribe, Eugene 1791-1861 . . . . .DLB-192
Scribner, Arthur Hawley 1859-1932 . . . . DS-13, 16
Scribner, Charles 1854-1930 . . . . DS-13, 16
Scribner, Charles, Jr. 1921-1995 . . . . Y-95
  Reminiscences DS-17
Charles Scribner's Sons DLB-49; DS-13, 16, 17
  Archives of Charles Scribner's Sons DS-17
Scribner's Magazine DS-13
Scribner's Monthly DS-13
Scripps, E. W. 1854-1926 . . . . .DLB-25
Scudder, Horace Elisha 1838-1902 . . . . DLB-42, 71
Scudder, Vida Dutton 1861-1954 . . . . .DLB-71
Scudéry, Madeleine de 1607-1701 . . . . . . .DLB-268
Scupham, Peter 1933- DLB-40
Seabrook, William 1886-1945 . . . . .DLB-4
Seabury, Samuel 1729-1796 . . . . .DLB-31
Seacole, Mary Jane Grant 1805-1881. . . . .DLB-166
The Seafarer circa 970 . . . . .DLB-146
Sealsfield, Charles (Carl Postl)
  1793-1864 . . . . DLB-133, 186
Searle, John R. 1932- DLB-279
Sears, Edward I. 1819?-1876 . . . . .DLB-79
Sears Publishing Company DLB-46
Seaton, George 1911-1979 . . . . .DLB-44
Seaton, William Winston 1785-1866 . . . . . .DLB-43
Martin Secker [publishing house]. DLB-112
Martin Secker, and Warburg Limited DLB-112
The "Second Generation" Holocaust
  Novel. DLB-299
Sedgwick, Arthur George 1844-1915. . . . . .DLB-64
Sedgwick, Catharine Maria
  1789-1867 . . . . DLB-1, 74, 183, 239, 243
Sedgwick, Ellery 1872-1960 . . . . .DLB-91
Sedgwick, Eve Kosofsky 1950- DLB-246
Sedley, Sir Charles 1639-1701 . . . . .DLB-131

Seeberg, Peter 1925-1999. . . . . .DLB-214
Seeger, Alan 1888-1916 . . . . .DLB-45
Seers, Eugene (see Dantin, Louis)
Segal, Erich 1937- Y-86
Segal, Lore 1928- DLB-299
Šegedin, Petar 1909-1998. . . . . .DLB-181
Seghers, Anna 1900-1983 . . . . DLB-69; CDWLB-2
Seid, Ruth (see Sinclair, Jo)
Seidel, Frederick Lewis 1936- Y-84
Seidel, Ina 1885-1974. . . . . .DLB-56
Seifert, Jaroslav
  1901-1986 . . . . DLB-215; Y-84; CDWLB-4
  Jaroslav Seifert Through the Eyes of
    the English-Speaking Reader Y-84
  Three Poems by Jaroslav Seifert Y-84
Seifullina, Lidiia Nikolaevna 1889-1954 . .DLB-272
Seigenthaler, John 1927- DLB-127
Seizin Press DLB-112
Séjour, Victor 1817-1874 . . . . .DLB-50
Séjour Marcou et Ferrand, Juan Victor
  (see Séjour, Victor)
Sekowski, Jósef-Julian, Baron Brambeus
  (see Senkovsky, Osip Ivanovich)
Selby, Bettina 1934- DLB-204
Selby, Hubert Jr. 1928-2004 . . . . DLB-2, 227
Selden, George 1929-1989 . . . . .DLB-52
Selden, John 1584-1654 . . . . .DLB-213
Selenić, Slobodan 1933-1995 . . . . .DLB-181
Self, Edwin F. 1920- DLB-137
Self, Will 1961- DLB-207
Seligman, Edwin R. A. 1861-1939. . . . . . . .DLB-47
Selimović, Meša
  1910-1982 . . . . DLB-181; CDWLB-4
Sellars, Wilfrid 1912-1989 . . . . .DLB-279
Sellings, Arthur (Arthur Gordon Ley)
  1911-1968 . . . . .DLB-261
Selous, Frederick Courteney 1851-1917 . .DLB-174
Seltzer, Chester E. (see Muro, Amado)
Thomas Seltzer [publishing house] DLB-46
Selvon, Sam 1923-1994 . . . . . DLB-125; CDWLB-3
Semel, Nava 1954- DLB-299
Semmes, Raphael 1809-1877 . . . . .DLB-189
Senancour, Etienne de 1770-1846 . . . . . . .DLB-119
Sena, Jorge de 1919-1978 . . . . .DLB-287
Sendak, Maurice 1928- DLB-61
Seneca the Elder
  circa 54 B.C.-circa A.D. 40 . . . . .DLB-211
Seneca the Younger
  circa 1 B.C.-A.D. 65 . . . . . DLB-211; CDWLB-1
Senécal, Eva 1905-1988 . . . . .DLB-92
Sengstacke, John 1912-1997 . . . . .DLB-127
Senior, Olive 1941- DLB-157
Senkovsky, Osip Ivanovich
  (Józef-Julian Sekowski, Baron Brambeus)
  1800-1858 . . . . .DLB-198
Šenoa, August 1838-1881 . . . DLB-147; CDWLB-4
Sentimental Fiction of the Sixteenth
  Century. DLB-318

Sepamla, Sipho 1932- DLB-157, 225
Serafimovich, Aleksandr Serafimovich
  (Aleksandr Serafimovich Popov)
  1863-1949 .... DLB-272
Serao, Matilde 1856-1927 .... DLB-264
Seredy, Kate 1899-1975 .... DLB-22
Sereni, Vittorio 1913-1983 .... DLB-128
William Seres [publishing house] DLB-170
Sergeev-Tsensky, Sergei Nikolaevich (Sergei
  Nikolaevich Sergeev) 1875-1958 .... DLB-272
Serling, Rod 1924-1975 .... DLB-26
Sernine, Daniel 1955- DLB-251
Serote, Mongane Wally 1944- ... DLB-125, 225
Serraillier, Ian 1912-1994 .... DLB-161
Serrano, Nina 1934- DLB-122
Service, Robert 1874-1958 .... DLB-92
Sessler, Charles 1854-1935 .... DLB-187
Seth, Vikram 1952- DLB-120, 271
Seton, Elizabeth Ann 1774-1821 .... DLB-200
Seton, Ernest Thompson
  1860-1942 .... DLB-92; DS-13
Seton, John circa 1509-1567 .... DLB-281
Setouchi Harumi 1922- DLB-182
Settle, Mary Lee 1918- DLB-6
Seume, Johann Gottfried 1763-1810 ...... DLB-94
Seuse, Heinrich 1295?-1366 .... DLB-179
Seuss, Dr. (see Geisel, Theodor Seuss)
Severianin, Igor' 1887-1941 .... DLB-295
Severin, Timothy 1940- DLB-204
Sévigné, Marie de Rabutin Chantal,
  Madame de 1626-1696 .... DLB-268
Sewall, Joseph 1688-1769 .... DLB-24
Sewall, Richard B. 1908-2003 .... DLB-111
Sewall, Samuel 1652-1730 .... DLB-24
Sewell, Anna 1820-1878 .... DLB-163
Sexton, Anne 1928-1974 ... DLB-5, 169; CDALB-1
Seymour-Smith, Martin 1928-1998 ...... DLB-155
Sgorlon, Carlo 1930- DLB-196
Shaara, Michael 1929-1988 .... Y-83
Shabel'skaia, Aleksandra Stanislavovna
  1845-1921 .... DLB-238
Shadwell, Thomas 1641?-1692 .... DLB-80
Shaffer, Anthony 1926-2001 .... DLB-13
Shaffer, Peter 1926- ... DLB-13, 233; CDBLB-8
Muhammad ibn Idris al-Shafi'i 767-820 .. DLB-311
Shaftesbury, Anthony Ashley Cooper,
  Third Earl of 1671-1713 .... DLB-101
Shaginian, Marietta Sergeevna
  1888-1982 .... DLB-272
Shairp, Mordaunt 1887-1939 .... DLB-10
Shakespeare, Nicholas 1957- DLB-231
Shakespeare, William
  1564-1616 ...... DLB-62, 172, 263; CDBLB-1
  The New Variorum Shakespeare Y-85
  Shakespeare and Montaigne: A Symposium
    by Jules Furthman Y-02

$6,166,000 for a *Book!* Observations on
  *The Shakespeare First Folio: The History
  of the Book* Y-01
Taylor-Made Shakespeare? Or Is
  "Shall I Die?" the Long-Lost Text
  of Bottom's Dream? Y-85
The Shakespeare Globe Trust Y-93
Shakespeare Head Press DLB-112
Shakhova, Elisaveta Nikitichna
  1822-1899 .... DLB-277
Shakhovskoi, Aleksandr Aleksandrovich
  1777-1846 .... DLB-150
Shalamov, Varlam Tikhonovich
  1907-1982 .... DLB-302
al-Shanfara fl. sixth century DLB-311
Shange, Ntozake 1948- DLB-38, 249
Shapcott, Thomas W. 1935- DLB-289
Shapir, Ol'ga Andreevna 1850-1916 ..... DLB-295
Shapiro, Karl 1913-2000 .... DLB-48
Sharon Publications DLB-46
Sharov, Vladimir Aleksandrovich
  1952- DLB-285
Sharp, Margery 1905-1991 .... DLB-161
Sharp, William 1855-1905 .... DLB-156
Sharpe, Tom 1928- DLB-14, 231
Shaw, Albert 1857-1947 .... DLB-91
Shaw, George Bernard
  1856-1950 .... DLB-10, 57, 190, CDBLB-6
  The Bernard Shaw Society Y-99
  "Stage Censorship: The Rejected
    Statement" (1911) [excerpts] DLB-10
Shaw, Henry Wheeler 1818-1885 .... DLB-11
Shaw, Irwin
  1913-1984 ..... DLB-6, 102; Y-84; CDALB-1
Shaw, Joseph T. 1874-1952 .... DLB-137
  "As I Was Saying," Joseph T. Shaw's
    Editorial Rationale in *Black Mask*
    (January 1927) DLB-137
Shaw, Mary 1854-1929 .... DLB-228
Shaw, Robert 1927-1978 .... DLB-13, 14
Shaw, Robert B. 1947- DLB-120
Shawn, Wallace 1943- DLB-266
Shawn, William 1907-1992 .... DLB-137
Frank Shay [publishing house] DLB-46
Shchedrin, N. (see Saltykov, Mikhail Evgrafovich)
Shcherbakova, Galina Nikolaevna
  1932- DLB-285
Shcherbina, Nikolai Fedorovich
  1821-1869 .... DLB-277
Shea, John Gilmary 1824-1892 .... DLB-30
Sheaffer, Louis 1912-1993 .... DLB-103
Sheahan, Henry Beston (see Beston, Henry)
Shearing, Joseph 1886-1952 .... DLB-70
Shebbeare, John 1709-1788 .... DLB-39
Sheckley, Robert 1928- DLB-8
Shedd, William G. T. 1820-1894 .... DLB-64
Sheed, Wilfrid 1930- DLB-6
Sheed and Ward [U.S.] DLB-46
Sheed and Ward Limited [U.K.] DLB-112

Sheldon, Alice B. (see Tiptree, James, Jr.)
Sheldon, Edward 1886-1946 .... DLB-7
Sheldon and Company DLB-49
Sheller, Aleksandr Konstantinovich
  1838-1900 .... DLB-238
Shelley, Mary Wollstonecraft 1797-1851
  .... DLB-110, 116, 159, 178; CDBLB-3
  Preface to *Frankenstein; or, The
    Modern Prometheus* (1818) DLB-178
Shelley, Percy Bysshe
  1792-1822 ...... DLB-96, 110, 158; CDBLB-3
Shelnutt, Eve 1941- DLB-130
Shenshin (see Fet, Afanasii Afanas'evich)
Shenstone, William 1714-1763 .... DLB-95
Shepard, Clark and Brown DLB-49
Shepard, Ernest Howard 1879-1976 .... DLB-160
Shepard, Sam 1943- DLB-7, 212
Shepard, Thomas I, 1604 or 1605-1649 ... DLB-24
Shepard, Thomas, II, 1635-1677 .... DLB-24
Shepherd, Luke fl. 1547-1554 .... DLB-136
Sherburne, Edward 1616-1702 .... DLB-131
Sheridan, Frances 1724-1766 .... DLB-39, 84
Sheridan, Richard Brinsley
  1751-1816 .... DLB-89; CDBLB-2
Sherman, Francis 1871-1926 .... DLB-92
Sherman, Martin 1938- DLB-228
Sherriff, R. C. 1896-1975 .... DLB-10, 191, 233
Sherrod, Blackie 1919- DLB-241
Sherry, Norman 1935- DLB-155
  Tribute to Graham Greene Y-91
Sherry, Richard 1506-1551 or 1555 ..... DLB-236
Sherwood, Mary Martha 1775-1851 .... DLB-163
Sherwood, Robert E. 1896-1955 ...DLB-7, 26, 249
Shevyrev, Stepan Petrovich
  1806-1864 .... DLB-205
Shiel, M. P. 1865-1947 .... DLB-153
Shiels, George 1886-1949 .... DLB-10
Shiga Naoya 1883-1971 .... DLB-180
Shiina Rinzō 1911-1973 .... DLB-182
Shikishi Naishinnō 1153?-1201 .... DLB-203
Shillaber, Benjamin Penhallow
  1814-1890 .... DLB-1, 11, 235
Shimao Toshio 1917-1986 .... DLB-182
Shimazaki Tōson 1872-1943 .... DLB-180
Shimose, Pedro 1940- DLB-283
Shine, Ted 1931- DLB-38
Shinkei 1406-1475 .... DLB-203
Ship, Reuben 1915-1975 .... DLB-88
Shirer, William L. 1904-1993 .... DLB-4
Shirinsky-Shikhmatov, Sergii Aleksandrovich
  1783-1837 .... DLB-150
Shirley, James 1596-1666 .... DLB-58
Shishkov, Aleksandr Semenovich
  1753-1841 .... DLB-150
Shmelev, I. S. 1873-1950 .... DLB-317
Shockley, Ann Allen 1927- DLB-33

Sholokhov, Mikhail Aleksandrovich
   1905-1984 . . . . DLB-272
Shōno Junzō 1921- DLB-182
Shore, Arabella 1820?-1901 . . . . DLB-199
Shore, Louisa 1824-1895 . . . . DLB-199
Short, Luke (see Glidden, Frederick Dilley)
Peter Short [publishing house] DLB-170
Shorter, Dora Sigerson 1866-1918 . . . . DLB-240
Shorthouse, Joseph Henry 1834-1903 . . . . . DLB-18
Short Stories
   Michael M. Rea and the Rea Award
     for the Short Story Y-97
   The Year in Short Stories Y-87
   The Year in the Short Story Y-88, 90–93
Shōtetsu 1381-1459 . . . . DLB-203
Showalter, Elaine 1941- DLB-67
Shreve, Anita 1946- DLB-292
Shteiger, Anatolii 1907-1944 . . . . DLB-317
Shukshin, Vasilii Makarovich
   1929-1974 . . . . DLB-302
Shulevitz, Uri 1935- DLB-61
Shulman, Max 1919-1988 . . . . DLB-11
Shute, Henry A. 1856-1943 . . . . DLB-9
Shute, Nevil (Nevil Shute Norway)
   1899-1960 . . . . DLB-255
Shuttle, Penelope 1947- DLB-14, 40
Shvarts, Evgenii L'vovich 1896-1958 . . . . . DLB-272
Sibawayhi circa 750-circa 795 . . . . DLB-311
Sibbes, Richard 1577-1635 . . . . DLB-151
Sibiriak, D. (see Mamin, Dmitrii Narkisovich)
Siddal, Elizabeth Eleanor 1829-1862 . . . . . DLB-199
Sidgwick, Ethel 1877-1970 . . . . DLB-197
Sidgwick, Henry 1838-1900 . . . . DLB-262
Sidgwick and Jackson Limited DLB-112
Sidney, Margaret (see Lothrop, Harriet M.)
Sidney, Mary 1561-1621 . . . . DLB-167
Sidney, Sir Philip
   1554-1586 . . . . DLB-167; CDBLB-1
   An Apologie for Poetrie (the Olney edition,
     1595, of *Defence of Poesie*) DLB-167
Sidney's Press DLB-49
Sierra, Rubén 1946- DLB-122
Sierra Club Books DLB-49
Siger of Brabant circa 1240-circa 1284 . . . . DLB-115
Sigourney, Lydia Huntley
   1791-1865 . . . . . . DLB-1, 42, 73, 183, 239, 243
Silkin, Jon 1930-1997 . . . . DLB-27
Silko, Leslie Marmon
   1948- DLB-143, 175, 256, 275
Silliman, Benjamin 1779-1864 . . . . DLB-183
Silliman, Ron 1946- DLB-169
Silliphant, Stirling 1918-1996 . . . . DLB-26
Sillitoe, Alan 1928- DLB-14, 139; CDBLB-8
   Tribute to J. B. Priestly Y-84
Silman, Roberta 1934- DLB-28
Silone, Ignazio (Secondino Tranquilli)
   1900-1978 . . . . DLB-264

Silva, Beverly 1930- DLB-122
Silva, Clara 1905-1976 . . . . DLB-290
Silva, José Asunció 1865-1896 . . . . DLB-283
Silverberg, Robert 1935- DLB-8
Silverman, Kaja 1947- DLB-246
Silverman, Kenneth 1936- DLB-111
Simak, Clifford D. 1904-1988 . . . . DLB-8
Simcoe, Elizabeth 1762-1850 . . . . DLB-99
Simcox, Edith Jemima 1844-1901 . . . . DLB-190
Simcox, George Augustus 1841-1905 . . . . . DLB-35
Sime, Jessie Georgina 1868-1958 . . . . DLB-92
Simenon, Georges 1903-1989 . . . . . DLB-72; Y-89
Simic, Charles 1938- DLB-105
   "Images and 'Images'" DLB-105
Simionescu, Mircea Horia 1928- DLB-232
Simmel, Georg 1858-1918 . . . . DLB-296
Simmel, Johannes Mario 1924- DLB-69
Valentine Simmes [publishing house] DLB-170
Simmons, Ernest J. 1903-1972 . . . . DLB-103
Simmons, Herbert Alfred 1930- DLB-33
Simmons, James 1933- DLB-40
Simms, William Gilmore
   1806-1870 . . . . DLB-3, 30, 59, 73, 248
Simms and M'Intyre DLB-106
Simon, Claude 1913-2005 . . . . DLB-83; Y-85
   Nobel Lecture Y-85
Simon, Neil 1927- DLB-7, 266
Simon and Schuster DLB-46
Simonov, Konstantin Mikhailovich
   1915-1979 . . . . DLB-302
Simons, Katherine Drayton Mayrant
   1890-1969 . . . . Y-83
Simović, Ljubomir 1935- DLB-181
Simpkin and Marshall
   [publishing house] DLB-154
Simpson, Helen 1897-1940 . . . . DLB-77
Simpson, Louis 1923- DLB-5
Simpson, N. F. 1919- DLB-13
Sims, George 1923-1999 . . . . DLB-87; Y-99
Sims, George Robert 1847-1922 . . . DLB-35, 70, 135
Sinán, Rogelio 1902-1994 . . . . DLB-145, 290
Sinclair, Andrew 1935- DLB-14
Sinclair, Bertrand William 1881-1972 . . . . . DLB-92
Sinclair, Catherine 1800-1864 . . . . DLB-163
Sinclair, Clive 1948- DLB-319
Sinclair, Jo 1913-1995 . . . . DLB-28
Sinclair, Lister 1921- DLB-88
Sinclair, May 1863-1946 . . . . DLB-36, 135
   The Novels of Dorothy Richardson
     (1918) DLB-36
Sinclair, Upton 1878-1968 . . . . . DLB-9; CDALB-5
Upton Sinclair [publishing house] DLB-46
Singer, Isaac Bashevis 1904-1991
   . . . . . . DLB-6, 28, 52, 278; Y-91; CDALB-1
Singer, Mark 1950- DLB-185
Singmaster, Elsie 1879-1958 . . . . DLB-9

Siniavsky, Andrei (Abram Tertz)
   1925-1997 . . . . DLB-302
Sinisgalli, Leonardo 1908-1981 . . . . DLB-114
Siodmak, Curt 1902-2000 . . . . DLB-44
Sîrbu, Ion D. 1919-1989 . . . . DLB-232
Siringo, Charles A. 1855-1928 . . . . DLB-186
Sissman, L. E. 1928-1976 . . . . DLB-5
Sisson, C. H. 1914-2003 . . . . DLB-27
Sitwell, Edith 1887-1964 . . . . DLB-20; CDBLB-7
Sitwell, Osbert 1892-1969 . . . . DLB-100, 195
Sixteenth-Century Spanish Epic, The DLB-318
Skácel, Jan 1922-1989 . . . . DLB-232
Skalbe, Kārlis 1879-1945 . . . . DLB-220
Skármeta, Antonio
   1940- DLB-145; CDWLB-3
Skavronsky, A. (see Danilevsky, Grigorii Petrovich)
Skeat, Walter W. 1835-1912 . . . . DLB-184
William Skeffington [publishing house] . . . DLB-106
Skelton, John 1463-1529 . . . . DLB-136
Skelton, Robin 1925-1997 . . . . DLB-27, 53
Škėma, Antanas 1910-1961 . . . . DLB-220
Skinner, Constance Lindsay
   1877-1939 . . . . DLB-92
Skinner, John Stuart 1788-1851 . . . . DLB-73
Skipsey, Joseph 1832-1903 . . . . DLB-35
Skou-Hansen, Tage 1925- DLB-214
Skrzynecki, Peter 1945- DLB-289
Škvorecký, Josef 1924- DLB-232; CDWLB-4
Slade, Bernard 1930- DLB-53
Slamnig, Ivan 1930- DLB-181
Slančeková, Božena (see Timrava)
Slataper, Scipio 1888-1915 . . . . DLB-264
Slater, Patrick 1880-1951 . . . . DLB-68
Slaveykov, Pencho 1866-1912 . . . . DLB-147
Slaviček, Milivoj 1929- DLB-181
Slavitt, David 1935- DLB-5, 6
Sleigh, Burrows Willcocks Arthur
   1821-1869 . . . . DLB-99
Sleptsov, Vasilii Alekseevich 1836-1878 . . . DLB-277
Slesinger, Tess 1905-1945 . . . . DLB-102
Slessor, Kenneth 1901-1971 . . . . DLB-260
Slick, Sam (see Haliburton, Thomas Chandler)
Sloan, John 1871-1951 . . . . DLB-188
Sloane, William, Associates DLB-46
Slonimsky, Mikhail Leonidovich
   1897-1972 . . . . DLB-272
Sluchevsky, Konstantin Konstantinovich
   1837-1904 . . . . DLB-277
Small, Maynard and Company DLB-49
Smart, Christopher 1722-1771 . . . . DLB-109
Smart, David A. 1892-1957 . . . . DLB-137
Smart, Elizabeth 1913-1986 . . . . DLB-88
Smart, J. J. C. 1920- DLB-262
Smedley, Menella Bute 1820?-1877 . . . . . . DLB-199
William Smellie [publishing house] DLB-154
Smiles, Samuel 1812-1904 . . . . DLB-55

Smiley, Jane 1949- DLB-227, 234

Smith, A. J. M. 1902-1980 .... DLB-88

Smith, Adam 1723-1790 .... DLB-104, 252

Smith, Adam (George Jerome Waldo
    Goodman) 1930- DLB-185

Smith, Alexander 1829-1867......... DLB-32, 55

    "On the Writing of Essays" (1862) ... DLB-57

Smith, Amanda 1837-1915 .... DLB-221

Smith, Betty 1896-1972................... Y-82

Smith, Carol Sturm 1938- Y-81

Smith, Charles Henry 1826-1903......... DLB-11

Smith, Charlotte 1749-1806 .... DLB-39, 109

Smith, Chet 1899-1973 ....DLB-171

Smith, Cordwainer 1913-1966 .... DLB-8

Smith, Dave 1942- DLB-5

    Tribute to James Dickey Y-97

    Tribute to John Gardner Y-82

Smith, Dodie 1896-1990............. DLB-10

Smith, Doris Buchanan 1934-2002....... DLB-52

Smith, E. E. 1890-1965................ DLB-8

Smith, Elihu Hubbard 1771-1798 .... DLB-37

Smith, Elizabeth Oakes (Prince)
    (see Oakes Smith, Elizabeth)

Smith, Eunice 1757-1823.............. DLB-200

Smith, F. Hopkinson 1838-1915.......... DS-13

Smith, George D. 1870-1920........... DLB-140

Smith, George O. 1911-1981 .... DLB-8

Smith, Goldwin 1823-1910............. DLB-99

Smith, H. Allen 1907-1976 .... DLB-11, 29

Smith, Harry B. 1860-1936........... DLB-187

Smith, Hazel Brannon 1914-1994....... DLB-127

Smith, Henry circa 1560-circa 1591 ..... DLB-136

Smith, Horatio (Horace)
    1779-1849.................. DLB-96, 116

Smith, Iain Crichton (Iain Mac A'Ghobhainn)
    1928-1998 .... DLB-40, 139, 319

Smith, J. Allen 1860-1924 .... DLB-47

Smith, James 1775-1839 .... DLB-96

Smith, Jessie Willcox 1863-1935......... DLB-188

Smith, John 1580-1631 .... DLB-24, 30

Smith, John 1618-1652 .... DLB-252

Smith, Josiah 1704-1781 .... DLB-24

Smith, Ken 1938- DLB-40

Smith, Lee 1944- DLB-143; Y-83

Smith, Logan Pearsall 1865-1946 .... DLB-98

Smith, Margaret Bayard 1778-1844 ..... DLB-248

Smith, Mark 1935- Y-82

Smith, Michael 1698-circa 1771 .... DLB-31

Smith, Pauline 1882-1959............. DLB-225

Smith, Red 1905-1982 ....DLB-29, 171

Smith, Roswell 1829-1892 .... DLB-79

Smith, Samuel Harrison 1772-1845....... DLB-43

Smith, Samuel Stanhope 1751-1819 ...... DLB-37

Smith, Sarah (see Stretton, Hesba)

Smith, Sarah Pogson 1774-1870 .... DLB-200

Smith, Seba 1792-1868 .... DLB-1, 11, 243

Smith, Stevie 1902-1971 .... DLB-20

Smith, Sydney 1771-1845 ....DLB-107

Smith, Sydney Goodsir 1915-1975 .... DLB-27

Smith, Sir Thomas 1513-1577........... DLB-132

Smith, W. Gordon 1928-1996 .... DLB-310

Smith, Wendell 1914-1972 ....DLB-171

Smith, William fl. 1595-1597 .... DLB-136

Smith, William 1727-1803.............. DLB-31

    A General Idea of the College of Mirania
    (1753) [excerpts]................ DLB-31

Smith, William 1728-1793............... DLB-30

Smith, William Gardner 1927-1974....... DLB-76

Smith, William Henry 1808-1872....... DLB-159

Smith, William Jay 1918- DLB-5

Smith, Elder and Company DLB-154

Harrison Smith and Robert Haas
    [publishing house] DLB-46

J. Stilman Smith and Company DLB-49

W. B. Smith and Company DLB-49

W. H. Smith and Son................ DLB-106

Leonard Smithers [publishing house] DLB-112

Smollett, Tobias
    1721-1771 .... DLB-39, 104; CDBLB-2

    Dedication to Ferdinand Count Fathom
    (1753)...................... DLB-39

    Preface to Ferdinand Count Fathom
    (1753)...................... DLB-39

    Preface to Roderick Random (1748) DLB-39

Smythe, Francis Sydney 1900-1949 ..... DLB-195

Snelling, William Joseph 1804-1848..... DLB-202

Snellings, Rolland (see Touré, Askia Muhammad)

Snodgrass, W. D. 1926- DLB-5

Snorri Hjartarson 1906-1986 .... DLB-293

Snow, C. P.
    1905-1980 .... DLB-15, 77; DS-17; CDBLB-7

Snyder, Gary
    1930- DLB-5, 16, 165, 212, 237, 275

Sobiloff, Hy 1912-1970 .... DLB-48

The Social Contract, Jean-Jacques
    Rousseau DLB-314

The Society for Textual Scholarship and
    TEXT........................ Y-87

The Society for the History of Authorship,
    Reading and Publishing............... Y-92

Söderberg, Hjalmar 1869-1941......... DLB-259

Södergran, Edith 1892-1923........... DLB-259

Soffici, Ardengo 1879-1964........ DLB-114, 264

Sofola, 'Zulu 1938- DLB-157

Sokhanskaia, Nadezhda Stepanovna
    (Kokhanovskaia) 1823?-1884.......DLB-277

Sokolov, Sasha (Aleksandr Vsevolodovich
    Sokolov) 1943- DLB-285

Solano, Solita 1888-1975................ DLB-4

Soldati, Mario 1906-1999 ....DLB-177

Soledad (see Zamudio, Adela)

Šoljan, Antun 1932-1993 .... DLB-181

Sollers, Philippe (Philippe Joyaux)
    1936- DLB-83

Sollogub, Vladimir Aleksandrovich
    1813-1882 .... DLB-198

Sollors, Werner 1943- DBL-246

Solmi, Sergio 1899-1981.............. DLB-114

Sologub, Fedor 1863-1927 .... DLB-295

Solomon, Carl 1928- DLB-16

Solórzano, Carlos 1922- DLB-305

Soloukhin, Vladimir Alekseevich
    1924-1997 .... DLB-302

Solov'ev, Sergei Mikhailovich
    1885-1942 .... DLB-295

Solov'ev, Vladimir Sergeevich
    1853-1900 .... DLB-295

Solstad, Dag 1941- DLB-297

Solway, David 1941- DLB-53

Solzhenitsyn, Aleksandr
    1918- DLB-302
    Solzhenitsyn and America Y-85

Some Basic Notes on Three Modern Genres:
    Interview, Blurb, and Obituary Y-02

Somerville, Edith Œnone 1858-1949 .... DLB-135

Somov, Orest Mikhailovich 1793-1833 .. DLB-198

Sønderby, Knud 1909-1966 .... DLB-214

Sone, Monica 1919- DLB-312

Song, Cathy 1955- DLB-169, 312

Sonnevi, Göran 1939- DLB-257

Sono Ayako 1931- DLB-182

Sontag, Susan 1933-2004 .... DLB-2, 67

Sophocles 497/496 B.C.-406/405 B.C.
    ....DLB-176; CDWLB-1

Šopov, Aco 1923-1982 .... DLB-181

Sorel, Charles ca.1600-1674 ....DLB-268

Sørensen, Villy 1929- DLB-214

Sorensen, Virginia 1912-1991.......... DLB-206

Sorge, Reinhard Johannes 1892-1916.... DLB-118

Sorokin, Vladimir Georgievich
    1955- DLB-285

Sorrentino, Gilbert 1929- DLB-5, 173; Y-80

Sosa, Roberto 1930- DLB-290

Sotheby, James 1682-1742 .... DLB-213

Sotheby, John 1740-1807 .... DLB-213

Sotheby, Samuel 1771-1842 .... DLB-213

Sotheby, Samuel Leigh 1805-1861 ...... DLB-213

Sotheby, William 1757-1833 .... DLB-93, 213

Soto, Gary 1952- DLB-82

Soueif, Ahdaf 1950- DLB-267

Souster, Raymond 1921- DLB-88

The South English Legendary circa
    thirteenth-fifteenth centuries DLB-146

Southerland, Ellease 1943- DLB-33

Southern, Terry 1924-1995 .... DLB-2

Southern Illinois University Press Y-95

Southern Literature
    Fellowship of Southern Writers Y-98

    The Fugitives and the Agrarians:
    The First Exhibition Y-85

"The Greatness of Southern Literature":
  League of the South Institute for the
  Study of Southern Culture and
  History Y-02
The Society for the Study of
  Southern Literature. Y-00
Southern Writers Between the Wars. . . . DLB-9
Southerne, Thomas 1659-1746 . . . . DLB-80
Southey, Caroline Anne Bowles
  1786-1854 . . . . DLB-116
Southey, Robert 1774-1843 . . . . . DLB-93, 107, 142
Southwell, Robert 1561?-1595. . . . . DLB-167
Southworth, E. D. E. N. 1819-1899. . . . . . DLB-239
Sowande, Bode 1948- DLB-157
Tace Sowle [publishing house]. DLB-170
Soyfer, Jura 1912-1939. . . . . DLB-124
Soyinka, Wole
  1934- DLB-125; Y-86, Y-87; CDWLB-3
  Nobel Lecture 1986: This Past Must
    Address Its Present Y-86
Spacks, Barry 1931- DLB-105
Spalding, Frances 1950- DLB-155
Spanish Byzantine Novel, The. DLB-318
Spanish Travel Writers of the
  Late Middle Ages DLB-286
Spark, Muriel 1918- DLB-15, 139; CDBLB-7
Michael Sparke [publishing house]. DLB-170
Sparks, Jared 1789-1866. . . . . DLB-1, 30, 235
Sparshott, Francis 1926- DLB-60
Späth, Gerold 1939- DLB-75
Spatola, Adriano 1941-1988. . . . . DLB-128
Spaziani, Maria Luisa 1924- DLB-128
Specimens of Foreign Standard Literature
  1838-1842 . . . . DLB-1
The Spectator 1828- DLB-110
Spedding, James 1808-1881 . . . . DLB-144
Spee von Langenfeld, Friedrich
  1591-1635. DLB-164
Speght, Rachel 1597-after 1630 . . . . DLB-126
Speke, John Hanning 1827-1864 . . . . DLB-166
Spellman, A. B. 1935- DLB-41
Spence, Catherine Helen 1825-1910 . . . . . DLB-230
Spence, Thomas 1750-1814 . . . . DLB-158
Spencer, Anne 1882-1975. . . . . DLB-51, 54
Spencer, Charles, third Earl of Sunderland
  1674-1722 . . . . DLB-213
Spencer, Elizabeth 1921- DLB-6, 218
Spencer, George John, Second Earl Spencer
  1758-1834 . . . . DLB-184
Spencer, Herbert 1820-1903 . . . . DLB-57, 262
  "The Philosophy of Style" (1852). DLB-57
Spencer, Scott 1945- Y-86
Spender, J. A. 1862-1942 . . . . DLB-98
Spender, Stephen 1909-1995 . . DLB-20; CDBLB-7
Spener, Philipp Jakob 1635-1705 . . . . DLB-164
Spenser, Edmund
  circa 1552-1599 . . . . DLB-167; CDBLB-1
  Envoy from *The Shepheardes Calender*. . . . DLB-167

"The Generall Argument of the
  Whole Booke," from
  The Shepheardes Calender DLB-167
"A Letter of the Authors Expounding
  His Whole Intention in the Course
  of this Worke: Which for that It
  Giueth Great Light to the Reader,
  for the Better Vnderstanding
  Is Hereunto Annexed,"
  from *The Faerie Queene* (1590) DLB-167
"To His Booke," from
  The Shepheardes Calender (1579) . . . DLB-167
"To the Most Excellent and Learned
  Both Orator and Poete, Mayster
  Gabriell Haruey, His Verie Special
  and Singular Good Frend E. K.
  Commendeth the Good Lyking of
  This His Labour, and the Patronage
  of the New Poete," from
  The Shepheardes Calender DLB-167
Sperr, Martin 1944- DLB-124
Spewack, Bella Cowen 1899-1990. . . . . . . DLB-266
Spewack, Samuel 1899-1971 . . . . DLB-266
Spicer, Jack 1925-1965. . . . . DLB-5, 16, 193
Spiegelman, Art 1948- DLB-299
Spielberg, Peter 1929- Y-81
Spielhagen, Friedrich 1829-1911 . . . . DLB-129
"Spielmannsepen" (circa 1152-circa 1500) . . . DLB-148
Spier, Peter 1927- DLB-61
Spillane, Mickey 1918- DLB-226
Spink, J. G. Taylor 1888-1962. . . . . DLB-241
Spinrad, Norman 1940- DLB-8
  Tribute to Isaac Asimov Y-92
Spires, Elizabeth 1952- DLB-120
The Spirit of Laws, Claude-Adrien
  Helvétius. DLB-314
The Spirit of Laws, Charles-Louis de Secondat, baron
  de Montesquieu. DLB-314
Spitteler, Carl 1845-1924 . . . . DLB-129
Spivak, Lawrence E. 1900-1994. . . . . DLB-137
Spofford, Harriet Prescott
  1835-1921 . . . . DLB-74, 221
Sports
  Jimmy, Red, and Others: Harold
    Rosenthal Remembers the Stars
    of the Press Box Y-01
  The Literature of Boxing in England
    through Arthur Conan Doyle. Y-01
  Notable Twentieth-Century Books
    about Sports DLB-241
Sprigge, Timothy L. S. 1932- DLB-262
Spring, Howard 1889-1965 . . . . DLB-191
Springs, Elliott White 1896-1959. . . . . . . DLB-316
Squibob (see Derby, George Horatio)
Squier, E. G. 1821-1888. . . . . DLB-189
Staal-Delaunay, Marguerite-Jeanne Cordier de
  1684-1750 . . . . DLB-314
Stableford, Brian 1948- DLB-261
Stacpoole, H. de Vere 1863-1951 . . . . . . DLB-153
Staël, Germaine de 1766-1817 . . . . . . DLB-119, 192
Staël-Holstein, Anne-Louise Germaine de
  (see Staël, Germaine de)
Staffeldt, Schack 1769-1826 . . . . DLB-300

Stafford, Jean 1915-1979 . . . . DLB-2, 173
Stafford, William 1914-1993 . . . . DLB-5, 206
Stallings, Laurence 1894-1968 . . . . DLB-7, 44, 316
Stallworthy, Jon 1935- DLB-40
Stampp, Kenneth M. 1912- DLB-17
Stănescu, Nichita 1933-1983 . . . . DLB-232
Stanev, Emiliyan 1907-1979 . . . . DLB-181
Stanford, Ann 1916-1987. . . . . DLB-5
Stangerup, Henrik 1937-1998 . . . . DLB-214
Stanihurst, Richard 1547-1618. . . . . DLB-281
Stanitsky, N. (see Panaeva, Avdot'ia Iakovlevna)
Stankevich, Nikolai Vladimirovich
  1813-1840 . . . . DLB-198
Stanković, Borisav ("Bora")
  1876-1927 . . . . DLB-147; CDWLB-4
Stanley, Henry M. 1841-1904 . . . . DLB-189; DS-13
Stanley, Thomas 1625-1678. . . . . DLB-131
Stannard, Martin 1947- DLB-155
William Stansby [publishing house]. DLB-170
Stanton, Elizabeth Cady 1815-1902. . . . . . DLB-79
Stanton, Frank L. 1857-1927 . . . . DLB-25
Stanton, Maura 1946- DLB-120
Stapledon, Olaf 1886-1950 . . . . DLB-15, 255
Star Spangled Banner Office DLB-49
Stark, Freya 1893-1993 . . . . DLB-195
Starkey, Thomas circa 1499-1538 . . . . DLB-132
Starkie, Walter 1894-1976 . . . . DLB-195
Starkweather, David 1935- DLB-7
Starrett, Vincent 1886-1974 . . . . DLB-187
Stationers' Company of London, The. . . . DLB-170
Statius circa A.D. 45-A.D. 96. . . . . DLB-211
Stead, Christina 1902-1983 . . . . DLB-260
Stead, Robert J. C. 1880-1959 . . . . DLB-92
Steadman, Mark 1930- DLB-6
Stearns, Harold E. 1891-1943 . . . . . . DLB-4; DS-15
Stebnitsky, M. (see Leskov, Nikolai Semenovich)
Stedman, Edmund Clarence 1833-1908 . . . DLB-64
Steegmuller, Francis 1906-1994. . . . . DLB-111
Steel, Flora Annie 1847-1929 . . . . . . DLB-153, 156
Steele, Max 1922- Y-80
Steele, Richard
  1672-1729 . . . . DLB-84, 101; CDBLB-2
Steele, Timothy 1948- DLB-120
Steele, Wilbur Daniel 1886-1970 . . . . DLB-86
Wallace Markfield's "Steeplechase". Y-02
Steere, Richard circa 1643-1721. . . . . DLB-24
Stefán frá Hvítadal (Stefán Sigurðsson)
  1887-1933 . . . . DLB-293
Stefán Guðmundsson (see Stephan G. Stephansson)
Stefán Hörður Grímsson
  1919 or 1920-2002 . . . . DLB-293
Steffens, Lincoln 1866-1936. . . . . DLB-303
Stefanovski, Goran 1952- DLB-181
Stegner, Wallace
  1909-1993 . . . . DLB-9, 206, 275; Y-93
Stehr, Hermann 1864-1940 . . . . DLB-66

Steig, William 1907-2003 .... DLB-61

Stein, Gertrude 1874-1946
.... DLB-4, 54, 86, 228; DS-15; CDALB-4

Stein, Leo 1872-1947................... DLB-4

Stein and Day Publishers DLB-46

Steinbeck, John 1902-1968
.... DLB-7, 9, 212, 275, 309; DS-2; CDALB-5

    John Steinbeck Research Center,
    San Jose State University........... Y-85

    The Steinbeck Centennial Y-02

Steinem, Gloria 1934- DLB-246

Steiner, George 1929- DLB-67, 299

Steinhoewel, Heinrich 1411/1412-1479...DLB-179

Steinn Steinarr (Aðalsteinn Kristmundsson)
1908-1958 .... DLB-293

Steinunn Sigurðardóttir 1950- DLB-293

Steloff, Ida Frances 1887-1989.......... DLB-187

Stendhal 1783-1842.................... DLB-119

Stephan G. Stephansson (Stefán Guðmundsson)
1853-1927.................... DLB-293

Stephen, Leslie 1832-1904 ......DLB-57, 144, 190

Stephen Family (Bloomsbury Group)........ DS-10

Stephens, A. G. 1865-1933 .... DLB-230

Stephens, Alexander H. 1812-1883....... DLB-47

Stephens, Alice Barber 1858-1932 ...... DLB-188

Stephens, Ann 1810-1886 .... DLB-3, 73, 250

Stephens, Charles Asbury 1844?-1931 .... DLB-42

Stephens, James 1882?-1950.... DLB-19, 153, 162

Stephens, John Lloyd 1805-1852 ... DLB-183, 250

Stephens, Michael 1946- DLB-234

Stephensen, P. R. 1901-1965 .... DLB-260

Sterling, George 1869-1926 .... DLB-54

Sterling, James 1701-1763 .... DLB-24

Sterling, John 1806-1844............... DLB-116

Stern, Gerald 1925- DLB-105

    "Living in Ruin".................. DLB-105

Stern, Gladys B. 1890-1973............. DLB-197

Stern, Madeleine B. 1912- DLB-111, 140

Stern, Richard 1928- DLB-218; Y-87

Stern, Stewart 1922- DLB-26

Sterne, Laurence 1713-1768 ... DLB-39; CDBLB-2

Sternheim, Carl 1878-1942 .... DLB-56, 118

Sternhold, Thomas ?-1549 .... DLB-132

Steuart, David 1747-1824 .... DLB-213

Stevens, Henry 1819-1886 .... DLB-140

Stevens, Wallace 1879-1955 ... DLB-54; CDALB-5

    The Wallace Stevens Society Y-99

Stevenson, Anne 1933- DLB-40

Stevenson, D. E. 1892-1973 .... DLB-191

Stevenson, Lionel 1902-1973 .... DLB-155

Stevenson, Robert Louis
1850-1894 ....DLB-18, 57, 141, 156, 174;
DS-13; CDBLB-5

    "On Style in Literature:
    Its Technical Elements" (1885) ... DLB-57

Stewart, Donald Ogden
1894-1980 .... DLB-4, 11, 26; DS-15

Stewart, Douglas 1913-1985........... DLB-260

Stewart, Dugald 1753-1828.............. DLB-31

Stewart, George, Jr. 1848-1906.......... DLB-99

Stewart, George R. 1895-1980 .... DLB-8

Stewart, Harold 1916-1995............ DLB-260

Stewart, J. I. M. (see Innes, Michael)

Stewart, Maria W. 1803?-1879 .... DLB-239

Stewart, Randall 1896-1964 .... DLB-103

Stewart, Sean 1965- DLB-251

Stewart and Kidd Company............ DLB-46

Sthen, Hans Christensen 1544-1610..... DLB-300

Stickney, Trumbull 1874-1904 .... DLB-54

Stieler, Caspar 1632-1707 .... DLB-164

Stifter, Adalbert
1805-1868 .... DLB-133; CDWLB-2

Stiles, Ezra 1727-1795 .... DLB-31

Still, James 1906-2001.............DLB-9; Y-01

Stirling, S. M. 1953- DLB-251

Stirner, Max 1806-1856 .... DLB-129

Stith, William 1707-1755 .... DLB-31

Stivens, Dal 1911-1997 .... DLB-260

Elliot Stock [publishing house] DLB-106

Stockton, Annis Boudinot 1736-1801 .... DLB-200

Stockton, Frank R.
1834-1902 ....DLB-42, 74; DS-13

Stockton, J. Roy 1892-1972............. DLB-241

Ashbel Stoddard [publishing house] DLB-49

Stoddard, Charles Warren 1843-1909 ... DLB-186

Stoddard, Elizabeth 1823-1902......... DLB-202

Stoddard, Richard Henry
1825-1903 .... DLB-3, 64, 250; DS-13

Stoddard, Solomon 1643-1729 .... DLB-24

Stoker, Bram
1847-1912........DLB-36, 70, 178; CDBLB-5

    On Writing *Dracula,* from the
    Introduction to *Dracula* (1897)....DLB-178

    Dracula (Documentary)............ DLB-304

Frederick A. Stokes Company DLB-49

Stokes, Thomas L. 1898-1958 .... DLB-29

Stokesbury, Leon 1945- DLB-120

Stolberg, Christian Graf zu 1748-1821 .... DLB-94

Stolberg, Friedrich Leopold Graf zu
1750-1819...................... DLB-94

Stone, Lucy 1818-1893............ DLB-79, 239

Stone, Melville 1848-1929 .... DLB-25

Stone, Robert 1937- DLB-152

Stone, Ruth 1915- DLB-105

Stone, Samuel 1602-1663 .... DLB-24

Stone, William Leete 1792-1844 .... DLB-202

Herbert S. Stone and Company DLB-49

Stone and Kimball DLB-49

Stoppard, Tom
1937- DLB-13, 233; Y-85; CDBLB-8

    Playwrights and Professors DLB-13

Storey, Anthony 1928- DLB-14

Storey, David 1933- DLB-13, 14, 207, 245

Storm, Theodor
1817-1888.............DLB-129; CDWLB-2

Storni, Alfonsina 1892-1938........... DLB-283

Story, Thomas circa 1670-1742.......... DLB-31

Story, William Wetmore 1819-1895 .. DLB-1, 235

Storytelling: A Contemporary Renaissance ... Y-84

Stoughton, William 1631-1701 .... DLB-24

Stout, Rex 1886-1975 .... DLB-306

Stow, John 1525-1605.................. DLB-132

Stow, Randolph 1935- DLB-260

Stowe, Harriet Beecher 1811-1896..... DLB-1,12,
42, 74, 189, 239, 243; CDALB-3

    The Harriet Beecher Stowe Center Y-00

Stowe, Leland 1899-1994 .... DLB-29

Stoyanov, Dimitr Ivanov (see Elin Pelin)

Strabo 64/63 B.C.-circa A.D. 25 ....DLB-176

Strachey, Lytton 1880-1932 ..... DLB-149; DS-10

    Preface to *Eminent Victorians* DLB-149

William Strahan [publishing house] DLB-154

Strahan and Company DLB-106

Strand, Mark 1934- DLB-5

The Strasbourg Oaths 842 .... DLB-148

Stratemeyer, Edward 1862-1930 .... DLB-42

Strati, Saverio 1924- DLB-177

Stratton and Barnard DLB-49

Stratton-Porter, Gene
1863-1924 .... DLB-221; DS-14

Straub, Peter 1943- Y-84

Strauß, Botho 1944- DLB-124

Strauß, David Friedrich 1808-1874..... DLB-133

The Strawberry Hill Press DLB-154

Strawson, P. F. 1919- DLB-262

Streatfeild, Noel 1895-1986 .... DLB-160

Street, Cecil John Charles (see Rhode, John)

Street, G. S. 1867-1936 .... DLB-135

Street and Smith DLB-49

Streeter, Edward 1891-1976 .... DLB-11

Streeter, Thomas Winthrop 1883-1965 .. DLB-140

Stretton, Hesba 1832-1911 .... DLB-163, 190

Stribling, T. S. 1881-1965............... DLB-9

Der Stricker circa 1190-circa 1250 ...... DLB-138

Strickland, Samuel 1804-1867........... DLB-99

Strindberg, August 1849-1912 .... DLB-259

Stringer, Arthur 1874-1950 .... DLB-92

Stringer and Townsend DLB-49

Strittmatter, Erwin 1912-1994 .... DLB-69

Strniša, Gregor 1930-1987 .... DLB-181

Strode, William 1630-1645............ DLB-126

Strong, L. A. G. 1896-1958 .... DLB-191

Strother, David Hunter (Porte Crayon)
1816-1888 .... DLB-3, 248

Strouse, Jean 1945- DLB-111

Strugatsky, Arkadii Natanovich
1925- DLB-302

Strugatsky, Boris Natanovich 1933- ... DLB-302

Stuart, Dabney 1937- DLB-105

"Knots into Webs: Some
    Autobiographical Sources" DLB-105

Stuart, Jesse 1906-1984 ..... DLB-9, 48, 102; Y-84

Lyle Stuart [publishing house] DLB-46

Stuart, Ruth McEnery 1849?-1917 .... DLB-202

Stub, Ambrosius 1705-1758 .... DLB-300

Stubbs, Harry Clement (see Clement, Hal)

Stubenberg, Johann Wilhelm von
    1619-1663 .... DLB-164

Stuckenberg, Viggo 1763-1905 .... DLB-300

Studebaker, William V. 1947- DLB-256

Studies in American Jewish Literature Y-02

Studio DLB-112

Stump, Al 1916-1995 .... DLB-241

Sturgeon, Theodore
    1918-1985 .... DLB-8; Y-85

Sturges, Preston 1898-1959 .... DLB-26

Styron, William
    1925- DLB-2, 143, 299; Y-80; CDALB-6

    Tribute to James Dickey Y-97

Suard, Jean-Baptiste-Antoine
    1732-1817 .... DLB-314

Suárez, Clementina 1902-1991 .... DLB-290

Suárez, Mario 1925- DLB-82

Suassuna, Ariano 1927- DLB-307

Such, Peter 1939- DLB-60

Suckling, Sir John 1609-1641? DLB-58, 126

Suckow, Ruth 1892-1960 .... DLB-9, 102

Sudermann, Hermann 1857-1928 .... DLB-118

Sue, Eugène 1804-1857 .... DLB-119

Sue, Marie-Joseph (see Sue, Eugène)

Suetonius circa A.D. 69-post A.D. 122 ..... DLB-211

Suggs, Simon (see Hooper, Johnson Jones)

Sui Sin Far (see Eaton, Edith Maude)

Suits, Gustav 1883-1956 .... DLB-220; CDWLB-4

Sukenick, Ronald 1932-2004 ..... DLB-173; Y-81

    An Author's Response Y-82

Sukhovo-Kobylin, Aleksandr Vasil'evich
    1817-1903 .... DLB-277

Suknaski, Andrew 1942- DLB-53

Sullivan, Alan 1868-1947 .... DLB-92

Sullivan, C. Gardner 1886-1965 .... DLB-26

Sullivan, Frank 1892-1976 .... DLB-11

Sulte, Benjamin 1841-1923 .... DLB-99

Sulzberger, Arthur Hays 1891-1968 ..... DLB-127

Sulzberger, Arthur Ochs 1926- DLB-127

Sulzer, Johann Georg 1720-1779 .... DLB-97

Sumarokov, Aleksandr Petrovich
    1717-1777 .... DLB-150

Summers, Hollis 1916-1987 .... DLB-6

Sumner, Charles 1811-1874 .... DLB-235

Sumner, William Graham 1840-1910 .... DLB-270

Henry A. Sumner
    [publishing house] DLB-49

Sundman, Per Olof 1922-1992 .... DLB-257

Supervielle, Jules 1884-1960 .... DLB-258

Surtees, Robert Smith 1803-1864 .... DLB-21

    The R. S. Surtees Society Y-98

Sutcliffe, Matthew 1550?-1629 .... DLB-281

Sutcliffe, William 1971- DLB-271

Sutherland, Efua Theodora 1924-1996 ... DLB-117

Sutherland, John 1919-1956 .... DLB-68

Sutro, Alfred 1863-1933 .... DLB-10

Svava Jakobsdóttir 1930- DLB-293

Svendsen, Hanne Marie 1933- DLB-214

Svevo, Italo (Ettore Schmitz)
    1861-1928 .... DLB-264

Swados, Harvey 1920-1972 .... DLB-2

Swain, Charles 1801-1874 .... DLB-32

Swallow Press DLB-46

Swan Sonnenschein Limited DLB-106

Swanberg, W. A. 1907-1992 .... DLB-103

Swedish Literature
    The Literature of the Modern
    Breakthrough DLB-259

Swenson, May 1919-1989 .... DLB-5

Swerling, Jo 1897-1964 .... DLB-44

Swift, Graham 1949- DLB-194

Swift, Jonathan
    1667-1745 .... DLB-39, 95, 101; CDBLB-2

Swinburne, A. C.
    1837-1909 .... DLB-35, 57; CDBLB-4

    Under the Microscope (1872) DLB-35

Swineshead, Richard floruit circa 1350 ... DLB-115

Swinnerton, Frank 1884-1982 .... DLB-34

Swisshelm, Jane Grey 1815-1884 .... DLB-43

Swope, Herbert Bayard 1882-1958 ...... DLB-25

Swords, James ?-1844 .... DLB-73

Swords, Thomas 1763-1843 .... DLB-73

T. and J. Swords and Company DLB-49

Swynnerton, Thomas (John Roberts)
    circa 1500-1554 .... DLB-281

Sykes, Ella C. ?-1939 .... DLB-174

Sylvester, Josuah 1562 or 1563-1618 ..... DLB-121

Symonds, Emily Morse (see Paston, George)

Symonds, John Addington
    1840-1893 .... DLB-57, 144

    "Personal Style" (1890) DLB-57

Symons, A. J. A. 1900-1941 .... DLB-149

Symons, Arthur 1865-1945 ...... DLB-19, 57, 149

Symons, Julian 1912-1994 ..... DLB-87, 155; Y-92

    Julian Symons at Eighty Y-92

Symons, Scott 1933- DLB-53

Synge, John Millington
    1871-1909 .... DLB-10, 19; CDBLB-5

    Synge Summer School: J. M. Synge
    and the Irish Theater, Rathdrum,
    County Wiclow, Ireland Y-93

Syrett, Netta 1865-1943 .... DLB-135, 197

The System of Nature, Paul Henri Thiry,
    baron d'Holbach (as Jean-Baptiste
    de Mirabaud) DLB-314

Szabó, Lőrinc 1900-1957 .... DLB-215

Szabó, Magda 1917- DLB-215

Szymborska, Wisława
    1923- DLB-232, Y-96; CDWLB-4

    Nobel Lecture 1996:
    The Poet and the World Y-96

T

Taban lo Liyong 1939?- DLB-125

al-Tabari 839-923 .... DLB-311

Tablada, José Juan 1871-1945 .... DLB-290

Le Tableau de Paris, Louis-Sébastien
    Mercier DLB-314

Tabori, George 1914- DLB-245

Tabucchi, Antonio 1943- DLB-196

Taché, Joseph-Charles 1820-1894 .... DLB-99

Tachihara Masaaki 1926-1980 .... DLB-182

Tacitus circa A.D. 55-circa A.D. 117
    .... DLB-211; CDWLB-1

Tadijanović, Dragutin 1905- DLB-181

Tafdrup, Pia 1952- DLB-214

Tafolla, Carmen 1951- DLB-82

Taggard, Genevieve 1894-1948 .... DLB-45

Taggart, John 1942- DLB-193

Tagger, Theodor (see Bruckner, Ferdinand)

Taiheiki late fourteenth century DLB-203

Tait, J. Selwin, and Sons DLB-49

Tait's Edinburgh Magazine 1832-1861 ...... DLB-110

The Takarazaka Revue Company Y-91

Talander (see Bohse, August)

Talese, Gay 1932- DLB-185

    Tribute to Irwin Shaw Y-84

Talev, Dimitr 1898-1966 .... DLB-181

Taliaferro, H. E. 1811-1875 .... DLB-202

Tallent, Elizabeth 1954- DLB-130

TallMountain, Mary 1918-1994 .... DLB-193

Talvj 1797-1870 .... DLB-59, 133

Tamási, Áron 1897-1966 .... DLB-215

Tammsaare, A. H.
    1878-1940 .... DLB-220; CDWLB-4

Tan, Amy 1952- DLB-173, 312; CDALB-7

Tandori, Dezső 1938- DLB-232

Tanner, Thomas 1673/1674-1735 .... DLB-213

Tanizaki Jun'ichirō 1886-1965 .... DLB-180

Tapahonso, Luci 1953- DLB-175

The Mark Taper Forum DLB-7

Taradash, Daniel 1913-2003 .... DLB-44

Tarasov-Rodionov, Aleksandr Ignat'evich
    1885-1938 .... DLB-272

Tarbell, Ida M. 1857-1944 .... DLB-47

Tardieu, Jean 1903-1995 .... DLB-321

Tardivel, Jules-Paul 1851-1905 .... DLB-99

Targan, Barry 1932- DLB-130

    Tribute to John Gardner Y-82

Tarkington, Booth 1869-1946 .... DLB-9, 102

Tashlin, Frank 1913-1972 .... DLB-44

Tasma (Jessie Couvreur) 1848-1897 ..... DLB-230

Tate, Allen 1899-1979 ...... DLB-4, 45, 63; DS-17

Tate, James 1943- DLB-5, 169
Tate, Nahum circa 1652-1715........... DLB-80
Tatian circa 830..................... DLB-148
Taufer, Veno 1933- DLB-181
Tauler, Johannes circa 1300-1361.......DLB-179
Tavares, Salette 1922-1994............. DLB-287
Tavčar, Ivan 1851-1923 .... DLB-147
Taverner, Richard ca. 1505-1575 .... DLB-236
Taylor, Ann 1782-1866................ DLB-163
Taylor, Bayard 1825-1878 ...... DLB-3, 189, 250
Taylor, Bert Leston 1866-1921.......... DLB-25
Taylor, Charles H. 1846-1921 .... DLB-25
Taylor, Edward circa 1642-1729 .... DLB-24
Taylor, Elizabeth 1912-1975........... DLB-139
Taylor, Sir Henry 1800-1886........... DLB-32
Taylor, Henry 1942- DLB-5
    Who Owns American Literature Y-94
Taylor, Jane 1783-1824................ DLB-163
Taylor, Jeremy circa 1613-1667 .... DLB-151
Taylor, John 1577 or 1578 - 1653 .... DLB-121
Taylor, Mildred D. 1943- DLB-52
Taylor, Peter 1917-1994 ...DLB-218, 278; Y-81, 94
Taylor, Susie King 1848-1912 .... DLB-221
Taylor, William Howland 1901-1966 ... DLB-241
William Taylor and Company.......... DLB-49
Teale, Edwin Way 1899-1980 ....DLB-275
Teasdale, Sara 1884-1933.............. DLB-45
Teffi, Nadezhda 1872-1952............. DLB-317
Teillier, Jorge 1935-1996 .... DLB-283
Telles, Lygia Fagundes 1924- DLB-113, 307
The Temper of the West: William Jovanovich.... Y-02
Temple, Sir William 1555?-1627 .... DLB-281
Temple, Sir William 1628-1699 .... DLB-101
Temple, William F. 1914-1989 .... DLB-255
Temrizov, A. (see Marchenko, Anastasia Iakovlevna)
Tench, Watkin ca. 1758-1833........... DLB-230
Tencin, Alexandrine-Claude Guérin de
    1682-1749..................... DLB-314
Tender Is the Night (Documentary) DLB-273
Tendriakov, Vladimir Fedorovich
    1923-1984 .... DLB-302
Tenn, William 1919- DLB-8
Tennant, Emma 1937- DLB-14
Tenney, Tabitha Gilman 1762-1837...DLB-37, 200
Tennyson, Alfred 1809-1892 .. DLB-32; CDBLB-4
    On Some of the Characteristics of
    Modern Poetry and On the Lyrical
    Poems of Alfred Tennyson
    (1831) DLB-32
Tennyson, Frederick 1807-1898 .... DLB-32
Tenorio, Arthur 1924- DLB-209
"The Tenth Stage," Marie-Jean-Antoine-Nicolas
    Caritat, marquis de Condorcet...... DLB-314
Tepl, Johannes von
    circa 1350-1414/1415.............DLB-179
Tepliakov, Viktor Grigor'evich
    1804-1842 .... DLB-205

Terence circa 184 B.C.-159 B.C. or after
    .... DLB-211; CDWLB-1
St. Teresa of Ávila 1515-1582.......... DLB-318
Terhune, Albert Payson 1872-1942 .... DLB-9
Terhune, Mary Virginia 1830-1922........DS-13
Terpigorev, Sergei Nikolaevich (S. Atava)
    1841-1895 .... DLB-277
Terry, Megan 1932- DLB-7, 249
Terson, Peter 1932- DLB-13
Tesich, Steve 1943-1996................. Y-83
Tessa, Delio 1886-1939 .... DLB-114
Testori, Giovanni 1923-1993
    ....DLB-128, 177
Texas
    The Year in Texas Literature Y-98
Tey, Josephine 1896?-1952............. DLB-77
Thacher, James 1754-1844 .... DLB-37
Thacher, John Boyd 1847-1909 .... DLB-187
Thackeray, William Makepeace
    1811-1863 .. DLB-21, 55, 159, 163; CDBLB-4
Thames and Hudson Limited.......... DLB-112
Thanet, Octave (see French, Alice)
Thaxter, Celia Laighton
    1835-1894 .... DLB-239
Thayer, Caroline Matilda Warren
    1785-1844..................... DLB-200
Thayer, Douglas H. 1929- DLB-256
Theater
    Black Theatre: A Forum [excerpts] ... DLB-38
    Community and Commentators:
    Black Theatre and Its Critics...... DLB-38
    German Drama from Naturalism
    to Fascism: 1889-1933 .... DLB-118
    A Look at the Contemporary Black
    Theatre Movement DLB-38
    The Lord Chamberlain's Office and
    Stage Censorship in England..... DLB-10
    New Forces at Work in the American
    Theatre: 1915-1925.............. DLB-7
    Off Broadway and Off-Off Broadway.. DLB-7
    Oregon Shakespeare Festival Y-00
    Plays, Playwrights, and Playgoers DLB-84
    Playwrights on the Theater DLB-80
    Playwrights and Professors DLB-13
    Producing *Dear Bunny, Dear Volodya*:
    The Friendship and the Feud........... Y-97
    Viewpoint: Politics and Performance,
    by David Edgar................ DLB-13
    Writing for the Theatre,
    by Harold Pinter DLB-13
    The Year in Drama Y-82–85, 87–98
    The Year in U.S. Drama Y-00
Theater, English and Irish
    Anti-Theatrical Tracts DLB-263
    The Chester Plays circa 1505-1532;
    revisions until 1575 .... DLB-146
    Dangerous Years: London Theater,
    1939-1945 .... DLB-10
    A Defense of Actors.............. DLB-263
    The Development of Lighting in the
    Staging of Drama, 1900-1945 .... DLB-10

Education..................... DLB-263
The End of English Stage Censorship,
    1945-1968 .... DLB-13
Epigrams and Satires DLB-263
Eyewitnesses and Historians DLB-263
Fringe and Alternative Theater in
    Great Britain DLB-13
The Great War and the Theater,
    1914-1918 [Great Britain] DLB-10
Licensing Act of 1737............... DLB-84
Morality Plays: *Mankind* circa 1450-1500
    and *Everyman* circa 1500 .... DLB-146
The New Variorum Shakespeare........ Y-85
N-Town Plays circa 1468 to early
    sixteenth century DLB-146
Politics and the Theater........... DLB-263
Practical Matters DLB-263
Prologues, Epilogues, Epistles to
    Readers, and Excerpts from
    Plays DLB-263
The Publication of English
    Renaissance Plays DLB-62
Regulations for the Theater........ DLB-263
Sources for the Study of Tudor and
    Stuart Drama.................. DLB-62
Stage Censorship: "The Rejected
    Statement" (1911), by Bernard
    Shaw [excerpts] DLB-10
Synge Summer School: J. M. Synge and
    the Irish Theater, Rathdrum,
    County Wiclow, Ireland Y-93
The Theater in Shakespeare's Time .. DLB-62
The Theatre Guild.................. DLB-7
The Townely Plays fifteenth and
    sixteenth centuries............ DLB-146
The Year in British Drama Y-99–01
The Year in Drama: London.......... Y-90
The Year in London Theatre........... Y-92
A Yorkshire Tragedy DLB-58
Theaters
    The Abbey Theatre and Irish Drama,
    1900-1945 .... DLB-10
    Actors Theatre of Louisville DLB-7
    American Conservatory Theatre...... DLB-7
    Arena Stage DLB-7
    Black Theaters and Theater
    Organizations in America,
    1961-1982: A Research List DLB-38
    The Dallas Theater Center DLB-7
    Eugene O'Neill Memorial Theater
    Center DLB-7
    The Goodman Theatre DLB-7
    The Guthrie Theater DLB-7
    The Mark Taper Forum DLB-7
    The National Theatre and the Royal
    Shakespeare Company: The
    National Companies DLB-13
    Off-Loop Theatres................ DLB-7
    The Royal Court Theatre and the
    English Stage Company DLB-13
    The Royal Court Theatre and the
    New Drama................... DLB-10

The Takarazaka Revue Company Y-91

Thegan and the Astronomer
fl. circa 850 .... DLB-148

Thelwall, John 1764-1834 .... DLB-93, 158

Theocritus circa 300 B.C.-260 B.C. DLB-176

Theodorescu, Ion N. (see Arghezi, Tudor)

Theodulf circa 760-circa 821 .... DLB-148

Theophrastus circa 371 B.C.-287 B.C. DLB-176

Thériault, Yves 1915-1983 .... DLB-88

Thério, Adrien 1925- DLB-53

Theroux, Paul 1941- DLB-2, 218; CDALB-7

Thesiger, Wilfred 1910-2003 .... DLB-204

They All Came to Paris DS-15

Thibaudeau, Colleen 1925- DLB-88

Thiele, Colin 1920- DLB-289

Thielen, Benedict 1903-1965 .... DLB-102

Thiong'o Ngugi wa (see Ngugi wa Thiong'o)

Thiroux d'Arconville, Marie-Geneviève
1720-1805 .... DLB-314

This Quarter 1925-1927, 1929-1932 .... DS-15

Thoma, Ludwig 1867-1921 .... DLB-66

Thoma, Richard 1902-1974 .... DLB-4

Thomas, Audrey 1935- DLB-60

Thomas, D. M.
1935- ... DLB-40, 207, 299; Y-82; CDBLB-8

The Plagiarism Controversy Y-82

Thomas, Dylan
1914-1953 .... DLB-13, 20, 139; CDBLB-7

The Dylan Thomas Celebration Y-99

Thomas, Ed 1961- DLB-310

Thomas, Edward
1878-1917 .... DLB-19, 98, 156, 216

The Friends of the Dymock Poets Y-00

Thomas, Frederick William 1806-1866 ... DLB-202

Thomas, Gwyn 1913-1981 .... DLB-15, 245

Thomas, Isaiah 1750-1831 .... DLB-43, 73, 187

Thomas, Johann 1624-1679 .... DLB-168

Thomas, John 1900-1932 .... DLB-4

Thomas, Joyce Carol 1938- DLB-33

Thomas, Lewis 1913-1993 .... DLB-275

Thomas, Lorenzo 1944- DLB-41

Thomas, Norman 1884-1968 .... DLB-303

Thomas, R. S. 1915-2000 ..... DLB-27; CDBLB-8

Isaiah Thomas [publishing house] DLB-49

Thomasîn von Zerclære
circa 1186-circa 1259 .... DLB-138

Thomason, George 1602?-1666 .... DLB-213

Thomasius, Christian 1655-1728 .... DLB-168

Thompson, Daniel Pierce 1795-1868 ..... DLB-202

Thompson, David 1770-1857 .... DLB-99

Thompson, Dorothy 1893-1961 .... DLB-29

Thompson, E. P. 1924-1993 .... DLB-242

Thompson, Flora 1876-1947 .... DLB-240

Thompson, Francis
1859-1907 .... DLB-19; CDBLB-5

Thompson, George Selden (see Selden, George)

Thompson, Henry Yates 1838-1928 ..... DLB-184

Thompson, Hunter S. 1939-2005 .... DLB-185

Thompson, Jim 1906-1977 .... DLB-226

Thompson, John 1938-1976 .... DLB-60

Thompson, John R. 1823-1873 .... DLB-3, 73, 248

Thompson, Lawrance 1906-1973 .... DLB-103

Thompson, Maurice 1844-1901 ...... DLB-71, 74

Thompson, Ruth Plumly 1891-1976 ..... DLB-22

Thompson, Thomas Phillips 1843-1933 ... DLB-99

Thompson, William 1775-1833 .... DLB-158

Thompson, William Tappan
1812-1882 .... DLB-3, 11, 248

Thomson, Cockburn
"Modern Style" (1857) [excerpt] DLB-57

Thomson, Edward William 1849-1924 .... DLB-92

Thomson, James 1700-1748 .... DLB-95

Thomson, James 1834-1882 .... DLB-35

Thomson, Joseph 1858-1895 .... DLB-174

Thomson, Mortimer 1831-1875 .... DLB-11

Thomson, Rupert 1955- DLB-267

Thon, Melanie Rae 1957- DLB-244

Thor Vilhjálmsson 1925- DLB-293

Þórarinn Eldjárn 1949- DLB-293

Þórbergur Þórðarson 1888-1974 .... DLB-293

Thoreau, Henry David 1817-1862 ... DLB-1, 183, 223, 270, 298; DS-5; CDALB-2

The Thoreau Society Y-99

The Thoreauvian Pilgrimage: The
Structure of an American Cult ... DLB-223

Thorne, William 1568?-1630 .... DLB-281

Thornton, John F.
[Repsonse to Ken Auletta] Y-97

Thorpe, Adam 1956- DLB-231

Thorpe, Thomas Bangs
1815-1878 .... DLB-3, 11, 248

Thorup, Kirsten 1942- DLB-214

Thotl, Birgitte 1610-1662 .... DLB-300

Thrale, Hester Lynch
(see Piozzi, Hester Lynch [Thrale])

The Three Marias: A Landmark Case in
Portuguese Literary History
(Maria Isabel Barreno, 1939- ;
Maria Teresa Horta, 1937- ;
Maria Velho da Costa, 1938-   ) DLB-287

Thubron, Colin 1939- DLB-204, 231

Thucydides
circa 455 B.C.-circa 395 B.C. DLB-176

Thulstrup, Thure de 1848-1930 .... DLB-188

Thümmel, Moritz August von
1738-1817 .... DLB-97

Thurber, James
1894-1961 ..... DLB-4, 11, 22, 102; CDALB-5

Thurman, Wallace 1902-1934 .... DLB-51

"Negro Poets and Their Poetry" DLB-50

Thwaite, Anthony 1930- DLB-40

The Booker Prize, Address Y-86

Thwaites, Reuben Gold 1853-1913 ...... DLB-47

Tibullus circa 54 B.C.-circa 19 B.C. DLB-211

Ticknor, George 1791-1871 .... DLB-1, 59, 140, 235

Ticknor and Fields DLB-49

Ticknor and Fields (revived) DLB-46

Tieck, Ludwig 1773-1853 .... DLB-90; CDWLB-2

Tietjens, Eunice 1884-1944 .... DLB-54

Tikkanen, Märta 1935- DLB-257

Tilghman, Christopher circa 1948 .... DLB-244

Tilney, Edmund circa 1536-1610 .... DLB-136

Charles Tilt [publishing house] DLB-106

J. E. Tilton and Company DLB-49

Time-Life Books DLB-46

Times Books DLB-46

Timothy, Peter circa 1725-1782 .... DLB-43

Timrava 1867-1951 .... DLB-215

Timrod, Henry 1828-1867 .... DLB-3, 248

Tindal, Henrietta 1818?-1879 .... DLB-199

Tinker, Chauncey Brewster 1876-1963 ....DLB-140

Tinsley Brothers DLB-106

Tiptree, James, Jr. 1915-1987 .... DLB-8

Tišma, Aleksandar 1924-2003 .... DLB-181

Titus, Edward William
1870-1952 .... DLB-4; DS-15

Tiutchev, Fedor Ivanovich 1803-1873 .... DLB-205

Tlali, Miriam 1933- DLB-157, 225

Todd, Barbara Euphan 1890-1976 .... DLB-160

Todorov, Tzvetan 1939- DLB-242

Tofte, Robert
1561 or 1562-1619 or 1620 .... DLB-172

Tóibín, Colm 1955- DLB-271

Toklas, Alice B. 1877-1967 .... DLB-4; DS-15

Tokuda Shūsei 1872-1943 .... DLB-180

Toland, John 1670-1722 .... DLB-252

Tolkien, J. R. R.
1892-1973 ...... DLB-15, 160, 255; CDBLB-6

Toller, Ernst 1893-1939 .... DLB-124

Tollet, Elizabeth 1694-1754 .... DLB-95

Tolson, Melvin B. 1898-1966 .... DLB-48, 76

Tolstaya, Tatyana 1951- DLB-285

Tolstoy, Aleksei Konstantinovich
1817-1875 .... DLB-238

Tolstoy, Aleksei Nikolaevich 1883-1945 .. DLB-272

Tolstoy, Leo 1828-1910 .... DLB-238

Tomalin, Claire 1933- DLB-155

Tómas Guðmundsson 1901-1983 .... DLB-293

Tomasi di Lampedusa, Giuseppe
1896-1957 .... DLB-177

Tomlinson, Charles 1927- DLB-40

Tomlinson, H. M. 1873-1958 ... DLB-36, 100, 195

Abel Tompkins [publishing house] DLB-49

Tompson, Benjamin 1642-1714 .... DLB-24

Tomson, Graham R.
(see Watson, Rosamund Marriott)

Ton'a 1289-1372 .... DLB-203

Tondelli, Pier Vittorio 1955-1991 .... DLB-196

Tonks, Rosemary 1932- DLB-14, 207

Tonna, Charlotte Elizabeth 1790-1846 ... DLB-163

Jacob Tonson the Elder
  [publishing house] DLB-170

Toole, John Kennedy 1937-1969 . . . . Y-81

Toomer, Jean
  1894-1967 . . . . DLB-45, 51; CDALB-4

Topsoe, Vilhelm 1840-1881 . . . . DLB-300

Tor Books DLB-46

Torberg, Friedrich 1908-1979 . . . . DLB-85

Torga, Miguel (Adolfo Correira da Rocha)
  1907-1995 . . . . DLB-287

Torre, Francisco de la ?-? DLB-318

Torrence, Ridgely 1874-1950 . . . . DLB-54, 249

Torres-Metzger, Joseph V. 1933- DLB-122

Torres Naharro, Bartolomé de
  1485?-1523? DLB-318

El Tostado (see Madrigal, Alfonso Fernández de)

Toth, Susan Allen 1940- Y-86

Richard Tottell [publishing house] DLB-170
  "The Printer to the Reader,"
    (1557) DLB-167

Tough-Guy Literature DLB-9

Touré, Askia Muhammad 1938- DLB-41

Tourgée, Albion W. 1838-1905 . . . . DLB-79

Tournemir, Elizaveta Sailhas de (see Tur, Evgeniia)

Tourneur, Cyril circa 1580-1626 . . . . DLB-58

Tournier, Michel 1924- DLB-83

Frank Tousey [publishing house] DLB-49

Tower Publications DLB-46

Towne, Benjamin circa 1740-1793 . . . . . . DLB-43

Towne, Robert 1936- DLB-44

The Townely Plays fifteenth and sixteenth
  centuries DLB-146

Townsend, Sue 1946- DLB-271

Townshend, Aurelian
  by 1583-circa 1651 . . . . DLB-121

Toy, Barbara 1908-2001 . . . . DLB-204

Tozzi, Federigo 1883-1920 . . . . DLB-264

Tracy, Honor 1913-1989 . . . . DLB-15

Traherne, Thomas 1637?-1674 . . . . DLB-131

Traill, Catharine Parr 1802-1899 . . . . DLB-99

Train, Arthur 1875-1945 . . . . DLB-86; DS-16

Tranquilli, Secondino (see Silone, Ignazio)

The Transatlantic Publishing Company . . . DLB-49

The Transatlantic Review 1924-1925 . . . . DS-15

The Transcendental Club
  1836-1840 . . . . DLB-1; DLB-223

Transcendentalism DLB-1; DLB-223; DS-5
  "A Response from America," by
    John A. Heraud DS-5
  Publications and Social Movements DLB-1
  The Rise of Transcendentalism,
    1815-1860 . . . . DS-5
  Transcendentalists, American DS-5
  "What Is Transcendentalism? By a
    Thinking Man," by James
    Kinnard Jr DS-5

transition 1927-1938 . . . . DS-15

Translations (Vernacular) in the Crowns of
  Castile and Aragon 1352-1515 . . . . . . DLB-286

Tranströmer, Tomas 1931- DLB-257

Tranter, John 1943- DLB-289

Travel Writing
  American Travel Writing, 1776-1864
    (checklist) DLB-183
  British Travel Writing, 1940-1997
    (checklist) DLB-204
  Travel Writers of the Late
    Middle Ages DLB-286
  (1876-1909) DLB-174
  (1837-1875) DLB-166
  (1910-1939) DLB-195

Traven, B. 1882?/1890?-1969? DLB-9, 56

Travers, Ben 1886-1980 . . . . DLB-10, 233

Travers, P. L. (Pamela Lyndon)
  1899-1996 . . . . DLB-160

Trediakovsky, Vasilii Kirillovich
  1703-1769 . . . . DLB-150

Treece, Henry 1911-1966 . . . . DLB-160

Treitel, Jonathan 1959- DLB-267

Trejo, Ernesto 1950-1991 . . . . DLB-122

Trelawny, Edward John
  1792-1881 . . . . DLB-110, 116, 144

Tremain, Rose 1943- DLB-14, 271

Tremblay, Michel 1942- DLB-60

Trent, William P. 1862-1939 . . . . DLB-47, 71

Trescot, William Henry 1822-1898 . . . . . . DLB-30

Tressell, Robert (Robert Phillipe Noonan)
  1870-1911 . . . . DLB-197

Trevelyan, Sir George Otto
  1838-1928 . . . . DLB-144

Trevisa, John circa 1342-circa 1402 . . . . . DLB-146

Trevisan, Dalton 1925- DLB-307

Trevor, William 1928- DLB-14, 139

Triana, José 1931- DLB-305

Trierer Floyris circa 1170-1180 . . . . DLB-138

Trifonov, Iurii Valentinovich
  1925-1981 . . . . DLB-302

Trillin, Calvin 1935- DLB-185

Trilling, Lionel 1905-1975 . . . . DLB-28, 63

Trilussa 1871-1950 . . . . DLB-114

Trimmer, Sarah 1741-1810 . . . . DLB-158

Triolet, Elsa 1896-1970 . . . . DLB-72

Tripp, John 1927- DLB-40

Trocchi, Alexander 1925-1984 . . . . DLB-15

Troisi, Dante 1920-1989 . . . . DLB-196

Trollope, Anthony
  1815-1882 . . . . . . DLB-21, 57, 159; CDBLB-4
  Novel-Reading: *The Works of Charles
    Dickens; The Works of W. Makepeace
    Thackeray* (1879) DLB-21
  The Trollope Societies Y-00

Trollope, Frances 1779-1863 . . . . DLB-21, 166

Trollope, Joanna 1943- DLB-207

Troop, Elizabeth 1931- DLB-14

Tropicália DLB-307

Trotter, Catharine 1679-1749 . . . . DLB-84, 252

Trotti, Lamar 1898-1952 . . . . DLB-44

Trottier, Pierre 1925- DLB-60

Trotzig, Birgitta 1929- DLB-257

Troupe, Quincy Thomas, Jr. 1943- DLB-41

John F. Trow and Company DLB-49

Trowbridge, John Townsend 1827-1916 . DLB-202

Trudel, Jean-Louis 1967- DLB-251

Truillier-Lacombe, Joseph-Patrice
  1807-1863 . . . . DLB-99

Trumbo, Dalton 1905-1976 . . . . DLB-26

Trumbull, Benjamin 1735-1820 . . . . DLB-30

Trumbull, John 1750-1831 . . . . DLB-31

Trumbull, John 1756-1843 . . . . DLB-183

Truth, Sojourner 1797?-1883 . . . . DLB-239

Tscherning, Andreas 1611-1659 . . . . DLB-164

Tsubouchi Shōyō 1859-1935 . . . . DLB-180

Tsvetaeva, Marina Ivanovna
  1892-1941 . . . . DLB-295

Tuchman, Barbara W.
  Tribute to Alfred A. Knopf Y-84

Tucholsky, Kurt 1890-1935 . . . . DLB-56

Tucker, Charlotte Maria
  1821-1893 . . . . DLB-163, 190

Tucker, George 1775-1861 . . . . DLB-3, 30, 248

Tucker, James 1808?-1866? DLB-230

Tucker, Nathaniel Beverley
  1784-1851 . . . . DLB-3, 248

Tucker, St. George 1752-1827 . . . . DLB-37

Tuckerman, Frederick Goddard
  1821-1873 . . . . DLB-243

Tuckerman, Henry Theodore 1813-1871 . . DLB-64

Tumas, Juozas (see Vaizgantas)

Tunis, John R. 1889-1975 . . . . DLB-22, 171

Tunstall, Cuthbert 1474-1559 . . . . DLB-132

Tunström, Göran 1937-2000 . . . . DLB-257

Tuohy, Frank 1925- DLB-14, 139

Tupper, Martin F. 1810-1889 . . . . DLB-32

Tur, Evgeniia 1815-1892 . . . . DLB-238

Turbyfill, Mark 1896-1991 . . . . DLB-45

Turco, Lewis 1934- Y-84
  Tribute to John Ciardi Y-86

Turgenev, Aleksandr Ivanovich
  1784-1845 . . . . DLB-198

Turgenev, Ivan Sergeevich
  1818-1883 . . . . DLB-238

Turgot, baron de l'Aulne, Anne-Robert-Jacques
  1727-1781 . . . . DLB-314
  "Memorandum on Local
    Government" DLB-314

Turnbull, Alexander H. 1868-1918 . . . . . DLB-184

Turnbull, Andrew 1921-1970 . . . . DLB-103

Turnbull, Gael 1928- DLB-40

Turner, Arlin 1909-1980 . . . . DLB-103

Turner, Charles (Tennyson)
  1808-1879 . . . . DLB-32

Turner, Ethel 1872-1958 . . . . DLB-230

Turner, Frederick 1943- DLB-40

Turner, Frederick Jackson 1861-1932 ... DLB-17, 186

A Conversation between William Riggan and Janette Turner Hospital ... Y-02

Turner, Joseph Addison 1826-1868 ... DLB-79

Turpin, Waters Edward 1910-1968 ... DLB-51

Turrini, Peter 1944- ... DLB-124

Tutuola, Amos 1920-1997 ... DLB-125; CDWLB-3

Twain, Mark (see Clemens, Samuel Langhorne)

Tweedie, Ethel Brilliana circa 1860-1940 ... DLB-174

A Century of Poetry, a Lifetime of Collecting: J. M. Edelstein's Collection of Twentieth-Century American Poetry ... YB-02

Twombly, Wells 1935-1977 ... DLB-241

Twysden, Sir Roger 1597-1672 ... DLB-213

Ty-Casper, Linda 1931- ... DLB-312

Tyler, Anne 1941- ... DLB-6, 143; Y-82; CDALB-7

Tyler, Mary Palmer 1775-1866 ... DLB-200

Tyler, Moses Coit 1835-1900 ... DLB-47, 64

Tyler, Royall 1757-1826 ... DLB-37

Tylor, Edward Burnett 1832-1917 ... DLB-57

Tynan, Katharine 1861-1931 ... DLB-153, 240

Tyndale, William circa 1494-1536 ... DLB-132

Tyree, Omar 1969- ... DLB-292

U

Uchida, Yoshiko 1921-1992 ... DLB-312; CDALB-7

Udall, Nicholas 1504-1556 ... DLB-62

Ugrešić, Dubravka 1949- ... DLB-181

Uhland, Ludwig 1787-1862 ... DLB-90

Uhse, Bodo 1904-1963 ... DLB-69

Ujević, Augustin "Tin" 1891-1955 ... DLB-147

Ulenhart, Niclas fl. circa 1600 ... DLB-164

Ulfeldt, Leonora Christina 1621-1698 ... DLB-300

Ulibarrí, Sabine R. 1919-2003 ... DLB-82

Ulica, Jorge 1870-1926 ... DLB-82

Ulitskaya, Liudmila Evgen'evna 1943- ... DLB-285

Ulivi, Ferruccio 1912- ... DLB-196

Ulizio, B. George 1889-1969 ... DLB-140

Ulrich von Liechtenstein circa 1200-circa 1275 ... DLB-138

Ulrich von Zatzikhoven before 1194-after 1214 ... DLB-138

'Umar ibn Abi Rabi'ah 644-712 or 721 ... DLB-311

Unaipon, David 1872-1967 ... DLB-230

Unamuno, Miguel de 1864-1936 ... DLB-108

Under, Marie 1883-1980 ... DLB-220; CDWLB-4

Underhill, Evelyn 1875-1941 ... DLB-240

Undset, Sigrid 1882-1949 ... DLB-297

Ungaretti, Giuseppe 1888-1970 ... DLB-114

Unger, Friederike Helene 1741-1813 ... DLB-94

United States Book Company ... DLB-49

Universal Publishing and Distributing Corporation ... DLB-46

University of Colorado
Special Collections at the University of Colorado at Boulder ... Y-98

Indiana University Press ... Y-02

The University of Iowa Writers' Workshop Golden Jubilee ... Y-86

University of Missouri Press ... Y-01

University of South Carolina
The G. Ross Roy Scottish Poetry Collection ... Y-89

Two Hundred Years of Rare Books and Literary Collections at the University of South Carolina ... Y-00

The University of South Carolina Press ... Y-94

University of Virginia
The Book Arts Press at the University of Virginia ... Y-96

The Electronic Text Center and the Electronic Archive of Early American Fiction at the University of Virginia Library ... Y-98

University of Virginia Libraries ... Y-91

University of Wales Press ... DLB-112

University Press of Florida ... Y-00

University Press of Kansas ... Y-98

University Press of Mississippi ... Y-99

Unnur Benediktsdóttir Bjarklind (see Hulda)

Uno Chiyo 1897-1996 ... DLB-180

Unruh, Fritz von 1885-1970 ... DLB-56, 118

Unsworth, Barry 1930- ... DLB-194

Unt, Mati 1944- ... DLB-232

The Unterberg Poetry Center of the 92nd Street Y ... Y-98

Untermeyer, Louis 1885-1977 ... DLB-303

T. Fisher Unwin [publishing house] ... DLB-106

Upchurch, Boyd B. (see Boyd, John)

Updike, John 1932- ... DLB-2, 5, 143, 218, 227; Y-80, 82; DS-3; CDALB-6

John Updike on the Internet ... Y-97

Tribute to Alfred A. Knopf ... Y-84

Tribute to John Ciardi ... Y-86

Upīts, Andrejs 1877-1970 ... DLB-220

Uppdal, Kristofer 1878-1961 ... DLB-297

Upton, Bertha 1849-1912 ... DLB-141

Upton, Charles 1948- ... DLB-16

Upton, Florence K. 1873-1922 ... DLB-141

Upward, Allen 1863-1926 ... DLB-36

Urban, Milo 1904-1982 ... DLB-215

Ureña de Henríquez, Salomé 1850-1897 ... DLB-283

Urfé, Honoré d' 1567-1625 ... DLB-268

Urista, Alberto Baltazar (see Alurista)

Urquhart, Fred 1912-1995 ... DLB-139

Urrea, Luis Alberto 1955- ... DLB-209

Urzidil, Johannes 1896-1970 ... DLB-85

U.S.A. (Documentary) ... DLB-274

Usigli, Rodolfo 1905-1979 ... DLB-305

Usk, Thomas died 1388 ... DLB-146

Uslar Pietri, Arturo 1906-2001 ... DLB-113

Uspensky, Gleb Ivanovich 1843-1902 ... DLB-277

Ussher, James 1581-1656 ... DLB-213

Ustinov, Peter 1921-2004 ... DLB-13

Uttley, Alison 1884-1976 ... DLB-160

Uz, Johann Peter 1720-1796 ... DLB-97

V

Vadianus, Joachim 1484-1551 ... DLB-179

Vac, Bertrand (Aimé Pelletier) 1914- ... DLB-88

Vācietis, Ojārs 1933-1983 ... DLB-232

Vaculík, Ludvík 1926- ... DLB-232

Vaičiulaitis, Antanas 1906-1992 ... DLB-220

Vaičiūnaite, Judita 1937- ... DLB-232

Vail, Laurence 1891-1968 ... DLB-4

Vail, Petr L'vovich 1949- ... DLB-285

Vailland, Roger 1907-1965 ... DLB-83

Vaižgantas 1869-1933 ... DLB-220

Vajda, Ernest 1887-1954 ... DLB-44

Valdés, Alfonso de circa 1490?-1532 ... DLB-318

Valdés, Gina 1943- ... DLB-122

Valdes, Juan de 1508-1541 ... DLB-318

Valdez, Luis Miguel 1940- ... DLB-122

Valduga, Patrizia 1953- ... DLB-128

Vale Press ... DLB-112

Valente, José Angel 1929-2000 ... DLB-108

Valenzuela, Luisa 1938- ... DLB-113; CDWLB-3

Valera, Diego de 1412-1488 ... DLB-286

Valeri, Diego 1887-1976 ... DLB-128

Valerius Flaccus fl. circa A.D. 92 ... DLB-211

Valerius Maximus fl. circa A.D. 31 ... DLB-211

Valéry, Paul 1871-1945 ... DLB-258

Valesio, Paolo 1939- ... DLB-196

Valgardson, W. D. 1939- ... DLB-60

Valle, Luz 1899-1971 ... DLB-290

Valle, Víctor Manuel 1950- ... DLB-122

Valle-Inclán, Ramón del 1866-1936 ... DLB-134

Vallejo, Armando 1949- ... DLB-122

Vallejo, César Abraham 1892-1938 ... DLB-290

Vallès, Jules 1832-1885 ... DLB-123

Vallette, Marguerite Eymery (see Rachilde)

Valverde, José María 1926-1996 ... DLB-108

Vampilov, Aleksandr Valentinovich (A. Sanin) 1937-1972 ... DLB-302

Van Allsburg, Chris 1949- ... DLB-61

Van Anda, Carr 1864-1945 ... DLB-25

Vanbrugh, Sir John 1664-1726 ... DLB-80

Vance, Jack 1916?- ... DLB-8

Vančura, Vladislav 1891-1942 ... DLB-215; CDWLB-4

van der Post, Laurens 1906-1996 ... DLB-204

Van Dine, S. S. (see Wright, Williard Huntington)

Van Doren, Mark 1894-1972 ... DLB-45

van Druten, John 1901-1957 ... DLB-10

Van Duyn, Mona 1921-2004 . . . . DLB-5	Verbitskaia, Anastasiia Alekseevna 1861-1928 . . . . DLB-295	Villegas de Magnón, Leonor 1876-1955. . . . . DLB-122
Tribute to James Dickey Y-97	Verde, Cesário 1855-1886 . . . . DLB-287	Villehardouin, Geoffroi de circa 1150-1215 . . . . DLB-208
Van Dyke, Henry 1852-1933 . . . . . DLB-71; DS-13	Vergil, Polydore circa 1470-1555 . . . . DLB-132	
Van Dyke, Henry 1928- DLB-33	Veríssimo, Erico 1905-1975 . . . . .DLB-145, 307	Villemaire, Yolande 1949- DLB-60
Van Dyke, John C. 1856-1932 . . . . DLB-186	Verlaine, Paul 1844-1896 . . . . DLB-217	Villena, Enrique de ca. 1382/84-1432 . . . . DLB-286
Vane, Sutton 1888-1963 . . . . DLB-10	Vernacular Translations in the Crowns of Castile and Aragon 1352-1515. . . . . . DLB-286	Villena, Luis Antonio de 1951- DLB-134
Van Gieson, Judith 1941- DLB-306	Verne, Jules 1828-1905. . . . . DLB-123	Villiers, George, Second Duke of Buckingham 1628-1687 . . . . DLB-80
Vanguard Press DLB-46	Verplanck, Gulian C. 1786-1870. . . . . DLB-59	
van Gulik, Robert Hans 1910-1967 . . . . .DS-17	Vertinsky, Aleksandr 1889-1957 . . . . DLB-317	Villiers de l'Isle-Adam, Jean-Marie Mathias Philippe-Auguste, Comte de 1838-1889 . . . . DLB-123, 192
van Itallie, Jean-Claude 1936- DLB-7	Very, Jones 1813-1880 . . . . DLB-1, 243; DS-5	
Van Loan, Charles E. 1876-1919 . . . . .DLB-171	Vesaas, Halldis Moren 1907-1995 . . . . . . DLB-297	Villon, François 1431-circa 1463? DLB-208
Vann, Robert L. 1879-1940 . . . . DLB-29	Vesaas, Tarjei 1897-1970 . . . . DLB-297	Vinaver, Michel (Michel Grinberg) 1927- DLB-321
Van Rensselaer, Mariana Griswold 1851-1934 . . . . DLB-47	Vian, Boris 1920-1959 . . . . DLB-72, 321	
	Viazemsky, Petr Andreevich 1792-1878. DLB-205	Vine Press. DLB-112
Van Rensselaer, Mrs. Schuyler (see Van Rensselaer, Mariana Griswold)		Viorst, Judith 1931- DLB-52
	Vicars, Thomas 1591-1638. . . . . DLB-236	Vipont, Elfrida (Elfrida Vipont Foulds, Charles Vipont) 1902-1992 . . . . DLB-160
Van Vechten, Carl 1880-1964 . . . . . . DLB-4, 9, 51	Vicente, Gil 1465-1536/1540? DLB-287, 318	
van Vogt, A. E. 1912-2000 . . . . DLB-8, 251	Vickers, Roy 1888?-1965 . . . . DLB-77	Viramontes, Helena María 1954- DLB-122
Varela, Blanca 1926- DLB-290	Vickery, Sukey 1779-1821 . . . . DLB-200	Virgil 70 B.C.-19 B.C. DLB-211; CDWLB-1
Vargas Llosa, Mario 1936- DLB-145; CDWLB-3	Victoria 1819-1901 . . . . DLB-55	Vischer, Friedrich Theodor 1807-1887. DLB-133
	Victoria Press DLB-106	
Acceptance Speech for the Ritz Paris Hemingway Award Y-85	La vida de Lazarillo de Tormes DLB-318	Vitier, Cintio 1921- DLB-283
	Vidal, Gore 1925- DLB-6, 152; CDALB-7	Vitrac, Roger 1899-1952 . . . . DLB-321
Varley, John 1947- Y-81	Vidal, Mary Theresa 1815-1873 . . . . DLB-230	Vitruvius circa 85 B.C.-circa 15 B.C. DLB-211
Varnhagen von Ense, Karl August 1785-1858 . . . . DLB-90	Vidmer, Richards 1898-1978 . . . . DLB-241	Vitry, Philippe de 1291-1361 . . . . DLB-208
Varnhagen von Ense, Rahel 1771-1833 . . . . DLB-90	Viebig, Clara 1860-1952 . . . . DLB-66	Vittorini, Elio 1908-1966 . . . . DLB-264
	Vieira, António, S. J. (Antonio Vieyra) 1608-1697 . . . . DLB-307	Vivanco, Luis Felipe 1907-1975 . . . . DLB-108
Varro 116 B.C.-27 B.C. DLB-211		Vives, Juan Luis 1493-1540 . . . . DLB-318
Vasilenko, Svetlana Vladimirovna 1956- DLB-285	Viereck, George Sylvester 1884-1962. . . . . DLB-54	Vivian, E. Charles (Charles Henry Cannell, Charles Henry Vivian, Jack Mann, Barry Lynd) 1882-1947 . . . . DLB-255
Vasiliu, George (see Bacovia, George)	Viereck, Peter 1916- DLB-5	
Vásquez, Richard 1928- DLB-209	Vietnam War (ended 1975) Resources for the Study of Vietnam War Literature DLB-9	Viviani, Cesare 1947- DLB-128
Vásquez Montalbán, Manuel 1939- . . . DLB-134		Vivien, Renée 1877-1909 . . . . .DLB-217
Vassa, Gustavus (see Equiano, Olaudah)		Vizenor, Gerald 1934- DLB-175, 227
Vassali, Sebastiano 1941- DLB-128, 196	Viets, Roger 1738-1811. . . . . DLB-99	Vizetelly and Company DLB-106
Vaugelas, Claude Favre de 1585-1650. . . . DLB-268	Vigil-Piñon, Evangelina 1949- DLB-122	Vladimov, Georgii 1931-2003 . . . . DLB-302
Vaughan, Henry 1621-1695 . . . . DLB-131	Vigneault, Gilles 1928- DLB-60	
Vaughan, Thomas 1621-1666 . . . . DLB-131	Vigny, Alfred de 1797-1863 . . . .DLB-119, 192, 217	Voaden, Herman 1903-1991 . . . . DLB-88
Vaughn, Robert 1592?-1667 . . . . DLB-213	Vigolo, Giorgio 1894-1983 . . . . DLB-114	Voß, Johann Heinrich 1751-1826 . . . . DLB-90
Vaux, Thomas, Lord 1509-1556 . . . . DLB-132	Vik, Bjorg 1935- DLB-297	Vogau, Boris Andreevich (see Pil'niak, Boris Andreevich)
Vazov, Ivan 1850-1921 . . . . . .DLB-147; CDWLB-4	The Viking Press DLB-46	
Véa, Alfredo, Jr. 1950- DLB-209	Vilde, Eduard 1865-1933 . . . . DLB-220	Voigt, Ellen Bryant 1943- DLB-120
Veblen, Thorstein 1857-1929 . . . . DLB-246	Vilinskaia, Mariia Aleksandrovna (see Vovchok, Marko)	Voinovich, Vladimir Nikolaevich 1932- DLB-302
Vedel, Anders Sørensen 1542-1616 . . . . . DLB-300		
Vega, Janine Pommy 1942- DLB-16	Villa, José García 1908-1997. . . . . DLB-312	Vojnović, Ivo 1857-1929 . . . . .DLB-147; CDWLB-4
Veiller, Anthony 1903-1965 . . . . DLB-44	Villanueva, Alma Luz 1944- DLB-122	Vold, Jan Erik 1939- DLB-297
Velásquez-Trevino, Gloria 1949- DLB-122	Villanueva, Tino 1941- DLB-82	Volkoff, Vladimir 1932- DLB-83
Veley, Margaret 1843-1887 . . . . DLB-199	Villard, Henry 1835-1900. . . . . DLB-23	P. F. Volland Company DLB-46
Velleius Paterculus circa 20 B.C.-circa A.D. 30. . . . . DLB-211	Villard, Oswald Garrison 1872-1949 . . DLB-25, 91	Vollbehr, Otto H. F. 1872?-1945 or 1946 . . . . .DLB-187
	Villarreal, Edit 1944- DLB-209	
Veloz Maggiolo, Marcio 1936- DLB-145	Villarreal, José Antonio 1924- DLB-82	Vologdin (see Zasodimsky, Pavel Vladimirovich)
Vel'tman, Aleksandr Fomich 1800-1870 . . . . DLB-198	Villaseñor, Victor 1940- DLB-209	Voloshin, Maksimilian Aleksandrovich 1877-1932 . . . . DLB-295
Venegas, Daniel ?-? DLB-82	Villedieu, Madame de (Marie-Catherine Desjardins) 1640?-1683 . . . . DLB-268	Volponi, Paolo 1924-1994 . . . . .DLB-177
Venevitinov, Dmitrii Vladimirovich 1805-1827 . . . . DLB-205	Villegas, Antonio de ?-? DLB-318	Voltaire (François-Marie Arouet) 1694-1778 . . . . DLB-314

"An account of the death of the chevalier de La Barre" DLB-314
Candide DLB-314
Philosophical Dictionary DLB-314
Vonarburg, Élisabeth 1947- DLB-251
von der Grün, Max 1926- DLB-75
Vonnegut, Kurt 1922- DLB-2, 8, 152; Y-80; DS-3; CDALB-6
 Tribute to Isaac Asimov Y-92
 Tribute to Richard Brautigan Y-84
Voranc, Prežihov 1893-1950 .... DLB-147
Voronsky, Aleksandr Konstantinovich 1884-1937 .... DLB-272
Vorse, Mary Heaton 1874-1966 .... DLB-303
Vovchok, Marko 1833-1907 .... DLB-238
Voynich, E. L. 1864-1960 .... DLB-197
Vroman, Mary Elizabeth circa 1924-1967 .... DLB-33

W

Wace, Robert ("Maistre") circa 1100-circa 1175 .... DLB-146
Wackenroder, Wilhelm Heinrich 1773-1798 .... DLB-90
Wackernagel, Wilhelm 1806-1869 ...... DLB-133
Waddell, Helen 1889-1965 .... DLB-240
Waddington, Miriam 1917-2004 .... DLB-68
Wade, Henry 1887-1969 .... DLB-77
Wagenknecht, Edward 1900-2004 .... DLB-103
Wägner, Elin 1882-1949 .... DLB-259
Wagner, Heinrich Leopold 1747-1779 .... DLB-94
Wagner, Henry R. 1862-1957 .... DLB-140
Wagner, Richard 1813-1883 .... DLB-129
Wagoner, David 1926- DLB-5, 256
Wah, Fred 1939- DLB-60
Waiblinger, Wilhelm 1804-1830 .... DLB-90
Wain, John 1925-1994 ... DLB-15, 27, 139, 155; CDBLB-8
 Tribute to J. B. Priestly Y-84
Wainwright, Jeffrey 1944- DLB-40
Waite, Peirce and Company DLB-49
Wakeman, Stephen H. 1859-1924 ...... DLB-187
Wakoski, Diane 1937- DLB-5
Walahfrid Strabo circa 808-849 .... DLB-148
Henry Z. Walck [publishing house] DLB-46
Walcott, Derek 1930- DLB-117; Y-81, 92; CDWLB-3
 Nobel Lecture 1992: The Antilles: Fragments of Epic Memory Y-92
Robert Waldegrave [publishing house] ... DLB-170
Waldis, Burkhard circa 1490-1556? DLB-178
Waldman, Anne 1945- DLB-16
Waldrop, Rosmarie 1935- DLB-169
Walker, Alice 1900-1982 .... DLB-201
Walker, Alice 1944- DLB-6, 33, 143; CDALB-6
Walker, Annie Louisa (Mrs. Harry Coghill) circa 1836-1907 .... DLB-240

Walker, George F. 1947- DLB-60
Walker, John Brisben 1847-1931 .... DLB-79
Walker, Joseph A. 1935- DLB-38
Walker, Kath (see Oodgeroo of the Tribe Noonuccal)
Walker, Margaret 1915-1998 .... DLB-76, 152
Walker, Obadiah 1616-1699 .... DLB-281
Walker, Ted 1934- DLB-40
Walker, Evans and Cogswell Company ... DLB-49
Wall, John F. (see Sarban)
Wallace, Alfred Russel 1823-1913 .... DLB-190
Wallace, Dewitt 1889-1981 .... DLB-137
Wallace, Edgar 1875-1932 .... DLB-70
Wallace, Lew 1827-1905 .... DLB-202
Wallace, Lila Acheson 1889-1984 .... DLB-137
 "A Word of Thanks," From the Initial Issue of *Reader's Digest* (February 1922) DLB-137
Wallace, Naomi 1960- DLB-249
Wallace Markfield's "Steeplechase" Y-02
Wallace-Crabbe, Chris 1934- DLB-289
Wallant, Edward Lewis 1926-1962 .... DLB-2, 28, 143, 299
Waller, Edmund 1606-1687 .... DLB-126
Walpole, Horace 1717-1797 ..... DLB-39, 104, 213
 Preface to the First Edition of *The Castle of Otranto* (1764) DLB-39, 178
 Preface to the Second Edition of *The Castle of Otranto* (1765) DLB-39, 178
Walpole, Hugh 1884-1941 .... DLB-34
Walrond, Eric 1898-1966 .... DLB-51
Walser, Martin 1927- DLB-75, 124
Walser, Robert 1878-1956 .... DLB-66
Walsh, Ernest 1895-1926 .... DLB-4, 45
Walsh, Robert 1784-1859 .... DLB-59
Walters, Henry 1848-1931 .... DLB-140
Waltharius circa 825 .... DLB-148
Walther von der Vogelweide circa 1170-circa 1230 .... DLB-138
Walton, Izaak 1593-1683 .... DLB-151, 213; CDBLB-1
Wambaugh, Joseph 1937- DLB-6; Y-83
Wand, Alfred Rudolph 1828-1891 ..... DLB-188
Wandor, Michelene 1940- DLB-310
Waniek, Marilyn Nelson 1946- DLB-120
Wanley, Humphrey 1672-1726 .... DLB-213
War of the Words (and Pictures): The Creation of a Graphic Novel Y-02
Warburton, William 1698-1779 .... DLB-104
Ward, Aileen 1919- DLB-111
Ward, Artemus (see Browne, Charles Farrar)
Ward, Arthur Henry Sarsfield (see Rohmer, Sax)
Ward, Douglas Turner 1930- DLB-7, 38
Ward, Mrs. Humphry 1851-1920 .... DLB-18
Ward, James 1843-1925 .... DLB-262
Ward, Lynd 1905-1985 .... DLB-22
Ward, Lock and Company DLB-106
Ward, Nathaniel circa 1578-1652 .... DLB-24

Ward, Theodore 1902-1983 .... DLB-76
Wardle, Ralph 1909-1988 .... DLB-103
Ware, Henry, Jr. 1794-1843 .... DLB-235
Ware, William 1797-1852 .... DLB-1, 235
Warfield, Catherine Ann 1816-1877 ..... DLB-248
Waring, Anna Letitia 1823-1910 .... DLB-240
Frederick Warne and Company [U.K.] DLB-106
Frederick Warne and Company [U.S.] DLB-49
Warner, Anne 1869-1913 .... DLB-202
Warner, Charles Dudley 1829-1900 ...... DLB-64
Warner, Marina 1946- DLB-194
Warner, Rex 1905-1986 .... DLB-15
Warner, Susan 1819-1885 .... DLB-3, 42, 239, 250
Warner, Sylvia Townsend 1893-1978 .... DLB-34, 139
Warner, William 1558-1609 .... DLB-172
Warner Books DLB-46
Warr, Bertram 1917-1943 .... DLB-88
Warren, John Byrne Leicester (see De Tabley, Lord)
Warren, Lella 1899-1982 .... Y-83
Warren, Mercy Otis 1728-1814 ...... DLB-31, 200
Warren, Robert Penn 1905-1989 ..... DLB-2, 48, 152, 320; Y-80, 89; CDALB-6
 Tribute to Katherine Anne Porter Y-80
Warren, Samuel 1807-1877 .... DLB-190
Die Wartburgkrieg circa 1230-circa 1280 ... DLB-138
Warton, Joseph 1722-1800 .... DLB-104, 109
Warton, Thomas 1728-1790 .... DLB-104, 109
Warung, Price (William Astley) 1855-1911 .... DLB-230
Washington, George 1732-1799 .... DLB-31
Washington, Ned 1901-1976 .... DLB-265
Wassermann, Jakob 1873-1934 .... DLB-66
Wasserstein, Wendy 1950- DLB-228
Wassmo, Herbjørg 1942- DLB-297
Wasson, David Atwood 1823-1887 .... DLB-1, 223
Watanna, Onoto (see Eaton, Winnifred)
Waten, Judah 1911?-1985 .... DLB-289
Waterhouse, Keith 1929- DLB-13, 15
Waterman, Andrew 1940- DLB-40
Waters, Frank 1902-1995 .... DLB-212; Y-86
Waters, Michael 1949- DLB-120
Watkins, Tobias 1780-1855 .... DLB-73
Watkins, Vernon 1906-1967 .... DLB-20
Watmough, David 1926- DLB-53
Watson, Colin 1920-1983 .... DLB-276
Watson, Ian 1943- DLB-261
Watson, James Wreford (see Wreford, James)
Watson, John 1850-1907 .... DLB-156
Watson, Rosamund Marriott (Graham R. Tomson) 1860-1911 .... DLB-240
Watson, Sheila 1909-1998 .... DLB-60
Watson, Thomas 1545?-1592 .... DLB-132
Watson, Wilfred 1911-1998 .... DLB-60
W. J. Watt and Company DLB-46

501

Watten, Barrett 1948- DLB-193	Weiss, Paul 1901-2002 . . . . DLB-279	West, Cornel 1953- DLB-246
Watterson, Henry 1840-1921 . . . . DLB-25	Weiss, Peter 1916-1982 . . . . DLB-69, 124	West, Dorothy 1907-1998 . . . . DLB-76
Watts, Alan 1915-1973 . . . . DLB-16	Weiss, Theodore 1916-2003 . . . . DLB-5	West, Jessamyn 1902-1984 . . . . DLB-6; Y-84
Watts, Isaac 1674-1748 . . . . DLB-95	Weiß, Ernst 1882-1940 . . . . DLB-81	West, Mae 1892-1980 . . . . DLB-44
Franklin Watts [publishing house] DLB-46	Weiße, Christian Felix 1726-1804 . . . . DLB-97	West, Michael Lee 1953- DLB-292
Waugh, Alec 1898-1981 . . . . DLB-191	Weitling, Wilhelm 1808-1871 . . . . DLB-129	West, Michelle Sagara 1963- DLB-251
Waugh, Auberon 1939-2000 . . . DLB-14, 194; Y-00	Welch, Denton 1915-1948 . . . . DLB-319	West, Morris 1916-1999 . . . . DLB-289
Waugh, Evelyn 1903-1966 . . . . DLB-15, 162, 195; CDBLB-6	Welch, James 1940- DLB-175, 256	West, Nathanael 1903-1940 . . . . DLB-4, 9, 28; CDALB-5
Way and Williams DLB-49	Welch, Lew 1926-1971? DLB-16	West, Paul 1930- DLB-14
Wayman, Tom 1945- DLB-53	Weldon, Fay 1931- DLB-14, 194, 319; CDBLB-8	West, Rebecca 1892-1983 . . . . DLB-36; Y-83
Weatherly, Tom 1942- DLB-41	Wellek, René 1903-1995 . . . . DLB-63	West, Richard 1941- DLB-185
Weaver, Gordon 1937- DLB-130	Wells, Carolyn 1862-1942 . . . . DLB-11	West and Johnson DLB-49
Weaver, Robert 1921- DLB-88	Wells, Charles Jeremiah circa 1800-1879 . . . . DLB-32	Westcott, Edward Noyes 1846-1898 . . . . DLB-202
Webb, Beatrice 1858-1943 . . . . DLB-190	Wells, Gabriel 1862-1946 . . . . DLB-140	The Western Literature Association. Y-99
Webb, Francis 1925-1973 . . . . DLB-260	Wells, H. G. 1866-1946	*The Western Messenger* 1835-1841 . . . . DLB-1; DLB-223
Webb, Frank J. fl. 1857 . . . . DLB-50	. . . . DLB-34, 70, 156, 178; CDBLB-6	
Webb, James Watson 1802-1884 . . . . DLB-43	H. G. Wells Society Y-98	Western Publishing Company DLB-46
Webb, Mary 1881-1927 . . . . DLB-34	Preface to *The Scientific Romances of H. G. Wells* (1933) DLB-178	Western Writers of America Y-99
Webb, Phyllis 1927- DLB-53		*The Westminster Review* 1824-1914 . . . . DLB-110
Webb, Sidney 1859-1947 . . . . DLB-190	Wells, Helena 1758?-1824 . . . . DLB-200	Weston, Arthur (see Webling, Peggy)
Webb, Walter Prescott 1888-1963 . . . . DLB-17	Wells, Rebecca 1952- DLB-292	Weston, Elizabeth Jane circa 1582-1612 . . .DLB-172
Webbe, William ?-1591 . . . . DLB-132	Wells, Robert 1947- DLB-40	Wetherald, Agnes Ethelwyn 1857-1940 . . . DLB-99
Webber, Charles Wilkins 1819-1856? DLB-202	Wells-Barnett, Ida B. 1862-1931 . . . . . DLB-23, 221	Wetherell, Elizabeth (see Warner, Susan)
	Welsh, Irvine 1958- DLB-271	Wetherell, W. D. 1948- DLB-234
Weber, Max 1864-1920 . . . . DLB-296	Welty, Eudora 1909-2001 . . . . . . DLB-2, 102, 143; Y-87, 01; DS-12; CDALB-1	Wetzel, Friedrich Gottlob 1779-1819 . . . . . DLB-90
Webling, Lucy (Lucy Betty MacRaye) 1877-1952 . . . . DLB-240		Weyman, Stanley J. 1855-1928 . . . . DLB-141, 156
	Eudora Welty: Eye of the Storyteller Y-87	Wezel, Johann Karl 1747-1819 . . . . DLB-94
Webling, Peggy (Arthur Weston) 1871-1949 . . . . DLB-240	*Eudora Welty Newsletter* Y-99	Whalen, Philip 1923-2002 . . . . DLB-16
	Eudora Welty's Funeral Y-01	Whalley, George 1915-1983 . . . . DLB-88
Webster, Augusta 1837-1894 . . . . DLB-35, 240	Eudora Welty's Ninetieth Birthday Y-99	Wharton, Edith 1862-1937 . . . . .DLB-4, 9, 12, 78, 189; DS-13; CDALB-3
Webster, John 1579 or 1580-1634? DLB-58; CDBLB-1	Eudora Welty Remembered in Two Exhibits Y-02	
The Melbourne Manuscript Y-86	Wendell, Barrett 1855-1921 . . . . DLB-71	Wharton, William 1925- Y-80
Webster, Noah 1758-1843 . . . . DLB-1, 37, 42, 43, 73, 243	Wentworth, Patricia 1878-1961 . . . . DLB-77	Whately, Mary Louisa 1824-1889 . . . . . . DLB-166
	Wentworth, William Charles 1790-1872 . . . . DLB-230	Whately, Richard 1787-1863 . . . . DLB-190
Webster, Paul Francis 1907-1984 . . . . DLB-265		*Elements of Rhetoric* (1828; revised, 1846) [excerpt] DLB-57
Charles L. Webster and Company DLB-49	Wenzel, Jean-Paul 1947- DLB-321	
Weckherlin, Georg Rodolf 1584-1653 . . . DLB-164	Werder, Diederich von dem 1584-1657 . . DLB-164	Wheatley, Dennis 1897-1977 . . . . .DLB-77, 255
Wedekind, Frank 1864-1918 . . . . DLB-118; CDWLB-2	Werfel, Franz 1890-1945 . . . . DLB-81, 124	Wheatley, Phillis circa 1754-1784 . . . . DLB-31, 50; CDALB-2
	Werner, Zacharias 1768-1823 . . . . DLB-94	
Weeks, Edward Augustus, Jr. 1898-1989 . . . . DLB-137	The Werner Company DLB-49	Wheeler, Anna Doyle 1785-1848? DLB-158
	Wersba, Barbara 1932- DLB-52	Wheeler, Charles Stearns 1816-1843 . . DLB-1, 223
Weeks, Stephen B. 1865-1918 . . . . DLB-187	Wescott, Glenway 1901-1987 . . . . DLB-4, 9, 102; DS-15	Wheeler, Monroe 1900-1988 . . . . DLB-4
Weems, Mason Locke 1759-1825 . . . DLB-30, 37, 42		Wheelock, John Hall 1886-1978 . . . . DLB-45
Weerth, Georg 1822-1856 . . . . DLB-129	Wesker, Arnold 1932- DLB-13, 310, 319; CDBLB-8	From John Hall Wheelock's Oral Memoir Y-01
Weidenfeld and Nicolson DLB-112		
Weidman, Jerome 1913-1998 . . . . DLB-28	Wesley, Charles 1707-1788 . . . . DLB-95	Wheelwright, J. B. 1897-1940 . . . . DLB-45
Weigl, Bruce 1949- DLB-120	Wesley, John 1703-1791 . . . . DLB-104	Wheelwright, John circa 1592-1679 . . . . . DLB-24
Weil, Jiří 1900-1959 . . . . DLB-299	Wesley, Mary 1912-2002 . . . . DLB-231	Whetstone, George 1550-1587 . . . . DLB-136
Weinbaum, Stanley Grauman 1902-1935 . . . . DLB-8	Wesley, Richard 1945- DLB-38	Whetstone, Colonel Pete (see Noland, C. F. M.)
	Wessel, Johan Herman 1742-1785 . . . . . . DLB-300	Whewell, William 1794-1866 . . . . DLB-262
Weiner, Andrew 1949- DLB-251	A. Wessels and Company DLB-46	Whichcote, Benjamin 1609?-1683 . . . . . . DLB-252
Weintraub, Stanley 1929- DLB-111; Y82	*Wessobrunner Gebet* circa 787-815 . . . . DLB-148	Whicher, Stephen E. 1915-1961 . . . . DLB-111
Weise, Christian 1642-1708 . . . . DLB-168	West, Anthony 1914-1988 . . . . DLB-15	Whipple, Edwin Percy 1819-1886 . . . . . DLB-1, 64
Weisenborn, Gunther 1902-1969 . . . . DLB-69, 124	Tribute to Liam O'Flaherty Y-84	Whitaker, Alexander 1585-1617 . . . . DLB-24
Weiss, John 1818-1879 . . . . DLB-1, 243	West, Cheryl L. 1957- DLB-266	Whitaker, Daniel K. 1801-1881 . . . . DLB-73

Whitcher, Frances Miriam
  1812-1852 .... DLB-11, 202
White, Andrew 1579-1656 .... DLB-24
White, Andrew Dickson 1832-1918 ...... DLB-47
White, E. B. 1899-1985 .... DLB-11, 22; CDALB-7
White, Edgar B. 1947- DLB-38
White, Edmund 1940- DLB-227
White, Ethel Lina 1887-1944 .... DLB-77
White, Hayden V. 1928- DLB-246
White, Henry Kirke 1785-1806 .... DLB-96
White, Horace 1834-1916 .... DLB-23
White, James 1928-1999 .... DLB-261
White, Patrick 1912-1990 .... DLB-260
White, Phyllis Dorothy James (see James, P. D.)
White, Richard Grant 1821-1885 .... DLB-64
White, T. H. 1906-1964 .... DLB-160, 255
White, Walter 1893-1955 .... DLB-51
Wilcox, James 1949- DLB-292
William White and Company DLB-49
White, William Allen 1868-1944 .... DLB-9, 25
White, William Anthony Parker
  (see Boucher, Anthony)
White, William Hale (see Rutherford, Mark)
Whitechurch, Victor L. 1868-1933 ..... DLB-70
Whitehead, Alfred North
  1861-1947 .... DLB-100, 262
Whitehead, E. A. (Ted Whitehead)
  1933- DLB-310
Whitehead, James 1936- Y-81
Whitehead, William 1715-1785 ...... DLB-84, 109
Whitfield, James Monroe 1822-1871 .... DLB-50
Whitfield, Raoul 1898-1945 .... DLB-226
Whitgift, John circa 1533-1604 .... DLB-132
Whiting, John 1917-1963 .... DLB-13
Whiting, Samuel 1597-1679 .... DLB-24
Whitlock, Brand 1869-1934 .... DLB-12
Whitman, Albery Allson 1851-1901 ..... DLB-50
Whitman, Alden 1913-1990 .... Y-91
Whitman, Sarah Helen (Power)
  1803-1878 .... DLB-1, 243
Whitman, Walt
  1819-1892 .... DLB-3, 64, 224, 250; CDALB-2
Albert Whitman and Company DLB-46
Whitman Publishing Company DLB-46
Whitney, Geoffrey
  1548 or 1552?-1601 .... DLB-136
Whitney, Isabella fl. 1566-1573 ...... DLB-136
Whitney, John Hay 1904-1982 .... DLB-127
Whittemore, Reed 1919-1995 .... DLB-5
Whittier, John Greenleaf
  1807-1892 .... DLB-1, 243; CDALB-2
Whittlesey House DLB-46
Wickham, Anna (Edith Alice Mary Harper)
  1884-1947 .... DLB-240
Wickram, Georg circa 1505-circa 1561 ... DLB-179
Wicomb, Zoë 1948- DLB-225
Wideman, John Edgar 1941- DLB-33, 143
Widener, Harry Elkins 1885-1912 ...... DLB-140
Wiebe, Rudy 1934- DLB-60

Wiechert, Ernst 1887-1950 .... DLB-56
Wied, Gustav 1858-1914 .... DLB-300
Wied, Martina 1882-1957 .... DLB-85
Wiehe, Evelyn May Clowes (see Mordaunt, Elinor)
Wieland, Christoph Martin 1733-1813 ... DLB-97
Wienbarg, Ludolf 1802-1872 .... DLB-133
Wieners, John 1934- DLB-16
Wier, Ester 1910-2000 .... DLB-52
Wiesel, Elie
  1928- DLB-83, 299; Y-86, 87; CDALB-7
  Nobel Lecture 1986: Hope, Despair and
  Memory Y-86
Wiggin, Kate Douglas 1856-1923 .... DLB-42
Wigglesworth, Michael 1631-1705 ...... DLB-24
Wilberforce, William 1759-1833 .... DLB-158
Wilbrandt, Adolf 1837-1911 .... DLB-129
Wilbur, Richard 1921- ... DLB-5, 169; CDALB-7
  Tribute to Robert Penn Warren Y-89
Wilcox, James 1949- DLB-292
Wild, Peter 1940- DLB-5
Wilde, Lady Jane Francesca Elgee
  1821?-1896 .... DLB-199
Wilde, Oscar 1854-1900
  . DLB-10, 19, 34, 57, 141, 156, 190; CDBLB-5
  "The Critic as Artist" (1891) DLB-57
  "The Decay of Lying" (1889) DLB-18
  "The English Renaissance of
  Art" (1908) DLB-35
  "L'Envoi" (1882) DLB-35
  Oscar Wilde Conference at Hofstra
  University Y-00
Wilde, Richard Henry 1789-1847 .... DLB-3, 59
W. A. Wilde Company DLB-49
Wilder, Billy 1906-2002 .... DLB-26
Wilder, Laura Ingalls 1867-1957 ...... DLB-22, 256
Wilder, Thornton
  1897-1975 .... DLB-4, 7, 9, 228; CDALB-7
  Thornton Wilder Centenary at Yale Y-97
Wildgans, Anton 1881-1932 .... DLB-118
Wiley, Bell Irvin 1906-1980 .... DLB-17
John Wiley and Sons DLB-49
Wilhelm, Kate 1928- DLB-8
Wilkes, Charles 1798-1877 .... DLB-183
Wilkes, George 1817-1885 .... DLB-79
Wilkins, John 1614-1672 .... DLB-236
Wilkinson, Anne 1910-1961 .... DLB-88
Wilkinson, Christopher 1941- DLB-310
Wilkinson, Eliza Yonge
  1757-circa 1813 .... DLB-200
Wilkinson, Sylvia 1940- Y-86
Wilkinson, William Cleaver 1833-1920 ... DLB-71
Willard, Barbara 1909-1994 .... DLB-161
Willard, Emma 1787-1870 .... DLB-239
Willard, Frances E. 1839-1898 .... DLB-221
Willard, Nancy 1936- DLB-5, 52
Willard, Samuel 1640-1707 .... DLB-24
L. Willard [publishing house] DLB-49
Willeford, Charles 1919-1988 .... DLB-226
William of Auvergne 1190-1249 .... DLB-115

William of Conches
  circa 1090-circa 1154 .... DLB-115
William of Ockham circa 1285-1347 .... DLB-115
William of Sherwood
  1200/1205-1266/1271 .... DLB-115
The William Charvat American Fiction
  Collection at the Ohio State
  University Libraries Y-92
Williams, Ben Ames 1889-1953 .... DLB-102
Williams, C. K. 1936- DLB-5
Williams, Chancellor 1905-1992 .... DLB-76
Williams, Charles 1886-1945 ... DLB-100, 153, 255
Williams, Denis 1923-1998 .... DLB-117
Williams, Emlyn 1905-1987 .... DLB-10, 77
Williams, Garth 1912-1996 .... DLB-22
Williams, George Washington
  1849-1891 .... DLB-47
Williams, Heathcote 1941- DLB-13
Williams, Helen Maria 1761-1827 ...... DLB-158
Williams, Hugo 1942- DLB-40
Williams, Isaac 1802-1865 .... DLB-32
Williams, Joan 1928- DLB-6
Williams, Joe 1889-1972 .... DLB-241
Williams, John A. 1925- DLB-2, 33
Williams, John E. 1922-1994 .... DLB-6
Williams, Jonathan 1929- DLB-5
Williams, Miller 1930- DLB-105
Williams, Nigel 1948- DLB-231
Williams, Raymond
  1921-1988 .... DLB-14, 231, 242
Williams, Roger circa 1603-1683 ...... DLB-24
Williams, Rowland 1817-1870 .... DLB-184
Williams, Samm-Art 1946- DLB-38
Williams, Sherley Anne 1944-1999 ..... DLB-41
Williams, T. Harry 1909-1979 .... DLB-17
Williams, Tennessee
  1911-1983 ..... DLB-7; Y-83; DS-4; CDALB-1
Williams, Terry Tempest 1955- ... DLB-206, 275
Williams, Ursula Moray 1911- DLB-160
Williams, Valentine 1883-1946 .... DLB-77
Williams, William Appleman 1921-1990 ... DLB-17
Williams, William Carlos
  1883-1963 ..... DLB-4, 16, 54, 86; CDALB-4
  The William Carlos Williams Society Y-99
Williams, Wirt 1921-1986 .... DLB-6
A. Williams and Company DLB-49
Williams Brothers DLB-49
Williamson, David 1942- DLB-289
Williamson, Henry 1895-1977 .... DLB-191
  The Henry Williamson Society Y-98
Williamson, Jack 1908- DLB-8
Willingham, Calder Baynard, Jr.
  1922-1995 .... DLB-2, 44
Williram of Ebersberg circa 1020-1085 ... DLB-148
Willis, John circa 1572-1625 .... DLB-281
Willis, Nathaniel Parker 1806-1867
  .... DLB-3, 59, 73, 74, 183, 250; DS-13
Willis, Ted 1918-1992 .... DLB-310
Willkomm, Ernst 1810-1886 .... DLB-133
Wills, Garry 1934- DLB-246

Cumulative Index

Tribute to Kenneth Dale McCormick Y-97
Willson, Meredith 1902-1984.......... DLB-265
Willumsen, Dorrit 1940- DLB-214
Wilmer, Clive 1945- DLB-40
Wilson, A. N. 1950- DLB-14, 155, 194
Wilson, Angus 1913-1991 ..... DLB-15, 139, 155
Wilson, Arthur 1595-1652 .... DLB-58
Wilson, August 1945- DLB-228
Wilson, Augusta Jane Evans 1835-1909 ... DLB-42
Wilson, Colin 1931- DLB-14, 194
  Tribute to J. B. Priestly Y-84
Wilson, Edmund 1895-1972............. DLB-63
Wilson, Ethel 1888-1980 .... DLB-68
Wilson, F. P. 1889-1963 .... DLB-201
Wilson, Harriet E.
  1827/1828?-1863? DLB-50, 239, 243
Wilson, Harry Leon 1867-1939 .... DLB-9
Wilson, John 1588-1667 .... DLB-24
Wilson, John 1785-1854 .... DLB-110
Wilson, John Anthony Burgess
  (see Burgess, Anthony)
Wilson, John Dover 1881-1969 .... DLB-201
Wilson, Lanford 1937- DLB-7
Wilson, Margaret 1882-1973 .... DLB-9
Wilson, Michael 1914-1978 .... DLB-44
Wilson, Mona 1872-1954 .... DLB-149
Wilson, Robert Charles 1953- DLB-251
Wilson, Robert McLiam 1964- DLB-267
Wilson, Robley 1930- DLB-218
Wilson, Romer 1891-1930 .... DLB-191
Wilson, Thomas 1524-1581 .... DLB-132, 236
Wilson, Woodrow 1856-1924 .... DLB-47
Effingham Wilson [publishing house].... DLB-154
Wimpfeling, Jakob 1450-1528 .... DLB-179
Wimsatt, William K., Jr. 1907-1975 ..... DLB-63
Winchell, Walter 1897-1972 .... DLB-29
J. Winchester [publishing house] DLB-49
Winckelmann, Johann Joachim
  1717-1768 .... DLB-97
Winckler, Paul 1630-1686 .... DLB-164
Wind, Herbert Warren 1916-2005 ...... DLB-171
John Windet [publishing house] DLB-170
Windham, Donald 1920- DLB-6
Wing, Donald Goddard 1904-1972 ..... DLB-187
Wing, John M. 1844-1917 .... DLB-187
Allan Wingate [publishing house]....... DLB-112
Winnemucca, Sarah 1844-1921 .... DLB-175
Winnifrith, Tom 1938- DLB-155
Winsloe, Christa 1888-1944........... DLB-124
Winslow, Anna Green 1759-1780 ..... DLB-200
Winsor, Justin 1831-1897 .... DLB-47
John C. Winston Company DLB-49
Winters, Yvor 1900-1968 .... DLB-48
Winterson, Jeanette 1959- DLB-207, 261
Winther, Christian 1796-1876 .... DLB-300

Winthrop, John 1588-1649.......... DLB-24, 30
Winthrop, John, Jr. 1606-1676 .... DLB-24
Winthrop, Margaret Tyndal
  1591-1647..................... DLB-200
Winthrop, Theodore
  1828-1861 .... DLB-202
Wirt, William 1772-1834 .... DLB-37
Wise, John 1652-1725................ DLB-24
Wise, Thomas James 1859-1937........ DLB-184
Wiseman, Adele 1928-1992 .... DLB-88
Wishart and Company................ DLB-112
Wisner, George 1812-1849............ DLB-43
Wister, Owen 1860-1938 ....DLB-9, 78, 186
Wister, Sarah 1761-1804.............. DLB-200
Wither, George 1588-1667............ DLB-121
Witherspoon, John 1723-1794......... DLB-31
  The Works of the Rev. John Witherspoon
    (1800-1801) [excerpts] DLB-31
Withrow, William Henry 1839-1908..... DLB-99
Witkacy (see Witkiewicz, Stanisław Ignacy)
Witkiewicz, Stanisław Ignacy
  1885-1939 .... DLB-215; CDWLB-4
Wittenwiler, Heinrich before 1387-
  circa 1414?.................... DLB-179
Wittgenstein, Ludwig 1889-1951 ...... DLB-262
Wittig, Monique 1935- DLB-83
Wodehouse, P. G.
  1881-1975......... DLB-34, 162; CDBLB-6
  Worldwide Wodehouse Societies Y-98
Wohmann, Gabriele 1932- DLB-75
Woiwode, Larry 1941- DLB-6
  Tribute to John Gardner Y-82
Wolcot, John 1738-1819.............. DLB-109
Wolcott, Roger 1679-1767 .... DLB-24
Wolf, Christa 1929- DLB-75; CDWLB-2
Wolf, Friedrich 1888-1953 .... DLB-124
Wolfe, Gene 1931- DLB-8
Wolfe, Thomas 1900-1938...................
  DLB-9, 102, 229; Y-85; DS-2, DS-16; CDALB-5
  "All the Faults of Youth and Inexperience":
    A Reader's Report on
    Thomas Wolfe's O Lost Y-01
  Emendations for Look Homeward, Angel.... Y-00
  Eugene Gant's Projected Works Y-01
  Fire at the Old Kentucky Home
    [Thomas Wolfe Memorial] Y-98
  Thomas Wolfe Centennial
    Celebration in Asheville Y-00
  The Thomas Wolfe Collection at
    the University of North Carolina
    at Chapel Hill Y-97
  The Thomas Wolfe Society.......... Y-97, 99
Wolfe, Tom 1931- DLB-152, 185
John Wolfe [publishing house] DLB-170
Reyner (Reginald) Wolfe
  [publishing house] DLB-170
Wolfenstein, Martha 1869-1906........ DLB-221
Wolff, David (see Maddow, Ben)
Wolff, Egon 1926- DLB-305

Wolff, Helen 1906-1994................ Y-94
Wolff, Tobias 1945- DLB-130
  Tribute to Michael M. Rea Y-97
  Tribute to Raymond Carver Y-88
Wolfram von Eschenbach
  circa 1170-after 1220 ....DLB-138; CDWLB-2
  Wolfram von Eschenbach's Parzival:
    Prologue and Book 3......... DLB-138
Wolker, Jiří 1900-1924............... DLB-215
Wollstonecraft, Mary 1759-1797
  .... DLB-39, 104, 158, 252; CDBLB-3
Women
  Women's Work, Women's Sphere:
    Selected Comments from Women
    Writers DLB-200
Women Writers in Sixteenth-Century
  Spain DLB-318
Wondratschek, Wolf 1943- DLB-75
Wong, Elizabeth 1958- DLB-266
Wong, Nellie 1934- DLB-312
Wong, Shawn 1949- DLB-312
Wood, Anthony à 1632-1695 .... DLB-213
Wood, Benjamin 1820-1900........... DLB-23
Wood, Charles 1932-1980 .... DLB-13
  The Charles Wood Affair:
    A Playwright Revived............. Y-83
Wood, Mrs. Henry 1814-1887......... DLB-18
Wood, Joanna E. 1867-1927........... DLB-92
Wood, Sally Sayward Barrell Keating
  1759-1855.................... DLB-200
Wood, William fl. seventeenth century ... DLB-24
Samuel Wood [publishing house]........ DLB-49
Woodberry, George Edward
  1855-1930 ....DLB-71, 103
Woodbridge, Benjamin 1622-1684....... DLB-24
Woodbridge, Frederick J. E. 1867-1940 ...DLB-270
Woodcock, George 1912-1995.......... DLB-88
Woodhull, Victoria C. 1838-1927 ...... DLB-79
Woodmason, Charles circa 1720-? DLB-31
Woodress, James Leslie, Jr. 1916- DLB-111
Woods, Margaret L. 1855-1945........ DLB-240
Woodson, Carter G. 1875-1950 ....DLB-17
Woodward, C. Vann 1908-1999 ....DLB-17
Woodward, Stanley 1895-1965 .... DLB-171
Woodworth, Samuel 1785-1842........ DLB-250
Wooler, Thomas 1785 or 1786-1853 .... DLB-158
Woolf, David (see Maddow, Ben)
Woolf, Douglas 1922-1992........... DLB-244
Woolf, Leonard 1880-1969 .....DLB-100; DS-10
Woolf, Virginia 1882-1941
  .... DLB-36, 100, 162; DS-10; CDBLB-6
  "The New Biography," New York Herald
    Tribune, 30 October 1927....... DLB-149
Woollcott, Alexander 1887-1943 .... DLB-29
Woolman, John 1720-1772 .... DLB-31
Woolner, Thomas 1825-1892 .... DLB-35
Woolrich, Cornell 1903-1968.......... DLB-226
Woolsey, Sarah Chauncy 1835-1905..... DLB-42
Woolson, Constance Fenimore
  1840-1894 ....DLB-12, 74, 189, 221

Worcester, Joseph Emerson
1784-1865 .... DLB-1, 235

Wynkyn de Worde [publishing house] ... DLB-170

Wordsworth, Christopher 1807-1885 .... DLB-166

Wordsworth, Dorothy 1771-1855 .... DLB-107

Wordsworth, Elizabeth
1840-1932 .... DLB-98

Wordsworth, William
1770-1850 .... DLB-93, 107; CDBLB-3

Workman, Fanny Bullock
1859-1925 .... DLB-189

World Literatue Today: A Journal for the
New Millennium Y-01

World Publishing Company DLB-46

World War I (1914-1918) DS-18

   The Great War Exhibit and Symposium
   at the University of South Carolina .. Y-97

   The Liddle Collection and First World
   War Research Y-97

   Other British Poets Who Fell
   in the Great War DLB-216

   The Seventy-Fifth Anniversary of
   the Armistice: The Wilfred Owen
   Centenary and the Great War Exhibit
   at the University of Virginia Y-93

World War II (1939–1945)
Literary Effects of World War II DLB-15

   World War II Writers Symposium
   at the University of South Carolina,
   12–14 April 1995 .... Y-95

   WW2 HMSO Paperbacks Society Y-98

R. Worthington and Company DLB-49

Wotton, Sir Henry 1568-1639 .... DLB-121

Wouk, Herman 1915- Y-82; CDALB-7

   Tribute to James Dickey Y-97

Wreford, James 1915-1990 .... DLB-88

Wren, Sir Christopher 1632-1723 .... DLB-213

Wren, Percival Christopher 1885-1941 ... DLB-153

Wrenn, John Henry 1841-1911 .... DLB-140

Wright, C. D. 1949- DLB-120

Wright, Charles 1935- DLB-165; Y-82

Wright, Charles Stevenson 1932- DLB-33

Wright, Chauncey 1830-1875 .... DLB-270

Wright, Frances 1795-1852 .... DLB-73

Wright, Harold Bell 1872-1944 .... DLB-9

Wright, James 1927-1980
.... DLB-5, 169; CDALB-7

Wright, Jay 1935- DLB-41

Wright, Judith 1915-2000 .... DLB-260

Wright, Louis B. 1899-1984 .... DLB-17

Wright, Richard
1908-1960 ..... DLB-76, 102; DS-2; CDALB-5

Wright, Richard B. 1937- DLB-53

Wright, S. Fowler 1874-1965 .... DLB-255

Wright, Sarah Elizabeth 1928- DLB-33

Wright, T. H. "Style" (1877) [excerpt] DLB-57

Wright, Willard Huntington (S. S. Van Dine)
1887-1939 .... DLB-306; DS-16

Wrightson, Patricia 1921- DLB-289

Wrigley, Robert 1951- DLB-256

Writers' Forum Y-85

Writing

A Writing Life Y-02

On Learning to Write Y-88

The Profession of Authorship:
Scribblers for Bread Y-89

A Writer Talking: A Collage Y-00

Wroth, Lawrence C. 1884-1970 .... DLB-187

Wroth, Lady Mary 1587-1653 .... DLB-121

Wurlitzer, Rudolph 1937- DLB-173

Wyatt, Sir Thomas circa 1503-1542 ..... DLB-132

Wycherley, William
1641-1715 .... DLB-80; CDBLB-2

Wyclif, John circa 1335-1384 .... DLB-146

Wyeth, N. C. 1882-1945 .... DLB-188; DS-16

Wyle, Niklas von circa 1415-1479 ...... DLB-179

Wylie, Elinor 1885-1928 .... DLB-9, 45

Wylie, Philip 1902-1971 .... DLB-9

Wyllie, John Cook 1908-1968 .... DLB-140

Wyman, Lillie Buffum Chace
1847-1929 .... DLB-202

Wymark, Olwen 1934- DLB-233

Wynd, Oswald Morris (see Black, Gavin)

Wyndham, John (John Wyndham Parkes
Lucas Beynon Harris) 1903-1969 .... DLB-255

Wynne-Tyson, Esmé 1898-1972 .... DLB-191

X

Xenophon circa 430 B.C.-circa 356 B.C. DLB-176

Y

Yamamoto, Hisaye 1921- DLB-312

Yamanaka, Lois-Ann 1961- DLB-312

Yamashita, Karen Tei 1951- DLB-312

Yamauchi, Wakako 1924- DLB-312

Yasuoka Shōtarō 1920- DLB-182

Yates, Dornford 1885-1960 .... DLB-77, 153

Yates, J. Michael 1938- DLB-60

Yates, Richard 1926-1992 ... DLB-2, 234; Y-81, 92

Yau, John 1950- DLB-234, 312

Yavorov, Peyo 1878-1914 .... DLB-147

Yearsley, Ann 1753-1806 .... DLB-109

Yeats, William Butler
1865-1939 .... DLB-10, 19, 98, 156; CDBLB-5

The W. B. Yeats Society of N.Y. Y-99

Yellen, Jack 1892-1991 .... DLB-265

Yep, Laurence 1948- DLB-52, 312

Yerby, Frank 1916-1991 .... DLB-76

Yezierska, Anzia 1880-1970 .... DLB-28, 221

Yolen, Jane 1939- DLB-52

Yonge, Charlotte Mary 1823-1901 ... DLB-18, 163

The Charlotte M. Yonge Fellowship Y-98

The York Cycle circa 1376-circa 1569 .... DLB-146

A Yorkshire Tragedy DLB-58

Thomas Yoseloff [publishing house] DLB-46

Youd, Sam (see Christopher, John)

Young, A. S. "Doc" 1919-1996 .... DLB-241

Young, Al 1939- DLB-33

Young, Arthur 1741-1820 .... DLB-158

Young, Dick 1917 or 1918-1987 .... DLB-171

Young, Edward 1683-1765 .... DLB-95

Young, Frank A. "Fay" 1884-1957 .... DLB-241

Young, Francis Brett 1884-1954 .... DLB-191

Young, Gavin 1928- DLB-204

Young, Stark 1881-1963 ...... DLB-9, 102; DS-16

Young, Waldeman 1880-1938 .... DLB-26

William Young [publishing house] DLB-49

Young Bear, Ray A. 1950- DLB-175

Yourcenar, Marguerite 1903-1987 ... DLB-72; Y-88

Yovkov, Yordan 1880-1937 .. DLB-147; CDWLB-4

Yushkevich, Semen 1868-1927 .... DLB-317

Z

Zachariä, Friedrich Wilhelm 1726-1777 .... DLB-97

Zagajewski, Adam 1945- DLB-232

Zagoskin, Mikhail Nikolaevich
1789-1852 .... DLB-198

Zaitsev, Boris 1881-1972 .... DLB-317

Zajc, Dane 1929- DLB-181

Zālīte, Māra 1952- DLB-232

Zalygin, Sergei Pavlovich 1913-2000 ..... DLB-302

Zamiatin, Evgenii Ivanovich 1884-1937 ... DLB-272

Zamora, Bernice 1938- DLB-82

Zamudio, Adela (Soledad) 1854-1928 .... DLB-283

Zand, Herbert 1923-1970 .... DLB-85

Zangwill, Israel 1864-1926 ...... DLB-10, 135, 197

Zanzotto, Andrea 1921- DLB-128

Zapata Olivella, Manuel 1920- DLB-113

Zapoev, Timur Iur'evich
(see Kibirov, Timur Iur'evich)

Zasodimsky, Pavel Vladimirovich
1843-1912 .... DLB-238

Zebra Books DLB-46

Zebrowski, George 1945- DLB-8

Zech, Paul 1881-1946 .... DLB-56

Zeidner, Lisa 1955- DLB-120

Zeidonis, Imants 1933- DLB-232

Zeimi (Kanze Motokiyo) 1363-1443 ..... DLB-203

Zelazny, Roger 1937-1995 .... DLB-8

Zenger, John Peter 1697-1746 .... DLB-24, 43

Zepheria DLB-172

Zernova, Ruf' 1919-2004 .... DLB-317

Zesen, Philipp von 1619-1689 .... DLB-164

Zhadovskaia, Iuliia Valerianovna
1824-1883 .... DLB-277

Zhukova, Mar'ia Semenovna
1805-1855 .... DLB-277

Zhukovsky, Vasilii Andreevich
1783-1852 .... DLB-205

Zhvanetsky, Mikhail Mikhailovich
1934- DLB-285

G. B. Zieber and Company DLB-49

Ziedonis, Imants 1933- CDWLB-4

Zieroth, Dale 1946- DLB-60

Zigler und Kliphausen, Heinrich
Anshelm von 1663-1697 .... DLB-168

Zil'ber, Veniamin Aleksandrovich
(see Kaverin, Veniamin Aleksandrovich)

Zimmer, Paul 1934- DLB-5

Zinberg, Len (see Lacy, Ed)

Zincgref, Julius Wilhelm 1591-1635 ..... DLB-164

Zindel, Paul 1936- DLB-7, 52; CDALB-7

Zinnes, Harriet 1919- DLB-193

Zinov'ev, Aleksandr Aleksandrovich
1922- DLB-302

Zinov'eva-Annibal, Lidiia Dmitrievna
1865 or 1866-1907 .... DLB-295

Zinzendorf, Nikolaus Ludwig von
1700-1760 .... DLB-168

Zitkala-Ša 1876-1938................DLB-175

Zīverts, Mārtiņš 1903-1990............ DLB-220

Zlatovratsky, Nikolai Nikolaevich
1845-1911 .... DLB-238

Zola, Emile 1840-1902 .... DLB-123

Zolla, Elémire 1926- DLB-196

Zolotow, Charlotte 1915- DLB-52

Zoshchenko, Mikhail Mikhailovich
1895-1958 ....DLB-272

Zschokke, Heinrich 1771-1848.......... DLB-94

Zubly, John Joachim 1724-1781 .... DLB-31

Zu-Bolton, Ahmos, II 1936- DLB-41

Zuckmayer, Carl 1896-1977........ DLB-56, 124

Zukofsky, Louis 1904-1978 .... DLB-5, 165

Zupan, Vitomil 1914-1987 .... DLB-181

Župančič, Oton 1878-1949...DLB-147; CDWLB-4

zur Mühlen, Hermynia 1883-1951....... DLB-56

Zweig, Arnold 1887-1968............. DLB-66

Zweig, Stefan 1881-1942 .... DLB-81, 118

Zwinger, Ann 1925- DLB-275

Zwingli, Huldrych 1484-1531 ....DLB-179

Ø

Øverland, Arnulf 1889-1968 .... DLB-297

ISBN 0-7876-8139-3

PQ
556
.Q64

2006